Dictionary *of* Evangelical Biography
1730–1860

This work is dedicated to
Andrew F. Walls and John D. Walsh

Dictionary *of* Evangelical Biography
1730–1860

VOLUME ONE

DONALD M. LEWIS, EDITOR

© 2004 by Donald M. Lewis

Hendrickson Publishers, LLC
P. O. Box 3473
Peabody, Massachusetts 01961-3473

ISBN 1-56563-935-9

Dictionary of Evangelical Biography, 1730–1860, two volumes.

Previously published in two volumes as *The Blackwell Dictionary of Evangelical Biography, 1730–1860*. Oxford: Blackwell, 1995.

Printed in the United States of America

First Printing — November 2004

Contents

Specialist Editors with fields of expertise

Dr Randall Balmer
Columbia University, New York City
(Eighteenth-century American middle colonies)

John Briggs
University of Keele, England
(British Baptists)

Dr David Bundy
Christian Theological Seminary, Indianapolis, Indiana
(The Holiness Movement; Continental Europe)

Professor R. H. Campbell
Newton Stewart, Scotland
(Scotland)

Dr Jonathan Cutmore
Erindale College, University of Toronto
(British entries)

Professor Robert E. Frykenberg
University of Wisconsin – Madison
(British India)

Dr E. Dorothy Graham
Birmingham, England
(Female Methodist preachers)

Professor Allen Guelzo
Eastern College, St David's, Pennsylvania
(American Episcopalians)

David J. Hall
Cambridge University Library, Cambridge, England
(British Quakers)

Dr David Hempton
The Queen's University of Belfast, Northern Ireland
(Ireland)

The Revd. Dr R. Tudur Jones
Bangor, Gwynedd, Wales
(Wales; British Congregationalists)

Dr William J. Leonard
Samford University, Birmingham, Alabama
(American Baptists)

Dr Peter Lineham
Massey University, Palmerston North, New Zealand
(New Zealand/South Seas)

Dr David N. Livingstone
School of Geosciences
The Queen's University of Belfast, Northern Ireland
(Scientists)

Professor Donald E. Meek
Department of Celtic, University of Aberdeen
(Celtic figures/Scottish highlands)

Professor Mark A. Noll
Wheaton College, Illinois
(American Congregationalists, Presbyterians)

Dr Stuart Piggin
Robert Menzies College, Sydney, Australia
(Australia)

Professor Arthur Pollard
North Cave, Brough, England
(British literary entries)

Dr George Rawlyk
Queen's University, Kingston, Ontario, Canada
(Canada)

Dr Russell E. Richey
The Divinity School, Duke University, Durham, North Carolina
(American Methodists)

Dr Andrew Ross
New College, Edinburgh, Scotland
(Southern Africa)

Dr Harold H. Rowdon
Lymington, Hampshire, England
(British Plymouth Brethren)

Dr W. John Roxborogh
Auckland, New Zealand
(Malaysia/Singapore/China)

Dr Horace Russell
Eastern Baptist Seminary, Philadelphia, Pennsylvania
(West Indies)

Professor Andrew F. Walls
New College, Edinburgh
(British Missionary societies; East and West Africa; the Middle East; South America)

Dr John D. Walsh
Jesus College, Oxford, England
(British Anglicans 1730–1820)

Professor W. Reginald Ward
Petersfield, Hampshire, England
(British Methodists)

Dr David Wills
Amherst College, Amherst, Massachusetts
(American Blacks)

Dr John Wolffe
The Open University, Milton Keynes, England
(British Anglicans post 1820)

Contributors

Kerry Abel
Carleton University, Ottawa

Alan R. Acheson
Ballycastle, Northern Ireland

C. Leonard Allen
Abilene Christian University, Texas

Martin A. W. Allen
Glasgow, Scotland

W. Loyd Allen
Southern Seminary, Louisville, Kentucky

Basil W. O. Amey
Harrow, England

Douglas Firth Anderson
Northwestern College, Orange City, Iowa

Lesley G. Anderson
London, England

John S. Andrews
Lancaster, England

Stephen W. Angell
Florida A and M University, Tallahassee, Florida

Alan Argent
London, England

Donald S. Armentrout
University of the South, Sewanee, Tennessee

Thomas Askew
Gordon College, Wenham, Massachusetts

C. Evans Bailey
Kingston, Jamaica

Frank Baker
Durham, North Carolina

Wesley D. Balda
Claremont, California

Randall Balmer
Barnard College, Columbia University, New York City

William S. Baker
Westminster Seminary, Philadelphia, Pennsylvania

Suzanne Wilson Barnett
University of Puget Sound, Tacoma, Washington

Jonathan Barry
Exeter University, England

Michael Bauman
Hillsdale College, Hillsdale, Michigan

David W. Bebbington
University of Stirling, Scotland

Oliver A. Beckerlegge
York, England

Roger Beckwith
Latimer House, Oxford, England

David Bell
University of New Brunswick

Judith Binney
University of Auckland

Robert Merrill Black
Trinity College, University of Toronto

Richard Charles Blake
Wokingham, Berkshire, England

Michael P. Boddy
School of Theology at Claremont, California

Geoffrey Bolton
University of Queensland, Australia

Ole E. Borgen
Asbury Theological Seminary, Wilmore, Kentucky

Henry Warner Bowden
Rutgers University, New Brunswick, New Jersey

Robert Boyd
Fort William, Scotland

Geoffrey R. Breed
Gillingham, England

Catherine A. Brekus
Chicago, Illinois

John H. Y. Briggs
University of Keele, England

Simon Bright
Hertfordshire, England

Charles W. Brockwell, Jr
University of Louisville, Kentucky

Raymond Brown
St Neots, England

Roger L. Brown
Cardiff, Wales

Stewart J. Brown
New College, Edinburgh, Scotland

Esther Bruland
Youngstown, Ohio

David Bundy
Christian Theological Seminary, Indianapolis, Indiana

Dietrich Buss
Biola University, La Mirada, California

Diana Butler
Westmont College, Santa Barbara, California

K. J. Cable
Randwick, Australia

Robert Calhoon
University of North Carolina at Greensboro

Clive Calver
London, England

Edward D. C. Campbell, Jr
Virginia State Library, Richmond, Virginia

R. H. Campbell
Newton Stewart, Wigtownshire, Scotland

P. S. E. Carson
Denstone College, Denstone, England

Grayson Carter
Brasenose College, Oxford

Hugh Cartwright
Free Church College, Edinburgh

Richard Carwardine
University of Sheffield, England

Nancy Cassels
Dundas, Ontario

Gordon A. Catherall
Liverpool, England

Wesley A. Chambers†

J. Robert Charles
Goshen, Indiana

P. Chassagne
Sunnybank, Queensland, Australia

Geoffrey Chew
Royal Holloway & Bedford New College, England

Eric G. Clancy
North Parramatta, Australia

Dudley Clarke
Hobart, Tasmania, Australia

Ernest F. Clipsham
Budleigh Salterton, England

Robert G. Clouse
Indiana State University, Terre Haute, Indiana

F. Roy Coad
Carshalton, Surrey, England

Milton J Coalter, Jr
Louisville Presbyterian Seminary, Kentucky

Judith Colwell
McMaster Divinity College, Hamilton, Ontario

Joseph Conforti
University of Southern Maine, Portland, Maine

Ralph Covell
Denver Conservative Baptist Seminary, Colorado

David A. Currie
Newtown, Pennsylvania

Gordon H. Cutler
Newport, Wales

Jonathan Cutmore
Erindale College, University of Toronto

Allan K. Davidson
St John's College, Auckland, New Zealand

Rupert E. Davies†

Paul R. Dekar
Memphis Theological Seminary, Memphis, Tennessee

Timothy J. Demy
Springfield, Virginia

Dennis C. Dickerson
Williams College, Williamstown, Massachusetts

Brian Dickey
Flinders University of South Australia

William DiPuccio
Marquette University, Milwaukee, Wisconsin

Ruth Doan
Hollins College, Roanoke, Virginia

Frederick W. Drake
Cambridge, Massachusetts

A. J. Durie
University of Glasgow

Michael Stone Edwards
High Wycombe, England

J. P. Ellens
Redeemer College, Ancaster, Ontario

Mary Ellis
Aberystwyth, Dyfed, Wales

Richard Ely
University of Tasmania, Tasmania

Ainslie T. Embree
Columbia University, New York City

Timothy Paul Erdel
Mishawaka, Indiana

W. J. Clyde Ervine
Etobicoke, Ontario

Eifion Evans
Pembroke Dock, Dyfed, Wales

Ian Farley
Lambeth, London, England

Sinclair Ferguson
Westminster Seminary, Philadelphia, Pennsylvania

Clive Field
University of Birmingham

Geoffrey Finlayson
University of Glasgow

Brian Fletcher
University of Sydney, New South Wales

Charles G. Flinn
Arlington, Virginia

Matthew D. Floding
Northwestern College, Orange City, Iowa

Charles W. Forman
*The Divinity School, Yale University,
New Haven, Connecticut*

Duncan B. Forrester
New College, University of Edinburgh

Ian Foster
Fitzwilliam College, Cambridge, England

Robert E. Frykenberg
University of Wisconsin – Madison

Christopher Fyfe
London, England

Jane Garnett
Wadham College, Oxford

John Garrett
Pacific Theological College, Suva, Fiji

Stewart D. Gill
Presbyterian Theological College, Victoria, Australia

Sheridan W. Gilley
University of Durham, England

Bryan Gilling
University of Waikato, Hamilton, New Zealand

Norman Girardot
Lehigh University, Bethlehem, Pennsylvania

Donald Goertz
Toronto, Ontario

Alasdair Bothwell Gordon
Aberdeen, Scotland

David A. Gowland
Dundee University

E. Dorothy Graham
Birmingham, England

Stephen R. Graham
North Park Theological Seminary, Chicago, Illinois

Elizabeth Grant
New College, Edinburgh

John Webster Grant
Victoria University, Toronto, Ontario

Christopher Grasso
Middleton, Connecticut

William B. Gravely
University of Denver

V. H. H. Green
Lincoln College, Oxford

Howard Gregg
Friends' Historical Society, London

Michael Griffiths
Guildford, Surrey, England

Allen Guelzo
Eastern College, St David's, Pennsylvania

Bruce L. Guenther
McGill University, Montreal

Paul E. H. Hair
University of Liverpool

David J. Hall
Cambridge University Library, England

Christopher Hancock
Selwyn Gardens, Cambridge, England

Nancy Hardesty
Greenville, South Carolina

Alan Harding
Potters Bar, Hertfordshire, England

Gillis Harp
Acadia University, Wolfville, Nova Scotia

George W. Harper
Alliance Bible Seminary, Manila, Philippines

Steven Harper
Lexington, Kentucky

John W. Harris
New College, Kensington, New South Wales, Australia

Darryl Hart
Westminster Theological Seminary, Philadelphia, Pennsylvania

Roger Hayden
Bristol, England

Alan J. Hayes
Edinburgh, Scotland

David N. Hempton
The Queen's University, Belfast

Charles R. Henery
Nashota House, Nashota, Wisconsin

Michael Hennell
South Wirral, England

R. Brian Higham
Llansamlet, Swansea, West Glamorgan, Wales

Myrtle Hill
The Queen's University, Belfast

David Hilliard
Flinders University, Adelaide, South Australia

A. J. Boyd Hilton
Trinity College, Cambridge, England

Bruce Hindmarsh
Christ Church, Oxford

Andrew Hoffecker
Grove City College, Pennsylvania

Robert Hooper
David Lipscomb University, Nashville, Tennessee

Wade A. Horton
Louisville, Kentucky

John Howes
Obirin University, Tokyo

Leslie Howsam
University of Windsor, Windsor, Ontario

Lydia Huffman Hoyle
Georgetown College, Kentucky

Arnold D. Hunt
Brighton, South Australia

Robert Hunt
Seminari Theoloji Malaysia, Kuala Lumpur

Mark Hutchinson
The Centre for the Study of Australian Christianity, Macquarie Centre, Australia

E. M. Jackson
St Martin's College, Lancaster, England

E. Wyn James
University of Wales, Cardiff, Wales

R. Watcyn James
Ammanford, Dyfed, Wales

Elizabeth Jay
Westminster College, Oxford

Geraint H. Jenkins
*Director, Centre for Advanced Welsh and Celtic Studies,
The National Library of Wales, Aberystwyth, Wales*

David J. Jeremy
Manchester Metropolitan University

E. Stanley John
Llanelli, Dyfed, Wales

James E. Johnson
Bethel College, St Paul, Minnesota

Wayne J. Johnson
University College of Ripon & York St John, York, England

Elwood Hugh Jones
Trent University, Peterborough, Ontario

Ieuan S. Jones
Swansea, West Glamorgan, Wales

R. M. Jones
Aberystwyth, Dyfed, Wales

R. Tudur Jones
Bangor, Gwynedd, Wales

Mark S. Joy
Jamestown College, Jamestown, North Dakota

David Kling
University of Miami, Coral Gables, Florida

William Kostlevy
Asbury Theological Seminary, Wilmore, Kentucky

John K. La Shell
Sykesville, Pennsylvania

Di Langmore
Australian National University, Canberra, Australia

Sione Latukefu
Pacific Theological College, Suva, Fiji

Terence R. Leach†

Arie Leegwater
Calvin College, Grand Rapids, Michigan

Jane Kate Leonard
University of Akron, Ohio

William J. Leonard
Samford University, Birmingham, Alabama

Donald M. Lewis
Regent College, Vancouver, British Columbia

Joe Liechty
Dublin, Ireland

Harold Lindsell
Lake Forest, California

Peter Lineham
Massey University, Palmerston North, New Zealand

Rob Linn
Blackwood, Australia

F. Linyard
Moravian Church House, London, England

Charles H. Lippy
Clemson University, Clemson, South Carolina

David N. Livingstone
The Queen's University of Belfast

Diane Lobody
Methodist Theological School in Ohio, Delaware, Ohio

K. Richard Lougheed
Université de Montréal, Canada

Deryck Lovegrove
St Mary's College, University of St Andrews, Scotland

Jessie G. Lutz
Harve de Grace, Maryland

James L. McAllister, Jr†

Gerald McDermott
Roanoke College, Salem, Virginia

Richard McEdward
Tacoma, Washington

N. MacIntosh
Coffeyville, Kansas

John R. McIntosh
Dollar, Scotland

B. Mack
Queen's University, Kingston, Ontario

Norris A. Magnuson
Bethel Theological Seminary, St Paul, Minnesota

Andrew Manis
Averett College, Danville, Virginia

K. R. Manley
Whitley College, Victoria, Australia

George Marsden
Notre Dame University, Indiana

V. Paul Marston
Preston, England

John Mason
London, England

Sondra Matthaei
St Paul School of Theology, Kansas City, Missouri

Donald E. Meek
University of Aberdeen

J. Graham Miller
Victoria, Australia

Randall Miller
St Joseph's University, Philadelphia, Pennsylvania

Edward H. Milligan
Reading, England

Bruce Milne
Vancouver, British Columbia

A. C. Milner
Australian National University, Canberra, Australia

David Milner
Norwich, England

William Mitchell
Sociedades Biblicas Unidas, Quito, Ecuador

David E. H. Mole
Brugge, Belgium

Robert Monk
McMurry University, Abilene, Texas

Gerald Moran
University of Michigan, Dearborn, Michigan

D. Densil Morgan
University College of North Wales, Wales

Nancy J. Morris
Honolulu, Hawaii

Alan F. Munden
Coventry, England

Derek B. Murray
Edinburgh, Scotland

Douglas M. Murray
Faculty of Divinity, University of Glasgow

Jocelyn Murray
London, England

Robert N. Nash
Judson College, Marion, Alabama

N. R. Needham
Rutherford House, Edinburgh, Scotland

Anthony G. Newell†

Richard Newman
New York Public Library

M. Nicholls
Spurgeon's College, London

Mark A. Noll
Wheaton College, Illinois

Geoffrey F. Nuttall
Birmingham, England

J. Steven O'Malley
Asbury Theological Seminary, Wilmore, Kentucky

John Oakes
University of British Columbia

Geoffrey A. Oddie
University of Sydney, New South Wales, Australia

Thomas H. Olbricht
Pepperdine University, Malibu, California

Goronwy Price Owen
Llanrwst, Gwynedd, Wales

W. T. Owen
London, England

John M. R. Owens
Massey University, Palmerston North, New Zealand

J. I. Packer
Regent College, Vancouver, British Columbia

Jean Paquette
Lander College, Greenwood, South Carolina

Calvin Parker
Mars Hill, North Carolina

L. Dale Patterson
University of Louisville, Kentucky

John Paul
University of Wisconsin – Madison

Kenneth N. Pearson
Vancouver, British Columbia

Peter Penner
Calgary, Alberta

Paul Perone
Toronto, Ontario

R. V. Pierard
Indiana State University, Terre Haute, Indiana

Stuart Piggin
Robert Menzies College, New South Wales

Colin Podmore
Council for Christian Unity, London, England

Richard W. Pointer
Westmont College, Santa Barbara, California

Steven Pointer
Trinity College, Deerfield, Illinois

Arthur Pollard
North Humberside, England

E. Daniel Potts
Lismore, New South Wales, Australia

Avril Powell
School of Oriental and African Studies, London, England

Andrew Pratt
Cape Girardeau, Missouri

Malcolm D. Prentis
Australian Catholic University, Strathfield, Australia

David T. Priestley
Edmonton Baptist Seminary, Alberta

Henry D. Rack
Manchester, England

Rick Railsback
Calvin College, Grand Rapids, Michigan

George Rawlyk
Queen's University, Kingston, Ontario

Margaret I. Reeson
Pearce, Australia

Marjorie E. Reeves
Oxford, England

Ian S. Rennie
Ontario Theological Seminary, Toronto, Ontario

John Reynolds
Oxford, England

William Ringenberg
Taylor University, Upland, Indiana

Dana L. Robert
Boston University School of Theology, Boston, Massachusetts

Elfed ap Nefydd Roberts
United Theological College, Aberystwyth, Dyfed, Wales

Allen B. Robertson
Halifax, Nova Scotia

Hans Rollmann
Memorial University of Newfoundland

Marcella Rollmann
Memorial University of Newfoundland

John B. Roney
Sacred Heart University, Fairfield, Connecticut

John Root
Alperton, Middlesex, England

E. Alan Rose
Hyde, Cheshire, England

Doreen M. Rosman
Rutherford College, The University of Kent at Canterbury

Andrew Ross
New College, University of Edinburgh

M. Ross
Sunnybank, Queensland, Australia

Harold H. Rowdon
Lymington, Hampshire, England

W. John Roxborogh
The Bible College of New Zealand, Auckland

Massimo Rubboli
Universita di Firenze, Florence, Italy

Colin A. Russell
Open University, Milton Keynes, England

Horace Russell
Eastern Baptist Seminary, Philadelphia, Pennsylvania

Roger Ryan
Southport, Merseyside, England

Paul E. Sangster
Broadstairs, Kent, England

Peter Schmitthenner
Mansfield University, Pennsylvania

David Schubert
Highgate, South Australia

Sally Schwartz
Marquette University, Milwaukee, Wisconsin

G. Scobie
University of Glasgow

Glen Scorgie
North American Baptist College, Edmonton, Alberta

Nigel A. D. Scotland
College of St Paul and St Mary, Cheltenham, England

Ian Sellers
Warrington, England

Eric J. Sharpe
University of Sydney, Australia

Bruce Shelley
Denver Seminary, Colorado

Christopher Smith
Philadelphia, Pennsylvania

Gary Scott Smith
Grove City College, Grove City, Pennsylvania

Jeffrey W. Smith
Andrews University, Berrien Springs, Michigan

Karen Smith
South Wales Baptist College, Cardiff, Wales

Mark A. Smith
Oxford, England

C. Jeffrey Spittal
Bristol, England

Brian Stanley
Trinity College, Bristol

Kenneth Stewart
Isle of Harris, Scotland

Kenneth J. Stewart
Prairie Bible College and Graduate School, Three Hills, Alberta

R. J. Stewart
MacMurray College, Jacksonville, Illinois

Robert Stewart
Willingboro, New Jersey

Mark S. Still
College of San Mateo, California

Harry Stout
Divinity School, Yale University, New Haven, Connecticut

Patrick Streiff
Centre Methodiste de Formation Theologique, Lausanne, Switzerland

Douglas M. Strong
Wesley Theological Seminary, Washington, DC

Timothy C. F. Stunt
Stowe School, Buckingham, England

Scott Sunquist
Trinity Theological College, Singapore

David Swift
Lincoln University, Pennsylvania

Richard Taylor
Springfield, Illinois

Thomas T. Taylor
Wittenberg University, Springfield, Ohio

Gerrit J. tenZythoff
Southwestern Missouri State University, Springfield, Missouri

Lynette Thistlethwayte
Roseville, New South Wales, Australia

Arthur D. Thomas, Jr
Wesley Theological Seminary, Washington, DC

D. Arthur Thomas
West Glamorgan, Wales

Joshua Thompson
Belfast, Northern Ireland

J. G. S. S. Thomson
Edinburgh, Scotland

William G. Travis
Bethel Theological Seminary, St Paul, Minnesota

Geraint Tudur
Penylan, Cardiff, South Glamorgan, Wales

Alex Tyrrell
La Trobe University, Bundoora, Victoria, Australia

Marguerite Van Die
Queen's University, Kingston, Ontario

Richard Vaudry
The University of Alberta and North American Baptist College, Edmonton, Alberta

John A. Vickers
Bognor Regis, Sussex, England

A. James Vincent
Chacewater, Truro, Cornwall, England

David A. Vlosak
Kalamazoo, Michigan

John Waller
Loughborough, Leicestershire, England

Andrew F. Walls
New College, Edinburgh, Scotland

W. Reginald Ward
Petersfield, Hampshire, England

James Warnock
Utah Institute of Biblical Studies, Salt Lake City, Utah

Susan E. Warrick
United Methodist Church General Commission on Archives and History, Madison, New Jersey

John F. Waukechon
Austin, Texas

Douglas Weaver
Brewton Parker College, Mt Vernon, Georgia

Timothy Weber
Southern Baptist Theological Seminary, Louisville, Kentucky

C. Edwin Welch
Lantzville, British Columbia

David Wells
Gordon-Conwell Theological Seminary, South Hamilton, Massachusetts

Woodrow Whidden
Andrews University, Berrien Springs, Michigan

Barrie White
Regent's Park College, Oxford

Luder Whitlock
Reformed Seminary, Jackson, Mississippi

John Wiers
Kirkwood City College, Cedar Rapids, Iowa

C. Peter Williams
Ecclesall, Sheffield, England

David W. Wills
Amherst College, Amherst, Massachusetts

Leland E. Wilshire
Biola University, La Mirada, California

Robert S. Wilson
Acadia Divinity College, Wolfville, Nova Scotia

John Wolffe
The Open University, Milton Keynes, England

A. Skevington Wood†

Helen Woolcock
Wooloowin, Queensland, Australia

David F. Wright
New College, University of Edinburgh

Donald I. Wright
University of Newcastle, New South Wales, Australia

A. T. Yarwood
New South Wales, Australia

Davis Young
Calvin College, Grand Rapids, Michigan

Charles Yrigoyen, Jr
The General Commission on Archives and Methodist History, Madison, New Jersey

Preface

This volume seeks to provide biographical treatment and to indicate the sources for study of figures of historical, literary or religious significance who flourished at any time between 1730 and 1860 and were associated with the evangelical movement in the English-speaking world. The need for such a work has been suggested by:

1. the lack of any one source of information on figures related to a significant period of Christian history in the West which is also organically related to that world-wide expansion which has transformed Christianity into a global religion in the twentieth century;
2. the acknowledgement that in English-speaking North America evangelicalism was the leading religious influence during this period and that in Britain, evangelicalism was important both within and without the established churches and outside the religious world altogether, and was in some ways responsible for some of the dominant characteristics of British society, particularly in the Victorian period;
3. the evident interest in the movement and its branches on the part of historians and social scientists as well as theologians, church historians, and many concerned Christians;
4. the quantity and quality of recent scholarly work which has been devoted to the movement, but to which no index or guide has been available.

The dictionary, by its entries and its full index, seeks to show at how many points the evangelicals touched, and often moulded, social and political life. As one would expect, the volume includes a large number of ordained ministers; but one of the greatest strengths of evangelicalism has always been its appeal to the laity and thus the work includes lay people of every conceivable occupation.

The dictionary also brings to the fore scores of evangelical women who have heretofore been largely unknown: Ellen Ranyard who pioneered in preventative health care in Britain through her 'Bible nurses'; Anne Dutton, an early Methodist poet who sparred with John Wesley over the finer points of Calvinism; and Elizabeth Evans, the woman preacher who served as George Eliot's model for Dinah Morris in ADAM BEDE.

In designing this volume, exhaustive treatment of well-known figures has been deemed less important than adequate treatment of the many neglected or minor persons; some subjects rate a brief entry simply because published work has drawn attention to them.

The Period and the Area to be Covered

The period 1730–1860 has been chosen, both to set a reasonable limit on what otherwise would be an impossibly large task and to reduce the difficulties of terminology. In penning an appeal to evangelical Anglican clergy in 1764, John Wesley did not hesitate in outlining his own view of what was the essence of evangelicalism: 'I Original Sin. II Justification by Faith. III Holiness of Heart and Life; provided their life be answerable to their doctrine' (N. Curnock, ed., *The Journal of John Wesley* (London, 1909–16) v: 61.) If only historians since Wesley found the task of definition so easy! It is significant that it was clear to Wesley that from the 1730s there had been a reasonably coherent historical phenomenon which he regarded as a distinct movement.

As Andrew Walls has argued, there has always been an evangelical faith; there have been many evangelical movements. Yet from the middle of the eighteenth to the middle of the nineteenth century there is a reasonably coherent historical phenomenon which can be called the Evangelical Movement. After this period, it becomes considerably more difficult to determine how the adjective should be applied or denied. The chosen period begins with the first clear manifestations of the evangelical revival, more or less contemporaneously in New England, Wales, Scotland and England, and ends with the 'Prayer Meeting Revival' of 1858–9, which in so many ways looks like the last wave of the eighteenth century movement.

The test applied to people whose life dates overlap the terminal dates has been: would their significance *after* 1730 or *before* 1860 have been sufficient to justify their inclusion? Thus Solomon Stoddard (the grandfather of Jonathan Edwards), for all his influence on the evangelicals, must be cut out, for his life's work was over by 1730. Similarly, while David Livingstone, who overlaps at the other end, is in, General Charles Gordon of Khartoum, is out; for had both died in 1860, one would have been the explorer who opened up central Africa, the other an unknown British army officer who served in China. More problematic for the editor have been figures such as Bishop J. C. Ryle who were rising stars by 1860 but whose place in the firmament was not firmly established until after that date. In such cases the figures have been given minor entries which concentrate on their careers up to the 1860 cutoff.

Within the period concerned, the 'English-speaking

world' includes Great Britain and all of Ireland, and Britain's colonial holdings: the American colonies (and subsequently the United States), Canada, Australia, New Zealand, parts of the South Seas, the African and West Indian territories and British India. Some who did not speak English are included if they had strong connections with, or exercised notable influence on evangelicalism (such as the Moravian, Count Zinzendorf). A number of key continental evangelicals have been included because of the important links that they had to the English-speaking world.

Who were the Evangelicals?

Contemporary scholars may be forgiven for being baffled by the sheer diversity of evangelicalism. This was a popular movement which touched a variety of people of vastly different backgrounds, politics, class, church affiliation, presuppositions and prejudices, none of which was necessarily lost as a result of it. The movement encompassed both peace activists and war heroes, ardent abolitionists and black insurrectionists as well as staunch defenders of slavery. It embraced High Calvinists and Low Arminians, the high born as well as many of 'the great unwashed'.

This disconcerting diversity tends to obscure the unifying elements which gave the movement its coherence. As Professor Walls has argued, between the dates selected there is a stream of Christian life in the English-speaking world which, despite the multiform tributaries and branches, displays certain distinctive features which mark it off from the rest of the landscape: the intensification of the Christian life associated with a deep sense of personal guilt and an overwhelming sense of forgiveness through Christ; the application of preaching to conversion and transformation; the growing conviction of the universal significance of the Christian message (with its inevitable outcome in the missionary movement); the moral radicalism which springs from a sense of personal accountability and the new pattern of church relations which produces both ecumenicity and schism as well as an enlarged conception of ministry and a burgeoning of that organ which the evangelicals transformed, the voluntary society.

Of course problems of definition have arisen and there have been a number of border-line cases. It has thus been necessary to define carefully the term 'evangelical' for the purposes of the dictionary. The four-fold definition which David Bebbington has offered in his work *Evangelicalism in Modern Britain. A History from the 1730s to the 1980s* (London: Unwin Hyman, 1989) has been found to be the most helpful. It encompasses and further clarifies the above-mentioned characteristics and has been the basis for inclusion and exclusion of figures in the dictionary. It has been defined as follows for contributors to this volume:

Evangelical Protestantism was a movement marked by: conversionism (involving a call to personal repentance and moral transformation); crucicentrism (evangelicals have centred their theology on the cross of Christ, the doctrine of the Atonement being central to their theological understanding); biblicism (the Bible being taken as the supreme authority in matters of faith and practice); and activism (a commitment to doing which springs from the moral radicalism rooted in a sense of personal responsibility).

Regarding entries in the dictionary, the label 'evangelical' has been accepted if the person in question: 1) conformed to Bebbington's criteria; or 2) seriously claimed to be an evangelical and identified with evangelicals; or 3) if he/she was clearly recognized as such by an evangelical community or publication. (Caution needs to be exercised here as sometimes evangelicals have claimed sheep not of their fold – as in the twentieth century case of C. S. Lewis.)

Merely exhibiting 'evangelical characteristics' – such as frequent association with evangelicals, participation in evangelical societies, the publication of books, tracts, or articles on topics of peculiar interest to evangelicals or by evangelical publishers or evangelical journals – would not by this definition lead to their inclusion in the dictionary.

Background to this Volume

This volume was first conceived in the mind of Andrew Walls while lecturing in West Africa in the early 1960s. From 1971 Dr Walls, who was by then Professor Walls, and chairman of the Religious Studies Department of the University of Aberdeen, gave the project considerable attention, and established a distinguished committee of British academics to serve as consulting editors. The original work was to be known as the *Biographical Dictionary of the Earlier Evangelical Movement* and focus specifically on British evangelicalism. It was anticipated that the volume would include some 3,170 entries and run to 1,250,000 words. The current volume exceeds this by almost 400 entries and has involved some 360 historians worldwide.

While under the editorship of Professor Walls, much of the day-to-day management of the work was in the hands of Andrew Brockett, the Secretary of the Editorial Board who had done a doctorate in East African colonial studies at Oxford. Standard histories of the evangelical movement in the United Kingdom were consulted in order to establish a preliminary list of subjects, and denominational specialists such as A. Skevington Wood (Wesleyan Methodists) and Oliver Beckerlegge (Free Methodists) acted as advisors on possible entries from specific faith communities. Because the work was to deal with British figures, only evangelicals in colonial America up to the time of the Revolution were to be included.

The committee undertook an exhaustive and exhausting search for possible subjects. The following sources were consulted for other candidates for inclusion: committee lists of the Church Missionary, Baptist Missionary, Wesleyan Missionary, and London Missionary societies; Irish Church Missions Committee; Church of Scotland

Missions; the British and Foreign Bible Society; the London City Mission; the Church Pastoral-Aid Society; the London Society for Promoting Christianity Amongst the Jews; the Railway Navvy Mission; the Canal Mission; the Protestant Reformation Society; the Lord's Day Observance Society; the Protestant Alliance; the Protestant Truth Society; the Religious Tract Society; and the Evangelical Alliance. Lists were compiled of CMS, BMS, and LMS Native Agents and indices of [Plymouth] Brethren figures compiled by H. H. Rowdon and R. Coad were used.

Specific attempts were made to identify figures in the following categories:

Countries: England; Scotland; Ireland; Wales; France; Italy; British India; colonial America
Specific areas of British evangelical strength: the Scottish Highlands; Cheshire; Lancashire; Yorkshire; Bristol and the West Country; Birmingham; Oxford; Cambridge
Occupational groups: architects; artists; the British navy and military; novelists, essayists and litterateurs; musicians; Members of Parliament; peers; public health figures; scientists; Scripture Readers [lay evangelists] in the armed forces; trade unionists; trade-and industry
Publications: *Christian Observer*; *The Eclectic Review*; *The Record*; *The Evangelical Magazine* (for its biographical articles and obituaries); *Banner of Truth*
Denominations: Anglicans; General Baptists; Strict Baptists; Congregationalists; the Countess of Huntingdon's Connection; the Church of Christ; the Church of Scotland; the Free Church of Scotland; Wesleyan Methodists; Primitive Methodists; Free Methodists; Moravians; Quakers; the Plymouth Brethren
Institutions: the universities of Oxford, Cambridge, and Durham; and various Anglican clerical societies (Eclectic, Elland and Matlock Bath).

By 1976 the committee had identified well over 2000 possible entries and commissioned hundreds of articles. By that time, however, the original publisher was re-considering the viability of the whole project. In 1975 Dr Brockett had left the United Kingdom to take up a position at Regent College in Vancouver. With his departure, the committee's work ground to a halt and it was feared that it was all to be in vain. In 1985 Dr Brockett suggested to the writer (who was by then teaching at Regent College) that he attempt a resurrection. Having done doctoral studies at Oxford on nineteenth-century British evangelicals, he was perhaps more aware than most historians of the potential significance of such a volume. He was soon convinced that this work would help to open up the field of evangelical history to a wide range of scholars and interested lay people. With the support and encouragement of Professor Walls, he agreed to take on the task.

The resurrection has been slow in coming. It has, in fact, taken almost ten years to effect. Regretfully only a few score of the original articles survived their burial and the project has had to be re-thought, re-planned and re-financed. Its original scope has been enlarged to include the whole of the English-speaking world rather than just Britain and the American colonies up to the point of American independence; as noted above, key European figures who served as links between the continent to the English-speaking world have also been included.

In order to identify new figures and rank them, some twenty-nine scholars were recruited to serve as specialist editors; among them are several who served on the original editorial committee (Professor Roy Campbell, John Briggs and Professor Arthur Pollard). Other non-British specialists were found to cover specific areas not contemplated in the original volume. The specialist editors listed at the beginning of the volume suggested new entries in their areas of expertise and undertook to read the entries in their fields. To these scholars this editor owes an enormous debt. The value and usefulness of the volume is due in large measure to their willingness to contribute freely of their time and advice. This volume does not claim to be comprehensive. Although strenuous efforts have been made to identify many heretofore unknown figures, some 900 minor figures have had to be excluded simply because of a lack of information. It is hoped that this volume will spur interest in local studies which will provide information on relatively unknown, but often quite important, regional figures.

In preparing the volume and reading and re-reading the hundreds of articles, the editor has been struck by the international connections of a movement which have often not been noticed by historians. Some attention has been given to the Trans-Atlantic evangelical world which existed in the eighteenth and nineteenth centuries but far more study is needed of the role which the evangelicals had in the creation of what has become known as the 'global village', not to mention the pioneering contributions they made to the study of linguistics and anthropology, the development of international trade and inter-cultural exchange.

Books, however, no matter how well conceived and organized, need a publisher. In 1986 the original publisher agreed to hand over all rights of publication to a new publisher provided that an appropriate one could be found. In 1988 Blackwell Publishers of Oxford offered to take on the work provided a substantial subvention could be raised. Altogether the editor has had to come up with a small fortune – well over one hundred thousand dollars in funding – to cover the subvention, the costs of two full-time secretaries for two years, numerous research assistants, travel, office expenses etc. Only an historian somewhat unaware of how much work this would involve would have been willing to take on such a venture!

Acknowledgements

It is with great gratitude that I want to thank two government agencies and the numerous foundations that have had a part in making this volume possible. The Canadian government has been most generous through the Challenge Programme of its Unemployment Insurance programme in funding a host of typists and researchers and also in supplying direct cash grants to support their work. I would especially like to thank the Right Honourable John Turner, for his assistance in securing such assistance and Mr Steve Bujnowicz, for the invaluable help he offered as Project Officer for Employment and Immigration Canada in facilitating the same. The Government of British Columbia is also to be thanked for the help given to the project through the Work/Study programme of the Province's Ministry of Advanced Education.

In terms of private foundations, debts to the following organizations for major gifts are gratefully acknowledged: the Institute for Advanced Christian Studies, Chicago; the Oswald Smith Foundation, Vancouver, British Columbia; the Spring Harvest, East Sussex, England; the Anglican Foundation, Toronto, Ontario; the Kirby Laing Foundation, London, England; the Drummond Trust, Stirling, Scotland; and the Hope Trust, Edinburgh, Scotland. The Cyril W. Black Charitable Trust, of London, England also contributed a modest sum. Furthermore, appreciation needs to be expressed to the Association of Theological Schools in the United States and Canada for a research grant from its Younger Scholars' Program.

Thanks are also due to the administration and to the Board of Governors of Regent College for providing ample office space for the project, excellent support services and for funding one and a half years of sabbatical time over the past eight years. The encouragement of Dr Carl Armerding, the Principal of Regent College and Dr Walter Wright, its current President, have been most appreciated. Members of the Regent staff should also be thanked: Sari Oloffs, Doug Bennett, Sarah Ahmadi, Michael Ho, Mary Lam, Elmer Dyck, and Art Mooney.

Appreciation should also be expressed to the following individuals who worked with me in Vancouver in the many tasks involved in producing this volume: Doug McDonald; Grey Pannell; Greg Dallimore; Greg Sturk; Maureen McKane; Marianna Kavanagh; Heather Reid; Stella Griffin; Joan Ryan; Chi Wing Ho; Hugh Stewart; Karen Kilgore; Kathryn Penner; and Ken Pearson.

I would also like to acknowledge the editorial team at Blackwell Publishers, Oxford for their patience and on-going assistance: Alyn Shipton, Alison Cowan, Sarah McNamee, and Denise Rea, and Carol Lucas, who patiently put hundreds of queries to me in her role as copy editor of this volume.

Special thanks also should be expressed to Professor Reg Ward for acting as my mentor under the Younger Scholars' Program of the Association of Theological Schools and to Andrew Brockett for first suggesting that I take on this task. I also want to thank two friends, both of whom have counselled and encouraged me in this endeavour: David Bebbington of the University of Stirling, and John Wolffe of the Open University.

A penultimate expression of gratitude is due to my supportive and encouraging wife who has herself been busy in the past eight years giving birth to three children.

Finally, I would express my deep and enduring appreciation of two of the most eminent historians of evangelicalism: Andrew Walls and John Walsh. Those who have had the honour of knowing them will fully appreciate why this volume is dedicated to them.

Dr Donald M. Lewis

How To Use This Dictionary

Bibliographies and Select Writings List

A bibliography has been appended to each article. References to articles in important biographical dictionaries are noted by their standard abbreviations. All bibliographical items are listed in alphabetical order by the author's last name or, in the case of standard reference works, by the abbreviation of that work.

Articles normally include a 'Selected Writings List' which provides readers with a guide to their major publications. These precede the Bibliographies.

Cross References

Figures in this volume have been extensively cross-referenced and these are indicated by SMALL CAPS the first time they appear within an article.

Figures who were known by more than one name are normally listed under both names (or in some cases more than two names). Readers are then directed to the heading under which the article appears.

Index

A full index of the figures by country of association, by denomination(s) and occupation has been included.

Place Names

Original place names have normally been used in this dictionary; for instance, the names of historic British counties have been employed. The abbreviation 'BNA' has been used to designate 'British North America' – which is intended as a generic descriptor for Britain's colonial holdings in North America prior to the American Revolution, and Canadian independence.

A

A.L.O.E. [A Lady of England] *See* TUCKER, CHARLOTTE MARIA

Abbott, Benjamin Jr (b. NJ, BNA, 1732; d. Salem, NJ, USA, 14 Aug. 1796). Methodist itinerant. He was the son of Benjamin Abbott, a wealthy landowner and Hannah Burroughs, both of whom died when Abbott was a boy. In accordance with his father's will, he was apprenticed to a hat-maker in Philadelphia, but left this to work on a plantation in southern New Jersey. He then purchased his own farm and married.

About 1765 he was troubled by a frightful dream which led to a short-lived religious interest. In 1772 his wife attended a Methodist meeting and persuaded him to join her. Abbott's dream returned to haunt him and was instrumental in his conversion, which was effected through the preaching of Abraham Whitworth, an English Methodist itinerant. This was soon followed by the conversion of his wife and six of their children. Abbott began immediately to itinerate and pioneered Methodist societies in New Jersey, Pennsylvania, Maryland and Delaware. He played a particularly important role in the expansion of Methodism during the American Revolution, being one of its most effective evangelists.

He served as a local preacher rather than as a recognized itinerant until April 1789 when he was received into the travelling ministry of the New Jersey conference; he was made Deacon in 1790 and Elder in 1793. Appointed to the Dutchess Circuit in New York state, he saw it grow from a handful of members to over 1300 in sixteen months. He continued to plant new Methodist societies in New York, Connecticut, New Jersey, Pennsylvania, Delaware and Maryland.

BIBLIOGRAPHY
AAP 7: 41–6
E. S. Bucke, et al, *History of American Methodism* (Nashville, 1964) 1: 43
EWM
J. Firrth, *Experience and Gospel Labours of the Rev. Benjamin Abbott* (New York, 1830)

DONALD M. LEWIS

Abdul Masih [Sheikh Salih] (b. Delhi, India, *c.* 1776; d. Agra, Uttar Pradesh, India, 27 March 1827). Notable Muslim convert, preacher, and scholar. Son of a Lucknow munshi and learned in Persian and Arabic, Abdul Masih served the King of Oude as custodian of the court jewels. Upset by a political murder, he went to his father in Kanpur. There he met HENRY MARTYN, whose neighbour his father was teaching. Martyn took him to DAVID BROWN, who baptized him in Calcutta.

Abdul Masih declined to accept a catechist's post until properly instructed, and instead worked for DANIEL CORRIE. Being ordained by Lutheran Church Missionary Society missionaries in Chinsurah gave him recognition and protection from persecution. In December 1813 he baptized 41 adults and 14 children in Agra, the first of many converts. His commentaries on Matthew, Romans and Hebrews were widely circulated. When Bishop Heber met Abdul Masih, he was so impressed that he ordained him in Agra. He died singing one of his own Hindustani hymns.

Although criticized by European missionaries as lethargic (he was overweight and frequently ill), Abdul Masih nevertheless gained access to Begum Sumroo and rulers in other important Muslim courts. His contribution as the first Indian Anglican priest in North India cannot be overestimated.

BIBLIOGRAPHY
CMS archives, University of Birmingham, England, letters and journal
Rajaiah Paul, *Triumphs of His Grace* (CLS Madras, 1967)

E. M. JACKSON

Abdy, William Jarvis (b. 1755; d. Horsley Down, Surrey, England, 16 April 1823). Anglican clergyman. Abdy graduated from Magdalene Hall, Oxford (BA 1779) and became Curate of Staines (Middlesex) (1778–80). He was lecturer at All Hallows, Lombard Street (1781) and later evening lecturer at St Mary-le-Bow, Cheapside (1800), but his main work was at St John's, Horsley Down, Southwark, for many years as curate (1782–1805) and then as rector (1805–23). He transferred to King's College, Cambridge for his MA degree (1794). He was an early member of the EcS (1783) and also of the CMS.

BIBLIOGRAPHY
Al. Cant., II.i: 3
C. Hole, *Early History of the CMS* (London, 1896)

ARTHUR POLLARD

Abeel, David (b. New Brunswick, NJ, USA, 12 June 1804; d. Albany, NY, USA, 4 Sept. 1846). Pioneer American missionary to China and south-east Asia. Abeel was associated with the Dutch Reformed Church in America. Completing religious instruction in the Theological Seminary at New Brunswick, New Jersey, in 1826, he was sent by the Seamen's Friend Society in 1829 as chaplain for foreign sailors at Canton. Until 1833 he reconnoitred south-east Asia for the ABCFM, preaching and distributing Christian tracts. In China again by 1839, he witnessed the Opium War and established a mission in Amoy, one of the new treaty ports, where he served until 1844. There he supplied Governor Hsü Chi-yü with maps and geographical information which helped Chinese interest in the geopolitical dimensions of the world outside China. He returned to America in 1845, his health shattered. Condemning female infanticide and footbinding in China, he helped inspire the formation of the Society for Promoting Female Education in the East (London, 1834) and the Woman's Board of the (Dutch) Reformed Church in America.

SELECT WRITINGS

D. Abeel, *Journal of a Residence in China* (New York, 1834)

BIBLIOGRAPHY

F. W. Drake, *China Charts the World* (Cambridge, MA, 1975)
G. R. Williamson, *Memoir of the Rev. David Abeel* (New York, 1848)

FRED W. DRAKE

Abington, Leonard James (b. London, 27 Nov. 1785; d. Hanley, Staffordshire, England, 7 Aug. 1867). Baptist minister and pottery manufacturer. A modeller and ceramic designer, he assisted Benjamin Wyatt in the decoration of Drury Lane Theatre after the fire of 1809, and was entrusted by Sir John Soane with much of the ornamental detail on the Bank of England, but his unwillingness to undertake Sunday work limited his career development. His grandmother had been a convert of GEORGE WHITEFIELD, but his father adopted Baptist views. In 1807, he married the daughter of a deacon at the Hammersmith Baptist Church where he had been baptized, but within a year he was a widower. He subsequently became a deacon of the Little Wild Street Church, marrying again in 1811. Advised to leave London for health reasons, in 1819 he took up employment in the potteries with Jacob Phillips, formerly a deacon at Little Wild Street. In 1820, with Phillips, he re-opened the Baptist chapel in Hanley which had been closed for 16 years, preaching regularly both there and in Burslem, as indeed also for the Congregationalists and the Methodists. He was also associated with the opening of the Baptist Chapel in neighbouring Newcastle-under-Lyme in the midst of the cholera crisis of 1832, and, on the urging of EDWARD IRVING, accepted the pastorate for some four years, until persuaded by the Hanley church to become pastor. He retired in 1863, after some 340 members had been added to the roll, but numbers remained modest because emigration caused continued depletion. Both pastorates were served gratuitously. For a period from 1824, as editor of the liberal newspaper, *The Pottery Mercury*, he was an advocate of political change; he also sought the abolition of Dissenter's disabilities, and the iniquities of the truck system, and more positively supported the work of the Society for the Diffusion of Useful Knowledge, contributing to the production of *The Penny Cyclopedia*. Along with other pottery manufacturers he was an active member of the Pottery Philosophical Society, and both wrote and lectured on a wide range of scholarly topics, welcoming advances in geology, assured that 'the investigations of Science would strengthen rather than weaken the evidence of Inspiration'. He also lectured at the Mechanics' Institute of which he was a founder and in 1836 helped to bring a lengthy strike in the pottery industry to an end. He worked for Phillips's successor, Joseph Mayer, up to 1831 when he entered into partnership with William Ridgway, and later his son, until his retirement in 1860, having benefited from a bequest of almost £10,000 in Joseph Mayer's will. Abington exercised a deep interest in the establishment of the EA, was one of the founders of the Hanley branch of the RTS, and with Josiah Wedgwood II and JOHN RIDGWAY of the Hanley auxiliary of the Bible Society, becoming a life governor of the parent society. He was also influential in establishing the Pottery auxiliary of the Sunday School Union which he served as president.

BIBLIOGRAPHY

Anon., *Personal Recollections of the Late Leonard James Abington of Hanley, Staffordshire* (Hanley, England, 1868)
D. Stuart, ed., *People of the Potteries* (Keele, England, 1985)

J. H. Y. BRIGGS

Acland, Sir **Thomas (Dyke)** (b. Porlock, Somerset, England, 29 March 1787; d. Broadclyst, Devon, England, 22 July 1871). Landowner, philanthropist and MP. At age seven, on the death of his father, Acland inherited his family's West Country estates. All his life, he was greatly influenced by the family chaplain, Joshua Stephenson, who was unmoved by the 'enthusiasm' (as he saw it) of the evangelicals or later by the Tractarians. Acland's mother, Henrietta, did not like evangelicals, believing they 'had a particular starch look' which marked them out the moment they came into a room. She believed that HANNAH MORE had a 'scrutinizing artful countenance' and was 'rather vulgar' in manner. However, she approved of his choice of Lydia Hoare (a third cousin) as his wife. Lydia's brother William lived on Clapham Common and her father, HENRY HOARE, though not himself a member of the Clapham Sect, was a friend of WILLIAM WILBERFORCE, HENRY THORNTON and Hannah More.

Acland went up to Christ Church, Oxford, in 1806; his mother wrote to him regularly with instructions including 'evangelicals must be avoided'; but to the end of his life he took no notice of this advice. Acland married Lydia in April 1808, and told his father-in-law that he was anxious 'to form a course in life which a wise man would not repent and which a Christian would not fear'.

Acland's lifelong friend, Sir ROBERT HARRY INGLIS, was close to the Clapham Sect and through him and the Hoare family, Acland developed a close friendship with Wilberforce and Henry Thornton. Unlike his mother, he admired Hannah More and it was through her that he met Alexander Knox, an unusually open-minded and influential Irish theologian, who with his friend Bishop Jebb of Limerick was a forerunner of the Tractarians.

In October 1812 Acland was elected Tory MP for Devon; he frequently upset his constituents by taking an independent line in the Commons. He spoke earnestly in favour of Catholic emancipation; against the extravagance of the Royal family; for LORD ASHLEY's factory acts; and against the slave trade which still flourished outside British territory.

Acland's main preoccupation in the 1820s was religious liberty and he applied his love of tolerance equally to Catholics and Nonconformists. At his estate at Killerton, Devon, Protestant and Catholic servants knelt together for family prayers. His missionary interests led him to support both the CMS and the SPG as well as the African Civilization Society. When Wilberforce retired from Parliament in 1825, Sir Walter Scott dubbed Acland the 'leader of the religious party in the House of Commons'. When he championed the cause of Catholic emancipation, an evangelical friend cut down Acland's picture from the wall, and Hannah More spoke severely of her 'recreant Knight'.

Acland's sons were all influenced by the Tractarians and this caused tension in the home, greatly distressing Lady Lydia, but not the tolerant Acland. He appreciated the religious verse of Keble but believed that Pusey and J. H. NEWMAN tended too strongly towards Rome. By the early 1840s, however, Acland was regarded by conservative Anglican evangelicals as having embraced Tractarianism. In 1845 he supported the controversial Maynooth Grant and he was one of only six MPs who publicly favoured state endowment of Roman Catholic clergy. In 1847 the evangelical *Record* newspaper expressed its earnest hope for his defeat in the general election. In spite of such a chilly reception among evangelicals, Acland continued his public support of the CMS.

In 1858, two years after his wife's sudden death, he withdrew from Parliament. Within three years the citizens of Exeter erected a statue to him which still stands in Northernhay Gardens.

BIBLIOGRAPHY
A. Acland, *A Devon Family* (Chichester, England, 1981)
Churchman's Monthly Review (December 1843)
DNB
Record (6 May 1843); (20 May 1847); (4 May 1854)

ROGER STEER AND DONALD M. LEWIS

Acrelius, Israel (b. Sweden, 1714; d. Sweden, 1800). Swedish Lutheran clergyman, ecclesiastical overseer of Swedish Lutherans in America, 1749–56, and historian of Swedes in colonial America. The Swedish Lutheran Consistory sent Acrelius to serve Swedish congregations at Racoon and Penns Neck in New Jersey in 1748. Reluctant to accept the post because of his lack of knowledge of English, he struggled to learn to preach in that tongue. He sought to stem the Anglicization of Swedes in the middle colonies and to deal with the disruptive influence of Swedish Moravians. Acrelius also made serious overtures to German Lutheran pastors in Pennsylvania with a 1751 oration (in Latin) on the unity of the spirit and a treatise two years later on the history of German Lutherans in Pennsylvania (also in Latin). The Lutheran Ministerium responded by electing him its presiding officer. Chronic ill health prompted his request to return to Sweden, finally granted in 1756. There he wrote his *History of New Sweden*, still a valuable source on religious and ethnic pluralism in the middle colonies.

SELECT WRITINGS
I. Acrelius, *History of New Sweden* (Philadelphia, PA, 1874)

BIBLIOGRAPHY
S. Geissler, *Lutheranism and Anglicanism in Colonial New Jersey* (Lewiston, NY, 1988)

ROBERT CALHOON

Acworth, James (b. Chatham, Kent, England, 1 Aug. 1798; d. Scarborough, Yorkshire, England, 13 Oct. 1883). Baptist minister and college principal. The eldest of the children of William Acworth, a prosperous businessman and Baptist deacon, he was educated from the age of eight at a boarding-school at Tenterden in Kent. He went to Bristol Baptist College in 1817 and then Glasgow University, where he took his MA (the university later awarded him an LL D). He was co-pastor and then in sole charge of the first Baptist church in Leeds from 1823. A new chapel was erected in South Parade and the church grew considerably. In 1835 he succeeded Dr WILLIAM STEADMAN as principal of the Baptist Academy in Bradford. As well as teaching theology he raised the general academic standard of ministerial training, improved the financial base, and led the move to the new college at Rawdon in 1859. Always a champion of religious freedom, Acworth opposed church rates and contended with equal earnestness for Roman Catholic emancipation and, surprisingly for those days, maintained that the state had no right in any way to enforce the observance of the Lord's Day. He was at the first meetings of what became the Liberation Society. He served as president of the Bradford Mechanics' Institute, on the committee of the BMS and is the only person to have served as president of the Baptist Union four times. Retiring to Scarborough in 1863 he was instrumental in forming a new Baptist church on open-communion principles and was the chairman of the first School

Board. Several of his sermons and addresses were published.

BIBLIOGRAPHY
Baptist Handbook 1884: 279–81
E. C. Starr, ed., *A Baptist Bibliography*, 25 vols (New York, 1947–76)

DAVID B. MILNER

Adam, George   (b. Glasgow, Scotland; d. Cathcart, Scotland, 6 April 1759). Minister of Cathcart (1738–59) and participated in the 1742 Cambuslang revival. He assisted GEORGE WHITEFIELD and WILLIAM MCCULLOCH at the second Communion of the summer of 1742, that of 15 August. He was deposed for immoral conduct in 1746, but his elders sought the removal of the sentence because of 'his exemplary character and great usefulness' and he was resettled in 1748.

BIBLIOGRAPHY
Fasti, 3
A. Fawcett, *The Cambuslang Revival* (London, 1971)

JOHN R. MCINTOSH

Adam, Thomas   (b. Leeds, England, 25 Feb. 1701; d. 31 March 1784). Anglican evangelical minister. The son of the town clerk of Leeds, educated there and in Wakefield, and Hart Hall, Oxford, Adam completed his BA in 1724 and became Vicar of the parish of Wintringham, Lincolnshire. Adam had a formal faith until 1736 when he read William Law's mystical writings. Then in 1748 his biblical study led him to an evangelical faith. After contact with SAMUEL WALKER in the 1750s he was drawn into a network of Anglican evangelical clergy and had a significant influence through his *Practical Lectures on the Church Catechism, Evangelical Sermons* and *Paraphrases and Annotations on ... St Paul's Epistle to the Romans*. His 'Private thoughts on religion' greatly influenced Coleridge. JOHN WESLEY consulted Adam about the legitimacy of itineracy in September 1755, but Adam stoutly defended the parochial system, and was deeply suspicious of perfectionism, although he rejected final perseverance.

SELECT WRITINGS
T. Adam, *An Exposition of the Four Gospels* (London, 1837)

BIBLIOGRAPHY
DNB

PETER J. LINEHAM

Adams, Newton   (b. East Bloomfield, NY, USA, 4 Aug. 1804; d. Amanzimtoti, Natal, South Africa, 16 Sept. 1851). American missionary doctor and educationalist. Trained as a doctor he went, having had no theological training, to South Africa with the pioneer ABCFM party.

His first mission was at Umlazi near Durban, where, in addition to medical work, he and his wife taught school for both children and adults. Because of the clash between the Afrikaner and the Zulu in 1838, he left Natal temporarily, but returned as soon as the situation allowed. In 1844 he was ordained, still without any formal theological training, and in 1847 founded what was to become Adams College at Amanzimtoti.

BIBLIOGRAPHY
R. Sheils, 'Newton Adams: Missionary in Natal 1835–1851', in *Historia* (December 1964)

ANDREW C. ROSS

Adams, Thomas   (b. probably Minchinhampton, Gloucestershire, England; d. August 1770). Whitefieldite itinerant. Adams was converted when GEORGE WHITEFIELD preached at Minchinhampton in Gloucestershire, his home village, about 1739, and became a lay preacher. He attended Whitefield's first English Association in 1743 and was employed as an exhorter even in Ireland, but particularly in Gloucestershire. He was a blunt evangelist, and some hearers responded violently, notably a mob which attacked his house at Minchinhampton in July 1743. Adams remained loyal to Whitefield when other preachers left the connexion, but he was drawn to seek a licence as a dissenting minister when the law failed to protect him in the Exeter riot of June 1745. His ministry became more local as the English Association collapsed, focused in the tabernacle he built at Rodborough, Gloucestershire, in 1750. However, Whitefield regularly preached in this circuit, while Adams occasionally supplied the tabernacle in London. His simple faith, earnestness and lack of doctrinal peculiarities made him popular among Calvinist Methodists. He wrote *The Character of the Almost and Altogether Christian* (1745). He was married twice, the second time in 1767 to his faithful servant. Whitefield left £50 to 'dear Tommy' in his will, but in fact Adams had pre-deceased him by one month.

BIBLIOGRAPHY
G. F. Nuttall, 'Rowland Hill and the Rodborough Connexion, 1771–1833', in Congregational History Society *Transactions*, 21, 3 (1972): 69–73.
C. E. Watson, 'Whitefield and Congregationalism', in Congregational History Society *Transactions*, 8, 4 (1922): 171–80; 8, 5 (1922): 237–45.

PETER J. LINEHAM

Adger, John Bailey   (b. Charleston, SC, USA, 1810; d. 1899). Presbyterian minister and missionary. One of the most influential leaders within southern Presbyterianism in the nineteenth century, Adger experienced a conversion while at Union College in 1826. After graduating from Princeton Theological Seminary, he and his wife went as missionaries through the agency of the ABCFM to the Armenian people in the Middle East from 1834 to 1846. When his wife inherited slaves, they returned to Charleston, South Carolina, where Adger organized and served a congregation of blacks. He also was professor of church history and polity at Columbia Theological Seminary from 1857 to 1874 and editor of the *Southern Presbyterian Review* from 1857 to 1885. Together with R. J. Breckinridge and J. H. THORNWELL, Adger was an advocate of *jure divino* presbyterianism and of the spirituality of the church, believing that the Bible offered explicit instruction as to the structure, governance, mandate and limits of the church's activities.

SELECT WRITINGS
J. B. Adger, *My Life and Times* (Richmond, VA, 1888)

BIBLIOGRAPHY
E. T. Thompson, *Presbyterians in the South*, 3 vols (Richmond, VA, 1963–73)

STEVEN R. POINTER

Adley, Wilson (b. Canterbury, Kent, England, *c.* 1790; d. 1887). CMS missionary to Ceylon (Sri Lanka). Adley studied (*c.*1819–23) as a probationer missionary under HENRY GAUNTLETT before being ordained (deacon 21 December 1823, priest 25 April 1824). In May of 1824 he was sent to Nellore, Ceylon and returned to England in February 1840 following the death of his wife (Lucy Coles, died June 1839). In 1841 he married Catherine Theodore Gauntlett and they returned to Ceylon. In March 1846 the Adleys returned to England and ended their association with the CMS. In 1857 Adley became Rector of Rudbaxton, Pembrokeshire, Wales.

BIBLIOGRAPHY
D. T. B[arry], *CMS Register of Missionaries and Native Clergy* (privately printed) (London, 1906)

DONALD M. LEWIS

Adlington, John (b. England; d. *c.* 1875) CMS missionary to north India. Adlington was apparently an orphan raised by the Reverend DANIEL CORRIE. On 14 April 1817 he was sent with L. BERNARD, E. SCHMID and DEOCAR SCHMID to India, proceeding to Benares where he was headmaster of Jay Narain's School. He was ordained by the Bishop of Calcutta (deacon 21 December 1825, priest 1828) but returned to England in 1828 and withdrew from the CMS. From 1832 to 1839 he served as chaplain to Worcester County Gaol and from 1839 to 1875 as chaplain of Worcester Union. There is no record of his having been married.

BIBLIOGRAPHY
D. T. B[arry], *CMS Register of Missionaries and Native Clergy* (privately printed) (London, 1906)

DONALD M. LEWIS

Agnew, Sir **Andrew** (b. Kinsale, Ireland, 21 March 1793; d. Edinburgh, Scotland, 12 April 1849). Landowner and MP. Agnew succeeded his grandfather as seventh baronet of Lochnaw in Wigtownshire, Scotland, in 1809. The estates he inherited had been neglected, and in 1821 Agnew had decided to go to live on the continent as an economy measure when he felt divinely led to live on his property. Until 1830 he devoted his time and resources to its improvement. In 1830 he became MP for Wigtownshire, supported the Reform Bill of 1832, and held the seat until 1837. Agnew was the first chairman of the Scottish Society for Promoting the Due Observance of the Lord's Day and he became the parliamentary leader of all measures to promote Sunday observance. He proposed a select committee of the House of Commons to examine the issue in 1832 and became its chairman but his annual attempts to secure the passage of a Bill to prohibit all labour on Sunday except on works of necessity and mercy did not succeed. Agnew continued to promote Sunday observance as strenuously after leaving Parliament, notably in trying to prevent the running of trains on Sundays. He bought shares in railway companies and exercised his rights as a shareholder to achieve his end, though with limited success.

Agnew was a leading supporter of the EA. His denominational affiliations were fluid. He was brought up in the Church of Ireland and always regarded himself as belonging to the Church of England. After the Disruption of the Church of Scotland in 1843, an event he deemed to be a deplorable necessity, he became an active supporter of the FCS.

BIBLIOGRAPHY
T. McCrie, *Memoirs of Sir Andrew Agnew of Lochnaw, Bart.* (London, 1850)

R. H. CAMPBELL

Aikman, John (b. Borrowstoneness, West Lothian, Scotland, 1759; d. Edinburgh, 6 Feb. 1834). Independent evangelist and pastor. As a young man Aikman went to Jamaica for a number of years. He was converted there and returned to Edinburgh to study divinity. Impatient to preach, he joined JAMES A. HALDANE in field preaching at Gilmerton, outside Edinburgh, and then accompanied him in travels in the Highlands and Islands in 1797 and 1798. He preached at the Circus, and in 1802, at his own expense he built a chapel in North College Street, Edinburgh, the predecessor of the present Augustine Church. He ministered there until his death without stipend. He also taught classes in Haldane's Academy, and continued to itinerate. For some years he edited the *Missionary Magazine*, and in 1800 helped edit a hymn-book for the tabernacle connection. He was instrumental in founding many congregational churches throughout Scotland.

BIBLIOGRAPHY
R. Kinniburgh, *Fathers of Independency in Scotland* (Edinburgh, 1851)

H. Escott, *A History of Scottish Congregationalism* (Glasgow, 1960)

W. McNaughton, *The Scottish Congregational Yearbook* (Glasgow, 1993)

DEREK B. MURRAY

Aitken, Robert (b. Crailing, Roxburgh, Scotland, 22 Jan. 1800; d. London, 11 July 1873). Anglican clergyman and pastoral evangelist. Aitken, the younger son of Crailing's schoolmaster, attended Jedburgh Grammar School and Edinburgh University. Having left Presbyterianism, he was ordained by the Bishop of Durham (Van Mildert) in 1823 to become Curate of Whitburn, near Sunderland, where he was teaching with success in the school his brother had founded. His wife's tubercular condition soon led him to a light-load curacy in the Isle of Man, where he became a gentleman farmer. In 1828 an evangelical conversion raised him to great heights of joyful assurance and evangelistic zeal. Plunging into aggressive evangelism, he preached for Methodists and after 1836 in his own chapels in London and Liverpool. In the 1830s he was England's premier evangelist, travelling widely and seeing thousands of 'Aitkenite' converts. Convinced, however, that his freelancing was schismatic to a degree, he returned to the Church of England, prepared to endure the three-year prohibition on his preaching in public that was then the standard discipline in cases like his. This requirement of silence was, however, waived in his case, and after brief parochial stints in Liverpool, Perranuthnoe (Cornwall), Leeds and Coatbridge near Glasgow, he became the first incumbent of the new parish of Pendeen, located in tin-mining country outside Penzance near Land's End. He served there for a quarter of a century, periodically emerging, however, to lead Anglican parishes in revivalist 'missions' (a term borrowed from Roman sources) that centred upon 'conversion work' through preaching and personal counselling. This type of event became increasingly common in England after 1850. Aitken dropped dead on Paddington platform while waiting for the train that would return him to West Cornwall after one such mission.

A big man of imposing presence and arresting sincerity, endowed with a vast bass voice, Spurgeonic resources of eloquence, a leader-like style and a majestically impetuous temperament, the mature Aitken had three passions: evangelism, holiness and unity. In the 1840s, as an admirer of JOHN HENRY NEWMAN, he framed his Methodist understanding of conversion as a journey into Christ-centred assurance with the Tractarian ideal of (1) dignity in worship; (2) the centrality of sacraments (baptism requiring conversion, and Holy Communion sustaining fellowship with Christ); (3) a distinctive and demanding clerical spirituality (he wore skull-cap and cassock in his Cornish parish, and would spend whole days in church praying for his people); and (4) goodwill towards Rome. His 'High Church evangelical' identity, which set him at a distance from both the evangelical party in the Church of England and the interdenominational EA, gave him entry into Anglican circles where the call to conversion rarely penetrated.

He was warm towards Cornish Methodists like WILLIAM (BILLY) BRAY, mentored the high-and-dry Tractarian clergyman WILLIAM HASLAM into evangelical vitality, fathered W. H. Hay Aitken, a tireless Anglican evangelist who preached over 23,000 sermons and, energetically helped by his second wife, a formidable daughter of a Scottish laird, kept his parsonage an open-house retreat centre for the spiritually needy. Waves of revival in his own congregation were frequent and powerful, and an organized band of lay helpers maintained ministry to all the parish's 3,000 inhabitants. Justification by faith, as the truth that shapes personal conversion, and the life of regeneration in union with Christ, were the staple themes of his teaching. His volume, *The Prayer Book Unveiled ...* (2nd edn 1867), sought to show Nonconformists that these doctrines are the dual focus of Anglican Prayer Book Christianity, in particular of the sacramental services. He lived and died a controversial figure within the Anglican spectrum, but a totally loyal churchman and a contented one.

BIBLIOGRAPHY
DNB
W. H. Haslam, *From Death into Life* (London, 1894)
D. Voll, *Catholic Evangelicalism* (London, 1963)
C. E. Woods, *Memoirs and Letters of Canon Hay Aitken* (London, 1928)

J. I. PACKER

Albright, Jacob (b. Fox Mountain, PA, BNA, 1 May 1759; d. Kleinfeltersville, PA, USA, 18 May 1808). Founder of the Evangelical Association. Albright grew up among German Lutherans near Pottstown, Pennsylvania and joined the Bergstrasse Lutheran Church in Lancaster County following his marriage to Catherine Cope in 1785. He quickly established himself as a successful farmer and tile manufacturer, earning the nickname 'the honest Tiler' for his trustworthy business practices.

The major turning point in Albright's life occurred in 1791 following the death of several of his children. Mired in deep depression, he found solace in the evangelical message and experienced a dramatic conversion in July 1791 under the spiritual tutelage of Adam Riegel, a lay preacher of the United Brethren in Christ. Albright was immediately impressed with his own need for Christian fellowship and his German neighbours' need for evangelical preaching. He joined the local Methodist class meeting and became a licensed Methodist exhorter in 1796.

Over the next 12 years, Albright evangelized widely among the German-speaking settlers of Pennsylvania, Maryland, and Virginia. His preaching emphasized conversion and the Wesleyan doctrine of entire sanctification. Convinced, however, that there was little place for his converts within the MEC, he began organizing them into separate classes in 1800. In 1803 Albright's followers ordained him a minister; four years later they held their first annual meeting and elected him bishop. Within another six months, Albright died, probably of tuberculosis. But the group he had founded carried on and developed into the denomination known in the nineteenth century as 'The Evangelical Association'.

BIBLIOGRAPHY
R. W. Albright, *A History of the Evangelical Church* (Harrisburg, PA, 1942)
J. B. Behney and P. H. Eller, *The History of the Evangelical United Brethren Church* (Nashville, TN, 1979)

RICHARD W. POINTER

Alden, Timothy (b. Yarmouth, MA, USA, 28 Aug. 1781; d. Pittsburgh, PA, USA, 5 July 1839). Congregationalist educator and missionary to Indians. After graduating from Harvard College in 1794 Alden taught school for some years and served from 1799 to 1805 as assistant pastor of the South Congregational Church in Portsmouth, New Hampshire. Resigning this ordained post, he proved to be an exceptionally gifted teacher during the next ten years. He dreamed of founding an institution of higher learning on the western frontier, and in 1815 he settled in Meadville, Pennsylvania, where he organized Allegheny College with himself as president. Instruction began two years later with students meeting in the president's house, but financial hardship plagued the fledgling school. Alden travelled extensively to raise funds and collect books, eventually producing a library of 7,000 volumes. Every summer he also evangelized among Seneca Indians, a tribe of the Iroquois League, and the Munsi Indians, a branch of the Delawares. In 1827 a series of his letters was printed as *An Account of Sundry Missions Performed Among the Senecas and Munsees*. Problems with the college continued to mount, however, and in 1831 Alden was forced to close it and turn to anticlimactic work in a number of boarding-schools. Always interested in history, he helped organize the American Antiquarian Society, served occasionally as librarian for the Massachusetts Historical Society, and prepared a library catalogue for the New York Historical Society.

BIBLIOGRAPHY
AAP
DAB
NCAB

HENRY WARNER BOWDEN

Alder, Robert (b. England, 1796; d. Gibraltar, 31 Dec. 1873). Methodist minister and Anglican clergyman. Sent out as a Wesleyan missionary in 1816 to combat New Light teaching in the Maritimes, Alder arrived at Yarmouth, Nova Scotia, and served in the Maritimes and Lower Canada until 1827. He then returned to England to become a secretary of the WMMS (1833–51) with primary responsibility for British North America. In 1847 he helped bring about, after much trial, a permanent union of the MEC (Upper Canada) and the English Wesleyan Methodist Conference. He was then made first president of the Canada Conference. Alder played important roles in founding Mount Allison University (1839) and in the North West mission (1840). Habitually deferential to the Anglican establishment, an admirer of its liturgy, and politically conservative, it is perhaps not surprising that in 1853 he fled Wesleyanism for ordination in the Church of England. He retired, much respected, as Canon of Holy Trinity Cathedral at Gibraltar.

BIBLIOGRAPHY
DCB

JONATHAN BURKE CUTMORE

Aldersey, Mary Ann (b. London, 24 June 1797; d. Adelaide, Australia, 30 Sept. 1868). Pioneer woman missionary in China. Born into an Anglican home, her parents attended JOHN EYRE's church but following Eyre's death helped to found a Congregational church with JOHN PYE SMITH as its first pastor. As a young woman Aldersey became interested in the China missions when ROBERT MORRISON took up residence in her neighbourhood of Hackney when on leave in 1824. Aldersey's interest drove her to contribute and to seek contributions for the China missions.

While soliciting funds, Aldersey was challenged to become a missionary herself. Her father refused permission for her to embark on such a seemingly perilous mission. Her departure was further delayed in 1832 following the death of her sister-in-law; between 1832 and 1837 she put aside her desires to be a missionary in order to care for her nieces and nephews until their father's remarriage. Aldersey finally began her missionary career in Batavia in 1837.

In 1843, Aldersey settled in Ningpo, China, where she began a 16-year career which included operating a school for Chinese girls, holding Bible classes, and distributing tracts. Aldersey differed from most missionaries not only by the fact that she was a single woman but because she belonged to no missionary society. As a personality she was formidable, eccentric, difficult and influential. She was the prototype for women missionaries who would become the mainstay of British and American missionary societies. Her epitaph was singularly appropriate: 'Why don't you go yourself?' In 1857 she retired to Australia to join her nieces who had opened a girls' school.

BIBLIOGRAPHY
E. Aldersey White, *A Woman Pioneer in China* (London, 1932)
CWM
J. C. Pollock, *Hudson Taylor and Maria* (London, 1962)

JEAN PAQUETTE

Aldis, John (b. Colchester, Essex, England, 11 May 1808; d. Frome, Somerset, England, 27 Sept. 1907). English Baptist minister. Of devout Congregational parentage, he became a Baptist by being set the task of answering the Baptist position in the Mutual Improvement Society attached to WHITEFIELD's Tabernacle. He persuaded his audience but failed to persuade himself. He was baptized at the Spencer Place Church soon after his seventeenth birthday and was persuaded by the Reverend John Peacock of the Maze Pond Church to train for the ministry. This he did at Horton College, where he adopted open-communion views, later marrying the daughter of the president, Dr WILLIAM STEADMAN – the kind of lady, it is recorded, who revelled in reading Mansel's Bampton Lectures on *The Limits to Religious Thought* – thereafter settling to a first pastorate in Manchester in 1830–7.

In 1837 he moved to the historic church at Maze Pond, near London Bridge, where he exercised an influential, gracious and elegant ministry. His son testified to the excellence of the congregational singing and the high intellectual and social character of many members of the congregation, only rivalled at that time by JOHN H. HINTON's congregation at Devonshire Square, north of the river. For much of this pastorate the Aldis family lived out on the Shirley Hills some miles out of London and the minister had therefore to complete all his pastoral duties between Saturday and Wednesday. He was one of the first to welcome C. H. SPURGEON on his arrival at the neighbouring church in New Park Street: in the middle of the Downgrade controversy Spurgeon specifically identified Aldis as one with whom he had no quarrel.

In 1853 Aldis moved to Reading and ministered there for 15 years. It was during this pastorate that his three sons caused something of a stir by being denied fellowships at Cambridge on account of their Nonconformity, notwithstanding their distinguished academic achievements, cases all too eagerly taken up by the Liberation Society. Vitally involved in the work of the Baptist Union, he was called to its presidency in 1866. A long life enabled him to ponder whether Baptists, in reacting against the rise of Tractarianism, had not made an idol of 'individualism, independence and freedom' at the expense of proper church order. His ministerial career concluded with nine years at George Street, Plymouth, where it was argued 'he did his best work'. In retirement he visited the Baptist mission in north India at the request of the BMS whose activities he had long supported.

BIBLIOGRAPHY
Baptist Handbook (London, 1908)
'Reminiscences of the Revd John Aldis', *BQ* V (London, 1930)

J. H. Y. BRIGGS

Aldred, John (b. Stutton, Suffolk, England, 12 Feb. 1818; d. Christchurch, New Zealand, 14 Jan. 1894). WMMS missionary to New Zealand. Brought up an Anglican, Aldred was converted among the Wesleyans and began preaching at 16. Well educated, he taught for a short period before ordination (4 September 1839) and joining the Wesleyan mission in New Zealand in 1840. He was the first Wesleyan minister to both Maoris and settlers in Wellington, Nelson and Canterbury provinces. His wife was a daughter of WALTER LAWRY.

Initially he was based in Te Aro Maor settlement in Wellington. Transferring to the European settlements, in both Nelson (1843) and Canterbury (1854) he established churches and schools. In addition he served at Hutt (1848), Wellington (1860) and Dunedin (1864). In the latter place he travelled extensively on the goldfields. An accident necessitated retirement (1867) in which he served as secretary of the district for 25 years, hospital visitor, advocate for the BFBS and the Women's Refuge.

BIBLIOGRAPHY
Scholefield

W. A. CHAMBERS

Aldridge, William (b. Warminster, Wiltshire, England, 1737; d. London, 28 Feb. 1797). Evangelical minister. He was born at Warminster, and sent to Trevecka College by Lady HUNTINGDON in 1768 when it opened. He unsuccessfully sought episcopal ordination in 1771, and was sent by Lady Huntingdon to Margate with Joseph Cook. Their evangelical activities in Kent were very successful. A number of connexion chapels were opened, and Aldridge took over a moribund Presbyterian meeting house at Dover with considerable success.

From Kent he was sent to Mulberry Gardens chapel in London about 1775. When Lady Huntingdon attempted to move him elsewhere, he left the connexion and became minister of the Independent congregation at Jewry Street. There he remained until his death in 1797. His reputation as a preacher was great, but he has left few printed works by which his sermons can be judged.

BIBLIOGRAPHY
DNB
Cheshunt College archives, Cambridge, England, original letters
W. Wilson, *Dissenting Churches*, 1: 129–32

EDWIN WELCH

Aleamotu'a, Josiah [Siosaia] Tupou (b. Tongatapu, Tonga, d. Tongatapu, Tonga, 18 November 1845). First Christian Tu'i Kanokupolu (temporal ruler of Tonga). Disillusioned by the failure of his gods, Aleamotu'a, the elderly chief and great-uncle of TĀUFA'ĀHAU, persuaded two Tahitian LMS teachers to remain with him at Nuku'alofa in 1826, Christian worship taking place there before the arrival of the missionary JOHN THOMAS. However, under duress from non-Christian chiefs, he ceased to attend worship until after his installation as

Tu'i Kanokupolu, 7 December 1827. He was baptized as Josiah on 18 January 1830. His conversion appeared to be largely politically motivated, as he advised Tāufa'āhau, then ruler of Ha'apai, and Finau 'Ulukālala, ruler of Vava'u, to turn Christian so the British would support them against their rivals. He was a weak ruler, but being Tu'i Kanokupolu, became the rallying point for the Christian minority. During the civil wars 1835–40 his residence at Nuku'alofa provided a safe haven for Christian refugees. After his death, Tāufa'āhau succeeded him.

BIBLIOGRAPHY
S. Lātūkefu, *Church and State in Tonga* (Canberra, 1974)

SIONE LĀTŪKEFU

Alexander, Archibald (b. Lexington, VA, BNA, 17 April 1772: d. Princeton, NJ, USA, 22 Oct. 1851). Presbyterian minister, educator, and author. Born of Scottish-Irish parents, Alexander was one of William Graham's many pupils at Liberty Hall Academy (later Washington and Lee University) who rose to prominence in Virginia, and then in American religious life. Acknowledging his educational and spiritual indebtedness to Graham, Alexander proceeded to establish a similar network for evangelical religion in the early national period. He professed faith in Christ during a revival in Lexington in 1789 and became an itinerant evangelist in Virginia and North Carolina though still in his teenage years. Successful pastorates in Charlotte County led to a call as president of Hampden-Sydney College in 1796 where he served until 1807, with the exception of 1801, when he toured New England to meet religious leaders across a broad theological spectrum.

In 1807 Pine Street Church in Philadelphia installed Alexander as pastor and Presbyterians elected him moderator of their General Assembly. He was convinced by observations of religious life in Virginia and his New England tour that private theological training of pastors was inadequate to meet growing needs of Presbyterian churches. Alexander's 1808 appeal at the General Assembly was one of the factors that resulted in the formation of Princeton Seminary and his appointment as its first professor in 1812. Alexander established its challenging curriculum on the writings of seventeenth-century Reformed theologian Francois Turretin and the Westminster confession of faith. Princeton's philosophical undergirding was Scottish common-sense realism which Alexander had learned from Graham. In addition to intellectual rigor Alexander placed equal emphasis on nurturing students' evangelical piety through weekly Sunday afternoon 'conferences' devoted to discussions of practical faith. He taught all courses until SAMUEL MILLER arrived in 1813 to take over church history and government, thus leaving theology courses to Alexander. Joined by his famous pupil CHARLES HODGE in 1822, Princeton's theology was perpetuated by two sons each from Alexander and Hodge and later by Benjamin B. Warfield.

Alexander established Princeton's prestige through publishing numerous carefully reasoned treatises. His works on Christian evidences, the canon, religious experience and moral science formed the basis of Princeton's teaching which his successors articulated in more detail. He also solicited funds for JOHN HOLT RICE, another Graham pupil, who laboured to establish a southern Presbyterian seminary in Virginia (eventually Union Seminary in Richmond). Alexander's foremost legacy was his indomitable spirit evidenced primarily in lively preaching by which he moulded not only the character of his institution but also of his many students and friends.

BIBLIOGRAPHY
AAP
J. W. Alexander, *Life of Archibald Alexander* (Philadelphia, PA, 1854)
DAB
DcAmReB
W. A. Hoffecker, *Piety and the Princeton Theologians* (Phillipsburg, NJ, 1981)
L. A. Loetscher, *Facing the Enlightenment and Pietism* (Westport, CN, 1983)
M. A. Noll, *The Princeton Theology, 1812–1921* (Grand Rapids, MI, 1983)

W. ANDREW HOFFECKER

Alexander, James Waddel (b. Louisa Co., VA, USA, 13 March 1804; d. Virginia Springs, VA, USA, 31 July 1859). Presbyterian minister, educator, and author. Eldest son and biographer of ARCHIBALD ALEXANDER, James graduated from the College of New Jersey in 1820, tutored and then pastored for two years in Virginia. He ministered in Trenton, New Jersey (1828–32), taught rhetoric at his alma mater (1833–44), pastored Duane Street Presbyterian Church in New York (1844–9), and taught ecclesiastical history and church government at Princeton Seminary for two years. Although Alexander was a good teacher, his heart longed for the pastorate: 'I miss my old women: and especially my catechumens, my sick rooms'. He returned to his former parish in New York in 1851.

A prolific author, Alexander wrote on the geography of the Bible, prepared an article for almost every number of the old *Princeton Repertory* and penned numerous children's works for the AASU in addition to several volumes of 'Discourses'. A contemporary likened Alexander's forty years of letters to his friend John Hall to Pepys' diary.

BIBLIOGRAPHY
J. Hall, *Forty Years of Letters* (Philadelphia, PA, 1860)
NCAB

W. ANDREW HOFFECKER

Alexander, Joseph Addison (b. Philadelphia, PA, USA, 24 April 1809; d. Princeton, NJ, USA, 28 Jan. 1860).

Seminary professor and author. Joseph Alexander, third son of ARCHIBALD and Janetta ALEXANDER, was born while his father pastored Philadelphia's Pine Street Church. Educated by his father, Alexander proved a precocious learner especially in languages. At ten he knew Latin and could read Old Testament texts in Hebrew. He graduated from Princeton with highest honours in 1826. Alexander never married. Continuing his linguistic studies for several years, including a year in Europe, Alexander joined Princeton Seminary's faculty (1834) as professor of biblical literature and after 1851 taught biblical and ecclesiastical history.

Alexander contributed to Princeton's prestige among Presbyterians through numerous publications. He contributed articles for the immensely popular, *Biblical Repertory* which he served as editor; was much in demand as a preacher; and authored biblical commentaries on Isaiah, Psalms, Matthew, Mark and Acts which established his scholarly reputation domestically and abroad. His biographer attributes Alexander with mastery of seven languages and at least a reading knowledge of 26.

BIBLIOGRAPHY
H. C. Alexander, *Life of Joseph Addison Alexander* (New York, 1870)
DAB

W. ANDREW HOFFECKER

Alexander, Michael Solomon (b. Posen, Germany [now in Poland], May 1799; d. near Cairo, 23 Nov. 1845). Anglican bishop. Alexander, raised as an orthodox Jew, was educated to become a teacher of the Talmud. Emigrating to England in 1820, he married Miss Levy in 1821. He was introduced to Christianity in Lambeth when a district visitor left a Bible at his lodgings. He and his wife became Christians independently, and he was baptized in 1825. After his 1827 ordination (in Dublin) he worked in Danzig and London for the LSPCJ. Later he taught at King's College, London, eventually becoming professor of Hebrew and rabbinical literature. There he was involved in revising the Hebrew New Testament and in translating the *Book of Common Prayer* into Hebrew. From that post he was called to the episcopate.

The Anglican bishopric in Jerusalem began through the initiative of King Frederick William IV of Prussia, who wished to obtain from Turkey (from 1839 in control of Palestine) greater religious freedom for Christians. His proposal that English Anglicans and German Lutherans should co-sponsor an episcopate, though opposed, was accepted and a relevant bill passed in the British Parliament in September 1841. The Crowns of England and Prussia were to make nominations alternately; from England Alexander was proposed, and he was consecrated in November 1841.

He arrived in Jerusalem in January 1842. During his three years there he ministered to Jews and Muslims; enterprises were begun which had to be concluded by his successor, SAMUEL GOBAT. Among them was the building of Christ Church, on Mount Zion.

BIBLIOGRAPHY
M. A. Gidney, *History of the London Society for the Propagation of Christianity Among the Jews from 1809 to 1908* (London, 1908)
ODCC
E. Stock, *History of the Church Missionary Society*, 3 vols (London, 1899)

JOCELYN MURRAY

Alexander, William Lindsay (b. Leith, Edinburgh, Scotland, 24 Aug. 1808; d. Musselburgh, Midlothian, Scotland, 20 Dec. 1884). Congregational divine. He was educated at the universities of Edinburgh and St Andrews and, although of Baptist extraction, he became a Congregationalist in 1826. In 1827 he studied at Glasgow Theological Academy under RALPH WARDLAW and GREVILLE EWING. After a period of classical tutoring at Blackburn Theological Academy, he commenced medical studies in 1831. In 1832 he became minister of Newington Independent Church, Liverpool moving to Edinburgh in 1834 to take up the charge of North College Street Congregational Church (which eventually became Augustine Congregational Church) where he remained until 1877. An eminent scholar, he served both as professor of theology and principal at the Edinburgh Congregational College; he was also a member of the Old Testament Revision Committee. In 1884, the year of his death, he was awarded the degree of LL D by Edinburgh University having previously received the degree of DD from St Andrews University in 1846.

BIBLIOGRAPHY
DNB

ALASDAIR BOTHWELL GORDON

Alexander, William Patterson (b. Paris, KY, USA, 25 July 1805; d. Oakland, CA, USA, May 1884). Congregational missionary. An 1830 graduate of Princeton Seminary, ordained the following year by the presbytery of Cincinnati, he arrived in Honolulu in May 1832 under appointment of the ABCFM. After an exploratory mission in the Marquesas, he returned to Hawaii, and embarked on a variegated career. From 1834 to 1843 he pastored a church on the island of Kauai, ministering to a congregation of 800–1,000. A boarding-school established during his tenure there led ultimately to the founding of Oahu College (1853). For the next 13 years, 1843–55, he headed a teacher-training school at Lahainaluna, Maui. In addition to his academic duties he did some land surveying for the Hawaiian government and supported land reform for the poor. He moved to Wailuku, Maui in 1855, pastored the church there until 1869, and taught at a newly founded theological school, 1863–74. He also travelled for the mission, both to the USA and to the Marquesas. His publications included a manual for pastors, school and Sunday school books, *The Evidences of Christianity*, and *A System of Theology*.

BIBLIOGRAPHY
ESM

WILLIAM G. TRAVIS

Alford, Henry (b. London, 7 Oct. 1810; d. Jan. 1871). Anglican clergyman, biblical critic, and periodical editor. He was the only son of Henry Alford, Rector of Ampton, Suffolk, an evangelical, the son and grandson of evangelical clergymen. His mother dying shortly after his birth, Alford spent much of his youth with his uncle, the Reverend Samuel Alford, also an evangelical, whose daughter, Fanny, he married in 1832.

Alford was educated first by a Congregational minister, from 1824 at Ilminster Grammar School, and in 1827 by John Bickersteth, an evangelical clergyman. He attended Trinity College, Cambridge (BA 1832, MA 1835, BD 1850, DD 1859), became a fellow, and in 1841–2 was Hulsean lecturer. Through membership in the Cambridge 'Apostles' conversazione society he established a lasting friendship with the poet Alfred Tennyson.

Alford was ordained deacon (1833), and priest at Winkfield, Wiltshire, his father's charge. He was Vicar of Launcells, Cornwall (1834), and of Wymeswold, Leicestershire (1835–53). A minister of Quebec Chapel, London (1853), he was also Dean of Canterbury (1857–71). He improved pastoral care, preaching and music in each of his appointments.

Alford's pioneering edition of the Greek New Testament (1849–61) introduced German scholarship into English textual studies. Unsympathetic to the rationalism of the German critics, he saw this great work as an attempt 'to furnish to ... students of Scripture fitting weapons for the coming struggle with infidelity' (Alford, 1873: 196). In his Greek New Testament notes Alford supported the premillennialist interpretation of biblical revelation, though he later doubted which school of eschatology was more correct. Under his editorship (1866–70) the *Contemporary Review* thrived as a literary journal and a forum for religious debate. He also contributed to the *Christian Observer*, *Christian Guardian*, *Edinburgh Review*, *Good Words*, and the *Sunday Magazine*.

Far from repudiating his evangelical heritage, though he took no leading role in any church party and was moderate on such questions as sabbath-keeping, Alford ably defended evangelical Protestantism against ritualism and rationalism. An accomplished scholar and editor, he ranks as an eminent divine of the Victorian Church. The British Library, the Bodleian Library, Lambeth Palace, and the National Library of Scotland hold a few of his letters.

BIBLIOGRAPHY
F. Alford, *Life, Journals, and Letters of Henry Alford* (London, 1873)
M. L. Maddox, 'Henry Alford and the *Contemporary Review*' (Univ. of Chicago, IL, PhD thesis, 1950)
WI, I and V

JONATHAN BURKE CUTMORE

Ali, Willayat (b. Agra, India; d. Delhi, India, 11 May 1857). Baptist evangelist and martyr. Ali came from a respectable, once wealthy Muslim family in Agra. He was influenced by Colonel Wheeler, and then converted. Following his baptism he was persecuted and imprisoned, but was bailed out by Presbyterian missionaries. For seven years he worked with the Reverend James Smith in Chitoor; and then, in 1845, he went to replace J. T. THOMPSON in Delhi. He led the Baptist church there, and then continued working as an evangelist after the arrival of John MacKay. His martyrdom on the first day of the Great Mutiny was recorded by his wife, Fatima, in *The Oriental Baptist* (October 1857). Trying to save John MacKay, he refused a chance to recant. Fatima and their seven children were saved by a sympathizer, Prince Mirza Hajee.

BIBLIOGRAPHY
R. Paul, *They Kept the Faith* (Lucknow, India, 1968)
M. A. Sherring, *The Indian Church During the Great Rebellion* (London, 1859)

E. M. JACKSON

Allan, Thomas (dates and places of birth and death are unknown). *Fl.* 1800–40. Methodist solicitor and political adviser. In 1803 Allan was appointed general solicitor for the Wesleyan Methodist connexion. He also became a standing member of the Committee of Privileges formed in the same year to look after Methodism's legal and political rights. Described as a 'man forgotten by history' Allan is revealed by his private papers to have been the most important layman in the connexion in the critical years between 1800 and 1840. His extensive private papers, now held by the John Rylands University Library of Manchester, shed new light on the Methodist response to Lord Sidmouth's bill against itinerant preaching in 1811 and on the popular Protestant resistance to the campaign for Catholic emancipation between 1812 and 1829. Allan also kept a wary eye on the impact of political radicalism on Methodist societies in the troubled years before the Peterloo massacre (1819) and on the growth of a high doctrine of the pastoral office within Wesleyanism.

Allan's most important achievement was his handling of the Methodist opposition to Sidmouth's bill and his successful negotiations with cabinet ministers resulting in the passage of a new Toleration Act in 1812. During these delicate negotiations Allan portrayed Wesleyan Methodism as Anglican in sympathy, Protestant in character, disciplined in ecclesiastical organization and sustainer of a stable social order. Allan had become convinced that Methodist preaching privileges depended on their loyalty and good order in a period of radical ferment and this was the dominant tone of the printed circulars sent out by the Committee of Privileges to all Methodist societies in the troubled second decade of the nineteenth century.

Although Allan championed the cause of greater religious toleration for Protestant Nonconformists in

1812 his papers show that he was also a vigorous supporter of the Protestant Constitution. He helped form the Protestant Union in 1813 and became its chief publicist, but he wisely conceded that Methodism 'as a body' should not become publicly embroiled in the issue of Catholic emancipation, notwithstanding the pleas of Irish Methodists for a firmer connexional response.

Toward the end of his life Allan became increasingly disillusioned with the professionalization of the Wesleyan ministry – including proposals for a Wesleyan theological college – and with the lack of primitive zeal in Methodist societies. He confessed to a friend in the London circuit that 'it has long been obvious that the lower classes generally speaking will not attend our chapels'. By 1840 he pessimistically concluded that a century of rapid Methodist expansion was drawing to an end.

Allan's importance lies in his behind-the-scenes activities as a political friend of popular evangelicalism. His task was not easy because Methodism came of age at a time of profound social, political and religious change. The complexity of the issues required nimble footwork. In 1811–12 Allan used the traditional friends of religious liberty, the aristocratic Whigs, to secure an enlarged toleration; from 1811 to 1819 he convinced governments of Methodism's inherent conservatism and loyalty as distinct from the disaffected working-class radicals; from 1812 to 1829 he built up contacts with the traditional enemies of religious toleration, the ultra-Tory Protestant constitutionists, to keep out the Catholics; and in 1839 he argued as a doctrinaire voluntaryist, an antecedent of Victorian liberalism, to prevent state money from going to High Church or Roman Catholic schools. Such consistency as may exist in these opinions is rooted in Allan's desire to promote the cause of evangelical Protestantism throughout the British Isles in the generation after the French Revolution.

BIBLIOGRAPHY
D. N. Hempton, 'Thomas Allan and Methodist Politics, 1800–1840', *History*, 67 no. 219 (1982): 13–31
W. R. Ward, *Religion and Society in England 1790–1850* (London, 1972)

DAVID N. HEMPTON

Allen, Benjamin (b. Hudson, NY, USA, 29 Sept. 1789; d. Atlantic Ocean, 13 January 1829). Episcopal clergyman. Born into a nominally Christian family, he left school at age 11 and worked briefly in his father's mercantile business and in other commercial pursuits. Interested in religion and literature, he was tutored by a Presbyterian minister and then studied at a local academy. In 1810 he published his first poetical work and came to achieve modest recognition before entering the theological seminary of the Associate Reformed Presbyterian Church in Newburgh, New York in 1812. The following year he withdrew from the seminary for health reasons.

In 1814, under the influence of Bishop RICHARD CHANNING MOORE, he entered the Episcopal Church. Becoming a lay reader in Charlestown, Virginia, he soon pastored seven congregations. He was ordained deacon in 1816 and priest in 1818. In 1821 he accepted the call to be Rector of St Paul's, Philadelphia, succeeding the popular JOSEPH PILMORE.

Under Allen's leadership, Philadelphia became a stronghold of evangelical Episcopalianism. He devoted particular attention to Sunday schools and Bible classes, as well as several benevolent institutions. In 1827 he aggressively but unsuccessfully campaigned for the election of an evangelical bishop in Pennsylvania. The same year he opened a book establishment, the Church Missionary House, and in 1828 published a militant evangelical sheet, *The Christian Warrior*. His sermons were said not to owe their attractiveness to mental vigour or literary elegance, but to his manifest sincerity. He defended freedom in the pulpit, declaring that his fellow evangelicals 'would stand on the liberty of prophesying until they stood before the judgement of God'.

BIBLIOGRAPHY
AAP
T. G. Allen, *Memoir of the Rev. Benjamin Allen*. (Philadelphia, 1832)

CHARLES R. HENERY

Allen, Cary (b. Cumberland Co., VA, BNA, 1767; d. Danville, KY, USA, 1795). Presbyterian revivalist and home missionary. Allen was raised in a religious home; nevertheless, he embraced the prevailing impiety of his peers while attending Hampden-Sydney College in Virginia. On vacation from school in 1787, Allen visited a Methodist meeting and experienced a dramatic conversion. Returning to the college, he helped precipitate a revival among the students. This revival is now viewed by historians as one of the first outbreaks of the Second Great Awakening. Allen entered the Presbyterian ministry, and was commissioned by his synod as an itinerating evangelist and home missionary for Virginia and the trans-Appalachian south-west. To the settlers, Allen preached a winsome evangelical message – his popularity credited to a certain 'sanctified eccentricity' in his personality. To the slaves, he proclaimed that 'the blessed Saviour shed his blood as much for you as for the white people'. In 1794, Allen accepted a settled pastorate in frontier Kentucky and died there unexpectedly at age 28.

BIBLIOGRAPHY
W. H. Foote, *Sketches of Virginia, Historical and Biographical* (Philadelphia, PA, 1856)

DOUGLAS M. STRONG

Allen, David Oliver (b. Barre, MA, USA, 14 Sept. 1799; d. Lowell, MA, USA, 19 July 1863). Congregational missionary. Graduate of Amherst College (1823) and Andover Seminary (1827), Allen arrived later that year in Bombay, where he served for the next 25 years. While he frequently made Gospel trips outside the city, his most influential work was done in Bombay. For five years he was secretary of the Bombay Tract and Book Society, then for twenty years beginning in 1832 he was closely identified with the BFBS. He also was interested in work with seamen, education, and temperance. His chief work for the Congregational mission was superintending its press for ten years and working with others on the translation of the Bible into Marathi. Completed in 1847, the next years were spent with the Bible Society working on a uniform translation. His health broke before the Marathi Bible was published in its complete form (1855), and in 1853 he was forced to leave India. His other publications include several Marathi tracts and some English language works translated into Marathi, and in 1856 a work entitled *India, Ancient and Modern.*

BIBLIOGRAPHY
DAB

WILLIAM G. TRAVIS

Allen, Ebenezer Brown (b. London, 1810; d. West Brompton, London, 19 Dec. 1886). Anglican clergyman. Allen was educated at Queens' College, Cambridge (BA, 1835) and served first as Curate of Salesbury (Lancashire) (1834–6), where his brother, SAMUEL JAMES ALLEN, had preceded him. He remained in Lancashire first as Perpetual Curate of Goodshaw (1836–9) and then of Bacup (1839–50), after which he moved to London as chaplain of the Royal Hospital for Consumption at Brompton (1850–73).

BIBLIOGRAPHY
Al. Cant., II.i: 34

ARTHUR POLLARD

Allen, Elizabeth [Vernon, Mrs John] (b. Kirkoswald, Cumberland, England, *c.* 1803; d. Macclesfield, Cheshire, England, 8 Jan. 1850). Primitive Methodist itinerant preacher. Daughter of John and Mary, Allen was converted as a child. She joined the Primitive Methodists when their missionaries visited the town and quickly took part in services where she was especially helpful with new converts. Her talent for public speaking made her greatly in demand for public worship. This led to opposition, but she persisted, becoming a local preacher at 21 and a travelling preacher in 1825. Allen itinerated in Hull, Louth, Grimsby, Pocklington, Preston Brook, including missions to Scotland and Ireland, Tunstall and Macclesfield. She often preached in the open air because of the great crowds attracted by the novelty of a woman preacher. In 1835 while at Macclesfield she married and retired from the active ministry, but continued as a local preacher. Allen was taken ill on 2 January and died on the eighth leaving a husband and two children.

BIBLIOGRAPHY
E. D. Graham, 'Chosen by God: the Female Itinerants of Early PM' (Birmingham Univ. Ph.D. thesis, 1987)

PMMag (1832–5, 1850)

E. DOROTHY GRAHAM

Allen, George (b. London, Nov. 1800; d. Sydney, 3 Nov. 1877). Wesleyan lawyer, philanthropist, and politician. Reaching Sydney in 1816, Allen turned to the law and was admitted a solicitor in 1822. He practised his profession successfully until 1854 and held a variety of directorships in leading companies. He was Mayor of Sydney in 1844/5, member of the Legislative Council (1845–73), member of the Denominational Board of Education, (1848- 66), the Council of Education, (1867–73) and the senate of the University of Sydney (1859–73). Allen served the NSW Benevolent Society (*circa* fifty years), the Sydney Infirmary (over thirty years), the WMMS, the BFBS, the RTS, the Bethel Union, the Wesleyan Contingent Fund and Chapel Building Committee. He was founder of the Wesleyan Methodist Sunday School Society (1834) and the Destitute Children's Asylum. His was a life of rich dedication to the church and other good causes.

BIBLIOGRAPHY
ADB
Sydney Morning Herald (6 November 1877)
Wesleyan Advocate (10 November 1877)

DON WRIGHT

Allen, Hugh (b. Cork, Ireland, 1 July 1806; d. London, 20 June 1877). Anglican clergyman. Allen was a product of Trinity College, Dublin (scholar 1834; BA 1835; MA BD DD 1861) and served first as minister of Douglas Chapel (Isle of Man) (1838–48) and afterwards moved to London as incumbent of St Jude's, Whitechapel. Here he exercised a notable ministry in the slums of the capital (1848–59), one comparable to the more celebrated W. W. CHAMPNEYS. The returns of the religious census in 1851 indicate that St Jude's (which had been consecrated in 1848) had 1,400 adults in the morning congregation while in the evening all the standing room was normally occupied, the sittings of 1,900 being exceeded by 300.

During Allen's time in London he was for a time lecturer at St George-in-the-East just when the riots occasioned by the ritualistic innovations of the rector, Brian King, were at their peak. King also sought to prevent Allen from lecturing. Allen was also lecturer at St Olave's Jewry (1856–9), after which he succeeded as Rector of St George the Martyr, Southwark (1859–77). He was also editor of the *London Messenger* in 1862.

BIBLIOGRAPHY
Boase, VI: 31
Ecclesiastical Census Returns (Home office 129/22/4/1/1)
D. M. Lewis, *Lighten Their Darkness* (Westport, CT, 1986)

ARTHUR POLLARD AND DONALD M. LEWIS

13

Allen, John (b. Chapel-en-le-Frith, Derbyshire, England, 10 June 1737; d. Liverpool, England, 28 Feb. 1810). Methodist itinerant. Of mixed Anglican and Presbyterian parentage, he had Methodist relatives and it was at nearby Chinley that he joined the society. Before his conversion he had belonged to a group of touring singers but left to become an exhorter and then a local preacher. In 1766 he was received on trial to travel, beginning in the Lancashire North circuit. In Staffordshire he was involved in pioneer evangelism and for three years served in London as one of JOHN WESLEY's more immediate associates. The remainder of his ministry was spent in the north of England. He rejoiced to see a marked revival in Leeds in 1793. Arthritic illness compelled him to retire in 1799. According to his obituary, he was a man of good report among all who knew him.

BIBLIOGRAPHY
AM (1779)
MM (1810, 1812)

A. SKEVINGTON WOOD

Allen, John (b. Farmington, ME, USA, 7 March 1795; d. East Livermore camp meeting, ME, USA, 31 Aug. 1887). Methodist holiness evangelist and camp meeting speaker. Born as the eighth of ten children to an impoverished Maine farmer, he received his education at Farmington Academy where he became certified to teach school. Allen taught at 'district' schools during the winters and worked as a farmer during the summers. He also worked as a stage driver. Religiously, Allen became a universalist. In 1820, he married Annah S. Hersey of Farmington and became a clothier. He joined the temperance movement (1824) and was converted at a camp meeting near Industry, Maine (July, 1825). He became an evangelist in Farmington and experienced sanctification at a Methodist camp meeting in 1826.

Allen was licensed as a local preacher (1828). After struggling to learn how to preach, he was ordained deacon at the Maine Conference (1835) and elder by Bishop E. HEDDING (1838). He then served circuits throughout Maine before transferring to the East Maine Conference (1854) where he served as tract agent. Allen became an ardent abolitionist. Rejoining the Maine Conference (1862), he enlisted (1863) as a chaplain in the United States Christian Commission under W. E. BOARDMAN. After the war, he served his church as an evangelist and temperance crusader until his retirement in 1876. Thereafter, he served as a holiness camp meeting evangelist.

Allen attended the first national holiness camp meeting at Vineland, New Jersey (July 1867) where he rededicated himself to the experience and doctrine of sanctification. Becoming an ardent proponent of holiness, he would later attend more than 370 camp meetings, preaching or exhorting at most. He conducted temperance meetings throughout New England. Not a scholarly person, he achieved recognition for his ability to vividly recite Bible passages, his wit and ability at repartee. His wife, who suffered from and could not support

his unorganized itinerant ministry, died (June 1875) and he married (1876) Sarah A. W. Fellows who died in the spring of 1881. Allen served as chaplain of the Maine House of Representatives (1879–80). His funeral, attended by more than 3,000 people, was preached by Charles Cullis at the East Livermore, Maine, camp meeting. Allen's will divided his money between the church of Dr Charles Cullis, the Freeman Camp Meeting Association, WILLIAM TAYLOR's Africa mission and his heirs.

BIBLIOGRAPHY
S. Allen, *The Life of Rev. John Allen* (Boston, MA, 1888)

DAVID BUNDY

Allen, Richard (né Richard) (b. 14 Feb. 1760; d. Philadelphia, PA, USA, 26 March 1831). First bishop of the African Methodist Episcopal (AME) Church. Born the slave of prominent Philadelphia lawyer and Delaware planter, Benjamin Chew, he was sold as a child, together with his parents and siblings, to Stokely Sturgis of Little Creek Hundred, Kent County, Delaware. Years later, his family was divided when Sturgis resold Allen's mother and three of her children. Methodism provided him a path to spiritual and temporal freedom. Of his conversion under Methodist influences in the late 1770s, he later wrote 'all of a sudden my dungeon shook, my chains fell off, and glory to God, I cried' (Allen, 1960: 15). Inner liberation found outward embodiment in January 1780 when Sturgis, convicted by the antislavery preaching of FREEBORN GARRETTSON, agreed to let Richard purchase his freedom.

In the early 1780s, after earning the money to pay Sturgis and adopting the surname Allen, he became a Methodist itinerant. Beginning in Delaware, New Jersey, and Pennsylvania, his travels took him from New York to South Carolina and included two months among Indians. In 1786, he settled in Philadelphia. His evangelistic success quickly convinced him the city's blacks needed their own place of worship, but his plans were blocked by white Methodist authorities and Philadelphia's leading blacks. A loyal Methodist, Allen was again frustrated when the Free African Society, a non-denominational mutual benefit association he and ABSALOM JONES founded in April 1787, first veered toward Quakerism, then in the early 1790s re-organized itself as a black congregation of the Protestant Episcopal Church. The celebrated 'gallery incident' (traditionally dated to 1787 but probably occurring in 1792 or 1793) when praying blacks were dragged from their knees for occupying the wrong section of the new balcony at St George's MEC, created a constituency of disaffected black Methodists that eventually enabled Allen to organize Bethel AME Church. It was dedicated by FRANCIS ASBURY in June 1794.

Persuaded that the 'Methodists were the first people that brought glad tidings to the colored people', Allen adhered throughout his life to Methodism's 'good old way' (Allen, 1960:30). He was equally convinced, however, that white Methodists had early gone astray and that black Methodists required considerable autonomy to work effectively among their own people. Though they had purchased the land and the building, and though Allen was ordained a local deacon by Asbury in April 1799, under the Methodist system Bethel's blacks controlled neither their property nor their pulpit. In January 1816, after more than two decades of recurrent conflict with white Methodist authorities, Allen and Bethel's trustees won, through the civil courts, complete independence. Three months later, they joined comparable black Methodist groups in Baltimore and elsewhere in the region to form the AME Church. Allen became the new denomination's first and, until 1828, its only bishop.

Allen's Methodism emphasized not only heartfelt piety, but economic self-help, community activism and social protest. The proprietor of several small businesses, Allen left at his death an estate valued at $80,000. Active in the Prince Hall Masons, he also collaborated closely with members of the Pennsylvania Abolition Society. In 1830, he decisively influenced the black social justice movement of the later ante-bellum period by convening at Bethel Church the first in a series of national black conventions.

SELECT WRITINGS
R. Allen, *Life Experience and Gospel Labours* (Philadelphia, PA, 1833; reprint edn., Nashville, TN, 1960)

BIBLIOGRAPHY
G. B. Nash, 'New Light on Richard Allen: The Early Years of Freedom', *William and Mary Quarterly*, 3rd series, 46 (1989): 332–40
A. J. Raboteau, 'Richard Allen and the African Church Movement', in L. Litwack and A. Meier, eds, *Black Leaders of the Nineteenth Century* (Urbana and Chicago, IL, 1988)

DAVID W. WILLS

Allen, Samuel James (b. London, 16 June 1798; d. Easingwold, Yorkshire, England, 29 April 1856). Anglican clergyman. Elder brother of EBENEZER BROWN ALLEN, Samuel was a member of Pembroke College, Cambridge (BA 1820; MA 1824), becoming Curate of Langho and Salesbury (Lancashire) in 1822 and thereafter, first of all, chaplain to Lord de Tabley at his seat at Over Peover (Cheshire) and then headmaster of Burnley Grammar School before moving to Easingwold as vicar (1839–56). He assisted THOMAS DUNHAM WHITAKER in his literary work and himself published *Lectures in Defence of the Church of England* as well as being nominated to preach before the university at Cambridge in 1833.

BIBLIOGRAPHY
Al. Cant., II.i: 34

ARTHUR POLLARD

Allen, William (b. London, 29 Aug. 1770; d. Lindfield, Sussex, England, 30 Dec. 1843). Quaker scientist and philanthropist. Son of a Quaker silk manufacturer, and educated at Rochester, he first worked in his father's business and later in the chemical establishment at Plough Court, London which he acquired on J. G. BEVAN's retirement in 1795. Experimenting in a laboratory which he built at Plaistow, he lectured at Guy's Hospital (1802–26) and by 1807 was a fellow of both the Linnaean and the Royal Societies. As a Quaker he was active against slavery. In 1811 he founded *The Philanthropist* in which social issues were debated including the educational controversy between Lancaster and Bell. Allen himself supported Lancaster and was treasurer of the BFSS. He worked with Jeremy Bentham and Robert Owen in the purchase of the New Lanark Mills in 1814 but disputes developed when Allen insisted on biblical instruction in the schools. After Owen's withdrawal in 1829 Allen continued to support the project until 1835. One of its most distinguished patrons was the DUKE OF KENT for whose estate Allen became a trustee when the Duke was found to be seriously in debt.

When Tsar Alexander I visited England in 1814 he met Allen and seemed sympathetic to his religious views. Soon after, Allen undertook the first of his several continental tours, preaching, investigating prisons and schools, meeting statesmen and rulers and advocating numerous social reforms. He was well received by the Tsar in Russia and, in 1822, at the Congress of Verona where he lobbied the participants for a condemnation of the slave trade. Sometimes accompanied by other Quakers like STEPHEN GRELLET and ELIZABETH FRY he made similar journeys in 1819, 1832, 1833, and 1840.

As a prominent evangelical Friend he resolutely opposed Elias Hicks's 'Inner Light' teaching and encouraged various churches of the continental *Réveil* which he visited after 1819. At the same time his philanthropic zeal was such that he abstained from eating sugar for 43 years in protest against slavery, and it was at his home that the Peace Society was founded in 1816.

SELECT WRITINGS
W. Allen, *Life of William Allen with Selections from his Correspondence*, 3 vols (London, 1847)

BIBLIOGRAPHY
E. C. Cripps, *Plough Court, the Story of a Notable Pharmacy 1715–1927* (London, 1927): 25–51
DNB
Friends of Humanity (Doncaster, England, 1965)
A. J. C. Hare, *The Gurneys of Earlham*, 2 (London, 1895): 108–17
B. Seebohm, ed., *Memoirs of the Life and Gospel Labours of Stephen Grellet* (London, 1860)
Society of Friends Biographical Catalogue (London, 1888): 7–14

TIMOTHY C. F. STUNT

Allin, Thomas (b. Broseley, Shropshire, England, 10 Feb. 1784; d. Longton, Staffordshire, England, 7 Nov. 1866). Methodist minister. Allin joined the MNC in 1800 in Hanley, entering its ministry in 1808. He was early seen to possess outstanding intellectual and moral gifts, and after only 14 years in the ministry was elected president of the conference in 1822, an office he held a second time in 1846. Allin was a voluminous author of theological and polemical works, such as *The Immateriality and Immortality of the Soul, The Character and Folly of Modern Atheism*, etc. Retiring through ill health from active circuit work after 25 years, he was appointed ministerial tutor; for 15 years he served as the connexion's corresponding secretary, and for 11 years its general secretary of missions. So highly was he held in esteem that in 1854 the connexion presented him with a gold watch and a purse of £800, the result of a widespread subscription list. In his last two years Allin suffered from a partial paralysis, and the Bible and hymn-book were his constant companions.

BIBLIOGRAPHY

S. Hulme, *Memoir of the Reverend T. Allin* (London, 1881)

G. J. Stevenson, *Methodist Worthies*, 6 vols, 4 (London, 1884–6): 600ff

H. Smith, *Sketches of Eminent Methodist New Connexion Ministers* (London, 1893)

G. Packer, ed., *Centenary of the Methodist New Connexion* (London, 1897)

Minutes (1867): 6ff

O. A. BECKERLEGGE

Alline, Henry (b. Newport, RI, BNA, 18 Apr. 1748; d. North Hampton, NH, USA, 2 Feb. 1784). New Light evangelist, hymn-writer, and anti-Calvinist theologian. Alline's formal schooling ended at age 12, when his parents joined a major northward migration of New England Yankees to a Nova Scotia made safe from the French by the fall of Quebec. The family set down on newly vacated Acadian land in the township of Falmouth on Minas Basin. Alline's parents, although New Light Congregationalist sympathizers, had little access to religious fellowship in their new surroundings. His autobiography leaves no doubt that his spiritual awakening was a solitary affair.

Alline was only nine when he began to read works of theology. Within a few years he could boast that he had read, studied and debated so much that 'I had acquired a great theory of religion, and spent much time disputing on the controverted points [of theology], such as election, reprobation, resurrection, baptism, &c'. After years of soul-searching the pivotal event in his life occurred on 26 March 1775. Alone and despairing he prayed continually until 'redeeming love broke into my soul ... with such power, that my whole soul seemed to be melted down with love ... and my will turned of choice after the infinite God' (*Beverley and Moody*, 1982: 46, 62). A year later, on a public fast day to mark the deepening crisis between Great Britain and her American colonies, Alline came out as an exhorter. Soon after he began to preach.

From the Fast Day in 1776 until his death at age 36, Alline's public career lasted only eight years. He preached on an ever-widening circuit in Nova Scotia and what became New Brunswick, triggering the greatest religious 'reformation' that any extensive part of Canada has ever seen. His dominant message was one of radical emphasis on a perceptible conversion experience and equally radical disdain for or indifference to the outward forms of religion, including ministerial hierarchy and the ordinances. Surviving sermons unite with contemporary witnesses in attesting to the power with which he preached this theme. The more than 500 published hymns and 'spiritual songs' that made him the most prolific North American hymn-writer of his day also evidenced a shrewd ability to convey his message in simple, memorable terms. Alline's admirers likened him to GEORGE WHITEFIELD and John the Baptist. Even the critics who denounced him as a ravager of churches did not dispute his success.

While the twin themes of inner conversion and purist rejection of outward religious forms were always dominant in his preaching, Alline came in the latter phase of his ministry to pay more attention towards the perpetuation of his insights. He gathered a total of eight 'gospel churches', for which he composed radically simplified articles of faith. He also ventured into the realm of print to publish two volumes of theology. Although in some degree influenced by the mystical writings of Jacob Boehme and William Law, the eccentric nature of Alline's theology also reflected its author's lack of access to formal education after age 12. Among Alline's insights was the notion that Adam pre-existed the Creation in spiritual form, that his nature was both male and female, that all persons were present spiritually with Adam at the Fall (hence, had sinned personally and not just by imputation), and that Christ's resurrection was spiritual rather than physical. JOHN WESLEY's characterization of Alline's theology as 'gold and dross shuffled together' won general assent among learned critics (Telford, 1931, VII: 182–3); yet it was not without influence. Alline passed his dying days among the nascent Freewill Baptists of northern New England. In Alline's writings the Freewills found an evangelical, non-Arminian critique of predestination and defence of free will that proved crucial in enabling them to formulate their point of distinction from the numerically dominant Regular Baptists.

In view of his indifference on the baptism issue, it is ironic that Alline's major nineteenth-century influence was on the two major Baptist groups of eastern Canada. The first Regular Baptist churches in the Maritime provinces were gathered, in great measure, by men who had their spiritual awakening under his labours. Even more directly, the Free Christian Baptist conferences took their formative inspiration from Alline's suspicion of the externals of religion and insistence on a theology of free will.

BIBLIOGRAPHY

D. G. Bell, *Henry Alline and Maritime Religion* (Ottawa, 1993) (gives full Alline bibliography)

The Life and Journal of the Rev. Mr. Henry Alline (Boston, MA, 1806) [repr. J. Beverley and B. M. Moody, eds., (Hantsport, NS, 1982)]

G. A. Rawlyk, *Ravished by the Spirit* (Montreal, Canada, 1984)

G. A. Rawlyk, ed., *Henry Alline: Selected Writings* (New York, 1987)

J. Telford, ed., *The Letters of John Wesley*, 8 vols (London, 1931)

D. G. BELL

Allison, Burgess (b. Bordentown, NJ, BNA, 17 Aug. 1753; d. Washington, DC, 20 Feb. 1827). Baptist minister, educator, and chaplain to Congress. Allison was baptized October 1769, educated under the care of SAMUEL JONES, and ministered within the Philadelphia Association. He opened a successful academy which was noted for pioneering discipline without the rod. He was acclaimed as a master of almost all branches of study, yet he lost his savings trying to fund his modifications to the steam engine. After retirement he served as chaplain to Congress and then to the Navy Yard.

BIBLIOGRAPHY
AAP
W. Cathcart, *Baptist Encyclopedia* (Philadelphia, PA, 1881)

WADE A. HORTON

Allison, Charles Frederick (b. Cornwallis, Nova Scotia, BNA, 25 Jan. 1795; d. Sackville, New Brunswick, BNA, 20 Nov. 1858). Sackville merchant and Methodist founder of Mount Allison Wesleyan Academy. Educated in Cornwallis, he became a business partner of his cousin William Crane of Sackville, New Brunswick. The firm of Crane and Allison developed a thriving export–import business on the Atlantic coast, stimulating not only shipbuilding but other enterprise as well.

In 1839 Allison offered land and money for the founding of Wesleyan Academy for boys. Launched in 1843, it was followed by a female academy in 1854, and a college in 1858, the year of his death. Mount Allison University owes its foundation to Allison. Clearly he would not have made this educational offer without his thorough conversion to Wesleyan Methodism in 1833. An observer remembered his words of 1839: 'The Lord hath put it into my heart to give this sum [£4,000] towards building a Wesleyan Academy – I know the impression is from the Lord, for I am naturally fond of money' (Penner, 1990: 32; Reid, 1984: 17). Allison gave evidence in his life and worship that on more than one occasion he sought the Wesleyan ideal of perfection.

BIBLIOGRAPHY
DCB
P. Penner, *The Chignecto 'Connexion'* (Sackville, Canada, 1990)
J. G. Reid, *Mount Allison University* (Toronto, 1984)

PETER PENNER

Allix, Richard Wager (b. 1790; d. Great Warley, Essex, England, 31 May 1827). Anglican clergyman. Allix was admitted scholar of St John's College, Cambridge on 1807 (BA 1811; MA 1814; BD 1821). He was much influenced by CHARLES SIMEON and was a supporter of the Bible Society, the CMS and the Jews' society. He served at St James, Latchford, Warrington (Cheshire), where he had a Sunday school of over 400 scholars. He became Rector of Great Warley (Essex) (1826–7), but died within a year. He is said to have been an earnest pastor, but also guileless and innocent and sometimes imposed upon.

BIBLIOGRAPHY
Al. Cant., II, i: 43
W. Beaumont, *History of Latchford* (Warrington, England, 1889)

ARTHUR POLLARD

Allon, Henry (b. Welton, near Hull, Yorkshire, England, 13 Oct. 1818; d. London, 16 April 1892). Congregational minister and editor. Brought up among the Wesleyans, Allon became a Congregationalist by conviction and was trained at Cheshunt College for their ministry. In 1844 he was ordained as assistant to Thomas Lewis at Union Chapel, Islington, succeeding him in 1852 and remaining in office till his death, the church being rebuilt as a great 'nonconformist cathedral' in 1877. Allon built up the church by dignified worship, where he made an important contribution in setting higher standards for all Nonconformists, quality preaching and attentive pastoral work. The first man to be called twice to the chair of the Congregational Union [1864 and 1881], he gave remarkable service to a wider nonconformity through the pages of the cultivated *British Quarterly Review*, which he served as joint editor from 1866 and sole editor from 1874 until its demise 12 years later; notwithstanding his general view of the philistinism of Dissent, Matthew Arnold congratulated Allon on the role of the *British Quarterly Review* in 'forming a public whose intellectual and spiritual growth is going on, or beginning'. Through this he came to be regarded as a representative Nonconformist and was consulted by Gladstone, for example, as to dissenting opinion. At the same time he shared the confidence of such evangelical leaders as Lord SHAFTESBURY from whom he received subscriptions for the work at Union Chapel and with SPURGEON, with whom he exchanged pulpits. While generally conservative and reverential, he gave support to progressive as well as to traditional colleagues. His chairman's address in 1864 caused some stir by describing verbal inerrancy as an indefensible doctrine. However, he still firmly upheld the Divine authorship of the Bible, and wrote in *The Evangelical Magazine* on 'The credibility of miracles' in answer to *Essay and Reviews*.

BIBLIOGRAPHY
DNB
W. B. Harwood, *Henry Allon* (London, 1894)
A. Peel, *Letters to a Victorian Editor* (London, 1929)

J. H. Y. BRIGGS

Allport, Josiah (b. Walsall, Staffordshire, England, 1784; d. Sutton-upon-Trent, Nottinghamshire, England, 16 Feb. 1867). Anglican clergyman, editor, and translator. The son of Joseph Allport, he was ordained (deacon 1811, priest 1812) and became the Perpetual Curate of Bream in Gloucestershire (1813–19), and of Atherstone, Warwickshire (1825–32). From 1829 to 1859 he was the minister of St James's, Ashted, Birmingham. Here he exercised a significant pastoral ministry in a poorly endowed church located in a densely populated working-class area which included a barracks to which he was chaplain from 1847. He succeeded in raising over £2,100 for repairs and enlargements to the church in the 1830s. In 1859 he became Vicar of Sutton-upon-Trent and remained there until his death.

Although he apparently never attended university, and in spite of his many pastoral responsibilities, Allport translated Bishop John Davenport's (1576–1641) *Expositio Epistolae Pauli ad Colossenses* (1831) and *Disputatio de Justitia* (1846) and edited Richard Baxter's (1615–91) *Key for Catholics* (1839) and Richard Sall's *True Catholic and Apostolic Faith* (1840). The key concern of his work was to maintain the catholicity of Anglicanism against Roman Catholic charges of schism. He also edited the monthly *Protestant Journal* from 1831 to 1834.

BIBLIOGRAPHY
Aris's Birmingham Gazette (28 June 1847, 7 March 1859)
Boase
Church Commissioners, benefice files
Crockford
GM (April 1867): 541

D. E. H. MOLE

Anderson, Alexander (b. Peterhead, Scotland, 4 Sept. 1808; d. Aberdeen, Scotland, 25 Oct. 1884). Educationalist and Baptist pastor. Alexander Anderson, the son of a doctor, graduated MA at St Andrews University in 1826, coming into contact with ROBERT HALDANE and settled as minister of Boyndie Parish Church, Banffshire in 1830. He became Free Church minister in Whitehills at the Disruption in 1843, and moved to Old Machar Free Church, Aberdeen in 1845. When he arrived at Baptist views in 1847 he demitted his charge and opened the gymnasium, which became a successful school. He also gathered a Baptist congregation in a chapel in George Street, Aberdeen which united with Crown Terrace Church in 1877.

BIBLIOGRAPHY
A. Anderson, *Statement on Principles of Spirituality in the New Testament Church* (Edinburgh, 1848)
—, *Science, Theology and Religion* (Edinburgh, 1874)
Anon., *The Centenary Brochure of the Free Communion Baptist Church* (Aberdeen, Scotland, 1939)
Fasti, 6: 279–81

DEREK D. MURRAY

Anderson, Christopher (b. Edinburgh, 19 Feb. 1782; d. Edinburgh, 18 Feb. 1852). Baptist pastor. Born into an Independent family, Anderson was converted in his late teens and hoped to join WILLIAM CAREY in India. Health forbade this and so he devoted his life to ministry in Britain. Having spent time with JOHN SUTCLIFF at Olney and at the Bristol Academy, he returned to Edinburgh, where he gathered a small church, on English Baptist lines, in 1808. In 1818 the congregation had grown sufficiently for it to be able to purchase Charlotte Chapel, formerly an Episcopalian meeting place. Anderson ministered to this church until shortly before his death. It was never large, but attracted many English Baptist students attending the university.

He never lost interest in India, and worked closely with ANDREW FULLER, Carey and others, being a staunch supporter of the Serampore Mission. He initiated mission and education in Ireland, and sent preachers into the Highlands of Scotland. The Itinerating Society which he founded became part of the Baptist Home Missionary Society in 1824. He was also a prime mover in the Edinburgh Gaelic School Society and a founder of the Edinburgh Bible Society. His main scholarly work is *The Annals of the English Bible*. Anderson was able to raise Scottish interest in the BMS, to promote evangelistic work in the Highlands and in Ireland, and to make well-considered contribution to Christian co-operation in education and evangelism.

SELECT WRITINGS
C. Anderson, *The Annals of the English Bible* (Edinburgh, 1835)

BIBLIOGRAPHY
H. Anderson, *Life and Letters of Christopher Anderson* (Edinburgh, 1854)
V. E. Durkacz, *The Decline of the Celtic Languages* (Edinburgh, 1983)

DEREK B. MURRAY

Anderson, David (b. London, 10 Feb. 1814; d. Clifton, Bristol, England, 5 Nov. 1885). First Anglican bishop of Rupert's Land, Canada. Anderson was educated at Edinburgh Academy and Exeter College, Oxford. He was ordained 1837 and served two curacies in Liverpool. Between 1841 and 1846 he was on the staff of St Bee's College. He then became the minister of a chapel in Kilburn, London and then briefly Perpetual Curate of All Saint's, Derby.

A bequest from Hudson's Bay Company trader James Leith provided the endowment for a Church of England bishopric in Rupert's Land, now north-western Canada. Anderson was consecrated as its first bishop on 29 May 1849. As bishop of a largely missionary diocese, Anderson was responsible for considerable extension of the work of the CMS including the ordination of twenty clergy, of whom eight were natives of the region. Anderson, however, while strongly supportive of the CMS, was never himself a CMS missionary. He established St John's Collegiate School as a centre for classical studies and religious training and played a role in the politics of the Red River settlement, generating frequent controversy in the process. As the first Church of England bishop in the Canadian north-west, he had an important role to play during a period of significant expansion.

In 1864, Anderson returned to England and became Vicar of Clifton, Bristol and having a large staff was able to be released for wider episcopal duties. During Bishop s. WALDEGRAVE's illness in 1869 Anderson was given full authority to perform all episcopal functions in the diocese of Carlisle. He continued to support the CMS mission in north-west America.

BIBLIOGRAPHY

DCB, 11

B. Heeney, *Leaders of the Canadian Church* (Toronto, 1943)

E. Stock, *The History of the Church Missionary Society* 2: (London, 1899) 313–32

W. S. Wallace, *The Macmillan Dictionary of Canadian Biography* (Toronto, 1963)

KERRY M. ABEL
ALAN FREDERICK MUNDEN

Anderson, John (b. Perthshire, Scotland, 1769; d. 1822). Itinerant evangelist and church founder in Perthshire. Anderson was associated with Auchnaguie, probably his residence near Tullymet. Converted in 1802, he was originally an Independent, training at a HALDANE class in Edinburgh (1804–6). He began preaching in Tullymet in July 1806, and founded an Independent church in August 1806. Ordained in 1807, he became a Baptist in 1808, followed by the majority of his church. Later supported by the Baptist Highland Mission, he remained Baptist pastor at Tullymet until his death.

BIBLIOGRAPHY

Baptist Highland Mission Report (1822–3)

D. E. Meek, 'The Independent and Baptist Churches of Highland Perthshire and Strathspey', *Transactions of the Gaelic Society of Inverness*, 56 (1988–90): 269–343

Tullymet Minute Book (Baptist Union of Scotland Archives, Glasgow)

DONALD E. MEEK

Anderson, John (b. Gibraltar, *c*. 1791; d. Liverpool, England, 11 April 1840). Methodist. He was converted in London at the age of 18, joined the Methodist Society, and entered the Wesleyan ministry in 1812. He speedily earned the reputation of a great evangelical preacher and missionary speaker. Dr Benjamin Gregory claimed: 'Next to [Theophilus] Lessey he was the most irresistibly eloquent Methodist preacher of the time.' He was appointed to the most prestigious circuits in Methodism. It was Anderson who organized the opposition against some of Methodism's rebels, such as JOSEPH RAYNER STEPHENS and SAMUEL WARREN. He was invited to publish a funeral sermon on the death of DR ADAM CLARKE in 1832, and *The Spirit of a Great People*, in 1839. There seems little doubt that he would have been elected a president of the Methodist Conference had he not died at the age of 49.

BIBLIOGRAPHY

B. Gregory, *Autobiographical Recollections* (London, 1903)

B. Gregory, *Side Lights on the Conflicts of Methodism . . . 1827–1852* (London, 1898)

G. Smith, *History of Wesleyan Methodism*, 3 vols, 5th edn (London, 1866, etc.)

WMM (1840)

FRANK BAKER

Anderson, John (b. Galloway, Scotland, 23 May 1805; d. Madras, India, 2 March 1855). First Scottish Church missionary to south India. Anderson was educated at the University of Edinburgh and Divinity Hall, Edinburgh, and subsequently received his call to the Indian mission field while suffering a long illness. He arrived in Madras on 22 February 1837 and opened the Central Institution on 3 April that year. The school was founded with a missionary purpose, as Anderson firmly believed in education as a means of reaching the caste population of India with the Christian message. The school grew so rapidly that it changed premises three times within ten years. (In 1867 it became a first grade college of Madras University and in 1877 was renamed Madras Christian College. It is now the most prestigious college in south India.)

Anderson early made a stand on the caste question and lost all his pupils when three untouchable (pariah) boys were admitted in 1838. However, this set-back was only temporary, though, in 1841, the baptism of the first converts led to another exodus of students and, again in 1845, the giving asylum to a newly converted Hindu girl ('Mooniatha') caused yet another exodus. Ultimately, despite contretemps of this nature, Anderson's zeal was rewarded by seeing his educational work in the area thrive. In 1847 he married Margaret Locher, a Swiss missionary, who helped him with unstinting energy. Anderson's efforts were characterized by his own unflagging energy and enthusiasm which enhanced the fame and influence of his school.

BIBLIOGRAPHY

G. Pittendrigh and W. Meston, *Mission of the United Free Church of Scotland* (Edinburgh, 1907)

LYNETTE E. L. THISTLETHWAYTE

Anderson, Rufus (b. North Yarmouth, ME, USA, 17 Aug. 1796; d. Boston, MA, USA, 30 May 1880). Mission theorist and secretary of the ABCFM. Anderson's father was a Congregational minister who introduced him to missions by taking him to the ordination service of the first Americans sent as overseas missionaries in 1812. In assisting his father to collect material for a proposed history of missions, Anderson became predisposed toward mission service even before his conversion in

1816. After graduation from Bowdoin College, he travelled abroad for his health and acted as a correspondent for the ABCFM, thus becoming familiar to the mission agency. In 1819 he entered Andover Theological Seminary and joined a secret society of students committed to becoming missionaries. But after graduation in 1822, instead of becoming a missionary, Anderson began to work full time for the American Board. His administrative work was so valuable that the Congregational Church ordained him an evangelist in 1826.

In 1832, Anderson became the board's foreign secretary, a position he held until his retirement in 1866. A superb administrator, he guided the ABCFM through its years of expansion and consolidation as the premier American mission agency. He put the board on a regular financial footing by organizing its supporters into auxiliaries. He corresponded with the missionaries and advised them on matters of both personal concern and mission policy. He worked closely with the prudential committee of the ABCFM in setting mission policy. During his tenure as secretary, Anderson made four investigative trips to the various mission fields. At the time of his retirement, he had appointed all but six of the over 1,200 active missionaries of the board.

While secretary, Anderson wrote thousands of letters to missionaries, numerous sermons and pamphlets, and many reports on missions. His first literary task at the ABCFM was to edit the *Missionary Herald*. His first book was the *Memoir of Catherine Brown* (1824). The most complete statements of his mission theory can be found in the tracts he wrote for the American Board, as well as a series of lectures published in 1869 as *Foreign Missions*. Following each trip abroad, he published reports on his activities and related policy recommendations. In 1861, he wrote and edited a *Memorial Volume of the First Fifty Years of the American Board of Commissioners for Foreign Missions*. After his retirement, Anderson devoted his time to writing and to lecturing at theological seminaries. In the final decades of his life, he wrote four volumes on the history of the board's missions in the Sandwich Islands (Hawaii), India, and among the churches of the Middle East.

Anderson is universally recognized as the most important mission theorist in American history. The policies that he articulated were influential throughout Protestantism well into the twentieth century. Simultaneously with his contemporary HENRY VENN, he developed the three-self theory of missions – that the goal of Christian mission was to plant self-supporting, self-governing, and self-propagating indigenous churches. The goal of mission was not to civilize or to educate people into becoming westernized Christians, but to convert the lost and to organize them into churches. The local churches thus created would support and govern themselves. The missionary would seek to raise up an indigenous ministry so that true self-support and governance could be attained as quickly as possible. Self-propagation, the ability and desire of each church to send its own missionaries, was to Anderson

the most important of the three selfs and the sign of a mature, scriptural church.

Anderson derived his basic mission theory from an evangelical understanding of Paul's work as a missionary in the New Testament. Paul's ministry concentrated on making converts, gathering them into churches, and then arranging for native pastoral ministry. Following the example of Paul, the missionary should not serve as a local pastor or spend time supervising institutional ministries, except as such activities supported the three-self goals. Rather, the missionary's primary task was to be an evangelist who relied on the verbal proclamation of the word to save sinners and to found three-self churches.

Consistent application of three-self theory meant that Anderson made difficult and often controversial decisions about the nature of existing mission work. His theories were at odds with prior American mission theory that believed that people must be 'civilized' before they could be evangelized. Thus Anderson opposed the sending of missionary colonists to share western culture. Educational, medical, industrial, and literary work were all secondary ministries for the missionary. Whenever Anderson detected that secondary ministries had supplanted evangelism as the work of missions, he objected. In 1854–5, he visited the mission stations in India and Ceylon, concerned at the low rate of conversions and the lack of a native pastorate. He concluded from his visit that the mission schools had become means of social advancement for the pupils rather than instruments for creating a native ministry. Consequently, he stopped the teaching of English in the schools and limited the curricula to what prepared people for Christian service, he decentralized missions for greater evangelistic effectiveness, and he insisted on the ordination of indigenous Christians. In 1863 he made another difficult decision when he provided for the closure of the Hawaiian mission. Deeming the islands converted, he ordered the western missionaries to withdraw in favour of indigenous pastors and self-supporting churches.

Another major emphasis in Anderson's mission theory was the role of the Holy Spirit in the mission of the church. Following JONATHAN EDWARDS and other millennialists, Anderson had great faith in the power of the Spirit to turn the world toward Christ. He looked and saw the 'fullness of time' in the spreading influence of the modern Protestant missionary movement. Missions both represented obedience to God's will and the fulfilment of biblical prophecy.

Anderson also played a key role in the mobilization of American women for foreign missions. He supported the higher education of women as a means to prepare them to work for the conversion of the world. As a child he attended an academy with ANN HASSELTINE JUDSON, one of the first missionary wives, and thus developed a lifelong concern for the training and mobilization of missionary wives. In 1839, he spoke at the second anniversary of America's first college for women, Mt Holyoke Female Seminary, established by MARY LYON to train women as educators and missionaries. But Anderson held to female subordination to men and discouraged women from founding their own mission-sending societies.

Rufus Anderson's mission principles were clear, simple, and valuable guidelines for the pioneer period of American foreign missions. As American missions matured, however, their concern for the socio-political context of the emerging churches led to a decline of interest in three-self principles. But Anderson is still admired by evangelicals for basing American mission work on biblical principles, for stressing church planting and an indigenous ministry, and for making cultural change secondary to evangelism in the mission of the church.

BIBLIOGRAPHY
R. P. Beaver, 'The Legacy of Rufus Anderson', *Occasional Bulletin of Missionary Research* (July, 1979): 94–8
—, ed. *To Advance the Gospel* (Grand Rapids, MI, 1967)
A. C. Thompson, *Discourse Commemorative of Rev. Rufus Anderson* (Boston, MA, 1880)

DANA L. ROBERT

Anderson [Andersen], Sven (b. Smørjaberg, Göteborg, Sweden, 14 Aug. 1746; d. Hopedale, Labrador, Canada, 28 Feb. 1816). Moravian missionary to the Labrador Inuit. Anderson, a harness-maker, was a Lutheran before he became a member of the Moravian church at Zeist on 1 July 1770. He arrived in Labrador on 16 Aug. 1775 and stayed there until his death.

BIBLIOGRAPHY
Public Archives of Canada, Ottawa, 'Catalogus der Missionare in Labrador', Records of the Moravian Mission in Labrador [1764–1944], Microfilm 511, Reels 11–12, fol. 15223–4
Kölbing

MARCELLA ROLLMANN

Anderson, Thomas Gummersall (b. Sorel, Quebec, BNA, 12 Nov. 1779; d. Port Hope, Ontario, Canada, 10 Feb. 1875). Indian agent. Apprenticed to a Kingston merchant, Anderson traded with Indians in the upper Mississippi valley, 1800–14. His honourable reputation and dedication to Indian welfare later aided missionaries such as Isaac Cloux, A. DANIEL GAVIN, Samuel Dentan, and others whom he helped place among them. Service during the War of 1812 gained him the rank of captain and employment in the Indian Department of the army, 1816–30, at Mackinac, Drummond Island, and Penetanguishene. With the transfer of responsibility for Indians to the civil government, Anderson was involved in plans to protect the Indians by settling and educating them in sites such as Manitoulin Island, although a support society founded by Bishop C. J. STEWART in 1834 was not effective. From 1845 to 1858 at and near, he was the chief official responsible for Indians in Upper Canada. Anderson's evangelical convictions were not

obtrusive, but his Christian example, sincerity, and sensitivity contributed greatly to the later strength of indigenous Anglican ministry in what became (1872) Algoma diocese.

BIBLIOGRAPHY
DCB

ROBERT MERRILL BLACK

Anderson, William (b. London, 1 Dec. 1769; d. Pacaltsdorp, Cape Province, South Africa, 24 Sept. 1852). LMS missionary and Griqua leader. Anderson was the son of a Scots merchant settled in London, and went to the Cape as one of the second party sent there by the LMS. He arrived in September 1800; in February 1801 he joined J. J. KIRCHERER and his Christian Khoi (Hottentot) community on the Sak River. After a brief month of 'training', Anderson went to the border country on the Orange River, where there was no effective authority, colonial or African. People of mixed Khoi-European ancestry (at that time referred to as Bastards), runaway slaves, people of Tswana origin, deserters from the Dutch East India Company Army, were gathered round various families of mixed racial origin who were rich in horses and guns. These groups were part brigand, part pastoralist.

Anderson gradually came to be accepted by the Kok family and their followers. His consistent, patient, loving concern played a key role in persuading them to attempt to follow a settled life. By 1805, they had established a settlement at Klaarwater, a little north of the Orange, which, in 1813, was named Griquatown by JOHN CAMPBELL. Under the leadership of the 'kaptyn', Adam Kok and his principal adviser, Barend Barends, a stable society developed which built its own churches and schools. Anderson was their close friend and devoted pastor throughout, loyal both to the Gospel and to the people.

Another similar mini-state formed around the Waterboer family which also attached itself to the LMS. The Griqua 'nation' came into being around these two families and their client groups. The 'Christianity and Civilisation' of the Griqua so impressed JOHN PHILIP when he got to know them in the 1820s, that he saw their development as the model for other African peoples.

In 1814 Anderson showed his loyalty to the Griqua in a confrontation with Lord Charles Somerset, Governor of the Cape. Somerset demanded that the Griqua should supply soldiers for the Cape Corps, his new colonial regiment. The Griqua, a free people living beyond the colony's frontier, refused his order. Anderson supported them and then refused to act as a recruiting agent for Griqua mercenaries, when ordered to do so by Somerset. The governor, who was angry with the LMS in any case, found this yet one more reason for his dislike of 'these arrant dissenters'. Under extreme pressure from the colonial authorities, the LMS withdrew Anderson from his post in 1820.

After a brief stay at Swellendam, he was sent by Philip to head the station at Pacaltsdorp. There, he and his wife, Maria Schonke, a devout Afrikaner whom he married in 1805, created what many considered a model missionary community among the Khoi and Bastards, the future so-called 'Cape Coloureds'. He retired in 1848, the year Maria died, but continued to live among his people until his death in 1852.

BIBLIOGRAPHY
T. A. Anderson, *The Story of Pacaltsdorp and Some Reminiscences* (Port Elizabeth, South Africa, 1957)
R. Ross, *Adam Kok's Griqua* (Cambridge, 1976)

ANDREW C. ROSS

Anderson, William (b. Durno, Scotland, 18 Oct. 1784; d. Bristol, England, 11 June 1833). Baptist minister and tutor at Bristol Baptist College. Of pious farming stock, Anderson's early education was received in Sabbath evening schools of the Church of Scotland. During his youth, he joined with an Independent congregation in Aberdeen, but was later baptized as an adult on 18 December 1803. In February 1804 he moved to London and became a member of the Baptist church at Little Wild Street. From Bristol Academy (1805–8) he was ordained in Dunstable in 1809 and remained there until 1825 when he returned to Bristol as tutor in classics and mathematics.

BIBLIOGRAPHY
BaptMag, 25 (1833): 445–50, 488–93

KAREN E. SMITH

Andrew, James O(sgood) (b. Wilkes County, GA, USA, 3 May 1794; d. New Orleans, LA, USA, 2 March 1871). MEC,So bishop in USA. He was the son of John Andrew, the first native Georgian to enter the Methodist ministry, and Mary [née Crosby]. The father later located and became a schoolteacher. Andrew joined the South Carolina Annual Conference on trial in 1812 and served on circuits which included territory in North Carolina, South Carolina and northern Georgia. He also served in the cities of Charleston, South Carolina, Wilmington, North Carolina, Columbia, South Carolina and Augusta and Savannah in Georgia.

He was a delegate to the General Conference, the legislative body for the denomination, in 1820, 1824, 1828 and 1832. He became a presiding elder in 1824. In 1832 he was the head of his delegation from South Carolina to the General Conference and it was at this conference he was elected bishop. His episcopal assignments included most of the annual conferences in the southern states of the United States and ranged as far west as Ohio, Kentucky and Missouri. He lived in Augusta, Georgia and later Oxford, Georgia.

Andrew was married three times. In 1816 he married Ann Amelia McFarlane, who died in 1842. In 1844 he married Mrs Leonora Greenwood, who died in 1854. In 1854 he married Mrs Emily Sims Childers.

His first wife owned a slave girl and boy who became Andrew's property upon her death. The laws of Georgia did not permit owners to free their slaves at that time, but Andrew declared the girl was at liberty to leave the state at any time when provision could be made for her livelihood elsewhere. But his second wife also owned slaves, which she had inherited from her first husband. Upon their marriage the bishop drew up legal papers renouncing ownership of the slaves and securing them to his wife. His concern for this was not only his dislike for slavery, but also the Methodist church had legislation prohibiting its clergy from owning slaves in states which allowed their manumission. The issue was complicated by the fact that the slave girl would not leave Georgia for free territory and the boy was considered too young to be on his own.

Abolition sentiment was running strong at the 1844 General Conference and Andrew became the focus around which the denomination argued. The nature of the debates focused on the polity issues raised by Andrew's case rather than by the case of morality and religion involved in the holding of people in bondage. Andrew was inclined to resign but the southern delegates opposed his idea and convinced him that greater evils would happen to the church if he did. The General Conference finally adopted a resolution requesting that Andrew not exercise his office as bishop until he could free his slaves, but that he would still be considered a bishop of the church. The southern delegates reacted strongly to this resolution. Andrew's case provided another piece to the background of the adoption of the Plan of Separation which resulted, in 1846, in the creation of the MEC,So, composed mostly of former southern annual conferences of the MEC. Andrew participated in these proceedings and became one of the founding bishops of the MEC,So.

Andrew was a sincere and well-loved individual who found himself in a time in American history when great decisions and great sacrifices needed to be made. Not a strong individual he became the pawn of competing sides in an alienating contest which had no winners.

BIBLIOGRAPHY
DAB
EWM
E. S. Bucke, ed., *History of American Methodism* (Nashville, TN, 1964)
A. H. Redford, *Organization of the Methodist Episcopal Church, South* (Nashville, TN, 1871)
G. G. Smith, *James Osgood Andrew* (Nashville, TN, 1882)

L. DALE PATTERSON

Andrew, William Wayte (b. Burton Latimer, Northamptonshire, England, 1805; d. Sawbridgeworth, Hertfordshire, England, 21 Nov. 1889). Anglican clergyman. After his father's bankruptcy Andrew was apprenticed to a draper, but then inherited substantial property.

He entered St Mary Hall, Oxford, in 1826 and graduated BA in 1830 and MA in 1834. During his time at Oxford he was converted following a hunting accident and read for orders with Arthur Roberts, Rector of Wood Rising (Norfolk) (1831–86). He was successively curate at Cromer and Gimingham (1831–4) and Witchingham (all in Norfolk) (1834), in this latter year marrying Ellen Wickes. From 1835 to 1887 he was Vicar of Ketteringham (also in Norfolk), for much of this time engaged in an acrimonious relationship with the local squire, Sir John Boileau. He was also Rural Dean of Humbleyard (1843–78). Andrew attracted outsiders to his own church and engaged in some itinerant ministry in neighbouring parishes. His views were Calvinistic, Protestant, millenarian, Sabbatarian and puritanical with that killjoy quality widespread among some nineteenth-century evangelicals who saw any relaxation – cards, dancing, even gardening – as dangerous worldliness.

BIBLIOGRAPHY
O. Chadwick, *Victorian Miniature* (London, 1965)

ARTHUR POLLARD

Andrews, Henry (b. England; d. Malta, 4 Sept. 1826). CMS missionary to Malta. Andrews, a printer, was sent on 26 December 1823 by the CMS to join WILLIAM JOWETT in Malta. Like THEOPHILUS C. DEININGER before him, he soon died. His wife (Jane Fleet) married Mr Hallock of the ABCFM.

BIBLIOGRAPHY
D. T. B[arry], *CMS Register of Missionaries and Native Clergy* (privately printed) (London, 1906)

DONALD M. LEWIS

Andrews, Lorrin (b. East Windsor, CT, USA, April 1795; d. Honolulu, HI, USA, 29 September 1868). Congregational missionary. A graduate of Princeton Seminary, Andrews went to Hawaii under the ABCFM in 1828. In 1831 he was assigned to establish the Lahainaluna Seminary, which opened that year with 25 students. Over the next ten years, and with the aid of several others, the school was put on a sound footing, later becoming the University of Hawaii. In addition to administrative and professorial duties, Andrews helped with translating the Bible into Hawaiian. A person with strong antislavery feelings, in 1842 Andrews resigned from the board because it received funds from slave states. After working briefly with a seaman's mission, he was appointed by the Hawaiian government in 1845 to serve as a judge in its judicial system, which he did for ten years. During these same years he served as secretary to the government's privy council. After his retirement from the government he continued his lifelong interest in literary matters, publishing a *Hawaiian Dictionary* of some 17,000 words, and doing research into the history, songs and literature of the Hawaiian people.

BIBLIOGRAPHY
ESM

WILLIAM G. TRAVIS

Andrews, Maria Grace. *See* SAFFERY, MARIA GRACE

Angas, George Fife (b. Newcastle-upon-Tyne, England, 1 May 1789; d. 15 May 1878). Baptist businessman. Son of Caleb (a coachbuilder) and Sarah Jameson Angas, his childhood was marred by illness. Because of his ailments he was largely self-taught. He took up his father's craft after schooling and eventually became a successful merchant and mahogany trader. Deeply affected by the power of religion during his youth, he became an ardent and zealous adherent to the Baptist cause. After the age of 18 he developed an active social conscience.

By the early 1820s he was the senior partner of Angas and Company, a large firm of shipowners and merchants which had been active in Central America from the turn of the century. Aggressive evangelism went hand in hand with their commercial activities. In 1821 Angas proposed to the BMS that it send a missionary to Honduras, and he largely financed the establishment of the Baptist mission there. He also became interested in seamen's missions and was a prime founder of the Newcastle Sunday school movement.

From 1832 he became actively involved in the colonization of South Australia – a province that was deemed to have a base of civil and religious liberty. He was founding director of the South Australian Company and founded three banks in Australia, acting as chairman of their London boards until he emigrated to South Australia in 1851. He also used his influence to assist the emigration of a group of German Lutheran dissidents to South Australia. He and his wife Rosetta (nee French) arrived in South Australia in 1851, but many of their family had emigrated earlier. His last years were spent in a public career and in the pursuit of evangelical Protestantism. He was ardently anti-Catholic and amassed a large personal estate before his death.

BIBLIOGRAPHY
E. Hodder, *George Fife Angas, Father and Founder of South Australia* (London, 1891)
D. Pike, *Paradise of Dissent*, (Melbourne, 1967)
W. R. Johnson, *A History of Christianity in Belize: 1776–1838* (Lanham, MD, 1985)

ROB LINN

Angas, William Henry (b. Newcastle-upon-Tyne, Northumberland, England, 6 Oct. 1781; d. Tynemouth, Northumberland, England, 9 Sept. 1832). Baptist minister and missioner to seamen. The Angas/Anguses were a significant Baptist family in the north-east. William Henry became the captain of one of his father's West Indiamen, after having been imprisoned by the French for a year and a half during the Napoleonic Wars. In

1809, he gave this up, and was baptized by JOHN RIP-PON at Carter Lane, Southwark. After a year's study in Edinburgh, he was ordained by this church in 1817, devoting himself to mission work among sailors of all nations. In 1820 he accompanied WILLIAM WARD to Holland to secure the interests of Dutch Baptists (Mennonites) in the work of the infant BMS, with which he associated his own missionary endeavours. Working from 1822 for the British and Foreign Seamen's Friend Society and Bethel Union (later, the British Sailors' Society), he established Sunday schools, libraries and Bible classes for sailors in the different seaports of Britain and the Channel Islands. His useful life was cut short by cholera in 1832 while working a station at South Shields.

BIBLIOGRAPHY
DNB
Baptist Magazine (1832)
F. A. Cox, Life of W. H. Angas (London, 1834)
E. W. Mathews, The King's Brotherhood (London, 1911)

J. H. Y. BRIGGS

Angus, Joseph (b. Bolam, Northumberland, England, 16 Jan. 1816; d. Hampstead, London, 28 Aug. 1902). Baptist biblical scholar. Angus was educated at Newcastle-upon-Tyne, then at Stepney College, London (to prepare for the Baptist ministry) and finally at Edinburgh University. In 1837 he succeeded JOHN RIPPON as pastor of New Park Street Chapel, Southwark, London, and in 1840 became one of the secretaries of the BMS. On JOHN DYER's tragic death in 1841 Angus became sole secretary and served for eight years, a most creative period for the society. In 1841 he married Amelia Gurney (daughter of W. B. GURNEY, the BMS treasurer) who shared his enthusiasm for missions and became one of the founders (in 1867) and secretaries of the Baptist Zenana Mission. Angus organized the BMS jubilee celebrations in 1842 raising a special fund of £33,000. During his secretaryship the society's headquarters were built in Moorgate Street, the African Mission was established and Calabar College founded in Jamaica. Angus was also used to settle some difficult financial problems connected with the society's work in the West Indies (Baptist Magazine 1846). In 1849 he became president of Stepney College at a difficult time in its history. He organized the removal of the college to Regent's Park, London, in 1856 and devoted his considerable administrative ability to several important projects such as the consolidation of the college's financial position and provision for the endowment of college lectureships. Greatly interested in Christian journalism, he served as a director and literary editor of the Baptist newspaper, The Freeman. His academic gifts were recognized by Brown University, Rhode Island, which awarded him an honorary DD and London University which appointed him as examiner in English language and literature 1859–69. He was a member of the first London School Board for ten years and also of the New Testament Revision Committee.

Angus was a prolific author and wrote books and pamphlets on a variety of important subjects. His first prize essay, The Voluntary System (1839), was a vigorous reply to lectures given in London by THOMAS CHALMERS in 1838. His Christ our Life (1855) indicates his essentially Christocentric outlook, and his Christian Churches (1863), a Congregational Union Bicentenary Essay, is a discussion of the nature, discipline and government of the church as expounded in the New Testament; it also reflects his firm commitment to Free Church principles. In 1879 he used a generous gift of £2,000 (mainly donated by former students to commemorate thirty years service) to establish an Angus lectureship, giving the first series himself. Subsequently published (Regeneration, 1897) the lectures reveal his suspicion of the type of Incarnational theology advocated by nineteenth-century writers like F. D. Maurice, F. W. ROBERTSON and others who suggested that since the advent of Christ all humanity has been regenerated, whether individuals make a personal confession of faith or not. Throughout his life he gave frequent expression to his continuing missionary interest (e.g. his 1871 BMS sermon 'Apostolic Missions') and his denominational concern (see his address to the 1872 Baptist Union Assembly on 'Our Progress, Statistical and Spiritual'). His most popular work, however, was as a biblical scholar and his famous Bible Handbook was used for many years as an introduction to biblical history, literature and interpretation. He retired from the presidency of the college in 1893. During his lifetime Angus acquired a large collection of valuable Baptist literature which he bequeathed to his college, and is now housed in the Angus Library, Regent's Park College, Oxford.

BIBLIOGRAPHY
BaptMag, 38 (1846): 704: (October 1902)
R. E. Cooper, From Stepney to St Giles (London, 1960)
DNB
G. P. Gould, Regent's Park College, A Centenary Record (London, 1910)
E. A. Payne, The Great Succession (London, 1938)

RAYMOND BROWN

Anthon, Henry (b. New York City, 11 March 1795; d. New York City, 5 Jan. 1861). Protestant Episcopal clergyman. A graduate of Columbia College in 1813, he studied for ordination under Bishop John Henry Hobart, and was ordained deacon by Hobart in Trinity Church, New York City, on 29 September 1816. He was placed in charge of St Paul's Church, Red Hook, New York, and was ordained priest on 27 May 1819 by Hobart, at the same time as Hobart consecrated a new church building for St Paul's. In 1821, he became Rector of Trinity Church, Utica, New York, and was elected a trustee of the General Theological Seminary. In 1829, he moved to New York City to begin work as Rector of St Stephen's Church, and then in 1831, moved again to become Rector of Trinity Church, New York City. But in 1836, he abandoned his original allegiance to Hobartian High-Churchmanship and vigorously embraced evangelical principles; and accordingly, he resigned the rectorship of Trinity Church and took up the humbler labours of St Mark's-in-the-Bowery, New York City.

Anthon's new-found evangelicalism brought him into the most celebrated conflict of his time in the Episcopal Church. In 1843, Arthur Carey, a graduate of General Theological Seminary who had fallen there under the spell of Anglo-Catholicism, was denied testimonials for ordination by his rector, Dr Hugh Smith, on the grounds that Carey could not certify that he was in accord with 'the doctrine or discipline of the Protestant Episcopal Church.' Bishop Benjamin T. Onderdonck of New York City summoned a special board of examiners, including Smith and Anthon, which recommended Carey's ordination as deacon. But Smith and Anthon vigorously dissented, and when Onderdonck ignored them and ordained Carey on 2 July 1843, Smith and Anthon rose during the ordination to read a public objection to Carey's ordination.

Carey died shortly thereafter, but the incident had serious repercussions throughout the Episcopal Church. Bishop Onderdonck was suspended from his office in 1845 for moral misconduct, but the charges were understood to have been related to his role in the Carey debacle; General Theological Seminary was subjected to a visitation by the Episcopal House of Bishops in 1844, and although the bishops grudgingly passed favourably on the seminary, suspicion of the school as an agency 'to Romanize the Church' remained. Anthon was driven by these incidents into more radical evangelical views, especially 'in regard to the necessity of Episcopacy to the very being of a Church,' and founded a newspaper, The Protestant Churchman to act as an organ for evangelical views in his diocese. He was also instrumental in the founding in 1847 of the Protestant Episcopal Society for the promotion of Evangelical Knowledge, in 1850 of the Pastoral Aid Society of the Diocese of New York, and in 1860 of the American Church Missionary Society. On Christmas Day, 1860, he was stricken during a Communion service at St Mark's, and died 11 days later.

BIBLIOGRAPHY
E. C. Chorley, Men and Movements in the American Episcopal Church (New York, 1950)
M. Eastburn, Tributes to the Memory of the Rev. Henry Anthon, D.D. (New York, 1862)

ALLEN C. GUELZO

Antliff, William (b. Caunton, Nottinghamshire, England, 6 Dec. 1813; d. 7 Dec. 1884). Primitive Methodist minister. Reared in a pious Methodist home, Antliff was a serious, curious and precocious child. Converted when he was nine, he joined the Primitive Methodists, and engaged in child-preaching in his early teens. In 1829, at the age of 16, he became a minister. Stationed in 15 circuits in 31 years, he preached primarily at Nottingham, Ashby-de-la-Zouch (where he became superintendent), and Oldham (1857–61). Ecumenical in style and approach, Antliff preached in the chapels of other denominations.

A product of self-help, and a voracious reader, Antliff was self-educated; he taught himself Latin, Greek and Hebrew. An early advocate of temperance, he was himself an abstainer. Antliff had a reputation for being stubborn, at times overbearing and opinionated (he was personally disliked by HUGH BOURNE), but he was a dignified, conservative individual, with an impressive, commanding appearance, clear academic reasoning and perceptive wit. Moreover, he was well spoken, with a graceful, fluent oratorical style.

He was a regular attender at the Primitive Methodist conference and renowned as a talented administrator, thus gaining a prestigious influence; he was twice elected president (in 1863 and 1865), and was three times appointed conference secretary. A prolific writer, originator of The Christian Messenger (1865), editor of the connexional magazine and other denominational volumes, Antliff was criticized for making the Primitive Methodist Magazine dull and stuffy, overburdening it with essays on theology and ecclesiastical history.

Facing opposition from traditionalist 'ranters', Antliff argued the need for the scholarly training of young ministers. Eventually, in 1869, Sunderland Theological Institute was established, with Antliff as its first college principal (1869–81). In 1870, he was awarded the honorary degree of Doctor of Divinity by Middletown Wesleyan University, Connecticut. Antliff was superannuated in 1881. One of the most prominent figures in the Connection, he was described by H. B. Kendall as probably one of the most influential and best known personalities of the middle, transitional period of Primitive Methodist history.

BIBLIOGRAPHY
Boase
J. Petty, The History of the PMC (London, 1864)
G. J. Stevenson, Methodist Worthies, 5 (London, 1886)

WAYNE J. JOHNSON

Anund Masih [né Parmanand] (b. Agra, India; d. Kurnaul, India). Brahman convert and evangelist. First influenced during a visit to Agra by JOHN CHAMBERLAIN, he was later employed as a schoolmaster in Meerut by Captain and Mrs M. M. SHERWOOD under the auspices of the CMS Corresponding Committee. He was baptized as Anund Masih in 1816 by HENRY FISHER, who employed him as a catechist. Fisher's letters (1824) to DANIEL CORRIE describe his 'good conduct' and his usefulness, but need of supervision.

Beginning in 1817, Anund Masih established contacts with heterodox, syncretistic and monotheistic sects around Delhi. He was later sent to Kurnaul and encouraged to write New Testament commentaries. In 1841 he left to itinerate around Agra, returning to Meerut in 1842. Meerut's CMS committee investigated and confirmed reports of his drunkenness, drug abuse and quarrelsomeness. In May 1843 Bishop DANIEL WILSON upheld the CMS committee's findings, considering his behaviour to be the result of too much responsibility and too little supervision. Despite his behaviour, there was no reason to doubt his sincerity or the value of his early work.

BIBLIOGRAPHY
CMS archives, University of Birmingham
M. E. Gibbs, *The Anglican Church in India 1600–1970* (Delhi, 1972)

E. M. JACKSON

Anundo, Chunder Mazumdar (b. India, *c.* 1811; d. *en route* to Islington, London, 1841). LMS catechist. The nephew of Brojomohum Mazundar, who had written tracts against idolatry, Anundo became interested in the New Testament and approached ALEXANDER DUFF in March 1831. Ignoring the opinions of his family, he became the fourth pupil of the General Assembly's institution to be baptized (June 1832).

ANTHONY NORRIS GROVES, a Plymouth Brethren missionary and acquaintance of Alexander Duff, took Anundo to England after promising to settle Anundo's massive debts. In 1834 Anundo joined a church in Bristol and met a Miss Bevan, whom he married there in 1841. The LMS returned Anundo to India. But he had become too anglicized for their evangelization programme, and failed to absorb theology, languages or sciences, despite intensive efforts by William Morton. Raised as a high caste (Brahman) Bengali, wishing to be an English gentleman, and rejected by his family, Anundo was incapable of earning a living or keeping out of debt. His career typifies problems of some high caste converts in Calcutta.

BIBLIOGRAPHY
Archives of the National Library of Scotland, Alexander Duff correspondence
LMS archives, CWM archives, Centre for Oriental and African Studies, London

E. M. JACKSON

Appleyard, John Whittle (b. Cirencester, Gloucestershire, England, 15 June 1814; d. King William's Town, Cape Colony, South Africa, 4 April 1874). Methodist missionary among the Xhosa and Tswana, linguist, Bible translator, and journalist. Son of the Reverend John Appleyard, he arrived in South Africa as a missionary in January, 1840. A brilliant linguist, he immediately plunged into the study of Xhosa. In 1850 his still, in some ways, unsurpassed *Kafir Language* was published, an historical introduction to, as well as a grammar of Xhosa. In 1854 he produced a new translation of the New Testament and, with a minimum of help from others, in 1864 the complete Xhosa Bible. This version produced a great deal of controversy which persisted for a hundred years, but his version has remained popular with some Xhosa speakers.

BIBLIOGRAPHY
L. A. Hewson, *An Introduction to South African Methodists* (Cape Town, 1950)
T. Smith, *Memoir of the Rev. John Whittle Appleyard* (London, 1881)

ANDREW C. ROSS

Aratoon, C(arapiet) C(hator). (b. Bussora, Persia, 1781; d. Calcutta, India, 24 Nov. 1857). Baptist missionary in India. A member of Calcutta's prosperous Armenian community, Aratoon was influenced by street preaching and joined the Serampore Baptist Church on 6 June 1808. Sent to Jessore, he baptized many Bengali converts and was ordained pastor in September 1809.

The BMS home committee required that Aratoon, before starting a new mission in Bombay (26 September 1812), be baptized, his full immersion as an infant being deemed insufficient. Aratoon deeply resented this decision. After five unsuccessful years in Bombay and then in Sura, he returned to street preaching in Calcutta. He also engaged in business ventures. In 1822 he joined the 'junior brethren' of the Lower Circular Road Baptist Chapel. After his death, the Calcutta Missionary Council acknowledged him as a beautiful, long-suffering soul and a patriarch among evangelists.

BIBLIOGRAPHY
Periodical Accounts of the Baptist Missionary Society (1808–17)
Serampore Mission Archives, Carey Library, Serampore College
William Ward's Journal, as transcribed by E. Daniel Potts, BMS archives

E. M. JACKSON

Archbell, James (b. Tadcaster, Yorkshire, England, *c.* 1798; d. Pietermaritzburg, Natal, South Africa, 30 March 1866). Methodist missionary, Voortrekker pastor, entrepreneur and politician. Almost nothing is known of Archbell's life in Britain. In 1819 he arrived in South Africa with his wife of a year, Elizabeth Haigh, to assist BARNABAS SHAW among the Namaqua north of the Orange. Instead, he set up a separate mission to the north of Shaw. In 1823 he was assigned to replace T. L. HODGSON. The latter's mission among the Tswana was meanwhile burned to the ground in a tribal conflict and Archbell accompanied Hodgson to restart a mission among Tswana-speaking people. From 1825 until 1833 he worked with the ba-Rolong and began to study the language seriously. He published a grammar of Tswana in 1826, a hymnary in 1832 and a service book in 1833. Later, in 1837, he published in Grahamstown, a much more substantial grammar. In 1833 he persuaded Moshweshwe of the Sotho to settle several thousand Rolong at Thaba Nchu. This soon led to bitter conflict when Archbell claimed that Moshweshwe had ceded sovereignty in this transaction, at a time when Moshweshwe needed help to defend his people from the Voortrekkers. While at Thaba Nchu, Archbell went out of his way to welcome and aid the Voortrekkers who wished him to become their minister.

After some months in England and the eastern Cape, he went, in 1841, to Natal, recently claimed by the Voortrekkers who faced a counter-claim by Britain. At first, Trekkers saw Archbell as their ally but eventually felt betrayed by him. In 1846 Archbell moved to Pietermaritzburg, the capital of the new colony, where he resigned from the ministry and began a career in journalism and politics. He was Mayor of Pietermaritzburg 1858–64. He remained an active Methodist layman. Despite a deep evangelical commitment, Archbell became a bitter critic of missions in South Africa, particularly of JOHN PHILIP. Some have claimed he was ruled by a desire for personal gain, escaping from obscure poverty by mission service which led to a prosperous career in journalism and colonial politics. What appears a much more convincing explanation is that he found it easy to minister to whites and that he was never able to relate to African people to whom he became increasingly antagonistic as the years went by.

BIBLIOGRAPHY
DSAB

ANDREW C. ROSS

Archer, Matilda [Corbett, Mrs Edward] (b. London c. 1815; d. Wednesbury, Staffordshire, England, 3 Aug. 1851). Primitive Methodist itinerant preacher. Archer, with her parents, James and Matilda, moved to Birmingham while she was still young. It was a religious household, enjoying family worship and Matilda was sent to Sunday school. Converted at 14 she joined the Wesleyan Methodists, becoming a Sunday school teacher, but in 1834 became a Primitive Methodist. She was appointed a teacher and prayer leader (1834–5); local preacher (1835–6) and travelling preacher (1836–7). Matilda itinerated in Darlaston, Burland, Ludlow and Ramsor. In 1841 she married and continued as a local preacher for nine years, living in Darlaston. Travelling to an appointment, in the winter of 1850, Matilda caught a cold, which affected her lungs and she died the following August.

BIBLIOGRAPHY
PMMag (1851)

E. DOROTHY GRAHAM

Armitage, Thomas (b. Pontrefact, Yorkshire, England, 2 Aug. 1819; d. Yonkers, NY, USA, 20 Jan. 1896). Baptist pastor and writer in New York. He emigrated to the United States on 3 September 1838 and pastored for ten years in the Methodist Church. In 1847 he became a Baptist. Armitage was installed as pastor of the Fifth Avenue Baptist Church in New York City on 1 July 1848. He received several degrees during his lifetime including an MA (Madison University, 1839), DD

(Georgetown College 1853) and D.Litt. (New York University, 1888). His primary influence on the evangelical movement rests in his efforts to revise the King James Version of the Scriptures and to translate the Bible into several languages, including Chinese, German, French, Italian, and Spanish. When the ABS refused requests from Baptists to provide such translations of scripture, Armitage helped to found the American Bible Union which undertook the work.

His published works include *Jesus His Self-Introspection*, written in 1878, and *Preaching*, written in 1880. His most widely read work is entitled *A History of the Baptists Traced by the Vital Principles and Practices* (1886).

BIBLIOGRAPHY
L. M. Lawson, ed., *Record of the Services of Dedication of the Bust and Tablet Erected in the Fifth Avenue Baptist Church of New York in Memory of Thomas Armitage* (New York, 1899)

ROBERT N. MASH

Armour, Samuel (b. at the 'Curragh', near Maghera, Londonderry Co., Ireland, 1785; d. Cavan, Ireland, 25 Feb. 1853). Anglican clergyman in Ontario. Samuel Armour received his MA from the University of Glasgow in 1807 and served as a Burgher or Original Secession minister in Doune, Perthshire from 1813 until he and his wife, Margaret (nee Douglas) emigrated to Upper Canada (now Ontario) in 1820. He taught school, 1820–32, in Newmarket, York (now Toronto) and Peterborough. As there were no Original Secession churches in Upper Canada, he read theology under the Reverend John Strachan (later Bishop of Toronto) and was ordained deacon, 2 September 1826, and priest, 1 September 1827. He was the first SPG missionary at Peterborough, 1826–33, and had SPG support while serving at nearby Cavan Parish, 1833–53, where he became rector. The Good Shepherd window at St John's Ida (in Cavan) is dedicated to their 'worthy, hospitable and zealous Rector, Mr Armour'.

Armour was an energetic and learned missionary in trying circumstances. In Peterborough, he was deterred from a plan of visiting parishioners to give catechism lessons; some objected it was 'innovation'. The same congregation provided no financial support, and he bought his own surplice, Bible, and prayer-book. His prized two volume Bible was edited by THOMAS HAWEIS, the evangelical theologian. In Cavan, in addition to Sunday services at the two churches, he preached during the week in remoter parts of Cavan, Emily and Ops townships, areas where the church would eventually prosper. His prayer to parishioners was 'May salvation by the cross of Christ be your chief desire and wish and the Bible be your companion'. His interest in teaching reinforced his evangelical approach.

BIBLIOGRAPHY
Archives, Diocese of Quebec, XIII, folio 44 ff
Church (Cobourg and Toronto, e.g. 30 June 1838)
F. M. Delafosse, *Centenary History* (Peterborough, Canada, 1927)

E. W. Dunlop, ed., *Our Forest Home Being Extracts From the Correspondence of the Late Frances Stewart* (Montreal, 1902)
E. H. Jones, *St John's Peterborough* (Peterborough, Canada, 1976)
Peterborough, Canada, St John's Parish Archives
SPG papers

ELWOOD HUGH JONES

Armstrong, John (b. Philadelphia, PA, USA, 27 Nov. 1798; d. Columbus, MS, USA, 15 Sept. 1844). Baptist teacher and pastor in North Carolina and Mississippi. The son of Robert and Mary Armstrong, he became a Baptist *circa* 1814. He received his BA in 1825 from Columbian College. Then he pastored for five years at the Baptist church in Newbern, North Carolina. In 1835 he became professor of ancient languages at Wake Forest College and spent several years raising funds for the school. In addition, he served the Baptist State Convention of North Carolina as Corresponding Secretary. Following two years of travel in France and Italy, he was installed as the pastor of the First Baptist Church of Columbus, Mississippi in 1840. He served the Columbus Association as its moderator and was significantly involved in the work of the Mississippi Baptist Convention. He retired to his plantation near Columbus in 1843.

BIBLIOGRAPHY
AAP

ROBERT N. NASH

Armstrong, John (b. Manchester, England, *c*. 1801). *Fl.* 1830s. CMS missionary to British Guiana. Armstrong trained briefly at the CMS training school at Islington (London) in 1826 and was sent with CHARLES CARTER as a lay missionary to Bartica Grove, British Guiana (now Guyana) on 24 October 1827. They were the first CMS missionaries to work in South America. Their mission is unclear, but they were likely sent out in response to a request for lay catechists to work on a particular plantation. Armstong returned to England on 7 August 1833 but went back to British Guiana on 13 March 1835. He withdrew from the CMS in 1836. In 1835 he married a woman by the name of Rickatson. A daughter of theirs served as a CMS missionary.

BIBLIOGRAPHY
D. T. B[arry], *CMS Register of Missionaries and Native Clergy* (privately printed) (London, 1906)

DONALD M. LEWIS

Armstrong, Nicholas (b. Tipperary, Ireland, 1802; d. Albury Heath, Surrey, England, 9 Oct. 1879). Anglican clergyman, controversialist, and Irvingite. Armstrong was a graduate of Trinity College, Dublin. He became Rector of St James's, Dublin, where he was part of the dynamic and Romantic Irish evangelical Anglicanism of the 1820s. Fearful of the renewed power of Irish Roman Catholicism, and of its threat to the Established Church, the Christendom concept of the state, and Protestant social ascendancy, he became active in the 'New' or 'Second Reformation' for the conversion of Irish Catholics. In this connection he linked himself with J. E. GORDON's British Reformation Society and its method of mass confrontational gatherings. Soon leaving the explosive Irish situation, he became rector of St Dunstan's-in-the-West, London. His activities in England caused *Fraser's Magazine* to place him 'at the head of the most popular orators of the day'. Espousing premillennialism, with its pessimistic prognosis of church and society, he came to believe that evangelical Anglicanism could not handle the forces of liberalism and Catholicism. As a result he joined the Catholic Apostolic Church with its claim of apostolic and charismatic power and its vision of a covenant nation. On 18 January 1834 he was ordained one of its 12 apostles.

BIBLIOGRAPHY
Al. Dub.
Boase
Fraser's Magazine (1837): 196
E. Miller, *The History and Doctrines of Irvingism*, 2 vols (London, 1878)
P. E. Shaw, *The Catholic Apostolic Church* (New York, 1946): 82

IAN S. RENNIE

Armstrong, Richard (b. McEwensville, PA, USA, 13 April 1805; d. Honolulu, HI, USA, 23 Sept. 1860). Presbyterian missionary. An 1830 graduate of Princeton Seminary, Armstrong was ordained by the Baltimore presbytery, but went to Hawaii under the ABCFM, beginning his work there in 1832. After a brief stay in the Marquesas Islands he returned to Hawaii, serving on Maui 1835–40, first at Haiku, then at Wailuku. In 1840 he took up duties in Honolulu at HIRAM BINGHAM's church, remaining in the parish ministry for eight years. While serving this church he was gradually drawn into service for the Hawaiian government. He did surveys for the government when it reformed its land policy and granted individual holdings to the Hawaiians. In 1847 he was appointed Director of Public Instruction. In 1851 he established a royal school for the education of young chiefs. From 1849 to 1858 he lectured on education, supervised the 500 village schools in the islands, the seminary at Lahainaluna, and the Hilo Boarding School. By his recommendation, the department was reconstituted as a board of education in 1855, and Armstrong served as its first president.

BIBLIOGRAPHY
ESM

WILLIAM G. TRAVIS

Arnold, John J. Müehleisen (b. Zell, Wurtemberg, Germany, 1817; d. Papendorf, Cape Town, South Africa, 9

Dec. 1881). Anglican clergyman. Born John J. Müehleisen, he trained at Basel Seminary and in 1841 went with John C. Muller as a CMS missionary to Abyssinia. He was ordained (deacon 17 April 1841, priest 31 July 1841) by Bishop MICHAEL SOLOMON ALEXANDER of Jerusalem. In 1844 he transferred to western India but in May of 1848 moved to England, closed his association with the CMS and took Arnold as his surname. He became chaplain to the Bishop of Gibraltar, served as chaplain at St Mary's Hospital, Paddington (1852–61), and was Curate of East Ham, Essex (1861–5). Returning to the Continent in 1865, he became consular chaplain at Batavia. He resigned in August 1870 but continued there until June 1871. Arnold was, lastly, Rector of St Mary's, Papendorf, Cape Town, from March 1876 until his death.

In 1859 he founded the Moslem Mission Society in England and was its honorary secretary 1860–5. Arnold published a number of lengthy evangelistic works in which he compared Christianity favourably to Islam. He was also responsible for *English Biblical Criticism* (2nd edn, 1864), a reaction to German Higher Criticism, and *Genesis and Science* (2nd edn, 1875), a creationist text.

BIBLIOGRAPHY
D. T. B[arry], *CMS Register of Missionaries And Native Clergy from 1804 to 1904* (privately printed) (London, 1906): 56
BLC
Boase

JONATHAN BURKE CUTMORE AND DONALD M. LEWIS

Arnold, John Motte (b. Acra, NY, USA, 15 Oct. 1824; d. Detroit, MI, USA, 5 Dec. 1884). Methodist clergyman and holiness advocate. After his father's death left the family with meagre funds, he attended Sunday school but was unable to afford more than five years of formal education. Despite this he became a voracious reader. In 1839, he and his mother moved to Michigan. At the Remeo, Michigan, camp meeting (May 1841), where he went to sell water melons, he fell under conviction. He was finally converted in a Methodist church (20 March 1842) and felt called to the ministry. After teaching school for a year (1848) in Rochester, Michigan, he began itinerant work as minister on the Birmingham, Michigan, circuit. In the fall of 1849, he was received into the conference on trial. He pastored in Litchfield, Port Huron, St Clair, Flint, Corunna, Owasso, Dexter and then Detroit.

In Detroit, he established a branch of the Western Book Concern (bookshop) which he managed until 1881. In 1863, he proposed a conference periodical, which eventually evolved into *The Michigan Advocate* which became *The Michigan Christian Advocate* and one of the nation's most influential holiness periodicals. He became associate editor (1876–9) and then editor (1879–84). He re-initiated the Detroit Sunday School Alliance (1877), and was one of the founders of the Bay View Camp Meeting Association (1875).

BIBLIOGRAPHY
M. A. Boughton, ed., *Selections From the Autobiography of Rev. J. M. Arnold, D.D. and From His Editorial Writings on the Doctrine of Sanctification* (Ann Arbor, MI, 1885)

DAVID BUNDY

Arnot, William (b. Scone, Scotland, 6 Nov. 1808; d. Edinburgh, 3 June 1875). Presbyterian/Free Church minister. The son of a farmer, Arnot worked on the land before going to Glasgow University in 1829. In 1839 he was ordained into the Church of Scotland, joining the Free Church at the Disruption. He was minister of St Peter's, Glasgow from 1839 to 1863 (the church moved site in 1850), when he went to the Free High Church, Edinburgh, where he served until his death. His preaching was particularly appealing to young men, and he wrote popular works addressing their dilemmas. He lectured frequently to the YMCA. He was a strong temperance advocate. He travelled widely, supplying the newly organized Free Church in Montreal (1845), and visiting the Continent and America under the auspices of the EA. He helped to promote the 1861 Glasgow revival and Moody and Sankey's visit to Edinburgh in 1873.

SELECT WRITINGS
Autobiography of the Rev. William Arnot, and Memoir by his Daughter, 3rd edn (New York, 1878)

BIBLIOGRAPHY
Boase

JANE GARNETT

Arthington, Robert (b. Leeds, England, 20 May 1823; d. Teignmouth, Devon, England, 9 Oct. 1900). Missionary philanthropist. The only son of Robert and Maria [nee Jowitt] of Hunslet Lane, Leeds, Robert junior was brought up in the evangelical Quaker faith of his parents. It is said that he studied at Cambridge University, but there is no record of his matriculation. His father was a prosperous brewer, but abandoned his business after being persuaded of temperance principles in 1846. His mother was disowned by the Leeds monthly meeting of the Society of Friends in 1838 after she had been baptized. A decade later, Arthington, having also been baptized, left the Friends. For a time he maintained close links with the Christian Brethren. Later he became associated with South Parade Baptist Chapel. On his father's death in 1864, Arthington inherited a fortune of £200,000. He never entered into business himself, but relied on prudent investment to maximize his inheritance.

Arthington's wealth was not used for his own comfort – he lived in austerity in a mansion on Headingley Hill – nor generally to support local philanthropic causes; he became known as 'the miser of Headingley'. Rather it was dedicated to the consuming passion for overseas missions which characterized his life from the

1850s to his death. The most frequent recipients of his largesse were the BMS and the LMS. As a premillennialist, Arthington believed in the urgent priority of pioneer evangelism, and much of his giving was conditional upon the willingness of missionary societies to embark on new projects in virgin territory. The BMS Congo mission and the Central Africa mission of the LMS, both begun in 1877, were the result of his initiative and money. The Arthington Aborigines Mission, established in 1889, pioneered work among the hill tribes of Mizoram, which laid the foundations for the extraordinary success of the Welsh Calvinistic Methodist Mission and the BMS in this part of north-east India.

Arthington left half of his residuary estate of approximately £1 million to the BMS, and two-fifths to the LMS. He was perhaps the most remarkable British missionary philanthropist of the nineteenth century.

BIBLIOGRAPHY
A. M. Chirgwin, *Arthington's Million* (London, no date)
S. Southall, 'An uncommon life', *Friends' Quarterly Examiner*, 35 (1901): 277–86
B. Stanley, 'The Miser of Headingley', *SCH(L)*, 24 (1987): 371–82

BRIAN STANLEY

Arthur, Sir **George** (b. Plymouth, Devon, England, 21 June 1784; d. England, 19 Sept. 1854). Colonial administrator. Born into a Plymouth merchant family, he saw service in the Napoleonic wars and was a major by 1812. In 1814 he became Superintendent of British Honduras, beginning a long career as colonial administrator. From 1824–36 he was Lieutenant-Governor of Van Dieman's Land (VDL), a convict colony; 1837–41 Lieutenant-Governor of Upper Canada; and 1842–7 Governor of Bombay. Efficiency-minded and autocratic, he did not suffer fools or liberals gladly. Around 1820 he became deeply convicted of personal sinfulness and the 'truth and power' of the Gospel. His family feared he had become a 'Methodist'. He had not, but often claimed churchmen were inferior to Methodists in ministering to the moral and religious needs of colonists and convicts.

Arthur corresponded with leading lay Evangelicals: WILLIAM WILBERFORCE, JAMES STEPHEN, THOMAS FOWELL BUXTON and ZACHARY MACAULAY. Thoroughly Erastian, he in effect maintained against Archdeacon (later Bishop) Broughton in VDL, and Archdeacon (later Bishop) Strachan in Upper Canada, that *he* was colonial pastor-in-chief. However he wielded the sword of mercy indirectly, remotely. His chief claim to evangelical originality was the 'system' of convict administration he created in VDL, a kind of out-of-doors Panopticon. Rigorous invigilation was to ensure bad conduct was punished, and good rewarded. Chaplains were to foster the development of 'mind' (by which Arthur meant feelings of degradation) in convicts. Thus 'minded', shamed as well as hurt by punishment, the convict would be led, step by step, to develop the 'inward regulator', which conforms

conduct to the laws of God and man. The 'system' recognized human freedom, but subtly, causing sheep and goats to select themselves. Arthur's punishment–redemption machine did not long survive his departure. His attitude to the children of convicts and native peoples was anxiously benevolent, but unimaginative. His removal of the remnants of the Aboriginal Tasmanians to Flinder's Island, seeking to convert them from hunter-gathering to farming and Christianity, brought about their near-destruction.

BIBLIOGRAPHY
A. G. L. Shaw, *Sir George Arthur, Bart, 1784–1854* (Melbourne, 1980)

RICHARD ELY

Arthur, William (b. Kells, Antrim, Ireland, 3 Feb. 1819; d. Cannes, France, 9 March 1901). Methodist author. Converted at age 16 Arthur began preaching in the same year. He was trained for the Wesleyan ministry at Hoxton Theological Institution (1837–9) and sailed for India to serve as a Wesleyan missionary in Mysore. In 1841 a serious ophthalmic disorder necessitated his return to England. For a limited period he served the Wesleyan Missionary Committee by advocating their work in the churches and then, as a gifted linguist, was sent to missionary service in France, working at Boulogne (1846) and Paris (1847). From 1848 to 1850 he had London pastoral appointments at Hinde Street (1849) and Great Queen Street (1850), and in 1851 became one of the secretaries of the Wesleyan Missionary Society and served for 17 years. Arthur remained a passionate enthusiast for overseas missions throughout his whole life. He was appointed principal of the newly built Methodist College, Belfast, in 1868, a post he held, despite increasingly poor health, for three years. He was appointed a member of the Legal Hundred (1856), was elected president of the Wesleyan Conference in 1866 and served as the denomination's Fernley lecturer (1883). He became a supernumerary minister in 1888. Arthur was for many years one of the secretaries of the EA. Serious throat trouble and poor eyesight limited his preaching ministry, but he became a gifted writer on a wide variety of subjects. A keen reader, he took an alert interest not only in contemporary theological developments but also in history, travel, philosophy, current affairs, biography, world religions, missionary experience and strategy, and wrote books on all these subjects.

His most influential book *The Tongue of Fire* (1856) offered an essentially practical interpretation of the doctrine of the Holy Spirit in relation to the Christian life and maintained that the Spirit's work was hindered by unbelief, foolish talking, sensual indulgences and even by a concern among preachers to produce a polished 'literary effect' in their sermons. He took fierce exception to the contemporary practice of reading a sermon manuscript from the pulpit. Such fears about mid-nineteenth-century evangelical preaching were seriously criticized by James Kendall in his *Pulpit Liberty* (London, 1857).

BIBLIOGRAPHY

J. H. J. Barker (ed. with intro.), *The Tongue of Fire*, abridged centenary edn (London, 1956)

T. B. Stephenson, *William Arthur* (London, 1907)

G. S. Wakefield, *Methodist Devotion 1791–1945* (London, 1966): 61–6

RAYMOND BROWN

Asbury, Daniel (b. Fairfax County, VA, BNA, 18 Feb. 1762; d. Catawba County, NC, USA, 15 April 1825). Methodist circuit rider. Asbury was one of the first Methodists to evangelize in the wilds of the South, including the Carolinas and Georgia. His adventurous spirit is attributed to his abduction by Shawnee Indians when he was 16 years old. Returning home at age 21, he became a Methodist convert and eventually a minister. Asbury was a powerful speaker with a deep religious experience.

BIBLIOGRAPHY

AAP: 127–9

WOODROW W. WHIDDEN AND JEFFREY W. SMITH

Asbury, Francis (b. Handsworth, Staffordshire, England, 20 or 21 Aug. 1745; d. Richmond, VA, USA, 31 March 1816). Second American Methodist bishop. Asbury was born in the parish of Handsworth, about four miles north of the city of Birmingham. His childhood was spent in a four-roomed cottage about two miles away, in the parish of Great Barr. His meagre schooling in the hamlet of Snails Green, at a shilling a week, was nothing like as important as the scholarly example of his mother Elizabeth, whom Asbury always remembered standing 'by a large window, poring over a book for hours together' (Clark, Manning Potts, and Payton, 1, 1958: 720); his gardener father, Joseph, left no such vivid memory. Asbury was able to read his Bible when he was six, and 'greatly delighted in the historical part of it'. He would 'pry into the Bible by twinkling firelight' on the wooden bench in the corner of the large fireplace while his mother chided him, 'Frank, you will spoil your eyes!' (ibid.: 720–1) His young friends nicknamed him 'Methodist parson'. Asbury Cottage was purchased by the World Methodist Council in 1959, was restored, refurnished, and is now maintained as a place of pilgrimage by the Corporation of West Bromwich.

When he was nearing 14 years of age, in 1750, his father bound him apprentice, but not to the Methodist blacksmith Henry Foxall, as tradition has it, but to John Griffin, whose trade was 'chape filing'. (A chape was a metal overlay fashioned for a belt buckle, a bucket handle, or even a scabbard, a subspecialty of the Staffordshire 'Black Country' hardware.) Griffin's workshop was congenial to religion, and he treated his apprentice 'more like a son or an equal' (Baker, 1976: 108). The Asbury home also became a centre for religious gatherings, and Elizabeth Asbury persuaded a devout visitor

to take young Frank under his wing. They forsook the ministrations of the 'blind priest' at the local parish church for the evangelical preaching sponsored by the EARL OF DARTMOUTH at All Saints' Church, West Bromwich. He was introduced to the writings of GEORGE WHITEFIELD and JOHN CENNICK, and then was encouraged by his mother to visit Wednesbury, already a focal point for a decade of Methodist revival and anti-Methodist persecution. He may well have been present on 4 March 1760, when JOHN WESLEY preached in the new 'preaching-house' at Wednesbury, and certainly came under the influence there of one of Wesley's most effective evangelists, ALEXANDER MATHER, and also of Mather's wife, who conducted regular prayer meetings in the area. He was about 16 when he 'experienced a marvelous display of the grace of God, which some might think was full sanctification' (Clark, Manning Potts, and Payton, 1, 1958: 125).

Soon he was accompanying his mother to the fortnightly women's devotional meetings which she conducted. He himself described the next stage: 'After I had been thus employed as a clerk for some time, the good sisters thought that Frank might venture a word of exhortation. So, after reading, I would venture to expound and paraphrase a little on the portion read.' He extended his tentative speaking efforts to meetings in their own cottage, and then to a friend's house in Sutton Coldfield. Alexander Mather was so impressed by the reports that while Asbury was still 17 he appointed him leader of the first Society Class at West Bromwich Heath, a fellowship class for twenty young men.

In 1763, at 18 he received official status as a local preacher, conducting his first public service at Manwoods cottage on the estate of Lord Dartmouth, a regular worshipper at the little Wednesbury Methodist preaching-house, where his tenants were instructed to address him as 'Brother Dartmouth'. (Prior to the War of American Independence Dartmouth served as Colonial Secretary for England, 1772–5.) Asbury later downplayed his own status at this time:

> Behold me now a local preacher! The humble and willing servant of any and every preacher that called on me by night or by day; being ready with hasty steps to go far and wide to do good, visiting Derbyshire, Staffordshire, Warwickshire, and indeed almost every place within my reach, for the sake of precious souls; preaching generally three, four, and five times a week, and at the same time pursuing my calling. (Ibid.: 722)

He would be up most mornings at 4 a.m. to finish his work in time to preach, and occasionally not return until midnight, walking both ways to his appointments. An old Methodist recollected him as 'a youth not quite out of his 'teens, with a voice like the roaring of a lion' (*PWHS*, 16: 76).

In 1764 the young men in his West Bromwich class built their own 'Society Room', and whenever possible young Asbury conducted Sunday morning services there at 8 a.m. to a congregation of men and women separated by a central pillar, in accordance with Wesley's instructions. They were joined by another young Staffordshire Methodist, RICHARD WHATCOAT of Quinton, who became a local preacher two or three years later, followed Asbury to America, and was elected a Methodist bishop there in 1800.

Having turned 21, in 1766, he was called upon to supply some of the appointments of an ailing itinerant, William Orpe, and did it to such good effect that at the 1767 Conference he was 'admitted on trial' as an itinerant preacher, and appointed to Bedford under the helpful supervision of James Glassbrook, whom he was to meet later as a Presbyterian minister in New York. The 1768 Conference received him into 'Full Connexion', and stationed him in the one-man circuit of Colchester, or Essex. He continued to have the normal Methodist preacher's experience of travelling around a circuit of two or three hundred miles, organizing new societies, settling disputes in old ones, preaching to groups large and small, in cottages or preaching-houses, accepting local hospitality, and only rarely sleeping in the same bed two nights in succession. He also had the normal preacher's experience of itinerating not only around a circuit, but around the circuits in general, never being able to put his roots down for long; on 26 October 1768, he informed his parents that he had been moved from Essex to south Wiltshire to serve under Nicholas Manners. In 1769 he was again appointed by Wesley to Bedford, under Richard Henderson, though with Northamptonshire as his own major responsibility. In 1770 he was stationed again in south Wiltshire, under John Catermole, but by that winter he already had 'strong intimations in my mind that I should visit America' (ibid.: 3) – probably from hearing about Wesley's search during 1770 for more preachers to join the two who had been sent in 1769. At the 1771 Conference, Asbury was one of five volunteers to go to America, the senior of the two accepted. He was only 26, however, and during his four years on country circuits had never been listed in the printed *Minutes* as one Wesley's senior 'Assistants', though his experience had been very varied.

He sailed from the tiny seaport of Pill, five miles northwest of Bristol, along with his colleague Richard Wright, on 4 September 1771, and reached Philadelphia on October 27. During the long voyage – after three days being 'very ill with the seasickness' (ibid.: 4) – he steeped himself in the writings of John Wesley. The voyage also furnished the occasion for him to follow Wesley's example by beginning a journal. Therein on 12 September he examined his own motives:

> Whither am I going? To the new world. What to do? To gain honour? No, if I know my own heart. To get money? No, I am going to live to God, and to bring others so to do ... The people God owns in England are the Methodists. The doctrines they preach, and the discipline they enforce, are, I believe, the purest of any people now in the world ... If God does not acknowledge me in America,

> I will soon return to England. I know my views are upright now – may they never be otherwise! (Ibid.: 4–5)

God did acknowledge him in America, nor did he ever return to England.

From the outset Asbury strove to implement Wesley's insistence upon the disciplined itinerancy of Methodism as opposed to the more comfortable settled ministry into which his 1769 Methodist predecessors – his seniors by six or seven years – had slipped, JOSEPH PILMORE in Philadelphia and RICHARD BOARDMAN in New York. He confided to his journal of 21 November:

> My brethren seem unwilling to leave the cities, but I think I shall show them the way. I am in trouble, and more trouble is at hand, for I am determined to make a stand against all partiality. I have nothing to seek but the glory of God; nothing to fear but his displeasure. (Ibid.: 10)

The further trouble which he sensed was at hand was because he had discovered a laxity in society discipline even in the cities, and was embarking on a 16-point plan of reform. Wesley supported him, however, and in 1772 appointed him temporary assistant over all the American work, including that of his senior colleagues. By 1773, however, Wesley had persuaded a still more senior preacher, with seven years' English experience as an assistant, THOMAS RANKIN, to take over from Asbury as general assistant. Like Asbury, Rankin firmly believed in the itinerancy, and himself practised it. (Throughout his 45 years in America Asbury never had a permanent home.) Although there were occasional points of friction between the two men, on the whole they worked well together, and Asbury never took major decisions without adding the proviso, 'unless Mr. Rankin has given orders to the contrary' (Clark, Manning Potts, and Payton, 3, 1958: 19).

Rankin added another essential element of English Methodism, by speedily summoning the first annual Conference of American Methodism, which assembled in Philadelphia on 14–16 July 1773. By the time of the second annual conference in May 1774, however, the developing anti-British sentiment convinced Rankin that he should return with some others to England, though Asbury's charge of desertion shamed him into remaining for a few more years. Asbury's main task became that of disciplining the less able of the native preachers who were volunteering for the task, and of recruiting and training others who might strengthen the ministerial ranks while maintaining the original Methodist evangelical enthusiasm and administrative discipline. On 1 September 1773, he confessed himself 'much distressed on account of so few preachers well qualified for the work, and so many who are forward to preach without due qualification' (Clark, Manning Potts, and Payton, 1, 1958: 91–2).

The declared policy of the British preachers was to remain politically neutral, but this became so difficult that by 1778 all had left except James Dempster, who eventually became a Presbyterian minister in New York, and Asbury himself, who went into hiding at Judge Thomas White's or John Fogwell's in Delaware, and for at least one day in a swamp (Williams, 1984: 46–8). He seems never to have renounced his British citizenship, but became increasingly sympathetic to American aspirations for political independence, and resolutely determined that Methodist churchmanship must be adapted to American needs. He managed to prevent a schism by some southern preachers, pending some positive action by Wesley.

For both British and American Methodism 1784 was a year of dramatic and far-reaching change, in all of which Asbury was concerned. Wesley legally incorporated one hundred of his representative preachers to take over the government of the British Methodist societies after his death, and nominated Asbury to fill the first vacancy which developed. He prepared a reformed *Book of Common Prayer* for use in America, *The Sunday Service of the Methodists*, of which Asbury presented a copy to George Washington. Wesley included therein a revised threefold ordinal, which replaced bishops and priests by superintendents and elders, as having the same functions but without the pomp and superstition. And in 1784 Wesley vicariously ordained Asbury as a 'Superintendent' through the agency of Dr THOMAS COKE, whom he had himself first elevated to that office – without using the word 'consecration'. Asbury insisted on summoning his American colleagues in conference to confirm or reject this British authorization. He wrote later: 'My real sentiments are union but no subordination; connexion but no subjection' (Clark, Manning Potts, and Payton, 3, 1958: 65). This conference, beginning on Christmas Eve, 1784, and continuing until 3 January 1785, in Baltimore, founded and organized the Methodist Episcopal Church, with two 'Superintendents', Coke and Asbury, and a 'Form of Discipline' solidly based on Wesley's 1780 'Large' *Minutes*, but with some important American revisions.

Although in their joint publications and proclamations Thomas Coke's name always preceded that of Francis Asbury, the American Methodists had no question that Asbury was their primary superintendent: Coke was unassimilated, and too often absent. The speedily translated title 'Bishop Asbury', however, induced universal love, respect, and even awe. After long consideration he wrote on 11 May 1805: 'I will tell the world what I rest my authority upon. 1. Divine authority. 2. Seniority in America. 3. The election of the General Conference. 4. My ordination by Thomas Coke, PHILIP WILLIAM OTTERBEIN, German Presbyterian minister, Richard Whatcoat, and THOMAS VASEY. 5. Because the signs of an apostle have been seen in me' (Ibid.: 469–70).

For thirty years Bishop Asbury made an annual tour of America from New England south along the Atlantic coast to Charleston, returning west of the mountains, his itineraries faithfully recorded in the headlines of his *Journal*. As his chief editor, Dr Elmer T. Clark, said in *The Encyclopedia of World Methodism*: 'He became the best-known man in America. He travelled more, knew more people, and had a better knowledge of the trails, towns,

and villages, than any other person' (*EWM*, 1: 162). Dr Clark's *Album of Methodist History* (pp. 163–4), records that he rode on horseback or by carriage 270,000 miles, preached 16,000 times, and ordained by his own hands 4,000 Methodist preachers. As Alexander Gordon testified in the (British) *Dictionary of National Biography*, 'Asbury's *Journal* shows him to have been a man of simple and winning character, administrative power, and pithy expression; his piety is both frank and deep.'

Asbury died unmarried on Sunday, 31 March 1816, after preaching his last sermon on 24 March at Richmond, Virginia. He was buried three times, first in the family burying ground of the log cabin home of George Arnold, near Spottsylvania, Virginia, where he collapsed and died on his way to the General Conference in Baltimore. When the General Conference assembled, on 2 May 1816, they ordered the corpse to be brought to Baltimore, where a 'vast procession' followed the disinterred body to a vault in Eutaw Street Church; the funeral sermon was preached by WILLIAM MCKENDREE, the sole remaining Methodist bishop. In 1854 the remains were removed to Mount Olivet Cemetery in Baltimore, to rest in the company of three other Methodist bishops, ENOCH GEORGE, JOHN EMORY, and BEVERLY WAUGH, along with ROBERT STRAWBRIDGE, JESSE LEE, and other early Methodist leaders. On 28 February 1919, by joint resolution of the Senate and the House of Representatives, Congress authorized the erection of public grounds in Washington, DC, of a memorial to Asbury, and a noble statue of the itinerant preacher on horseback was duly dedicated on 15 October 1924. His true stature, his true mission, was thus recognized nationally.

BIBLIOGRAPHY
F. Baker, *From Wesley to Asbury* (Durham, NC, 1976): 105–41
E. T. Clark, J. Manning Potts and J. S. Payton, eds, *The Journal and Letters of Francis Asbury*, 3 vols (Nashville, TN, 1958)
EWM
PWHS
L. C. Rudolph, *Francis Asbury* (Nashville, TN, 1966)
E. S. Tipple, *Francis Asbury* (New York, 1916)
W. H. Williams, *The Garden of American Methodism* (Wilmington, DE, 1984)

FRANK BAKER

Ash, Edward (b. Bristol, England, 12 Aug. 1797; d. Cotham, Bristol, England, 23 Dec. 1873). Physician and biblical scholar. Born into a Bristol Quaker family (he was first cousin to ROBERT CHARLETON), he qualified MD in 1825, practising for 12 years in Norwich, where he was profoundly influenced by the ministry and personal friendship of JOSEPH JOHN GURNEY. He was recorded a minister in 1834. In 1835–7 he was, with Gurney, on a committee appointed to visit Manchester meeting in connection with dissensions centring round ISAAC CREWDSON.

On retirement in 1837 he returned to Bristol. He wrote *Explanatory Notes and Comment on the New Testament* (1849–50) and was assiduous in conducting Bible classes especially for the young. The official reprinting of Robert Barclay's *Apology for the True Christian Divinity* (1676) 'to some portions of which he strongly objected' led to his issuing an anonymous pamphlet (1849) and to resigning his membership in 1852. He continued to attend Quaker meetings, however, and did not induce others to leave. He rejoined in 1863 and was again recorded a minister in 1871.

BIBLIOGRAPHY
E. Ash, *A Retrospect of My Life* (Bristol, England, 1874)
Annual Monitor (New York, 1875): 198–209

EDWARD H. MILLIGAN

Ash, John (b. Dorset, England, *c.* 1724; d. Pershore, Worcestershire, England, 10 April 1779). Particular Baptist minister. Baptized in Loughwood, Dorset, he was admitted to Bristol Academy 12 June 1748 and ordained pastor of the Pershore Baptist Church in June 1751. He was active in the Midland Baptist Association, as moderator and author of Association Letters. He was a close friend of CALEB EVANS with whom he edited the first Baptist hymn-book, *A Collection of Hymns Adapted to Public Worship* (1769), using a selection of Baptist hymnwriters, including ANNE STEELE and BENJAMIN BEDDOME, bringing emotional warmth and sensitivity to Baptist worship. Ash's evangelical Calvinism is epitomized in *The Perfecting of the Saints* (1778). As lexicographer he introduced stress marks to aid pronunciation.

SELECT WRITINGS
J. Ash, *Grammatical Institutes* (London, 1766)
—, *The Easiest Introduction to Dr Lowth's English Grammar* (London, 1768)
—, *The New and Complete Dictionary of the English Language* (London, 1775)

BIBLIOGRAPHY
DNB
N. S. Moon, *Education for Ministry* (London, 1979)
G. F. Nuttall, 'John Ash and the Pershore Church', *BQ* XXII (1968)
S. A. Swaine, *Faithful Men* (London, 1884)
G. H. Taylor, 'The Reverend John Ash', *BQ* XX (1963)

ROGER HAYDEN

Ashley, Lord. *See* SHAFTESBURY, the seventh Earl of

Ashley-Cooper, Anthony. *See* SHAFTESBURY, the seventh Earl of

Ashton, William (b. Heaton Norris, Lancashire, England, 13 July 1817; d. Barkley West, Cape Province, South Africa, 29 March 1897). Missionary, translator, and printer. Ashton, a skilled carpenter and bookkeeper, studied for the ministry at Airedale College. After ordination, the LMS sent him to South Africa in 1843 to work with ROBERT MOFFAT. From 1843 to 1864 and

again from 1871 to 1876 he worked with Moffat at Kuruman. In the interval he ran a station at the present day Delportshoop. After leaving Kuruman in 1876 he spent his remaining years at Barkley West.

From 1850 he devoted seven years to aiding Moffat translating the Bible into seTswana. He felt that this work was never fully appreciated. He also differed with Moffat and later again with the latter's son 'J. S.' over-reliance on African teachers and preachers to which, like DAVID LIVINGSTONE and JOHN MACKENZIE, Ashton was deeply committed.

BIBLIOGRAPHY
Boase
DSAB

ANDREW C. ROSS

Ashton, William (Easterly) (b. Philadelphia, PA, USA, 18 May 1793; d. Philadelphia, PA, USA, 26 July 1836). Baptist pastor and teacher in Pennsylvania. He was baptized shortly after his birth at Christ Church Cathedral in Philadelphia. In 1809 he joined the Second Baptist Church of Philadelphia and was baptized again by immersion. Licensed and ordained in 1814, he served for ten years as the pastor of Baptist churches in Hopewell, Pennsylvania and in Philadelphia. He also founded a seminary for women in Philadelphia. He received an MA from the College of New Jersey in 1830.

In 1823 Ashton was installed as pastor of the Third Baptist Church of Philadelphia. He also continued his teaching load at the seminary. In addition, he offered weekly instruction at no charge to young men who were preparing for the ministry. Following a lengthy illness, he resigned as pastor on 23 February 1835. Ashton served as the first president of the Baptist General Association of Pennsylvania and as a member of the Board of the General Missionary Convention in the United States of America for Foreign Missions, the first national Baptist organization in America.

BIBLIOGRAPHY
AAP

ROBERT N. NASH, JR.

Ashwell, Benjamin Yate (b. Birmingham, England, 1810; d. Auckland, New Zealand, 29 Sept. 1883). CMS missionary to New Zealand. Trained at Islington 1–2, Ashwell journeyed in November 1833 with his wife, Harriet, to Sierra Leone as a CMS lay missionary. Invalided home in 1834, in 1835 he was sent to New Zealand. Despite his lifelong evangelistic eagerness, because of his temperamental instability he was not readily assigned his own station. He worked under ROBERT MAUNSELL at Maraetai 1839–42, making long exploratory journeys and initiating Christian communities inland. In 1842, Ashwell established his own station near Taupiri, at Pepepe, then Kaitotehe. Deaconed in

1848 and priested in 1853, he remained until ejected in 1863 by interracial warfare. One of the few missionaries to return to his former station he persisted sporadically throughout the 1860s and then 1872–9, also visiting hospitals and prisons. Unexpectedly successful as a missionary, he established a flourishing work and highly regarded school, all effectively lost in the conflict and subsequent Maori depopulation of the Waikato.

BIBLIOGRAPHY
Scholefield
A. H. McLintock, ed., *An Encyclopedia of New Zealand*, 1 (Wellington, 1966): 100

BRYAN D. GILLING

Ashworth, John (b. Rochdale, Lancashire, England, 8 July 1813; d. Rochdale, Lancashire, England, 26 Jan. 1875). Author, lecturer, and philanthropist. Ashworth was the son of John and Alice Ashworth, woollen weavers. He started his working life as a weaver and later became a house-painter. After membership of a Wesleyan Sunday school he joined the Wesleyan Methodist Association in 1836. Childhood privations left a keen determination to serve the poorest sections of Rochdale society. His strong evangelical faith found many outlets for practical work. He created or supported many agencies for the relief of poverty and for moral and spiritual improvement. In 1848 he founded a ragged school, and ten years later he opened the Chapel for the Destitute which drew its first congregation from a nearby lodging house. Ashworth supervised the chapel until his death.

Besides his tracts on particular types of hardship and pacifism, he was a prolific writer of narratives. He first attracted public attention outside his locality in the *United Methodist Free Churches Magazine* of 1861. During the next ten years he acquired a reputation as a result of *Strange Tales from a Humble Life*, a collection of 61 stories based on his experiences of local characters and incidents especially in connection with the Chapel for the Destitute. The popularity of this work, some three million copies of the tales were published, led to the appearance of a sequel entitled *Simple Records*.

BIBLIOGRAPHY
A. L. Calman, *Life and Labours of John Ashworth*, 3rd edn (Manchester and London, 1876)
DNB

D. A. GOWLAND

Atherton, William (b. Lamberhead Green, near Wigan, Lancashire, England, 1775; d. London, 26 Sept. 1850). Methodist minister. He entered the Wesleyan ministry in 1797, at the age of 21. After a year in the Grimsby circuit, from 1799 he spent ten years in Scotland. In this land of sermon-tasters and limited itinerancy, he learned habits of close study and logical thought, as well as developing a speaking style which was (as his conference obituary noted) both 'peculiarly forcible, epigrammatic, and racy' (*WMM*, 1851: 914), and 'full-fraught with evangelical theology' (ibid.). From 1802 onwards he served as the superintendent minister of his circuits. In 1810, after another two years as superintendent in Edinburgh (where he had been stationed in 1801), he came south of the border to superintend the Sunderland circuit, and then to guide its offshoot, the Durham circuit. From 1814 for a decade he served the normal two or three years in different parts of the country (mainly in northern circuits) without the responsibilities of the superintendency, which he took up again in Wakefield in 1825.

In 1818 he ventured into print, 'improving' the death in 1817 of Princess Charlotte, daughter of the unpopular Prince Regent (later King George IV). His chief claim to literary fame, however, was a sketch of the life of Lady DARCY MAXWELL (c. 1742–1810), an evangelical Scots Methodist, and great friend of JOHN WESLEY; Atherton had known her well during his years in Scotland. This was published in three instalments of the *Wesleyan Methodist Magazine* for 1816 – some 15,000 words. In 1821 John Lancaster, who had been more fortunate than Atherton in securing Lady Maxwell's voluminous diary and manuscripts, published her biography, which went through two editions. In 1839, after Lancaster's death, Atherton re-arranged, abridged, and revised this work, incorporating some of his own biographical material; this went through two further editions. In that same year of 1839 he also contributed to the Centenary of Wesleyan Methodism 'a sermonic address' on *Wesleyan Methodism, in its Character, Agencies, and Religious Effectiveness*.

At the age of fifty, in 1827, Atherton was successively associated with various London circuits, and became a familiar figure in Wesleyan Conference debates, daring to oppose the dominance of JABEZ BUNTING. At the 1834 Conference a veteran president of that august body chided the members for the outbursts of applause following speeches by both Bunting and Atherton. On that occasion Atherton had spoken against undue subservience to the Church of England: 'What has it done for Methodism? It gave us Wesley; but not as a boon. It cast him out as a pestilent fellow. We might as well say that we are indebted to the Church of Rome for Luther' (Hurst, 1901: 1362). In 1846, 'his ministerial jubilee', the conference elected Atherton as their president, by 208 votes out of the 251 cast. He 'discharged its onerous duties with impartiality, vigour, and kindness' (Anon., 1891: 66).

Atherton figures frequently in Dr Benjamin Gregory's publication (1898), and his lengthy obituary appears in the Wesleyan *Minutes* of 1851. Thomas E. Brigden, who penned the three volumes on British Methodism for Bishop John Fletcher Hurst's *History of Methodism* (1901) characterized him thus: 'William Atherton was an original, pungent, forceful preacher, who lived to see his son become solicitor-general for England' (Hurst, 1901: 1331).

BIBLIOGRAPHY
Anon., *Wesley and His Successors* (London, 1891)
B. Gregory, *Side Lights on the Conflicts of Methodism . . . 1827–1852* (London, 1898)
J. F. Hurst, *History of Methodism* (London, 1901)
WMM (1851)

FRANK BAKER

Atkinson, Miles (b. Ledsham, Yorkshire, England, 28 Sept. 1741; d. Leeds, England, 6 Feb, 1811). Anglican clergyman. Atkinson was the son of Christopher Atkinson (1713–74), the evangelical Rector of Thorp Arch (Yorkshire) who for a time was assisted by JOSEPH MILNER. His brother Christopher (1754–95) was Vicar of St Edward's, Cambridge (1781–5) and Wethersfield (Essex) (1785–95). Atkinson received his early education from his father and then proceeded to Peterhouse, Cambridge (BA 1763). He became Curate of Leeds Parish Church (1764–7) and headmaster of Drighlington School (1764–71), having expected to become lecturer at Halifax where, however, the vicar opposed his appointment. He then hoped to become first incumbent of a new church at Aberford, but he lost the presentation through a defect in the act authorizing the church. He returned to Leeds as lecturer (1768–70), his evangelical views now firmly fixed as a result of reading PHILIP DOD-DRIDGE's *Rise and Progress of Religion in the Soul*. In 1771, he joined the Elland Clerical Society and became one of its first tutors of ordinands. He may indeed have suggested the idea of such training. He was morning lecturer at Whitchurch (near Leeds) (1773–80), Rector of Walton-on-the-Hill (Lancashire) (1780–8), Vicar of Leek (1785–1803) and of Kippax (1783–1811) where he set up Sunday schools for over 2,000 children. In 1791 he began building St Paul's, Leeds (consecrated 1793), of which he was minister (1793–1811). It was DYKES [Dikes] of Hull who preached his funeral sermon.

Atkinson appears to have been pious from his youth. He was diligent in his study of the Bible and in prayer, both individually and within his family. His preaching is described as 'plain and practical', insisting not only on personal commitment but also on social duty, this latter reinforced in his own case by ministry at the infirmary and in visiting the sick.

Atkinson's sons were Christopher (1773–1843) who was Perpetual Curate of Elland (1802–43) and Curate of St Paul's, Leeds, succeeding his father (1811–43), and Thomas (1780–1870) who became Perpetual Curate of Thornton (near Bradford) (1804–15) and Hartshead (near Dewsbury) (1815–66), the latter by exchange with PATRICK BRONTË. Both were graduates of Cambridge and evangelicals.

BIBLIOGRAPHY
Al. Cant., II.i: 54
M. Atkinson, *Practical Sermons* (with memoir) (London, 1812)
C. A. Hulbert, *A Review of the Origin and History of the Elland Clerical Society* (Huddersfield, England, 1868)

ARTHUR POLLARD

Atkinson, William Mayo (b. Powhatan, VA, USA, 22 April 1796; d. Winchester, VA, USA, 24 Feb. 1849). Presbyterian minister. Graduated from the College of New Jersey (Princeton) in 1814, he practised law in Petersburg, Virginia until 1833. Atkinson was converted in 1822 in Petersburg, joined the local Presbyterian church and served as an elder of the congregation. Long under the belief that he should enter the ministry, he was ordained in 1834, and assigned to the Virginia Bible Society. After supplying vacancies for a few years he accepted the call to the Presbyterian church in Winchester, where he remained until 1846, when he took up duties with the Board of Education of the Presbyterian Church, retiring in 1848.

BIBLIOGRAPHY
AAP

WILLIAM G. TRAVIS

Atlay, John (b. Sheriff Hutton, Yorkshire, England, Dec. 1736). Wesley's book steward. Converted at the age of 22, Atlay joined the Methodists and became an itinerant preacher in 1763. After ten years in Yorkshire and Scottish circuits, JOHN WESLEY stationed him in London to act as book steward and keep the accounts. By 1785 he showed signs of disenchantment, possibly because he was not among the 'Legal Hundred' preachers named in Wesley's 1784 deed of declaration; he began to attend Moravian services and started a sideline as a coal merchant. In the dispute between Wesley and the Dewsbury trustees, who sought power to dismiss unsatisfactory preachers, Atlay encouraged the trustees. After the 1788 Conference, Wesley withdrew preachers from Dewsbury and Atlay left the bookroom (after apparently overvaluing the stock) and became the minister at Dewsbury. The arrangement was short-lived and in 1791 Atlay was again in London after an attempt to set up a circuit of his own in the north-east of England. JOHN PAWSON alleged that he had adopted the heretical views of Nicholas Manners (an itinerant 1759–84).

BIBLIOGRAPHY
L. Tyerman, *The Life and Times of . . . John Wesley*, 3rd edn (London, 1876) 3: 552–9

E. ALAN ROSE

Atmore, Charles (b. Heacham, Norfolk, England, 17 Aug. 1759; d. London, 30 June 1826). Wesleyan minister. The son of a ship's captain, Charles was brought up by an uncle and aunt after the early death of his mother. He was converted under the ministry of JOSEPH PIL-MORE, joined the Methodist society in June 1779, and became a local preacher. Early in 1781 he was called out as an itinerant by JOHN WESLEY and served as the junior minister in the Norwich circuit until appointed to the Grimsby circuit at the conference of that year.

Wesley named him as a member of the original 'Legal

Hundred' and in 1786 ordained him for work in Scotland. He played an active role in connexional events after Wesley's death, was president of the conference in 1811 and was actively involved in the establishment of the WMMS. His best-known work is his *Methodist Memorial* (Bristol, 1801).

BIBLIOGRAPHY
DNB
WMM (1845): 1–18, 105–23, 209–28, 313–32, 417–40, 521–48

JOHN A. VICKERS

Atwater, Lyman (Hotchkiss) (b. Cedar Hill, CT, USA, 3 Feb. 1813; d. Princeton, NJ, USA, 17 Feb. 1883). Professor at the College of New Jersey and Princeton Seminary. A descendent of a prominent New Haven, Connecticut family, Atwater trained for the ministry first at Yale College, graduating with honours in 1831, and then at Yale Divinity School. In 1835, he was ordained pastor of the First Congregational Church, Fairfield, Connecticut, where he served for 19 years. Atwater spent the rest of his life in Princeton, New Jersey, teaching moral philosophy at the College of New Jersey and apologetics at Princeton Seminary. A prolific writer, Atwater's significance rests upon his numerous contributions to the *Princeton Review*, which he edited with CHARLES HODGE. Reflecting the wide-ranging nature of moral philosophy, Atwater wrote on theology, apologetics, biography, history, education, philosophy, ethics, and economics. He was especially forceful in defending Old School Presbyterianism against CHARLES G. FINNEY's revivalism, NATHANIEL W. TAYLOR's New Divinity, and HORACE BUSHNELL's mediating theology.

BIBLIOGRAPHY
DAB
'Lyman Atwater', *Biblical Repertory and Princeton Review*, 1 (1870): 94–6

D. G. HART

Aubrey, Thomas (b. Cefn-coed-y-cymmer, Merthyr Tydfil, Wales, 13 May 1808; d. Rhyl, Clwyd, Wales, 16 Nov. 1867). Welsh Wesleyan Methodist minister. He was the son of Thomas and Anne Aubrey and came from a working-class industrial background. He was accepted into the Wesleyan ministry in 1826. Between then and 1865 he served Welsh-speaking circuits in Wales, London and Liverpool. He was the outstanding Welsh Wesleyan preacher of his generation and proved also to be an able, if autocratic, administrator but a powerful advocate of Welsh interests in the central committees of the denomination. He was a warm, but critical, admirer of the teaching and methods of the American CHARLES G. FINNEY (1792–1875) and was one of the first to make them known in Wales. Aubrey's greatest distinction was as a preacher. Although he tended, especially in his early

career, to obscurity and overelaborate analysis of his themes, he possessed a rare ability to reach the hearts and consciences of his auditors.

BIBLIOGRAPHY
DWB
J. Peter and Gweirydd ap Rhys, ed., *Enwogion y Ffydd* (London, no date)
A. Thomas, *Works*, 3 vols (Bangor, Wales, 1887)
A. H. Williams, *Welsh Wesleyan Methodism, 1800–58* (Bangor, Wales, 1935)

R. TUDUR JONES

Ault, William (b. West Bromwich, Staffordshire, England, 1786; d. 1 April 1815). Pioneer Wesleyan missionary to Ceylon. The son of a shoemaker whose family had suffered in the Wednesbury riots of the 1740s and were friends of the Asburys, he showed an early love of books and had read the Bible through six times by the time he was seven. His father trained him in his own trade; but in 1808 he became a Wesleyan itinerant, after four years as a local preacher. He served in the Dewsbury, Preston, Stockport and Congleton circuits before being ordained and sent out with THOMAS COKE as a missionary to Ceylon (now Sri Lanka).

His wife, Sarah, whom he had married before sailing, died during the voyage. In Ceylon, he was stationed at Batticaloa, an isolated town on the east coast, where he found himself the first Christian preacher to work among the local Tamils. Apart from the small garrison, his nearest compatriot was the Anglican chaplain at Trincomalee. Despite the isolation, appalling climatic conditions and a diet largely confined to rice and fish, he was soon preaching in Tamil to neighbouring villagers and organizing schools. But early in 1815 he was taken ill, and a few weeks later became the first Methodist missionary to die in Asia. There are commemorative tablets to him in Batticaloa and at the Pettah church in Colombo.

BIBLIOGRAPHY
Bulletin of the West Midlands Branch of the Wesley Historical Society, 1, pts 2–4
G. G. Findlay and W. W. Holdsworth, *The History of the Wesleyan Methodist Missionary Society* (London, 1925), V
Minutes of the Wesleyan Conference, 1816
W. J. T. Small ed., *A History of the Methodist Church in Ceylon, 1814–1964* (Colombo, no date)

JOHN A. VICKERS

Auna (b. Raiatea, Society Island, South Seas; d. Leeward Islands, Society Island, South Seas, 1835). LMS missionary to Hawaii from Huahine, Leeward Islands, and Tahiti. Auna, son of a chief on the Leeward Island of Raiatea, was an early LMS convert in Tahiti. A member of the Arioi sacred society of singers and dancers in the old religion and a warrior under King Pomare II, he was led to Christ by the Welsh missionary JOHN

DAVIES. Under the able WILLIAM ELLIS of the LMS on the Leeward Island of Huahine, he became a deacon in the church. In 1822, he and his wife, with five other Tahitian couples, took ship with Ellis to Honolulu. There the first company of ABCFM missionaries, which began in Hawaii in 1820, was having problems with the language and culture. Ellis, already proficient in Tahitian, helped them with Hawaiian, a cognate language. Auna and his colleagues accompanied Kaahumanu, the imposing Queen Mother and widow of the Hawaiian conqueror Kamehameha the Great, in touring major Hawaiian islands. They told how Christian faith had changed Tahiti. Auna's journal survives. He stayed in Hawaii until March 1824, then returned to Tahiti with his homesick wife. A leader with finesse, radically transformed by knowledge of Christ, he was a key figure in the early growth of the churches in Tahiti and Hawaii. He and his companions opened a door for later achievements of the ABCFM.

BIBLIOGRAPHY
J. Garrett, *To Live Among the Stars* (Geneva and Suva, 1982)

JOHN GARRETT

Auriol, Edward (b. London, 27 Feb. 1805; d. London, 10 Aug 1880). Anglican clergyman. Auriol was descended from a Huguenot family and educated at Westminster School and Christ Church, Oxford (BA, 1828; MA, 1832). After ordination he was curate at Roydon, Hertfordshire and then Little Horwood, Buckinghamshire. He made his reputation as a preacher while he was curate of two churches in Hastings. He was briefly Rector of Newton Valence, Hampshire, before the Simeon Trustees appointed him as Rector of St Dunstan's in the West (1842–80) and was made a prebendary of St Paul's Cathedral. Twice personal tragedy struck his life. In 1847 his son aged 17 was drowned in Lake Geneva, and in 1864 his wife died of typhoid fever.

Though he was shy and retiring he was a highly respected evangelical whose counsel was widely sought. 'If you ever want good, sound counsel, go to Auriol' (H. M. VILLIERS) (Tate and Bayley, 1880: 13). Auriol was regarded by Eugene Stock as 'the nestor of the Evangelical party' (Stock, 1899: 3: 30, 259) and 'the wisest of all the Evangelical clergy' (Stock, 1909: 178). He was the archetypal committee man and involved in a number of causes. He was a member of the CMS committee and subcommittees, a Simeon Trustee and a trustee of numerous evangelical livings. He supported those in training for the ministry and was a council member of Wycliffe Hall, Oxford and on the joint committee of Wycliffe Hall and Ridley Hall (Cambridge). Auriol described himself as 'an old fashioned churchman' (Church Congress, 1873: 59) who was a deeply committed premillennialist and an active member of the Church Association council.

BIBLIOGRAPHY
Al. Ox.
Boase
Official Report of the Church Congress Held at Bath (London, 1873)
E. Stock, *The History of the CMS* (London, 1899)
—, *My Recollections* (London, 1909)
G. E. Tate and E. Bayley, *Two Sermons . . . on the Occasion of the Death of the Revd E. Auriol* (London, 1880)

ALAN FREDERICK MUNDEN

Austin, Abraham (b. Sutton Coldfield, Warwickshire, England, 25 Dec. 1749; d. London, 5 July 1816). Baptist minister and educator. From a prosperous farming and timber-merchant family, he was trained for the Anglican ministry, but family deaths caused him to be apprenticed to a Birmingham grocer instead. Piously brought up, it was reading JAMES HERVEY that introduced him to 'vital religion', and led to his establishment in 1770 of an independent evangelical congregation to which he ministered. About 1776 he became convinced of Baptist views and following conversations with a Mr Hickling, General Baptist minister in Coventry, was baptized at the Melbourne Church in Derbyshire. Fifteen members of his Sutton congregation came to share his views and formed a New Connexion congregation in Sutton which soon planted daughter causes in Bloxwich and Birmingham. Austin began a cordial friendship with DAN TAYLOR who ordained him in 1785 on his call to the Fetter Lane Chapel in London, the burning down of which three years later provided opportunity for its replacement by a more handsome edifice, which in 1814 was purchased and vested in Particular Baptist trustees. His preaching ministry there was described as 'judicious, evangelical and experimental'. In 1807 one of Austin's members was refused appointment as a schoolmaster on the grounds of his Baptist convictions which prompted Austin to establish a Baptist Free School whose cause was canvassed in the *Evangelical Magazine*. Austin shared in the deliberations of the London Baptist ministers and was appointed to the General Body of Dissenting Ministers in London.

BIBLIOGRAPHY
J. Ivimey, *History of the English Baptists*, IV (London, 1830)
A. S. Langley, *Birmingham Baptists* (London, 1939)

J. H. Y. BRIGGS

Austin, David (b. New Haven, CT, BNA, 19 March 1760; d. Bozrah, CT, USA, 5 Feb. 1831). Congregational minister and millennialist. The son of a wealthy merchant, Austin graduated from Yale in 1779, studied with JOSEPH BELLAMY, and was licensed in 1780. He pastored the First Presbyterian Church of Elizabethtown, New Jersey (1788–97), and the Congregational Church of Bozrah, Connecticut (1815–31).

Austin is chiefly remembered for his obsession with premillennial views of eschatology. He rejected not only the more conventional postmillennial views of the day;

but, after a severe bout with scarlet fever left him partially deranged, he prophesied that Christ would visibly return on 15 May 1796. Dismissed by the New Jersey presbytery, Austin returned to New Haven in 1797 and purchased buildings and a wharf to be used by American Jews as a way station to the Holy Land to await the Messiah's imminent return. Apart from a four-volume collection of American sermons, nearly all of Austin's literary output focused on millennial themes.

BIBLIOGRAPHY
AAP, 2
R. Bloch, *Visionary Republic* (New York, 1985)
BSGYC, 4
DAB, 1
J. W. Davidson, 'Searching for the Millennium', *NEQ*, 45 (1972): 241-61

DAVID W. KLING

Austin, Samuel (b. New Haven, CT, BNA, 7 Oct. 1760; d. Glastonbury, CT, USA, 4 Dec. 1830). New England Congregational divine. After volunteer service at age 16 in the American Revolutionary army, he spent three years teaching school, and in 1780 prepared to study law. But in 1781, he obtained admission on advanced standing to Yale College, and after graduating from there in 1783, he studied theology with JONATHAN EDWARDS, JR in order to prepare for the Congregational ministry. He was licensed to preach on 12 October 1784, and finally accepted a call two years later to the Fair Haven Church in New Haven, Connecticut, and was ordained on 9 November 1786. His pastorate there was brief: he had imbibed from Edwards the Younger many of the extremist principles of the New Divinity, including its moral rigorism and its contempt for the conditional membership policy in the New England churches known derisively as 'the half-way covenant'. Consequently, Austin was dismissed from the Fair Haven Church on 19 January 1790.

He was, however, called almost at once to the First Church of Worcester, Massachusetts, where he found a more congenial congregation which was willing, at his demand, to abandon the 'half-way covenant'. He stayed there until 1815, when he accepted the presidency of the University of Vermont at Burlington, which had been virtually shut down during the War of 1812. But he proved ill adapted to the demands of running a college, and in 1821 he returned to pastoral ministry at the Second Church in Newport, Rhode Island [which had once been pastored SAMUEL HOPKINS, one of the principal architects of the New Divinity]. Failing health finally forced his retirement in 1825. He moved back to Worcester, then to Northampton (in 1827), and then finally to Glastonbury, Connecticut, in 1828.

In addition to over thirty sermons and tracts, Austin published a volume of *Dissertations upon Several Fundamental Articles of Christian Theology* in 1826 and two polemical works on baptism, *An Examination of the . . . Rev. Daniel Merrill, on the Mode and Subjects of Baptism* (1805)

and *A View of the Economy Church of God* (1807). His most important publication, however, was his edition of the works of JONATHAN EDWARDS (1808–9), which formed the first comprehensive edition of Edwards's writings.

BIBLIOGRAPHY
AAP
F. B. Dexter, *Biographical Sketches of the Graduates of Yale College*, 1 (New York, 1907)

ALLEN C. GUELZO

Averell, Adam (b. Mullan, County Tyrone, Ireland, 7 May 1754; d. Clones, County Cavan, Ireland, 16 Jan. 1847). Leader of the Irish Primitive Wesleyan Methodists. At the time of his birth, his father was agent to a wealthy relative who was later Bishop of Limerick. Educated at Trinity College, Dublin, he became private tutor in a baronet's family. He was ordained deacon in 1777, but without a cure. He met JOHN WESLEY in Dublin but, with certain qualms, lived as a conventional clergyman. After his evangelical conversion he took a curacy with Dr Ledwick at Aghavoe in 1789, but resigned two years later to undertake the gratuitous itinerant ministry which established him as a leader of Irish Methodism. His home base was Tentower in the the Queen's county parish of Killermogh.

The journal which he kept between 1792 and 1807 is a main source for this formative period in Irish history. It reveals how necessary were the interrelated episcopal reforming activity and evangelical awakening, both then in their infancy. It also shows how cool were the relations between Averell and the early evangelical Church of Ireland clergy, particularly those in Ossory, his home diocese. He denounced them as 'Calvinists' and deplored their regularity, while they rejected his view of the innate corruption of the Established Church. Earlier he had, however, both discovered and enjoyed fellowship with 'awakened' clergy in isolated situations in the south, most of them perpetual curates. Averell's journal also reveals that, although only in deacon's orders, he regularly celebrated the Holy Communion, holding that he did not need 'man's ordinance' to qualify him. Curiously enough, then, it was he who took the lead when the Irish Primitive Wesleyan Methodists (not to be confused with the English Primitive Methodists) broke from the Irish Conference on the ground that no Methodist preacher as such should administer the sacrament. Both the consistency and necessity of the action are open to question: the motive was to avoid a final breach with the establishment where Protestants were a minority.

After the split in 1818 Averell was elected president of the Primitive Wesleyan Methodist Conference. He was re-elected annually until 1841. The attachment of his followers to the Established Church was symbolized in the annual attendance of Averell and his preachers at Communion in St Patrick's Cathedral, Dublin. Like GIDEON OUSELEY, the leader of the main wing of Irish Methodism, Averell was a man of fearless character, strong convictions and tireless energy. If the weakness of his position was that he belonged neither to the Methodists nor to the Church of Ireland evangelicals, its strength was the devotion to his Master's cause which he maintained to the end of a long life.

BIBLIOGRAPHY
J. H. Cooke, *PWHS*, 34, 6 (1964): 135–40
DNB
R. H. Gallagher, *PWHS*, 34, 5 (1964): 126
F. Jeffrey, *PWHS*, 34, 4 (1963): 73–5
A. Stewart and G. Revington, *Memoir of the Rev. Adam Averell* (no place, 1849) regularly 'doctor' the sources
Wesley Historical Society (Irish Branch), Aldersgate House, 13 University Road, Belfast, manuscript 'Journal of Rev. Adam Averell, 1792–1807'

ALAN R. ACHESON

Avery, David (b. Norwich [now Franklin], CT, BNA, 5 April 1746; d. Sheperdstown, VA [now WV], USA, 16 February 1818). Military chaplain and Congregationalist minister. After brief stints as missionary among the Oneida Indians and minister in western Massachusetts, Avery was among the first to volunteer as a chaplain in the Continental Army. He graduated from Yale in 1769 and was ordained in 1771, bearing himself with what observers called a manner that was Edwardsian in sentiment and Whitefieldian in warmth. His service with troops during the revolution lasted from April, 1775, to February, 1780, one of the longest tours of duty on record. In addition to providing daily prayers and regular services, Avery presided at fast days and thanksgiving services, comforted the sick and wounded, and counselled the dying. Through these various means he emphasized the need for moral reform and used such exhortations to defend political liberty and the war effort. His subsequent years were less fruitful, consisting of sporadic, contentious ministerial appointments. Avery was quarrelsome and rigid, characteristics that produced personal as well as doctrinal difficulties in the Massachusetts and Connecticut churches he served. Since he still preached occasionally in later years, a Presbyterian congregation near his daughter's home invited him to be its minister. He died the day before installation proceedings could begin.

BIBLIOGRAPHY
AAP
BSGYC

HENRY WARNER BOWDEN

Axley, James (b. 1776; d. Madisonville, TN, USA, 22 February 1838). Methodist preacher. Details of Axley's family background are unknown. He was born either in North Carolina or in Cumberland County, Virginia. He was an itinerant preacher from 1804 to 1822, serving in Indiana, Ohio, Kentucky, Tennessee, North Carolina, and Louisiana. From 1811 to 1821 he was presiding elder over Methodist districts. After locating (ceasing to travel a circuit under episcopal appointment) for reasons of health in 1822, he made his family's living as a farmer but continued a preaching ministry. Axley is a classic figure from the heroic era of USA Methodism (1784–1835). Though without early education, he was literate and his knowledge of the English Bible, as well as the Methodist doctrinal standards and hymn-book, was extensive. His recall of these sources was powerful, and in elocution he was dramatic and idiosyncratic. An Axley sermon during the 1820 General Conference was recalled as late as mid-century.

Indifferent to people's opinions of him, Axley had a reputation for severity and unyielding opinions. Slavery, whisky, tobacco, fashion, and Masonry were among his favorite pulpit targets. In Louisiana he starved because of his antislavery bellicosity. Axley evidenced how the Methodist preachers saw Paul and themselves the purest models of Christian ministry. He spoke of the apostle as a travelling preacher who was a bishop, or at least a presiding elder, and who opened new circuits, regulated the societies, and appointed preachers.

BIBLIOGRAPHY
EWM
A. H. Redford, *The History of Methodism in Kentucky*, II (Nashville, TN, 1869)
M. Simpson, *Cyclopedia of Methodism* (Philadelphia, PA, 1878)

CHARLES W. BROCKWELL, JR

Aycliffe, Jane (b. Rowde, Wiltshire, England, *c.* 1815; d. Hungerford, Berkshire, England, 29 Nov. 1837). Primitive Methodist itinerant preacher. Born into a farming family. When the Primitive Methodists visited Ramsbury, Aycliffe went out of curiosity to hear them and was converted a few days later, joining them on 1 January 1831. Apprenticed to a dressmaker she remained behind when her family emigrated to the USA in 1835. Aycliffe became a local preacher (1835–6) and a travelling preacher in June 1836. She was noted for her faith, prayers and powerful singing voice. Within a few months she caught a violent cold and died at her brother's home.

BIBLIOGRAPHY
PMMag (1838)

E. DOROTHY GRAHAM

Ayre, John (b. Spalding, Lincolnshire, England, Feb. 1801; d. London, 20 May 1869). Parker Society secretary and editor. The son of Robert Ayre, a Lincolnshire merchant, Ayre was sent to school at Oakham, near Leicester. From there he proceeded in 1818 to Caius College, Cambridge (BA 1823; MA 1827) where he was a scholar and a prizeman. Bathurst, Bishop of Norwich, ordained him deacon in 1824 and priest in 1826. Ayre's residence at Oakham had placed him in the vicinity of

LEGH RICHMOND, and of Richmond's daughter Henrietta, whom he married in July 1825. His association with Richmond bore further fruit in a lifelong appointment, from 1832, as domestic chaplain to Richmond's admirer, ROBERT JOCELYN, the third Earl of Roden. Two years later he became the incumbent of St John's, Hampstead, London, a church he served for twenty years.

In 1840, when, under the auspices of LORD ASHLEY, the Parker Society was formed to reprint the early English Protestant writers, Ayre was appointed its general secretary and librarian (until 1853). He edited for the society the works of Becon, Horne, Jewel, Sandys, and Whitgift. Various evangelical publishers – including Burns, R. B. SEELEY, and JOHN HATCHARD – saw fit to publish his sermons. He also issued a popular edition of his father-in-law's famous *Annals of the Poor*, enlarged, illustrated, and with a brief life. Ayre was a friend and scholarly associate of THOMAS HARTWELL HORNE, and was an early supporter of the evangelically conducted *Church of England Magazine* (founded 1836). A letter of his, to Sir Robert Peel, is in the British Library.

BIBLIOGRAPHY
Al. Cant.
BLC
Boase

JONATHAN BURKE CUTMORE

B

Babington, Thomas (b. 18 Dec. 1758; d. 21 Nov. 1837). Banker, philanthropist and abolitionist. Educated Rugby and St John's College, Cambridge, he studied law at Lincoln's Inn (1778), becoming Sheriff of Leicester 1780–1. The squire of Rothley Temple, Leicestershire, he served as MP for Leicester 1800–18. In 1787 he married Jean, sister of ZACHARY and COLIN MACAULAY. Babington was a member of the Clapham Sect and an intimate friend of HENRY THORNTON and WILLIAM WILBERFORCE. He helped Wilberforce prepare the parliamentary case against the abolition of the slave trade, reading papers to detect contradictions and collecting answers which corroborated Wilberforce's assertions. He was Wilberforce's most constant companion in the division lobby of the House of Commons. Babington was on a number of parliamentary finance committees. He was also concerned about the plight of the poor. In Parliament he called for a more adequate bread assize to help them and for the endowment of smallholdings.

He belonged to some twenty charitable and religious societies and was vice-president of eleven; he also authored a work entitled *Christian Education*. Babington became a director of the Sierra Leone Company in 1805. He was in favour of Catholic emancipation and was one of the chief 'conspirators' in the 1813 campaign to open India to missionaries. Babington gave up his seat in 1818 and became a partner in the Leicester bank with John Mansfield.

BIBLIOGRAPHY

Sir R. Coupland, *Wilberforce* (re-issued London, 1945)

J. Pollock, *Wilberforce* (London, 1977)

R. G. Thorne, *The House of Commons 1790–1820* (London, 1986), III: 100

PENELOPE CARSON

Bachman, John (b. Rhinebeck, NY, USA, 4 Feb. 1790; d. Charleston, SC, USA, 24 Feb. 1874). Lutheran minister and natural scientist. Bachman was the driving force in modernizing the Lutheran Church in ante-bellum South Carolina. After serving three Lutheran parishes in New York, he accepted a call to St John's Lutheran Church, Charleston, in 1815, where he remained pastor until his death. As president of the South Carolina Synod of the Lutheran Church from 1824–33 and 1839–40, he led the movement for a Lutheran seminary in the state: 'an enlightened age required an intelligent ministry', he argued; 'religion will scarcely make any really beneficial advances if its advocates and defenders are men of narrow unfurnished minds'.

Though associated with the movement to Americanize Lutheranism, he opposed revivalism as contrary to Lutheran dependence on catechetical training and the sacraments. But his understanding of conversion – confessed at the time of his daughter's conversion – was thoroughly evangelical. In response to Lutheran abolitionist resolutions adopted in 1857, he wrote what his biographer calls 'the most extensive defense of slavery to come from the pen of a Lutheran clergyman in the South'.

BIBLIOGRAPHY

H. G. Anderson and R. M. Calhoon, eds., *A Truly Efficient School of Theology* (Columbia, SC, 1981)

R. M. Bost, 'The Rev. John Bachman and the Development of Southern Lutheranism' (Yale, Ph.D. thesis, 1963)

ROBERT CALHOON

Backhouse, James (b. Darlington, Co. Durham, England, 8 July 1794; d. York, England, 21 Jan. 1869). Quaker missionary, social reformer, and naturalist. Born into a Quaker business family, in 1816 Backhouse, with his brother, purchased a plant nursery which prospered. He married in 1822, but his wife Deborah Lowe died five years later. Deeply interested in the effects of convict transportation and the condition of Aborigines, Backhouse in 1831 was accredited as minister by the London yearly meeting to travel, as missioner, to the Australian colonies and South Africa. His companion/secretary was a Quaker shopkeeper, George Washington Walker. Backhouse's two children remained with relatives; his business in his brother's care. He and Walker itinerated through the Australian colonies, 1832–8. Ever active and alertly observant, they systematically distributed Bibles, tracts and BFSS schoolbooks. They established Quaker meetings in Sydney and Hobart. Backhouse collected many botanic specimens for Kew Gardens. Hence, Backhousia, a genus of myrtaceous shrub. In South Africa from mid-1838, they proved busy as ever, learning Afrikaans and travelling thousands of miles by covered wagon inspecting missions, but also observing the effect of the emancipation of the slaves. In 1840 Walker returned as a settler to Van Diemen's Land, while Backhouse resumed secular life in England. In 1843, 1844 and 1862 Backhouse published extensive studies based mainly on his voluminous travel reports to the London yearly meeting.

BIBLIOGRAPHY
ADB
S. Backhouse, *Memoir of James Backhouse* (York, England, 1870)

RICHARD ELY

Backus, Azel (b. Norwich, CT, BNA, 13 Oct. 1765; d. Clinton, NY, USA, 9 Dec. 1817). Congregationalist minister and first president of Hamilton College. After a period of infidelity in his youth, Backus was converted at age 17 through the influence of his uncle, CHARLES BACKUS. Following graduation from Yale in 1787, teaching school at Withersfield, Connecticut, and studying theology with his uncle, he was licensed to preach in 1789. In 1791 he succeeded the renowned theologian and educator, JOSEPH BELLAMY, as the pastor of the Congregationalist church in Bethelem, Connecticut. For the next 21 years, Backus served this congregation, operated a college preparatory school and was very involved in the civic affairs of Bethelem. A popular and respected preacher, he was invited to give the eulogy for the governor of the state in 1797 and to deliver the annual election sermon before the state legislature in 1798. Disturbed by Thomas Jefferson's deism, he critiqued the Vice-President by comparing him with David's rebellious son Absalom. In 1806 and again in 1807 he was arraigned in court for allegedly libelling President Jefferson. The case never went to trial. In the fall of 1812 he became the president of newly founded Hamilton College located in Hamilton, New York. He served effectively in this capacity until his sudden death in 1817. He received the DD degree from Princeton in 1810. His publications include 'Absalom's Conspiracy' (1798), his inaugural address at Hamilton, and two ordination sermons.

BIBLIOGRAPHY
AAP
DAB
NCAB

GARY SCOTT SMITH

Backus, Charles (b. Norwich, CT, BNA, 5 Nov. 1749; d. Somers, CT, USA, 30 Dec. 1803). Congregational minister. A Yale graduate (1769), Backus prepared for the ministry under LEVI HART whose Edwardsian New Divinity theology he thoroughly imbibed. In 1773 Backus began preaching in Somers to a congregation formerly divided by the radical political views of the Reverend Samuel Ely. Ordained in 1774, he remained in Somers until his death.

Backus engaged in a busy rural ministry. He declined professorships at Yale and Dartmouth, opting for his own 'parlor seminary' where he trained nearly fifty men for the ministry, including ALVAN HYDE, LEONARD WOODS of Andover Seminary, President ZEPHANIAH S.

MOORE of Amherst College, and President H. Davis of Hamilton. A keen advocate of sane and sober revivals, Backus's parish experienced four periods of awakening. In addition, he defended the supernatural inspiration of the Bible in *Five Discourses on the Divine Authority of Scripture* (1797), and restated New Divinity views on the will and conversion in *The Scripture Doctrine of Regeneration* (Hartford, 1800). AZEL BACKUS was his nephew.

BIBLIOGRAPHY
AAP, 2: 61–8
BSGYC, 3
R. Rabinowitz, *The Spiritual Self in Everyday Life* (Boston, MA, 1989)
R. Shiels, 'The Connecticut Clergy in the Second Great Awakening' (Boston Ph.D. thesis, 1976)

DAVID W. KLING

Backus, Isaac (b. Norwich, CT, BNA, 9 Jan. 1724; d. Middleborough, MA, USA, 20 Nov. 1806). Baptist pastor and champion of religious liberty in the American colonies during the revolutionary era. Backus was the fourth child of Samuel Backus and Elizabeth Tracy Backus, members of the ruling elite of Puritan Connecticut. As a New England farm boy, he imbibed the principles of Calvinism and learned that religious training and the laws of the state maintained the good order of society.

The threat to these social foundations began in Norwich during 1741 with the coming of the Great Awakening revivalists. First Isaac's mother's faith was renewed. Then, in August under the influence of JAMES DAVENPORT, 17-year-old Isaac was converted. The experience came, however, without the usual emotion and ecstasy. He was mowing alone in a field, when, as he testified, 'I was enabled by divine light to see the perfect righteousness of Christ . . . with such clearness, that my soul was drawn forth to trust him for salvation'.

Not long after his conversion Backus felt called of God to join the ranks of the revivalists, often called 'New Lights' or 'Separates'. He plunged into the work of itinerant evangelism in the towns of south-eastern New England. In the Titicut parish, he found a gathering of converts who were anxious to have a New Light pastor. Early in 1748 they invited Backus to become their minister. He accepted and on 13 April was ordained.

Slowly, however, he came to Baptist beliefs in this New Light Congregational church. After agonizing prayer and intense Bible study, he, along with six fellow church members, was immersed on profession of faith in Christ on 22 August 1751. For five years the Titicut church tried to live in peace as a mixed fellowship. But Backus followed his conscience and, with his wife and four others, formed a Baptist church, the First Baptist Church in Middleborough, MA. After ordination as the church's pastor, he remained in the church for the rest of his life.

Freed at last of his indecision, Backus plunged into more evangelistic tours, pastoral responsibilities, and most importantly, the cause of religious freedom. Late in his career he compiled a summary of his journeys from his arrival at Titicut in January 1748 until December 1802. It revealed 918 trips exceeding ten miles, for a total of 68,000 miles, mostly on horseback.

In 1767, New England Baptists formed the Warren Association to advance their cause, which often centred on their taxation for the support of the established Congregational churches. Two years later the association created the Grievance Committee and charged it with the task of advocating religious freedom throughout New England. Backus became the key member of this committee. He wrote tracts, drew up dozens of petitions, obtained factual evidence of persecution, appeared in court as a witness, worked on committees to formulate policies, and carried on a constant warfare of words in newspapers, public disputes, and private letters. The imprisonment of his mother, brother, and uncle in the Norwich area, after he had left, and his own deep pietistic convictions produced in him a passionate opposition to the established system.

Basic to the Baptist position was the belief that all direct connections between the state and institutionalized religion must be broken in order that America might become a truly Christian country. Backus, like Jefferson and Madison, believed that 'Truth is great and will prevail'. But unlike his 'enlightened colleagues', by truth he meant the revealed doctrines of Scripture. His fundamental assumption was that 'God had appointed two different kinds of government in the world which are different in their nature and ought never to be confounded'. One is civil, the other ecclesiastical. 'Our civil legislature', said Backus, does not function as 'our representatives in religious affairs'. They were elected as representatives for civil or secular affairs, and when they act in ecclesiastical affairs, they meddle in matters upon which their constituents did not empower them to legislate. Furthermore, legislative power is inappropriate for faith. 'Religion is a voluntary obedience unto God which force cannot promote.'

By resisting established churches the revivalists like Backus never intended to surrender their dream for a Christian America. They had found in the Great Awakening the answer to their needs. The kingdom of God would come to America if a majority of the citizens could be persuaded to submit voluntarily to the laws of God. Revivals were God's means to that end.

In 1773 Backus's most important tract, *An Appeal to the Public for Religious Liberty Against the Oppression of the Present Day*, appeared. Many regard it as the best exposition of the eighteenth-century evangelical concept of separation of church and state. Historians, however, have found his attempt at writing history (Backus, 1969) a valuable source.

In 1774 New England Baptists sent Backus and JAMES MANNING to Philadelphia to present a memorial (or appeal) to the First Continental Congress, asking for a declaration of full religious liberty. They were able to meet with the Massachusetts delegates, but found that John and Samuel Adams defended the Massachusetts system. In 1780 Backus continued his efforts for religious liberty by lobbying the delegates chosen to draft a state constitution. He even drew up a proposed bill of rights, but the new proposed constitution, finished on 2 March 1780, did not totally separate church and state, retaining the principle of compulsory religious taxation.

For all these reasons, Backus has come to be regarded as the pre-eminent evangelical champion of religious freedom in the revolutionary period. He lived to see the birth of the United States and found comfort in the nation's adoption of the First Amendment guaranteeing religious freedom.

SELECT WRITINGS
I. Backus, *An Appeal to the Public for Religious Liberty Against the Oppression of the Present Day* (Boston, MA, 1773)
—, *A History of New England, with Particular Reference to . . . Baptists*, 3 vols (Boston and Providence, 1777–96; revised edn Newton, MA, 1871; New York, 1969)

BIBLIOGRAPHY
DAB
DARB
S. Grenz, *Isaac Backus: Puritan and Baptist* (Macon, GA, 1983)
A. Hovey, *A Memoir of the Life and Times of the Rev. Isaac Backus* (Boston, MA, 1859)
T. B. Maston, *Isaac Backus* (Rochester, NY, 1962)
W. G. McLoughlin, *Isaac Backus and the American Pietistic Tradition* (Boston, MA, 1967)
—, ed., *Isaac Backus on Church, State, and Calvinism* (Cambridge, MA, 1968)
—, ed., The Diary of Isaac Backus, 3 vols (Providence, RI, 1979)

BRUCE L. SHELLEY

Bacon, John (b. London, 24 Nov. 1740; d. London, 7 Aug. 1799). Sculptor. The son of a skilled cloth-maker, Bacon was apprenticed at the age of 14 to a china manufacturer. From clay modelling he progressed to marble, and after attending evening classes at the newly opened Royal Academy gained royal patronage. The leading sculptor of his day, he became an academician in 1778. His funeral monuments can be found in churches throughout England including Westminster Abbey and St Paul's Cathedral.

Brought up in a dissenting home, Bacon gradually moved to Anglicanism, although he was buried at WHITEFIELD's Tabernacle. The six children of his first marriage were baptized by Dissenters, the six of his second into the Church of England. A close friend of leading evangelicals, Bacon was a member of the first CMS committee and one of the few laymen invited to join the EcS.

BIBLIOGRAPHY
R. Cecil, *Memoir of John Bacon Esq. RA* (London, 1801)
DNB
A. Graves, *The Royal Academy of Arts* (London, 1905–6) 1: 87–8
A. C. Johnson, *John Bacon RA* (London, 1961)
D. M. Rosman, *Evangelicals and Culture* (London, 1984): 158–60

DOREEN M. ROSMAN

Bacon, John (b. London, England, 13 March 1777; d. Bath, England, 14 July 1859). Sculptor. John Bacon junior was trained by his father (JOHN BACON), entered the Royal Academy School at the age of 12, and achieved early success as a sculptor. Between 1792 and 1824 he exhibited regularly at the Academy and was given prestigious commissions. A popular speaker at CMS and BFBS meetings, he was vice-president of three charitable societies and on the governing bodies of others. He published some of his BFBS material and memoirs of his sister and daughter. His diaries which are in private hands show that he was a highly introspective man who suffered from intense religious depression. Unable to cope with financial and professional pressures, he retired early in 1824, carving only family memorials thereafter for his wife and one of several daughters who predeceased him. An address to the Exeter Diocesan Architectural Society in 1842 and his *Letter to Sir Robert Peel* (London, 1843) confirm that his interest in the arts continued.

BIBLIOGRAPHY
F. K. Brown, *Fathers of the Victorians* (Cambridge, 1961): 355
DNB
A. Graves, *The Royal Academy of Arts* (London, 1905–6) 1: 88–9
D. M. Rosman, *Evangelicals and Culture* (London, 1984): 160–1

DOREEN M. ROSMAN

Bacon, Leonard (b. Detroit, MI, USA, 19 Feb. 1802; d. New Haven, CT, USA, 24 Dec. 1881). Congregationalist minister, controversialist and reformer. The son of missionaries to native Americans in the Old Northwest Territory, Bacon succeeded NATHANIEL W. TAYLOR as minister of the prestigious First Congregational Church in New Haven, Connecticut, following his education at Yale College and Andover Theological Seminary. This was the sole pastorate of his career; he was the active minister from 1825 to 1866 and then pastor emeritus until his death. Additionally, he taught at Yale Divinity School during his retirement years.

Theologically sympathetic to the 'New Haven School' and nicknamed 'the fighting parson', Bacon's influence was, nonetheless, irenic and conciliatory as he intervened in several ante-bellum theological disputes to prevent division within New England Congregationalism. He also was active in the campaign against slavery, though he supported gradual emancipation and not the abolitionist cause.

BIBLIOGRAPHY
DAB
W. Walker, *Ten New England Leaders* (New York, 1901)

STEVEN R. POINTER

Badley [Baddeley], **John** (b. England, *c.* 1706; d. Hayfield, Derbyshire, England, Sept. 1764). Anglican minister and Vicar of Hayfield. Little is known of Badley (his name is variously spelled, but this is how he signed himself in his will) prior to his arrival at Hayfield in 1748. He is said to have belonged to a family of yeoman farmers with estates in Staffordshire. His brother Anthony was a cider merchant in Kingswinford. In October 1748 JOHN BENNET wrote to JOHN WESLEY reporting that Badley had recently been converted and was now preaching as an evangelical. The town was up in arms but Badley was undeterred. He formed societies on Methodist lines and utilized lay leaders, but was opposed to separation from the Established Church and allowing too great liberty to Methodist preachers. Latterly he distanced himself somewhat from Wesley, who had once cited him along with WILLIAM GRIMSHAW as an example of effective evangelistic ministry.

BIBLIOGRAPHY
AM (1779)

A. SKEVINGTON WOOD

Bagster, Samuel (b. 26 Dec. 1772; d. Old Windsor, Berkshire, England, 28 March 1851). Bible publisher. The son of George and Mary Bagster he was educated at Northampton. After an apprenticeship he began as a bookseller in 1794 in the Strand. Three years later he married Eunice Birch. In 1800 their son SAMUEL BAGSTER was born. In 1816 he moved to Paternoster Row. The publishing firm that he founded became famous for editions of polyglot Bibles, which had hitherto been rare and costly.

He published a Hebrew Bible, then the Septuagint. In 1816 he published *The English Version of the Polyglot Bible* with over 60,000 parallel references, mainly selected and all verified by himself. He supervised the production in detail. His *Biblia Sacra Polyglotta Bagsteriana* appeared in four volumes between 1817 and 1828. It comprised prolegomena by Samuel Lee, the pointed Hebrew Old Testament, the Samaritan Pentateuch, the Septuagint, the Vulgate, the Authorized Version, the Textus Receptus, and the Peshito. An edition of a French, Italian, Spanish, and German Bible was entirely destroyed by fire except for 23 copies of the New Testament. A folio edition of the 1817–28 polyglot was published in 1828 and reprinted later, presenting eight languages at the opening of the volume. Two other forms of the English Bible began the 'Facsimile Series'. In 1821 an octoglot edition of the Church of England liturgy appeared, containing English, French, German, Italian, Spanish, ancient Greek, modern Greek, and Latin versions.

In 1822 the orientalist William Greenfield was engaged as a proofreader of Bagster's learned publications. In 1827 Greenfield edited for Bagster his *Comprehensive Bible*, with 4,000 notes, 500,000 references, and other useful information. He also edited Bagster's *Syriac New Testament* (1828–29), *Hebrew New Testament* (1830), *Polymicrian Greek Lexicon* (1829), and *Schmidt's Greek Concordance* (1829).

In 1841 Bagster published *The English Hexapla*, giving the following English versions of the New Testament: Wycliffe (1380), Tyndale (1534), Cranmer (1539), the Genevan (1557), the Anglo-Rhemish (1582), and the Authorized Version (1611). There was also the Greek text of Scholz and (in an 1872 edition) an historical account of the English translations.

As a publisher of valuable and handsomely produced aids to the study of the Scriptures Bagster deserves to be remembered. His son Jonathan (1813–72) succeeded him as senior partner. The firm remained independent until 1973, when it was bought by Marshall, Morgan & Scott (later part of Marshall Pickering which is now a HarperCollins imprint).

BIBLIOGRAPHY

[Anon.,] *The Centenary of the Bagster Publishing House* (London, 1894)
S. Bagster, *Samuel Bagster of London* (London, 1972)
DNB

JOHN S. ANDREWS

Bagster, Samuel (b. 19 Oct. 1800; d. London, 1 July 1835). Printer and author. The eldest son of SAMUEL BAGSTER, he attended the Reverend JAMES HINTON's school in Oxford, before being articled in his father's bookshop in 1815. In 1824 he set up as a printer on his own account in Bartholomew Close, London. His business developed slowly at first but then steadily. In 1834 he printed a small octavo, *The Management of Bees* which was published by his father and William Pickering. Now superseded but in its day much appreciated as being full of useful information, it was reprinted in 1838 and 1865. Towards the end of his life Bagster occupied himself with bee-keeping and poultry-breeding.

In 1657 Samuel Purchas, the son of the author of *Purchas his Pilgrimage* and other travel books, had issued a quarto entitled *A Theatre of Politicall Flying Insects*. The first part dealt with the history and management of bees, and the second comprised theological and moral reflections on the subject. Bagster reprinted the bulk of this second part in the same style and format and in the same year (1834) as his own practical handbook under the title, *Spiritual Honey from Natural Hives*.

Also in 1834 Bagster contributed to his father's polyglot series, *The Treasury of Bible Knowledge*. This formed the second part of the *Treasury Bible* and consisted of more than 500,000 scripture references and parallel passages from various commentators, with many illustrative notes. His manuscript of a series of questions on the Gospels for Sunday school use remained unfinished and unpublished. Many of the polyglot Bibles and other learned works of his father's firm were printed by him.

He had, as early as 1822, joined the Baptist church in Blackfriars. After his death the Reverend John Broad, a Baptist minister, paid tribute to his amiable and devout disposition and to the active part that he had taken in the antislavery and temperance movements. He had

written several temperance pamphlets. Bagster spent the last part of his life in Shepherd's Bush, which was then rural, and died there childless aged 34. His widow survived until 1879.

BIBLIOGRAPHY

J. Broad, *Memoir of the Life and Christian Experience of Samuel Bagster, Jr* (London, 1837)
DNB

JOHN S. ANDREWS

Bailey, Benjamin (b. Dewsbury, York, England, c. 1780; d. Sheinton, Shropshire, England, 3 April 1871) CMS missionary, Kottayam, India. Originally a woolstapler, Bailey arrived in Kottayam 4 May 1816. Apart from one furlough (May 1831 to July 1834), he worked in the state of Travancore until ill health forced his 1850 retirement. He founded the CMS Kottayam station, built Holy Trinity Church (now the cathedral church of the Church of South India's Madya Kerala diocese), and developed an extensive mission. He produced Malayalam/English and English/Malayalam dictionaries, edited the Malayalam Bible and *Book of Common Prayer*, and helped develop the educational system. In 1816 he married Elizabeth Ella (died 19 June 1859), the first person to organize education for Syrian Christian women, a very difficult task because of the custom of very early marriages.

During his February 1819 visit, Bishop Middleton observed good relationships with the Syrian Orthodox Christians, but not with the Jacobite Syrian Metran, who prevaricated over the missionaries' proposed reforms, and who ordained boys not trained in the new CMS College. Bailey appears not directly responsible for the 1836 end of this tenuous cooperation, after which Syrian congregations were received into the Anglican fellowship.

BIBLIOGRAPHY

M. E. Gibbs, *A History of the Anglican Church in India 1600–1970* (Delhi, 1972)
E. Stock, *The History of the Church Missionary Society* I (London, 1899)

E. M. JACKSON

Bailey, Joseph (b. Dewsbury, Yorkshire, England, c. 1797; d. Cotta, Ceylon, 19 March 1844). CMS missionary to Ceylon [Sri Lanka]. Bailey was the brother of BENJAMIN BAILEY, an early CMS missionary to India, and of Sarah Archer Bailey (wife of THOMAS DAWSON). He studied as a probationer missionary under the Reverend E. Parkin of Dewsbury and Reverend ANDREW BRANDRAM and was ordained (deacon and priest 1820) by the Archbishop of York. On 5 June 1821 he went to Ceylon to join the CMS party that had been sent to Ceylon in 1817 (*see* SAMUEL LAMBRICK, ROBERT MAYOR, BENJAMIN WARD, JOSEPH KNIGHT) and THOMAS BROWNING who went out in 1820. He served first at Nellore and from 1823 in Cotta.

In November 1824 he returned to England, perhaps because of his wife's health. He married Sophia Parkin, who died 23 September 1825. In 1834 he married Octavia Bulmer (died 1864), sister of John A. Bulmer. With almost 24 years experience, Bailey was one of the longest-serving CMS missionaries in Ceylon.

BIBLIOGRAPHY
D. T. B[arry], *CMS Register of Missionaries and Native Clergy* (privately printed) (London, 1906)

DONALD M. LEWIS

Bailey, Wesley (b. Readsborough, VT, USA, 26 Feb. 1808; d. Decorah, IA, USA, 23 Feb. 1891). Methodist editor, political abolitionist and ecclesiastical reformer. When Bailey was five years old, his father, Elijah, withdrew from the MEC to found the Reformed Methodist Church, a small sect that insisted on a democratically congregational polity. Subsequently, the family moved to Fayetteville, New York, where Wesley became a Reformed Methodist minister, edited the denominational paper, and jointly published an abolitionist paper with LUTHER MYRICK, the originator of the 'Union church' movement. In 1842, Bailey was invited to edit another antislavery paper in Utica, New York. This paper, *The Liberty Press*, became the unofficial organ of the Liberty Party, an avowedly Christian political party. Bailey was also one of the organizers of the abolitionist Wesleyan Methodist Connexion in Utica in 1843. He was the chairman (superintendent) of the Utica district of the Wesleyan Methodists while simultaneously continuing his duties as a political editor and campaigner. Later, Bailey edited papers for the temperance movement and the Republican party.

BIBLIOGRAPHY
D. M. Strong, 'The Application of Perfectionism to Politics', *Wesleyan Theological Journal*, 25 (Spring 1990): 1

DOUGLAS M. STRONG

Baillie, John (b. Edinburgh, Scotland, 23 Aug. 1816; d. Wivenhoe, Essex, England, 17 June 1890). Church of Scotland, Free Church and Anglican minister. Educated at the Edinburgh high school, he obtained the gold medal in philosophy at the University of Edinburgh (BA 1839). Baillie served in three denominations. He was ordained in the Church of Scotland as minister of Fogo (1841–3). At the Disruption in 1843 he joined the Free Church, which he served at Fogo until 1854. In 1857 he entered Gonville and Caius College, Cambridge (BD 1868; DD 1876) and in the same year was ordained deacon by the Bishop of London. From late 1860 and from 1863 he ministered at Percy Chapel, London, and from 1866 until his death as Rector of Wivenhoe, near Colchester. Most of Baillie's numerous biographical, pastoral, evangelistic, and premillennialist tracts were published by the evangelical firms Nisbet, Hatchard, and Seeley.

BIBLIOGRAPHY
Al. Cant.
Boase

JONATHAN BURKE CUTMORE

Bainbridge, Thomas (d. Croydon, Surrey, England, 8 Jan. 1830). English lawyer. Bainbridge was a London lawyer and a prominent lay supporter of the CMS in its formative years. He was a close friend of his minister, RICHARD CECIL, the cultured incumbent of St John's, Bedford Row (1780–1808). He served on the CMS governing committee from 1806 to 1813 and from 1814 to 1830 and left the society a legacy of £792.

BIBLIOGRAPHY
C. Hole, *Early History of the Church Missionary Society* (London, 1896): 621–2

DONALD M. LEWIS

Baines, Edward (b. Walton-le-Dale, Lancashire, England, 5 Feb. 1774; d. Leeds, England, 3 August 1848). Publisher and MP. He was the second son of Richard Baines and his wife Jane (née Chew). Richard, from Yorkshire, was a grocer who turned cotton manufacturer and land agent for the Earl of Derby after falling out with the Tory corporation of Preston. Edward imbibed his father's liberal convictions. He attended Hawkeshead and Preston grammar schools. After learning to weave he commenced at the age of 16 an apprenticeship with a local printer. This was completed in Leeds with Messrs Binns & Brown, printers and booksellers and proprietors of the *Leeds Mercury*.

In 1801 he took over and edited that newspaper, with the aid of a £1,000 loan from a group of reformers, mostly Unitarians. It became the strongest voice of orthodox dissent and the North's new capitalist classes, its weekly circulation rising from 700 in 1801 to 10,000 in the 1840s. Baines, nicknamed 'the Franklin of Leeds', challenged the gentlemen wool merchants, predominantly Anglican and Tory, who ruled the corporation of industrializing Leeds. He battled for more open local government and in the 1820s fought tithes, church rates and university tests and supported Catholic emancipation. He became a national figure in 1830 when his influence won a prestigious Yorkshire parliamentary seat for Henry Brougham, the reforming Whig. Representing Leeds in Parliament from 1834 to 1841, Baines advocated the ballot, some extension of the suffrage, the removal of religious disabilities and free trade. Although the *Mercury* published RICHARD OASTLER'S sensational letter on 'Yorkshire slavery' in 1830, Baines opposed the Ten Hour Movement and the shortening of the factory day, fearing both state intervention and reduced working-class family incomes. In his last years he attacked state intervention in education.

He engaged in land reclamation and estate development on Chat Moss, Lancashire. In middle age he wrote topographical histories of Yorkshire and Lancashire, a history of the French revolutionary wars, and another of the reign of George III. His involvement in improvement schemes ranged from the Lancasterian Society to Mechanics Institutions to railway, insurance, and utility companies. Baines worshipped for many years with both the Unitarians of Mill Hill Chapel and the Congregationalists of Salem Church, Leeds. Through his wife's influence he became a member of Salem on 3 January 1840, following an inner conversion experience. He married in 1798, against her father's wishes, Charlotte, daughter of Matthew Talbot, a Leeds currier and later secretary of Leeds General Infirmary, and a devout Congregationalist. They produced six sons, including MATTHEW TALBOT BAINES and (Sir) EDWARD BAINES, and five daughters, and a dynasty of newspaper editors, pillars of 'Bainesocracy'.

BIBLIOGRAPHY
(Sir) E. Baines, *The Life of Edward Baines Late MP for the Borough of Leeds* (London, 1851)
C. Binfield, *So Down to Prayers* (London, 1977)
DNB
Leeds Mercury, 5 (12 August 1848)
G. I. T. Machin, *Politics and the Churches in Great Britain, 1832 to 1868* (Oxford, 1977)

DAVID J. JEREMY

Baines, Sir Edward (b. Leeds, England, 28 May 1800; d. Burley, Hampshire, England, 2 March 1890). Publisher and MP. The second son of EDWARD BAINES and his wife Charlotte, he attended a private school at Leeds and New College, Manchester. He became a Sunday school teacher in Salem Independent Church, Leeds, at 15 but not a church member until he was 28. He retired as Sunday school superintendent on being elected MP.

At 15, too, he joined his father in the editorial offices of the *Leeds Mercury*. The investigative aspects of journalism especially attracted him. With his father he attended reform meetings, culminating in the 'Peterloo massacre' of 1819 and unmasked the Home Secretary's spy system. From the 1820s he progressively succeeded his father as editor of the *Mercury*, eventually shaping it into one of the 'authoritative organs' of the Liberal party. His upbringing and years of travel and data collection at home and abroad in the 1820s made him an advocate of industrialism, free trade and self-improvement as well as political reform. His *History of the Cotton Industry of Great Britain* (1835) became and remains a standard text. He wrote pamphlets attacking the Corn Laws and supporting Catholic emancipation.

Education increasingly concerned Baines. An early sponsor of Mechanics Institutions, he became president of the West Riding Union in 1837. Among Dissenters he was prominent in thwarting plans to extend state control over education, especially in 1843 and 1847, in the long-running Voluntaryist controversy. However, while a member of the Taunton Commission into secondary education, he publicly switched sides in 1867, thereby losing much Nonconformist backing. He spoke and

wrote on behalf of the Sunday school movement. In old age he chaired the Yorkshire College (later Leeds University), 1880–7.

Representing Leeds in Parliament, 1859–74, he became a back-bencher to whom, for example, Gladstone turned for advice on dissenting issues. Baines's efforts for a modest extension of the franchise were superseded by the Second Reform Act (1867). Thereafter he pitched into questions stirring the Nonconformist conscience: the abolition of church rates (1868); the disestablishment of the Church of Ireland (1869); and the repeal of university tests (1871). Yet he was never a predictable Nonconformist. From 1837 he wrote and spoke in defence of total abstinence temperance, though voted against the prohibitionists' Permissive Bill of the 1860s, later favouring the less drastic 'local option' proposal. On pacifism he had publicly opposed Cobden at the outset of the Crimean War. In addition he opposed Home Rule for Ireland and criticized trade unions. Binfield characterizes his position as that of 'comfortless moderation'.

On retirement he contributed an essay on the history of the woollen trade to *Yorkshire Past and Present* (1875) published by his brother Thomas. Baines was knighted in 1880. He married in 1829 Martha (died 1881) only daughter of Thomas Blackburn of Liverpool. They had three sons and four daughters.

BIBLIOGRAPHY
C. Binfield, *So Down to Prayers: Studies in English Nonconformity, 1780–1920* (London, 1977)
DNB
D. Frazer, 'Edward Baines' in P. Hollis (ed.), *Pressure from Without in Early Victorian England* (London, 1974)
Leeds Mercury (3 March 1890)
G. I. T. Machin, *Politics and the Churches in Great Britain, 1832 to 1868* (Oxford, 1977)
G.R. Searle, *Entrepreneurial Politics in Mid-Victorian Britain* (Oxford, 1993)

DAVID J. JEREMY

Baines, Matthew Talbot (b. Leeds, England, 17 Feb. 1799; d. Westminster, England, 23 Jan. 1860). MP. He was the eldest son of EDWARD BAINES. Educated at grammar schools at Leeds, Manchester and Richmond, he won a scholarship to Trinity College, Cambridge, graduating in classics and mathematics as a senior optime in 1820. He was called to the Bar (Inner Temple) in 1825, practising on the Northern circuit and becoming recorder of Hull (1837) and a Queen's Counsel (1841). A Whig and later a Liberal, he represented Hull in Parliament, 1847–55, and Leeds, 1855–9. President of the Poor Law Board under Russell and Aberdeen, 1849–52 and 1852–5, he then served Palmerston as Chancellor of the Duchy of Lancaster with a seat in the Cabinet, 1855–8. He was sworn of the Privy Council. Ill health forced his retirement in 1859. He was recalled as 'one of the wisest of counsellors': which may sum up his role as an evangelical leader. In 1833 he married the only child of L. Threlfall of Lancaster; she, their son and daughter survived him.

BIBLIOGRAPHY
DNB
Leeds Mercury (24 January 1860)

DAVID J. JEREMY

Baird, Robert (b. near Pittsburgh, PA, USA, 6 Oct. 1798; d. Yonkers, NY, USA, 15 March 1863). Presbyterian minister, author, and leader of voluntary organizations. Baird's parents were of Scotch-Irish descent, and his father served in the revolutionary army. He was educated at Washington and Jefferson colleges (1816–18), and then received a degree from Princeton Theological Seminary in 1822. Ordained to the Presbyterian ministry in 1822, he directed the Princeton Academy for the next five years and thus launched a career of advocacy for public education. He married Fermine Du Brisson, a young woman of Huguenot descent, in 1824. As agent for the New Jersey Missionary Society, he travelled throughout the state attempting to supply each family with a Bible. He developed an interest in Sunday schools, and served as general agent of the ASSU from 1829 to 1834. Travelling throughout the United States, he founded schools, wrote voluminous reports and articles for religious periodicals, and became a widely recognized spokesperson for the Sunday school cause. In 1834 he accepted a position from a group that sought to promote Protestantism in France, and for 29 years he laboured to that end. While living in Paris and working for the Protestant cause, he promoted temperance in Europe, based on the model of the American Temperance Society. He made numerous journeys, crossing the Atlantic eighteen times, and carried the message to cities such as Rome, Moscow, and Stockholm. His own organization became known as the American and Foreign Christian Union and marked his own drift into ecumenical activities. A prolific author, he wrote extensively about voluntary societies, evangelicalism, and the American church scene. In regard to the latter, his *Religion in America* from 1843 was one of the first and best nineteenth-century discussions of the churches in the United States.

SELECT WRITINGS
R. Baird, *A View of the Mississippi Valley* (Philadelphia, PA, 1832)
—, *A Memoir of Anna Jane Linnard* (Philadelphia, PA, and Boston, MA, 1835)
—, *Histoire des Societes de Temperance des Etats-Unis d'Amérique* (Paris, 1836)
—, *Visit to Northern Europe or Sketches, Descriptive, Historical, Political and Moral of Denmark, Norway, Sweden, and Finland, and the Free Cities of Hamburg and Lubeck* (New York, 1841)
—, *The Christian Retrospect and Register . . .* (New York, 1851)

JAMES E. JOHNSON

Baker, Amelia Dorothea (née Kohlhoff). (b. Tanjore, India, 1801; d. Kottayam, India, 5 April 1888). Missionary wife and widow. She was the niece of J. C.

KOHLHOFF and thus one of the third generation in a famous Lutheran missionary family. She married the CMS clergyman HENRY BAKER when she was only 18. Soon after her marriage she commenced a school for girls at Kottayam, and continued it after his death in 1866 until her own death in 1888. Only in the length of service (seventy years) does this stand out from the largely unacknowledged contributions of countless missionary wives and widows, especially in India. Her oldest son, Henry Baker Jr, served in South India 1843–78, and his widow, Frances Kitchen Baker, likewise worked on after her husband's death. Three daughters married CMS missionaries and four granddaughters taught at Kottayam and nearby schools; the last was Isabel Amelia Baker (born 1847), dying only in 1939. Well over a score of the Kohlhoff and Baker families served the church in south India in five generations, over almost two hundred years.

BIBLIOGRAPHY
D. T. B[arry], *CMS Register of Missionaries and Native Clergy from 1804–1904* (privately printed) (London, 1906)
E. Dalton, *The Baker Family in India* (Kottayam, India, 1963)

JOCELYN MURRAY

Baker, Charles (b. Tamworth, Staffordshire, England, c. 1803; d. Auckland, New Zealand, 6 Feb. 1875). CMS missionary in New Zealand. Baker trained at the CMS College at Islington (London) from 1826 and on 14 July 1827 was sent to New Zealand. From 1828 he served at Kerikeri and then at Paihia, and from 1839 at Waikare. In 1843 he served at Uawa and from 1854 at Waiapu. He was ordained (deacon 1853, priest 1860) by Bishop WILLIAM WILLIAMS. He served the CMS in New Zealand for over 46 years. He married Hannah Maria Bailey.

BIBLIOGRAPHY
D. T. B[arry], *CMS Register of Missionaries and Native Clergy* (privately printed) (London, 1906)

DONALD M. LEWIS

Baker, Daniel (b. Midway, Liberty County, GA, USA; d. Austin, TX, USA, 10 Dec. 1857). Presbyterian minister. Baker entered Hampden-Sydney College in 1811 and was converted through the influence of MOSES HOGE, and became a Presbyterian. He also established a close friendship with WILLIAM CLAIBORNE WALTON. In 1813 he transferred to Princeton College, becoming a student leader of the Princeton College revival of 1814–15. Following graduation in 1815, he studied theology under WILLIAM HILL and was licensed to preach by Winchester presbytery in Virginia during the autumn of 1816. In that year he married a Virginian, Elizabeth McRobert.

He held various pastorates in Presbyterian churches in Harrisonburg, Virginia; Washington, DC; Savannah, Georgia; Tuscaloosa, Alabama; and Holly Springs, Mississippi. While pastoring Second Presbyterian Church in

Washington, DC (1822–7), he preached regularly to Presidents John Quincy Adams and Andrew Jackson. A successful Old School evangelist, he was often called the 'WHITEFIELD of the South'. Over 2,500 people were said to have been converted in his evangelistic services. Baker used a modification of the new measures of revivalism advocated by FINNEY in such a way as to conform to the orthodox Calvinism of his church. Though thoroughly Reformed, Baker did not preach paralysing notions about sinners' complete inability to respond to God's grace. He noted, 'I am a Calvinist, but I am no fatalist.' His revival methods included anxious seats, protracted meetings, inquiry meetings, and sunrise prayer groups.

He was the founding president of Austin College in Huntsville, Texas in 1853. His revival sermons were published in 1854 and reprinted in England in 1875 at the suggestion of Dwight L. Moody. His name has been perpetuated in Daniel Baker College, which was established in Brownwood, Texas in 1889.

SELECT WRITINGS
D. Baker, *Revival Sermons* (Philadelphia, PA, 1854)

BIBLIOGRAPHY
W. M. Baker, *The Life and Labors of Daniel Baker* (Philadelphia, PA, 1858)
DAB
Alfred Nevin, ed., *Encyclopedia of the Presbyterian Church in the United States* (Philadelphia, PA, 1884), s.v., 'Baker, Daniel'
A. D. Thomas, *The Second Great Awakening in Virginia and Slavery reform* (Richmond, VA, 1981)

ARTHUR DICKEN THOMAS, JR

Baker, Henry (b. Walton, Essex, England, *c.* 1794; d. Kottayam, India, 1866). CMS missionary to India. The son of a wealthy farmer, Baker abandoned a £1,400 inheritance to become a missionary in Travancore, arriving there 15 December 1817. Apart from one furlough (1833–5), he worked there until his death. First stationed at Kottayam, he established the CMS mission at Pallam in 1822.

Baker married Amelia Dorothea Kohlhoff, niece of J. C. KOHLHOFF (*see* AMELIA D. BAKER). Their son trained at the CMS College in Islington, and then joined his parents as a missionary. In 1848 Baker responded to the tribal Hill Arrians' pleas for Christian teaching. Former members of the Syrian Orthodox churches who had joined the CMS mission churches were dismayed when ninety Hill Arrians were baptized in 1857. They considered themselves high caste (Thurston, *The Castes and Tribes of Southern India*, Madras, 1908) and refused to worship with the Hill Arrians. Baker established a firm base for the congregations but could not heal this rift.

BIBLIOGRAPHY
W. S. Hunt, *History of the Anglican Church in Travancore and Cochin* (Kottayam, India, 1920)
E. Dalton, *The Baker Family in India* (Kottayam, India, 1963)

E. M. JACKSON

Baker, Moses (b. *c.* 1758; d. 1826). Native Baptist leader, Jamaica. He arrived in Jamaica from New York in 1783, and worked in Kingston as a barber. Under the influence of GEORGE LIELE, he and his wife were baptized and began a house church in Kingston. In 1788 he was invited by I. L. WINN, a Quaker and owner of the Adelphi Estate, St James, to instruct his slaves in 'religious and moral principles'. From this base he founded the church at Crooked Spring, the second Baptist church in Jamaica, in 1791. Baker corresponded with Dr JOHN RIPPON of London and Dr JOHN RYLAND of the Bristol Academy, pleading the cause of the slaves, and for help. After 26 years Ryland sent out JOHN ROWE, a student from Bristol, and first Baptist missionary to Jamaica, in 1814. Despite a successful ministry Baker's reputation was under constant attack from missionaries of the mainstream societies, but contemporary Moravian and Baptist missionaries reveal that he was an orthodox evangelical. Whatever the weaknesses of the native Baptist movement, they were exacerbated by the restrictive legislation set up to crush the movement.

BIBLIOGRAPHY
BaptMag (1814): 41; (1815): 165–9
EM (1803): 361–71
Periodic Accounts of the Baptist Mission, 5: 505

GORDON A. CATHERALL

Bakewell, John (b. Brailsford, Derbyshire, England, 1721; d. Lewisham, London, 18 March 1819). Methodist preacher and hymn-writer. Converted in youth through reading Thomas Boston's *Human Nature in its Fourfold State* (1720) he became an ardent evangelist. Despite opposition he started to preach in 1744. Moving to London he met the WESLEYS, AUGUSTUS M. TOPLADY, MARTIN MADAN, and JOHN W. FLETCHER. Bakewell became one of Wesley's preachers in 1749. After some years directing the Greenwich Royal Park Academy he resigned in favour of his son-in-law, James Egan, and spent much time preaching wherever other Methodist preachers were not available. He was buried in his ninety-eighth year in City Road near John Wesley. Bakewell had many links with early Methodism, and the New Testament Greek scholar W. F. Moulton (1835–98) was his great-grandson (Telford, 1935).

THOMAS OLIVERS wrote 'The God of Abraham praise', it was said, at Bakewell's house in Westminster. Bakewell himself wrote several hymns; but only one (and his authorship is not certain) has survived. The earliest version of 'Hail, thou once despisèd Jesus' appeared in the anonymous pamphlet, *A Collection of Hymns addressed to the Holy, Holy, Holy, triune God* (1757). Expanded and altered especially by Madan and Toplady, it has since appeared in some form in many hymn-books.

BIBLIOGRAPHY
Julian: 108, 479–80
J. Stelfox, *Brief Sketch of the Late Mr John Bakewell, of Greenwich* (Belfast, 1864)

J. Telford, *The New Methodist Hymn-Book Illustrated in History and Experience*, 2nd edn (London, 1935): 135–6

R. Watson and K. Trickett, ed., *Companion to 'Hymns & Psalms'* (Peterborough, England, 1988): 154–5, 566

JOHN S. ANDREWS

Baldwin, Thomas (b. Bozrah, CT, BNA, 23 Dec. 1753; d. Waterville, ME, USA, 29 Aug. 1825). Baptist pastor and promoter of missions. He was the only son of Thomas and Mary Baldwin. Following his father's death, the family moved from Connecticut to Canaan, New Hampshire where Baldwin studied law and served in the legislature. He became a Baptist in 1780 and was ordained 11 June 1783. He worked for seven years as an itinerant evangelist in Vermont and New Hampshire.

In 1790 he became pastor of the Second Baptist Church, Boston, remaining there until his death. He was awarded an MA (Brown University, 1795) and DD (Union College, 1803). He founded one of the earliest Baptist periodicals, the *Massachusetts Baptist Missionary Magazine* and was the primary force behind the establishment of the General Missionary Convention in the United States of America for Foreign Missions, the first national Baptist organization in America. He served as its first recording secretary and then as its president until his death. He was a trustee of Brown University, Waterville College, and Columbian College. He wrote several works and many of his sermons were published.

BIBLIOGRAPHY
AAP

T. Armitage, *A History of the Baptists* (New York, 1887)

D. Benedict, *A General History of the Baptist Denomination in America* (New York, 1848)

J. L. Boyd, *A History of the Baptists in America Prior to 1845* (New York, 1947)

ROBERT N. NASH

Balfour, John Hutton (b. Edinburgh, 15 Sept. 1808; d. Edinburgh, 11 Feb. 1884). Scottish botanist and educator. Balfour was named after his relative, James Hutton, the geological theorist. Educated at the universities of St Andrews and Edinburgh and at the Paris medical school, he became Doctor of Medicine in 1832.

Robert Graham's famous lectures in Edinburgh interested him in botany. He became proficient in the subject and accepted the botanical chair at Glasgow University in 1841, which he held until 1845 when he succeeded Graham at Edinburgh. He retired in 1879. Balfour made no significant contribution to botanical knowledge but was an enthusiastic and engaging lecturer. He was an honoured member of many scientific societies and served as a journal editor and textbook writer.

Balfour gloried in the evidence of God's hand in nature in *Phyto-Theology* (1851), *Plants from the Bible* (1857), *Lessons from Bible Plants* (1870), and he contributed to McCrie's *Bass Rock* (1848). He was secretary of the Edinburgh auxiliary of the CMS, was on the committee of the Edinburgh Medical Missionary Society, of the RTS (Scotland), of the Scottish Reformation Society and was very prominent in the Edinburgh auxiliary of the EA.

BIBLIOGRAPHY
Boase

R. G. C. Desmond, 'Balfour, John Hutton', *Dictionary of Scientific Biography*, ed. C. C. Gillespie (NY, 1970–90) II: 423

DNB

Oliver and Boyd, *Edinburgh Almanac* (1853)

JONATHAN BURKE CUTMORE

Ball, Edward (b. Hastings, Sussex, England, 1793; d. Burwell, near Newmarket, Suffolk, England, Nov. 1865). British MP. The son of Richard Ball and Elizabeth Thwaites Ball, he was educated at Bromley, near Newmarket. Ball served as Deputy-Lieutenant of Cambridge in 1852 and in the same year became MP for Cambridgeshire. A Whig Dissenter, probably a Congregationalist, he opposed the Maynooth Grant, advocated the abolition of church rates and supported non-sectarian education 'based upon the Word of God'. Ball retired from Parliament in January 1863.

BIBLIOGRAPHY
Boase

GM (December 1865): 802

Stenton

JONATHAN BURKE CUTMORE

Ball, Hannah (b. High Wycombe, Buckinghamshire, England, 13 March 1734; d. High Wycombe, Buckinghamshire, England, 16 Aug. 1792). Pioneer of Sunday schools. A lacemaker's daughter, she was influenced by reading THOMAS WALSH's sermons and converted in 1765 through JOHN WESLEY with whom she frequently corresponded. The following year she began to keep a diary, later published as her memoirs. In 1769 she started a Sunday school which anticipated the venture of ROBERT RAIKES. She reported that they were a wild little group but seemed eager to learn. Samuel Wells, Wesley's assistant in the Oxfordshire circuit, supported her. It has been claimed that she was the originator of Sunday schools, but Catherine Warren of Haverfordwest may well have been the first in the field. A new chapel was opened in High Wycombe in 1779. Her sister, Ann, superintended the school after Hannah's death.

BIBLIOGRAPHY
DNB

J. Cole, ed., *Memoirs of Miss Hannah Ball* (York, England, 1796)

A. SKEVINGTON WOOD

Ball, John (b. Aylesbury, Buckinghamshire, England, 27 Aug. 1799 (ordination papers, Oxford); d. Reading, Berkshire, England, 17 Dec. 1865). College tutor and

Anglican clergyman. Son of James (gentleman) and Elizabeth Ball, John became a Christian early in life. Educated at Merchant Taylors' School, London, he was scholar and fellow of St John's College, Oxford, 1818–35. Ordained in 1822, for some years Ball was one of a small group of fellows of St John's forming a significant element in contemporary evangelicalism at Oxford. Having served as curate to his friend JOHN NATT, from 1834 till death he was Vicar of St Laurence's, Reading, Berkshire, remaining unmarried. Of deep personal piety, Ball was a staunchly protestant evangelical, firm but tolerant, an unobtrusive yet zealous pastor, not least in Sunday schools.

BIBLIOGRAPHY
Reading Mercury (28 December 1865) obituary
J. S. Reynolds, *Evangelicals at Oxford* (Oxford, 1953; Appleford, England, 1975)
V. Sillery, *St. John's College Biographical Register 1775–1875* (Oxford, 1987)

J. S. REYNOLDS

Ball, Mary [Barksworth, Mrs T.] (b. Belper, Derbyshire, England, 10 April 1810; d. Grimsby, Lincolnshire, England, 11 Feb. 1860). Primitive Methodist (PM) itinerant preacher. Converted at approximately ten years old, she became a PM member. Ball taught in the Sunday school, became a local preacher at 15 and a travelling preacher in 1822. She worked unofficially in Belper for 22 months and then in Louth, Grimsby and Whitby, before retiring to marry. She continued as a local preacher and class leader. In June 1859 Ball underwent a mastectomy, but died the following February after much suffering. PM was established early in Belper, so Ball may be the only female itinerant to have been through a PM Sunday school.

BIBLIOGRAPHY
PMMag (1860)

E. DOROTHY GRAHAM

Ball, Richard (b. probably Bridgwater, Somerset, England, *c.* 1794; d. Clifton, Bristol, England, 10 May 1862). Quaker seceder. Reared in the Quakers he had moved to Taunton by 1835. In his *Holy Scripture, the Test of Truth*, he supported ISAAC CREWDSON in the Beaconite controversy. In 1837 he and his wife were baptized respectively at Taunton by BENJAMIN WILLS NEWTON and at Bristol by HENRY CRAIK. His *Dissuasive Considerations ... [from] Joining the Established Church* (1837) was aimed at Quakers as he had joined the Brethren. In the 1850s as a secretary of the Chinese Association, he edited *The Gleaner in the Missionary Field*, later being described by J. HUDSON TAYLOR's biographers as 'a man of literary gift as well as spiritual insight'. In Bristol (where he moved in 1850) he was an elder at Bethesda Chapel and it was he who conducted the funeral service of ANTHONY NORRIS GROVES.

BIBLIOGRAPHY
Boase
[Harriet Groves], *Memoir of the Late Anthony Norris Groves* (London, 1857): 511
The Inquirer, 1 (1838): 64
H. and G. Taylor, *Hudson Taylor in Early Years* (London, 1912): 90

TIMOTHY C. F. STUNT

Ball, William (b. Bridgwater, Somerset, England, 1 Jan. 1801; d. Scotland, 30 July 1878). Quaker minister. Ball travelled extensively in the British Isles in the ministry over almost fifty years and attended business meetings diligently. His 19 published works included five selections of his articles from Quaker periodicals and many hymns and poems. While he was evangelical in his ministry he was anxious too to preserve Friends' traditions and dependence on the immediate guidance of the Holy Spirit. He became influential in the yearly meeting in London. Ball was noted as an individual of marked intellectual independence and originality, characteristics found difficult by some contemporaries. He was not recorded as a minister until 1846, 18 years after he had first prayed aloud in meeting. That delay was a deep trial to him.

BIBLIOGRAPHY
Biographical Catalogue ... London Friends Institute (London, 1888)
Dictionary of Quaker Biography (typescript, Friends' House Library, London)
J. Smith, *A Descriptive Catalogue of Friend's Books*. 2 vols and supplement, (London, 1867, 1893)

DAVID J. HALL

Bampton, William (b. Bourne, Lincolnshire, England, 1787; d. Pūrī, India, 17 Dec. 1830). Baptist New Connexion missionary pioneer. Converted under the ministry of W. Taylor, New Connexion minister in Boston, Linconshire (who in his last illness confessed 'his unshakable reliance on the efficacy of the Saviour's atonement'), Bampton went into ministerial service. In 1811 he became assistant minister at Sutterton; in 1814 the sole pastorate at Gosberton; and in 1818, he settled as minister at Great Yarmouth, Norfolk. His offer to serve the new General Baptist Missionary Society was unanimously accepted and he was ordained in May 1821 as one of the new society's first missionaries. Starting work in the Orissa field of India, he, with JAMES PEGGS, founded the work at Cuttack. After a short while he was despatched to begin a Christian witness at Pūrī, the site of the temple of Jagganāth. In this task he surmounted many difficulties including the deepest poverty and widespread disease. Here he baptized the first convert in Orissa. While determined to stand against the worship of Jagganāth, he was committed to seeking every possible means for the conversion of Hindu people. Pledged to means of conciliation wherever possible, he even went so far as to adopt native dress, believing that by so doing he removed an unnecessary obstacle to the reception of his message: 'my object', he confessed, 'is to conciliate the people in order to promote their salvation'.

BIBLIOGRAPHY
J. H. Wood, *A Condensed History of the New Connexion* (London, 1847)

J. H. Y. BRIGGS

Banerjea, K(rishna) M(ohun)   (b. Navagram, India, 24 May 1813; d. India, 11 May 1888). Indian scholar, theologian and evangelist. Born an orthodox Kulin Brahman, Banerjea was educated in the Hindu classics by his maternal grandfather Ramjoy Vidyabushan, a Sanskrit scholar. He attended David Hare's primary schools, and then entered Hindu College (February 1824). There he met and was influenced by poet and freethinker Michael Derozio. He later became an avowed atheist. Banerjea edited his own paper, 'The Enquirer', beginning May 1831, and taught at one of Hare's schools.

After he met ALEXANDER DUFF, Banerjea agreed to study Christianity and, after much resistance, requested baptism. He became an Anglican, a catechist, and a superintendent of the CMS school on Amherst Street, Calcutta. Archdeacon THOMAS DEALTRY persuaded him to enter Bishop's College to prepare for ordination. In 1839 he was ordained to Christ Church, Cornwallis Square, where he preached to congregations of 200–500 students. One he influenced was Michael Madhusadan Dutt, now regarded as one of the greatest Bengali poets. In 1868 he joined Bishop's College as second professor, but resigned his canonry at the new cathedral upon discovering that European canons were being paid more than Indian canons.

Banerjea became a writer and a campaigner for social reform, especially for women's rights. He opposed the 1868 Indian Christians' Marriage Act, which allowed converts to remarry if their wives refused to live with them, and argued for the rights of deserted Hindu wives. He was also active in the 'Bengal Renaissance,' a flowering of Bengali literature and arts, as well as editing Hindu scriptures. In 1876 Banerjea received an honorary doctorate from Calcutta University. His influence stretched far beyond Bengal. Today his theology is required reading for Indian theological students. A full bibliography of his works contains more than 45 titles.

BIBLIOGRAPHY
T. V. Philip, *Krishna Mohun Banerjea* (Madras, India, 1982)
R. Paul, *Triumphs of His Grace* (Madras, India, 1968)

E. M. JACKSON

Bangs, Nathan   (b. Stratford, CT, USA, 2 May 1778; d. New York City, USA, 3 May 1862). Methodist itinerant, apologist, historian, and Methodist Missionary Society founder. The son of Lemuel and Rebecca [née Keeler] Bangs, he began a career as a teacher and surveyor in Upper Canada in 1799. In 1801 Bangs was licensed as a Methodist itinerant and commenced 12 years of ministry in Upper Canada (now Ontario) and Lower Canada (now Quebec). Indeed, Bangs is generally credited with being the founder of Methodism in Lower Canada. Bangs' labours in bringing the Methodist Gospel to Canada would instil in him an abiding commitment to evangelism and missions. While serving in Canada in 1806, he married Mary Bolton of Edwardsburg, Upper Canada.

During his years in Canada, Bangs wrote the first of several theological treatises that vigorously defended Methodism's advocacy of free grace, free will, and form of episcopal polity. His works, especially *The Errors of Hopkinsianism Detected and Refuted* (1815), also contained acerbic attacks on Calvinist doctrine. For example, Bangs was particularly hostile to the Calvinist notion of predestination or election. In his mind, the idea that God alone determined who would receive salvation and that human assent to divine grace offered in Jesus Christ played no role whatsoever, undermined all human moral responsibility. As well, Bangs felt that predestination was contrary to ordinary human experience, repugnant to human reason, and without any basis in scripture. Again and again he insisted that salvation was available to all who of their own free will would accept it as the gift offered by God in Christ. The same line of thinking led him to reject the popular notion that salvation was a permanent condition; for Bangs, the Christian life was one of constant struggle against forces that would lure believers away from faith. What one once accepted by faith, one could just as easily abandon through an act of will. Hence it is no surprise that in the 1840s and 1850s, when PHOEBE PALMER and others led the crusade for American Methodism to reclaim JOHN WESLEY's emphasis on scriptural holiness and sanctification, Bangs wholeheartedly endorsed their efforts. If the Christian experience was a continuing battle against temptation, it was for Bangs also an ongoing pursuit of holiness.

In 1819, Bangs was instrumental in founding the Methodist Missionary Society that promoted Methodist expansion both in North America and overseas. For 16 years, he served without compensation as its corresponding secretary and treasurer. Then from 1836 to 1841 he had formal appointment as the society's salaried corresponding secretary. His work with the missionary society and his history of missions (published in 1832) earned him the popular sobriquet, 'father of the missionary work of the Methodist Episcopal Church'. But Bangs harboured an imperialist understanding of the missionary enterprise that in time would be generally repudiated. In the annual reports that he drafted for the society – and he wrote all but one from the society's founding through 1841 – a recurring theme is the necessity of conversion to Christianity as a precursor of becoming civilized, and civilization meant the adoption of Euro-American cultural and religious ways.

In addition to his work with the missionary society,

Bangs became an agent of the fledgling Methodist Book Concern when he returned to the United States in 1820. Although charged primarily to turn Methodism's publishing arm into a profitable venture, Bangs made a more enduring contribution through his endeavours as editor of the monthly *Methodist Review* (*Methodist Quarterly Review* after 1832). At that time, religious periodicals were a primary forum for airing opposing views on controversial issues within and between denominations. Methodism was no exception. Hence Bangs was quickly drawn into an internal debate over the nature of bishops' authority in the MEC. He hewed a conservative course in the controversy, strongly supporting FRANCIS ASBURY's insistence on granting bishops considerable administrative power (particularly in the appointment of presiding elders) and refusing to print essays supporting the so-called 'reformist' position that wanted to restrict episcopal authority and develop a more democratic and less hierarchical polity for the church. After the 1828 General Conference re-affirmed episcopal powers, the controversy led to the schism that resulted in the organization of the MPC in 1830. But the position Bangs defended became the standard for the MEC. Bangs also used the pages of the *Methodist Review* to champion the necessity of continual evangelism and Methodist expansion; many articles promoting evangelism were written by Bangs himself. As well, Bangs frequently reprinted material by British Methodist writers, making the *Methodist Review* an important means of reminding American Methodists of the international character of the Wesleyan movement.

Largely self-educated, Bangs nevertheless was a tireless proponent of setting educational standards for those seeking to become Methodist itinerants. Aversion to formal theological education was strong in American Methodism. Many believed that an intensive personal experience of conversion was the primary qualification for effective ministry. Others regarded seminary education as theologically dangerous and a potential source of heretical doctrine. But in the 1840s, successive General Conferences began to standardize the course of study expected of candidates for the itinerary and to support the establishment of theological schools. Once again, Bangs' position became normative for the denomination.

Bangs' major historical work was a four volume history of American Methodism. Stylistically cumbersome, it contains a wealth of factual information about early Methodist developments in the United States that remains a valuable source for contemporary analysts. Bangs's history is clearly triumphalist, for he was aware that by the mid-nineteenth century Methodism had become the numerically largest Protestant denomination in the United States, and he reviewed its development with considerable pride. But the story Bangs unfolds is also uncritical, for he failed to take adequate account of the controversy over slavery that was paramount within American Methodism at the time he was writing and that would split the MEC in the United States into two regional denominations just four years after the publication of the final volume.

Bangs' support of formal education took another form in 1841 when he undertook a one-year tenure as acting president of Wesleyan University in Connecticut, one of American Methodism's early ventures in higher education. Ten years as a pastor of several congregations in New York City followed before he retired in 1852. Generally regarded as the most influential writer among American Methodists of his generation, Bangs died in 1862. WILLIAM M. BANGS was his son.

SELECT WRITINGS

N. Bangs, *The Errors of Hopkinsianism Detected and Refuted* (New York, 1815)
—, *The Reformer Reformed* (New York, 1816)
—, *Methodist Episcopacy Vindicated* (New York, 1820)
—, *Letters to Young Ministers of the Gospel* (New York, 1826)
—, *An Authentic History of . . . Missions* (New York, 1832)
—, *The history of the Methodist Episcopal Church . . .* 4 vols (New York, 1838–41)

BIBLIOGRAPHY

DAB
DCA
DcAmReB
EWM
NCAB, 9: 429–30
A. Stevens, *The Life and Times of Nathan Bangs, D.D.* (New York, 1862)
A. H. Tuttle, *Nathan Bangs* (New York and Cincinnati, OH, 1909)
J. G. Wilson and J. Fiske, eds, *Appleton's Cyclopaedia of American Biography* (New york, 1894–96)

CHARLES H. LIPPY

Bangs, William McKendree (b. New York City, 15 Dec. 1810; d. New York City, Sept. 1852). Methodist preacher, teacher and scholar. The son of NATHAN BANGS, he was educated first by his father and then at the Grammar School of Columbia College (1825–7) and the University of Ohio (1827–9). In spite of his religious upbringing, he did not become personally committed to his faith until August 1827 when he heard the preaching of the Reverend Dr Durbin. At about this time he was licensed as an exhorter and soon authorized to preach. Following his graduation he was appointed Professor of Languages at Augusta College in Kentucky. In 1831 he was recognized as an itinerant preacher.

In 1834 he suffered from 'inflammatory rheumatism' and his health never fully recovered. He did, however, manage to make significant theological contributions to the *Methodist Quarterly Review*. Bishop ELIJAH HEDDING thought him the most able theological thinker in American Methodism.

BIBLIOGRAPHY

AAP 7: 773–6
M. Simpson, ed., *Cyclopaedia of Methodism* (Philadelphia, PA, 1882)

DONALD M. LEWIS

Banister, Robert (d. Liverpool, England, 1829). Anglican clergyman. Banister had studied at St Catherine's College, Cambridge (BA 1785). He subsequently held curacies at Upholland (Lancashire), St John's, St Paul's, and St Peter's, Liverpool and might have become first incumbent of Christ Church, Liverpool but for differences with its builder and proprietor, Houghton, and the Bishop of Chester. Richard Walker and other prominent citizens built All Saints which was opened in 1798, where Banister ministered for the rest of his life. He sat loosely to Anglican disciplines, the church remaining unconsecrated in his lifetime while he himself had no episcopal licence. He modified the liturgy to meet his requirements and admitted Dissenters to his pulpit. Nevertheless, he exercised great influence among Liverpool evangelicals and was said to have been 'probably the most popular minister' in the city.

BIBLIOGRAPHY
D. Thom, *Liverpool Churches and Chapels* (Liverpool, England, 1854)

ARTHUR POLLARD

Banks, Charles Waters (b. Ashford, Kent, England, 9 Feb. 1806; d. South Hackney, London, 25 March 1886). Printer, publisher, and Strict Baptist minister. Banks was minister at St John's Chapel, Northgate, Canterbury, Kent, 1839–40; all his later pastorates were in London. A keen railway traveller, he constantly visited country churches, preaching at anniversaries. He concentrated on the development of a cheap and sound religious press, establishing in 1845 *The Earthen Vessel*, which he edited until his death. *The Earthen Vessel*, a monthly publication circulating among Strict Baptists, was unlike the *Gospel Standard* in that it did not adopt a dogmatic view on 'the eternal generation of the son.' *The Earthen Vessel* was followed by: in 1850, *The Anti-popish Reviewer and Protestant Lamp for the Christian Churchman* (anti-Catholic propaganda); from March 1851, *Cheering Words*, the first halfpenny monthly tract magazine; in 1852, *The Baptist Almanack* listing Strict Baptist, Baptist and Congregational chapels and ministers, mostly in London; in 1855 *The Christian Cabinet*, the first penny weekly Christian newspaper, and in 1861, *The Gospel Times*, a weekly Protestant paper. A staunch conservative, his '*A Baptist Minister's Appeal* . . . (London, 1868) excited much controversy.

BIBLIOGRAPHY
A. M. Banks, *The Reverend Charles Waters Banks* (London, 1890)
The Baptist Handbook (1887): 94–5
Boase
Earthen Vessel (1854): 118–19
The Times (31 March 1886): 10

GEOFFREY RALPH BREED

Bannerman, James (b. Manse of Cargill, Perthshire, Scotland, 9 April 1807; d. Edinburgh, 27 March 1868).

He was educated at Perth Academy and Edinburgh University, licensed by the presbytery of Perth in 1830 and ordained and inducted to the charge of Ormiston in 1833; he adhered to the Free Church in 1843.

In 1849, Bannerman was appointed professor of apologetics and pastoral theology at New College, Edinburgh. A very able and distinguished scholar in the Reformed tradition, his work 'Inspiration, The Infallible Truth and Divine Authority of the Holy Scriptures', published in 1865, was written (in his own words) at a 'time of transition in the history of religious opinion'. The volume helped to clarify some of the main issues and contemporary attitudes in the debate over the inspiration of the Bible. While he remained an exponent of orthodox teaching until his dying day, Bannerman's support for plenary rather than verbal inspiration was undoubtedly of considerable significance in the longer term. He was awarded the degree of DD by Princeton College in 1850.

SELECT WRITINGS
J. Bannerman, *Apologetic Theology* (Edinburgh, 1851)
—, *Inspiration. The Infallible Truth and Divine Authority of the Holy Scriptures* (Edinburgh, 1865)
—, *The Church of Christ* (Edinburgh, 1868)
—, *Sermons* (with Memoir) (Edinburgh, 1869)

BIBLIOGRAPHY
W. Ewing ed., *Annals of the FCS, 1843–1900* (Edinburgh, 1914)
Fasti

ALASDAIR BOTHWELL GORDON

Barber, John (b. Kinder, Peak District, Derbyshire, England, 16 Dec. 1757; d. Bristol, England, 28 April 1816). President of the Methodist Conference. As a rough young farm labourer he sought to improve himself by attending evening school, and proved an apt student. He was hired by Mr Greaves of Woodlands, a Methodist class leader, after promising never to swear another oath, a promise which he faithfully kept. An earthquake in 1777 warned him of his mortality, and the sermon of a local preacher convinced him of his own sinfulness. On Easter Sunday, 19 April 1778, he was converted, and became a steady member of Mr Greaves's class, taking every opportunity of attending prayer meetings, and even warning strangers 'to flee from the wrath to come'. He moved to Chinley to lodge with a Methodist schoolmaster named Mathews, with whom he practised his new trade as a weaver, but at the same time exercised his spiritual gifts and eager mind as a Methodist local preacher.

It is difficult to piece together the specific steps by which he entered the Methodist ministry. One of WESLEY'S assistants (later known as superintendent ministers) prophesied, 'he will make a great preacher'. After making a pilgrimage to Macclesfield to hear Wesley preach (possibly on Good Friday, 29 March 1782) another assistant dragooned him into preaching at 5.00 a.m. the following morning, apparently to the great satisfaction of Wesley, who later that year appointed him to serve in the newly formed Birmingham circuit. (His name, however, is not listed in the 1782 *Minutes*, and James Rogers, supposedly the assistant who urged Barber to preach at Macclesfield, was not stationed there until later that year. Edward Oxley, John Barber's painstaking biographer in 1817–18, understandably lamented the fact that he never followed up his intention of preparing an autobiography.)

John Wesley's approval of John Barber was demonstrated by the fact that he was accepted into full connection with the Methodist Conference to begin his first minuted appointment, at Northampton in 1783, where his advocacy was the means of the new Methodist preaching-house at Whittlebury being opened free of debt. The following year Barber was named in the Deed of Declaration by which Wesley legally defined the Methodist Conference, one of a handful of men among the hundred preachers who had been in full connection no more than a year. When the preacher appointed for the important charge at Edinburgh died at the beginning of the conference year, John Wesley wrote on 15 September 1787, to George Holder in Whitby: 'Upon mature deliberation I judge it most advisable that John·Barber should remove to Edinburgh (for I can trust him in any part of Great Britain), and that you should supply his place at York' (Telford, 1931). On 19 May 1788, at 3.30 in the morning, John Wesley 'ordained brother Barber' for his continuing ministry in that city for another year. Summing up Barber's ministry on 31 January 1791, a few weeks before his own death, Wesley wrote, 'Mr. Barber has the glory of God at heart.'

As a Methodist itinerant preacher Barber served widely and effectively. In Huddersfield, for example, where he was stationed 1794–6, 'he found a large society nearly torn to pieces by dissensions; through his prudence and firmness, however, the mischief was considerably counteracted, and a glorious revival of religion immediately succeeded'. Twice he was appointed president of the Methodist Conference, in 1807 and 1815. He was a leading member of the Committee of Privileges, by means of which, from its formation in 1803, legal protection was secured for Methodist ministers from parliamentary pressure aimed at disenfranchizing them and their societies. During his later years his wife tried to dissuade him from preaching, to which he replied: 'Ah, my dear, in the pulpit I forget all my sufferings.' Barber died suddenly, aged 59, during his second year of presidential office.

BIBLIOGRAPHY
MM (1816): 430, 706–7; (1818): 241–8, 321–8
J. Telford, ed., *The Letters of John Wesley* 8 vols (London, 1931)

FRANK BAKER

Barber, Suzannah [probably née Perry] (b. Nottingham, England, *c.* 1776; d. New Mills, Derbyshire, England, 26 June 1851). Primitive Methodist (PM) itinerant preacher. Converted to Wesleyan Methodism at 18, she joined the PMs when they visited Nottingham, becoming a local preacher and then a travelling preacher. Barber faced much opposition and persecution. She was imprisoned for preaching in Huddersfield (16 July 1820) with William Taylor. She was one of the earliest PM preachers and a PM for about forty years. She married J. Barber and reverted to local preacher status.

BIBLIOGRAPHY
H. B. Kendall, *The Origin and History of the PM Church*, 1 (London, 1904)
PMMag (1851)

E. DOROTHY GRAHAM

Barber, Thomas (b. County Fermanagh, Ireland, 3 December 1751; d. Monaghan, Ireland, 7 November 1825). Methodist preacher. He was one of about twenty young men who entered the ministry under the influence of JOHN SMITH (1713–74). Smith's exhortations were sharpened when Barber heard JOHN WESLEY himself preach at Sidaire on 25 May 1778. He began a freelance preaching itinerary in northern Londonderry, which incorporated the beginnings of the first Gospel challenge to ADAM CLARKE, who was later introduced to Wesley by John Bredin. In 1779 Barber was received on trial in the Methodist itinerancy, and served simply but faithfully as pastor and preacher in many circuits throughout much of Ireland. In preaching he often employed, to helpful advantage the mannerism of occasionally stopping and addressing individual members of his congregation. John Wesley named him in 1784 as one of the 'Legal Hundred' constituting his official conference. When in 1811 Dr ADAM CLARKE spent a whole month in what he described as a 'preaching pilgrimage' throughout Ireland, before presiding over the Irish Conference, only two members of the Legal Hundred still resided in Ireland, of whom one was Thomas Barber. He had retired to Monaghan in 1808, however, where he died in 1825.

BIBLIOGRAPHY
C. H. Crookshank, *History of Methodism in Ireland*, 1 (Belfast, 1885)
R. H. Gallagher, *Pioneer Preachers of Irish Methodism* (Belfast, no date)
G. Smith, *History of Wesleyan Methodism* 5th edn 1 (London, 1866): 465–72

FRANK BAKER

Barclay, George (b. Kilwinning, Ayrshire, Scotland, 12 March 1774; d. Kilwinning, 20 July 1838). A pioneer of Baptist home missionary activity in Scotland. Barclay was converted at the age of twenty and trained as an Independent preacher at HALDANE classes in Dundee and Glasgow, then returned to work in Kilwinning in April 1802. In 1803 he was baptized in Edinburgh by Dr CHARLES STUART, and in December 1803 founded a

Baptist church on the 'English' single-pastor model (in 1822 the church moved to the more populous town of Irvine, becoming Irvine Baptist Church). He influenced CHRISTOPHER ANDERSON, whom he met when in Edinburgh, and with whom he later established an itinerant society. In 1823 he became the secretary of this society, reconstituted as the Baptist Evangelical Society of Scotland, a precursor of the Baptist Home Missionary Society for Scotland. His church supported candidates for Baptist home mission, sending the first Scottish student to Bradford Baptist Academy in 1804. Barclay had a strong supportive interest in WILLIAM CAREY's mission to India, and his son, William Carey Barclay, served as a printer at Serampore. In 1837 he played an important role in the reconciliation between Serampore and the home committee. He wrote a number of books and pamphlets, including *Memoirs of James Neil, Shipmaster, Irvine* (Irvine, 1821), *Essays on Doctrinal and Prophetic Subjects* (Edinburgh, 1828) and *Strictures on Two Sermons by the Rev. McLeod Campbell of Row* (1829).

BIBLIOGRAPHY
D. Bebbington, ed., *The Baptists in Scotland* (Glasgow, 1988): 33–5, 135, 284
A. B. Thomson, 'Some Baptist Pioneers in Scotland During the Eighteenth Century and the Early Years of the Nineteenth', *Scottish Baptist Year-Book* (1902): 24–31

DONALD E. MEEK AND DEREK B. MURRAY

Barclay, Hugh (b. Glasgow, Scotland, 18 Jan. 1799; d. Craigie, near Perth, Scotland, 1 Feb. 1884). Scottish judge. The son of a Glasgow merchant, Barclay was admitted to the faculty of procurators in 1821 and rose to local prominence, first as sheriff substitute for western Perthshire in 1829, then for the whole county in 1833. He was made sheriff in the year before his death. His professional reputation rested mainly on his *Digest of the Law of Scotland* (1852–3), for many years a standard. He was also the author of related works and was a contributor to professional journals.

Throughout his life Barclay was active in the Church of Scotland as a temperance, Sabbatarian, and Sunday school advocate, which opinions he supported in print. He also bears responsibility for two other curious works, neither of which made a lasting impression: *A Basket of First Fruits* (1868), a collection of doggerel 'Poems in Verse'; and an inventive attempt to demonstrate *Heathen Mythology Corroborative or Illustrative of Holy Scripture* (1884). He was a member of the EA from its foundation.

BIBLIOGRAPHY
DNB
Anon., *Sheriff Barclay*, reprinted from the *Perthshire Advertiser*, (Edinburgh, 1884)

JONATHAN BURKE CUTMORE

Barclay, Robert (b. Croydon, Surrey, England, 4 Aug. 1833; d. Reigate, Surrey, England, 11 Nov. 1876.)

Ecclesiastical historiographer. As the younger son of John Barclay (1797–1838), he was descended from the Quaker apologist, Robert Barclay (1648–90). After preparatory school at Epping in Essex, he was sent to the Friends' School at Hitchin, Hertfordshire. In 1847 he moved to a school at Tottenham in Middlesex. He did well in botany, chemistry and electrical experiments.

In 1850 he left school to go to Bristol, where he joined a Quaker firm. Five years later he bought a manufacturing stationery concern in London. In 1857 he married Sarah Matilda, eldest daughter of Francis Fry of Bristol, a bibliographer of the English Bible. Their home was at Tottenham, and they had nine children, six of whom survived him. In 1860 he patented an 'indelible writing paper' for the prevention of forgery and described the process of manufacture in a communication to the Society of Arts. His brother-in-law, J. D. Fry, became a partner in his firm in 1867. Deteriorating health in 1873 made him and his wife move to Reigate, where he spent the rest of his life.

While still at school at Tottenham he deepened his Christian commitment and met with a few other boys for prayer and Bible study. During his early years in Bristol he studied the Greek Testament in his spare time. At home and on his many European holidays he supported evangelistic work. From about 1857 onwards he regularly read the Bible to his employees before the start of work, and he strongly supported the public reading of it in Friends' meeting. He held that the early Friends were the first home mission association and wanted them to become again an aggressive Christian church. He opposed birthright membership of the society.

His major work on *The Inner Life of the Religious Societies of the Commonwealth* appeared in January 1877, shortly after his death. His widow published 36 of his sermons preached in Quaker meetings and missions besides extracts from his diary and his letters, all revealing a deep faith. 'To the rich and poor', she wrote in her introduction, 'R.B. preached boldly Jesus Christ and Him crucified' (Barclay, 1878). Although a loyal Friend, he attended Wesleyan class meetings and Baptist church meetings and was commended by C. H. SPURGEON.

SELECT WRITINGS
R. Barclay, *Sermons, With a Brief Memoir*, ed. by his widow [S.M. Barclay] (London, 1878)

BIBLIOGRAPHY
DNB

JOHN S. ANDREWS

Bardsley, James (b. near Oldham, Lancashire, England, 1808; d. Southport, Lancashire, England, 20 May 1886). Anglican clergyman. Bardsley was baptized in Lees on 16 April 1809. In his youth he worked as a factory lad, and married a daughter of the proprietor. Deaconed in 1833, priested 1834, he held curacies at

Haworth, Keighley, Bierley, Bowling and Burnley before going to Manchester (1849) to be incumbent of St Philip's, Bradford Road. He helped to promote the Ten Hours Bill and remained popular with working men. From 1857 to 1880 he was Rector of St Ann's, Manchester, where he organized midday services for businessmen. He was Honorary Canon of Manchester Cathedral from 1871 to 1880. He actively supported the Systematic Beneficence Society. A founder of the Church of England Temperance Society, he was also vice-president of the United Kingdom Alliance. He was known for his conservatism and fervent evangelicalism, and also for his spirit of interdenominationalism.

BIBLIOGRAPHY
Boase
J. Garnett and A. C. Howe, 'Churchmen and Cotton Masters in Victorian England', in *Business and Religion in Britain*, ed. D. J. Jeremy (Aldershot, England, 1988): 72–94

JANE GARNETT

Bardsley, Samuel (d. Delph, Lancashire, England, 19 Aug. 1818). Methodist preacher. At the time of his death the oldest preacher in the connexion, Samuel Bardsley entered the ministry in 1768 and served the length and breadth of the country and as far north as Inverness, and was one of the 'Legal Hundred' appointed in 1784.

He was a man of unblemished character, truly devoted and zealous; possessed of a great natural simplicity, uniform piety and strict integrity; and was described as being 'firm in his adherence to all the great truths and duties of the Gospel taught among us'. His sermons, couched in simple language, were a blessing to many. He was a great friend of JOHN WESLEY who regularly addressed him in his letters as 'Dear Sammy', and who held him in high regard, often relying on him for advice and support. Taken ill on the way home from the Leeds Conference, he died at the inn where he was to spend the night.

BIBLIOGRAPHY
EWM
MM (1818): 348

OLIVER A. BECKERLEGGE

Bärenbruck, George Theophilus (b. Prussia; d. Stettin, Prussia, 6 May 1833). CMS missionary in south India. Bärenbruck trained at the Berlin Mission Seminary under Professor JOHANNES JÄNICKE and responded to the request from the CMS for German missionaries in the absence of English recruits. He was ordained to Lutheran orders but received further training as a probationer missionary under Reverend A. Westoby, of Emberton, Buckinghamshire. On 15 December 1817 he was sent to Madras and then in 1823 moved to the CMS Mission at Tranquebar and again in 1824 to Mayaveram. In May 1831 he returned to Europe and withdrew from

the CMS. His wife (née Behrens) bore him a son, John Theophilus George who also served with the CMS in India.

BIBLIOGRAPHY
D. T. B[arry], *CMS Register of Missionaries and Native Clergy* (privately printed) (London, 1906)

DONALD M. LEWIS

Barff, Charles (b. South Cave, Yorkshire, England, 1792; d. Sydney Australia, 23 June 1866.). LMS missionary in the Pacific Islands. Barff was a farmer, a bricklayer and a plasterer who associated with the Calvinistic Methodists. He received some training at the Homerton Academy, London, before serving with the LMS. He arrived at Papetoai, Moorea on 17 November, 1817. On 25 July 1818 he moved to Huahine, where he and WILLIAM ELLIS developed the educational programme which had been inaugurated by JOHN DAVIES. Barff travelled extensively throughout the Pacific islands and was responsible for printing the Samoan translation of St Matthew's Gospel. After a journey to England he returned to his station in 1848. Ill health hindered his activity and in 1855 he was permitted to retire. Nevertheless Barff was later reinstated to his former charge in 1859. He continued to work on the island until March 1864 when growing infirmity necessitated his removal to Sydney, Australia.

BIBLIOGRAPHY
N. Gunson, *Messengers of Grace* (Melbourne, 1978)
R. Lovett, *The History of the London Missionary Society 1795–1895* (London, 1899)
RMD, 4th edn (London, 1923)

R. WATCYN JAMES

Barham, the first Baron. *See* MIDDLETON, CHARLES

Barham, Baroness, of Barham Court and Teston, Kent, England [née Middleton, Diana; Edwardes, Mrs D., subsequently Noel, Mrs D.] (b. 18 Sept. 1762; d. Fairy Hill, near Swansea, Glamorganshire, Wales, 12 April 1823). Patroness of preachers. Diana was the only child of CHARLES MIDDLETON, created Baron Barham in 1805. She married (21 December 1780) Gerard Noel Edwardes, who in 1798 changed his surname to Noel. Diana, the mother of 18 children, took them to mix with the Prince of Wales and his circle at Brighton. In 1813, on succeeding to her father's peerage, she took up residence in the Gower Peninsula in south Wales, where she promoted evangelistic work. Advised by DAVID CHARLES of Carmarthen, she was the patroness of WILLIAM GRIFFITHS. The chapels of 'Lady Barham's Connexion' were eventually conveyed to the Calvinistic Methodists.

BIBLIOGRAPHY
A. N. Jones, *Gower Memories of William Griffiths* (Aberayron, Wales, 1957)
Peerage, 1: 424

DAVID WILLIAM BEBBINGTON

Baring, Charles Thomas (b. 11 Jan. 1807; d. Wimbledon, Surrey, England, 14 Sept. 1879). Anglican bishop. A member of the banking family of that name, Baring was educated privately and then at Christ Church, Oxford, where he graduated BA with a double first in classics and mathematics in 1829 (MA 1832; DD 1856). He worked first in Oxford (serving from 1842 to 1844 with SAMUEL WALDEGRAVE as a curate of St Ebbe's), before becoming Vicar of Kingsworthy (Hampshire), and moving to All Saints, Marylebone in 1847, a year after marrying as his second wife, Caroline Kemp, whose father developed Kemp Town in Brighton. He became a chaplain to the Queen in 1850, and in 1856 Rector of Limpsfield, Surrey. A year later he was nominated Bishop of Gloucester, and in 1861 was translated to Durham, succeeding a fellow evangelical, H. M. VILLIERS, who had himself moved from Carlisle only a year before but then died prematurely. Baring occupied the see of Durham till February 1879, dying just over six months later.

His work at Durham was chiefly notable for church extension to cater for the increasing manufacturing and mining population, as a result of which 102 new parishes were formed, 110 churches built, and 138 additional parish clergy appointed. He was very much the bishop of his diocese, playing little part in national affairs. He found, however, that Durham was too much for one man, and in the 1878 Act extending the episcopate he secured permission for the establishment of a see of Newcastle.

He was considered as 'perhaps the most distinct Low Church bishop on the Bench' (Arnold, 1875: 374). At Gloucester he condemned special Lenten services as High Church practice, and in his 1860 charge he advocated revision of the Liturgy, especially in respect of the use of the word 'regeneration' in the service of baptism, and of the expression of eternal hope in the burial service of those whose lives made such hope seem hardly likely. He also spoke out against the abolition of church rates.

Baring criticized the 'spirit of scepticism pervading the scientific publications, the popular periodical literature, and even the theological writings' of his time (*CO*, 1864: 517), but he did not favour the imposition of a general inhibition on Colenso by the English bishops. Indeed, he had little time for the corporate opinion of the church, declaring at Convocation that he did 'not regard the voice of Convocation as the voice of the Church' (14 May 1861).

Within his own diocese he called for more frequent celebration of Holy Communion and prescribed a minimum of eight occasions per year as well as asking for two sermons per Sunday. He would not, however, tolerate ritual which he thought contrary to the prayer-book, and indeed he refused to license offending curates, often

at the cost of ecclesiastical harmony. Arnold claimed that Durham was 'fast winning itself the character of being the most perturbed diocese in the country' (Arnold, 1875: 372). Indeed, a copy of Arnold which I consulted has the pencilled word 'over' inserted within 'Bishop Baring', presumably by someone who disliked his alleged autocratic tendencies.

BIBLIOGRAPHY
F. Arnold, *Our Bishops and Deans* (London, 1875)
CO, 63 (1864)
DNB
B. E. Hardman, 'The Evangelical Party in The Church of England, 1833–1865' (Cambridge Univ. Ph.D. thesis, 1964)

ARTHUR POLLARD

Baring, George (b. 23 Sept. 1781; d. 4 Oct. 1854). Anglican clergyman. The son of Sir Francis Baring, banker, and brother of THOMAS BARING he was educated privately. Baring made an early fortune at Canton while employed by the East India Company. Returning to England he was ordained in the Church of England, becoming Vicar of Winterbourne-Stoke, Wiltshire, 19 November 1814 and was Curate of Dunston, Somerset, under T. T. BIDDULPH.

In November 1815, Baring resigned his living and became leader of the Western Schism, a secession from the Church in and around the West Country. He then moved to Taunton, and purchased the Octagon Chapel where he rebaptized a number of his fellow Seceders. His 'connexion' then began to expand. In 1817, he moved to Exeter where he constructed a substantial chapel and became a popular preacher. In March 1819, he fled to the continent to escape bankruptcy.

BIBLIOGRAPHY
G. Carter, 'Evangelical Seceders from the Church of England, c. 1800–50' (Oxford Univ. Ph.D. thesis, 1990): 164–218
Index Ecclesiasticus: 8

GRAYSON CARTER

Baring, Sir **Thomas** (b. 12 June 1772; d. 3 April 1848). MP. The eldest son of Sir Francis Baring, founder of the Baring Bank and chairman of the East India Company and brother of GEORGE BARING, he was educated privately. He married Mary Ursula, daughter of Charles Sealy, barrister, of Calcutta. He served as MP for Wycombe, Buckinghamshire, 1806–32 and for Hampshire, June–December 1832. Among his children were: Francis Thornhill Baring, first Lord Northbrook; Sir THOMAS BARING, MP and banker; and CHARLES THOMAS BARING, Bishop of Gloucester and Bristol, and Durham. He was a supporter of the LSPCJ.

In 1815, Baring participated in the Western Schism, a secession from the Church of England in and around the West Country. His luxurious home at Stratton Park, Micheldever, Hampshire, became the early headquarters of the Seceders, where they met in convocation to settle doctrinal disputes. It remains uncertain whether he ever formally seceded from the church.

BIBLIOGRAPHY
Annual Register, 1848
G. Carter, 'Evangelical Seceders from the Church of England, *c*. 1800–50' (Oxford Univ. Ph.D. thesis, 1990): 164–218
G. E. Cokayne, *Complete Baronetage*, 6 vols (Exeter, England, 1906) 5:286
C. Marsh, *The Life of the Rev. William Marsh, D.D.* (London, 1867): 109–22

GRAYSON CARTER

Baring, Sir **Thomas** (b. 7 Sept. 1799; d. Bournemouth, Hampshire, England, 18 Nov. 1873). Banker, MP, and philanthropist. He was the second son of Sir THOMAS BARING and brother of Sir Francis Thornhill Baring, the first Lord Northbrook. His grandfather was Francis Baring, the founder of the banking house of Baring Brothers and Company, who was described in his day as 'the first merchant in Europe'. He was educated at Winchester and became a partner in the family business. He was chairman of Lloyds Bank, a director of the Bank of England, and served as Tory MP for Great Yarmouth (1835–7) and later for Huntingdon (1844–73). In both 1852 and 1858 he declined being Chancellor of the Exchequer in Derby's administrations. On his death he left an estate of £1.5 million.

During his lifetime he was a generous art patron and supporter of evangelical causes. He retained the family interest in the LSPCJ, of which his father had been president from 1815 until his death, and was very committed to the CPAS. His brother CHARLES THOMAS BARING was Rector of All Souls, Langham Place, London, and successively Bishop of Gloucester and of Durham.

BIBLIOGRAPHY
DNB

IAN S. RENNIE

Barker, **Joseph** (b. Bramley, Leeds, England, 11 May 1806; d. Omaha, NE, USA, 15 Sept. 1875). Methodist minister. Barker was a child of Wesleyan parents, and joined the MNC in his youth, entering its ministry in 1829. He had outstanding gifts of mind and oratory, and gave valuable help to young men training for the ministry. In public lectures and discussions he defended the faith successfully against the disciples of Robert Owen, winning thereby a wide reputation which fed his ambition and self-assertive independence. He soon began to question items of Christian faith and practice – the validity of baptism and of the Lord's Supper, and the doctrine of the Trinity; and he queried the right of ministers to receive a promised stipend; but he strenuously advocated total abstinence, the abolition of slavery, and Chartism: he was put on trial for sedition and conspiracy in 1848.

From step to step he was carried forward from a nebulous Arianism to a more definite Socinianism, through deism to compete atheism. Having been expelled by the Conference in 1841, his popularity caused a loss to the Connexion of 29 societies and 4,348 members. He continued to lecture in exposition of his atheism with outstanding bitterness. In Newcastle he and his party had wrested the chapel from the Connexion and made the town the centre of his operations. WILLIAM COOKE, then stationed in Newcastle, was unwilling to engage in public debate, but undertook it when he found the havoc wrought by Barker. In the ensuing ten-day debate in 1845 Barker was thoroughly defeated, but that did not prevent him engaging in Halifax in 1854 in another ten-day debate with Brewin Grant, in which again he was worsted. He went to America but knew little peace or happiness. On his return to Britain in 1860 he visited Cooke, when they talked, sang hymns, and prayed together; and Cooke continued to keep in touch with Barker until the latter returned to his former faith. Thenceforward Barker lectured both in Britain and America on his reconversion and in defence of the faith, though he seems never to have appreciated the extent of the damage he had done. But for the rest of his life he held fast his Christian convictions, and a letter to Cooke shortly before his death gave the clearest evidence of his faith. He died leaving £1,000 to the Primitive Methodists. He was a voluminous author in all phases of his life.

SELECT WRITINGS
J. Barker, *History and Confessions of a Man As Put Forth by Himself* (Wortley, England, 1846)
—, *Teachings of Experience* (London, 1869)
—, *The Life of Joseph Barker Written by Himself* (London, 1880)

BIBLIOGRAPHY
DNB
G. J. Stevenson, *Methodist Worthies*, 4: 611 ff
W. J. Townsend, *James Stacey* (London, 1891): 18–42

O. A. BECKERLEGGE

Barnard, **Thomas** (b. Pontefract, Yorkshire, England, *c*. 1685; d. Leeds, England, 20 May 1750). Anglican clergyman. Son of Thomas Barnard of Pontefract, he was educated at Leeds Grammar School and St John's College, Cambridge (BA 1708/9; MA 1713). He was ordained and returned to his old school as headmaster in 1712, and remained there until his death.

Barnard's evangelical credentials are questioned by some historians. It is clear that he became a close friend of Lady ELIZABETH HASTINGS and assisted her in her charitable work. Her nephew George Hastings became his pupil and boarded with him. George's mother, Lady HUNTINGDON, consulted Barnard about her spiritual well-being, and he played an important part in her conversion to Methodism in July 1739. He wrote several long letters of advice to her. Despite this, when he came to write his *Historical Character of . . . Lady Elizabeth Hastings* in 1742 he attacked the Methodists and denied that she had ever been one. His change of heart can possibly be attributed to the marriage of BENJAMIN INGHAM and Lady MARGARET HASTINGS, which was unpopular in Yorkshire.

BIBLIOGRAPHY
Al. Cant.
Leicestershire Record Office, original letters

EDWIN WELCH

Barnes, Albert (b. Rome, NY, USA, 1 Dec. 1798; d. Philadelphia, PA, USA, 24 Dec. 1870). Presbyterian minister, author, and New School leader. Barnes left home during his youth to attend school in Fairfield, Connecticut. He enrolled at Hamilton College with the intention of a career in law, graduating in 1820. While at Hamilton, he developed an interest in religion, joined the Presbyterian church, and decided on a career in the ministry. He graduated from Princeton Theological Seminary in 1824, took a church in Morristown, New Jersey, and was ordained in 1825. In these early years of his ministry, Barnes formulated a theology compatible with the New School emphasis, which featured an adjustment in historic Calvinism to address the conditions of modern America. In 1829 he preached a sermon called 'The Way of Salvation' which put him at odds with the Old School (or traditionalists), particularly regarding the doctrine of original sin. When the First Presbyterian Church of Philadelphia called Barnes in 1830, some of the presbytery, including Dr ASHBEL GREEN, opposed him and brought charges against him, which were ultimately adjudicated by the General Assembly in 1831. For the next few decades he was a leading spokesperson for the New School in the theological debate.

Along with other activists in America's Second Great Awakening, Barnes not only denied that people were guilty of Adam's sin, but he claimed that sinfulness arose from the exercise of the will. He also taught that the Atonement, which offered free grace to all who sought it, was unlimited. This teaching put the burden on sinners to repent since it was they who had to choose rather than God determining the outcome. Barnes' views became controversial for a second time when he published a commentary on the book of Romans, and in 1835 Dr George Junkin preferred charges against him for departing from the Westminster Confession. Barnes was again acquitted since the New School held the majority in the General Assembly of 1836. Division over Barnes' views was one reason for the Presbyterian division into New and Old School factions (1837), a split not healed for 33 years.

Barnes supported revivalism and social reform, taking a stand on slavery, temperance reform, Sunday closing laws, and Christian education. His later years were devoted to writing, and his 11 volumes of commentaries on the New Testament, Isaiah, and the Psalms sold over a million copies. He served as director of the Union Theological Seminary almost from its beginnings, provided continuing leadership to the New School, and retired from his Philadelphia church in 1868. He lived to see the Presbyterian church reunited in 1870, with the event taking place in the Philadelphia church where he had laboured for so many years.

SELECT WRITINGS
A. Barnes, *Life at Three-Score and Ten* (Philadelphia, PA, 1871)

BIBLIOGRAPHY
S. J. Baird, *History of the New School* (Philadelphia, PA, 1868)
G. Junkin, *The Vindication, Containing a History of the Trial of the Rev. Albert Barnes* (Philadelphia, PA, 1836)
G. M. Marsden, *The Evangelical Mind and the New School Presbyterian Experience* (New Haven, CT, 1970)

JAMES E. JOHNSON

Barnes, Daniel Henry (b. Canaan, Columbia Co., NY, USA, 25 April 1785; d. Union, Columbia Co., NY, USA, 27 Oct. 1828.) Baptist minister and teacher in New York. The son of Reverend Elisha Barnes, he was an honours graduate of Union College in 1809. He then studied Hebrew extensively for six months. In 1811, Barnes became the principal of Poughkeepsie Academy and in 1813 was licensed to preach by the Poughkeepsie Baptist Church. From 1815 to 1819 he administered the Classical School of Union College until he became a 'Professor of Languages' at the Baptist Theological Seminary in New York (later moved to the Hamilton Institution). In 1824, Barnes was named associate principal of the New York High School for Boys. Barnes preached frequently but never pastored a church. FRANCIS WAYLAND was among his students. Barnes was a participant in the making of Webster's Dictionary and he often wrote for *Silliman's Journal* in the field of geological science.

BIBLIOGRAPHY
AAP, 6
W. Cathcart, *Baptist Encyclopedia* (Philadelphia, PA, 1881)

C. DOUGLAS WEAVER

Barnes, Thomas (b. Farnworth, Lancashire, England, 1813; d. Farnworth, England, 1872). British MP. The son of a magistrate of Lancashire, James Rothwell Barnes, Thomas made his fortune in cotton spinning. He was a Deputy-Lieutenant of Lancashire and was MP for the industrial riding of Bolton, Lancashire (1852–7; 1861–8). A Radical, he supported the ballot, triennial Parliaments, and the separation of church and state. He is mentioned in the correspondence of John Stuart Mill. A Congregationalist, he was a founder of Quinton Congregational Church, Shropshire. Barnes was a member of the EA.

BIBLIOGRAPHY
Evangelical Christendom (1847): 54
Stenton

JONATHAN BURKE CUTMORE

Barneth, John Charles (b. Bernsdorff, Silesia, Poland, *c.* 1766; d. Fantimania, West Africa, 2 Feb. 1810). Lutheran clergyman and CMS missionary. Barneth trained under JOHANNES JÄNICKE at the Berlin Seminary and responded to the appeal from the CMS for missionaries in 1803. He offered to serve with G. R. NYLÄNDER in 1806 but was turned down because of his wife's ill health. He spent two years in England, being educated briefly by WILLIAM DAWES and then THOMAS SCOTT. Following his wife's death, he took Lutheran orders and on 10 July 1809 the CMS sent him to Fantimania. Like so many other early CMS missionaries in West Africa, he survived only a few months.

BIBLIOGRAPHY
D. T. B[arry], *CMS Register of Missionaries and Native Clergy* (privately printed) (London, 1906)

DONALD M. LEWIS

Barnett, Francis (Augustus) (d. Clifton, Bristol, England, 27 Dec. 1883). Manufacturer, father of Samuel Augustus Barnett. Barnett was the son of Samuel Augustus Barnett, a wealthy Bristol timber merchant, after whom he named his first son, who became a prominent Church of England canon, social reformer and founder of Toynbee Hall in East London (1844–1913, *DNB*). In 1839 Francis Barnett married Mary Gilmore, the daughter of a Bristol shipowner. Barnett made his name as the original manufacturer of iron bedsteads, a notable development in the mass production of consumer goods.

His children caricatured him as a Victorian evangelical patriarch. Cold and domineering in his relations with his wife and children, habitually, sometimes peevishly subordinating his family's needs to his own, yet towards employees and customers he was generous and fairminded. So concerned was he to maintain his public reputation for rectitude that he refused to produce hollow bedstead legs. They were, he reasoned, a kind of deception.

A committed Tory, he entertained strong prejudices against 'free-thinking'. As a result he strenuously resisted his eldest son's desire to attend university. When he finally gave in – sending his son to Wadham College, Oxford – it was only because an 'unbending Tory and a rigid evangelical', B. P. SYMONS, was warden (Barnett, 1918, I: 169).

BIBLIOGRAPHY
H. O. Barnett, *Canon Barnett, His Life, Work, and Friends*, 2 vols. (London, 1918)

JONATHAN BURKE CUTMORE

Barrett, Alfred (b. Attercliffe, Yorkshire, England, 17 Oct. 1808; d. London, England, 26 Oct. 1876). Methodist minister and college principal. Barrett joined the Wesleyan Methodists at 15 and entered into a family business career during which he held services for employees in their homes. Ordained in 1832 he was stationed from then until 1858 chiefly in poor industrial areas of the north of England though also for three years (1852–4) at Great Queen Street Chapel, London, where administrative ability greatly reduced a heavy burden of debt.

In 1858 he became house governor of Richmond College, Surrey, where he remained ten years. He regularly led students on evangelizing excursions to nearby villages. Unremitting habits of work throughout his life steadily aggravated an inherent tendency to melancholic depression which made his last years ones of illness and seclusion during which he never even attended the annual Methodist Conference.

BIBLIOGRAPHY
Boase

JEFFREY SPITTAL

Barrett, Henry (b. England; d. Sierra Leone, 10 May 1819). CMS missionary to Sierra Leone. Barrett trained as a schoolmaster before volunteering to go to Sierra Leone with the CMS. He travelled out with Mr and Mrs THOMAS JESTY on 29 January 1819 and served in Kissey. Barrett lasted only three months. There is no record of his being married. His willingness to serve in Sierra Leone is remarkable in view of the fate of other early CMS missionaries (*see* M. RENNER, P. HARTWIG, J. G. PRASSE, J. C. BARNETH, J. QUAST, C. H. MEISSNER, H. MEYER, J. H. SCHULZE, C. JOST and T. Jesty).

BIBLIOGRAPHY
D. T. B[arry], *CMS Register of Missionaries and Native Clergy* (privately printed) (London, 1906)

DONALD M. LEWIS

Barrett, John Casebow (b. probably Bath, Somerset, England, c. 1811; d. 26 Feb. 1881). Anglican clergyman. Son of William Barrett of Bath, he entered Christ Church, Oxford (1828) and proceeded BA (1833) and MA (1837). Ordained (deacon 1834, priest 1835) to the Anglican ministry, he was curate of St John's, Hull, before succeeding EDWARD BURN as Perpetual Curate of St Mary's, Birmingham (1837). He remained in this position until his death.

Barrett's effective (although somewhat florid) preaching drew large congregations. Initially he experienced some difficulties which are alluded to in his sermon 'A Minister's Trials' (1846) and in a local newspaper. His congregation supported him through these difficulties. Later in life, however, the congregation declined with the exodus of the middle classes to the suburbs. Although not a deep thinker, he was exceptionally effective as a preacher. Several of his printed sermons can be found in the Birmingham Collection of the Birmingham Central Reference Library.

BIBLIOGRAPHY
Al. Ox.
Boase

Birmingham Daily Gazette (28 February 1881)
Birmingham Daily Post (28 February 1881)

D. E. H. MOLE

Barritt, Mary [Taft, Mrs Zechariah] (b. Hay, Lancashire, England, *c.* Aug. 1772; d. Sandiacre, Nottinghamshire, England, 26 March 1851). Wesleyan Methodist preacher. Barritt, daughter of John, a non-believer, and Mary, a Methodist, came from a farming family. Converted at an early age Mary felt the importance of communicating her faith to others. Her preaching was attended by conversions and revivals. When she was 19 her superintendent minister threatened to expel her if she persisted in 'exhorting', but she felt she ought to obey God rather than men. Barritt received many invitations and travelled extensively throughout the north of England effecting many conversions in spite of much opposition and a number of her converts became travelling preachers and missionaries. She also attended the Conferences in Leeds and Manchester chiefly in order to meet the itinerants who were sympathetic to women preaching. In 1802 she married ZECHARIAH TAFT, an itinerant who was very supportive of her work and encouraged her to preach in the face of fierce controversy, which led to the 1803 Conference resolution against women preaching. He wrote three pamphlets on the subject. In 1827 Barritt published an account of her work as a revivalist and this, with later information, shows that she was virtually another itinerant in her husband's circuits.

SELECT WRITINGS
M. Taft, *Memories of the Life of . . . Mrs Mary Taft* (London, 1827)

BIBLIOGRAPHY
L. F. Church, *More About the Early Methodist People* (London, 1949)

E. DOROTHY GRAHAM

Barry, John (b. Bandon, Co. Cork, Ireland, 18 Sept. 1792; d. Montreal, Lower Canada, 21 June 1838). Methodist missionary in Jamaica. Born into a Church of Ireland family with Huguenot roots, Barry came under Methodist influence in 1809 and soon became a local preacher. He became interested in Methodist missions and was commissioned by the WMMS to serve in Jamaica from 1825 to 1831. He also served in Toronto and Montreal 1832–4 before being posted to Bermuda where his health broke down in 1836.

In a career dogged by recurring controversies, Barry made a significant contribution to Methodist missions in Jamaica in the years leading up to the slave uprising in 1831. Barry was vigorously opposed to slavery and came perilously close to infringing the WMMS's 'no-politics rule' in a series of legal cases in the late 1820s. In a published letter to the Secretary of State for the Colonies in 1830, and under cross-examination before a parliamentary select committee, Barry denounced slavery and defended the actions of Christian missionaries in Jamaica. He was in Jamaica during the slave uprising in December 1831 and was fortuitously posted to Bermuda only a few weeks after the slaves were emancipated in 1834. Barry was a man of strong convictions and humane inclinations who seemed to revel in the controversies surrounding Methodist missionary expansion in the early nineteenth century.

BIBLIOGRAPHY
N. W. Taggart, *The Irish in World Methodism 1760–1900* (London, 1986)

DAVID N. HEMPTON

Barry, Robert (b. *c.* 1759, Kinross, Scotland; d. Liverpool, Nova Scotia, BNA, 3 Sept. 1843). Wesleyan lay exhorter, Loyalist merchant, and educator. Barry arrived in New York from Fratton, England, as an impressed seaman in New York, *circa* 1774. During the revolution he attended Trinity Anglican Church, and exhorted in the Methodists' John Street Chapel. He joined the Loyalist exodus to Shelburne, Nova Scotia, in 1783. After teaching for two years he joined his brother in the A & R Barry firm to engage in transatlantic trade. Robert Barry later moved to Liverpool, Nova Scotia, where he continued to support new Wesleyan chapels, exhort, and aid missionaries. Between 1783 and 1790 he corresponded with JOHN WESLEY on Anglican-Methodist tensions, American MEC preachers, and the ministry to blacks (free and slave). Protestant evangelicalism's impact on the province was enhanced greatly by the lay leadership which such merchants as Robert Barry provided.

BIBLIOGRAPHY
A. B. Robertson, 'John Wesley's Nova Scotia Businessman: Halifax Methodist Merchants 1815–1855' (Queen's Univ. Ph.D. thesis, 1990)

ALLEN B. ROBERTSON

Barth, Christian Gottlob (b. Stuttgart, Germany, 31 July 1779; d. Calw, Germany, 12 Nov. 1862). Pastor, theologian, author, editor, publisher, songwriter, and missions advocate. During studies at Tübingen (1817–19), his attention was given to Pietist theologians and theological issues. In 1819 he founded a student missionary society, the Studentenmissionsverein and published *Ueber die Pietisten mit Besonderer Rucksicht auf die Wüttembergischen und Ihre Neuesten Verhältnisse* (Tübingen, 1819). After his studies, he served as assistant pastor in various centres and travelled extensively in northern Germany, the Netherlands and the Alsace. Already a prolific author he founded (1824) a mission periodical, *Calwer Missionsblatt*. As pastor at Möttlingen (1834–8), he led efforts to prepare for the end of the world predicted by J. A. BENGEL. A second mission periodical, *Monatsblätter für Öffentliche Missionsstunden*, was

63

established in 1839, a third specifically for children, *Kindermissionsblatt*, was started in 1842, and finally, *Beleuchtungen der Missionssache* (1842–52) was published. His mission, social and Pietist interests had a great influence on J. C. BLUMHARDT who succeeded him as pastor in Möttlingen and his mission efforts significantly influenced the development of mission theory and organizations in Germany and Switzerland.

His international influence was due to the various commentaries, Bible stories, mission stories and histories of Germany and the world. These were translated into English, Swedish, modern Greek, Dutch, French, Marathi, Tahi, Amharic, and various African languages including Swahili. These were designed for didactic purposes and served as school texts on five continents. Those translated into English include: *Biblical History in the Words of Holy Scripture* (Reading, PA, no date – 19 edns by 1880); *A Brief History of the Church of Christ* (London, 1837); *An Expository and Practical Commentary on the Books of Scripture, Arranged in Chronological Order, Forming a Handbook of Biblical Elucidation, For the Use of Families, Schools and Students of the Word of God* (London, 1865); *General History of the World* (London, 1840); and, *Setma the Turkish Girl* (Philadelphia, PA, 1869).

BIBLIOGRAPHY
P. Breymaier, 'Barth, Christian Gottlob', *Evangelisches Gemeindelexikon* (Wuppertal, Germany, 1978): 48
G. Hering, 'Barth, 1. Chr. Gottlob', *Religion in Geschichte und Gegenwart*, 2nd edn, 1 (1909): 923–4
W. Kopp, *Christian Gottlob Barth's Leben und Wirken* (Calw, Germany, 1886)
H. Sundert, 'Barth, Dr. Christian Gottlieb (*sic*)', *Realencyklopädie für Protestantische Theologie und Kirche*, 2 (1897): 418–20

DAVID BUNDY

Bartlett, Thomas (b. Henley, Oxfordshire, England, 1789; d. Burton Latimer rectory, Northamptonshire, England, 28 May 1872 [not 1864, as *DNB*]). Anglican clergyman and author. Son of Thomas Bartlett, gentleman, Thomas Jr went up to St Edmund Hall, Oxford, in 1809, while DANIEL WILSON was vice-principal. Ordained deacon at Salisbury in 1812, he became curate to Dr WILLIAM MARSH, at Basildon, Berkshire. Ordained priest at Wells in 1814, he was assistant minister to DANIEL WILSON at St John's Bedford Row, London. He was Vicar of Kingston, Kent, 1816–52, and in 1828 he became domestic chaplain to the second Marquess of Cholmondeley (*see* GEORGE HORATIO CHOMONDELEY). By 1832 he was one of the six preachers of Canterbury Cathedral. After two years as Rector of Chevening, Kent, to which he was presented by Archbishop SUMNER, he became Vicar of Luton, Bedfordshire, a more demanding, town parish. He was Rector of Burton Latimer, Northamptonshire, a village with an earlier evangelical tradition, 1857 till death.

Bartlett married 1) 1814 Catherine Sarah Cowper, colateral descendant of Bishop Joseph Butler (1692–1752); 2) Lucinda Grace, daughter of the Reverend H. Hoare,

vicar of Framfield, Sussex. His principal work was a *Memoir* of Butler (1839), using unpublished sources, supplemented (1842) by an index to the *Analogy*. Other numerous publications, one a defence of the CMS, show an evangelical outlook.

BIBLIOGRAPHY
Al. Ox.
Crockford (1860)
DNB
G. H. Townsend, ed., *Men of the Time*, 7th edn (London, 1868); 8th edn (London, 1872)

J. S. REYNOLDS

Bascom, Henry Bidleman (b. Hancock, NY, USA, 27 May 1796; d. Louisville, KY, USA, 8 Sept. 1850). Methodist preacher, editor, college and university president, and bishop. Bascom's parents, Alpheus and Hannah Houk Bascom, were very poor. In 1808 they moved to Little Valley, New York and in 1812 to Maysville, Kentucky. They settled in Brown County, Ohio. Bascom attended school only from age 6 to age 12. Throughout his ministry he gave poor people attention and respect.

Bascom was converted at 14 and became a Methodist at 15. As he accompanied circuit rider James Gilmore in the spring and summer, 1811, young Gilmore tutored him in Methodist doctrine. Also that year Bascom was invited to reside with Mr William Connelly and given access to his host's fine library. He was licensed to preach at 16, and admitted on trial to the Ohio Conference at 17 (1813). For seven years he rode circuits in both this and the Tennessee Conference. He was the first man to serve the Methodist church in Louisville as a station (single) church rather than being part of a circuit (1818–20). A petition for his continuance was signed, even by non-Methodists, but the Methodist Episcopal *Discipline* required his removal after two years. When the Kentucky Conference was organized in 1820 he joined it, but transferred back to Ohio in 1822.

Bascom's itinerant years were stressful. Preachers already in the conference put newcomers to the test before personally accepting them. Bascom appeared a young dandy, and was a crowd pleaser as well, so the veterans made his way especially hard. He was held in on trial status unduly long and was elected to elder's orders in 1818 by one vote. In 1816 he wrote, but did not submit, a letter of resignation from the conference. He believed his immediate post-Louisville appointment was designed to drive him out of conference. Next, he was sent to another circuit, as the third man. This was too much for a popular pulpit orator who had enjoyed the prestige of a station appointment in what was then one of the major cites of the USA. He transferred back to his home Ohio Conference. There his appointment was to the same circuit where his itinerant ministry had begun ten years before.

In his years of rejection Bascom was befriended by Bishop WILLIAM MCKENDREE. In the 1790s McKendree at first sympathized with the JAMES O'KELLY movement and declined to take an appointment. Bishop FRANCIS ASBURY patiently counselled him and brought his loyalty and talents back to the majority body of Methodists. In the 1810s McKendree played a similar supportive role with young Bascom, who likewise matured into a major figure in the church. In turn, Bascom was ever the encourager of young ministers.

The break in Bascom's career came in 1823 when, on nomination of Henry Clay, he was elected chaplain of the United States House of Representatives. This was the first of a series of six appointments which took him finally to the Methodist episcopacy. He was not popular with the House, but during his 18 months based in Washington, DC he made many preaching tours. Then he was president of newly founded Madison College at Uniontown, Pennsylvania, 1827–9. From 1829 to 1831 he served as agent for the American Colonization Society. In 1832 he was elected professor of moral science and belles-lettres in Augusta College, Augusta, Kentucky. He was president of Transylvania University, Lexington, Kentucky from 1842 to 1849, and simultaneously from 1846 editor of the new *Southern Methodist Quarterly Review*. The second General Conference of the MEC,So, at St Louis in 1850, elected him bishop on the second ballot by a large majority. Bascom was the only bishop this conference chose.

From 1828 Bascom was a delegate to every General Conference (Methodist Episcopal – 1828, 1832, 1836, 1840, and 1844; MEC,So – Louisville Convention 1845, 1846, 1850). Around 1835 Bascom was offered the presidency of Augusta College, and about 1839 or 1840 was elected to the presidency of Louisiana College and then to the presidency of Missouri University. He declined all three. Transylvania University in Lexington, Kentucky, where he was president from 1842 to 1849, had been offered by its trustees to the Kentucky Conference of the MEC and they in turn offered it to the General Conference. When the north-south separation occurred the first General Conference of the MES,So (1846) adopted Transylvania as 'the university of the southern connection'. The unsuccessful relationship, however, ended in 1850.

Never the recipient of an earned academic degree, Bascom was given an MA and five doctorates *honoris causa*. The first of four Doctorates of Divinity came from Wesleyan University, Middletown, Connecticut in 1838. In 1845 LaGrange College in Alabama made him Doctor of Laws.

He did not live to make his contribution as a bishop. He presided over a single annual conference, became sick in early August, and died some five weeks later. Some of his symptoms were cholera-like, but his condition was never diagnosed specifically. He is buried in Eastern Cemetery, Louisville, Kentucky.

On 7 March 1839 Bascom married Miss E. Van Antwerp of New York City. Of their three children, a daughter and two sons, the younger boy died in infancy. All biographical sources are enigmatically terse about this aspect of Bascom's life.

Bascom's career is amazing for one with so little formal education. He read widely, averaging 100 pages daily, even in his busiest years of activism and administration, and he was gifted with an excellent memory for what he read. Bascom early demonstrated unusual gifts for public speaking. Even after leaving circuit ministry he travelled widely and preached. Eventually, his name drew street overflow audiences. In the decade of his residence outside Kentucky (1822–32) he became one of the most famous preachers in the USA.

Ultimately, Bascom's entire professional achievement is seen rooted in the verbal skills which enabled his rise to national prominence in the 1820s. His popularity as a preacher was owing to an emotionally charged and profusely embellished rhetorical style. Another noted Methodist leader of the day once said that Bascom's effect would have been greater 'had it contained a third less of accumulated thought and brilliant imagery'. Bascom preferred the controlled speaking environment of the worship service or the small group interaction of the committee. He did not participate much in the open field debate of the conference session.

Bascom was also respected by his partisans as a writer of documents of ecclesiastical statecraft. He authored the 'Address' of the slavery compromise minority of the Tennessee Conference to the 1820 General Conference. At the 1844 General Conference where the decision was taken for the MEC to divide, Bascom's southern colleagues asked him to write their 'Protest' to the conference's vote to restrict the ministry of Bishop JAMES O. ANDREW. One year later at the Louisville (Kentucky) Convention which formally established the MEC,So, Bascom wrote the 'Report' which the convention sent to the public. In 1846 he chaired the MEC,So's commission to meet with a similar body from the MEC to settle the details growing out of the separation. Finally, he was the first editor of the *Southern Methodist Quarterly Review*.

During his lifetime Bascom published two titles: *Methodism and Slavery* and *Sermons*. The *Sermons* sold 20,000 copies. His *Works* were published posthumously (4 vols, 1855). *Methodism and Slavery* relates his personal intellectual history on the topic and is a classic statement of the southern view of both slavery and the Bishop James O. Andrew case. Bascom's position on slavery was like that of many southern Methodists. Convinced by hearing Bishop FRANCIS ASBURY in 1812 make the case for compromise with slavery for the sake of evangelistic opportunity in the south, Bascom unswervingly defended the view that the institution of slavery could not and should not be challenged by the church.

Personally, he judged slavery an out and out evil. On the other hand, it was so powerful – 'a household reality' – he did not think the church could end it. He defended the church's failure to challenge the institution because as a civil matter it was outside the church's jurisdiction, and if Methodists did challenge it their church could not survive in the south. He also worked for the colonization movement because he did not think free

African-Americans could be socially assimilated as persons with full civil rights.

Bascom was the kind of leader whose impact is powerful when combined with personal presence, especially the Daniel Webster-like physiognomy others saw in him. He was very much a man of his day in the history of USA Methodism. His leadership seems to have paralleled what another bishop said of his preaching, 'You had the extemporaneous utterance agreeing with the mood of the moment'.

Had Bascom lived into the Reconstruction era he would probably have become a figure in the memory of southern USA Methodists comparable to Bishop Holland N. McTyeire. Also, the Methodist bishop's appointive power would have allowed him to do much to determine the leadership of the denomination in the second half of the nineteenth century.

SELECT WRITINGS
H. B. Bascom, *Methodism and Slavery* (Frankfort, KY, 1845)
—, *Sermons*, 2 vols (Nashville, TN, 1849)

BIBLIOGRAPHY
AAP
DAB 2 (1929)
N. B. Harmon, ed., *Encyclopedia of World Methodism* (Nashville, TN, 1974)
M. M. Henkle, *The Life of Henry Bidleman Bascom* (Louisville, KY, 1856)
A. A. Redford, *The History of Methodism in Kentucky*, 3 vols (Nashville, TN, 1868–70)

CHARLES W. BROCKWELL, JR

Bassett, Christopher (b. Aberthaw, Glamorgan, Wales, 27 Feb. 1752; d. Bristol, England, 8 Feb. 1784). Welsh Methodist cleric. The son of the Glamorgan agent of the dean and chapter of Gloucester, and an influential Welsh Methodist convert, Bassett was educated at Jesus College, Oxford, and ordained as curate to WILLIAM ROMAINE at St Anne's, Blackfriars, London, 1775. Illness caused his return to south Wales to serve the curacy of St Fagans, near Cardiff, 1778. Here he established a Welsh Methodist meeting house, and itinerated with the Methodists throughout Wales. These activities caused him to be passed over for the vicarage of Cardiff, even though it was in the patronage of his father's employers. His early death was much lamented by WILLIAM WILLIAMS of Pantycelyn, and by DAVID JONES of Llangan, who published a booklet about his life.

BIBLIOGRAPHY
R. L. Brown, 'Christopher Bassett and the Living of Cardiff', *Morgannwg*, 33 (1989): 37–54
DWB

ROGER L. BROWN

Bateman, James (b. Bury, Lancashire, England, 18 July 1811; d. Springbank, Worthing, England, 27 Nov. 1897). Orchid cultivator and botanical illustrator. His father, John Bateman, a Manchester industrialist, was a strong church and state Tory and a munificent patron of local Anglican churches.

Bateman was educated at Lincoln College, Oxford, and migrated to Magdalene (BA 1834; MA 1845). He became the pre-eminent authority on orchids, creating a vogue for them through his lectures, articles, and by developing methods of northern cultivation. He is most famous for his *Orchidaceae of Mexico and Guatemala* (1837–43), an elephant folio, the largest botanical book ever published. It contains forty plates by Bateman (produced at a cost of £200 each) and delightful vignettes by Cruikshank. He was elected fellow of the Linnean Society (1833) and of the Royal Society (1838).

Bateman was on the executive of the Church Association (1870–80), was editor of the evangelical weekly, *The Rock*, and for a time of the *English Churchman*. In the 1870s he was on the LSPCJ committee and spoke at its anniversary meetings.

BIBLIOGRAPHY
P. Hayden, *Biddulph Grange* (London, 1989)
H. L. Malchow, *Agitators and Promoters in the Age of Gladstone and Disraeli* (New York, 1983)

JONATHAN BURKE CUTMORE

Bateman, Josiah (b. 1803; d. 8 May 1893). Anglican clergyman. Bateman was educated at Queens' College, Cambridge (BA, 1828) and became Curate of Burslem, Staffordshire, a large manufacturing parish, 1828–30, and St Sepulchre, London, 1830–2.

Asked by DANIEL WILSON, soon after his appointment as Bishop of Calcutta, to become his chaplain, he spent 1832–8 in India, also becoming Wilson's son-in-law and biographer. In 1838 he became Vicar of Marlborough, and from 1840 to 1855 was Vicar of the Yorkshire industrial centre of Huddersfield, where he had the oversight of a number of daughter churches and curates. An indefatigable worker, he also supervised some thirty voluntary district visitors. The parish church regularly had 2,000 in attendance. During the Chartist uprisings he conducted special evening services with crowds of 'operatives' in attendance. A warm-hearted man, he maintained reasonably good relations with Dissenters, did not attack Roman Catholics, and led the local clergy in active support of LORD ASHLEY, RICHARD OASTLER and the factory reform movement. Exhausted for a time after his ministry at Huddersfield, he subsequently served until his death at North Cray, Margate, and Southend, in his spare time writing a biography of the Reverend HENRY VENN ELLIOTT.

BIBLIOGRAPHY
Al. Cant.
Boase
Senex (Josiah Bateman), *Clerical Reminiscences* (London, 1880)
E. Stock, *History of the Church Missionary Society*, 3 vols (London, 1899)

J. T. Ward, *The Factory Movement, 1830–1855* (London, 1962)

IAN S. RENNIE

Bateman, R(ichard) T(homas) (b. Haverfordwest, Dyfed, Wales, *c.* 1712; d. London, *c.* 1760). Rector of Llysyfran, Dyfed (then Pembrokeshire) and St Bartholomew the Great, London. Described as a man of high birth and unusual natural endowments, he met WHITEFIELD and the WESLEYS when at Jesus College, Oxford, although he is not to be confused with Edmund Bateman mentioned in Wesley's diary. Graduating in 1738 he eventually identified himself fully with the revival largely through the influence of his curate in Wales, HOWELL DAVIES. He opened his London pulpit to his Oxford friends. His churchwardens complained but Bishop Gibson upheld him. He attended early meetings of the Calvinistic Methodist Association and the Wesleyan Conference and preached for Lady HUNTINGDON. He prayed with Lord St John at his deathbed and was a friend and correspondent of Joseph Williams of Kidderminster. In 1756 he volunteered as a naval chaplain. Latterly his intimacy with the Wesleys was somewhat diminished.

A. SKEVINGTON WOOD

Bateman, Thomas, (b. Chorley, near Nantwich, England, 1799; d. Nantwich, England, 1897). Primitive Methodist pioneer. Thomas was converted as a young man by the preaching of JOHN WEDGWOOD, a relation of Josiah Wedgwood the potter and a Primitive Methodist evangelist, in 1819. He began to preach in 1821 and laboured hard with George Taylor in building up the Burland branch (formerly the Cheshire Mission) of the Primitive Connexion, and in opening up work in North Wales and Shropshire. Throughout his long career as a farmer and land surveyor he had the satisfaction of seeing the Branch subdivided into 15 circuits. He was president of conference in 1857 and 1867 and his *Journals and Life of John Wedgwood* are important historical documents. In later Victorian times he was one of the lay grandees of Primitive Methodism: his personal fiefdom embraced the whole of Cheshire and beyond, and his conservatism alienated the younger advocates of change.

BIBLIOGRAPHY
Anon., *Earnest Men, Sketches of Eminent Primitive Methodists* (London, 1872)
G. J. Stevenson, *Methodist Worthies*, 6 vols (London, 1884–6)

IAN SELLERS

Bates, George Ferne (b. 1775; d. South Mimms, Middlesex [now Hertfordshire], England, 18 Nov. 1841). Anglican clergyman. He was the son of Henry Bates, Rector of Freckenham, Suffolk and appears to have been the nephew of Dr Benjamin Bates, a London medical doctor (died 1828). Bates was educated at Queens' College, Cambridge (BA 1805; MA 1808) where he first became involved with the CMS and became a close friend of HENRY MARTYN. (Martyn's *Letters and Journals* mention Bates either by name or simply as 'B'; Martyn stayed in the home of Dr Bates when in London on CMS business.)

He was ordained (deacon 1805; priest 1806) and served as: lecturer of St Giles, Cripplegate in London (1808); Vicar of South Mimms, Middlesex (*circa* 1812–15); and Rector of West Malling, Kent (1815–41).

BIBLIOGRAPHY
Al. Cant.
C. Hole, *History of the Church Missionary Society* (London, 1892): 622–3

DONALD M. LEWIS

Bates, Stewart (b. Silverhill, Londonderry, Ireland, May 1794; d. Glasgow, 7 Nov. 1856). Reformed Presbyterian minister. Bates studied at the University of Glasgow (MA 1815). He was brought up in the Presbyterian Church of Ireland but entered the Reformed Presbyterian Church. He ministered at Strathmiglo in Fife, to a congregation which had not been regularly constituted, before being ordained to the Reformed Presbyterian Church at Kelso in 1823. From 1838 until his death he was minister to the West Campbell Street congregation, Glasgow. While at Kelso he encouraged the Reformed Presbyterian Church to undertake foreign missionary work. Bates was given the degree of DD.

SELECT WRITINGS
T. Bateman, *Approved Workmen* (Glasgow, 1827)
—, *The Church's Obligations and Encouragement to Missionary Enterprise* (Edinburgh, 1831)
—, *The Sin and Danger of Union Between the . . . Church and an Immoral . . . Government* (Glasgow, 1841)
—, *The Sabbath and Religious Liberty* (Glasgow, 1849)
—, *Perils of the Present Time* (Glasgow, 1851)

R. H. CAMPBELL

Bather, Edward (b. Meole Brace, Shropshire, England, 1779; d. Meole Brace, Shropshire, England, 3 Oct. 1847). Bather was educated at Shrewsbury Grammar School, Rugby and Oriel College, Oxford (BA 1803; MA 1808). He followed his father as Vicar of Meol Brace (1804–47) and was appointed archdeacon of Salop by Bishop HENRY RYDER in 1828. In the same year he married as his second wife Mary, daughter of Samuel Butler, headmaster of Shrewsbury and Ryder's successor as Bishop of Lichfield, and thus became in due course uncle to Samuel Butler, the agnostic author of *The Way of All Flesh*. Bather was famous as a preacher, and besides the 14 charges of his archdeaconship he published *Sermons, Chiefly Practical* (3 vols, 1827–40) and posthumously *Hints on the Art of Catechising* (1848).

BIBLIOGRAPHY
DNB

ARTHUR POLLARD

Batty, Thomas (b. Mapleton, near Hull, Yorkshire, England, 31 Aug. 1790; d. Dudley, England, 2 April 1856). Primitive Methodist minister. As a youth Thomas entered the Royal Navy. He was converted in 1813 and joined the Wesleyans but in 1821 was persuaded by the Primitive Methodists to conduct missions, first in Driffield and then Silsden. Afterwards between 1821 and 1822 he opened up Blackburn, Preston, Wigan, Padiham and Accrington. In 1823 he became the leader of the 'great Weardale revival', founding new causes here, and in Allendale, Teesdale and the Eden Valley, quadrupling the membership of the Westgate branch. In his later circuit ministry he was crippled by asthma and retired to Dudley in 1852. Thanks to the biography by JOHN PETTY, the denomination's leading historian, Thomas became one of the best known of the early Primitive Methodist pioneers.

BIBLIOGRAPHY
Obituary, *Minutes of the Primitive Methodist Conference* (1857)
J. Petty, *Memoir of the Life and Labours of Thomas Batty* (London, 1857)

IAN SELLERS

Baxter, George Addison (b. 22 July 1771, Rockingham County, VA, BNA; d. 24 April 1841, Hampden-Sydney, VA, USA). College educator, Reformed theologian, and proslavery writer. While president and Rector of Washington College, Lexington, VA (1779–1829), Baxter taught moral philosophy, wrote a favourable account of the controversial Kentucky camp meetings in 1802, and led the New Monmouth and Lexington Presbyterian Churches into various revivals of religion during his pastorate (1799–1831). When professor of theology at Union Theological Seminary in Virginia (1831–41), he made the seminary into a bastion of orthodox Reformed theology and sectionalism.

An opponent of abolitionism and a supporter of gradual emancipation, Baxter succeeded in having GEORGE BOURNE deposed from the Presbyterian ministry in 1818 for his call for immediate emancipation, defended slavery for the present in *Essay on the Abolition of Slavery*, and advocated having the Old School party in the Presbyterian Church exscind New School synods with objectionable theological and abolitionist views.

BIBLIOGRAPHY
AAP
A. D. Thomas, *The Second Great Awakening in Virginia* (Richmond, VA, 1981)

ARTHUR DICKEN THOMAS, JR

Baxter, John (d. Antigua, Leeward Island, 7 Nov. 1805). Pioneer Methodist missionary. A shipwright in Chatham dockyard, and a local preacher, in 1778 Baxter responded to a request for dock workers to go to English Harbour, Antigua, recognizing the opportunities the position would give him for evangelism. He arrived on 2 April, taking up the work of NATHANIEL GILBERT which had been taken over by two black women, Mary Alley and Sophia Campbell. At his first service he had thirty hearers, but 400–500 the following day. He soon had 1,500 members in his care and built his first chapel in 1783. On Christmas Day 1786 THOMAS COKE arrived unexpectedly and met Baxter on his way to take an early morning service.

He gave up his post as under-storekeeper at £400 per annum in order to enter the ministry. Subsequently he went to St Vincent in 1787, opened a mission to Carib Indians in 1788, and on one occasion in the 1790s he was murderously assaulted. But he won the respect of the white inhabitants, some of whom attended his services and raised no objection to his preaching to slaves on their estates.

BIBLIOGRAPHY
W. D. Lawson, *Wesleyan Local Preachers* (Newcastle-upon-Tyne, England, 1874): 281–7

OLIVER A. BECKERLEGGE

Baxter, Matthew (b. Alston, Cumberland, England, 1 Jan. 1812; d. Oxford, New Zealand, 1 May 1893). Free Methodist minister. Under the influence of JOHN FLESHER he entered the Primitive Methodist ministry about 1834, but after two years joined the Wesleyan Methodist Association, taking his church in Scarborough with him. He was soon sent out to Jamaica to organize the Association's churches there. After nine years he returned, and became president of the Wesleyan Methodist Association in 1856, editor and book steward 1854–9, and connexional secretary in 1860. With JAMES EVERETT he edited the United Methodist Free Churches' hymn-book in 1860, and was the author of several books, including the valuable *Memorials of Free Methodism*. In 1868 he went to New Zealand to strengthen the mission there, remaining there till his death.

BIBLIOGRAPHY
O. A. Beckerlegge, *Bibliography of the UMFC* (Westcliff-on-Sea, England, 1988)
O. A. Beckerlegge, *United Methodist Ministers and their Circuits* (London, 1968)
G. J. Stevenson, *Methodist Worthies*, 6 (Edinburgh, 1896): 939
UMFC Minutes, 1893: 15

OLIVER A. BECKERLEGGE

Baxter, Nadir (b. c. 1800; d. after 1847). Anglican lawyer and 'universal secretary'. A senior partner in the prominent firm of Baxter, Rose and Norton (parliamentary solicitors), he represented an important lay development in evangelical Anglicanism which began in the 1820s. As the Second Evangelical Awakening faded the lay leadership provided by the Clapham Sect and its associates passed from the scene. Almost by default a new group of lay leaders emerged, almost all of whom were London lawyers. More back-room men than public figures, and more administrators than exciting leaders of vision, their power base was in the committee rooms of the evangelical societies. As voluntary societies continued to increase, so did their influence, and they gave themselves to the maintenance and development of the various ministries of evangelism, missions and philanthropy.

Among these lawyers were JOHN BRIDGES, CHARLES BRODRICK, WILLIAM DUGMORE, W. A. GARRATT, WILLIAM GRANE, E. V. Sidebottom, J. M. STRACHAN, and, of course, Nadir Baxter, who did much to coordinate and encourage. This work was made easier by the fact that they all had their offices around Fleet Street in the vicinity of the Inns of Court, where more of the evangelical societies also established their premises. A further item of importance was that another member of this group was ALEXANDER HALDANE, the proprietor of the evangelical Anglican newspaper, the *Record*. Although he was not a committee man, and was probably of a higher social class than most, he was greatly respected by this band of lawyers. He actively participated in the lawyers' prayer group which he had initiated, and when he spoke of his vision of a new form of evangelical Anglicanism they were ready to listen.

The lawyers were perhaps not universally interested in the finer points of Calvinism, the inspiration of the Bible or millennial theories. But they were deeply concerned about the maintenance of the Church of England and England as a Protestant nation. Here Haldane struck a resonant chord among most Anglican evangelicals. Their leaders for the last generation had not given expression to this conviction, but with liberal theology, renascent Roman Catholicism, and new forms of political life ready to weaken the Church of England and destroy the Christendom state, many Anglican evangelicals, including Baxter and his legal friends, were eager for someone to articulate their concerns. Thus they aligned themselves to a considerable extent with Recordite evangelicalism.

Baxter's committee involvement indicated this orientation. While he remained as secretary of the Colonial Church Society and was founding secretary of the Church Pastoral-Aid Society, he was particularly involved with the new societies which emerged to defend church and state. He was secretary of the Association of the Friends of the Church of England, a key member of the Lay Union for the Defence of the Established Church, a stalwart of the Christian Electors' Committee, one of the founders of the Lord's Day Observance Society, a life member of the Reformation Society and an organizer of the Protestant Association. ROBERT DUDLEY BAXTER, who became one of his law partners, appears to have been Nadir's younger brother.

BIBLIOGRAPHY
Rec.

IAN S. RENNIE

Baxter, Robert Dudley (b. Stoke Golding, Leicestershire, England, 1802; d. London, 8 Oct. 1889). Solicitor and disillusioned Irvingite. The third son of Dudley Baxter, he practised as a solicitor in Doncaster from 1823 to 1845 during which time he organized the London and York railway company (afterwards the Great Northern). In 1845 he moved to London to join NADIR BAXTER (apparently his brother) as head of Baxter, Rose and Norton (parliamentary solicitors). His brilliant powers of concentration enabled him to steer the Great Northern Railway Bill (1846) through Parliament in spite of great opposition. He contested two parliamentary elections unsuccessfully.

In 1831 he attended EDWARD IRVING'S services in London where for a while he was a respected prophet until May 1832 when he retired. His account of his experiences and of his discovery that he was deluded provides an important source for the historian of Irvingism. Although disillusioned with Irvingism, he remained active in evangelical causes.

His eldest son Robert Dudley Baxter (1827–75) was a solicitor and author and his second son Michael Paget Baxter (1834–1910) was a well-known evangelical clergyman whose millennial speculations led him to the conclusion that Louis Napoleon was the destined monarch of the world.

SELECT WRITINGS
R. Baxter, *Narrative of Facts* (London, 1833)

BIBLIOGRAPHY
Al. Cant.
Boase
Christian Herald and Signs of our Times (23 October 1889)
R. A. Davenport, *Albury Apostles* (London, 1974): 54–61
E. Miller, *History and Doctrines of Irvingism*, 1 (London, 1878): 74–81

TIMOTHY C. F. STUNT

Bayford, John (b. 1773; d. 1844). Student of prophecy and Irvingite. A proctor in Doctors' Commons, Bayford was active in the LSPCJ and sponsored JOSEPH WOLFF'S missionary travels. His *Messiah's Kingdom* (1820) was influential in the calling of the Albury conferences in which Bayford (identified as 'Evander' in HENRY DRUMMOND'S *Dialogues*) participated. His prophetic utterance at Albury in January 1833 led to Drummond's recognition as apostle. He was then appointed elder of a congregation in Brighton which he had established in the previous year. In Chelsea, as a member of the congregation of his son-in-law, HENRY JOHN OWEN, Bayford again prophesied – this time during public worship – on 25 August 1833. His intervention almost emptied the chapel and led to Owen's removal. In later years he seems to have been inactive in the Catholic Apostolic community.

BIBLIOGRAPHY
Bodleian Library, Oxford, S. Newman-Norton, ed., A Biographical Index of those associated with the Lord's work (manuscript facs b.61)
L. E. Froom, The Prophetic Faith of our Fathers, 3 (Washington, DC, 1946): 409–13
E. Miller, The History and Doctrines of Irvingism, 1 (London, 1878): 137, 139–40

TIMOTHY C. F. STUNT

Baylee, Joseph T. (b. 1808; d. Shepscombe, Gloucestershire, England, 7 July 1883). Anglican clergyman, founder of St Aidan's Theological College, Liverpool. Baylee was educated at Trinity College, Dublin (BA 1834; MA 1848; BD and DD 1852). While Perpetual Curate of Holy Trinity, Birkenhead (1842–64), he secured permission from Bishop J. B. SUMNER of Chester in 1846 to begin private theological classes. For the next ten years Baylee so successfully developed the work, preparing ordinands for ministry, that in 1856 St Aidan's College was built. Baylee continued as principal until 1869, moving in 1871 to become Vicar of Shepscombe, Gloucestershire. St Aidan's continued as a theological institution.

While principal of St Aidan's, Baylee was a celebrated figure in Liverpool. His influence extended beyond theological education, however, through his prolific literary advocacy of the evangelical Anglican cause. A leader of the movement, he championed Protestant orthodoxy against Roman Catholics and Unitarians alike, and proved himself a doughty defender of the evangelical cause. Among his many published works and sermons are accounts of his controversies with Bishop Joseph Brown (Roman Catholic Bishop of Apollonia), Matthew Bridges, and EDWARD MIALL, and works of evangelical Anglican apologetics, such as The Institutions of the Church of England are of Divine Origin, and a number of general studies of the Bible.

SELECT WRITINGS
J. T. Baylee, The Institutions of the Church of England are of Divine Origin (London, 1838)
—, Introduction to the Study of the Bible, 3 vols (London, 1870)
—, Verbal Inspiration, the True Characteristics of God's Holy Word (London, 1870)

BIBLIOGRAPHY
Boase
DNB

CHRISTOPHER D. HANCOCK

Bayley, Cornelius (b. Ashe, Shropshire, England, 1751; d. Manchester, England, 2 April 1812). Anglican clergyman. Bayley displayed precocious piety in his daily habit of fervent prayer at the age of six. He was educated at

and later became a master at Whitchurch Grammar School. He registered at Trinity College, Cambridge as a 'ten-year man' in 1781 (BD 1792; DD 1800). He received his doctorate for his Hebrew scholarship. He had published An Entrance into the Sacred Language (1782) and this remained so acceptable as to be reissued after his death. He was curate to JOHN W. FLETCHER at Madeley and RICHARD CONYERS at Deptford before building St James's, Manchester with a seating capacity of 1,400 and remaining incumbent till his death (1787–1812).

He held a regular Tuesday evening meeting for young people and one on Wednesdays for adults, and he also set up the first Sunday school in Manchester. His main doctrinal emphasis was upon the fruits of righteousness as evidence of faith. His funeral sermon was preached by JOHN CROSSE of Bradford, who took the living and installed Henry Heap as curate so that Bayley's widow and daughter might still enjoy an income.

BIBLIOGRAPHY
Al. Cant., II.1:194
CO, XI (1812)
DNB
C. Hulbert, Memoirs of Seventy Years (London, 1852)

ARTHUR POLLARD

Bayley, John Robert Laurie Emilius (b. Westminster, London, England, 16 May 1823, d. Scotland, 4 Dec. 1917). Anglican clergyman. Bayley was the son of Sir John Bayley of Westminster, and studied at Eton (where he captained the cricket team) and Trinity College, Cambridge. He was ordained (deacon 1846, priest 1847) and served in Wheatley in Nottinghamshire 1847–9, then in East Claydon, Buckinghamshire, and as Perpetual Curate of Woburn in Bedfordshire 1853–6, but achieved recognition as Rector of St George's, Bloomsbury in London from 1856 to 1867 and of St John's Paddington from 1867 to 1889. These became bustling evangelical parishes. He was awarded a BD in 1862. In 1871 he succeeded his father as baronet and in 1887 he inherited a Scottish title as Laurie of Maxwelltown in Denbighshire and retired to live on his estates. He was a learned preacher and served as a council member for Ridley Hall. He opposed High Church ceremonialism, and wrote a catechism which was translated into Urdu and a commentary of the book of Galatians. He married a Miss Rice of Dane Court in Kent.

BIBLIOGRAPHY
Crockford
F. W. G. Bullock, The History of Ridley Hall (Cambridge, 1941)

PETER J. LINEHAM

Bayley, William Butterworth (b. 1782; d. 1860). East India Company servant. Bayley was one of the East India Company civil servants to become a student at Lord Welleley's College of Fort William. An Urdu scholar, he gradually worked his way up the official hierarchy to become the Governor-General's chief secretary in 1819. In 1821 he was appointed to the Supreme Council and in 1828, became Acting Governor-General. A friend of WILLIAM CAREY, he supported the Baptist schools and used his influence with the Bengal government to smooth the path for missionaries. He was instrumental in persuading Lord Moira to support the LMS schools in Chinsurah but failed to get a government sponsorship for a mission in Rungpore. He became president of the Calcutta School Book Society (1817–30) and a member of the Calcutta Diocesan Committee of the SPCK. He also became a member of the Bengal government's General Committee of Public Instruction. Bayley wrote a pamphlet: 'On the Advantages to be expected from an Academical Institution in India', and published a volume of *Miscellaneous Essays* (1802).

BIBLIOGRAPHY
M. A. Laird, *Missionaries and Education in Bengal 1793–1837* (London, 1972)

PENELOPE CARSON

Bayly, Mary (née Saunders) (b. Market Lavington, near Devizes, England, 4 March 1816; d. 13 Dec. 1899). Charity worker. Bayly founded in 1853 the first 'Mothers Society' in the slum of the Potteries, Notting Dale, by bringing together a number of working-class women for scripture readings and simple instructions in home management, needlework, cookery and child care. Mrs Bayly described her social methods in *Ragged Homes, and How to Mend Them* (1859) and *Mended Homes, and What Repaired Them* (1861); and by 1863 there were three such meetings in the Potteries, under the management of a ladies' committee, and another connected with the parish church of St James. Out of this work with her husband Captain George Bayly and the local LCM, there arose a ragged school (opened by Lord SHAFTESBURY in 1858), and the temperance Workingmen's Hall (opened in 1861) and Latymer Road Mission which ultimately included a coffee-house, evening shelter for ragged and destitute boys, and a convalescent home for boys and girls. Mrs Bayly was influenced by Mrs CATHERINE MARSH's *English Hearts and English Hands* (1858), and her Workingmen's Hall is contemporary with those of Mrs Wightman and Adeline Cooper, and was a model for Mrs LOUISA DANIELL's institute for soldiers at Aldershot. Mrs Bayly was a strong defender of the ministry of women, and more especially of the Mildmay deaconesses. She was a close friend of Mary Sewell and wrote her life story.

BIBLIOGRAPHY
Boase
F. M. Gladstone, *Notting Hill in Bygone Days* (London, 1924): 138–9, 151–2
K. J. Heasman, *Evangelicals in Action: an Appraisal of Their Social Work in the Victorian Era* (London, 1962): 32–3, 261
—, 'The Influence of the Evangelicals upon the Origin and Development of Voluntary Institutions in the Second Half of the Nineteenth Century' (Univ. of London Ph.D. thesis, 1960): 38, 254, 294, 582, 616, 683
P. T. Winskill, *The Temperance Movement and its Workers*, 3 (Edinburgh, 1892): 88

SHERIDAN WAYNE GILLEY

Bayne, John (b. Greenock, Scotland, 16 Nov. 1806; d. Galt, Canada West, 3 Nov. 1859). Presbyterian clergyman in British North America and Free Church leader. Educated at the universities of Glasgow and Edinburgh, Bayne was ordained in 1834 and appointed to British North America under the auspices of the GCS. He was admitted to Galt in 1835 where he remained for the rest of his life. Visiting Scotland in 1842–3 he witnessed the events leading up to the Disruption of 1843. Returning to Canada West he played a leading role in the formation of a Free Church in Canada. His advocacy of Free Church principles (particularly the Headship of Christ) helped delay the union between the Free Church and the United Presbyterian Church which finally occurred in 1861.

BIBLIOGRAPHY
DCB, VIII
G. Smellie, *Memoir of the Rev. John Bayne* (Toronto, 1871)

RICHARD W. VAUDRY

Beamish, Henry Hamilton (b. 1796; d. Lillingstone Dayrell, Buckinghamshire, England, 23 Feb. 1872). Anglican clergyman and Protestant controversialist. Beamish was descended from an old Anglo-Irish Protestant family long settled in County Cork. He graduated BA from Trinity College, Dublin, in 1816, was ordained as an Anglican minister in 1819, became a Freeman of Cork City in 1823, and succeeded his father Samuel as Vicar of Kinsale in 1826. In 1829 he also became Rector of Taxas (now Tisaxon), and in 1830, as secretary of the Irish Society, he undertook a mission to convert Irish Roman Catholic immigrants in London, preaching in a church in West Street, St Giles's, and in other Anglican churches in the metropolis. This contact with London determined his subsequent career, and in 1832, he resigned the living of Kinsale to begin his thirty-year ministry as Perpetual Curate of Trinity Chapel, Conduit Street, London where his vigorous preaching attracted a fashionable congregation, which included the Duke of Devonshire. As chaplain to the second and third Earls of Bandon, and as the author of numerous anti-Catholic tracts and treatises, he enjoyed a considerable reputation as a Protestant propagandist both in England and Ireland, and was untiring in his duties as a public speaker and preacher for Protestant causes, especially at the May meetings in London. In the last decade of his life he retired to the country, where he held a succession of livings with a Protestant tradition, as Vicar of Old Cleeve, Somerset (1862–5) and Wimbish (1865–9), and Rector of Lillingstone Dayrell (1869–72).

BIBLIOGRAPHY
Boase
Burke's Irish Family Records (London 1976): 92–3
G. D. Burtchaell and T. U. Sadleir, *Alumni Dublinenses* (London, 1924): 52
The Record (28 February 1872)

SHERIDAN GILLEY

Beardsall, Francis (b. Sheffield, Yorkshire, England, 6 Sept. 1799; d. at sea, 1842). Baptist minister and temperance reformer. The son of an innkeeper who drank to excess, he became a class leader and local preacher among the Methodists before his baptism as a believer at Hull in 1828. Trained at Loughborough under the Reverend T. Stevenson, he held New Connexion General Baptist pastorates in Leicestershire before moving to Manchester, 1834–42. Arguing that the wine of the Bible was unfermented, he campaigned against the use of alcohol in Communion services and himself manufactured non-fermented grape juice for this purpose. His wider temperance advocacy saw him as editor of the *Temperance Star*, and the publisher of the first temperance hymn-book in 1837. Known as the 'Bible wine controversialist' of the 1830s, he died in mid-Atlantic, on board the 'Henry Bliss,' *en route* for 'that land of liberty ... where his mind would not be pained by a people's suffering, the result of heartless oppression.'

BIBLIOGRAPHY
Baptist Union Handbook (1843): 20

J. H. Y. BRIGGS

Beauchamp, William (b. Kent County, DE, BNA, 26 April 1772; d. Paoli, IN, USA, 7 Oct. 1824). Methodist preacher and editor. Beauchamp's father was a Methodist local preacher and Beauchamp served as an itinerant minister from 1794 to 1801 in Pennsylvania, New York, and Massachusetts and from 1822 to 1824 in Missouri and Indiana. In youth he had some formal education and learned Latin. Later in life he learned Greek and Hebrew, as well. In 1790 he was the first schoolmaster in Wood County, West Virginia where his family had recently moved.

From 1801 to 1822 Beauchamp lived first in Nantucket, Massachusetts, then Wood County, West Virginia (1807), Chillicothe, Ohio (1815), and Mt Carmel, Illinois (1817). He was highly respected as a local preacher. At Chillicothe he privately published the *Western Christian Monitor*, the only successful USA Methodist periodical prior to 1818. He had already published *Essays on the Truth of the Christian Religion*. These publications defended the Trinity and other evangelical teachings which had come under attack. Mt Carmel was a planned Methodist settlement which he served as surveyor, inventor, pastor, and teacher. The final year of his ministry was as presiding elder over nearly all of Indiana. He was a member of the 1824 General Conference where he came within two votes of election to the episcopacy.

Beauchamp was both an intellectual and a leader. He was able quickly to establish strong congregations and lead them in erecting houses of worship. One of the most celebrated frontier Methodist preachers of the early 1800s, he was called 'the Demosthenes of the West'. His ministry demonstrates the significance of the local preacher for the success of early USA Methodism. Many preachers dropped out of the itinerancy owing to health considerations or, as in his case, to provide for their families, but continued to render great service as evangelists and pastors. Beauchamp's near-election as bishop is unique for a person who had been so long out of the travelling ministry.

BIBLIOGRAPHY
E. S. Bucke ed., *History of American Methodism* (Nashville, TN, 1964)
EWM
A. H. Redford, *The History of Methodism in Kentucky* (Nashville, TN, 1869)
A. Stevens, *The History of the Methodist Episcopal Church* (Nashville, TN, 1864)

CHARLES W. BROCKWELL, JR

Beaufort, Duchess of. See SOMERSET, CHARLOTTE SOPHIA [née Leveson-Gower].

Beaumont, John (b. near Holmfirth, Yorkshire, England, 1761; d. Macclesfield, Cheshire, England, 8 Nov. 1822). Methodist preacher and composer. The son of a farmer and music teacher, who taught him singing, the bass viol, and musical rudiments, he sang in public aged six and toured the north of England as a child prodigy. At 16 he encountered the Wesleyans at Mexborough, and abandoned music until the 1790s. Admitted on trial as a preacher at the 1786 Conference, he served in circuits in the north of England until 1821.

He published anthems and hymn tunes in a moderately florid style, but avoiding conflicting texts in different voices. His 1801 volume contains a portrait dated 1 April 1795 showing him at the organ in the 'new Chapel' at Newark, besides 'Observations on the Abuses of Singing' perhaps responding to the continuing opposition to anthems in conference (1796, 1799). He was one of the first Methodists to work for an improved appreciation of music.

SELECT WRITINGS
J. Beaumont, *Four Anthems Adapted for Public Worship* (London, [1793])
—, *The Nature of the Work of God* (Nottingham, England, 1796)
—, *The New Harmonic Magazine* (London, 1801)

BIBLIOGRAPHY
J. T. Lightwood, 'John Beaumont, Preacher-Musician', *The Choir*, 13 (1924): 85–8

GEOFFREY CHEW

Beaumont, Joseph (b. Castle Donnington, Leicestershire, England, 19 March 1794; d. Hull, Yorkshire,

England, 21 Jan. 1855). Wesleyan minister. The son of the Reverend JOHN BEAUMONT (died 1822), Joseph was converted while at Kingswood School, came under the influence of MELVILLE HORNE at Macclesfield, but chose to follow his father into the Wesleyan ministry. After working briefly in a chemist's shop, he went to his first circuit in 1813 and was received into full connection in 1817.

During his first Edinburgh ministry 1821–4, he began to study medicine, receiving an MD during a second period there, 1833–6. He made a special study of heart disease, from which he himself suffered. Periods of ill health, beginning in his twenties, caused him to consider resigning from the ministry.

His wife was sister-in-law to the pioneer China missionary, ROBERT MORRISON, and Joseph became known for the passionate eloquence of his missionary advocacy. His liberal political stance led him to support the Reform Act 1832 and he was active in the long struggle against clerical dominance in the Wesleyanism of the 1830s and 1840s, culminating in the Fly-Sheet Controversy of 1849. He opposed the expulsion of JAMES EVERETT at the 1849 Conference and himself faced an attempt by the leaders of the Hinde Street circuit to degrade him from his superintendency. His publications included two series of YMCA lectures, *The Acquisition of Knowledge* (1848) and *Divine Revelation* (1852).

BIBLIOGRAPHY

J. Beaumont Jr, *The Life of the Rev. Joseph Beaumont By His Son* (London, 1856)
DNB
R. Wrench, *A Biographical and Critical Sketch* (London, 1859)

JOHN A. VICKERS

Beaver, Herbert (b. England, 1800; d. Fort Beaufort, Cape Colony, South Africa, 21 May 1858). Anglican clergyman. Educated at Queen's College, Oxford (BA 1821), he was ordained (deacon 1822, priest 1823); from 1825 to 1835 he served as an army chaplain in St Lucia, British West Indies [now the West Indies]. In 1835 Beaver was invited by George Simpson, the superintendent of the Hudson's Bay Company in North America, to become the 'chaplain and missionary for the education and religious instruction of the Indians' at Fort Vancouver. Here Beaver provoked the hostility of the chief factor, John McLoughlin (a Roman Catholic), by challenging his jurisdiction over the fort's school, and by castigating 'fur-trade' marriages. Beaver's attitude of social superiority and his exaggerated and acrimonious reports and letters to BENJAMIN HARRISON exacerbated this personal feud. Beaver's discursive reports and letters reveal much about life in Fort Vancouver, but reflect little concern for local Indians. After two years, Beaver returned to England in an unsuccessful effort to indict McLoughlin. Little is known of his subsequent ministry except that after spending four years in a country parish, he recommended several military chaplaincies in Cape Colony, South Africa.

SELECT WRITINGS

H. Beaver, *Reports and Letters of Herbert Beaver, 1836–1838*, ed. T. E. Jessett (Portland, OR, 1959)

BRUCE L. GUENTHER

Beck, Johann Ludwig (b. New Herrnhut, Greenland, 19 June 1737; d. Kloster, Graubünden, Germany, 1802). Moravian deacon and missionary to the Greenland and Labrador Inuit. Beck, a bag-maker, grew up in a Moravian environment and became a member of the Moravian church on 3 August 1749. He first arrived in Labrador on 25 July 1773, was ordained deacon on 9 June 1777, and left the mission field to return to Germany in 1797.

BIBLIOGRAPHY

Public Archives of Canada, Ottawa, 'Catalogus der Missionare in Labrador', Records of the Moravian Mission in Labrador [1764–1944], Microfilm 511, Reels 11–12, fol. 15195–6
Kölbing

MARCELLA ROLLMANN

Beck, Johann Tobias (b. Balingen, Württemberg, Germany, 22 Feb. 1804; d. Tübingen, Germany, 28 Dec. 1878). University professor and theologian. After studies at Tübingen (1822–6), Beck served as pastor at Waldthann (1827–9) and Mergenheim (1829–36). In 1836 he was invited to Basel as professor, and under the influence of C. G. BLUMHARDT founded the 'Verein zur Beforderung christlich-theologischer Wissenschaft und christlichen Lebens' to encourage Pietist theological scholarship. In 1843, Beck was named professor of systematic theology at Tübingen and morning preacher at the Stiftkirche, both positions which he held until his death. He was well known as a preacher and numerous volumes of sermons were published. He wrote about theology, for example the *Einleitung in das System der christlichen Lehre* (Stuttgart, 1838; 2nd ed. 1870) and was a pioneer in pastoral psychology: *Die christliche Menschenliebe, das Wort und die Gemeinde Christi* (Basel, 1842) and *Umriss der biblischen Seelenlehre* (Stuttgart, 1843) the third edition of which (1873) was translated into English as *Biblical Psychology* (Edinburgh, 1877). A number of biblical commentaries were published posthumously.

Beck was a key figure in the development of biblicism (a verbal inspiration view of scripture) in Württemberg Pietism through his influence on generations of students at Tübingen. He was concerned to base all doctrines, pastoral science and spirituality on the biblical witness alone with minimal illustrative reference to the larger traditions of interpretation in the church. He avoided critical scholarly issues. Beck's theological influence extended throughout Europe and North America, many of his works being translated into English, Swedish and other languages.

BIBLIOGRAPHY
F. Liebetrut, *J. T. Beck und seine Stellung zur Kirche* (Berlin, 1858)
B. J. Riggenbach, *Johann Tobias Beck, ein Schriftgelehrter zum Himmelreich* (Basel, 1888)
A. Schlatter, *Beck's theologische Arbeit* (Stuttgart, Germany, 1904)
G. Sentzke, *Die Theologie Johann Tobias Becks und ihr Einfluss in Finnland*, 2 vols (Helsinki, 1949, 1957)
C. Sturhahn, *Rechtfertigungslehre nach Beck mit Berucksichtigung von Ebrard's Sola* (Leipzig, Germany, 1890)

DAVID BUNDY

Beckhauer, Charles William (b. Saxony, Germany, c. 1798; d. Sierra Leone, 28 June 1823). CMS missionary to Sierra Leone. Beckhauer studied at Basel Seminary and took Lutheran orders at Stuttgart Cathedral on 5 August 1821 along with J. MAISCH, J. T. REICHARDT and G. W. E. METZGER. He then studied the National School system in England and on 8 November 1822 was sent by the CMS to Sierra Leone and was stationed at Freetown and York. He died within eight months of his arrival. His willingness to serve in Sierra Leone is remarkable in view of the fate of other early CMS missionaries (*see* M. RENNER, P. HARTWIG, J. G. PRASSE, J. C. BARNETH, J. QUAST, C. H. MEISSNER, H. MEYER, J. H. SCHULZE and C. JOST). He appears not to have been married.

BIBLIOGRAPHY
D. T. B[arry], *CMS Register of Missionaries and Native Clergy* (privately printed) (London, 1906)

DONALD M. LEWIS

Beckley, Robert (b. London, England). *Fl.* 1820s. CMS missionary to Sierra Leone. Beckley trained as a schoolmaster at the Central School of the National School Society and was sent out with his wife and JAMES LISK on 5 January 1820 and served at Freetown. His wife died on 27 November 1820. In 1821 he served at Kissey and Kent. In 1822 he married HANNAH JOHNSON, sister of W. A. B. JOHNSON and one of the first 'female missionaries' to serve with the CMS. It is not known what became of either of the Beckleys.

BIBLIOGRAPHY
D. T. B[arry], *CMS Register of Missionaries and Native Clergy* (privately printed) (London, 1906)

DONALD M. LEWIS

Beckwith, General John Charles (b. Halifax, Nova Scotia, Canada, 2 Oct. 1789; d. Torre Pellice, Italy, 19 July 1862). Anglican benefactor and missionary. An officer in the British Army, he was seriously wounded at Waterloo in 1815. The painful experience changed his spiritual life, and the nominal Anglican became a committed Christian.

After a visit to the Waldensian valleys in 1827, the retired lieutenant-colonel (later major-general) devoted himself to the material and spiritual welfare of the 'Israel of the Alps'. To improve education, he founded more than one hundred parish schools in towns and isolated villages and, in concert with Canon W. S. GILLY, the College of the Holy Trinity in Torre Pellice. In his vision, a renewed Waldensian church, disengaged from the liberal reformed tradition and French culture embraced by their elite and oriented towards an Anglican heritage, would have to respond to the challenge of the evangelization of Italy.

BIBLIOGRAPHY
A. G. Ashdown, *The General With A Wooden Leg* (Bognor Regis, England, 1980)
D. Jehier, 'Per una Nuova Biografia del Generale Carlo Beckwith', *Bulletin de la Société d'Histoire Vaudoise*, 38 (1917): 82–90
J. P. Meille, *Le Général Beckwith* (Lausanne, 1872) [English trans., *Among the Waldenses*, Nelson, England, 1876]
'O Sarete Missionari o non Sarete Nulla'. Charles Beckwith 1789–1989 (Torre Pellice, Italy, 1991)

MASSIMO RUBBOLI

Beddome, Benjamin (b. Henley, Oxfordshire, England, 23 Jan. 1717; d. Bourton-on-the-Water, Gloucestershire, England, 3 Sept. 1795). Baptist minister and hymnwriter. The son of John and Rachel [née Brandon], he was baptized in London in 1739 at the Baptist church at Prescott Street. He studied under the direction of BERNARD FOSKETT at the Bristol Academy, and later at the Independent Academy at Miles End in London. In July 1740, he began a 55-year pastorate at the Baptist church at Bourton-on-the- Water, but was not ordained until 1743. He wrote over 800 hymns which were published in a collection entitled *Hymns Adapted to Public Worship* (1817). He also published a catechism in 1752 which was reprinted in 1776.

BIBLIOGRAPHY
J. Ivimey, *History of the English Baptists*, 4 (1830): 461–9
J. Rippon, *The Baptist Annual Register*, 2 (1794): 314–28

KAREN E. SMITH

Bedell, Gregory Townsend (b. Staten Island, NY, USA, 28 Oct. 1793; d. Baltimore, MD, USA, 30 Aug. 1834). Protestant Episcopal clergyman. Nephew of the evangelical Episcopal bishop, RICHARD CHANNING MOORE, and the offspring of devout Episcopal parents, he was educated at the Episcopal Academy in Chesire, Connecticut. Despite poor health, he entered Columbia College, graduating in 1811. He was ordained deacon by Bishop J. H. Hobart on 4 November 1814, and assumed his first pastoral charge in Hudson, New York, in 1815. His talents as a preacher, together with 'his peculiar vivacity of spirit, and cheerful pleasantry in conversations', won him early popularity in New York. But in 1818, Hobart arranged to transfer him to the charge of an Episcopal congregation in Fayetteville, North Carolina, ordaining him presbyter for that purpose in July 1818. In 1822, he was recalled to the North as Rector of St Andrew's Church, Philadelphia, where his preaching in the 'language of affectionate and earnest expostulation' recruited 334 communicants for the church in a year's time. 'Nearly every day in the year there was some religious meeting in connection with St Andrew's Church'. He instituted frequent weekday lectures and prayer meetings, promoted revivals of 'religious sensibility', and encouraged intradenominational cooperation, especially in the work of the ABS and the ASSU. His labours, however, told severely on his health, and despite a medical vacation in the summer of 1834, he collapsed and died while on return to Philadelphia.

Bedell published several small books for the ASSU, as well as several devotional volumes, and was also an editor of the *Episcopal Recorder*. A posthumous collection of sermons, with a memoir, was published by S. H. TYNG in 1835.

SELECT WRITINGS
G. T. Bedell, *Sermons of Rev. Gregory T. Bedell, D.D.*, ed. S. H. Tyng, 2 vols (Philadelphia, PA, 1835)

ALLEN C. GUELZO

Bedford, Peter (b. Kelvedon, Essex, England, 26 July 1780; d. Croydon, Surrey, England, 1 Dec. 1864). Quaker philanthropist. Coming to London as a young man he entered the business of a Spitalfields silk manufacturer, becoming partner and finally sole proprietor. Poverty in the neighbourhood led him to help organize and manage the Brick Lane soup kitchen, to establish savings banks, and to set up probably the first infants' school in England (under the influence of the Swiss educationist Wilderspin). He was particularly concerned for young delinquents and had a wide and shrewd knowledge of the Spitalfields criminal underworld.

He was never recorded a minister but as an elder frequently accompanied ministering Friends on their travels, and on four occasions (1822, 1840, 1845, 1852) visited the Continent in this capacity. On retirement (1836) he settled at Croydon. He appears to have been theologically closer to eighteenth-century Quietism than to his contemporary evangelicals but shared to the full their philanthropic preoccupations.

BIBLIOGRAPHY
London Friends Institute, *Biographical Catalogue* (London, 1888): 64–6
W. Robinson, ed., *Friends of a Half Century* (London and Ashford, England, 1891): 73–9
W. Tallack, *Peter Bedford, the Spitalfields Philanthropist* (London, 1865)

EDWARD H. MILLIGAN

Beecham, John (b. Barnoldby le Beck, Lincolnshire, England, 5 Nov. 1787; d. London, 22 April 1856).

Methodist missionary secretary. Converted in 1812 at Waltham, near Grimsby, through a zealous Methodist, John Beecham was instrumental in forming a Methodist society in the neighbouring village of Ashby. At the Wesleyan Methodist Conference of 1815, he was taken into full connexion. He served successively in Lincolnshire, Yorkshire, and Lancashire circuits. The Leeds Organ Case of 1828 led to his defence before the Liverpool South quarterly meeting of the authority of conference; this was published in 1829 as *An Essay on the Constitution of Wesleyan Methodism*.

In 1831, recognition of his talent and interest in overseas missions, particularly by JABEZ BUNTING, led to his appointment as one of the general secretaries to the WMMS. Missionary expansion was gaining rapid momentum. Beecham proved throughout 25 years' service an assiduous secretary, always well-briefed, with a keen eye for detail and a sure grasp of the whole work. He was active in strengthening missionary work in the West Indies, especially in school provision, and rejoiced in the emancipation of the slaves. He took a particular interest in South and West Africa and wrote a detailed study of the Ashanti and the Gold Coast. He was deeply committed to Australasia. As a proponent of affiliated conferences, he supported the creation in 1854 of the Australian Conference with responsibility for New Zealand, the Friendly Islands, and Fiji. He upheld the rights of aboriginal peoples against colonial exploitation, giving evidence before parliamentary committees. He repeatedly urged on the Colonial Office the maintenance of the Treaty of Waitangi (1840). He helped to establish in 1852 the French Methodist Conference, having presented the case for autonomy since 1835. Shortly before his death, he undertook an exhausting journey to North America, visiting the Canadian Conference, and assisting in the formation of the Eastern British American Conference.

Apart from his work for overseas missions, he was closely associated with important developments at home, including the establishment of the Wesleyan Theological Institution and the Centenary Fund. In 1850, he was elected president of conference. A personal friend and colleague of Jabez Bunting, he maintained the 'high' Wesleyan concept of the ordained ministry and the authority of conference. He deeply respected the legacy of 'Mr Wesley'; publishing an edition of his sermons with a biography. Much correspondence is contained in the Methodist archives, School of Oriental and African Studies, London, and John Rylands University Library, Manchester.

BIBLIOGRAPHY
DNB
Watchman (30 April 1856)
W. R. Ward, *Early Victorian Methodism* (Oxford, 1976)
Wesleyan Methodist Magazine (July 1856)

JOHN WALLER

Beecher, Catharine Esther (b. East Hampton, NY, USA, 6 Sept. 1800; d. Elmira, NY, USA, 12 May 1878). Educator, author, and moral philosopher. The firstborn of the Reverend LYMAN BEECHER and Roxana (Foote) Beecher, Catharine shared her revivalist father's millennial vision for America. She proposed to realize it by means of education. She founded the Hartford Female Seminary, considered a model for serious female education, and authored textbooks, advice books, and religious works.

Beecher asserted that women, as mothers and teachers, were especially suited to be the moral educators of children – the next generation who would shape American culture and destiny. She worked to train and place single women as missionary teachers who would bring moral education, Christian influence, and basic literacy to the American frontier. She was also a leader in the field of domestic science, promoting it as a means of elevating women's work in the domestic sphere. In addition to her published works, manuscript sources are available at Yale University, Radcliffe College, and the Stowe-Day Library in Hartford, Connecticut.

BIBLIOGRAPHY
NAW
K. Sklar, *Catharine Beecher* (New Haven, CT, 1973)

ESTHER BYLE BRULAND

Beecher, Lyman (b. New Haven, CT, BNA, 12 Oct. 1775; d. Brooklyn, New York, 10 Jan. 1863). Congregational and Presbyterian clergyman. The son of David Beecher, a blacksmith, and a mother who died during his birth, Beecher was raised by his uncle on a farm near New Haven, Connecticut and entered Yale College in New Haven in 1793. In 1795 TIMOTHY DWIGHT became the new president of the college and began aggressively preaching against the French Enlightenment thinking then popular with Yale students. Beecher was one of Dwight's early converts and the two became lifelong friends. Beecher always saw his own ministry as a continuation of Dwight's in both style and substance.

After graduating in 1797, Beecher spent a further year studying under Dwight and was licensed as a Congregational clergyman. However, in 1798, he accepted a call to the East Hampton Presbyterian Church on Long Island and thereby clearly exemplified the *de facto* alliance between Presbyterians and Congregationalists that had been consolidated by the Plan of Union of 1801 (which encouraged joint action in home missionary work). Beecher remained in the village of East Hampton for 11 years. Although hampered by financial need and by limited contact with the rest of the country, he faithfully sought to promote a revival in his congregation. After several years revival finally came.

In 1806 he attracted national attention with an attack on duelling, which reflected horror at the death of Alexander Hamilton in a duel with Aaron Burr Jr (1756–1836). (Burr, who served as US Vice-President from 1801 to 1805, was the son of AARON BURR, a Presbyterian minister and president of Princeton College.) Beecher preached against duelling in a sermon before his congregation and then before synod. His condemnation was soon printed and over 40,000 copies were distributed.

In 1810 Beecher accepted a call to a more lucrative position as pastor of the Congregational church in Litchfield, Connecticut. Litchfield boasted a famous law school where several leading American politicians trained. Here Beecher staunchly defended Congregationalism's status as Connecticut's established church until its demise in 1818. He was eventually reconciled to the separation of church and state and finally supported the voluntary principle. During his Litchfield tenure, Beecher began to advocate abstinence from alcohol; his *Six Sermons On Intemperance* (1827) brought him renown at a time when this issue was beginning to attract the attention of the American evangelical community.

In 1826, at the height of controversy between Unitarians and Trinitarians, Beecher became the pastor of the Hanover Street Congregational Church in Boston. He was anxious to challenge Unitarianism where it had been born by both assaulting its heterodoxy and promoting revivals. Moderately successful in Boston, Beecher, however, also came under scrutiny from conservatives who believed that his attempts to defend Calvinism against Unitarianism actually compromised traditional orthodoxy. His theology appeared to resemble that of NATHANIEL W. TAYLOR of Yale, which was then being challenged by theologians like CHARLES HODGE of Princeton Seminary in New Jersey. While in Boston, Beecher moved from opposition to cautious acceptance of the revivalistic 'New Measures' practised by CHARLES G. FINNEY. Beecher also hired and gave free reign to the famous musician and hymn-composer Lowell Mason who was to have a significant impact upon American church music.

Beecher was convinced of the strategic importance of the new western settlements for the future growth of evangelical churches. Thus, in 1832, he accepted the concurrent positions of pastor at the Second Presbyterian Church in Cincinnati and the presidency of the fledgling Lane Theological Seminary, a small Presbyterian school in the same city. Lane, always on the brink of financial ruin during this period, required much travel by Beecher to recruit students and solicit funds. Generally successful in these endeavours, Beecher kept Lane afloat during difficult times; one year he had to recruit a whole incoming class on short notice when no students matriculated.

Among his most popular addresses during his recruitment trips were those which appealed to eastern evangelicals to save the West from the twin evils of infidelity and Roman Catholicism. Many of these were later published as *A Plea for the West* (1835). In 1834, shortly after Beecher spoke in Boston, a mob of anti-Catholic protesters burned the Ursuline convent in Charlestown, Massachusetts. Many blamed Beecher's oratory for the incident.

While in Cincinnati, Beecher experienced two difficult struggles. First, in 1833, the issue of slavery erupted at Lane Seminary. After a lengthy debate the radical abolitionist students who were led by THEODORE D. WELD withdrew when the board attempted to silence them. Beecher's attempt to mediate between the abolitionist and proslavery factions lost him the support of the former group led by LEWIS TAPPAN and ARTHUR TAPPAN (who had been key supporters).

Second, in 1835 Beecher faced a heresy trial. Joshua Wilson, a conservative Old School (or traditionalist) minister, accused Beecher of violating the standards set out in the Westminster Confession of Faith on the issues of original sin, inability and election. Although his subscription to the confession was loose, Beecher was exonerated by presbytery and synod. However, conservative Old School theologians were always convinced that Beecher's views were close enough to those of N. W. Taylor to be suspect. Such differences contributed to the 1837 division of American Presbyterianism into 'Old School' and 'New School' branches.

Beecher retired from his pastoral duties in 1843 and from the presidency of Lane Seminary in 1851. He spent the remainder of his life with his children in Boston and Brooklyn preparing his papers for publication. Beecher is notable because he exemplified the theology and ethos of the evangelical wing of New England Congregationalism and New School Presbyterianism. Mostly concerned with the fundamental evangelical doctrines and always emphasizing the need to preach to the heart for conversion, his theology was ambiguous enough to raise suspicions about his orthodoxy according to strict Reformed standards. Yet Beecher was a clear example of the direction taken by much of American evangelicalism in the later nineteenth century.

Beecher married: (1) Roxana Foote (1775–1816) in 1799 and had nine children by her; (2) Harriet Porter (1790–1835), in 1817 by whom he had four other children; (3) Lydia Beals Jackson (1789–1869) in 1836, by whom he had no issue. All of his sons entered the Christian ministry and several of the offspring of his first marriage became well known in their own right: CATHARINE (1800–78) as a champion of female higher education, Edward (1803–95) as an educator and abolitionist, HARRIET BEECHER STOWE (1811–96) as author of the influential antislavery novel, *Uncle Tom's Cabin* (1852) and Henry Ward (1813–87) as one of the most popular preachers in late-Victorian America. None of his children, however, followed completely his evangelical theology. The fact that several of them did not have the dramatic conversions that their father had long promoted was an ongoing concern to him. In a very real sense the legacy of Beecher's family is as significant in the shifting patterns of American evangelicalism as is his place in the history of American Christianity.

SELECTED WRITINGS

L. Beecher, *The Autobiography of Lyman Beecher*, ed. B. M. Cross (Cambridge, MA, 1961)

—, *Works* (Boston, MA, 1852–3)

BIBLIOGRAPHY

M. Caskey, *Chariot of Fire* (New Haven, CT, 1978)
S. Henry, *Unvanquished Puritan* (Grand Rapids, MI, 1973)
M. Rugoff, *The Beechers* (New York, 1981)

JOHN R. WIERS

Begg, James (b. New Monkland, Lanarkshire, Scotland, 31 Oct. 1808; d. Edinburgh, 29 Sept. 1883). Presbyterian minister and social reformer. The son of a parish minister, Begg was educated at the University of Glasgow and ordained to the ministry of the Church of Scotland in 1830. In 1835, be became minister of Liberton, then a suburb of Edinburgh. He emerged to prominence in the evangelical party during the 'The Years Conflict' between the Church of Scotland and the British government over the issues of patronage and the church's spiritual independence. At the Disruption of the Church of Scotland in 1843, Begg joined the new Free Church and became minister in the Edinburgh suburb of Newington, where he stayed for the remaining forty years of his ministry.

During the 1840s, Begg had become increasingly interested in social questions. As convener of the Free Church Home Mission and Church Extension Committee from 1847 to 1857, he worked to strengthen Free Church efforts for reclaiming the lapsed urban masses, while his own congregation organized and conducted a model urban mission in a deprived district of Edinburgh. Begg's evangelical concerns led him to examine the environmental factors that hindered the spread of the Gospel, and after 1848 he became a leading advocate of social reform. In 1850, he took the principal role in founding the Scottish Social Reform Association, which pressed for sanitary reforms, land reform, temperance and reform of the poor relief and prison systems. That same year, he began to campaign for the establishment of a national system of education. During the later 1850s, he pressed for an expansion of the franchise and for a degree of home rule for Scotland.

His major efforts, however, were directed towards the problems of working-class housing. He was convinced that the lack of adequate housing for the urban labouring orders was not only a danger to health, but was also an obstacle to religion. Crowded into single-room apartments, families were unable to respect the ordinary decencies of life, while individuals had no opportunity for private prayer. Deplorable environmental conditions, he recognized, thwarted moral and spiritual development. He pressed the Free Church to interest itself in urban working-class housing, and advocated cooperative building societies and property investment companies to enable workers to own their own homes. In 1861 he took a prominent part in the formation of the Edinburgh Co-operative Building Company, which was owned and managed by the workers. His concern for housing also included rural farm labourers, and he became a zealous opponent of the bothy system and pressed landowners to erect decent family cottages for the labourers on their estates. He became known as 'tribune of the people', a champion of the rights and interests of the Scottish nation.

Begg combined these commitments to social and political reform with a conservative Calvinism and an extreme anti-Catholicism. He became especially vehement in his attacks on Roman Catholicism following the restoration of the hierarchy in England in 1850. In 1851, he was one of the founders of the *Bulwark*, an anti-Catholic monthly magazine, which he edited for 21 years. His hatred of Roman Catholicism became an obsession, which grew to overshadow many of his liberal and reformist views and diminish his influence as a social reformer.

During the 1860s, his High Calvinist views put him increasingly out of touch with the majority opinion in the Free Church, which was moving toward more liberal views in theology. Begg's support became restricted to the group of conservative Free Church Calvinists in the Highlands, known as Begg's 'Highland Host'. He strongly opposed the movement which began in 1863 to unite the Free Church and the liberal United Presbyterian Church. Such a union, Begg argued, would be contrary to the conservative Calvinist principles on which the Free Church had been founded at the Disruption of 1843. Although the large majority in the Free Church supported the union movement, Begg and his 'Highland Host' managed to thwart the union by threatening legal action in the civil courts to claim all the Free Church property if the Free Church joined with the United Presbyterians. Rather than risk an expensive and potentially divisive legal struggle, the majority admitted defeat and withdrew from the union negotiations in 1873.

Committed to a literalist interpretation of scripture and opposed to the 'Higher Criticism', Begg and his 'Highland Host' played a leading role in deposing the celebrated biblical scholar, William Robertson Smith, from his chair at Aberdeen Free Church College in 1880. This was to prove one of the last conservative victories. Begg died in 1883. Deprived of their eloquent and imposing leader, the conservative Calvinist party in the Free Church became increasingly marginalized and the Free Church again moved toward union with the United Presbyterians.

BIBLIOGRAPHY
DNB
S. Mechie, *The Church and Scottish Social Development* (London, 1960): 119–35
T. Smith, *Memoirs of James Begg*, 2 vols (Edinburgh, 1885, 1888)

STEWART J. BROWN

Beighton, Thomas (b. Ednaston, Derbyshire, England, Dec. 25, 1790; d. Penang, Malaysia, April 14, 1844). LMS missionary in Penang. He was a Congregational minister before being accepted by the LMS. He arrived in Malacca in 1818. In April, 1819 he moved to Penang. He sought to attract the interest of Muslim Malays by opening schools with educated Muslims as teachers. In 1826 he organized a church with British soldiers and four Malay-speaking Chinese.

He translated, wrote, and published numerous tracts, many of which were offensive to the Muslim population. Despite their wide readership, the successful schools (140 pupils by 1826), and continual visitation there were no converts in over twenty years of ministry. He was a pioneer in ministries among Muslims but his use of tracts and schools, while popular, did not prove successful in winning converts.

BIBLIOGRAPHY
J. H. Haines, 'A History of Protestant Missions in the Nineteenth Century, 1815–1881' (Princeton Theological Seminary, Th.D. thesis, 1962)
L. O'Sullivan, 'The London Missionary Society: A Written Record . . . ', *Journal of the Malaysian Branch of the Royal Asiatic Society*, 57, 2 (1984): 61–104
J. Sibree, *A Register of Missionaries, Deputations, Etc.*, (London Missionary Society, London, 1925)

ROBERT HUNT

Beilby, William (b. Sheffield, England, 13 April 1783; d. Edinburgh, 30 May 1849). Before studying medicine in Edinburgh he engaged in the linen trade in Dublin for ten years. He graduated MD in 1816, specializing in midwifery. He became physician accoucheur to the New Town dispensary, and in 1844 was president of the Royal College of Physicians. Dr Beilby was a founder of the Edinburgh Medical Missionary Society in 1841, and its president from 1844 until shortly before his death.

Interested in the work of the EA, he was a member of Elder Street (now Canonmills) Baptist Church and a confidant of Dr Innes, the pastor. He was noted for introducing spiritual conversation into his medical work.

BIBLIOGRAPHY
W. Beilby, *A Selection from the Papers of the Late Dr Wm Beilby FRCPE*, ed. W. Innes, with a memorial sketch by J. Angel James (Edinburgh, 1850)
DNB
Edinburgh Medical Missionary Society, *Jubilee Memorial* (Edinburgh, no date)

DEREK B. MURRAY

Belcher, Joseph (b. Birmingham, England, 5 April 1794; d; Philadelphia, PA, USA, 10 July 1859). Baptist minister and author. Belcher is said to have written more works on religious subjects than any other author in the century. The editor of ANDREW FULLER's works, he wrote biographies of GEORGE WHITEFIELD, ROBERT RAIKES, WILLIAM CAREY, and the HALDANES among many other works. A leading light in the Baptist Home Missionary Society, he held pastorates from 1818 to 1844 at Somersham, Folkestone, Chelsea, and Greenwich, combining the enthusiasms of the revivalist with the statistical concern of the administrator. From 1832, he became editor of the unsectarian periodical, *The Revivalist*, which purported to give news of developments in America as a way of stirring sluggish Calvinist churches into new life. Through its pages the teachings of CHARLES FINNEY and other revivalists were communicated to an English audience. 1832 was also the year in which this enthusiast for revivalism became secretary to the revitalized Baptist Union. The changes of 1832 partly arose out of a careful statistical survey of Baptist churches which Belcher published in *The Baptist Magazine* for that year comparing 1832 with 1790, finding in those forty years a threefold increase, though growth in the provinces had been more pronounced than in London. The life of the new Baptist Union was fragile to start with and Belcher did well to shape it into becoming a more effective denominational instrument, serving until 1840. He emigrated to North America in December 1844, serving successively in New York; Halifax, Nova Scotia; Philadelphia; Maine; and Michigan before returning to Philadelphia in 1851, where, without particular church commitments, he devoted all his time to writing, principally for the American Baptist Publication Society.

BIBLIOGRAPHY
Boase
J.H.Y. Briggs, *English Baptists in the Nineteenth Century* (Didcot, England, 1994): 214ff
R. Carwardine, 'The Evangelist System, Charles Roe, Thomas Pulsford and the Baptist Home Missionary Society' *BQ* (1980)
The Freeman (3 August 1859)

J. H. Y. BRIGGS

Belfrage, Henry (b. Falkirk, Stirlingshire, Scotland, 24 March 1774; d. Rose Park House, near Falkirk, Scotland, 16 Sept. 1835). United Secession minister. He was the fourth son of John Belfrage, a long-serving Burgher Secession minister, and of Jean Whyte, a corn merchant's daughter. Belfrage responded to intense parental pressure by becoming at age ten a child preacher known as 'the wee minister'. He used study as a means of escape from the feverish piety and displaced ambition that characterized his home life. At age four or five he began to attend Falkirk grammar school. At age 13 he entered Edinburgh University, and in 1789 the Secession Divinity Hall, Haddington. He showed strength in ancient languages, having read Latin 'grammatically' by age six.

Licensed to preach in July 1793, Belfrage received calls from no less than three congregations. Bowing to Belfrage's stated will, in June 1794 the synod assigned him as assistant pastor to his father at Falkirk. He succeeded to full ministry upon his father's death in May 1798. Belfrage's assiduousness in pastoral visitation was astounding. He made annual visits to each of his 2,000 or so parishioners and held annual diets for the examination of their progress in Christian faith and practice.

His numerous pastoral writings, emotively pietistic, were highly regarded in Nonconformist evangelical circles, while his *Shorter Catechism* became a standard in Calvinist households and Sunday schools worldwide. Belfrage also gained prominence through regular contributions to religious periodicals, in particular to the *Pulpit*, the *Christian Instructor*, and the *Evangelical Magazine*. In the 1830s he was a co-editor of the latter journal. Belfrage was a friend of HENRY W. MONCRIEFF, to whom he was distantly related, and to whose influence he owed his honorary DD, conferred by St Andrews in 1824.

BIBLIOGRAPHY
DNB
EM (1836): 1–7
J. McKerrow and J. Macfarlane, *Life and Correspondence of Henry Belfrage* (Edinburgh, 1837)

JONATHAN BURKE CUTMORE

Belham, William Green (b. King's Lynn, Lincolnshire, England, 24 March 1797; d. Ramsgate, Kent, England, 22 Jan. 1854). Primitive Methodist preacher in Lincolnshire. Brought up an Anglican by his parents, Belham was converted as a consequence of the despair he suffered resulting from a friend's death by drowning. A shipwright by trade, Belham joined the Wesleyans in 1815, becoming a local preacher and class leader in Gainsborough, Lincolnshire. After hearing the Primitive Methodist, WILLIAM BRAITHWAITE, give a service in 1820, Belham joined the Primitive Methodist Connexion in 1821. He immediately became a travelling preacher, and ministered in the Scotter, Loughborough and Welton areas until 1825, and from then until his death he pioneered the Norwich district of East Anglia, including the Swaltham circuit. He helped build a small chapel and began a Sunday school in his home town of King's Lynn. Belham was the victim of much persecution. In 1825, he took part in the first camp meeting to be held in Witney, Oxfordshire, where he and his companions were met by a barrage of eggs. He was a Primitive Methodist for 33 years.

BIBLIOGRAPHY
PM Mag (1854)

WAYNE J. JOHNSON

Bell, Alexander (Montgomery) (b. Paisley, Renfrewshire, Scotland, 4 Dec. 1808; d. Edinburgh, 19 Jan. 1866). Legal author. The son of John Bell, a Paisley industrialist, he was educated at the local grammar school and at Glasgow University. He became a Writer to the Signet in 1835 and practised conveyancing as a partner in the Edinburgh firm of Dundas and Wilson.

Bell was best known as professor of conveyancing at Edinburgh University, a post he held from 1856. His lectures, which appeared posthumously in printed form, became the standard manual for generations of Scottish lawyers. A man of 'quiet and retiring habits', he played no prominent role in church affairs. He was, however, a member of the British EA and served on the committee of the Edinburgh auxiliary.

BIBLIOGRAPHY
DNB
Evangelical Christendom (1847): 54
Oliver and Boyd, *Edinburgh Almanac* (1865)

JONATHAN BURKE CUTMORE

Bell, George *Fl.* 1760s. Wesleyan schismatic. A corporal in the Life Guards, Bell was converted in London about 1758, and gained a Methodist ticket in 1760. In February 1761 he and two others urged London Methodists to attain perfection. THOMAS MAXFIELD, JOHN WESLEY's London preacher, encouraged the trio's noisy prayer meetings, which excited Methodists all over England. Bell impressed Wesley by his fervent devotion when they met in October 1762, but Wesley transferred the prayer meetings to the Foundery to control them. Bell increasingly claimed unique spiritual privileges and the power to heal miraculously, and in November 1762 claimed that the world would end on 28 February 1763. Wesley was nervous about this, and Bell moved his prayer meetings to the Snowsfields chapel, and then on 4 February withdrew from Methodism. When nearly 200 of his London society followed suit, Wesley denounced Bell in a letter to the *London Chronicle* and the government evidently arrested him, but crowds gathered to await 28 February. Little more is known about Bell, but he is said to have subsequently become an infidel and then a radical reformer.

BIBLIOGRAPHY
T. Maxfield, *Vindication*, (London, 1767)
J. Telford, ed., *The Letters of John Wesley*, 8 vols (London, 1931)
J. Wesley, *Journal*, ed. N. Curnock, 8 vols (London, 1909)

PETER J. LINEHAM

Bell, James (b. Jedburgh, Roxburghshire, Scotland, 1769; d. Campsie Fells, near Glasgow, 3 May 1833). Geographer. He was educated by his father, Thomas Bell (*DNB*), a Relief minister at Glasgow. Bell spent much of his life as a weaver, but in 1806, having been a voracious reader from youth, he became a tutor in the classic languages. In 1830 he published a *System of Geography*. It was greatly admired by Scottish contemporaries but was overlooked elsewhere and is not remembered today.

Bell was a pious Christian, faithful to his father's Calvinist legacy. He deeply believed in 'the corruption of human nature, and saw the necessity of man's justification by faith alone'. Though humble and tolerant, when necessary he could argue theology 'with great vigour and effect'.

BIBLIOGRAPHY
Alli
J. O. Thorne, ed., *Chambers Biographical Dictionary*, revised edn (Edinburgh and London, 1969): 112
DNB

JONATHAN BURKE CUTMORE

Bellamy, Joseph (b. Cheshire, CT, BNA, 19 Feb. 1719; d. Bethlehem, CT, USA, 6 March 1790). New England Congregational clergyman. One of the major figures in the development of New England theology between 1750 and 1850, Bellamy was graduated from Yale College in 1735, and seems to have undergone a dramatic conversion experience shortly thereafter. He turned to theological study, and was fitted for the ministry by his own minister, Samuel Hall, and by JONATHAN EDWARDS of Northampton. He was licensed by the New Haven Association in 1737, and agreed to supply the pulpit of the newly organized Congregational church in Bethlehem, Connecticut, where he was ordained on 22 April 1740.

With the arrival of the Great Awakening in New England in 1740, Bellamy embarked on an extensive round of itinerant preaching, delivering 454 sermons in over 200 communities in Connecticut, Massachusetts, and New York. But his confidence in the usefulness of itinerant preaching was undermined by the increasingly fanatical measures employed by other itinerants in Connecticut, and in 1742 he abandoned itinerant preaching altogether and concentrated his attention on his parish work in Bethlehem.

Bellamy was fully as disappointed in the theology of the itinerants as he was in their tactics, and in 1750, he published *True Religion Delineated* as his judgement on both the 'Old Light' enemies of the Awakening and its radical 'Antinomian' adherents. Bellamy insisted on the validity of the moral law and the obligation and ability of all Christians to obey it (as against the 'Antinomians'), and the equal validity of grace, being available to all people (as against the 'Old Lights'). In order to further promote the supremacy of grace, Bellamy resorted to a governmental (and consequently, unlimited) construction of the Atonement, and attacked the 'Half-Way Covenant' custom of predicating membership and Communion status upon baptism; in order to promote his insistence on law, Bellamy taught the infusion (rather than the imputation) of Christ's righteousness as the basis of justification, and set up a rigorous standard of 'disinterested benevolence' as the measure of Christian behaviour.

Bellamy's other major publications in the 1750s and 1760s mark him, along with SAMUEL HOPKINS, as a major interpreter of Jonathan Edwards and a leader in the creation of the 'consistent Calvinism' known as the New Divinity. Through his close contacts with JOHN ERSKINE, he was awarded the DD of the University of Aberdeen in 1768; and although offered the pulpit of the First Presbyterian Church in New York City in 1753, Bellamy chose to spend all of his life in the comparatively rural isolation of Bethlehem.

BIBLIOGRAPHY
AAP
Anon., *The Works of Joseph Bellamy*, 2 vols, with a memoir by Tryon Edwards (Boston, MA, 1853)
Hartford Seminary (Hartford, CT) manuscripts
Presbyterian Historical Society (Philadelphia, PA) manuscripts

M. R. Valeri, 'Joseph Bellamy: Conversion, Social Ethics, and Politics in the Thought of an Eighteenth Century Calvinist' (Princeton Univ. Ph.D. dissertation, 1985)

ALLEN C. GUELZO

Bellett, J(ohn) G(ifford) (b. Dublin, 19 July 1795: d. Dublin, 10 Oct. 1864). Brethren writer. Born into a wealthy Anglo-Irish family, he was educated at Exeter Grammar School and at Trinity College, Dublin, where he was classical prizeman. He read law in London, was called to the Bar in Dublin (1821), but practised little. Converted to an evangelical faith while a student, he became a close friend of JOHN NELSON DARBY, participated in the Powerscourt conferences, and associated with the Brethren in Dublin where he resided most of his life. He remained loyal to Darby but tried to exercise a moderating influence. A man of gracious spirit, his writings possess a warm, devotional quality. He wrote books on *The Patriarchs*, *The Evangelists*, *The Son of God*, and *A Short Meditation on the Moral Glory of the Lord Jesus*. The last-named is a minor devotional classic.

BIBLIOGRAPHY
Pickering

HAROLD H. ROWDON

Beman, Amos (Gerry) (b. Colchester, CT, USA, 1812; d. New Haven, CT, USA, 29 June 1874.) Black Congregational minister. Beman went to high school in Middletown, Connecticut, where his father had recently founded the Cross Street African Methodist Episcopal Zion Church. In 1838 after several years of teaching in a black school in Hartford and one year of study at Oneida Institute, a radical college in upper New York State, young Beman became the first black minister of the Temple Street African Congregational Church in New Haven.

During a twenty year ministry, Beman publicized the educational achievements of Connecticut blacks, challenged a racist legislator to debate the inferiority or equality of blacks, and urged their right to vote. By the latter 1850s Beman also travelled for the American Missionary Association, encouraging struggling parishes, black and white.

BIBLIOGRAPHY
D. E. Swift, *Black Prophets of Justice: Activist Clergy Before the Civil War* (Baton Rouge, LA, and London, 1989).

DAVID E. SWIFT

Beman, Nathan (S. S.) (b. New Lebanon, NY, USA, 26 Nov. 1785; d. Carbondale, IL, USA, 6 Aug. 1871). Presbyterian minister, evangelist, educator. A graduate of Middlebury College, Vermont 1807, Beman taught at an academy, tutored at his Alma Mater, was ordained in 1810, and pastored the First Presbyterian Church, Portland, Maine from 1810 to 1812. After a decade in Mount Zion, Georgia, where he established an academy, Beman accepted a call as minister of the First Presbyterian Church in Troy, New York in 1823. In 1845, following several years as its vice-president 1842–5, he was elected president of Rensselaer Polytechnic Institute, a position he held until 1865.

Beman was a prominent leader and defender of New School Presbyterianism. An eloquent preacher and effective evangelist, he supported 'new measures' revivalism, promoted home mission colleges, and signed the Auburn Declaration – the New School's attempt to prove its fidelity to historical Presbyterianism. Typical of fellow northern Protestant 'theocrats', Beman attacked all forms of prelacy, and ardently supported moral reform, abolitionist, and Union causes.

BIBLIOGRAPHY
DAB, 2
O. Peterson, *A Divine Discontent* (Macon, GA, 1986)

DAVID W. KLING

Benezet, Anthony (b. 11 Feb. 1714, St Quentin, France; d. 3 May 1784, Philadelphia, PA, USA). Quaker educator and humanitarian. In order to escape religious persecution, Benezet's Huguenot parents emigrated to Holland in 1715, then to London, where Benezet joined the Quakers at age 14. In 1731, the family moved to Philadelphia. John Stephen Benezet wanted his son to follow in his footsteps as a merchant, but the younger Benezet soon sought an occupation more in accord with his religious disposition. This he found in 1739 when he was employed as a teacher, first in Germantown and, three years later, at the William Penn Charter School. He established an advanced school for girls in Philadelphia in 1755. He was renowned for his learning, impeccable manners, religious piety and refusal to use corporal punishment. Benezet published a child's primer that he claimed was the first one designed to 'mend the heart ... by raising in the tender mind, principles of compassion and tenderness'.

As a philanthropist and social reformer, he obtained food, money and shelter for homeless Acadians exiled from Nova Scotia by the British, and he worked to obtain more just terms for American Indians in their land dealings with colonial authorities. He wrote a tract against the 'mighty destroyer', i.e. excessive consumption of liquor. A dedicated peacemaker, he wrote a pacifist tract at the time of the American Revolution. But the main focus of his humanitarian efforts was the emancipation and betterment of enslaved African-Americans. There was no more determined opponent of slavery and the slave trade than Benezet. He wrote more than half a dozen tracts combining African history with arguments against slavery from 1759 to 1784. His most important work was *A Short Account of that Part of Africa Inhabited by Negroes* (1762), although his subsequent pamphlets in 1766 and 1771 added a wealth of corroborating detail. On behalf of antislavery, he corresponded with diverse politicians, intellectuals and religious leaders including JOHN WESLEY, PATRICK HENRY, GRANVILLE SHARP, THOMAS CLARKSON, WILLIAM WILBERFORCE, Abbé Raynal and Queen Charlotte of England. Clarkson and Wesley became active opponents of slavery largely because of Benezet's influence. In 1775, he founded the first antislavery society in America. He circulated petitions and lobbied the Pennsylvania legislature in favour of mass manumissions and in 1780 the legislature responded by enacting a measure for the gradual emancipation of slaves.

Benezet used a formidable range of arguments in opposition to slavery. Drawing on his experience of teaching African-Americans in the evening for many years, he asserted the intellectual equality of persons of African and European descent. The blacks he had taught have 'as great variety of talents as among a like number of whites'. Benezet highly praised African societies, citing many authorities in regard to the industriousness, productivity, just government and religious piety prevalent in Africa. The slave trade, he charged, was attributable to the 'selfish avarice' of the European enslavers, who distributed weapons and fomented wars in order to have a large supply of captives that could be transported to the Americas.

Like all fervent evangelicals of his time, Benezet had a definite conviction of the reality of human sin. Human weakness, he stated, 'cannot be restored to its original purity, but through the efficacy of the Blood of Jesus Christ'. But real Christianity required Christian practice, not just Christian profession. He warned slave traders who claimed to be Christian that their actions violated the commandment to 'love thy neighbour as thyself'. Their actions must result in 'the utmost Scorn and Detestation of the Christian name'. Benezet favoured Christian missions to Africa, but only after slavery and the slave trade had been eliminated. A master who manumitted slaves, stated Benezet, was required to make certain that his former servants were economically independent before he was discharged of his duty. He believed that free blacks should be 'mixed amongst the whites' in America, '& by giving them property amongst us, make them parties & interested in our welfare & security'. Benezet's humility was evidenced in the epitaph he desired for himself: 'Anthony Benezet was a poor creature, and, through divine favour, enabled to know it.'

BIBLIOGRAPHY
H. Barbour and J. W. Frost, *The Quakers* (Westport, CT, 1988): 145–7, 292–3
G. S. Brookes, *Friend Anthony Benezet* (Philadelphia, PA, 1937)
R. Bruns, ed., *Am I Not a Man and a Brother* (New York, 1983)
DAB
DCA
R. Vaux, *Memoirs of the Life of Anthony Benezet* (York, England, 1817)

STEPHEN W. ANGELL

Bengel, Johann Albrecht (b. Winnenden bei Stuttgart, Germany, 24 June 1687; d. Stuttgart, Germany, 2 Nov. 1752). Pietist theologian and exegete. After studies at the Stuttgart Gymnasium, he entered the Stift at Tübingen (1703–8). He was especially influenced by the writings of Pietist theologians J. Arndt, J. Spener and the Spener tradition. One year was spent as Vicar in Metzingen. In 1713, Bengel travelled throughout Germany visiting universities and Pietist centres to observe scholarly methods and meet scholars. In November 1713, he became an instructor at the Monastic School of Denkendorf where he spent 28 productive years as a scholar and professor. In 1741 Bengel became prelate at Herbrechtingen. Then, in 1749, he was named to the consistory and as prelate of Alpirsbach, which had its living in Stuttgart. One year before his death, the faculty of theology at Tübingen conferred (1751) on Bengel a doctoral degree.

As a scholar Bengel made contributions in the areas of New Testament criticism and exegesis, as well as theology. In 1734, he published *Apparatus Criticus ad Novum Testamentum* (Tübingen, 1734) which established the text of the New Testament on the basis of a collation of numerous manuscripts. He was the first to group manuscripts into 'families' according to the tendencies of their readings. He was also the first to argue that it was not the number of manuscripts supporting a given reading that was determinative, but the quality of the reading. As well, Bengel established the rule, which has become a scholarly consensus, that the most difficult reading is the one to be preferred. On the basis of Bengel's theoretical and textual study, all subsequent New Testament textual criticism would be built. These innovations provoked significant opposition among conservative churchmen and scholars. Related to this effort was the *Richtige Harmonie der Vier Evangelisten, da die Geschichten, Werke und Reden Jesu Christi Unsers Herrn, in Ihrer Geziemand Natürlichen Ordnung . . .* (Tübingen, 1736) which comprised a chronologically based harmony of the Gospels.

Bengel's *Gnomen Novi Testamenti in Quo ex Nativa Verborum vi, Simplicitas, Profunditas, Concinnitas, Salubritas Sensuum Coelestium Indicatur* (Tübingen, 1742) was a brief commentary on the New Testament. The theological structures of the work are determined by Pietist foci. However, in this work, Bengel sought to establish the theological issues by appeal to the historical and grammatical data. This volume was eventually translated into German and English. It served as the base for JOHN WESLEY's *Notes on the New Testament* (London, 1755). Wesley drew heavily upon Bengel's work and updated it in light of his own reading. Through that revision, Bengel influenced Wesleyan, Holiness and Pentecostal exegesis.

Also important, albeit less influential in the long term, was a commentary on the *Apocalypse, Eklärte Offenbarung Johannis und Viel Mehr Jesu Christi* (Frankfurt, 1740), which also offered a new translation on the basis of a new critical edition of the text. This method, if not the analysis, would remain paradigmatic for historical critical commentaries. A series of sixty sermons on the

Apocalypse was also published: *Sechtig Erbauliche Reden Über die Offenbarung Johannis* (Stuttgart, 1748). Related to his interest in the *Apocalypse* was Bengel's concern about biblical chronology and predictive elements in the Bible. He wrote two major treatises addressing these concerns which attempted to combine the findings of theology, astronomy and historical studies to clarify theoretical problems which the Pietists had inherited from Joachim of Fiore: *Cyclus Cive de Anno Magno Solis, Lunae Stellarum, Consideratio ad Incrementum Doctrinae Propheticae Atque Astronomiae* (Ulm, 1745) and *Ordo Temporum a Principio per Periodos Oeconomiae Divinae Historicas Atque Propheticas ad Finem Usque Ita Deductus ut Tota Series et Quarumvis Partium Analogia . . . ex Scriptura V. et N.T . . . Documento* (Stuttgart, 1741). In these he established the chronology of the world from the biblical texts, and did not hesitate to predict future details of the life of the Church and world, including the 'Millenial Reign of Christ' which he indicated would begin in 1836. These works made him the founder of what has been called the 'Biblical-Prophetic School' in Protestant theology.

Bengel became involved in the process of differentiating between the Würtemberg and Herrnhut Pietist traditions. His *Abriss der so Gennanten Brüdergemeine* (Stuttgart, 1751), examined the doctrinal tendencies of Count ZINZENDORF and his followers, to sort out 'the good and the bad'. It was a dignified but severe critique of the separatist tendencies of eastern German Pietism. He was committed to maintaining a Pietist witness within the Established Church and within the mainstream of Protestant theology.

Bengel influenced not only the Wesleyan tradition, but all subsequent Pietist and evangelical traditions, as well as the development of biblical textual criticism as a scholarly tradition.

SELECT WRITINGS
J. A. Bengel, *Hinterlassen Predigten*, hrsg. J. C. F. Burk (Reutlingen, Germany, 1839)

BIBLIOGRAPHY
K. Aland, ed., *Pietismus und Bibel* (Witten, Germany, 1970)
J. C. F. Burk, *Dr. J. A. Bengel's Leben und Wirken* (Stuttgart, Germany, 1831)
F. Delitzsch, *Biblisch-Propehetische Theologie* (Leipzig, Germany, 1845)
M. Greschat, ed., *Orthodoxie und Pietismus* (Stuttgart, Germany, 1982)
G. Mälzer, *Die Werke der Württembergischen Pietisten des 17, und 18, Jahrhunderte* (Berlin, New York, 1972)
—, *Johann Albrecht Bengel, Leben und Werk* (Stuttgart, Germany, 1970)

DAVID BUNDY

Bennet, John (b. Hexworthy, Cornwall, England, *c*. 1675; d. North Tamerton, Cornwall, England, Oct. 1750). Anglican clergyman. Bennett entered Queens' College, Cambridge in 1693 (BA 1696/7; MA 1726), where he was contemporary of the Wesleys' father, Samuel. He became Perpetual Curate of North Tamerton in 1705, adding Tresmere in 1720 and Laneast in 1731 and holding all three until his death. Up to 1742 Bennett was a typical sporting parson, but in 1742 he was converted by GEORGE THOMSON's preaching of *sola fide* salvation. Like Thomson, he welcomed JOHN and CHARLES WESLEY and GEORGE WHITEFIELD to Cornwall and himself engaged in local itinerancy.

BIBLIOGRAPHY
CO (1877): 65
G. C. B. Davies, *The Early Cornish Evangelicals, 1735–60* (London, 1951)

ARTHUR POLLARD

Bennet, John (b. Chinley, Derbyshire, England, 1 March 1715; d. Chinley, England, 24 May 1759). Wesleyan itinerant and Independent minister. The son of a Presbyterian farmer, Bennet was converted through the preaching of DAVID TAYLOR on 1 January 1742, and in March 1743 became an itinerant preacher, developing a 'round' in Lancashire, West Yorkshire, the peak districts of Derbyshire and Cheshire, partly where Taylor had been before, although most of his sixty preaching places were new, for this was one of the earliest incursions of Methodism into the north. Initially Bennet preached as an Independent, although he had met JOHN WESLEY in 1742 through the good offices of the Countess of HUNTINGDON. However he attended the first Wesleyan Conference in 1744 and was named an assistant to Wesley from 1746. From 1749 he was responsible for Wesley's Cheshire circuit. About this time he pioneered the use of quarterly meetings, which subsequently became a characteristic feature of Wesleyan polity. His ministry benefited from Wesley's support and his theology became Arminian, and Wesley benefited from Bennet's advice about developments in the region. Nevertheless his Independent origins led him to expect a remarkable degree of freedom of thought and action. His pattern of ministry was to make links with those who had been awakened, draw them into societies, supply hymn-books, and preach generally in hired rooms, but occasionally in the open air.

Falling sick while visiting Newcastle on connexional business in 1746, he was nursed to health by GRACE MURRAY, who was in charge of the female house there, and gradually a romantic attachment between them grew. On 3 October 1749 CHARLES WESLEY presided at their wedding even though Grace had been pledged to John Wesley – a match which Charles was determined to avert. This move stung John Wesley, not only because of the loss of a bride, but also because in his view Bennet had betrayed him. Thereafter Wesley was less tolerant of Bennet's contact with WHITEFIELD and indications that he was developing Calvinist sympathies. His hostility pushed Bennet into the Calvinist camp, and on 31 December 1751 he renounced the Wesleyan connexion, accusing John Wesley of 'popery'. Most but not all of his societies remained faithful to Wesley, but he retained the support of the majority at Bolton and some other large societies, and continued a round which included Stockport and Woodley. Then he abandoned itinerating and removed to Warburton (Cheshire), and the erstwhile Methodist society there became an Independent church and he was probably ordained in November 1754. Indifferent health and a depressive personality may have inhibited the full flourishing of his work, but Bennet was one of the first Methodists to contribute to the emergence of a 'new' Dissent. He died in 1759 but his wife lived until 1803.

BIBLIOGRAPHY
H. D. Rack, 'Survival and Revival: John Bennet, Methodism and the Old Dissent', in *Protestant Evangelicalism* ed. K. Robbins, *Studies in Church History*, Subsidia 7 (Oxford, 1990)

PETER J. LINEHAM

Bennett, James   (b. London, 22 May 1774; d. London, 4 Dec. 1862). Congregational minister and historian. Unhappy with a business career he sought work in Bath, lodging with a family, part Moravian, part Methodist. There at 19 he was converted and WILLIAM JAY's preaching confirmed his call to the ministry. Bennett began preaching in November 1792 in the nearby villages and also then started a devotional diary.

He studied under DAVID BOGUE and in 1796 was called to serve a church at Romsey, Hampshire. The meeting house there was soon replaced by a new chapel where he preached for 17 years. He was a founder of the LMS, and worked with JAMES A. and ROBERT HALDANE on their evangelistic tours. He recommended JOHN ANGELL JAMES as minister to his future church at Birmingham when Bennett himself declined their invitation. In 1813 Bennett had spoken in favour of an independent society for the evangelization of London.

Also in that year he became principal of Rotherham college, and minister of Masbro' Chapel. Suffering breakdowns in health in 1821 and 1827, he accepted the call to the church at Silver Street, London, in 1828. A new chapel was built nearby in Falcon Square in 1842 while in 1840 Bennett became chairman of the Congregational Union. He knew several missionaries, including the young DAVID LIVINGSTONE who attended his church while studying in London. Bennett retired in 1860, dying two years later.

Bennett did much to raise the status of Nonconformity through his preaching and scholarship. His most important work is *The History of Dissenters* (written with David Bogue, 4 vols, London, 1808–12). He married Sarah Cowley in 1797 and was father of Sir Risdon Bennett.

BIBLIOGRAPHY
DNB
D. W. Lovegrove, *Established Church, Sectarian People* (Cambridge, 1988): 154

K. W. Wadsworth, *Yorkshire United Independent College* (London, 1954): 87–92

ALAN ARGENT

Benson, Christopher (b. Cockermouth, Cumberland, England, 16 Jan. 1788; d. Ross-on-Wye, Herefordshire, England, 26 March 1868). Anglican clergyman and writer. After school at Eton, Benson proceeded to Trinity College, Cambridge (BA 1805; MA. 1815). His first appointment was as Curate of St John's and St Nicholas's, Newcastle-upon-Tyne in 1811. In 1817 he preached before the university a series of sermons on baptism during the time of the controversy arising from Bishop Mant's views on the subject. These were subsequently published as *A Theological Enquiry into the Sacrament of Baptism and the Nature of Baptismal Regeneration* (1817).

Benson was establishing a reputation in Cambridge and besides being made a fellow of Magdalene in 1820, he was appointed in the same year first Hulsean lecturer (thirty years after the bequest was made to support work on Christian evidences). He again held this position in 1822, in which year also he was appointed by Lady BETTY HASTINGS to the vicarage of Ledsham (Yorkshire) (1822–7). He was also Vicar of St Giles-in-the-Fields (1824–6).

On his appointment as Canon of Worcester in 1825 he shortly thereafter became Vicar of Cropthorne in that diocese (1826–40) and also of Lindridge subsequently (1842–9). His major activity at this period, however, was as Master of the Temple (1826–45). From this pulpit he preached a series of *Discourses upon Tradition and Episcopacy* (1839), one of the earliest criticisms of the reliance upon tradition by JOHN HENRY NEWMAN, Pusey and other Tractarians. Indeed, Benson may well have been the first person to use this name for the adherents of the Oxford Movement. These sermons involved him in a controversy with F. Merewether, Rector of Cole Orton. Benson whose works also included *The Chronology of Our Saviour's Life* (1819) has been described as belonging to 'the broader evangelical school' (*DNB*).

BIBLIOGRAPHY
Al. Cant., II.i:235
DNB

ARTHUR POLLARD

Benson, Joseph (b. Mamerby, Cumberland, England, 25 Jan. 1748; d. London, 16 Feb. 1821). Wesleyan minister and connexional editor. Benson came from farming stock, but showed early signs of a studious nature. His father intended him for the church and he was given a thorough grounding in Hebrew and the classics by the local Presbyterian minister. At 16 he became a teacher at Gamblesby. Experiencing an evangelical conversion under the influence of a Methodist cousin, Joshua Watson, he sought out JOHN WESLEY, who was so impressed by him that he immediately made him classics master at Kingswood School.

Benson still had thoughts of ordination and preached from time to time to the Kingswood colliers. In 1769 he entered St Edmund Hall, Oxford, but his Methodist leanings prevented his being ordained by the Bishop of Worcester. After serving for a while as headmaster of the COUNTESS OF HUNTINGDON's college at Trevecca, in 1771 he eventually entered the Wesleyan itinerancy.

Benson was a rather sober character, of solemn appearance and manner – a feature which extended even to his courting of Sarah Thompson, whom he married in 1780. (Witness his love letters, edited by M.M. Jamison [Emory University, 1945].) Moral earnestness characterized most of his writings; and his preaching, though marked by simplicity and a passionate sincerity, was laboured. He was twice president of the conference, 1798, 1810, and also served as its secretary in 1805 and 1809. Despite his early disappointments, he remained a leader of the High Church Methodists opposed to separation from the church, and two of his sons entered the Anglican priesthood.

Wesley found in young Joseph a kindred spirit and corresponded with him extensively during the last twenty years of his life. His eagerness to 'redeem the time' and his studiousness caused Wesley to give him the uncharacteristic advice to avoid too much study. Despite this he maintained to the end the habits of his Kingswood days and was regularly to be found in his London study as early as 5 a.m. and as late as 11 p.m.

At the end of his second London ministry the three-year rule prevented his being re-appointed to the London circuit in 1803. Instead, he was made connexional editor, which enabled him to spend the rest of his ministry in the capital. In this capacity, he modernized and gave a new lease of life to the *Methodist Magazine* and edited collected editions of the works of JOHN W. FLETCHER 1806–8 and John Wesley 1809–13. His other publications include a commentary on the Bible, 1810, a number of sermons and *A Defence of the Methodists, in Five Letters Addressed to the Rev. Dr. Tatham* (London, 1793), *A Farther Defence of the Methodists . . .* (London, 1793), *A Vindication of the People Called Methodists . . .* (London, 1800), and *The Life of the Rev. John William de la Flechere . . .* (London, 1804).

BIBLIOGRAPHY
DNB
J. Macdonald, *Memoirs of the Rev. Joseph Benson* (London, 1822)
R. Treffry, *Memoirs of the Rev. Joseph Benson* (London, 1840)

JOHN A. VICKERS

Bentinck, Lord William (Cavendish) KB, GCB, GCH [Knight Grand Cross of the Guelphic Order of Honour] (b. London, 14 Sept. 1774; d. Paris, France, 17 June 1839). Army officer, MP, and Governor-General of India. The not particularly intellectual second son of the third Duke of Portland, William Bentinck entered the Coldstream Guards at age 17. He also served as his family's nominee for Nottinghamshire MP (1796–1803, 1816–26) until his appointment as Governor of Madras 1803–7 and as envoy to the court of Sicily 1811–15. To Bentinck's chagrin, the East India Company held him responsible for the Vellore mutiny, ostensibly a symbol of injudicious evangelical influence in India, and recalled him. Bold constitutional initiatives in Sicily and Italy also ended in his recall. Although a potential leader of radical reform in Parliament, Bentinck retreated to experiments in drainage of the fens.

Bentinck married Lady Mary Acheson, sister of Sir Archibald Acheson (*see* the second EARL OF GOSFORD) and Lady OLIVIA SPARROW. It was the evangelicalism of his wife's family – particularly his sister-in-law, the formidable Lady Olivia – which led Bentinck to join the BFBS. This influence was reflected in his term as Governor-General of India 1828–35. Though nicknamed 'The Clipping Dutchman' for his economies in that office, Bentinck also had the courage to legislate the abolition of *sati*, to supress the *Thags*, and to secure rights of property and employment to Christian converts from Hinduism and Islam. Forced by ill health to resign in March 1835, Bentinck returned to England, to become, in 1837, MP for radical, industrial Glasgow and to refuse a peerage.

BIBLIOGRAPHY
C. H. Philips, *The Correspondence of Lord William Cavendish Bentinck* (Oxford, 1977)
J. Rosselli, *Lord William Bentinck* (London, 1974)

NANCY G. CASSELS

Bentley, Roger (d. Oct. 1795). Anglican clergyman. Educated at Sidney Sussex College, Cambridge, Bentley was ordained 20 September 1760 in York. JOHN THORNTON, a wealthy friend of early Methodists and evangelicals, attempted to find livings for several of Bentley's contemporaries. Thornton first attempted to place Bentley in the parish of Cottingham near Hull, in 1767. The Bishop of Chester, patron of the living, wrote to the Archbishop of York, enquiring whether there was 'anything of a methodistical cast' about Bentley. The bishop was anxious not to present 'an improper person' under which the category of 'methodistical' clergy evidently fell. Bentley did not get the living.

By 1769 Thornton had succeeded in having Bentley made Vicar of St Giles, Camberwell in Surrey. In 1789, Bentley suffered a stroke and his son-in-law, John King (born 1766), took over. In 1790, on the death of Thornton, Bentley was made a trustee of Thornton's Trust by his will. Bentley died in 1795, and Camden Chapel, Peckham, was founded after his death 'by those of his congregation who were dissatisfied with the preaching of his successor which was not of that Evangelical character to which they had been accustomed'. The chapel remained part of the parish and Christ Church, Old Kent Road, appears also to have been an evangelical addition to the parish because of its patronage by Miss Hyndman's Bounty later.

BIBLIOGRAPHY
Al. Cant.
Clergy List (London, 1851)
DNB
J. D. Walsh, 'The Yorkshire Evangelicals in the Eighteenth Century: with Especial Reference to Methodism' (Cambridge Univ. Ph.D. thesis, 1956)

WESLEY D. BALDA

Benton, John (b. Wyrley Bank, Staffordshire, England, 1785; d. 1856) Primitive Methodist minister. John was converted at the age of 19 in 1805. At first he preached for the Wesleyans but fell in with HUGH BOURNE who persuaded him to become a Primitive itinerant in 1810. In 1811 he handed over to Bourne a number of societies which he had established and these became the nucleus of the Darlaston circuit. A passionate evangelist he refused to be bound by the Tunstall Non-Mission Law, and led revival work in Staffordshire where the Ramsor circuit arose out of his labours, through into Derbyshire in the 'great revival' of 1817–18 (it was while he was preaching in the open air in Belper that the Primitives were first called Ranters) and thence into Nottingham, Grantham and Leicester. A coal-pit owner and landowner he had independent means and published an edition of the *Small Hymn Book* (Warrington 1818), but later, afflicted by throat trouble, caused by his efforts to quell a panic at a camp meeting, he ceased to itinerate.

BIBLIOGRAPHY
G. Herod, *Historical and Biographical Sketches* (London, no date but 1855)
PMMag (1908): 795f

IAN SELLERS

Benton, Joseph A(ugustine) (b. Guilford, CT, USA, 7 May 1818; d. Oakland, CA, USA, 8 April 1892). Congregationalist pastor, author, and educator. Benton attended Yale College and Theological School, where he became a theological disciple of NATHANIEL W. TAYLOR. He journeyed to California as part of the Gold Rush of 1849. Settling in Sacramento, he organized and pastored the First Church of Christ (1849–63). In 1851 he became one of the founding editors of the San Francisco *Pacific*, the Pacific Coast's earliest permanent religious periodical. Two years later, Benton published *The California Pilgrim*, a Bunyanesque moralistic critique of the cosmopolitan society of California. Benton spent the latter decades of his life (1869–90) as a member of the founding faculty of the Pacific Theological Seminary, the oldest Protestant seminary west of the Mississippi River. Manuscript and published material of Benton is available in the archives of the Pacific School of Religion, Berkeley, California, and in the California State Library, Sacramento, California.

BIBLIOGRAPHY
H. E. Hgue, *Christian Seed in Western Soil* (Berkeley, CA, 1965): 7, 11, 33, 56, 231, 233–9

DOUGLAS FIRTH ANDERSON

Berkhout, James John Teding van (b. Amsterdam, 4 Dec. 1814; d. Amsterdam, 25 July 1880). Dutch jurist, scientist, and seminary professor. After studies in the philosophy faculty of the Athenaeum in Amsterdam (1831–3), Berkhout studied at the University of Leiden where he graduated in 1839 with a doctorate in law with the thesis entitled 'De Mutata a Guilielmo IV Regiminis Forma in Republicae Foederati Belgii Provinciis Post Rerum Conversionem Anni 1747' (Leiden, 1839). In 1843 Berkhout received a doctorate in mathematics and natural science with the thesis 'Dissertatio Physica Inauguralis, de Fluxubus Thermo-Electricis, Acusmagneticae ope Observatis' (Leiden, 1843).

He established himself as a lawyer in Amsterdam with his brother P. J. Teding van Berkhout. In sympathy and correspondence with the positions articulated by GUILLAUME GROEN VAN PRINSTERER, and ABRAHAM KUYPER, he entered the political and ecclesial arenas. Active in the *Revéil*, he served as professor of logic and Dutch history at the independent and innovative Scottish Reformed Seminary in Amsterdam (1851–61). He was, for a number of years, a member of the Amsterdam City Council.

In 1873 he was elected to the Tweede Kamer (Second Chamber) of the Dutch Parliament where he remained until his death in 1880. Despite the teaching and political activity he was active in scholarly work publishing *De Vraag, of de Methode, in de Natuurkundige Wetenschap Gebruikt, Bruikbaar Kan Geacht Wordern Voor Andere Wetenschappen* (Amsterdam, 1866) and a volume on educational theory entitled *Gedachten en Wenschen Omtrent de Inrichting Van Het Wiskundig Onderwijs op de Scholen* (Amsterdam, 1866). He was also a frequent contributor to newspapers and other periodical publications.

BIBLIOGRAPHY
B. de Gaay Fortman, 'Teding van Berkhout, James John', *Nieuw Nederlandsch Biographisch Woordenboek*, 6 (1933): 1109–10
M. E. Kluit, *Het Reveil in Nederland, 1815–1865 en Daarbuiten* (Amsterdam, 1970)
R. Kuiper, *Zelfbeeld en Wereldbeeld* (Kampen, Netherlands, 1992)
H. J. W. Mulder, *Groen van Prinsterer, Staatsman en Profeet* (Franeker, Netherlands, 1973)

DAVID BUNDY

Bernard, Sir **Thomas** (b. Lincoln, Lincolnshire, England, 27 April 1750; d. Royal Leamington Spa, Warwickshire, England, 1 July 1818). Philanthropist. The second surviving son of Sir Francis Bernard (1712–79, *DNB*), governor of Massachusetts Bay colony, he was educated at Harvard and was for a time his father's private secretary. He returned to England, studied law and was called to the Bar at the Middle Temple in 1780. He accumulated a fortune as a conveyancer and married a wealthy heiress. Bernard retired early to dedicate his considerable energy and wealth to philanthropic causes. He co-founded with WILLIAM WILBERFORCE and others the Society for Bettering the Condition of the Poor (1796), which then became virtually identified with him, so dominant was he in its affairs. He was prominent as well in over a score of other evangelical societies, especially the Foundling Hospital, and the Philanthropic, Marine, Stranger's Friend, and British and Foreign Bible societies. He was strenuous in his support of Henry Bankes's efforts to repeal the salt duties. Indeed, few social welfare or religious schemes in his period did not benefit from his valued assistance.

BIBLIOGRAPHY
Annual Biography and Obituary (1819): 116–39
F. K. Brown, *Fathers of the Victorians* (Cambridge, 1953)
GM (July 1818): 82–83

JONATHAN BURKE CUTMORE

Bernau, John Henry (b. Stople, Pomerania, *c.* 1805; d. 14 June 1890). CMS missionary to British Guiana [now Guyana]. Bernau trained at the Basel Seminary and from 1832 at the CMS training school at Islington (London). He was ordained (deacon 1833, priest 1834) by the Bishop of London and was sent out to Berbice in 1835 and then in 1837 apparently was assigned to work with CHARLES CARTER and JOHN ARMSTRONG who had been serving as lay missionaries at Bartica Grove since 1827. He served there until May 1853, apart from a two-year furlough in England (July 1845 to June 1847). From 1856 he served as minister of All Saints' Church, Belvedere. Bernau wrote of his experience in *Missionary Labours in British Guiana*. He married: 1) Anna Maria Pasche in 1831 (died 1845); 2) Maria Stephen in 1847 (died 1891).

BIBLIOGRAPHY
D. T. B[arry], *CMS Register of Missionaries and Native Clergy* (privately printed) (London, 1906)

DONALD M. LEWIS

Berridge, John (b. Kingston, Nottinghamshire, England, 1 March 1716; d. Everton, Bedfordshire, England, 22 January 1793). Anglican clergyman. Berridge, a man of imposing presence, strong voice, and witty expression, was one of the few and earliest of Anglican peregrinating preachers. He attracted great crowds to his performances, but some of more reserved temperament like ROBERT HOUSMAN found in him 'the uncouth extravagances of a fermentitious faith' (Housman, 1841: xxv). JOHN WESLEY considered him 'one of the most simple as well as most sensible men', while a more modern commentator, speaking of his preaching style, described it as 'plain; the points in his argument boldly underlined; the

language simple, colloquial, and sometimes jocular, but never trifling' (Smyth, 1940: 182). Something of the power which Berridge sought may be inferred from a letter to CHARLES SIMEON: 'When you open your Commission, begin with ripping up the Audience, and Moses will lend you a Carving Knife, which may be often whetted at his Grind-Stone. Lay open the universal sinfulness of nature'; but he went on: 'When your Hearers have been well harrowed, and the clumps begin to fall ... Let them know that all the Treasures of Grace are lodged in Jesus Christ, for the use of poor needy sinners' (*Arminian Magazine*, September 1794, XVII: 496–8, quoted in Smyth, 1940: 276–8).

Berridge entered Clare Hall, Cambridge, in 1734 (BA 1738; MA 1742) and held a resident fellowship till 1755, for the last six years being also Curate of Stapleford. He was preferred to the college living of Everton in 1758, where he remained for the rest of his life. He experienced an evangelical conversion around Christmas 1757. Of the preceding period he wrote: 'I preached of sanctification very earnestly for six years in a former Parish and never brought one soul to Christ. I did the same at this Parish for two years, without any success at all; but as soon as ever I preached Jesus Christ and Faith in his Blood, the Believers were added to the Church continually' (Whittingham, 1838: 356–7). Berridge's position appears to have been Arminian until about 1768–9, but, following an illness, he adopted Calvinistic views which were somewhat moderated later.

Not long after his conversion Berridge met both Wesley and GEORGE WHITEFIELD, the latter of whom declared that 'Mr Berridge who was lately awakened promises to be a burning and a shining light' (Tyerman, 1876: 410). He visited Whitefield's tabernacle in Tottenham Court Road, London, every year; and within three weeks of meeting Wesley in June 1758 he began to itinerate, sometimes with his friend William Hicks of Wrestlingworth. Besides preaching four times each Sunday at Everton, beginning at seven in the morning, Berridge travelled around his own and adjoining counties, delivering between 10 and 12 sermons and regularly riding over 100 miles per week. His invasion of other parishes called down upon him the censure of his bishop, but this in no way moderated his diligence.

In this preaching he appears to have deliberately sought emotional effects. Thus in one letter he speaks of 'the presence of the Lord [being] wonderfully among us. There was abundance of weeping and strong crying' (Whittingham, 1838: 50), while an eyewitness describes the 'mixture of various sounds, some shrieking, some roaring aloud. The most general was a loud breathing, like that of people, half strangled and gasping for life ... Great numbers wept without any noise; others fell down as dead; some sinking in silence; some with extreme noise and violent agitation' (Whittingham, 1838: 46). These displays of mass emotionalism were particularly evident in the periods 20–4 May and 9–23 July 1759.

Berridge was unmarried and had quite strong views on the subject. Thus he wrote to Lady HUNTINGDON: 'Matrimony has quite maimed poor Charles [Wesley] and might have spoiled John [Wesley] and George [Whitefield] if a wise Master had not graciously sent them a brace of ferrets ... Eight or nine years ago, having been grievously tormented with housekeeping, I truly had thought of looking out for a Jezebel myself' (23 March 1770 in Whittingham, 1838). Seeking assistance in prayer, he found direction against it in Jeremiah 16:2!

Berridge's own beliefs are contained in his *The Christian World Unmasked: Pray Come and Peep* (1773), a long quasi-dialogue written in what even his admiring critic, J. C. RYLE, has to admit is 'a very unrefined style'. It was answered by JOHN W. FLETCHER of Madeley in the first two parts of his *Fifth Check to Antinomianism*. Berridge numbered among his friends and correspondents JOHN THORNTON, JOHN NEWTON and HENRY VENN, while Simeon preached his funeral sermon. His tombstone in Everton Church contains a brief biography, not altogether accurate in its dates, but recording how Berridge was 'born in sin February 1716. Remained ignorant of [his] fallen state till 1730. Lived proudly on faith and works for salvation till 1754 ... Fled to Jesus alone for refuge, 1756'.

BIBLIOGRAPHY
DNB
R. F. Housman, *The Life and Remains of Robert Housman* (London, 1841)
J. C. Ryle, *The Christian Leaders of the Last Century* (London, 1868)
C. H. E. Smyth, *Simeon and Church Order* (Cambridge, 1940)
L. Tyerman, *The Life and Times of George Whitefield*, 2 vols, II (London, 1876)
R. Whittingham, ed., *The Works of J. Berridge ... with Memoir* (London, 1838)

ARTHUR POLLARD

Best, Thomas (b. Cradley, Worcestershire, England, 23 June 1787; d. Sheffield, England, 10 March 1865). Anglican clergyman. After Birmingham Grammar School Best proceeded to Worcester College, Oxford (BA 1810; MA 1816). He was a successor to JONATHAN STUBBS as curate of Uttoxeter and then became Archdeacon EDWARD SPENCER's curate at Chipping Campden. He was preferred to the incumbency of St James, Sheffield (1817–65) where he spent the rest of his life in a diligent ministry which included three lectures weekly. He also preached against the theatre. He is said to have been a simple, scholarly man, proficient in Greek and Hebrew.

BIBLIOGRAPHY
Al. Ox. I: 103
CO, new series, 330: 475

ARTHUR POLLARD

Bethune, Joanna [née Graham] (b. Fort Niagara, Canada, 1 Feb. 1770; d. New York, 28 July 1860). Teacher and leader in the Sunday school movement. Daughter of British army surgeon John Graham and Isabella Marshall (*see* ISABELLA GRAHAM) Joanna was reared in Scotland. She studied education for two years in Rotterdam, supported by evangelical reformer Lady GLENORCHY. She then taught in Isabella's school in Edinburgh. In 1789 they moved to New York. There Joanna joined the Presbyterian Church and in July 1795 married merchant Divie Bethune. In 1806 Joanna founded the Orphan Asylum Society, serving on its board for fifty years.

In 1803 the Bethunes, with Mrs Graham, founded several Sunday schools in New York. In 1816, prompted by the work of ROBERT RAIKES, Mrs Bethune organized the Female Union Society for the Promotion of Sabbath-Schools. The society merged with the ASSU, founded in 1824, under the Bethunes' leadership. After Divie's death in 1824, Joanna devoted herself to childhood education, founding the Infant School Society in New York in 1827.

BIBLIOGRAPHY
G. Bethune, *Memoirs of Mrs Joanna Bethune* (New York, 1863)
NAW

NANCY A. HARDESTY

Bethune, John (b. Parish of Sleat, Skye, Scotland, 1751; d. Williamstown, Glengarry, Upper Canada, 23 Sept. 1815). Presbyterian minister. Bethune was the founder of Montreal's first Presbyterian church and the first Presbyterian preacher in Upper Canada (Ontario). He was educated at King's College, Aberdeen University. In 1773 he emigrated to South Carolina as a licentiate of the Church of Scotland. At the outbreak of the American War of Independence in 1776 the North Carolina Highlanders formed a regiment loyal to the King and Bethune became their chaplain. After a short imprisonment he moved to Nova Scotia where on 30 September 1782 he married Veronica Wadden from Switzerland; they had four sons and three daughters. At the end of the war he settled in Montreal along with other United Empire Loyalists and formed St Gabriel Street Church. In 1787 he moved to Glengarry County, Upper Canada, and began a fruitful ministry among Scottish Highlanders. He quickly organized churches in Williamstown, Martintown, Summerstown, Cornwall and Lancaster. He was buried at Williamstown.

BIBLIOGRAPHY
Fasti
J. MacKenzie, 'John Bethune: The Founder of Presbyterianism in Upper Canada', in *Called To Witness*, ed. W. S. Reid, 1 (Toronto, 1975)

STEWART D. GILL

Betts, William Keeling (b. Colchester, Essex, England, c. 1800; d. England, Nov. 1865). CMS missionary to Sierra Leone and Jamaica. Betts studied for a year

(1824–5) as a probationer missionary under Reverend W. Plume of Baxford and then received some training at the newly established CMS College (1825). He was ordained (deacon and priest 1825) by the Bishop of London and on 12 January 1826 was sent to Sierra Leone, serving there (with two furloughs to England) until 1833. In April 1834 he went to Jamaica where the CMS had unsuccessfully attempted to start a work in 1825 (*see* THOMAS JONES and HENRY C. TAYLOR) and again in 1827 (*see* E. COLLINS and W. MANNING). In 1835 he was joined by C. L. F. HÄNSEL. Betts returned to England in 1840 and closed his connection with the CMS. From 1860 Betts was Rector of Felbrigge with Metton, Norfolk.

Betts married: 1) Mary Paul (died Sierra Leone, March 1826), the sister of James Paul, Hannah and Eliza; 2) Mary Anne Moore (widow of CHRISTOPHER TAYLOR) on 20 February 1829 (died 4 Nov. 1838).

BIBLIOGRAPHY
D. T. B[arry], *CMS Register of Missionaries and Native Clergy* (privately printed) (London, 1906)

DONALD M. LEWIS

Bevan, Bridget (b. Derllys Court, Carmarthenshire, Wales, 1698; d. Laugharne, Carmarthenshire, Wales, 11 Dec. 1779). Patron of Welsh circulating schools. The youngest daughter of John Vaughan, who was involved in the supervision of the SPCK's schools in Carmarthenshire, she was baptized 30 October 1698. In 1721 she married Arthur Bevan (died 1743), a barrister and MP for Carmathen (1727–41).

When GRIFFITH JONES established his circulating schools during the 1730s, she became his chief patron and adviser. Following the death of his wife, she invited him to make his home at her house in Laugharne, where he remained until his death in 1761. Her patronage of the schools continued, and in her will she bequeathed £10,000 to secure their future. The will was contested and the money withheld by the Chancery Court. However, during her lifetime, her contribution to the development of the circulating schools was immense.

BIBLIOGRAPHY
DWB

GERAINT TUDUR

Bevan, (Emma) Frances [née Shuttleworth] (b. Oxford, England, 25 Sept. 1827; d. Cannes, France, 13 Feb. 1909). Translator of German hymns. Her father, P. N. SHUTTLEWORTH, became the anti-Tractarian Bishop of Chichester. Despite that, Frances was at first a High-Churchwoman. After marrying the evangelical Anglican R. C. L. BEVAN in 1856 she associated with Open Brethren. Her convictions resembled his except that she withdrew more completely from the world. She was a good artist and a gifted author. She spoke French and German

well and, when over seventy, still rose every morning at 8.30 to read Hebrew.

From 1858 onwards she published several collections, mainly paraphrases from the German mystics and pietists, e.g. 'Sinners Jesus will receive'. *Hymns of Ter Steegen, Suso and Others* (2 vols London, 1894–7, reprinted 1920) contained many of her translations, e.g. 'As the bridegroom to his chosen' (now in at least five current British hymn-books) and original hymns, e.g. 'The Gospel according to Paul'. A stanza from this inspired Brethren missionaries: 'Christ, the Son of God, hath sent me / Through the midnight lands; / Mine the mighty ordination / Of the piercéd Hands' (*Hymns of TSS*, 1, 1894: 142). She wrote often anonymously or over the initials of one of her several houses. 'Midst the darkness, storm, and sorrow' (an original hymn) was signed 'P[rinces] G[ate]' and therefore misattributed to Paul Gerhardt. Much of her work was devotional poetry rather than congregational hymnody.

BIBLIOGRAPHY
J. S. Andrews, 'As the bridegroom to his chosen', *Hymn Society Bulletin*, no. 118 (Spring 1970): 84
—, 'Frances Bevan, Translator', *EQ*, 34 (1962): 206–13; 35 (1963): 30–8
—, 'Sinners Jesus will receive', *EQ*, 55 (1983): 223–30
Julian: 139, 1506

JOHN S. ANDREWS

Bevan, Favell Lee [Mrs Thomas Mortimer] *see* MORTIMER, FAVELL LEE [née Bevan]

Bevan, George (b. Fosbury, Wiltshire, England, 22 Sept. 1782; d. Hampstead, London, England, 12 Dec. 1819). Anglican clergyman. He was the fifth son of SILVANUS BEVAN and was educated at Trinity College, Cambridge (BA 1813) and admitted to Lincoln's Inn, 21 January 1805. He married Ann, daughter of Andrew Buchanan of Glasgow on 22 September 1816. He was ordained and became Curate of Stratton Park, Hampshire.

Bevan participated in the Western Schism of 1815 and was rebaptized, May 1816, by immersion by GEORGE BARING at the Octagon Chapel, Taunton, where he became a minister. In 1818, he published a work defending his highly unorthodox Trinitarian doctrines. In the following year, he published a second work, and denied (to the *Christian Observer*) the charge of antinomianism. He remained estranged from the Church of England, dying prematurely in 1819.

BIBLIOGRAPHY
Al. Cant.
Burke's
GM (1819)
G. Carter, 'Evangelical Seceders from the Church of England, *c.* 1800–50' (Oxford Univ. D.Phil. thesis, 1990): 164–218

GRAYSON CARTER

Bevan, Joseph Gurney (b. London, 18 Feb. 1753; d. Stoke Newington, London, 12 Sept. 1814). Quaker minister and writer. Bevan retired from his father's business as a chemist and druggist in 1794 to devote most of his energies to the Society of Friends. An elder for many years he was essentially evangelical, conservative, and very influential, especially as a writer. He became clerk of the London yearly meeting in 1794. He played an important part in the controversy with the American visitor Hannah Barnard who was charged with denying the authority of scripture. His publications included *A Refutation of Some of the More Modern Misrepresentations of the Society of Friends . . .* [with] *A Summary of the History, Doctrine and Discipline of Friends* (London, 1800) prepared for the Meeting for Sufferings with the latter part also translated into French, Italian and German.

BIBLIOGRAPHY

Anon., *Extracts From the Letters and Other Writings of the Late Joseph Gurney Bevan Preceded by a Short Memoir of his Life* (London, 1821)
DNB
Dictionary of Quaker Biography (typescript, Friends' House Library, London)
J. Smith, *A Descriptive Catalogue of Friends' Books*, 2 vols (London, 1867)

DAVID J. HALL

Bevan, Robert Cooper Lee (b. 9 Feb. 1809, Walthamstow, Essex, England; d. East Barnet, Hertfordshire, England, 22 July 1890). Banker and philanthropist. The son of David Bevan and the brother of F. L. MORTIMER, he was educated at Harrow and Trinity College, Oxford, which he left when his father had a stroke. Aged twenty, he became a partner and eventually chairman of Barclays, the family bank. A Justice of the Peace for Middlesex, he was the leader of the City of London Private Bankers and, 1874–90, chairman of the Committee of London Clearing Bankers. In 1836 he married Lady Agneta Elizabeth Yorke, like himself an evangelical Anglican. The daughter of an admiral and the sister of the fourth Earl of Hardwicke, she was descended from two Lord Chancellors. She died in 1851 leaving him with four sons and two daughters. In 1856 he married EMMA FRANCES SHUTTLEWORTH, daughter of P. N. SHUTTLEWORTH.

At the age of 27, partly through the preaching of BAPTIST W. NOEL and his mother's and his sister's influence, he underwent a conversion which resulted in his abandoning favourite pleasures such as hunting. He worked with Lord SHAFTESBURY to improve working conditions. He was a co-founder and treasurer of the EA and supported many religious and philanthropic societies, including the CMS, the LCM, and the YMCA. He wrote over his initials three short works: *Accommodated Texts* (London, 1854), *Christ and Temptation* (London, 1879), and *Texts Misquoted and Misapplied* (London, 1877).

In the general election of 1847 Bevan ran for Parliament against Lord John Russell, the Whig Prime Minister, in the City of London. Although unsuccessful, Bevan was effective in forcing Russell to pledge not to bring forward any further endowment of Roman Catholicism in the wake of the Maynooth Controversy of 1845.

BIBLIOGRAPHY

J. S. Andrews, 'The Recent History of the Bevan Family', *EQ*, 33 (1961): 81–92
[E. F. Bevan], *A Few Recollections of Robert Lee Bevan* (London, 1892)
Boase
C. Calver, 'A Critical Investigation into the Developing Activities of the British Organization of the Evangelical Alliance' (London Bible Coll., forthcoming thesis)
A. N. Gamble, *A History of the Bevan Family* (London, 1924): ch. 6
ILN (2 August 1890): 134
P. W. Matthews, *History of Barclays Bank* (London, 1926): 45
The Times (24 July 1890): 9
J. Wolffe, *The Protestant Crusade in Great Britain* (Oxford, 1991): 225

JOHN S. ANDREWS AND DONALD M. LEWIS

Bevan, Silvanus (b. London, 3 Aug. 1743; d. Brighton, England, 25 Jan. 1830). Banker and philanthropist. The Quaker, Silvanus Bevan (1691–1765), set up a pharmacy in London. He was joined by his brother Timothy (1704–86), who married Elizabeth. Of their sons three were named Silvanus, two of whom died in infancy.

According to the digest register of the Friends London and Middlesex quarterly meeting the survivor was born on 3 August 1743, not 3 October (*pace* Gamble 1924: 44). He was educated at Hackney, probably at a Quaker school. After two years at the pharmacy he joined what eventually became Barclays Bank. In 1769 he married a 17-year-old Quaker, Isabella Wakefield, who died soon afterwards. In 1773 he married a non-Quaker, Louisa Kendall, and was disowned by the society. Among their descendants were F. L. MORTIMER and R. C. L. BEVAN.

Silvanus was known as a successful banker and a keen huntsman, who farmed much of his own property. He generously supported many evangelical and philanthropic causes (Brown, 1961: 236, 241–2, 342, 405). Brown thought it worth noting (429) that one such cause was *not* supported by him. Bevan's Christian name was misspelled by Brown. Jenkins's 'Sylvanus' (1884: 190) might be intended for the fellow of the Royal Society who contributed to the Society's *Philosophical Trans.* in 1743 [but cf. the reference to 'Silvanus' (1743–1830) in Frost's footnote to Jenkins].

BIBLIOGRAPHY

J. S. Andrews, 'The Recent History of the Bevan Family', *EQ*, 33 (1961): 81–92
F. K. Brown, *Fathers of the Victorians* (Cambridge, 1961)
A. M. Gamble, *A History of the Bevan Family* (London, [1924])
Information from Friends House Library, Euston Road, London
J. Jenkins, *Records and Recollections of James Jenkins (1753–1831)*, ed. J. W. Frost (New York, 1984): 189–90
'The Quaker Family of Bevan', *JFHS*, 22 (1925), 15–17

JOHN S. ANDREWS

Bevan, Thomas (b. near Aberaeron, Dyfed, Wales, 1795; d. Tamatave, Madagascar, 31 Jan. 1819). Pioneer missionary to Madagascar. A member of Neuadd-lwyd Independent Church, he was trained for the ministry in a school run by his minister, Dr THOMAS PHILLIPS. After being accepted by the LMS he had further training at Gosport. He was ordained at his home church for overseas service on 21 August 1817. He married Miss Mary Jones of Pen-yr-alltwen, Neuadd-lwyd, and together sailed with DAVID JONES and his wife on 9 February 1818, arriving at Port Louis, Mauritius on 3 July. On 8 August he and David Jones made a short first visit to Madagascar. He returned there with his family arriving at Tamatave on 27 December 1818 to find Mrs David Jones and her child had died of fever. The child of the Bevans died on 20 January 1819, followed by Thomas Bevan on 31 January and his wife on 3 February.

BIBLIOGRAPHY
G. P. Griffith, *Cenhadon Cymreig* (Cardiff, 1897)
LMS Register of Missionaries 1796–1923, 4th edn (London, 1923)

IEUAN S. JONES

Bevan, William (b. Islington, London, 3 Sept. 1812; d. Canonbury, London, England, 4 June 1874). Congregational minister. From an Anglican background he adopted Congregational principles and joined Union Chapel, Islington, and trained for the Congregational ministry at Highbury. During his early ministry he revived ailing churches in Wellingborough, Northamptonshire (1835–7), and in Liverpool (1837–47). He moved to London in 1847 at the request of Sir CULLING EARDLEY to be secretary to the embryonic EA, which he gave a sound administrative base (1847–9). Returning to his primary calling of the pastorate, he served in Wolverhampton from 1849 retiring because of ill health in 1860, but this restored he revived the church in Bow (1867–74), which under his ministry grew from 49 to 345 members. He sat on the committee of Hackney College.

BIBLIOGRAPHY
Congregational Year Book, 1875

J. H. Y. BRIGGS

Beverley, Robert Mackenzie (b. Beverley, Yorkshire, England, *c.* 1796; d. Scarborough, Yorkshire, England, 3 Nov. 1868). Seceder and polemicist. Son of William Beverley he was educated briefly and unhappily at Eton, and was admitted as a pensioner at Trinity College, Cambridge in 1814 (at age 18), taking his LL B in 1821. Induced by his gambling father to sign away any claim on the family estate, he was subsequently both impoverished and embittered. In the quest for a spiritual church he turned to Dissent and in the 1840s was associated with Brethren like the HOWARD brothers but eventually,

disillusioned by their strife, attended no place of worship. His pamphlets against the Establishment, one of which was described in *The Times* as 'invidious, envenomed and offensive', were notorious in their time. He was a Justice of the Peace and Deputy-Lieutenant for the East Riding of Yorkshire.

BIBLIOGRAPHY
Al. Cant.
R. M. Beverley, *Posthumous Letters of the Rev. Rabshakeh Gathercoal* (London, 1837) [The copy in the Bodleian, Oxford contains two autograph letters and a manuscript biographical note by Eliot Howard.]
Greater London Record Office, Howard Papers Acc. 1017/1524–37

TIMOTHY C. F. STUNT

Bexley, Lord. *See* VANSITTART, NICHOLAS

Bicheno, James (b. *c.* 1752; d. Newbury, Berkshire, England, 9 April 1831). Baptist minister and writer on prophecy. Little is known of his early years. In 1768, he joined Robert Robinson's church, in Cambridge, where he worked as a glover. Within 18 months he had been expelled, though the reason is not clear. It was another four years before he was restored to fellowship. Meanwhile, he had been 'kidnapped into America', sold to a planter and reduced to extreme misery. After his restoration he felt called to the ministry, though the Cambridge church was not prepared to recommend him to Bristol Academy until April 1776. A man of considerable gifts, Bicheno made a great impression on the Falmouth church during his college course. Early in 1780, he accepted an invitation to the pastorate at Newbury, where he stayed for 27 years. From 1811 till 1819 he served the Cote church, retiring thence to Newbury. A 'paralytic affection' in August 1824 deprived him of his powers of speech and movement for the rest of his life. Scanty information is available concerning his public ministry, his main interest being the interpretation of prophecy. His best known work on the subject was *The Signs of the Times.* He believed that he was living in the days described in Revelation 16: 13–15, and that the Second Coming of Christ was imminent.

BIBLIOGRAPHY
BaptMag (1831)
W. J. Lewenden, *Notes on Newbury Baptists* (Newbury, England, 1940)
E. A. Payne, *The Baptists of Berkshire* (London, 1951)
Whitley, *BB*

E. F. CLIPSHAM

Bicheno, James Ebenezer (b. Newbury, Berkshire, England, 1785; d. Hobart, Tasmania, Australia, 15 Dec. 1851). Author and colonial administrator in Australia. The only surviving son of the Reverend JAMES BICHENO, he wrote an early essay on *Benevolence* attacking the current administration of the Poor Laws (1817, republished 1824). His *Philosophy of Criminal Jurisprudence* (1819) attacked the severity of contemporary penalties arguing that the colonies should not be 'burdened with the refuse of our prisons'. Called to the Bar in 1822, he worked on the Oxford circuit. He served on a commission under Archbishop Whateley to investigate the conditions of the Irish poor, appending to its final report of 1836 the judgement that there could be no solution to Ireland's problems without a large measure of self-help. In 1830 he had written *Ireland and Its Economy*. In September 1842 he was appointed colonial secretary in Van Dieman's Land and seems to have fulfilled his duties to the joint satisfaction of imperial authority and the colonists. He also undertook botanical observations and from 1825–32 was secretary of the Linnaeum Society.

BIBLIOGRAPHY
DNB
R. C. Walton 'Two Baptist Pamphleteers', *BQ*, X (1940): 209–14

J. H. Y. BRIGGS

Bickersteth, Edward (b. Kirkby Lonsdale, Westmoreland, England, 19 March 1786; d. Watton, Hertfordshire, England, 28 Feb. 1850). Anglican clergyman, author, and missionary statesman. Born into the cultivated home of a country surgeon, Bickersteth was educated at the local grammar school until aged 14. He then followed a brother to London, working first at the Post Office before becoming an articled law clerk. In 1812, he set up practice as a solicitor with his brother-in-law, THOMAS BIGNOLD, in Norwich, though thoughts of ordination had already been entertained. During his decade in London, Bickersteth, who had been raised as an earnest Anglican, gradually imbibed evangelical convictions and involved himself in the missionary activism of his spiritual mentors, HENRY BUDD and JOSIAH PRATT. Underpinning Bickersteth's evangelicalism was both theological reading, and a rigorous spiritual discipline drawn from traditional Anglicanism and evangelical pietism.

Having initiated a CMS auxiliary in Norwich against considerable odds, Bickersteth was invited by CMS to head an investigation into its mission work in Sierra Leone. Though lacking a university degree, Bickersteth was ordained a deacon by the accommodating Bishop Bathurst of Norwich and later ordained priest by HENRY RYDER, the evangelical Bishop of Gloucester. On returning from his epoch-making visit to West Africa, Bickersteth became CMS deputation secretary and head of its missionary training college. Though not a natural orator, Bickersteth stirred the British public's interest in mission by his passion, persuasion and deep integrity. He was a pioneer in the development of nationwide, grass-roots support for the multitude of religious societies mushrooming in Britain during the first quarter of the nineteenth century, an innovation in English social life, exploited to the full by the Anglican evangelicals, but bitterly opposed by the 'High and Dry' Anglicans. Thus Bickersteth was not only a major spokesman for overseas mission, but also a key itinerant ambassador for evangelicalism at home. In 1824 he succeeded Pratt as principal secretary at CMS. When he left CMS in 1830 he had become nationally and internationally known as an evangelical leader.

From 1816 onwards, Bickersteth's reputation (and personal income) was increasingly enlarged by his success as an author. Most of his devotional material sold in the hundreds of thousands, at home and abroad. Though he was not an original thinker, he was a competent distiller of theological issues, able to draw on the riches of the Patristic Fathers, the Protestant Reformers, classical Anglican divines and evangelical expositors. He drew also from medieval and Catholic devotional material.

A Scripture Help, his first publication, was written to aid the new recipients of cheap Bibles produced by the BFBS. The tone was popular and practical: 'Far would the writer be from finding fault with the labours of the learned, to whom we are so much indebted ... whilst they do not neglect the practical application of the truth' (Bickersteth, 1816: 134). In later editions Bickersteth nowhere commits himself to a precise doctrine of scriptural inspiration, though this issue was the subject of great debate in evangelical circles.

Bickersteth's *Treatise on the Lord's Supper* (1822), presented a thoughtful commentary on the Anglican liturgy, but also a plea for a more central place for this sacrament in congregational life and in the spiritual experience of the individual. Not a mere memorial, the supper was 'a participation, a communication, or enjoyment of the body and blood of Christ', a real Communion which, Bickersteth admitted, too many evangelicals tended to undervalue.

Bickersteth's most sophisticated volume was *The Christian Student*. Written as a guide to theology, he argued for the necessity of a ministry which combined learning with evangelical piety. The theological curriculum outlined included Hebrew, Greek, the Fathers, the Reformers, dissenting and Anglican writers, Biblical criticism, historical, controversial and pastoral theology. He provided a 100-page reading list of daunting ecumenical and international scope. Though decidedly evangelical in his principles, Bickersteth was no obscurantist: 'we must not condemn books altogether because in some, perhaps in points of more or less importance, they may oppose our own views ... Even from those who have fundamentally erred, some rays may be gathered not to be despised' (Bickersteth, 1826: 376).

Those words present us with a key to Bickersteth's evangelicalism. Though he differed from many of his fellow Anglicans, and from Dissent, though he was to be a leading protestor against Tractarianism, Roman Catholicism, and both theological and political liberalism, he always did so out of principle rather than prejudice. By 1830, Bickersteth had become, perhaps the leading Anglican evangelical spokesman to the nation, promoting a balanced, non-doctrinal, Jesus-centred, Anglican- based, ethical evangelicalism, as taught by CHARLES SIMEON at Cambridge and as presented by the *Christian Observer* to the cultured religious elite.

During the 1820s Bickersteth had been afternoon lecturer at Wheler Chapel, Spitalsfield, and in 1829, despite his heavy CMS responsibilities, became its minister. Happy after a gruelling itinerant ministry to be a pastor, he developed a thorough-going preaching, sacramental and catechetical ministry. His experience in inner-city London made Bickersteth acutely aware of the inadequacies of the Anglican parochial system and open to the need for a more aggressive evangelism, using lay agents if need be.

In 1830, however, Bickersteth left the pressures of industrial London for a lucrative living in Hertfordshire. This removal from CMS and from the capital marked a significant change not only in Bickersteth's ministry but in his outlook. By the late 1820s evangelical Anglican optimism had been shattered by a sharp critique of its accommodating policy, springing largely from the Scottish evangelicals, EDWARD IRVING and ROBERT HALDANE. Whereas Bickersteth and the Anglican evangelicals had assumed a postmillennial scheme, where world missionary success among both Jews and Gentiles would lead inevitably to the reign of peace, Irving and his circle insisted that Christ would return imminently and in judgement. As CMS finances faltered in 1828, as Parliament passed the Catholic Emancipation Act in 1829, to which the Protestant constitutionalist Bickersteth was opposed, as the cholera epidemic spread in Britain during 1831, as the BFBS splintered that same year over the limits of accommodation, as political agitation increased surrounding the Great Reform Acts of 1832 and as a series of European revolutions mounted, so did evangelical postmillennial confidence collapse, and Bickersteth's views change. No longer confined by his CMS links, he increasingly took an independent line. Though he continued to support the BFBS, he was an initial supporter of the splinter Trinitarian Bible Society. Though it was opposed by the Bishop of London, and suspected by many of the Anglican evangelical clergy, Bickersteth supported the interdenominational LCM. Though leading Anglicans protested against the use of lay agents by the new CPAS, Bickersteth defended the society even when many evangelicals hesitated. Though almost all his fellow evangelical clergy steered clear, Bickersteth was the Anglican architect of the international and interdenominational EA. Though premillennialism had been tainted by the Irvingites and evangelical extremists of the 1820s, Bickersteth emerged as its leading Anglican promoter in the mid-1830s.

Bickersteth's voluminous publications on prophecy, while they distanced him initially from the mainstream 'Christian Observer school' were yet written in a practical and devotional spirit. Focusing on the second coming of Christ, Bickersteth helped make premillennialism a respectable subject of inquiry in mainline ecclesiastical circles. He used his belief in the imminence of the second Advent to insist on both personal holiness and national righteousness. Indeed the urgency of the social reforms

promoted by Lord Ashley (later Lord SHAFTESBURY) sprang directly from the eschatological ethics of his mentor Bickersteth.

Bickersteth continued until his death as a tireless pastor, and promoter of church societies, a founder of the LCM, the CPAS, the EA, Irish Church Mission and the Parker Society. However, he increasingly became depressed and defensive in the 1840s. In the age of liberalism, Tractarianism, the Catholic revival, trade unionism, class conflict and physical and spiritual deprivation in the slums, Bickersteth's optimism gave way to dark foreboding. Somewhat despairing of the ability of the state church to convert the nation, he looked for the battle to be won against the forces of infidelity and popery through a united international Protestantism. He wrote in 1844:

> in promoting the union of the churches we hasten the time when the world should believe in the Lord Jesus ... Already the interchange of Christian feeling has been full of benefit. It is a privilege to have communion with such men as Monod and Grandpierre, Gaussen, and D'Aubigne, Tholuck, Krummacher; and to fight with them against every form of apostasy, error and sin.
> (Bickersteth, 1844: 158).

By the middle of the century, the Anglican evangelicals had become large and powerful. Bickersteth had been a major architect of their success. However, evangelicalism had become too diverse to have one unquestioned leader. Bickersteth was respected by all – it was he and the Archbishop of Canterbury who were invited to preach at CMS's fiftieth anniversary. Nevertheless, his sympathies were too catholic, his mind too independent, and his spirit too gentle to be the ecclesiastical party leader. Bickersteth was the founder of a long family line of influential church leaders, missionaries and hymnwriters, including his son Bishop Edward Henry Bickersteth of Exeter.

SELECT WRITINGS

E. Bickersteth, *A Scripture Help* (London, 1816)
—, *Treatise on the Lord's Supper*, 2nd edn (London, 1826)
—, *The Christian Student* (London, 1826)
—, *The Promised Glory of the Church of Christ* (London, 1844)

BIBLIOGRAPHY

T. R. Birks, *Memoir of the Revd Edward Bickersteth*, 2 vols (London, 1851)
DNB
W. J. Clyde Ervine, 'Doctrine and Diplomacy: Some Aspects of the Life and Thought of the Anglican Evangelical Clergy 1797–1837' (Cambridge Univ. Ph.D. thesis, 1979)
M. Hennell, *Sons of the Prophets* (London, 1979)

W. J. CLYDE ERVINE

Bickersteth, Robert (b. Acton, Suffolk, England, 24 Aug. 1816; d. Ripon, Yorkshire, England, 15 April 1884). Bishop of Ripon 1857–84. He was the son of

John Bickersteth, Vicar of Acton, and his wife Henrietta. Originally bound for a career in medicine, Robert came under the influence of HENRY MELVILL's preaching ministry in London's Camden Chapel and was ordained deacon in the Church of England in 1841. After curacies in Sapcote, Reading and Clapham, he was the incumbent of St John's Clapham Rise (1845–51), and then Rector of St Giles-in-the-Fields (1851–7), 'the largest and most degraded parish in London'. It was during his time in London that Bickersteth developed his interest in evangelism among the English working classes and Irish Roman Catholics which came to dominate much of the rest of his life. On Lord SHAFTESBURY's advice Bickersteth was appointed by Palmerston to the see of Ripon, a relatively new diocese which encompassed the densely populated textile towns of the West Riding of Yorkshire.

During his time there Bickersteth was an uncompromising opponent of ritualism, biblical criticism and secularism, and was an ardent advocate of popular preaching, religious education and church building. Under his control the number of church sittings, baptisms, confirmations, and elementary and Sunday school pupils kept pace with the rapidly growing population of the West Riding. He conducted regular visitations of the clergy and tried to stimulate in them a more vigorous preaching ministry. Bickersteth had to cope with well-established centres of High Church ritualism within his own diocese. He made no secret of the fact that he disapproved of such practices, but on the whole he seems to have disliked indolent clergymen more than the activities of the earnest ritualist priests. In that sense Bickersteth's evangelicalism was principled but rarely vindictive, and he had no time for building up parties for polemical purposes.

Bickersteth succeeded his uncle EDWARD BICKERSTETH, rector of Watton, as honorary secretary of the Society of Irish Church Missions, a fervently evangelistic and deeply controversial voluntary organization led by ALEXANDER DALLAS. In the first flush of enthusiasm, and after several visits to Connemara in the west of Ireland, Bickersteth told an audience in London's Exeter Hall in 1852 that the work of the mission 'had wrung from the Romish hierarchy the unwilling admission that their power in Ireland is fast approaching destruction'. More realistically, Bickersteth's vigorous support of evangelicalism in Ireland led him to disapprove of governmental concessions to Irish Roman Catholicism, including the disestablishment of the Church of Ireland, against which he spoke in the House of Lords in 1869.

Bickersteth's chief contribution to evangelicalism was his unremitting concern for the religious welfare of the English labouring poor. He was aware that the appalling physical condition of the poor in English industrial towns and cities made it difficult for teachers, clergymen or city missionaries to have much impact on their moral and religious problems. As with many mid-Victorian evangelicals he relied upon a mixture of self-help liberalism and evangelical paternalism to reclaim the labouring classes for the Church of England. While his zeal could not be faulted, he was profoundly aware that ecclesiastical energy and efficiency would not of themselves reverse the tide of working-class infidelity. Nevertheless, at a time when the Church of England could ill afford anything else, Bickersteth was a working bishop whose indefatigable exertions played an important part in the limited and temporary restoration of Anglican fortunes in the second half of the nineteenth century.

BIBLIOGRAPHY

M. C. Bickersteth, *A Sketch of the Life and Episcopate of Robert Bickersteth, D.D.* (London, 1887)

D. N. Hempton, 'Bickersteth, Bishop of Ripon: the Episcopate of a Mid-Victorian Evangelical', *NH*, 17 (1981): 183–202

DAVID N. HEMPTON

Bicknell, Henry (b. Dorset, England, 1766; d. Papara, Tahiti, 7 Aug. 1820). Early LMS missionary in the South Seas. Bicknell was associated with Lady Huntingdon's Connexion. A carpenter by trade, he was deemed to be a suitable missionary, since directors of the LMS thought that his trade could be usefully employed in 'civilizing' the natives of the South Seas. Not only was he among the first detachment of missionaries to arrive on Tahiti (1797), he also remained on the island in 1798 to continue evangelistic work when other missionaries believed that the mission should be abandoned. Bicknell was also the first missionary to leave the island to return to England with the sole purpose of finding a wife. Following a successful journey which commenced 28 May 1808 he and his bride Mary Ann (née Bradley) arrived on Eimeo in July 1811 and Pomare II, the 'king' of Tahiti and Eimeo shared their home. Bicknell officiated at the first baptism on the island on 16 May 1819, and not surprisingly Pomare II was the first candidate for baptism to be baptized. When the islands were divided as missionary stations Bicknell left Matavai for Papara, Tahiti where he died less than two years later of dysentery. Bicknell, according to Lovett was a diligent, consecrated and energetic missionary.

BIBLIOGRAPHY

R. Lovett, *The History of the London Missionary Society 1795–1895* (London, 1899)

N. Gunson, *Messengers of Grace* (Melbourne, 1978) (This volume provides a useful 'Calendar of Manuscript Sources').

RMD, 4th edn (London, 1923)

R. WATCYN JAMES

Bicknell, Henry Edgeworth (b. *c.* 1786; d. London, 20 Feb. 1879). Senior civil servant and supporter of missionary societies. Serving under several Lord Chancellors, Bicknell held for many years the post of senior registrar at the High Court of Chancery. He served on the first committee of the CPAS and for most of the years 1834–49 was a member of the interdenominational committee of the RTS. Bicknell was one of many laymen of stature who, in the shadow of more prominent figures such as MPs like LORD ASHLEY, were depended upon to give week-by-week leadership in the missionary societies.

BIBLIOGRAPHY
Annual Reports of the Religious Tract Society (London, 1834–50)
Boase
E. J. Speck, ed., *The Church Pastoral-Aid Society* (London, 1881)

D. B. HINDMARSH

Biddle, William Phillips (b. Princess Anne, VA, USA, 7 Jan. 1787; d. Newberne, NC, USA, 8 Aug. 1853). Baptist minister. William Phillips Biddle was largely a self-educated man. He was ordained 28 February 1808 and pastored several churches through eastern Virginia and North Carolina, and was active in the formation and activities of the North Carolina State Convention. A wealthy farmer, he preached gratuitously. Unfortunately, at the close of his life, those churches which had benefited from his largesse were ill prepared to meet financial realities.

BIBLIOGRAPHY
W. Cathcart, *Baptist Encyclopedia* (Philadelphia, PA, 1881)

WADE A. HORTON

Biddulph, Thomas (b. *c.* 1735; d. probably Bath, Somerset, England, 30 Aug. 1790). Anglican clergyman. Biddulph was the son of Francis, of Madresfield, Worcester, but little is known of his early education or how he came within the orbit of evangelicalism. GEORGE WHITEFIELD and THOMAS JONES urged him to seek ordination and he was educated at Magdalen Hall, Oxford (matriculated March 1759 at age 23) but did not take a degree. Ordained in 1760, he became curate of Colwall, Herefordshire. From there he moved to Worcester ministering both there and later in a nearby town. Using small group meetings in his home he saw 'many awakened' (Wills, 3, 1784: 42). His first wife, Martha (née Tregenna; died 1783) and her sister (died 1766), both appear to have been converts of SAMUEL WALKER and were particularly helpful to Biddulph's ministry in Worcester.

In 1770 Biddulph moved to become Vicar of Padstow and thereafter he confined his work to Cornwall. Toward the end of his life a painful illness cut short his preaching ministry. His son was THOMAS T. BIDDULPH.

BIBLIOGRAPHY
Al. Ox.
J. S. Reynolds, *Evangelicals at Oxford* (Appleford, England, 1975)
T. Wills, *The Spiritual Register*, 3 vols (London, 1784)

DONALD M. LEWIS

Biddulph, Thomas Tregenna (b. Claines, Worcestershire, England, 5 July 1763; d. Bristol, England, 10 May 1838). Anglican clergyman and writer. Biddulph's father, THOMAS BIDDULPH, an associate of JAMES HERVEY and THOMAS HAWEIS and influenced by the Calvinism of Lady HUNTINGDON's preachers, was Incumbent of Bengeworth near Evesham (1769–71), and then of Padstow (Cornwall) till his death. Thomas Tregenna Biddulph was educated at Truro under GEORGE CONON and at Queen's College, Oxford (BA 1784; MA 1787). He was first of all curate to his father at Padstow (1785) and then at Ditcheat (1786), St Mary-le-Port (1787), Wansborough (Wiltshire) (1788) and again at St Mary-le-Port (1789) before becoming incumbent of his father's former living at Bengeworth (1793–1803). Latterly in this period he placed WILLIAM DAY as his curate-in-charge, and Biddulph himself became Curate of Congresbury and Wick St. Lawrence (1798), then Perpetual Curate of St James, Bristol and Durston (1799) which he held for over thirty years.

Biddulph regularly preached three sermons each Sunday and he also established a Friday evening meeting. He introduced a new edition of *Portions of the Psalms of David* (1802), set up a Sunday school, and a kitchen and clothing store. As late as 1830 he introduced the St James's District Visiting Society. He was also prominent in the inauguration of the Bristol Female Penitentiary Society (1801) and the Bristol Church of England Tract Society (1811), for which he himself wrote several tracts.

Biddulph became a country member of CMS within months of its establishment in 1799 and was a founder member of the Bristol Church Missionary Association in 1813. He helped to found the Birmingham and Bath associations and travelled widely for the society in the west of England. He was clerical secretary of the Bristol auxiliary of BFBS from 1813 to his death, a supporter of evangelical work among the Irish and of PRS, and he also presided at the inaugural meeting of the Bristol branch of CPAS. He built St Matthew's, Kingsdown (1835), of which his son Theodore became first vicar, being succeeded on his death in 1837 by John Bryant Clifford (1837–80).

Special mention must be made of Biddulph's work as first secretary and treasurer of the Bristol Clerical Education Society, whose members included William Tanday (St Werburgh's, Bristol), ROBERT HAWKER (Charles, Plymouth), and ROBERT JARRATT (Wellington, Somerset). Like its sister society at Elland it supported pensioners for university study before ordination. These included SAMUEL C. WILKES (later editor of *CO*), W. H. HAVERGAL (C. Astley, Worcestershire and father of Frances Ridley Havergal), Robert Brodie (Mangotsfield), John Cawood (Bewdley) and HUGH STOWELL. Led by Biddulph, the society established *The Christian Guardian* (originally entitled *Zion's Trumpet*) in 1795.

Biddulph was a prolific writer, remembered now only for his contribution to the baptismal controversy in 1815, arising from Richard Mant's assertion that regeneration was simultaneous with baptism. In his *Baptism, A Seal of the Christian Covenant* (1816) Biddulph argued that regeneration is possible without baptism and can exist before baptism. Moreover, baptism conveys no spiritual gift to the unbeliever. The sacrament, Biddulph claimed, makes the recipient a member of the church and is evidence of the seal of divine pardon and salvation, infant baptism being thus the means of leading to the beginnings of faith through church membership. Spiritual regeneration is to be seen as a change of nature, whereas baptism is merely a change of state. Nevertheless, in *A Search After Truth* (1818) Biddulph upheld infant baptism against the views of his own curate at Durston, GEORGE BARING, arguing that it was the promise of remission of sins to children of believers. He also engaged in controversy with the Irvingites in *Conversion, not Miracle, the Standing Test of Divine Influence in the Christian Church* (1836), in which he rejected the idea that some are justified from eternity together also with the notion of imputed sanctification.

Biddulph was a strong church and state man, staunchly Protestant, opposed both to Roman dogma, especially the *opus operatum* doctrine, and to Catholic emancipation. He also resisted parliamentary reform. HANNAH MORE regarded him as a High Calvinist, but his rejection of supralapsarianism suggests that he should more reasonably be considered moderate.

BIBLIOGRAPHY
Al. Ox., I: 107
DNB
L. P. Fox, 'The Work of the Reverend Thomas Tregenna Biddulph' (Cambridge Univ. Ph.D. thesis, 1953)

ARTHUR POLLARD

Biddulph, Zachary Henry (b. Bristol, England, 1790; d. Backwell, Somerset, England, 21 Nov. 1842). Anglican clergyman. One of the 14 children of THOMAS TREGENNA BIDDULPH, Vicar of St James, Bristol, and his wife Rachel (née Shrapnel), and the brother of the prolific author, Theopholis Biddulph, Vicar of St Matthew's Bristol, he studied at Magdalen College, Oxford, from 1809, and then served as a fellow of the college, gaining a BD. In March 1827 he became Curate of Backwell in Somerset, in 1831 Vicar, and in 1828 also became Vicar of New and Old Shoreham by Sea in Sussex, through the patronage of his college. Like the rest of his family he was an evangelical Calvinist, diligent in promoting schools and missionary interest in his parishes.

BIBLIOGRAPHY
J. T. Barclay, *A Burning and a Shining Light* (London, 1843)
A. B. Packham, *The Story of Shoreham* (Hove, England, 1921)

PETER J. LINEHAM

Bigelow, Russell (b. Chesterfield, NH, USA, 24 Feb. 1793; d. Columbus, OH, USA, 1 July 1835). Distinguished pioneer minister of the MEC. He was converted in Vermont when he was nine years of age. With his parents, he moved to Worthington, Ohio in 1812.

He received his license to exhort at age 19, and was admitted on trial in 1814. Until his death he served the Ohio Conference as preacher, missionary to the Wyandotte Indians, presiding elder, and Chaplain of the Ohio State Prison in Columbus. He is remembered for excellence in preaching and his positive influence among the people he served.

BIBLIOGRAPHY
CM

STEVE HARPER

Bignold, Thomas (Jr) (b. Norwich, Norfolk, England, 3 April 1787; d. Norwich, England, 15 July 1867). Lawyer. Bignold was the son of Thomas Bignold, the founder of Norwich Union Insurance. While studying law, he was strongly influenced by EDWARD BICKERSTETH. T. R. BIRKS' *Memoir of the Reverend Edward Bickersteth* (London, 1851) recounts their friendship as law students and Bickersteth's marriage to Bignold's sister in 1812.

As young lawyers, both men were active in the Norwich CMS association which led Bickersteth to become an Anglican clergyman. Bignold veered towards the Baptists, joining their congregation at St Mary's, Norwich, in 1815 and supporting Whig reform campaigns as well as local groups such as the Moravian Missions. In 1833 the St Mary's congregation excluded him for adultery but he remained influential at local antislavery meetings until the 1840s. His first wife died in 1837 and, although he remarried, his later years passed in comfortable obscurity.

His son, Edward Samuel (1821–96) became a lawyer and coroner at Norwich. Another son, Thomas Frank (1837/8–1887) became a judge in the Bengali Civil Service. His younger brother was Sir Samuel Bignold.

BIBLIOGRAPHY
C. B. Jewson, *The Baptists in Norfolk* (London, 1957)
Norfolk and Norwich Record Office, MS4281, St Mary's Baptist Church, Wilkins Papers 1789–1832

R. J. RYAN

Billings, William (b. 7 Oct. 1746; d. 26 Sept. 1800). A composer of hymn tunes and a singing master in his native Boston. Billings published the first book of hymns, or of any totally American music, printed in North America. Engraved by Paul Revere and released in 1770, *The New England Psalm-Singer* was followed in 1778 by the more influential *The Singing Master's Assistant or Key to Practical Music*, which appeared in new editions in 1779 and 1780. Other books were: *Music in Miniature* (1770); *The Psalm Singer's Amusement* (1781); *The Suffolk Harmony* (1794).

Despite his meagre formal educational or musical training, Billings' love of music and singing motivated him to improve the choral experience of New England churches during a time of transition. Choirs were being introduced and rote, or 'lining-out', singing of metred psalms was giving way to congregational hymn-book singing. Billings adapted hymn tunes written by others as well as composing new ones, often more rhythmic than the older style hymnology. To aid singing on pitch Billings introduced the pitch pipe and violoncellos. Organs would not be used in New England parishes until the nineteenth century.

Leaving the tanning trade, Billings became a singing teacher and trainer of choirs in Boston, especially at the Old South Church and the Brattle Street Church. He organized musical societies in nearby towns; one of his societies still exists. Nevertheless, Billings could not earn a living from his music, worked at menial jobs and died poor. Given his handicaps, Billings's contributions to American church music are especially noteworthy; he was blind in one eye, had a withered arm and a rasping voice. Faith, persistence and a love of music sustained him.

BIBLIOGRAPHY
DAB
D. P. McKay and R. Crawford, *William Billings of Boston* (Princeton, NJ, 1975)
F. J. Metcalf, *American Writers and Compilers of Sacred Music* (New York, 1925)
H. Nathan, *William Billings* (Detroit, MI, 1976)

THOMAS A. ASKEW

Bingham, Charles William (b. 28 Sept. 1810; d. Melcombe, Dorset, England, 1 Dec. 1881). Anglican clergyman. Bingham was the youngest son of William Bingham (1771–27 May 1810), an Anglican minister and fellow of New College, Oxford, who died several months before his son's birth. Bingham was educated at Winchester and New College, Oxford (matriculated 1828; BA 1833; MA and fellow (1836). He became Vicar of Sydling St Nicholas (Dorset) (1838–46) and Rector of Bingham's Melcombe (or Melcombe Horsey) in the same county (1842–81). During his long incumbency of this latter place he was also Rural Dean of Whitchurch (1863) and latterly Prebendary of Salisbury (1876–81). He was CMS secretary for Dorset (1848–50 and 1867–81) and a member of the Dorset Clerical Meeting (see HENRY MOULE). He was a frequent contributor to *Notes and Queries* and translated Calvin's *Commentaries on the Four Last Books of the Pentateuch* (4 vols, 1852, 1855) for the Calvin Society.

BIBLIOGRAPHY
Al. Ox. I: 109
Boase I: 279
Burke's
J. S. Reynolds, *The Evangelicals at Oxford 1735–1871* (Abingdon, England, 1975) Additional Contents: 103

ARTHUR POLLARD

Bingham, Hiram (b. Bennington, VT, USA, 30 Oct. 1789; d. New Haven, CT, USA, 11 Nov. 1869). Congregational missionary to Hawaii. Bingham seemed destined to farm his family's land but his conversion in 1811 and graduation from Andover Seminary in 1819 led him to join the pioneer company of missionaries bound for Hawaii. The *Thaddeus* completed a difficult 164-day voyage around Cape Horn with the sighting of Hawaii, 30 March 1820. Bingham led the mission for twenty tempestuous years. His accomplishments included the conversion of key members of the Hawaiian ruling chiefs which led in turn to success among the commoners, and a key role in reducing the Hawaiian language to written form; his trials came in the form of conflicts with merchants and seamen who preferred premissionary Hawaii. As other companies came to reinforce the first missionary group, Bingham gradually found himself out of step with the times. He was a difficult man. 'I never knew a man who had such a compound of vanity, self-importance, forwardness, obstinacy, self complacency and at the same time true kindness,' lamented fellow missionary Richard Armstrong (Armstrong to R. Chapman, 18 July 1844. Library of Congress). The health of his wife Sybil failed and Bingham returned to the United States in 1840. Hawaii missionaries did not press for his return. With Bingham an American family dynasty was founded which has continued a commitment to social change and public service.

BIBLIOGRAPHY
DAB
H. Bingham, *A Residence of Twenty-One Years in the Sandwich Islands* (New York, 1847)

NANCY J. MORRIS

Binney, Hibbert (b. Halifax, Nova Scotia, BNA, 1793; d. Newburg, Berkshire, England, 6 June 1857). SPG missionary and Anglican clergyman. Born into a family of colonial government officials, Binney decided early in favour of the Anglican ministry. His time as a teacher (1811–15) brought him under strong Wesleyan Methodist influence. Evangelical leanings in sermons and pastoral work marked his subsequent clerical career such that he felt the ill will of Cape Breton governor Ainslie while in charge of St George's Church, Sydney. Binney removed with his wife Amelia (née Stout) in 1823 to England where for 19 years he served as Rector of St Nicholas Church, Newburg. His son, Hibbert Newton Binney (1819–87), a Tractarian, was fourth Bishop of Nova Scotia.

BIBLIOGRAPHY
Obituary, *Church Times* (Halifax, Nova Scotia, Canada, 27 June 1857)
H. T. White, *A Funeral Sermon* (Newburg, England, 1857)

ALLEN B. ROBERTSON

Binney, Thomas (b. Newcastle-upon-Tyne, Northumberland, England, 30 April 1798; d. London, 24 March

1874). Congregational preacher and writer. 'The great Dr Binney', called both the 'representative and architect of nineteenth-century dissent', asked in his will that no biography of him should be written! Apprenticed by his Presbyterian parents to a bookseller, he became a Congregationalist and trained for the ministry at Wymondley. Short pastorates in Bedford and Newport in the Isle of Wight were preliminary to a forty-year ministry at The Weigh House Church in the City of London. A fierce opponent of church establishments, his vivid statement that the Church of England, which he carefully distinguished from Episcopalianism, 'a great national evil . . . destroys more souls than it saves' caused a great stir which he exploited in subsequent pamphlets. The growth of ritualism within the Established Church did nothing to assuage his worries which found expression in contributions to the Gorham debate on baptismal regeneration, though here his criticisms turned not only on the sacramentalists but, like C. H. SPURGEON later, also upon prayer-book evangelicals. Although he generally resisted becoming a 'political dissenter', he supported ROBERT VAUGHAN in campaigning for secular education funded by the state. He made his pulpit among the most influential in London employing a more direct, intimate, less ponderous and affected style than then obtained, limiting the length of his sermons to no more than forty minutes. Placing renewed stress on adoration, he also encouraged greater dignity in Congregational worship. The author of *The Ultimate Objective of the Evangelical Dissenters* (1834), he supported the foundation of the EA, but sought to bring peace to the Congregational Union when its future was imperilled when T. T. Lynch was hounded by the conservative zealot, JOHN CAMPBELL, in the Rivulet Affair. In his preaching Binney also sought to address everyday affairs, thus for example his course of sermons on money. He published a pamphlet in 1855 addressed to young men, which for the first 12 months sold at a rate of 100 copies per day, entitled *Is It Possible To Make the Best of Both Worlds?* Binney offered a positive answer, the logic offered being – 'the Evangelical form of Christian ideas, . . . best produces that faith, . . . which, by way of natural consequence, secure those things, . . . which contribute to the satisfaction and embellishment of life', the evangelical passport to success.

Elected in 1848 to the chair of the Congregational Union, in whose formation he was intimately involved, he worried about its later bureaucratic development. In his chairman's address he made the oft-quoted remark on the mission of Congregationalism: 'Our special mission is neither to the very rich nor to the very poor. We have a work to do upon the thinking, active influential classes'. At the Weigh House, however, Binney's congregation was encouraged to undertake missionary work amongst an inner-city population through schools, the domestic mission, Sunday schools and ragged schools. For a time secretary of the Colonial Missionary Society, he made an influential visit to Australia in 1857 and was away from his pulpit for almost two years. His theology was transitional: never a Calvinist, he stressed the broad purposes of the love of God as demonstrated in the salvation offered through Christ in a way which made him deny the eternal torment of the wicked, though he offered no alternative theory.

SELECT WRITINGS
T. Binney, *Sermons Preached in the King's Weigh House* [edited by H. Allon and including a Biographical and Critical Sketch] (London, 1875)

BIBLIOGRAPHY
DNB
E. P. Hood, *Thomas Binney, His Mind, Life and Opinions* (London, 1874)
R. T. Jones, *Congregationalism in England 1662–1962* (London, 1962)
E. Kaye, *The History of the King's Weigh House Church* (London, 1968)
J. Stoughton, *Thomas Binney, A Memorial* (London, 1874)

J. H. Y. BRIGGS

Bion, Ruprecht (b. St Gallen, Switzerland, 1818; d. Monghyr, India, 11 June 1898). Pioneer missionary in East Bengal. A Swiss national, Bion was apprenticed as a merchant. But as early as 1839, he became convinced of a call to missionary service. For this he prepared at the Basel Missionary Institute from 1841 to 1846. For five years he served with his close colleague, F. Süpper, near Dacca. Then, convinced of the correctness of the Baptist position, he sought believer's baptism for himself and a transfer of the work for which he was responsible to the BMS. He continued in East Bengal, based in Dacca, for a further 35 years. Funds for his work being largely raised by subscription from among officials of the British raj, only a small part of his support came from church-raised missionary funds. He was so dutiful in his village itinerancy that he eventually became known as the 'Apostle of East Bengal'. His pioneering work in Commilla, Mymensingh and the Garo Hills, was eventually taken over by Australian Baptists. Only twice was he absent from India: once for a visit to Britain and Switzerland, and again for travel to Australia in order to negotiate the transference of the work. He remained in India after retirement, living for more than a half century in the subcontinent.

BIBLIOGRAPHY
Baptist Handbook (1899)
BMS Archive, Angus Library, Regent's Park College, Oxford, letters

J. H. Y. BRIGGS

Bird, Charles Smith (b. Liverpool, England, 28 May 1795; d. Lincoln, England, 9 Nov. 1862). Anglican clergyman. The son of a pious West India merchant, Bird was educated at Macclesfield and articled as a solicitor, but, influenced by ROBERT P. BUDDICOM, he decided to seek orders and entered Trinity College, Cambridge (scholar, 1818; BA and fellow 1820; MA 1827). He took private pupils, including T. B. (Lord) Macaulay and the three sons of CHARLES R. SUMNER, with whose brother JOHN B. SUMNER he became acquainted at Reading Clerical Club. He was Curate of Burghfield (1823–7), Sunday curate at Sulhamstead (1839–42), Curate of Fawley (near Henley) (1842–3), Vicar of Gainsborough (1843–59) and Chancellor of Lincoln (1859–62).

Bird opposed the Maynooth Grant, the Irish education measures, the Dissenters' Chapel Bill and the admission of Jews to Parliament. He was a frequent contributor to the *Christian Observer* and a prominent participant in the Tractarian controversy, his first contribution being *The Oxford Tract System Considered With Reference to the Principle of Reserve in Preaching* (1838), a dissection of Tract 80. This was followed by an attack on the idea of development in *A Plea for the Reformed Church* (1841), followed by the more extensive *A Second Plea* (1843) with quotations from JOHN HENRY NEWMAN on Athanasius illustrating the Romeward movement of his thought. In *The Sacramental and Priestly System Examined* (1854) Bird took issue with R. I. Wilberforce for his acceptance of development, the apostolic succession and the exaltation of the visible church at the expense of Christ. He also engaged with the Roman Catholics in *Transubstantiation Tried by Scripture and Reason* (1839) and *Romanism not Primitive* (1850) as well as delivering a lecture on Mariolatry and the doctrine of the Immaculate Conception at Islington in 1849. He also foresaw some of the problems ahead, censuring Benjamin Jowett in 1855 for a distorted view of redemption ('All is *Love*, and nothing else, in his scheme') and finding 'neology . . . sapping the foundations of our religion'. Bird was also a keen entomologist and fellow of the Linnaean Society.

BIBLIOGRAPHY
C[laude] S. Bird, *Sketches from the Life of the Rev. Charles Smith Bird* (London, 1864)
DNB
P. Toon, *Evangelical Theology 1833–1856* (London, 1979)

ARTHUR POLLARD

Bird, Edward (b. England, 1792; d. Wyton, Huntingdonshire, England, 15 May 1858). Anglican clergyman and sabbatarian. The third son of Robert and Lucy Bird of Barton House, Warwickshire and Taplow Hill, Berkshire, he was closely related to WILLIAM WILBERFORCE, ABEL SMITH, and CHARLES RICHARD SUMNER and JOHN BIRD SUMNER.

A scholar of Magdalene College, Cambridge (BA 1815), he studied law (admitted to Lincoln's Inn, 1819) and was called to the Bar (1824). He practised at the Supreme Court of Calcutta (1825–9). Following the death of his first wife and their only child, he returned to England and was ordained to a curacy at Boroughbridge in Yorkshire (1830–2). While there he married Dora Lawson. He exercised a fruitful ministry at Maidenhead, Berkshire (1832–4), but later as Rector of Tattenhall, Cheshire (1834–42) and as Rector of St Thomas's,

Birmingham (1842–7), his tactless enforcement of Sunday observance led to his being stoned in the streets. The Birmingham clergy (mostly evangelicals) publicly dissociated themselves from his actions. His health was adversely affected, but once recovered he accepted the living of Wyton (1847–58). His daughter Isabella (Mrs Bishop) achieved fame as a traveller in the East.

BIBLIOGRAPHY
Al. Cant.
Aris's Birmingham Gazette (5 May 1847)
E. Bird, *Substance of a Farewell Sermon* (London, 1847)
GM (June 1858): 681

D. E. H. MOLE

Bird, Golding (b. Downham, Norfolk, England, 9 Dec. 1814; d. Tunbridge Wells, Kent, England, 27 Oct. 1854). Physician and medical scientist. After a stint as a London pharmacist, in 1838 he obtained the degree of MD through St Andrew's University; in 1840 he was licensed by the London College of Physicians. Bird made a name for himself as a lecturer, from 1836, at Guy's Hospital and through research and publications in urinary pathology. He was a member of learned societies, enjoyed a lucrative medical practice and a national reputation.

As a director of Christian Medical associations in London and Edinburgh, along with J. H. BALFOUR, J. H. GLADSTONE and others, Bird prominently represented evangelical Christianity in medical circles; he promoted medical missions and defended the practice of bedside evangelism.

BIBLIOGRAPHY
J. H. Balfour, *Biographical Sketch of . . . Dr. Golding Bird* (Edinburgh, 1855)
DNB

JONATHAN BURKE CUTMORE

Bird, Mark Baker (b. London, 1807; d. Jersey, Channel Islands, England, 23 Aug. 1880). Methodist missionary, builder, and writer. Converted as a youth, Mark became a church member at 18 and a local preacher at twenty. He entered the Methodist ministry (1832) and was appointed to the Evesham circuit (1833). He was sent as a missionary to Jamaica (1834–8) but became ill and returned to England to work in the Ipswich circuit. On regaining his health, he was the first Methodist missionary to be stationed in the Cayman Islands (1839). Three months later he began his formidable work in Haiti (1839–79), where he became chairman of the district.

He was a hard-working, self-sacrificing, committed evangelical servant of the church, who was truly devoted to the people of Haiti. He and his family miraculously survived the devastating earthquake of 7 May 1842 in Cap Haïtien. Constant political insurrections/revolutions severely tested his faith. When half the city of Port-au-Prince was destroyed by fire (1869), he had to rebuild the chapel, manse and school. He wrote, *The Black Man or Haitian Independence, deduced from Historical Notes*. When he departed from Haiti (1879), the Church had 213 members, 2,300 adherents, 4 local preachers, 10 Sunday school teachers, 137 Sunday school scholars, and 289 students in the Methodist day schools.

BIBLIOGRAPHY

Minutes (London, 1881): 13–14

G. G. Findlay and W. W. Holdsworth, *The History of the Wesleyan Missionary Society*, II (London, 1921): 494–509

L. J. Griffiths, *History of Methodism in Haiti* (Port-au-Prince, Haiti, 1991)

LESLEY G. ANDERSON

Bird, Robert M(erttins) (b. Taplow Hill, Buckinghamshire, England, *c*. 1788; d. Torquay, Devon, England, 22 Aug. 1853). Director of the land settlement of 1833 in North India. Robert M. Bird was educated privately and at the East India Company College at Haileybury. Beginning in 1808 in the judicial line under the company's administration, Bird changed to the revenue service. Having made himself an expert as revenue commissioner of Gorakhpur district, WILLIAM C. BENTINCK as Governor-General appointed Bird senior member of the Board of Revenue, North-West provinces in 1832. When he retired in 1842 he was likened by some of his peers as the English Todarmal (a great Hindu administrator under Akbar). Bird's land settlement minutes in the India Office Records remain unedited.

Related to WILLIAM WILBERFORCE, the Birds of Taplow Hill came under the influence of the 'Clapham Sect'. In India Bird first married Jane Grant Brown, daughter of DAVID BROWN, one of CHARLES SIMEON's appointments to India's chaplaincy service. Robert supported his sister's missionary work in North India and the cause of the CMS throughout his career.

BIBLIOGRAPHY

P. Penner, *The Patronage Bureaucracy in North India* (Delhi, 1986): 8–11, 253

J. Rosselli, *Lord William Bentinck* (Berkeley, CA, 1974): 256–9

PETER PENNER

Birks, Thomas Rawson (b. Staveley, Derbyshire, England, 28 Sept. 1810; d. Cambridge, England, 19 July 1883). Professor of moral philosophy and Anglican clergyman. Born into a Non-conformist farming family on the estates of the Duke of Devonshire, Birks was educated first locally at Chesterfield and then at the Dissenting College in Mill Hill near London. Funding being provided, he entered Trinity College, Cambridge, and graduated with the highest honours (second wrangler and second Smith's prizeman) in January 1834. Fellow of the college from 1834 to 1844 (winning the Seatonian poetry prize in 1843–4), Birks became a member of

the Church of England in 1834 and was appointed tutor and curate to the former secretary of the CMS, EDWARD BICKERSTETH at Watton. There he emerged increasingly as a powerful controversialist in debates surrounding the millennium (Birks was a premillennialist) and the state of the departed.

In 1844 Birks married Bickersteth's daughter and moved to become Rector of Kelshall, Hertfordshire where he remained until 1864 actively engaged in literary work (but for a period after the death of his first wife in 1856) and the evangelical cause (being the honorary secretary of the EA from 1850 to 1871). During this period his most significant published works were an edition of Paley's *Horae Paulinae* (1850), *Horae Evangelicae* (1852), *Modern Rationalism* (1853), *The Inspiration of the Holy Scriptures* (1853), and the first edition of his later expanded *The Bible and Modern Thought* (1861) at the behest of the RTS. His works were marked by a pugnacious biblical defence of evidential religion and a growing apologetic concern for a thoughtful response to modern scientific enquiry.

In 1866 Birks moved back to Cambridge, married for a second time, and became perpetual curate at CHARLES SIMEON's former church, Holy Trinity, a position he held until ill health forced his resignation in 1877. Identified as a leader of scholarly evangelicalism, Birks emulated Simeon's pastoral ministry among members of the university and city and was controversially appointed as a conservative successor to F. D. Maurice as Knightsbridge professor of moral [theology and] philosophy on 30 April 1872, a position he held until his death. Prominent in the university, Birks was a theological examiner in 1867–8, a member of the board of theological studies, Ramsden preacher in 1867, and frequently 'select preacher' to the university. A stroke in 1875 and a second in 1877 did not curtail significantly his literary output, but a third in 1880 caused lasting paralysis and an end to his intellectual endeavours, though he lived another three years.

During his second period in Cambridge Birks' publications continued to focus upon the impact of modern criticism and scientific enquiry upon the Bible and the Christian faith but incorporated a specific focus in the realm of ethical theory and practice. Hence, in 1872, for example, his inaugural professorial lecture was on 'The Present Importance of Moral Science', and other works included *Scripture Doctrine of Creation* and *The Philosophy of Human Responsibility*. In addition to these, other major works of this period included *A Commentary on the Book of Isaiah* (1871), *First Principles of Moral Science* (1873), *Modern Utilitarianism* (1874) and *Supernatural Revelation* (1879). These, together with especially his lectures in 1876 on 'The Uncertainties of Modern Physical Science' and 'Modern Physical Fatalism and the Doctrine of Evolution', reveal Birks as neither ill-informed with respect to contemporary thought nor hesitant to engage with it critically. As he said, for example, characteristically of Herbert Spencer's 'First Principles', they [are] 'radically unsound, full of logical inconsistency and contradiction, and flatly opposed to the fundamental doctrines of Christianity and even the very existence of modern science'.

Birks had eight children by his first wife, one of whom followed him as a fellow of Trinity College, Cambridge. His *Memoir of the Rev. Edward Bickersteth* continues to be a significant source for the early history of the evangelical movement and especially the CMS.

BIBLIOGRAPHY
Boase
T. Cooper, ed., *Men of the Time*, 11th edn (London, 1884)
DNB
M. Hennell, *Sons of the Prophets* (London, 1979)
K. Hylson-Smith, *Evangelicals in the Church of England: 1734–1984* (Edinburgh, 1989)
P. Toon, *Evangelical Theology: 1833–1856* (London, 1979)
T. H. Ward, ed., *Men of the Reign* (London, 1885)

CHRISTOPHER D. HANCOCK

Birney, James Gillespie   (b. Danville, KY, USA, 4 Feb. 1792; d. Eaglewood, NJ, USA, 25 Nov. 1857). Presbyterian abolitionist leader and Liberty Party candidate for president. Birney was raised in Kentucky as the son of a prosperous slave owner. Educated at Transylvania University and the College of New Jersey (Princeton), Birney practised law in Kentucky and Alabama. Persuaded that slavery was evil, he worked with the American Colonization Society for gradual emancipation, but by 1834 was convinced of the need for immediate abolition. He manumitted his slaves at his own expense and tried to convince other slave owners (particularly fellow Presbyterians) to do likewise, with little success. He also wrote an influential tract, *The American Churches the Bulwarks of American Slavery*, which stated that evangelical Christians were largely responsible for the perpetuation of slavery. Birney's activities brought him to the attention of certain prominent Northern abolitionists, who asked him to be executive secretary of the American Anti-Slavery Society. In 1839, a large number of abolitionists became committed to direct political action. They organized the Liberty Party based on uncompromisingly Christian principles, and Birney was induced to run as their presidential candidate. This he did in both 1840 and 1844, receiving only a small percentage of the total votes cast. In 1845, Birney fell off a horse and was partially paralysed, ending his public career. During his last years he lived in the reform-minded community of Eaglewood, New Jersey, and became something of a religious freethinker.

BIBLIOGRAPHY
W. Birney, *James G. Birney and His Times* (New York, 1890)
DAB
B. Fladeland, *James Gillespie Birney* (Ithaca, NY, 1955)

DOUGLAS M. STRONG

Birrell, Charles Morton   (b. Kirkcaldy, Fife, Scotland, 5 Jan. 1810; d. London, 10 Sept. 1880). Baptist minister.

A Scotsman and a commercial agent in early life, Charles was converted in St Petersburg, Russia by WILLIAM KNIBB, trained for the Baptist ministry, and spent his whole pastoral career serving the congregation at Pembroke Chapel, Liverpool (1838–72). A rather unusual Baptist minister, retiring, aloof and progressive in outlook, he presided over an open-membership, open-communion church which attracted a 'high' and cultured type of Nonconformity. He was part-time secretary of the Baptist Union from 1879 to 1883, president in 1871 and helped found the Baptist Annuity Fund (1882). He married Henrietta Grey, the daughter of Dr HENRY GREY of Edinburgh. She was a feminist and a cousin of Josephine Butler. Their son, Augustine, became a well-known politician and man of letters. Charles wrote several biographies of Baptist worthies and other works.

BIBLIOGRAPHY
W. Graham, *A Memoir of C. M. Birrell* (London, 1913)

IAN SELLERS

Birt, Isaiah   (b. Coleford, Gloucestershire, England, 6 Sept. 1758; d. Hackney, London, England, 1 Nov. 1837). Baptist minister. The son of a Baptist minister, he suffered persecution as a youngster for not being christened. From the church at Usk in Monmouthshire, he entered Bristol College in 1780, establishing a lifelong friendship with ROBERT HALL. He had notable first pastorates at Devonport, where WILLIAM STEADMAN became his co-pastor (1784–1813) when the church had grown to the extent that it needed to use two separate chapels. From here he undertook mission work and church planting in the surrounding villages and towns, sometimes encountering hostility which was later confounded by popular support. Clerical opposition and difficulties over Baptist burials in Saltash led to the publication of his *A Vindication of the Baptists* (1793). His son described him as 'one of those who hailed the commencement of the French Revolution as the day-break of liberty for continental Europe', regarding 'the war that was waged against the infant republic, as a royal crusade against the liberties of mankind'. He especially condemned the way in which the French wars were made an argument for infringing the British constitution, and accordingly came under surveillance from government agents. A committee member of the RTS, and heavily involved with the BMS, in 1792 he spent two months in Dublin at the invitation of the Evangelical Society formed there to secure the revival of religion. After turning down many other calls, in 1815 he moved to Cannon Street, Birmingham where the church, adding daughter Sunday schools, ragged schools and missions, prospered under his warm evangelical ministry until ill health caused his retirement to Hackney in 1827, where he was instrumental in gathering a congregation in neighbouring Shoreditch. JOHN HOWARD HINTON was his son-in-law. His son, Caleb, who studied law at Cambridge but as a Dissenter did not graduate, went on to study theology at Bristol and Edinburgh. President of the Baptist Union in 1836, the following year Caleb responded to a call from Broadmead, Bristol, which bore the name of F. W. NEWMAN, the Cardinal's brother, then a Baptist, as one of its signatories.

BIBLIOGRAPHY
J. Birt, 'Memoir of the Late Rev. Isaiah Birt', *Baptist Magazine*, (1838): 54
S. A. Swaine, *Faithful Men* (London, 1884): 99, 260

J. H. Y. BRIGGS

Birt, John (b. Plymouth, Devon, England, 1787; d. Oldham, Lancashire, England, 1862). Baptist minister and author. Son of ISAIAH BIRT prominent West Country Baptist, John Birt was educated at Bristol College and began his ministerial career in Hull where he also produced his first significant publication, *The Conversations of Eratus and Trophimus on the Doctrine of Distinguishing Grace* (1813). In 1819 Birt moved to Manchester and began work on *A Summary of the Principles and History of the Papacy* (London, 1823) which became something of a popular standard. In 1841 he began his final and perhaps most successful pastorate at the Manchester Street Church in Oldham. Birt had a major impact on the church, presiding over a significant increase in its membership and extending its influence generally in the town. He also made his mark on the national scene when at the 1847 EA conference he attempted to prevent the adoption of the doctrine of eternal punishment as one of the foundational tenets of the alliance.

BIBLIOGRAPHY
J. Eavans, *Lancashire Authors and Orators* (Manchester, England, 1859)
Oldham Chronicle (1 November 1862)

M. A. SMITH

Biss(e), Henry (b. England, 1792; d. 1859). Anglican clergyman. The son of James Biss(e) of Hereford, he was educated at Worcester College, Oxford (BA 1814; MA 1817; fellow 1816–51). Bisse was ordained (deacon 1815, priest 1816), becoming Curate of Headington, Oxford, 1815–6 and Curate of St Ebbe's, Oxford, 1825–6.

In November 1828, Biss(e), with J. C. PHILPOT, came into conflict with the authorities at Worcester for 'having exposition and prayer in the Common Room at a party of their friends'; he was, consequently, refused a testimonial to the Bishop of Salisbury for the living of Kennington, Berkshire. In August 1829, he became Chaplain of Southampton Penitentiary; Rector of Hope Mansell, Herefordshire, 1838–50 and Winford, Somerset, 1850–8.

BIBLIOGRAPHY
Al. Ox.
Clergy List (London, 1857)
Index Ecclesiasticus: 17
J. S. Reynolds, *The Evangelicals at Oxford 1735–1871* (Appleford, England, 1975)

GRAYSON CARTER

Biss, John (b. 10 Jan. 1776; d. at sea, 5 Feb. 1807); and Hannah [née Osmund] (b. *c.* 1776; d. Digah, Bihar, India, 13 Jan. 1818). Baptist missionaries to India. John and Hannah Biss (married 1801) were to sail to India with RICHARD and Rhoda MARDON, WILLIAM and Eleanor MOORE, and JOSHUA and Elizabeth ROWE on 3 January 1804, but were delayed. Like Mardon, Biss was from ISAIAH BIRT's Devonport congregation and was educated by JOHN SUTCLIFF in Olney.

A daughter was born just before their departure and sons were born in Serampore (1805 and 1806), by which time Biss was suffering from a fatal liver disease. Biss died on his return voyage to Philadelphia. Hannah returned with her family to teach in Serampore in May 1809. On 18 February 1813 she married William Moore, now a widower, in Digah, Bihar, bearing him two daughters before dying in childbirth. Like her, her descendants did ecumenical missionary work into the 1920s.

BIBLIOGRAPHY
Obituary, *Friend of India* I (1818): 16
Journal in *Periodical Accounts Relative to the Baptist Missionary Society* VII–XII (Dunstable, England, 1806): 461 f.

E. M. JACKSON

Black, Adam (b. Edinburgh, 20 Feb. 1784; d. Edinburgh, 24 Jan. 1874). MP and publisher. The son of Charles Black, an Edinburgh builder, he was educated at the High School before being apprenticed to an Edinburgh bookseller. He worked in London for a time but returned to Edinburgh in 1808 where he established his own bookselling business, and later, with a nephew, set up the firm Adam and Charles Black. In 1827 the firm obtained the copyright of the *Encyclopedia Britannica* and in 1851 that of Scott's Waverley novels.

In politics Black advocated reform of the burghs and repeal of the Test and Corporation Acts. He became a member of the first Edinburgh town council after the passage of the Reform Act in 1832, becoming city treasurer. He was twice elected Lord Provost of Edinburgh and declined a knighthood offered in recognition of his management of civic affairs. He was elected president of the Philosophical Institution at its foundation in 1845 and, succeeding Lord Macaulay, served as Liberal MP for Edinburgh from 1856 to 1865. Black was a deacon of Augustine Congregational Church, Edinburgh.

BIBLIOGRAPHY
DNB
H. Escott, *A History of Scottish Congregationalism* (Glasgow, 1960)

ALAN ARGENT

Black, Alexander (b. Aberdeen, Scotland, 1789; d. Edinburgh, 27 Jan. 1864). Minister. Educated at the University of Aberdeen, he was ordained to the ministry of the Church of Scotland at Tarves, Aberdeenshire, in 1818 and became professor of divinity at Marischal College, Aberdeen. In 1839 he went to the east on behalf of the Church of Scotland to investigate the possibilities of setting up a mission to Jews. He was a man of wide erudition, with notable linguistic abilities, and, having joined the FCS in 1843, was appointed professor of New Testament exegesis at New College, Edinburgh, in the following year, holding the chair until 1856.

R. H. CAMPBELL

Black, David (b. Perth, Perthshire, Scotland, 23 May 1762; d. Edinburgh, 25 Feb. 1806). Church of Scotland minister. Black was ordained to the parish of St Madoes, near Perth, in 1785 and transferred to Lady Yester's parish in Edinburgh in 1794. He assisted in the formation of the Edinburgh Missionary Society in 1796 and hosted a prayer meeting in his home for those interested in spreading the Gospel. The meeting served as a sending base for the controversial lay preaching tour throughout Scotland of JAMES A. HALDANE and his associates in 1797. Despite Black's sympathies with their evangelistic efforts, he did not join them in leaving the Established Church.

SELECT WRITINGS
D. Black, *Sermons* [with memoir] (Edinburgh, 1808)

BIBLIOGRAPHY
Fasti, 1: 82–3
A. Haldane, *The Lives of Robert Haldane of Airthrey, and of His Brother, James Alexander Haldane*, 3rd edn (London and Edinburgh, 1853)

DAVID A. CURRIE

Black, William (b. Huddersfield, Yorkshire, England, 10 Nov. 1760; d. Halifax, Nova Scotia, BNA, 8 Sept. 1834). Pioneer Methodist missionary of Atlantic Canada. The son of William Black and Elizabeth Stocks, he received a good elementary education at Otley while living with an uncle. In 1775 the Blacks, like many other Yorkshire families, emigrated to the Cumberland area of Nova Scotia. Some settlers who had come under the influence of JOHN WESLEY held house meetings there, and at one of these in 1779 Black was converted. Nova Scotia was then in the throes of a revival brought about by the preaching of the New Light Congregationalist

HENRY ALLINE among New England settlers who constituted a majority of the population. In 1781 Alline visited Cumberland, and shortly thereafter Black embarked on a travelling mission to these settlers and to the loyalists who followed them into the province. The two movements, similar in their emotional effects, collided when Black objected to Alline's mysticism and to his insistence that conversion ensured ultimate salvation.

Recognizing the limitations of his experience, Black secured in 1784 the cooperation of the newly organized MEC in the United States and most notably the services for several years of the outstanding preacher FREEBORN GARRETTSON. For a time, because of his youth and Garrettson's qualities of leadership, Black was somewhat in the background. In 1789, however, the American Conference ordained him and appointed him presiding elder for eastern British North America. In 1800, when aid from the United States had largely dried up and he turned to the British Conference, he became chairman of the Nova Scotia district. In 1812, worn out by constant travel, he retired.

Black's administrative methods reflected the isolation in which they evolved. He failed to apply the full Methodist discipline, establish a genuine itinerancy, or recruit leaders to carry on his work. During most of his career he himself was the settled pastor of the Halifax congregation. As 'Bishop' Black, however, he was universally and rightly acknowledged as the agent through whom Methodism had been introduced to Atlantic Canada and from whom it derived much of its distinctive character. This Methodism, in contrast with that of central Canada, was unobtrusive, deferential to secular authority, and firmly anchored in British traditions.

BIBLIOGRAPHY
DCB
M. Richey, *A Memoir of the Late Rev. William Black* (Halifax, Nova Scotia, Canada, 1839)
T. Jackson, *The Lives of Early Methodist Preachers*, 4th edn, 6 vols (London, 1871–5)

JOHN WEBSTER GRANT

Black, William (Henry) (b. Kintore, Aberdeenshire, Scotland, 7 May 1808; d. London, 12 Apr. 1872). Scholar and Adventist minister. Emigrating to Surrey in 1825 as a family tutor, Black soon established himself in the metropolis as a man of learning. He became a clerk at the Public Record Office and was eventually promoted to assistant keeper. Without peer as an antiquarian and bibliographer, he catalogued important bodies of manuscripts at the Ashmolean Library, the British Museum, and elsewhere.

From 1840 Black was minster to a small Seventh-Day Adventist congregation in Whitechapel, London (inimitably described in Davies's *Unorthodox London*). His sermons were learned, in keeping with a man who 'thought in Latin, said his prayers in Hebrew, and read his New Testament in Greek'. Black was a founder of the Palestinian Archaeological Association and of the

Anglo-Biblical Institute. A number of his manuscript letters are at the British Library, and a diary (1844–6) is in Chetham's Library, Manchester.

BIBLIOGRAPHY
C. M. Davies, *Unorthodox London* (London, 1875): 227–37
DNB

JONATHAN BURKE CUTMORE

Blackburn, Ann [probably née Armstrong] (b. Flintham, Nottinghamshire, England, *c.* 1797; d. 12 Aug. 1827). Primitive Methodist (PM) itinerant preacher. Converted in May 1820 Blackburn became a travelling preacher the same year. She was one of the earliest PM female itinerants, ministering in the Hull, especially well received in Huddersfield, and Pocklington circuits. Extracts from her Journal in the *PM Magazine* give some idea of the work of early PM preachers. Blackburn married Joseph Blackburn of Denby Dykeside, Yorkshire on 2 February 1822 and reverted to local preacher status.

BIBLIOGRAPHY
H. B. Kendall, *The Origin and History of the PM Church*, 1 (London, 1904)
PMMag (1821, 1829)

E. DOROTHY GRAHAM

Blackburn, John (b. The Minories, London, 1791; d. Holford Square, London, 16 June 1855). English Congregational minister. Blackburn spent periods as a Sunday school teacher and as a theological student at the Baptist College, Stepney, before becoming a Congregationalist and entering the Hoxton Academy. He worked as a missionary for the Irish Evangelical Society in Sligo; and in September 1815 he was ordained pastor of the Church of Christ, Finchingfield, Essex. In 1819, the Claremont chapel was built in an increasing neighbourhood in Pentonville, and Blackburn often preached in the chapel between 1820 and 1822 when he became its pastor. He then began a long and powerful metropolitan ministry in which he rose to high office in his church, as an originator and secretary of both the Christian Instruction Society of 1825 and the Congregational Union of 1831, and as editor of the *Congregational Magazine and Congregational Year Book*. His strong evangelicalism made him a leader of the opposition to the Maynooth Grant in 1845, and an enthusiastic propagandist for the EA of 1846, and he worked hard to commit his church to support it, partly out of his interest in Ireland. His death was hastened by an unlucky commercial speculation.

BIBLIOGRAPHY
Boase
J. Waddington, *Congregational History (1850–1880)*, 4 (London, 1880): 198–202

SHERIDAN GILLEY

Blackford, Mary Berkeley Minor (b. Fredericksburg, VA, USA, 2 Dec. 1802; d. Alexandria, VA, USA, 13 Nov. 1896). Episcopal laywoman and opponent of slavery. The daughter of General John Minor and Lucy Landon Carter, she was educated at home. On 12 October 1825 she married William Matthews Blackford, a lawyer and newspaper editor. Although a devout Episcopalian, she attended the services of other Protestant denominations when she could not attend her own church. The subtitle of her biography by one of her sons describes her work: 'who taught her sons to hate Slavery and to love the Union' (Blackford, 1954). She and her husband freed all their slaves and, at their own expense, sent most of them to Liberia. Even though she was opposed to slavery, and she and her husband and sons were opposed to secession, she did not protest when the war came and her five sons joined the Confederate army. She was also one of the earliest advocates for temperance reform. She was a person of great strength of character and social power in Virginia.

BIBLIOGRAPHY
L. M. Blackford, *Mine Eyes Have Seen the Glory* (Cambridge, 1954)

DONALD SMITH ARMENTROUT

Blackman, Charles (b. England, 1798; d. 16 March 1853, St John's, Newfoundland). Anglican clergyman and educator. Blackman, an avowed evangelical, first came to Newfoundland as tutor to the son of Governor Charles Hamilton. He returned to England and was ordained priest in 1822. Upon his arrival in Newfoundland as missionary with the SPG, Blackman became a close associate of his fellow evangelical Bishop A. G. SPENCER, who appointed the ambitious clergyman first principal of the Theological Institute at St John's, the future Queen's College. He later lost this position for espousing evangelical and ecumenical causes not congenial to the Tractarian successor of Bishop Spencer, Edward Feild. Before Bishop Spencer's translation to the see of Jamaica, Blackman, in 1842, was made a perpetual curate of St Thomas's garrison church, the centre of Newfoundland's anti-Tractarian Anglicans and opponents of Bishop Feild. The evangelical stamp of this church is still a pervasive ecclesiastical force in St John's today.

BIBLIOGRAPHY
DCB
DNLB
ENL
F. Jones, 'The Early Opposition to Bishop Feild of Newfoundland', *CCHS Journal*, 16 (1974): 30–41
—, 'Religion, Education and Politics in Newfoundland, 1836–1875', *CCHS Journal*, 12 (1970): 64–76

HANS ROLLMANN

Blackman, Learner (b. Great Egg Harbor, Gloucester Co, NJ, USA, 19 June 1781; d. Cincinnati, OH, USA, 7

June 1815). Methodist preacher. He was the son of David Blackman. Blackman was converted in 1797 under the Methodist preaching of his brother-in-law, JOHN COLLINS. He was admitted to the Philadelphia Annual Conference in 1800. He transferred to the Western Conference in the autumn of 1801, and in 1805 was sent to Natchez to aid the mission begun by TOBIAS GIBSON. His three years in Mississippi were successful.

From 1806 Blackman presided over districts in Mississippi, Tennessee and Kentucky. This service was interrupted by a period in the army as chaplain to the Tennessee volunteers in the War of 1812 (January–March, 1813). He was a delegate to the 1808 General Conference and was elected to the 1812 and 1816 conferences as well. He married Mrs Elizabeth Elliott, a widow from Sumner County, Tennessee on 22 June 1813. They had no children. He drowned in the Ohio River when, crossing from Cincinnati on a flatboat, their horses became frightened and plunged into the water taking Blackman with them. The Blackmans were returning to Tennessee from a visit with the Collins members of his family.

Blackman experienced great evangelistic success. His quarterly meetings were attended by thousands. A charismatic speaker, he was said to use words as one who 'dipped his pencil in living light'. Blackman always expected immediate results from his preaching. 'I am alarmed when sinners are not converted', he wrote.

BIBLIOGRAPHY
J. G. Wilson and J. Fiske, eds, *Appleton's Cyclopedia of American Biography* (New York, 1887)
EWM
A. H. Redford, *The History of Methodism in Kentucky*, I (Nashville, TN, 1868): 437–49

CHARLES W. BROCKWELL, JR.

Blackwood, Lady **Alicia** (née Lambart) (b. 1818; d. Bovingdon, Hertfordshire, England, 30 July 1913). Crimean war nurse and memorialist. She was the daughter of the Earl of Kilcoursie, and of a sister of Lord CAVAN. In 1849 she married the Reverend Dr James Stevenson Blackwood (died 1882). She and her husband, together with two Swedish women, Emma and Ebba Almroth, landed at Scutari in December 1854. There Lady Blackwood and the Almroth sisters relieved Florence Nightingale and successfully organized and cared for the soldiers' wives and children, a great many of whom were present in the camp. Her husband served as an army chaplain. Lady Blackwood's memoirs of this period are very revealing of conditions at Scutari and are an important source for Nightingale scholars.

At the end of the war the Reverend Blackwood became Vicar of Middleton Tyas, Yorkshire but later moved to London where he was a prominent figure in evangelical circles. A co-founder of the EA, he attended its Geneva conference in 1862. He wrote a book of sacred poems (1881) and a volume on Psalm 99 (1880).

BIBLIOGRAPHY
Alli
A. Blackwood, *A Narrative of . . . a Residence on the Bosphorus Throughout the Crimean War* (London, 1881)
The Times (1 August, 6 September 1913)

JONATHAN BURKE CUTMORE

Blackwood, James Stevenson. *See* **Blackwood**, Lady **Alicia**

Blacow, Richard (b. Barton, Lancashire, England, 1765; d. Liverpool, England, 1846). Anglican clergyman. Blacow was educated at Kirkham School and Trinity College, Cambridge (scholar, 1786; BA 1788; MA 1814). Originally intended for the law and indeed admitted to Lincoln's Inn in 1788, he changed course and became Incumbent of West Derby (Liverpool) (1798–1846) and then first minister of St Mark's in that city (1803–46). JOSIAH PRATT regarded him as the 'chief hope' by which CMS might get a footing in Liverpool (1813), but Blacow was pessimistic about its chances. He was a man of distinctive, even 'peculiar views', accused of 'lugging party politics into sermons' as well as 'urging indiscriminate war with dissentient sects', while his ardour in enforcing his views was said to throw his congregation into tears – but 'for awe rather than love'. Blacow was more than once prosecuted for libel and during the troubles over George IV's rejection of Queen Caroline he was committed for trial at Lancaster Assizes.

BIBLIOGRAPHY
Al. Cant., II.i: 284
G. R. Balleine, *A History of the Evangelical Party in the Church of England* (London, 1951)
C. Hole, *The Early History of CMS* (London, 1896)
R. McMoney, ed., *The Hermes* 9 (Liverpool, 1822–3)

ARTHUR POLLARD

Blaikie, William (Garden) (b. Aberdeen, Scotland, 5 Feb. 1820; d. North Berwick, East Lothian, Scotland, 11 June 1899). Free Church biographer and periodical editor. He was the son of James Blaikie, a prominent advocate who became Lord Provost of Aberdeen; ALEXANDER KEITH, the premillennialist writer, was his uncle. A brilliant scholar at Aberdeen Grammar School under James Melvin (*DNB*), Blaikie also attended Marischal College, Aberdeen, and Edinburgh University. He received an honorary DD from Edinburgh (1864) and the LL D from Aberdeen (1872).

Licensed in 1841 in the Church of Scotland, in 1842 he was ordained at Dunblane. Upon the 1843 Disruption most of his congregation followed him into the Free Church, and from 1844–68 he was Free Church minister at a mission church, Pilrig, Edinburgh. In that capacity Blaikie concerned himself with various popular causes, including temperance work, home missions, and church extension; the social welfare of local working-class inhabitants especially occupied him. He arranged for the building of model houses and produced *Six Lectures to the Working Classes . . .* (1849). Updated in 1863 as *Better Days for Working People*, it obtained an international audience for his sympathetic, if paternalist, views.

For the balance of his career he was professor of apologetics and pastoral theology at New College, Edinburgh, was Cunningham lecturer in 1888, and Free Church moderator for 1892. He was also chief founder (1875) of the World Alliance of Reformed and Presbyterian Churches (now the World Alliance of Reformed Churches) and was its president in 1892.

Blaikie gained national influence through his editorship of various periodicals: the *Free Church Magazine* (1849–53); the *Sunday Magazine* (1873–4); and the *Catholic Presbyterian* (1879–83). From November 1860 to August 1863 he was also editor of the Free Church *North British Review*, a reputable literary journal, 'liberal in politics and Christian in tone'. Its circulation and the quality of its articles, which had recently suffered, recovered under his intelligent direction.

Besides minor works of theology, homiletics, biblical history, and pastoral care, Blaikie also wrote competent biographies of DAVID BROWN, Robert Rollock, THOMAS CHALMERS, Andrew Chrichton, and ISLAY BURNS. The *DNB* article on Chalmers was his and, most notably, he was author of *The Personal Life of David Livingstone* (1880), a valuable work because compiled from original sources.

SELECT WRITINGS
N. L. Walker, ed., *Autobiography of W. G. Blaikie* (London, 1901)

BIBLIOGRAPHY
DNB

JONATHAN BURKE CUTMORE

Blair, Andrew (b. Northern Ireland, *c.* 1748; d. Dublin, 8 April 1793). Methodist preacher. Very little is known of his birth and early years, except that he was very studious from youth. WILLIAM MYLES claims that he first heard a Methodist preach in 1768, which would be about the time when a Methodist society was formed in his presumed place of birth, Old Cleens in Magheraboy in the Augher circuit, in the south of Ulster. [Crookshank's statement about Old Cleens is difficult to verify from Samuel Lewis, *Topographical Dictionary of Ireland*, 1846.] In 1767 John Dillon had been appointed as JOHN WESLEY's assistant in the Augher circuit, and he was enthusiastic in establishing class meetings, a regular preaching schedule, and ventures into new areas. Dillon wore himself out, but JOHN SMITH proved almost indestructible, and continued to bear spiritual fruit throughout Ulster, especially in the counties of Fermanagh and Tyrone. In 1771 there was a revival at Old Cleens, and Mrs Blair was converted, along with her son Andrew,

and joined the society. In 1778 he was admitted on trial into the Methodist itinerancy, together with the future Methodist historian, William Myles: Blair was stationed in Armagh, Myles in Castlebar, both in junior positions. Successively Blair was stationed in Londonderry and Sligo. In the Sligo circuit, 1780–1, he became very friendly with the Reverend James Creighton, Curate of Swanlinbar, who later became one of Wesley's clerical helpers in Methodism.

In 1782 Blair was brought into full connexion and sent to Dublin, from which he was removed at Christmas to Cork, to help fill an emergency caused by the sudden death there of RICHARD BOARDMAN. In 1784 John Wesley demonstrated his confidence in Blair by appointing him to the 'Legal Hundred' of his preachers, and sent him to assist James Rogers, just remarried to his second wife, Hester Ann Roe (*see* H. A. ROGERS), at Dublin. When John Wesley visited them in April 1785 he reported: 'I found . . . two such preachers, with two such wives, [as] I know not where to find again.' Under their supervision the Dublin society underwent a needed reform, followed by a revival. Rogers found Blair as a fellow labourer 'suitable in every respect', and wanted to keep him for another year. Wesley, however, felt that Blair's proven gifts as preacher and administrator merited a removal to England. He was sent as the assistant in charge of Birmingham (for two years), Chester, Birmingham again, and then Leeds.

At the 1790 Conference, building committees were appointed for both Great Britain and Ireland, and Andrew Blair's was the first name (apparently the chairman) for Ireland, supported by ADAM CLARKE and two others. Blair was appointed assistant to Cork that year, Clarke to Dublin. Clarke's health suffered, however, and he returned to England in 1791. Blair took over in Dublin, but became seriously ill during the second year of his superintendency. He died in his middle years on Monday, April 8, leaving behind his wife Mary and their four young children. The testimony to him by a younger contemporary, CHARLES ATMORE (1801), is perhaps more revealing than the brief conference obituary: 'In conversation he was a pattern of ease, modesty, and good sense; and all his conversations were directed to the glory of God, and to the edification of souls. His public discourses were well digested, solid, and lively, and were generally attended with divine unction'.

BIBLIOGRAPHY
C. Atmore, *Methodist Memorial* (Bristol, England, 1801): 54–7
C. H. Crookshank, *History of Methodism in Ireland*, 2 vols (Belfast, 1885; London, 1886)
R. H. Gallagher, *Pioneer Preachers of Irish Methodism* (Belfast, no date)
G. Smith, *History of Wesleyan Methodism*, 3 vols, 2 (London, 1857–61): 267–8

FRANK BAKER

Blair, James (b. Cairneyhill, Fife, Scotland, 19 September 1797; d. Bridge of Allan, Stirlingshire, Scotland,

9 April 1859). Scottish Baptist evangelist. James Blair was the son and grandson of Secession ministers. In 1819 he married the daughter of a 'staunch Baptist' and ·this led him to believer's baptism in 1822. He worked as a teacher and was ordained over a small Baptist congregation in Saltcoats, Ayrshire in 1829. He was supported by the Baptist Home Missionary Society for Scotland from 1836, and itinerated widely in the south-west of Scotland. He founded a new church in Ayr in 1837. Moving to Dunfermline in 1840, he changed decisively from Scotch Baptist principles and formed a new Baptist church in 1841. He associated with F. JOHNSTONE and the Baptist Union, being its agent in the Borders and later Stirling and Dundee. During his largely itinerant ministry he practised as a homeopathic doctor.

SELECT WRITINGS
J. Blair, *The Scottish Evangelist* (Glasgow, 1860)

DEREK B. MURRAY

Blair, Samuel (b. Ulster, Ireland, 14 June 1712; d. Faggs Manor, PA, BNA, 5 July 1751). Presbyterian minister in New Jersey and Pennsylvania. Samuel Blair came to America in his early youth. Educated at the 'Log College' in Neshaminy, Pennsylvania, he was licensed by the presbytery of Philadelphia 9 November 1733. In 1734 he became pastor of the churches of Middletown and Shrewsbury, New Jersey.

Called by the Faggs Manor church in New Londonderry, Pennsylvania (near modern Cochranville), in 1739, he began his ministry there in November. Revival began at Faggs Manor in March 1740 under a visiting preacher while Blair was on a preaching mission in New Jersey. The revival continued after his return, and Blair became, with GILBERT TENNENT, a main supporter of the New Side in the Presbyterian division of 1741. He established the Faggs Manor academy for the training of ministers on the model of the Log College. Among its graduates was SAMUEL DAVIES. Blair was involved as a trustee in the forming of the College of New Jersey (later Princeton). A strong Calvinist and an impressive preacher, he wrote a narrative of the revival at Faggs Manor.

BIBLIOGRAPHY
DAB
W. B. Noble, *A History of Faggs Manor United Presbyterian Church, 1730–1980* (Cochranville, PA, 1980)

WILLIAM S. BARKER

Blair, William (b. Lavenham, Suffolk, England, 28 Jan. 1766; d. London, 6 Dec. 1822). Surgeon, bibliophile and collector of Bibles. The son of William Blair, MD, Blair qualified as a surgeon under J. Pearson of Golden Square and began to practise in Bloomsbury and develop his interest in evangelical institutions. A member of the

Royal College of Surgeons and surgeon to the Lock Hospital, he edited the *London Medical Review and Magazine*. Blair wrote several medical works, including a defence of vaccination. He was a member of the BFBS Committee for 17 years, from 1806 until his death, serving on several subcommittees and taking a particular interest in editorial and publishing matters. His collection of Bibles in various editions was invaluable to the BFBS for collating their first few foreign language versions. With the collections of GRANVILLE SHARP and others, the bequest of Blair's Bibles and New Testaments to the society formed the nucleus of their library.

BIBLIOGRAPHY
DNB
A. S. Herbert, *Historical Catalogue* (London, 1968)
L. Howsam, *Cheap Bibles* (Cambridge, 1991)

LESLIE HOWSAM

Blake, William Hume (b. Kiltegan, Ireland, 10 March 1809; d. Toronto, Ontario, Canada, 15 Nov. 1870). Lawyer, politician, and judge. The son of a Church of Ireland clergyman, Blake was educated at Trinity College, Dublin (BA 1828) and emigrated to Upper Canada in 1832 with a group that included his brother, Reverend Dominick Edward Blake and Reverend BENJAMIN CRONYN. Settling first in the London area, Blake moved to Toronto in 1834 where he began his legal studies. Called to the Bar of Upper Canada in 1838 he soon established himself as a very successful lawyer and played an important role in helping to re-organize the Upper Canadian judicial system in the 1840s. He became involved in provincial politics as a supporter of the Reform Party, was elected to the Assembly in 1848, and held the position of Solicitor-General in the Baldwin-Lafontaine administration. In 1850 he was appointed to the bench as Chancellor of Upper Canada; a position he held until 1862. He later served as a judge in the Court of Error and Appeal. He had also acted as first professor of law in King's College, Toronto (1843–8) and as chancellor of the University of Toronto (1853–6). His son, Samuel Hume Blake was the leading evangelical Anglican layman in late nineteenth-century Toronto.

BIBLIOGRAPHY
DCB, IX

RICHARD W. VAUDRY

Blakeney, Richard Paul (b. Roscommon, Ireland, 2 June 1820; d. Bridlington, Yorkshire, England, 31 Dec. 1884). Anglican clergyman and anti-Catholic controversialist. Blakeney was descended from an old Norfolk family settled in County Roscommon, Ireland, and graduated a BA Hons in theology from Trinity College, Dublin in 1842. In 1843 he was ordained deacon to the curacy of St Paul's, Nottingham (priested 1844), where he at once discovered his gift for polemical argument with Roman Catholics, which bore fruit from 1844 in his Nottingham Tracts and his *Awful Disclosure of the Iniquitous Principles taught by the Church of Rome* (1846); and in 1854, in a *Protestant Catechism*. His vehement anti-Catholicism would seem to be related to 'some imperfectly documented personal tragedy, relating to his wife, for which he held the Roman Catholic Church responsible' (Wolffe, 1991: 109). He became involved in the Reformation Society in the late 1840s and was soon one of the powerful clerical personages dominating the Society by the 1850s. JOHN HOPE persuaded Blakeney to write a series of short tracts designed to teach standard Protestant responses to Catholic arguments in polemical debates; these were collected and published as the *Manual of the Romish Controversy* (Edinburgh, 1851) and *Popery in its Social Aspect* (Glasgow, 1852). He was also a strong supporter of the Church Association (formed 1865) which opposed Anglo-Catholic 'ritualism'.

Blakeney built up two new parishes, as Perpetual Curate of Hyson Green, near Nottingham (1844–52), and of Christ Church, Claughton, near Birkenhead (1852–74), which was in an area with many Orangemen and Irish evangelical clergymen. He combined warm friendships with Scottish Presbyterians and Dissenters with a strong Anglican churchmanship declared in his work *The Book of Common Prayer in its History and Interpretation* (1865), and in his restoration of the Priory Church of Bridlington, Yorkshire, where he was vicar from 1874, and where he has his memorial. Despite his honours, academic and ecclesiastical (LL B and LL D of Trinity College, Dublin, 1852; DD of Edinburgh, 1868; Rural Dean of Bridlington, 1876; Canon of York, 1882), Blakeney was loved by rich and poor as a faithful and devoted shepherd of souls, like his brother Canon John Edward Blakeney (born 7 December 1824; died 12 January 1895) Vicar of Sheffield, who shared his views, and who was a church builder and ecclesiastical administrator, and who had a more exclusively pastoral career.

BIBLIOGRAPHY
Boase
Burke's Irish Family Records (London, 1976): 124–5
DNB
The Church Portrait Journal (May 1880)
The Record (30 January 1885)
J. Wolffe, *The Protestant Crusade in Great Britain 1829–1860* (Oxford, 1991)

SHERIDAN GILLEY

Blanchard, Jonathan (b. Rockingham, VT, USA, 19 Jan. 1811; d. Wheaton, IL, USA, 14 May 1892). Presbyterian/Congregationalist minister, college president, and social activist. A practical-minded farmer's son who loved poetry, Blanchard was converted at age 16, decided for the ministry as a student at Middlebury College, Vermont, and enrolled in 1834 at Andover Theological Seminary, Massachusetts.

Andover's want of Christ-centred piety and neutrality on slavery dismayed Blanchard, who turned abolitionist and left school in 1836 to lecture for the American Anti-Slavery Society. In 1838 the spiritual struggle for the West drew him to Cincinnati, where he graduated from Lane Seminary and became pastor of the Sixth Presbyterian Church. Intent on organizing unseen realities into practical programmes, Blanchard won repute as a revivalist, reformer and churchman. He married another Vermonter, Mary Avery Bent, in 1838; they had 12 children.

Blanchard turned Congregationalist after becoming president of Knox College, Illinois, in 1846, but his sharp personality, decided opinions on social reform, and denominational preferences led to his ouster in 1858. In 1860 he moved to Wheaton, Illinois, where he founded Wheaton College, serving as president until succeeded by his son in 1882. Colleges were, for Blanchard, public extensions of the church engaged in preparing evangelical leaders to work toward a perfect society. That lifelong vision of social perfection continued to inform Blanchard's last crusade as he laboured until his death for the National Christian Association opposed to Secret Societies, which he helped establish in 1867, and its newspaper, *The Christian Cynosure*.

BIBLIOGRAPHY
DAB
C. S. Kilby, *Minority of One* (Grand Rapids, MI, 1959)
R. S. Taylor, 'Seeking the Kingdom: A Study in the Career of Jonathan Blanchard, 1811–92' (Northern Illinois Univ. Ph.D. diss., 1977)

RICHARD S. TAYLOR

Blanshard, Thomas (b. *c.* 1765; d. 20 Feb. 1824). Methodist minister. Blanshard entered the Wesleyan Methodist ministry in 1795, spent two years in Shrewsbury, a year each in Swansea, Liverpool, Stourport, Horncastle, Harrow, two in Louth, one in Bradford (Wiltshire), two in Witney, and then one in Northampton. Since 1804 JOSEPH BENSON had been editor of the Wesleyan Methodist Book Room. Again from 1804, Benson's business colleague, the junior book steward, had been Robert Lomas, who by 1808 was suffering from 'a violent fever on his brain'. The conference thanked Lomas profusely for his services and (somewhat strangely, as it may seem) appointed him 'General Auditor of all our accounts' until his untimely death at the age of 41 in 1810.

In 1808 Blanshard was appointed to succeed Lomas as book steward. He proved a faithful and efficient officer in overseeing Wesleyan Methodist publishing throughout the remaining editorship of Joseph Benson, and on through the three years of his successor, JABEZ BUNTING. At the outset of his term he organized the removal of the book room and his own residence to 14 City Road. Other forms of modernization were initiated, and in 1811 the *Magazine* begun by JOHN WESLEY in 1778 was doubled in size and price. During his fifteenth year in this arduous but rarely romantic career Blanshard was already failing physically, but his pastoral heart refused to accept retirement as a supernumerary. Instead he attempted to take over the superintendency of the Loughborough circuit, but survived only a few months, suffering all the time. Blanshard laid no claim to literary merit, his only known printed work being an 1816 catalogue of the publications of John Wesley and his preachers, together with a selection of the other stock of the book room, 'some of the most excellent and useful books now extant'. His official obituary testified that he had discharged his book room duties 'with scrupulous and strict fidelity', and that he was 'a man of inflexible integrity, and of sincere piety, and his ministry was sensible and edifying'. With this he would have been content.

FRANK BAKER

Bleby, Henry (b. probably England; d. 1878). Methodist minister. Bleby, with his wife and young baby, arrived in Jamaica from England in 1832. During his 46 years of ministry in the West Indies, the first third of which was spent in Jamaica, Bleby travelled to nearly every part of West Indian Methodism. He is especially remembered for his active identification with the antislavery movement in Jamaica and he provided valuable resource material for the abolition movement in England through his book *Death Struggle of Slavery* as well as many pamphlets and letters.

He served as district chairman in St Vincent, Demerara, and the Bahamas where he established Queen's College to provide secondary and advanced education. Bleby had three sons who became missionaries, one of whom, William F. G. Bleby, was to become chairman of the Bahamas district of the Methodist Church.

BIBLIOGRAPHY
G. G. Findlay and W. W. Holdsworth, *The History of the Wesleyan Methodist Missionary Society*, 5 vols, 2 (London, 1921–4)
P. Samuel, *The Wesleyan Methodist Missions in Jamaica and Honduras* (London, 1850)

EVANS BAILEY

Bliss, Thomas R. (b. Oxford, England, *c.* 1738; d. Bideford, Devon, England, 13 Jan. 1802). Vicar of Ashford and Yarnscombe, Devon. Baptized 17 April 1738, he was the son of Nathaniel Bliss, Rector of St Ebbe's, Oxford, and university professor who became the Astronomer Royal. Converted under THOMAS HAWEIS, he matriculated from Merton College in 1755, migrated to Christ Church in 1758, and graduated BA in 1759. Ordained deacon (1760) and priested (1762), he assisted WILLIAM GRIMSHAW at Haworth before being licensed in 1766 as Curate of Broadwoodwidger, Devon. In 1770 he was instituted to his livings which he held until his death. He resided at Ashford until he retired to Bideford in 1792 on health grounds. He itinerated on occasion for Lady HUNTINGDON but ensured that his parishes were cared for in his absence. A voracious reader, especially of evangelical writers, he left 14 manuscript volumes of extracts.

BIBLIOGRAPHY
EM (1802)

A. SKEVINGTON WOOD

Bloomfield, Lord Benjamin, (first) Baron (b. Newport, Tipperary, Ireland, 13 April 1768; d. London, 15 Aug. 1846). Soldier, courtier, diplomat, and MP. Bloomfield's military career started at the age of 13. Posted in Brighton in 1806, he attracted the attention of the Prince of Wales, who attached him to his household. In 1815, now a major-general, Bloomfield was knighted and in 1817 became the Prince's private secretary for the duration of the Regency. From 1812 to 1815 he was MP for Plymouth. While serving as minister plenipotentiary to Stockholm (1822–30) he was made an Irish peer. In 1828 the deaths of his mother and daughter prompted him to join the Wesleyan congregation in Stockholm. On his return he became commandant of the Woolwich garrison where he founded schools for soldiers' children. A tract, entitled *A Coronet Laid at the Feet of Jesus as Illustrated by the Conversion of the Late Lord Bloomfield* (1856) by the Stockholm Wesleyan minister GEORGE SCOTT makes clear his significance to the evangelical cause.

BIBLIOGRAPHY
Georgiana, Lady Bloomfield, *Memoir of Benjamin Lord Bloomfield* (London, 1884)
DNB

ELISABETH JAY

Blumhardt, Carl Henry [né Karl Heinrich] (b. Stuttgart, Würtemberg, Germany, 1808; d. Tonbridge, Kent, England, 2 June 1883). Anglican missionary in India. He was a nephew of C. G. BLUMHARDT, the founder of the Basel Mission, and the brother of J. C. BLUMHARDT and studied at Basel Seminary. Like so many other 'Würtembergers' he offered to work with the [English] CMS. He received Anglican orders in 1835, and in 1836 he was sent to the new work in Abyssinia (Ethiopia), where he learned enough Amharic to publish an Amharic vocabulary and a new edition of the New Testament. In 1839 he was transferred to India where he served at Krishnagar until 1877.

In and around Krishnagar there had started in 1838 a remarkable people movement which resulted in over 3,000 baptisms. Bishop DANIEL WILSON quickly located several missionaries in Krishnagar itself, and a divinity school was established. Despite stable and faithful work from Blumhardt and his colleagues, the church at Krishnagar proved a disappointment. Adequate instruction seems to have been lacking, and the missionaries failed to recognize and deal with caste and communal differences among the converts who came from Hindu and Muslim backgrounds. Blumhardt retired to England shortly after the death of his wife in 1876. A son and a daughter also served as missionaries in Krishnagar.

BIBLIOGRAPHY
M. E. Gibbs, *The Anglican Church in India 1600–1970* (London, 1972)
E. Stock, *History of the Church Missionary Society*, 3 vols (London, 1899): 314–16.

JOCELYN MURRAY

Blumhardt, Christian Gottlieb (b. 29 April 1779, Stuttgart, Germany; d. 19 Dec. 1838, Basel, Switzerland). A Founder of the Basel Mission. Born as the eldest child into a devout Pietist shoemaker's family, Blumhardt was graduated from the 'Gymnasium' at Stuttgart before beginning theological studies at Tübingen in October 1798. After a series of spiritual struggles, he left the university in 1803 and was called to be the successor of C. F. A. STEINKOPF as secretary of the Deutsche Christentumsgesellschaft in Basel. There he worked with his friend C. F. SPITTLER to edit the monthly revivalistic periodical *Sammlungen für Liebhaber Christlicher Wahrheit*. The publication developed the central themes of Schwabian Pietism reflecting on the 'Kingdom of God' and the implications of the concept for the social, political and religious life of the Christian. He wrote extensively for the periodical and handled the correspondence of the organization. From this platform he was frequently invited to lead pastors' conferences. He also participated in the founding of the Basel Bibelgesellschaft (31 October 1804) on the model of the BFBS.

The recently married Blumhardt accepted a call first as vicar (1807–9) and then as pastor (1809–16) at Burg, Württemberg. He remained, however, in close contact with Basel, and when it was decided to establish a school for educating missionary candidates, Spittler invited Blumhardt to return as director. Back in Basel (on 17 April 1816), he also became editor of the *Evangelisches Missionsmagazin* (1816–38). As the only international ecumenical and independent (of ecclesial control) German missions periodical it exercised significant influence throughout Europe. The Basel Mission cooperated extensively during its first decade with the British and Dutch mission organizations and most missionaries served within those contexts. However, Blumhardt felt that German mission organizations should send their own missionaries and so, in 1821, he began to dispatch German missionaries, especially to the German colonies in south Russia. Others went to Georgia, Persia, Africa and India, the latter by permission of the East India Company. Missionaries were also sent to the German diaspora in the United States, Canada, Australia and Brazil. These had formative influences on the development of the Lutheran Church in those areas.

In April 1828, Blumhardt also began to edit the *Evangelisches Heidenbote*, a more popular missions periodical. This served as the source for the French missions periodical edited by A. VINET, *Gazette des Missions Evangeliques*. That year he also began the publication of his master work, the three (in five) volume history of Christian mission entitled *Versuch Einer Allgemein Missionsgeschichte der Kirche Christi* (Basel, 1828–37; French translation, 1838), which discussed the expansion of the church from the Apostolic period up to the Reformation. This global and ecumenical historiographical effort was a significant departure from the more limited and ideologically defined efforts. Better known to English readers was the translation of *Handbuch der Missionsgeschichte und Missions Geographie* (Basel) entitled *Christian Missions* (1846) which also developed the ecumenical missionary vision of Blumhardt. These commitments contributed significantly to the Basel Mission not identifying with the German Lutheran Confessional movement. Through his organizational work, historiographical writing, editorial work and international mission diplomacy, Blumhardt exercised a formative influence on mission history, theory and practice, not only in Basel, but through the world.

SELECT WRITINGS
C. G. Blumhardt, *Grundlinien einer Hausordnung für die Evangelische Missions-Anstalt zu Basel* (Basel, 1818; 2 edn Basel, 1888)
—, *Vergleichende Bemerkungen über Uie Familien- Verwandtschrift der Indischen Sprachen, in Besonderer Beziehung auf Drei und Dreissig Beigefügte Orientalische Übersetzungen des Gebets des Herrn* (Basel, 1919)
—, *Lazarus, den Kranke, Sterbende und Auferweckte* (2. aufg. Basel, 1827)
—, *Vie de D. Zeisberger, Missionaire de l'Eglise des Frères de Moravie* (Neuchâtel, Switzerland, 1844)
—, *Christian Missions; or A Manual of Missionary Geography and History*, 2 vols (London, 1846)

BIBLIOGRAPHY
A. Ostertag und H. Sundert, 'Blumhardt, Christian Gottlieb', *Realencyklopadie fur Protestantische Theologie und Kirche*, 3 (1897): 262–4
W. Schlatter, *Geschichte der Basler Mission, 1815–1915*, 1 (Basel, 1916)
H. H. Schrey, 'Blumhardt, ev. Theologen', *Neue deutsche Biographie*, 2 (1953): 334

DAVID BUNDY

Blumhardt, Johann Christoph (b. Stuttgart, Germany, 16 July 1805; d. Bad Boll, Germany, 25 Feb. 1880). Pastor, healing movement leader, and reformer. Born into a working-class family early in the Napoleonic era, Blumhardt experienced the turmoil of the occupation of Germany. He received a historical and philological formation at the Stuttgart Gymnasium. He studied at Schönthal Seminary (1820–4) and the University of Tübingen (1824–9), where he worked under F. C. Bauer, among others. His pastoral career began at Dürmenz (1829). From 1830 to 1837, at the instigation of his missiologist uncle C. G. BARTH, he taught at the Basel Evangelical Mission Institute (theological and philological subjects as well as mathematics and practical studies). Returning to pastoral duties, he was assistant at Iptingen (1837) and then successor of C. G. Barth at Möttlingen (1838–52).

At Möttlingen, he encountered a 28-year-old woman, Gottliebin Dittus (1815–72, married name became Brodersen) who had been diagnosed as being possessed by demons and sent to him for care. Using depth psychology as it was then understood, he worked with the woman regarding her inner conflicts. Finally in 1843, with the words, 'Jesus is Victor', Dittus achieved healing. This event stunned parishoners who responded in Revivalist-Pietist fashion, confessing and repenting of sins. Narratives of the healing and revival spread throughout Europe. Many came to be healed, and many were. In 1845, he was forbidden by the church to practice faith-healing. For four-and-a-half years he endured the mistrust and disapproval of ministerial colleagues and superiors.

Finally in 1852, the consistory made it possible for him to purchase the bath [Bad] at Boll. There he established (1852–80) an internationally influential healing centre with the help of his two sons, Theophil and Christoph. He was active in pastoral counselling and worked for the renewal of the church on a Pietist model. A gifted theologian, his reflections on his experience, ministry, the church and the 'kingdom of God' had a profound influence on Reformist theologians, including Karl Barth. The tales of Möttlingen also became paradigmatic for the British and American healing movements of the late nineteenth century and, eventually, of Pentecostalism. His son, Christoph Friedrich Blumhardt (1842–1919) was his successor at Bad Boll. Unpublished papers may be consulted at the Blumhardt-Forschungsstelle Stuttgart.

SELECTED WRIINGS

J. C. Blumhardt, *Gesammelte Werke* hrsg. C. F. Blumhardt (Karlsruhe, Germany, 1886–8)
—, *Gesammelte Werke* hrsg. P. Ernst and J. Scharfenberg (Göttingen, Germany, 1968–74)

BIBLIOGRAPHY

W. Guest, *Pastor Blumhardt and his Work* (London, 1881)
L. Ragaz, *Der Kampf um das Reich Gotts in Blumhardt, Vater und Sohn* (Zürich, 1922)
M. T. Schulz, *Johann Christoph Blumhardt* (Göttingen, Germany, 1984)
—, 'Blumhardt, Johann Christoph', *TRE*, 6 (1980): 721–7
F. Zundel, *Johann Christoph Blumhardt* (Heilbronn, Germany, 1880)

DAVID BUNDY

Blundell, Thomas (b. Kettering, Northamptonshire, England, 1752; d. Luton, Bedfordshire, England, 1 July 1824). Baptist minister and founding member of the BMS. Originally a weaver by trade, Blundell became a Particular Baptist minister. He was baptized by ANDREW FULLER in Kettering on 2 October 1785. He entered Bristol Baptist Academy in 1792 to train for the pastoral ministry. From August 1791 he supplied the pulpit at the village of Arnesby in Leicestershire in succession to ROBERT HALL, Sr. The church called him to the pastorate in 1793. Blundell was one of the 14 persons who gathered in Kettering on 2 October 1792 to form the 'Particular Baptist Society for Propagating the Gospel

amongst the Heathen' (the BMS). He subsequently ministered at Luton (1804–12?) and Keighley (1820–4). Blundell's publications include a collection of sermons (1806) and a study of the seven vials of Revelation (1810).

BIBLIOGRAPHY

Whitley, *BB*
BQ, 1 (1922–3): 286
E. A. Payne, *The First Generation* (London, no date): 13–14

BRIAN STANLEY

Blunt, Henry (b. Dulwich, England, 12 Aug. 1794; d. Streatham, Surrey, England, 20 July 1843). Anglican clergyman and popular preacher. Blunt was educated at Merchant Taylors' School and Pembroke College, Cambridge. He was ordained to a college fellowship and from 1820 was Vicar of Clare, Suffolk. There he was converted to evangelicalism and took private pupils.

In 1824 he became Curate of St Luke's, Chelsea and two years later declined FRANCIS CLOSE's invitation to become Curate of Holy Trinity, Cheltenham. In 1832 Blunt became the first Rector of Holy Trinity, Upper Chelsea and was also the Chaplain to the Duke of Richmond. He resigned through ill health in 1835 and became Rector of Streatham, Surrey.

Blunt was a popular evangelical preacher and 'drew around him what was perhaps the most influential congregation in London' (G. R. Balleine). He was an early supporter of *The Record* and with other evangelicals planned a counterblast to the *Tracts for the Times*. He published numerous volumes of sermons and a parish magazine, *The Poor Churchman's Evening Companion*.

BIBLIOGRAPHY

DNB

ALAN FREDERICK MUNDEN

Boardman, George Dana (b. Livermore ME, USA, 8 Feb. 1801; d. Tavoy, Burma 11 Feb. 1831). American missionary in Burma. In 1819 Boardman matriculated at what was later named Colby College, and the next year made public profession of faith and joined the Baptist Church at Waterville. In 1822 he graduated at the head of his class. The death of James Colman, one of the first to answer ADONIRAM JUDSON's call for missionary volunteers, and then the death of his sister Harriet, moved him to offer to take Colman's place. In May 1823 the standing committee of the Baptist Triennial Convention voted to send him to Burma.

Boardman attended Andover Theological Seminary for two years. On 16 February 1825 he was ordained by the Waterville Baptist Church; on 3 July he was married to Sarah Hall [see SARAH HALL BOARDMAN JUDSON] in the First Baptist Church of Salem. They sailed from Philadelphia on the *Asia*, arriving in Calcutta over four months later. Judson was then in prison at Ava.

The Boardmans studied Burmese in Calcutta and remained there until March 1827 because of Mrs Boardman's health. During that time Sarah Ann was born. In April 1827, the Boardmans went to Amherst where they met Adoniram Judson for the first time. Next month they settled at Moulmein, where Judson and Jonathan Wade with his wife joined them after the closure of the Amherst station. Here they faced robbers, fire, insects and disease, but the work grew steadily, and they built a *zayat* (house of worship).

A station was opened at Tavoy, and the Boardmans were assigned there. They left Moulmein on 28 March 1828, taking with them Ko Tha Byu, a Karen murderer who been bought by Mrs Judson and converted. Boardman baptized him at Tavoy on 16 May. At Tavoy the Boardmans opened several schools. Their son, George Dana, was born in 1828. Boardman found a Karen teacher who had an English copy of the *Book of Common Prayer* with Psalms. In January 1829, two Karens invited Boardman to visit their people. He and Ko Tha Byu received a warm welcome.

In the Tavoy revolt of 1829, the Boardman dwelling was wrecked. Their daughter died, Mrs Boardman was forced away by sickness for a time, and Boardman himself developed illness of the lungs. Meanwhile Ko Tha Byu was preaching among the Karens, who responded remarkably. Early in 1831 it became apparent Boardman was failing. A new couple, the Masons, arrived 23 January. A week later the Boardmans and Mason went to visit the Karens, but it was evident that Boardman was dying. He watched Francis Mason baptize 34 converts. The following day, 11 February, he died on the way back to Tavoy, where he was buried beside Sarah. His wife lived to 1845, marrying Adoniram Judson in 1834.

Of Boardman and his ministry Judson wrote in his diary: 'One of the brightest luminaries of Burma is extinguished ... Such a death, next to that of martyrdom, must be glorious, in the eyes of heaven.' His papers are in the American Baptist Foreign Mission Society Archives, Brown University and Andover-Newton Seminary.

BIBLIOGRAPHY
A. King, *Memoir of G. D. Boardman* (Boston, MA, 1848)
F. Mason, *The Karen Apostle* (Boston, MA, and London, *c.* 1843)
J. C. Robbins, *Boardman of Burma* (Philadelphia, PA, 1940)
R. G. Torbet, *Venture of Faith* (Philadelphia, PA, 1955)

HAROLD LINDSELL

Boardman, Richard (b. 1738; d. Cork, Ireland, 10 April 1782). Methodist preacher. Boardman was one of JOHN WESLEY's 'sons in the gospel', an itinerant Methodist lay preacher from 1763. In 1769, recently widowed, he joined JOSEPH PILMORE as one of the first two volunteers officially sponsored by Wesley to be missionaries to America. This action was in response to appeals from American Methodists to be supplied with preachers. They arrived at Philadelphia in October. Boardman

served in the colonies until January, 1774, New York and Philadelphia being the centres of his activity.

Wesley had made Boardman his assistant for America. FRANCIS ASBURY, who joined Boardman and Pilmore in 1771, was very critical of the former for not extending the mission more vigorously. Wesley replaced Boardman as assistant, first with Francis Asbury, then with THOMAS RANKIN. When the first American Methodist Conference met in Philadelphia in 1773, Boardman was in attendance but did not receive an appointment because he had already decided to leave America. He returned home owing to the deteriorating relations between Britain and America. Except for a year in London, seven of his remaining eight years of ministry were given to Ireland. He is buried in the graveyard of St Fin Barre's Cathedral, Cork. Boardman was remembered as an able preacher, successful evangelist, and warm colleague.

BIBLIOGRAPHY
E. S. Bucke, ed., *The History of American Methodism*, I (Nashville, TN, 1964)
EWM
M. Simpson, *Cyclopedia of Methodism* (Philadelphia, PA, 1880)
A. Stevens, *History of the Methodist Episcopal Church*, I (New York, 1864)

CHARLES W. BROCKWELL, JR.

Boardman, Sarah Hall. See JUDSON, SARAH HALL BOARD-MAN

Boardman, William Edwin (b. Smithfield, NY, USA, 11 Oct. 1810; d. London, 4 Feb. 1886). Presbyterian minister and evangelist, holiness and healing advocate. Converted (*circa*1831) he married Mary (February 1837) and continued in various business ventures before financial and family crises caused him to rededicate himself to Christ (*circa*1840). After a short sojourn in Stirling, Illinois, they moved to Potosi, Wisconsin (1842–3). In a Methodist church he experienced sanctification. He became involved in the life of the local church, where the main competition came from Mormon evangelists, and at the insistence of the congregation, he was ordained. He also became a supporter of the Wisconsin Anti-Slavery Society.

Boardman then studied at Lane Theological Seminary in Cincinnati (1843–6). After consultation with Henry Ward Beecher in Indianapolis, he established a church in Greenfield, Indiana. This was followed by study at Yale. While in New Haven, he was engaged by the ASSU to establish 'Mission Sunday Schools' in the West. In 1852, the Boardmans moved to Detroit. However, in 1854, the ASSU experienced financial problems and Boardman resigned.

The family then moved to Gloucester City, New Jersey, where Mary wrote the first draft of *The Higher Christian Life* and William revised it, publishing it under his name (1858). This volume sought to explain the doctrine and experience of sanctification without the specialized jargon of the Methodist Church and Holiness Movement;

it sold several hundred thousand copies in both North America and England. It was also translated, in whole or in extracts, throughout Europe and Asia. The volume became the basis of their future evangelistic work in the USA and Europe after the American Civil War.

However the book raised considerable hostility in Presbyterian circles, and the Boardmans went to California in 1859. Their abolitionist sentiments made life difficult after the outbreak of the Civil War and they returned to New England (March 1862). There he became secretary of the United States Christian Commission, a branch of the YMCA which attempted to minister to soldiers. He worked in the field (1862–6).

The Boardmans toured Europe in 1868 and wrote *He that Overcometh, or a Conquering Gospel* (Boston, 1869). In 1869, business interests brought him again to Europe where he met WILLIAM PENNEFATHER and spoke at the Mildmay Conference. On the model of Mildmay, he attempted to organize an ecumenical 'Association for Holding Union Holiness Conventions' (1870) in the USA which enjoyed ephemeral success among the Presbyterians and wrote *Gladness in Jesus* (Boston, 1870). From 1870 to 1872, the Boardmans engaged in a 'faith ministry' throughout the USA, but exhausted, they went to England and Germany (1873) travelling with Charles Cullis, whose work he described in *Faith Work Under Dr Cullis* (Boston, 1873). He became involved in holiness meetings in London, both at Mildmay and with the prayer breakfasts organized by T. B. Smithies, in cooperation with R. P. Smith, WILLIAM ARTHUR, Samuel Morley and Robert Morgan. A series of conferences for the 'Promotion of Scriptural Holiness' were organized at Mildmay and throughout Britain, including the Broadlands, Oxford and Brighton meetings from which Keswick evolved. In Glasgow, he preached in the church of ANDREW A. BONAR.

After a brief return to the USA (1876), the Boardmans returned to England where he continued his involvement with holiness and, increasingly, healing ministries, focusing on 'evangelizing among the Christians'. Ministry in Sweden among the Baptists brought positive responses. Out of these experiences came *The Lord that Healeth Thee* (London, 1880). He became the centre of the European healing movement among the 'higher life' groups, in cooperation with J. C. BLUMHARDT, O. Stockmeyer, C. Cullis and others. The International Healing Conference (1880) brought together healing evangelists from Europe and North America. Cooperating at 'Bethshan' (the healing centre) were M. Baxter and E. Sisson. He wrote extensively for holiness, revivalistic and healing periodicals throughout the world.

BIBLIOGRAPHY
M. Boardman, *The Life and Labours of the Rev. W. E. Boardman*, with a preface by Mark Guy Pearse (New York, 1887)
D. Bundy, *Keswick* (Wilmore, 1975; reprinted New York, 1984)
——'Keswick and the Experience of Evangelical Piety', in *Modern Christian Revivals*, ed. E. Blumhofer and R. Balmer (Urbana, IL, 1993): 118–44

DAVID BUNDY

Boase, Charles William (b. London, 8 June 1804; d. Albury, Surrey, England, 7 June 1872). Banker and Irvingite. Educated at Helston Grammar School, he entered in 1821, the Dundee New Bank of which his father HENRY BOASE (1763–1827) was a proprietor. From 1829 to his retirement in 1867 he was manager of the bank during which time it was merged with the Royal Bank of Scotland. He took an active part in the municipal life of Dundee and after the town's bankruptcy in 1842 he was made a trustee by the creditors. In 1836 he was ordained a priest and in 1851 a bishop in the Catholic Apostolic Church. On retirement he moved to Edinburgh and took charge of that church's evangelism throughout Scotland. Both he and his brother GEORGE C. BOASE married daughters of William Lindsay. His written works include *A Century of Banking in Dundee* (1866) and a valuable account of the Irvingite movement, *The Elijah Ministry* (1867). He must not be confused with his identically named nephew (1828–95) who edited the *Registrum Collegii Exoniensis*.

BIBLIOGRAPHY
Boase
C. W. Boase, G. C. Boase and F. Boase, *An Account of the Families of Boase and Bowes* (Truro, England, 1893): 12–16, 26–8, 34–5, 94–7

TIMOTHY C. F. STUNT

Boase, George Clement (b. London, 25 Aug. 1810; d. near Stirling, Scotland, 23 July 1880). Banker and Irvingite bishop. Educated at Exeter Grammar School and Queens', Cambridge, in 1830 he joined the Dundee New Bank where in 1840 he followed his brother CHARLES W. BOASE in a managerial position until his retirement in 1867. He was ordained a priest in the Catholic Apostolic Church in 1836 and a bishop in 1859. On retirement he moved to Brighton where he was responsible for the community founded by his relative (through marriage), JOHN BAYFORD. He must not be confused with his identically named nephew (1829–89) who contributed to the *Dictionary of National Biography*.

BIBLIOGRAPHY
C. W. Boase, G. C. Boase and F. Boase, *An Account of the Families of Boase and Bowes* (Truro, England, 1893): 34–5

TIMOTHY C. F. STUNT

Boase, Henry (b. Madron, Cornwall, England, 3 June 1763; d. Alverton, Penzance, Cornwall, England, 8 April 1827). Banker and philanthropist. An eminent London banker, with government support he led City opposition to the 1810 Bullion Committee report and produced pamphlets on the subject.

He was a co-founder of the BFBS, a supporter of the LMS. He lived in Penzance from 1811 where he operated a bank and became mayor. He contributed anti-Catholic articles to the *Christian Guardian* (1816). The correspondent of CHARLES of Bala, SHARP, Hardcastle, and other notables, his papers (British Library Additional Manuscripts 29281) are invaluable. An Anglican himself, two of his children became Irvingites.

BIBLIOGRAPHY
C. W. Boase, G. C. Boase and F. Boase, *An Account of the Family of Boase* (Truro, England, 1893)
DNB

JONATHAN BURKE CUTMORE

Boaz, Thomas   (b. Scarborough, Yorkshire, England, 10 August 1806; d. London, 13 Oct. 1861). Missionary and social reformer in India. A rough Yorkshireman of Quaker extraction, Boaz was criticized for his 'rough sailor's ways' and his 'wild unscholarly sermons.' Ordained 18 June 1834, he arrived in Calcutta in December 1834. He repaired schisms at the LMS's Union Chapel (*see* HENRY TOWNLEY) that were caused by his predecessor, ROBERT COTTON MATHER, and turned it into an important contributor to mission finances.

In 1842 Boaz almost single-handedly stopped the West Indies sugar plantations' trade in indentured labourers, but a lack of support in England foiled his efforts for a permanent end to this disguised form of slavery. Boaz promoted other social issues on an ecumenical basis, was secretary of various ecumenical charities, started a Bethel Mission to sailors, and worked as editor of the *Calcutta Christian Observer*. During his 1847–9 furlough he raised money to rebuild the LMS college at Bhowanipore, laying its foundation stone in 1851. Boaz also fought for better conditions of service for missionaries. King's College, Aberdeen recognized his work with an honorary LL D.

He married Elizabeth Smith (September 1849) and landed with her in Calcutta on 3 January 1850. Elizabeth was a valuable missionary, and ran the Union Chapel for several months when Boaz was ill in Darjeeling. His ill health forced their return to Britain in January 1859. Elizabeth had two sons by Thomas, and died on 30 November 1884.

BIBLIOGRAPHY
E. Boaz, *The Mission Pastor, Memorials of the Rev. Thomas Boaz, by His Widow* (London, 1862)

E. M. JACKSON

Bockett, John   (d. London, 13 May 1871). Merchant and BFBS treasurer. Bockett lived in Clapham Common. Research in London directories of the 1820s and 1830s suggests that he earned his considerable wealth as a distiller and brandy merchant in Blackfriars. His early retirement was explained in his BFBS obituary: 'Having from conscientious scruples given up a lucrative business which he thought to be detrimental to the best interests of his fellow-creatures, and in doing so sacrificed a large amount of property rather than perpetuate an evil of appalling magnitude' he engaged in philanthropic work.

He served the BFBS Committee for all but two of the years 1834 to 1861, then succeeded JOHN THORNTON as treasurer until 1869. When Bockett died in 1871 he left the society a substantial legacy.

BIBLIOGRAPHY
BFBS Monthly Reporter (July 1871)
L. Howsam, 'The Bible Transaction', (York Univ. Ph.D. thesis, 1988)

LESLIE HOWSAM

Boden, James   (b. Chester, Durham, England, 13 April 1757; d. Chesterfield, Derbyshire, England, 4 June 1841). Congregational minister. Trained at Homerton, he became the first minister of Hanley Tabernacle, Staffordshire, and a considerable church planter in Staffordshire. One of 'the strong earnest Evangelical breed', 'a scriptural Calvinist, making a practical use of the doctrines of grace, preaching Christ crucified as the power of God unto salvation', he edited a hymn-book, was a founder of the LMS, a committee member of the RTS, and from 1796 to 1839 exercised a strong ministry in Sheffield.

BIBLIOGRAPHY
J. Morison, *The Fathers and Founders of the London Missionary Society*, 2nd edn (London, 1844): 522–8

J. H. Y. BRIGGS

Boehm, Martin   (b. Lancaster County, PA, BNA, 30 Nov. 1725; d. Lancaster County, PA, USA, 23 March 1812). Mennonite and United Brethren in Christ bishop. A son of Jacob and Barbara (Kendig), Boehm was educated at home in both German and English. In 1756 he was chosen by lot and ordained a Mennonite minister, and in 1761 was ordained bishop. A conversion experience while ploughing, *circa* 1758, radically altered his life. Travelling among Germans in Pennsylvania, Maryland, and Virginia and holding large meetings at his farm, Boehm influenced and was influenced by a variety of evangelicals. On 10 May 1767 PHILIP W. OTTERBEIN proclaimed 'we are brothers', which eventually led to the United Brotherhood of evangelical German preachers in 1789 and the creation of the United Brethren in Christ on 25 September 1800.

Boehm's evangelical preaching and association with non-Mennonites resulted in excommunication in 1775. That year he organized a Methodist class; his wife, Eve (Steiner), was among the first members. Boehm had eight children; the youngest, Henry, became a Methodist minister.

BIBLIOGRAPHY
DAB
A. Sangrey, *Martin Boehm* (Ephrata, PA, 1976)

SALLY SCHWARTZ

Bogue, David (b. Coldingham, Berwickshire, Scotland, 18 Feb. 1750; d. Brighton, England, 25 Oct. 1825). Congregational historian and educationalist. Trained for the ministry of the Church of Scotland in Edinburgh, he became Congregational minister in Gosport, Hampshire, where in 1780 he opened one of the new academies for ministerial training that closely related education and evangelism and embraced itinerancy as part of the students' preparation. He did not, however, relax the demands for proper academic study, being highly critical of those evangelical academies which offered only 'a half education'. In later years, however, the function came largely to be the preparation of men for missionary service overseas, service denied Bogue himself through failure to secure the consent of the East India Company.

In 1781 he helped found the Hampshire Association of Independent Churches, the first of the new county associations to be founded, designed to spearhead a new concern for home mission. At the same time, inspired by WILLIAM CAREY's initiative, he believed that paedo-baptists should also play their part in overseas missions, and by calling meetings, and writing in the *Evangelical Magazine*, secured the founding of the LMS. The author of the famous pronouncement concerning 'the funeral of bigotry', he was also a founder of other interdenominational enterprises including the RTS and the Bible Society, and yet was an early champion of the idea of a union of Congregationalist churches and ministers some twenty years before that was secured. He campaigned for the repeal of the Test Acts, outlined a plan for a dissenting university in 1812, and with JAMES BENNETT wrote *A History of the Dissenters, 1689–1808*, 4 vols (London, 1808–12).

BIBLIOGRAPHY
J. Bennett, *Memoirs of the Life of the Rev. David Bogue, D.D.*, (London, 1827)
DNB

J. H. Y. BRIGGS

Böhler, Peter (b. Frankfurt am Main, Germany, 31 Dec. 1712; d. London, 27 April 1775). Moravian bishop. Peter was the fourth child of Johann Konrad Böhler, brewer and comptroller of the Corn Office at Frankfurt, and his wife Antonetta Elizabetha Hanf. Educated at the Frankfurt Gymnasium, he proceeded in 1731 to the University of Jena with a view to theological studies. Under Buddeus, Jena theology had established a mediating position between orthodoxy and Pietism, and under Walch developed a reputation for systematics and polemics. For some years revivals had been breaking out among students at Jena which Count ZINZENDORF sought to further by sending AUGUST SPANGENBERG there. Almost immediately Böhler was converted in one of Spangenberg's meetings; when the latter went to Halle and Zinzendorf came to provide pastoral oversight in his place, Böhler formed a lifelong attachment to him, and began to preach in the neighbourhood.

After a brief stay in the University of Leipzig in 1734,

he returned to Jena where the revival was rapidly gaining ground, and producing many adherents and evangelists for the Moravian community. Proceeding to Herrnhut in 1735, he was instrumental in the conversion of Georg Schulius, became tutor to Zinzendorf's son, and, when the Count was exiled from Saxony, found him temporary accommodation in Frankfurt. In 1737 he was received into the Moravian community, and ordained to its ministry (December 1737).

He was appointed by Zinzendorf to take charge of the small Moravian cause in Savannah with a view to promoting a mission for blacks, and to travel out via England with Schulius and FREDERICH WENZEL NEISSER (destined for Georgia) and Abraham Richter, who was to visit a small German group in London. Böhler was also to make a diplomatic visit to Oxford where Zinzendorf had long desired contacts. Since none of the party spoke English, their immediate concern was with the German community. JOHN WESLEY, who in Georgia had applied for membership of the Moravian Church was now in England, met the Moravians at the house of Francis Wynantz, the German merchant who was their London agent, got them lodgings near JAMES HUTTON's house where he was staying, and provided contacts in Oxford. He also gave an introduction to the world of London religious societies which they had not come to cultivate, and for which they were ill-fitted by their lack of English. Delays in his passage to America, however, enabled Böhler to speak effectively at these meetings with the help of translators of his German and Latin.

On 24 April 1738 he founded what became the Fetter Lane Society on a Moravian model, wrote its first rules, and left for Portsmouth. Richter remained behind to keep an eye on the German work, and the English contacts in both London and Oxford. The Fetter Lane Society remained in contact with cells of religious revival (and of disorder, like the French Prophets) throughout the country, Moravian influence being steadily intensified by visits from Zinzendorf, COSSART and many others. Paradoxically this development was hindered by the man on whom Böhler had most influence, John Wesley.

Böhler, like Spangenberg earlier, caught Wesley at his weakest point, his lack of existential certainty as to the concurrent testimony of scripture and reason. Convinced before the end of April 1738 that the transition from works to faith occurred in the 'new birth', experienced in instantaneous conversion, and supported by scripture and living witnesses, he was not yet certain that it had occurred in himself. John was nursed by Böhler into a Moravian-style experience of 'heart-warming' which proved an inadequate guide to his conversion as a whole. And it was John who, after a visit to Herrnhut in the summer of 1738 which did not lead to admission to the Moravian community, turned against them and divided the Fetter Lane Society.

Böhler arrived in Georgia as war with Spain (entrenched in Florida) was about to break out, found that in a colony whose founders had attempted to create a slave-free society there were few people to convert, and quickly had to bury his first convert, Schulius. When war broke out, Böhler took his tiny non-combatant remnant into Savannah, where he met GEORGE WHITEFIELD. The latter had purchased 5,000 acres on the forks of the Delaware for a black school and a refuge for English debtors; he proposed that the Moravian remnant go into the wilderness to build the school. Cooperation with Whitefield proved difficult, but the move led to the purchase of a neighbouring estate on which, with the assistance of another emigrant party, the famous settlement at Bethlehem was created.

Böhler returned to the continent via England early in 1741, and was brought back for a successful period of preaching in Yorkshire where the Moravians were now well entrenched and the revival was in full swing. In 1742 Böhler took charge of another group of immigrants from Germany, and escorted them to Pennsylvania whence they proceeded to Bethlehem. Böhler exercised an itinerant ministry in the region, and for a time joined Zinzendorf in his ill-fated attempt to create a congregation of God in the Spirit among the Pennsylvania Germans. In November 1744 he handed over charge of the American mission to Spangenberg, and returned to Germany. On 10 January 1748 he was consecrated the sixteenth bishop of the new Moravian line.

He seems to have had no influence upon the Moravian negotiations in England for legal recognition and political privileges, and was deeply grieved by the community's financial crisis in the early 1750s. When Spangenberg returned to Europe in 1753, Böhler crossed to take charge of the American mission for the third time. Here he provided pastoral care for settled congregations and attempted evangelism among the Indians. Until the death of Zinzendorf in 1764 his life was divided between work in America and attendance at the community's synods in Europe. He then returned permanently to Europe and was reconciled with Wesley just before his death. He suffered a stroke after preaching in the Fetter Lane Chapel in 1775, and died eight days later. He was survived by his wife, Elizabeth née Hobson, whom he married in 1742; she was buried at Fulneck in 1781. The characteristics of Böhler were a quiet humility and a capacity to expound the Gospel to educated and untutored hearers in a variety of languages.

BIBLIOGRAPHY
Böhler's brief autobiography, 'Lebenslauf von Petrus Böhler' was printed in Mitteilungen aus der Brüder-Gemeine zur Förderung Christlicher Gemeinschaft, 5 (1931): 154–66
J. F. Lockwood, Memorials of the Life of Peter Böhler (London, 1868)
C. J. Podmore, 'The Fetter Lane Society, 1738', PWHS, 46 (1988): 125–53
G. A. Wauer, Die Anfänge der Brüderkirche in England (Leipzig, Germany, 1900)

W. R. WARD

Bolton, James (Jay) (b. near Weymouth, England, 11 Feb. 1824; d. Kilburn, Middlesex, England, 8 April 1863). Anglican clergyman and children's preacher. He was the son of an American preacher, Robert Bolton of Pelham, New York, and of Anne Jay, eldest child of WILLIAM JAY of Bath. In 1836 his family returned to the USA where he received his early education. Attendance at Corpus Christi, Cambridge (BA 1848) brought him back to England. As superintendent of the Jesus Lane Sunday school, Bolton was among the 'Jesus Lane lot', the group of undergraduates who formed the Cambridge Prayer Union (a distant forerunner of Inter-Varsity Fellowship). He was ordained priest in 1849 and obtained his first curacy at Saffron Walden, Essex (1849–51), where he underwent a religious conversion. Bolton submitted relevant portions of his daily journal to the Christian Observer (July 1850: 773–5) as evidence of the necessity of sudden conversion. A lively debate followed with the Christian Observer editorializing against the notion.

In 1852, following two years in London as a curate at St Michael's, Pimlico, he was made Perpetual Curate of St Paul's Episcopal Chapel, Kilburn, Middlesex, where he stayed for his few remaining years. He was also domestic chaplain to H. G. F. R. MORETON, second Earl of Ducie. Bolton frequently contributed to popular Christian family journals, such as the Christian Treasury and the Sunday Scholars Magazine. Evangelical contemporaries uniformly considered him to have been without peer as a children's evangelist.

SELECTED WRITING
J. J. Bolton, Selected Sermons (London, 1863)

BIBLIOGRAPHY
CO, 63 (October 1863): 123–25
DNB

JONATHAN BURKE CUTMORE

Bomberger, J(ohn) H(enry) A(ugustus) (b. Lancaster, PA, USA, 13 Jan. 1817; d. Collegeville, PA, USA, 19 Aug. 1890). German Reformed clergyman, college president, editor, and controversialist. The only member of the first graduating class of Marshall College (Mercersburg, Pennsylvania) in 1837, Bomberger went on to study at the German Reformed Theological Seminary at Mercersburg. He was ordained by the German Reformed Church in 1838 and served pastorates in various Pennsylvania churches. His longest pastorate was at the Race Street Church in Philadelphia (1854–70). He was the founder and editor of the Reformed Church Monthly (1868–77), a publication which strongly opposed the liturgical emphases of the Mercersburg Theology. In 1870 he became president of Ursinus College at Collegeville, Pennsylvania, serving there until his death. His published works include: a revised translation of Kurtz's Text-Book of Church History (2 vols, 1860–2), The Protestant Theological and Ecclesiastical Encyclopedia (2 vols, 1858–60) – a condensation of the first six volumes of Johann Jakob Herzog's Realencyklopädie; and The Revised Liturgy, a History and Criticism of the Ritualistic Movement in the German Reformed Church (1867).

BIBLIOGRAPHY
DCA
DAB

STEPHEN R. GRAHAM

Bonar, Andrew Alexander (b. Edinburgh, 1810; d. Glasgow, 31 Dec. 1892). Preacher and author. Born on 29 May (Boase) or 29 August 1810 (*DNB*) as the seventh son of James Bonar (1757–1821), Depute-Solicitor of Excise in Edinburgh, he was the brother of JOHN JAMES BONAR and HORATIUS BONAR. Like himself both became gifted preachers. Andrew was a Latin medallist at the city's high school and university. He was licensed as a Church of Scotland preacher on 1 July 1835. After serving in Jedburgh, Roxburghshire, and St George's, Edinburgh, he was ordained a minister of Collace, Perthshire, on 23 September 1838. Deeply concerned with evangelizing the Jews he and his friend, R. M. MCCHEYNE, were sent to Palestine by the Church of Scotland in 1839. The two men wrote a *Narrative of a Mission of Inquiry to the Jews* (Edinburgh, 1842), which led to the establishment of a notable work. Both also took part in a movement which culminated in 1838–9 in the revival at Kilsyth near Glasgow (in which W. C. Burns was also involved).

After the Disruption in 1843 Bonar remained in Collace preaching in a tent until a Free Church was built. On 4 December 1856 he started a new Free Church in Finnieston, Glasgow, where he remained until his death. On 22 April 1874 he became a DD of the University of Edinburgh, and in May 1878 moderator of the General Assembly of the Free Church.

Apart from his preaching Bonar is remembered for his books. Some have become devotional classics, for example, his *Memoir and Remains of Robert Murray McCheyne* (Dundee, 1843) and his edition of Samuel Rutherford's *Letters* (Edinburgh, 1848). His shorthand diary covering the period 1828 to 1892 was extended and edited by his daughter, Marjory, who published it as his *Diary and Letters* (London, 1894). It soon became a best seller. His *Commentary on the Book of Leviticus, Expository and Practical* (London, 1894; reprinted 1972), with its detailed allegorizing of the offerings, was popular for many years. Beside many short memoirs, pamphlets, and tracts, he wrote *Christ and His Church in the Book of Psalms* (London, 1859) and *Palestine for the Young* (London, 1865).

SELECT WRITINGS
A. A. Bonar, *Reminiscences*, ed. M. Bonar (London, 1895)

JOHN S. ANDREWS

Bonar, Archibald (b. Cockpen, Scotland, 23 Feb. 1753; d. Cramond, West Lothian, Scotland, 8 April 1816). Church of Scotland minister. Descended from three generations of Church of Scotland ministers with evangelical sympathies, he impressed GEORGE WHITEFIELD, a family acquaintance, with his spiritual maturity as a youth. After brief stints at churches in Fife and Glasgow, Bonar came in 1785 to the parish of Cramond, near Edinburgh, where he spent the remainder of his life. He was a strong proponent of revival and missions throughout his ministry. He sought to encourage spiritual renewal in his parish by preaching on the importance of 'vital religion' and through regular parochial visitation and catechizing. Although a firm adherent to the Church of Scotland, he also supported local interdenominational organizations. He and his lawyer brother James (the father of HORATIUS BONAR) were keystones of the Edinburgh Missionary and Bible societies and writers for such early Scottish evangelical periodicals as the *Missionary Magazine* and the *Religious Monitor*.

SELECT WRITING
A. Bonar, *Sermons*, 2 vols (London, 1815 and 1817) [memoir by James Bonar prefixed to vol. 2]

BIBLIOGRAPHY
DNB
Fasti, 1: 12–13

DAVID A. CURRIE

Bonar, Horatius (b. Edinburgh, 19 Dec. 1808; d. Edinburgh, 31 July 1889). Hymn-writer and preacher. Bonar was of the fifth generation of Church of Scotland ministers. His father, James, was Depute-Solicitor of Excise in Edinburgh and an elder in Lady Glenorchy's Chapel, where THOMAS JONES exercised a powerful ministry. His godly mother was originally Marjorie Maitland. Two of his brothers, ANDREW ALEXANDER BONAR and JOHN JAMES BONAR, were also great preachers. He was educated at the Edinburgh High School and under THOMAS CHALMERS at the university, where ROBERT MURRAY MCCHEYNE was a fellow student.

After being licensed as a preacher in 1833 Bonar became missionary assistant to the Reverend John Lewis at St James's, Leith, in Midlothian. In 1837 he was ordained parish minister in Kelso, Roxburghshire. At the Disruption in 1843 he left the Church of Scotland, but remained in Kelso as a minister of the newly formed FCS, of which he became a leader. That year he married Jane Katherine Lundie, daughter of a former minister of Kelso. Five of his children died in infancy. His influence grew owing to his gifted preaching throughout Scotland, his extensive correspondence, and many publications. In 1853 he became a DD of Aberdeen University. In 1866 he was called to the newly established Chalmers Memorial Free Church, Grange, Edinburgh, and in 1883 elected moderator of the Free Church General Assembly. His ministerial jubilee was celebrated in 1888, the year before his death.

His sermons and tracts, his devotional and biblical books are now forgotten. So are *The Border Watch, The Christian Treasury* and his other religious magazines. He was, however, one of the few Scottish hymn-writers to find widespread acceptance outside Scotland. At the outset of his ministry hymns were not used in the regular services of his church in Leith (the Free Church as a whole was not to approve their use until 1872); but the metrical Psalms did not appeal to his young people. So he wrote hymns for them to popular tunes.

Over his lifetime he wrote more than 600 hymns. Lack of revision left stylistic blemishes, to which he was indifferent. Characteristic of his work as a whole was the simplicity and devotional warmth of two widely used hymns, one of evangelism and one on the Lord's Supper: 'I heard the voice of Jesus say' and 'Here, O my Lord, I see Thee face to face'. The influence of EDWARD IRVING upon the young Bonar later made the Second Advent feature in many of his hymns as well as in his spoken and written ministry (e.g. in his *Quarterly Journal of Prophecy*, 1848–73). Premillenarian sentiments in some hymns have prevented their wider circulation.

Nevertheless, 85 of his hymns were annotated and 110 more recorded as (arguably) 'in common use' by Julian, who cited the collections in which they had been published or reprinted. Although most are passing out of use, many are still sung on both sides of the Atlantic. Besides those already quoted the most enduring are 'Fill Thou, my life, O Lord my God', 'Glory be to God the Father', 'Go, labour on: spend and be spent', 'Not what these hands have done', and 'Thy way, not mine, O Lord'.

SELECT WRITINGS
H. Bonar, *Fifty-Two Sermons* (Grand Rapids, MI, 1954)
—, *Hymns of Faith and Hope*, 3 series (London, 1857–66)
—, *Hymns: Selected . . . by H. N. Bonar*, 2 vols (London, 1904–8)

BIBLIOGRAPHY
J. Bonar, 'Horatius Bonar', in *The Hymns and Hymn Writers of 'The Church Hymnary'* ed. J. Brownlie (London, [1899]): 225–32
DNB
G. L. Gibb, *Horatius Bonar and his Hymns* (Edinburgh, 1989)
Julian: 161–2, 1506–7, 1761
A. W. Medley, 'Horatius Bonar', *Evangelical Library Bulletin*, 82 (Spring 1989): 2–6
New Cambridge Bibliography of English Literature, 3 (Cambridge, 1969): 511

JOHN S. ANDREWS

Bonar, James (b. 1801; d. 11 July 1867). Scottish solicitor. He was the eldest brother of ANDREW A. BONAR. On his father's death, he assumed his place as head of the family when only 19. By profession he was a Writer to the Signet (the highest grade of the profession of solicitor as practised in Scotland). An elder at Lady Glenorchy's Chapel from 1830, he laboured in many religious and philanthropic societies, including the Edinburgh City Mission, the Orphan Hospital, the SPCK in the Highlands and Islands, and the Edinburgh and Leith Seamen's Friend Society. He was secretary to the Senatus of New College. He wholeheartedly supported the Free Church after the Disruption, employing his legal talents in its defence.

BIBLIOGRAPHY
G. R. Davidson, *Disruption Worthies*, ed., J. A. Wylie (Edinburgh, 1881)

DONALD M. LEWIS

Bonar, John (b. near Alloa, Clackmannan, Scotland, 4 Nov. 1722; d. Perth, Scotland, 21 Dec. 1761). Preacher and theologian. The son of John and Jean Bonar he was the grandfather of HORATIUS BONAR. When in 1729 his father was ordained minister in the Shetland Islands he was sent to his grandfather's manse near Linlithgow. After attending the parish school there he matriculated at the University of Edinburgh on 27 April 1742. He was licensed as a preacher by the Church of Scotland on 5 June 1745, and ordained on 22 August 1746 as minister of Cockpen, near Dalkeith. There in November 1746 he married Christian Currier.

In 1756 he declined a call from the Abbey Church of Jedburgh, but accepted one from the Collegiate Church of Perth. He became a persuasive preacher of the gospel. His publications included: *Observations on the Conduct and Character of Judas Iscariot* (Edinburgh, 1750; reprinted 1822); the *Nature and Necessity of a Religious Education* (Edinburgh, 1752); a controversial *Analysis of the Moral and Religious Sentiments Contained in the Writings of Sopho [i.e. Henry Home, Lord Kames] and David Hume* (Edinburgh, 1755); *Nature and Tendency of the Ecclesiastical Constitution in Scotland* (Edinburgh, 1760); and *Triumph of Faith* (London, 1767).

BIBLIOGRAPHY
DNB

JOHN S. ANDREWS

Bonar, John (b. Cramond, near Edinburgh, 22 July 1801; d. Edinburgh, 20 Dec. 1863). Preacher and author. The son of ARCHIBALD BONAR, he was educated at the University of Edinburgh. He was licensed in the city by the Church of Scotland on 30 April 1823 and ordained 11 July 1826. He was minister of Larbert and Dunipace from March 1826 to May 1843, when at the Disruption he joined the FCS. In 1846 he was the convener of the Committee for Colonial and Continental Missions in the Free Church. After a brief ministry in Aberdeen he served the Renfield Street Church in Glasgow from 1848 to 1854. The University of Edinburgh awarded him its DD in 1857. He was author of *The Established Church of Scotland As It Was and As It Is* (1845) and an eight-page pamphlet issued by the Stirling Anti-Erastian and Non-Intrusion Association, *Reasons for Religious People Taking a Lively Interest in the Present Position of the Church of Scotland* (Dundee, no date).

BIBLIOGRAPHY
Boase

JOHN S. ANDREWS

Bonar, John James (b. Edinburgh, 25 March 1803; d. Greenock, near Glasgow, 7 July 1891). Preacher and author. The elder brother of HORATIUS BONAR he was educated in Edinburgh at the high school and university. He was licensed as a Church of Scotland preacher on 25 April 1827 and ordained a minister of St Andrew's, Greenock on 20 August 1835. At the Disruption in 1843 he joined the FCS. On 20 April 1883 the University of Edinburgh awarded him a DD. He celebrated his jubilee on 8 June 1885. Like his brothers Horatius and ANDREW ALEXANDER BONAR he was a gifted preacher. He wrote several religious handbooks, including *Books of the Bible, Fourfold Creation of God, Mosaic Ritual* and *Outline of Prophetic Truth.*

BIBLIOGRAPHY
DNB

JOHN S. ANDREWS

Bond, Thomas Emerson Sr (b. Baltimore, MD, USA, Feb. 1782; d. New York, March 1856). Methodist physician and editor. Born into a Methodist family, Bond studied medicine at the University of Pennsylvania and established a large medical practice in Baltimore, Maryland. In 1807 he declined a Professorship of Medicine at the University of Maryland because of ill health.

In 1824 he was licensed as a Methodist preacher and took up his pen in 1827 to write *An Appeal to the Methodists* to counter the growing reform movement within American Methodism. He briefly edited *The Itinerant*, an anti-reform publication, and was elected editor of the New York *Christian Advocate*, serving from 1840–8 and 1852–6. Although a strong supporter of African colonization, he opposed discussion of slaveholding in the *Advocate*.

BIBLIOGRAPHY
EWM
E. S. Bucke, et al, *The History of American Methodism*, 3 vols (Nashville, 1964)
M. Simpson, ed., *Cyclopaedia of Methodism* (Philadelphia, PA, 1882)

DONALD M. LEWIS

Bond, William (Bennett) (b. Truro, England, 10 Sept. 1815; d. Montreal, Canada, 9 Oct. 1906). Educator and bishop. A Newfoundland merchant, Bond came to Quebec with MARK WILLOUGHBY and was ordained in 1840. In 1853, disaffected laity from Trinity Chapel enticed Bond to St George's Church, Montreal. Becoming rector in 1861, he also became famous nationally. In Bishop Fulford's time he was called 'the other bishop of Montreal'; in Bishop Oxenden's, made archdeacon (1870) and dean (1872). His election as Bishop of Montreal (1878) was contested because he had received Methodist communion, but consecration followed in 1879. Bond was elected fifth metropolitan in 1901, and second primate in 1904.

An 'evangelical warhorse', Bond's convictions coloured the character and policy of his diocese for generations. Famous for administrative skills, he advocated self-support, scripture-based education, and domestic missions. His precritical convictions formed a major obstruction to the spread of liberal thought in Canadian Anglicanism, but he was not a controversialist. His papers are in the Montreal diocesan archives.

BIBLIOGRAPHY
L. N. Tucker, 'William Bennett Bond', in *Leaders of the Canadian Church*, ed. W. B. Heeney, I, (SPCK, 1920): 171–99

ROBERT MERRILL BLACK

Bonser, James (b. Kinoulton, Nottinghamshire, England, *c.* 1800; d. 1828). Primitive Methodist evangelist. James was converted during the revival which swept through Nottinghamshire in 1817. With Thomas Brownsward he missioned South Staffordshire in 1820, then Manchester, Liverpool, Chester, Oakengates, Shrewsbury in 1822, where he continued the work begun by Sarah Spittle, and Bridgenorth. In 1823 he headed the Western Mission into South Shropshire, Worcestershire and Gloucestershire till it stretched to the area already being missioned by the Brinkworth circuit. Worn out by his labours, and at odds with his colleagues, he retired from the work in 1826, joined the Wesleyans and died prematurely two years later.

IAN SELLERS

Boone, William Jones (b. Walterborough, SC, USA, 1811; d. Shanghai, 17 July 1864). Missionary bishop in China. After ordination and marriage to Sarah Amelia De Saussure, he sailed to Batavia, [now Jakarta, Indonesia] in 1837 under the newly formed Board of Foreign Missions of the Protestant Episcopal Church. Ill health forced him to move to Macao in 1840, where he began his ministry among the Chinese people. When he had completed one year of teaching in Macao at the school run by the Morrison Education Society, he and his wife, along with DAVID ABEEL, went to Gulangsu, the small island off Amoy on the south China coast, in 1842. Within a very short time, Mrs Boone died, and he returned to America with their children early in 1843. While in America in 1844, he remarried, received the DD degree, and also was consecrated as Missionary Bishop for China. The Boones returned to China in April 1845, living in Shanghai as a more central site for carrying out his administrative duties.

Along with his ecclesiastical duties, Boone was appointed as a Shanghai delegate to the Committee of Delegates, commissioned to produce the Delegate's Version of both the New Testament and Old Testament. When this committee could not agree on the term in Chinese for God, he became the member of the American committee which produced an alternative version.

Bishop Boone served for one year (1862–3) as the

British chaplain in Shanghai. His many Chinese writings include a translation of Matthew and John into the Shanghai dialect. His second wife died in Suez on 20 January 1864.

BIBLIOGRAPHY
M. Boone, *The Seed of The Church in China* (Philadelphia, PA, 1973)
K. Latourette, *A History of Christian Missions in China* (London, 1929)
A. Wylie, *Memorials of Protestant Missionaries* (Shanghai, 1867): 99–102

RALPH R. COVELL

Booth, Abraham (b. Blackwell, Derbyshire, England, 20 May 1734; d. London, 27 Jan. 1806). Baptist minister and writer. Booth's earliest religious associations were with the evangelical General Baptists of the East Midlands among whom he was converted and baptized. Despite the strength of his early Arminian convictions he became a convert to Calvinism, ministering to the small Particular Baptist congregation at Sutton Ashfield. His new views found expression in *The Reign of Grace* (1768), for which HENRY VENN wrote the preface. In 1769, he became pastor of the church in Prescott Street, London, with the COUNTESS OF HUNTINGDON present at his ordination. He remained there for the rest of his life. His sermon on 'Commerce in the Human Species' (1792) was regarded by THOMAS CLARKSON as an important reinforcement of the campaign against slavery.

Theologically, he was closer to the Hyper-Calvinists than to FULLER, whom he accused of abandoning true Calvinism. Nevertheless, he supported the BMS and was active in the formation of a society for itinerant village evangelism, believing the Gospel to contain 'a complete warrant for the ungodly to believe in Jesus Christ'. This was the theme of his *Glad Tidings to Perishing Sinners* (1796). A strong opponent of infant baptism and of open Communion, his *Paedobaptism Examined* (1784) brought him into conflict with EDWARD WILLIAMS. In support of Williams, ROBERT HALL JR advocated the opening of the communion table to all believers in his *Terms of Communion* (1815). This was primarily directed at 'the venerable Mr. Booth, in his treatise styled "An Apology for the Baptists" (1778).

Unostentatious and a man of simple tastes, Booth hated flattery and deceit. He was a firm believer in religious liberty, though somewhat dogmatic in stating his own views, particularly in his later years. Though he was essentially a family man and a pastor, Andrew Fuller regarded Booth as 'the first counsellor of our denomination,' a judgement confirmed by several others.

BIBLIOGRAPHY
DNB
E. A. Payne, 'Abraham Booth, 1734–1806' *BQ* XXVI (1975): 28–42
J. Rippon, *A Short Memoir of the Rev. Abraham Booth* (London, 1806)

Whitley, *BB*

E. F. CLIPSHAM

Booth, William (b. Nottingham, England, 10 April 1829; d. London, 20 Oct. 1912). Founder of the Salvation Army. (Career to 1860) Booth was brought up a Wesleyan, converted at the age of 15 and soon began preaching. He moved to London in 1849 and in 1851 joined the Wesleyan Reformers, to whom he ministered at London and Spalding. Through the mediation of E. H. RABBITS, he was accepted as a candidate for the MNC ministry early in 1854 and after some months under WILLIAM COOKE (features of whose methods were later to be reproduced in Booth's training scheme for his officers) was appointed to the London circuit. For three years he conducted successful missions in many areas, which served to develop his revivalist techniques and confirm his call to this type of work. The MNC Conference subsequently insisted that he follow a regular ministry and this led to his resignation from their ministry in 1861.

BIBLIOGRAPHY
H. Smith, 'William Booth and the Methodist New Connexion', *The United Methodist* (18 March 1920): 1–2
W. R. Ward, 'William Booth', *Gestalten der Kirchengeschichte*, ed. M. Greschot 9 ii, (Stuttgart, Germany, 1985): 233–43

E. ALAN ROSE

Borlase, Henry (b. Helston, Cornwall, England, 15 Feb. 1806; d. Plymstock, Devon, England, 13 Nov. 1835). Anglican Seceder and Brethren leader. Educated at Ottery St Mary and Trinity College, Cambridge (1823–8, twenty-ninth wrangler) he was licensed in August 1831 as Curate of St Keyne, Liskeard, but resigned in late 1832 believing that the Church of England was apostate and hence that separation was no schism. Possibly influenced by RICHARD HILL (also of Helston) he joined B. W. NEWTON as a leader in the Plymouth assembly. In straightened circumstances, he taught classics, and later married Caroline Pridham (sister-in-law of Derwent Coleridge). From 1834 he edited the *Christian Witness*. His early death deprived the Brethren of one of their most gifted exponents.

BIBLIOGRAPHY
W. W. R. Ball and J. A. Venn, *Admissions to Trinity College Cambridge*, 4 (London, 1911): 229
G. C. Boase, *Collectanea Cornubiensia* (Truro, England, 1890)
H. Borlase, *Papers Connected with the Present State of the Church* (London, 1836)
F. R. Coad, *History of the Brethren Movement* (Exeter, England, 1968): 34, 64–5, 117, 254–5
Devon County Archives, Exeter, England. Curates Licence Book 4, MS 95: 10
DNB
S. P. T(regelles) ed., *Answers (by Borlase et al.) to the Questions*

considered at ... Plymouth on 15 Sept. 1834, 2nd edn (Plymouth, 1847)

TIMOTHY C. F. STUNT

Bosanquet, Samuel Richard (b. London, 1 April 1800; d. Dingestow Court, Monmouth, Monmouthshire, Wales, 27 Dec. 1882). Barrister and author. He was the eldest son of a wealthy banker, Samuel Bosanquet of Forest House, Waltham forest, Essex and nephew of the influential judge, Sir John Bernard Bosanquet (*DNB*). Bosanquet was educated at Eton and Christ Church, Oxford (BA 1822; MA 1829) and studied law at the Inner Temple in London (1826), becoming one of the revising barristers appointed with the passing of the Reform Act in 1832.

Bosanquet's significance lies in the fact that he frequently wrote leading articles for *The Times* of London and for the *British Critic*. A staunch Tory paternalist, in the late 1830s he argued strongly for the Poor Law Amendment Act but by the early 1840s he had come to oppose any poor law. In 1841 he expanded two articles which had appeared in the *British Critic* in his *The Rights of the Poor and Christian Almsgiving Vindicated*. Strongly sympathetic toward the poor he argued that an increasing number of wage earners could not subsist on their earnings; his solution, however, was to call on private philanthropy rather than state intervention. His 1843 work entitled *Principia* was violently antiliberal, and linked Britain's national degeneracy and apostasy with biblical prophecy. Bosanquet's social views appear to be similar to those of R. B. SEELEY, M. T. SADLER and CHARLOTTE ELIZABETH TONNA.

Bosanquet also wrote works of Christian ethics, producing his *New System of Logic* (1839) and on biblical prophecy. His brother was James Whatman Bosanquet (*DNB*).

BIBLIOGRAPHY
Boase
DNB
D. M. Lewis, *Lighten Their Darkness* (Westport, CT, 1986): 151–62

DONALD M. LEWIS

Bost, Ami (b. Geneva, 10 June 1790; d. La Force, Dordogne, France, 24 Dec. 1874). Evangelist and pastor. Educated by Moravians at Neuwied and the Genevan Academy, Bost was consecrated as pastor in 1814. A key figure in the *Réveil*, Bost was a suffragan pastor in the Jura-Bernois, seceded in 1818 and served with the London Continental Society in and around Switzerland returning to Geneva in 1824 as a joint-pastor of the Bourg-de-Four Assembly. In 1826 he was acquitted in the courts of slandering the clergy in a pamphlet defending the dissidents, but his independence led him to withdraw from the pastorate and turn to evangelism as an agent of the Scottish Continental Society. In the 1830s his charismatic tendencies seem to have been attracted briefly to Irvingism leading him to visit Albury in 1835, but in 1840 he was reconciled to the Established Church in Geneva which was now more favourable to the *Réveil*. Moving to France he served at Asnières (1843–6) and at Melun (1846–9). After more peripatetic work he retired to his son's home at La Force. A gifted musician and outspoken individualist, six of his sons became pastors.

SELECT WRITINGS
A. Bost, *Mémoires ... du Réveil Religieux des Eglises de la Suisse et de la France*, 3 vols (Geneva, 1854, 1855)

BIBLIOGRAPHY
A. Westphal, *John Bost et sa Cité Prophétique* (La Force, France, 1937) 14–20, 83

TIMOTHY C. F. STUNT

Boston, Edmund (b. Dedham, Essex, England, *c.* 1807; d. Sierra Leone, 8 June 1830). CMS missionary to Sierra Leone. Boston studied briefly at the CMS College at Islington in 1827 before being sent out with THOMAS HEIGHWAY on 18 November 1827 to Sierra Leone. Boston died after about two and a half years of service. His willingness to serve in Sierra Leone is remarkable in view of the fate of other early CMS missionaries. In 1828 he married Jane Hickson (died 17 March 1841). Following his death she married another CMS missionary, William Young.

BIBLIOGRAPHY
D. T. B[arry], *CMS Register of Missionaries and Native Clergy* (privately printed) (London, 1906)

DONALD M. LEWIS

Boston, Thomas [the younger] (Ettrick, Selkirkshire, Scotland, 3 Apr. 1713; d. Jedburgh, Roxburghshire, Scotland, 13 Feb. 1767). Co-founder of Scottish Relief Church. He was the third son of Thomas Boston, the elder (1677–1732). Boston senior was a learned, popular, evangelical preacher and author. He was one of the 'twelve apostles' condemned during the *Marrow* controversy (1722); he alone protested the light sentence given to Professor Simpson for teaching anti-Trinitarian doctrine at Glasgow (1729); and he consistently opposed patronage and denounced the evils inherent in a national established church. The younger Boston inherited his father's principles and theology. He received his early education at home after which he attended the Grammar School of Hawick and Edinburgh University. He was licensed by the presbytery of Selkirk August 1732 and ordained to Ettrick (his father's church) 4 August 1733. He was released from Ettrick in 1748 to transfer to Oxnam, Roxburghshire, where he was admitted 10 August 1749.

In 1755 the pulpit at Jedburgh near Oxnam became

vacant. The majority of the town wanted Boston, and so rejected both of the patron's presentees. The second was particularly despised (all but five in the town declared themselves against him), but the General Assembly ordered that he be settled. At this juncture a delegation from Jedburgh proposed to Boston that he become pastor of a new church, separate from the establishment. He consented, and a meeting house was erected within about six months. His resignation was given to the presbytery on 7 December 1757, and he was inducted at Jedburgh two days later.

Boston patterned the new church after the Presbyterian Dissenters in England. He declared himself willing to hold Communion with faithful ministers of the Church of Scotland who opposed the forcible settlement of ministers over reluctant congregations, but he removed himself from the ecclesiastical jurisdiction of the national church. The General Assembly responded by forbidding establishment pastors from participating with him in any ministerial endeavours. Nevertheless, his popular stand against patronage and his powerful preaching procured for him a wide influence. 'Bogue of Gosport, . . . who was qualified to judge, said, . . . that Thomas Boston, next to Whitefield, was the most commanding preacher he had ever heard' (Struthers, 1843: 150).

He conducted his first Communion season alone, but at the second he was joined by THOMAS GILLESPIE. In 1761 these two and THOMAS COLIER formed the Presbytery of Relief with Boston as the first moderator. In 1765 a large congregation in Glasgow applied for membership in the Relief Church. There were few Relief ministers capable of managing such an influential charge, so they attempted to call Boston. He initially refused, but later consented to consider a joint pastorate with his son, Michael. When he came to Glasgow to preach, his health was very poor, and the congregation voted to delay the call (October 1766). Boston was chagrined, and he resented the subsequent interference of his friends Gillespie and James Baine (Relief minister in Edinburgh). Before the matter could be settled, Boston had died. He was an effective champion of a free church and open communion.

SELECT WRITINGS

T. Boston, *Select Discourses on a Variety of Practical Subjects* (Glasgow, 1768), some of which are included in *Select Sermons, by Thomas Boston . . . and James Baine . . . with an Introductory Essay by N. M'Michael* (Edinburgh, 1850). (The essay is not biographical.)

—, *Essays on Theological Subjects* (1773)

BIBLIOGRAPHY

T. Boston, the elder, *Memoirs* in *the Complete Works of the Late Rev. Thomas Boston, Ettrick*, 12 (London, 1853; reprinted Wheaton, IL, 1980)

DNB

Fasti, 2

G. Struthers, *The History of the Rise, Progress, and Principles of the Relief Church* (Glasgow, 1843)

JOHN K. LA SHELL

Bostwick, Shadrach (b. Maryland, DE, BNA, *c*. 1767–9; d. Canfield, OH, USA, 1837). Physician and Methodist preacher. Bostwick served 14 years in the Methodist Episcopal itinerancy (1791–1805). Most of his travelling, including five years as a presiding elder, was in Maryland, Delaware, New Jersey, New York, Connecticut and Massachusetts. In 1803 he was sent to north-eastern Ohio, the first regularly appointed Methodist preacher in the Western Reserve. He had learned medicine and practised it simultaneously with his preaching ministry.

Bostwick's in-laws, the Daniel Diver family, resided in the region and he left the itinerancy in 1805. Bostwick was among the large number of former itinerants whose continued work as local preachers was critical to the long-term success of early American Methodism. Bostwick was praised by such Methodist Episcopal leaders as Bishop ELIJAH HEDDING. His preaching was remembered as intellectually and theologically powerful.

BIBLIOGRAPHY

J. M. Barker, *History of Ohio Methodism* (Cincinnati, OH, 1848)

E. M. Bucke, ed., *The History of American Methodism*, II (Nashville, TN, 1964)

M. Simpson, ed., *Cyclopedia of Methodism* (Philadelphia, PA, 1880)

CHARLES W. BROCKWELL, JR

Boucher, John (baptized Tynemouth, Northumberland, England, 5 Aug. 1777 (ordination papers, Oxford); d. Kirk Newton, Northumberland, 12 Nov 1818). Anglican clergyman. Son of James (Lieutenant-Governor, Tynemouth Castle) and Jane Boucher, he entered St John's College, Oxford, in 1795, with leanings towards a smart life; but he became a Christian. He was Ingledew fellow of Magdalen College, 1802–9. Ordained in 1801, Boucher was appointed Rector of Shaftesbury, Dorset, and Vicar of the extensive parish of Kirk Newton, Northumberland, in 1802. Known for pastoral concern and learning, he worked mainly at Kirk Newton, dying suddenly of an 'acute disorder'. Two volumes of his sermons were published as a memorial of 'a most estimable character'. Archdeacon Singleton lamented 'the excellent Mr Boucher'.

SELECT WRITINGS

J. Boucher, *Sermons*, 2nd edn (London, 1821); review C. O. (1821)

BIBLIOGRAPHY

J. S. Reynolds, *Evangelicals at Oxford* (Oxford, 1953; Appleford, England, 1975)

V. Sillery, *St. John's College Biographical Register 1775–1875* (Oxford, 1987)

K. H. Vickers, *History of Northumberland*, XI (Newcastle-upon-Tyne, England, 1922)

J. S. REYNOLDS

Boudinot, Elias (b. Philadelphia, PA, BNA, 2 May 1740; d. Burlington, NJ, USA, 24 Oct. 1821). Presbyterian layman and philanthropist. Elias Boudinot, an influential lawyer, American patriot, and political leader, considered Christian service the primary avocation of his life. Boudinot was born to a family descended from French Huguenots and baptized by the revivalist GEORGE WHITEFIELD. As a young boy he moved from Philadelphia to Princeton, New Jersey, where later he apprenticed as a lawyer. Boudinot early advocated the cause of American independence, became George Washington's chief officer for the care and exchange of military prisoners and then was the mainstay of New Jersey's delegation in the US Congress in the first years under the Constitution. From 1795 to 1805 Boudinot served as the Director of the United States Mint.

Boudinot's religious and philanthropic activities were even more notable than his political accomplishments. He became a trustee of the College of New Jersey in 1772 and for the rest of his life devoted great energy to the school. After a ruinous student rebellion in 1807, it was Boudinot whom the other trustees asked to articulate their defence of Christian learning. Boudinot was also active on behalf of his Presbyterian denomination. Yet he was far from narrowly sectarian as friendly relations with Episcopalians, Lutherans, and even Roman Catholics attest. From the 1790s Boudinot spoke out against slavery. His eager support of the new American voluntary societies was crowned by his election as the first president of the ABS (1816). His will included benefactions for Princeton College, Princeton Theological Seminary, the Presbyterian Church, the New Jersey Bible Society (to buy spectacles for the elderly), several local agencies for the poor, Magdalen societies in New York and Philadelphia, the ABCFM, the Moravian Indian mission and a number of Indian schools. As an older man, he ventured into print with a vigorous rebuttal of Tom Paine's rationalism entitled *The Age of Revelation* (1801), and a biography of colonial revivalist WILLIAM TENNENT (1810). He also published apocalyptic speculations and a work suggesting that native Americans were descended from the ten lost tribes of Israel. Boudinot's biographer recorded the truth in noting that he was regarded 'without a peer as the foremost Christian layman of the United States' (Boyd, 1952: 261).

BIBLIOGRAPHY
G. A. Boyd, *Elias Boudinot* (Princeton, NJ, 1952)
DAB
M. A. Noll, 'The Response of Elias Boudinot to the Student Rebellion of 1807', *Princeton University Library Chronicle*, 43 (1981): 1–22

MARK A. NOLL

Boudinot, Elias (b. near Rome, GA, USA, c. 1802; d. Park Hill, Indian Territories [now OK], USA, 22 June 1839). Cherokee evangelist and tribal spokesperson. Named Galagina in his native language, this young convert was sent to study in New England where he adopted the name of a New Jersey Presbyterian political leader and philanthropist who was a patron of the school (*see* ELIAS BOUDINOT [1740–1821]). Upon his return in 1823, he collaborated with SAMUEL A. WORCESTER in translating the New Testament into Cherokee. For seven years he also edited the *Cherokee Phoenix*, the first newspaper ever printed for any American Indian tribe. In its pages he advanced the causes of public education, Christian morality, and national solidarity. He preached widely, advocating acceptance of Christian principles and the advantages of white culture. This was an effective message because Cherokees were highly successful in acculturation. His influence was extensive until 1835 when he, along with several other prominent leaders, acquiesced to pressure from the Federal government and signed the Treaty of New Echota. This agreement ceded native lands and agreed to removal beyond the Mississippi River. The resultant 'Trail of Tears' (1838) produced much suffering among his people at the hands of land-hungry whites and indifferent government supervision. Boudinot's evangelical witness became suspect in the eyes of many, and shortly thereafter he was murdered by vengeful tribesmen who viewed him as a traitor.

BIBLIOGRAPHY
DAB
DARB
R. H. Gabriel, *Elias Boudinot, Cherokee and his American* (Norman, OK, 1941)
W. G. McLoughlin, *Cherokee Renascence in the New Republic* (Princeton, NJ, 1986)

HENRY WARNER BOWDEN

Bouffler, Mary (b. London; d. Sierra Leone, 1 June 1820). First CMS female missionary. Bouffler and HANNAH JOHNSON, were the first females to be appointed in their own right as missionaries by the CMS. (Previously wives had accompanied their husbands but had not been appointed by the CMS.) A schoolmistress and a member of the London congregation of EDWARD BICKERSTETH, she sailed on 5 January 1820 for Sierra Leone with Hannah Johnson. Their willingness to serve in Sierra Leone is remarkable in view of the fate of other early CMS missionaries (*see* M. RENNER, P. HARTWIG, J. G. PRASSE, J. C. BARNETH, J. QUAST, C. H. MEISSNER, H. MEYER, J. H. SCHULZE and C. JOST).

BIBLIOGRAPHY
D. T. B[arry], *CMS Register of Missionaries and Native Clergy* (privately printed) (London, 1906)

DONALD M. LEWIS

Boultbee, Thomas Pownall (b. Liverpool, Lancashire, England, 7 Aug. 1818; d. Bournemouth, Hampshire, England, 30 Jan. 1884). Anglican clergyman, Principal of London College of Divinity. Boultbee was educated at Uppingham School and St John's College, Cambridge, and after ordination and a college fellowship became curate to FRANCIS CLOSE. From 1853 Boultbee was a theological tutor at Cheltenham College. The evangelical ethos of the school was maintained through Close's chairmanship of the directors and Boultbee's teaching.

In 1863 Boultbee was appointed the first principal of the London College of Divinity, situated at Kilburn and from 1866 at Highbury, London. Boultbee made a significant contribution to the theological education of the evangelicals and gave papers on ordination training at church congresses. He was rewarded by becoming a prebendary of St Paul's Cathedral and LL D. Boultbee was the author of a number of theological textbooks, notably *A Commentary on the Thirty-Nine Articles*.

BIBLIOGRAPHY
G. C. B. Davies, *Men for the Ministry* (London, 1963)
DNB
The Record, 1 Feb. 1884

ALAN FREDERICK MUNDEN

Bourne, George (b. Westbury, England, 13 June 1780; d. New York City, 20 Nov. 1845). Presbyterian and Dutch Reformed minister, and abolitionist. Educated at Homerton Seminary in England, Bourne went from there to Virginia and Maryland. He briefly held a pastorate in Virginia in 1814, where direct contact with slavery led to a strong reaction, making him among the first in the USA to advocate immediate emancipation, in *The Book and Slavery Irreconcilable* (1816). Compelled to leave the southern states he moved to Pennsylvania, then to New York, then to Quebec, 1825–8, where he became an opponent of Catholicism. Back in New York by 1830, but without a church, he joined the Garrison wing of abolitionism. In 1833 he became a member of the Dutch Reformed Church, doing pulpit supply and writing articles and books. He was among the delegates present at the formation of the Anti-Slavery Society in 1833 in Philadelphia, and continued his writing through the decade. Among other opponents, he censured clergy who defended slavery. Bourne, however, was not in favour of increased women's rights. At the time of his death in 1845 he was employed by the *Christian Intellegencer* in New York.

BIBLIOGRAPHY
DAB

WILLIAM G. TRAVIS

Bourne, Hugh (b. Fordhays, Staffordshire, England, 3 April 1772; d. Bemersley, Staffordshire, England, 11 Oct. 1852). Co-founder of the Primitive Methodist Connexion. Reared in a pious environment, in a moorland tenant farming family, Bourne was influenced by the spirituality of his mother, Ellen. The family moved to Bemersley in 1788, where Hugh, a carpenter by trade, worked with his uncle as a wheelwright. He endured religious struggles as an adolescent, searching for spiritual awareness. It was through reading Quaker Methodist and other works on Christian experience, (such as

JOHN WESLEY's *Sermons* and *Letters on the Spiritual Manifestation of the Son of God* by J. W. FLETCHER of Madeley, Shropshire), that moved Bourne with meaning and power, removed the doubt which had affected him and resulted in his conversion. Bourne joined the Wesleyan Methodists in 1799.

The origins of Primitive Methodism can be traced to Christmas day, 1800. Bourne had travelled to buy some timber in the nearby mining village of Harriseahead, in the desolate and isolated countryside of North Staffordshire, a peripheral area, empty of the influence of both the Established Church and dissident religion. While there, Bourne met his cousin, Daniel Shubotham, a troubled collier and boxer of some infamous repute, and engaged him in 'conversation preaching'. Shubotham's conversion sparked off a local revival in the village in 1801, in which Bourne engaged in cottage prayer meetings (untypical for Wesleyanism at that time), with a reputation for lively lay participation. The fire spread southwards into the townships of Tunstall and Burslem by 1804, to result in the conversion of the notorious reprobate WILLIAM CLOWES.

All this, however, was being conducted without the supervision or oversight of the Burslem Wesleyan circuit authorities, who were worried by the aggressive style of such evangelism and by the popular practice of conducting camp meetings, a device of spreading the Gospel which had been introduced into England through the personal witness and revelation of the eccentric American peacher, LORENZO DOW. Heavily influenced by Dow's accounts of the remarkable effect of camp meetings held in the frontier regions of the United States, Bourne decided to hold his own camp meeting (in competition with the local wakes), on 31 May 1807, at Mow Cop, on the Staffordshire/Cheshire border. Rather than being the cause, as has been interpreted by many historians, the camp meeting was a symbol of the fissure which existed between the ecclesiastical bureaucrats of Wesleyanism, and the rough-hewn evangelists of Harriseahead. Bourne's rejection of the authority of the conference directive forbidding camp meetings resulted in his expulsion, in June 1808, by the Burslem quarterly meeting.

Despite Primitive Methodist notions of providence, and ideas of historical inevitability, it had never been Bourne's intention to form a separate denomination. Through circumstances, and the logical effect of mass expulsions, the Camp Meeting Methodists as they came to be called (led by Bourne), and the Clowesites, merged in 1811 to form what became the Primitive Methodists. It became a movement primarily of labouring people, seeking to re-invigorate the Old Methodism, to reinstil the 'popular' revivalism of John Wesley's original fire. A constitution was devised and rules were formed. From 1814, true to their origins, and with Bourne's blessing, local members, ignoring the restrictive call which had caused a lull in Primitive Methodist fortunes, swept across into west Derbyshire and south Cheshire, like a moorland brush fire. This marks the early history of Primitive Methodism up to 1819, as it spread into the

East Midlands and on through Yorkshire and East Anglia. In 1819 Bourne called the first Primitive Methodist conference, held at Nottingham, and established the denominational *Primitive Methodist Magazine*.

Bourne was able, through his own financial resources, to spend the rest of his life constantly travelling around the country, acting like a patriarch, keeping together these loose and disparate groups, seeing his movement grow into the largest new denomination in England since the birth of Methodism. Bourne was superannuated against his own wishes in 1842 (aged seventy). He spent the next ten years, until his death, just as energetically engaged, in moving from circuit to circuit. And in 1844, Bourne travelled to Canada and the United States, to inspect the mission stations, as well as repaying his debt to Lorenzo Dow. Renowned for his abstinence, and his comments on temperance, Bourne became more active in the temperance cause during these later years, travelling the country, mistakenly claiming that he was the father of teetotalism (H. B. Kendall criticized Bourne for displaying shallow arrogance in elevating his own position within the Primitive Methodist Connexion, and easily adopting new causes and ideas as if they were his own).

Bourne wrote on topics such as baptism and present salvation; he compiled and edited the *Primitive Methodist Hymnbook*, prepared conference minutes, wrote an *Ecclesiastical History*, and a history of the Primitive Methodists, an *Autobiography*, and was editor of the *Primitive Methodist Magazine* for twenty years. He was never a true preacher like William Clowes; his style was for conversational preaching. Despite possessing toiling energy, and gifts of organization and order, administrative ability, and strict discipline, Bourne was an unremarkable man, due to his own timidity and placid shyness as well as his occasional misjudgment and gullibility; although his temper was more pronounced in his later years (he provoked an unpleasant and unnecessary rift with Clowes). He was eccentric in his repeated tendency to wear moorland dress in an urban environment.

Bourne had been a powerful patriarchal figure to thousands of Primitive Methodists. Upwards of 16,000 were gathered at Bourne's funeral procession in 1852 in Tunstall, which served symbolically to bind together the societies peppered around the country. William Clowes had died a year earlier; within the space of 18 months both the great patriarch and the populist of Primitive Methodism had passed away. Bourne was buried at the Primitive Methodist shrine at Englesea Brook, Cheshire. Primitive Methodism, with its more democratic organization, was able, unlike its parent body, not only to survive but to thrive without the presence of its leaders. The deaths of Bourne and Clowes did not cause faction and schism as John Wesley's had done. That is testimony to the movement that Bourne helped to create. Remaining unmarried, Bourne was faithful and devoted to the cause of Primitive Methodism; to give an account of Bourne's life is to tell the story of the Primitive Methodist Connexion.

BIBLIOGRAPHY
Boase
DNB
G. Herod, *Historical and Biographical Sketches* (London, 1851)
J. Petty, *The History of the PMC* (London, 1864)
G. J. Stevenson, *Methodist Worthies*, 5 (London, 1886)
J. Walford, *Memoirs of the Life and Labours of the Venerable Hugh Bourne*, 2 vols (London, 1855–6)
WBDC
J. T. Wilkinson, *Hugh Bourne, 1772–1852* (London, 1952)

WAYNE J. JOHNSON

Bourne, James (b. Fordhays, Staffordshire, England, 8 Feb. 1781; d. Bemersley, Staffordshire, 15 Jan. 1860). Co-founder of the Primitive Methodist Connexion. Brother of HUGH BOURNE, and co-founder of the Primitive Methodist Connexion, Bourne was converted when he was young, influenced by the conversion of his mother. Bourne suffered from a lack of education due to his working on his parents farm in Bemersley, which they had moved to in 1788. Bourne had an especially close relationship with Hugh, his brother and guardian. In the early years of the Harriseahead revival Bourne aided his brother, but became more involved in the material activities of the denomination; he gave money for travelling ministers, provided land for the building of chapels, including the first Primitive Methodist chapel, at Tunstall in 1811, and indeed, owned the chapels themselves. He was the connexional printer and book steward for a number of years. He established the book room and printing press.

Bourne was made bankrupt in 1843, which, it has been discovered, was due to his excessive moneylending, a practice which his obituary writer believed Bourne 'plunged into with an infatuation truly astonishing'. This event had a deteriorating effect on Bourne; he lost his friendships and in his physical appearance he degenerated 'from hale and hearty to a withered, decrepit old man'. Ironically, he died in poverty, but was known primarily for 'promoting the material development of Primitive Methodism'.

BIBLIOGRAPHY
Boase
PM Mag (1862)

WAYNE J. JOHNSON

Bowden, Elizabeth (b. England). *Fl.* 1820s. First CMS female missionary to North America. Bowden was only the fifth female to be sent as a missionary by the CMS and the first to be appointed to North America. (Previously wives had accompanied their husbands but had not been appointed by the CMS.) She appears to have been a schoolmistress. On 1 June 1822 she was sent to work under the direction of JOHN WEST at Red River (near modern-day Winnipeg) but in 1823 married George Harbidge, another schoolteacher at the mission school.

Her case is not unique. Eight of the first ten 'female missionaries' sent out by CMS married in the field, often only a few months after their arrival; of the two who did not marry, one died *en route* and the other shortly after her arrival. In seven out of the eight cases the women were married within two years of being sent out. In the nineteenth century this high marriage rate was a continuous problem for mission officials (both male and female) who felt that their investment in single female missionaries was not paying the sort of dividends they had anticipated and desired.

BIBLIOGRAPHY

D. T. B[arry], *CMS Register of Missionaries and Native Clergy* (privately printed) (London, 1906)

DONALD M. LEWIS

Bowden, Thomas (b. Devonshire, England, 1778; d. Singleton, New South Wales, Australia, 13 Sept. 1834). Methodist pioneer and schoolmaster. He early became a Methodist, and was schoolmaster in Great Queen Street, London. Recommended by WILLIAM WILBERFORCE and JOSEPH BUTTERWORTH, he was invited by the Reverend SAMUEL MARSDEN to take charge of the Female Orphan School, Sydney. He arrived in Sydney on 28 January 1812, and on 6 March he organized the first Methodist class meeting in New South Wales. He penned a powerful appeal to the Wesleyan Methodist Church in England for a minister to be sent to Sydney 'to proclaim His salvation to perishing sinners'. In 1815 the Reverend SAMUEL LEIGH arrived. Thomas was appointed master of the Male Orphan School in 1819. After 1825 he devoted himself to farming and religious interests. There is manuscript material relating to him in Mitchell Library, Sydney.

BIBLIOGRAPHY

ADB 1

J. Colwell, 'The Lay Pioneers of Australian Methodism', *The Methodist* (15 July 1911; 5 August 1911)

ERIC G. CLANCY

Bowdler, John [Jr] (b. London, 4 Feb. 1783; d. London, Feb. 1815). Barrister at Law, devotional and theological writer, and protege of the Clapham Sect. Son of John Bowdler the elder, a High Churchman, Bowdler grew up in a religious, though not an evangelical family. From his youth, however, he embraced an evangelical faith. Bowdler attended grammar school at Sevenoaks and the Hyde Abbey School and was later placed at Winchester College. He was articled to a solicitor at age 17 and was called to the Bar in 1807. For much of 1810 through 1812, Bowdler was forced to reside in southern Europe because of ill health. In 1815, shortly after the death of HENRY THORNTON, who had treated him as a son, Bowdler himself died.

Through CHARLES and ROBERT GRANT he came into contact with the Clapham Sect and corresponded with leading evangelicals. He contributed to *The Christian Observer*, his major articles appearing under the pseudonym 'Crito'. Several of them were published by his father in 1816. He wrote 'On the Atonement', 'On the Eternity of Future Punishments', 'On Prayer', and many others. In his introductory 'Memoir' of his son, Bowdler the elder sought to exonerate him from the charge of 'enthusiasm', thus misleading some persons as to his son's evangelical faith.

That such a talented and spiritually-minded young man should perish so young was felt deeply in the evangelical community. Respectful references to his sanctity and ability appear in *The Christian Observer* at least until 1840.

SELECT WRITINGS

J. Bowdler, Jr, *Select Pieces in Verse and Prose* (London, 1816)

BIBLIOGRAPHY

CO xviii (1818): 696; xl (1840): 443; and xlii (1842): 6

R. I. Wilberforce, *Life of William Wilberforce* (London, 1838)

RICK D. RAILSBACK

Bowen, Elias (b. Warwick, MA, USA, 6 June 1791; d. Cortland, NY, USA, 25 October 1870). Methodist minister, Free Methodist minister, and abolitionist. Converted at the age of 12, Bowen eventually joined the MEC and was licensed to preach in 1813. He sought and received the experience of entire sanctification in 1834 and he remained a strong advocate of the Wesleyan doctrine of Christian perfection for the rest of his life. Bowen served the MEC as a presiding elder for 24 years and was a delegate to seven General Conferences.

An abolitionist, in 1836 Bowen voted against resolutions censuring ORANGE SCOTT for his lectures against slavery. In 1859, Bowen published a book detailing Methodist complicity with slavery and the church's failure to become 'an asylum for the oppressed'. Bowen's dissatisfaction with cultural, experiential, and theological changes within the MEC resulted in his joining the Free Methodist Church in 1869. He was the author of that denomination's first history, *History of the Origins of the Free Methodist Church* (1871). Correspondence of Elias Bowen is located at Cornell University, Ithaca, New York.

BIBLIOGRAPHY

Earnest Christian (January, 1871)

Free Methodist (10 November, 1870)

WILLIAM KOSTLEVY

Bowen, John (b. Fishguard, Pembrokeshire, Wales, 21 Nov. 1815; d. Freetown, Sierra Leone, 28 May 1859). Missionary bishop. Born into a prominent Pembrokeshire family, Bowen farmed in Canada where he was 'converted' in 1842. Ordained in 1846 after studying at

Trinity College, Dublin, he became curate at Knaresborough, undertook an extended tour for the CMS in Syria, Cairo and Jerusalem, and served as Rector of Orton Longleville, Hertfordshire (1853–7), spending part of this time in helping the Christians of Nablus, Jordan. His extensive experience of pioneer work prompted his appointment as Bishop of Sierra Leone. He died in this 'white man's grave' two years after his appointment, but not before he had begun a policy of indigenization for his diocese, which was continued by his successors.

SELECT WRITINGS

J. Bowen, *The Memorials of John Bowen, Compiled From His Letters and Journals* (published by his sister) (London, 1862)

ROGER L. BROWN

Bowen, Thomas Jefferson (b. GA, USA, 2 Jan. 1814; d. 1875). Baptist missionary in Yoruba country. The son of a farmer, having fought in wars against native Americans and Mexicans, he experienced a religious conversion in 1840. After reading an account of the Wesleyan Methodist mission in the Yoruba country (modern Nigeria), he persuaded the Foreign Missions Board of the Southern Baptist Convention to send him there, with the ultimate aim of founding a mission among the Hausa. He arrived in Badagry in 1850. Detained there for a year and a half by wars in the adjacent countries, he learnt Yoruba, and eventually established a mission at Ijaye. He went home in 1853, returning with colleagues, and moved the mission to Ogbomosho. He went home finally in 1856, and published his *Adventures and Missionary Labours* (1857), giving a sympathetic view of the Yoruba. He also published a grammar and dictionary of the Yoruba language, building on CROWTHER's foundations. He went briefly as a missionary to Brazil, and during the American Civil War was, also briefly, a chaplain in the Confederate army. He spent the rest of his life as a preacher, increasingly deranged by insanity, which had already manifested itself in Africa, and died in obscurity and neglect.

SELECT WRITINGS

T. J. Bowen, *Adventures and Missionary Labours*, ed. E. A. Ayandele (London, 1968)

BIBLIOGRAPHY

J. F. A. Ajayi, *Christian Missions in Nigeria 1841–1891* (London, 1965)

CHRISTOPHER FYFE

Bowley, Mary [Mrs John Peters] *see* PETERS, MARY [née Bowley]

Bowley, William (b. India, 1780s; d. Chunar, India, 10 Oct. 1843). Pioneer CMS evangelist. Son of a British soldier and Indian mother, Bowley was a fifer in a European company of the East India Company's (EIC) army before going into business. Although Bowley lived 'in European habits', he was proud of his Indian mother, and tolerated no racism.

A fluent speaker of Urdu and Hindi, Bowley was converted through the influence of DANIEL CORRIE. Receiving Lutheran ordination in 1820 and Anglican orders in 1825, he itinerated on the Buxar-Chunar-Benares axis. Later, while stationed by the CMS at Agra, Bowley came into conflict with ABDUL MASIH. T. T. THOMASON later took him to Benares to superintend schools. Bowley main work, however, was focused partly on street evangelism, and partly on aiding the EIC army's drummer boys and the sepoys of the EIC.

Bowley built up churches from 1814 to 1843. The CMS archives contain his journals and 130 of his letters. He left all he possessed to the CMS on the condition they maintain what he had built and grant his Indian widow an adequate pension. This was accepted by the CMS, although HENRY VENN was concerned that it would set a precedent.

E. M. JACKSON

Boyce, James (Petigru) (b. Charleston, SC, USA, 11 Jan. 1827; d. Pau, France, 29 Dec. 1888). Southern Baptist educator and seminary founder. Boyce was the first child of Ker and Amanda Boyce, one of the wealthiest families in South Carolina. He was educated at Charleston College (1843–5), Brown University (1845–7), and Princeton Seminary (1849–51). During his undergraduate years, Boyce experienced an evangelical conversion and soon decided to enter the Baptist ministry. Devoted to Reformed theology, he was influenced significantly by Baptist FRANCIS WAYLAND at Brown and Presbyterian CHARLES HODGE at Princeton.

In 1855, after two years as a pastor, Boyce became professor of theology at Furman University. He was a leading proponent of theological education in the Southern Baptist Convention and was one of the founding faculty of the Southern Baptist Theological Seminary, organized in Greenville, South Carolina, in 1859. Boyce spent the rest of his life teaching theology and promoting the seminary's work. He envisioned an institution which trained scholars but was open to all persons called to ministry regardless of their educational backgrounds.

BIBLIOGRAPHY
ESB

BILL J. LEONARD

Boyce, William Binnington (b. Beverly, Yorkshire, England, 9 Nov. 1803; d. Sydney, Australia, 8 March 1889). Methodist missionary, linguist, Bible translator and mission administrator. He entered the Methodist ministry in 1829 and was sent to the eastern Cape, where he worked among the Xhosa as well as the British '1820' settlers. He developed a deep lifelong friendship with WILLIAM SHAW.

In 1834 he published *A Grammar of Kafir* and was the first linguist to understand the 'euphonic concord', the key to all Bantu languages; with Shaw he completed a translation of Luke into Xhosa. From 1833 to 1843 he was deeply involved in the political controversies surrounding the conflict with the colony which the Xhosa called the War of Hintza, and published, in 1838, his *Notes on South African Affairs*. The *DSAB* says it 'was characterized by its factual accuracy and objectivity' but is seen by some other authorities as an apologia for the British '1820' settlers.

In 1843 he returned to England and was then, in 1845, appointed general superintendent of Wesleyan missions in Australia. He was instrumental in the creation of the Australasian Conference of the Methodist Church of which he was president in 1855 and 1856. In 1858 he was appointed secretary of the Methodist Missionary Society and retired from that post and returned to Sydney in 1876.

BIBLIOGRAPHY
G. G. Findlay and W. W. Holdsworth, *The History of the Wesleyan Methodist Missionary Society* (London, 1922)
D. Williams, 'The Missionaries on the Eastern Frontier of the Cape Colony' (Univ. of Witwatersrand, unpublished Ph.D. thesis, 1959)

ANDREW C. ROSS

Boyd, Archibald (b. Londonderry, Ireland, 1803; d. Exeter, Devon, England, 11 July 1883). Anglican clergyman, Dean of Exeter. Boyd was educated at Foyle College, Londonderry and Trinity College, Dublin (BA 1823, MA 1834, BD and DD 1868). He was ordained (deacon 1828 and priest 1829) and became well known as a controversialist and author during his curacy at Derry Cathedral between 1828 and 1842.

Between 1842 and 1859 he was the Perpetual Curate of Christ Church, Cheltenham and from 1857 an honorary canon of Gloucester. He worked with FRANCIS CLOSE in supporting evangelical causes and one of his curates was F. W. ROBERTSON. Boyd was a born orator, a scholarly and eloquent preacher and 'a firm but moderate Evangelical' (*DNB*). Between 1859 and 1867 he was the Vicar of St James's, Paddington, London, where he preached to large congregations.

In 1867 Boyd became Dean of Exeter and was responsible for the restoration of the cathedral and conflict with Protestants over the introduction of an ornate stone reredos. He died at the deanery after a long illness and left a considerable fortune.

BIBLIOGRAPHY
R. Glover, *The Golden Decade of a Favoured Town* (London, 1884)
DNB

ALAN FREDERICK MUNDEN

Boys, Thomas (b. Sandwich, Kent, England, 1792; d. London, 2 Sept. 1880). Anglican clergyman. Boys

graduated from Trinity College, Cambridge in 1813 (MA 1817). The next year, as a paymaster in the Peninsular war, he was wounded and while convalescing produced a successful Portuguese translation of the Bible and editions of some of the classics. Ordained priest in 1822, he was curate at Crayford from 1816, and Vicar of Holy Trinity parish, Hoxton, London (1848–80).

The *Jewish Expositor*, the semi-official organ of the LSPCJ, was for a time edited by Boys. In its pages, he and LEWIS WAY, HENRY DRUMMOND, and other members of the prophetic Albury Group, offered the evangelical world nothing but gall and vinegar. Pentecostalism, premillennialism, the 'verbal' view of biblical inspiration, and a more rigid Calvinism were advocated by them with such acerbity and vehemence that in 1831 the LSPCJ moved to quash the *Expositor*. Boys was expelled from the society and dismissed from the LSPCJ missionary seminary at Hackney, where he had been sole tutor since 1830.

He then largely retired from controversy. He was professor of Hebrew at Islington Missionary College (from 1836) and in 1849 to 1865 contributed 'My Peninsular Medal' and five other articles to *Blackwood's Magazine*. (His letters to William Blackwood are in the National Library of Scotland.) Though he lived out his last years in virtual seclusion, he kept his name alive by offering valuable notices on Chaucer to *Notes and Queries*.

BIBLIOGRAPHY
DNB
T. P. Platt, *Thomas Boys* (London, 1832)
I. S. Rennie, 'Evangelicalism and English Public Life' (Univ. of Toronto Ph.D. thesis, 1962): 59, 121

JONATHAN BURKE CUTMORE

Brackenbury, Robert Carr (b. Panton House nr Wragby, Lincolnshire, England, 1752; d. Raithby Hall, Raithby by Spilsby, Lincolnshire, England, 11 Aug. 1818). Methodist preacher, poet, and philanthropist. Brackenbury, the eldest surviving son of a wealthy landowner, was educated at Felsted and St Catherine's College, Cambridge, where he underwent a spiritual crisis. He had a large estate in Lincolnshire and built Raithby Hall, with a chapel over its stables in 1779. JOHN WESLEY 'opened' the chapel, having met Brackenbury in 1776. Exact details of Brackenbury's conversion are unknown, but he began preaching immediately after leaving Cambridge.

Highly regarded by Wesley, and a member of the Legal Hundred, he travelled with him on numerous tours. His first wife having died in 1782, he went in 1783 to the Channel Islands, responding to a request for a Methodist preacher. Despite sustained, often violent, opposition, he succeeded in establishing Methodist societies before leaving in 1790. While recuperating his health and spirits he was asked to go to the Isle of Portland, where he was again successful. In 1795 he married Sarah Holland. He continued to travel, preaching in many areas, until his death.

Among Brackenbury's friends and correspondents

were ALEXANDER KILHAM, his some-time assistant; THOMAS COKE, whose executor he became, and whose edition of Wesley's *Hymns* was prepared at Raithby; ADAM CLARKE, THOMAS JACKSON; JOSEPH BENSON; JABEZ BUNTING; JAMES EVERETT; ROBERT HALL; Lady Mary Fitzgerald; HENRY MOORE; Thomas Roberts; WILLIAM WILBERFORCE and JAMES MONTGOMERY. Raithby Hall became famous for its hospitality. In its fine library Thomas Jackson saw the works of many English theologians, 'Episcopal, Puritan and Nonconformist' and 'a considerable amount of general literature, historical, poetic and philosophic'. It reflected Brackenbury's interest in the millennium, angels and other matters, and was used by preachers stationed locally, who were greatly influenced by Brackenbury.

Excessive modesty led Brackenbury to direct that no memoir should be written; he wished all his papers destroyed. His widow obeyed, even destroying Brackenbury's letters collected from their recipients. She long delayed erecting his memorial in Raithby church, with its epitaph by Montgomery:

> Silent be human praise,
> The solemn charge was thine;
> And widowed love obeys,
> And here upon thy shrine
> Inscribes the monumental stone
> With, Glory be to God alone.

Sarah Brackenbury died in 1847, having spent her widowhood supporting causes associated with Brackenbury and Methodism. In 1859 Mrs Smith's brief and inaccurate account of Brackenbury was published. A later would-be biographer gave up in the face of opposition and scarcity of material.

Brackenbury was highly regarded as a preacher, but few of his sermons survived. One at least was published; others may have appeared anonymously. He published four volumes of verse and James Montgomery published his *On the Holy Angels*. Brackenbury's modesty led to his financial support of chapel building and other philanthropic work being largely unrecorded.

BIBLIOGRAPHY
T. R. Leach, 'The Will of Robert Carr Brackenbury', *PWHS*, xxxiii, 1962
—, 'The Preaching Squire – Robert Carr Brackenbury', *The Lincolnshire Historian*, II, 11 (1964)
—, 'The Methodist Squire of Raithby', *Journal of Lincolnshire Methodist History Society*, I, 13, 14 and 15 (1969–70)
—, *The Life of Robert Carr Brackenbury* (unpublished manuscript)

TERENCE R. LEACH

Bradburn, Samuel (b. Gibraltar, 5 Oct. 1751; d. London, 26 July 1816). Methodist itinerant. Dubbed the Methodist Demosthenes on account of his pulpit oratory, he was a soldier's son who was apprenticed to a shoemaker when his family settled in Chester. After hearing Methodist preachers he was converted in his home while reading an evangelical book. Encouraged by both WESLEY and FLETCHER, he began to itinerate in 1774 in the Liverpool circuit. He exercised a vigorous and at times controversial ministry both in England and Ireland. He formed a close relationship with CHARLES WESLEY; JOHN WESLEY described them as twin souls.

Along with HENRY MOORE he was charged with disturbing the peace of the Bristol society by favouring ordination and opening Portland Chapel for services during church hours with the administration of the sacraments. Taking his stand as a new planner, he strongly believed that the voice of the Methodist people should prevail and suspected the 'spirit of bigoted high churchmen' (Manuscript letter to Rodda, MARC). After his ordination in 1792 he published a pamphlet *The Question, Are the Methodists Dissenters?* in which he contended that the majority of them were mild Presbyterians in their views. In 1794 he supported the abortive Lichfield proposal to create an order of superintendents and surfaced in 1795 with a further scheme of travelling bishops which proved equally unacceptable. He was, however, named as one of the nine who drew up the compromise Plan of Pacification adopted in 1795. He was elected conference president in 1799.

BIBLIOGRAPHY
DNB
Memoirs (London, 1816)
MM (1816)

A. SKEVINGTON WOOD

Bradbury, James (b. Mayfield, Staffordshire, England, 22 Sept. 1805; d. Croydon, Surrey, England, 26 Jan. 1892). LMS missionary to India. Bradbury arrived at the LMS secondary school in Bhowanipore (10 February 1837), learned Bengali, preached to pilgrims at Sagor Island (1840–1), and was sent in 1842 to the Chinsurah mission built up by ROBERT MAY and George Mundy. There he met his wife, 'Miss Lucie Margot,' who arrived as a volunteer with A. F. LACROIX (in 1842). She greatly improved the schools and persuaded Muslim girls to attend. The FCS Mission bought the station in 1849 and the Bradburys were ordered to Berhampore. Poor health sent Mrs Bradbury and her four children back to Europe in January 1857. Bradbury followed four months later.

After their 1858 return, Bradbury, an independent mission strategist, often fought over policy with Calcutta brethren and the LMS. He resisted centralization; favoured a mufussal vernacular ministry, and, from 1851 to 1854, fought to retain the Berhampore station. In 1858 Edward Storrow falsely accused him of accumulating savings of Rs 20,000 in breach of LMS regulations. He returned to England in 1870.

BIBLIOGRAPHY
LMS archives, School of Oriental and African Studies, London; also on microfiche (IDC, Leiden, Netherlands)

E. M. JACKSON

Bradbury, Mrs. *See* BRADBURY, JAMES

Bradford, Joseph (b. England, *c.* 1741; d. Hull, England, 28 May 1808). Methodist itinerant and Wesley's personal travel companion. Blandford, Dorset, has been conjectured as his birthplace, without firm evidence. After serving in the Cornwall West and Bristol circuits he accompanied WESLEY for 11 years as co-evangelist, prayer partner, secretary, and nurse. After an illness in 1781 he returned to the stations before resuming his former duties from 1787 until Wesley's death. He was entrusted with Wesley's letter read at the first conference after his passing. One of the committee which drew up the Plan of Pacification in 1795, he was conference president in that year and in 1803. He favoured the old plan for the constitution of Methodism, but recommended the establishment of provincial conferences with a general conference at longer intervals. Mental derangement finally led to his tragic end.

BIBLIOGRAPHY
C. A. Bradford, *The Life of the Rev. Joseph Bradford* (London, 1931)

A. SKEVINGTON WOOD

Bradley, Charles (b. Halstead, Essex, England, Feb. 1788; d. Cheltenham, Gloucestershire, England, 16 Aug. 1871). Anglican clergyman. Bradley was educated at Wallingford, married early and then for a time was a member of St Edmund Hall, Oxford, at that time a distinctly evangelical college. He left without taking a degree and was appointed Curate of High Wycombe (1812–25), a post with which he combined much private tuition. He knew a number of prominent evangelicals, one of whom, Bishop HENRY RYDER, promoted him to the vicarage of Glasbury (Brecknockshire, Wales) (1825–71), but friendship with another, WILLIAM WILBERFORCE, led to his appointment to St James, Clapham (1829–53), where he consolidated his reputation as a preacher. He published several volumes of sermons, beginning with a volume in 1818, then another in 1825 and a third in 1831, followed by *Practical Sermons* (2 vols, 1836, 1838), *Sacramental Sermons* (1842) and *Sermons on the Christian Life* (1853), most of which ran to several editions. A selection (ed. Reverend G. J. Davies) appeared in 1884.

Bradley was as prolific in his family as he was in his writings, fathering around twenty children from his two marriages. These included G. G. Bradley, Dean of Westminster and once famous as the reviser of the Latin grammar for long known as Bradley's Arnold, A. C. Bradley, the famous Shakespearean scholar, and Herbert Bradley, the moral philosopher. One of Bradley's grandsons records that Bradley was held in much less affection than the other grandfather, Archdeacon BENJAMIN PHILPOT.

BIBLIOGRAPHY
Boase, I: 174
A. G. Bradley, *Our Centenarian Grandfather* (London, 1922)
DNB

ARTHUR POLLARD

Bradley, Dan Beach (b. Marcellus, NY, USA, 18 July 1804; d. Bangkok, Thailand, 23 June 1873). American missionary pioneer to Siam (Thailand). Bradley exemplifies much of the early Protestant missionary approach and theology: medical, social, educational and political service with evangelism. A Presbyterian medical doctor with the ABCFM, he ministered to slaves of the king who had smallpox. He also helped teach the future king, Rama IV (Mongkut). Bradley dispensed medicine from his house to nearly 100 patients per day, giving each a portion of scripture or a Christian tract which he translated or wrote.

He arrived in Siam on 18 July 1835 and returned to the United States only once (1847–9) in his 35-year career in Siam. On his way to Bangkok, Bradley stopped off in Singapore and purchased a printing press which would provide his means of support. The press proved to be invaluable not only to provide income for the ABCFM work in Siam, but also in printing scripture portions, Christian tracts, the first newspaper (the *Bangkok Calendar*), and the first government document: a royal proclamation outlawing opium (1838).

Bradley accomplished many firsts for Siam. Besides the printing press, Bradley also did the first inoculations (1835) and the first vaccinations (smallpox, 1840). He performed the first modern surgical operation, amputating a monk's arm in 1837. Bradley's tireless service for both rich and poor helped earn respect and freedom for Christian missionaries in Siam.

BIBLIOGRAPHY
D. C. Lord, *Mo Bradley and Thailand* (Grand Rapids, MI, 1969)
K. E. Wells, *History of Protestant Work in Thailand: 1828–1958* (Bangkok, 1958)

SCOTT W. SUNQUIST

Braidwood William (b. Edinburgh, 27 Feb. 1751; d. Edinburgh, 13 Oct. 1830). Business man and Scottish Baptist elder. Converted in a Church of Scotland fellowship meeting, Braidwood joined the Old Scots Independent Church in Edinburgh and in 1778 was baptized in the Scottish Baptist Church by ACHIBALD MCLEAN. He was soon called to the eldership in which he continued until his death, and became an important writer for his church. He began business as an ironmonger, and became the first manager of the Caledonian Insurance Company. He lived in George Square and occupied a prominent position in Edinburgh business society.

BIBLIOGRAPHY
W. Jones, ed., *Works of William Braidwood* (London, 1838)
G. Yuille, ed., *History of the Baptists in Scotland* (Glasgow, 1926)

DEREK B. MURRAY

Brainerd, David (b. Haddam, CT, BNA, 20 April 1718; d. Northampton, MA, BNA, 9 Oct. 1747). Presbyterian missionary to Delaware Indians. Young Brainerd was deeply affected by the Great Awakening, a revival movement that took shape in his formative years. He had, by his own description, a melancholy disposition, brooding even at an early age on fears of death. His father died when he was eight years old, his mother when he was 14, and he turned inward for religious consolation. Predestinarian doctrines afforded little solace, however, and he struggled with almost pathological obsession over spiritual matters. Still, the evangelical message expounded by such preachers as GEORGE WHITEFIELD offered new hope. By 1739 he came to acknowledge grace as stemming from a sovereign God and subsequent works of merit as flowing from that source as well. Thereafter he determined to be a witness to this transforming truth which his own experience confirmed.

That same year, at the age of 21, Brainerd entered Yale College to prepare for the ministry. He did well in his studies, but pious zeal caused him to clash with school authorities. During his third year he remarked that one of the instructors had no more grace than a chair. The college president demanded an apology; Brainerd refused; expulsion and denial of a degree followed. Thus hampered, Brainerd persisted in efforts to spread the Gospel. In 1742 he obtained a commission from the SSPCK to serve as missionary among the Mohican Indians at Kaunaumeek, a small station on the Hudson River.

Brainerd's missionary activities were not a marked success. Throughout his brief career he rarely stayed in one place long enough to master a native dialect, understand aboriginal customs, or gain acceptance from those he sought to convert. His residence among the Mohicans, for instance, lasted less than a year. After being ordained in 1744 by the presbytery of New York, he moved to a site called 'Forks of the Delaware' where the Lehigh River flows into the larger stream. He hoped to build a Christian Indian community there, but most natives had already abandoned the area. Thwarted in that design, he spent his few remaining years trying to find another effective missionary approach. Physically weak, he experienced frequent bouts of illness and psychological depression. These mental burdens added to his difficulties in locating a place for fruitful evangelistic effort.

Brainerd spoke through an interpreter whenever he visited the Munsis or the Unamis, both subgroups of the Delaware tribe. He went on furlough frequently and visited the Wyoming and Susquehanna valleys in Pennsylvania, pursuing his vision of an ideal community of believers which always eluded him. By June of 1745 he concentrated his work among small bands of Delawares at Crosswicks and Cranbury in central New Jersey. This native remnant led a marginal existence, peddling home made wares to their more prosperous neighbours. Decimated by disease and reduced to poverty by whisky traders, they presented Brainerd with an opportunity for the kind of missionary contribution he longed to make. His desultory visits did not lay sufficient groundwork for much influence, but these locations formed the nucleus of evangelical efforts that continued after his initial work.

In August of 1745 Brainerd's meetings began to attract as many as seventy Indians at a time, some of them travelling forty miles to hear the message of salvation. Signs of a religious awakening began to appear, and the travelling preacher baptized more than 25 converts including Moses Tattamy, his trusted interpreter. In the spring of the following year Brainerd celebrated the first Lord's Supper for these native communicants. Still unsettled, he continued to travel and to take convalescent leave among friends on Long Island and in Massachusetts. He left his missions for the last time in November of 1746 and died of tuberculosis less than a year later at the home of his fiancee, Jerusha Edwards.

Brainerd was an SSPCK missionary for four years. He spent a total of 16 months in New Jersey, the scene of his most productive labours. His converts totalled no more than fifty, and they received Communion from him only three times. But JONATHAN EDWARDS, his prospective father-in-law, memorialized the young man by publishing his journal. The printed diary became a minor classic, epitomizing selfless Puritan virtue and stimulating others to volunteer for missionary endeavour. This posthumous influence was greater than any tangible results achieved during his lifetime.

BIBLIOGRAPHY
AAP
DAB
J. Edwards, 'The Life of David Brainerd', in ed., N. Pettit, *The Works of Jonathan Edwards*, Vol. 7 (New Haven, CT, 1985)
D. Wynbeek, *David Brainerd* (Grand Rapids, MI, 1961)

HENRY WARNER BOWDEN

Brainerd, John (b. Haddam, CT, BNA, 28 February 1720; d. Deerfield, NJ, USA, 18 March 1781). Presbyterian missionary to Delaware Indians. Successor to DAVID BRAINERD, his older and more famous brother, John received an SSPCK commission in 1748. He worked in New Jersey among native charges for almost three decades thereafter, fighting against an old Indian propensity for roving across ancestral lands and a new one for liquor. Abstinence and farming were his remedies, in addition to Gospel precepts. By 1758 the colony bought up all Delaware land claims and settled natives on a bleak reservation called Brotherton. Serving as superintendent and guardian, Brainerd eked out a living despite poor support from government and missionary organizations. The population under his care fell to less than sixty by 1774, of whom no more than a dozen were qualified to receive Communion. Since these few required little of his time, Brainerd expanded his work to include destitute whites in the southern half of the colony. Turmoil during the revolution worsened conditions, but Brainerd held fast to Indian friends throughout their fateful decline. In the last four years of his life he organized seven churches among whites and preached regularly at twenty other stations in the district. No one replaced him at those places or at the decaying Brotherton mission after his death.

BIBLIOGRAPHY
AAP
DAB
T. Brainerd, *The Life of John Brainerd* (Philadelphia, PA, 1865)

HENRY WARNER BOWDEN

Braithwaite, Anna (b. Birmingham, England, 27 Dec. 1788; d. Kendal, Westmorland, England, 18 Dec. 1859). Quaker minister. Anna was the daughter of Charles and Mary Lloyd of Birmingham. She married Isaac Braithwaite of Kendal in 1808. Her family and connections were not solely Quaker; her sister Priscilla for example married the Anglican clergyman Christopher Wordsworth, brother of the poet. Anna was much influenced by JOSEPH GURNEY BEVAN. She first offered vocal ministry in 1814 and was recognized as a minister in 1815. Numerous visits in the ministry followed, to meetings, to the families of Friends and, beginning in Yarmouth in 1819, to speak at public meetings held for a general audience. She acted as assistant clerk to the women's yearly meeting in London in 1815 and 1817 and as its clerk in 1819, 1821, 1822, and 1823.

Between 1823 and 1829 she made three visits to the USA in the ministry and in 1827 was present in the Philadelphia yearly meeting when the separation occurred. Though her son JOSEPH BEVAN BRAITHWAITE scarcely refers to the Beacon controversy in his biography of her she sympathized with ISAAC CREWDSON and became ultra-evangelical, sharing with her husband the view that Friends depended too heavily on the doctrine of the Inner Light.

BIBLIOGRAPHY
J. B. Braithwaite, *Memoirs of Anna Braithwaite* (London, 1905)
Dictionary of Quaker Biography (typescript, Friends' House Library, London)

DAVID J. HALL

Braithwaite, Joseph Bevan (b. Kendal, England, 21 June 1818; d. London, 15 Nov. 1905). Quaker minister and barrister. Braithwaite's parents Isaac and ANNA BRAITHWAITE were notable Friends who travelled widely in the ministry. After schooling in Kendal, Bevan was articled to a local solicitor, moving in 1840 to London where he became a barrister in 1843 and gradually built up a busy practice. He was much involved in the Society of Friends throughout his life though the period of his greatest influence and his important contribution to the work of BFBS fall outside this dictionary's period.

Braithwaite first attended the yearly meeting in London in 1834. There he met J. J. GURNEY who presented him with a number of books towards the nucleus of his large personal library, particularly concerned with New Testament studies. He began his lifetime's serious biblical study while articled to the Kendal solicitor from 1834 to 1840, making use of his knowledge of Greek and Hebrew. At the time of the Beacon controversy in the 1830s many of his relatives, including five siblings, and his friends left the society. He contributed anonymously to the voluminous literature on the side of the extreme evangelicals who were to leave the society and also acted as amanuensis to the controversial American minister Elisha Bates.

By 1840 Braithwaite was on the verge of resignation from the society and had planned to be baptized by the evangelical clergyman BAPTIST W. NOEL. In the course of the yearly meeting he changed his mind, attributing this to the testimonies of deceased ministers read in that meeting. Thereafter he adopted the moderate evangelical position taken by J. J. Gurney. He was acknowledged as a minister in 1844 and the next year began extensive travels in the ministry which were to span 39 years. A mark of his early standing among Friends was the invitation in 1849 to edit the *Memoirs of Joseph John Gurney* (2 vols, Norwich, 1854). In 1851 he married Martha Gillett junior, also a minister, who shared his work on Gurney's *Memoirs*. Later he played an important role in the General Conference of Yearly Meetings held in Richmond, Indiana in 1887 and is considered largely responsible for the drafting of the Declaration of Faith issued by that conference.

BIBLIOGRAPHY
Dictionary of Quaker Biography (typescript, Friends' House Library, London)
A. B. Thomas, *J. Bevan Braithwaite* (London, 1909)

DAVID J. HALL

Braithwaite, William (d. Yorkshire, England). Primitive Methodist apostle of North Lincolnshire. Active in one of the fertile areas for Primitive Methodism, North Lincolnshire, Braithwaite was famous for his converting work at open-air and cottage meetings, often walking over 450 miles in a month. Sent to Lincolnshire, to the Gainsborough (or Scotter) circuit, he became a pioneering and legendary travelling preacher, firmly rooted as he was in the local popular tradition and folklore of the area. Known as 'hell-fire Dick' for his rousing, fiery, Old Testament sermons, 'Billy' Braithwaite evinced a rough, muscular Christianity, 'full of God and holy fire'. He had a well-defined preaching style; his voice gradually rose, while his bodily movements became more visible, froth would form on his lips, as he 'spoke of the devil throwing the wicked into hell like a man throwing faggots into a bonfire'. He was known to rise from supper and pray forgiveness for self-indulgence, 'for taking too much tea'.

BIBLIOGRAPHY
PM Mag (1895)

WAYNE J. JOHNSON

Bramwell, John (b. Birstall, Yorkshire, England, 1794; d. Durham, England, Nov. 1882). Wesleyan layman. Bramwell was the son of the Wesleyan itinerant preacher and revivalist, WILLIAM BRAMWELL. He was articled to John Ward (1771–1857) a Methodist solicitor in Durham and became his partner for 16 years in a developing practice before setting up on his own. He was appointed Recorder of Durham 1860–82. An advanced Liberal, he was elected Mayor of Durham in 1840 and on four subsequent occasions and in 1843 helped to secure John Bright's election as MP for the city. He prompted progressive policies both locally and nationally. He had great oratorical gifts and served as a Wesleyan local preacher from 1826. He became disillusioned with Wesleyanism in 1834 but the estrangement was temporary.

BIBLIOGRAPHY
G. E. Milburn, 'Piety, Profit and Paternalism' in *PWHS*, 44, 3 (1983): 45–92

E. ALAN ROSE

Bramwell, William (b. Elswick, Lancashire, England, Feb. 1759; d. Leeds, Yorkshire, England, 13 Aug. 1818). Wesleyan Methodist minister and revivalist. The tenth of the 11 children of George and Elizabeth Bramwell, both practising Anglicans, Bramwell endured a sickly childhood before becoming an apprentice to a currier in Preston. It was in Preston that he joined the Methodists and met JOHN WESLEY himself, soon becoming a class leader and local preacher. Called to the ministry, into the Kent circuit, between the conferences of 1785 and 1786, he subsequently travelled in the following – mostly northern – circuits; Lynn (1787), Blackburn (1788), Colne (1789), Dewsbury (1791), Birstall (1793), Sheffield (1795), Nottingham (1798), Leeds (1801), Wetherby (1803), Hull (1804), Sunderland (1806), Liverpool (1808), Sheffield (1810), Birstall (1812), London West (1814), Newcastle-upon-Tyne (1815), and Salford (1817). He died the day after the conclusion of the 1818 Conference, being seized by an apoplectic fit as he was preparing to take the early morning mail coach from Leeds to Manchester, and his funeral took place at Westgate Hill, near Leeds.

Bramwell's enduring significance is as probably the most successful revivalist of the immediate post-Wesley generation, whose methods foreshadowed those of Charles Finney and whose labours were evidently highly regarded in America (there were no fewer than 11 numbered New York editions of Sigston's memoir, some in several different issues, by 1853). In association with ANN CUTLER (1759–95), better known as 'Praying Nanny', he enjoyed particular success during the Great Yorkshire Revival of 1792–6; for example, during the first year of his ministry in the Birstall circuit there was a 58 per cent increase in membership. Bramwell never rose to a high position in the Methodist connexion, although he had been designated as the chairman of the Manchester district on the eve of his death. This failure to ascend

beyond the level of an itinerant was probably due to three factors: his occasional acts of disloyalty to the Wesleyan establishment, including his identification with ALEXANDER KILHAM's cause during his first period in Sheffield and, in 1803, his temporary resignation from the ministry in a forlorn attempt to unite and lead dissident Wesleyan revivalist groups in Leeds, Manchester and Macclesfield; to the more divisive elements in his theology, especially his commitment to immediate conversion and his claim to possess the power of discernment of spirits; and to perceived negative traits in his personality such as his extreme asceticism and disciplinarianism.

Bramwell's published output was relatively small, his best-known title being *A Short Account of the Life & Death of Ann Cutler* (Sheffield, 1796, with numerous British and American reprints to 1847). His longest work was a translation from the French of d'Oyley's *The Salvation Preacher* (Nottingham, 1800). Bramwell destroyed his extensive personal diary during the course of his ministry in the Hull circuit, and the principal sources of his life are therefore the reminiscences of relatives and friends and his surviving letters. Both categories of evidence feature prominently in the published biographies.

BIBLIOGRAPHY
C. W. Andrews, *William Bramwell, Revivalist* (London, [1909])
J. L. Baxter, 'The Great Yorkshire Revival, 1792–6', *A Sociological Yearbook of Religion in Britain*, 7, ed. M. Hill (London, 1974): 46–76
W. Dawson, *The Sudden Death of Mr William Bramwell* (Leeds, England, 1818)
[J. Everett], *Wesleyan Takings*, 3rd edn, 1 (London, 1841): 33–43
T. Harris, *The Christian Minister in Earnest* (London, 1846)
Memoirs of the Life and Ministry of the Rev. William Bramwell by members of his family (London, 1848)
J. Sigston, *A Memoir of the Life and Ministry of Mr Wm. Bramwell*, 2 vols (London, 1820–2)

CLIVE D. FIELD

Brandram, Andrew (b. 1791; d. Brighton, Sussex, England, 26 Dec. 1850). BFBS Church of England secretary. After a distinguished career at Oriel College, Oxford (where he received the MA with a double first in 1815), Brandram became curate of Beckenham, Kent, and in 1822 replaced JOHN OWEN as Anglican secretary to the BFBS. With dissenting secretary GEORGE BROWNE, he managed the society's transition from a controversial pan-evangelical organization to its emergence as a prosperous and complex Victorian institution. Soon after his appointment, Brandram's diplomacy was tested in several disputes, notably the question of circulating the Apocrypha, 1825. He travelled widely for the society, organizing and activating local auxiliaries. 'To eminence in learning, he conjoined a masculine mind, an uncompromising spirit, active habits, strong affections, and devoted piety' (Stoughton, 1884: 2, 377). He died in office, leaving a wife and children.

BIBLIOGRAPHY
J. Stoughton, *History of Religion in England* (London, 1884)

LESLIE HOWSAM

Brantley, William T(heophilus) (Sr) (b. Chatham Co., NC, USA, 23 Jan. 1787; d. Augusta, GA, USA, 28 March 1845). Baptist minister and editor in Georgia. Converted at the age of 15, Brantley graduated from South Carolina College in 1808. He became Rector of Richmond Academy in Augusta, Georgia (1809) before serving as pastor of the Baptist church in Beaufort, South Carolina (1811–18). In 1819, he returned to the academy and helped establish First Baptist, Augusta (1821). Considered one of the powerful preachers of his era, Brantley also was pastor of first Baptist Church of Philadelphia (1826–37) and First Baptist Church of Charleston, South Carolina (1837–45). He also served as president of the College of Charleston. In Philadelphia, he was editor of *The Columbian Star*, changing its name to *The Christian Index*. He moved the paper to Georgia and JESSE MERCER became editor.

BIBLIOGRAPHY
S. Boykin, *History of Georgia Baptists with Biographical Compendium* (Atlanta, GA, 1881)

C. DOUGLAS WEAVER

Brasen, Christoph (b. Ripen, Jutland, Denmark, 6 Jan. 1738; d. on the coast of Nain, Labrador, 15 Sept. 1774). Moravian deacon and missionary to the Labrador Inuit. Brasen, a Danish surgeon, was a Lutheran before he became a member of the Moravian Church on 7 May 1769. He had acquired firsthand knowledge of the Moravian missionary effort in Greenland and was ordained deacon on 19 March 1771. Brasen was chosen as the leader of the Labrador Moravian contingent that established Nain in August of 1771. He served as superintendent of the mission from 1771 until 1774, when he died tragically in a shipwreck on the coast of Nain. The dramatic boat accident, in which GOTTFRIED LEHMANN also lost his life and which JENS HAVEN and CHRISTIAN LISTER survived, is detailed at length in Jens Haven's German autobiography. Brasen and Lehmann were buried at Nain on 25 September 1774.

BIBLIOGRAPHY
Public Archives of Canada, Ottawa, 'Catalogus der Missionare in Labrador', Records of the Moravian Mission in Labrador [1764–1944], Microfilm 511, Reels 11–12, fol. 15195–6
'Lebenslauf des Bruders Jens Haven', *Gemeinnachrichten* (1844): 900–25
Kölbing

MARCELLA ROLLMANN

Bray, John (*fl.* 1738–44). Pioneer English evangelical. Prominent by January 1738 in new religious societies in London, John Bray, a brazier, headed the members of the Moravian-style band PETER BÖHLER formed there in April. In May, CHARLES WESLEY sought and found faith in Bray's house, under Bray's guidance, and for four months followed Bray's advice. Bray also impressed John Byrom.

Bray's house in Little Britain was the venue for meetings of up to 100 people, the Wesleys' normal London lodging (May 1738–September 1739) and the new society's centre (September–October 1738) until superseded by the Fetter Lane meeting room. An influential member, Bray's volatility was damaging – when he briefly lost his faith (September 1738) or turned to the French Prophets (April–June 1739). In August 1739 GEORGE WHITEFIELD refused to take him to America. From December Bray led support for 'Stillness', eventually taking it to extremes and leading opposition to the Wesleys. After they withdrew in July 1740 (Bray's attempts at pacification having failed) contact ceased. Bray's last prominent evangelical guest was WILLIAM SEWARD.

Bray continued to host leading Moravians, requesting closer fellowship in November 1740, but after they took over the society in March 1741 he lost influence. After Böhler's anniversary lovefeast in Bray's house for John Wesley and other founder members, Bray was sent to apologize for Wesley's treatment in 1740. Unsuccessful in the society's elections for a president and two stewards in August, Bray was subsequently given very minor offices.

By December Bray was expressing discontent. Renewed friendly contact with the Wesleys followed. His criticisms multiplied after the first English Moravian congregation was formed in May 1742. The Moravians opposed his nomination to the select Little Conference. Bray left the society in August, and in February 1743 forbade his wife to attend. Meetings still held in his house were moved.

Bray flirted with old religious societies and with CHARLES WESLEY, but hoped for agreement with ZINZENDORF – in vain. In May he discussed his grievances – the society's separation from the Church of England and his relegation from leadership – with the Fetter Lane Elders' Conference. This and later Moravian attempts at reconciliation failed, while the Wesleys' incipient separatism prevented Bray from joining them. Bray supplied the hostile letter from AUGUST SPANGENBERG which Bishop Gibson used against the Moravians in his anti-Methodist *Observations*.

Financial collapse (perhaps due in part to loss of Moravian trade) forced Bray to move from Little Britain that autumn. Moravian attempts to help failed, and when his sister had to move out in November 1744, Bray disappeared from history.

C. J. PODMORE

Bray, William (Billy) (b. Twelveheads, Truro, Cornwall, England, 1 June 1794; d. Twelveheads, Truro, Cornwall,

England, 25 May 1868). Eccentric Bible Christian. Of Methodist parents, but losing his father when he was very young, he lived with his grandfather till he was 17 years of age, when he moved to Devonshire, falling into bad company and becoming a drunkard. But the memory of the truths he had been taught tormented him, and for some time towards the end of 1823, after his return to Cornwall, he was in agony. After struggling in prayer he was suddenly made aware of divine mercy and pardon, and immediately witnessed to his workmates in the mine as to what God had done for him.

The rest of his life was spent in God's service. A tin miner all his days, living on the meanest of wages, he often took time off work to engage in evangelistic work in which he was amazingly successful, his success being largely due to his eccentricity, his infectious joy in his faith, and his ready tongue. In his joy and simple faith, and the naturalness of his conversation with his heavenly Father, he has been described as the last of the Cornish saints. With his own hands he built three chapels (which he called 'fishing nets') one of which is still in use, and in these, as wherever he went, he knew constant conversions, even preaching to his doctor on his deathbed. His biography by F. W. Bourne, *The King's Son*, first appeared in 1871 and is still being reprinted.

BIBLIOGRAPHY
F. W. Bourne, *The King's Son*, (London, 1871)
C. J. Davey, *The Glory Man* (London, 1979)

OLIVER A. BECKERLEGGE

Breadalbane, second Marquess and fifth Earl of [Campbell, John] [Also Lord Glenorchy] (b. Dundee, Angus, Scotland, 26 Oct. 1796; d. London, 8 Nov. 1862). Landowner and peer. Previously known by the courtesy title of Lord Glenorchy, he succeeded his father in 1834. He was a major landowner, especially in Perthshire, centred on his great house of Taymouth Castle, to which he made major additions. Breadalbane was an active Liberal politician and supporter of the Reform Bill of 1832. His major significance in religious affairs came through his support for the FCS at the Disruption in 1843. He delayed giving his support until the last, leading to some accusations, probably unfair, that he had difficulty in coming to decisions on complex issues. More probably, he hoped for some response from the government which would have prevented the break in the Established Church. Few landowners supported the Free Church and almost no other major one, so his support proved immensely valuable. It countered criticism and direct opposition from some aristocratic quarters and, more directly, led to generous financial assistance, especially to the building of New College, the theological college of the Free Church. Though supporting the Free Church, Breadalbane continued to exercise his right of patronage in the Established Church, but he did so in accordance with the wishes of the congregations.

R. H. CAMPBELL

Brealey, George (b. North Tawton, Devonshire, England, 4 Sept. 1823; d. Weston-super-Mare, Somerset, England, 6 March 1888). Brethren evangelist and founder of the Blackdown Hills Mission. Converted in youth, and a shoemaker by trade, he was influenced by the revivalist Reginald Radcliffe to engage in part-time evangelism. In 1863, when about to leave England to become a missionary in the West Indies, his attention was drawn to the spiritual needs of the villages of the Blackdown Hills in south-west England. He devoted almost all the rest of his life to rural evangelism in that area, seeing five chapels built or re-opened, and several Sunday and day schools established. He was followed as superintendent of the mission by his son, Walter, and grandson, Douglas.

BIBLIOGRAPHY
W. J. H. Brealey, *Always Abounding* (London, 1897)
Pickering
R. H. White, *Strength of the Hills* (Exeter, England, 1964)

HAROLD H. ROWDON

Breay, John George (b. Devonport, Devon, England, 9 April 1796; d. Birmingham, England, 5 Dec. 1839). Anglican clergyman. Breay was raised by his evangelical mother, his father having died within a year of Breay's birth. Educated at Plymouth Grammar School until 1809, he worked as a clerk then studied for the ministry under John Cawood of Bewdley (1814–16) and Walter Smith, Curate of Almondbury, West Yorkshire (1816–19). Ordained (deacon 1819, priest 1820), he held curacies at Ruddington, Nottinghamshire (1819–23) and Rothley, Leicestershire (1823–6).

In 1825 he was admitted as a pensioner at Queens' College, Cambridge, but continued with his pastoral work and was offered the temporary incumbency of Haddenham, Cambridgeshire, by Archdeacon J. H. BROWNE of Ely (1826). In 1832 Archdeacon HODSON invited him to Birmingham. He succeeded Hodson as incumbent of Christ Church (1833) and as Prebendary of Lichfield (1835). Apart from a short period in Cambridge (1834) to graduate (BA), he remained in Birmingham until his death by fever.

Breay was an extremely conscientious and energetic pastor with a wholehearted and intense devotion to his duties. At Christ Church he developed an extensive network of parochial organizations, and paid particular attention to careful confirmation preparation and to guiding the congregation in the principles of worship. After his death his widow and friends published his correspondence and a memoir, memorial sermons, notes of his own sermons, and 39 lectures on Moses.

BIBLIOGRAPHY
Al. Cant.

D. E. H. MOLE

Breckinridge, John (b. Cabell's Dale, KY, USA, 4 July 1797; d. Lexington, KY, USA, 4 August 1841). Presbyterian minister in Kentucky. Named after his father, the attorney-general in Thomas Jefferson's Cabinet, John was reared without religious influences. But after graduating from the College of New Jersey in 1818 and studying at Princeton Seminary, he overcame family opposition to a career in the ministry. Upon being licensed to preach in 1822, he served as chaplain of Congress until 1823 when he became pastor of the McChord church in Lexington, Kentucky. He led opposition to New School Presbyterianism through the *Western Luminary*, which he edited. Throughout the 1830s he held administrative posts in the Presbyterian Church and taught pastoral theology at Princeton Seminary. Poor health contributed to Breckinridge's early death which occurred while pastor of a church in New Orleans. A skilful polemicist, Breckinridge is remembered for his publicized debates in the 1830s with John Hughes, later Archbishop of New York, over the merits of Protestantism and Catholicism.

BIBLIOGRAPHY
Anon., 'John Breckinridge', *Biblical Repertory and Princeton Review*, 1 (1870): 108–13
DAB

D. G. HART

Breeden, Henry (b. Southwell, Nottinghamshire, England, 11 Aug. 1804; d. Leeds, England, 24 Nov. 1878). Methodist minister. On the secession in Derby in 1832 of the group taking the name Arminian Methodists, he became their minister and was their president in 1833–5. On their joining the Wesleyan Methodist Association in 1837 he became a minister of that church, holding several offices, and becoming president of the Wesleyan Methodist Association Assembly in 1848. He was at all times an ardent and successful evangelist, his converts running into thousands; it was indeed a desire for passionate evangelism that ran counter to the prevailing Wesleyan temper that was one of the causes of the secession in 1832.

SELECT WRITINGS
H. Breeden, *Striking Incidents of Saving Grace* (autobiography) (London, 1878)

BIBLIOGRAPHY
UMFC Minutes (1879): 13 ff

O. A. BECKERLEGGE

Brennand, David (b. Leeds, England; d. Sierra Leone, 29 June 1817). CMS missionary to Sierra Leone. Brennand trained as a schoolmaster before volunteering to go to Sierra Leone with the CMS. He was sent to Kissey on 14 January 1817 travelling out with J. B. CATES and died shortly after his arrival. He appears to have been unmarried. Few of the early CMS missionaries to Sierra Leone lasted much longer than he.

BIBLIOGRAPHY
D. T. B[arry], *CMS Register of Missionaries and Native Clergy* (privately printed) (London, 1906)

DONALD M. LEWIS

Brenner, Peter (b. England). *Fl.* 1830s. CMS missionary to Malta. Brenner, a printer, was sent on 12 April 1828 by the CMS to work at the CMS press in Malta (*see* WILLIAM JOWETT). The press had suffered a number of set-backs because of the high mortality rate of personnel (*see* HENRY ANDREWS and THEOPHILUS C. DEININGER) and the difficulty in keeping recruits once they were in Malta (*see* JOHN HARTLEY and AUGUSTUS KÖLNER). Brenner, however, remained there, although in September 1842 he ended his association with the CMS and was taken up by the Basel Missionary Society. In 1840 Brenner married a lady by the name of Carew.

BIBLIOGRAPHY
D. T. B[arry], *CMS Register of Missionaries and Native Clergy* (privately printed) (London, 1906)

DONALD M. LEWIS

Brenton, Edward Pelham (b. Rhode Island, BNA, 20 July 1774; d. 6 April 1839). Captain Royal Navy, naval historian, and philanthropist. Son of a loyalist admiral whose property was sequestrated during the American Revolution, Edward was the younger brother of the better known JAHLEEL BRENTON. After serving in the navy during the Napoleonic war, he became a noted historian on the basis of his *Naval History of Great Britain from 1783 to 1822* (London, 1823) and *Life and Correspondence of John, Earl of St. Vincent* (London, 1838). With the help of Jahleel, he planned to save London boys from juvenile delinquency by taking over seventy of them in to a home in Hackney where they would receive some education and training to prepare them for a new life in South Africa, but the scheme collapsed after attracting much criticism. The *Memoir of Captain Edward Pelham Brenton* (London, 1842) was written by Jahleel in defence of his brother's reputation.

RICHARD C. BLAKE

Brenton, Sir Jahleel (b. Rhode Island, BNA, 22 Aug. 1770; d. England, 3 April 1844). British vice-admiral. Son of a loyalist admiral whose property was sequestrated during the American Revolution, Jahleel was the elder brother of EDWARD PELHAM BRENTON. Early service in the Swedish navy was followed by rapid advance in the Royal Navy. As flag captain to Admiral SAUMAREZ he took part in the battles of Algeciras and the Straits

(1801). In 1803 he surrendered his frigate after a ten-hour defence when grounded off Cherbourg. Held prisoner of war in France until 1806, he was tireless in his efforts to secure good treatment for British sailors held in detention by the French. In 1810 he fought a successful frigate action off Naples, was wounded, made a baronet and subsequently Knight Commander of the Bath. Rarely afloat thereafter, he was Resident Commissioner at the Cape of Good Hope 1814–22 and Lieutenant-Governor of Greenwich Hospital 1831–40, reaching admiral's rank in 1830.

Through his writings, *An Appeal to the British Nation on behalf of Her Sailors* (London, 1838) and *The Hope of the Navy* (London, 1839), he argued persuasively for seamen's welfare and their evangelization. His son was Sir L. CHARLES L. BRENTON.

BIBLIOGRAPHY
DNB
M. A. Lewis, *Napoleon and his British Captives* (London, 1962)
H. Raikes, *Memoir of Admiral Sir Jahleel Brenton* (London, 1846)

RICHARD C. BLAKE

Brenton, Sir **(Lancelot) Charles (Lee)** (b. *c.* 1807; d. Ryde, Isle of Wight, England, 13 June 1862). Seceder and pacifist. The only son of Vice-Admiral Sir JAHLEEL BRENTON, he was educated at Oriel College, Oxford 1824–8. He was deaconed in 1830 and during 1831 he served curacies in Oxford, Kelly (Devon) and Stadhampton (Oxfordshire) where he resigned in December when scruples over the burial service led him to secede. He soon associated with Brethren, ministering with W. Morshead at Bath where he sided with DARBY against NEWTON in 1847. His translation of the Septuagint appeared in 1844 when he also succeeded to the baronetcy on the death of his father, whose *Memoir* he published in 1855 with a pacifist introduction. He married Anna Chester whose brother was killed in the Crimean War – an episode which Brenton condemned.

BIBLIOGRAPHY
P. Brock, 'The Peace Testimony of the Early Plymouth Brethren,' *ChH* (1984) 53: 40–2
Devon County Archives, Exeter, England, Curates, Licence Book 4, *MS* 95: 8
Lambeth Palace Archives, London, Brenton's Letters to C. P. Golightly (7 August 1833, 14 September 1834, 29 January 1846) *MS* (1804): 79–84
C. L. Shadwell, *Registrum Orielense* (Oxford, 1902) 2: 369
T. C. F. Stunt, 'John Henry Newman and the Evangelicals', *JEH*, 21 (1970): 70–1

TIMOTHY C. F. STUNT

Brettell, Jeremiah (d. 4 Dec. 1828). Methodist preacher. Having been brought to an experience of God through Methodist preaching, he felt called himself to become an evangelist, and became a travelling preacher in 1774. For 36 years he exercised his ministry with acceptance and success, until bodily infirmity compelled him to become a supernumerary.

A man of deep piety, integrity and blameless life, his preaching of the gospel and visitation of the sick rendered his ministry a blessing to many. His relation to JOHN BRETTELL is uncertain.

BIBLIOGRAPHY
C. Atmore, *The Methodist Memorial* (Bristol, 1801): 65–7
MM (1829): 642

OLIVER A. BECKERLEGGE

Brettell, John (b. Stourbridge, Worcestershire, England, 1742; d. 1796). Methodist preacher. Little is known of him, save that he was early converted to Christ, meeting with the opposition of his parents. But he joined the Methodist society in Birmingham in his early twenties, becoming a local preacher in *circa*1766. In 1771 he became a travelling preacher and continued so for 26 years, during which time his labours were blessed to many, until ill health, culminating in his death, cut short his labours in his middle age. His Christian experience was very evident in his last illness.

BIBLIOGRAPHY
C. Atmore, *The Methodist Memorial* (Bristol, 1801) 65–7
MM (1829): 642

OLIVER A. BECKERLEGGE

Brewster, Sir **David** (b. Jedburgh, Roxburghshire, Scotland, 11 Dec. 1781; d. Allerly, Scotland, 10 Feb. 1868). Leading Free Churchman and scientist. His father was a schoolmaster and classical scholar who desired all his sons to be ministers in the Church of Scotland. David entered Edinburgh University in 1794, received an honourary MA in 1800, and was licensed to preach in 1804 but, unlike his three brothers, was never ordained. His living came from his literary and academic work, and he achieved international renown for his experiments and work on optics.

He was a private tutor from 1799 to 1807, and edited various journals including the *Edinburgh Magazine* and *Scots Magazine* from 1802 to 1806, and the *Edinburgh Encyclopedia* from 1807 to 1830. His honours included the LL D from Aberdeen and MA from Cambridge (1807), a knighthood (1831), the DCL from Oxford (1832), the FRS (1848) and various important scientific prizes in France as well as Britain. He failed in attempts to gain a professorial chair, but became principal of St Andrews College (1838) and later principal of Edinburgh University (1859). The poor income from his various inventions, particularly the popular kaleidoscope, led to dissatisfaction with the patent laws, as well as with the limited opportunities for scientific careers.

In 1843, following an Act of Protest signed by some 200 representative ministers and elders in the Church of Scotland including Brewster, over 400 ministers left the Established Church in protest at the system of patronage by which ministers were appointed. In this 'Disruption' Brewster was a leader, and a friend of THOMAS CHALMERS who was a key Free Churchman. Brewster's name is also on the original provisional committee of proposers for the EA which met for the first time in Liverpool in 1845.

On a personal level, Brewster was always orthodox, though, according to his daughter's biography he seems to have felt a lack of spiritual experience in his life until towards its later stages when he received a full assurance of salvation. His Christian pacifist and anti-Sabbatarian views were unusual, and he also wrote a book arguing that God had made other inhabited worlds.

Brewster believed of nature that: 'Into its deepest mysteries we are invited to dive, and if we make Reason our guide, and Imagination our footstool, we may rest assured that truths that are demonstrated will never rush into collision with truths that are revealed.'

BIBLIOGRAPHY
DSB
M. M. Gordon, *The Home Life of Sir David Brewster* (Edinburgh, 1869)

V. PAUL MARSTON

Bridge, Thomas Finch Hobday (b. Harwich, Essex, England, 20 December 1807; d. St John's, Newfoundland, 28 February 1856). Anglican clergyman, educator, and archdeacon of the diocese of Newfoundland and Bermuda. Bridge, ordained priest in 1831, came to Newfoundland in 1832 as chaplain to Governor Thomas Cochrane and remained in St John's as the right-hand man of Bishop AUBREY GEORGE SPENCER, for whom he conducted fund-raising missions in England and whose examining chaplain and ecclesiastical commissary he became. Bridge was also the superintendent of the evangelical Newfoundland Church Society and, later, chairman of the Protestant Education Board of St John's. Upon the translation of Bishop Spencer to Jamaica and the accession of the Tractarian bishop Edward Feild, Bridge, from 1850 on, served as archdeacon of the diocese.

From the extant pamphlets and sermons, Bridge appears as an evangelical who saw Anglicanism in the colonies as the realization of the divine commission with educational and charitable obligations, and his own work among the sick during the cholera epidemic of 1855–6 has been praised as exemplary. Whether Bridge's quick adjustment to and service under the Tractarian Bishop Feild exhibited features of duplicity and opportunism, as was alleged by his clerical opponents, will have to await a more thorough biographical treatment of this Victorian clergyman.

SELECT WRITINGS
T. F. H. Bridge, *The Two Religions* (London, 1841)

BIBLIOGRAPHY
DCB
DNLB
ENL
F. Jones, 'The Early Opposition to Bishop Feild of Newfoundland', *CCHS Journal*, 16 (1974): 30–41

HANS ROLLMANN

Bridges, Charles (b. Northampton, Northamptonshire, England, 24 March 1794; d. Hinton Martell, Dorset, England, 2 April 1869). Anglican clergyman. The fourth son of John Bridges and the nephew of NATHANIEL BRIDGES, he was educated at Christ's Hospital and Queens' College, Cambridge (BA 1818; MA 1831). He was ordained (deacon 1817, priest 1818) to a curacy at Wortwell, Norfolk but only remained for a month and subsequently served two further curacies before becoming Vicar of Old Newton, Suffolk in 1823. There much of his writing was completed and he published biblical expositions, biographical works and numerous sermons. His significant treatise on *The Christian Ministry* was published in 1829 (8th edn, 1854). He was an early supporter of the CMS and preached the annual sermon in 1847. From 1849 Bridges was the incumbent of two Dorset parishes – Melcombe Regis (Weymouth) and Hinton Martell on the presentation of Lord Ashley (*see* Lord SHAFTESBURY). Bridges was a member of the Dorset Clerical Society. He died the day after the foundation stone of the new church at Hinton Martell was laid and it was erected in his memory.

BIBLIOGRAPHY
Al. Cant.
Boase
DNB
T. Hill, *Letters and Memoir of Walter Augustus Shirley* (London, 1849)
H. C. G. Moule, *Memoirs of a Vicarage* (London, 1914)

ALAN FREDERICK MUNDEN

Bridges, John (b. 1787; d. 1865). Lawyer. An alderman of the City of London, and brother of the well-known clergyman and author, CHARLES BRIDGES, he was an active participant in the life of the congregation of the evangelical Anglican stronghold of St John's, Bedford Row. He was closely involved with the group of lawyers, represented by NADIR BAXTER and CHARLES BRODRICK, who did so much to direct the work of the evangelical societies, and thus of the evangelical section of the Church of England as a whole. In the fields of evangelism and missions he was active on the committees of the CPAS, Irish Church Missions and CMS where he served as honourary solicitor; in the defence and extension of the national church on the committees of the Established Church Society and the evangelical organization founded in 1838 for church extension in the diocese of London, which would vest patronage in trustees; in opposition to Roman Catholicism on the committees of PRS, the Protestant Association, the anti-Maynooth Committee and the Anti-Papal Aggression Committee, and in support of the confessional state on the committees of the LDOS and the Christian Electors' Committee. He also wrote a biography of the political leader of Sabbatarianism, Sir ANDREW AGNEW.

BIBLIOGRAPHY
Record
E. Stock, History of the Church Missionary Society, 3 vols (London, 1899)

IAN S. RENNIE

Bridges, Nathaniel (b. 1750; d. Willoughby, Warwickshire, England, 1834). Anglican clergyman. He was the son of Brooke Bridges, clergyman, of Orlingbury, Northamptonshire. Bridges was educated at University College, Oxford and at Magdalen College, Oxford, (BA 1770, MA 1773, BD 1780, DD 1784, fellow 1775–93). He was ordained deacon and priest (1778) becoming Vicar of Toot Bladon, Oxfordshire and then of North Moreton, Berkshire. He was Rector of Wadenhoe, Northamptonshire, 1783–92 (exchanged, 1792, for Hatton, Warwickshire); of Orlingbury, Northamptonshire, 1783–1805; and of Willoughby, 1792–1834. He was also lecturer at St Nicholas', Bristol, 1799–1834, and St Mary Redcliffe, Bristol, 1806–34.

Between 1775 and 1783, Bridges was Oxford's most influential evangelical. A friend of Samuel Parr and Dr Routh, he was (GM, 1834) 'distinguished by a compass of mind, a vivacity of thought, and a strength of memory which are almost proof against the presence of old age; pointed originality of language served him as a medium of communication upon all subjects'. His memorial inscription at Willoughby was more succinct: 'By nature a man of talent, by education a man of learning, by grace a man of God'. CHARLES BRIDGES was his nephew.

BIBLIOGRAPHY
Al. Ox.
J. Reynolds, The Evangelicals at Oxford, 1735–1871 (Appleford, England, 1975)

GRAYSON CARTER

Bridgman, (Elijah) Coleman (b. Belchertown, MA, USA, 22 April 1801; d. Shanghai, 2 Nov. 1861). First American missionary to China. Son of a farmer, he graduated from Amherst College in 1826 and completed his education at Andover Theological Seminary in 1829. A Congregationalist, he was sent out by the ABCFM, arriving at Canton in 1830. There he collaborated with WILLIAM MILNE's convert, Liang Fa, on Christian tracts that helped inspire the Taiping Rebellion. He devoted his thirty-year career in Canton, Macao, Hong Kong, and Shanghai to the introduction of religious and secular information, modern education, and Western medicine. His translations into Chinese include the Bible and the first detailed history of the United States (1838). As founder and editor of the Chinese Repository (1832–51) and first president of the North China Branch of the Royal Asiatic Society (1857–9), he became America's first scholar of China and an influential publicist for the China mission.

BIBLIOGRAPHY
P. R. Bohr, 'Liang Fa's Quest for Moral Power', in Christianity in China, ed. S. W. Barnett and J. K. Fairbank (Cambridge, MA, 1985): 35–46
E. J. G. Bridgman, ed., The Life and Labors of Elijah Coleman Bridgman (New York, 1864)
F. W. Drake, 'Protestant Geography in China: E. C. Bridgman's Portrayal of the West', in Christianity in China, ed. S. W. Barnett and J. K. Fairbank (Cambridge, MA, 1985): 89–106

FRED W. DRAKE

Bridgman, Eliza Jane [née Gillett] (b. Derby, CT, USA, 6 May 1805; d. Shanghai, 10 Nov. 1871). Missionary and pioneer educator of females in China. After more than twenty years as a teacher and principal in boarding-schools for young women in Connecticut and New York, she was sent by the American Episcopal Mission as a missionary teacher to China. Shortly after her arrival in April 1845, she married E. C. BRIDGMAN, the first American missionary to China, and joined in his work for the ABCFM, apparently becoming a Congregationalist. She devoted her entire career in China to improve the lives of Chinese women and to establish primary and secondary schools for Chinese girls in Canton, Shanghai, and Peking. By 1904 the Bridgman Academy inspired the creation of China's first women's college, North China Union College for Women, an antecedent of Yenching University. After her husband's death she edited and published his letters and journal to depict his life's work in China.

SELECT WRITINGS
E. J. G. Bridgman, Daughters of China (New York, 1852)
—, ed., The Life and Labors of Elijah Coleman Bridgman (New York, 1864)

FRED W. DRAKE

Briggs, Martin C(lark) (b. Rome, NY, USA, 23 Jan. 1823; d. Newark, CA, USA, 14 Jan. 1902). Methodist pastor, lecturer, and editorialist. Upon graduation from the Concord (Massachusetts) Biblical Institute in 1850, Briggs was sent in support of WILLIAM TAYLOR and others in the establishment of Methodism in California. In addition to fulfilling various preaching assignments, Briggs gained a reputation in the region as an outspoken speaker and editorialist for temperance, sabbath observance, and the abolition of slavery. In 1851–2, he served as founding co-editor of the San Francisco California Christian Advocate. Briggs also was actively involved in launching what became the University of the Pacific. The institution is the oldest Protestant college on the

Pacific coast, and Briggs briefly served as its president (1854–6). During the American Civil War, he led California's delegation to the party convention which nominated Abraham Lincoln for a second term as US president.

BIBLIOGRAPHY

R. D. Hunt, 'Martin C. Briggs: "Methodist Trumpeter" of California', *California Historical Society Quarterly*, 31 (1952): 1–11

DOUGLAS FIRTH ANDERSON

Briggs, William (b. *c.* 1722; d. *c.* 1788). Methodist lay assistant to John Wesley. Too little is known about Briggs, JOHN WESLEY's secretary at his London Methodist headquarters, the Foundery, for a generation, and our loss is the greater because he is also our closest link to the family of VINCENT PERRONET, 'the grandfather of Methodism', and 'the Archbishop of the Methodists'. He was the son of the Reverend Henry Briggs, DD (1687–1748), Rector of Holt, Norfolk, and chaplain to King George II. The membership lists for the Foundery Society (many in the hand of John Wesley) show that on 1 March 1743, Briggs became a member of band no. 4 for single men. Far more important, both for Briggs and the general welfare of the Foundery Society, on 25 December 1743, when after lengthy deliberation Wesley drew up a list of the spiritual elite of the society, he included among the 97 names in the Select Society that of William Briggs. Some weeding out of the names was needed, but Briggs continued as one of Wesley's most trusted lay helpers.

On 1 January 1744, Briggs became the leader of band no. 3 for single men, and maintained that responsibility through 1745. For a year or two it seemed probable that Wesley might enlist him as an itinerant preacher. It was most likely he who wrote the account of a spiritual pilgrimage signed 'W. B.' quoted in John Wesley's journal of 27 December 1744, and certainly the following day Briggs was serving as a pastoral helper to CHARLES WESLEY in Newcastle, going into some detail about the experience in a moving letter to John, and describing himself as 'your son and servant in the Lord, W. Briggs'.

Gradually, however, John Wesley requisitioned his pastoral and organizing talents in the Foundery. On 21 February 1744, RICHARD VINEY had noted in his journal that the Foundery family then included 'Thos. Butts, Clerk and Secretary' and 'Wilm. Spencer, Secretary's Assistant and Messenger in outward things.' Shortly thereafter Briggs was sharing Butts' responsibilities. In November 1746 he was given the leadership of the 'trial bands'. In the same month the list of 'stewards' for the Foundery school were Briggs, Samuel Watkins – probably one of the men who first invited Wesley to organize the Foundery Society – and Thomas Butts. Briggs was in charge of two of the twenty-two corps of the Foundery Sick Visitors. Briggs also, rather than Butts, attended the 1748 London Conference as a 'Steward', and in that capacity received JOHN BENNET's reports of Methodist affairs from the north later that year.

It seems likely that from 1746 onwards Briggs accompanied the Wesleys on some of their preaching visits to Shoreham for the vicar. At least he became sufficiently familiar with the Shoreham family for the printing of a notice in the *Gentleman's Magazine* for 28 January 1749, announcing the marriage of Elizabeth, daughter of the Reverend Vincent Perronet of Shoreham to 'William Briggs, Esq., of the Custom House, Secretary to Messrs. Wesley'. (It is not known how long Briggs had been employed by the Custom House, but John Bennet's letter to Wesley of 22 October 1748, had been addressed to him 'at the Custom-house, London', in Thames Street, adjoining the Tower on the east, and just over a mile south-east of Wesley's Foundery.)

In the autumn of 1749 there was an estrangement between Wesley and Briggs, possibly linked with Wesley's espousal of GRACE MURRAY, which Charles Wesley had frustrated by marrying her off to John Bennet on 3 October 1749. In a letter to Bennet of 3 November Wesley implied some criticism of Briggs in the affair, and on 5 December Briggs wrote to Bennet about Wesley, 'I can have no comfort in his company ... But when God breaks that stubborn sinew in his neck, then I shall love him better than ever.' On 19 March 1750, before leaving Bristol for travels in Wales and Ireland, Wesley wrote what was apparently an attempt at a reconciling letter to Briggs, enclosing his heart-broken poem on the loss of Grace Murray, assigning some blame to Briggs' father-in-law, Vincent Perronet, and suggesting that Briggs himself had been ensnared into disunity by Satan's devices. Briggs replied in a very lengthy letter on 5 April 1750, acknowledging his own lack of harmony with Methodism: 'I impute the cause partly to you, partly to myself, and partly to the devil.' He claims: 'I love, I honour, I reverence you for your great worth, wisdom, and high office ... , yet I have not that *fellowship* with you as I once had with Thomas Scipio' – another unmarried band member at the Foundery. He continued at some length with a critical appraisal of Wesley's Christian faith as few would have been bold enough or honest enough to do: 'I think you have the *knowledge* of all *experience*; but not the *experience* of all you *know* ... You have the *appearance* of all Christian graces; but they do not, I think, spring from a *deep experience* or change of *nature*.' He freely admits, however, that perhaps the only cause of the strangeness between them may be in himself, or the 'many, subtle, and strange' devices of Satan, and ends, 'Excuse or reprove all that is amiss in your weak, but affectionate charge, but obedient servant, W. Briggs.' The breach was healed, and Briggs was chosen to represent Wesley in his marriage agreement with Mary Vazeille on 9 February 1751. Two years later Wesley divested himself of all financial responsibilities in London by giving Briggs and Thomas Butts power of attorney to manage all his secular activities at the Foundery, especially the publishing business. They circulated a printed document to Methodist societies throughout the nation instructing them, in Wesley's name, to appoint book agents; they stated that henceforth book money must be sent to London quarterly, and not given to preachers; that they should settle their accounts with Mr Butts, and send orders for books 'to us only (directing for Mr Briggs, in Hoxton Square, London).' Within a year or two Butts seems to have left Wesley's employ to concentrate on music publishing. For a time (as on 24 December 1754) Robert Windsor, another early Foundery band member, teamed up with Briggs in administering Wesley's financial affairs. In November 1759, however, another book steward took over, Samuel Franks, until 1773. It seems likely that William Briggs' worldly career, a responsible position at the Ordnance Office in the Tower of London, demanded more time and offered greater financial rewards, the latter being especially desirable in view of his growing family responsibilities.

Elizabeth Briggs apparently suffered a miscarriage in 1750, and then bore a girl on 7 February 1751, another Elizabeth – 'Betsy' to John and Charles Wesley, for whom she was a favourite correspondent, especially when she was nursing her grandfather on his Shoreham deathbed in 1785, at the age of 91. On 30 April 1788, she married her grandfather's temporary curate, who became one of Wesley's City Road Chapel 'readers', Reverend Peard Dickenson. Another favourite Briggs daughter correspondent of John Wesley was born around 1753, Philothea (Wesley's 'Philly'). Wesley, indeed, in a letter of 30 November 1774, to Miss Jane Catherine March of Moorfields, with whom Philly often stayed, paid a remarkable tribute to these two teenagers' spiritual maturity: 'I do not care whether they are of five or five-and-thirty years' standing . . . When I look at Miss Betsy Briggs or Miss Philly Briggs I am ready to hide my face: I am ashamed of having set out before they were born.' On 29 August 1781, Philothea Briggs married (at Shoreham) THOMAS THOMPSON, a merchant and banker of Hull. He was an ardent supporter of the Methodist Missionary Society, and also one of the first Methodist Members of Parliament, as well as the father of Thomas Perronet Thompson (1783–1869), a well-known general and politician.

Strangely enough, although his family survived in a blaze of Methodist glory, especially in Wesley's City Road Chapel, well into the nineteenth century, it is difficult to document his own death, apart from a statement in Peard Dickenson's *Memoirs* (p. 58): 'On April 30, 1788, I was married to Miss Elizabeth Briggs, daughter of the late Mr. William Briggs of London, and granddaughter to the Rev. Mr. Perronet.' Brigg's widow survived until 1822, dying at Walthamstow, Essex, a member, sick visitor, and class leader of the Methodist Society for almost sixty years, though paralysed for the last six of her 71 years.

BIBLIOGRAPHY
DNB
Private correspondence in the collection of Prof. Frank Baker, Duke University, Durham, NC, USA
G. J. Stevenson, *City Road Chapel, London, and Its Associations* (London, 1872)

FRANK BAKER

Brisco, Thomas (b. *c*. 1731, Upton, near Chester, England; d. Chester, England, 1797). Methodist itinerant. Specific details of his birth and death cannot be established and little is known of his early life. He was a childhood friend of ROBERT ROBERTS (1731–99), in whose conversion he played a part (*circa*1752). William Myles (1812: 446), lists Brisco as beginning his ministry in 1751.

The account book of the Manchester Round shows Brisco bringing in moneys (for the connexional year 1753) in March 1754, and receiving travelling charges in March 1756. Other clues show him itinerating in Bristol in 1757. In 1758 he was stationed in Ireland and was again in Ireland in 1760 and 1762. JOHN WESLEY seems to have supported his securing of a preaching license under the terms of the Toleration Act while he was present at the London Conference in August 1767.

Brisco rarely stayed more than a year in one circuit, though on at least four occasions he was appointed assistant in charge, 1766 (Athlone), 1767 (Birstall), 1768 (Lancashire North), and 1772 (Staffordshire). He was also restationed in Birstall for two years, 1781 and 1782, and in 1783 Wesley appointed him as a member of the 'Legal Hundred' comprising the official Methodist Conference. Although an unremarkable itinerant preacher, Brisco was included in John Wesley's last will, made 20 February 1789, designated to share with three other preachers 'whatever money remains in my bureau and pockets at my decease'.

In his later years Wesley relied greatly on Brisco, though perhaps even more so upon his wife. Wesley told SARAH CROSBY on 3 March 1780: 'Sister Brisco is a good leader, either for a band or a class.' On 12 March, 1782, Wesley wrote commending him for his work and added a reminder about his valuable wife (whose personal and family name we have been unable to discover): 'I hope you give Sister Brisco full employment. She may be of great use.' She appears in several other of Wesley's letters where he commends her talents in working with children.

By 1786 Brisco had superannuated at Chester. He was commemorated by a somewhat unusual obituary:

Thomas Brisco was a man of many afflictions, being subject to extreme nervous debility, so that for many years he could not take a Circuit. His disorder was first occasioned by lying in a damp bed, and by poor accommodations in the country parts of Ireland. He was a sensible, well-read man, and by no means a weak preacher; but, owing to his great feebleness of body, he wanted that energy which would have rendered his discourses more useful. He was uniformly steady in his attachment to Methodism, and died happy in the Lord. (*Minutes*, 1798)

BIBLIOGRAPHY
C. Atmore, *The Methodist Memorial* (Bristol, England, 1801): 17
T. Jackson, ed., *Early Methodist Preachers*, 6 vols, 4th edn (London, 1871-2) 2: 264–5
Minutes (1798)

W. Myles, *A Chronological History of the People Called Methodists* (London, 1812)
WHS, 27: 30–2

FRANK BAKER

Broaddus, Andrew Sr (b. Caroline Co., VA, BNA, 4 Nov. 1770; d. 1 Dec. 1848). Baptist educator, hymn composer, and preacher. One of 12 children, he was the son of John Broaddus, a Virginia Episcopalian and farmer. Against his father's wishes, Broaddus became a Baptist and was baptized 28 May 1789. Largely self-educated, he displayed significant intellectual abilities. Ordained in 1791, he taught at school and served numerous rural churches in central Virginia, refusing various invitations to become pastor of larger, urban congregations.

Broaddus was the author of numerous books including responses to certain controversial works of Thomas Paine and ALEXANDER CAMPBELL. He was also a hymnwriter of some renown, editing three hymn-books used extensively among Baptists in the American South. His hymnals included: *Collection of Sacred Ballads*, 1790; *The Dover Selection of Spiritual Songs*, 1828; and *The Virginia Selection of Psalms, Hymns, and Spiritual Songs*, 1836. A frequent contributor to Virginia's *Religious Herald*, Broaddus was well known as a preacher and Bible teacher. His son, Andrew Broaddus, Jr, was also a prominent Virginia pastor.

BIBLIOGRAPHY
ESB

BILL J. LEONARD

Brock, William (b. Honiton, Devon, England, 14 Feb. 1807; d. St Leonards, Sussex, England, 13 Nov. 1875). Baptist pastor. Born the son of a Baptist tradesman, Brock was apprenticed to a watchmaker, becoming a journeyman in Hertford in 1828. In 1829 he was baptized at Highgate Baptist Church. He studied at Stepney College from September 1830. His first pastorate was at Norwich (1833–48). He became pastor of the new Bloomsbury Chapel, London in 1848, brought there by Sir SAMUEL MORTON PETO, the building contractor and then MP for Norwich, who had established the chapel.

Accessibility was Brock's aim and his achievement. He was a powerful preacher, drawing frequently on current events. He organized special services, and missionary and philanthropic initiatives, and built up a large following, both in Bloomsbury and more widely. He was noted for his mission to young people, and played an important role as lecturer to the YMCA. He was among the first ministers to preach in London theatres, and also participated in the first midnight meeting for prostitutes. In the 1860s he helped to form the London Association of Baptist Churches, and in 1869 was president of the Baptist Union. He saw the political sphere as an important part of his responsibilities; he spoke against the principle of establishment, and was involved in the antislavery campaign. He worked closely with evangelicals of different denominations, and, although sceptical of the EA, was a keen advocate of united evangelical action.

BIBLIOGRAPHY
C. M. Birrell, *The Life of William Brock* (London, 1878)
Boase
F. Bowers, *Called to the City* (London, 1989)
DNB
G. W. McCree, *William Brock, First Pastor of Bloomsbury Chapel* (London, 1876)

JANE GARNETT

Brockhaus, Carl (b. Himmelwert bei Plettenberg, Germany, 7 April 1822; d. Elberfeld, Germany, 9 May 1899). Pastor, author, and organizer of the Christliche Versammlung in Deutschland (Darbyist Brethren in Germany). Brockhaus experienced (1845) an evangelical conversion as a public school teacher in Breckerfeld bei Hagen, Germany. He became a widely recognized preacher and organizer. After leaving teaching in 1850 he devoted himself to full-time evangelistic work and served as secretary of the Evangelisches Brüderverein in Elberfeld. He embraced the theology of JOHN NELSON DARBY. The periodical, *Botschafter des Heils in Christo* (today *Die Botschaft*), was founded to propagate that persuasion. He became fast friends with Darby (after 1854) and they travelled together, with Brockhaus as translator. Most of German Darbyist literature was published by the Brockhaus publishers. Among those publications was a translation of the Bible (New Testament 1855; Old Testament 1871) prepared by Brockhaus, Darby and others. Brockhaus also contributed significantly to Darbyist hymnody, writing 62 of 147 hymns for the *Kleinen Sammlung Geistlicher Lieder* (Elberfeld, no date). His willingness to cooperate with other Christian groups influenced the German Darbyists to be less sectarian than in other countries.

SELECT WRITINGS
C. Brockhaus, *Alles in Christo* (Elberfeld, 1859, with many reprintings)

BIBLIOGRAPHY
E. Eylenstein, 'Carl Brockhaus, ein Beitrag zur Geschichte der Entstehung des Darbyismus', *Zeitschrift für Kirchengeschichte* 47 (1928): 275–312
H. Hermes, *H. H. Grafe und Seine Zeit* (Witten/Ruhr, Germany, 1933)

DAVID BUNDY

Brodhead, John (b. Smithfield, Northampton County, PA, BNA, 22 Oct. 1770; d. 7 April 1838). American Methodist preacher and US Congressman. Brodhead was born to Luke Brodhead, Revolutionary War veteran and Pennsylvania magistrate, and Elizabeth Harrison. He was converted at the age of 22 and entered the itineracy in 1794. For 44 years he served in Maine, Rhode Island, and New Hampshire as preacher and presiding elder. He was chaplain to the New Hampshire legislature, a state Senator, and a member of Congress (1829–33).

A meeting at Brodhead's home in Newmarket, New Hampshire led to the formation of Wesleyan Academy in 1817, which moved to Wilbraham, Massachusetts in 1825. Brodhead also helped found *Zion's Herald*, the weekly newspaper of New England Methodism. In 1801, Brodhead married Mary Dodge of Ipswich, Massachusetts. At his death, he left his widow, six sons and six daughters.

BIBLIOGRAPHY
AAP
Nolan B. Harmon, ed., *Encyclopedia of World Methodism* (Nashville, TN, 1974)

SUSAN E. WARRICK

Brodie, Elisabeth [the last Duchess of Gordon] (b. London, 20 June 1794; d. Huntly Lodge, Scotland, 31 Jan. 1864). Philanthropist. A Brodie of Brodie, of covenanting stock, she early was influenced by EBENEZER ERSKINE'S 'The Assurance of Faith' and experienced an evangelical conversion. On 11 December 1813 she married George Gordon, Marquis of Huntly (from 1827 fifth Duke of Gordon). His death in 1836 gave her greater freedom to express her devotion. Though an Episcopalian aristocrat naturally hostile to the separation of church and state, and situated in Strathbogie, a moderate stronghold in the pre-1843 Scottish church conflict, her sympathies lay with the non-intrusion party. The evangelical leaders were her personal friends and often conducted worship in her home. She entertained ministers sent to preach in Strathbogie and encouraged evangelistic tours and open-air preaching, especially at feeing markets. Before and after the Disruption she held monthly conferences of evangelical ministers at Huntly Lodge which contributed to a revival of religion throughout the north-east parishes represented there. In 1846 she concluded that the Church of England discipline was not scriptural and joined the FCS, faithfully and attractively representing the evangelical cause and the church to her social peers. She played an important role in the spiritual pilgrimage of the evangelist, BROWNLOW NORTH, and strongly supported the 1859 revival in Scotland.

BIBLIOGRAPHY
DNB
A. Moody Stuart, *Life and letters of Elisabeth, last Duchess of Gordon*, 2nd edn (London, 1865)
H. M. Williamson, in *Disruption Worthies: A Memorial of 1843*, ed. J. A. Wylie (Edinburgh, no date)

HUGH M. CARTWRIGHT

Brodrick, Charles [sixth Viscount Midleton] (b. Cahirmore, County Cork, Ireland, 14 Oct. 1791; d. 2 Dec. 1863). Lawyer. Son and heir of the Most Reverend and Honourable Charles Brodrick, Archbishop of Cashel, he represented the increasingly strong links between Irish and English evangelical Anglicanism, which tended to make the issues and attitudes of the 'troubled island' normative for their confreres across the Irish Sea. He was educated at Eton, at St John's College, Cambridge (MA 1812) and at Lincoln's Inn, and called to the Bar in 1819. He was a nephew of the Honorable William Brodrick, MP, and thus a cousin of the Reverend and Honourable W. J. BRODRICK. He was part of the group of London lawyers, personified by NADIR BAXTER and JOHN BRIDGES, who dominated the committees of many of the evangelical Anglican societies. He was a leading member of the CMS committee for many years, and also of the committee of the CPAS. In seeking to widen the scope of evangelicalism, he was one of those who, between 1833 and 1838, sought to introduce evangelical influence into the counsels of the SPCK, under the leadership of another lawyer, GEORGE ROCHFORT CLARKE. In 1848 he succeeded to the title of sixth Viscount Midleton. His cousin William John Brodrick succeeded him as the seventh Viscount Midleton.

BIBLIOGRAPHY
Al. Cant.
E. Stock, *History of the Church Missionary Society*, 3 vols (London, 1899)

IAN S. RENNIE

Brodrick, William John [seventh Viscount Midleton] (b. 8 July 1798; d. 29 Aug. 1870). Anglican clergyman, Dean of Exeter. Son of the Honourable William Brodrick, MP and Lord of the Treasury 1807–12, he was also nephew of Charles Brodrick, Archbishop of Cashel. He depicted the increasing penetration of the aristocracy and the gentry by the evangelical Anglicans, and their shift from a leadership primarily associated with the business world to one which asserted a more ancient and conservative outlook. He studied at Balliol College, Oxford (BA 1820). He was Rector of Castle Rising, Norfolk, until 1839, when he was appointed Rector of Bath by the Simeon Trust, as part of their programme to secure the ecclesiastical patronage of key provincial towns, and appoint evangelical clergy. On arrival he found himself in conflict with the National School Society, insisting that the clergy must have final authority over schools in their parish. He preached the prestigious CMS annual sermon in 1843, thus being marked out as an evangelical leader. He became Canon of Wells in 1855, and in one of the Palmerston appointments favourable to evangelicals, became Dean of Exeter 1861, where he remained until 1867, having succeeded his cousin CHARLES BRODRICK to become seventh Viscount Midleton in 1863.

SELECT WRITINGS
W. Brodrick, *The Case Stated Between the Committee of the Bath District National Schools and the Rev. W. J. Brodrick, Rector of Bath* (Bath, England, 1840)

BIBLIOGRAPHY
Al. Ox.
E. Stock, *History of the Church Missionary Society*, 3 vols (London, 1899)

IAN S. RENNIE

Bromley, James (b. 1785; d. 1860). Wesleyan minister and reformer. Bromley entered the ministry in 1811. As a friend and supporter of SAMUEL WARREN he opposed the suspension of J. R. STEPHENS at the Conference of 1834. A year later he himself was censured for supporting the Warrenite faction. During the Flysheet Controversy of 1849 he again sided with the connexional rebels and opposed the expulsion of EVERETT, DUNN, and Griffiths. He himself was expelled the following year for refusing to acknowledge the jurisdiction of a special district meeting called to examine the charges brought against him.

His published works include a *Brief Account of the External Evidences of Christianity* (Huddersfield, 1829), several polemical tracts in 1849–50, and *Proposed Data for the Constitution of a Christian Church* (London, 1855).

BIBLIOGRAPHY
B. Gregory, *Sidelights on the Conflicts of Methodism 1827–1852* (London, 1898)
Minutes of the Wesleyan Conference (London, 1850): 174–83

JOHN A. VICKERS

Brontë, Patrick (b. Emnath, Drumballyroney, Ireland, 17 March 1777; d. Haworth, West Yorkshire, England, 7 June 1861). Anglican clergyman and minor author. Patrick Brontë was the eldest of ten children of Hugh Prunty or Brunty. He took the name of Nelson's Italian dukedom on entering St John's College, Cambridge, in October 1802, where he went under the encouragement of the man to whose family Brontë had been tutor, THOMAS TIGHE, evangelical Rector of Drumballyroney from 1778 after himself being at St John's and a fellow of Peterhouse, Cambridge. Brontë graduated BA in 1806 and during his stay at Cambridge where he had been supported by WILLIAM WILBERFORCE and HENRY THORNTON he came to know HENRY MARTYN, though one of his closest friends was John Nunn (1783–1861), who later served at Colchester, St Chad's, Shrewsbury and finally became Vicar of Thorndon (Essex).

Patrick Brontë served his first curacy in Essex, at Wethersfield, where JOSEPH JOWETT, professor of civil law at Cambridge and friend of CHARLES SIMEON, was vicar. He stayed there from 1806 to 1809, towards the end of which period he was invited to Glenfield by THOMAS ROBINSON of Leicester, but went instead to Wellington (Shropshire), where his fellow curate and subsequently lifelong friend was WILLIAM MORGAN. In December 1809 Patrick Brontë became curate to JOHN BUCKWORTH at Dewsbury (Yorkshire) and in 1811 took charge of nearby Hartshead, moving to Thornton (near

Bradford) by exchange with Thomas Atkinson (nephew of HAMMOND ROBERSON and incumbent of Hartshead from 1815 to 1866, who died on 28 February 1870) and finally becoming Perpetual Curate of Haworth in February 1820, a position he held till his death in 1861. He married Maria Branwell, of Cornish Methodist stock, on 29 December 1812. She bore him six children (Maria, Elizabeth, Charlotte, Branwell, Emily and Anne), all of them were very young when she died shortly after they had arrived in Haworth.

In 1811 Brontë published a collection of *Cottage Poems*, which have been described as 'pious sentiments in a plain garb'. Another volume, *The Rural Minstrel*, followed in 1813, and in 1815 came *The Cottage in the Wood*. Finally, in 1818 there appeared the narrative tale, *The Maid of Killarney*, a discursive piece allowing Patrick Brontë to give expression to his views on topical and social questions with insistence on civil obedience and dislike of Roman Catholicism.

In politics Brontë was a staunch Tory and took a strong line together with his friend, Hammond Roberson, against the Luddite machine-breakers in the riots of 1811 (see Charlotte Brontë's treatment of this subject in her novel *Shirley*). His Toryism assisted his Irish Protestantism in his support of the Establishment and especially in his opposition to Romanism. This latter is present as late as 1851 where, in reference to the Roman aggression in claiming territorial sees in Britain, he writes of 'popery, that ghastly Incubus of the human mind'.

We have no record that Brontë underwent a specific and historically identifiable spiritual conversion, but in Morgan's *The Pastoral Visitor* he wrote in 1815 of conversion as 'a spiritual and universal change . . . effected by the agency of the Holy Ghost . . . wrought suddenly or gradually. Its effects will be manifested in the heart and life. The understanding will be enlightened to discover the evil of sin, the need of a Saviour, the excellency of religion, the vanity of the world, and the importance of eternal things'. In an oft-quoted letter to J. C. FRANKS, Vicar of Huddersfield, Patrick Brontë, seeking a curate, made it clear that he had no sympathies with Calvinism and its 'appalling doctrines of personal election and reprobation' and that he was 'fearful of evil consequences to the hearers from the enforcement of final perseverance'. Aided though he was by the CPAS, his curates were neither Calvinist nor even evangelical. It is evident that the first, the attractive William Weightman, held high views of church order, and Arthur Bell Nicholls, the last and Charlotte's husband, certainly did not have evangelical sympathies.

Of Brontë's daughters, the famous writer-sisters, it is impossible to identify anything particularly Christian in Emily, who at one moment can claim entire union with the Deity as the 'God within my breast' and then more characteristically exhibit the pagan determinism (inverted and subverted Calvinism) that pervades *Wuthering Heights*. Anne and Charlotte are explicitly Christian, even if not obviously orthodox. Both went through a phase of Calvinistic depression, Anne the more acutely (even comparing herself to COWPER), but their treatment of Christian topics, more especially of eternal destiny, suggests that both espoused universalism, claiming that even the most sinful (Huntingdon in *The Tenant of Wildfell Hall* is the exemplar) will after purgation attain to salvation, a curious approximation indeed to Romanist belief, the more so in Charlotte's case as she retained through life her father's hostility to that faith. Her universalism is most movingly expressed in the noble sentiments of Helen Burns who, rejecting notions of punishment and hell, declares: 'I hold another creed, which no one ever taught me ... but in which I delight ... for it extends hope to all; it makes Eternity a rest – a mighty home, not a terror and an abyss' (*Jane Eyre*, chap. 6).

BIBLIOGRAPHY
A. B. Hopkins, *The Father of the Brontës* (Baltimore, MD, 1958)
J. Lock and W. T. Dixon, *A Man of Sorrow* (London, 1965)
A. Pollard, 'The Brontës and Their Father's Faith' in *Essays and Studies*, 37, new series, (1984): 46–61
W. W. Yates, *The Father of the Brontës* (Leeds, England, 1897)

ARTHUR POLLARD

Brook, William (John) (b. Ashburnham, Sussex, England, 1776; d. Brighton, Sussex, England, 21 Sept. 1811). Anglican clergyman and Secessionist. Brook was the son of William Brook of Ashburnham, Sussex. He was educated at Wadham College, Oxford (BA 1798) and ordained in 1800 becoming Curate of St Nicholas's, Brighton. While curate, Brook preached frequently before the Prince Regent. Influenced by WILLIAM HUNTINGTON in late 1803, when required to read the burial service over an apostatized parishioner, Brook seceded. His followers then erected Providence Chapel, Brighton, where he served as minister until his premature death in 1811.

BIBLIOGRAPHY
R. F. Chambers, *Strict Baptist Chapels*, 5 vols, 2 (London, 1963): 122
J. W. Middleton, *An Ecclesiastical Memoir of the First Four Decades of the Reign of George the Third* (London, 1822)
T. Wright, *The Life of William Huntington, S. S.* (London, 1909)

GRAYSON CARTER

Brooke, Henry (b. Co. Cavan, Ireland, 6 Nov. 1738; d. Dublin, 6 Oct. 1806). Wesleyan painter and mystic. Brooke was the son of a clergyman of the Church of Ireland and the nephew of Counsellor Henry Brooke, and was taught to paint in Dublin. In 1761 he exhibited in London but subsequently returned to Dublin. He joined the Methodists in April 1765, having corresponded with JOHN WESLEY from 1762. Brooke became Wesley's Dublin confidante and host and was a minor benefactor in Wesley's will, and he arranged for Wesley to issue an expurgated edition of his uncle's famous novel *The Fool of Quality*. Although his painting had some recognition, Brooke is more notable for his mystical approach to evangelical religion. William Law's writings led him to faith, and although he assured Wesley that he accepted the simple biblicism of Methodist preachers he encouraged deeper 'inward religion', and corresponded with many 'seekers after light'. He married Anne Kirchoffer in 1767; she died in 1805. His son William Henry also became an artist.

BIBLIOGRAPHY
DNB
I. D'Olier, *Memoirs of the Life of the Late Excellent and Pious Mr Henry Brooke* (Dublin, 1816)
W. G. Strickland, *A Dictionary of Irish Artists* (Dublin, 1913)

PETER J. LINEHAM

Brooks, Henry (b. London, *c.* 1795; d. Sierra Leone, 4 May 1825). CMS missionary to Sierra Leone. Brooks was a lieutenant in the Royal Navy before his ordination (deacon 26 September and priest 9 October 1824) by the Bishop of London. On 3 November 1824, within weeks of his being deaconed, Brooks (along with CHARLES KNIGHT) was sent with his wife to Regent, Sierra Leone, by the CMS. Like Charles Knight and a host of other early CMS missionaries to Sierra Leone, he lasted only a few months. It is not known what became of his wife.

BIBLIOGRAPHY
D. T. B[arry], *CMS Register of Missionaries and Native Clergy* (privately printed) (London, 1906)

DONALD M. LEWIS

Brooks, William (*fl.* 1808–32). Lay supporter of the CMS. A member of St John's Chapel, Bedford Row, London, where DANIEL WILSON was pastor and JOSIAH PRATT his assistant, Brooks served on the CMS committee in 1813.

BIBLIOGRAPHY
C. Hole, *The Early History of the Church Missionary Society* (London, 1896)

D. B. HINDMARSH

Brotherton, Joseph (b. Whittington, Derbyshire, England, 22 May 1783; d. Manchester, England, 7 Jan. 1857). MP and reformer. In 1819, aged 36, he retired with a small fortune from textile manufacturing in Manchester, to be pastor of a Bible Christian church which he had joined 14 years before. In 1832 he became MP for Salford which he represented until his death. He actively supported many benevolent and educational schemes, opposed the Corn Laws, and backed LORD ASHLEY's Ten Hours Bill, arguing the case from his own experiences. Advocating abstinence from meat and alcohol, he was respected for his few needs and good temper.

BIBLIOGRAPHY
T. H. Ward, *Men of the Reign of Queen Victoria* (London, 1885)
Stenton, 1: 50

TIMOTHY C. F. STUNT

Broughton, Thomas (b. Oxford, England, 1712; d. London, 21 Dec. 1777). Oxford Methodist, Anglican clergyman, and SPCK secretary. Baptized 3 September 1712, he joined the Holy Club while at University College, Oxford, and continued to meet when elected a fellow of Exeter (1734), graduating BA (1737). After service at Cowley, near Uxbridge, and at the Tower of London, he obtained lectureships in the capital before being appointed the SPCK secretary in June 1743, a post which he held for 34 years. He initiated the work of the society in Wales and the Isle of Man. Recommended by HENRY VENN, he accepted the living of Wotton, Surrey, in 1752, and from 1755 was also Rector of All Hallows, Lombard Street, London. He was drawn towards the Moravians, although he resisted MOLTHER's emphasis on stillness. His views on assurance, imputed righteousness, and baptismal regeneration on occasion puzzled some of his evangelical friends.

BIBLIOGRAPHY
DNB

A. SKEVINGTON WOOD

Brown, Alexander (b. 1758; d. 28 March 1836). Minister. Second son of JOHN BROWN of Haddington and brother of John Brown of Whitburn, he was ordained to the Burgher congregation at Inverkeithing, where he remained in spite of calls from churches in Stirling, Glasgow and Aberdeen. Both he and his congregation resisted any move and the local presbytery acceded to their requests.

R. H. CAMPBELL

Brown, Alfred (Nesbitt) (b. Colchester, Essex, England, 23 Oct. 1803; d. Tauranga, New Zealand, 7 Sept. 1884). CMS missionary in New Zealand. Brown was among the first to train at the CMS's Islington College which opened in London in 1825. He was ordained (deacon 1827, priest 1828) by the Bishop of London and arrived in New Zealand in 1829, teaching missionary children until 1833. He opened a mission station at Matamata in the Waikato in 1835, withdrawing in 1836 because of continued harassment and intertribal conflict. Wiremu Taminhana Tarapipipi, a notable chief, and later a leading figure in the Maori King movement, was influenced by Brown's teaching and was baptized by him in 1839.

Brown moved to Te Papa, Tauranga in 1838, becoming Archdeacon of Tauranga in 1844. He oversaw missionary work in the Bay of Plenty and eastern Waikato, itinerating between Maori settlements, preaching, baptizing and seeking to promote peace amongst Maori and with the settlers. His first wife Charlotte (died 1855) made a significant contribution in teaching, extending hospitality and supporting other missionary wives.

The New Zealand wars of the 1860s undermined the work of the mission, particularly the stationing of colonial troops at Te Papa. Like other missionaries, Brown was caught up in the conflict of loyalties, trying to minister to the needs of settlers and troops as well as maintaining good relationships with Maori, many of whom were rejecting both European government and missionary Christianity. After the conflict, much of Te Papa was taken over by the colonial government for the settlement of Tauranga. Brown bought the mission buildings in 1873 and they remain in family hands, an outstanding example of colonial missionary influence. Brown endowed the Marsh scholarship at St John's College, Auckland in 1846 in memory of his son, Alfred Marsh Brown.

BIBLIOGRAPHY
D. T. B[arry], *CMS Register of Missionaries And Native Clergy from 1804 to 1904* (privately printed) (London, 1906)
DNZB
N. V. Hall, *I Have Planted* (Palmerston North, New Zealand, 1981)

ALLAN K. DAVIDSON

Brown, Antoinette Louisa [Mrs Blackwell] (b. Henrietta, NY, USA, 20 May 1825; d. Elizabeth, NJ, USA, 5 Nov. 1921). First ordained woman minister. Antoinette Brown's parents were converted at the famous Rochester, New York, revival of CHARLES G. FINNEY. At the early age of nine, Antoinette made her own confession of faith and joined the local Congregational church. She went to Finney's revivalistic college in Oberlin, Ohio, completing the theological course in 1850. For two years thereafter, Brown lectured on social reform issues such as temperance, abolitionism and women's rights. As an evangelical feminist, she rejected the unorthodox, anarchistic ideas which were common among some of her feminist contemporaries. Believing that she was called to be a public preacher of the Gospel, Brown was ordained at the Congregational church in South Butler, New York, on 15 September 1853, becoming the first ordained woman minister. After only one year at South Butler, however, Brown became unsettled in her faith and resigned her position. Eventually she became a Unitarian. In 1856, she married Samuel Blackwell.

BIBLIOGRAPHY
E. Cazden, *Antoinette Brown Blackwell* (Old Westbury, NY, 1983)
DCA
N. A. Hardesty, *Women Called to Witness* (Nashville, TN, 1984)
NAW

DOUGLAS M. STRONG

Brown, C(harles) P(hilip) (b. Calcutta, 10 Nov. 1798; d. London, 12 Dec. 1884). Madras civil servant. Son of

DAVID BROWN, the first evangelical Anglican minister in India, C. P. Brown attended Haileybury College, 1814–16. In 1816 he was appointed to the Madras Civil Service and attended the College of Fort St George, Madras, 1817–20. Between 1820 and 1834 he was an administrative or judicial officer in the Telugu-speaking districts of the Madras presidency. After a three-year furlough in England, he held various positions in Madras – most notably Postmaster General – from 1838 until his retirement in 1854. During his retirement in England he was professor of Telugu at the University College, London, 1864–1878.

Best known for his scholarship on Telugu, Brown produced several dictionaries, a grammar, and various texts on that language. These texts and his own scriptural translation efforts greatly facilitated revision of the Telugu Bible during the late nineteenth century. His great fame today comes from recognition that, by his efforts, Brown may have rescued Telugu culture and literature from extinction.

BIBLIOGRAPHY
DNB
G. N. Reddy and Bangorey, ed., *Literary Autobiography of C. P. Brown* (Tirupati, India, 1978)

PETER L. SCHMITTHENNER

Brown, David (b. East Riding of Yorkshire, England, *c.* 1762; d. Calcutta, 14 June 1812). Bengal chaplain. Educated at Milner's School in Hull and Magdalen College, Cambridge, 1782–5, he was influenced by CHARLES SIMEON, through whose contacts he was ordained deacon in 1785 and appointed head of the Orphan Institution, Calcutta. Arriving in India in 1786, Brown was officially attached to the East India Company, serving initially as a military chaplain, and then as presidency chaplain from 1794 until his death. He also was the first provost of the College of Fort William, 1800–7.

As the first evangelical Anglican minister in India, Brown stimulated a Christian revival among Europeans in Calcutta. In 1787, together with CHARLES GRANT, he proposed a Protestant mission for Bengal, which stimulated British interest in missionary activity. He became a trustee of the Old (Mission) Church, Calcutta – which Grant purchased in 1787 – and ministered to its congregation until 1808. In 1805, Brown and CLAUDIUS BUCHANAN joined the Serampore Baptist missionaries in forming a translation fund; but differences with the Baptists eventually led Brown to support rival translation efforts and run a scriptural translation school in his suburban Calcutta home. His home was also a nerve centre for early Anglican evangelical activity in India. He helped establish the Calcutta auxiliary of the BFBS in 1811 and served as its first secretary. Brown helped lay the foundations of British evangelical activity in India. He was survived by his wife and nine children, including CHARLES PHILIP BROWN, the eminent Telugu scholar.

BIBLIOGRAPHY
DNB
[Charles Simeon, ed.], *Memorial Sketches of the Rev. David Brown* (London, 1816)

PETER L. SCHMITTHENNER

Brown, David (b. Aberdeen, Scotland, 17 Aug. 1803; d. Aberdeen, Scotland, 3 July 1897). Free Church minister and postmillennialist writer. Brown was educated at Aberdeen grammar school and at Marischal College, Aberdeen University (MA 1821). He was licensed in the Church of Scotland in 1826, and was ordained in 1836.

In 1830 Brown's 'poetic temper' attracted him to EDWARD IRVING. For two years he acted, under the title of 'missionary', as Irving's assistant minister at the National Scotch Church in London. Finally unable to believe in glossolalia and faith healing himself, Brown, as he later told Irving, exercised his intellect and withdrew from this 'grand man'. He was therefore in company with others of his generation – notably HUGH STOWELL, DANIEL WILSON, and HUGH MCNEILE – who after a brief flirtation with Irvingism retreated into the evangelical mainstream.

Brown then dedicated himself to regular service in the Church of Scotland. In 1835 he was minister to the remote village of Ord, Isle of Skye. Upon the Disruption (1843) his powerful intellect and reputation for excellent preaching were recognized in his appointment to St James's Free Church, Glasgow. In 1857 he was elected professor of church history, exegesis, and apologetics in the Free Church College, Aberdeen, and, in 1875, as its principal (to 1897). He was moderator of the Free Church Assembly in 1885.

Brown is best remembered as the author of *Christ's Second Coming* (1843, often reprinted), which, until B. B. Warfield, was the classic statement of postmillennialist thought. His supposition that Christ will return in person – an innovation upon eighteenth-century formulations – suggests the abiding influence of his Irvingite premillennialist phase. Along similar lines, he also produced *The Restoration of the Jews* (1861), and *The Apocalypse* (1891).

Testifying to his excellent scholarship, he was on the New Testament Revision Committee (1870–80) and was co-author with R. JAMIESON and A. R. Fausett of a *Commentary . . . on the Old and New Testaments* (1864), long esteemed and now of historical value. He was an active participant in the EA from its foundation.

BIBLIOGRAPHY
W. G. Blaikie, *David Brown* (Edinburgh, 1898)
Boase

JONATHAN BURKE CUTMORE

Brown, George (b. Alloa, Scotland, 29 Nov. 1818; d. Toronto, Ontario, Canada, 9 May 1880). Founder of the Toronto *Globe* newspaper and politician. Educated at the High School and Southern Academy of Edinburgh, Brown emigrated to New York City with his father PETER BROWN in 1837. In 1843 they moved to Toronto where they established the *Banner*, a paper which combined advocacy of the Free Church cause with that of Reform politics. A second, more exclusively political paper, the *Globe*, was founded the following year, and it soon became the most powerful newspaper in British North America.

Brown first entered Parliament in 1851 and was a major force in politics for the next 15 years. Like his father Peter, George's combination of an evangelical Protestantism and a liberal political philosophy shaped his public vision. He was a leading spokesman for the Protestants of Canada West (now Ontario) in his opposition to perceived Roman Catholic aggression and French Canadian domination of the political union. He was also a vociferous critic of the vestiges of church establishment which bolstered the High Church Anglican position in Canada West. He worked tirelessly in support of a confederation of all British North American provinces and was a warm supporter of the temperance, Sabbatarian and antislavery causes. He died 9 May 1880 after having been shot by a disgruntled former *Globe* employee. The Brown papers are housed at the Public Archives of Canada, Ottawa.

BIBLIOGRAPHY
J. M. S. Careless, *Brown of the Globe*, 2 vols (Toronto, 1959)
J. S. Moir, 'George Brown – Christian Statesman' in *Called to Witness*, vol. 2 ed., W. S. Reid, (Hamilton, Canada, 1980)

RICHARD W. VAUDRY

Brown, Hugh Stowell (b. Douglas, Isle of Man, England, 10 Aug. 1828; d. Liverpool, England, 24 Feb. 1886). Baptist pastor. The son of a very Low Church Anglican clergyman, in 1839 Brown went to England, worked for the Ordnance Survey, then as a railway engineer. In 1841 he became a teetotaller and a Rechabite. In 1844 he went home to prepare for ordination into the Church of England, but abandoned this course, and returned to England, where in 1846 he became a Baptist. From 1848 he was pastor of Myrtle Street Chapel, Liverpool. He was known for his breadth of practical experience; his sermons were direct and effective. He was powerful in denouncing tricks of trade. In 1854 he began Sunday afternoon services for working men in the Concert Hall, and in 1861 the church established a workman's bank. He lectured frequently to young men's associations all over the country. A political radical, he was among those to popularize Cromwell in the 1850s.

BIBLIOGRAPHY
Boase
W. S. Caine, ed., *Hugh Stowell Brown, His Autobiography, His Commonplace Book, and Extracts From His Sermons and Addresses* (London, 1887)

JANE GARNETT

Brown, James (b. *c*. 1730; d. Bath, Somerset, England, 6 Feb. 1791). Leading evangelical among Bristol and Somerset Anglican clergy. Born to a Cirencester family, he attended Trinity College, Oxford 1748–52. When curate to WALTER CHAPMAN at Bradford-on-Avon he was awakened by Joseph Williams of Kidderminster. Possibly through Chapman, he became usher of Bristol Grammar School and a Bristol minor canon by 1759, then lecturer at St Nicholas by 1763. In 1761 he became Vicar of West Harptree, Somerset, resigning this and his Bristol posts in 1764–5 to become Rector of Portishead and, in 1771, Vicar of Kingston near Taunton, as well as chaplain to the Duke of Athol. He supported JAMES ROUQUET as his replacement at West Harptree, and, together with RICHARD HART, they worked closely with the Countess of HUNTINGDON evangelizing the Bristol area. He was also friendly with JOHN WESLEY and JOHN W. FLETCHER of Madeley, and recommended their writings to Dr THOMAS COKE, who first met Wesley in August 1776 at Brown's Kingston vicarage, where he served later as curate. Jacob Easterbrook acted as Brown's curate at Portishead 1776–8 and in 1788 he appealed to Brown and his friend RICHARD SYMES, to assist him in exorcising George Lukins, but they refused. In 1778 his daughter married Sir HARRY TRELAWNY.

BIBLIOGRAPHY
A. B. Sackett, *James Rouquet and His Part in Early Methodism* (Wesley Historical Society publications no. 8, 1972)

JONATHAN BARRY

Brown, John (b. Woodplumpton, near Preston, Lancashire, England, 8/19 July 1712; d. Gracehill, Antrim, Northern Ireland, 13 May 1794). Moravian minister. A London merchant's clerk and then a woollen draper, Brown was 'awakened' by GEORGE WHITEFIELD's preaching (September 1737), met PETER BÖHLER and F. W. NEISSER (spring 1738), and 'found power to believe' at a meeting conducted by CHARLES WESLEY in June of that year. He accompanied JOHN WESLEY to Herrnhut.

In 1739 Brown preached in Yorkshire for BENJAMIN INGHAM (praying extempore unlike Ingham). They quarrelled and separated in October, many of Brown's followers turning to JOHN NELSON, but were reconciled in June/July 1741. A founder member of the Yorkshire Moravian congregation (May 1742), Brown is listed as warden of the London congregation's married choir (October). He worked in Yorkshire (1743 and later), Bedford (assisting JACOB ROGERS, 1743–4) and Ockbrook, Derbyshire (from 1744). In the later 1740s he became estranged from the Moravians, ceasing to work for them for a time.

In Northern Ireland from 1750, Brown served in Ballymena (1752), Drumargan (1753), Cootehill (1754–6, 1759, 1776–90), Lisnamara (1759–74) and Ballinderry (1774–6), building chapels in Ballymena, Cootehill and Lisnamara. He was ordained deacon on 12 May 1758 while living in Herrnhut (1756–8). Brown married Jane

Moore (1718–53) in June 1742 and Sarah Harden in December 1758.

C. J. PODMORE

Brown, John (b. Carpow, Perthshire, Scotland, 1722; d. Haddington, East Lothian, Scotland, 19 June 1787). Scottish seceding minister. His father (also John) was a poor but pious weaver and salmon fisher who taught himself to read. He completed only a few quarters of school including one month of Latin, but his thirst for knowledge was prodigious. When eight or ten, he memorized the catechisms of Vincent and Flavel and the Larger Westminster Catechism. His father died in 1733, and his mother (Catherine Millie) shortly thereafter. On the death of his parents, he became a herd boy.

Soon afterwards his spiritual concerns were quickened by four bouts of fever, and he eagerly absorbed Puritan classics on conversion by Joseph Allein, William Guthrie and William Gouge as well as the letters of Samuel Rutherford. In an effort to ensure his salvation he dedicated himself to pray six times each day if herding, or three times if not. After a fresh attack of fever in 1741, he determined to hear sermons while his sheep rested at noontide, since he had no other opportunity for public worship. These messages turned him from legalism to a clearer understanding of God's grace.

During his years with the sheep, he used to go to neighbouring ministers at midday to receive assignments. He quickly mastered all they set before him, but though he wanted to learn Greek, he was too shy to ask for instruction. Therefore, he set himself to learn it on his own without even the aid of a grammar. He learned the sounds of the Greek alphabet by comparing names in Greek and English. He then proceeded to deduce verb, noun and adjective inflections. Having made some progress, he desired to have his own Greek Testament, so one evening in 1738 he left his sheep with a friend and walked 24 miles to St Andrews. The bookseller, seeing only a country lad with bare feet, asked, 'What would you do wi' that book? You'll no can read it'. 'I'll try to read it', was the humble response. A professor from St Andrews University, who happened to be present, asked the bookseller to bring a Greek Testament. 'Boy', he said, 'if you can read that book, you shall have it for nothing.' Brown met the challenge and by afternoon was back, studying in the midst of his flock (Mackenzie, 1918: 34–5). During his herding days, he also taught himself Hebrew, though in this case he had the benefit of a grammar.

Brown's learning excited jealousy among some ministerial students who rumoured (1741) he had received his unusual ability from Satan. This was a serious charge because the statutes against witchcraft had only recently been repealed. Because of persecution he determined to change his residence, but he could not join another church without a certificate from the officers of his own congregation. This they would not give, so he became a travelling pedlar. In 1745 he volunteered to defend the government against Prince Charles Stuart. After the uprising, he returned to peddling until the elders and deacons of his church granted him a certificate (1746). Only his minister, ALEXANDER MONCRIEFF, remained adamant and refused to sign.

With freedom to relocate, he became a schoolmaster at Gairney Bridge and later at Spittal. In the spring of 1747 the Secession church split over the issue of the Burgess Oath. Moncrieff took the narrower view; Brown sided with EBENEZER and RALPH ERSKINE. For the next three years he studied philosophy and theology under EBENEZER ERSKINE and James Fisher. He was licensed in 1750 and was unanimously called to Haddington in 1751. It was a poor parish; his stipend never rose above £50, but he avoided debt and still distributed at least ten per cent of his income to the poor.

Brown took an active part in the affairs of the Burgher Synod. He was elected moderator for 1753 and held a number of other posts in the synod and in the presbytery of Edinburgh. He introduced two innovations into the observance of the Lord's Supper; he permitted children to be present, and he celebrated it twice a year. He believed that the traditions surrounding annual Communion tended to obscure the primitive simplicity of the supper. From 1767 until his death he served as Burgher professor of divinity, a position for which he was well qualified. To his mastery of Latin, Greek and Hebrew he added Arabic, Persian, Syriac, Ethiopian, French, Spanish, Italian, Dutch and German. Approximately thirty students came to study with him each year during August and September. The rest of the year students were guided by ministers in their respective presbyteries.

Brown was married twice (Janet Thompson, 1753; Violet Croumbie, 1773). He had children by both wives. Several of his descendants distinguished themselves in the ministry, in science and in literature.

His reputation, based on his numerous writings, spread beyond the borders of Scotland. He corresponded with the Countess of HUNTINGDON, and in 1784 was invited to become a professor in the Dutch Reformed college in New York. Though a learned man, he sought to speak 'as if I had never read a book but the Bible' (Mackenzie, 1918: 108). His writing was also intended to edify ordinary Christians. He published two short catechisms, the first designed to teach the essentials of salvation to children, the second a preparation for admission to the Lord's table. His *Dictionary of the Holy Bible* continued to be updated for at least a hundred years. The *Self-Interpreting Bible* established the author's worldwide reputation. It was frequently revised and was valued in Scottish homes alongside Bunyan's *Pilgrim's Progress* and Boston's *Four-fold State*. The three authors were memorialized together by Robert Burns:

For now I'm grown sae cursed douse,
I pray an' ponder butt the house;
My shins, my lane, I there sit roastin
Perusing Bunyan, Brown, and Boston.
(Burns's letter to J. Tennant in Kinsley, 1968: 225)

However, Brown never realized any appreciable income

from his books, preferring to keep their price within the reach of the poor. M'Kerrow and Mackenzie list over thirty publications plus numerous tracts.

Brown never lost the humble spirit which marked him as a youth. His brief memoirs and his dying advice to his children stress his great sinfulness and the abounding grace of God.

SELECT WRITINGS

J. Brown, *Two Short Catechisms Mutually Connected* (Edinburgh, 1764)

—, *Sacred Tropology* (Edinburgh, 1768)

—, *A Dictionary of the Holy Bible* (Edinburgh, 1769)

—, *A General History of the Christian Church, from the Birth of Our Saviour to the Present Time* (Edinburgh, 1771)

—, *The Self-Interpreting Bible* (Edinburgh, 1778)

—, *A Compendious History of the British Churches in England, Scotland, Ireland, and America* (Glasgow, 1784)

BIBLIOGRAPHY

J. and E. Brown, eds, *Select Remains of the Rev. John Brown* (London, 1789); and the Memoir by W. Brown attached to the 1856 Edinburgh edition

J. Brown, *Dr. John Brown's Letter to the Rev. J. Cairns, D.D.*, 2nd edn (Edinburgh, 1861)

DNB

J. Kinsley, ed., *The Poems and Songs of Robert Burns*, 3 vols, I (Oxford, 1968)

R. Mackenzie, *John Brown of Haddington* (1918; reprinted London, 1964)

J. M'Kerrow, *History of the Secession Church*, 2nd edn (Glasgow, 1845)

JOHN K. LA SHELL

Brown, John (b. Glasgow, Lanarkshire, Scotland, 9 May 1778; d. Langton, Scotland, 25 June 1848). Minister of Gartmore (1805–10), Langton (1810–43), and of Langton Free Church of Scotland (1843–8). Nineteenth-century Scottish evangelical minister and Presbyterian apologist. An early supporter of the evangelical party in the Church of Scotland, he was a regular contributor to Dr ANDREW M. THOMSON's *Edinburgh Christian Instructor*. In 1842 he participated in a delegation to the Prime Minister, Sir Robert Peel, on the situation in the Church. He joined the Free Church in 1843 and was to have been moderator of the 1849 FCS General Assembly.

His most significant publications were *A Vindication of Presbyterian Church Government in Reply to the Independents* (Edinburgh 1805), a standard work on the subject, and *The Exclusive Claims of Puseyite Episcopalians to the Christian Ministry Indefensible* (Edinburgh 1842). He also published against Socinianism and Arianism, on the election of ministers, and a report of the 1842 deputation.

BIBLIOGRAPHY

DNB

T. Brown, *Annals of the Disruption* (Edinburgh, 1893)

W. Ewing, ed., *Annals of the Free Church of Scotland*, 1 (Edinburgh, 1914)

Fasti, 1

JOHN R. McINTOSH

Brown, John [of Broughton Place] (b. Whitburn, Lothian, Scotland, 12 July 1784; d. Edinburgh, 13 Oct. 1858). Scottish Secession divine. He was a grandson of the more famous JOHN BROWN of Haddington and a son of John Brown of Whitburn; although a less distinguished scholar than his famous grandfather, he was of a warmer nature and maintained connections with other Christian traditions. He studied at Edinburgh University 1797–1800 and received further theological education 1800–4 under the saintly GEORGE LAWSON of Selkirk, who had succeeded to John Brown of Haddington's position as sole professor of the Associate Synod.

He was inducted to his first pastoral charge of Biggar Associate Church in 1806 and remained there some 16 years. During his time at Biggar, he built up a justifiable reputation as an expositor of scripture; at a time when much expository preaching was either very formal or purely devotional Brown returned to true expository preaching, opening up the Bible in a consecutive, doctrinal and practical manner.

In 1822 he was called to minister to the United Associate congregation worshipping in Rose Street, Edinburgh and in 1829 he moved to the pastorate of Broughton Place Church in the New Town of the same city. The handsome classical building which housed Brown and his congregation of 1,500 (and which still stands) was popularly known in Edinburgh as 'Dr John Brown's Chapel'. It was at Broughton Place that Brown's ministry was most influential. A contemporary (Professor Masson) wrote of him:

> At that time there was no more venerable man in Edinburgh. People turned in the street to observe his dignified figure as he passed, and strangers who went to hear him were struck no less by the beauty of his appearance, the graceful fall of the silver locks round his fine head and sensitive face, than by his Pauline earnestness. (Masson in MacEwen, 1895: 111)

In 1830 he was awarded the degree of DD by Jefferson College, Pennsylvania. In 1834 he was appointed as Scotland's first professor of exegetical theology in the United Associate Synod; by this time, the training for Secession ministers had altered and there were four professors, of whom Brown was one, who also held full-time pastoral charges. Students came to study in the synod hall in Queen Street, Edinburgh over the summer months, working for the remainder of the year under the supervision of their home Presbyteries. Brown was able to use his expository gifts for the benefit of his students and, in later life, he was able to publish much of this material in commentary format; even today, some of his works are still available in print.

Among his more influential works are 'Discourses and Sayings of Our Lord Jesus Christ' and 'Expository Discourses on I Peter'; among his commentaries are works on Romans, Galatians, Hebrews and II Peter. C. H. SPURGEON wrote of him 'We always think of Brown as a Puritan born out of due time. Everything he has left us is solid gold. He is both rich and clear, profound and perspicuous'. Equally, expounding scripture seems to have been Brown's greatest delight; writing of his work on Hebrews he said 'Happier hours than those which I have spent in composing these expository discourses I can scarcely expect to spend on this side of the grave'.

In 1841, Brown became involved in a controversy of which he was never to be entirely free. The Reverend James Morison of Clerk's Lane, Kilmarnock and a former student of Brown's was indicted for heresy in that he held and preached a universal view of the Atonement. This was not denied by Morison but Brown, while not agreeing with everything that Morison said, spoke on his behalf and suggested that 'there ought to be room in the United Secession Church for men who held views similar to Mr Morison . . .', although he also stated that Morison was certainly in error 'in certain respects'. As it happened, Morison effectively deposed himself and went on to form the Evangelical Union in 1843. As Morison attributed at least some of his views to Brown's teaching and since Brown was perceived as having taken Morison's side at the trial, he had laid himself open to the suspicion of the Hyper-Calvinists, led by Dr Andrew Marshall of Kirkintilloch. To them, Brown's view at least tended in the direction of Amyraldianism, sometimes known as Universal Calvinism, and they charged him before the synod on 12 counts of teaching unsound doctrine. In 1845 he was finally cleared of all such charges.

Interestingly, Brown and Marshall were allies in another matter – the movement which sought to disestablish the Church of Scotland and move towards what later came to be known as the 'voluntary principle'. Brown was so strongly against any church/state connection that he refused to pay the annuity tax levied on citizens of Edinburgh to pay the stipends of the minister of the Burgh Churches. Rather than pay this tax, he allowed his goods to be poinded and sold by the civil authorities. He had a son, also named John, a medical doctor and the author of 'Rab and His Friends' and other works.

BIBLIOGRAPHY
DNB
J. Brown, MD, *Letter to John Cairns* (Edinburgh, 1869)
A. R. MacEwen, *Life and Letters of John Cairns* (London, 1895)

ALASDAIR BOTHWELL GORDON

Brown, John (b. Torrington, CT, USA, 9 May 1800; d. Charlestown, VA, USA, 2 Dec. 1859). Radical abolitionist. Raised in a strict Calvinist home, Brown embraced the religious and moral convictions of his parents regarding the sovereign Providence of God and the evils of slavery. As a teen, he made a formal profession of faith, joined the Congregational Church of Judson, Ohio, and concluded that his Christianity required him to help runaway slaves reach Canada and freedom.

Later, his barn in Richmond, Pennsylvania, served as a station for the underground railroad.

Brown married twice and fathered twenty children. He moved his family repeatedly between the 1820s and the 1850s, mostly due to a long series of business failures as a tanner, land speculator, and shepherd. He remained a staunch Calvinist but he grew disillusioned with white Christianity's failure to treat blacks equally and after 1840 never attended church regularly.

Brown's lifelong abolitionism grew more radical in the 1850s. Persuaded that neither political legislation nor moral suasion could rid the nation of its greatest evil, he determined that violent force alone could free the slaves. Such extraordinary means were justified by the righteousness of the cause. Thus, when the fight over free soil broke out in Kansas in the mid-1850s, Brown eagerly followed five of his sons westward to engage in the 'holy war' against the South's slave power. The Browns employed various guerilla tactics, including the massacre of five proslavery men at Pottawatomie in May 1856.

By 1857, Brown had decided on a new ploy – incite a slave revolt in the South. With the financial aid and moral backing of the 'Secret Six', a group of north-eastern abolitionists, he announced his plan for an invasion of the South to a convention of his followers at Chatham, Canada West [now Ontario], in May 1858. Within another year, he had picked Harpers Ferry, Virginia as the site where his war for slave liberation would begin. On October 16, Brown and his men seized the federal armoury and expected area slaves to flock to their cause. But none did and within 36 hours Brown's forces were overtaken by US Marines led by ROBERT E. LEE, later the leading southern general in the US Civil War. Brown was tried and executed but not before convincing himself that God would use the Harpers Ferry raid to provoke a national crisis over slavery that would ultimately bring an end to the peculiar institution.

Major manuscript collections may be found in the Boyd B. Stutler Collection, Charleston, West Virginia, the John Brown papers at the Library of Congress, and the Kansas State Historical Society in Topeka.

BIBLIOGRAPHY
DAB
S. B. Oates, *Our Fiery Trial* (Amherst, MA, 1979)
—, *To Purge This Land With Blood*, 2nd edn (New York, 1984)
J. Rossbach, *Ambivalent Conspirators* (Philadelphia, PA, 1982)

RICHARD W. POINTER

Brown, J(ohn) T(urland) (b. Bugbrooke, Northamptonshire, England, 1 Jan. 1819, d. Northampton, 11 June 1899). English Baptist minister. Brown exercised a remarkable ministry at College Street, Northampton from 1843 to 1894, it being said that he exercised more influence on the churches of the Northamptonshire Association than many a bishop of the Established Church, but his influence was that of service rather than that of office. From a farming family, Brown was converted and baptized when he was not yet 14, and soon began to preach in neighbouring villages. Called to the ministry from the church at Bugbrooke, at the age of 17, he entered Bristol College for training but was expelled after only three months at the college. Under the guidance of J. P. MURSELL of Leicester he therefore studied under Mr Cyrus Edmonds (son of ROBERT HALL's successor at Cambridge) in Leicester, where under the influence of Mursell and EDWARD MIALL he became involved in the work of the Liberation Society, which influenced him in favour of active Christian citizenship throughout his ministry. He intended to continue his studies at a Scottish university but was diverted by a call to the church at Oakham, Rutland, 1839–43. He served as a committee member of the BMS from 1854 and was an ever eager advocate of its interests. With Dr E. B. UNDERHILL he formed a special commission to visit the churches in Jamaica in 1859. In 1877 he was president of the Baptist Union and was active in home missions.

BIBLIOGRAPHY
BaptMag (1890, 1899)

J. H. Y. BRIGGS

Brown, Joseph (b. Suffolk, England, 1800; d. Richmond Hill, London, 13 Aug. 1867). Anglican clergyman. Brown was a graduate of Queens' College, Cambridge (BA 1829; MA 1833). He was Vicar of St Paul's, Mill Hill (1833–44), Perpetual Curate of St Matthias, Bethnal Green (1844–9) and Rector of Christ Church, Southwark (1849–67). During all these years of service in London he was active in social work, being the inspiration behind the foundation of the Homes for Servants Out of Place and the Albert Institution at Blackfriars. He also played a prominent part in the establishment of the Cholera Orphan House at Ham Common. He published *Narratives and Sermons for Schools* (1856) and *Hymns and Psalms for Divine Worship* (1859).

BIBLIOGRAPHY
Boase, I: 436

ARTHUR POLLARD

Brown, Morris (b. Charleston, SC, BNA, 8 Jan. 1770; d. Philadelphia, USA, 9 May 1849). Bishop of African MEC. Born free of mixed parentage, Brown joined the MEC in Charleston as a youth. Its large African contingent, in a dispute over their burial ground, withdrew, and, in 1816, joined the new African Methodist denomination in Philadelphia. Bishop RICHARD ALLEN ordained Brown deacon in 1817 and elder in 1818. Repression after the DENMARK VESEY plot destroyed his congregation. Brown moved north to assist Allen until elected bishop in 1828. Under his leadership the denomination moved westward and into Canada, debated women's right to preach, established *The A. M. E. Church Magazine*

(1841–8) and sent delegates to the EA in London (1846). In Charleston Brown assisted slaves to purchase their freedom and was punished for breaking laws governing black worship. He served on the Vigilance Committee of Philadelphia, a part of the underground railroad. Morris Brown College in Atlanta carries his name.

BIBLIOGRAPHY
DAB
DCA
R. W. Logan and M. R. Winston, eds, *Dictionary of American Negro Biography* (New York, 1985)

WARREN NAPIER
WILL GRAVELY

Brown, Obadiah B. (b. Newark, NJ, USA, 20 July 1779; d. 2 May 1852). Baptist minister. Educated as a Presbyterian and self-taught, Brown taught school in his early years. He became a baptist *circa* 1803. He studied under William Van Horn for the ministry and was called to be pastor of the First Baptist Church, Washington in 1807. He held that position until 1850 while working for the Federal government. Brown is remembered as a member of the board of trustees for Columbian College, as a tireless advocate of missions, and as chaplain to Congress.

BIBLIOGRAPHY
W. Cathcart, *Baptist Encyclopedia* (Philadelphia, PA, 1881)

WADE A. HORTON

Brown, Peter (b. Edinburgh, Scotland, 29 June 1784; d. Toronto, Canada West, 30 June 1863). Journalist. Brown worked as a merchant and civic official in Edinburgh before emigrating to New York City in 1837. There he began his journalistic career, writing occasionally for the *Albion* and in 1842 establishing his own paper, the *British Chronicle*. The following year he ceased publishing the *British Chronicle*, moved to Toronto and established *The Banner*. He had taken a lively interest in the events leading up to the Scottish Disruption of 1843 and became a firm supporter of the Free Church. In Toronto, largely through the instrumentality of *The Banner* he played a key role in the formation of the Canadian Free Church. Brown was also active in the Anti-Slavery Society of Canada and the Toronto City Mission. His outlook combined a Whig political philosophy with a warm-hearted evangelicalism. He acted as a watchdog over the interests of the Protestant community in Toronto and was the most visible and articulate lay spokesman for early evangelical Presbyterianism in Canada.

BIBLIOGRAPHY
DCB, 9
R. W. Vaudry, 'Peter Brown, the Toronto *Banner* and the Evangelical Mind in Victorian Canada', *Ontario History*, 77, 1 (1985): 3–18

RICHARD W. VAUDRY

Brown, Robert James (b. Aberdeen, Scotland, 23 Dec. 1792; d. Aberdeen, Scotland, 7 Dec. 1872). FCS minister. He was the third son of William Laurence Brown (1755–1830), principal of Aberdeen University. Brown was educated at Aberdeen (MA 1808) and was ordained minister at Drumblade, Aberdeenshire in 1821. He served there until 1827 when he was made professor of Greek at Aberdeen. He left the Established Church upon the Disruption of 1843 but retained his professorship until his retirement in 1860. He was moderator of the Free Church General Assembly in 1846. Brown was a member of the EA.

BIBLIOGRAPHY
Boase
T. Brown, *Annals of the Disruption* (Edinburgh, 1892): 808

JONATHAN BURKE CUTMORE

Brown, Samuel (b. Haddington, East Lothian, Scotland, 1779; d. Haddington, Scotland, 13 July 1839). Pioneer of circulating libraries. A son of JOHN BROWN (1722–87) he was largely self-educated and reared by an uncle, John Croumbie, a chapman, ironmonger and drysalter in Haddington. After a crisis of faith he became a moderate Calvinist. He succeeded to Croumbie's business, married Elizabeth Duncan of Edinburgh, and joined his father's church. He managed the Haddington Tract Society, supported the East Lothian Bible Society, and founded and taught in his own Sunday school. He was a founder and president of the Haddington School of Art (a Mechanics' Institute), 1821–39, and Provost of Haddington, 1833–6. He also campaigned for the abolition of slavery.

Although he did not originate circulating libraries, he started a library in Haddington as early as 1817. Two-thirds of his books were moral or religious. They were designed to nurture faith, promote enlightenment and show the application of science to everyday life. From 1831 onwards with the help of missionary societies he sent books to Jamaica and other countries.

After his death his scheme faded away at home and overseas, but his administrative arrangements were basically those adopted a century later by the Carnegie UK Trust for the infant county libraries.

BIBLIOGRAPHY
S. Brown, *Some Account of Itinerating Libraries and Their Founder* (Edinburgh, 1856)
L. G. Durbidge, 'Pioneer Itinerator', *Times Literary Supp.* (6 March 1969): 246
—, 'Samuel Brown' (Loughborough Univ. of Tech., MA thesis, 1972)
—, 'Itinerating Libraries', *Encyclopedia of Library and Information Science*, 13 (New York, 1975): 154–60

JOHN S. ANDREWS

Brown, Sarah [Firbank, Mrs C.] (b. Hunmanby, Yorkshire, England, 17 April 1812; d. probably London, 20 Aug. 1879). Primitive Methodist itinerant preacher.

Brown's grandfather was one of JOHN WESLEY's class leaders. When the Primitive Methodists visited the East Riding she was an early convert, becoming a local preacher at 17 and an itinerant (1833). During her two years in the Hull circuit, especially in the Westmorland/Cumberland missions where she was one of the first PM preachers, she travelled long distances, often preaching three times a Sunday. In January 1835 Brown married and retired, continuing as a local preacher, being particularly in demand for chapel and Sunday school anniversaries. She died after much suffering, leaving behind her husband and nine children.

BIBLIOGRAPHY
PMMag (1881)

E. DOROTHY GRAHAM

Brown, William (b. Leuchars, Fife, Scotland, 1800; d. St Andrews, Scotland, 19 July 1868). Church of Scotland minister. He was educated at the universities of St Andrews, of which he became a DD in 1842, and Aberdeen. After Argentina became independent, parties of Scottish Presbyterians settled there and Brown was encouraged by THOMAS CHALMERS to go and minister to them. The presbytery of Glasgow ordained him to this work in 1826. From 1828 Brown ministered to a congregation formed by a merger of two groups of Presbyterians near Buenos Aires. In 1835 his congregation erected what is claimed to have been the first Scots Church in South America. Brown left in 1850 and became professor of divinity at St Andrews.

R. H. CAMPBELL

Brown-Westhead, Joshua Procter (b. Manchester, England, 1807; d. Woverley, Worcestershire, England, 25 July 1877). Merchant and MP. He was born Joshua Procter Westhead, and added the name of Brown in fulfilment of the testamentary wishes of his uncle, John Brown, High Sheriff of Worcestershire.

He held various public offices in his locality, as Justice of the Peace for Staffordshire and Worcestershire, and Deputy-Lieutenant of Worcestershire from 1852. He had entered Parliament in 1847 as Member for Knaresborough, which he represented for five years. Later he sat for York from 1857 to 1865, and again from 1868 to 1871. As an active Liberal MP, he voted for the disestablishment of the Irish Church, the introduction of voting by ballot, and the setting up of courts of conciliation for industrial disputes. He was a member of the Wesleyan Methodist Church, and his career exemplifies the alliance of Wesleyanism and Liberalism in the second half of the nineteenth century.

RUPERT E. DAVIES

Browne, George (b. c. 1789; d. Weston-super-Mare, England, 5 Sept. 1868). Congregational minister and

BFBS secretary. Browne ministered to the Independent congregation at Clapham and developed an interest in the BFBS, attending committee meetings and becoming acquainted with its business. In 1833 he became dissenting secretary. With the Anglican secretary, ANDREW BRANDRAM, he managed the society during a period of tremendous growth, committing much energy to organizational work with local auxiliaries; together with the secretaries he steered the BFBS through a controversial reduction in the price of Bibles in 1840. Browne was devoted to the ecumenical principle of the society. Despite his dissenting views, he was thought to be more like a Church dignitary than Brandram, and remembered as 'a good man, a diligent worker, respected by everybody'. Browne was ill in 1850 but delayed his retirement until 1854 because of Brandram's death and the golden jubilee celebrations. In retirement he wrote a *History of the British and Foreign Bible Society* (1859).

BIBLIOGRAPHY
W. Canton, *History of the BFBS* (London, 1904)
L. Howsam, *Cheap Bibles* (Cambridge, 1991)

LESLIE HOWSAM

Browne, John (b. Riverstown, Co. Cork, Ireland, 15 Nov. 1794; d. Cheltenham, Gloucestershire, England, 25 July 1857). Anglican clergyman. Browne was educated at Eton College, Trinity College, Dublin and Trinity College, Cambridge where he graduated LL B in 1818. At Cambridge he knew FRANCIS CLOSE and was probably a follower of CHARLES SIMEON. After ordination (deacon 1819, priest 1820) he was Curate of Castle Bromwich, Warwickshire, and from 1828 as Curate of Holy Trinity, Cheltenham (where he succeeded THOMAS TRUEBODY THOMASON).

Browne was regarded as an outstanding preacher and second only to Close in the ministerial hierarchy of Cheltenham. Both men were involved in church extension and in educational enterprises. Their opposition to Tractarianism was noted in the local newspaper; that 'High and rampant would it be if the shining light of a Close, or a Browne, could be removed' (*Cheltenham Journal*, 14 May 1844). As a mark of their affection, his parishioners presented him with a parsonage house. Browne edited three volumes of the sermons of HENRY BLUNT.

BIBLIOGRAPHY
Cheltenham Journal (14 May 1844, 1 August 1857)

ALAN FREDERICK MUNDEN

Browne, John Henry (b. Maidstone, Kent, England, 1779; d. Cotgrove, Northamptonshire, England, 2 Nov. 1858). Anglican clergyman. Educated at Oakham and Louth, Browne was admitted to Pembroke College, Cambridge but subsequently migrated to St John's (scholar, 1800; BA 1803; MA 1806; fellow 1808–14). He became Perpetual Curate of Thrumpton (Nottinghamshire)

(1804–11), then rector of Cotgrove (1811–58). He was made Archdeacon (1816–58) and Prebendary of Ely (1817–58). As archdeacon he carried disciplinary responsibilities, not least in respect of alterations to churches. He was thus involved in the controversy about the introduction of a stone altar in the Round Church at Cambridge. He also corresponded with C. P. Golightly, who initiated the Martyrs' Memorial monument scheme at Oxford. Browne denounced Pusey's views as 'flagrant and atrocious dishonesty'.

BIBLIOGRAPHY
Boase, I: 445
P. Toon, *Evangelical Theology 1833–1856* (London, 1979)

ARTHUR POLLARD

Browne, Moses (b. 1704; d. Blackheath, London, 13 Sept. 1787). English Anglican clergyman and Poet. Brown was a poet greatly patronized by Edward Cave, the editor of *Gentleman's Magazine*, who awarded him a prize for the best theological poem submitted. Encouraged to seek ordination by JAMES HERVEY, he became Hervey's curate at Collingtree in 1753. In the same year he was appointed to the rectory of Olney by Lord DARTMOUTH, but because of the size of his family – he had 13 children – he had to accept the chaplaincy of Morden College in plurality, with JOHN NEWTON serving as his curate at Olney 1764–80. Among his published works are religious poetry, sermons and theological translations. Cecil described him as 'an evangelical minister and good man', and Southey whilst speaking of his poetry remarks that he was 'not negligent of his vocation as a fisher of men'.

BIBLIOGRAPHY
DNB
R. Southey, *Life and Works of William Cowper*, 15 vols (London, 1835–7)

J. H. Y. BRIGGS

Browne, William Henry (b. Mallow, Ireland, 1800; d. Launceston, Australia, 18 June 1877). Australian Anglican chaplain. Son of Henry, a barrister, Browne studied medicine and, after his conversion, theology at Trinity College, Dublin (BA 1822, LL D 1828). Priested in 1825, he found that his Irish curacy offered little scope for his enthusiasm and missionary zeal. In 1828, he took up a chaplaincy at Launceston, Van Diemen's Land (later Tasmania).

Browne ministered in northern Tasmania for forty years, initially over a huge area, later in the growing town of Launceston. Much of his early work lay with the convicts, for whom he composed a prayer manual. His restless energy found outlets in wider concerns for the welfare of the community: interdenominational cooperation, antitransportation, savings banks, education, and Bible societies. He opposed vigorously the first bishop's Tractarian policies but was never a 'party' man. Indeed, on retiring as a parish minister, Browne was made archdeacon by the High Church second bishop. A resolute individualist who revelled in controversy, Browne espoused many causes. This argumentative evangelical Irishman had many opponents but few enemies.

BIBLIOGRAPHY
ADB
Al. Dub.
Boase

KENNETH J. CABLE

Browning, Colin Arrott (b. 1791; d. Woolwich, England, 23 Oct. 1856). Surgeon-Superintendent of convict ships to Australia. He entered the Royal Navy in 1813 and received the degree of MD from Edinburgh University medical college 12 years later. Between 1831 and 1849 he made eight voyages from England to Australia as Surgeon-Superintendent of convict ships, developing an enlightened and efficient system for his ships. He described his methods in *England's Exiles* (London, 1842) and *The Convict Ship* (London, 1844). The prisoners were divided into manageable groups; some were given posts of responsibility as petty officers, schoolmasters and medical assistants; all were encouraged to extend their education. He kept firm discipline without recourse to flogging, and he achieved high standards of health and literacy. Bible reading and Christian instruction formed a major part of his educational purpose. Before his retirement from the navy he became Deputy Inspector of Hospitals.

BIBLIOGRAPHY
ADB
DNB

RICHARD C. BLAKE

Browning, Thomas (b. Stroud, Gloucestershire, England; d. at sea, 7 July 1838). CMS missionary to Ceylon (Sri Lanka). Browning studied as a probationer missionary under the Reverend Dr JOHN WILLIAMS and was ordained (deacon 1819, priest 1820) by the Bishop of Gloucester. On 19 May 1820 he went to Kandy, Ceylon to join the CMS party sent to Ceylon in 1817 (*see* SAMUEL LAMBRICK, ROBERT MAYOR, BENJAMIN WARD and JOSEPH KNIGHT). He served for some 18 years. He died the day before his boat was to arrive in England. He married Mary Stephens, who remarried a Captain McAlpine.

BIBLIOGRAPHY
D. T. B[arry], *CMS Register of Missionaries and Native Clergy* (privately printed) (London, 1904)

DONALD M. LEWIS

Brownlee, John (b. Wishaw, Lanarkshire, Scotland, 1 May 1791; d. King William's Town, Cape Colony, South Africa, 24 Dec. 1871). LMS missionary and linguist. Brownlee was a skilled artisan before studying theology at Glasgow. He volunteered his services to the LMS in 1814 and was ordained for missionary service on 30 September 1816.

After his arrival at Cape Town in June 1817 he went to work among the Xhosa people on the Tyume river. He resigned after only a few months because of the notorious disorder in which the mission was at that time, and he was offered the post of missionary and government agent among the Xhosa of Ngqika. He accepted the offer and settled, in 1820, near the present day town of Alice in the Ciskei. He was joined, the next year, by the first three missionaries of the Glasgow Missionary Society.

However, in 1821, Dr JOHN PHILIP succeeded in persuading him to return to the LMS, and in January 1822, Brownlee settled where the modern King William's Town now stands. Despite three bitter frontier wars he worked there among the Xhosa people and the incoming Mfengu until his retirement in 1867. He was highly respected by many Xhosa people, NTSIKANA for example told his flock to go to Brownlee after his death.

BIBLIOGRAPHY
B. F. Holt, *Greatheart of the Border* (South Africa Missionary Museum, 1976)

ANDREW C. ROSS

Brownlow, William Gannaway (b. Wythe County, VA, USA, 29 August 1805; d. Knoxville, TN, USA, 29 April 1877). Methodist preacher, newspaper editor, Governor of Tennessee, and United States Senator. Joseph A. and Catherine Gannaway Brownlow migrated from Virginia to eastern Tennessee, settling near Knoxville. They both died within three months of each other in 1816 and William was then reared by Catherine's relatives.

Brownlow enjoyed few formal educational advantages. He was trained to be a carpenter, but literary and public career interests moved him in other directions. He was a Methodist travelling preacher from 1826 to 1836 in the Holston Conference, serving in western North Carolina and eastern Tennessee. His outspokenness led to his being censured by the conference in 1831. This same session, however, made him a delegate to the 1832 General Conference. He married Eliza Ann O'Brien in 1836.

Between 1838 and 1861 'Parson Brownlow' edited Whig newspapers in Elizabethton, Jonesboro, and Knoxville respectively. The *Knoxville Whig* became the most influential paper in eastern Tennessee. His fundamental political commitment was to the Union. He described himself as a 'Federal Whig of the Washington and Hamilton type'. Only during the Civil War did he adopt emancipation as well. He ran against Andrew Johnson for nomination to Congress in 1843.

Brownlow's house was the last one in Knoxville under

the USA flag. His paper was suppressed in October, 1861 and he fled to the mountains on the North Carolina border. He was captured and held until March 1862. Brownlow returned home with the Union forces in the fall of 1863. He participated in reconstituting pro-USA government in Tennessee and was elected governor by acclamation of the Union central committee in 1865. His 1867 re-election was by a large majority, though he was afflicted with palsy and unable to campaign.

The Ku Klux Klan grew powerful among the disenfranchised former Confederates. Brownlow requested but was denied Federal troops to handle this problem, so he organized a state guard and declared martial law in nine counties.

Brownlow was elected to the United States Senate in 1869. Poor health limited him to a single term. His Senate career was not distinguished, but the final bill he introduced was for the purchase of property in Nashville for Fisk University, a school for African-Americans. Brownlow sold the *Knoxville Whig* when he went to the Senate. Now he bought it back and resumed a vigorous editorship of it until just before his death.

'Parson Brownlow' published five books: *Helps To the Study of Presbyterianism* (1834); *A Political Register, Setting Forth the Principles of the Whig and Locofoco Parties in the United States, With the Life and Public Services of Henry Clay* (1844); *Americanism Contrasted With Foreignism, Romanism, and Bogus Democracy* (1856); *The Great Iron Wheel Examined, and an Exhibition of Elder [J. R.] Graves, its Builder* (1856), and *Sketches of the Rise, Progress, and Decline of Secession* (1862).

BIBLIOGRAPHY
DAB
EWM

CHARLES W. BROCKWELL, JR

Bruce, Philip (b. Kings Mountain, NC, BNA, 25 Dec. 1755; d. Giles County, TN, USA, 10 May 1826). Methodist circuit rider and presiding elder. Born to parents of Huguenot background, Bruce was converted as a youth, along with his mother through the efforts of pioneer Methodist preachers. After serving in the Continental Army during the American Revolution, he began his career as a travelling preacher in 1781. His ministry spanned 36 years and at the time of his death he was the oldest travelling preacher in the United States, with the exception of FREEBORN GARRETTSON. Most of his work was in Virginia, the Carolinas and Georgia. Typical of many early circuit riders, he never married.

His distinction as a circuit riding evangelist and presiding elder led, on two occasions, to his coming within three votes of being elected a bishop. Bruce was a prolific evangelist, renowned for his self-sacrificing labours, affection for his fellow preachers, and ecclesiastical judgment. His preaching, though devoid of 'striking characteristics', sometimes halting, and somewhat hobbled by a 'feeble' voice, reputedly displayed sound judgment. His

theology was quite typical of the times in its conversionist appeal and appreciation for emotive responses from his auditors. It seems that Bruce's greatest contribution to early American Methodism was his gift for persistence and numerical fruitfulness as a travelling preacher.

BIBLIOGRAPHY
AAP, 7: 73–6
M. H. Moore, *Sketches of the Pioneers of Methodism in North Carolina and Virginia* (Nashville, TN, 1884): 180–95

WOODROW W. WHIDDEN

Brückner, Gottlob (b. Saxony, Germany, 19 July 1783; d. Java, 9 July 1857). German missionary to Java. Son of a pious Lutheran farmer, Brückner was converted through JOHANNES JÄNICKE about 1803 and in 1806 entered his seminary. In February 1808 Jänicke sent Brückner and John Supper to Rotterdam at the request of the Netherlands Missionary Society (NMS). Joined in April 1811 by Joseph Kam, in September 1811 they were sent to learn from the Moravians at Zeist. In October 1812 they arrived in London where the LMS sent them to DAVID BOGUE's seminary at Gosport. The LMS appointed them to Java as the British had temporarily taken over the Dutch East Indies where the governor, Sir Stamford Raffles, was sympathetic to missions.

Ordained by a Dutch Reformed minister in London, Brückner, Kam and Supper sailed on 1 January 1814, arriving in Batavia on 26 May. With the support of Raffles and WILLIAM ROBINSON, of the BMS, they established an auxiliary of the BFBS. Brückner then proceeded to Semarang on the north coast of central Java. In December 1814 he married the daughter of a Dutch clergyman.

On a trip to Jogjakarta he met THOMAS TROWT who was working on a Javanese New Testament. Through Trowt, Brückner became convinced of Baptist doctrine and was baptized by immersion on 7 April 1816. As a result Brückner's salary as a government chaplain ceased, as did his connection with the LMS. Trowt died in October and the translation work was halted.

With the restoration of Dutch rule in 1816, the colonial officials sought to ban missionary work. Supper died; Kam and Brückner were allowed to remain. Brückner associated with the BMS and turned to translation. By 1823 he completed the New Testament and in 1828 travelled to Serampore where, with JOSHUA MARSHMAN's help, a Javanese New Testament, tracts and grammar were printed.

However, the BMS suggested Brückner abandon Java as they were unable to reinforce his efforts because of Dutch opposition and there had been no conversions. In 1847 it finally withdrew its support. In 1839, however, a copy of one of Brückner's tracts or perhaps Mark's Gospel, led to the conversion of a Muslim leader in a village. Brückner visited the group in 1842 but declined to baptize them leaving the NMS to incorporate the group into the Dutch Reformed Church.

BIBLIOGRAPHY
D. Bentley-Taylor, *The Weathercock's Reward* (London, 1967)
I. Fletcher, *LMS in the Malay Archipelago* (London, 1952)
E. Payne, *The First Generation* (London, 1936)
—, *South East from Serampore* (London, 1945)
J. Sibree, *Register of LMS Missionaries* (London, 1923)

MICHAEL GRIFFITHS

Brunsdon, Daniel (b. Pershore, Worcestershire, England, 1 June 1777; d. Serampore, Bengal, India, 3 July 1801). Baptist pioneer missionary. Converted as a teenager, baptized by Dr JOHN RYLAND, and trained for the ministry by JOHN SUTCLIFF at Olney, Brunsdon sailed to Bengal with the Marshman family, WILLIAM WARD, and his fiancée Miss Hirons of Fairfield, Gloucestershire. He died from an enlarged spleen and mercury poisoning after making little progress in Bengali. In 1830 J. C. MARSHMAN had to refute a charge that Brunsdon was deliberately poisoned (an accusation which may have emanated from JOHN CHAMBERLAIN, also a suitor for Mrs Brundson's hand).

Mrs Brunsdon, who was instrumental in the conversion of Rasu, KRISHNA PAL's wife, and stayed on to work with HANNAH MARSHMAN in Serampore, married James Rolt, a builder, convert and active lay worker in 1803, bore two more sons (in addition to Daniel Brunsdon Jr) and returned permanently to England in 1813.

BIBLIOGRAPHY
BMS Archives, London, W. Ward, Journal, as transcribed by E. Daniel Potts
Periodical Accounts relative to the proceedings of the BMS

E. M. JACKSON

Brunton, Henry (b. Selkirk, Scotland, *c.* 1775; d. Karass, North Caucasus, March, 1813). Missionary linguist in West Africa and Tartary. When accepted by the Edinburgh Missionary Society in 1797, Brunton was married, with children, and was in training as a minister at the theological hall of the Associate Synod. In late 1797, he and a colleague PETER Grieg (or GREIG) were sent to Sierra Leone, whose governor, ZACHARY MACAULAY, directed them to Rio Pongas, 200 miles to the north, to begin a mission in Susu country, an area under Islamic influence. Because of ill health Brunton returned to Sierra Leone in 1799 and to Britain in 1800. Despite his short stay in Africa, and the difficult conditions of the Rio Pongas mission (Greig was murdered), Brunton had acquired a respectable knowledge of the Susu language, and he welcomed an invitation from the CMS to prepare Susu material. In 1800–8, he published at Edinburgh a series of catechisms, a grammar, and a vocabulary; these were used to a limited extent by the CMS Mission on the Rio Pongas 1806–16.

In 1802, Brunton accompanied Alexander Patteson on a mission to Russia, which led to the establishment of a mission station in the North Caucasus. At Karass,

near Georgievsk, Brunton worked among the Nogai Tatar, another people under Islamic influence. Accompanied by his family, he was assisted by several Scotsmen and a Susu youth: as the best educated member of the party, Brunton concentrated on linguistic work. A press was provided by BFBS and from 1806 Brunton published catechisms and Gospel translations in Tatar. A problem with drink brought him into 'disgrace' just before he died in 1813.

His Tatar work was based on earlier studies. But his Susu work was original: his grammar was the most detailed study to date of any West African language, and for long served as an introduction to the Mande language family. The grammar included an intelligent discussion of mission strategy in relation to semi-Islamized peoples.

BIBLIOGRAPHY
W. Brown, *History of the Propagation of Christianity* (Edinburgh, 1823)
C. Hole, *Early History of CMS* (London, 1896)
P. E. H. Hair, 'Susu studies and literature 1799–1900', *Sierra Leone Language Review*, 4 (1965): 38–53
—, 'A Scottish Missionary in the Caucaus' in *SIMBS*, 13 (1973): 28–30
M. V. Jones, 'The Sad . . . Story of Karass', *Oxford Slavonic Papers*, 8 (1975): 53–81

P. E. H. HAIR

Bryan, Andrew (b. Goose Creek, SC, BNA, 1716; d. Savannah, GA, USA, 6 Oct. 1812). African Baptist founder in Georgia. A slave to Jonathan Bryan, who was converted by GEORGE WHITEFIELD in 1740, Andrew and his wife, Hannah, were baptized by GEORGE LIELE. With permission, Bryan began to preach on plantations, and in Savannah. Twice imprisoned with his brother Samson, he and fifty other slave Christians were severely whipped for holding unauthorized meetings. Bryan proclaimed that he 'would freely suffer death for the cause of Jesus Christ'. Released to his owner, he was permitted to hold daytime services at Brampton plantation.

In 1788, the white Baptist, Abraham Marshall, and black Baptist, Jesse Peter, ordained Bryan and baptized 45 blacks to form a church. Bryan purchased property in 1793 to house a growing congregation – First African Baptist which had 1,500 members at his death. He helped found the Savannah River Association and three other African Baptist congregations.

BIBLIOGRAPHY
D. Benedict, *A General History of the Baptist Denomination in America* (Boston, MA, 1813)
A. Gallay, *The Formation of a Planter Elite* (Athens, GA, 1989)

LINDA GLENN

WILL GRAVELY

Bryan, Hugh (b. SC, BNA, 1699; d. Husbah Neck, SC, BNA, 31 Dec. 1753). Whitefield convert and lay evangelical leader in colonial South Carolina. Bryan was a middle level member of the Carolina planter aristocracy near the Georgia border. Yamasee Indians took him prisoner for a year when he was 16. A slave uprising in and a disastrous military expedition against Spanish Florida, both in 1739, filled white settlers in Bryan's neighbourhood with anxiety, and at this juncture first Bryan's wife Catherine, a pious Anglican, and then Bryan himself became evangelical converts – she after reading WHITE-FIELD and he after journeying to Georgia to hear the evangelist. Taking Whitefield's advice to preach to slaves seriously, Bryan perceived in 1741, in part because blacks told him so, that God was about to visit his wrath on South Carolina unless the populace repented. Briefly jailed for uttering these thoughts, Bryan apologized. With his brother, Jonathan, he spent the rest of his life building a biracial evangelical community on his plantation in which slavery functioned only nominally.

BIBLIOGRAPHY
H. H. Jackson, 'Hugh Bryan and the Evangelical Movement in Colonial South Carolina', *Wm. & Mary Q.*, 48 (1986): 594–614

ROBERT CALHOON

Bryan, William. See O'BRYAN, WILLIAM

Buchan, tenth Earl of. *See* ERSKINE, HENRY DAVID

Buchan, George (b. Edinburgh, 29 May 1775; d. Kelloe, Berwickshire, Scotland, 3 Jan. 1856). Civil Servant, landowner, and philanthropist. Brother of General Sir George Buchan of Peninsular War fame, he was related to prominent Scots including the Earls of Buchan and Lord President Dundas. Shipwrecked off the Madagascar coast while *en route* to a post with the Madras Civil Service in 1792, and captured by a French privateer, he became chief secretary to the government in Madras. His conversion took place after returning to the family estate of Kelloe, Berwickshire, in 1809.

He gave himself to philanthropy, promoting Sabbath schools and circulating libraries, maintaining home missionaries, engaging as an elder in pastoral and charitable visits, and entertaining itinerating evangelical clergy. In the General Assembly of the Church of Scotland he was prominent in support of those who formed the FCS in 1843. He wrote pamphlets supporting the non-intrusion of undesired ministers, opposing duelling, and illustrating from his own experience the particular providence of God.

BIBLIOGRAPHY
A. Spence, in *Disruption Worthies*, ed. J. A. Wylie (Edinburgh, no date)

HUGH M. CARTWRIGHT

Buchanan, Claudius (b. Cambuslang, Scotland, 12 March 1766; d. Broxbourne, Hertfordshire, England, 9 Feb. 1815). East India Company chaplain and missionary publicist. He attended Inverary Grammar School 1773–9, was a tutor in western Scotland 1779–82 and 1784–6, a student at Glasgow University 1782–4, 1786–7, and a law clerk in London 1786–91.

He was encouraged by JOHN NEWTON to enter the Anglican priesthood and assisted by HENRY THORNTON secured a place at Queens' College, Cambridge in 1791. He was one of the first evangelical students to receive private tuition from CHARLES SIMEON (BA 1795, deacon 1795). He became John Newton's curate. Through Simeon's friendship with CHARLES GRANT he was appointed an East India Company chaplain in 1796, and ordained priest in 1796.

He was stationed at Barrackpore 1797–9 and Calcutta 1799–1808. A close friend of DAVID BROWN, he assisted him at the Mission Church in Calcutta. He established contacts with BMS missionaries at Serampore, defending WILLIAM CAREY's work before the governor, Lord Mornington (Marquis Wellesley) in 1799. Buchanan recommended the training of young civil servants on their arrival in India and was asked by Wellesley to draw up plans for a college. In the resulting College of Fort William, Buchanan was vice-provost and professor of Greek, Latin and English classics, 1800–6. He became its chief administrator and apologist, promoting it in three volumes of student's essays, *Primitae Orientales* (Calcutta, 1802–4) and a collection of papers and statutes, *The College of Fort William* (London, 1805). To draw attention to the college and his belief in the need to Christianize and civilize India, Buchanan offered £2,670 for prize essays and poems in British universities and schools in 1803 and 1805. Eight books and a number of poems were published, bringing the missionary cause before the British public.

In his *Memoir of the Expediency of an Ecclesiastical Establishment for British India* (London, 1805) Buchanan advocated the extension of episcopacy to India and Anglican involvement in the conversion of Indian people. He was extremely critical of European life in India, Indian people and their religions. Buchanan also sought to promote the translation of the Bible into Asian languages in connection with the BFBS and BMS. His schemes alienated the Baptists by threatening to place their work under Anglican supervision.

He undertook two extensive journeys in India, 1806–7, 1807–8. Buchanan investigated Indian religious practices, Christian missionary activity, visited the Syrian Christians, collected ancient Jewish and Christian manuscripts and promoted the distribution of Bibles. Before leaving India he addressed a memorial to the governor attacking government restrictions on missionary activity and charging it with attempts to censor missionary publications.

In 1808 Buchanan returned to Britain. His actions and attitudes were the centre of a controversy raging in pamphlets, reviews and the deliberations of the East India Company. He continued to focus attention on India through his *Christian Researches in Asia* (London, 1811) and his sermons, notably 'The Star in the East' (1809).

His publications went through numerous editions both in Britain and the United States.

Buchanan collated the Biblical manuscripts he had collected in India, depositing them in Cambridge University Library and engaging Thomas Yeates to complete this work. In 1810 he became Curate-in-Charge of Ouseburn, Yorkshire. He proposed a visit to the Holy Land and Asia Minor in 1811 to investigate the translation of the Bible and the extension of Christianity. Declining health prevented this and his plans were taken up by WILLIAM JOWETT.

He played an active part in the campaign to promote bishops and access for missionaries in India, during the debate over the renewal of the East India Company's charter in 1813. His 'Prospectus of an Ecclesiastical Establishment for India' became the basis of the SPCK's representations. Encouraged by JOSIAH PRATT and the CMS he published *Colonial Ecclesiastical Establishment* (London, 1813). He defended his views on India in *An Apology for Promoting Christianity in India* (London, 1813). In 1814 Buchanan prepared the charge for the first CMS missionaries sent to India. He also worked with the BFBS in superintending the printing of a Syriac New Testament.

The outstanding missionary publicist of his day, Buchanan stimulated Christian involvement in India and the extension of episcopacy to colonial territories at a time when missionary activity was considered by many to be suspect. His perspective of other cultures and religions was limited by his own narrow theological and cultural outlook. He was awarded honorary doctorates from the universities of Glasgow, Aberdeen, St Andrew's, Dublin and Cambridge.

BIBLIOGRAPHY
A. K. Davidson, *Evangelicals and Attitudes to India 1786–1813* (Appleford, England, 1990)
DNB
H. Pearson, *Memoirs of the Life and Writings of The Rev. Claudius Buchanan* 2 vols (Oxford, 1817)

ALLAN K. DAVIDSON

Buchanan, Dugald (b. Ardoch, Strathyre, Perthshire, Scotland, 1716; d. 2 July 1768). Celebrated Gaelic religious poet, belonging to the foundational stage of the evangelical movement in the Highlands. Son of a miller, Buchanan became a tutor to a local family, but moved to Stirling to continue his education. Apprenticed thereafter to a carpenter in Kippen and later at Dumbarton, he did not complete his apprenticeships, largely because of his restless nature. By the early 1740s, the religious impressions which were evident even in his boyhood had deepened noticeably, and he became conscious of his own sinfulness. In 1742 he heard GEORGE WHITEFIELD preaching at Cambuslang, during the revival, but he did not find peace until his conversion in 1744. His spiritual search is documented in a diary which he wrote in English, following Puritan models. Marrying in 1749, he

settled on his father's farm. A year later he abandoned farming, and became an itinerant teacher.

Buchanan's talents lay in teaching and preaching. In 1753 he was settled as a teacher at Kinloch Rannoch in the estate of Strowan, forfeited after the Jacobite Rebellion of 1745. Combining the duties of teacher and catechist from 1755, Buchanan had a major role in 'civilizing' the estate after the rebellion, and was instrumental in planting schools.

Buchanan's Gaelic poetry reflects his calling as preacher and teacher, since it has a strong didactic element. His eight surviving poems establish his reputation as a skilful craftsman of verse, although his themes are far from being original. He is sometimes heavily indebted to Isaac Watts, whom he translates and paraphrases *in extenso* in 'Mòrachd Dhè' ('The Greatness of God'). The influence of the English 'Graveyard School' of poets (represented in England by Edward Young and in Scotland by Robert Blair) is apparent in his poem 'An Claigeann' ('The Skull'), in which he provides vignettes of possible owners of a skull found in a graveyard. His chief concerns as a poet are: (1) the majesty of God and the suffering of Christ; (2) the accountability of man and his impending judgement, a theme pursued in a long 'epic ballad' on 'Là a' Bhreitheanais' ('The Day of Judgement'); (3) the transience of life and the need for timely repentance, developed with great skill in his 'symbolic' poem 'An Geamhradh' ('The Winter'); and (4) the practice of Christian virtues and spiritual, rather than physical, prowess, befitting the Christian warrior whom he depicts in 'An Gaisgeach' ('The Hero'), an adaptation of Watts' poem, 'True Monarchy, 1701'.

Buchanan's style is terse, conveying Biblical teaching by means of vivid imagery, drawn mainly from the natural world of Perthshire. The effect is both homely and dramatic; the cataclysm accompanying Christ's Second Coming is 'like a moor-burn going up the steep slopes'. In 'An Geamhradh', the characteristics of a crisp Perthshire winter – feathery snowfalls, lead-like hailstones, blue slabs of ice – introduce his picture of death. Unlike the lazy bees and flies, only those who make adequate preparation beforehand can survive this last enemy. Buchanan was also a notable Gaelic scholar, and supervised the printing of the Scottish Gaelic New Testament in 1767.

BIBLIOGRAPHY
D. MacLean ed., *The Spiritual Songs of Dugald Buchanan* (Edinburgh, 1913)
L. MacBean, *Buchanan, the Sacred Bard of the Scottish Highlands* (London, 1919)
D. E. Meek, 'Images of the Natural World in the Hymns of Dugald Buchanan and Peter Grant', *Scottish Gaelic Studies* (forthcoming)
D. S. Thomson, *An Introduction to Gaelic Poetry* (Edinburgh, 1990): 205–7

DONALD E. MEEK

Buchanan, George (b. Perthshire, Scotland, 1762; d. Upper Canada [now Ontario], 1836). Minister of the

Relief Church in Scotland and Canada and an itinerant preacher in the West Highlands. Licensed by the Relief presbytery of Perth, Buchanan served two seasons on the Relief Church's mission to Argyllshire in 1798, accompanying J. MCDERMID and D. MCNAUGHT. He was minister of the Relief Church at Strathkinness, Fife, from 1800 to 1808. He also served as minister of the Relief congregation at Dysart, Fife, and apparently ministered latterly in Edinburgh. Buchanan emigrated to Beckwith, Lanark County, Upper Canada, in 1822. Sometimes called 'Dr Buchanan', he possessed medical skills which were used in the community. He also established a small school at Beckwith, and travelled extensively in Upper Canada. He and his family made a major contribution to the development of the Beckwith settlement.

BIBLIOGRAPHY
J. B. Campbell, *The Pioneer Pastor* (Toronto, 1900)
J. S. McGill, *A Pioneer History of the County of Lanark* (Bewdley, Ontario, 1968)
D. E. Meek, 'Evangelical Missionaries in the Early Nineteenth-Century Highlands', *Scottish Studies*, 28 (1987): 21

DONALD E. MEEK

Buchanan, Isaac (b. Glasgow, Scotland, 21 July 1810; d. Hamilton, Ontario, Canada, 1 Oct. 1883). Merchant, politician, and writer. Educated at the Glasgow Grammar school, Buchanan was apprenticed to William Guild and Co., a Glasgow firm of West India merchants. In 1830 he emigrated to British North America as a representative of the firm but soon afterwards established the first of his many businesses and quickly became a leading member of the Upper Canadian business community. He first entered politics in 1841 but sat only intermittently in the Parliament of the United Province of Canada during the next 25 years. He supported the Free Church cause in 1843–4 and did much to secure its formation in Canada, giving generously to the construction of churches. He also wrote extensively on economic questions.

BIBLIOGRAPHY
DCB, XI
D. McCalla, *The Upper Canada Trade 1834–72* (Toronto, 1979)
R. W. Vaudry, *The Free Church in Victorian Canada, 1844–61* (Waterloo, Canada, 1989)

RICHARD W. VAUDRY

Buchanan, James (b. Paisley, Renfrewshire, Scotland, 14 April 1804; d. Edinburgh, 19 April 1870). Scottish minister, theological professor, author, and church leader. After studies at Glasgow and Edinburgh, he was ordained at Roslin, 1827, translated to North Leith, 1828, and to the High Church (St Giles), Edinburgh, 1840. He adhered to FCS at the Disruption and was translated to St Stephen's, Edinburgh, March 1845. He was appointed professor of apologetics in May 1845 and

of systematic theology in 1847 in New College, Edinburgh, and became DD of Princeton 1844 and LL D of Glasgow 1852. Passionate and persuasively evangelical in his preaching, he was used in many conversions, especially in North Leith. He chaired his church's Foreign Missions Committee, resisted the growing German theological influence and opposed moves for union with the United Presbyterian Church.

Persistent ill health, and the use of assistants, gave him comparative leisure for writing during his pastoral ministry. His writings, reflecting his varied interests and occupations, include *Preparatory Discourses to Lectures on Civil Establishments of Religion* (1835), *Comfort in Affliction* (1857), *The Office and Work of the Holy Spirit* (1842), *Faith in God and Modern Atheism Compared* (1855), *Analogy Considered as a Guide to Truth and Applied as an Aid to Faith* (1864), and *The Doctrine of Justification* (1866).

BIBLIOGRAPHY
R. G. Balfour, in *Disruption Worthies*, ed. J. A. Wylie (Edinburgh, no date)
DNB
J. Ewing, *Annals of the FCS 1843–1900* (Edinburgh, 1914)
Fasti

HUGH M. CARTWRIGHT

Buchanan, Robert (b. St Ninian's, Stirling, Scotland, 15 Aug. 1802; d. Rome, 31 March 1875). Disruption worthy. After studies at the Universities of Glasgow and Edinburgh he was licensed to preach by the presbytery of Dunblane in 1825. He was ordained and inducted to Gargunnock in 1827, translated to Saltoun in 1830 and to the Tron Church, Glasgow in 1833. Though opposed to a 'voluntary' church, he moved the Independence Resolutions in the 1838 General Assembly of the Church of Scotland, declaring its spiritual jurisdiction independent of all state control. In 1840, he was awarded the degree of DD by Glasgow University. In 1843, he signed the Deed of Demission and adhered to the FCS. The first minister of the Free Tron Church, Glasgow and the historian of the Disruption, he was also a social reformer, champion of the poor, an educationalist, scholar and a respected evangelical leader. He was convener of the Free Church Sustentation Fund Committee, 1847–75, became minister of Glasgow Free College Church in 1857 and moderator of the Free General Assembly in 1860.

BIBLIOGRAPHY
DNB
R. Buchanan, *The Ten Years Conflict* (Edinburgh, 1849)
N. L. Walker, *Robert Buchanan, D.D.* (Edinburgh, 1877)

ALASDAIR BOTHWELL GORDON

Buck, M(ary) C(larissa) (b. Newbold, Derby, England, 5 Jan. 1810; d. Leicester, England, 19 July 1876). Primitive Methodist itinerant preacher. Her parents were poor, honest, industrious and moral, who entertained the Primitive Methodists when they first visited Coleorton and services were held there for 15 years until a chapel was built. Buck received little formal education, but made great efforts to 'improve herself'. Converted at the annual lovefeast and watch meeting at Griffydam Wesleyan Methodist Chapel, she joined the Primitive Methodists, becoming an exhorter (1831) and then a local preacher. She was a hired local preacher (1835) and became an itinerant (1836) and ministered in the Burland, Kidderminster, Wrockwardine Wood, Darlaston, and Leicester circuits. Manuscripts in local Record Offices show she was extremely popular and in great demand, but she resigned in 1847 because the strain of the itinerancy was undermining her health and also she felt her real calling was to take special services and anniversaries throughout the connexion.

Although settled in Leicester, for the next 25 years she travelled extensively. It was reported that at times her sermons were too long. The 1866 Conference granted her an annuity of £20. In 1872 she suffered a paralytic stroke. She was buried in Leicester cemetery.

BIBLIOGRAPHY
E. D. Graham, 'Chosen by God: the female itinerants of Early PM' (Birmingham Univ. Ph.D. thesis, 1987)
H. B. Kendall, *The Origin and History of the PM Church*, 2 (London, 1904)
PMMag (1842–3, 1852–4, 1877)

E. DOROTHY GRAHAM

Buckworth, John (b. Colsterworth, Leicestershire, England, 16 Jan. 1779; d. Dewsbury, Yorkshire, England, 2 April, 1835). Anglican clergyman. Buckworth began life as apprentice to a chemist in Sleaford (Lincolnshire) where he underwent an evangelical conversion on 23 December 1798 and was thereafter recommended to THOMAS ROBINSON of Leicester as a suitable candidate for the ministry. He entered St Edmund Hall, Oxford (BA 1805; MA 1810), where one of his contemporaries was DANIEL CORRIE, later Bishop of Madras. Buckworth became curate to MATTHEW POWLEY at Dewsbury on his ordination in 1804. Powley was already ill and on his death Buckworth succeeded as vicar (1806–35). Among Buckworth's early curates in his widespread parish was PATRICK BRONTË at Hartshead.

Buckworth himself did not enjoy good health and often had to spend the winter in milder climes and less polluted atmosphere than Dewsbury provided. He made several visits to Torquay, but in 1813 he ministered at St Chad's, Shrewsbury. For over twenty years he edited *The Cottage Magazine* to which Brontë contributed. He was also active in the work of CMS, sending three men – James and BENJAMIN BAILEY and WILLIAM GREENWOOD from his parish to the mission field, preaching for the society and succeeding THOMAS SCOTT as the society's host and tutor to men preparing for orders. He was assisted in this latter work after 1814 by THOMAS ROGERS, who had recently retired after 19 years as headmaster of Wakefield Grammar School. Buckworth was responsible for three new churches in his parish – at Hanging Heaton (1823), Earsheaton and Dewsbury Moor (both 1827).

SELECT WRITINGS
J. Buckworth, *Memoirs of the Rev. John Buckworth* (London, 1836)

BIBLIOGRAPHY
Al. Ox.: 185
C. Hole, *The Early History of CMS* (London, 1896)

ARTHUR POLLARD

Budd, Henry (b. Newbury, Berkshire, England, 25 Sept. 1774; d. Essex, England, 27 June 1853). Anglican clergyman. Brought up an Anglican, educated at Winchester, and St John's, Cambridge, Budd was ordained priest in 1797, assuming that ministerial responsibilities meant the reading of the Liturgy and the preaching of morality.

From 1801 to 1831 Budd was chaplain at the Bridewell Hospital, London, and from 1808–55, Rector of White Roding, Essex. On beginning his London ministry, he abandoned his life of elegant trifling out of a new sense of pastoral responsibility. Contact with evangelical clergy encouraged study of the Bible and the English Reformers. Budd subsequently became a thoughtful evangelical preacher, active in BFBS, CMS and a founder of the Prayer Book Society. The scholarly Budd promoted the theology of the Anglican Reformers and Hooker, becoming the key figure behind the forming of the Parker Society in 1840.

Concerned by evangelical suspicion of liturgy and baptism, Budd published his controversial *Infant Baptism the means of National Regeneration* (1827). He argued that the baptismal promises were the foundation of the whole Anglican liturgical and pastoral superstructure. The evangelicals ignored Budd's strictures about their sacramental weakness, and under pressure from the Oxford Movement, 'Buddism' was dismissed.

In later years, Budd complained of evangelicalism's low-church attitude and theological shallowness. Equally depressed by political change, he increasingly interpreted the signs of the times from an imminent premillennial perspective. On the day of his death, his namesake (see below) became the first ordained native Canadian.

BIBLIOGRAPHY
Anon., *A Memoir of the Rev. Henry Budd* (London, 1855)

W. J. CLYDE ERVINE

Budd, Henry (b. c. 1812; d. The Pas, Manitoba, Canada, 2 April 1875). CMS missionary and first Cree Indian ordained by the Church of England in North America. Budd was the son of a Cree father and a mixed-blood mother. Apparently orphaned, he was brought to Red

River in 1821 by JOHN WEST and educated briefly at West's new school there. When he was baptized in 1822, he was given his name in honour of HENRY BUDD, the rector at West's home parish in England.

For a time, Budd worked for the Hudson's Bay Company, but in 1836 he married, settled at Red River, and began to assist at the CMS mission school. In 1840 he was sent to establish a mission in the Cumberland district to the north, choosing The Pas as its site. JAMES HUNTER joined him as the missionary in charge in 1844. Budd was ordained deacon in 1850 and priest in 1853. He continued to work in the Cumberland district, assisting Hunter in translation work and establishing a new mission at Nepowewin.

Budd had at least six children, one of whom attended the CMS college at Islinston briefly as probably the only North American Indian ever enrolled there. Henry Budd became a symbol to many evangelicals of the promise of the north-west America mission. He was, however, the first of only a handful of Indian missionaries ordained in the region.

BIBLIOGRAPHY
DCB, 10
W. B. Heeney, *Leaders of the Canadian Church: Second Series* (Toronto, 1920)

KERRY M. ABEL

Buddicom, Robert Pedder (b. Liverpool, England, 1781; d. Great Alne, Warwickshire, England, 2 July 1846). Anglican clergyman and writer. The son of a Liverpool surgeon, Buddicom was educated at Sedbergh and entered Pembroke College, Cambridge in 1801, but transferred to Queens' (BA 1806; MA 1809; fellow 1807). His father contributed £1,000 to the building of the iron-framed church of St George's, Everton, to which Buddicom was elected first minister in 1815, defeating the corporation's favoured nominee by seventy votes to ten. Everton was then an exclusive suburb inhabited by the rich merchants of Liverpool. He was held in high esteem for his piety, saintliness and diligence, notable in this last regard for the attention he gave to the establishment of church schools. In 1840 he became principal of St Bees (Cumberland) and vicar till his death six years later. He raised the numbers of students in the college from 25 to 100. He was succeeded at Everton by W. W. Ewbank, but took with him as his assistant his curate there, DAVID ANDERSON, subsequently Bishop of Rupertsland.

Buddicom wrote against Unitarians in *The Atonement Indispensable to the Necessities of Guilty Men* (1839) and against Roman Catholics in *The Inspired Scriptures the Only Infallible Rule of Faith* (1838) and *Baptism and the Supper of the Lord Are the Only Sacraments* (1840) as well as publishing several volumes of sermons.

BIBLIOGRAPHY
Al. Cant., II,i: 436
H. G. Hampton, *The History of St George's, Everton* (Liverpool, England, 1856)

The Hermes; A Literary, Moral and Scientific Journal, 5 (Liverpool, England, 1822–3)

ARTHUR POLLARD

Bull, Frederick (b. *c*. 1714; d. London, 10 Jan. 1784). Baptist, Lord Mayor and MP. The son of a gentleman, he also inherited property from his mother. By 1744 he was trading on his own account as a London tea merchant, joining in partnership from 1757 with Samuel Moody. In the 1760s each partner was earning in excess of £1,000 a year. He is conspicuous in being, as a known Dissenter, an alderman, sheriff, 1771–2 and Lord Mayor of the city, 1773–4, and its representative in Parliament, 1773–84, thus underlining the fact that the Test and Corporation Acts did not, as commonly supposed, exclude from Parliament, while Indemnity Acts, passed in many years following 1726 indemnified Dissenters from the penalties of serving on corporations.

Bull was a member at Little Prescot Street, under the ministry of ABRAHAM BOOTH from 1766. He was a generous supporter of the Bristol Education Society, having family associations with Wellington, Somerset. He was a collaborator of the radical John Wilkes, Horace Walpole judging him in 1773 'entirely his creature'. From his election to the city council he was strongly antiministerialist; identified as 'a personal link between Baptists and Radical London'. In 1771 he had become treasurer of the Society of Supporters of a Bill of Rights, and was elected to Parliament at a by-election in 1771 on a reformist programme of demanding shorter Parliaments, the exclusion of placemen, the requirement of all members to take an oath against bribery, restoration of the American liberties – for taxation without consent was robbery – and relief for Ireland. A supporter then of the North American colonists at the time of the Boston tea party, he opposed Catholic Relief and made a strong anti-government speech in the Commons at the time of the Gordon Riots in favour of the many petitions presented by the large number of Protestant Associations that had been established. (Lord George Gordon had been an occasional hearer of the Reverend JOHN MARTIN of the Grafton Street Baptist Church but Martin declined to lend support to Gordon's Protestant Association.)

BIBLIOGRAPHY
D. W. Bebbington, 'Baptist MPs in the Seventeenth and Eighteenth Centuries', BQ, XXVIII (1980): 261–2
J. Ivimey, *History of English Baptists*, IV (London, 1830): 42–6 (includes text of his anti-Catholic speech in the Commons)
L. Namier and J. Brooke, *The History of Parliament* II (London, 1964): 129–30
E. A. Payne, 'Abraham Booth', BQ, XXVI (1975): 34

J. H. Y. BRIGGS

Bull, George (Stringer) (b. Stanway, Essex, England, 12 July 1797; d. Almeley, Herefordshire, England, 20 Aug. 1865). Anglican clergyman, philanthropist, factory reformer, and Poor Law opponent. Born the sixth son of John Bull, Rector of Pentlow and Tattingstone in Suffolk, he joined the navy at the age of ten (as was customary for intending officers). He left it six years later. After study at the CMS Missionary House he was accepted by the CMS in 1818 as a schoolmaster at the Christian Institution in Sierra Leone. After only 18 months service he suffered ill health and returned to England in 1820. Although not formally educated he studied under his father and an uncle at Inworth and was ordained to a curacy in Hessle in the East Riding of Yorkshire (deacon 23 March 1823, priest 1824). In 1825 he married Mary Coulson, the daughter of a Hull merchant.

In October 1826 Bull became Curate of Bierley near Bradford. Here he soon became concerned because children were too exhausted to benefit from the meagre education offered by his Sunday schools. Close examination of the state of things in his own parish, at length convinced him of the validity of the campaign (which he first regarded as exaggerated) launched by RICHARD OASTLER at the instigation of the Bradford manufacturer JOHN WOOD on behalf of the factory children. In the early 1830s he therefore began to involve himself with the 'Ten Hours Movement' which aimed to restrict the hours of child labour to a maximum of ten a day. In 1832 he was among those who gave evidence on the matter to a Parliamentary select committee.

When MICHAEL T. SADLER, MP, main House of Commons sponsor of the 'Ten Hours Bill', lost his seat, the task of finding a successor was left to Bull as secretary of the West Riding Short Time Committee. He eventually succeeded in persuading LORD ASHLEY, the heir to the earldom of Shaftesbury, to take on the task. In addition to briefing Ashley, Bull organized and spoke at many major meetings in places as far apart as Newcastle and London. Bull found it an uphill struggle to convince the British public who readily accepted that 'laissez-faire' economics were divinely sanctioned. The victory was eventually won in 1847.

Bull left Bradford for Birmingham in 1840 following a dispute with JOHN WOOD, who was his patron, over St James's Church which had been built under his supervision with private funds. His departure from Yorkshire ended the phase of his life which brought him public recognition and for which he was dubbed 'The Ten Hours Parson'. When he left Birmingham tribute was paid to his 'colossal work' in promoting the education, social and spiritual welfare of the people. Bull was always a staunch Tory and a defender of the Established Church. He was a vigorous opponent of the 1834 Poor Law, a temperance campaigner and a lifelong advocate of education. He retired to Herefordshire in 1864 and died the following year.

Bull wrote no book but was a prolific pamphleteer; most of the forty-odd that survive are in the Oastler Collection in the Goldsmith's Library at London University, Columbia University, New York City, or the Reference Library at Bradford Public Library.

BIBLIOGRAPHY
Aris' Birmingham Gazette (2 April 1864)
J. C. Gill, The Ten Hours Parson (London, 1959)
—, Parson Bull of Bierley (London, 1963)
E. Hodder, The Life and Work of the Seventh Earl of Shaftesbury, (London, 1886)
J. T. Ward, The Factory Movement 1830–55 (London, 1962)

NIGEL SCOTLAND

Buller, James (b. Helston, Cornwall, England, 6 Dec. 1812; d. Christchurch, New Zealand, 6 Nov. 1884). Wesleyan minister in New Zealand. From a Baptist background, Buller joined the Wesleyans on his conversion, aged twenty. He and his wife emigrated to Australia in 1835 and he joined the New Zealand mission in 1836 as tutor to NATHANIEL TURNER's children.

Ordained in 1837, his influence in the Kaipara district contributed to preventing the Maori attack on Auckland and to the founding of Auckland Methodism. From 1854 to 1875 he served European settlers as chairman of the Auckland, Wellington and Canterbury Districts, using his administrative skills in planting churches and schools to cater for the rapidly increasing population. He was president of the Australasian Wesleyan Conference (1864), inaugurated the first New Zealand Conference (1874) and was its president in 1875. In 1878 he published his memoirs, Forty Years in New Zealand. He was a highly respected minister.

BIBLIOGRAPHY
B. Gadd, The Rev. James Buller (PWHS [New Zealand] 1966)
Scholefield

W. A. CHAMBERS

Bulmer, Agnes (b. Lombard Street, London, 31 Aug. 1775; d. Ryde, Isle of Wight, England, 30 Aug. 1836). Methodist poet. She was the third daughter of Elizabeth and Edward Collinson, pious Methodist ironmongers, personal friends of JOHN WESLEY, who privately baptized their baby. She grew up a model child, her favourite study, after the Bible, being Edward Young's Night Thoughts, which she began reading at 12 years of age. In 1789 she received her first Methodist class ticket from Wesley's own hands, her first class leader being HESTER ANN ROGERS. Her first noteworthy poem was 'On the Death of the Rev. Charles Wesley [By Miss A.C. in the thirteenth year of her age]', printed in the Arminian Magazine for October 1788 (p. 557). Surely referring to this John Wesley wrote to her: 'My dear maiden, Beware of pride, beware of flattery; suffer none to commend you to your face; remember, one good temper is of more value in the sight of God than a thousand good verses. All you want is to have the mind that was in Christ, and to walk as Christ walked.'

In 1793 she married Joseph Bulmer, born at Rothwell near Leeds in 1761, who came to London in 1780, prospered as a merchant, and served as one of the stewards of Wesley's City Road Chapel for many years before his death in 1822. He was a generous contributor to Methodist causes, with special concern for children and missionary work. His young wife continued to contribute verse to the *Methodist Magazine* and *Youth's Instructor*. One of her poems, written for the laying of the foundation stone of Oxford Road Wesleyan Chapel in Manchester, 'Thou who hast in Zion laid / The true foundation-stone', was in 1830 incorporated as hymn 737 in the supplement to the Wesleyan hymn-book.

Her memoir by Mrs Rowley, a daughter of Dr ADAM CLARKE, stressed her devout diffidence, and her 'uniform practice of introducing religious truths in every conversation with her friends', but to do so with such feeling and lucidity that they were both interested, instructed, and inspired. Clarke and his wife first met her when she was twenty, and Mary Clarke noted that 'she was one of the most interesting young women she ever met with', while the doctor himself averred: 'That woman astonishes me. She takes in information just as a sponge absorbs water . . . Whether it be philosophy, history, or theology, she seizes upon it, and makes it all her own.' WILLIAM MACLARDIE BUNTING claimed that she was 'one of the most intellectual and holy women, probably, whose presence ever adorned this world.' After the death of her husband she took on the pastoral responsibilities of a class leader at City Road, as well as being a diligent and welcomed sick visitor.

In 1833 Rivingtons published for her the massive *Messiah's Kingdom: a poem in twelve books* (486 pages), which Mrs Rowley delicately described as 'of too lofty and sublime a character to meet the tastes of superficial readers'. Her *Scripture Histories* were published posthumously in six parts during 1837–8 and W. M. Bunting edited her *Select Letters* in 1842. Her greatest claim to evangelical fame, however, was her *Memoirs of Mrs. Elizabeth Mortimer, with Selections from her Correspondence*, published in the year of her death, 1836, which passed through several editions both in England and America. This is especially important because it introduces the young woman – far better known by her maiden name as ELIZABETH RITCHIE – who nursed John Wesley during his closing months, and wrote the best known account of his death. In 1801 Elizabeth Ritchie married Harvey Walklake Mortimer, Esquire, and eventually closed a long life of devotion and good works as a Methodist in the London area on 9 April 1835. Her book is greatly enriched by much important Methodist correspondence.

BIBLIOGRAPHY
A. R. Collinson, *Memoir of Mrs. Agnes Bulmer, . . . to which is subjoined Mrs. Bulmer's Last Poem, "Man the offspring of divine benevolence"* (London, 1837)
DNB
Methodist Magazine (1840): 801–10
G. J. Stevenson, *City Road Chapel and Its Associations* (London, 1872)

FRANK BAKER

Bulpit(t), James (b. in London, England, *c.* 1775; d. in Prince Edward Island, BNA, 1849). Methodist missionary to Newfoundland and Prince Edward Island. Bulpit, ordained a Methodist minister in 1799, served as successor to the itinerant WILLIAM THORESBY in Carbonear, Conception Bay, Newfoundland, where his wife also conducted a school associated with the mission. He returned to England in 1806 but continued his missionary service to British Eastern America the subsequent year in Prince Edward Island, where he remained until his death in 1849.

BIBLIOGRAPHY
DNLB
W. Wilson, *Newfoundland and its Missionaries* (Cambridge, MA, 1866): 179–80

HANS ROLLMANN

Bulteel, Henry (Bellenden) (b. Plymstock, Devon, England, 14 Sept. 1800; d. Plymouth, England, 28 Dec. 1866). Seceder and Plymouth Brother. The fourth son of Thomas Hillersdon Bulteel of Plymstock, and descended from the Huguenot family of Bultayle he was educated at Eton (1815–18) where he lost one eye in an accident, and at Brasenose College, Oxford (1818–22). A great oarsman, notorious for his rowdiness especially during the Queen Caroline riots, he became a fellow of Exeter in 1823 and was ordained in 1824 taking a country curacy. In January 1826 he returned to Oxford as tutor and bursar at Exeter, and lecturing on Aeschylus. He was by now reading THOMAS SCOTT's *Commentaries* and other evangelical literature. In the summer, hearing ROBERT HAWKER of Plymouth, he gained assurance of his salvation and his Calvinism began to be a cause of some embarrassment to the Rector of Exeter. As curate-in-charge at St Ebbe's from December 1826 he exercised a powerful and increasingly radical ministry among some students (including W. E. Gladstone) to the annoyance of the university authorities.

He vacated his fellowship in 1829 by marrying Eleanor, niece of James Sadler, a pioneer hot-air balloonist, and daughter of a pastry cook. In 1829–30 he helped in the campaign which removed J. H. NEWMAN from the CMS secretaryship at Oxford. In February 1831 he preached a university sermon of High Calvinism to a packed congregation in St Mary's condemning Anglican Erastianism and the indiscriminate giving of testimonials for ordination. Having publicly declared that the Anglican Church was all but apostate Bulteel now toured the West Country with W. TIPTAFT preaching in dissenting chapels and in the open air. On 14 August, during a service in his Oxford garden he publicly destroyed the Bishop of Oxford's letter withdrawing his licence. Gladstone detected a 'soreness of spirit' (Foot: 386).

In October after meeting E. IRVING in London he returned to Oxford 'satisfied of the genuineness of the miraculous healings and tongues, and convinced moreover of their doctrines of general redemption' (Bodleian

Library, Oxford, Hill's diary). During this phase which lasted until May 1833, various well attested healings occurred. Those cured included Bulteel's sister-in-law, Mary Sadler and Charlotte Charriere with whom Bulteel had prayed shortly before her recovery. He believed that the cures were 'connected with the fact of my having been cast out the carnal church.'

In February 1832 he was baptized in Hinton's Baptist meeting house and in June a new chapel was opened for him at the rear of Pembroke College. Here he served an Independent congregation (popularly known as *Bulteelers*) until 1845 and was loosely associated with Brethren though his position was not typical. By 1844 he favoured a local episcopacy appointed by a regional presbyterate. After 1850 he lived at Plymouth where he was identified with former Brethren (his cousin J. L. HARRIS and H. W. SOLTAU) at Ebrington Street. Later (1862) he preached occasionally with S. P. TREGELLES in Compton Street Chapel.

SELECT WRITINGS
For Bulteel's works see *DNB* and the British Library Catalogue

BIBLIOGRAPHY
Al.Ox.
Boase
C. W. Boase, *Registrum Collegii Exoniensis* (Oxford, 1893): 114
Bodleian Library, Oxford, John Hill diary, St Edmund Hall manuscripts, 67/8/65a
C. Charisere (sic), M. Sadler and H. B. Bulteel, 'Accounts of Miraculous Cures,' *MW*, 5 (1831): 218–21
DNB
Exeter College Archives; Fellows' Registers and Library Register A.1.7–8; D.4.2
M. R. D. Foot, ed., *The Gladstone Diaries*, 1 (Oxford, 1968)
W. E. Gladstone, *Gleanings*, 8 (London 1879): 211
J. S. Reynolds, *The Evangelicals at Oxford 1735–1871* (Oxford, 1975): 97–9 [inaccurate account but useful references]
H. H. Rowdon, *The Origins of the Brethren* (London 1967): 61–9
John Rylands Library, Manchester; Letters from Tregelles to Newton (1862–7) CBA 7181
T. C. F. Stunt, 'John Henry Newman and the Evangelicals,' *JEH*, 21 (1970): 70–4 [includes full references]

TIMOTHY C. F. STUNT

Bultitude, Elizabeth (b. Hardwick, England, 12 Aug. 1809; d. Norwich, Norfolk, England, 14 Aug. 1890). Primitive Methodist (PM) itinerant preacher. Bultitude came from a very poor Wesleyan Methodist family, so she had no formal education. When she was 13 her father died and the family moved to Norwich where they lived at starvation level. Bultitude was converted at a PM camp meeting held on Mousehold Heath (14 May 1826), but did not join them till 1829. On 20 December 1830 she received 'a note to preach', in March was an exhorter, by June a local preacher and in June 1832 an itinerant. Bultitude worked chiefly in East Anglia. She was remembered as having a 'large round rubicund face in a poke bonnet', using 'ejaculatory prayers with many fervent repetitions' and as a stickler for propriety. On

superannuation (1862) she received an annuity and settled in Norwich, where she continued to preach and attend her class. After a long, painful illness she died in her own home.

Bultitude itinerated longest – 28 years – and was the last of the PM female itinerants, but there is remarkably little information extant about her ministry other than in manuscripts of Minutes and Accounts in Local Record Offices which usually merely record preaching appointments and salary payments. As Bultitude was the only female itinerant 'to die in the work' she is the only one to have an obituary in the *PM Minutes*.

BIBLIOGRAPHY
E. D. Graham, 'Chosen by God: the female itinerants of Early PM' (Birmingham Univ. Ph.D. thesis, 1987)
PMMag (1891)

E. DOROTHY GRAHAM

Bumby, John (Hewgill) (b. Thirsk, Yorkshire, England, 17 Nov. 1808; d. Hauraki Gulf, New Zealand, 26 June 1840). Superintendent of New Zealand Wesleyan Missions. Converted at 15, Bumby was ordained (1829) and gave promise of a distinguished career in northern circuits. To celebrate the centenary of Methodism in 1839, the British Conference planned to strengthen Wesleyan missions in the South Seas. Bumby was appointed superintendent for New Zealand. He was barely thirty years old. His first task in New Zealand was to survey the field and prepare for additional staff. With JOHN HOBBS he circumnavigated the North Island. Native teachers were left at Port Nicholson and Kapiti Island to prepare for resident missionaries. He visited Sydney where he secured the services of JAMES WATKIN to fill the opening offered by John Jones at Waikowaiti. At the district meeting of 1840 placements were made which extended Wesleyan missions south from Kawhia along the west coast of the North Island and the east coast of the South Island. On the journey back to Mangungu Bumby visited Maraetai, and then on 26 June he set out by canoe. Somewhere between Motutapu and Tiritiri Matenga the canoe capsized. Bumby and 12 companions were drowned. In 15 months Bumby laid down the lines of Wesleyan development in New Zealand.

BIBLIOGRAPHY
A. Barrett, *Life of the Rev. John Hewgill Bumby* (London, 1852)
Scholefield

W. A. CHAMBERS

Bunting, Jabez (b. Manchester, England, 13 May 1779; d. London, 16 June 1858). British Methodist leader. The son of a radical Manchester tailor, and educated by two Unitarians, Bunting evolved from revivalist origins into the leading exponent of the High Wesleyan doctrine of the ministry, and a connexional politician who resolutely opposed many of the public causes espoused by the

Unitarians of his heyday. Taken up by one of the leading Manchester doctors, the Unitarian Thomas Percival, Bunting was educated by him for the medical profession; but in 1794 he had undergone a Methodist conversion, and in 1799 he entered the Wesleyan Methodist itinerancy.

The paradoxical character of his career was early manifest. As a youthful revivalist he had developed a preaching talent which carried him quickly to the best circuits in the connexion; but, in his second appointment at Macclesfield (1801–3), he encountered revivalists who were separating from Wesleyanism, as the Wesleyans had mostly separated from the Church of England, and turned harshly against them for the rest of his life. Also at Macclesfield he revealed administrative talents, and in his next appointment (London, 1803–5) he had, in addition to the usual circuit duties, responsibility for rectifying confusion in the accounts of the foreign missions and the connexional publishing organization. If circuit management suffocated the revivalist in Bunting, administration gradually suffocated his preaching career. His apogee as a preacher came in 1812 with a conference sermon on 'Justification by Faith' in a series intended for the instruction of young preachers; after his death the connexion declined to publish his collected sermons. Yet Bunting's evolution into a bureaucrat, faceless but ferocious if challenged in conference, had a religious root and was evoked in part by religious needs. The problem was that Wesley's personal oversight had been replaced by no institutional development adequate to the needs of a now rapidly expanding community.

Bunting's achievement was to turn Methodism into a very actively governed body, and one governed substantially from London, away from the great centres of Methodist strength. The signs of this were new central institutions such as the Methodist Missionary Society (1813) and the Theological Institution (1834), the creation of standing and *ad hoc* committees of conference (on which prominent laymen were invited to serve) to control the raising and expenditure of funds, the exertion of the corporate authority of the pastorate in conference upon the local church authorities of the church, and constant negotiations with government about public order and slavery, colonial administration and missions, education and chapel trusts, not to mention the ecclesiastical diplomacy generated by the Protestant crusade in Ireland, the EA and the Disruption in the Scottish Church.

The pressure for this administration advance came not only from church growth but also from pastoral, political and financial difficulties. The problems which Bunting had encountered with revivalists were repeated in Methodist relations with other non-ecclesiastical agencies, the Sunday schools and cottage prayer meetings, and became acute in decayed town-centre chapels where ministerial authority, unsupported by the influence of substantial laymen who had migrated to the suburbs, could not solve or circumvent important problems of discipline. These problems were greatly exacerbated after the Napoleonic Wars by the spread of popular radicalism

and by the burden of debt upon the connexion at a time of falling prices, and also by the central repercussions of local financial indiscipline. Bunting was brought to the front of the ministry (he was president for the first time in 1820, serving also in 1828, 1836 and 1844, and secretary of conference for very many years) by his simple answer to unavoidable problems – the re-establishment of discipline in the flock and in the ministry by the collective action of the pastorate – and the toughness of his determination to confront them. This policy was underpinned by the development of the High Wesleyan doctrine of the pastoral office, and by training and ordaining preachers in ways new to Methodism, but familiar in older branches of the church.

Bunting's emphasis upon ministerial rule put a greater strain on the health of ministers in key positions (his own included) than it could bear, and led to Reform secessions in the late 1820s, mid-1830s and late 1840s, which halted the progress of the Wesleyan connexion, and developed a radical Methodist alternative form of constitutional organisation and spiritual enterprise. Against conference and ministry the Reformers stressed lay and circuit rights, and clung to informal agencies – revivalism, Sunday schools, teetotalism. In 1851 Bunting was made a supernumerary before the question of a fifth presidential term could arise.

In 1804 he married Sarah Maclardie who died in 1835 and in 1837 he married a minister's widow, Mrs Martin. His eldest son, WILLIAM MACLARDIE BUNTING (1805–66), became a Methodist minister, but retired in 1849 on grounds of health before his father.

SELECT WRITINGS
J. Bunting, *Sermons*, 2 vols (London, 1861–2)

BIBLIOGRAPHY
DNB
T. P. Bunting, *The Life of Jabez Bunting* (London, 1859–87)
W. R. Ward, ed., *The Early Correspondence of Jabez Bunting, 1820–29*, Camden 4th series, 11 (London, 1972)
W. R. Ward, *Religion and Society in England, 1790–1850* (London, 1972)
W. R. Ward, ed., *Early Victorian Methodism* (London, 1976)

W. R. WARD

Bunting, T(homas) Percival [Percy] (b. 1810; d. 1886). Second son and biographer (2 vols, London, 1859–87) of Jabez Bunting, the most celebrated Wesleyan minister of his day, and christened after Thomas Percival, the unitarian doctor who befriended Jabez in his youth. A Manchester solicitor, and for long a member of the fashionable Oxford Road Chapel, he fought wholeheartedly beside his father in the great Methodist constitutional conflicts of the 1830s and 1840s and remained the leading lay figure in connexional committees after his father's death. It was symptomatic of larger changes in the Wesleyan connexion that in 1871 Percy Bunting championed the admission of lay representatives to conference, against which he and his father had fought, a system adopted in 1876.

SELECT WRITINGS
T. P. Bunting, *Lay Representation in the Wesleyan Conference* (London, 1871)

BIBLIOGRAPHY
W. R. Ward, *Early Victorian Methodism* (London, 1976)
—, *Religion and Society in England 1790–1850* (London, 1972)

W. R. WARD

Bunting, William Maclardie (b. Manchester, England, 23 Nov. 1805; d. London, 13 Nov. 1866). Wesleyan Methodist preacher and hymnodist. Bunting was the eldest son of the Reverend Dr JABEZ BUNTING, the dominant Wesleyan leader during the first half of the nineteenth century. Bunting received an extensive schooling including spells at the two Methodist schools, Woodhouse Grove and Kingswood. In 1824 he became an itinerant preacher. His active ministry, however, was cut short by ill health in 1843. His public activities ranged from support for Protestant Toryism in the 1830s to involvement in the EA in later life.

His early interest in music and poetry remained an abiding passion. He wrote his first published hymn as a teenager, and subsequently composed a number of other hymns three of which are in the *Methodist Hymn Book* (1933).

BIBLIOGRAPHY
DNB
G. S. Grove, ed., *Memorials of the Late Rev. William M. Bunting* (London, 1870)

D. A. GOWLAND

Bunyer, James (b. London, *c.* 1800; d. Sierra Leone, 20 April 1823). CMS missionary to Sierra Leone. Bunyer trained as a schoolmaster at the Central School of the National School Society before volunteering to go to Sierra Leone with the CMS. He and his wife were one of three couples (*see* J. GERBER, and W. H. SCHEMEL) sent out on 8 November 1822 along with C. W. BECKHAUER. He lasted a few months; his wife (Mary Woolston, died 22 June) only two more than he. Six of the original seven were dead by May 1825. The Bunyers' willingness to serve in Sierra Leone is remarkable in view of the fate of other early CMS couples (*see* M. RENNER, P. HARTWIG, J. G. PRASSE, J. C. BARNETH, J. QUAST, C. H. MEISSNER, H. MEYER, J. H. SCHULZE and C. JOST).

BIBLIOGRAPHY
D. T. B[arry], *CMS Register of Missionaries and Native Clergy* (privately printed) (London, 1906)

DONALD M. LEWIS

Burch, Thomas (b. Tyrone Co., Ireland, 30 Aug. 1778; d. 22 Aug. 1849). Minister of the MEC. He was converted in 1801 in Ireland under the preaching of GIDEON OUSELEY, eminent and successful Irish Methodist missionary. In 1805 he was admitted on trial in the Pennsylvania Conference, where he was elected to the first delegated General Conference of 1812. His itineracy also included the Canadian part of the New York Conference during the war with Great Britain. He was stricken suddenly with heart disease and died only ten days after preaching his last sermon.

BIBLIOGRAPHY
CM

STEVE HARPER

Burchell, Thomas (b. Tetbury, Gloucester, England, 25 Dec. 1799; d. London, 16 May 1846). Baptist missionary in Jamaica. He was converted in Shortwood Baptist Church, Nailsworth 1816 and was encouraged to apply to the BMS Committee which accepted him on 25 November 1816. Five days later he entered the Bristol Academy. A month after his wedding to a Miss Lusty, in October 1822 he sailed for Jamaica, arriving in January 1824, finally settling in Montego Bay. Ill health forced his return to England 1826, during which time he made his views on slavery public in an open letter. His return to Jamaica 1827 included a court appearance, due to the letter. He was in England again in 1831 due to illness. On his return to Jamaica in 1832 a revolt was in progress and he was arrested. He escaped home via America. He toured the British Isles advocating abolition. He went back to Jamaica in 1834, was involved in extensive church planting and every aspect of education, including a theological college, the establishment of a free village system and a hospital.

BIBLIOGRAPHY
W. F. Burchell, *Memoir Of Thomas Burchell* (London, 1848)
G. A. Catherall, 'Thomas Burchell: Gentle Rebel', *BQ*, 21, (London 1966)

GORDON A. CATHERALL

Burckhardt [Burghardt], **Christian Friederich** (b. Oberlunersdorf, Upper Lusatia, Poland, 2 Aug. 1743; d. Nain, Labrador, 28 July 1812). Moravian deacon and missionary to the Labrador Inuit. Burckhardt, a hunter by profession, was Lutheran before he became a member of the Moravian Church on 3 August 1777 and was ordained deacon on 12 May 1784. He commenced his work in Labrador on 21 August 1784. He served in the mission stations of Hopedale, Okak, and Nain, and in 1794 replaced CHRISTIAN LUDWIG ROSE as superintendent.

BIBLIOGRAPHY
Public Archives of Canada, Ottawa, 'Catalogus der Missionare in Labrador', Records of the Moravian Mission in Labrador [1764–1944], Microfilm 511, Reels 11–12, fol. 15197–8
Kölbing

MARCELLA ROLLMANN

Burder, George (b. London, 5 June 1752; d. London, 29 May 1832). Congregational minister, secretary of the LMS, editor of the *Evangelical Magazine*, founder of the RTS, the BFBS, and the Warwickshire Association. His father was a deacon of Fetter Lane Church and his mother had been converted by GEORGE WHITEFIELD. He had displayed artistic talents, becoming a student at the Royal Academy, and taking lessons from ISAAC TAYLOR, an engraver. At 21 he set up in business as an engraver. The young Burder, already a Christian in judgement, was inspired by the preaching of WILLIAM ROMAINE, J. W. FLETCHER of Madeley and George Whitefield. He began preaching in 1776 in a Staffordshire farmhouse owned by his father, adjoining Bromstead Heath, near Newport. The house was full, with many outside, and Burder's preaching affected all the hearers, some to tears. One week later the congregation had so increased that the people gathered under an oak tree. In yet another week 500 people heard Burder preach at the farm. Therefore he took to itinerant preaching in the surrounding villages, encountering some resistance.

At Brewood in Staffordshire in 1777 a mob hammered at the barn doors when he was speaking and began to throw stones. One Sunday in 1778 he was at Gnosall with Captain JONATHAN SCOTT when their preaching occasioned a riot. In court the rioters claimed they had championed the Church of England and were acquitted. In London he also began preaching in both town and suburbs and here he felt called to decide on his future. He greatly admired the evangelical clergy of the Church of England, and felt an attachment to the Calvinistic Methodists always, yet he decided on principle to follow his call to the ministry among the Congregationalists, for whom he became an ardent apologist. Nevertheless he retained an affection and respect for evangelical Christians in all the churches.

With no formal theological education he was ordained at Lancaster in 1778 and was pastor there for six years, preaching often in the surrounding villages. In 1781 he preached at Burslem, Hanley (where the Tabernacle Chapel was soon to be built) and Newcastle-under-Lyme and in that year also he married Sarah Harrison of Newcastle. In 1783 he moved to West Orchard Chapel, Coventry where he remained almost twenty years and, from there, took his preaching into Warwickshire, Staffordshire and Nottinghamshire. At Coventry he founded Sunday schools in 1785, attempting unsuccessfully to work with local Anglicans, and encouraging such schools also at Kidderminster and elsewhere.

While at Coventry Burder's preaching in the countryside opened new opportunities. He realized that 'the rustic and untaught' felt a great need for simple, devotional literature which he aimed to provide in the eight volumes of his *Village Sermons* (the first two volumes being published in Coventry). Plain, lucid, direct and evangelical, the *Village Sermons*, 100 in all, contrasted with much contemporary pomposity and attained an enormous popularity. They displayed their author's zeal and delight in preaching and rendered him a literary hack of

his age, second only to JOHN WESLEY. His sermons proved useful not only to rural readers but also to itinerant preachers and the Anglican clergy. These sermons were widely circulated in Britain and America and several were translated into other European languages. Burder later produced a volume of *Sea Sermons*, and one of *Cottage Sermons*, as well as *Sermons for the Aged*.

Burder had stated that 'a great part of Staffordshire is in total darkness and many places seem resolved that the light shall never make an entrance among them'. In July 1790 Burder and Reverend James Moody of Warwick preached at the opening of a chapel in Lichfield. However support dwindled and in 1796 the building was closed. In 1802 with the encouragement of newcomers the chapel was reopened and Burder wrote two pamphlets in answer to high church criticisms of the venture. The dissenting cause in Lichfield survived and grew. A young man's suicide in 1808 was blamed, by the jury at the coroner's inquest, on his hearing William Salt's preaching the day before at the Independent chapel. Burder again took up his pen to defend the cause in *A Vindication of the Dissenters in Lichfield*.

In 1795 Burder applied for a room at Gnosall to be registered as a place of worship and, in the following year, he repeated this act for a modest chapel whose erection he had prompted at Bromstead Heath. Burder, himself, exemplified the evangelical awakening in the west midlands of England.

In 1793 Burder was one of the founders of the Warwickshire Association for the Spread of the Gospel at Home and Abroad (later the Warwickshire county union of the Congregational Union). This association of churches was eager to support foreign missions and in the vestry of Burder's Coventry chapel was collected the first money, donated to the LMS. Indeed in 1795 Burder was among those gathered in London to found the LMS and he was appointed one of the first directors of the society.

Burder's term of office as secretary of the LMS witnessed several significant developments, among which were the establishment of ROBERT MORRISON in China, ROBERT MOFFAT in South Africa, WILLIAM T. RINGELTAUBE in south India, and John Wray in Demerara. Missions were established in Benares and Calcutta, work begun in Madagascar, and consolidated in the Pacific islands. In addition, missions were started but later abandoned in Malta, Malacca, Java and elsewhere. A dozen men were sent to the West Indies where sensitivity over slavery was high. Wray's successor, JOHN SMITH, enjoyed great success with the blacks, but after an uprising in 1823, was sentenced to be hanged on the flimsiest evidence. The LMS published the facts, arousing great public interest in England and gaining the praise of WILLIAM WILBERFORCE for both the missionary and the society, but Smith died in prison in 1824. The work of the society, carefully and enthusiastically steered by Burder, did much also to further the cause of slavery emancipation in the British colonies.

In June 1803 Burder moved to London to accept the unanimous call to the ministry of Fetter Lane Chapel, made simultaneously with the invitation to become unpaid secretary of the LMS, in succession to JOHN EYRE of Homerton. Burder served in that post until 1827 when he was elected a life director. In 1799 on the closure of his London bookseller, Burder devised and founded the RTS for which he wrote more sermons and tracts than any other contributor, these works also being translated into many languages. Again in succession to JOHN EYRE, he edited from 1803 the *Evangelical Magazine* for more than twenty years and in 1804 he helped to establish the BFBS. In 1806 he was one of the preachers of the Merchants' Lecture.

During Burder's editorship the *Evangelical Magazine* maintained its defence of Nonconformity and evangelical Christianity but moved from a non-denominational position to one closely associated with the Congregationalists. He always valued learning and found time for regular study throughout his life.

Burder was one of the most influential men of his day. In 1826, on the fiftieth anniversary of his first sermon, he claimed to have preached almost 10,000 sermons. In his later years Caleb Morris assisted him but Burder nominally remained minister at Fetter Lane until his death. From 1830 he refused to accept a stipend and, although blind for the last two years of his life, he continued to preach until March 1832. He died aged 79 and was buried in the family grave at Bunhill Fields. After the death of his first wife in 1801, Burder married again but his second wife predeceased him in 1824. His son, Henry Forster Burder (1783–1864), wrote his *Memoir* and was chairman of the Congregational Union in 1844. George Burder wrote also on *The Welsh Indians* (early emigrants to America) and a *Life of Rev. John Machin* (his first wife's relative), and edited the works of Bunyan, John Owen, Matthew Henry, Isaac Watts, and Cotton Mather, among others.

BIBLIOGRAPHY
D. Bogue and J. Bennett, *The History of Dissenters* III (London, 1839): 426–33
H. F. Burder, *Memoir of George Burder* (London, 1833)
DNB
R. Lovett, *History of the London Missionary Society* I (London, 1899): 18–25
A. P. F. Sell, 'George Burder and the Lichfield Dissenters' in *Transactions of the South Staffordshire Archaeological and Historical Society* XIII (Stafford, England, 1971–2): 52–60
W. R. Ward, *Religion and Society in England 1790–1850* (London, 1972): 49–50, 300

ALAN ARGENT

Burditt, Thomas (b. Leicester, England, 8 March 1811; d. Rawdon, Yorkshire, England, 20 Feb. 1881). Baptist minister and educator. Of a devout family, he was apprenticed in business with the Dawson family. Baptized in 1829 by THOMAS PRICE at Devonshire Square, Bishopsgate, he entered Stepney College in 1836 and the following year made a visit to Germany with one of the tutors. Leaving college in 1840, he settled as minister at Long Sutton, Lincolnshire. During his ministry there, with tutors and students at Stepney, he founded the *Baptist Record* of which he became first editor. This short-lived periodical was of a weighty literary kind with many distinguished authors contributing. In 1845 he moved to Zion, Cambridge, and in 1853 succeeded NATHANAEL HAYCROFT at Saffron Walden, Essex. His most fruitful years were those spent from 1853 to 1866 at Haverfordwest, West Wales, where he served both as co-pastor in the chapel and classical tutor in the college. He was heavily involved in the work of the British Schools Society and saw three good suites of building erected in the town. His pastorate at Tenby was interrupted by a visit to his sons in North America, where the pastoral needs of the continent so impressed him that he did not immediately return to Wales but undertook pastoral work in Nova Scotia instead. His last pastorate was at Rawdon in Yorkshire from 1875–81.

BIBLIOGRAPHY
Baptist Handbook (1882)

J. H. Y. BRIGGS

Burdon-Sanderson, Richard (b. Jesmond, near Newcastle, England, 31 March 1792; d. probably Plymstock, Devon, 1865). Seceder. The younger son of Sir Thomas Burdon he attended Durham Grammar School and Oriel College, Oxford, of which he became a fellow in 1813. Impressed by Keble and Whately, and a friend of D. WILSON and H. DRUMMOND he was an exact churchman with evangelical sympathies. As secretary of ecclesiastical presentations to his uncle Lord Chancellor Eldon he found the system to be corrupt and resigned, retiring from the legal profession. In 1826 he unexpectedly inherited his father's estate and moved back to Northumberland where in 1837 he was persuaded by the Honourable Paul Methuen, a Plymouth Brother from Clifton, to be baptized by immersion. In 1848 he moved to Plymstock and was associated with Open Brethren. Many of his progeny had outstanding intellects.

BIBLIOGRAPHY
C. Binfield, 'Jews in Evangelical Dissent' in M. Wilks, ed., *Prophecy and Eschatology* (Oxford, 1994): 251
E. S. H[aldane], ed., *Mary Elizabeth Haldane* (London, [1925]): 4–94
F. Maurice, *Haldane, 1856–1915* (London, 1937): 10–11

TIMOTHY C. F. STUNT

Burgess, Richard (b. 1796; d. Brighton, Sussex, England, 12 April 1881). Anglican clergyman. According to a report prepared for the editor of *The Times* of London in 1844, Burgess was a convert from Roman Catholicism and had trained for the Roman Catholic priesthood. He was ordained (deacon 1820, priest 1823) by Bishop Vernon-Harcourt of York and admitted to St John's College, Cambridge in 1824 (matriculated 1834;

BD 1835). In 1828 he served as domestic chaplain to Lord Alymer and was chaplain to the English residents at Geneva and from 1831 to 1836 was chaplain to an Anglican congregation at Rome. In 1836 Earl Cadogan appointed him Rector of Upper Chelsea which he held from 1836 to 1869, and was a Prebendary of St Paul's Cathedral from 1850.

He sought to resist the secularization of the state and was a strong supporter of a distinctly Anglican school system. Under Bishop Blomfield's administrative reforms, he became secretary of the London Diocesan Board of Education. *The Times* reporters noted that he 'Is extremely popular and influential with the Bishop and the principal laity of the diocese. Very decidedly low church – and is quite prepared to recommend reportedly the strongest measures with a view to put down 'the heresy' [Tractarianism].

BIBLIOGRAPHY
Al. Cant.
DNB
Bodleian Library, Oxford, 'The Principal Clergy of London ... prepared for Mr Delane, editor of *The Times*' (1844) Additional manuscript *c*.290

DONALD M. LEWIS

Burke, William   (b. Loudon County, VA, BNA, 13 January 1770; d. Cincinnati, OH, USA, 1855). Methodist preacher and presiding elder. Burke's family moved from Virginia to west of the Allegheny Mountains soon after the American Revolution. Converted in 1790, he entered the Methodist itinerancy in 1791. His ministry was mostly in Kentucky, Tennessee, and Ohio. Even after his marriage in 1796 he continued under appointment, thus becoming the first of the western itinerants to be married.

No hardship or physical danger stopped Burke. He was also a great debater in defence of Methodist discipline and doctrine. He was very effective in Kentucky against the JAMES O'KELLY schism of the 1790s. He also debated Baptists about baptism and Presbyterians about predestination. He was a leader in the great Cane Ridge, Kentucky revival in 1801. Burke was a member of the General Conferences of 1804 and 1808.

Burke was suspended from the Ohio Conference in 1813 and expelled from the Church in 1820. His offence, insubordination to a presiding elder, was treated too harshly and the Methodists thus discarded one of their champions. The General Conference of 1836, acting at the suggestion of Bishop WILLIAM MCKENDREE, restored his credentials. Burke adhered to the southern cause in the 1844–5 sectional schism of the MEC. He served from 1814 to 1842 as post-master in Cincinnati. He also served as one of the judges of the county.

BIBLIOGRAPHY
EWM
A. H. Redford, *The History of Methodism in Kentucky* (Nashville, TN, 1868–70)

M. Simpson, *Cyclopedia of Methodism* (Philadelphia, PA, 1880)
W. W. Sweet, *Circuit Rider Days Along the Ohio* (New York, 1923)
J. Young, *Autobiography of a Pioneer* (Cincinnati, OH, 1857)

CHARLES W. BROCKWELL, JR

Burks, Mary   (b. England, 2 Feb. 1796; d. East Stockwith, Nottinghamshire, England, 22 Jan. 1837). Primitive Methodist itinerant preacher. Burks, eldest of four children of poor industrious parents, often went with her mother to an Independent chapel and was religiously inclined, but doubted that God would hear her prayers. Burks had contact with the Wesleyan Methodists, but working in Hull she was converted by the Primitive Methodists (1818), soon becoming a local preacher and then an itinerant (1822). She itinerated in Scotter, Lincoln, Grimsby, Louth, Malton and York. Burks was very impressive (over 6 ft tall) with a powerful voice and forceful personality. Local records and *PM Minutes* show that by 1834 she was ill with a bladder disorder and retired from the active itinerancy (1836), returning to East Stockwith to live with her father. Burks acted as class leader and took services whenever her health permitted; she is said to have petitioned the Hull quarterly meeting (1828), unsuccessfully, to buy her an ass to ride to her appointments!

BIBLIOGRAPHY
J. Davison, *The Vessel of Beaten Gold, . . .* (Grimsby, 1840)
E. D. Graham, 'Chosen by God: the female itinerants of Early PM' (Birmingham Univ. Ph.D. thesis, 1987)
PMMag (1837)

E. DOROTHY GRAHAM

Burls, William   (b. London, 6 March 1763; d. London, 26 June 1837). Baptist merchant and mission supporter. Burls was educated at the Blue Coat school at Christ's Hospital, London. Apprenticed to John Hankinson, Burls so impressed with his reliability and ability that the merchant business eventually passed to him. William in 1795 joined the Baptist church at Carter Lane, Southwark and became a deacon in 1802. For many years Burls acted as the London agent for BMS becoming confidant and supporter of ANDREW FULLER. He served as treasurer and chairman of BMS often allowing missionaries to draw their bills on his name. After the disastrous fire at Serampore, India in 1812 Burls collected over £1,000 in London. He was active in many evangelical societies, such as the committee of the BFBS (1809–24) and was founding treasurer of the Baptist Irish Society formed in 1814 for evangelism among the Irish. JOHN DYER, secretary of BMS, aptly called him 'the excellent Mr Burls'.

BIBLIOGRAPHY
BaptMag, 29 (1837): 425–31
E. A. Payne, *The Excellent Mr. Burls* (London, 1943)

K. R. MANLEY

Burn, Edward (b. Killileagh, Co. Down, Ireland, 29 Nov. 1762; d. Birmingham, England, 20 May 1837). Anglican clergyman. Son of Charles Burn, he was educated for the ministry at the Countess of HUNTINGDON's college at Trevecca. He entered St Edmund Hall, Oxford in 1784 (BA 1790, MA 1791). Following ordination he became assistant curate and lecturer under John Riland at St Mary's, Birmingham, succeeding him as incumbent (1810). For a time he was minister of St James's, Ashted (Birmingham) and later was Rector of Smethcott, Shropshire. Although he initiated a public controversy (which encouraged a good deal of ill-feeling with Joseph Priestley) he mellowed in later years and was generally on good terms with Dissenters, and his death was mourned by both Churchmen and Dissenters. He was a good extempore preacher, the author of several pamphlets and sermons. In Birmingham he was the founder secretary of the CMS auxiliary and largely responsible for the formation of the BFBS auxiliary (1806). He married and had children.

BIBLIOGRAPHY
Al. Ox.
Aris's Birmingham Gazette (22 May and 19 June 1837)
Birmingham Journal (1 July 1837)
DNB
GM (October 1810): 381 and (July 1837): 97
J. S. Reynolds, *Evangelicals at Oxford* (Oxford, 1953): 63

D. E. H. MOLE

Burnett, (Frances) 'Fanny' (Elizabeth) [née Dickens] (b. Portsmouth, Hampshire, England, Nov. 1810; d. near London, 2 Sept. 1848). Sister of Charles Dickens. Burnett's attractive singing voice inspired her parents to send her to the Royal Academy of Music (RAM) (1823–7), much to the chagrin of Charles who through family penury was forced to work at a blacking warehouse. Still, Charles and Fanny were very close; their friendship survived even her conversion to evangelical Christianity. That came about in the context of her relationship with a fellow RAM student, Henry Burnett (1811–93), with whom, in the period 1835–7, she occasionally performed on stage. They married in 1837 and for a time Henry acted in company with the great tragedian William Macready.

Fanny and Henry, who had been exposed to evangelical influences in youth – she through her schooling under William Giles, the son of a Baptist minister, he through his pious grandmother – in the late 1830s were converted under the guidance of James Griffin, a Manchester Congregationalist. As a consequence, in 1841 Henry left the theatre for good.

Fanny's awakening spirituality is recorded in letters to Griffin, which he published in 1883. She died of tuberculosis after two years of suffering, her brother sublimating his grief through the death of Paul Dombey in his novel *Dombey and Son*.

BIBLIOGRAPHY
J. Griffin, *Memories of the Past* (London, 1883)

JONATHAN BURKE CUTMORE

Burnett, George (b. Aberdeen, Scotland, *c.* 1734; d. Elland, Yorkshire, England, 8 July 1793). Vicar of Elland. From a wealthy family and related to Gilbert Burnet, bishop and historian, he was invited by his godfather, GEORGE CONON, headmaster of Truro Grammar School, to join the staff. Called to the ministry under the influence of SAMUEL WALKER, he matriculated from Christ Church, Oxford, in 1755 along with his friend THOMAS HAWEIS. Opposition to evangelicals was intensifying and he left. He taught languages in London but was eventually ordained after some difficulties. He apparently served as curate in Padstow before going in 1759 as curate to HENRY VENN in Huddersfield and subsequently Perpetual Curate of Slaithwaite. In 1761 he accepted Elland where he maintained a staunch witness for over thirty years, refusing preferment. In his vicarage the EIS was formed in 1777 to raise funds for the education of evangelical candidates for the ministry.

BIBLIOGRAPHY
GM (1793)

A. SKEVINGTON WOOD

Burnham, Mark (b. Cobourg, Upper Canada 12 July 1804; d. Peterborough, Ontario, Canada, 12 May 1877). Anglican clergyman in Upper Canada. The only son of the Honourable Zaccheus Burnham, he was educated at John Strachan's school and Queen's College, Oxford (BA 1829; MA), was ordained a deacon (1829) and a priest (1833). Burnham was an SPG missionary in St Thomas, Upper Canada, 1829–52 and rector in Peterborough, Canada West, 1852–7, when he retired to manage his estates. Burnham was generous in his support of three evangelical churches, in Otonabee, Warsaw and Ashburnham. He possessed a fine private library and published *Notes on the Prayer Book*.

Bishop Strachan, proud of his former student, was impressed with Parson Burnham's immense influence 'from his teaching and example'. Others noted his congregations were divided; Burnham on one occasion quit his position in St Thomas but was intercepted by the bishop and ordered back. At St John's Church in Peterborough, he oversaw major restoration work but was unable to overcome the serious debt in the parish. For all his love of books, Burnham's sermons failed to inspire, but he had very strong ideas on the solemnity of the prayer-book service. He loved music in the services, but had serious disagreements with the choir in St Thomas. He opposed Gothic church architecture and remained an advocate of no central aisle, and all the implications; no church processions, and music and ceremony secondary to the message of the prayer-book and Gospel.

BIBLIOGRAPHY
S. D. Clark, *Church and Sect in Canada* (Toronto, 1971) orig. 1948

F. M. Delafosse, *Centenary History* (Peterborough, Canada, 1927)

E. H. Jones, *St John's Peterborough* (Peterborough, Canada, 1976)

C. O. Ermatinger, *The Talbot Regime . . .* (St Thomas, Canada, 1904)

ELWOOD HUGH JONES

Burns, Dawson. *See* BURNS, JABEZ

Burns, Sir **George** (b. Glasgow, 10 Dec. 1795; d. Wemyss Bay, Renfrewshire, Scotland, 2 June 1890). Shipowner and philanthropist. The youngest son of Dr John Burns, minister of the Barony of Glasgow, he was educated at the High School of Glasgow and began his commercial career in the Glasgow office of the New Lanark cotton mills. In 1818 he entered into partnership with his brother JAMES BURNS and traded as J. and G. Burns. In 1824 he started his main business interest of steam shipping, in which he was the driving force, and appropriately the firm's name was changed to G. and J. Burns. Burns pioneered passenger shipping routes from the Clyde to the west coast of Scotland but they were given up in favour of the trade with Ireland which grew at the time of large-scale migration from Ireland to the west of Scotland. In 1840 Burns provided Samuel Cunard with the capital and encouragement needed to start the transatlantic mail service and the Burns family became one of the major shareholders in Cunard.

As a young man Burns worked closely with THOMAS CHALMERS at both the Tron and St John's churches in Glasgow. His religious and philanthropic activities continued unabated thereafter, especially after his retiral from active business in 1860, bringing him into contact with most of the leading evangelical figures of the day, notably Lord SHAFTESBURY. Unusually, Burns provided a chaplain for his own vessels. George Burns became an Episcopalian and took a leading role in the dispute between those Episcopalians in Scotland – known generally as English Episcopalians and evangelical in churchmanship – who refused on doctrinal grounds to accept the ministrations of the bishops of the Scottish Episcopal Church. His generosity helped establish English Episcopal congregations in Glasgow and the west of Scotland. He was created a baronet in 1889.

BIBLIOGRAPHY
E. Hodder, *Sir George Burns, Bart. His Times and Friends* (London, 1890)

R. H. CAMPBELL

Burns, Islay (b. Dun, Forfarshire, Scotland, 16 Jan. 1817; d. Glasgow, 20 May 1872). FCS minister. Burns was the sixth child of a Church of Scotland minister and the brother of WILLIAM CHALMERS BURNS. He was educated at the parish church, Kilsyth, later at the Aberdeen grammar school, and at Marischal College, Aberdeen University. He studied theology at the University of Glasgow where he also excelled in classics and mathematics.

In June 1843 he was ordained at St Peter's Free Church, Dundee, succeeding ROBERT MURRAY MCCHEYNE. Burns maintained a lifelong interest in working class missions. Prior to 1841 he was a home missionary in the parish of St George's, Edinburgh, under ROBERT S. CANDLISH. His expertise in that area of service is reflected in an article he wrote for the *North British Review* (February 1859: 202–27). Further, in an 1871 *Sunday Magazine* article he promoted the Glasgow Foundry Boys Society and personally officiated at working boys' Sunday services.

In 1864 Burns was narrowly elected to the chair of systematic theology at the Free Church College, Glasgow and the previous year Aberdeen awarded him the degree of DD.

BIBLIOGRAPHY
W. G. Blaikie, 'Memoir' in *Select Remains of Islay Burns* (London, 1874)
Boase
DNB

JONATHAN BURKE CUTMORE

Burns, Jabez (b. Oldham, Lancashire, England, 18 Dec. 1805; d. Paddington, London, 31 Jan. 1876). New Connexion Baptist minister and temperance advocate. The son of an Oldham chemist, his mother named him after JABEZ BUNTING. He was in print for more than fifty years and in the pulpit for rather longer, establishing a reputation not only in Great Britain but in Australia and the United States. He attended grammar school and was employed as a bookseller, joining the MNC. After coming to London, where he lived with his young family in real poverty, he underwent believer's baptism at the General Baptist Chapel in the Borough. In late 1829 he accepted a call to become an itinerant working with a Scottish evangelistic agency. Centred first on Edinburgh and Leith and later on Perth, he travelled many miles on horseback but suffered a broken leg when in 1834 a steam coach in which he was travelling between Glasgow and Paisley blew up.

In the following year he was called to lead a new New Connexion General Baptist cause which had been established in Church Street, Marylebone, in London. This small congregation, as it then was, could only offer a small salary which Burns supplemented with his pen, producing, for example *The Christian's Daily Portion*, of great use to heads of households conducting family prayers, *The Pulpit Cyclopedia, Christian Philosophy*, as well as *Retrospect of Forty-Five Years' Ministry*. He influenced others through his editing of *The Preacher's Magazine and Pastor's Monthly Journal* (1839–44) and the profusion of sermon outlines that flowed from his pen amidst a great profusion of other publications. With J. J. Goadby in

1847, he was sent by the New Connexion to visit the Free Will Baptists in North America with whom they shared a common evangelical Arminianism; in 1872 he preached and lectured his way across the republic. He received a DD from the Wesleyan University of Connecticut and an LL D from Bates; added more than a thousand souls to the membership at Church Street during his forty-year pastorate; was one of the earliest members of the EA; and was, in 1850, only the second General Baptist to be appointed to the chair of the Baptist Union. Claimed as the first clergyman to advocate teetotalism from the pulpit, he was a tireless temperance advocate, signing the pledge in May 1836, and being the principle organizer of the World Temperance Convention which met in August 1846. A friend of THOMAS COOK, in 1869 he accompanied his pioneer tour to Egypt and Palestine preparing a *Help-Book for Travellers to the East*, for the use of future travellers.

His son, Dawson Burns (1828–1909), inherited both his father's energy and religious and temperance interests. Publishing his first temperance article at the age of 12, at 17 he was assistant secretary of the National Temperance Society and a year later its secretary and editor of the *Temperance Chronicle*. Trained at the Leicester Academy of the New Connexion, he had a first pastorate in Salford (1851–3). In 1853 he helped to found the United Kingdom Alliance and served for over a quarter of a century as its metropolitan superintendent. A master of statistics, he was a formidable organizer of petitions and of pressure group activity. In 1874 he joined and later succeeded his father in the work at Church Street, continuing until 1881 when he again resigned the pastorate for temperance work. 'Enthusiastically devoted to the promulgation of the Gospel of Jesus', he was a leading opponent of the amalgamation of the General and the Particular Baptists, but accepted this with good grace himself becoming a personal member of the Baptist Union.

BIBLIOGRAPHY
Baptist Handbook, (1877, 1910)
DNB

J. H. Y. BRIGGS

Burns, James (b. Glasgow, Scotland, 25 June 1789; d. Cardross, Perthshire, Scotland, 6 Sept. 1871). Merchant and philanthropist. The sixth son of Dr John Burns, minister of the Barony of Glasgow, he was educated at the University of Glasgow. He was associated with his younger brother, GEORGE BURNS, both as merchants and as shipowners. James's role in the business was always less enterprising, though he provided the necessary stability and balance to his brother's more adventurous undertakings. He took little part in the shipping enterprises and remained responsible for the trade in general produce. James Burns was an unassuming man. He took practically no part in public life but contributed generously to evangelistic and philanthropic

work in Glasgow and district. In 1843 he joined the FCS and became one of its strong supporters.

BIBLIOGRAPHY
R. H. Campbell, *Memoirs and Portraits of One Hundred Glasgow Men* (Glasgow, 1886)

R. H. CAMPBELL

Burns, James Drummond (b. Edinburgh, Scotland, 18 Feb. 1823; d. Mentone, France, 27 Nov. 1864). Presbyterian clergyman and hymn-writer. Educated at Edinburgh High School and University, where he studied under THOMAS CHALMERS, at the Disruption he went with the Free Church and became minister at Dunblane. Ill health led him to serve as chaplain in Madeira for a number of years, returning to build up the new Presbyterian Church in Hampstead in 1855. The author of two volumes of verses, he wrote the article on hymns in the *Encyclopaedia Britannica*; 'Hushed was the evening hymn' is perhaps the most commonly used surviving hymn of his.

BIBLIOGRAPHY
DNB
Julian

J. H. Y. BRIGGS

Burns, Robert (b. Barrowstowness, Scotland, 13 Feb. 1789; d. Toronto, Ontario, Canada, 19 Aug. 1869). Presbyterian clergyman and educator. Educated at the University and Divinity Hall in Edinburgh, Burns was ordained and admitted to St George's, Paisley in 1811, where he remained until the Disruption of 1843. He entered the Free Church and ministered to Free St George's for the next two years. An active Church of Scotland evangelical he edited the *Edinburgh Christian Instructor and Colonial Religious Register* from 1838 to 1840 and was involved in a variety of philanthropic activities and ecclesiastical controversies. His concern with the religious needs of Scottish emigrants to British North America (BNA) prompted him to help organize the GCS. He served as its principal secretary from its beginning in 1825 until it merged with the Church of Scotland's Colonial Committee in 1840.

Following the Disruption of 1843 the FCS dispatched a group of ministers and elders to North America in an attempt to elicit moral and financial support for their cause. Burns played a prominent part in this deputation and his two month tour of the British provinces was an important factor in the formation of a Canadian Free Church.

In 1845 he returned to BNA to take up the position of minister of Knox Church, Toronto and interim professor of divinity at Knox College. In 1847 the two positions were divided and Burns remained in the pastorate. In 1856 he was once again appointed to the college, this time as professor of church history and Christian evidences. In addition to his pastoral and college responsibilities Burns was an indefatigable traveller on behalf of the Free Church, conducting numerous missionary tours throughout the province of Canada West (Ontario). There is a collection of Burns papers in the United Church Archives, Toronto.

BIBLIOGRAPHY
DCB, IX
R. W. Vaudry, *The Free Church in Victorian Canada, 1844–61* (Waterloo, Canada, 1989)

RICHARD W. VAUDRY

Burns, Thomas (b. Mauchline, Ayrshire, Scotland, *c.* 10 April 1796; d. Dunedin, New Zealand, 23 Jan. 1871). Pioneer Presbyterian minister in New Zealand. A nephew of Robert Burns the poet, Burns attended Haddington Grammar School where EDWARD IRVING was one of his teachers. He studied at Edinburgh University, was licensed in 1822, and worked as a tutor until 1826. He was popular as minister of Ballantrae (1826–30) and Monkton (1830–43). In 1843 he joined the Disruption. WILLIAM CARGILL and Burns promoted a Free Church settlement in New Zealand; meanwhile he served as minister of Portobello near Edinburgh (1846–8).

Burns sailed for New Zealand on the 'Philip Laing' arriving at Port Chalmers in April 1848. His Free Church 'Geneva in the South Seas' was quickly undermined by the influx of settlers who rejected his ideal. An active pastor in harsh pioneering conditions, Burns promoted high moral standards in the community. He led the establishment of Presbyterian organization in southern New Zealand, as the founding moderator of Dunedin presbytery in 1854, and of the synod of Otago and Southland in 1866. A significant educational pioneer, he helped found public schools, Sunday schools, high schools for boys (1863) and girls (1871), and the first university in the country (1869) serving as its first chancellor. He was awarded a DD by the University of Edinburgh in 1861. Among his detractors he was thought of as narrow minded, but he was a successful and deeply respected leader among his own people.

His wife Clementina was the daughter of J. F. Grant, an Anglican minister. One daughter, Jane, married William Bannerman, another leading minister in Otago.

BIBLIOGRAPHY
DNZB
A. H. McLintock, *The History of Otago* (Dunedin, New Zealand, 1949)
E. N. Merrington, *A Great Coloniser* (Dunedin, New Zealand, 1929)

ALLAN K. DAVIDSON

Burns, William Chalmers (b. Kilsyth, Stirlingshire, Scotland, 1 April 1815; d. Niuchuang, China, 4 April 1868). Evangelist and pioneer Presbyterian missionary in China. Converted while training for law in Edinburgh and called to missionary service while a theology student at Glasgow, Burns stood in for his friend ROBERT MURRAY MCCHEYNE in St Peter's, Dundee, in 1839 and became a central figure in revivals there, in his home town of Kilsyth and in Perth. He developed considerable gifts as a preacher and personal evangelist, and tested these in Ireland and for two years in Canada before accepting a call to China from the Presbyterian Church of England. He was ordained as an evangelist in April 1847 and left for Hong Kong two months later.

Burns worked in Canton, Amoy, Swatow, Shanghai and elsewhere. He used every opportunity to develop his language ability, translated Bunyan's *Pilgrim's Progress*, wrote a number of hymns in Chinese and compiled a hymnbook. He developed a spartan lifestyle and insisted on freedom to determine his own pattern of outreach. In JAMES HUDSON TAYLOR he found a colleague with a similar spirituality and adventurous commitment to evangelism. They worked closely together particularly from December 1855 to July 1856 and shared views on Chinese dress, itineracy and much else.

Those who later joined Burns in the English Presbyterian Mission did not find him easy, but his example and death inspired others to service in China. His appeal to the Presbyterian Church of Ireland to work in Manchuria was taken up in 1869.

BIBLIOGRAPHY
E. Band, *Working His Purpose Out* (London, 1948)
A.J. Broomhall, *Hudson Taylor and China's Open Century. Book Two: Over the Treaty Wall* (London, 1982)
A. Clark, *China's Man of the Book* (London, 1968)
I. Burns, *Memoir of the Rev. William C. Burns* (London, 1885)

W. JOHN ROXBOROGH

Burpé, Richard E. [anglicized spelling 'Burpee'] (b. York Co., New Brunswick, BNA, 1809; d. Jacksonville, FL, USA, 26 Feb. 1853). First foreign missionary from British North America. A Fredericton, New Brunswick merchant, Burpé was converted and baptized at Brunswick Street Baptist Church in November 1829. Licensed to preach 1836, he was ordained at St George, New Brunswick, on 7 September 1837. For some time he pastored the church at St Andrews. The Nova Scotia and New Brunswick churches began preparation for foreign mission work in 1838. In 1839 Burpé was appointed their first foreign missionary. He attended Acadia College and graduated BA in 1844.

He married Laleah Johnstone. They arrived Akyab, Burma by October 1845 and established a mission among the Karen people at Mergui. By 1846 he had contracted a pulmonary infection (probably tuberculosis) from which he never recovered. He sailed for Canada December 1849 and arrived at Halifax May 1850. During 1851–2 Burpé visited Maritime churches on behalf of the foreign missions. In an effort to ameliorate his disease he went to Florida where he died.

BIBLIOGRAPHY
Baptist Missionary Magazine (Boston, 1846–50)
Christian Messenger (Halifax, Canada, 1845–53)
Christian Visitor (Saint John, Canada, 1851–3)
I. E. Bill, *Fifty Years with the Baptist Ministers and Churches of the Maritime Provinces of Canada* (Saint John, Canada, 1880)
B. M. Moody, 'Burpee, Richard E.', *Dictionary of Canadian Biography* VII (Toronto, 1985)
G. C. Warren, *Canada's Pioneer Missionary* (Toronto, 1944)

JUDITH COLWELL

Burr, Aaron (b. Fairfield, CT, BNA, 4 Jan. 1715; d. Princeton, NJ, BNA, 24 Sept. 1757). Presbyterian minister and second president of the College of New Jersey. After graduating from Yale in 1735, Burr remained in New Haven for graduate study under the auspices of the Berkeley Foundation. In the course of that year he experienced a spiritual awakening that prompted a shift in theology. 'Before this', he recounted, 'I was strongly attached to the Arminian scheme, but then was made to see those things in a different light, and seemingly felt the truth of the Calvinian doctrines'. Infused with a resolve to devote his life to the ministry, Burr briefly served churches in Greenfield, Massachusetts, and Hanover, New Jersey, and then, in December 1736, began a long tenure as minister of the First Presbyterian Church in Newark, New Jersey.

Burr enjoyed good relations with GEORGE WHITE-FIELD, the TENNENTS, and other leaders of the Great Awakening, although he was not uncritical of revival excesses. In a 1742 letter to JOSEPH BELLAMY, Burr appeared to refute GILBERT TENNENT's famous Nottingham sermon, 'The Danger of an Unconverted Ministry', when he criticized those who separated 'from their minister under a notion of his being unconverted'.

Upon the death of JONATHAN DICKINSON, the College of New Jersey's first president, in 1747, the college students removed to Newark, where they sat under the tutelage of Burr, an expert in classical languages. Burr was appointed president of the college in 1748, and held both positions – pastor at Newark and president of the college – simultaneously until 1755, when he devoted his full energies to the college. He supervised the move to Princeton in 1756, but his tireless efforts on behalf of the institution soon took a toll on his health. He fell ill in August 1757 and died a month later.

BIBLIOGRAPHY
AAP, 3: 68–72
DAB

RANDALL BALMER

Burr, Esther Edwards (b. Northampton, MA, BNA, 13 Feb. 1732; d. Princeton, NJ, BNA, 7 April 1758). Daughter, wife, mother and diarist. She was the third of JONATHAN and SARAH EDWARDS's eleven children; wife of AARON BURR, second president of the College of New Jersey (later called Princeton College), mother of Aaron Burr Jr, Thomas Jefferson's Vice-President.

Converted in her teens, she married Burr in 1752 and bore Aaron Jr in 1756. Aaron Sr died in 1757. When a smallpox epidemic broke out at Princeton in early 1758, she and her father were inoculated. He died of the inoculation on March 22, she of an unknown cause two weeks later.

Her recently published journal (a series of letters written between 1754 and 1757 to friend Sarah Prince, daughter of Boston minister THOMAS PRINCE) demonstrates that she participated in the emergence of private documents as a female literary genre. Her bright and lively prose places her in a tradition of American women writers from Anne Bradstreet to HARRIET BEECHER STOWE. Her resolute evangelical convictions marked her as a worthy daughter of her father and mother.

BIBLIOGRAPHY
C. F. Karlsen and L. Crumpacker, eds, *The Journal Of Esther Edwards Burr 1754–1757* (New Haven, CT, 1984)

GERALD R. MCDERMOTT

Burton, Asa (b. Stonington, CT, BNA, 25 March 1752; d. Thetford, VT, USA, 1 May 1836). Congregational minister and theologian. A year after his birth, Burton's family moved to Preston, Connecticut where he grew up under the Edwardsian New Divinity preaching of LEVI HART. After graduating from Dartmouth (1777), he returned to study theology with his former pastor. Typical of his generation of abstemious, missionary-minded New Divinity men, Burton sought a frontier outpost, and so accepted a pastorate with the tiny rural congregation of Thetford, Vermont. During the next half century Burton endured disease and danger, built up his congregation through revivals, prepared about sixty men for the ministry, and published his theological views in *Essays on Some of the First Principles of Metaphysicks, Ethics, and Theology* (1824).

Hailed in its time as 'one of the great influential philosophical books of the world,' the *Essays* represent one of the last attempts by an Edwardsian to rescue New England Calvinism from obliterating freedom of the will. Convinced that JONATHAN EDWARDS's unity of the faculties of will and understanding led to determinism, Burton posited a third faculty, that of 'taste' (or the 'heart' or 'moral faculty') – as the primary cause of action. Burton's 'faculty psychology' placed him at odds with other New Divinity men such as NATHANAEL EMMONS whose philosophical immaterialism led him to posit an 'exercise' scheme which upheld both God's immediate agency and man's freedom to sin. Burton's views did, however, find favour with other New Divinity men such as LEONARD WOODS and BENNET TYLER who, in their defence of Burton's tripartite scheme, appealed more to the empiricism of Scottish 'common sense' philosophy and less to the immaterialist views of Edwards. By defending the freedom of the will upon the ground of intuition and self-evident 'facts,' Woods and Tyler, influenced by Burton's

Essays, unintentionally contributed to the demise of Edwardsianism as force within New England Calvinism.

SELECT WRITINGS
A. Burton, *The Life of Asa Burton Written by Himself*, ed. Charles Latham, Jr (Thetford, VT, 1973)

BIBLIOGRAPHY
AAP, 2
A. Guelzo, *Edwards on the Will* (Middletown, CT, 1989)
J. Haroutunian, *Piety Versus Moralism* (1932; New York, 1970)
J. Hoopes, *Consciousness in New England* (Baltimore, MD, 1989)
B. Kuklick, *Churchmen and Philosophers* (New Haven, CT, 1985)

DAVID W. KLING

Burton, John (b. Nottingham, England, 1773; d. Leicester, England, 1822). Baptist Sunday school worker and publisher. Born in Nottingham, he removed to Leicester in 1813, the year after he had helped compile the *Nottingham Sunday School Union Hymn Book*. He wrote many poems for children and is designated in the British Library Catalogue, the Leicester Schoolmaster. He wrote a spelling and grammar book for schools and secured ROBERT HALL to write a preface to one of his works.

BIBLIOGRAPHY
Julian
E.C. Starr, *A Baptist Bibliography* (London, 1954)

J. H. Y. BRIGGS

Busby, Sampson (b. Rainton, Yorkshire, England, 16 February 1790; d. in New Brunswick, BNA, 31 March 1850). Methodist missionary to Newfoundland and Prince Edward Island. Busby, a convert to Methodism from the Church of England, was ordained in London, England, in 1812. He went as a missionary to Carbonear, Conception Bay, Newfoundland in 1812. The missionary career of Busby mirrors that of his predecessor JAMES BULPIT, both of whose wives conducted school in Newfoundland and who subsequently (Busby from 1817 on) served churches in Prince Edward Island.

BIBLIOGRAPHY
DNLB
ENL
W. Wilson, *Newfoundland and its Missionaries* (Cambridge, MA, 1866): 182–3

HANS ROLLMANN

Bush, Robert (Wheler) (b. Bristol, England, 24 Oct. 1819 [ordination papers, Oxford]; d. London, 2 Oct. 1908). Clerical schoolmaster and Anglican clergyman. Son of John (gentleman) and Catherine Sarah Bush, and perhaps influenced spiritually by their rector T. T. BIDDULPH, Robert matriculated from Lincoln College,

Oxford (1838), becoming scholar (1839–47) and fellow (1844–7) of Worcester College, also university prizeman. He was a private tutor (1842–4) at Oxford. Ordained in 1844, Bush was appointed senior classical master at Rossall School (founded 1844), Lancashire. From 1846 to 1879 he was headmaster of Islington Proprietary School, assisting at various London churches from 1857. In 1870 he became Rector of St Michael, Wood Street, London. From 1880 till death he was Rector of St Alphege, London Wall.

BIBLIOGRAPHY
T. W. Ashworth, *Rossall Register 1844–94*, 3rd edn (Manchester, England, 1895)
J. S. Reynolds, *Evangelicals at Oxford* (Oxford, 1953; Appleford, England, 1975)
The Times (5 and 6 October 1908)

J. S. REYNOLDS

Bushnell, Horace (b. Bantam, CT, USA, 13 Aug. 1802; d. Hartford, CT, USA, 18 June 1876). New England Congregational Minister and theologian. Bushnell graduated from Yale College in 1827 and studied at Yale Law School (1829–31). In 1831 he experienced conversion and changed his professional aspirations from law to the ministry. At the Yale Divinity School, from which he graduated in 1833, Bushnell studied under NATHANIEL W. TAYLOR and was introduced to the moderate evangelical Calvinism of the New Haven theology. In 1833, Bushnell was ordained as minister of the North Church in Hartford, Connecticut, which he served until he retired from the pastoral ministry in 1859. During the last two decades of his life, Bushnell continued to publish works explaining the liberal evangelicalism with which he has become so closely identified.

Bushnell's sermons and major publications moved Congregational religious thought further from its Calvinist origins. At the same time he drew on the Romantic movement's emphasis on feelings and intuitive knowledge to modify the traditional New England Congregational use of theological systems and logic to defend and explain evangelical religious positions. Indeed, Bushnell argued that religious language should be seen as poetic, not literal, because spiritual experience could not be conveyed in logical linguistic statements or systems. For such views Bushnell was accused of heresy by the Connecticut Association of Congregational Ministers in 1850, a charge that he survived.

Bushnell is best known for his advocacy of 'Christian nurture'. He de-emphasized the importance of revivals and the need for dramatic conversions to promote the spiritual and moral transformation of America. He urged parents to make the home a centre of Christian nurture, where children would be raised never knowing themselves to be other than Christian. Such views suggest Bushnell's place as a transitional figure between the moderate Calvinism of his teacher Nathaniel Taylor and the liberal evangelicalism of the Social Gospel.

BIBLIOGRAPHY
W. R. Adamson, *Bushnell Rediscovered* (Philadelphia, PA, 1966)
B. M. Cross, *Horace Bushnell* (Cambridge, MA, 1958)

JOSEPH CONFORTI

Bushnell, Jedediah (b. Saybrook, CT, BNA, 26 Nov. 1769; d. Cornwall, VT, USA, 25 August 1843). Congregationalist missionary and minister. Following an apprenticeship of five years to a tanner and shoemaker, Bushnell at age 21 established his own business. After working at this trade for two years, he was converted and felt called to the ministry. He graduated from Williams College in 1797, having financed his education through making shoes and teaching school. He then studied theology under the direction of a minister from Sheffield, Massachusetts and was licensed to preach. For the next five years he was highly effective as an evangelist while serving with the Connecticut Missionary Society, primarily in the western sections of New York and Vermont. His success as a missionary was due chiefly to his personal piety and his plain, direct preaching.

In 1803 Bushnell became the pastor of the Congregationalist church in Cornwall, Vermont, which was one of the state's largest, most active congregations. During his 33 years of ministry, his church experienced 14 years of revival. As a pastor, Bushnell preached evangelistic sermons, visited each family three or four times a year, excelled in comforting the sick and dying, helped resolve disputes and quarrels between family members and between neighbours, and ministered effectively to youth. After being dismissed by his congregation in 1836 as a result of his stand on several controversial issues, Bushnell served as an itinerant minister to several congregations in the vicinity of Cornwall.

A committed Calvinist who regularly preached on major points of Reformed theology, Bushnell played an active role in the benevolent societies established by the Second Great Awakening which helped to revitalize evangelical Protestantism in much of the USA during the first forty years of the nineteenth century. He helped to found the Vermont Missionary Society, served as a trustee of Middlebury College, and inspired many men to become ministers. He was also an editor of and contributor to *The Advisor*, a Congregationalist monthly magazine published in Middlebury, Vermont.

BIBLIOGRAPHY
AAP

GARY SCOTT SMITH

Bushyhead, Jesse (b. Cherokee Nation, USA, Sept. 1804; d. Westville, OK, USA, 17 July 1844). Cherokee minister, interpreter, lobbyist, and Chief Justice. A Cherokee Baptist preacher, educated by the Presbyterians, Bushyhead worked as an interpreter and itinerant preacher for EVAN JONES. Bushyhead became the first ordained Cherokee minister and founded the first indigenous Cherokee church at Amohee, Tennessee. He was appointed as a Justice to the Cherokee Supreme Court and later served as Chief Justice. Described as the most noble looking and eloquent man in the Cherokee nation, he was active as a lobbyist to Congress in opposition to removal. In 1844, abolitionists of the northern United States published false information that Bushyhead owned slaves, and challenged his employment by the Baptist Mission Board. This action called forth the 'Alabama Resolutions' which prompted the split of 1845, between Southern and Northern Baptist Churches. Bushyhead died in 1844 of 'Prairie fever' before word of the controversy reached him.

BIBLIOGRAPHY
W. McLoughlin, *Cherokees and Missionaries, 1789–1839* (New Haven, CT, 1984): 162, 326, 339
W. N. Wyeth, *Poor Lo!* (Philadelphia, PA, 1896): 60–2

WADE A. HORTON

Butler, Elizur (b. Norfolk, CT, USA, 11 June 1794; d. Park Hill, Indian Territory [OK], USA, 4 Feb. 1857). Medical missionary among the Cherokee. Although he never attended college, Butler practised medicine for a time in New Marlboro, Massachusetts. In 1820, the ABCFM sent him to work among the Cherokee in Georgia. He served at Brainerd Mission (1821–4) and Haweis Mission (1824–31). In 1831, Georgia required all those working among the Indians to swear allegiance to the state. Butler and several other missionaries refused. Convicted of violating the Oath Law, Butler and SAMUEL A. WORCESTER were imprisoned. The US Supreme Court, in *Worcester v. Georgia*, 1832, declared the state law invalid. Upon release from prison, in January 1833, Butler returned to his work among the Cherokee, moving with the tribe to the Indian Territory in 1838. There he worked at the Dwight, Park Hill, and Fairfield missions, and finally at the Cherokee Female Seminary at Park Hill, until his death.

BIBLIOGRAPHY
DCA
ESM
W. G. McLoughlin, 'Civil Disobedience Among the Missionaries to the Cherokees, 1829–1839', *JPH*, 51 (1973): 116–139
W. G. McLoughlin, *Cherokees and Missionaries, 1789–1839* (New Haven, CT, 1984)
R. S. Walker, *Torchlights to the Cherokees* (New York, 1931)

MARK S. JOY

Butler, John (b. London). CMS missionary in New Zealand. Butler was a probationer missionary trained by Reverend John Bishop of Paddington, London. He was ordained (deacon 1818) by the Bishop of Gloucester and on 15 December 1818 he went (along with his son SAMUEL BUTLER) as the first Anglican clergyman to New Zealand. On 14 November 1823 he returned to England and in February 1825 withdrew from the CMS.

BIBLIOGRAPHY
D. T. B[arry], *CMS Register of Missionaries and Native Clergy* (privately printed) (London, 1906)

DONALD M. LEWIS

Butler, Samuel (b. London). CMS missionary in New Zealand. Butler was a probationer missionary trained by Reverend John Bishop of Paddington, London. On 15 December 1818 he went (along with his father JOHN BUTLER) as a CMS lay missionary to New Zealand. In 1819 he went to Parramatta Seminary, New South Wales and in 1821 to Kidderkidder. His association with the CMS ended in New Zealand on 28 February 1823. Nothing is known of him thereafter.

BIBLIOGRAPHY
D. T. B[arry], *CMS Register of Missionaries and Native Clergy* (privately printed) (London, 1906)

DONALD M. LEWIS

Butler, Thomas (b. Shrewsbury, Shropshire, England, 28 Nov. 1806; d. probably Shrewsbury, 29 Dec. 1886). Anglican clergyman. Son of one Samuel, headmaster of Shrewsbury and subsequently Bishop of Lichfield and father of another, the author of *The Way of All Flesh*, Thomas Butler, who was also brother-in-law to Archdeacon EDWARD BATHER, differed from both parent and offspring in his strong and narrow evangelical views which were bitterly satirized in the character of Theobald Pontifex in his son's novel. Butler was educated under his father at Shrewsbury and then at St John's College Cambridge (BA 1829; MA 1832). Beginning as assistant to his father and curate to Bather at Meole Brace, he was preferred to the living of Langar-with-Bramston (1834–76), becoming in due course Canon of Lincoln (1868–86) and retiring to Shrewsbury in 1876. Butler objected to his son's personal habits and his agnosticism, but *The Way of All Flesh*, though finished in the father's lifetime, was not in fact published, until after the son's death, in 1903.

BIBLIOGRAPHY
Mrs R. S. Garnett, *Samuel Butler and his Family Relations* (London, 1926)
P. Raby, *Samuel Butler, A Biography* (London, 1991)

ARTHUR POLLARD

Butler, William (b. Dublin, Ireland, 30 Jan. 1818; d. Old Orchard, ME, USA, 16 Aug. 1899). Methodist Episcopal missionary. Butler began preaching in Wesleyan Methodist meetings soon after his 1838 conversion. He received an education at Hardwick Street Mission Seminary and Training School (Dublin) and Didsbury College (near Manchester) graduating 1844. He joined the Irish Conference (1844) and was ordained elder

(1848). He married Julia Anne Crompton, who died *circa* 1853.

In 1850, Butler moved to the USA, to the New York Conference and then to the New England Conference. On 23 November 1854 he married Clementina Rowe. The Butlers served as missionaries to India from 25 September 1856 to 18 January 1865. He chose to make North India the centre of his Methodist Episcopal mission. His experiences of the Sepoy Rebellion (1857) and the founding of his mission were chronicled in *The Land of the Veda* (New York, 1872). After tensions with the mission board and missionaries over funding, governance and management, he returned to New England (1865–9). His return to India for a visit in 1883–4 was described in *From Boston to Bareilly and Back* (New York, 1885).

From 1869 to 1872, Butler was secretary of the American and Foreign Christian Union. He served as founding superintendent of the Mexico Mission of the MEC (1872–9), narrating his activities in the virulently anti-Catholic *Roman Catholicism and the Reformation of Mexico* (Belfast, 1883) and *Mexico in Transition from the Power of Political Romanism to Civil and Religious Liberty* (New York, 1892).

Butler was radically opposed to the 'self-supporting' mission efforts of WILLIAM TAYLOR. He promoted a colonial model in which missionaries lived like foreign rulers. His experiences in India made him a vigorous supporter of the 'Christian' Empire. His writings show little appreciation of or sensitivity to local cultures.

BIBLIOGRAPHY
W. C. Barclay, *History of Methodist Missions*, 3 (New York, 1957)
C. Butler, *William Butler, Founder of Two Missions of the Methodist Episcopal Church* (New York and Cincinnati, OH, 1902)
W. Butler, *A Compendium of the Missionary Bible and Tract Institutions of Evangelical Christendom* (Boston, MA, 1851)

DAVID BUNDY

Butscher, Leopold (b. Überlingen, Germany, *c.* 1777; d. Freetown, Sierra Leone, 17 June 1817). CMS missionary, Sierra Leone. One of the German Lutherans recruited by the CMS in its early years, he went to Sierra Leone in 1806 to work in the mission to the Susu in the Rio Pongas country (modern Guinea). There was little hope of converting the Susu, partly through the growing influence of Islam in the area, partly from the hostility of the small settled population of European and Eurafrican slave traders, so the missionaries concentrated on teaching children (including the slave traders' children). In 1815 he was transferred to Freetown as colonial chaplain. Contrary to the usual Anglican practice, but more in keeping with his own Lutheran background, he held joint communion services with the Wesleyan missionary. When the CMS opened a Christian institution on Leicester Mount, above Freetown, to train missionaries and teachers (later reorganized as Fourah Bay College) he had charge of it until his death.

BIBLIOGRAPHY
C. Fyfe, *A History of Sierra Leone* (London, 1962)

CHRISTOPHER FYFE

Butt, Mary Martha. See SHERWOOD, MARY MARTHA

Butterworth, John (b. Goodshaw, Rossendale, Lancashire, England, 13 Dec. 1727; d. Coventry, Warwickshire, England, 24 April 1803). Baptist minister. His father, Henry Butterworth, was a blacksmith and John was one of five sons; four of them entered the Baptist ministry. He became minister of the Particular Baptist Church, Cow Lane, Coventry, in 1753, where he remained for fifty years. His *Serious Address* (1790), written under the pseudonym Christophilus, opposed the Unitarian views of Joseph Priestley. A gifted Bible student, he produced a concordance and dictionary which was reprinted on several occasions; in 1790 JOHN RIPPON described it as 'the most full and concise of any before published' (*Baptist Annual Register*, 1790: 119). After Butterworth's death it was edited by ADAM CLARKE, an indication of its continuing appeal in the early nineteenth century. His son, JOSEPH BUTTERWORTH, was successively MP for Coventry and Dover, and although a supporter of the BMS, had become a Wesleyan.

SELECT WRITINGS
J. Butterworth, *A Serious Address to the Rev. Dr. Priestly ... Wherein the Doctor's Sentiment of the Person of Christ is Considered* (by Christophilus) (Coventry, England, 1790)

BIBLIOGRAPHY
BQ, 3: 141, 283
DNB
TBHS, 6: 152–3; 7: 191

RAYMOND BROWN

Butterworth, Joseph (b. Coventry, England, 12 Aug. 1770; d. London, 30 June 1826). Methodist publisher and MP. He was the son of the Reverend JOHN BUTTERWORTH, Baptist minister of Coventry. He early became a Methodist, and founded the famous law publishing firm in London. He figured prominently in evangelical philanthropic circles; leading supporters of the BFBS, antislavery and other movements gathered at his house. He regretted the growth of the High Wesleyan doctrine of the Pastoral Office, and the Methodist claim to independent church status. However, in 1803 he pressed conference to found the Committee of Privileges, to defend Methodist rights at law, and was one of its first members. He remained much in demand for political and legal advice. He was an independent MP for Coventry 1812–18, and for Dover 1820–6. Manuscript material relating to his political activities survives in the Methodist Church Archives, John Rylands University Library of Manchester.

BIBLIOGRAPHY
DNB

W. R. WARD

Buxton, Sir Edward North (second baronet) (b. London, 16 Sept. 1812; d. Colne House, Cromer, Norfolk, England, 11 June 1858). British MP. The eldest son of Sir THOMAS FOWELL BUXTON, he matriculated at Trinity College, Cambridge in 1830. In 1836 he married his cousin, Catherine Gurney, the second daughter of Samuel Gurney. Buxton was a Whig MP for South Essex (1847–52). In 1857 he was returned for East Norfolk, even though he was absent at the time in Nice and had not himself put his name forward. However, he accepted and held the seat until his death. He was a moderate reformer.

Buxton was especially active in the African Civilization Society, the LCM, the Ragged Schools Union, the CMS, and the LDOS. He spent much of the 1850s in Italy attempting to reconcile Italian and Waldensian Protestant missionaries, then in competition in the evangelistic field.

BIBLIOGRAPHY
Al. Cant.
GM, 50 (1858): 190
N. Pope, *Dickens and Charity* (New York, 1978): 104, 116, 184, 206, 244
Stenton

JONATHAN BURKE CUTMORE

Buxton, Sir (Thomas) Fowell (b. Earls Colne, Essex, England, 6 April 1786; d. Overstrand, Norfolk, England, 19 Feb. 1845). Baronet, brewer, emancipator, and MP. He was the eldest son of Thomas Fowell Buxton some time High Sheriff of Essex. He was educated at private schools and in 1803 entered Trinity College, Dublin, and graduated as a gold medalist in 1807. He inherited from his father his passion for field sports, especially shooting. He was six feet four inches tall and became known as 'Elephant' Buxton. His father died when he was six, and Buxton was brought up with the five other children by his mother, Anna Buxton (née Hanbury). 'She treated me as an equal, conversed with me and led me to express my opinions without reserve ... Throughout my life I have acted and thought for myself.' Mrs Buxton hoped that her son might inherit an Irish estate and, therefore, entered him for Trinity College, Dublin. Before going to university Buxton had become engaged to his cousin, Hannah Gurney of Earlham Hall, Norfolk, who was three years older than he was. SAMUEL HOARE, who married Louise Gurney, one of Hannah's sisters, became Buxton's closest friend. Buxton distinguished himself academically by winning several university prizes. On 7 May 1807, he married Hannah at Tarsburgh Friends Meeting House, both families being members of the Society of Friends. The following year the Buxtons moved to London.

The hope of an estate in Ireland having failed to materialize, Buxton was prepared to accept a place in the management of Truman's Brewery in Brick Lane, Spitalfields. In three years he was on the board and the firm became Truman, Hanbury and Buxton. From 1808 till they moved to Hampstead, the Buxtons lived in a house in Brick Lane. For worship they attended the Friends Meeting House in Bishopsgate. In 1811 Buxton was back in Norfolk visiting two evangelical Anglican clergy, EDWARD EDWARDS, Rector of St Edmund's, North Lynn, and Robert Hankinson (see ROBERT E. HANKINSON), Curate of St Margaret's, King's Lynn, both of whom were friends of JOHN VENN and CHARLES SIMEON who were founder members of the CMS. They urged Buxton to attend Wheler Street Chapel, Spitalfields, where JOSIAH PRATT, secretary of CMS took Sunday duty. The move for Buxton was revolutionary. He said later 'It was much and of vast moment that I learned from Mr Pratt.' Later he wrote to Pratt, 'Whatever I have done in my life for Africa, the seeds of it were sown in my heart, in Wheler Street Chapel.' The truths that Pratt preached, Buxton came to accept during a severe illness in 1813. In 1816 Buxton wrote in his diary: 'We went to Wheler Chapel where Mr Pratt gave us one of his best sermons ... S. Hoare and I stayed for the sacrament, which I entered into more I think than I ever did before.'

At the brewery Buxton overhauled the business methods of the enterprise with great efficiency, persuading the clerks to adopt more modern methods of book-keeping. Although he ceased to be general manager, he maintained for the rest of his life a broad oversight of the business. Buxton himself believed in the regulation of the liquor trade. He once said 'I could brew one hour, do mathematics the next, and shoot the next; each with my whole soul.' It is significant that of those who subscribed to CMS, among his contemporaries were the names of Barclay, Samuel Hoare, ARTHUR GUINNESS, Perkins and Whitbread, and ROBERT HANBURY (Buxton's cousin), all of them brewers.

By 1815 the Buxtons had four children; they decided to move from Spitalfields to Hampstead. Five years later he moved out of London and eventually built for himself Northrepps Hall near Overstrand in Norfolk. About the same time Buxton and Hoare told their sister-in-law, ELIZABETH FRY, that they too wanted to be involved in prison reform. The opportunity came for Buxton when in 1818 he was elected as Tory MP for Weymouth. He later became a Whig, making prison reform his chief concern. The aim of Sir James Mackintosh and Fowell Buxton was to remove from the statute book all crimes demanding the penalty of death, apart from murder.

In 1821 WILLIAM WILBERFORCE invited Buxton to share the leadership of the abolitionists; by 1823 Buxton was sole leader. Though his first motion against slavery mentioned gradual abolition of slavery, its extinction in British dominions was its aim and this was achieved in a little over 11 years. The same methods were used as against the slave trade, petitions to Parliament from all over the country and massive publicity including up-to-date facts in the monthly Anti-Slavery Reporter edited by

ZACHARY MACAULAY. The arrival of a Whig government in 1830 helped forward the pace of abolition which came on 28 August 1833. Wilberforce died when the issue was no longer in doubt. Liberation came the following August. After the wedding of his daughter, Priscilla, Buxton wrote: 'The bride has just gone – everything has passed off to admiration, AND – there is not a slave in the British colonies.' On 7 July 1840 Buxton was created a baronet in recognition of his public service.

Buxton's concern for Africa did not supplant his concern for the evangelization of London; he became first treasurer of the LCM in 1835, however, the final period of his life was devoted to Africa. Buxton's vision for Africa included an expedition up the River Niger to prepare for 'agricultural, commercial and missionary settlements' which would bring to Africa the benefits of western civilization. 'It is the Bible and the plough that must regenerate Africa.' By 1840 a model farm had been set up at Lokaja on the Niger and new societies in Britain gave lavish support to the expedition, but it all ended disastrously. On 20 August three steamships provided by the government entered the Niger, but fever broke out. Forty-two, all Europeans, died, government support was withdrawn and Buxton abandoned the venture. Two years later he was dead. Fifty thousand inhabitants of Africa and the West Indies subscribed to the statue erected in Westminster Abbey in his memory.

The Buxtons have been one of the leading evangelical families in Britain; its members have served as politicians, clergy and missionaries all over the world. His eldest son, Sir EDWARD NORTH BUXTON, inherited the baronetcy.

BIBLIOGRAPHY

T. Binney, Sir Thomas Fowell Buxton Bart (London, 1853)
C. Buxton, Memoirs of Sir Thomas Fowell Buxton (London, 1925)
DNB
M. M. Hennell, Sons of the Prophets (London, 1979)
E. Stock, History of CMS (London, 1899)

MICHAEL MURRAY HENNELL

Buyers, William (b. Dundee, Scotland, 1804; d. near Allahabad, India, 4 Oct. 1865). LMS missionary pioneer in India. Educated in Aberdeen and at University College, London, Buyers was ordained 16 February 1831 and arrived in Benares in January 1832. He worked with the notoriously difficult ROBERT COTTON MATHER from 1837 to 1838, and suffered a physical and nervous breakdown in April 1840.

With J. A. SCHURMANN, Buyers translated the New Testament into Urdu 'in a style suited to the lower orders of the people'. JOHN CAMPBELL thought the translation too literal and unintelligible. On furlough (1843–5), Buyers wrote Letters from India, a hard-hitting book about north India missions which provoked his temporary severance from the LMS. He returned to work on his own in Benares (1845) until re-engaged by the LMS (1850), whereupon his family joined him.

During the mutiny, Buyers's wife (Eliza Ann Walker of Aberdeen, married in Calcutta July 1833) stayed at her mission rather than join the evacuation to Calcutta. She succumbed to dysentery during the siege of Benares in October 1857, and is listed among the martyrs in the mutiny. Buyers resigned in 1863 but stayed on in India for the rest of his life.

BIBLIOGRAPHY
LMS Benares mission papers, CWM archives, School of Oriental and African Studies, London

E. M. JACKSON

Buzacott, Aaron (b. South Molton, Devon, England, 4 March 1800; d. Sydney, Australia, 20 Sept. 1864). LMS missionary on Rarotonga. Before being trained at Hoxton Academy and Hoxton Mission College Buzacott was a farm labourer, and a versatile craftsman. Between 1827 and 1828 he served on Tahiti and was ordained. His name is usually associated with Rarotonga where he served between 1828 and 1846 and again between 1852 and 1857. Buzacott was the first to establish a Christian church at Avarua on Rarotonga. He travelled extensively throughout the Pacific region and was a fluent speaker of the islanders' language. Having printed most of the Old and some of the New Testament on the island he returned to England where between 1847 and 1851 he oversaw the printing of the whole Rarotongan Bible on behalf of the Bible Society. He was, according to Lovett, regarded by many as 'the model missionary'.

BIBLIOGRAPHY
N. Gunson, *Messengers of Grace* (Melbourne, 1978) (provides a useful Calendar of 'Manuscript Sources')
R. Lovett, *The History of the London Missionary Society 1795–1895* (London, 1899)
RMD, 4th edn (London, 1923)

R. WATCYN JAMES

Byington, Cyrus (b. Stockbridge, MA, USA, 11 March 1793; d. Belpre, OH, USA, 31 Dec. 1868). Missionary and linguist among the Choctaw Indians. Born into a frontier family, Byington had little formal education but eventually mastered Greek and Latin, and prepared for a career in law. He practised law from a time before his conversion in 1813. Deciding to pursue the ministry, he entered Andover Theological Seminary, graduating in 1819. After serving briefly with the ABS, in 1820 he was sent by the ABCFM to work among the Choctaw at Eliot Mission in Mississippi. He was ordained as a Congregationalist minister in 1827. His most significant achievements were in the study of the Choctaw language, and the preparation of a grammar and dictionary of the language, as well as translations of portions of the Bible. He remained at Eliot until 1859, when the last remnants of the Choctaw tribe were forced to move to the West. Moving with the Indians, he served at the Stockbridge Mission in the Indian Territory until 1866, when he retired to Ohio due to poor health.

BIBLIOGRAPHY
DAB
ESM

MARK S. JOY

Byrd, William (b. Virginia, BNA, 28 March 1674; d. Virginia, BNA, 26 Aug. 1744). Virginia planter, political leader, and diarist. In 1984, historian Jon Butler made the striking suggestion that evangelicalism in the American South owed much to the Anglican evangelists who during the seventeenth and early eighteenth centuries built beachheads of piety in the region which made revivalism after 1740 possible.

The second William Byrd is a prime example of this Anglican proto-evangelicalism. Educated at the Middle Temple in London, he inherited the substantial estates of his father and namesake in 1704 and in 1708 became a member of the Royal Council in Virginia. He built a handsome plantation house, Westover, and installed the best library in the colony. Exploring the Virginia-North Carolina borderline, he wrote a classic description of the region. His extensive diaries record his daily routine of prayer, reading the classics, dealing irritably with spouses, children, neighbours, and slaves, and sexual escapades during frequent visits to England. His diaries reveal a complex spirituality: rational, mystical, troubled, emotional, and thoroughly Trinitarian.

BIBLIOGRAPHY
P. U. Bonomi, *Under the Cope of Heaven* (New York, 1986)
K. A. Lockridge, *The Diary and Life of William Byrd II* (Chapel Hill, NC and NY, 1987)

ROBERT CALHOON

C

Cadman, William (b. Billinge, Lancashire, England, 13 May 1815; d. London, 12 May 1891). Anglican clergyman. Cadman was educated in his native place under SAMUEL HALL and proceeded to St Catherine's College, Cambridge (BA 1839; MA 1842). He served simultaneously as Curate of Brent Eleigh (to Richard Snape) and of Lavenham, Suffolk (to Richard Johnson) (1839–44). He then moved as curate to H. M. VILLIERS at St George's, Bloomsbury (1844–6) and thus began what was to be his life's work in the metropolis. He migrated south of the river to become vicar of St George's, Southwark (1852–9), a very different place from Park Chapel, Chelsea, where he had served as lecturer under J. C. MILLER (1846–52). There he had given his support to the CMS, the CPAS and the Jews' Society. Though he continued his interest in these societies, the work at Southwark brought more urgent problems immediately to hand.

St George's covered a large slum area of some 30,000 people. Cadman divided the parish into six districts, each with its own curate, and, helped by the CPAS and the Scripture Readers' Association as well as the LCM and the Ragged School Union, he recruited over 200 voluntary workers as district visitors and the like. He had over a thousand people at some of his weekday meetings. In 1856 he extended the church to take over 1,300 sittings, and in 1857 the daughter church of St Paul's was opened.

When he moved to Holy Trinity, Marylebone (1859–91), he found himself in another very different social sphere, for this parish of 14,000 souls contained within it such wealthy areas as Portland Place, Harley Street and Wimpole Street. He instituted daily prayer and weekly Communion. The parish made substantial contributions to Bishop Tait's London Fund for churches, mission rooms, clergy and lay agents.

Cadman was select preacher at Cambridge (1871–2), a prebendary of St Paul's (1874–83), Canon of Canterbury (1883–91), chaplain to Archbishop Benson (1886) and rural dean and proctor in convocation (1869–91). He was also a Simeon Trustee (1863–91) and a Hyndman Trustee.

BIBLIOGRAPHY
Al. Cant. II.i: 487
L. E. Shelford, *Memoir of the Reverend William Cadman* (London, 1899)

ARTHUR POLLARD

Cadogan, Hon. William Bromley (b. London, 22 Jan. 1751; d. Reading, Berkshire, England, 18 Jan. 1797). Anglican clergyman. Cadogan, the second son of the Earl of that name, was educated at Westminster School and Christ Church, Oxford (BA 1773; MA 1776). Through family connections he succeeded WILLIAM TALBOT in the valuable living of St Giles, Reading (1774–97), offered to him by the Lord Chancellor. In 1775 he obtained the family living of St Luke's, Chelsea, even though, not being of MA status, he was strictly ineligible to hold two cures, a difficulty overcome by the conferment of a Lambeth degree by Archbishop Cornwallis.

Cadogan antagonized his Reading parishioners initially by dismissing his evangelical curate, JOHN HALLWARD. Though not having experienced an evangelical conversion, Cadogan was nonetheless a diligent pastor, active in visiting, baptizing, distributing Bibles and prayer-books and in generosity to the poor. He was also a strict Sabbatarian. A severe illness in 1782 led to more distinctly evangelical views, though before this there was an interesting contrast – at Reading he was disliked for not being 'Methodist' enough, at Chelsea for being too much so.

He divided his time by spending one half of the year at Chelsea, the other at Reading with visits to the place where he was not resident once a month. Latterly Chelsea was left largely in the care of his curate, ERASMUS MIDDLETON, who had been one of the six students expelled from St Edmund Hall, Oxford, for holding 'Methodist' views in 1768. Cadogan was a forceful, if somewhat monotonous, preacher, and in personality said to be testy, abrupt and autocratic. CHARLES SIMEON preached his funeral sermon.

BIBLIOGRAPHY
Al. Ox., I: 208
W. B. Cadogan, *Discourses* with Memoir by R. Cecil (London, 1798)
C. Smyth, *Simeon and Church Order* (Cambridge, 1940)

ARTHUR POLLARD

Cadwaladr, Dafydd (b. Llangwm, Denbighshire, Wales, 1752; d. Bala, Merionethshire, Wales, 9 July 1834). Welsh Calvinistic Methodist preacher. Before his marriage in 1777 to Judith Humphreys, when he settled at Penrhiw, Bala, he was employed on the land. Aged 28 he began to preach at the instigation of JOHN EVANS of

Bala. He was regarded as an exceptionally scriptural preacher, having an uncommon gift to reach the understanding of the meanest listeners. He was also a local poet of some repute and published elegies for THOMAS CHARLES and his wife, Dafydd Edward and John Evans.

BIBLIOGRAPHY
DWB
O. Thomas, *Cofiant y Parch. John Jones, Talsarn* (Wrexham, no date)

GORONWY PRYS OWEN

Cairns, Adam (b. Longforgan, Scotland, 29 Jan. 1802; d. Melbourne, Australia, 30 Jan. 1881). Australian Presbyterian minister. Educated at St Andrews and Edinburgh, Cairns was licensed to preach in the Church of Scotland in 1824. From 1825 to 1827 he assisted HENRY MONCRIEFF at St Cuthbert's in Edinburgh, and in 1828 was ordained at Manor. He was then minister at Dunbog (1833–7) and from 1837 at Cupar. Upon the Disruption of 1843 he remained at Cupar, but now as the Free Church minister.

In 1847, poor health having driven him south, he organized the Free Church at Gibraltar. In 1853 Cairns led a delegation to Australia to establish new congregations in the colonial Free Church, just then burgeoning because of the gold rush. He served a large and influential congregation at Melbourne and was the first principal of the Theological Hall. Largely as a result of his efforts the union of the Presbyterian churches was effected (1859), the Scotch College (university and grammar school) was built, and a beginning was made on a national school system. He was an influential social and moral reformer, after THOMAS CHALMERS' example. With the collapse of his health in 1865, he returned briefly to Scotland, but soon after resumed his colonial ministry until his retirement in 1876. Cairns was the leading representative of Australian Presbyterianism in the high Victorian age.

BIBLIOGRAPHY
ADB
Boase
T. Brown, *Annals of the Disruption* (Edinburgh, 1892): 568–76

JONATHAN BURKE CUTMORE

Cairns, (First) Earl [Sir Hugh McCalmont] (b. Cultra, County Down, Ireland, 27 Dec. 1819; d. Bournemouth, Hampshire, England, 2 April 1885). Lord Chancellor, leader of the Conservative Party in the Lords, Crown law officer, and MP. Educated at Belfast (Royal) Academy and Trinity College, Dublin, he became a barrister of the Middle Temple in 1844, migrated to Lincoln's Inn and acquired a large practice. He achieved early eminence as a Chancery barrister, and became Queen's Counsel in 1856. In 1852 he was elected MP for Belfast, and impressed in debate with his powers of reasoning and

eloquence. He was appointed Solicitor-General in Lord Derby's administration, 1858–9. He was considered the equal, as a front bench orator of his party, of Disraeli, Edward Lytton and Lord Stanley, while *The Times* prophesied that, given his early rise to the first rank in his profession, he might look forward to 'the highest legal distinction' (2 March 1858).

On Lord Derby's return to power, he was Attorney-General from June to November 1866, when he was appointed Lord Justice of Appeal in Chancery, and a Privy Councillor. In 1867 he became Baron Cairns of Garmoyle, in the County of Antrim, and in March 1868, Lord Chancellor. He held this office until the fall of Disraeli's ministry in December 1868. Thus within three years he had passed through three great legal offices, and risen from being a practising barrister to the highest seat in the law, the Woolsack. During 1869, he became leader of the Conservative Opposition in the Lords. He was not yet fifty. He became Lord Chancellor again in Disraeli's ministry, 1874–80, being created Earl Cairns in 1878. He worked in close harmony with his great friend and political opponent, Lord Selborne.

He received the honorary degrees of LL D of both Cambridge and Dublin in 1862, and DCL of Oxford in 1863, and was elected chancellor of the University of Dublin in 1867.

For all his greatness in the law and government of the UK, he was never divorced from his Irish roots and loyalties. He married Mary Harriet, eldest daughter of John McNeile of Parkmount, County Antrim, in 1856. He was prominent in debate on the Liberals' Irish Land bills, and with William Alexander, Bishop of Derry and William Connor Magee, Bishop of Peterborough, made up a trio of brilliant Irish orators in the Lords who opposed their Irish Church bill. With HUGH MCNEILE, he was one of two county Antrim evangelicals who achieved national importance, but like RODEN, he remained a man of unaffected humility. Both taught a Sunday school class throughout their lives, while Cairns spent the half hour before Cabinet meetings in prayer. His philanthropy was felt in Belfast. It was fitting, then, that in its memorial to him, the Church of Ireland Young Men's Society (of which he was a founder) should quote, as a comment on his life: 'The people that do know their God shall be strong and do exploits'.

BIBLIOGRAPHY
DNB
The Times (3 April 1885)

ALAN R. ACHESON

Cairns, John (b. Ayton, Scotland, 23 Aug 1818; d. Edinburgh, 12 March 1892). Presbyterian minister. After studying at the University of Edinburgh, of which he later became an honorary DD and LL D, and in Berlin, he was ordained in 1845 to a leading Secession congregation in Berwick. Cairns entered the United Presbyterian Church of Scotland when it was formed in 1847 and became its leading figure in the later nineteenth century. In spite of efforts to attract him to various prestigious appointments in his church and elsewhere, Cairns remained in Berwick until 1876 when he moved to Edinburgh on becoming a full-time professor, and later principal, of the United Presbyterian divinity hall.

Cairns' philosophical accomplishments, influenced by Sir William Hamilton, equipped him to engage in the theological controversies of the time, though he never published the major works which might have been expected from him. He was a strong supporter of the EA and encouraged, and was much influenced by, a visit of Moody and Sankey to Berwick in 1874, but he supported the acceptance by his denomination in 1879 of a declaratory statement allowing liberty of opinion in interpreting its formularies on matters not entering into the substance of the faith. The alternative would have been a change in the formularies which was unacceptable to Cairns as he himself did not share the doubts and criticisms which others in his denomination were raising against them.

Cairns was a strong advocate of closer union among Presbyterians. He tried to promote union between his own church and the FCS in the 1860s and advocated disestablishment as a means to achieving greater unity.

BIBLIOGRAPHY
A. R. MacEwen, *Life and Letters of John Cairns, DD, LL D.* (London, 1898) lists his publications in an appendix

R. H. CAMPBELL

Calcraft, John Hales (b. Rempstone, Dorsetshire, England, 13 Sept. 1796; d. Rempstone, 13 March 1880). Landed gentleman and MP. Of a squirearchical family Calcraft was prominent both in the public life of his native county and in social work in London, in which latter capacity he was identified with the Metropolitan City Mission and the District Visiting Society. He was MP for Wareham (Dorset) from 1820 to 1826, 1832 to 1841 and 1857 to 1859. During his second period in parliament he supported the emancipation of slaves in 1833. In Dorset he served as a magistrate, Deputy-Lieutenant and High Sheriff.

BIBLIOGRAPHY
Boase, I: 512
D. M. Lewis, *Lighten Their Darkness* (Westport, CT, 1986)

ARTHUR POLLARD

Calder, Charles (b. Croy, Inverness, Scotland, 1 Dec. 1748; d. Urquhart, Ross-shire, Scotland, 1 Oct. 1812). Church of Scotland parish minister. Third ministerial son of James Calder, minister of Croy (Diary, *Banner of Truth*, 1974), and grandson of two ministers, he was converted before he was 11, graduated MA Aberdeen 30 March 1767, and was ordained minister of Urquhart (Ferintosh) 12 May 1774. On 8 July 1779 he married

Margaret Brodie, aunt of ELISABETH BRODIE, the last Duchess of Gordon. His son James went to India and his daughters married ALEXANDER STEWART, minister in Moulin, Edinburgh and Dingwall, and Angus Mackintosh, minister at Tain. His preaching was undemonstrative, he was frequently ill, and he greatly underestimated his ability and usefulness, but his ministry drew many hearers from surrounding moderate parishes, promoted a local revival of religion, resulted in the establishment of prayer and fellowship meetings and interest in recently formed missionary societies, and led several young men into the ministry. His holy life and Christ-centred preaching (dismissed by some as 'the piper of one tune') left an impression of God. He contributed to Sinclair's *Statistical Account*. Three sermons with brief biography were published by Malcolm MacGregor, Edinburgh, 1877.

BIBLIOGRAPHY
Fasti

HUGH M. CARTWRIGHT

Caldwell, David (b. Lancaster, PA, BNA, 22 March 1725; d. Greensboro, NC, USA, 25 Aug. 1824). Presbyterian minister and educator. Born into a Ulster Scots family and a graduate of the College of New Jersey in the class of 1761 (at the age of 36), Caldwell came to North Carolina in 1765 as a Presbyterian minister. There he married Rachel Craighead, daughter of the leading Presbyterian minister in North Carolina; the couple settled in present-day Greensboro where he became minister at Buffalo Church and at Alamance Church, a day's ride to the east. He held these pulpits for nearly sixty years.

In 1767 he opened a Log College, a classical and theological school which was one of the best in the region. During the political uprising known as the Regulator Revolt in 1770–1, he mediated between the regulators and the royal governor. At the start of the American Revolution he preached a sermon on 'The Character and Doom of the Sluggard' that a recent historian regards as one of the most sophisticated versions of Whig, republican, and Calvinist ideology (Calhoon, 1988: 93–5). His role in rallying people to the American cause in a region sharply divided between patriots and Tories led to his house being ransacked and library destroyed by Tory partisans in 1781.

BIBLIOGRAPHY
R. M. Calhoon, *Evangelicals and Conservatives in the Early South, 1740–1861* (Columbia, SC, 1988)
E. W. Caruthers, *A Sketch of the Life and Character of the Reverend David Caldwell* (Greensboro, 1842)

ROBERT CALHOON

Caldwell, James (b. Charlotte Co., VA, BNA, April 1734: d. Elizabeth, NJ, USA, 24 Nov. 1781). Militant revolutionary minister. James Caldwell, son of David Caldwell, an immigrant originally from Scotland and then Ireland, traced his background to Huguenot origin. Young Caldwell graduated from the College of New Jersey (1759), and following ordination in 1761 assumed the pastorate of the First Presbyterian Church in Elizabeth, New Jersey. He married Hannah Ogden in 1763.

A gifted preacher, Caldwell spoke eloquently from his pulpit for patriotic causes which resulted in rewards offered for his capture. He served as chaplain in revolutionary forces, and doctors treated wounded in his church before a refugee torched it in 1780 forcing the family to escape to Union, New Jersey, for safety. Later in the same year Mrs Caldwell died from a shot fired on the family home. Caldwell lived up to his reputation as 'Soldier Parson' by urging his men to use hymn-book pages as wadding in the battle of Springfield (1780) by saying, 'Now put Watts into them, boys'. In 1781 a sentry shot and killed him over a dispute regarding a package in Caldwell's possession. The soldier was tried and executed for murder.

BIBLIOGRAPHY
AAP
DAB
E. Kempshall, *Caldwell and the Revolution* (Elizabeth, NJ, 1880)

W. ANDREW HOFFECKER

Caldwell, Robert (b. near Belfast, Ulster: 7 May 1814; d. Kodaikanal, South India, 28 August 1891). Missionary, missionary bishop, and scholar (ethnographer, historian, and philologist). From an impoverished family, he began working at age nine, when his family moved to Glasgow. Largely self-educated, he studied art in Dublin (1829–33). A religious experience prompted his returning to Glasgow and becoming active in a Congregational church. A scholarship to Balliol College, Oxford, was invalidated by discovery of his being born in Ireland. In 1834, after being accepted by the LMS, he was sent to Glasgow University. There, while studying Greek and Latin, he came under the influence of a Greek professor (David Stanford or Daniel Sanford?), who was a pioneer in comparative philology. Sanford encouraged him to read theology critically; and thereafter, he began to ponder the merits of Anglicanism.

After graduation with distinction, ordination as a Congregational minister, and commissioning into missionary service, Caldwell embarked on the 'Mary Ann'. On the ship, he met and learned much from C. P. BROWN, the Madras Civil Servant who was becoming a renowned Telugu scholar. Arriving in Madras (8 January 1838), three years were devoted to learning Tamil. In February 1841, having concluded that the Church of England was the least un-Christian church and the SPG the least unacceptable missionary society, he trekked up to 'Ooty' (Ootacamund), in the Nilagiri Hills, where he was ordained by Bishop George Spencer of Madras. On his way back to Madras, he visited the aged J. C. KOHLHOFF

at Thanjavur. By December, he had settled in Idayankudi (Tirunelveli District). Already working under the SPG in Tirūnelveli were Caemmerer (Jr) at Nazareth and Heyne at Mudalur, both of whom were India-born SPCK German missionaries trained at Bishop's College, Calcutta. Caldwell remained at Idayankudi, 'Shepherd's Abode', for most of the next fifty years. Within three years, older congregations were being revitalized. The 'mass movement' of conversions among Shanar (Nadar) people, first begun in the 1790s and being revived in every decade thereafter, brought over 2,000 new inquirers into local churches. The old Halle system of instruction before baptism, first introduced in Tranquebar over a century earlier, was reinforced. Nine schools were re-established or strengthened. His marriage (in March 1844) to Eliza Mault, the India-born eldest daughter of a senior LMS missionary, greatly increased his effectiveness. Eliza immediately started a boarding-school for girls, introducing home-making and lacemaking so as to enable literate Tamil Christian women to achieve personal, social and financial independence.

Caldwell's scholarly contributions to Tamil culture were wide-ranging and profound. His first book, *The Tinnevelly Shanars* (Madras, 1849; London, 1850) became increasingly controversial. The ethnographic descriptions of this community, while of increasing value to historians, offended the more prominent and upwardly mobile members of the community. As they became more respectable, Shanars who called themselves Nadars, objected to any suggestion that their roots were less than fully Aryan. Petitions to the SPG and the Archbishop of Canterbury expressed outrage at the notion that Nadars came from low or polluting occupations. Caldwell became best known, especially in Europe, for his *Comparative Grammar of the Dravidian, or South Indian Family of Languages* (first published in 1856). This work, subsequently revised and enlarged, established his reputation as a leading Orientalist. It remains a standard authority and is still in print. He was the first to argue that south India's four main languages – Tamil, Telugu, Kannada and Malayalam – had 'a common origin' and were 'a separate family' altogether distinct from the Aryan family of languages. The implications of his theory were far-reaching. By arguing that these Dravidian languages of the south were different from those derived from Sanskrit and that their cultures and polities had existed prior to the arrival of Brahmans in the south, going so far as to suggest intrinsic differences in physical anthropology, religion and social structures, Caldwell may even have laid the foundations for anti-Brahman cultural and political movements in this century. No less significant were Caldwell's other scholarly contributions. Among these, *A Political and General History of the District of Tinnevelly, in the Presidency of Madras, From the Earliest Period to its Cession to the English Government in 1801* (Madras, 1881) was perhaps his greatest single work. He also published *Lectures on the Tinnevelly Mission* (London, 1881); *On Communicating Religious Instructions to Non-Christians in Mission Schools of India* (Madras, 1881); and, finally, *Reminiscences of Bishop Caldwell* (Madras,

1894), edited posthumously by his son-in-law, Reverend J. L. Wyatt. At the same time, in the process of producing these works, Caldwell uncovered many rare manuscripts. Finally, he helped to revise the Tamil *Book of Common Prayer*, both in 1842 and 1872; and, from 1858 to 1869, he played a part helping the Madras branch of the BFBS's production of a revised version of the Tamil Bible.

Caldwell's piety and scholarship eventually led to his elevation to a higher office. But when the decision was made to create a separate bishopric for Tirunelveli, both Robert Caldwell and EDWARD SARGENT were put forward for the new position (there then being no Indian thought to be qualified). This double nomination led to complications. Only after passage of the Colonial Clergy Act of 1874, were both finally consecrated, in Calcutta (11 March 1877), as assistant bishops. Neither appointment was fully satisfactory. Both missionaries were aging and could not travel very far. As the number of European missionaries declined, the Native Church Council became restive and strove for increasing autonomy. Moreover, ever since the days of the Rhenius Schism, Tamil Christians connected to the SPG and the CMS had been divided, and partially polarized. This situation persisted even though the two bishops remained on excellent terms with each other. The final amalgamation of these two branches into a single diocesan structure did not occur until after the death of Sargent in October 1887. Caldwell, who by then had been preoccupied with a theological school in Tuticorin since 1881, was persuaded to retire.

Caldwell's final years were spent in Kodaikanal. It was there, where he had erected St Peter's Church many years earlier, that he died. His body was returned to Idayankudi and buried under the altar of the magnificent church building he had constructed. Mrs Caldwell remained in Kodaikanal until her death, on 18 June 1899; and her body was also returned to lie beside that of her husband. At least one daughter, married to J. L. Wyatt of the SPG, continued in missionary service. A statue of Caldwell stands on the esplanade in Madras as a tribute to his contributions to the culture and to the people of Tamilnadu.

BIBLIOGRAPHY
A. P. Appasawmy, *A History of the CMS in Tinnevelly* (Madras, India, 1923)
K. N. Arooran, *Tamil Renaissance and Dravidian Nationalism: 1905–1944* (Madurai, India, 1980)
DIB
DNB
M. E. Gibbs, *The Anglican Church in India: 1600–1970* (Delhi, 1972)
S. Neill, *A History of Christianity in India: 1707–1858* (Cambridge, 1985)

R. E. FRYKENBERG

Calthorpe, Frederick Gough [fourth Baron Calthorpe] (b. London, 14 June 1790; d. Elvetham Park, Hampshire, England, 2 May 1868). MP and peer. Born the fourth son of Henry, first Baron Calthorpe, he entered Christ Church, Oxford in 1808. In 1823 he married Lady Charlotte Sophia Somerset, eldest daughter of the sixth Duke of Beaufort and Lady CHARLOTTE SOPHIA SOMERSET. He was MP for Hindon, Wiltshire (1818–26) and Bramber, Sussex (1826–31) and served as: a Metropolitan Commissioner in lunacy; a councillor of King's College, London; High Sheriff and Deputy-Lieutenant of Staffordshire (1848).

In 1851 he succeeded his brother GEORGE CALTHORPE. He continued the third Baron's work in founding St James's Church, Edgbaston (Birmingham) (1851–2), and opened Calthorpe Park (1857) for the people of Birmingham. In politics was 'a Whig in the Commons, and in the Lords a very moderate Palmerstonian Liberal'. He was succeeded by his eldest son.

BIBLIOGRAPHY
Al. Ox.
Birmingham Collection, BCRL, s.v. Calthorpe, Edgbaston
Boase
Burke's
GM (May 1868): 777–8

D. E. H. MOLE

Calthorpe, George [third Baron Calthorpe] (b. 22 June 1787; d. Lyon, France, 27 Sept. 1851). Anglican aristocrat. Third son of Henry, first Baron Calthorpe and Frances, second daughter of General Benjamin Carpenter, he was admitted fellow-commoner at St John's College, Cambridge in 1804 (MA 1808) and succeeded to the peerage on the death of his brother Charles (1807).

A cousin of Barbara Spooner (wife of WILLIAM WILBERFORCE) and of her brother Archdeacon WILLIAM SPOONER, Calthorpe was a supporter of evangelical societies and was one of the original Simeon Trustees (1817). A moderate in politics, he voted for Catholic emancipation, against the Reform Bill of 1831 (but for it in 1832); he took little part in votes in later life although he inclined towards the Tories. He founded St George's and St James's churches in the parish of Edgbaston (Birmingham), where he was the principal landowner. He died unmarried and was succeeded by his brother, FREDERICK CALTHORPE.

BIBLIOGRAPHY
Al. Cant.
Birmingham Collection, BCRL, s.v. Calthorpe, Edgbaston
Boase
Burke's
GM (May 1868): 777–8

D. E. H. MOLE

Calvert, James (b. Pickering, Yorkshire, England, 3 Jan. 1813; d. Hastings, Sussex, England, 8 March 1892). Wesleyan missionary in Fiji. The son of a farmer, James was initially apprenticed to a printer and bookbinder. He joined the Wesleyan Methodists at the age of 18. Accepted by the British Wesleyan Conference as a candidate for the ministry in 1837, he studied at the Wesleyan Theological Institution at Hoxton and, with his friend JOHN HUNT, was appointed by the Wesleyan Methodist Missionary Society to the new mission field in Fiji. Before leaving England in April 1838 he married Mary Fowler and was ordained at Hackney. In Fiji Calvert was based mainly at Lakeba in the Lau group and at Viwa on Vanua Levu. Through his personal courage he achieved great influence with the chiefs. However, he was unpopular among the white traders of Fiji, who regarded him as a political manipulator. After 17 years in Fiji without a break, the last of the early missionaries, he went to England in 1856 to see DAVID HAZLEWOOD's translation of the Old Testament through the press. His history of the mission, with Thomas Williams's account of the islands and their inhabitants, was published in London in 1858 as *Fiji and the Fijians*. In 1861 he resumed work in Fiji and was chairman of the district until his retirement from the mission in 1865. In response to an appeal for ministers for the diamond fields, he worked in South Africa from 1872 to 1880. In 1886 he revisited Fiji and was delighted to find 'a nation of Methodists' (Rowe, 1893: 268). After the death of Mary (1882) he married the widow of the Reverend Andrew Kessen (1889).

BIBLIOGRAPHY

G. S. Rowe, *James Calvert of Fiji* (London, 1893)
R. Vernon, *James Calvert, or from Dark to Dawn in Fiji* (London, 1890)

DAVID HILLIARD

Cambridge, Alice (b. Bandon, Ireland, 1 Jan. 1762; d. Nenagh, Ireland, 1 Jan. 1829). Female preacher. Although her father belonged to the Church of Ireland and her mother was Presbyterian, it was among the Methodists that she found spiritual comfort following the latter's death in 1780. After her own conversion she turned her attention to the encouragement of others, praying and exhorting at public meetings throughout the country. Although she was excluded from the Methodists by the ban on female preaching imposed by the 1802 Conference, she determined to continue preaching. She held a series of public meetings in Dublin and Cork, and was particularly successful on visits to Ulster where she drew large crowds to the open-air meetings arranged by Presbyterians and Anglicans, as well as the Methodists who re-admitted her as a member in 1811. She is one of the few examples of females preaching to both sexes in early nineteenth-century Ireland.

BIBLIOGRAPHY

C. H. Crookshank, *Memorable Women of Irish Methodism in the Last Century* (London, 1882)
J. J. McGregor, *Memoir of Miss Alice Cambridge* (Dublin, 1832)

MYRTLE HILL

Cameron, Archibald (b. Balnald, Fortingall parish, Perthshire, Scotland, 1778; d. 1843). Independent and later Baptist preacher at Lawers, Perthshire. Cameron, the son of a farmer, John Cameron, was converted in May 1803, at the time of a revival under the leadership of the Independent HALDANE preacher, JOHN FARQUHARSON. He then joined the Independent church at Lawers, and became co-pastor with WILLIAM TULLOCH. He became a Baptist at the same time as Tulloch in 1808, and was his co-pastor at Lawers until Tulloch removed to Renfrew in 1814; thereafter he continued as pastor of the Baptist church at Lawers. He preached extensively in the district, and maintained a meeting at Fortingall.

BIBLIOGRAPHY

D. E. Meek, 'The Independent and Baptist Churches of Highland Perthshire and Strathspey', *Transactions of the Gaelic Society of Inverness*, 56 (1988–90): 269–343
First Yearly Report of the Baptist Union of Scotland (Cupar, Scotland, 1844): 17

DONALD E. MEEK

Cameron, Duncan (b. Lawers district, Perthshire, Scotland, 1801; d. Bruce Co., Ontario, Canada, 1868). Schoolmaster and later Baptist itinerant preacher in Scotland and Canada. Nephew of ARCHIBALD CAMERON, Cameron was exceptionally talented, and his schooling was aided by the benevolence of the Perthshire laird, Stewart of Garth. He was schoolmaster at Lawers from 1826 to 1837. With HALDANE's support, he became pastor of the Baptist church at Lawers, with further responsibility for the churches at Killin and Aberfeldy, in the period 1837–57. Employed formally by the Baptist Home Missionary Society for Scotland, he was active as a preacher in Breadalbane, Glenlyon and Rannoch. In 1857 he emigrated to Breadalbane, Glengarry County, Ontario, where he became pastor of Breadalbane Baptist Church from 1857 to 1860. In 1860 he moved west to Tiverton, Bruce County, becoming assistant to WILLIAM FRASER, and itinerating in Kincardine, Glammis and North Bruce districts from 1863 until his death.

BIBLIOGRAPHY

D. E. Meek, 'The Independent and Baptist Churches of Highland Perthshire and Strathspey', *Transactions of the Gaelic Society of Inverness*, 56 (1989–91): 269–343
Report of the Baptist Home Missionary Society for Scotland (1857): 6–7
Tiverton Baptist Church brochure (1905)
G. Yuille, ed., *History of the Baptists in Scotland* (Glasgow, 1926): 268

DONALD E. MEEK

Cameron, George (Thomas) (b. Shifnal, Shropshire, England, 28 May 1821 (ordination papers); d. High Holden, Kent, England, 23 June 1902). Anglican clergyman. Third son of evangelical parents, Charles Richard Cameron (minister of St George's, Donnington Wood) and Lucy Lyttleton (Butt), authoress (*DNB*; for both, Boase, 1), grandson of Dr George Butt (*DNB*), and related to Julia Cameron, photographer (*DNB*), George studied at Christ Church, Oxford, 1839–43. Ordained at London in 1844, Cameron was Curate of St Peter's, Saffron Hill, 1844–6, then to a family friend, H. B. W. CHURTON, at Icklesham, Sussex. Probably through Churton's influence, Cameron moved (1847) to be Curate-in-charge of St Ebbe's, Oxford, a densely populated, poor parish. Living at 35, Pembroke Street (1851), he appealed for (1852) and built (1853) a rectory. From 1854 to 1860 he was also chaplain of Merton College. He lost his wife in 1856, their child in 1859 (tablet: St Ebbe's). He had given St Ebbe's a settled lead, following a long period of shorter ministries; but his health giving way, he needed lighter work.

After a year as rector at Bonnington, Kent, in 1861 Cameron became Vicar of Heckington, Lincolnshire, where he provided more frequent services and married again. Soon he had to organize rebuilding the nave of his church (1864), where a reredos was erected in 1892 to commemorate his ministry. He also edited a second edition of his mother's *Life* (1873). But he was a diligent pastor, who spent much time supervising his Sunday schools (290 scholars by 1871, though a third of the inhabitants were Nonconformists). Following his second wife's death, he retired (1894) to Kent. Dr C. H. Waller (*DNB*), principal of St John's Hall, Highbury, 1884–98, was his nephew.

Cameron married (1) 1854 (*GM*) Emily Marian Sophia Short (died 1856); (2) 1861 Marion Elizabeth Goe (1836–93), sister of F. F. Goe, Bishop of Melbourne. His portrait and photograph are at Heckington.

SELECT WRITINGS
G. T. Cameron, *Sermon, St Ebbe's* (Oxford, 1856)
— *Farewell Sermon, St Ebbe's* (Oxford, 1860)

BIBLIOGRAPHY
J. S. Reynolds, *Evangelicals at Oxford* (Oxford, 1953; Appleford, England, 1975)
Information from Reverend G. Spencer, Vicar of Heckington; Mrs Sardeson
M. Woods, ed., *Heckington in the Eighteen Seventies* (Sleaford, England, 1975)

J. S. REYNOLDS

Campbell, Alexander (b. near Ballymena, Co. Antrim, Ireland, 12 Sept. 1788; d. Bethany, VA, USA, 1866). Founder of a reform movement out of which evolved the Disciples of Christ and the Churches of Christ. Schooled under his father THOMAS CAMPBELL and at the University of Glasgow (for ten months), Alexander and his family came to western Pennsylvania in 1809 to join his father who had preceded them in 1807. Upon arrival Campbell discovered that his father had just published a manifesto, 'The Declaration and Address', laying down the challenge to reject all human opinions in religion and to take 'the Divine word alone for our rule'. With this goal, father and son left Presbyterianism and formed an independent congregation at Brush Run which was to form the nucleus of a new reform movement.

Between 1813 and about 1830 Campbell's fledgling movement was associated with the Baptists. He edited and largely wrote a journal, *The Christian Baptist* (1823–9), through which his views spread widely. Beginning with his 'sermon on the Law' of 1816, however, controversy with the Baptists steadily mounted until a break occurred. As if to mark the break, Campbell in 1830 began a new journal, *The Millennial Harbinger*; it remained for nearly forty years the leading voice of his Disciples of Christ or Christian Church. After the 1832 union of Campbell's 'Disciples' and the 'Christian' movement led by BARTON W. STONE, the movement grew rapidly so that by 1860 it could claim about 200,000 adherents, making it the fifth largest Protestant body in the United States.

Campbell's fame and influence spread through his success as a debater and polemicist. He engaged in much publicized debates on Christian baptism (with John Walker, 1820; W. L. McCalla, 1823; and N. L. Rice, 1843), Christian evidences (with the sceptic Robert Owen, 1829), and Roman Catholicism (with Bishop John Purcell, 1837), among others. With a great flair for polemics, he took on the 'kingdom of the clergy', Protestant creedalism, the Protestant voluntary associations, and the experimental piety of frontier Calvinism.

Campbell claimed that his reform movement was 'unlike any ever pled in Europe or America since the great Apostasy'. The heart of that uniqueness, he claimed, was the restoration of the 'ancient gospel' and its essential corollary, 'the ancient order of things'. Rediscovery of both rested upon a particular approach to the Bible – what he termed its 'true and rational' reading. Influenced heavily by John Locke and the moderate Scottish Enlightenment, this approach was patterned after the new scientific empiricism with its stress upon the inductive accumulation of 'facts'. Campbell demanded that people confine themselves to the 'plain declarations recorded in the Bible', eschewing all the elaborate vocabulary of traditional theology. By rejecting all theological 'speculation' and all extra-biblical words and confining oneself to bare scriptural 'facts', the Bible would become an open book. In the same way that Baconian science, by confining itself to facts, had brought clarity and harmony to nature, so the 'divine science of religion', following the same method, would bring clarity and harmony to a badly divided Christian religion.

On this basis Campbell set forth the elements of the 'ancient gospel': 'gospel facts [death, burial, resurrection of Christ], faith, repentance, baptism, remission of sins, reception of the Holy Spirit, sanctification, the resurrection, and eternal life'. Though most Christian sects accepted these facts, each one ordered them differently due to its own theory. The 'ancient gospel' was simply the New Testament ordering of these facts. New Testament preaching began with testimony to the gospel facts; this testimony, without any other supernatural agency, produced faith; and faith led a person to 'obey the gospel', that is, to repent of sins and be baptized for remission of sins. Reception of the Spirit then followed. In this way people long distressed by the terrors and uncertainties of the 'anxious seat' could take matters into their own hands – they could believe, obey, and find immediate certainty of forgiveness.

By the 'ancient order of things' Campbell meant the original pattern of church order visible in Acts of the Apostles and the Epistles. This portion of the New Testament provided a precise and uniform code of laws for the church. It stipulated congregational autonomy, weekly observance of the Lord's supper, a plurality of elders and deacons in each congregation, and a simple pattern of worship. Any practice lacking an apostolic command or example was simply an illicit novelty.

Together 'the ancient gospel and order of things' presented an astounding prospect: the collapse of the many warring sects and the union of believers in one great body. If believers would 'purify their speech' and 'abandon every word and sentence not found in the Bible', nothing would be left but the gospel facts and division simply could not exist. As a result, Campbell envisioned the dawning of a millennial age of peace, harmony, and Christian triumph over the world. By the early 1830s, flushed with the rapid growth of his movement, he had little doubt that this millennial march was underway. Even though by the late 1850s – faced with the intransigence of pluralism and the impending Civil War – his hopes had dimmed, Campbell's millennialism stands as one of the most robust and comprehensive postmillennial visions of that age.

Campbell's career exemplified the new Democratic spirit at work in the young American republic. Seeking to make Christian faith of, by, and for the common people, he stressed that each person possessed the right, indeed the duty, to read the Bible for himself or herself without the superintendence of mediating elites. In his primitivist appeals, he vigorously cast off the weight of history and tradition. He caught up the optimistic, utopian hopes of the age in his confidence that Christian unity actually could be achieved. His success resulted, in large part, because he gave people a simple, rational program promising such an achievement.

SELECT WRITINGS
A. Campbell, *The Christian System, in Reference to the Union of Christians, and a Restoration of Primitive Christianity, as Plead in the Current Reformation* (Bethany, WV, 1835)

BIBLIOGRAPHY
DAB
DcAmReB
R. Humbert, ed., *Compendium of Alexander Campbell's Theology* (St Louis, MO, 1961)
Lectures in Honor of the A. Campbell Bicentennial, 1788–1988 (Nashville, TN, 1988)
R. Richardson, *Memoirs of Alexander Campbell*, 2 vols (Cincinnati, OH, 1868, 1870)

C. LEONARD ALLEN

Campbell, Sir **Alexander Thomas Cockburn.** *See* COCKBURN-CAMPBELL, Sir ALEXANDER THOMAS

Campbell, **A(rchibald) H(amilton)** (b. Scotland, *c.* 1819; d. Toronto, Ontario, Canada, *c.* 1885). Prosperous Ontario lumberman and founding life member of the Church Association of the Diocese of Toronto. A. H. Campbell, a recent emigrant from Scotland, bought the largest lumber mill in Upper Canada (now Ontario) at an 1858 Peterborough auction, and acquired 'St Leonard's', an Ashburnham mansion. He moved to Toronto by 1875, partly because of his religious interests. Even before the founding of the Church Association of the Diocese of Toronto in 1873, Campbell led initiatives to make laity more aware of their obligation to support the church financially and to assure clergy of decent salaries. Campbell was on the executive of the Church Association until it was dissolved in 1879 as part of the deal to break a deadlock in the episcopal election. As such he hoped 'members of our Church may be brought once more to rejoice in that simplicity of worship, purity of doctrine, and humble faith in the finished work of Christ, which were marks of the Primitive Church.' (Church Association, *Occasional paper* V, p. 1) He also played a key role in fights against ritualism, and appears to have been a key player in the establishment, in 1876, of St Luke's Church in Ashburnham, partly in protest of planned architectural changes at St John's Church, Peterborough.

BIBLIOGRAPHY
A. Hayes, ed., *By grace co-workers: Building the Anglican diocese of Toronto 1780–1989* (Toronto, Anglican Book Centre, 1989)
E. Jones and B. Dyer, *Peterborough: the electric city* (Burlington, ON, 1987)

ELWOOD HUGH JONES

Campbell, John. *See* BREADALBANE, second Marquess and fifth Earl of

Campbell, John (b. Edinburgh, March 1766; d. London, 4 April 1840). Pastor, philanthropist and director of the LMS. Campbell's parents died when he was very young and he was brought up by a pious uncle in Edinburgh. He attended the Royal High School where he was a classmate of Sir Walter Scott's.

He was profoundly affected by the HALDANE brothers and became one of their assistants, doing a great deal of itinerant preaching in the Highlands. In 1793 he was one of the founders of the RTS of Scotland, which predated the London-based body, and later he helped to found the Magdalene Society of Edinburgh. He began a settled ministry in 1802 when he was called to be minister of Kingsland Chapel in London.

In London he persuaded a number of pious businessmen to fund the bringing of young Africans to Britain for education and began writing popular books for young people which he continued to do into old age.

Except for his years in Africa he also edited a Christian magazine for young people 'The Youth's Magazine'.

An ardent supporter of the LMS he became one of its directors and, in 1812 on the death of VAN DER KEMP, he was sent to South Africa by the society to inspect the work there and report back. Although the Governor, Sir John Craddock had been very critical of the society he appeared to be won over by Campbell and was consistently helpful to him. Campbell undertook a series of journeys to visit outside and inside the colony, everywhere the society was working or had worked. By ox-waggon and on foot he covered 5,000 kilometres. He went north of the Orange River where only a few whites had gone hitherto, to visit the Griqua and Tswana peoples, as well as crossing into what is today Namibia, to visit the Namaqua. He was profoundly impressed by Adam Kok's Griqua and their missionary WILLIAM ANDERSON. Indeed, he was so impressed by this nascent Christian state that on his return to London he had a complete set of decimal coins minted for Kok, the first autonomous currency in southern Africa.

He arrived back in London in May 1814, and immediately began writing *Travels in South Africa* which was published in 1815 and went through three editions in rapid succession. He had hardly settled back into his work at Kingsland Chapel when he was called again by the LMS to go to South Africa, this time with a fellow director of the society, Dr JOHN PHILIP. Philip was to stay on as resident director in South Africa. Campbell's task was again to travel throughout the whole area reviewing the work and the staff. He was then to consult with Philip about the policy to be followed before he returned to report in London.

After his return he published volume 2 of *Travels in South Africa* in 1822. In this volume Campbell included one of the most accurate, hitherto, maps of southern Africa. Although Campbell was never to return to Africa, it stayed with him the rest of his life. In the constant stream of publications, mostly aimed at young people, which he continued to produce despite his duties as pastor at Kingsland, Africa was, more often as not, essential to the story. Perhaps the most famous among the ten substantial works he produced in this period was *African Light Thrown on a Selection of Scripture Texts* (London, 1835).

BIBLIOGRAPHY
R. Philip, *The Life, Times, and Missionary Enterprises of the Rev. John Campbell* (London, 1841)

ANDREW C. ROSS

Campbell, John (b. Kerriemuir, Scotland, 5 Oct. 1794; d. London, 26 March 1867). Congregational journalist and controversialist. Variously described as 'the stormy petrel of Victorian Congregationalism' (Peel) and 'Bombastes, Furioso, Brag and Co.' (Miall) he was, nevertheless Congregationalism's ablest journalist. A blacksmith before undertaking theological studies at both St Andrews and Glasgow, he was ordained at Kilmarnock in 1827, but two years later succeeded MATTHEW WILKS in the joint pastorates of Moorfields Tabernacle and Tottenham Court Road Chapel, London. He soon became a formidable editor of new denominational journals, the *Christian Witness* from 1844, *The Christian's Penny Magazine* from 1846, as well as the privately-owned *British Banner* from 1848, from when he virtually retired from the pastoral ministry.

Through his pen he perceived it to be his duty to ensure the safety of the Ark, warning the denomination not only about the dangers of popery and Puseyism, natural theology and the new thinking coming out of Germany, but also attacking the dissenting use of Gothic architecture, new fashions in church music, novel-reading, Bible-printing monopolies (which reduced their price by two-thirds), Wesleyanism, established churches, lukewarm Nonconformity, and the EA. Not surprising he had already provoked a large number of enemies before he took the major part in attacking T. T. Lynch's collection of hymns entitled *Hymns for Heart and Voice*. Published in 1855, these were represented as being more naturalistic than evangelical. Campbell's stance brought him into conflict with many denominational leaders including THOMAS BINNEY. This led to the Congregational Union, which nearly foundered in the process, severing its ties with Campbell's journals in 1857. He retired in 1865 to write his autobiography and a biography of GEORGE WHITEFIELD but these were never completed.

BIBLIOGRAPHY
DNB
R. Ferguson and A. M. Brown, *Life and Labours of John Campbell, D.D.* (London, 1867)
A. Peel, *These Hundred Years . . . 1831–1931*, (London, 1931): especially 129–142, and 216–235

J. H. Y. BRIGGS

Campbell, John (b. India, 1804). Educational pioneer in Calcutta. Born to a Bengali Christian mother in India, Campbell's father took him to Tain, Scotland to attend the Royal Academy and King's College, Aberdeen. Campbell arrived in Calcutta 11 July 1833, and worked in villages near Krishnapore. From 1834 onwards, he took charge of Kidderpore's LMS English School. This institution had been amalgamated with the Alipore boarding-school and moved to neighbouring Bhowanipore.

Campbell first, introduced a modern, science-based syllabus; second, gave a strong emphasis to Bengali language instruction; and third, integrated classes so as to provide low caste boys with the stimulus of high caste Hindus. Campbell also added a Bengali language theological class for evangelists. His students, unlike those of ALEXANDER DUFF, did not lose their Bengali roots. As a result of Campbell's policies, a self-supporting Bengali church composed of educated Christians who appointed their own pastor sprang up in the 1850s. Campbell almost single-handedly pushed the LMS into changing its education policy.

Mrs Campbell also experimented, creating an effective education system for girls. In 1844 she had to return to Scotland and was granted a pension in recognition of her independent work. John Campbell, found guilty of adultery, had his name removed from the reports of his itineration with A. F. LACROIX. In April 1846 he left Calcutta to start a school in Singapore.

BIBLIOGRAPHY
CWM archives, School of Oriental and African Studies, London, correspondence of the Calcutta District Council
M. A. Laird, *Missionaries and Education in Bengal 1793–1837* (Oxford, 1972)

E. M. JACKSON

Campbell, John McLeod (b. Ardmaddy House, Argyll, Scotland, 4 May 1800; d. Rosneath, Dunbartonshire, Scotland, 27 Feb. 1872). Scottish theologian. Brought up in the manse at Kilninver, Argyll, Campbell's close relationship with his father would be reflected later in his emphasis upon the fatherly love of God. After studying at the universities of Glasgow and Edinburgh, he became minister of Row (or Rhu) in Dunbartonshire in 1825. Campbell formed close friendships with other like-minded churchmen including THOMAS ERSKINE of Linlathen, EDWARD IRVING, and F. D. Maurice. He was deposed from the ministry of the Church of Scotland by the General Assembly in 1831 for teaching that assurance was of the essence of the faith and that the atonement was universal, views considered to be at variance with the Westminster Confession of Faith, the Kirk's subordinate standard. From 1833 until 1859 Campbell ministered to an independent congregation at Blackfriars Street in Glasgow formed by a group of his friends and supporters. In 1856 he produced his major theological work, *The Nature of the Atonement*. His outlook came to be widely accepted within the Scottish church and he was awarded the degree of DD by Glasgow University in 1868.

During his ministry at Row, Campbell thought that his congregation suffered from a serious lack of assurance of salvation. In his view the Calvinist doctrine of predestination led to holiness, truth and love being desired, not for their own sakes, but as evidences of election. Campbell taught that the primary characteristic of God is love rather than justice and that Christ's saving work is an expression, not a precondition, of God's forgiveness. Christ had not come to change the Father's mind but to reveal his true nature. Campbell's concern about assurance led him to believe in the universal scope of the atonement, that Christ died for all people.

In addition Campbell sought to relate the atonement to the incarnation and he spoke of the work of Christ in both a manward and a Godward aspect. Christ not only reveals God to man but also responds on behalf of humanity to God. Campbell was unhappy with a penal view of the atonement and he developed instead a clue

he had found in the writings of JONATHAN EDWARDS, that to atone for sin Christ either had to undergo an equivalent punishment or to express an equivalent sorrow and repentance. Campbell expounded the latter alternative, what has come to be known as his theory of vicarious repentance, that Christ made a perfect confession of sin, saying 'Amen' to the righteous judgement of God. As man Christ knew the full extent of humanity's need of forgiveness and as God he knew the full extent of the Father's mercy. Campbell also emphasized the prospective aspect of the atonement, that Christ offered a life of perfect sonship to the Father, a life of love, trust and prayer, in which the believer can share by the power of the Holy Spirit.

Campbell's linking of the incarnation and the atonement and his exposition of the universal scope of Christ's work was a significant breakthrough in Scottish theology. He helped to bring about the change in the relationship of the Presbyterian churches to the Westminster Confession and stimulated the free presentation of the Gospel to all people.

SELECT WRITINGS
J. M. Campbell, *Christ the Bread of Life* (London, 1851)
—, *The Nature of the Atonement* (Cambridge, 1856); 4th edn (London, 1959)
—, *Thoughts on Revelation* (London, 1862)
Reminiscences and Reflections, ed. D. Campbell (London, 1873)

BIBLIOGRAPHY
D. Campbell, ed., *Memorials of John McLeod Campbell D.D.*, 2 vols (London, 1877)
J. McIntyre, *Prophet of Penitence* (Edinburgh, 1972)
J. Macquarrie, 'John McLeod Campbell 1800–72', *The Expository Times* 83, 9 (1972): 263–8
J. B. Torrance, 'The Contribution of McLeod Campbell to Scottish Theology.' *Scottish Journal of Theology* 26 (1973): 295–311
G. M. Tuttle, *John McLeod Campbell on Christian Atonement* (Edinburgh, 1986)

DOUGLAS M. MURRAY

Campbell, Margaret, Lady **Cockburn** [née Malcolm]. *See* COCKBURN-CAMPBELL, MARGARET, Lady [née Malcolm]

Campbell, Thomas (b. near Newry, County Down, Ireland, 1 Feb. 1763; d. Bethany, VA, USA, 4 Jan. 1854). Presbyterian minister and co-founder of the Disciples of Christ. Son of Archibald Campbell, Thomas was educated at the University of Glasgow and the seminary of the Anti-Burgher branch of the Seceder Presbyterian Church at Whitburn, Scotland. In the years that followed he taught school and preached for Seceder congregations in Ireland. He served as pastor of the church at Ahorey (near Armagh) from 1798 until his migration to America in 1807. In 1798 Campbell and ministers from four denominations, disturbed by the fondness for 'partyism' among Presbyterians and others, formed the ecumenical Evangelical Society of Ulster. Campbells' own

Anti-Burgher church censured his participation and he withdrew. He remained a strong voice for unity in Irish Presbyterianism but his efforts bore little fruit.

Upon settlement in Washington, Pennsylvania, Campbell found the sectarian tensions equally distressing. Charged by his presbytery for indiscriminately administering the sacraments, Campbell eventually withdrew from the Presbyterians and formed in 1809 the Christian Association of Washington. He published a platform for unity, 'The Declaration and Address', that became the founding manifesto of the Disciples movement. Deploring division between Christians as a 'horrid evil', Thomas proclaimed that 'the church of Christ upon earth is essentially, intentionally, and constitutionally one', and that unity could be realized if believers would 'reduce to practice that simple original form of Christianity, expressly exhibited upon the sacred page'. Thomas' leadership soon gave way to his son ALEXANDER CAMPBELL. By 1860 the Campbell movement had become the fifth largest Protestant denomination in America.

BIBLIOGRAPHY

DAB

DCAmReB

A. Campbell, *Memoirs of Elder Thomas Campbell* (Cincinnati, OH, 1861)

L. McAllister, *Thomas Campbell* (St Louis, MO, 1954)

D. Thompson, 'The Irish Background to Thomas Campbell's *Declaration and Address', Journal of the United Reformed Church History Society*, 3/6 (May 1975)

C. LEONARD ALLEN

Campbell, William (b. Port of Menteith, Perthshire, Scotland, 1793; d. Tullichewan, Scotland, 2 Apr. 1864). Merchant and philanthropist. His family assumed the name of Campbell instead of McOran on moving to Glasgow. He was a general merchant with his brother James and their firm of J. and W. Campbell pioneered the system of fixed prices, aiming at small profit and quick turnover. He acquired the estate of Tullichewan near Loch Lomond. Campbell took little part in public life (though his nephew was Sir Henry Campbell-Bannerman, the prime minister) but he supported many religious and philanthropic societies in the west of Scotland. He was one of the young businessmen in Glasgow who came under the influence of THOMAS CHALMERS and became an active supporter of the FCS in 1843. He was a close associate of Sir ANDREW AGNEW in advocating Sunday observance.

BIBLIOGRAPHY

R. H. Campbell, *Memoirs and Portraits of One Hundred Glasgow Men* (Glasgow, 1886)

R. H. CAMPBELL

Campbell, William (b. Old Kirkpatrick, Dumbartonshire, Scotland, 28 May 1799; d. Islington, London, 14 Dec. 1878). Pioneer missionary to India. A church member in Glasgow, Campbell trained at Gosport and sailed (destination Bangalore) in June 1824. He studied Kannada, and established Tamil day schools. Campbell believed in the mission compound system, with schools, orphanages and a Christian village. Brahman opposition to the establishment of Kannada medium schools was fierce; eight families who had sent their children to the schools felt persecution and settled round Campbell's bungalow (for consequences see BENJAMIN RICE). In 1835 Campbell returned to England and resigned from the LMS (1836) to become, in 1841, the pastor of a Congregational church in Croydon.

He wrote an idealized account of his views in a controversial book, *British India in its Relation to the Decline of Hinduism and the Progress of Christianity*. In an enlarged edition (1858) he railed against the British government's educational policy, blaming it for the Mutiny. He argued that more Indian ministers should be trained and quickly given full independence.

E. M. JACKSON

Candlish, John (b. Bellingham, Northumberland, England, 1816; d. Cannes, France, 17 March 1874). English Baptist manufacturer, newspaperman, and MP. The son of a Scottish smallholder, he was apprenticed to a Sunderland draper and himself traded as such 1836–41. In fact the model of his biography was very much that of the Victorian self-help hero who through diligence and hard work raised himself to both wealth and influence. In 1842 he became joint-proprietor of the Tory *The Sunderland Beacon*, and in 1843 set up as a coal merchant, soon adding to this the secretaryship of the Sunderland Gas Company. The Free Trade agitation converted him from conservatism to radicalism.

In 1844, he entered on one of the two major business activities of his life in starting as a shipbuilder. To this he added the manufacture of glass bottles; by 1853 his bottle works at Seaham Harbour was reckoned the largest in Europe. So great was the confidence of the work force in his management that in a financial crisis in 1864 they offered to continue to work without wages.

From 1848 until his death he sat continuously on the town council, energetically attacking venerable abuses and promoting schemes of municipal improvement. He was twice mayor and later an alderman. He was also chairman of the Board of Guardians, a magistrate, a commissioner of the River Wear, and a deputy-lieutenant of the county. In 1851 he founded the *Sunderland News*. He contested Sunderland unsuccessfully in the Liberal interest in 1865, but sat for the borough from 1866 to 1873. His speeches in the House of Commons, where he was conspicuous for his diligent attendance, were in favour of greater economy in public expenditure and the removal of all hindrances to shipping. He showed himself a 'Liberal of the advanced kind', successfully extending the 1867 Reform legislation from houses to parts of houses, opposing the Contagious Diseases

Acts, and, against his party, opposing the opening up of the Lord Lieutenancy in Ireland to Roman Catholics.

Brought up in the evangelical section of the Church of Scotland he early became a member of Sans Street Baptist Church, Sunderland, where he showed himself strong on the doctrines of grace, with 'a firm and appreciative grasp of the broad aspects of the Evangelical system'. He disliked academic sermons, preferring them to be 'full of Christ', emphasizing that the Gospel was not a theme for speculation but rather good tidings of salvation. Though for a time excluded from the church at a time of pastoral dissension under a weak minister, he was later re-admitted. His personal discipline was conspicuous and his endeavours to be in his pew on a Sunday, notwithstanding absences in London and abroad, set a good example. His philanthropy was never broadcast but involved support of the orphans homes, the reformatory and the ragged schools. A painful illness led him to seek recuperation in Cannes where he died at the early age of 57; his own desire for a private funeral was countermanded, his funeral necessarily becoming a public occasion.

BIBLIOGRAPHY
BaptMag (May 1874)
Boase
Stenton

J. H. Y. BRIGGS

Candlish, Robert Smith (b. Edinburgh, 23 March 1806; d. Edinburgh, 23 Oct. 1873). Prominent FCS minister. Due to considerable family poverty and poor health, his early education was fragmentary. However, in 1818 Candlish entered Glasgow University and, having graduated MA with distinction, entered the Divinity Hall in 1823. After a short time in Eton as tutor, he was licensed by the Glasgow presbytery in 1828 and, in the following year, commenced the first of two brief assistantships. His undoubted gifts attracted the attention of the prominent congregation at St George's Church, Edinburgh and, following a further brief assistantship there, he was inducted as minister in 1834. The congregation, already strong, expanded rapidly and his proposal for church extension resulted in the establishment of St Luke's Church in 1837.

In 1840, widespread recognition of his attainments as a preacher and theologian led to his nomination for the chair of biblical criticism in Edinburgh University. Hugh Millar questioned whether 'in Britain or in the world an individual could be found better qualified for a chair of biblical criticism than the minister of St George's' (Wilson, 1880: 129). He was, however, rejected by the House of Lords on the grounds that he was a 'law-breaker'. This accusation referred to his refusal to heed an interdict from the Court of Session, issued during the period prior to the Disruption between the church and the state in 1843, forbidding ministers to preach in Strathbogie.

It was the massive contribution made by his pamphlets and speeches to the success of the Disruption movement which earned his first doctorate from Princeton Seminary in 1841. (He was to receive a second from Edinburgh University in 1864.) Following the death of THOMAS CHALMERS in 1847, he was appointed junior professor of theology in New College. However, the sudden death of his designated successor in St George's prompted him to reconsider his own appointment with the result that he resigned from the post in 1848 to resume his former pastoral office. In 1862, he was appointed principal of New College and he continued as principal and pastor until his death.

Candlish is perhaps best remembered as a preacher. In this capacity, his biographer claims that he came to be recognized as 'second to none in the Church of Scotland' (Wilson, 1880: 130). Several volumes of sermons were published, some of them posthumously, and many of them – particularly his expositions of Genesis and First John – are still read today.

His contribution to the foundation and subsequent growth of the FCS is generally considered to be second only to that of Chalmers. Throughout the ten year period prior to the Disruption, he played an active, persuasive role in the General Assembly to secure church independence. In 1839, he went to London as one of a deputation to discuss these issues with MPs. He toured extensively in Scotland and England in order to popularize disruption principles. The remarkable success of the church's education scheme, which saw the FCS supporting over 500 schools within five years of its formation, was due in great measure to his energy and organizational ability.

Candlish also figured prominently in the first Union Controversy, 1863–73, the first part of a controversy which was ultimately to issue in the secession of the vast majority of the FCS into a new union with the United Presbyterian Church (UPC) in 1900, known as the United Free Church of Scotland. Candlish favoured this union. He did not consider either the adherence of the FCS to the Establishment Principle or the adherence of the UPC to the double-reference theory of the atonement to be insuperable barriers to the proposed union because he did not believe the former necessarily propounded nor the latter explicitly condemned by Westminster Confession of Faith.

SELECT WRITINGS
J. Candlish, *Contributions Towards the Exposition of the Book of Genesis* (Edinburgh, 1842)
—, *Fatherhood of God* (Edinburgh, 1865)
—, *The First Epistle of John* (Edinburgh, 1866)

BIBLIOGRAPHY
A. Beith, *A Highland Tour with Dr Candlish* (Edinburgh, 1874)
DNB
W. Wilson, *Memorials of R.S. Candlish D.D.* (Edinburgh, 1880)

KENNETH STEWART

Canfield, Eli Hawley (b. Arlington, VT, USA, 8 June 1817; d. Arlington, VT, USA, 3 June 1898). Episcopal minister. Descendant of the founders of the first Episcopal parish in Vermont, he was educated in the district schools of his native state and briefly taught school in Bristol, Pennsylvania. In 1844 he graduated from the Virginia Seminary in Alexandria and was ordained, becoming rector of St Peter's church, Delaware City, Ohio. In 1849 he was called to the rectorship of Christ Church, Brooklyn, New York, where he exercised a notable evangelical ministry of twenty years. However, his promotion of pulpit interchange with non-episcopal ministers was reproved by the Bishop of New York. He afterward located in North Adams, Massachusetts, and then spent the last 25 years of his life in Vermont.

BIBLIOGRAPHY
H. Carleton, ed., *Genealogical and Family History of State of Vermont* (New York, 1903)

CHARLES R. HENERY

Capadose [also **Capadoce**], **Abraham** (b. Amsterdam, 22 Aug. 1795; d. Den Haag, The Netherlands, 16 Dec. 1874). Scientist. His parents were Portugese Jews who immigrated to The Netherlands. Capadose studied medicine at Leiden where he was heavily influenced by Willem Bilderdijk. After reading the Bible with his friend ISAAC DA COSTA, they converted to Christianity and on 22 October 1822 they and Da Costa's wife were baptized. Capadose quickly entered the lists for conservative religious causes. In 1823 he published a treatise against vaccination, using Luke 5: 31 to argue against the practice. Capadose was instrumental in blocking H. Brasz's ordination as elder in the Reformed Church, arguing in a pamphlet that he was a heretic (1825). His militant attacks, supported by a minimum of evidence, caused deep rifts in the *Réveil* movement.

In 1829 he married Jeanne van der Hoeven. The couple moved to The Hague in 1833 where Capadose was offended by the use of music in worship, against which he wrote the pamphlet, *Ontheiliging van het Huis Gods* (The Hague, 1833). The same year he wrote the first volume of the study of the divinity of Christ, *De goddeklijkheid van Christus* (Den Haag, 1833–43). A tour of *Réveil* sites in Switzerland resulted in the publication of an extensive correspondence with Swiss reveil leaders published as *Conversion du Dr A. Capadoce* (Neuchatel, 1837). His wife died in Switzerland in 1837.

In 1839, Capadose married Hendrick Jacoba Abrahams. He became very active in Christian missions to the Jews. He founded (1853) the Nederlandsche Vereeniging voor het Uitsenden van Zendelingen (Dutch Association for the Sending of Missionaries). Intensely interested in ecumenical and revivalist activities, he was a major influence in the Dutch branch of the EA. A committed member of the Dutch Abolitionist Society, he worked diligently also for slavery's abolition. Capadose is perhaps best remembered for his stand against vaccination, a struggle which he continued up to his death with a series of pamphlets criticizing the practice.

BIBLIOGRAPHY
'Capadoce, Dr Abraham', *Nieuw Nederlandsch Biographisch Woordenboek*, 6 (1933): 266–268
J. L. van Essen, 'De Betrekkingen tussen Willem Bilderdijk en Abraham Capadose', *Lucerne; Gereformeerd Interfacultair Tijdskrigt*, 5 (1969): 270–88
M. E. Kluit, *Het Reveil in Nederland, 1815–1865 en Daarbuiten* (Amsterdam, 1970)
R. Kuiper, *Zelfbeeld en Wereldbeeld* (Kampen, Netherlands, 1992)
G. J. tenZythoff, *Sources of Secession* (Grand Rapids, MI, 1987)

DAVID BUNDY

Capers, William (b. St Thomas's Parish, SC, USA, 26 Jan. 1790; d. Anderson Court House, SC, USA, 29 Jan. 1855). Missionary to slaves and bishop of the MEC,So. Capers was born outside Charleston, South Carolina, to the Methodist slaveholder William Capers and Mary Singletary Capers. He encountered some difficulty in finding and following a calling: he entered, left and re-entered South Carolina College, then he set about the study of law. In 1808, a profound series of religious experiences gave new direction to his life. Soon licensed as a Methodist preacher, Capers travelled with William Gassaway before taking on his own circuits and then locations in South Carolina, North Carolina, and Georgia. In addition to being elevated to deacon and elder, Capers filled a number of roles in the MEC, including missionary to the Creek Indians (1821–23), editor of the *Wesleyan Journal* (1825–7) and the *Southern Christian Advocate* (1836–45), official representative messenger to English Methodists (1828), professor at South Carolina College (1835), delegate to General Conferences (1820, 1824 and 1832–44) and secretary of the Southern Missionary Department of the Methodist Church (1840–4). His most significant work though, devolved upon him because of his southern identity and his interest in religion among slaves.

In 1829, Charles Cotesworth Pinckney, on behalf of several plantation owners, requested the services of an exhorter or preacher to oversee the religious instruction of their slaves. The South Carolina Conference appointed three preachers and placed Capers in a supervisory position over the 'missions to the slaves' in South Carolina. Capers organized the missions into circuits and also developed a special catechism for use with slaves. Capers's concern for the spiritual welfare of black southerners was clear; his understanding that religious teaching would only be possible if the lessons were carefully tailored to please the masters was equally clear. His slave catechism, for example, emphasized the virtues of humility and obedience – not the liberating words of Jesus. Building upon this compromise, Capers exercised a powerful influence in extending religious teaching to slaves.

Capers's other major public role also grew out of his association with the South and with slavery. Chosen in 1840 to prepare an address to British Methodists about the American Church and slavery, Capers took a position as spokesman on that subject just as it began to tear through American Methodism. Thus Capers came to the General Conference of 1844 prepared – and expected – to speak for the South and to confront the question of whether northern and southern Methodists could find common ground. Capers understood, as did other Methodists, that the immediate question was whether Bishop JAMES O. ANDREW could remain a Methodist bishop when he had married into ownership of slaves. For Capers and others, Andrew's case symbolized larger issues, including especially the acceptability of the institution of slavery but also the extent of episcopal power. Capers also associated his defence of Bishop Andrew with his defence of his missions to the slaves. Although Capers claimed to be working for a peaceful resolution of the differences between North and South, there was little room for compromise. Capers moved from the committee for 'pacification' in the Church to a southern 'Committee on Division'. Soon after the creation of the Methodist Episcopal Church, South, Capers became a bishop. From that position, he continued the work with which he had become so closely identified. He put forth a plan for 'Evangelizing the People of Color'. He spoke for religious worship of both races together; he deprecated both the 'sort of Negro religion' and the 'insipid' white religion that would result from separating the races.

Capers found no other major role to play within or beyond the episcopacy. Identified to the end with biracial religious community and with evangelizing slaves, he died of heart disease in 1855.

BIBLIOGRAPHY
DAB
D. A. Reily, 'William Capers: An Evaluation of His Life and Thought' (Emory Univ. Ph.D. thesis, 1972)
W. M. Wightman, Life of William Capers (Nashville, TN, 1858)

RUTH ALDEN DOAN

Capper, Joseph (b. c. 1778, Nantwich, Cheshire, England; d. 10 Jan. 1860, Tunstall, Staffordshire, England). Primitive Methodist Chartist. Capper's fame derives from his political activity during the reform and Chartist agitation in the Potteries of the 1830s and 1840s, where he worked as a blacksmith. Supposedly converted to Primitive Methodism at the first camp meeting at Mow Cop in 1807, it is not in fact known whether Capper was a member of the Primitive Methodist society, or whether he was expelled for his troubles. Tradition has it that he became a local preacher, travelling huge distances on Sundays and weekday evenings, preaching the Gospel, teaching morality and temperance, as well as commenting with his 'sledgehammer'-like tongue, on factory conditions and the hypocrisy of institutional religion – his venom for the Established Church being increased by his failure to receive payment for work done on a Tunstall church spire. Encouraged to speak at numerous Chartist rallies, Capper soon became a notable figure in the agitation, although with his shop in the Market Place of Tunstall serving as a focus of community, he was already one of the most prominent figures in the town. He was arrested in August 1842, following disturbances in Hanley after one of the meetings he was asked to address. Charged with sedition and conspiracy, the aged Capper was imprisoned for two years in Stafford Gaol. He returned to Tunstall broken in spirit and health.

Capper has enjoyed generous historical mileage. Many labour historians have portrayed him as being representative of a Primitive Methodist local preacher, thus imposing an excessive political radicalism upon early Primitive Methodism. But Joseph Capper's beliefs were different from the bulk of Primitive Methodists. His was a muscular-social Christianity, an extension of his belief into society. Like other Primitive Methodists, the Bible had provided his only learning, and Capper's daily speech contained the symbolic force of Scripture, but as the chronicler, Henry Wedgwood comments, to Capper the Bible 'spoke different lessons than are taught in our churches. To him it told of all men being equal, without distinction of class, of aristocracy, or of princes'. With his beliefs, infused with political sentiment, Capper sought to apply his Christian beliefs to the 'world', to attempt to create God's kingdom 'on earth, as it is in heaven'. Capper, however, was too impatient to wait for either divine intervention or the benevolence of the rich, whichever came first.

BIBLIOGRAPHY
J. Epstein and D. Thompson, The Chartist Experience (London, 1982)
W. Payne, Stafford Goal and its Associations (London, 1887)
C. Shaw, When I was a Child (London, 1903)
H. Wedgwood, People of the Potteries (Bath, England, 1970 reprint)

WAYNE J. JOHNSON

Cardale, John Bate (b. London, 7 Nov. 1802; d. Albury, Surrey, England, 18 July 1877). Solicitor and Irvingite apostle. Educated at Rugby, he was the son of a wealthy solicitor, William Cardale (1777–1826) to whom he was articled in 1818 becoming head of the practice on his father's death. He went to observe the glossolalia in Scotland in 1830 and returned convinced of their reality, the more so when his wife began to prophesy in 1831. When his own minister, BAPTIST NOEL, preached against the gifts he joined the congregation of EDWARD IRVING whom he assisted in his defence against charges of heresy before the London presbytery in 1832. After an utterance by HENRY DRUMMOND, Cardale was recognized as the first of the restored apostolate. He probably saw most clearly the insufficiency of prophetic utterance as a basis for stable church order and was influential in the re-organization of the community in 1835 and the drafting of the liturgy in 1842. A gifted administrator and writer he was tireless in visiting the scattered congregations of the community. The title 'Pillar of the Apostles' was not given to him inappropriately.

BIBLIOGRAPHY
Boase
R. A. Davenport, *Albury Apostles* (London, 1974): 36–9
DNB
J. Lancaster, 'John Bate Cardale, Pillar of Apostles' (thesis, St Andrews University, 1978)
D. J. Tierney, 'The Catholic Apostolic Church: a study in Tory Millenarianism' *HR* 63 (1990): 289–316

TIMOTHY C. F. STUNT

Carey, Charlotte Emilia [née Rumohr] (b. Denmark, 1761; d. Serampore, India, 30 May 1821). Second wife of WILLIAM CAREY. A lifelong invalid, this diminutive, aristocratic lady travelled to India for her health's sake in 1800. In Serampore, Carey taught her English and led her to Christ; he baptized her in June 1802. They married in May 1808, six months after his first wife died, in spite of opposition from his colleagues.

Charlotte committed herself wholeheartedly to supporting activities of the Serampore Mission. Carey prized her knowledge of European languages, her serenity, and active mind. Their 13 years of marriage were a source of great comfort to him, after his tragic domestic circumstances between 1793 and 1807. This effectively anchored 'the father of the Serampore mission' to the 12-mile stretch of river between the Danish settlement of Serampore and the growing cosmopolitan capital of British Calcutta. The *modus vivendi* of his most productive years in India can be credited to her influence. This contrasted greatly with his spartan life in England and Bengal during the 1780s and 1790s.

BIBLIOGRAPHY
S. P. Carey, *William Carey D.D.* (London, 1923): 274–5
G. Smith, *The Life of William Carey, D.D.* (London, 1885): 181–4

A. CHRISTOPHER SMITH

Carey, Dorothy [née Plackett] (b. Northamptonshire, England, 1755; d. Serampore, India, 8 Dec. 1807). First wife of WILLIAM CAREY. Born in England's rustic Midlands, her Puritan father was a leading Dissenter in the village of Hackleton. Carey, a shoemaker's apprentice to her brother-in-law, married her in 1781, several years before he became a Baptist.

During the first twenty years of their marriage, when Carey was a cobbler, a journeyman shoemaker, a lay preacher, a Baptist pastor, and supervisor of an indigo-works in Bengal, she brought up seven children mostly in precarious, poverty-stricken circumstances. The illiterate country lass was unprepared for pioneer mission work in India. Three of her infants died by 1794. Massive 'culture shock' overwhelmed her and she became mentally deranged. From 1800, in Serampore, she was locked up in a bedroom for the sake of safety. This tragic development bore down heavily on Carey's heart and mind. As a result, he was very much disinclined to accept personal praise for anything he achieved on the mission field.

BIBLIOGRAPHY
J. R. Beck, *Dorothy Carey, The Tragic Untold Story of Mrs William Carey* (Grand Rapids, MI, 1992)

A. CHRISTOPHER SMITH

Carey, Eustace (b. Paulerspury, Northamptonshire, England, 22 March 1791; d. London, 19 July 1855). Baptist missionary. Nephew of WILLIAM CAREY, Eustace was the third son of Thomas and Mary Carey. He was baptized by JOHN RYLAND, Jr, in Northampton on 7 July 1809. Later that year he began theological studies in JOHN SUTCLIFF's Academy at Olney. In 1812 he entered Bristol Baptist Academy to prepare for service with the BMS in Bengal. He married Mary Fosbrook of Leicester on 9 December 1813. They sailed for India in February 1814. After a period of language study with his uncle at Serampore, Carey became joint pastor of the Lal Bazaar church in Calcutta, employing his gifts as a preacher in Bengali in work among the indigenous population.

After 1815 relations between the 'junior brethren' of the BMS in Calcutta and the Serampore Trio deteriorated as the former imbibed the suspicion with which the BMS home committee now viewed the Serampore missionaries. As a result, Carey and his Calcutta colleagues formed a separate missionary union at Calcutta, and in 1818 withdrew from the Lal Bazaar church to found a new church on the Circular Road. For the remainder of his missionary career, Carey's relationship with his uncle was strained by the 'Serampore controversy'.

In 1824 ill health forced Carey to leave Bengal. In his later years he served the BMS in Britain as a full-time deputation agent. At the invitation of the BMS, he wrote the first biography of William Carey, published in 1836.

BIBLIOGRAPHY
Mrs E. Carey, *Eustace Carey* (London, 1857)
DNB

BRIAN STANLEY

Carey, Felix (b. Moulton, Northamptonshire, England, 1786; d. Serampore, India, 10 Nov. 1822). Baptist missionary and Orientalist. The eldest son of WILLIAM CAREY, Felix accompanied his parents to India in 1793. He was baptized by his father at Serampore in 1800 and, under the tutelage of WILLIAM WARD, developed into a brilliant Bengali scholar. He studied medicine at the Calcutta General Hospital in order to minister to the needs of the Serampore missionaries, but in 1807 was sent with JAMES CHATER to establish mission work in Burma. Felix employed his medical knowledge to introduce smallpox vaccination in Burma, and wrote a Bengali textbook on anatomy and physiology, *Vidyahara Vali*, which was intended to be the first volume of a Bengali encyclopedia. He was responsible for translating various English literary and historical works into Bengali, published a Burmese grammar, and compiled a Burmese dictionary, which was published in 1826.

An unstable personality, he had a disappointing missionary career, although the work in Burma survived to be taken over by ADONIRAM JUDSON. In December 1814 Carey left Burma to become ambassador from the King of Burma to the East India Company in Calcutta. There his grandiose lifestyle was a cause of pain to his father. After seven months he was re-called in disgrace from his post, and spent some years in Assam. In 1818 he returned to Bengal, and assisted his father in the Serampore biblical translations. He died of cholera.

BIBLIOGRAPHY

F. A. Cox, *History of the Baptist Missionary Society from 1792 to 1842*, 2 vols, 1 (London, 1842): 167–8, 179, 183–4, 193–4, 201–2, 242
DNB
E. D. Potts, *British Baptist Missionaries in India 1793–1837* (Cambridge, 1967): 65–6, 98, 198

BRIAN STANLEY

Carey, Jabez (b. Hackleton, England, May 1793). Baptist missionary, third son of WILLIAM CAREY. Previously hostile towards religion, in 1812 he was baptized, married, and ordained (in three days). Trained as a lawyer, Carey responded to Lord Hastings's call for teachers in Amboyna. He organized schools on the island and by 1815 had enrolled 303 scholars and visited many of the former Dutch colony's islands. By 1815 he was preaching in Malay and translating Watts's Catechism into Malay. He left when the colony was returned to the Dutch in 1817, deciding a permanent BMS station there was impractical.

From January 1819 to 1837, after studying at the Benevolent Institution in Calcutta, Carey organized a 'Lancastrian school' in Ajmeer, Rajastan, as part of an imperial programme for 'civilising the predatory hordes'. The government objected to his use of assigned scripture reading, even though there was little other literature available. WILLIAM CAREY advised him to find alternate means to introduce Christianity. In 1837 Carey returned to Calcutta to work as a sessions judge.

BIBLIOGRAPHY

Periodical Accounts relative to the Baptist Missionary Society (Bristol, England, 1817): vols xxx January–June 1815; vols xxxi–xxxii, June 1816. vol. xxxiii [which begins September 1817 – there is a gap in the record]
Review of the Mission (Serampore, India, 1817)
J. C. Marshman *The Life and Times of Carey, Marshman and Ward* II (London, 1859): 263 f

E. M. JACKSON

Carey, Jonathan (b. Mudnabatty, Bengal, India, Nov. 1796; d. Calcutta, India). Baptist attorney. The youngest son of WILLIAM CAREY, Jonathan spoke Bengali from infancy and studied Chinese with JOSHUA and JOHN CLARK MARSHMAN. He rejected a career as a missionary and, in 1814, chose the legal profession. Given a £600 loan by the Serampore Mission to buy a practice, during the 1820s 'Serampore Controversy' this loan provoked much controversy, even though he repaid it. After becoming an attorney at the Calcutta Supreme Court, he married the daughter of the late Reverend SAMUEL PEARCE of Cannon Street Chapel, Birmingham (WILLIAM WARD's friend). During the 1830s and 1840s he represented the Calcutta Baptists and the LMS district council in several legal disputes. He became a respected member of the Lower Circular Road Baptist Church.

E. M. JACKSON

Carey, Mary (b. Paulerspury, Northamptonshire, England, 1765; d. 1839). Baptist supporter of mission. Mary grew up in Northamptonshire and at 19 was baptized in the River Tove by Thomas Skinner of Towcester. At 24, she became speechless and paralyzed except for the use of one limb. She lived with Ann and William Hobson, her elder sister and brother-in-law. Despite her disability, Mary corresponded with her more famous brother, WILLIAM CAREY. Her letters provided encouragement, inspiration, news of home and theological reflection. By maintaining a strong link to Great Britain, Mary helped the BMS develop a home base, prompting her pastor, F. W. Gotch of Kettering, to observe, 'Her work in her affliction, in its way, was as great as that which her great brother wrought'.

BIBLIOGRAPHY

E. Carey, *Memoir of William Carey* (London, 1837)
J. N. Harding, 'Mary Carey' in A. S. Clement, ed., *Great Baptist Women* (London, 1955)
BMS archives, manuscript collection, Carey Collection

PAUL R. DEKAR

Carey, William (b. Paulers Pury, Northamptonshire, England, 17 Aug. 1761; d. Serampore, India, 9 June 1834). BMS missionary in India. Son of a handloom weaver and sometime schoolmaster, at 14 William was apprenticed to a shoemaker. His contacts and study of the Bible and other religious writings during this time decided him to become a Baptist, one with a strong missionary, evangelistic bent. First serving as pastor of a small church in Moulton, he soon moved to Leicester where, in 1792, he finished writing and published one of the best known missionary calls of all time: *An Enquiry into the Obligations of Christians to use means for the conversion of the Heathens* .... With the aid of ANDREW FULLER, later in the same year William constrained 13 colleagues to found at Kettering the BMS – the Particular Baptist Society for Propagating the Gospel Among the Heathen – thus beginning the modern era of Protestant missionary work.

Accompanied by his wife (DOROTHY CAREY) and children and JOHN THOMAS, William sailed for Calcutta on 13 June 1793. After some months familiarizing himself with the people and country, he set up as an indigo planter near Malda in Northern Bengal where he began translating the New Testament into Bengali. In 1799 JOSHUA MARSHMAN and WILLIAM WARD left England for India to join William in his work, but were forced by a hostile East India Company government to settle instead in the small Danish colony of Serampore (Frederiksnagar), north of Calcutta. Early in the new year William joined them, and so began the mission which in a short time earned praise from almost the whole evangelical Christian world.

William excelled in languages. His linguistic skills – which had led him, even before leaving England, to acquire some grasp of Latin, Greek, Hebrew, Italian, French, and Dutch – soon won him a government appointment to teach Bengali and shortly afterwards, Sanskrit and Marathi at the newly founded College of Fort William. He therefore had easy access to the pandits at the college and their assistance, in turn, made it possible for him, to translate the entire Bible into Bengali, Oriya, Marathi, Hindi, Assamese, and Sanskrit and parts of it into 24 other languages. In addition, during his 40 years in India William wrote, again with the assistance of learned Indian pandits, grammars in Bengali, Sanskrit, Marathi, Panjabi, Telugu, and Kanarese as well as editing, with J. C. MARSHMAN, a grammar in Bhotia and compiling dictionaries in Bengali, Sanskrit, and Marathi. His enthusiasm for Indian languages was manifest in his success in encouraging others, Indian and European, to write books in Bengali and to translate various Indian works into English. He himself translated part of the Hindu epic Ramayana. Such efforts led authorities on Indian literature to call him a father of modern Bengali.

William also became a staunch advocate of social reform. He urged the government to outlaw such practices as infanticide and sati and, appropriately, in late 1829 as the government's official translator he was the one who translated into Bengali the edict banning sati.

In addition, William's scientific work won him merit. He established an outstanding botanical garden at Serampore, identified several new Indian plants (beginning with Carea Saulea in 1796), advocated in published articles the conservation of forests, and founded (1820) the Agricultural Society of India. His contribution in editing and publishing William Roxburgh's Hortus Bengalensis and Flora Indica has been widely acknowledged. Having already been awarded an honourary doctorate from Brown University, in 1823 William was elected a fellow of the prestigious Linnaean Society in London and a member of both the London Horticultural and the Geological societies.

Being the best known member of the partnership often referred to as the 'Serampore Trio', sometimes William is wrongly credited with the achievements of Marshman and Ward. That he was able to devote so much time to his own very fine accomplishments was made possible by his good fortune in having senior colleagues equally as capable and hardworking. On his long stays in Calcutta he could be assured that the multiplicity of mission activities flourished in the hands of Marshman (and his wife HANNAH MARSHMAN) and Ward.

His personal success in achieving the objective of his Enquiry is hard to measure. A younger colleague JOHN MACK, in his published funeral sermon for Carey declared that while he had never heard of an Indian converted to Christianity by William's own activities in preaching and evangelizing, his work in other fields, especially his translations, 'was instrumental in the conversion of many'.

The most important group of Carey manuscripts is in the BMS Collection now held by the Angus Library, Regent's Park College, Oxford, including his correspondence with the BMS and others, and a journal (13 June 1793 to 2 October 1794).

BIBLIOGRAPHY
S. P. Carey, William Carey, 8th edn (London, 1934)
E. D. Potts, British Baptist Missionaries in India 1793–1837 (Cambridge, 1967)

E. DANIEL POTTS

Carey, William [Jr] (b. Moulton, Northamptonshire, England, 22 June 1787; d. India, 1852). Missionary and second surviving son of WILLIAM CAREY. WILLIAM WARD arrived in Serampore to find William Carey, Jr, and his older brother FELIX CAREY swearing, playing with the servants and visiting brothels. Ward brought him to repentance, persuaded him to attend school, and saw to his training as a printer. JOSHUA MARSHMAN delayed Carey's baptism until 1803, on the grounds that he knew too little theology.

Carey worked as an assistant to IGNATIUS FERNANDEZ at Dinadjpur and then at Sadamahal, made an arduous exploratory journey to Bhutan with WILLIAM ROBINSON, and then was ordained in Serampore, 22 August 1808. On 1 August 1808 he married Mary Kincey (baptized 16 September 1809), daughter of Mrs Gunn of the Free School, Calcutta, and a relative by marriage of DANIEL CORRIE. Mary was the sister of Felix Carey's first wife Margaret. They moved to Cutwa (Katwa) to rebuild JOHN CHAMBERLAIN's mission, and quietly increased its influence. With his father's help, William Jr introduced potatoes, coffee, and cotton into the area. Mary Carey became devoted to CHARLOTTE CAREY (née Ruhmohr), and worked on girls' educational projects. She is buried with her parents-in-law in Serampore (died 16 September 1859).

BIBLIOGRAPHY
BMS Archives, London, Ward's Journal

E. M. JACKSON

Cargill, David (b. Brechin, Angus, Scotland, 20 June 1809; d. Vavau, Tonga, 25 April 1843). Wesleyan missionary in Fiji. Born into a Presbyterian family, the son of a banker, he graduated MA in classics from the University of Aberdeen. While a student he joined the Wesleyan Methodists. In 1832 he was accepted for the

Wesleyan ministry and, having offered to the WMMS for missionary service, was appointed to the South Pacific. In September 1832, before leaving England, he married Margaret Smith in Aberdeen. After a year in Tonga, in 1835 Cargill was assigned with WILLIAM CROSS to found a Wesleyan mission in Fiji. As the only trained linguist in the mission, he devised an orthography of the Fijian language and wrote its first grammar and dictionary. After the death of Margaret in Fiji in 1840 he revisited England and in November 1841 married Augusta Bicknell. Many of Cargill's fellow missionaries found him difficult to work with and they were critical of his heavy drinking of spirits. He died of an overdose of laudanum.

SELECTED WRITINGS
D. Cargill, *Memoirs of Mrs Margaret Cargill* (London, 1841)
—, *The Diaries and Correspondence of David Cargill, 1832–1843*, ed. A. J. Schutz (Canberra, 1977)

BIBLIOGRAPHY
M. Dickson, *The Inseparable Grief* (London, 1976)

DAVID HILLIARD

Cargill, William (b. Edinburgh, 28 Aug. 1784; d. Dunedin, New Zealand, 6 Aug. 1860). Merchant and pioneer in New Zealand. Cargill served in the Napoleonic wars rising to the rank of Captain. With George Rennie and THOMAS BURNS he promoted a Scottish settlement in New Zealand. In March 1848 he arrived in Otago. He led the early settlement, becoming first provincial superintendent 1853–60, and MP for Dunedin Country 1855–60. Autocratic and opposed to those outside the Free Church, he gave significant but conservative leadership under difficult circumstances.

BIBLIOGRAPHY
T. Brooking, *And Captain of their Souls* (Dunedin, New Zealand, 1984)
DNZB

ALLAN K. DAVIDSON

Caries, Zacharias George (b. Schleswig, Denmark (now in Germany) 28 Feb. 1717; d. Dublin, 28 Dec. 1772). Moravian minister and missionary to Jamaica. Caries arrived in England in 1749 and worked with the Moravian Church in Ireland and Wiltshire. The brothers William Foster and Joseph Foster-Barham had invited JOHN CENNICK to work among the slaves on their estates in Jamaica. When Cennick declined, they asked that Caries might be assigned to the task. He was ordained a deacon and sailed for Jamaica with Thomas Shallcross and Gottlieb Haberecht, 4 October 1754, arriving on 9 December.

Although contact with the slaves was very limited, by 1756 there were 77 baptized Christians and 400 receiving instruction. Differences of opinion on missionary method with CHRISTIAN HEINRICH RAUCH who came to join Caries in 1756 caused Caries to return to Ireland in 1759. He continued to work among the young men and as a preaching assistant in a number of British Moravian churches until he died in Dublin, 1772. Although Caries's ministry in Jamaica was short he was the pioneer of Christian mission to the slaves there.

BIBLIOGRAPHY
J. Hastings and B. MacLeary, *Seedtime and Harvest* (Jamaica, 1979)

FRED LINYARD

Carlile, Ann Jane (b. Ruskey, County Monaghan, Ireland, 8 April 1775; d. Dublin, 14 March 1864). Philanthropist and temperance pioneer. The youngest daughter of David Hamill, she married Presbyterian minister Francis Carlile in 1800. Widowed 11 years later, she eventually moved to Dublin where she became a member of the Female Gaol Committee. She is said to have visited all the prisons in the city, accompanying ELIZABETH FRY when she visited Ireland in 1827. Convinced by her association with female prisoners that alcohol was the root cause of much personal and social distress, she founded her first temperance society in Dublin in 1830, and spent the remainder of her life in the furtherance of this cause. She travelled extensively throughout Britain, speaking in prisons and Sunday schools and at public meetings, and is credited with giving the title 'Band of Hope' to the juvenile temperance societies which she ardently promoted. Her philanthropic work, which focused particularly on women and children, was ended only by infirmity in old age.

BIBLIOGRAPHY
F. Sherlock, *Ann Jane Carlile* (London, 1897)

MYRTLE HILL

Carlile, James (b. Paisley, Scotland, 1784; d. Dublin, 31 March 1854). Presbyterian minister, writer, and educationalist. The eldest son of a successful businessman and magistrate, he decided to enter the ministry after hearing ROWLAND HILL preach in London. He trained at the universities of Glasgow and Edinburgh and received his licence to preach in Paisley in 1811. Two years later he was invited to the Scot's Church at Mary's Abbey, Dublin, which had become an important centre of evangelical influence under the leadership of Benjamin McDowell. Once settled in Dublin, Carlile's support for Christian cooperation was soon in evidence. In 1814 he helped found the Irish Evangelical Society, an interdenominational body, which promoted evangelistic preaching in the south and west of Ireland, and in 1818 he became secretary of the Hibernian Bible Society.

Carlile was twice moderator of the Presbyterian Church in Ireland, and his ability to combine religious zeal with a degree of moderation and tolerance was an important counterforce to the rigidity displayed by some of his colleagues in the Synod of Ulster. During the Arian controversy which erupted in the 1820s he rejected the extreme views of the opposing sides. While his own theological position was strictly orthodox, he opposed the enforced dismissal of Arians from the synod, urging a middle course which would allow the objectionable doctrine to die a natural death.

In 1830 he was appointed resident Commissioner to the Irish Board of Education, a position which embroiled him in the debate between evangelical, Roman Catholic and government views on the use of the Scriptures in the schoolroom. Working with Archbishops Whately and Murray, and responsible for preparing and editing school books, his major opponent within Presbyterianism was HENRY COOKE, for whom the national system of education represented unacceptable concessions to Catholicism. Although Carlile believed that a non-sectarian but religious education system would undermine Catholicism, his views were not well received at a time when anti-Catholic sentiment was high. The new system was no more acceptable to Catholics than to the majority of Protestants, and Carlile resigned from this difficult post in 1839, devoting the next 12 years of his life to missionary work among Roman Catholics in Birr.

Carlile's dislike of exclusivist policies meant that in this period of denominational consolidation he was often out of step with the majority, but both his evangelicalism and his orthodoxy were expressed with single-minded conviction. He was a considerable scholar and author of numerous theological works.

BIBLIOGRAPHY
DNB
R. J. Rodgers, 'James Carlile, 1784–1854' (Queen's Univ., Belfast, Ph.D. thesis 1973)

MYRTLE HILL

Carment, David (b. Keiss, Caithness, Scotland, 28 Sept. 1772; d. Rosskeen, Ross-shire, Scotland, 26 May 1856). Scottish preacher, ecclesiastic, and educationist. His family originated in Irongray, his grandfather being baptized in covenanting times by John Welsh. Educated initially by his schoolmaster father, he graduated from Aberdeen 1795, financing himself by tutoring in South Uist, where he learned Gaelic. He studied divinity while teaching at Strath, Skye, was licensed to preach in April 1799, and subsequently converted while tutoring in Scalpay, Skye. He became assistant minister in Croy, Inverness, March 1803, minister of Duke Street Gaelic Chapel, Glasgow, April 1810, and of Rosskeen, March 1822. In 1843 he led his 2,000-strong congregation into the FCS.

A powerful though untypically terse and humorous preacher, he saw revival in 1840. A leading Church of Scotland evangelical before 1843, he actively supported many religious and charitable institutions in Glasgow, and in the extensive rural parish of Rosskeen he secured the provision of five schools and distributed numerous BFBS Gaelic and English scriptures, requiring payment according to means from all but the poorest.

SELECT WRITINGS
D. Carment, *The Fiery Cross* (Edinburgh, 1842)

BIBLIOGRAPHY
J. Carment, in *Disruption Worthies of the Highlands* (Edinburgh, 1877)
W. Ewing, *Annals of the FCS 1843–1900* (Edinburgh, 1914)
Fasti

HUGH M. CARTWRIGHT

Carpenter, Charles Wesley (b. New York City, 16 Dec. 1792; d. Plattekill, NY, USA, 10 May 1853). Methodist minister. Carpenter's parents were members of the John Street Methodist Church in New York City. As a teenager he had a conversion experience while attending a revival meeting in Brooklyn conducted by EZEKIEL COOPER and in 1812 he was licensed to preach in the MEC by FREEBORN GARRETTSON. Two years later Carpenter was admitted to trial membership in the New York Conference and was assigned to a New York circuit. He was ordained deacon in 1820 and elder in 1826. He served the New York Conference as an itinerant and stationed minister for most of his career and was an elected delegate to the Methodist General Conference.

BIBLIOGRAPHY
AAP
Minutes

ROBERTA J. STEWART

Carpenter, Coles (b. Westchester Co., NY, USA, 17 March 1784; d. Cambridge, NY, USA, 17 Feb. 1834). MEC minister. He was born to devout Methodist parents who carefully trained him in religion. He was converted at age 17 and admitted on trial in the New York Conference in 1819. He served prominent appointments in that conference until the Troy Conference was organized in 1832. In 1833 he was appointed presiding elder of the Troy district, where he laboured until his death. He is remembered for his effective preaching and his lack of fear of dying.

BIBLIOGRAPHY
CM

STEVE HARPER

Carr, Ann (b. Market Rasen, Lincolnshire, England, 4 March 1783; d. Leeds, Yorkshire, England, 18 Jan. 1841). Revivalist. Carr, the daughter of Thomas and Rebecca, was converted at 18 and became a Wesleyan Methodist. She met SARAH ELAND and together they conducted revivals and were attracted to Primitive Methodism. Carr moved to Hull and preached for the Primitive Methodists there. Then she, Sarah Eland and MARTHA WILLIAMS were sent to Leeds, probably acting as revivalists, under the authority of the circuit. They were popular, but soon caused controversy because they would not accept circuit discipline, so they seceded and started the Female Revivalist Society. Ann Carr's Chapel in the Leylands, Leeds, was opened in 1825 and soon became noted for its social work. They obtained other premises to further their work. In November 1840 Carr became ill and on her death bequeathed all the property to Martha Williams, on the understanding that she carried on the work.

BIBLIOGRAPHY
D. C. Dews, ed., *From Mow Cop to Peake, 1807–1932* (Leeds, England, 1982)
Z. Taft, *Biographical Sketches of ... Holy Women ...* 1 (London, 1825)
M. Williams, *Memoirs of the Life of ... Ann Carr ...* (Leeds, England, 1841)

E. DOROTHY GRAHAM

Carr, Edward (*fl.* 1770–1811). Anglican clergyman and Seceder. Carr was educated at Trinity College, Dublin (BA 1770) and became Curate of New Ross in the diocese of Ferns. He seceded from the United Church of England and Ireland in 1811 after objecting to certain aspects of the baptismal and burial services which seemed to him to imply 'popish' doctrines.

BIBLIOGRAPHY
Al. Dub.
A. R. Acheson, 'The Evangelicals in the Church of Ireland, 1784–1859' (Queen's Univ. of Belfast, Ph.D. thesis, 1967)
J. B. Leslie, *Ferns Clergy and Parishes* (Dublin, 1936)

GRAYSON CARTER

Carrington, Lord. *See* SMITH, ROBERT

Carroll, John (Saltkill) (b. Saltkill's Island, New Brunswick, BNA, 8 Aug. 1809; d. Toronto, Ontario, 13 Dec. 1884). Canadian Methodist minister and author. The son of a saddler from Ireland and a well-born New Brunswick woman, he was largely self-educated. In 1823 he was converted under Methodist auspices. Ordained elder in 1833, he served mainly prominent circuits in what are now Ontario and Quebec until superannuation in 1870. He was on one occasion co-delegate (vice-president) of the Canadian Wesleyan conference. He is remembered chiefly for *Case and His Cotemporaries*, in which he reminded fellow Methodists of the hardships of pioneer saddlebag preachers and of the remarkable conversions that had taken place in what he pictured as a heroic period of signs and wonders. In his later years his simple, 'happy' faith made him an honoured if anachronistic symbol of the period he had celebrated.

SELECT WRITINGS
DCB
John Carroll, *Case and His Cotemporaries*, 5 vols (Toronto, 1867–77)

—, *Salvation! O the Joyful Sound*, ed. J. W. Grant (Toronto, 1967)

JOHN WEBSTER GRANT

Carson, Alexander (b. Annahone, near Stewartstown, Co. Tyrone, Ireland, *c.* Sept. 1776. d. Belfast, Ireland, 24 August 1844). Baptist author and controversialist. Carson received his early education in the classics at a private school in the village of Tullyhogue, near Cookstown. He studied at Glasgow University for the Presbyterian ministry graduating MA (licensed by Tyrone Presbytery, Synod of Ulster, May 1798; ordained Tobermore, 11 December 1798). In 1805 he adopted the congregational principle of church government, seceded from the Synod of Ulster followed by two-thirds of his congregation, and published his *Reasons for Separating from the Synod of Ulster*.

Between 1807 and 1809 he abandoned infant baptism in favour of believer's baptism, and identified his church with the Baptist community. A close friend of JAMES and ROBERT HALDANE, he collaborated with Robert in his commentary on Romans.

His *Baptism in Its Mode and Subjects* (1831), was quickly recognized as a major contribution to the contemporary debate on infant baptism, and was widely read in the USA. In 1841 Bacon College, Kentucky and Jackson University each conferred an LL D on him.

His collected works (5 vols Dublin 1847–63) have an historical value, being concerned with burning issues of his day, including Arianism, Roman Catholicism, inspiration of the Scriptures, the Atonement, Divine Providence, civil obedience, the Irish education debate of the 1820s, and the quarrel between the BMS and the BFBS over corrections to translations of the Bible. They are marked by independent thought, sound logic, and a lucid style.

An evangelical Calvinist, he wrote,

> According to my doctrine [the sinner] cannot believe till God opens the eyes of his understanding; he cannot do good works till he believes. It is his first duty to believe. You will not, says Christ, come unto me, that you may have life. As long as he is in this state the Scriptures keep the gospel before him; charge him to believe it; condemn him if he believes it not. The Scriptures assure us that faith is the gift of God; they assure us, nevertheless, that want of it is man's sin. How it is beyond man's power, and yet his duty, is not for me to establish.
> (Carson, 1847: I. 108)

His defence of the BMS brought invitations to speak on its behalf and to preach one of four BMS jubilee sermons in Surrey Chapel, London on 12 October 1842. Entitled, 'The Propagation of the Gospel, with encouragements to the vigorous prosecution of the Work' (in W. Carson, 1847: 425–54) it is a good example of Carson's evangelical Calvinism.

BIBLIOGRAPHY
R. A. Boggs, *Alexander Carson of Tobermore* (Belfast, 1969)
Carson's Works, 1 (Dublin, 1847)
DNB
D. P. Kingdon, 'The Theology of Alexander Carson' in the *Irish Baptist Historical Society Journal*, 2 (1969/70)
G. C. Moore, *The Life of Alexander Carson, LL.D.* (New York, 1851)
J. Thompson, 'Baptists in Ireland 1792–1922: A Dimension of Protestant Dissent' (Oxford Univ. D. Phil. thesis, 1988)
T. Witherow, *Three Prophets of Our Own* (Reprinted, Draperstown, N. Ireland, 1990)

JOSHUA THOMPSON

Carter, Charles (b. Shepscomb, Gloucestershire, England, *c.* 1805). *Fl.* 1830s. CMS missionary to British Guiana. Carter trained briefly at the CMS training school at Islington (London) in 1826 and was sent out with JOHN ARMSTRONG as a lay missionary to British Guiana [now Guyana] on 24 October 1827. Their mission is unclear, but they were likely sent out in response to a request for lay catechists to work on a particular plantation. On 29 July 1838 Carter was ordained a deacon by the Bishop of Barbados and on 29 August 1839 he returned to England, closed his connection with the CMS and transferred to the authority of the colonial church. He appears to have been unmarried.

BIBLIOGRAPHY
D. T. B[arry], *CMS Register of Missionaries and Native Clergy* (privately printed) (London, 1906)

DONALD M. LEWIS

Cartwright, James Boardman (b. 1798; d. Bethnal Green, London, 8 Feb. 1861). Anglican clergyman. Cartwright was a member of Queens' College, Cambridge (BA 1821; MA 1824). His life's work was devoted to evangelizing the Jews. He was Curate of St John's, Bethnal Green and minister of the Jews' Chapel in that area of London (1831–61). He was an active participant with the LSPCJ and in the 1850s he superintended the work of the LCM two Jewish missionaries, both of them Germans. In addition, he was chaplain and principal of the Hebrew College (1853–9).

BIBLIOGRAPHY
Al. Cant, II, i: 531

ARTHUR POLLARD

Cartwright, Peter (b. Amherst County, VA, USA, 1 Sept. 1785; d. Pleasant Plains, Sangamon County, IL, USA, 25 Sept. 1872). Pioneer Methodist circuit rider and politician. Cartwright's father had been a soldier in the Revolutionary War. His mother was an orphan. Cartwright's family moved to Kentucky in 1790 travelling with hundreds of others who crossed the mountains in the first years following the end of the war. In 1793, the family finally settled at Rogues' Harbor, Logan County in western Kentucky near the Tennessee border. The area was called Rogues' Harbor because of its large number of outlaws who preferred living on the edge of the American frontier.

Cartwright had a very informal education. He learned to read, write and do simple mathematics from a former Methodist minister, now a part-time teacher and doctor. By his own account, he also became interested in horse-racing and playing cards. In 1801, when he was 16, Methodists and Presbyterians held a camp meeting near the Cartwright home. The meeting was a direct result of the Cane Ridge meeting which had happened earlier in the year. Many in the area came and Cartwright was converted during the sessions. He then joined the local MEC, Ebenezer, and in May 1802 received his exhorter's licence.

In the fall of 1802 his family moved north and west toward the mouth of the Cumberland River in Kentucky. As the family was setting out young Cartwright was charged to begin a new circuit in the area. After a brief period of additional schooling he laid out a plan for the new circuit. In the fall of 1803 he was appointed to go out as a travelling preacher, along with an older minister on to the Red River circuit. After being on the circuit for a 'quarter', roughly a quarter of a year, Cartwright was appointed to the Waynesville circuit. It was on this circuit that he would begin to develop the rough-and-ready style which would make him famous as a frontier preacher. Cartwright enjoyed travelling on the frontier and soon stories developed about his swimming swollen rivers, fleeing from Native Americans, fighting ruffians when necessary (even during church services), as well as his quick wit and good-natured but combative style.

His early ministry included: Red River circuit in Kentucky; Waynesville circuit in Kentucky and part of Tennessee; Salt River and Shelbyville circuit, also in Kentucky and in part of southern Indiana; and the Scioto circuit in Ohio. Early in his travels he was encouraged to study by his presiding elder, WILLIAM MCKENDREE, later a bishop. McKendree selected books, both theological and literary, for Cartwright to read and examined him over them every quarter. In later years Cartwright felt that McKendree's influence had been more important in his education than any of his previous instructors.

In 1806 he was ordained deacon by Bishop FRANCIS ASBURY and in the fall of 1808 he was ordained an elder by the newly elected Bishop McKendree. In the late summer of 1808, 'after deliberation and prayer', Cartwright decided it was his duty to marry and married Frances Gaines on 18 August 1808, which was also her nineteenth birthday. He continued to serve circuits in and around the Ohio River, primarily in the state of Kentucky. In 1812, the Western Conference of the MEC, which covered all of the territory west of the Allegheny Mountains was divided into two new conferences, the Ohio and the Tennessee. Cartwright appears to have been placed in the Tennessee Conference. He was made a presiding elder for the Wabash district. This meant that he had responsibility over the travelling preachers in his area, was supposed to keep track of them, assist when necessary and advise the bishop concerning appointments. The district covered parts of southern Indiana, south-eastern Illinois, and the central and western part of Kentucky. From 1813 until 1816 he was presiding elder of the Green River district. Green River covered essentially the same area as the Wabash had but the Indiana and Illinois region had been removed and attached to other northern districts. Beginning in 1816 Cartwright was elected a delegate to the General Conference of the MEC, the legislative body of the denomination. He was a delegate at the next 12 General Conferences. As delegate to the General Conferences of 1840 and 1844 he saw the rising division in the denomination and participated in the great debates which led to the division of the denomination, a division which he always felt was wrong.

As early as 1813 Cartwright was uneasy about developing relationship between the church and the institution of slavery. He always felt that the early position held by the denomination, which was to speak out against slavery and to discourage its ministers and members from participating in it, had always been a wise course. During this time he saw the church membership grow as did his dislike for slavery. Not only was he against the practice of slavery, but also a leader in the early movement against drinking.

In 1823 Cartwright became convinced that he needed to leave Kentucky for new lands. He wished to 'get entirely clear of the evil of slavery', as well as to raise his children where work was not 'thought a degradation', to find a place with cheaper land so that his family could settle near as they grew, and he wished to take the gospel to the frontier. He and his family travelled to Illinois and found a new place to live in Sangamon County, Illinois. In the fall of 1824 Cartwright officially transferred from the Kentucky Conference into the newly created Illinois Conference. From 1826 until 1869 he was a presiding elder of several different districts. As presiding elder he encouraged circuits to be started in Iowa.

Feeling there was too much corruption in the state government and wanting to help keep Illinois a state free of slavery, he ran, and was elected, for the Illinois legislature in 1828 and 1832. His 1832 opponent was Abraham Lincoln. Cartwright's only political loss was in 1846 when he ran for the US Congress, this time losing to Lincoln. While in the legislature he worked on committees to improve roads and schools.

In the 1830s Cartwright met with Joseph Smith shortly after he and his followers had been expelled from Missouri. He engaged the Mormon leader in debate which ended in an argument and the two parted.

It is easy to see Cartwright in legendary terms. To some extent he encouraged such ideas in his autobiography and reminiscences. Yet he was typical of many of the frontier Methodist ministers who moved westward with the expanding population. He felt his call sent him out among the people who had little religion in a wild landscape. Yet, while he freely engaged in revivals, camp meetings, scuffles with ruffians and challenges, as well as challenging members of other denominations, he was a complex individual. He felt strongly enough about his beliefs to leave the slave states and move into free territory. He worked as a legislator to ensure safe roads and better education. For him the gospel touched every aspect of a person's life, whether it was preaching, helping to take care of his family or involvement with politics. Cartwright was both typical and unique.

SELECT WRITINGS
P. Cartwright, *Autobiography of Peter Cartwright*, ed. C. L. Wallis (Nashville, TN, 1956)
—, *Fifty Years as Presiding Elder* (Cincinnati, OH, 1871)

BIBLIOGRAPHY
DAB
EWM
NIDCC

L. DALE PATTERSON

Cartwright, Robert (b. Wellington, England, 15 Dec. 1771; d. Goulburn, Australia, 14 Dec. 1856). Australian Anglican chaplain. Born in Shropshire of a landed family, Cartwright spent his early years in travel and commerce. Marriage in 1796 to a devout Methodist, as well as other religious influences, led him into a fervent evangelical faith, a brief spell at the pietist St Edmund's Hall, Oxford and, in 1806, ordination to the diaconate by the Archbishop of York. While curate at Bradford, Cartwright was sought out by SAMUEL MARSDEN for service in the penal colony of New South Wales. He received a chaplain's commission and priest's orders and reached Sydney in 1810.

Cartwright ministered in the rural Hawkesbury region, preaching in barns and granaries and under trees to convict gangs, settlers and soldiers. Although troubled by financial problems – he had to provide for 11 children – he worked with zest. Before a church was completed, he asked to be moved to Liverpool. This district was on the edge of settlement and Cartwright grew interested in the vast lands to the south. He also became concerned for the aboriginal inhabitants, drew up a scheme for a residential mission and workstation and offered to be its conductor. The plan was eventually implemented but not with Cartwright. Instead, he took charge of the male orphan school in addition to his parish duties.

In 1836 Cartwright was moved to the principal Sydney church. Already saddened by the imprisonment of a son (a terrible blow for the old convict chaplain), Cartwright had no liking for a fashionable town congregation. He thought of retiring to England but, on the death of his wife, changed his mind. Instead, he moved in 1838 to the south-western region, which he had helped to explore years before. He stationed himself at Collector, married a landowner's daughter, built a little church and undertook an itinerant mission over a vast area of newly opened country. Cartwright, in his element as a pioneer parson, became the apostle of the Riverina.

Age and the advance of settlement eventually restricted his work but, in 1855, the new bishop, confirming a bushranger converted by Cartwright, found the old chaplain 'a venerable, apostolic man aged 86 . . . he has stood up for evangelical truth amid many adverse elements . . . The only sign of age he shews is being very deaf, but he is as shrewd and clear in mind as ever he was' (Barker, manuscript diary).

BIBLIOGRAPHY
ADB
Mitchell Library, Sydney, Australia, manuscript diary of Mrs J.S. Barker, vol 2

KENNETH J. CABLE

Carus, William (b. Liverpool, England, 1802; d. Bournemouth, England 27 Aug. 1891). Anglican clergyman. Carus entered Trinity College, Cambridge in 1821 (scholar 1825; BA 1827; MA 1830; fellow 1829; dean 1832–50) and after ordination became Curate of St Michael's, Cambridge, under JAMES SCHOLEFIELD. From 1832–7 he was curate and lecturer at Holy Trinity under CHARLES SIMEON, whose memoirs he composed. He contributed extensively to the rebuilding of Holy Trinity in 1843. He was also lecturer at Great St Mary's (1832, 1844–51) and in later years three times select preacher before the university (1854, 1859, 1861). His Sunday evening meetings for undergraduates attracted large numbers. He was one of the original Simeon's Trustees and served until 1890. Just after he left Cambridge the Carus Greek Testament Prize was established in his honour in 1853.

Carus had met Bishop CHARLES SUMNER at Lowestoft in 1833. The latter preferred him to a canonry of Winchester (1851–85) and appointed him as Vicar of Romsey (1851–4), after which he moved successively to St Maurice, Winchester (1854–60) and Christ Church, Winchester (1860–70) which he built.

His biographer speaks of him as 'an *attractive* christian' with a genial manner and a loving spirit (Bullock, 1891: 17), who gave 'four words as keynotes to [one's] ministry – Charity, Humility, Industry, Purity'. Carus saw the church as a union of believers, no matter what the outward organization might be, but at the same time he spoke of 'The Christian *Ministry*', not of sacrificing priests. At a time when the Church, and Anglican evangelicals not least, were often suspicious of science, Carus expressed admiration for the geologist ADAM SEDGWICK who considered that 'Revelation and true science can never be at variance'.

BIBLIOGRAPHY
Al. Cant., II. i: 531
C. Bullock, *Speaking Years* (London, 1891)

ARTHUR POLLARD

Carus Wilson, Roger. *See* CARUS WILSON, WILLIAM

Carus Wilson, William (b. Heversham, Westmorland, England, 7 July 1791; d. London, 30 Dec. 1859). Anglican clergyman, religious author and philanthropist. Carus Wilson is now remembered as the model for Charlotte Brontë's rancorous portrait of him as the sanctimonious and hypocritical Brocklehurst in *Jane Eyre*, the product of hers and her sisters' bitter experience of the Clergy Daughters' School at Cowan Bridge. He was the eldest son of William Wilson Carus who on succeeding to the Casterton estates in Westmorland (now Cumbria) added Wilson to his surname. The father had been influenced by CHARLES SIMEON at Cambridge and it was to Trinity College, after tuition by JOHN FAWCETT of Carlisle, that he sent his son in 1810. William Carus Wilson graduated BA in 1815 and MA in 1818. In 1815 he married Anne, daughter of Major-General Charles Neville. In the same year he applied for and was refused clerical orders by Law, Bishop of Chester, apparently for believing that grievous sin after baptism is unforgivable, contrary to Article 16 of the Thirty-Nine Articles. The Archbishop of York, however, was more amenable and Carus Wilson was preferred to the family living of Tunstall (Lancashire) (1816–28) and to that of nearby Whittington (1825–57) together with the perpetual curacy of Casterton (1833–56). At the beginning of his ministry he also had short spells as chaplain first to Lord Galway and then to the Duke of Sussex. He was one of the original Simeon's Trustees and continued in this patronage work till 1850. He succeeded to the family estates in 1851, but around this time increasing ill health, especially sciatica, compelled him to winter in Nice and finally in 1855 to move to Eglinton House, Ventnor, in the Isle of Wight.

Carus Wilson was active in education, founding no less than four schools. Despite the epidemic and suffering that engulfed the Brontë children among others Cowan Bridge prospered with ninety pupils in 1825. It moved to Casterton in 1833 and had 130 girls in 1843, among them another future novelist, Emma Jane Warboise, who gave a very different picture from that of the Brontës in her *Thorneycroft Hall* and who said of Carus Wilson: 'A kinder man I never knew'. In 1833 also he commenced the building of a chapel to serve Casterton.

In addition to all this, he was active in religious publication with tracts and periodicals, the latter comprising the monthly *Friendly Visitor* (begun 1819), *The Children's Friend* (begun 1824) and *The Teacher's Visitor* (around 1833). His writings illustrate one side of nineteenth-century evangelicalism to excess, namely, an undue concentration on sin and its hell-fire consequences. He edited *The Christian Guardian* for many years and published a number of selections of hymns and psalms. Beginning with members of the Sardinian Army in Nice, Carus Wilson was active also in later years in evangelistic and pastoral work among soldiers and sailors in Portsmouth, where he set up the first Soldiers' Institute, efforts for which he is commemorated in St John's Church, Newport, Isle of Wight, with a monument 'Erected by the

Non-Commissioned officers and privates of the British Army in token of their love and gratitude'. His one-time curate and later Bishop of Rochester, A. W. THOROLD, remarked on Carus Wilson's 'energy and moral courage [and] . . . a mighty power of love to God and man'.

Two of his three brothers were clergymen, the one, Roger (1792–1839) being his exact contemporary at Trinity, Cambridge, and subsequently vicar of the fast-growing Lancashire port and cotton-town of Preston from 1817 to his death; and the other, Edward (1795–1860) of Queens', Cambridge after acting as curate to William was Vicar of Crosby Ravensworth (Westmorland) from 1836 to 1848.

BIBLIOGRAPHY
CO (March 1860): 145 ff
J. M. Ewbank, The Life and Times of William Carus Wilson 1791–1859 (Kendal, England, 1959)

ARTHUR POLLARD

Carver, James (b. Wymondham, Norfolk, England, 1790; d. London, 12 Jan. 1866). Anglican clergyman. Carver was educated at Holt and Corpus Christi College, Cambridge (BA 1812; MA 1815). Most of his ministry was spent in London, where he was chaplain to the Lord Mayor and the Court of Aldermen of the City (1826–62), during which time he also held other chaplaincies, among them the Debtors' Prison, Newgate and the Lying-In Hospital, City Road.

BIBLIOGRAPHY
Al. Cant. II. i: 533
CO, LXV: 248

ARTHUR POLLARD

Carvosso, Benjamin (b. Gluvian, Cornwall, England, 29 Sept. 1789; d. Tuckingmill, Cornwall, England, 2 Oct. 1854). Methodist preacher. Accepted by the English Wesleyan Conference as a probationer in 1814, Carvosso volunteered for the mission field and joined the New South Wales Mission on 20 May 1820 serving in the Windsor, Sydney and Parramatta circuits. He helped launch the first Australian religious journal, The Australia Magazine, and was involved in a struggle with the parent Missionary Committee over the relationship of the Wesleyan Church in NSW with the Church of England and with the Missionary Committee itself. He ministered in Hobart from 1825 until his return to the English Conference in 1830. Manuscript material relating to his Australian work may be found scattered through the papers of the (English) WMMS. Carvosso was noted both for his devotion and his evangelical fervour.

BIBLIOGRAPHY
ADB
G. Blencowe, The Faithful Pastor (London, 1857)

D. I. WRIGHT

Carvosso, William (b. near Mousehole, Cornwall, England, 11 March 1750; d. Dowstall, Mylor, Cornwall, England, 13 Oct. 1834). Businessman and Methodist class leader. Converted as a young man through the spiritual influence of his sister (who had become a Christian through Methodist preaching), Carvosso joined the Methodists at Mousehole and soon claimed their experience of 'entire sanctification'. His son and biographer said: 'Of all the Wesleyan tenets none was received by my father more heartily than the doctrine of Christian perfection'. Carvosso became an enthusiastic promoter of class meetings in the area; his own society grew from one small class to 11 with nearly 200 members. 'He was never harsh in meeting a class but he would blend great fidelity with fervent melting compassion.' He retired from business in order to devote himself to local evangelism and pastoral care, and gave his last twenty years to full-time Christian work in Cornwall. His biography is a fascinating description of an ideal class leader in early nineteenth-century Wesleyanism; he engaged in personal evangelism, regular visiting of the sick, and constantly urged Methodists to enter into the experience of 'perfection'. He was a great lover of Wesley's hymns ('a body of divinity'). Carvosso served as society steward and trustee, and became an encouraging correspondent though until the age of 65 was unable to write more than his name.

BIBLIOGRAPHY
B. Carvosso, The Efficacy of Faith in the Atonement of Christ exemplified in a Memoir of Mr Wm Carvosso (London, 1836)
MM 35: 156

RAYMOND BROWN

Cary, Lott (b. Charles City County, VA, USA, c. 1780; d. Monrovia, Liberia, 10 Nov. 1828). Baptist minister and missionary. Born a slave on the tobacco plantation of William A. Christian, Cary went to work in Richmond in 1804 as a hired laborer. By 1813, he saved $850 to purchase his freedom and that of his children. Cary was baptized at First Baptist Church. In 1813, he received a licence to preach. Subsequently, he was ordained and helped form the Richmond African Baptist Missionary Society to enable freed slaves to return in Africa. Cary stated,

I am an African, and in this country [United States], however meritorious my conduct and respectable my character, I can-not receive the credit due to either. I wish to go to a country where I shall be estimated by my merits, not by my complexion, and I feel bound to labor for my suffering race.
(Gurley: 148)

Under the aegis of the American Colonization Society, in 1821, Cary settled at Monrovia, where he founded the Providence Baptist Church, schools and a missionary society. An effective preacher and teacher, Cary emerged as a leader in the colony. From 1827 to 1828 Cary served as Vice-Governor and, for six months, Acting-Governor of Liberia. He dealt competently with administrative problems and lay the constitutional foundations of modern Liberia. He died by accident while preparing to defend the colony against raids. In 1897, American Baptists recalled the man and his vision by establishing the Lott Cary Foreign Mission Society.

BIBLIOGRAPHY
DANB
M. M. Fisher, 'Lott Cary, The Colonizing Missionary', *Journal of Negro History,* 7 (1922): 380–418
L. Fitts, *Lott Carey* (Valley Forge, PA, 1978)
R. R. Gurley, *Life of Jehudi Ashmun . . . with an Appendix, Sketch of the Life of the Rev. Lott Cary* (Washington, DC, 1835)
HDL

PAUL R. DEKAR

Case, William (b. Swansea Township, MA, USA, 27 Aug. 1780; d. Alderville, Canada West, 19 Oct. 1855). Methodist itinerant and missionary to the American Indians. The eldest son of George Case, a Massachusetts farmer, William Case was converted in 1803 and two years later was admitted on trial as an itinerant minister by the New York Conference of the MEC. His first appointment was to the Bay of Quinte circuit in Upper Canada (after 1841 Canada West), and except for the period 1810–15, Case lived and worked in Canada until his death in 1855. Ordered a deacon in 1807 and an elder in 1808, he quickly rose to a prominent position in the Methodist itinerancy in his newly adopted land. Upon his return to Upper Canada from New York after the War of 1812–15, he became presiding elder of the Upper Canada District, an area which at the time stretched from Detroit to Kingston.

Case was one of the first to recognize that as a result of the anti-American feeling engendered by the War of 1812, Methodism in Canada needed to sever its ties with the parent American body. Accordingly, at the General Conference of 1824 he successfully encouraged the formation of a separate conference in Upper Canada. He was appointed presiding elder in the new conference and when an independent Canadian MEC was established in 1828, Case was elected general superintendent *pro tempore* and superintendent of Indian missions.

From this time on, two concerns would absorb his attention: the need to work out an amicable and permanent arrangement with the British Wesleyans, who by 1832 were entering into competition with the Methodist Episcopals, and secondly, the formation and welfare of Indian missions.

In 1832, largely under the urging of the powerful ADOLPHUS EGERTON RYERSON, the newly independent MEC in Canada made the decision to end rivalry with the British Wesleyans, and the following year the two bodies joined in union. Case strongly contested this decision and his plea for continuing independence appeared vindicated when the union proved abortive

and was dissolved in 1840. However, by that date, Case had come to the conclusion that the future of his beloved Indian missions lay with the Wesleyans, and therefore he threw his lot in with the British group after the dissolution. With more of his colleagues, he had come to distrust the influence of the powerful Ryerson brothers, in particular Egerton, who had played the leading role in promoting the 1833 union. However, when in 1847 the two branches of Methodism re-united, this time on a permanent basis, Case was willing to forget past animosities and rejoiced that stability had finally been achieved.

Throughout these troubled years, he continued to devote himself single-mindedly to his work among the Indians. As white settlers pushed into Upper Canada, the native population found its existence to be increasingly precarious, and Case became convinced that its only hope lay in a planned adoption of Christianity and western civilization. To this end, he strongly encouraged the cooperation of native converts, and one of these, a Mississauga of mixed race, PETER JONES, converted under his preaching in 1827, became the first native Indian minister in Upper Canada and a lifelong collaborator. To encourage the Christianization and acculturation of the Indians, Case in 1826 established a model community on Grape Island in the Bay of Quinte. Here in a strictly regulated way of life, Indian men and women were instructed in agriculture, crafts and housekeeping, and encouraged through religious services and camp meetings to accept the Gospel. It was here that Case met the two women he would successively marry. Both were teachers to the natives; Hester Ann Hubbard became his wife in 1829, and after her premature death, he married Eliza Barnes in 1833.

At the time of the 1833 union, Case had been demoted from general superintendent *pro tempore* to 'General Missionary to the Indian tribes', with the specific task of translating the Scriptures into the Indian languages. In that capacity he established a new model settlement at Alderville near Rice Lake through the combined financial assistance of the British Wesleyan Missionary Society and the provincial government. Alderville quickly became a show-piece of successful native acculturation. Each native family was given a fifty-acre farm, house, and garden; an industrial school was opened in 1839, and by the time of Case's death, it boasted 43 boarders and 35 day students, who were taught basic science and arithmetic, as well as the manufacturing of cloth.

Thanks to a journal which he kept from April 1808 to August 1809, some of Case's own inner life has been recorded. Humble, diffident, at times given to self-doubt, but fired by a strongly mystical faith, Case lacked the qualities requisite for political prominence in the expanding Methodist denomination in Upper Canada. However, his simple experimental preaching and his utter devotion to evangelization, especially of the native population, made him a revered minister. Fittingly, his last public effort, and only publication (in addition to numerous letters) was a jubilee sermon delivered to the 1855 conference, 'All the paths of the Lord are mercy and truth unto such as keep his covenant and his testamonies'.

When Case died unexpectedly in 1855 of injuries received by a fall from his horse, his denomination eulogized him for his 'labours of love for half a century', and fittingly, he was buried in Alderville among the native people to whom he had devoted most of his long ministry. Many of his letters are collected by his chief biographer, John Carroll, in *Case and His Cotemporaries*. A member of the second generation of Methodist itinerants, Carroll would nostalgically depict William Case as the model representative of 'the heroic age of Methodism in Canada'.

BIBLIOGRAPHY
J. Carroll, *Case and His Cotemporaries*, 5 vols (Toronto, 1866–77)
DCB 8
G. French, *Parsons and Politics* (Toronto, 1962)

MARGUERITE VAN DIE

Cashel, Bishop of. *See* DALY, ROBERT

Cates, John Brereton (b. England; d. Sierra Leone, 23 July 1819). CMS missionary to Sierra Leone. Cates trained as a schoolmaster at the Central School of the National Society before volunteering to go to Sierra Leone with the CMS. He was sent to Wilberforce on 14 January 1817 travelling out with DAVID BRENNAND and died after two and a half years of service, considerably longer than Brennand who died after six months. He appears to have been unmarried. Few of the early CMS missionaries lasted as long as he.

BIBLIOGRAPHY
D. T. B[arry], *CMS Register of Missionaries and Native Clergy* (privately printed) (London, 1906)

DONALD M. LEWIS

Catlin, Jacob (b. Harwinton, CT, BNA, 29 March 1758; d. New Marlborough, MA, 12 April 1826). Congregational minister. Catlin graduated from Yale (1784), then studied for the ministry under STEPHEN WEST of Stockbridge, Massachusetts. He was ordained at New Marlborough in 1787 where he remained for the duration of his life. A rural country pastor, Catlin prepared men for college, witnessed several revivals in his congregation (1798, 1815), was a trustee of Williams College, and was actively involved in the groundwork of several religious societies, including the ABS.

Catlin was a second generation Edwardsian of New Divinity theological sympathies who, together with a band of like-minded pastors, made New Divinity theology dominant in north-west Connecticut and western Massachusetts from 1775 to 1825. Catlin published one major theological treatise, *A Compendium of the System of Divine Truth* (1818), a restatement of Calvinistic New Divinity theology.

BIBLIOGRAPHY
AAP, 2: 260–5
R. Birdsall, *Berkshire County* (New Haven, CT, 1959)
J. Conforti, *Samuel Hopkins and the New Divinity Movement* (Grand Rapids, MI, 1981)

DAVID W. KLING

Caughey,   James (b. Ulster,   Ireland,   *c.* 1810; d. Highland Park, NJ, USA, 30 Jan. 1891). Methodist revivalist in Britain, Canada and the United States. Little is known of Caughey's early years and education. During his youth his Scottish-Irish parents emigrated from Ulster to the United States. By 1830 he was at work in a flour mill in Troy, upstate New York, where he was converted during one of the revivals sweeping the 'Burned-Over District'. He soon entered the ministry of the MEC, within the bounds of the Troy Conference. His work in the small but developing communities of upstate New York and northern New England grounded him in the technicalities of revivals and camp meetings. He won invitations to preach further afield, in Montreal and other parts of Canada. In 1841, unknown in Britain, he crossed the Atlantic. Within a few years he had established himself as the 'King of the Revivalist Preachers' in the Methodist churches of the industrial and urban areas of central and northern England. By 1847, when he returned to America, his revival campaigns boasted some 20,000 justified by faith and 9,000 'entirely sanctified'.

Caughey's successes, at a time of connexional stagnation, sprang from a forceful personality and confident handling of revival techniques. He preached some six to ten sermons a week throughout his active life. His commanding height, keen eyes, and strong features gave him great pulpit presence. A powerful and attractive voice captivated even critical hearers. He was not an original thinker and avoided speculative divinity. He presented the essentials of evangelical doctrine in novel, arresting but simple ways, and made the 'blessing of purification' an integral part of his preaching. A master of audience psychology, he often alarmed members of his congregation (unnamed but carefully targeted) with the prediction 'This year thou shalt die'. He made particularly effective use of the American call to the altar: while the congregation sang hymns and shouted hallelujahs, he moved from pew to pew inviting the anxious forward to the penitents' bench to 'get liberty'.

JABEZ BUNTING and the politically conservative 'High Church' party in the Wesleyan establishment, sensitive to the connexion's advancing social status, frowned at revivalist excitement, questioned the elements of contrivance in Caughey's *modus operandi*, charged him with frightening 'mushroom converts' into temporary religious life, and sought to end his irregular itinerancy. In 1846 the Wesleyan Conference moved against him. While Caughey spent the next year working outside Wesleyanism, his supporters took up their pens on his behalf. Though there was no immediate schism (Caughey himself counselled against it), Wesleyans were on the verge of the great *Fly Sheets* disruption, in which the two parties, conservatives and democratic reformers, closely resembled the forces earlier arranged behind and against the American.

Caughey's fame preceded him to America. The condensed American version of his *Letters*, describing his major English revivals, raced through numerous reprints. Over the next decade the demand for his services grew in the towns and cities of Canada and the north-eastern United States, particularly from churches concerned to promote holiness doctrine. In 1857 he returned to England for two further years, once more to the North and Midlands, once more converting thousands. But now he worked within the congregations of reformed Methodism, especially the United Methodist Free Churches, many of whose leaders were Caughey's spiritual children. In August 1862, towards the end of his third visit, his remarkable physical constitution began to give way. He made a fourth and final visit in the mid-1860s before retiring in broken health to Highland Park, New Jersey, after nearly 35 years of revivalist itinerancy.

Having no Victorian biographer and leaving no memoirs, Caughey has languished undeservedly in the shadow of CHARLES FINNEY and Dwight Moody. But his was as much a household name as theirs. WILLIAM BOOTH was only the most notable of the tens of thousands who attributed their religious awakening to his influence. No visiting American *denominational* preacher achieved in nineteenth-century Britain what Caughey did. LORENZO DOW was a much less disciplined revivalist; Finney's greater influence within British Dissent derived from his publications, not his visits; Moody's campaigns were inter- or extra-denominational and derived their strength from a very different strategy. Caughey's ministry on the 'urban frontier' on both sides of the Atlantic, but especially in Britain where native springs of spontaneous revivals were drying up, was well suited to a period of consolidation within Methodism. Most of his converts were regular churchgoers, from unsophisticated middle-class and aspiring working-class backgrounds, some of whom had backslidden from an earlier profession of faith. He blended the old and the new. His revivals recalled the pentecostal excitements of primitive Wesleyanism; his emphasis on sanctification suggested a return to Wesleyan standards. But he also gave revivalism a more premeditated, professional, manipulative character. Every act was directed to soul-saving; his triumphs were those of the paid revival technician.

SELECT WRITINGS

J. Caughey, *Letters on Various Subjects*, 5 vols (London, 1844–7)
—, *Revival Miscellanies* (London, no date)
—, *Methodism in Earnest*, ed. D. Wise (Boston, MA, 1850)
—, *Earnest Christianity Illustrated* (London, 1857)
—, *Glimpses of a Life in Soul-Saving* (New York, 1868)

BIBLIOGRAPHY

P. Bush, 'The Reverend James Caughey and Wesleyan Methodist Revivalism in Canada West, 1851–1856', *Ontario History*, 79, 3 (1987): 231–50
R. Carwardine, *Transatlantic Revivalism* (Westport, CT, 1978)
J. Kent, *Holding the Fort* (London, 1978)

RICHARD JOHN CARWARDINE

Caulfield, Charles   (b. 1738; d. 1818). Anglican clergyman. A scion of the house of Charlemont, he was the son of the Hon. and Revd Charles Caulfield, Rector of Abroe. A scholar of Trinity College, Dublin in 1757, he returned to Armagh diocese, serving as Rector of Forkhill 1772–5, and of Killyman 1775–1818. He supported the Methodists, inviting their preachers to his house and acting as host to JOHN WESLEY during his Irish tours of 1785 and 1789. His son, Hans Caulfield, Rector of Kilmanagh, was a founder member of the Ossory Clerical Association, and his grandson, Charles Caulfield, the first Bishop of Nassau.

BIBLIOGRAPHY

C. H. Crookshank, *History of Methodism in Ireland* I (Belfast and London, 1885)
J. B. Leslie, *Armagh Clergy and Parishes* (Dundalk, Ireland, 1911)

ALAN R. ACHESON

Cavan, eighth Earl of (Lambart, Frederick John William, styled Viscount Kilcoursie till 1837 when he succeeded to the earldom) (b. Eaglehurst, Hampshire, England, 30 Dec. 1815; d. Weston-super-Mare, Somerset, England, 15 Dec. 1887). Brethren peer. Cavan was a strong Tory evangelical whose religious and charitable activities are well documented from 1860, when he took up residence at Milton near Weston-super-Mare. Cavan relieved the poor at Milton, and built an iron-room in which he normally conducted services. For many years, he led Friday evening prayer meetings in the Assembly Rooms in Weston-super-Mare, became a trustee of Holy Trinity Church, preached at the Gospel Hall, and evangelized the thousands of excursionists, and visitors on the Weston beach and esplanade of a summer's evening, by the wayside, and in the railway station. He spoke at mission services throughout England and Scotland, and was among those who welcomed Moody and Sankey to Edinburgh in 1874.

Despite his title, he had no connection with Ireland, except his patronage of the Irish Society and the Scripture Reader's Society for Ireland, until he acquired a property on the island of Achill, where he tried to get roads made, and to promote fisheries. By his efforts a beautiful little pier was built, and he endeavoured to establish a steamer service, which would help the people to a ready market for their fish. As a friend of Lord Radstock and a trustee of the Mildmay Conference, Cavan was a prominent member of an inner circle of evangelical noblemen and gentlemen, and like Lord SHAFTESBURY, whom he resembled except in his habitual cheerfulness, was a convinced millenarian living in daily hope of the Second Coming. He executed the duties of his rank as a Lieutenant-Colonel of the Second Somerset Militia and Deputy-Lieutenant and Justice of the Peace for Somerset and his life shows a characteristically Victorian union between a traditional aristocratic sense of public duty and a deeply felt faith.

In 1838 he married the Honourable Caroline Augusta Littleton, third daughter of Baron Hatherton, who shared his faith and good works. His son and heir was an extreme High Churchman.

BIBLIOGRAPHY
Boase
The Christian (6 January 1888)
V. Gibbs, ed., *The Complete Peerage* 3 (London, 1913): 120
L. E. O'Rorke, *The Life and Friendships of Catherine Marsh* (London, 1917): 223
The Weston-Super-Mare Gazette (21 December 1887, 24 December 1887)

SHERIDAN GILLEY

Cecil, Richard (b. London, 8 Nov. 1748; d. London, 15 Aug. 1810). Anglican clergyman. Richard Cecil's father, a gentleman and East India Company scarlet-dyer, intended that his son should follow a business career. Ill health curtailed Cecil's city employment, and in 1773 at the age of 24 he entered Queen's College, Oxford, to prepare for ordination. Although at one time highly critical of evangelical teaching, Cecil admired his dissenting mother and had gradually come to faith himself. The idea of ordination came from his Anglican father, who promised to buy him a living if he remained loyal to the Church of England.

Cecil was ordained deacon in 1776 and priest in 1777, the year in which he gained his BA; an MA from Sidney Sussex College, Cambridge, followed in 1790. During a brief curacy in Rauceby and Cranwell (Lincolnshire), he was asked to take temporary charge of three Leicestershire churches (Thornton, Bagworth, and Markfield), pending the ordination of the intended incumbent whom he converted to evangelical faith. From 1777 to 1797/8 he held the livings of St Thomas's and All Saints Lewes, but the damp Sussex air so exacerbated his rheumatic tendencies that he placed them in the charge of carefully chosen curates. He moved to Islington in London where he exercised a preaching ministry by obtaining lectureships at various city churches: Orange Street Leicester Fields, Long Acre, St Margaret's Lothbury, Christ Church Spitalfields. His most prestigious responsibility was St John's, Bedford Row, the largest Anglican proprietary chapel in London, of which he was minister from 1780 to 1808, personally financing repairs to the building. Friends persuaded him to accept the livings of Bisley and Chobham (1800–10) in Surrey but his health was declining and he was often in pain. In 1798 a serious attack of what appeared to be sciatica prevented him from preaching for some time and nine years later he suffered a slight stroke. This was followed by more debilitating paralysis in 1808, which threatened his reasoning powers, made him depressed, and eventually led to his death.

Cecil is widely regarded as one of the most cultured of evangelicals. He inherited from his father a wide-ranging love of books: a catalogue of his library is held with his diary for 1804–7 and other papers at Ridley Hall, Cambridge. 'The stores of his mind were copious', wrote DANIEL WILSON. 'There was scarcely a branch of literature or science with which he had not some acquaintance' (Wilson, 1810: 22–3). From his youth he had been passionately interested in painting and he was a keen violinist. However, he renounced his violin, unable to restrict himself to 15 minutes practice a day, and eventually gave up art exhibitions and even general reading, lest they distract him from pastoral responsibilities. His conversation, writing and preaching continued to reflect his knowledge of the arts.

Many of Cecil's sermons were published for it was as a preacher that he was most renowned. The High Church *British Critic* described him as 'a very profound and original thinker' (4, 1828: 257), and further testimony abounds:

> He did not talk upon subjects as other men did . . . he viewed things with a different eye, with deeper penetration, and on a wider scale . . . . I never left him . . . without receiving ideas and impressions which I never had before. (Jerram, 1855: 264–5)

> Images and illustrations were at his command, and rendered his discourses not only instructive, but absolutely fascinating . . . . To confine himself to dry argumentative discussion was impossible: he was not, he could not be didactic. The genius of the man broke through on every occasion, and gilded and adorned the topics he handled . . . . He was, not merely one of the most eminent preachers of his day, but one of a totally different order from others, a completely original preacher. (Wilson, 1810: 35–6)

Original though he was, Cecil possessed many traits characteristic of Anglican evangelicals, and this may have enhanced his influence. He was suspicious of 'the world' and believed that religious interests should take precedence over all else. He objected to histrionic preaching and had a high view of ministerial authority. However, he did not claim all the emoluments that were his due lest he antagonize the people. Sympathetic to good order in worship, he was one of several clergymen to publish editions of the Psalms. He sat on the first CMS committee, and was a founder member of the clerical discussion group, the EcS, which met in St John's vestry. He published memoirs of fellow members, JOHN NEWTON and JOHN BACON, and from 1806 to his death wrote for the *Christian Observer*. The letters published in his *Remains* (Cecil, 1811, 1) reveal his happiness as a family man, but like many evangelicals he was an over-anxious parent, scrutinizing his children's every action. He also laughed at their foibles. Six of his eleven children survived him.

SELECT WRITINGS
R. Cecil, *Works . . . with a memoir of his life . . . and a view of the author's character*, ed. J. Pratt, 4 vols (London, 1811)

BIBLIOGRAPHY
Al. Cant.
Alli
C. Cecil, *Memoirs of Mrs Hawkes . . . including remarks in conversation and extracts from sermons and letters of the late Richard Cecil* 2nd edn (London, 1838)
DNB
Gentleman's Magazine, 80 (1810) 2: 135–6, 196–7, 320
C. Jerram, *Memoirs*, ed. J. Jerram (London, 1855): 45–6, 236–7, 244–67
Julian
M. L. Loane, *Oxford and the Evangelical Succession* (London, 1950)
POBC
J. H. Pratt, *Eclectic Notes* (London, 1856)
D. Wilson, *The Blessedness of the Christian in Death* (London, 1810)

DOREEN M. ROSMAN

Cennick, John (b. Reading, England, 12 Dec. 1718; d. London, 4 July 1755). Calvinist and Moravian Methodist. His father's family were Quaker and perhaps of Bohemian extraction, and his mother had a Non-Juror background, but Cennick abandoned religion when he went to London until, attending church in Reading on 6 September 1737, he overcame a deep depression and found faith. Then he read GEORGE WHITEFIELD's journal, and decided to visit CHARLES KINCHIN, the evangelical Vicar of Dummer near Oxford. Here he met the WESLEYS and George Whitefield. In March 1739 John Wesley visited Cennick's society in Reading, and Cennick was invited to help at Kingswood. On 14 June 1739 he preached there in the open air at the urging of local people without reproof from Wesley, and was thus the first authorized Methodist lay preacher. For 18 months Cennick was employed at Kingswood, and his gentle pastoral work and competent teaching made him popular with the miners. He led a mission to rural Gloucestershire in the summer of 1740.

In the growing debate over Calvinism, he sympathized with Whitefield, alarmed by Wesleyan ideas of Christian perfection, and the demand for groans from people under conviction. In December 1740 he challenged Wesley, and then contacted Whitefield and formed a separate society. Wesley hastily purged his society, and in March 1741 expelled Cennick. Cennick opened a Calvinist tabernacle in Kingswood in June 1741. That summer he preached along the Welsh border in the company of HOWEL HARRIS, and many were converted, but there was violence in Swindon and Stretton and a mob dragged him through the streets. Cennick organized the converts into the 'Wiltshire Association', and by 1742 he and his association had become leading members of Whitefield's English Association.

He based himself at Tytherton, and was a diligent pastor and evangelist throughout the south of England. In Exeter a serious riot was provoked by his visit in May 1745. While preaching in London he met many Moravians including ZINZENDORF. As debates over Antinomianism divided Whitefield's supporters, he emphasized imputed righteousness, and was accused of Antinomianism. He sought escape by preaching in Ireland, but bad weather stopped him at Holyhead in October 1745. Instead, on 20 November 1745, he sought admission to the Moravian Brethren, and offered his Wiltshire societies to the Moravians – an offer confirmed by his societies' stewards on 18 December 1745.

This secession was a serious blow to Calvinist Methodism in England, yet the Moravians thought him 'very methodistical' when he visited Germany in December 1745. Zinzendorf sent him to Dublin in June 1746, and his preaching attracted intense interest from Catholics. A Moravian society was formed in Dublin in March 1747, and over the next five years Cennick preached throughout the east and north of Ireland. Perhaps 220 religious societies were formed through this work. He was ordained into Moravian deacon's orders in London in September 1749, and in 1753 he preached in Leominster and Haverfordwest, forming societies there.

In June 1747 he married Jane Briant. He wrote and published many vivid and homely sermons, and one of the first hymn-books of the revival, *Sacred Hymns for the Children of God* (1741). Financial embarrassment, criticisms of the Moravians and ill health strained his relations with the Moravians in the 1750s, and he died on a visit to London in 1755.

Cennick was one of the greatest evangelists of the revival, provoking dramatic conversions and fierce opposition wherever he preached. His emphasis on religious experience drew him to the Moravians in their 'quietist' period, but his theology was more Calvinist than Moravian.

SELECT WRITINGS
J. Cennick, *The Life of Mr J. Cennick*, 2nd edn (Bristol, England, 1745)

BIBLIOGRAPHY
F. Baker, *John Cennick (1718–55) A Handlist of his Writings* (Leicester, England, 1958)
DNB Supplement
J. E. Hutton, *John Cennick. A Sketch* (London, [1906])
V. W. Couillard, *The Theology of John Cennick* (Nazareth, PA, 1957)

PETER J. LINEHAM

Chalmers, Thomas (b. Anstruther, Fife, Scotland, 17 March 1780; d. Edinburgh, 31 May 1847). Presbyterian minister, political economist, and theologian. The son of a merchant of modest means, he was born in the small east Fife coastal burgh of Anstruther and educated at nearby St Andrews University, where he trained for the ministry in the established Church of Scotland. In 1802, he became minister of the rural Fifeshire parish of Kilmany. He was, however, more interested in the intellectual culture of the later Scottish Enlightenment than in the parish ministry. He neglected his parish while he lectured on mathematics and natural philosophy in St Andrews, arguing, in a pamphlet published in 1805, that after completing all his parish duties, a minister had five days a week of 'uninterrupted leisure' for whatever interests he wished to pursue. His efforts to gain literary fame and academic preferment failed, and in 1809, he was struck down with consumption. During his prolonged illness, he experienced a religious conversion.

In 1811, he reappeared on the religious scene in Fife in the new guise of impassioned evangelical preacher. He began to associate with the evangelical party in the Church of Scotland, and became a zealous advocate of missionary societies, particularly the BFBS. He also directed attention to his parish, taking an active role in parish education, house-to-house visiting and poor relief, and finding a new appreciation for the traditional communal values of rural Scotland.

His fame grew and in 1814, he became minister of the Tron church in Glasgow, where he attracted a large and prosperous congregation. Combining the learning of the Scottish Enlightenment with the passionate emotion of the evangelical revival, his preaching proved extremely popular among the educated public, while his published sermons and discourses had great commercial success. His *Discourses* of 1817, for example, in which he endeavoured to reconcile the biblical account of sin and redemption with the latest scientific teachings on the extent and nature of the universe, sold over 20,000 copies within a year. During a visit to London in 1817, he was lionized by the ruling elites and developed lasting friendships with leaders of the evangelical movement in England, including WILLIAM WILBERFORCE and ZACHARY MACAULAY.

Amid the economic distress that followed the end of the Napoleonic wars, Chalmers became increasingly concerned with the problems of the urban parish ministry in Glasgow. The clergy, it seemed, were becoming little more than chaplains to prosperous congregations, while the parish system was breaking down and the labouring orders were sinking into irreligion, ignorance, poverty and vice. He became convinced that only by reviving the parochial structures of the national church in the urban areas could a sense of community be revived and the condition of the labouring orders be permanently improved. In 1819, he persuaded the town council and magistrates of Glasgow to give him a free hand to conduct a parish experiment in St John's, a new parish of some 10,000 inhabitants in a working-class district.

At St John's, Chalmers endeavoured to adapt the traditional rural parish system to the new environment of the industrial city. His St John's system included the subdivision of the large urban parish into 25 territorial districts or 'proportions', and systematic and 'aggressive' house-to-house visiting by elders, deacons and Sunday school teachers. To each proportion, Chalmers assigned an elder, a deacon and one or more Sunday school teachers. The elders provided moral and spiritual guidance, and sought to revive a traditional discipline among the parishioners. The deacons were responsible for the care of the poor. They encouraged self-help and communal sharing among relatives and neighbours, and worked to eliminate any need for legal poor relief, which Chalmers believed demoralized the poor. Finally, Sunday school teachers organized neighbourhood Sunday schools and visited the children's homes to encourage parental interest in their children's education. Chalmers also established quality weekday schools, with modest fees, for the children of the parish, and he instituted informal Sunday evening worship for the labouring poor. The aim of the St John's programmes was to create in the crowded urban parish a sense of community, similar to that Chalmers had known in his rural parish of Kilmany.

The St John's experiment aroused considerable controversy, especially for its efforts to abolish legal poor relief in the industrial city. Critics viewed this as unrealistic and potentially harmful to urban paupers. Chalmers, however, was convinced that his experiment was a success, and had demonstrated a solution to the problems of irreligion and social dislocation in the industrial city.

In 1823, Chalmers left the Glasgow parish ministry for the chair of moral philosophy at St Andrews University. Five years later, in 1828, he became professor of divinity at the University of Edinburgh. As a professor, he continued to advocate his parish community ideal through his lectures and extensive publications in moral philosophy and political economy. He was concerned by the increasing emphasis on individual self-interest by economists and politicians, and by the increasing class tensions in industrial society. Only an effective parish system, he believed, could preserve industrial society from revolution and elevate the condition of the labouring orders. And this effective parish system, he further believed, could be achieved only through a well-endowed national established Church, informed by evangelical zeal and sympathetic to the aspirations of the people. He became a leading opponent of the movement after 1829 among Scottish Dissenters to disestablish the Church of Scotland. While he believed in religious toleration – and had strongly supported Catholic emancipation in 1829 – he also believed that religious liberty was compatible with a strong and well-endowed national church.

In 1834, Chalmers became the convener of the Church Extension Committee of the Church of Scotland, and began a campaign to increase radically the number of parish churches and schools. His aim was to organize the whole of Scotland's growing population into small parishes of no more than 2,000 inhabitants, in which a Christian communal discipline and cooperation would be revived through evangelical preaching and the work of elders, deacons and sabbath school teachers. Scotland would become a 'godly commonwealth' of closely knit parish communities. The churches and schools were to be built through voluntary contributions and then to receive a partial endowment from the State. By 1841, the campaign had erected over 220 new churches. To Chalmers's great disappointment, however, the British government refused to provide a grant for endowing the new churches. The Government was convinced that Scotland already had enough churches to meet demand and that Chalmers's 'Godly commonwealth' ideal threatened the religious liberties of Dissenters.

Relations between the Church of Scotland and the British government were further strained by the increasingly heated controversy over patronage. In 1834, the Church of Scotland had attempted to deal with the institution of lay patronage, which for long had been a divisive force in Scottish Presbyterianism. By law, patrons (who did not need to be members of the Church of Scotland) had the right to present candidates to vacant parish livings within their gift – regardless of the wishes of the congregation. With the 'Veto Act' of 1834, the Church of Scotland sought to remedy the grievance by giving the male communicants in parishes the right to veto a patron's undesirable candidate. The aim was to strengthen the popular element in the Church. 'Vetoed' candidates, however, began appealing to the civil courts, which supported their claims to the church livings. In 1838, the House of Lords declared the church's 'Veto Act' to be an illegal encroachment on the rights of patrons, and ordered presbyteries to ordain candidates presented by patrons regardless of the feelings of the parishioners. The result was a bitter conflict between church and state, with Chalmers leading the evangelical antipatronage party in the church. For Chalmers, the 'intrusion' of unpopular patronage appointees into parish churches undermined efforts to strengthen Christian communities. Further, by ordering church courts to perform the spiritual act of ordination, the state was claiming sovereignty over the church in spiritual matters, and challenging the fundamental doctrine of the church's spiritual independence.

At the Disruption of May 1843, Chalmers led over a third of the clergy and nearly half the lay members out of the Established Church to form the FCS. His hope was now to create a free national 'establishment' that would duplicate the parochial and educational structures of the Church of Scotland, and work without state interference to create the Godly commonwealth. Within a few years, the Free Church had erected over 800 churches and 500 schools, and was the second largest denomination in Scotland. Chalmers became professor of divinity and principal of the Free Church College in Edinburgh. Despite this success, however, Chalmers soon grew discouraged over the failure of the Free Church to have an impact on the growing irreligion and misery in the cities. He devoted his final years to setting up a model urban mission operation in Edinburgh and to organizing an interdenominational campaign for building churches and schools in deprived urban districts, arguing that the evangelical mission to the unchurched urban masses was far more important than even the interests of the Free Church.

SELECT WRITINGS

T. Chalmers, *Discourses on the Christian Revelation, viewed in Connexion with Modern Astronomy* (Glasgow, 1817)

—, *The Civic and Christian Economy of Large Towns*, 3 vols (Glasgow, 1819–26)

—, *On the Power, Wisdom and Goodness of God, Bridgewater Treatise*, 2 vols (London, 1833)

BIBLIOGRAPHY

S. J. Brown, *Thomas Chalmers and the Godly Commonwealth in Scotland* (Oxford, 1982)

W. Hanna, *Memoirs of Dr Chalmers*, 4 vols (Edinburgh, 1849–52)

New College Library, Edinburgh, Chalmers Papers

DNB

H. Watt, *Thomas Chalmers and the Disruption* (Edinburgh, 1943)

STEWART J. BROWN

Chamberlain, John (b. Welton, Northamptonshire, England, 24 July 1777; d. at sea, 6 Dec. 1821). BMS missionary in India. John was a farmer until studying at Olney for the ministry. After being accepted by the BMS, he travelled via New York to Serampore, arriving in January 1803. A troubled, contentious person, whose personality would have prevented his being chosen for missionary service today, John's activities at Serampore, and at various mission stations between there and Delhi, were surrounded by controversy: his 'thundering and vehemence of stile' while preaching to Indians, as WILLIAM WARD put it, 'rather frightens . . . than convinces them'. Much of his work, especially after he struck a young Brahmin with a cane at Katwa in 1807, was confined to preaching to European soldiers at Agra, Berhampore, and elsewhere. A collection of his letters (1802–21) is in the Angus Library, Regent's Park College, Oxford.

BIBLIOGRAPHY

C. B. Lewis, *John Chamberlain* (Calcutta, 1876)

E. D. Potts, *British Baptist Missionaries in India, 1793–1837* (Cambridge, 1967)

E. DANIEL POTTS

Champion, George (b. Winchester, CT, USA, 3 June 1810; d. Santa Cruz, US Virgin Islands, 17 Dec. 1841). ABCFM missionary to the Zulu. Champion graduated from Yale and then from Andover Newton Seminary near Boston. In December 1834, he sailed for South Africa, a member of the ABCFM pioneer party. While the Americans were detained in Cape Town because of the Frontier War, he was deeply influenced by JOHN PHILIP.

Champion reached Natal in December 1835 and concentrated on learning Zulu and trying to get Dingane to permit mission work among his people. In August, 1836, he and his wife visited Dingane and finally got the King's permission; however, Champion had to leave again because of the Zulu–Boer conflict in March 1838. He hoped to return but his health forced him to remain in the USA where for two years he served a church in Dover, Massachusetts, till ill health forced his retiring to the Caribbean where he died.

BIBLIOGRAPHY
A. R. Booth, ed., *Journal of the Reverend George Champion, American Missionary in Zululand, 1835–1839* (Cape Town, 1967)

ANDREW C. ROSS

Champneys, (William) Weldon (b. London, 6 April 1807; d. Lichfield, Staffordshire, England, 4 Feb. 1875). Anglican clergyman in East London. Born into a clerical family, he was educated privately, and then at Brasenose College, Oxford, where he became a fellow and junior bursar. He was ordained in 1830 and served a brief curacy at Dorchester, Oxfordshire. Either here, or previously at Oxford, he experienced conversion. He returned to Oxford as Curate of St Ebbe's, where both his ministry to the poorest parts of the parish, and his use of undergraduates as visitors were to shape his later ministry.

In 1837 he became Vicar of St Mary's, Whitechapel, a parish with a population of over 30,000 and containing some of East London's worst slums. He became perhaps the most effective slum clergyman of the mid-century, so that attendances of 100 a Sunday before his arrival had risen to a remarkable total of over 10,000 (including Sunday schools and district churches) by the time of the 1851 Religious Census. Champneys explanation for such growth was 'the gospel, very simply preached in the parish church'. He could hardly have referred to the strengths of his own character – described in Bullock's obituary as 'practicality and friendliness', and which are borne out by the impressions of the person left by his writings: *Parish Work* (London, 1866), a manual for clergy; *Facts & Fragments* (London, 1864) and *The Spirit & the Word* (London, 1862), two collections of pastoral anecdotes; and many shorter pieces.

Such writings also reveal Champneys as an important innovator of pastoral methods for slum parishes. Most significant were: 1) an emphasis on education. He founded well over twenty day, ragged and Sunday schools. He also showed considerable ability as a teacher of all ages in his parish work, where he placed major emphasis on confirmation preparation as a means of evangelism, and of laying the foundations of Christian living. 2) Lay visitors. He made extensive use of London City Missionaries, Scripture Readers and others, including those of Irish and Jewish background. By 1853 there were 13 Scripture Readers. 3) Church planting. Champneys built three new churches in his parish: St Paul's, Dock Street, a church for sailors; St Mark's, which was unendowed, depended on pew rents, and seems never to have been well-attended; St Jude's, which by contrast was an early example of a West End congregation providing for the building of an East End church, and had congregations of 1,400 and 2,200 in the 1851 Census. (It later fell on hard times: its poor condition on the arrival in 1873 of Canon Barnett, the founder of Toynbee Hall, has been well recorded by historians; its earlier effectiveness, widely ignored.)

Champneys was also vigorously involved in the needs of the local community – he founded a shoe-black brigade, savings bank, coal club, and young men's institute.

He was a member of the Health of Towns Association, and took the initiative in founding the Whitechapel Association to improve conditions in the area. Allegations that evangelicals of the day avoided 'structural' issues need to be qualified by Champneys' role in supporting an Act of Parliament to regulate the employment of 'coal-whippers' in the docks, so that they were no longer taken on in public houses. However, like his associate, Lord SHAFTESBURY, Champneys' attitude to social questions was always that of a compassionate and conscientious traditionalist. He could be vigorous in denouncing the injustices caused by the rise of industrialism, and the isolation of social classes with the growth of suburbs; he was increasingly critical of attempts to rectify such situations by the poor themselves.

In 1860 he became Vicar of St Pancras parish church in London, and in 1867 became Dean of Lichfield – a post he held until his death in 1875. Champneys was a founder member of both the Oxford Evangelical Trust and the staunchly protestant Church Association, and he was a supporter of the CPAS, CMS, YMCA and RTS. His younger brother was Edward Free Champneys (1809-October, 1845) secretary of the CPAS from March 1843 until his death.

BIBLIOGRAPHY
C. Bullock, 'Biographical Sketch', in *The Story of the Tentmaker, W. Weldon Champneys* (London, 1875)
DNB

JOHN B. ROOT

Chance, William (b. Birmingham, England, 29 August 1788; d. 8 Feb. 1856). Merchant and philanthropist. The fourth son of William Chance, a hardware merchant in Birmingham, he began his commercial life as a merchant trading with America. In the early 1830s he joined his elder brother Robert Lucas Chance in his glass firm in Smethwick. While conservative and prudent in business, he held an enthusiasm for philanthropy and social work. He devoted a great deal of his time to civic affairs: he was High Bailiff of Birmingham from 1829 to 1830, a member of the committee of the Chamber of Commerce, a Justice of the Peace, churchwarden of St Thomas's, governor of the Queen's College, director of the Birmingham Banking Company, and a generous supporter of education, social reform and missionary work. He married Phoebe (1811), the daughter of James Timmins, and had several children, including his eldest son Sir James Timmins Chance, first baronet.

BIBLIOGRAPHY
Aris's Birmingham Gazette (11 February 1856)
Burke's
J. F. Chance, *A History of the firm of Chance Brothers & Co.* (London, 1919)
W. W. Wilson, *A History of the Church of England Cemetery, Birmingham* (Birmingham, England, 1910): 15

D. E. H. MOLE

Chapin, Calvin (b. Springfield, MA, BNA, 22 July 1763; d. Wethersfield (now Rocky Hill) CT, USA, 16 March, 1851). Congregational minister and one of the founders of ABCFM. Chapin was the son of Edward Chapin of Chicopee, Massachusetts, and his wife Eunice Colton Chapin. He was graduated from Yale College in 1788. While teaching in Hartford, Connecticut, he experienced a call to the pastoral ministry. He then studied theology under NATHAN PERKINS and was licensed to preach by the Hartford North Association in October 1791. After his licensure and four years as a tutor at Yale, Chapin was ordained the pastor of the Stepney Parish, Wethersfield, Connecticut, where he remained until his retirement. He married Jerusha, a daughter of JONATHAN EDWARDS, and raised three children.

Chapin is particularly noted for his influence beyond his pastoral charge. He was a trustee of the Missionary Society of Connecticut, helped found the Connecticut Bible Society and the Connecticut Society for the promotion of good morals, along with being active in the temperance reform movement. In 1810, he was one of five to organize the ABCFM and was its recording secretary for thirty years. He also served for many years on the board of visitors of Andover Seminary and the Corporation of Yale College.

In 1816, received the degree of DD from Union College. He was noted for his 'exuberant and boundless wit' which one friend called 'the involuntary and irrepressible sallies of his boundless good nature'.

BIBLIOGRAPHY
AAP
DAB
E. P. Parker, *Appreciation of Calvin Chapin D.D. of Rocky Hill, Connecticut* (Providence, Rhode Island, 1908)

LELAND EDWARD WILSHIRE

Chapman, Charles (b. *c.* 1822). (*Fl.* 1830–50). Anglican Seceder. Chapman was probably educated at Trinity College, Oxford (BA 1844, MA 1848) and became Chaplain of Tresco and Breyer, in the Scilly Isles.

Around 1850, when evangelical emotions were running at fever pitch over the still undecided Gorham affair, Chapman seceded from the Church of England, denouncing the doctrine of baptismal regeneration as 'a monstrous error' which had 'unequivocally' been established in the Anglican formularies. On 7 July 1850, he, along with Mrs Chapman and nine others, was rebaptized by immersion at Countership Chapel, Bristol, by the Reverend Thomas Winter.

BIBLIOGRAPHY
Al. Ox.
Baptist Magazine (August 1850): 480–3

GRAYSON CARTER

Chapman, Robert (Cleaver) (b. Elsinore, Denmark, 4 Jan. 1803; d. Barnstaple, Devonshire, England, 12 June 1902). Solicitor and Brethren leader. The son of Thomas Chapman, a wealthy merchant, he was educated in Yorkshire, served articles in London, qualified as a solicitor, and practised on his own account. He was converted in 1823 through the preaching of JAMES HARINGTON EVANS, once an Anglican curate but since 1818 Minister of John Street Chapel, Bedford Row, London, an independent evangelical chapel built for him by HENRY DRUMMOND. Under Harington Evans's guidance, Chapman commenced preaching and district visitation.

Qualms of conscience about some aspects of his legal work, coupled with a call to the pastorate of Ebenezer Chapel, Barnstaple (where he had relatives), led to his removal from London in 1832 to the Devonshire town with which his name would become inseparably linked. Under the influence of Harington Evans he had already adopted views which, in developed form, are characteristic of Brethren. At Barnstaple, he stipulated that scripture should be the sole standard of Christian doctrine, and it was not long before believer's baptism (though still, of course, practised) ceased to be a test for communion, and time was set aside for open worship before the observance of the Lord's Supper. Although Chapman tried to secure unanimous acceptance of these changes, a small minority seceded and later claimed possession of the chapel. Chapman relinquished the chapel in about 1838 and a few years later built a new one in Grosvenor Street which became known as 'The Room'.

By the end of 1832, at the latest, Chapman had made the acquaintance of JOHN NELSON DARBY, GEORGE MÜLLER and other Brethren leaders. Barnstaple became the centre of widespread Brethren activity in the villages and small towns of north Devon. Chapman became the confidant and adviser of other Brethren leaders, especially George Müller, and Barnstaple became one of the leading Brethren assemblies. Chapman tried, without much success, to act as mediator during the estrangement of Darby from BENJAMIN WILLS NEWTON, Müller, and others.

Chapman, who was an accomplished linguist, made several evangelistic visits to Spain and Portugal. In 1863 he accompanied W. Gould and G. Lawrence and their wives who were going to Spain as missionaries from the Barnstaple area, and in 1871 he spent about eight months in Spain, during which time he visited H. Payne, another missionary from Barnstaple. He also conducted a three-month preaching tour of Ireland in 1848.

A man of deep spirituality, gracious spirit and an almost ascetic way of life, Chapman never married. His capacity for spiritual friendship extended not only to men such as William Hake, a schoolmaster, whose memorial, *Seventy Years of Pilgrimage*, Chapman edited, but also to ELIZABETH PAGET, a saintly woman who is one of several influential Brethren women. Chapman wrote numerous devotional booklets and hymns. His *Choice Sayings* circulated widely among Brethren.

BIBLIOGRAPHY
W. H. Bennett, *Robert Cleaver Chapman of Barnstaple* (Glasgow, circa 1902)

F. Holmes, *Brother Indeed* (London, 1966)
R. L. Peterson and A. Strauch, *Agape Leadership* (Littleton, CO, 1991)

HAROLD H. ROWDON

Chapman, Walter (b. Bath, Somerset, England, 1711; d. Shirehampton, Somerset, 25 April 1791). Oxford Methodist and vicar of Bradford on Avon, Wiltshire. Baptized 25 June 1711, he entered Pembroke College, Oxford, in 1729. Attached to the WESLEYS and WHITE-FIELD in the Holy Club, he was also a friend of JAMES HERVEY. After graduation (BA 1732, MA 1735) he served in Bath as Master of St John's Hospital. A canon of Bristol Cathedral from 1745, he conducted Bishop Butler's funeral service as subdean in 1752. His Wiltshire living, accepted in 1754, was in the gift of the Bristol dean and chapter. From his parish he evangelized the area and preached for Lady HUNTINGDON in Bath despite opposition. HOWELL HARRIS, who resumed his public ministry in 1763 through his influence, regarded him as a significant evangelical leader. Some mistakenly refer to him as 'William'. Extant letters are merely signed, W. Chapman.

A. SKEVINGTON WOOD

Charles, David (b. Llanfihangel Abercywyn, Wales, 11 Oct. 1762; d. Carmarthen, Wales, 2 Sept. 1834). Preacher, Welsh-language hymn-writer and theologian. Charles, eighth child of Rees Charles's second marriage, was a younger brother of THOMAS CHARLES. Apprenticed to a rope factory in Carmarthen, he eventually became manager and owner. Although converted at the age of 15 on reading RALPH ERSKINE's sermons, he did not begin preaching until he was 46. He played a key role in the formation of the Welsh Calvinistic Methodist's Confession of Faith 1823 and in setting up the denomination in southern Wales. Some dozen of his hymns are included in current hymnals, two of which on Providence are considered among the finest hymns in the language. Volumes of his sermons were published, in Welsh (1840 and 1860) and in English (1846).

BIBLIOGRAPHY
G. P. Owen, *Ffrydiau Gorfoledd* (Carmarthen, Wales, 1977)
D. W. Williams, 'Y Ddau David Charles – Emynwyr Tref Caerfyrddin', *Bwletin Cymdeithas Emynau Cymru* 1,8 (1975): 213–31

R. M. JONES

Charles, Thomas (b. Longmoor, Llanfihangel Abercywyn, Carmarthenshire, Wales, 14 Oct. 1755; d. Llanycil, Wales, 5 Oct. 1814). Methodist clergyman. Charles was son of Rice and Jael Charles. As a lad he was sent to a school at Llanddowror, where he became friendly with a pious old man, Rees Hugh, one of GRIFFITH JONES's converts. He entered the Nonconformist

Academy at Carmarthen in 1769, and was there for six years. In 1773, he heard DANIEL ROWLAND preaching at Newchapel, Pembrokeshire, and the sermon was the means of changing his life completely. He entered Jesus College, Oxford in 1775 and graduated there. He was ordained deacon in 1778 and priest in 1780. He served various curacies in Somerset – Sparkford, South Barrow, Lovington and Milborne Port – until 1783.

He made many friends in Oxford, men of evangelical views such as JOHN NEWTON of Olney, JOHN MAYOR, EDWARD GRIFFIN and SIMON LLOYD of Bala. After leaving Oxford he visited Wales; he preached his first sermon in Llanfihangel Abercywyn (Rees Hugh, his old mentor heard him there), visited Llangeitho and heard Rowland preach, and spent some time there with Simon Lloyd at Bala in Merioneth. It was there that he first met Sally Jones, whom he married in 1783. It was she who brought him back to Wales. After his marriage he assisted in various parishes – Llangynog, Llandegla and Bryneglwys, and Shawbury (Salop). In 1784 he was appointed curate of Llanymawddwy. He laboured zealously there and was approved and well-loved by the parishioners, but owing to his friendship with the Methodists he was given notice to quit by the incumbent. The upshot was a resolution on his part to become associated with the Methodists. A Methodist society had been established in Bala in 1745, and survived although weak in numbers and influence until 1784, when Thomas Charles cast his lot with them and became their leader. Mrs Charles owned a business in the town, and the shop became the means of his support for the rest of his life.

Daniel Rowland once said that Charles 'was God's gift to North Wales'. Very soon, after settling down at Bala, he made his influence felt and in a few years the town became the centre of Methodist activity in North Wales. His experience at Llanymawddwy had shown him that the people were illiterate. Griffith Jones's circulating schools had broken down, and he resolved to open similar schools in North Wales. He trained a number of teachers, wrote new manuals, and with the help of the Methodist societies he established schools where young and old might be taught to read the Scriptures. In time he became convinced that the schools could be held on Sundays. He was not the innovator of Sunday schools, but the movement he launched has stood the test of time. He wrote a catechism *The Christian Instructor*, published a monumental *Biblical Dictionary*, organized catechetical assemblies, founded a religious periodical *The Spiritual Treasury*, and established a printing press in Bala to publish religious literature. The schools flourished and became a feature in the life of churches of all denominations in Wales; they profoundly affected the common people.

Charles was a member of the SPCK, a society which had printed and circulated 10,000 copies of Welsh Bibles in 1799. The Sunday schools had created a new demand for the Scriptures. As a member of the RTS, Charles saw an opportunity to provide a regular supply of Bibles for his people in their own tongue, and (with others) he exerted his influence to establish the BFBS in 1804; one of the first publications of the new society was an edition of the New Testament in Welsh.

Before the end of the eighteenth century Charles was one of the prime leaders of the Welsh Calvinistic Methodists. He took a leading part in the expulsion of PETER WILLIAMS in 1796. Under his leadership many changes occurred. The local societies were given the right to choose their own elders, but confirmed afterwards by the association. This was a major step, of course, towards a Presbyterian form of church government. Rules were revised and new regulations adopted, chapels multiplied all over the principality and the Calvinistic Methodists flourished.

It must be remembered that the Methodist societies were still nominally within the Church of England. There were enough clergy of the Established Church to administer the sacraments to society members, and lay preachers of extraordinary powers had been nurtured within the movement. However, during the first decade of the nineteenth century, there grew a demand to ordain these lay preachers. Charles at first was unwilling to take this crucial step, but rather than see the movement disintegrate, he bowed to the demands of the societies. He prepared a form of ordination (which is still used) and a number of able and devout brethren were solemnly ordained in 1811 at Bala and Llandeilo Fawr (Carmarthenshire). This was a breaking point in the relationship between the Church of England and the Methodist societies. A few beneficed clergy resisted and stayed with their people.

Charles was only 56 years of age in 1811, but in a few years his health began to fail. He died after a brief illness, and was buried at Llanycil churchyard, within a mile of his home. The whole of Wales lamented his early death.

BIBLIOGRAPHY
D. E. Jenkins, *The Life of Thomas Charles of Bala*, 3 vols (Denbigh, Wales, 1908)

GOMER M. ROBERTS

Charlesworth, John (b. Ossington, Nottinghamshire, England, 1782; d. London, 22 Apr. 1864). Anglican clergyman. He was the son of John, Rector of Ossington, and grandson of another clergyman. Nothing is known of his education; he emerges at the age of 22 apprenticed to a surgeon in Clapham, Surrey.

HENRY THORNTON encouraged him to pursue a clerical career and Charlesworth was ordained in 1809, serving as curate of Happisburgh, Norfolk from 1809 to 1814. In 1814 Thornton presented him to the rectorship of Flowton, Suffolk, which he held for thirty years. From 1816 he studied at Cambridge, first at St Catharine's, and from 1822 at Queens' (BD 1826). He was also Rector of Blakenham Parva, near Ipswich (1819) and of St Mildred's, Bread Street, London (1844–64). Charlesworth played an energetic, if minor, role in the slavery abolition campaign and in evangelical societies: the

CMS, BFBS, RTS, CPAS, and the LSPCJ. As in his early years when he was secretary of the East Suffolk auxiliary of the LMS, so into mid-century when he was a clerical examiner for the LCM, Charlesworth exemplified a willingness to cooperate closely with Dissent, something which was then uncommon among Anglican evangelicals.

A friend of men more notable than himself, letters of THOMAS CLARKSON and WILLIAM MARSH, and revealing anecdotes of CHARLES SIMEON and EDWARD BICKERSTETH, are preserved in his biography. MARIA LOUISA CHARLESWORTH was his daughter.

BIBLIOGRAPHY
Boase
T. Cooper, ed., 'Charlesworth, Maria', *Men of the Time* 10th edn (London, 1879)
DNB, under Charlesworth, Maria Louisa (1819–1880)
J. P. Fitzgerald, *The Quiet Worker For Good* (London, 1865)
GM (1864): 803

JONATHAN BURKE CUTMORE

Charlesworth, Maria Louisa (b. Blakenham Parva, Suffolk, England, 1 Oct. 1819; d. Nutfield, Surrey, England, 16 Oct. 1880). Children's writer. Miss Charlesworth lived with her clergyman father until his death in 1864. She was always a tireless parish visitor; in later life she conducted numerous weekly Bible readings (some posthumously published) and mothers' meetings.

She wrote tracts, pamphlets, Bible stories, a missionary work, devotional books, sketches of her parish visitation experiences, a very popular children's narrative (*Ministering Children*, 1854), a less successful sequel (1867), and five novels. Although her didactic drive overwhelmed her modest literary skills, Miss Charlesworth accurately rendered conditions in villages and country towns, describing poverty and advocating voluntary measures for its amelioration: for her, material relief and practical kindness took precedence over unvarnished evangelism, but she emphasized the necessity for a conscious personal conversion.

BIBLIOGRAPHY
DNB
A. G. Newell, 'Studies in Evangelical Popular Prose Literature: Its Rise and Decline' (Liverpool Univ. Ph.D. thesis, 1976): 539–51

A. G. NEWELL

Charleton, Robert (b. Bristol, England, 15 April 1809; d. Ashley Down, Bristol, England, 5 Dec. 1872). Quaker manufacturer. Concerned for the education of the poor, he built and maintained schools in the Kingswood district of Bristol. He was a pioneer of total abstinence. About 1830 his religious views were affected by reading Archbishop Leighton (1611–84). During 1841–3 he accompanied Samuel Capper to Ireland, helping in tent meetings.

British Friends sent him, JOSEPH STURGE and Henry Pease to Russia in an effort to avert the outbreak of the Crimean War. He returned there in 1858 on a Quaker deputation to present 'A Plea for Liberty of Conscience'; the group also visited Finland and Denmark.

He was recorded a minister in 1860, actively promoted the Friends Foreign Mission Association (1868) and, like his cousin EDWARD ASH, opposed passages in Robert Barclay's *Apology for the True Christian Divinity* (1676) as unsound, his *Thoughts on Barclay's Apology* (1868) provoking controversy with conservative Quakers.

BIBLIOGRAPHY
Annual Monitor (1874): 18–50
DNB
A. F. Fox, *Memoir of Robert Charleton* (London, 1873)
W. Robinson, ed., *Friends of a Half Century* (London and Ashford, England, 1891): 96–100

EDWARD H. MILLIGAN

Chase, Philander (b. Cornish, NH, BNA, 14 Dec. 1775; d. Jubilee, IL, USA, 20 Sept. 1852). Bishop and educator, Protestant Episcopal Church, USA. Chase converted from Congregationalism to Episcopalianism as a student at Dartmouth College through reading a prayer-book. Ordained as priest in 1799, he served as a missionary in New York and Louisiana, a rector in Connecticut, and in 1818, was elected first bishop of Ohio. Between 1831 and 1835, he went into semi-retirement. In 1835, he became Bishop of Illinois – a position he retained until his death.

He was a committed evangelical and established Kenyon College in 1824 with the assistance of Church of England evangelicals at Gambier, Ohio against the wishes of the High Church party. Kenyon was extremely successful, and in the nineteenth century, it was a significant centre for the training of evangelical clergy. Chase's authoritarian manner, however, did not suit many of his faculty. Under pressure in 1831, he resigned his positions as Kenyon's president and as Bishop of Ohio.

For five years, Chase resided on a small farm. In 1835, Illinois Episcopalians elected him as their first bishop. He accepted and started his missionary activities once again. In 1839, he began Jubilee College, a second western evangelical Episcopal college. In 1843, he became presiding bishop of the Episcopal Church. He vigorously opposed Tractarianism and urged action against New York's Bishop Onderdonk for his ordination of Arthur Carey. Chase was badly injured in a carriage accident in 1845, and from that time until his death, he preached sitting in a chair.

SELECT WRITINGS
P. Chase, *Reminiscences*, 2 vols (Peoria, IL, 1841–1; Boston, MA, 1848)

BIBLIOGRAPHY
AAP
DAB
DcAmReB
L. Chase Smith, *The Life of Philander Chase* (New York, 1903)

DIANA HOCHSTEDT BUTLER

Chater, James (b. Bourton-on-the-Water, Gloucestershire, England, 1779; d. at sea, 2 Jan. 1829). Baptist missionary in Burma and Sri Lanka. A former student at Bristol Academy, Chater was denied government permission to become a permanent member of the Serampore Mission in India. Departing for Rangoon (Burma), with FELIX CAREY, in 1807 he founded the mission later taken over by ADONIRAM JUDSON. In 1812 the Chaters moved to Colombo (Sri Lanka). With the assistance of a Dutch convert, Hendrick Siers, Chater established a number of small churches in the Sinhala-speaking areas around the capital. Preparing, with the aid of others, a Sinhala grammar and a new translation of the Bible, he also organized 13 schools, attended by up to 600 children. Chater died while on his way home to England.

BIBLIOGRAPHY
F. A. Cox, *History of the Baptist Missionary Society* (London, 1842)
E. A. Payne, 'James Chater', in *The First Generation* (London, 1936)

E. DANIEL POTTS

Cheap, Andrew (b. London, 1775; d. Knaresborough, Yorkshire, England, 28 Aug. 1851). Anglican clergyman. Cheap was admitted as a fellow-commoner at Trinity Hall, Cambridge (LL B 1808), on transfer from Magdalen Hall, Oxford. He was already vicar of Knaresborough (1804) and became Rector of Elvington, Yorkshire (1809–41).

BIBLIOGRAPHY
Al. Cant. II. ii: 21
CO, I: 861

ARTHUR POLLARD

Cheever, George B(arrell) (b. Hallowell, ME, USA, 17 April 1807; d. Englewood, NJ, USA, 1 Oct. 1890). Congregationalist pastor, reformer, and author. The son of Nathaniel Cheever, a publisher and printer in Hallowell, Maine, he graduated from Bowdoin College in the class of 1825, which included Henry W. Longfellow and Nathaniel Hawthorne, and from Andover Seminary in 1830. Following ministry in Newburyport, Boston, and Salem in Massachusetts, Cheever pastored the Allen Street Presbyterian Church in New York from 1838 to 1844 and the Church of the Puritans, Union Square, New York from 1846 to 1867. Through his sermons, his editorship of *The New York Evangelist*, and his many essays in *The Independent* and other religious periodicals, Cheever, along with CHARLES FINNEY, led evangelicals in attacking what they considered to be the primary theological and social evils of the mid-nineteenth century. Throughout his long ministry Cheever fought against Unitarianism, Catholicism, the use of liquor, sabbath desecration, materialism, and especially slavery.

A strong abolitionist, he penned a dozen books and pamphlets decrying human bondage including *God Against Slavery* (1857), *Fire and Hammer of God's Word Against the Sin of Slavery* (1858), and *The Guilt of Slavery and the Crime of Slave-Holding, Demonstrated from the Hebrew and Greek Scriptures* (1860). Cheever argued that slavery was both an individual and a national sin, that the 'higher law' of God demanded its abolition, and that ministers were God's chosen agents for eradicating it. He also strongly supported equal education and full citizenship for blacks. In 1860 he journeyed to England to recruit support among British Christians for the emancipation of slaves in the United States. The next year he preached several times at meetings of the Senate and the House of Representatives, arguing that blacks were entitled to citizenship and representation.

Cheever's views on social reform issues substantially influenced Northern opinion. His 23 books and 50 pamphlets, reviews, and addresses discuss a wide range of topics including biography, literature, theology, travel, politics, and religion. Theologically, he was an evangelical exponent of New England Theology.

BIBLIOGRAPHY
G. I. Rockwood, *Cheever, Lincoln and Causes of the Civil War* (Worcester, MA, 1936): especially 40–55
T. Smith, *Revivalism and Social Reform* (Baltimore, MD, 1982)

GARY SCOTT SMITH

Chevalier, Thomas (b. London, 3 Nov. 1767; d. London, 9 June 1824). Surgeon, translator and Baptist deacon. Of Huguenot stock, he was trained as a surgeon, and surprisingly for a Dissenter graduated at Cambridge. Professor of surgery and anatomy at the London College of Surgeons, he wrote on the history and practice of medicine, and was appointed surgeon extraordinary to the Prince of Wales. For many years a deacon at the Keppel Street Baptist Chapel, he was also esteemed as the translator of Pascal and Bossuet, and also wrote the preface to Bagster's Polyglot Bible.

BIBLIOGRAPHY
DNB

J. H. Y. BRIGGS

Chichester, the third Earl of. *See* PELHAM, HENRY THOMAS

Childe, Charles Frederick (b. Shropshire, England, 17 Dec. 1807; d. Cheltenham, Gloucestershire, England, 17 Dec. 1897). Anglican clergyman. Childe held a scholarship at St John's College, Cambridge but transferred to Emmanuel (BA 1832; MA 1837). His first curacy was with JAMES SCHOLEFIELD at St Michael's, Cambridge (1833–7), from which he moved to be perpetual curate of St Paul's Walsall and headmaster of Walsall Grammar School (1837–9). Then for nearly twenty years he was principal of the CMS College, Islington (1839–58), after which he became Rector of Holbrook, Suffolk (1858–84).

BIBLIOGRAPHY
Al. Cant. II. ii: 28–9

ARTHUR POLLARD

Chiniquy, Charles (Pascal Télesphore) (b. Kamouraska, Lower Canada, 30 July 1809; d. Montreal, 16 Jan. 1899). Ex-priest, anti-Catholic writer, and lecturer. Chiniquy was ordained as a Roman Catholic priest in 1833 in Quebec City. Famous as the 'Apostle of Temperance', he achieved stunning success in procuring abstinence pledges. Chiniquy also led efforts to attack French Protestant missions in Quebec and to foster ultramontanism. In 1851 he was sent to St Anne, Illinois, as priest among French-Canadian immigrants. Obstinate refusal to submit to the Chicago bishop resulted in Chiniquy's 1858 excommunication. He and most of the parish became Presbyterians in 1860. Chiniquy quickly developed evangelical beliefs and piety. Till age 89, he alternated between pastoring St Anne's, leading Quebec missions, and engaging in lecture tours of Europe and Australia. Jesuit conspiracy, Catholic schools, the confessional and ritualism were key targets in his aggressive talks and books. His oratory in French or English, even in old age, drew large crowds, and also frequent mob attacks. Called the Luther of Canada, he was a champion for religious liberty against Catholic censorship. Chiniquy was among the most published anti-Catholic writers. Most histories, however, view Chiniquy as a preacher of hate, a traitor to his faith and to French Canada, a habitual liar, seducer, embezzler and egotist.

BIBLIOGRAPHY
DCB
P. Laverdure, 'Creating an Anti-Catholic Crusader', *JRH*, 15, 1 (1988): 94–108
R. Lougheed, 'The Controversial Conversion of Charles Chiniquy' (Univ. de Montréal Ph.D. thesis 1994)
M. Trudel, *Chiniquy* (Trois-Riviéres, Canada, 1955)

K. RICHARD LOUGHEED

Cholmondeley, George Horatio [second Marquess of Cholmondeley] (b. Paris, 16 Jan. 1792; d. Cholmondeley Castle, Nantwich, Cheshire, England, 8 May 1870). MP, peer, and landowner. Cholmondeley is an example of evangelicalism penetrating the English aristocracy during the Second Evangelical Awakening *c.* 1785–1825.

He inherited the vast lands of the family in Chesire, as well as Houghton Hall and its estate in Norfolk through his maternal grandfather, Robert Walpole, the first Earl of Orford. His father had been known as a Regency rake. His first wife died within a few years of marriage, and he then married one of the eight evangelical daughters of the Duke and Duchess of Beaufort (*see* CHARLOTTE SOPHIA SOMERSET).

Cholmondeley was MP for the family riding of Castle Rising, Norfolk (1817–21). In 1821 he entered the House of Lords in his father's barony of Newburgh and in 1827 he succeeded his father as second Marquess of Cholmondeley. Ford K. Brown, *Fathers of the Victorians*, lists him as a contributor to at least 23 societies and patron of eight. He was president of the Society for the Relief of Distressed Widows, the Friendly Female Society, the London Hibernian Society for the evangelization of Ireland, and the Metropolitan City Mission. He was vice-president of the CPAS, 1837–60, and was an active supporter of the Naval and Military Bible Society, and the General Society for Promoting District Visiting. He was succeeded by his younger brother, WILLIAM HENRY HUGH CHOLMONDELEY.

BIBLIOGRAPHY
Boase
V. Gibbs, ed., *The Complete Peerage* (London, 1910–57)

IAN S. RENNIE

Cholmondeley, William Henry Hugh [third Marquess of Cholmondeley] (b. London, 31 Aug. 1800; d. Houghton Hall, Rougham, Norfolk, England, 16 Dec. 1884). MP and peer. He was the second son of George James, fourth Earl and first Marquess of Cholmondeley. His older brother was GEORGE HORATIO CHOLMONDELEY. Cholmondeley was educated at Eton and Christ Church, Oxford (matriculated 1818) but did not take a degree. He married his cousin Maria Emma Georgina on 28 February 1825 by whom he had eight children, only two of whom survived him. He succeeded his brother as MP for Castle Rising (1822–32) and represented South Hampshire (1852–7), inheriting the title in 1870. In addition to the Cholmondeley castle in Cheshire, he also owned a house in Piccadilly, London, and Houghton Hall in Norfolk, the former seat of Sir Robert Walpole.

A friend of Lord SHAFTESBURY and Lord Chichester (*see* H. T. PELHAM), he was a supporter of a number of evangelical causes centred on Exeter Hall. He was one of the founders of the Scripture Readers Association (1845), and was vice-president of the CPAS (1848–60), and of the Young Men's Society for Aiding Missions. He also had the gift of five benefices and was alternate patron of two others.

BIBLIOGRAPHY
Boase
D. M. Lewis, *Lighten Their Darkness* (Westport, CT, 1986)
The Times (18 December 1884)

DONALD M. LEWIS

Chown, Joseph Parbery (b. Kingsthorpe, Northamptonshire, England, 9 Dec. 1821; d. London, 16 July 1886). Baptist minister and philanthropist. Of an ancient dissenting family, his father was a deacon of the Kingsthorpe church and a local preacher; he had a basic elementary education in day school while his spiritual formation continued from Sunday school into Bible class. After some youthful deviation, he was baptized in the river near Kingsthorpe, at the age of 19 began preaching, and was soon called to the pastorate at Ravensthorpe which he served for over a year until convinced of his need for further theological education which he secured at the Horton Academy, Bradford. Here he completed only half of his course before receiving a call in 1848 to Sion Chapel in neighbouring Bradford, which he accepted on condition that he could continue with as many classes as was feasible.

Chown increased the church's membership from 301 to 817 in a 27-year pastorate, gross additions being some 1,311. His own confidence in the Holy Spirit's ability to reach the hearts of men and women through preaching led to an impressive and powerful pulpit ministry, which three times required an extension of the chapel premises, before the removal to Harris Street in 1873, as well as the establishment of a thriving daughter church. Supporting this was his prioritizing the prayer meeting within his congregation, and his diligence in pastoral visitation. He was active in support of Sunday schools, for which new accommodation had to be provided at Sion and branch schools opened, and in the temperance movement which he viewed 'as only tributary to something higher and better to lead the way for the enjoyment of that saving religion in which men shall be blessed for eternity as well as for time'.

In 1854, the communion table at Sion was opened to members of other evangelical denominations. In 1864 Chown who had briefly served as joint secretary of the Yorkshire Association, became secretary of the Northern Education Society now removed to Rawdon but he declined Rochester University's offer of a DD, although holding America in great affection, having made a four-month extensive tour in 1865. Believing evangelism to be the supreme task of the church, Chown did not lightly become embroiled in controversial issues, but was a leader in the Saturday Half-Holiday movement, was concerned about the operation of the Contagious Diseases Act, and supported Savings Banks and Friendly Societies. He served as a founder member of the Board of the Fever Hospital and was for a short time a Poor Law Guardian. In the heyday of Nonconformist concern about the life of the city, a large number of men from Sion served in the municipal life of Bradford.

From the beginning of his ministry Chown had given himself to popular lecturing, initially for the Mechanics' Institute, sometimes to enormous audiences; the series of lectures for working men which he initiated in St George's Hall in 1866 not only secured him a wide hearing but also raised considerable sums for the town's charities. These lectures so established his name that Chown was soon in demand in other cities, including

London for the popular services and lectures organized at the Exeter Hall, as well as for the YMCA. His own testimony was that his approach to secular subjects, and small asides during their progress, had a decided evangelistic impact.

In 1871 he became President of the Yorkshire Association, but four years later came to the conclusion that the invitation to the congregation which WILLIAM BROCK had brought into being at Bloomsbury in London, was a summons he could not reject. C. H. SPURGEON took part in welcoming him to London. A long-serving member of the committee of the BMS, he now became chairman of its Candidates Committee. In 1879 he was elected president of the London Baptist Association. Already a member of the Baptist Union Council, in 1883 he became its president, delivering a thoroughly Christocentric address, but after his presidential year his health began to decline and at the end of 1885 he resigned from Bloomsbury, and died in the middle of the following year after a full and disciplined life of Christian ministry.

BIBLIOGRAPHY
The Baptist (July 1886): 42–4
Baptist Handbook (1887)
Boase
F. Bowers, 'Bloomsbury Chapel, 1848–1905' (Univ. of London, M. Phil. thesis, 1985)
The Freeman (16 July 1886): 464–5
D. Milner, 'J.P. Chown, 1821–86', *BQ*, XXV (1973): 15–40

J. H. Y. BRIGGS

Christaller, Johann Gottlieb (b. Winnenden, Germany, 19 Nov. 1827; d. Stuttgart, Germany, 16 Dec. 1895). Basel missionary and linguist, Gold Coast. At an early age he decided to become a missionary and entered the Basel Mission Seminary. There he displayed such outstanding scholarship and linguistic skill that he was sent by the Mission Board to the Gold Coast (modern Ghana) in 1853, solely to work on the Twi language which he had already begun to study in Basel. He was in the Gold Coast, moving round the various Basel Mission stations, until 1868. From the numerous Twi (Tshi) dialects he chose that of Akwapim to be the 'common book language' (or literary medium), and began translating the New Testament and other religious works into it. Eventually, aided by David Asante and Theophilus Opoku, he translated the whole Bible, published in 1871. He then published his magisterial *A Grammar of the Asante and Fante Language* (1875) and *Dictionary of the Asante and Fante Language called Twi* (1881), works that have never been superseded, despite later changes in orthography. He also published *A Collection of 3600 Tshi Proverbs* (1879) which, with his *Dictionary*, contained a mass of information about Fante culture.

Thus he helped to impress Gold Coast Africans, hitherto schooled to see English as the necessary literary and cultural medium, with an appreciation of their own culture. In retirement he edited a journal, *The Christian Messenger*, to encourage those who were not proficient in English to write in their own native language.

BIBLIOGRAPHY
L. H. Ofosu-Appiah, ed., *Encyclopaedia Africana, Dictionary of African Biography*, (New York, 1977)
D. Kimble *A Political History of Ghana* (Oxford, 1963)

CHRISTOPHER FYFE

Christie, Amelia (Martha) [née Bowman; Plenderleath, Mrs Amelia] (b. Nova Scotia, Canada, *c.* 1808; d. Bath, Somerset, England, 13 May 1898). Benefactor. From the merchant class, Bowman was noted for the 'refined and friendly' zeal she focused on charitable enterprises. In 1835 at Montreal, she married widower and landowner William Plenderleath (later CHRISTIE) and had a major influence on the religious and educational lives of their thousands of tenants. After her husband's death in 1845 and her departure for England in 1858, Christie exerted her influence through estate agent William McGinnis, whose papers are in the National Archives of Canada.

Christie was a powerful, if seldom visible, defender of evangelicalism in Quebec. For fifty years she braved the waters of church politics, and her determination is the force behind the foundation of an Anglican mission to the French Canadians at Sabrevois in 1847, its schools, and its transfer to the Colonial and Continental School Society in 1852. She also advocated the cause of anglophone education in rural Quebec, and was the sole support of several schools.

BIBLIOGRAPHY
R. W. Black, 'A Crippled Crusade . . . 1835–68' (Th.D. thesis, Toronto, 1989)
National Archives of Canada, Morgan Papers, MG 29, D61, vol. 5: (1727–31)

ROBERT MERRILL BLACK

Christie, William Plenderleath [Plenderleath, William] (b. England, 13 Dec. 1780; d. Blackrock, Ireland, 4 May 1845). Landowner, benefactor. Natural son of an officer, he served in his father's regiment 1793–1810. He twice married into Montreal's merchant class and assimilated its interests, using his connections and political office to establish evangelicals in Indian missions, and seeking to secure habitant loyalty by planting missionaries and Protestants on lands he controlled. Inheriting his father's Canadian estates in 1835, he took the name Christie and promptly increased support for the National British North America School Society, founded Trinity Chapel in Montreal, paid salaries for many evangelical agents, and dedicated lands to religious ends.

Christie's support is behind much evangelical activity in Quebec, 1820–45, although his personality and views did not endear him to many and he was forced to work through agents. He advocated proselytism; the Feller mission at Grande Ligne was dependant on his support 1836–45, but he declined to head the French Canadian Missionary Society (1839). He left Canada in 1843 for medical reasons.

BIBLIOGRAPHY
R. M. Black, 'A Crippled Crusade . . . 1835–68' (Toronto, Th.D. thesis, 1989)
DCB, VII, 184–5

ROBERT MERRILL BLACK

Christopher, Alfred (Millard William) (b. 14, Great Coram Street, Bloomsbury, London, 20 Aug. 1820; d. 4, Norham Road, Oxford, 10 March 1913). Schoolmaster and Anglican clergyman. Sixth son and twelfth child of George Christopher, wine-merchant, and Caroline (Ashington) of Morton House, Chiswick Mall, Middlesex, at the age of two Alfred went to live with his childless aunt Caroline and her husband Thomas Millard at Downend, Gloucestershire. In 1834 Alfred returned home, becoming a boarder at Hall Place School, Bexley, Kent, where he remained for five years and developed a love of cricket. Before going up to Cambridge, he spent three months as a pupil of the Reverend Charles Goodhart, minister of St Marys' proprietary chapel, Reading, where he came briefly under evangelical influence. In 1839 he matriculated from St John's College, Cambridge, migrating to Jesus College as a scholar the following year. He played cricket for Cambridge in 1843 and was also nineteenth wrangler (in that year said to have been equivalent to a first). At Oxford he was admitted MA *ad eundem* 1860, and incorporated from Trinity College, where his uncle Millard was a benefactor, in 1872.

In 1844 Christopher married a first cousin, Maria Frances Christopher (1816–1904), and from then till 1849 was a successful principal of La Martinière, Calcutta, a school for Anglo-Indians. One of his sisters had already been a continuing evangelical influence in his life; but it was during these years that Christopher was converted. He felt that he could not give his pupils the necessary means to overcome evil without Christ, and that he himself needed Jesus as Saviour. Encouraged by the Bishop of Calcutta, Dr DANIEL WILSON, Christopher returned home with a view to ordination.

Made deacon by Dr C. R. SUMNER, Bishop of Winchester, he was curate (to Canon J. D. Hales) at St John's, Richmond, Surrey, from 1849 to 1855. From 1851, owing to illness in his vicar's family, he was in charge of the parish, living at the vicarage. While there a cholera epidemic broke out, which called for courage and a sympathetic but determined leadership. Christopher was also unofficial chaplain to local girls' schools, including apparently the Royal Naval School. From 1855 to 1859, still living in Richmond, he was an association (area) secretary of the CMS, travelling widely, and effectively increasing interest in missionary work.

In 1859, E. P. HATHAWAY, was searching in vain for a minister to fill an important vacancy at St Aldate's Oxford. Hearing that Christopher would be suitable, he was able to meet and nominate him before the appointment lapsed. This led to a long and successful ministry to town and gown alike. Undergraduates were soon attracted. In 1862 Christopher largely rebuilt St Aldate's

church, to provide more room for his growing congregation. In 1865 he built new schools. Hitherto Christopher's Bible readings for undergraduates on Saturday evenings had been held in the dilapidated old rectory in Pembroke Street. (Christopher himself lived in North Oxford.) In 1869 he built in the garden a rectory room, thereafter the scene of many memorable meetings, and still in use. In 1878 he built a new rectory. In 1891 he built St Matthew's, Grandpont, as a daughter church, which soon filled, and in 1894 St Matthews' schools. A tireless visitor in the parish, and a notable distributor of tracts, Christopher engaged a succession of good curates, including Dr W. H. Griffith Thomas, theologian and author. Annual missionary breakfasts for undergraduates, with well-known speakers, became an established institution. In 1886 Christopher was collated honorary canon of Christ Church. A strong Protestant, he was a member of the committee of the Church Association from its foundation in 1865. In 1881 he was made a council member of the newly founded Wycliffe Hall.

Christopher had become deaf in India, but with the aid of a well-known ear trumpet, he smilingly overcame the difficulties this entailed. Partly owing to the arrival in Oxford of a younger man, F. J. Chavasse, who succeeded Canon H. LINTON at St Peter-le-Bailey in 1878, in later years Christopher's undergraduate following diminished. In 1884 a successful but distressing libel action, against a clerical brother-in-law of his wife, attracted wide sympathy. However, Christopher's enthusiasm for Christian faith, and his remarkable energy, rising early and working late, supported by lay workers as well as curates, enabled him to serve as rector until 1905. Amusing stories about his single-mindedness only added to his reputation. The death of Mrs Christopher in 1904 was the first intimation that it might be right to resign.

Christopher went to live, in 1905, with a granddaughter, in North Oxford. At 4 Norham Road he continued to hold small gatherings for Bible study on Sunday afternoons for a few undergraduates, among them the Lawrence brothers, including T. E. Lawrence 'of Arabia'. Christopher had influenced generation after generation of young men in the university, as well as countless parishioners, and at his passing in 1913 tributes from church leaders and others were unanimously appreciative. Thus the Regius Professor of Hebrew, Dr S. R. Driver, representing a decidedly different school of thought, spoke in Christ Church cathedral of 'his deep spirituality, his devotion to his Lord and Master, his ardent love of souls, his affectionate sympathy, his transparent sincerity' which 'impressed all who knew him, and secured him the respect and regard of all shades of opinion'.

BIBLIOGRAPHY
Burke's
A. C. S. Christopher (son), *The Family of Christopher* (Exeter, England 1933)
A. C. Downer, *A Century of Evangelical Religion in Oxford* (London, 1938)
J. S. Reynolds, *Canon Christopher* (Abingdon, England, 1967)

—, *Evangelicals at Oxford* (Oxford 1953; Appleford, England, 1975)

J. S. REYNOLDS

Chubbock, Emily   *See* JUDSON, EMILY CHUBBOCK

Church, Charles (b. Whitehaven, Cumberland, England, 1785; d. at sea, 15 Apr. 1822). Anglican minister and missionary. Church was educated at St Bees School and Trinity College, Cambridge. On being ordained he returned to his native diocese and became a curate at Beckermet then perpetual curate of Hensingham. In 1814 he was converted while preparing a series of addresses on regeneration. This transformed his ministry and his influence spread to nearby Whitehaven. Previously he had criticized the Bible Society: now he was its keen supporter.

In 1816 he responded to a call for chaplains for the East India Company. But his ministry in India was very brief. Between 1817 to his death he worked in three places, Cuddalore, Vizagapatam and Madras. Illness dogged his family. His three children became ill and one died. Church caught dysentery and died on the return journey home.

BIBLIOGRAPHY
J. Hough, *Memoir of an Indian Chaplain, the Rev. Charles Church MA* (London, 1859)

ALAN FREDERICK MUNDEN

Churchey, Walter (b. Brecon, Brecknockshire, Wales, 7 Nov. 1747; d. Hay, Brecknockshire, Wales, 3 Dec. 1805). Attorney and would-be religious poet. A schoolfellow of THOMAS COKE, he lived for most of his life at Hay-on-Wye: 'a lawyer with large family and a slender purse, a good, earnest, conceited old Methodist, who, unfortunately for his wife and children, had more delight in writing poetry than he had employment in preparing briefs' (Tyerman, 1870–1: 579). Coke's efforts to arrange for him to take Orders came to nothing and later in life he was influenced by the millenarianism of Richard Brothers. He entertained and corresponded with JOHN WESLEY and claimed to have suggested to him to idea of his *Arminian Magazine*. Against the advice of both COWPER and Wesley he published several volumes of mediocre religious verse. He married Mary Bevan of Clyro, one of his six children, Walter, becoming town clerk of Brecon, 1814–40. He was buried in the Priory churchyard at Brecon.

BIBLIOGRAPHY
DNB
DWB
J. H. Temple, 'Walter Churchey', *PWHS*, 38, 5 (1972): 152–3
L. Tyerman, *The Life and Times of the Revd John Wesley*, 3 vols, III (London, 1870–1)

JOHN A. VICKERS

Churchill, John Winston Spencer [Lord Blandford] [seventh Duke of Marlborough] (b. Garboldisham Hall, Norfolk, England, 2 June 1822, d. London, 5 July 1883). English MP and peer. Lord Blandford, as he was known from birth, was educated at Eton and Oriel College, Oxford, served as a lieutenant in the first Oxfordshire Yeomanry, and took his seat in the House of Commons as member for Woodstock in 1844. In the Commons he supported Peel in the abolition of the Corn Law and the Maynooth Grant, to the outrage of his father, the sixth Duke. In the late 1840s he was evidently touched by evangelicalism and was seen by the *Record* as the natural leader of the evangelical party in the Commons when his cousin Anthony Ashley Cooper [*see* Lord SHAFTESBURY] took his seat in the Lords in 1851. As a private member he introduced legislation to redistribute episcopal incomes, creating suffragan bishops and subdividing large parishes, and vainly advocated Christian instruction in Indian schools.

In 1857 he succeeded to the dukedom. Under Disraeli he served as Lord President of the Council 1867–8 taking a particular interest in education, and had limited success as Viceroy of Ireland 1876–80. He was noted for his charity, although he had to sell some of the treasures of Blenheim Palace. Rowse (1958: 215) unkindly calls him 'a full-blown Victorian prig'. He married Lady Frances Tempest, daughter of the third Marquis of Londonderry and Lord Randolph was their second son.

SELECT WRITINGS
Lord Blandford, *A letter to the Hon. Sir George Grey, Bart, on Some Points connected with the Past and Proposed Legislation for the Church of England* (Westminster, England, 1856)
Marquis of Blandford, *The Management of Episcopal and Capitular Property* (London, 1853)
—, *Education (India)* (London, 1860)

BIBLIOGRAPHY
DNB
Record (3 July 1851)
A. L. Rowse, *The later Churchills* (London, 1958)

PETER J. LINEHAM

Churton, (Henry Burgess) Whitaker (b. Middleton Cheney rectory, Northamptonshire, England, 20 Sept. 1810; d. Icklesham vicarage, Sussex, England, 5 April 1891). College tutor and Anglican clergyman. Son of Ralph (Rector of Middleton Cheney, Archdeacon of St David's, of an old clerical family) and Mary (Calcot), Whitaker was educated at St Paul's (1819–22) and Charterhouse, London. Scholar of Balliol College, Oxford, 1828–33, he took a first class (*literae humaniores*) and became fellow of Brasenose College (1833–43), where (accounted by Pusey 'the best Hebraist of his day') he served as Hebrew and divinity lecturer from 1837, being contemporary with W. W. CHAMPNEYS. One pupil was apparently F. W. ROBERTSON, later of Brighton. Ordained at Oxford in 1835 (ordination papers missing), he became Curate-in-charge of St Ebbe's, Oxford, 1838–42, succeeding J. GARNIER. His 5.30 a.m. services for work people were well attended. He promoted a district church in the parish (Holy Trinity, built 1844), in aid of which his edition of Gerhard's *Meditations* (1840) was sold. Otherwise he published little.

Briefly Rector of St George's-in-the-East, London, 1842–4, Churton's former principal at Brasenose, A. T. Gilbert, as Bishop of Chichester, made him Prebendary of Colworth (1842–91), Vicar of Icklesham, Sussex (1844–91), where smuggling was an inherited problem, and Rural Dean of Hastings ii (1845–80). Serious ill health in 1846 did not preclude a long incumbency. While examining chaplain to Gilbert (1845–70) and subsequently to Durnford, he was influential in training diocesan ordinands. Known as an unusually saintly and scholarly pastor, who held melodious family prayers several times a day, in 1848–9 he not only restored Icklesham church, building a school, but erected a chapel-of-ease at Rye Harbour, with another school. He kept in touch with the wider church, his friends including (besides C. A. HEURTLEY) Keble and Pusey. He himself was 'a most able expounder of Holy Scripture', preaching effectively in the slums of Seven Dials during the London Mission of 1871.

Churton married (1842) Anna Maria (1828–79), daughter of Thomas Clarke, a notably evangelical Vicar of Micheldever, Hampshire, by whom he had a son Theodore (Archdeacon of Hastings). Churton also had three distinguished clerical brothers, of whom Thomas was one of the 'Four Tutors' at Oxford (1841). Another, Edward (Archdeacon of Cleveland), as father-in-law of his curate William Inge (Provost of Worcester College, Oxford, 1881–1903) became grandfather of 'the gloomy dean', W. R. Inge, Dean of St Paul's 1911–34 (*DNB*).

BIBLIOGRAPHY
Anon. (friends), *Theodore Churton* (London, 1918)
G. T. Cameron, *Life of Mrs Cameron*, 2nd edn (London, 1873)
W. R. Churton, funeral *Sermon*, with *Memoir* (Cambridge, 1891)
Information from Mr V. Churton; Mr A. S. Boyce, Icklesham
M. H. de Massue de Ruvigny, *Blood Royal of Britain* (London, 1903)
J. S. Reynolds, *Evangelicals at Oxford* (Oxford, 1953; Appleford, England, 1975)

J. S. REYNOLDS

Clap, Thomas (Stephen) (b. Scituate, MA, BNA, 26 June 1703; d. New Haven, CT, BNA, 7 Jan. 1767). Congregational minister and president of Yale College. After earning degrees at Harvard (BA 1722, MA 1725), Clap was pastor of the First Church in Windham, Connecticut, until called to Yale in 1740. Although he strengthened Yale's curriculum (especially in mathematics and science), and enlarged its student body, Clap was never far from controversy. He welcomed GEORGE WHITEFIELD's first revival tour in 1740, but quickly turned against the excesses of the 'Great Awakening' and supported a 1742 law against itinerant preaching.

A leader of Connecticut's 'Old Light' opposition to Whitefield in the mid-1740s, Clap switched allegiances a decade later to secure support for his plan to make Yale a fortress for Calvinist 'orthodoxy' against incursions by Anglicans and Arminians. Campus riots against his rigid policies drove him from office in 1766. Clap's *Annals, or History of Yale College* (1766) continues to be an important resource, even though it bends facts about the college's founding to fit his political agenda.

BIBLIOGRAPHY
F. Dexter, 'Thomas Clap and his Writings', *New Haven Colony Historical Society Papers*, V (1894): 247–74
S. Nissenbaum, ed., *The Great Awakening at Yale College* (Belmont, CA, 1972)
L. Tucker, *Puritan Protagonist* (Chapel Hill, NC, 1962)

CHRISTOPHER GRASSO

Clark, Davis Wasgatt (b. Mount Desert, ME, USA, 12 Feb. 1812; d. Cincinnati, OH, USA, 23 May 1871). Methodist bishop and editor. Clark was educated at Maine Wesleyan Seminary, Readfield, Maine and Wesleyan university, Middleton, Connecticut where he graduated in 1836. He served as professor of moral philosophy and principal of Amenia Seminary, Dutchess County, New York, 1836–43 and as a pastor in the New York Conference, 1843–53. In 1853, he became editor of the *Ladies Repository*, a magazine which was published in Cincinnati, Ohio. He was appointed bishop in 1864.

Although an abolitionist, Clark opposed the Wesleyan Methodist separation in 1843 and urged abolitionists to work quietly within the church. Following the Civil War, he took an active role in organizing a number of annual conferences of the MEC in the South. He served as president of the MEC's Freedmen's Aid Society. Fascinated by death, in part attributable to the early deaths of his own children, Clark wrote two books contemplating death, *Death-Bed Scenes* (1855) and *Man All-Immortal* (1864). He also wrote a controversial biography of Methodist Bishop ELIJAH HEDDING, *Life and Times of Bishop Hedding* (1855). In this work, Clark antagonized advocates of Christian perfection by indicating that the bishop had never publicly professed to have experienced entire sanctification. As a consequence attacks on Clark's orthodoxy, including one written by NATHAN BANGS, appeared in *Christian Advocate Journal* and in *The Beauty of Holiness*. Personal papers of Clark are located at the Cincinnati Historical Society, Cincinnati, Ohio.

BIBLIOGRAPHY
D. Curry, *Life-Story of Rev. Davis Wasgatt Clark, Bishop of the Methodist Church* (New York, 1873)
EWM
F. D. Leete, *Methodist Bishops* (Nashville, TN, 1984): 43–4

WILLIAM KOSTLEVY

Clark, John (b. Hartford, NY, USA, 30 July 1797; d. Chicago, IL, USA, 11 July 1854). Early American frontier missionary. He was born of Baptist parents and out of economic necessity was employed from the time he was eight years old. In 1815, he was apprenticed for three years to a tanner. Deep spiritual turmoil in 1817 led him to a Methodist class meeting and his conversion. After receiving his exhorter's licence, he was released from his apprenticeship early by his employer who believed Clark was called to preach.

Clark received his local preacher's licence in 1819 and was admitted to the New York Conference in 1820. He was ordained deacon in 1822 and married Sarah Foote the next year. From 1821 to 1828, he served Leyden, Montgomery, Pittstown, Warren, and Sandy Hill and Glen Fall's circuits. After serving in Middlebury, Vermont, he was named presiding elder of the Plattsburg district in 1828.

Clark had long been interested in the mission to the Indians. At the 1832 General Conference which extended the work to Indians, Clark volunteered for mission service. Through extensive travels and visits with the Indians, his ministry led to many conversions as he established several schools and missions in Wisconsin and Minnesota, including those at Sault Ste Marie and Kewowenon. He was held in great respect by all those with whom he worked.

In 1841, Clark's missionary zeal led him to an assignment as presiding elder to the Rutersville district, an area of Texas plagued by raiding bands of Mexicans and Indians. At the 1844 General Conference, he voted with the Northern majority against slavery. It was an issue that divided the Methodist Church and precipitated Clark's transfer to the Poultney, Troy and Albany Districts in New York following General Conference.

In 1852 he transferred to the Rock River Conference and was appointed to Clark Street Church in Chicago. It was there that he influenced Mrs Eliza Garrett to donate $100,000 for founding Garrett Biblical Institute. In 1854, his last mission was assisting cholera victims. Clark then died of the disease himself and was buried in Aurora, Illinois.

Clark was an untiring worker in spreading the Christian message through missions in the American West. 'Devotion to God and his cause' was his motto. Not only did he travel widely among the Indians, but his speeches generated interest and financial aid for the missions. His stand against slavery and his ministry to victims of cholera, which ultimately took his own life, stand in testimony to his devotion to ministry.

BIBLIOGRAPHY
AAP
W. C. Barclay, *History of Methodist Missions* (New York, 1949, 1950)
EWM
B. M. Hall, *The Life of Rev. John Clark* (New York, 1856)
M. B. Macmillan, *The Methodist Church in Michigan* (Grand Rapids, MI, 1967)
MQR
MR

W. C. S. Pellowe, R. A. Brunger, and J. Marvin, *History of Methodism in the Upper Peninsula* (Adrian, MI, 1955)

SONDRA H. MATTHAEI

Clark, John (b. Gateshead, England, 19 Dec. 1809; d. 2 July 1880). BMS missionary to Jamaica. Clark grew up in the Thrapston church where his mother Mary was a member. He moved to London and worked as a printer with Haddon of Castle Street where the BMS accounts were printed. He joined the Devonshire Square Baptist Church where THOMAS PRICE was pastor. He moved to Bedford and attended the Old Bunyan Meeting from which he was accepted by the BMS in March 1835.

Arriving in St Anns Bay, Jamaica on 7 August 1835 he began as assistant to James Coultart. When Coultart died the following year Clark was put in charge. He took up residence at Brown's Town where the stayed for fifty years. He was foremost in the criticism of the apprenticeship system calling it a halfway house of slavery. His home became the base of the investigation and through this friendship developed with JOSEPH STURGE and William Harvey. He was instrumental in setting up in its place the Free Village System in which the freed slave was able to purchase and own his own home. With Sturge's help he created a fund from which emancipated persons could borrow at low interest. THOMAS CLARKSON was also in communication with him. His aim was to create a free land-owning peasantry in the Dry Harbor Mountains along the lines of Samuel Smiles and John Cobb. In each village there was a school and a church with the houses radiating from them. He also developed among the membership a responsibility for Africa and in 1843 several members from the church went there on the *Chilmark*. Later in the century, the church continued to provide missionaries through the Grattan Guinness organization when the BMS withdrew. In his time he founded ten villages which are now large towns.

SELECT WRITINGS
J. Clark, *Northampton Biographies*, XXII (Northampton, England, 1892)

HORACE RUSSELL

Clark, John Alonzo (b. Pittsfield, MA, USA, 6 May 1801; d. Philadelphia, PA, USA, 27 Nov. 1843). Protestant Episcopal clergyman. Born in Massachusetts but raised in upstate New York in an old Episcopal family (two of his brothers were Episcopal clergymen), Clark 'became interested in his personal salvation' in 1816, and was confirmed by Bishop J. H. Hobart. He graduated from Union College in 1823 and from General Theological Seminary in New York City in 1826. He was ordained deacon by Bishop Hobart on 12 April 1826, and served several of Hobart's missionary stations in New York until 1829, when he was made assistant Rector of Christ Church, New York, under the oversight of the church's evangelical rector, Dr Thomas Lyell.

In 1832, Clark accepted the call of Grace Church, Providence, Rhode Island, to become rector, and despite feeble health, he speedily built up the parish from 41 to 157 communicants by the use of weekly lectures and 'meetings in private homes' for preaching and evangelism. His successes called him to the attention of St Andrew's Church, Philadelphia, in 1835, where he was installed as successor to GREGORY TOWNSEND BEDELL. There, among his other labours, he wrote *A Walk About Zion* (1836), a spirited justification of the Episcopal Church as a truly evangelical church.

After only two years, illness forced upon him a nine-month sabbatical in Europe which he used to write a two-volume travelogue, *Glimpses of the Old World* (1838). But his recuperation was brief, and in 1843, the onset of his final illness compelled his resignation from St Andrew's. In addition to three volumes of evangelical essays and addresses (*The Pastor's Testimony*, 1834, *Gathered Fragments*, 1836, *Gleanings By the Way*, 1842) which he published during his lifetime, a volume of sermons, *Awake Thou Sleeper* (1844), was published posthumously. From 1838, he was the co-editor of the *Episcopal Recorder*.

BIBLIOGRAPHY
E. C. Chorley, *Men and Movements in the American Episcopal Church* (New York, 1950)
W. B. Sprague, *Annals of the American Pulpit*, 5 (New York, 1857)
S. H. Tyng, 'Memoir', in *Glimpses of the Old World* (London, 1847 edn)

ALLEN C. GUELZO

Clark, Thomas March (b. Newburyport, MA, USA, 4 July 1812; d. Newport, RI, USA, 7 Sept. 1903). Fifth Episcopal bishop of Rhode Island. He was the son of Thomas March Clark and his second wife Rebecca Wheelwright. Both the Clark and Wheelwright families were Presbyterian, and he was raised in a Calvinist environment. After schooling in Newburyport and Framingham, Massachusetts, he attended Phillips Academy, Andover. At 14 he entered Amherst College, but dropped out, and in 1828 entered Yale, graduating in 1831. For two years, 1831–3, he was head of the high school in Lowell, Massachusetts. He then decided to prepare for the Presbyterian ministry and studied for two years, 1833–5, at Princeton Theological Seminary.

He was licensed to preach by the Presbytery of Newburyport, Massachusetts, and for a few months supplied the pulpit at Old South Church, Boston (a Congregational church). By this time he was moving away from the 'old Calvinism' of Princeton. While at Old South Church he became dissatisfied with the lack of liturgical substance in Presbyerian worship and decided to enter the Episcopal ministry. He was ordained deacon on 3 February 1836 and priest on 6 November 1836, by Bishop ALEXANDER VIETS GRISWOLD of the Eastern Diocese. He was Rector of Grace Church, Boston, 1836–43, Rector of St Andrew's Church, Philadelphia, 1843–6,

assistant minister of Trinity Church, Boston, 1846–50, and Rector of Christ Church, Hartford, 1850–4. Much to his surprise he was elected Bishop of Rhode Island, and was consecrated on 6 December 1854 at Grace Church, Providence. He was bishop for 49 years, and from 7 February 1899 until his death was presiding bishop of the Episcopal Church, being the senior bishop by consecration. He was a moderate evangelical and in the later years of his episcopate was sympathetic to the Broad Church movement. He received an honorary DD from Union College in 1857 and an honorary LL D from Cambridge University in 1867.

BIBLIOGRAPHY
DAB

DONALD SMITH ARMENTROUT

Clarke, Adam (b. Moybeg, Londonderry, Ireland, c. 1760; d. London, 26 Aug. 1832). Wesleyan preacher, Biblical commentator, theologian, linguist and scholar. The exact year of Clarke's birth is uncertain. His father, John Clarke, MA was a schoolmaster, Church of Ireland minister and farmer in an effort to care for his family in Ireland. Frequent moves and poverty caused Adam Clarke to develop slowly as a student, but eventually he would, by age twenty, be adept in mathematics and several languages. He was converted in a Methodist context (1778) and, together with his mother, joined a Methodist society. His academic prowess was then turned toward the study of the Bible. He began exhorting in society meetings and preached his first sermon at New Buildings, Ireland, 19 June 1782.

He came to JOHN WESLEY's attention and he was sent to Kingswood School for continued education. However, unhappy in the restrictive context, he stayed only one month and was assigned as the Methodist preacher in Bradford, Wiltshire (September 1782). This was followed by successful assignments to Cornwall and to the Channel Islands (because of his abilities with French) where he introduced Methodism to Alderney, as well as Liverpool (1793–5) where the society doubled under his leadership. An able preacher, Clarke was elected president of the Wesleyan Conference in 1806, 1814, and 1822.

In 1795, Clarke was assigned to London (where he would remain for most of his life) so that he could develop his scholarly interests, while being in charge of the entire London circuit, a responsibility which required walking up to twenty miles each day. He taught himself Hebrew, Syriac, Arabic, Persian, Sanscrit, Armenian, Coptic and Ethiopic as well as Greek, Latin and Hebrew and became thoroughly aware of the literature in the language. The natural sciences also attracted his attention. He contributed to the *Eclectic Review* from its beginning in 1804, and worked with the BFBS to produce editions in Middle Eastern languages.

These and other scholarly publications brought him recognition and national prestige unusual in Methodist circles. In 1807 he received a MA from King's College,

University of Aberdeen and the LL D (1808). He eventually became a fellow of the Royal Asiatic Society and the Antiquarian Society, as well as a member of the Geological Society of London, the EcS and the American Historical Institute. Among the early publications were the six volume *A Bibliographical Dictionary Containing a Chronological Account ... of Books ... in All Departments of Literature* (London, 1802–4) which provided bibliography, anecdotes and evaluated translations. It was supplemented by *The Bibliographic Miscellany* (2 vols, London, 1806) and *An Account of the English Translations of all the Greek and Roman Classics and Ecclesiastical Writers* (London, 1806). He also provided a new edition and translation of Wesleyan favourite, C. Fleury, *A Short History of the Ancient Israelites* (Liverpool, 1802). Clarke was requested by the House of Commons (1808) to re-edit Thomas Rymer's *Foedera*, a collection of state papers in the national archives, of which he edited the first two volumes.

Clarke was interested in missions. He did evangelistic work among immigrants in London, supported missionaries to the Shetland Islands, including SAMUEL DUNN, and raised funds to build chapels. He wrote *A Short Account of the Introduction of the Gospel into the British Isles* (London, 1815) and *Christian Missions* (London, 1837) as well as *The Love of God to a Lost World, Demonstrated by the Incarnation and Death of Christ, A Discourse on John iii. 16* (London, 1818).

Although he wrote on various theological and ethical subjects, his most significant contribution was the eight volume commentary, *The Holy Bible ... with a Commentary and Critical Notes* (London, 1810–25). With this work Clarke became embroiled in a controversy over Christology. He maintained the divinity of Christ but denied the concept of 'eternal sonship'. This elicited critiques by Methodists HENRY MOORE, RICHARD WATSON and Richard Treffry and clouded his relationships with his church.

After his death, caused by cholera, Clarke's library and manuscripts were sold at auction [*Catalogue of the Valuable and Extensive Library, Ancient Inscriptions and Mosaics which will be sold at auction, of the late Adam Clarke* (London, 1833), and the Sotheby sale, *Catalogue of the ... European and Asiatic Manuscripts of the Late Dr A. Clarke* (London, 1836)]. Samuel Dunn edited *The Miscellaneous Works of Adam Clarke* (13 vols, London, 1836–7). Despite the doctrinal controversy, several of Adam Clarke's works went through numerous editions after his death in both England and North America. Some were translated into Welsh and German. His influence on the development of the doctrine of sanctification in the American Holiness movement was significant as his understanding of the instantaneous character of the experience became standard.

SELECT WRITINGS

A. Clarke, *An Account of the Infancy, Religious and Literary Life of Adam Clarke, LL D ... Partly Written by Himself and Continued by One of His Daughters* (London, 1833)
—, *Memoirs of the Wesley Family* (London, 1823)

BIBLIOGRAPHY
S. Dunn, *The Life of Adam Clarke* (London, 1863)
J. W. Etheridge, *The Life of Rev. Adam Clarke* (London, 1858)
R. H. Gallagher, *Adam Clark* (Belfast, 1963)
D. McCarthy, 'Early Wesleyan Views of Scripture,' *Wesleyan Theological Journal*, 16 (1981): 95–105
I. Sellers, *Adam Clarke, Controversialist* (St Columb Major, England, 1976)
W. H. Vermillion, 'The Doctrinal Use of Scripture in the Wesleyan Movement,' *Wesleyan Theological Journal*, 16 (1981): 51–67

DAVID BUNDY

Clarke, Edward Daniel (b. Willingdon, Sussex, England, 5 June 1769; d. London, 9 March 1822). Anglican clergyman, scientist, and traveller. Coming from Tonbridge School, Clarke entered Jesus College, Cambridge (BA 1790; MA 1794; LL D 1803; fellow, 1795–1806; tutor 1803–6). Clarke was restlessly curious and active. Up to the time of his marriage in 1806 he travelled with various companies not only in the European countries of the Grand Tour but throughout Scandinavia right up to Lapland and deep into Russia, all the time collecting on a vast scale – 'Plants, minerals, antiquities, statistics, geography, customs, insects, animals, climates, everything I could observe and preserve I have done'. His most spectacular prize was a two-ton marble statue from Eleusis (Greece), lost in and then rescued from a shipwreck off Beachy Head. He became professor of mineralogy (1808) and university librarian (1817).

Clarke was ordained in 1805 and served as Rector of Harlton (Cambridgeshire) (1806–22) and of Yeldham (Essex) (1810–22), being also Curate of All Saints Cambridge (1819). He wrote a pamphlet against Herbert Marsh's strictures on the newly proposed Cambridge auxiliary of the Bible Society in 1812.

BIBLIOGRAPHY
DNB

ARTHUR POLLARD

Clarke, George (b. Wymondham, Norfolk, England, 27 Jan. 1798; d. Waimate North, New Zealand, 29 July 1875). CMS missionary in New Zealand. A gunsmith and carpenter, Clarke trained as a teacher. Together with his wife, Mary, he sailed to Australia in 1822 where he worked in the New South Wales Aboriginal government settlement at Blacktown. Arriving in New Zealand in 1824 he was stationed at Kerikeri, the home of the great Ngapuhi chief, Hongi Hika. While he refused to aid Hongi's warlike ambitions, Clarke had considerable respect for him. Clarke commenced a school, teaching basic subjects, carpentry and blacksmith skills. He played a leading part in establishing the CMS station and farm at Waimate North in 1830 which was important for both training Maori and supporting the mission. One of the most able lay missionaries, Clarke also acted as CMS New Zealand secretary.

Appointed with the approval of his colleagues as 'chief protector of the aborigines' after the annexation of New Zealand in 1840, he found himself in the ambiguous position of having to defend Maori interests and to try and secure Maori land for the growing settler community. A strong supporter of Maori rights and critic of the colonists, he tried to promote peace, but outbreaks of violence at Wairau in 1843 and in the Bay of Islands 1844–5 indicated his powerlessness. He worked closely with Governors Hobson, Shortland and FitzRoy but in 1846 Grey abolished his office and worked to undermine missionary influence. He resumed work as CMS secretary, but was dismissed in 1849 over the issue of missionaries' land holdings. Clarke was a successful farmer, justice of the peace, member of the first Auckland Provincial Council, civil commissioner in the Bay of Islands and from 1865 a judge of the Native Land Court. Firmly identified with the evangelical and humanitarian interests of the missionaries, Clarke had a deep understanding of Maori affairs.

His son, George (1823–1913), was a Maori interpreter. After training in England he served as a Congregational minister in Hobart for 52 years, and as Chancellor of the University of Tasmania from 1898 to 1907. Another son, Edward Blomfield Clarke (1831–1900), ministered among the Maori, serving as Anglican Archdeacon of Waimate from 1870 to 1900.

BIBLIOGRAPHY
A. H. McLintock, ed., *An Encyclopedia of New Zealand*, 3 vols. 1 (Wellington, New Zealand, 1966): 353–4
Church Gazette (September 1875): 102–3
DNZB

ALLAN K. DAVIDSON

Clarke, (George) Rochfort (b. Chesterton, near Bicester, Oxfordshire, England, 1801; d. London, 29 Sept. 1889) Anglican lawyer. Clarke was the second son of George Clarke of Chesterton and was educated at St John's College, Cambridge (BA 1825, MA 1828). He trained for the law at Lincoln's Inn and the Inner Temple in London. One of the famous group of London evangelical lawyers of his day, he shared most of their convictions, but tended to operate with his own agenda and approach for the extension of evangelical faith. He first came to prominence by drafting Sir ANDREW AGNEW's Sunday observance bill of 1833. In seeking to force an evangelical agenda on the SPCK, he published highly coloured accounts of the monthly meetings in the *Record* newspaper from 1833 to 1838. When this led to a reprimand from Bishop Blomfield, he did nothing to ingratiate himself with episcopal authority as the previous generation of evangelical Anglicans would likely have done. Although a founding member of the CPAS, when it conceded that lay assistants would only be employed directly by clergy rather than by the society itself, he bitterly attacked the clerical members, in a spirit if not of anti-clericalism, at least of qualified egalitarianism. He also spoke and wrote against Roman Catholicism and Tractarianism.

BIBLIOGRAPHY
Boase
J. Bridges, *Memoir of Sir Andrew Agnew* (Edinburgh, 1849)
D. M. Lewis, *Lighten Their Darkness* (Westport, CT, 1986): 42–5
Record

IAN S. RENNIE

Clarke, John (b. Kelso, Roxburghshire, Scotland, 12 Oct. 1802; d. Jamaica, 28 Sept. 1879). Missionary linguist in West Africa and missionary in Jamaica. Clarke, son of a Presbyterian farm labourer, joined the Baptist church in 1823 at Berwick-on-Tweed; while preparing himself for missionary labour he taught at a village school. In 1829, the BMS sent him to Jamaica, where he served various churches as minister, working principally among the population of African descent. In 1839, while visiting Britain for health reasons, he agreed to accompany Dr G. K. PRINCE on a missionary reconnaissance of the West African coast. In 1840–2 Prince and Clarke surveyed the island of Fernando Po and the neighbouring mainland coasts, and in 1845 Clarke led a pioneering party of Jamaican Baptists, of both European and African descent, to the island where a mission station was opened. This Baptist mission was soon extended to the mainland, on the Cameroon coast, where the leading missionaries were J. MERRICK, an Afro-Jamaican, and ALFRED SAKER. Clarke himself returned from Africa in 1847 because of ill health but in 1848 published at Berwick two works on African languages. In 1852 he returned to Jamaica, serving there until his death in 1879. His other publications included an account of the life of J. MERRICK, and a history of the Baptist missionaries in Jamaica, with a section on his own life.

Clarke's *Introduction to the Fernandian language* was one of the earliest works on North West Bantu. In this work, and again in the *Specimens of Dialects . . . in Africa*, Clarke presented evidence of a relationship between the languages of the Cameroon coast and those of the Congo and South Africa, and thus contributed to the development of the concept of 'Bantu'. The *Specimens* lists vocabularies of some 100 African languages, in various dialects, more than half of which Clarke had collected himself, apparently in the main when in Jamaica. Unfortunately Clarke's assiduity in collecting was not matched by his ability either as a linguist or as an arranger of material. Nevertheless, the *Specimens* would have been useful at the time if it had not been out-classed almost immediately by KOELLE's *Polyglotta Africana* (1854); but it remains of interest to historians of African languages.

BIBLIOGRAPHY
S. Ardener, 'Biographical note' in J. Clarke, *Specimens of dialects* (Berwick-on-Tweed, 1848), reprinted, ed. E. Ardener (no place, 1972)

P. E. H. HAIR

Clarkson, John (b. Wisbech, Cambridgeshire, England, 4 April 1794; d. Woodbridge, Suffolk, England, 2 April 1828). Naval officer and governor. Brother of THOMAS CLARKSON, opponent of the slave trade, he entered the Royal Navy, aged 12. He was promoted lieutenant in 1783, and retired on half pay. In 1791 he was sent to Nova Scotia by the directors of the newly formed Sierra Leone Company to recruit settlers from among the free black Loyalist population. In 1792 he brought nearly 2,000 of them to Sierra Leone where he was appointed governor. He endeared himself to the settlers, themselves evangelical Christians, by his strong religious principles, and his passionate sympathy for them. His readiness to champion their grievances against the company led to his dismissal in 1793. He then went into business in Essex, and was a founder member of the Society for the Promotion of Universal Peace. His papers are in the British Library.

BIBLIOGRAPHY

C. Fyfe, ed., *'Our Children Free and Happy'* (Edinburgh, 1991)

E. G. Wilson, *John Clarkson and the African Adventure* (London, 1980)

CHRISTOPHER FYFE

Clarkson, Robert Goodlow Harper (b. Gettysburg, PA, USA, 19 Nov. 1826; d. Omaha, NE, USA, 10 March 1884). Protestant Episcopal bishop. As the grandson of the first clergyman ordained by Bishop William White for the newly organized Protestant Episcopal Church, Clarkson was raised in a 'conservative and retrospective' Episcopal family, and graduated from Pennsylvania College (later renamed Gettysburg College) in 1844. He studied theology under the tutelage of Maryland Bishop W. R. Whittingham and soon-to-be-bishop J. B. Kerfoot at Whittingham's diocesan seminary, St James College, in Hagerstown, Maryland. He was ordained deacon by Whittingham on 13 June 1848, and was placed in charge of St James's Church, Chicago, Illinois. Finally ordained priest on 5 January 1851 by Bishop PHILANDER CHASE, he remained Rector of St James's until 1865, when 'his strong practical sense, the absence of all affectation, and his unbounded sympathy and zeal' led to his election by the Episcopal House of Bishops as a missionary bishop for Nebraska and the Dakota Territory. He was consecrated in St James's Church on 15 November 1865. When Nebraska was organized as a separate diocese in 1868, Clarkson was elected its first bishop; however, he retained provisional jurisdiction over the Dakota Territory until 1883. His enormous energy and enthusiasm as an administrator and pastor were widely admired.

BIBLIOGRAPHY

H. Harrison, *Life of the Right Reverend John Barrett Kerfoot* (New York, 1886)

H. C. Potter, 'Bishop Clarkson' in *Reminiscences of Bishops and Archbishops* (New York, 1906)

ALLEN C. GUELZO

Clarkson, Thomas (b. Wisbech, Cambridgeshire, England, 28 March 1760; d. Playford Hall, near Ipswich, Suffolk, England, 26 Sept. 1846). Antislavery agitator. The son of the Reverend John Clarkson, headmaster of Wisbech Grammar School, he was educated at St Paul's School, London where in 1780 he had been awarded an exhibition and at St John's College, Cambridge. He had a distinguished academic career, winning in 1785 the Members' Prize for a Latin essay the theme of which was *'anne liceat invitos in servitutem dare?'* (Is it lawful to make slaves of others against their will?), a topic which was henceforth to determine the future direction of his life. The essay was read in the Senate House at Cambridge to great applause. He was ordained a deacon in the Church of England but never proceeded to priest's orders, directing all his energies to the antislavery agitation.

The translation into English of his Cambridge essay as *An Essay on the Slavery and Commerce of the Human Species* caught the attention of other critics of slavery, among them GRANVILLE SHARP and WILLIAM WILBERFORCE. He joined the committee, mainly consisting of Quakers, which was set up in May 1787 to work for the suppression of the slave trade, visiting the ports, Bristol and Liverpool, from which the slave ships sailed, to secure evidence. In 1789 he visited Paris to interest the French government but as a result of the outbreak of the French Revolution he met with little success. In spite of the agitation, Wilberforce's measure for banning the import of slaves was defeated in Parliament by 163 to 88 votes, and Clarkson's efforts had so affected his health that in 1794 he had to retire temporarily from the campaign. In 1805 he returned to active propaganda which helped to bring about in 1807 a bill for the abolition of the slave trade. Wordsworth began the sonnet with which he commemorated the event with the words 'Clarkson, it was an obstinate hill to climb.'

Clarkson turned to writing, producing an illuminating and sympathetic study of the Quakers (1806), a biography of William Penn (1813) and his most important publication, a history of the abolition of the slave trade. In 1816 he settled at Playford Hall near Ipswich but continued to take an active part in antislavery agitation, visiting European countries to persuade their governments to follow suit, in 1818 interviewing the Tsar Alexander I at Aix-la-Chapelle. He and Wilberforce became vice-presidents of the Anti-Slavery Society, which was founded in 1823, and ten years later the Emancipation Bill abolished slavery in all British possessions (accomplished in stages by 1838). Clarkson presided over the first World Anti-Slavery Conference in London in 1840 and published *A Letter to the Clergy of various Denominations and to the Slaveholding Planters in the Southern Parts of the United States of America* (1841).

Clarkson only took up theological topics twice, once on the pre-Mosaic revelation and again in a tract on baptism directed against 'Puseyism'. While he worked closely with evangelicals, it is difficult to identify him with certainty as an evangelical although his deathbed confession clearly fit the evangelical stereotype: 'All my works and righteousness are as filthy rags. I trust only in the Atonement, the sacrifice, the blood shed on the cross for washing away my sins and entrance into Heaven.'

Manuscript material on him can be found in: the British Library (Add. manuscripts 41267A); St John's College, Cambridge (Correspondence); the Henry E. Huntingdon Library, San Marino, California (T. Clarkson Correspondence); Rhodes House Library, Oxford (British and Foreign Anti-Slavery Society Papers); and the Royal Commission on Historical Manuscripts, London.

SELECT WRITINGS

T. Clarkson, *Letters on the Slave-trade, and the State of the Natives in those Parts of Africa which are Contiguous to Fort St Louis and Goree* (London, 1791)

—, *The History of the Rise and Progress and Accomplishment of the Abolition of the African Slave Trade by the British Parliament* (London, 1808)

—, *The Mitigation of Slavery* (London, 1814)

—, *The Practicality, Safety and Advantages of Negro Emancipation* (Bristol, England, 1830)

Thomas Clarkson's Interviews with Alexander I of Russia . . . in 1815 and 1818 as told by himself, with a preface by P. H. Peckover (London, 1930)

BIBLIOGRAPHY
DNB
E. L. Griggs, *Thomas Clarkson* (London, 1936)

V. H. H. GREEN AND DONALD M. LEWIS

Clason, Patrick (b. Dalziel, Lanarkshire, Scotland, 13 Oct. 1789; d. Edinburgh, 30 July 1867). Presbyterian minister. The third son of Reverend Robert Clason, minister of Dalziel, he was educated privately and at the universities of Glasgow and Edinburgh. He was licensed to preach by the presbytery of Hamilton in 1813; in 1815, he was ordained and inducted to the charge of Carmunnock and was translated in 1824 to St Cuthbert's Chapel of Ease (afterwards Buccleuch Church), Edinburgh. An unsuccessful candidate for the chair of divinity in the University of St Andrews in 1830, he was awarded the degree of DD by Glasgow University in 1836. He signed the Deed of Demission in 1843, adhering to the FCS and, in the same year, became first minister of Free Buccleuch Church and also joint clerk to the Free Church General Assembly. He held both offices until his death.

BIBLIOGRAPHY
W. Ewing, ed., *Annals of the FCS, 1843–1900* (Edinburgh, 1914)
Fasti

ALASDAIR BOTHWELL GORDON

Clayton, Charles (b. Cambridge, England, 13 July 1813; d. Stanhope, Co. Durham, England, 18 Oct. 1883). Anglican clergyman. Clayton was educated at the Perse School, Cambridge and entered Gonville and Caius College in 1832 (scholar, 1833; BA, 1836; MA, 1839; fellow, 1838–66). He was also Hebrew lecturer (1842–4) and Greek lecturer (1842–6). With his friend JAMES SCHOLEFIELD he was secretary of the Cambridge auxiliary of the CMS, and he was also secretary of the university Prayer Union in 1850 and its chairman in 1853. Before that he had been curate of St John's, Chatham (1837–45) and secretary of CPAS (1845–51), but undoubtedly his most influential years were those which he spent as CHARLES SIMEON's and WILLIAM CARUS's successor as Vicar of Holy Trinity, Cambridge (1851–65). During this period he opposed the Bachelor's Ball, the festivities on the installation of the Duke of Devonshire as High Steward in 1862 and the choral festival at Great St Mary's in 1865. He was preferred by Bishop ROBERT BICKERSTETH to a canonry of Ripon (1864–83) and to the wealthy living of Stanhope (1864–83), of which area he was also rural dean (1880–3). He was said to be well liked in Cambridge for his genial character.

BIBLIOGRAPHY
Al. Cant., II. ii: 62

ARTHUR POLLARD

Clayton, John (b. Manchester, England, 9 Oct. 1709; d. Manchester, England, 25 Sept. 1773). Early associate of JOHN WESLEY. Clayton was the son of a Manchester bookseller. After education at Manchester Grammar School, at the early age of 15 he matriculated at Brasenose College in Oxford, proceeding BA in 1729, MA in 1732, and becoming a tutor at Brasenose. His chief claim to evangelical fame is his support of John Wesley. In 1729 Wesley had been recalled from parish work in Lincolnshire to serve as a tutor in Lincoln College, Oxford. In addition to overseeing the studies of his students, he also became the leader of a handful of serious friends of his brother, CHARLES WESLEY, becoming their spiritual director and organizing their charitable and educational activities among the poor and the inmates of the Oxford prisons. During the following year or two their numbers and their methodical piety increased sufficiently to earn them various nicknames, including 'The Holy Club' and 'Methodists'. On 20 April 1732, Clayton introduced himself to Wesley, and was invited to John's rooms. After discussing the Methodist activities, their regular devotions, their frequent communion, their service to the poor, Clayton 'immediately and heartily closed with' their whole design.

By Clayton's advocacy Wesley became even more eager to discover and to imitate the practices of the Early Church and made a special point of observing the 'stationary fasts' on every Wednesday and Friday, which seemed to have been an apostolic practice. During John Wesley's absences John Clayton became the Methodist factotum in Oxford. Two lengthy reports to Wesley survive, of 1 August and 5–6 September 1732, describing their dispensing of charity, their teaching in schools and prisons, their attempts to settle disputes and to conduct religious gatherings, and his own extension of their social work to St Thomas's workhouse, and his efforts to enlist religious leaders and groups in other colleges. Everywhere he urged early rising, fasting, and constant communion.

On 29 December 1732, Clayton was ordained deacon to serve the cure of Sacred Trinity Chapel, Salford, near Manchester, a hotbed of nonjuring supporters of the Stuart family. Wesley preached three times for Clayton on 3 June 1733, and warmed to his illustrious fellow citizens, especially Dr John Byrom, whose shorthand both the Wesleys and several of their Oxford followers learned. Clayton also introduced Wesley to 'good Dr Deacon', Thomas Deacon (1697–1753), consecrated a nonjuring bishop about 1733. In 1734 Deacon published his *Compleat Collection of Devotions*, attempting to restore the rituals of the apostolic church, and in an appendix included an extract from Wesley's manuscript 'Essay upon the Stationary Fasts'. Deacon agreed with Clayton (25 July 1733), however, in suspecting Wesley's attempt to organize a society: 'Observing the stations and weekly communion are duties which stand upon a much higher footing than a rule of a society.' Clayton remained enthusiastic in his High Church practices, his service to the poor, and his devoted teaching of an academy in Salford, but his evangelism was aimed at a deeper devotion rather than personal salvation, and on 3 September 1733, he urged Wesley, 'Dear sir, pray for me that I may press forward in the path of perfection.'

In 1740 he was appointed a chaplain of the Manchester Collegiate Church (later the Cathedral), in which he was buried in 1773. On Good Friday, 27 March 1752, Wesley's Manchester *Journal* records, 'I went to the old church where Mr Clayton read prayers, I think the most distinctly, solemnly, and gracefully of any man I have ever heard.' But Clayton seems never to have had any association with Wesley's rising Methodist society there.

BIBLIOGRAPHY
DNB
L. Tyerman, *The Oxford Methodists* (London, 1873): 24–56

FRANK BAKER

Clayton, John (b. Clayton Green, Chorley, Lancashire, England, 5 Oct. 1754; d. Upminster, Essex, England, 22 Sept. 1843). Congregational Minister. The only son of a bleacher, he had nine elder sisters and was educated at Leyland grammar school where religious loyalties led to fights between Protestants and Catholics. At 14 he was apprenticed to his brother-in-law, a chemist, in Manchester but, after four years, he visited his sister in London and was converted by the preaching of WILLIAM ROMAINE at Blackfriars. The Countess of HUNTINGDON placed him in her college at Trevecca. He took charge of the Countess's church at Tunbridge Wells and with her encouragement contemplated Episcopal ordination but, after reading Towgood's *Letters On Dissent*, he decided to her chagrin in favour of Nonconformity.

He became assistant about 1777 to the eccentric Sir Harry Trelawney, minister of a church near his estate at West Looe, Cornwall. Clayton was disappointed to discover Sir Harry's Arian views and the family's disturbed state, occasioned by Trelawney's unfortunate marriage. Clayton accepted the call to the King's Weigh House Church, London, and after a brief probationary period in 1778 became pastor there, remaining for 49 years. In 1784 he took the church out of the Presbyterian and into the Congregational fold. In 1793 he was appointed one of the preachers of the Merchants' Lecture. His fellow ministers admired his applying discipline to a member who travelled in his coach and attended the theatre on Sundays.

He retired to Upminster but, in July 1837, led the deputation of dissenting ministers in the presentation of their loyal address to Queen Victoria. The oldest dissenting minister in London, he died in 1843.

He married in 1779 Mary Flower. They had five children. The Claytons, father and sons, were characterized by gentlemanly conduct and had many friends in their own and other denominations.

His eldest son was John Clayton, the younger (born London, 13 May 1780; died Bath, England, 3 Oct. 1865). He trained at Homerton, settled at Kensington, then moved to Camomile Street, London which church moved in 1818 to Poultry Chapel where he pastored for 30 years. In 1808 an action was brought against him by his uncle, Benjamin Flower, who edited the *Cambridge Intelligencer*. Clayton had circulated his father's statement, accusing Flower of forgery. Minimal damages were awarded to Flower. Briefly, Clayton was one of two secretaries of the LMS. He was a founder of Mill Hill school.

Another son was George Clayton (born London, 9 April 1783; died Upminster, England, 14 July 1862) who trained at Hoxton, was assistant pastor at Above Bar, Southampton, 1802–4, and pastor of York Street, Walworth, 1804–54 where, among his congregation, was Robert Browning.

A third son was William Clayton (born Islington, England, 22 July 1785; died Mill Hill, England, 15 March 1838) also a Congregational Minister. He trained at Hoxton, ministered at Newbury, Berkshire and Edmonton, in 1807 and 1807–31 at Saffron Walden. He was chaplain of Mill Hill school, 1831–38.

BIBLIOGRAPHY
T. W. Aveling, *Memorials of the Clayton Family* (London, 1867)
C. Binfield, *So Down to Prayers* (London, 1977): 10
DNB
E. Kaye, *The King's Weigh House Church* (London, 1968): 47–61, 92

ALAN ARGENT

Clayton, Richard (b. Hexham, Northumberland, England, 9 March 1802; d. Newcastle upon Tyne, England, 8 Oct. 1856). Anglican clergyman. He was the fifth son of Nathaniel Clayton; his father and brother each served as town clerk of Newcastle. He was educated at the Percy Street Academy and University College, Oxford (BA 1823; MA 1826).

He was ordained by the Bishop of Durham (deacon 1825, priest 1826) to the curacy of Wark, near Hexham. From 1826 he was the master of St Thomas's Hospital, Newcastle, and also chaplain from 1836. During his early ministry at St Thomas's he was converted through the then chaplain, ROBERT WASNEY. St Thomas's Chapel became the centre of evangelicalism in the city and Clayton supported the CMS, the LSPCJ and the CPAS. He opposed Tractarianism, and united with Nonconformists over sabbath observance, opposition to the races and in the creation of the city mission. After his death the Clayton Memorial Church (now Jesmond Parish Church) was erected in his memory.

BIBLIOGRAPHY
A. F. Munden, 'The origin of Evangelical Anglicanism in Newcastle upon Tyne', *Archaeologia Aeliana*, 5th series, 11 (1983): 301–7

ALAN FREDERICK MUNDEN

Cleaveland, John (b. Canterbury, CT, BNA, 11 April 1722; d. Ipswich, MA, USA, 22 April 1799). Separate Congregational minister. In 1744, during his senior year at Yale and at the height of controversy between Congregational 'Old Lights' and 'New Lights' during the Great Awakening, John and his brother were expelled for attending an 'unauthorized' religious meeting of separatists. After studying briefly with PHILEMON ROBBINS, he ministered to a Separate church in Boston (1745–6), then accepted a permanent settlement from a newly formed Separate group at Ipswich's Second Parish (Chebacco). Ordained in 1747, Cleaveland pastored this rural parish until his death.

In 1763–4, his affective preaching triggered a revival which resulted in the addition of ninety members. At about the same time, Cleaveland engaged in theological controversy with J. Mayhew over the latter's 'Arminianism'. He served as chaplain in both the French and Indian and revolutionary wars, and joined with New Lights in zealously defending the sacred cause of independence. Called 'perhaps *the* grand separatist of New England' by A. Heimert, Cleaveland's career, like that of so many others, was profoundly shaped by the Great Awakening.

BIBLIOGRAPHY
AAP, 1: 458–61
C. C. Goen, *Revivalism and Separatism in New England, 1740–1800* (New Haven, CT, 1969)
A. Heimert, *Religion and the American Mind* (Cambridge, MA, 1966)
C. Jedrey, *The World of John Cleaveland* (New York, 1979)

DAVID W. KLING

Cleghorn, Thomas (b. near Edinburgh, 3 Mar. 1818; d. Edinburgh, 13 June 1874). Scottish advocate and Whig writer. The son of Alexander Cleghorn, collector of customs at Edinburgh, he was educated at the High School and the university. The association of Whiggism with the legal profession and the evangelical party in the Scottish church are well exemplified in his career. He was co-author of a history of the liberal Speculative Society (1854) and edited the *Journal* of Henry Cockburn, the Whig memorialist. A legal adviser to the Free Church, he was also a contributor to its literary journal, the *North British*.

Cleghorn, who was called to the Bar in 1839, became advocate depute and Sheriff of Argyllshire, and was a registrar of friendly societies. A member of the EA, he was active in the Free Church's foreign missions, Jews, and colonial committees and attended the 1860 Liverpool Conference on missions.

BIBLIOGRAPHY
Boase
[D.M.], *Memorial Sketch of Thomas Cleghorn* (Edinburgh, 1881)

JONATHAN BURKE CUTMORE

Cleland, John Fullarton (b. Edinburgh, 21 August 1821; d. Adelaide, Australia, 1901). LMS missionary to China. Cleland attended Cheshunt College and was ordained as a Congregational minister in London in December 1845. Assigned to China by the LMS he planned to follow the traditional pattern of learning Chinese and then preaching. Unfortunately, when Cleland arrived in Hong Kong in 1846, he was needed to oversee the mission press, the mission school and to minister in the European chapel. In 1848 he moved to Canton where he cooperated with Dr BENJAMIN HOBSON. The number and nature of his responsibilities made it impossible to study Chinese. His disappointment turned to discontent when he found himself caught in the middle of an acrimonious dispute between JAMES LEGGE (LMS) and KARL GUTZLAFF. In 1850, Cleland left China and the LMS, eventually settling in Australia.

BIBLIOGRAPHY
Council for World Mission Archives held in the School of Oriental and African Studies, London
J. Sibree, *A Register of Missionaries, Deputations, Etc.* (LMS, London, 1925): 476

JEAN PAQUETTE

Clephane, Elizabeth Cecilia (Douglas) (b. Edinburgh, Scotland, 18 June 1830; d. Melrose, Roxburghshire, Scotland, 19 Feb. 1869). Hymn-writer. She was a daughter of Andrew Douglas Clephane, Sheriff principal of Fife and Kinross, her mother belonging to the family of which the Earls of Home are the heads. After her father died she lived at Ormiston, East Lothian, then at Melrose. A chill in youth left her in poor health. She was gentle, retiring, and generous to the poor and suffering. A member of the FCS, she wrote at least eight hymns, published posthumously in *The Family Treasury* (1872–4). 'Beneath the Cross of Jesus' is in many current British and American hymn-books. 'There were ninety and nine', 'one of the really fine hymns . . . among the luxuriant vegetation of the Gospel Songs' (Routley, 1952: 217), had appeared earlier. It attracted little attention until I. D. Sankey improvised his tune for it immediately after a sermon by D. L. Moody on the lost sheep.

BIBLIOGRAPHY
Julian: 238–9, 1162
J. Moffatt, ed., *Handbook to 'The Church Hymnary'* (Oxford, 1927): 232, 234, 299–300
E. Routley, *Hymns and Human Life* (London, 1952)

JOHN S. ANDREWS

Clifford, Herbert John (b. *c.* 1790; d. 1855 or 6). British naval officer and supporter of mission. He entered the navy in 1802 and was commissioned lieutenant in 1811. As an officer on the *Lyra* during Lord Amherst's embassy to China 1816–17 he visited Okinawa, then known to Europeans as Great Loo-Choo (or Lieu-tchieu) Island, and compiled a vocabulary of the local language. He later served as an inspecting commander in the Coast Guard. After his conversion, Clifford was keen to see Britain's maritime influence used for the worldwide spreading of the Gospel. To this end, he and a group of naval officers planned a mission to Okinawa as a prelude to the evangelization of Japan. When the CMS declined to take up the challenge, they formed their own mission, sent a Jewish evangelist, Dr Bettelheim, to the island and supported him for several years. Health problems and local opposition combined to undermine the mission which closed in 1861.

BIBLIOGRAPHY
W. R. O'Byrne, *A Naval Biographical Dictionary*, 2 vols (London, 1849)
B. Hall, *Account of a Voyage to the West Coast of Corea and the Great-Loo Choo Island*, (London, 1818) incorporating Clifford's 'Loochoo Vocabulary' as an appendix
Navy List
4th Report of the Loo Choo Naval Mission for 1848 (London, 1849) in CMS archives
E. Stock, *History of the Church Missionary Society*, 3 vols (London, 1899)

RICHARD C. BLAKE

Close, Francis (b. Corston, Wiltshire, England, 11 July 1797; d. Penzance, Cornwall, England, 18 Dec. 1882). Anglican evangelical leader, incumbent of Cheltenham and Dean of Carlisle. Close was educated at Midhurst Grammar School and Merchant Taylors' School. He was converted while he was a private pupil of JOHN SCOTT of Hull. At Cambridge, Close came under the influence of CHARLES SIMEON whom he described as 'my affectionate

father, my generous patron and my wise and helpful counsellor'. Close graduated from St John's College (BA 1820) and was married and ordained (deacon, 1820; priest, 1821). He served curacies at Church Lawford, near Rugby, Willesden and Kingsbury, Middlesex and Holy Trinity, Cheltenham. In 1826 Simeon appointed him as the Perpetual Curate of Cheltenham.

Close consolidated and expanded the evangelicalism established by his predecessor, CHARLES JERVIS. Close appointed evangelicals as his curates, incumbents of district churches and as staff of educational establishments. He erected four district churches each with its own infant and National School. Other educational establishments were founded (like Cheltenham College) or revived (like Cheltenham Grammar School). Close was the active chairman of the directors of Cheltenham College and its evangelical stance was lost only after the constitution was changed in 1862. After Close's death the Dean Close Memorial School maintained the tradition lost at Cheltenham College.

The most significant educational enterprise was in the training of teachers first in the network of schools and then at 'The Church of England Training School'. This institution which opened in 1847 gained widespread support from evangelicals who valued Close's involvement. Alongside his parochial and educational work Close promoted home and overseas mission, was a convinced Sabbatarian and opponent of horse-racing. Though his 30-year rule at Cheltenham was unfavourably regarded by his opponents who criticized the activities of Close and his military friends as 'the Lieutenant General Close brigade', he had the support of at least half of the population of the town.

On becoming Dean of Carlisle in 1856 Close worked alongside Bishops VILLIERS and WALDEGRAVE in promoting evangelicalism, and after they had gone he was the leader of the evangelicals in the diocese. Close transferred all of his earlier concerns to the north – apart from his involvement in education. He established himself through his preaching ministry, chairing endless meetings and in supporting numerous worthy causes and institutions. He was responsible for the erection of two city churches and involved in the erection of a third. At Carlisle his direct involvement with the poor turned him into a convinced teetotaller.

Since the 1830s Close had strongly opposed Romanism inside and outside the Church of England – within the Cambridge Camden Society, the writings of the Tractarians, the SPG and elements within the National Society. In Carlisle his energies were mainly directed against the English Church Union; in the cathedral he dismissed the precentor, and in the city he opposed the establishment of an oratory. Alongside this he was an active member of the Church Association. Close's first wife, Diana, died in 1877, and in 1880 he married Mary, the widow of a wealthy landowner.

He was an outstanding example of evangelical piety, had a good sense of humour and was extremely fond of his pets. He resigned from the deanery in the summer of 1881 and settled in Penzance where he died. He was buried in Carlisle. Close was a leading follower of Simeon and modelled his preaching and teaching on the style of his patron. While Close adopted a critical stance towards Romanism, he remained at heart a Christian pastor deeply involved in the promotion of the gospel in Cheltenham and Carlisle.

BIBLIOGRAPHY
DNB
M. Hennell, *Sons of the Prophets* (London, 1979)
A. F. Munden, 'The Anglican Evangelical Party in the Diocese of Carlisle in the Nineteenth Century with particular reference to the ministries of Bishop Samuel Waldegrave and Dean Francis Close' (Durham Univ. Ph.D. thesis, 1987)

ALAN FREDERICK MUNDEN

Close, John Marjoram (b. *c.* 1780; d. Hastings, Sussex, England, 2 Feb. 1857). Army officer and evangelist. He was the son of the Reverend Henry Jackson Close, a distinguished agriculturalist (died 1806) and the older brother of FRANCIS CLOSE. He entered the Royal Artillergy on 6 March 1795 and was made captain in 1802, major in 1813, and retired on half pay in 1819.

His conversion appears to have been effected through the preaching of ROBERT STORRY. He was only about 39 years old when he retired and he dedicated the remainder of his life to the evangelization of British soldiers and sailors in his capacity as the secretary of the Naval and Military Bible Society. He was also a strong supporter of the CMS.

BIBLIOGRAPHY
C. Hole, *History of the Church Missionary Society* (London, 1892): 624–5

DONALD M. LEWIS

Clow, James (b. Chartershall, Stirling, Scotland, 26 May 1790; d. Queenscliff, Victoria, Australia, 15 March 1861). Presbyterian minister and chaplain to the East India Company in Bombay. Educated at Blackford School and St Andrews and Edinburgh universities. He was licensed by the presbytery of Kirkcaldy on 21 July 1813. In 1815 he went to Bombay as a chaplain with the East India Company and married on 13 April 1819 Margaret Morison. They had two sons and six daughters. Because of ill health he resigned in 1833 and returned to Scotland.

Late in December 1837 he settled in Melbourne, Australia and formed the first Presbyterian congregation. This work was taken up by JAMES FORBES in January 1838. He was never the minister of a settled congregation in Australia but he greatly assisted the other Presbyterian ministers in the colony and when the Presbyterian Church of Victoria was formed in 1859 he was elected the first moderator.

BIBLIOGRAPHY
ADB
Fasti
A. Hamilton, *Personal Life of James Clow* (Melbourne, 1937)

STEWART D. GILL

Clowes, Francis (b. Heacham, Norfolk, England, 10 Jan. 1805; d. London, 7 May 1873). Baptist minister, college tutor, and journalist. Clowes's father was ejected from his farm for his religious and political views (opinions the son also adopted). In 1827 he was admitted to Bristol Baptist College to train for the ministry. Five years ministry in Bristol were followed by fifteen years as classical tutor at the Baptist College in Horton, Bradford. During this period he was active in the Liberal Party and helped to establish two popular journals: *The Church* and *The Appeal*. He conducted a debate, by pamphlet, on the subject of baptism. On moving to London in 1854 he became an editor of *The Sun* newspaper and the Baptist paper, *The Freeman*.

BIBLIOGRAPHY

Baptist Handbook 1874: 264–5
E. C. Starr, ed., *A Baptist Bibliography* 25 vols (New York, 1947–76)
R. Taylor, 'English Baptist Periodicals, 1790–1865', *BQ* 27, 2 (1977): 80

DAVID B. MILNER

Clowes, William (b. Burslem, Staffordshire, England, 12 March 1780; d. Hull, Yorkshire, England, 2 March 1851). Primitive Methodist co-founder and populist. A potter by trade (his mother, Ann, was descended from the famous Wedgwood ceramics family), Clowes was apprenticed when he was ten. Clowes was also a notable dancer, boxer, gambler and all-round ruffian (he was a regular patron of the local public houses and dancing rooms), undoubtedly influenced in his early childhood both by his drunken and violent father, Samuel, as well as by the grim, soulless, smoky dark surroundings of Burslem. Marriage in 1800 did not change his ways, and he travelled around (escaping imprisonment and a press-gang in Hull) but was converted back in Tunstall in 1805, through attending a prayer meeting and lovefeast where he felt the need for a change in his moral conduct, renounced his old life and paid off his considerable debts. He joined the Burslem Wesleyan Methodists, became a member of JAMES STEELE's class, and began holding prayer meetings in his own home.

Together with HUGH BOURNE, whom he had befriended in 1804, Clowes visited the mystical 'old man of the forest', JAMES CRAWFOOT of Delamere, whom, Clowes acknowledges in his *Journal*, was influential in his own spiritual development, and who linked Bourne and Clowes to the independent Methodist groups peppered around the North Midlands.

Clowes co-led the first ever camp meeting in England, on Mow Cop, near Harriseahead (on the border of Cheshire and Staffordshire), on 31 May 1807, and as a result was expelled in 1810 at the quarterly meeting of the Burslem circuit because of his association with Bourne and because of his refusal to desist from holding 'irregular' meetings. As a result of this violation of conference regulations, he led a separate groups of loyal followers, the 'Clowesites'. Alongside Hugh Bourne, James Steele, and James Crawfoot, Clowes founded the Primitive Methodist Connexion (PMC) in 1811. What needs to be stated is the sincerity of the leaders; there had been no intention for union among most of the distinct and disparate groups, although, because of forced pressure from the parent Wesleyan body, a separate denomination was formed.

As co-founder of the PMC, Clowes' rougher and freer personality acted as a necessary contrast to Bourne's placid timidity, caution, and love for discipline and order. One of the most respected and forceful preachers in the PMC, Clowes was renowned for his strong, passionate, excited vitality. Diminutive in stature, Clowes was bold, strong and loud. A gifted, adventurous, self-confident evangelist, Clowes laboured in the north of England, particularly in Hull, the largest Primitive Methodist circuit. Due to ill health, Clowes had already preached on a part-time basis from 1827 onwards, by a special arrangement with the Hull Circuit Quarterly Committee. Clowes continued to preach until his superannuation in 1842. His own journal closes in 1842 at the time of his superannuation, although he continued to hold class meetings in Hull. He married twice.

SELECT WRITINGS
W. Clowes, *The Journals of William Clowes* (London, 1884)

BIBLIOGRAPHY
G. Herod, *Historical and Biographical Sketches* (London, 1851)
J. Petty, *The History of the PMC* (London, 1864)
J. T. Wilkinson, *William Clowes, 1780–1851* (London, 1951)

WAYNE J. JOHNSON

Coade, Eleanor (b. Exeter, Devon, England, 24 June 1733; d. Camberwell, London, 18 Nov. 1821). Female Baptist entrepreneur. Coade was 'One of the bright stars of the Georgian decorative and architectural world', remarkable for successfully exploiting her invention for fifty years with royal appointments to both George III and George IV. Her father was a wool-finisher associated with the George Meeting in Exeter, but Eleanor first appears in business as a linen-draper in London in 1766. Three years later she established the Lambeth factory that manufactured the 'stone' that bears her name, a pottery body that so perfectly imitates natural stone (as in Buckingham Palace, St George's Windsor, and the Royal Naval College) as not to be detected. In statuary work, she collaborated closely with the evangelical sculptor, JOHN BACON. A woman entrepreneur of some

significance, from about 1792 she was 'a most benevolent, useful member' of JAMES UPTON's chapel in Blackfriars. In her will bequests focused on helping the poor and the spreading of the Gospel, including a benefaction for the Baptist chapel at Lyme Regis and a number of bequests to be distributed through named clergymen.

BIBLIOGRAPHY
BaptMag (1822)
A. Kelly, *Mrs Coade's Stone* (Upton-upon-Severn, England, 1990)

J. H. Y. BRIGGS

Coan, Titus (b. Killingworth, CT, USA, 1 Feb. 1801; d. Hilo, HI, USA, 1 Dec. 1882). ABCFM missionary to Hawaii. Son of a Connecticut farmer, Coan began his career as a schoolmaster. He attended Auburn Theological Seminary 1831–3, and after ordination accepted a call from the ABCFM to explore the feasibility of a mission to Patagonia. Subsequently, with his bride Fidelia in 1835 Coan accompanied the seventh company of missionaries to Hawaii. He was stationed in Hilo where he spent most of the rest of his life. Much influenced by the revivals of CHARLES FINNEY which he had attended in New York, Coan changed the tenor of missionary endeavour in Hawaii by presiding over a Hawaiian 'Great Awakening'. By 1841 his Hilo-Puna congregation had grown to 7,000, the largest Protestant congregation in the world. Coan's astonishing success led to serious dissension when conservative veteran missionaries in Hawaii, slow to admit Hawaiians to the church without evidence of true conversion, criticized Coan's noisy and emotional revival sermons and his hasty church admissions. An independent-spirited man, Coan weathered the dispute.

In secular life Coan was an avid volcano watcher and his reports on eruptions remain important records of enduring importance. After his first wife's death, Coan married Lydia Bingham, youngest daughter of HIRAM BINGHAM in 1873. Coan's church, Haili Church of Hilo, continues today in the spirit of its founder as one of Hawaii's most vigorous and enthusiastic.

SELECT WRITINGS
T. Coan, *Life in Hawaii* (New York, 1882)

BIBLIOGRAPHY
DAB

NANCY J. MORRIS

Coates, Dandeson (d. London, 23 April 1846). Lay secretary, CMS. Becoming a member of the CMS Committee in 1817, he soon began to donate a considerable amount of his time in applying his business skills to the administrative needs of the society. In 1820 he commenced to live a bachelor existence at the CMS headquarters in Salisbury Square, where he would reside for the rest of his life. In 1824, upon the retirement of JOSIAH PRATT, he was appointed assistant secretary, the title being changed to lay secretary in 1830. Having been a member of the committee, as well as having become an administrator, he concerned himself as much with missionary policy as with financial, legal and bureaucratic affairs. And with his devotion to the society, his powers of work, and his constant presence, he had immense influence on the CMS in the years between Pratt and HENRY VENN, when there was no comparably able clerical secretary.

In common with most evangelical Anglicans he was wary of the influence of non-evangelical bishops. While the clergy might tend to stress their freedom given by such medieval anomalies as patronage and parson's freehold in the face of an unsympathetic diocesan, Coates emphasized the voluntary nature of the CMS. It was in the Church of England, but was not official, and was certainly not under the direction of bishops or archbishops. While many of his lay confreres were active in their attempt to resist the transformation of the United Kingdom from a Christian society to a secular nation, a particular concern of his was to see that Great Britain acted as a Christian nation in relation to its colonial subjects, and in his case particularly to the natives of New Zealand. He strongly objected to plans for settlement, as expressed in his 1837 pamphlet, *The Principles, Objects, and Plan of the New-Zealand Association Examined, in a Letter to the Right Hon. Lord Glenelg, Secretary of State for the Colonies.* And when settlement appeared inevitable, he successfully pressed for government wardship of native peoples, which CHARLES GRANT and JAMES STEPHEN, Secretary for the Colonies and Under-Secretary respectively, and both descendants of the Clapham Sect, were eager to guarantee.

BIBLIOGRAPHY
E. Stock, *History of the Church Missionary Society*, 3 vols (London, 1899)

IAN S. RENNIE

Coats, Thomas (Paisley, Renfrewshire, Scotland, 18 Oct. 1809; d. Scotland, 15 October 1883). Industrialist and philanthropist. Thomas Coats was the fourth of ten sons of James Coats, founder of the Paisley thread industry and shared in the prosperity of nineteenth-century Paisley. He belonged to the Baptist branch of the family, and was president of the Baptist Union of Scotland in 1873–4. He was generous to the BMS and to education for the ministry among Baptists in Scotland. He was also a generous benefactor of his native town, helping to found the School Board, and initiating the Paisley Observatory. He was a noted collector of Scottish coins. After his death the great Thomas Coats Church (Baptist) was raised in his memory.

BIBLIOGRAPHY
Anon., *Jubilee Book of the Thomas Coats Memorial Church* (Paisley, Scotland, 1944)

D. W. Bebbington, ed., *Baptists in Scotland* (Glasgow, 1988)

DEREK B. MURRAY

Cochran, James C(uppaidge) (b. Windsor, Nova Scotia, BNA, 17 Sept. 1798; d. Halifax, Nova Scotia, Canada, 20 June 1880). Anglican clergyman and editor. He was the son of Dr William Cochran, first president of King's College, Windsor. He was ordained priest in 1824, after completing his education at King's. He was among the many young people influenced by the evangelical preaching of Isaac Temple and HIBBERT BINNEY. For his first 28 years of ministry he served as Rector at Lunenburg, Nova Scotia. From 1835 to 1840 he was also editor of the short-lived *Colonial Churchman*, a fortnightly newspaper published by a local clerical society. In 1852 Cochran moved to Halifax to become editor of the *Church Times* – another attempt to establish a regular diocesan publication. Three years later he became Rector of Salem Chapel, a parish started among the poor in Halifax. Bishop Hibbert Binney dismissed him in 1866 after he refused to replace his black Geneva gown with a white surplice while preaching. He and his followers started Trinity Free Church where he stayed until his retirement in 1875. He was well-known for his involvement in humanitarian and philanthropic endeavours.

BIBLIOGRAPHY
DCB

BRUCE L. GUENTHER

Cockburn-Campbell, Sir **Alexander Thomas** (d. Albany, West Australia, 1871). Magistrate and Brethren leader. About the time of his marriage to his cousin, Margaret Malcolm (*see* MARGARET COCKBURN-CAMPBELL), on 20 June 1827 Sir Alexander took the simpler name of 'Campbell' (Roach, 1974: 19). He was actively associated with the beginnings of the Brethren movement in England. Seeking to return to primitive Christian simplicity he insisted that the servants joined him at table; once when he was late they began without him (Neatby, 1901: 41–2). He became resident magistrate in Albany, Australia, where he died in 1871.

BIBLIOGRAPHY
W. B. Neatby, *A History of the Plymouth Brethren* (London, 1901)
A. Roach, *The Little Flock Hymn Book* (Morganville, NJ, 1974): 19–20

JOHN S. ANDREWS

Cockburn-Campbell, Lady **Margaret** [née Malcolm] (b. 1808; d. Alphington, near Exeter, Devon, England, 6 Feb. 1841). Hymn-writer. She was the eldest daughter of General Sir John Malcolm (1769–1833), 'a sincere and devout Christian' (Chambers, 6, 1854: 567). On 20 June 1827 she married her cousin, SIR ALEXANDER THOMAS

COCKBURN-CAMPBELL, one of the early Brethren. Her hymns were lithographed for private circulation before some were included in J. G. DECK's *Psalms and Hymns and Spiritual Songs*, (London, 1842). The only hymn now sung is 'Praise ye, Jehovah, praise the Lord most holy', which is in the Presbyterian *[Revised] Church Hymnary* (London, 1927).

BIBLIOGRAPHY
R. Chambers, ed., *A Biographical Dictionary of Eminent Scotsmen*, new edn, 9 vols (Glasgow, 1853–5)
DNB, s.v. 'Malcolm, Sir John'
Julian: 202, 900, 905, 1299
Sir J. W. Kaye, *The Life and Correspondence of . . . Sir John Malcolm*, 2 vols (London, 1856)
A. Roach, *The Little Flock Hymn Book* (Morganville, NJ, 1974): 19–20

JOHN S. ANDREWS

Cocke, John Hartwell (b. Surry County, VA, USA, 19 Sept. 1780; d. Fluvanna County, VA, USA, 1 July 1866). Planter, slavery and temperance reformer, and brigadier-general. While studying at the College of William and Mary (1794–9), he adopted deism. He became a gentleman planter in Fluvanna County where he built his palladian mansion 'Upper Bremo'. He married on 25 December 1802 Ann Blaus Barraud. During the War of 1812, he was promoted to brigadier-general, commanding Virginia soldiers guarding Richmond, 1814–15.

Before she died in 1816, his wife pleaded with him to embrace Christianity. He found deism insufficient to meet the crisis of her death and experienced a conversion. His second marriage in 1821 to Louisa [née Maxwell] Holmes (*see* LOUISA H. COCKE), a Presbyterian evangelical, strengthened his piety. Cocke preferred to remain a non-sectarian evangelical until he was received into the Baptist Church in 1858. Besides supporting Bible, tract, and Sunday school societies, he served on the ABCFM.

The 'Puritan-cavalier' championed a variety of unpopular social reforms. He became first president of the American Temperance Union (1836–43). He condemned making tobacco the principal crop and published *Tobacco* (1860) to prove it ethically and economically 'the bane of Virginia husbandry'.

From its organization until his death, Cocke laboured as senior vice-president of the American Colonization Society, organized to settle the slavery problem peacefully by colonizing manumitted slaves in Liberia. He represented that white evangelical minority in the South which condemned slavery. As master of 178 slaves, Cocke devised a plan in 1837 to train his slaves for freedom by giving them the opportunity of earning their manumission on his recently acquired cotton plantation in Greene County, Alabama. Even if slaves earned the required money, Cocke made their freedom conditional upon evidence of their moral fitness. Before the Civil War commenced, Cocke deemed only 14 graduates of the Alabama experiments morally worthy for Liberian colonization.

He was associated with Thomas Jefferson in founding the University of Virginia and sat on its Board of Visitors (1819–52). He victoriously fought Jefferson, who had Unitarian sympathies, over the appointment of Thomas Cooper as Professor of science and law due to Cooper's unorthodox views of religion. After Jefferson's death, Cocke succeeded in establishing a university chapel and in appointing an evangelical, WILLIAM H. MCGUFFEY, as moral philosophy professor. Cocke's voluminous correspondence is deposited at the University of Virginia.

BIBLIOGRAPHY
M. B. Coyner, *John Hartwell Cocke* (Charlottesville, VA, 1964)
C. Eaton, *The Mind of the Old South* (Baton Rouge, LA, 1964)

ARTHUR DICKEN THOMAS, JR

Cocke, Louisa Holmes [née Maxwell] (b. Norfolk, VA, USA, 5 July 1788; d. Fluvanna County, VA, USA, 15 May 1843). Presbyterian plantation mistress, temperance and slavery reformer. The daughter of James and Helen [née Calvert] Maxwell, in 1807 she married Dr Robert Holmes and resided in Petersburg, Virginia until his death in 1810. Thereafter she lived with her brother, William, who had become a Presbyterian after undergoing a religious awakening. It was through him that she experienced an evangelical conversion and became active in numerous evangelical benevolent societies.

On 19 July 1821 she married General JOHN HARTWELL COCKE, becoming stepmother to his six children and mistress of 178 slaves on the 3,000-acre Bremo Plantation in Fluvanna County, Virginia. They had no children of their own. Sharing her husband's commitment to benevolent societies, she accompanied him to meetings of the American Temperance Union and the American Colonization Society.

Her 32 diaries (1816–43), now a part of the Cocke Deposit at the University of Virginia, are an important source for the history of evangelical women in the Old South. They reveal her deep commitment to the education of slave children, in spite of strong social disapproval.

BIBLIOGRAPHY
M. B. Coyner, Jr, 'John Hartwell Cocke of Bremo' (Univ. of Virginia, Ph.D. dissertation, 1964)
D. Scott, 'Louisa Maxwell Holmes Cocke 1788–1843', *The Bulletin of the Fluvanna County Historical Society*, no. 53 (Spring 1992)
J. L. Urbach, 'God and Man in the Life of Louisa Maxwell Holmes: A Search for Piety and Place in the Old South' (Florida State Univ. Ph.D. dissertation, 1983)

ARTHUR DICKEN THOMAS, JR

Cockran, William (b. Chillingham, Northumberland, England, 1796 or 1797; d. Portage la Prairie, Red River Settlement, Canada, 1 Oct. 1865). CMS missionary, Cockran was apparently born into a Presbyterian family but joined the Church of England as a youth. He was ordained (deacon 1824, priest 1825) by the Bishop of London. On 4 June 1825 he was sent to the CMS Red River mission as an assistant to DAVID JONES.

Soon after his arrival, Cockran concluded that the CMS policy of evangelization was doomed to fail in North West America unless the Indians were first taught the arts of 'civilization'. He decided to convert the mission gardens at Upper Church (now the site of St John's Cathedral, Winnipeg) into a demonstration farm; in 1829 he established a second project at Lower Church (St Andrew's). Three years later Cockran changed the programme at JOHN WEST's old Indian school to teach 'industrial' skills. He founded another mission farm for the people of Chief Peguis' band in 1836 which was later known as St Peter's.

After twenty years at Red River, Cockran was finding himself constantly at odds with Hudson's Bay Company officials who were opposed to his projects of bringing Indians to farm at Red River. Personal animosities played an ugly role as well; HBC officers and their wives were publically disdainful of Cockran and his wife, who had reputedly been employed as a maid before their marriage.

After a year's temporary retirement to Toronto in 1846, the Cockrans returned to Red River and continued to extend the work of the CMS. They oversaw the construction of the stone church which still stands at St Andrew's (1846–9) and three churches for new settlers in and around Portage la Prairie. In 1853, Cockran was appointed Archdeacon of Assiniboia by Bishop DAVID ANDERSON. Cockran's son Thomas was ordained in 1852 and two of his daughters married CMS missionaries in the North West American mission.

Cockran was a commanding figure who approached his religious work with an intensity which both angered and intimidated many people at Red River. Nevertheless, he is remembered particularly for his role in the experimental mission at St Andrew's.

BIBLIOGRAPHY

D. T. B[arry], *CMS Register of Missionaries and Native Clergy from 1804 to 1904* (privately printed) (London, 1906)
DCB, 9
Manitoba Library Association, *Pioneers and Early Citizens of Manitoba* (Winnipeg, Canada, 1971)

KERRY M. ABEL

Code, J(ohn) M(arsden) (b. probably Ireland, 1805; d. 16 April 1875). Anglican clergyman and Brethren leader. Educated at Trinity College, Dublin, and ordained into the Church of England, Code served as curate at Westport, Co. Mayo, Ireland. He was one of several Westport clergy who came under the spell of JOHN NELSON DARBY and resigned (February 1836). He spent some time in Cork, but later moved to Bath (becoming known as 'Code of Bath').

During the internal dissensions of 1845–9, Code urged moderation, and refused to follow Darby's line.

According to Neatby (1901: 326) his was the first signature to a statement issued by 'Open' Brethren leaders in 1872 professing 'the ordinary principles of evangelical orthodoxy'.

BIBLIOGRAPHY

W. B. Neatby, *A History of the Brethren Movement* (London, 1901)

HAROLD H. ROWDON

Codman, John (b. Boston, MA, USA, 3 Aug. 1782; d. Dorchester, MA, USA, 23 Dec. 1847). Congregational minister. Born into a prominent Boston family, Codman attended Harvard College, receiving the AB in 1802. Although his intention had been to take up a career in the law, he yielded to his father's dying request that he enter the ministry, sailing for Edinburgh in 1805 to pursue his studies in theology. Upon his return to Boston in 1808, he was almost immediately called to the pastorate of Dorchester's newly formed Second Parish Church, where he was to remain until his death. A staunch Calvinist, Codman was a prominent combatant in the Unitarian-Trinitarian civil war that racked early-nineteenth-century Massachusetts Congregationalism. His refusal to open his pulpit to theological liberals, thus breaking with the traditional practice of indiscriminate ministerial exchange, and his participation with JEDIDIAH MORSE and ABIEL HOLMES in the organization in 1809 of Boston's Park Street Church, orthodoxy's citadel, were among the opening salvos of that conflict.

BIBLIOGRAPHY

W. D. Orcutt, *Good Old Dorchester* (Cambridge, MA, 1908)

GEORGE W. HARPER

Codner, Samuel (b. Teignmouth, Devon, England, 1776; d. Devon, 5 August 1858). Newfoundland merchant and founder of the Society for the Education of the Poor in Newfoundland. Codner, a West Country fish merchant engaged in Newfoundland trade was based in St John's from the 1780s. An Anglican he was involved in British charitable causes but felt that for the stability of Britain's colonial presence in Newfoundland and as a bulwark against Roman Catholicism on the island as well as for the professional and personal development of its inhabitants, the education of the poor had to be placed upon a more secure institutional footing. Consequently, with prime ministerial support, he founded in 1823 the Society for the Education of the Poor in Newfoundland. Codner travelled incessantly in seeking to promote the society. The society flourished through Governor Cochrane's outspoken support and during the following twenty years established 45 schools and educated an estimated 12,000 pupils. Codner's evangelical activities were animated by plain Christian charity, anti-Catholicism, and British imperialism, intentions and motives which mutually supported each other and which contributed to Codner's considerable success.

BIBLIOGRAPHY
DCB
DNLB
ENL
P. McCann, 'The Newfoundland School Society 1823–1836: Missionary Enterprise or Cultural Imperialism?' in *'Benefits bestowed'?: Education and British Imperialism*, ed. J. A. Mangan, Studies in Imperialism, ed., John M. MacKenzie (Manchester and New York, 1988): 94–112

HANS ROLLMANN

Coetlogon, Charles Edward de (b. London, 1746; d. London, 16 Sept. 1820). Anglican clergyman. Son of the Chevalier Dennis de Coetlogon, MD, he was educated at Christ's Hospital and Pembroke College. Cambridge (BA 1770, MA 1773). The notebook which he kept in college (Dr Williams's Library) shows that he was already an evangelical and encouraged his fellow students to form a religious society.

In 1770 he was ordained deacon at Canterbury on the title of Curate of Marden, Kent. He was ordained priest in 1772, and soon after became MARTIN MADAN's assistant at the Lock Hospital chapel. He become well known as an evangelical preacher and was appointed the Lord Mayor's chaplain for 1789. In 1794 he was presented to the vicarage of Godstone in Surrey, which he retained until his death.

He also published many theological works, defending Calvinism and attacking the 'abominations of the Church of Rome'. He supported all Calvinist denominations and even preached to the Cambridge Baptist congregation.

BIBLIOGRAPHY
DNB

EDWIN WELCH

Cogswell, William (b. Atkinson, NH, USA, 5 June 1787; d. Gilmantown, NH, USA, 18 April 1850). Congregational minister. Born into a family of eight children of a doctor turned judge, Cogswell was graduated from Dartmouth in 1811. He taught at Atkinson and Hampton Academies even as he studied theology, chiefly with Dr Worcester of Salem. Ordained in 1815, he became pastor of South Church, Dedham, Massachusetts. He married Joanna Strong and they had three children. ln 1829 he resigned the pastorate to become general agent of the American Education Society. ln 1832 he became secretary and editor of the society's *Quarterly Journal and Register*, and a trustee of Andover Seminary.

Cogswell resigned as Secretary in 1841 and became a Trustee of Dartmouth, as well as professor of history and national education. He founded the Northern Academy of Arts and Sciences. In 1844, he accepted the presidency and chair of Christian Theology at Gilmanton

Seminary, in New Hampshire. The death of his promising 21-year-old son in 1848 was a heavy blow.

He published 'Reports of the American Education Society', 1833–40. He took a lively interest in state histories and edited for some years the *New Hampshire Repository* and *American Quarterly Register*. Other of his published works are: *A Manual of Theology and Devotion, Christian Philanthropist*, and *Harbinger of the Millennium*. He held MA degrees from Harvard and Brown (1816) and the DD from Williams (1833).

BIBLIOGRAPHY
AAP
J. G. Wilson and J. Fiske, eds, *Appleton's Cyclopedia of American Biography* (New York, 1891)

DIETRICH G. BUSS

Coke, Thomas (b. Brecon, England, 28 Sept. 1747; d. at sea, 4 May 1814). Anglican priest, American Methodist bishop, and pioneer of overseas missions. Coke was the only son of a prosperous apothecary who gave him a good education. He became a gentleman commoner at Jesus College, Oxford, taking his BA in 1768 and MA in 1770. In 1775 he obtained his DCL with the support of the Prime Minister, Lord North. Meanwhile he had been ordained priest in 1772 and was serving as curate at South Petherton, Somerset.

Under the influence of the writings of JOHN W. FLETCHER he became increasingly evangelical in sympathy and practice and on 13 August 1776 rode over to Kingston St Mary near Taunton to meet JOHN WESLEY. Wesley sent him back to his parish duties, but opposition to his ministry came to a head the following Easter; he was driven from the parish and decided to throw in his lot with the Methodists. He quickly became Wesley's chief assistant and was entrusted with many administrative responsibilities. These culminated in the drafting of the Deed of Declaration (1784), giving legal status to the Methodist Conference and ensuring the continuance of the Methodist connection after Wesley's death.

In the same year Coke issued his first appeal for overseas missionary work. This was increasingly to be his main concern. For the moment, however, his attention was diverted by the need to re-organize the Methodist work in North America in the wake of the Revolutionary War. In September 1784, at Bristol, Wesley departed from Anglican usage and discipline by ordaining two of his preachers and setting apart Coke as 'Superintendent' of American Methodism. Coke there upon set out on the first of nine visits to the American mainland and at the 'Christmas Conference' in Baltimore later that year the MEC was organized. FRANCIS ASBURY was ordained by Coke and elected as fellow superintendent (soon changed to 'Bishop').

During this and subsequent visits Coke travelled widely through the 13 States of the Atlantic seaboard. As a British citizen who divided his time between the two countries, he was never fully accepted by the American

Methodists or by Asbury. Nevertheless, he played a significant part in shaping the American Church and its discipline.

With the death of Wesley, Coke expected to have a key role in determining the future of British Methodism. Though passed over in favour of WILLIAM THOMPSON as first president of the conference, he was actively involved in the development of Methodism from a society into a new denomination. He was eventually elected president in 1797 and again in 1805. He also presided regularly over the Irish Conference, at which he had several times represented Wesley.

His concern for the wider mission of the church was expressed in a series of missionary appeals and in a tireless campaign of begging for subscriptions. Although the WMMS was not formally inaugurated until after his death, he laid its foundations. Almost single-handed and over nearly thirty years, he first created and then sustained an expanding work overseas. In 1786–7, the first of his four tours of the West Indies led to the placing of missionaries in several islands. An abortive attempt to establish a mission among the Fulas to the north of the new colony of Sierra Leone failed partly because Coke's enthusiasm exceeded his judgement of character in choosing missionaries. Towards the end of his life, however, a mission was begun in Sierra Leone itself, as well as in Gibraltar and at the Cape.

From 1804 on, Coke was aided by a missionary committee, but the burden of responsibility continued to rest on his shoulders. His own fortune and the property that came to him through two marriages late in his life were largely devoted to this cause. At the same time, from 1806 on he was involved in the establishment of home missions in areas hitherto unaffected by the Methodist movement.

In the course of a busy and peripatetic existence, Coke found time for a considerable amount of writing, much of it ephemeral. Among his more substantial publications were a Bible commentary, a history of the West Indies and a revised version of Samuel Wesley's poem on the life of Christ. He was responsible, in collaboration with HENRY MOORE, for the official biography of John Wesley and also published a number of sermons and several 'extracts' from his Journals, describing his visits to America and the Caribbean.

As early as 1784 he had been in correspondence with CHARLES GRANT of the East India Company about the prospects for a mission to India. This was put aside for many years because of other claims on his time and resources; but eventually, in 1813, after several years of impassioned persuasion on his part, the Wesleyan Conference authorized such a mission. Coke himself set out at the end of December, heading a party of six missionaries, but died at sea and was buried in the Indian Ocean, leaving his young companions to launch the mission without his support.

Criticism of Coke throughout his lifetime – and frequently reiterated since – centred chiefly on his personal ambition and his indiscretion. As an educated person with influential associations from his years at Oxford, he found it natural to adopt a position of leadership, if not an attitude of superiority, among the Methodist preachers on both sides of the Atlantic. This naturally bred resentment. At times he was given to hasty judgement and intemperate utterance, both in the pulpit and elsewhere. His enthusiasm for the mission of the church led him to vacillate in his attitude towards the Church of England in which he had been nurtured. For the most part after 1784, and especially after Wesley's death, he sided with those who wanted to sever Methodism's links with the parent church. But on three separate occasions – once in America (1791) and twice in England (1799 and 1813) he attempted, without authority from his fellow Methodists, to effect a reconciliation between the two bodies. In the long interval between Wesley's catholicity and twentieth-century ecumenism, this was an indiscretion which neither side found it easy to excuse.

SELECT WRITINGS

T. Coke, *A Plan of the Society for the Establishment of Missions among the Heathens* (1783/4) (Letter of appeal in Drew University Library)

—, *An Address to the Pious and Benevolent, Proposing an Annual Subscription for the Support of the Missionaries in the Highlands and Adjacent Islands of Scotland, the Isles of Jersey, Guernsey and Newfoundland, the West Indies, and the Provinces of Nova Scotia and Quebec* (London, 1786)

—, [with Henry Moore] *The Life of the Rev. John Wesley, A.M. Including an Account of the Great Revival of Religion, In Europe and America, of Which He Was the First and Chief Instrument* (London, 1792)

—, *A Commentary on the Holy Bible*, 6 vols (London, 1801–3)

—, *A History of the West Indies, containing the natural, civil and ecclesiastical history of each island*, 3 vols (London, 1808–11)

—, *The Life of Christ, a Poem* (London, 1809)

—, *Extracts of the Journals of the late Rev. Thomas Coke, L.L.D.* (Dublin, 1816)

BIBLIOGRAPHY

J. A. Vickers, *Thomas Coke, Apostle of Methodism* (London and Nashville, TN, 1969)

F. Baker, *From Wesley to Asbury* (Durham, NC, 1976): 142–61

Earlier lives by J. Crowther (Leeds, 1815), S. Drew (London, 1817), J. W. Etheridge (London, 1860) and W. A. Candler (Nashville, TN, 1923)

JOHN A. VICKERS

Coker, Daniel [né **Wright, Isaac**] (b. eastern shore of Maryland, USA, 1780: d. Sierra Leone, 1846). A founder of the African Methodist Episcopal Church and founder of the West African Methodist Church. Son of a white indentured servant, Susan Coker, and a black slave, Edward Wright, he was raised with his white half-brothers from his mother's first marriage. He served as their valet at school in order to get an education. As a young man he escaped to New York where he changed his name to avoid slave hunters. Here he was also converted, became a Methodist and began to preach.

In 1801 he moved to Baltimore where, financed by

four free blacks, Quaker abolitionist John Needles purchased his release (Michael Coate, a ME minister, also provided help). He joined a separate Black Methodist society, and in 1808 was ordained a deacon of Baltimore's Sharp Street Methodist Church by FRANCIS ASBURY. From 1802 to 1816 he taught at the African Academy School, the first school for blacks in Blatimore in which a black teacher taught. His *Dialogue Between a Virginian and an African Minister* (Baltimore, 1810), an elegant argument for emancipation, was perhaps the first pamphlet published by an African-American in the United States.

Coker was soon involved in the controversy between white and black Methodists in the North over segregationist policies within the church. Having become the leader of the African Bethel Church in Baltimore after secession from Sharp Street Church (which was controlled by white elders), he was elected representative to RICHARD ALLEN's 1816 meeting in Philadelphia to organize the African Methodist Episcopal Church (AME Church). Coker was elected its first Bishop, but inexplicably resigned the position the next day, Allen taking his place. Nevertheless, Coker's church in Baltimore flourished as a member of the AME Church, growing to over one thousand members. In 1818 he was expelled from the church but the reasons for this are not clear; he was reinstated the following year.

In 1820 he became a missionary to Liberia and Sierra Leone and ran the Maryland Colonization Society operation there; he later organized Methodist societies in collaboration with the Wesleyan Methodist Church. He founded the West African Methodist Church in Sierra Leone, and probably died there. A 'brilliant, erratic man', Coker played a key role in forming black denominations in both Africa and America.

BIBLIOGRAPHY
J. Coan, 'Daniel Coker: 19th Century Black Church Organizer, Educator and Missionary,' *Journal of the Interdenominational Theological Center* 3 (Fall 1975): 17–31
DCA
W. Gravely, 'African Methodism and the Rise of Black Denominationalism,' in R. Richey and K. Rowe, eds., *Rethinking Methodist History* (Nashville, TN, 1985): 111–24
L. Murphy, J. Melton and G. Ward, eds, *Encyclopedia of African American Religions* (New York and London, 1993): 187–8
H. Richardson, *Dark Salvation* (Garden City, NY, 1976)

KENNETH N. PEARSON

Colbert, William (b. Poolesville, MD, BNA, 20 April 1764; d. Stroudsburg, USA, PA, 1835). American Methodist itinerant preacher. Converted under Methodist preaching, Colbert became a circuit rider in Maryland in 1790. He was ordained elder in the Baltimore Methodist Episcopal Conference in 1792. Itinerating in Delaware, Maryland, New Jersey, Pennsylvania, and New York, Colbert came into conflict with Bishop FRANCIS ASBURY after he married Elizabeth Stroud on 1 November 1804 and asked for relief from changing

assignments each year. In 1807, he received a missionary appointment in Pennsylvania. Gradually he retired from the travelling ministry, lived near Stroudsburg, Pennsylvania and filled part-time pastoral functions.

His unpublished journal records his ministerial routine, preaching patterns, spiritual state, and commitment to social reform, especially the abolition of slavery. Deeply attached to African Methodists, Colbert boarded often with RICHARD and SARAH ALLEN in Philadelphia and preached regularly at the (Mother) Bethel African Church. While there in 1805–6, he laboured feverishly but unsuccessfully to prevent a breach between St George's Church and Bethel. His accounts of black testimonials in lovefeasts and class meetings demonstrate the significant African presence in early Methodism. His journal for 1790–1833 is held in the Garrett-Evangelical Theological Seminary in Evanston, Illinois.

BIBLIOGRAPHY
N. B. Harmon, ed., *The Encyclopedia of World Methodism* (Nashville, TN, 1974)

JEANNE KNEPPER
WILL GRAVELY

Cole, Charles (b. Wellow, Somerset, England, 1733; d. 1813). English Baptist minister. In 1756 he was baptized and received into membership by the church at Bradford in Wiltshire under the care of Richard Haines. He served the congregation at Whitchurch in Hampshire for many years and actively engaged in village preaching. Cole is a good example of an eighteenth-century Baptist minister who readily embraced other evangelicals. In 1789, under the leadership of Cole, the congregation at Whitchurch sent a formal letter to JOHN NEWTON expressing appreciation for his sermons. While Newton was widely respected, it is notable that a small congregation under the leadership of Cole would go so far as to send a formal letter to him and to write that they sent 'a mite towards encouraging your heart and strengthening your hands in God's service'.

SELECT WRITINGS
C. Cole, *A Three-fold Alphabet of New Hymns 1) On the Public Ministry of the Word 2) On Baptism 3) On the Lord's Supper* (London, 1789)

BIBLIOGRAPHY
'A memoir of Charles Cole' *BaptMag* (1814)

KAREN SMITH

Cole, Nathan (b. Kensington [now in Berlin], CT, BNA, 15 Feb. 1711; d. Kensington, USA, 1783). New England Separatist. Cole was a carpenter, farmer and an unconverted church member. On the morning of 23 October 1740 word spread that GEORGE WHITEFIELD was to preach in Middletown, and Cole dropped his work to attend. His description of the multitudes rushing to hear the evangelist is the opening scene in his always vivid, 'The Spiritual Travels of Nathan Cole'. The 'Travels' illustrate a pattern of conversion common during the Great Awakening – deep conviction, followed by despair of salvation, and finally assurance. In 1747 Cole separated from the state Congregational church over their practice of admitting the unconverted to the Lord's Supper. For a time several dissenters met at his home, but they were unable to secure a minister, and the group dwindled away. In 1764 he joined the Separatist congregation of EBENEZER FROTHINGHAM. The following year he wrote his 'Travels' in which he claimed that at his conversion he had seen a vision of this very church with angels hovering over it. Two bound volumes of manuscripts exist at the Connecticut Historical Society in Hartford.

BIBLIOGRAPHY
M. J. Crawford, 'The Spiritual Travels of Nathan Cole', *Wm. & Mary Q.*, 33 (1976): 89–126

JOHN K. LA SHELL

Colenso, Elizabeth [née Fairburn] (b. Kerikeri, New Zealand, 29 Aug. 1821; d. Otaki, New Zealand, 2 Sept. 1904). CMS missionary and translator. The daughter of Sarah and William Fairburn, CMS lay missionaries in New Zealand, Elizabeth was raised to be very fluent in Maori and had an outstanding linguistic flair. Unhappily married to WILLIAM COLENSO in 1843 (largely because Bishop Selwyn wanted a schoolteacher in Waimate), she bore two children in remote Ahuriri, leaving in 1853 after William's adultery became public knowledge.

Two periods of mission school teaching, at Kaitotehe 1854–60 and Paihia 1869–76, bracketed a London sojourn largely spent preparing the text and correcting the proofs of the first Bible in Maori. She was later invited to join the Melanesian Mission, learned Motu, and served as a translator and teacher on Norfolk Island 1876–98. She continued to prepare translations for the mission in her retirement.

BIBLIOGRAPHY
DNZB
C. Macdonald, M. Penfold and B. Williams, eds, *The Book of New Zealand Women* (Wellington, New Zealand, 1991)

BRYAN D. GILLING

Colenso, William (b. 7 or 17 Nov. 1811, Penzance, Cornwall, England; d. 10 Feb. 1899, Napier, New Zealand). CMS missionary to New Zealand. A printer, Colenso was recruited for a CMS press at Paihia, arriving in 1834. In 1835 he produced the first book printed in New Zealand, Philippians and Ephesians in Maori. In 1837 he printed 5,000 copies of the Maori New Testament.

Colenso yearned to be a missionary, but his dogmatism made the CMS and Bishop Selwyn reluctant. A loveless arranged marriage to Elizabeth Fairburn in 1843

preceded his ordination as deacon (22 September 1844) and missionary posting to Ahuriri. Much effort went into important pioneering journeys and botanical study, but self-righteousness and despotism marred his tireless evangelism. Adultery with a Maori servant resulted, in 1852, in the collapse of his marriage, severance from the CMS and Anglican ministry, and ridicule by Maori observers.

From 1859 Colenso entered provincial, then national politics, also inspecting schools 1872–8. He continued to produce many important scientific, linguistic and historical writings, being restored as deacon in 1894.

BIBLIOGRAPHY
A. G. Bagnall and G. C. Petersen, *William Colenso* (Wellington, New Zealand, 1948)
D. T. B[arry], *CMS Register of Missionaries and Native Clergy* (privately printed) (London, 1906)
DNZB

BRYAN D. GILLING

Colier [**Collier**], **Thomas** (b. Fife, Scotland; d. Colingsburgh, Fife, 19 July 1769). Minister of the Scottish Relief Church. Though born in Scotland, he first ministered in England among the Dissenters at Ravenstondale, Northumberland. In 1761 he was recommended by THOMAS BOSTON and THOMAS GILLESPIE to the new congregation at Colingsburgh. The General Assembly had imposed an unwanted minister on the church in Kilconquhar, Fife, so dissatisfied elders and a great majority of the parishioners constituted themselves an independent church, erected a meeting house, and settled Colier as their pastor. In these actions they followed the methods of English Independents. A few weeks later, on 22 October 1761, Gillespie and Boston came to Colingsburgh for Colier's formal induction. That same day three ministers and an elder from each of their churches constituted themselves into a presbytery of Relief. Colier 'left behind him the reputation of having been a minister of rare talents, and of liberal enlightened principles' (Struthers, 1843: 243).

BIBLIOGRAPHY
G. Struthers, *The History of the Rise, Progress and Principles of the Relief Church* (Glasgow, 1843)

JOHN K. LA SHELL

Collet, Elizabeth [née Tonkin] (b. Gwinear, Cornwall, England, 9 May 1762; d. England, *c.* 1820). Collet early had a religious outlook, encouraged by dreams. When she was 16 she joined a Wesleyan Methodist class, led by ANN GILBERT. Visiting Feock in 1782, when the preacher could not come, Collet was urged to speak, which reluctantly she did, very effectively. Other invitations followed and in spite of opposition she preached. When her husband built a chapel at St Erme, Collet preached at the opening. Her happy home life was reflected in her ministry.

BIBLIOGRAPHY
L. F. Church, *More About the Early Methodist People* (London, 1949)
Z. Taft, *Biographical Sketches of ... Holy Women ... 2* (London, (1828)

E. DOROTHY GRAHAM

Collingwood, William (b. Greenwich, London, 23 April 1819; d. Bristol, England, 25 June 1903). Watercolourist and Brethren leader. Grandson of Samuel, printer to Oxford University, Collingwood was educated privately and at the Cathedral School, Oxford. He specialized in 'baronial interiors' and in landscape (especially mountain scenery, his chief love). In 1839 he settled in Liverpool, where he became a member of the academy, and was elected to the Royal Society of Painters in Watercolours in 1855. In 1844 he started a Brethren congregation, later building them a hall, and leading them for forty years. A close friend of GEORGE MÜLLER, he moved to Bristol in 1890, becoming a member of the Bristol Academy. He was a friend of John Ruskin, his son being Ruskin's private secretary and biographer; his grandson was R. G. Collingwood, the Oxford philosopher and archaeologist.

ROY COAD

Collins, Brian Bury (b. Stamford, Lincolnshire, England, 1754; d. 1807). Anglican clergyman. Collins was educated at St John's College, Cambridge (scholar 1775; BA, 1776; MA, 1780), where he formed a friendship with HENRY COULTHURST. A number of bishops refused him orders because of his field-preaching for JOHN WESLEY, but he was eventually accepted and became curate to DAVID SIMPSON at Christ Church, Macclesfield (1781–2). He continued however, to exercise an itinerant ministry both for Wesley and Lady HUNTINGDON, a work in which he could more freely indulge after inheriting the estate of his uncle, Thomas Irwin Bury at Blankney (Lincolnshire), whose name he then assumed. His correspondence was edited by A. M. Broadley in *Proceedings of the Wesley Historical Society*, vol. IX.

BIBLIOGRAPHY
Al. Cant. II. ii: 98
A. Leedes Hunt, *David Simpson and the Evangelical Revival* (London, 1927)

ARTHUR POLLARD

Collins, Ebenezer (b. London, *c.* 1800; d. England, 6 Feb. 1875). CMS missionary in Jamaica and Sierra Leone. Collins trained at the CMS college at Islington (London) from 1825 and on 14 October 1827 was sent to Jamaica to restart the CMS work there that had been attempted by THOMAS JONES and HENRY C. TAYLOR. He returned from Jamaica on 1 August 1833 and in December 1833 transferred to the work in Sierra Leone, for which place he sailed in 1834.

Collins returned from Sierra Leone in October of 1837, probably for health reasons and was ordained (deacon and priest 1839) by the Bishop of London before going out to Sierra Leone again on 25 November 1839. In March of 1841 he returned to England and left the CMS. He then served in various curacies in Devon and Somerset. In 1846 he married Mary Pearse.

BIBLIOGRAPHY
D. T. B[arry], *CMS Register of Missionaries and Native Clergy* (privately printed) (London, 1906)

DONALD M. LEWIS

Collins, John (b. Gloucester County, NJ, BNA, 1 Nov. 1769; d. Maysville, KY, USA, 21 Aug. 1845). Methodist preacher. Collins' religious background was Quaker, but in June or July of 1794 he was 'awakened' to his need of religion through a near fatal illness. After a protracted struggle of soul he became an active member of the Methodist Church.

Some time following his Methodist conversion he sensed deep convictions of a calling to ministry. After considerable resistance he began preaching and for some years laboured as 'local preacher' in New Jersey. In the year 1803, he and his family settled on a farm in southern Ohio's Clermont County. He joined the Methodist Conference in 1807 and was appointed to the Miami circuit. All of his active ministry was spent in Ohio until his retirement in 1837. Collins served mainly as a circuit rider, though he did occasionally act as a 'Presiding Elder'. His ministerial notoriety was based on his considerable skills as a moving preacher and he was reputedly the most prolific Methodist evangelist in 'the West'.

His preaching eloquence greatly accentuated the themes of redemptive love (to God and Man) and grace, augmented with unabashed emotive appeals. Said not to be a 'classical scholar', he did have a reputation as a 'deep thinker', acquainted with history and English literature, and rich in 'Biblical knowledge'.

BIBLIOGRAPHY
AAP, 7: 263–7
M. Simpson, ed., *Cyclopedia of Methodism* (Philadelphia, PA, 1878)

WOODROW W. WHIDDEN

Collins, Judson Dwight (b. Rose County, NY, USA, 12 April 1823; d. Unadilla, MI, USA, 13 May 1852). First American Methodist missionary to China. Born into a devout Methodist family, Collins graduated in the first class from the University of Michigan in July 1845. He was appointed professor of natural and moral science at the holiness Methodist Albion College, Michigan (1845–7) and was taken into the Michigan Conference on trial in 1846.

Collins sought appointment to China. Told that the church had no immediate intention of establishing a mission there, he requested a ticket and volunteered to go on a self-supporting basis. Funds were solicited and received, including $1,000 from Dr WALTER C. PALMER. Together with Moses and Jane Atwater White, he sailed from Boston on 15 April 1847.

After less than 6 months in Foochow, Collins established a school for boys (28 February 1848) and began a Sunday school (5 March 1848). By May 1849, three schools for boys were functioning. A school for girls was opened on 30 December 1850. Collins and White also distributed literature provided by the ABCFM and the LMS. Collins opposed printing biblical texts, but the popularity of such literature led to Methodist publishing efforts in China. Preaching stations were established and a house refurbished and dedicated on 27 October 1852 as a small chapel.

Decimated by typhoid fever, he departed for the United States of America on 22 April 1851, hoping to recover. His diary is preserved at the Methodist Detroit Conference Historical Society Archives at Adrian, Michigan.

BIBLIOGRAPHY
W. C. Barclay, *History of Methodist Missions*, 3 (New York, 1957)
S. J. Harrision, 'Collins, Judson Dwight', *Encyclopedia of World Methodism*, 1 (Nashville, TN, 1974): 542–3
W. N. Lacy, *A Hundred Years of China Methodism* (Nashville, TN, 1948)

DAVID BUNDY

Collins, William (b. Glasgow, Scotland, 12 Oct. 1789; d. Rothesay, Buteshire, Scotland, 2 Jan. 1853). Presbyterian publisher and philanthropist. Born into a labouring family, Collins was educated at his parish school, worked briefly as handloom weaver, and then as a clerk at a Glasgow cotton mill. There he evangelized among the mill workers, organizing a Sunday school and teaching reading, writing and arithmetic in the evenings. He became the protege of the Church of Scotland evangelical minister and social reformer, STEVENSON MACGILL, minister of the Tron parish in Glasgow, who in 1813 convinced Collins to open a private school in Glasgow.

In 1814, Collins, now an elder in the Tron parish church, played a leading role in bringing the celebrated evangelical preacher, THOMAS CHALMERS, to the Tron as the replacement for MacGill, who had been appointed to a chair at Glasgow University. Collins became one of Chalmers's most zealous parish workers, organizing Sunday schools and regularly visiting homes in deprived areas. In 1819, with Chalmers's encouragement and financial backing, Collins set up a publishing firm in partnership with Chalmers' brother, Charles. A bold entrepreneur and tireless worker, Collins soon made the new press a major force, particularly in publishing evangelical works and Bibles. Charles Chalmers soon grew weary of the publishing business and in 1826 sold his partnership to Collins – who continued to expand the

enterprise, laying the foundations for one of the world's great publishing concerns.

Collins also became active in philanthropic work. After 1829, he travelled widely as a temperance lecturer. In 1834, stirred by a remark by his dying daughter concerning the unchurched poor in Glasgow, he began a campaign to erect twenty new parish churches in Glasgow, reaching his goal by 1841. He worked tirelessly for church extension, popular education, the abolition of slavery, the expansion of savings banks and the prohibition of Sunday trains. At the Disruption of 1843, Collins followed Chalmers and much of the evangelical party out of the established Church of Scotland, following a prolonged conflict with the state over patronage. He became a prominent member and generous benefactor of the new Free Church.

In 1846, Collins experienced a painful break with his long-time friend and mentor, Chalmers. Following the death of his wife in 1848, Collins left the management of the publishing firm to his only son, while he moved to Rothesay and devoted his final years to a mission for the poor and the support of various philanthropic causes.

BIBLIOGRAPHY
D. Keir, *The House of Collins* (London, 1952)

STEWART J. BROWN

Collyer, William Bengo (b. Blackheath, England, 14 April 1782; d. Peckham, Surrey, England, 9 Jan. 1854). Congregational minister. Collyer was the son of Thomas Collyer, a builder of Deptford. He entered Homerton college at 13, beginning his lifelong ministry at 19 at Peckham and being ordained in 1801. The church grew and the new Hanover chapel opened in 1817. Collyer ministered also, 1814–26, to the church at Salters' Hall. The Dukes of Kent and Sussex occasionally attended his church.

BIBLIOGRAPHY
DNB
Julian
R. T. Jones *Congregationalism in England 1662–1962* (London, 1962)

ALAN ARGENT

Colman, Benjamin (b. Boston, MA, BNA, 19 Oct. 1673; d. Boston, MA, BNA, 29 Aug. 1747). Congregational minister. After two degrees from Harvard (BA 1692, MA 1695), four years of preaching in England, and ordination by the London presbytery (4 August 1699), Colman returned to Boston to become the first minister of the Brattle Street Church. To the horror of Increase and Cotton Mather, the *Brattle Street Manifesto* (1699) announced that the new church would no longer require conversion relations for admittance to the Lord's Supper and would permit the Scriptures to be read without comment. Twenty years later, however, Colman joined with the Mathers to defend the medical procedure of inoculation. In 1740, he was the first to open his pulpit to GEORGE WHITEFIELD, and although Colman would criticize the excesses of JAMES DAVENPORT, he never turned against the revival movement.

Colman is considered an important transitional figure in the history of New England theology and prose style. His irenic, ecumenical temperament and his lucid, urbane manner have been called 'Calvinist sentimentalism' and 'implicit Arminianism'. He proclaimed adherence to the Westminster Confession, but avoided theological hairsplitting about topics like irresistible grace and limited atonement. For his prosperous congregation, he stressed 'holy mirth' more than fear and trembling, and Christian nurture more than cataclysmic conversion. In over a hundred published works including his *Practical Discourses upon the Parable of the Ten Virgins* (1707), he supplanted the apocalyptic foreboding of the Puritan past with a vision of a reasonable world made joyful through grace.

BIBLIOGRAPHY

T. Batson, 'Arminianism in New England' (George Washington Univ. Ph.D. thesis, 1974)
P. Miller, *The New England Mind, From Colony to Province* (Cambridge, MA, 1953)
SGH, IV: 120–37
T. Toulouse, *The Art of Prophesying* (Athens, GA, 1987)

CHRISTOPHER GRASSO

Colquhoun, John Campbell (b. Edinburgh, 23 Jan. 1803; d. London, 17 April 1870). MP and writer. Colquhoun was the eldest son of Archibald Campbell Colquhoun, Lord Clerk Register, and his wife Mary Ann, the daughter of the Reverend William Erksine, an Episcopalian minister. He was educated at Edinburgh High School and Oriel College, Oxford (BA, 1823). On his father's death in 1820 he inherited his property at Killermont, near Glasgow. On 10 September 1827 he married Henrietta Maria, eldest daughter of Thomas, second Lord Lilford. His wife's influence appears to have drawn his personal loyalties over to the Church of England, but he considered himself to be also 'connected by many ties of residence and cordial regard with the Church of Scotland'.

Colquhoun first entered Parliament in 1832 as a Radical, sitting for his home constituency of Dumbartonshire. He had close ties with THOMAS CHALMERS and the evangelical party in the Church of Scotland and, in 1834, he was responsible for obtaining parliamentary legislation to implement the General Assembly's Chapels Act and create *quoad sacra* parishes. The measure was vaguely drafted and in 1839 it was effectively invalidated by decisions of the Court of Session. Nevertheless Colquhoun continued to seek a compromise in the deepening conflict in the Church of Scotland: although sympathetic to the case of the Non-Intrusionists he considered their secession to be 'a great national calamity'.

Meanwhile his growing conviction that Established Churches were a powerful evangelistic agency and an essential bulwark of Protestantism led him during the mid-1830s to a change in his political loyalty. He did not contest the 1835 General Election, but played a major part, both as orator and organizer, in the campaign of anti-Catholic meetings in defence of the Church of Ireland held between 1834 and 1836. In 1837 Colquhoun returned to Parliament, now a Tory representing the Kilmarnock Burghs. According to Disraeli, he was 'anxious only for the diffusion of the Gospel' and, at this period, believed Sir Robert Peel 'to be the very prophet of the Lord'. In this 'Protestant' phase of the Tory party's history Colquhoun became an influential figure and was even seen by Thomas Chalmers as a potential latter-day WILLIAM WILBERFORCE.

His career received a setback when he lost his seat in the 1841 General Election in the face of the overall Tory triumph. He was returned for Newcastle-under-Lyme at a by-election in 1842, but Peel left him on the back benches nursing frustrated ambition. In 1845 Colquhoun's personal resentments blended with Protestant principle to produce an explosion of hostility to the prime minister. He took a prominent part in opposing the Maynooth Act, published articles and pamphlets forcefully attacking the record of the government, and organized the National Club as a focus for those seeking a more consistent and religiously based Conservatism. This bid for leadership proved to be abortive; Colquhoun had overplayed his hand, and his health failed at the critical juncture of 1846–7. The initiative in setting the direction of the post-Peel Conservative Party passed to others.

Meanwhile he retired from Parliament in 1847 and, although more than two decades of life remained to him, he was now troubled by recurrent illness. He continued to be a powerful force in the counsels of the National Club, and later took an active role in the Irish Church Missions and the Church Association. He also turned his hand to writing, both topical pamphlets and historical works, notably *William Wilberforce* (1866). A small collection of Colquhoun's papers survives, and there is important evidence relating to him in the Chalmers and the Disraeli Papers.

SELECT WRITINGS

J. C. Colquhoun, *Memorials of H.M.C.* (London, 1870)

BIBLIOGRAPHY

S. J. Brown, *Thomas Chalmers* (Oxford, 1982)
DNB
J. Wolffe, *The Protestant Crusade in Great Britain, 1829–1860* (Oxford, 1991)

JOHN WOLFFE

Colton, Walter (b. Rutland, VT, USA, 9 May 1797; d. Philadelphia, PA, USA, 22 Jan. 1851). Chaplain, journalist and author. He was educated at Yale College and Andover Theological Seminary before ordination as a Congregational minister in 1827. After service as a professor and school chaplain, he edited a Washington,

DC, newspaper opposing President Andrew Jackson's Indian removal policies. In 1831 he was commissioned as a chaplain in the United States Navy where he served until his death. Throughout his naval career he continued his journalistic endeavours for social reform. From 1846 to 1849 he ministered in California and in addition to his chaplaincy duties served as alcalde (mayor and chief magistrate) of Monterey, California, engaging in legal, journalistic and reform endeavours. When California gold was discovered in 1848, Colton's accounts published in United States newspapers added momentum to the gold rush.

A staunch advocate of naval reform, Colton was an outspoken critic of flogging, the grog ration, and the poor living and working conditions of seamen. His efforts to create better environments ashore and afloat paralleled those of the American Seamen's Friend Society of which he was a strong supporter. He was also a prolific writer on social issues such as duelling, African colonization, gambling, alcohol and asylums. His more important writings include *Three Years in California*, *The Sea and the Sailor*, and *Remarks on Duelling*.

BIBLIOGRAPHY
DAB
T. J. Demy, 'An Analysis of the Life and Ministry of Walter Colton (1797–1851): Congregational Minister and United States Navy Chaplain' (Dallas Theological Seminary Th.D. dissertation, 1990)

TIMOTHY J. DEMY

Colvin, John Russell (b. Calcutta, 29 May 1807; d. Agra, India, 9 Sept. 1857). Private secretary to Governor-General Lord Auckland and Lieutenant-Governor of the North West Provinces, 1853–57. Son of a Calcutta merchant, Colvin was educated at St Andrews University in Scotland and Haileybury College, the East India Company's school north of London. He rose rapidly in the company's secretariat, serving as Auckland's secretary during the tumultuous Afghan War (1839–41). At the same time he was placed influentially to support the ongoing but controversial land settlement directed by ROBERT M. BIRD. He succeeded JAMES THOMASON as Lieutenant-Governor in 1853 and died in Agra during the mutiny, having been overwhelmed by those events.

This does not detract from his achievements in less turbulent times as a competent administrator and a constant supporter of evangelical causes in the North West Provinces. He particularly approved of the Christian institutions fostered by the activities of HENRY CARRE TUCKER, who was Commissioner of Benares at the time of the mutiny.

BIBLIOGRAPHY
DIB
C. Hibbert, *The Great Mutiny* (Middlesex, England, 1986): 153–163
P. Penner, *The Patronage Bureaucracy in North India* (Delhi, 1986): 254

PETER PENNER

Compere, Lee (b. England, 1790; d. TX, USA, 1871). BMS missionary to Jamaica. Raised by an elderly aunt because he was orphaned at an early age, he had a sister, Jane, ten years his senior who was interested in missions and her influence led to Lee's conversion. He was baptized by JOHN RYLAND and attended Bristol Academy. There he met Suzanne Voysey, a well-to-do Londoner and they married in 1815. They travelled to Jamaica and gathered a group on the Lodge Estate in Old Harbor. Soon a call came to him to organize a group of GEORGE LIELE'S and Sweigle's members in Kingston. He organized them into a church at East Queen Street under BMS auspices in 1816. He, however, could not subscribe to BMS rules not to condemn slavery and when Henry Tripp, another missionary, bought a slave, Compere condemned him and an altercation developed. Coeval with this, both his wife and he succumbed to fever and they decided to catch the first ship to United States. They landed at Charleston in 1817.

Compere preached in Sumter District until 1822, encouraged by RICHARD FURMAN and William Johnson, and was a founding member of the South Carolina Baptist convention. He worked in Georgia and east Alabama concentrating on the Creek Indians and being funded by wealthy cotton planters. He conducted schools and missions between 1823 and 1839 but his support of Indian claims made him a controversial figure. This brought him into conflict with his funding agents and the Indian agent, Colonel John Crowell, and so he applied to the Trienniel Convention for support. This was meagre but with what he obtained together with his wife's wealth, they survived. He resigned in 1832 to give himself totally to the Indians and their cause. He moved to Mississippi in 1833 and during the next thirty years developed a strong work. During the Civil War he lived in Tennessee where his library and personal papers were destroyed by federal troops. After the war he preached in Arkansas and then moved to Texas where he died.

BIBLIOGRAPHY
Lee Compere (150th Anniversary pamphlet) (Halstead, England, 1968)
South Western Baptist Seminary, Fort Worth, TX, Compere papers

HORACE RUSSELL

Conder, John (b. Wimpole, Cambridgeshire, England, 3 June 1714; d. Homerton, London, 30 May 1781). Congregational minister and educator. Described by Isaac Watts as 'the most learned man I ever knew', he was, himself, the product of the King's Head Society, a society set up under the patronage of WILLIAM COWARD to promote evangelical orthodoxy in the Congregational ministry. It was to his academy, eventually to be settled at Homerton, that the society sent men for evangelical education after 1754, when Conder moved to London from his Cambridge pastorate to take charge of the academy conjointly with the pastorate of the Pavement Chapel.

BIBLIOGRAPHY
DNB
R. Tudur Jones, *Congregationalism in England, 1662–1962* (London, 1962)

J. H. Y. BRIGGS

Conder, Josiah (b. Aldersgate, London, 17 Sept. 1789; d. St John's Wood, London, 27 Dec. 1855). Congregational bookseller, journalist, and hymn-writer. He wrote his first article at ten, concluding his formal education at 13 to work in his father's bookselling business, which he took over in 1811, an education in itself. By this time, however, he had made the acquaintance of such Congregational litterateurs as JAMES MONTGOMERY and the TAYLORS of Ongar. In 1814 he acquired *The Eclectic Review* which he edited so expertly until 1837 seeking to make it a journal that combined piety with learning. Certainly a study of its pages would suggest that there was a more cultured aspect to early nineteenth-century Nonconformity than Matthew Arnold was prepared to recognize. Conder was also the first editor of the weekly, *The Patriot*, established in 1832 in the middle of the reform crisis to persuade orthodox dissenters to seek 'a larger share in the representation of their country', continuing as editor until his death. In 1838 he proposed the establishing of a society devoted to securing religious equality which would combine together churchmen and Dissenters, and for five years he sat on the council of the Religious Freedom Society which was dissolved in 1843, not having the cutting edge of the fiercely sectarian Liberation Society. Conder, perhaps the most distinguished layman of his generation, also wrote for other journals and authored a number of longer works, including his two volumes on *Protestant Nonconformity* issued in 1818, and, with little help, the thirty volumes of the remarkably comprehensive *The Modern Traveller*. He also penned a number of hymns which remain in common use, and edited *The Congregational Hymn Book*.

He maintained a formidable literary correspondence not only with other dissenting writers but with men such as Robert Southey, who said of Conder's work: 'I wish my co-adjutors in the Quarterly had thought half so much upon poetry and understood it half so well'. A modern critic argues that the *Eclectic* was ten years ahead of the field in its appreciation of Coleridge. His son, Eustace R. Conder (born St Albans, Hertfordshire, 1 April 1820; died Bournemouth, Hampshire, 6 July 1892) became one of Yorkshire's leading Free Churchmen, sustaining a thirty-year long pastorate at East Parade Church, Leeds; widely regarded as both 'saint and scholar', he became chairman of the Congregational Union in 1873. His Congregational Lecture on *The Basis of Faith* was rewarded with the award of an Edinburgh DD.

BIBLIOGRAPHY
E. R. Conder, *Josiah Conder, a Memoir* (London, 1857)
DNB

J. H. Y. BRIGGS

Coney, James (b. London, *c.* 1795). CMS missionary to Sierra Leone. Coney trained as a schoolmaster under the Reverend J. Bishop and on 3 November 1824 was sent by the CMS to Sierra Leone and stationed at Kissey. His wife (formerly Mrs Cooper) died 1 May 1825, a few months after their arrival, whereupon Coney returned to England (11 June) and ended his association with the CMS.

BIBLIOGRAPHY
D. T. B[arry], *CMS Register of Missionaries and Native Clergy* (privately printed) (London, 1906)

DONALD M. LEWIS

Congleton, (second) Lord [Parnell, John (Vesey)] (b. London, 16 June 1805; d. 23 Oct. 1883). Peer and Brethren leader. Eldest son of the former Sir Henry Brooke Parnell, a leading Irish MP, he was converted while a student in Edinburgh through reading Paul's epistle to the Romans. After declining his father's offer of an army commission, he was left a substantial legacy by an uncle. While visiting Dublin, he became acquainted with the earliest Brethren and was one of those who joined ANTHONY NORRIS GROVES in Baghdad (1830) and accompanied him to India. From 1837 he resided mainly in London and exercised a wide ministry among Brethren.

A man of gentle disposition, his was a moderating influence. Like most Brethren of his time he lived austerely (giving away half his income), but he was one of the few to play a part in political life. Occasionally he took his seat in the House of Lords, where he sat on the cross benches, voted on occasions and once spoke.

BIBLIOGRAPHY
H. Groves, *Memoir of Lord Congleton* (London, 1884)

HAROLD H. ROWDON

Conington, John (b. Boston, Lincolnshire, England, 10 June 1825; d. Boston, England, 23 Oct. 1869). English university reformer. The son of an evangelical rector, Conington was a prodigy and enjoyed much success at Rugby and Oxford. He matriculated at University College, Oxford, migrated to Magdalen, took prizes, and graduated BA (1847). He was elected fellow at University College and became professor of Latin at Corpus Christi (1854). His translation of Virgil (1866) is still admired.

From 1845 to 1854 Conington enjoyed a considerable reputation at the university as a leader, with his great friend, Goldwin Smith (1823–1910, *DNB*), in the call for university reforms. He wrote on that topic in the 'Morning Chronicle' and the *North British Review*, and on classics and church polity in the *Edinburgh*, *Quarterly*, and *Contemporary* reviews. In 1854, influenced by the evangelical Henry Latham (*DNB*, under 'Latham, John'), and at the time depressed by thoughts of eternal punishment, Conington abruptly and permanently converted to evangelical Christianity. His subsequent conservatism caused dismay and resentment among his liberal associates. In 1869 he died suddenly at the home of his father, of blood poisoning.

BIBLIOGRAPHY
DNB
H. J. S. Smith, Memoir in *Miscellaneous Writings of John Conington* (London, 1872)

JONATHAN BURKE CUTMORE

Connor, James (b. Dublin, *c.* 1798). CMS missionary to the Middle East. Connor was raised as a Moravian and educated at Lincoln College, Oxford (scholar; BA 1817). He was ordained (deacon 29 June 1817) by the Bishop of Gloucester and sent on 12 November 1817 to Malta proceeding on to Constantinople [now Istanbul] on 18 November 1818. He returned to England in February 1821 when his association with the CMS ended. He later was the Rector of Knossington, Leicestershire.

BIBLIOGRAPHY
Al. Ox.
D. T. B[arry], *CMS Register of Missionaries and Native Clergy* (privately printed) (London, 1906)

DONALD M. LEWIS

Conon, George (b. probably Scotland, 1698; d. 1775). Schoolmaster. A Scotsman and a Presbyterian, graduate of Aberdeen University, Conon was appointed headmaster of Truro Grammar School in 1728, where his strict standards of integrity impressed among others SAMUEL WALKER, who confessed that he 'had little knowledge and less practice of vital Christianity' till he met Conon. In 1756 he brought GEORGE BURNETT from Aberdeen as his assistant. Later, Burnett would become Vicar of Elland and a major figure in the Clerical Society there. One of Conon's best-known pupils was THOMAS HAWEIS. His firm evangelical faith led Walker to call him 'the father of the revival in these parts' and did not fail to arouse opposition to the extent even of attempts to turn him out of his post in 1758.

BIBLIOGRAPHY
G. C. B. Davies, *The Early Cornish Evangelicals 1735–60* (London, 1951)

ARTHUR POLLARD

Conyers, Richard (b. Lastingham, Yorkshire, England, Feb. 1725; d. Deptford, England, 23 April 1786). Anglican clergyman. Conyers was educated at Coxwold (North Yorkshire) and entered Jesus College, Cambridge in 1742 (BA 1745; MA 1749; LLD 1767), where HENRY VENN was a contemporary. He was Curate of Kirby Misperton (1745–50) and Rector (1763–8). He was also Rector of Helmsley (1756–62), holding the curacy of Kirkdale (1756–62), after which he was preferred by his brother-in-law, JOHN THORNTON, to Deptford (1775–86).

Conyers experienced a conversion entirely free of human agency, when after reading of the 'unsearchable riches of Christ' (Ephesians 3:8) and in despair not realizing what these might be, he found salvation on Christmas Day 1758 as he juxtaposed Hebrews 9: 20 ('Without shedding of blood there is no remission') and 1 John 2: 7 ('The blood of Jesus Christ cleanseth us from all sin').

He established domestic prayer meetings and scripture expositions at which he excelled, and the number of his communicants reached 1800. His visitors included HENRY VENN, MARTIN MADAN and JOHN WESLEY, who noted Conyers' move into Calvinism, though recognizing him as 'a deeply serious man who would fain reconcile Arminians and Calvinists'. To the sorrow of his people at Helmsley he moved to Deptford following the death of his wife. There he delivered four lectures a week, but he was obstructed by his afternoon lecturer, and his success was also hampered by an idiosyncratic, nervous style of delivery. He was struck down in the pulpit and was led away with the words: 'I am going to my master', and died the same afternoon. His funeral sermon was preached by THOMAS SCOTT.

BIBLIOGRAPHY
Al. Cant., I.i: 382
J. D. Walsh, 'The Yorkshire Evangelicals in the Eighteenth Century' (Cambridge Ph.D. thesis, 1956)

ARTHUR POLLARD

Cook, Archibald (b. Island of Arran, Buteshire, Scotland, baptized 19 Oct. 1788; d. Daviot, Inverness-shire, Scotland, 6 May 1865). Highland evangelist. The brother of FINLAY COOK, he matriculated at Glasgow in 1817 and was licensed to preach by the Church of Scotland in 1822. In 1823 he was ordained to the mission church of Berriedale-Bruan, Caithness. When his brother left Inverness, the congregation invited him on probation. He promptly alienated over half the congregation by the severity of his countenance and sentiments – he was a gloomy man who habitually employed eternal damnation as a sermon theme. As a result, the minority built the 'North Church' for him in 1837. He joined the Free Church with his congregation in 1843. In 1844 he transferred to Daviot, but not before Daviot and the North Church fought a tug-of-war over him that had to be settled in court. A charismatic, if not a learned or eloquent, preacher, for his many admirers Cook spoke the Gospel impressively from the heart.

BIBLIOGRAPHY
J. R. Mackay, 'Memoir of Archibald Cook,' in *Sidelights on Two Notable Ministries* (Inverness, Scotland, 1970)

JONATHAN BURKE CUTMORE

Cook, Charles (b. London, 31 May 1787; d. Lausanne, Switzerland, 21 Feb. 1858). Methodist missionary in France. Son of a coach-builder who was an evangelical Anglican, Charles Cook was converted through his sister Frances and Methodist preachers. He sought to enter the Methodist ministry and was appointed to Waltham Abbey, near London, in 1817.

In 1818, the Wesleyan Methodist Conference appointed him to work in France. He entered a mission begun in 1791 in Normandy by Channel Islanders William Mahy and Jean de Quetteville. He began his ministry near Caen with Martin Rollin, pastor of the Reformed Church. In 1819, he was introduced to evangelical pastors in the 'Midi' and decided to join them, thus becoming closely associated with the early 'Réveil' in French Protestantism. From 1821 to 1828, he was stationed at Caveirac and Congénies, near Nîmes, apart from a Palestinian interlude in 1824. As assistant to the Reformed pastor at Caveirac, Cook wished the Methodist mission to act within the Reformed Church as an evangelical society free to develop class meetings and pursue an itinerant ministry. His own zest to evangelize entailed extensive journeyings.

In 1826, he married Julie Marzials, daughter of the evangelical pastor of Montauban. After a short stay at Niort, he served the Methodist mission at Paris from 1829 to 1833. Returning to Congénies, he rejoiced in widespread revival and a growing thirst for holiness. From 1836 to 1841, he exercised a fruitful ministry at Nîmes. In 1841, there began a theological debate between Cook, an evangelical Arminian, steeped in the sermons of JOHN WESLEY, and CÉSAR MALAN, a strict Calvinist. A year later, Cook published L'Amour de Dieu pour Tous les Hommes.

From 1842, he was stationed at Lausanne. The Swiss experience was marked by fruitful contacts, especially with ALEXANDRE VINET, but also suffering. In 1844, his wife died after the birth of their eleventh child (of whom six had died in infancy). In 1847, he was expelled from Switzerland. The canton of Vaud supported official Protestantism and was intolerant of dissident groups. Such persecution paralleled experiences in France. There, too, as a body not officially recognized by the state, Methodists were in a difficult, often precarious position, especially under the Second Empire.

He returned to France in 1847 with pastorates at Nîmes and Paris. In 1852, he was fittingly nominated first president of the newly constituted Methodist Conference. With numbers rapidly increasing, the Methodist body was now quite distinct from the Reformed Church; doctrinally, the distinctive Arminian emphasis contrasted with both Calvinist orthodoxy and the rationalist tendencies of liberal pastors within the Reformed Church. There was greater freedom vis-à-vis the Missionary Society in London although financial dependency remained.

A tall man, with a disciplined devotional life, Cook was a formative influence for over thirty years. He was an active correspondent with London, much of which is contained in the School of Oriental and African Studies' Methodist archives, and a regular attender at British Conferences. He was greatly respected by colleagues drawn from the Channel Islands, France, and England. His two sons, Jean-Paul and Emile, were zealous Methodist ministers. Above all, he was a tireless evangelist. After his death at Lausanne in 1858, MERLE D'AUBIGNÉ wrote: 'The great work which John Wesley performed in the British dominions, Charles Cook has carried on – though in a lesser degree – on the Continent.' That the term 'methodist' came to have a wide evangelical application in France, is evidence of the contribution to the 'Réveil'. Well known in worldwide evangelical circles, he was a keen supporter of the EA from 1846 and was awarded an honorary doctorate in theology in 1850 by the Wesleyan University, New York.

BIBLIOGRAPHY
G. G. Findlay and W. W. Holdsworth, *History of the Wesleyan Methodist Missionary Society*, 4 (London, 1922)
M. Lelièvre, *Vie de Charles Cook* (Paris, 1897)
T. Roux, *Le Méthodisme* (Paris, 1940)

JOHN WALLER

Cook, Finlay (b. Island of Arran, Scotland, 1778; d. Reay, Caithness, Scotland, 12 June 1858). Highland evangelist. The brother of ARCHIBALD COOK, he was educated at Glasgow where he was much influenced by Dr JOHN LOVE of Anderston. Between university terms Cook was employed as an evangelist in Robert Owen's Lanark cotton mills. He was ordained by the Church of Scotland to the Achreny mission, Halkirk, in 1817 and six years later was called to the mission charge at Cross, on the Isle of Lewis. Under his ministry the island witnessed an extraordinary revival. From 1829 to 1833 Cook preached in the parish of Ness, Isle of Lewis, after which he transferred to the East Church, Inverness. In 1835 he was admitted to the Reay congregation, which he served until his death. At the Disruption Cook went out with the bulk of his congregation. He was famous throughout the Highlands for his pithy sayings and for his engaging, emotional delivery.

BIBLIOGRAPHY
J. Kennedy, 'Memoir of Finlay Cook', in *Sidelights on Two Notable Ministries* (Inverness, Scotland, 1970)

JONATHAN BURKE CUTMORE

Cook, Thomas (b. Melbourne, Derbyshire, England, 22 Nov. 1808; d. Leicester, Leicestershire, England, 18 July 1892). Baptist layman and pioneer travel agent. Because his father died when he was four leaving his mother in relative poverty, Cook was apprenticed to his uncle, a wood turner, but found his first employment with JOSEPH WINKS, a New Connexion General Baptist pastor-publisher. Cook became a Baptist, joined the church at the age of 18, and in 1828 was appointed General Baptist missionary and Bible reader to the county of Rutland, where in a single year he travelled almost 2,700 miles, most of them on foot, to carry out his duties. On marriage he returned to wood turning to support his family and his missionary labours, settling in Market Harborough and undertaking evangelistic work in the surrounding villages.

Converted by Father Matthew to the temperance cause, he founded *The Children's Temperance Magazine* in 1840, the first journal of this sort; he also became similarly hostile to smoking and published *The Anti-Smoker*. On 5 July 1841 he chartered his first train between Leicester and Loughborough to take supporters to a temperance meeting, and was requested to repeat the experiment for temperance groups and Sunday schools over the next three years, leading to him giving up his wood-turning business for full-time travel agency in 1845. This he based on Leicester, where his wife ran a temperance guest-house and where he built a Temperance Hall. The travel business so succeeded that in 1865 its headquarters were moved to London. In 1871 he took his son into partnership and at the age of seventy retired, relationships between father and son proving rather strained.

As the scope of travel expanded from England to Europe to worldwide trips, Cook took the opportunity to visit the work of both the BMS and the General Baptist Missionary Society about which he wrote reports for *The Missionary Chronicle*. Such travel also provided the experience which led him to found and endow the New Connexion mission in Rome, but his support of overseas missions extended to Asia and the Americas, while he showed special interest in the Near East supporting projects in Nazareth, Jaffa and Beirut.

A generous supporter of the work of the New Connexion both with his time and with his money, he gave school premises to the three churches where he had been a member: Archdeacon Lane, Leicester, Market Harborough and Melbourne, where he also endowed almshouses. He also provided libraries to soldiers in India, Sunday schools in England and the inhabitants of Iona. He funded the re-publication of *The Barton Memorials*, concerning New Connexion origins.

BIBLIOGRAPHY
Baptist Union Magazine, (1893)
D. J. Jeremy, ed., *Dictionary of Business Biography*, 5 vols (London, 1984–6)
DNB

J. H. Y. BRIGGS

Cook, Valentine Jr (b. Monroe Co., WV, BNA, 1765; d. KY, USA, 1820). Early American circuit rider and educator. He was the fifth son of Valentine Cook Sr, and the grandson of John Hamilton Cook, of London, England. This grandfather was the first cousin of Captain James Cook, the explorer. (Valentine Sr emigrated to America prior to the Revolution.) Valentine Jr experienced conversion and became a Methodist despite early parental opposition. He showed promise in the little schooling that he received, and entered Cokesbury College in 1786, remaining for one or two years. He eventually mastered German and also learned some Latin and Greek.

Cook was admitted to the Methodist Episcopal itineracy in 1788 and ordained Deacon in 1790, riding preaching circuits in Maryland, Virginia and Pennsylvania. From 1792 to 1793 he publicly disputed with Calvinists, most notably with John Jamieson, minister of the Seceder Church; thousands witnessed an open-air debate between them held near Pittsburgh on 12 June 1793. Cook's supporters were convinced that he had vindicated Methodism before its Calvinistic objectors.

From 1793 to 1799 he was presiding elder for several districts; he moved to Kentucky in 1798 and in the following year married Tabitha Slaughter, the niece of Kentucky's governor. They had several children.

In 1799 Cook was named principal of the newly-established Bethel Academy, but the school soon failed and in 1800 he retired from the itineracy to settle in Logan County. He spent the rest of his life farming, hunting, teaching and conducting camp meetings and revivals. An effective preacher, Cook is widely credited with introducing in 1797 the 'Mourner's Bench', whereby at the end of the service those seeking salvation were invited forward to be prayed with and counselled. This differed from earlier Methodist practice when 'seekers' had knelt where they had been seated and had waited for people nearby to minister to them. Hurst said of him: 'He was one of the most powerful revivalists of his day, and even after his location was in great demand for camp meetings' (Hurst, 1902, II: 622). Cook died shortly after conducting a camp meeting in Kentucky.

BIBLIOGRAPHY
AAP 7: 150–60
WEM
J. Hurst, *The History of Methodism: American Methodism* 2 vols (New York, 1902) II: 622–3

KENNETH N. PEARSON

Cooke, Henry (b. Maghera, County Antrim, Ireland, 11 May 1788; d. Belfast, Ireland, 13 Dec. 1868). Presbyterian leader. The son of John MaCook, a tenant farmer, he was educated locally until the age of 14. He then entered Glasgow University, completing the undergraduate course in 1805 without taking a degree. Two divinity sessions completed his theological training, and he was licensed to preach by the presbytery of Ballymena in 1808.

Cooke resigned from his first post at Duneane, County Antrim, because of differences with his latitudinarian senior minister and during his second appointment, at a rural congregation in Donegore, January 1811 to July 1818, he began to make an impression as a public orator, with highly successful charity sermons in both Belfast and Dublin. He continued his studies in Glasgow and in Dublin, the hub of evangelical activity, and also undertook Presbyterian missionary work in Carlow and

Stratford. It was while minister of Killyleagh, whose call he accepted in September 1818 that he first became known as the 'Champion of Orthodoxy', entering the field as a vigorous opponent of theological liberalism in opposition to a visiting Unitarian missionary in the spring of 1821. His attacks on the Reverend Smethurst's theology were enthusiastically received in the towns and villages of Ulster, and his campaign brought him to the notice of both sides of the Presbyterian theological divide as well as to the attention of the general public. His reputation was also enhanced in evangelical circles by a promotional tour of Scotland in 1824 on behalf of the Synod of Ulster's Home Mission, and he was appointed moderator in the same year.

Cooke used his new position to carry the campaign for doctrinal orthodoxy into the Synod of Ulster where he claimed that the Belfast Academical Institution, training ground for Ulster Presbyterian ministers, was a hotbed of Arianism. But while his influence eased the passage of a resolution for greater synodical control over the appointment of professors in the institution, moderates within the synod at this stage rejected any further attempts to impose more rigidly uniform doctrinal standards.

However, the growth of evangelicalism in Ulster encouraged the closer identification of theological with political liberalism, and Cooke was increasingly able to claim that his own orthodox and conservative views represented those of the wider Presbyterian community. His 'plain and powerful' speaking as he travelled on foot and horseback through Ulster won him considerable popular support from those who, made anxious by the political advances of the Roman Catholic church in Ireland, interpreted his vigorous defence of orthodoxy as a defence of Protestantism itself. His personal involvement with ardent defenders of the Protestant constitution and supporters of the Reformation movement helped to strengthen the link in the public mind between evangelical religion, doctrinal orthodoxy and anti-Catholicism. Cooke's main role in the development of evangelical Presbyterianism was to insist on the predominance of such conservative convictions at the highest level of the Presbyterian church.

Thus the annual general meetings of the Synod of Ulster in 1827, 1828 and 1829 became the forum for heated debates between Cooke and the Arian party, led by Reverend Henry Montgomery. Montgomery was an able opponent, representing a long tradition of Presbyterian liberalism, but Cooke's call for public profession to the full trinitarian doctrine by all ordinands seemed both politically and theologically expedient in the tense political climate of the late 1820s.

In 1830, in recognition of the growing support for Cooke both within and outside the synod the Arian party pre-empted expulsion by withdrawing to set up their own Remonstrant Synod. The 'purification' of the synod continued in 1835 with a resolution requiring full subscription to the Westminster Confession of Faith, and its increasingly rigid doctrinal requirements also led to a final breach with the Belfast Academical Institution in 1841.

Although not always so successful in determining synodical policy, Cooke's popular acclaim was undoubted. Following his victory against the Arians, his admirers had a new church especially built for him in May Street in Belfast. While he remained minister of this church until 1867, Cooke's central concern in the following decades was not with pastoral work but with the defence of evangelical Protestantism from the mounting dangers of secularism, liberalism and Catholicism.

He led the Presbyterian opposition to a national system of education introduced in Ireland in 1831 and challenged by churchmen of all denominations. The principle of combined secular and separate religious instruction embodied in the new system was an attempt to end accusations of proselytism, but was interpreted by many evangelicals as a denial of the free use of the Bible in schoolrooms and as a concession to the Roman Catholic priesthood. Cooke spoke at demonstrations and rallies throughout Ulster and again exercised his oratorical skills in the Synod of Ulster on behalf of evangelical principles. As a result of such agitation, the national educational system was subjected to a series of compromises which eventually left the tradition of denominational schooling virtually intact.

The combination of Whig concessions to Catholicism and the evangelical presentation of popery as dangerous to the fundamental liberties of the empire promoted a politico-religious conservatism which often surpassed denominational loyalties. Thus in 1834 Cooke appeared on a platform at Hillsborough alongside leading Anglicans to proclaim the 'banns of a sacred marriage' between the divided churches of Ulster. His defence of the Established Church both on this occasion and again in 1867 when disestablishment loomed near, was based on his belief that the Church of Ireland was an important bulwark against Romanism. However, he was not, on either occasion, speaking as an official representative of the Synod of Ulster and many of his colleagues bitterly opposed his public support for both Tory politics and church ascendancy. The meeting at Hillsborough was nevertheless an important display of popular Protestant unity which further enhanced Cooke's reputation as an ardent defender of the Protestant cause.

He appeared frequently on the platform of Exeter Hall in London alongside the evangelical nobility and other popular anti-Catholic spokesmen, and during the debate on voluntaryism in the Presbyterian Church re-affirmed his commitment to the principle of state support for religious institutions. In 1841, at the height of the repeal agitation, he attempted a more direct confrontation with the enemy by challenging Daniel O'Connell, then on a visit to Belfast, to a public debate. O'Connell's refusal to accept the challenge was triumphantly claimed as a victory for conservatism and unionism.

Cooke's high public profile often kept him from his May Street pulpit, but his influence in the Presbyterian Church remained significant. He was moderator of the General Assembly in 1841 and again in 1862, and was appointed Presbyterian dean of residence in the newly opened Queen's College in 1849. In the assembly's college which opened in 1853 he was given the chair of sacred rhetoric. Apart from extensive public preaching and lecturing engagements, he also published numerous sermons, pamphlets and articles.

It is a commonplace in Presbyterian history that Cooke was responsible for the revival and extension of a newly evangelistic church, and while this underestimates long-term trends in religious history, the ousting of the Arians did eliminate time-consuming preoccupations with doctrine and promoted a full-blown evangelicalism. Cooke is also credited with turning the tide of political liberalism in Ulster Presbyterianism, but his political conservatism rarely went unchallenged and was on more than one occasion rejected. His main contribution to Ulster protestant culture was the utilization of his oratorical eloquence, his popular influence and his evangelical convictions on behalf of Irish unionism, thus providing a model of 'the archetypal Ulster Protestant political parson' for future beleaguered generations.

BIBLIOGRAPHY
DNB
R. F. G. Holmes, *Henry Cooke* (Belfast, 1981)

MYRTLE HILL

Cooke, William (b. Burslem, Staffordshire, England, 2 July 1806; d. London, 25 Dec. 1884). MNC minister and theologian. Cooke's parents were publicans; in his early childhood his widowed mother remarried and moved to nearby Hanley, a stronghold of the MNC, whose Sunday school Cooke attended. Here he was converted in adolescence and showed such promise and ability that he entered the MNC and ministry at the age of twenty. He received some formal education at a local school but was largely self-taught. He walked to preaching appointments reading under an umbrella when it rained. His early ministry met with marked success and his reputation was enhanced by his effective re-organization and expansion of the ailing MNC Mission in Ireland, 1836–41.

In 1843 he went with reluctance to Newcastle-upon-Tyne, where the MNC circuit had been ravaged by the influence of the charismatic but unorthodox JOSEPH BARKER, expelled from the New Connexion ministry two years earlier. Cooke bested Barker in a notable and widely reported ten-day debate in 1845 and regained control of local chapels alienated by Barker's supporters. This success established Cooke as the leading figure of his denomination and launched him on a long career of theological authorship, which brought him fame far beyond his own communion. He wrote over sixty works, mostly popular and apologetic in purpose, of which the most important was *Christian Theology*, which ran into five editions.

A throat affliction caused his withdrawal from the normal ministry and from 1849 he lived in London. He was editor and book steward until 1870 and pastor of a church in Forest Hill 1875–80. As early as 1840 he had shown his practical concern for ministerial education by devising a course of study for Irish probationer ministers and from 1849 until the opening of the MNC theological college in Sheffield in 1864, selected ministerial students lodged his home where they received both practical and theological guidance in their studies. In this way, the young WILLIAM BOOTH received training and was encouraged in his revivalist preaching. More than twenty years after their public confrontation, Cooke was instrumental in guiding Joseph Barker back to the Christian faith. He was president of the MNC Conference in 1843, 1859 and 1869 and toured America and Canada in 1872. The Methodist Archives in Manchester, England, hold many of his letters on Overseas Missions and connexional matters.

BIBLIOGRAPHY
Boase (where he is wrongly said to be a Free Methodist)
S. Hulme, *Memoir of the Rev. William Cooke, D. D.* (London, 1886)
POBC

E. ALAN ROSE

Cookman, George G (b. Hull, England, 21 Oct. 1800; d. 1841). Methodist minister, orator, and chaplain of the US Senate. Raised in a wealthy and devout English Methodist home, he travelled to America in 1821 for his father's business. In 1825 he returned to America hoping to become a missionary to African-Americans. In 1826 he joined the Philadelphia Conference of the MEC and served as a pastor in Pennsylvania, Maryland, New Jersey and the District of Columbia. Cookman's popularity among African-Americans was noted by Frederick Douglass who observed that during Cookman's ministry in Maryland he quietly encouraged slave owners to emancipate their slaves. In 1839 he was elected chaplain of the United States Senate. An orator of note, Cookman's son, Albert, became a prominent Methodist minister while a second son, John, became a Methodist minister and a founder of the Christian and Missionary Alliance Church.

BIBLIOGRAPHY
EWM, 1: 581
H. B. Ridgaway, *The Life of Albert Cookman* (New York, 1874).

WILLIAM KOSTLEVY

Cooper, Anthony Ashley *See* SHAFTESBURY, the seventh Earl of

Cooper, Edward (b. Sonning, Berkshire, England, 1770; d. Hamstall, Ridware, Staffordshire, England, 1835). Anglican clergyman. Cooper was the son of Dr Edward Cooper and his wife Jane (née Leigh), through whom he was also cousin to the novelist Jane Austen.

He graduated from Oxford and served as Curate of Harpsden (Oxfordshire) (1793–9) when his relative, Mrs Leigh of Stoneleigh Abbey, offered him the living of Hamstall Ridware (1799–1835). He published a prophetic work, *The Crisis*, and several volumes of sermons (1804, 1809, 1816), the last of which caused Jane Austen to remark that Cooper was 'fuller of regeneration and conversion than ever – with the addition of his zeal in the cause of the Bible society' (Letter to Cassandra Austen, 8 September 1816). This she said, despite having recanted in 1814 the dislike she had expressed of the evangelicals in 1809. Her remark, 'I am by no means convinced that we ought not all to be Evangelicals', may help to explain the seriousness of *Mansfield Park* (1814) by comparison with most of her other novels.

BIBLIOGRAPHY

J. E. Austen-Leigh, *Memoir of Jane Austen* (London, 1870)

R. W. Chapman, ed., *Jane Austen's Letters*, 2nd edn (Oxford, 1952)

ARTHUR POLLARD

Cooper, Ezekiel (b. Caroline County, MD, BNA, 22 Feb. 1763; d. Philadelphia, PA, USA, 21 Feb. 1847). American preacher and editor. He was the son of Richard and Ann Cooper, whom he describes as 'plain people, in easy and plentiful circumstances in life'; he was raised an Anglican. When Cooper was about 14, FREEBORN GARRETTSON preached to two companies of soldiers on the Cooper property. His father was dead, and his mother had married an officer in the Revolutionary army. Cooper writes of himself: 'He was "a violent enemy to the Methodists as a people, who he supposed were enemies to the country".' Garrettson's sermon made a great impression upon the young boy, who then wished to become a Christian. After periods of depression, renewal, doubt, and despair, he was converted. He records that he felt such 'confidence in the merits of Christ and the mercy of God', that 'I laid hold of the promise, felt my burden remove, and a flood of peace, love, and joy break forth in my soul'. He soon felt a call to preach and sought advice from several Methodist preachers. Garrettson made him class leader in Talbot County. Cooper still hesitated to become a Methodist preacher. However, in 1784, FRANCIS ASBURY tried his abilities on the Caroline County circuit.

At the conference in 1785 he was admitted on trial, in full connexion in 1787, ordained deacon and finally ordained elder in 1789. Cooper served in this ministry with distinction for 64 years. In 1785 he was appointed to a circuit comprising all of Long Island, and in 1786 to East Jersey. Then followed appointments to Trenton, Baltimore, Annapolis, Alexandria, Virginia, and Charleston, South Carolina. Next followed New England where he served with the famed JESSE LEE; appointed presiding elder for the Boston district, from 1793 to 1794. Later in 1794 he came to New York and then Philadelphia in 1795. During an epidemic of yellow fever in Philadelphia in 1796, Cooper faithfully served the people. He writes, 'But as I was stationed here as a preacher, I resolved to put my trust in the Lord and stand by the dear people in the days of adversity and distress.'

With the appointment to Wilmington, Delaware, followed the task of serving as chairman of the book committee, which met in Philadelphia. When JOHN DICKINS, the editor and general book-steward, died in September 1798, Asbury appointed Cooper to take over, but he refused; 'but for various reasons, I then did not accept the appointment – and indeed, being aware of the many and great difficulties of the station, I did not intend to accept it at all'; but he was not able to resist for long, 'In the month of June last, [1799], Bishop Asbury, and the Philadelphia Conference, unanimously (excepting my own dissenting vote and one other) made choice of me to conduct the business; and they prevailed with me to accept the place; but I consented with considerable reluctance. My yielding was principally in compliance with the wishes of my brethren,. . .' (Cooper). For various reasons several attempts were made to move Cooper and the book business to another city. At the meeting of the Philadelphia Conference in 1803 in Smyrna, Delaware, it was decided to move the Book Concern to Baltimore. Cooper refused to make the change and was rebuked for this by Asbury himself. However, it soon became clear that Baltimore was not the best place for such endeavours and the General Conference of 1804 decided its move to New York with Cooper as 'Editor and General Book Steward'. He served in this capacity until 1808, when he again became an itinerant, serving Wilmington, Delaware, followed by two years as conference missionary. In 1812, he was in Baltimore, but located in 1813. He re-entered the conference in 1820 and served St George's Church, Philadelphia, but took a supernumerary's relation shortly thereafter.

Cooper was a man to attract attention, being over six feet tall with large frame, sharp features and a large wen on his right jaw. He never married, was extremely frugal, a principle which helped him turn the finances of the Book Concern from having no assets to showing assets of $45,000 when he left. He was a recognized church leader, an effective preacher with a language that was rich and glowing, but simple. As a debater he was unequalled, logical and convincing. During 1790–1, he wrote letters to several newspapers, attacking the evil of slavery. He died in Philadelphia and was buried at the door of Old St George's Church according to his own wishes.

BIBLIOGRAPHY

AAP

DAB

EWM

MM

E. Cooper, 'To the Preachers and Members of the Methodist-Episcopal Church', *Methodist Magazine for the Year 1798* 2 (Philadelphia, 1798): n.p.

G. A. Phoebus, *Beams of Light on Early Methodism in America*, (New York, 1887)

J. P. Pilkington, *The Methodist Publishing House*, 1 (Nashville, TN, 1968–)

W. Simpson, ed., *Cyclopaedia of Methodism* (Philadelphia, PA, 1880)

OLE E. BORGEN

Cooper, Jane (b. Hingham, Norfolk, England, 1738; d. 23 Nov. 1762). Methodist writer. At the age of 20 Cooper had to leave her Norfolk home to work in London. Greatly impressed by GEORGE WHITEFIELD's printed sermons she 'went to all the Methodist places of worship' she knew and was converted in 1758. Her letters (published by JOHN WESLEY in 1764) illustrate the importance of the Lord's Supper, Christian Perfection (though she confessed she 'did not much like the term'), prayer, good works, and a creative attitude to suffering among mid-eighteenth-century Methodists. Wesley referred to her as 'that saint of God, Jane Cooper, all sweetness, all gentleness, all love' and commended her spirituality as 'a pattern of all holiness'.

SELECT WRITINGS

J. Cooper, *Letters Wrote by Jane Cooper* (Bristol, England, 1764), preface by John Wesley

BIBLIOGRAPHY

J. Wesley, *Journals and Diaries: Bicentennial edition*, eds W. R. Ward and R. P. Heitzenrater, 18–24 (Oxford, 1975, later Nashville, TN)

J. Wesley, *The Letters of John Wesley*, ed. J. Telford, 8 vols (London, 1931)

RAYMOND BROWN

Cooper, John (b. Hull, Yorkshire, England, 16 Mar. 1813; d. Carlisle, Cumberland, England, 25 July 1896). Anglican clergyman and Archdeacon of Westmorland. Cooper was educated at Shrewsbury School and Trinity College, Cambridge and was made a college fellow. He held various academic appointments as tutor and senior dean of his college, and from 1843 to 1858 was Vicar of St Andrew-the-Great. In 1841 his sister Frances married CHARLES PERRY, later Bishop of Melbourne. From 1858 Cooper was the Vicar of Kendal, and from 1865 Archdeacon of Westmorland.

Cooper was a fine horseman, had a lively sense of humour and was well known for his hard work. Bishop SAMUEL WALDEGRAVE described him as 'a very modest but able, good and safe man'. With CLOSE he helped to maintain the evangelical tradition in the diocese after the death of Waldegrave. Cooper remained a bachelor and died at Carlisle and was buried at Kendal.

BIBLIOGRAPHY

S. Cooper Scott, *Things That Were* (London, 1923)

ALAN FREDERICK MUNDEN

Cooper, Thomas (b. Leicester, Leicestershire, England, 20 March 1805; d. Lincoln, Lincolnshire, England, 15 July 1892). Chartist and New Connexion Baptist lay preacher. Born in poverty, he became successively cobbler, schoolmaster, musician, and journalist. At the age of 16 he had joined the Mutual Improvement and Adult Sunday School Society run by his friend, the General Baptist publisher, J. F. WINKS. Converted in the 1820s in Gainsborough among the Primitive Methodists, he became a Wesleyan lay preacher, but soon came into conflict with the authoritarianism of the itinerant minister. Incensed by the wretched condition of the Midlands' stockingers, he became a Chartist, from 1841 editing their periodical, *The Midlands Counties Illuminator*. At this time he was judged 'one of the foremost of the more extreme party among the Chartists'. He was arrested for his speech to the striking miners and potters in Hanley in the Plug Plot Riots of 1842 and though acquitted on the charge of arson was subsequently arrested and found guilty of sedition and conspiracy, for which he was sentenced to two years' imprisonment in Stafford Goal, where he wrote his epic poem *The Purgatory of Suicides*.

After his release he quarrelled with Feargus O'Connor and took no further part in Chartism but lectured in the interest of radical free thought, much influenced by Strauss' *Leben Jesu*, attacking all varieties of Christian belief and Sabbatarianism in particular. Under the gentle influence of the author of *Alton Locke* (Charles Kingsley), he refound Christian faith, dramatically announcing this in the middle of a radical lecture in 1856, though as yet his conversion was only to theism rather than Biblical Christianity which occurred two years later. In June 1859 he joined the New Connexion General Baptists after baptism at the Friar's Lane Chapel in Leicester. He lectured widely on their behalf, and more generally, advocating the truth of Christian Evidences. Receiving a fraternal letter from him, the General Baptist Association of 1860, mindful of his influence among working men and the difficulties of winning them to Christ, resolved to try and secure his services for some months each year to engage in evangelistic work with their churches; one outcome of this was the help he gave in reviving the Baptist Church in Lincoln which subsequently adopted his name.

The puzzled testimony of the secular historian is that he spent the last thirty years of his life 'preaching the Gospel to all of the earth that he could reach.' As well as a number of apologetic writings, he published his autobiography, *The Life of Thomas Cooper, Written by Himself* in 1873. Shortly before his death he was awarded a state grant of £200.

BIBLIOGRAPHY

Baptist Union Magazine (1892)
Boase
G. D. H. Cole, *Chartist Portraits* (London, 1965)
DNB

J. H. Y. BRIGGS

Cooper, William (b. Boston, MA, BNA, 20 March 1694; d. Boston, MA, BNA, 13 Dec. 1743). Congregational minister. Born into a prominent Boston family,

Cooper graduated from Harvard College in 1712. After further studies in theology at that institution, in 1715 he was invited to become BENJAMIN COLMAN's colleague at the Fourth Parish ('Brattle Street') Church, to which position he was ordained in 1716. In spite of the fact that his father had been something of a theological liberal, and although the Brattle Street Church was itself rather unconventional, Cooper was a thoroughly conventional Calvinist and a protege of Cotton Mather. A warm supporter of the Great Awakening, he joined Colman in extending the invitation that first brought GEORGE WHITEFIELD to New England. A friend of JONATHAN EDWARDS, he remained a backer of the revival even after zealots and opponents had combined to snuff it out, engaging in a pamphlet war with Jonathan Ashley, an Old Light, and even breaking off his long-standing friendship with the Old Lights' leading voice, Charles Chauncy.

BIBLIOGRAPHY
SGH

GEORGE W. HARPER

Copley, Esther (b. probably Eythorne, Kent, England, 1786; d. 1851). Baptist authoress. Her father, surnamed Beuzeville, was a prosperous London merchant who subsequently lived at Henley-on-Thames. Although a member of JAMES HINTON's congregation in Oxford, her first marriage was to an Oxford curate named Hewlett. After his death she married Hinton's successor, William Copley, who had been trained by .WILLIAM STEADMAN. Mrs Copley's reputation as a domestic authoress was already considerable before her second marriage in 1827 to a man then aged 31 and ten years her junior. In addition to pious biography, sacred history and domestic tracts (with titles such as A Catechism of Domestic Economy, Cottage Comforts – by 1864 in its 24th Edition – Hints for Happy Homes, Kind Words from the Kitchen, The Young Servants' Friendly Instructor), Mrs Copley wrote on preventing cholera and in favour of the abolition of slavery. Some of her works were published by the RTS and a number of titles proved very successful in America where they were frequently reprinted. Following his Oxford pastorate (1825–39), Copley removed to Eythorne in Kent.

BIBLIOGRAPHY
Baptist Manual (London, 1858)
British Museum General Catalogue of Printed Books (London, 1965–)
National Union Catalogue of Pre 1956 Imprints (Chicago, IL, 1968)

J. H. Y. BRIGGS

Cornelius, Elias (b. Somers, NY, USA, 31 July 1794; d. Hartford, CT, USA, 12 Feb. 1832). Congregational minister, missionary fund-raiser, and secretary of ABCFM. After his graduation from Yale in 1813, he pursued theological studies under TIMOTHY DWIGHT and LYMAN BEECHER. He was licensed to preach by the South Association of Litchfield, Connecticut, on 4 June 1816 and was sent out, under the ABCFM, to raise funds for missions to the Indians in the south-west. After a year in New Orleans as an evangelist, he returned to Boston. In 1818, he married Mary Hooker Cornelius.

After pastorates at Goshen and Norwich, Connecticut, he accepted a call to the Tabernacle Church in Salem, Massachusetts, where he could devote three months a year to raising funds for missionary work. As secretary to the AES, in a six-year period, he raised $120,000–150,000 in missionary support. A month after being chosen as the secretary of ABCFM, he died suddenly at age 38. In 1826, the degree of DD was conferred upon him by Dartmouth College.

BIBLIOGRAPHY
AAP
J. G. Wilson and J. Fiske, eds, Appleton's Cyclopaedia of American Biography (New York, 1887)
B. B. Edwards, Memoir of Dr Cornelius (New York, 1833)

LELAND EDWARD WILSHIRE

Cornish, Samuel (Eli) (b. DE, USA, 1795; d. New York City, Nov. 1858). Black Presbyterian minister and pioneer black journalist. Born free in Delaware, Cornish went to Philadelphia in 1815 for more schooling. After being tutored by white Presbyterian clergy, he became an evangelist in New York City's black ghetto and founded the First Colored Presbyterian Church.

In 1827 Cornish became the founding editor of Freedom's Journal, the first black newspaper in America. In that post and in 1837 as editor of the Colored American, he defended American blacks against their white detractors. He attacked the American Colonization Society, founded by whites in 1816 to promote the migration of African-Americans back to Africa. Recognizing slavery as the root cause of black degradation, Cornish insisted that free blacks should be educated and granted employment, not colonized.

When the American Anti-Slavery Society was founded in 1833, Cornish and THEODORE WRIGHT, now pastor of New York City's First Colored Presbyterian Church, were placed on the society's Board of Managers. In the anti-abolition riots in New York City in 1834, Cornish joined leading white abolitionists in defending the Anti-Slavery Society and blaming racist white newspaper editors for fomenting the rioting.

By the late 1830s, when the younger black journalist, CHARLES RAY, led the way toward the founding of an antislavery third political party, Cornish drew back and ceased to be an aggressive defender of blacks' civil rights.

BIBLIOGRAPHY
D. E. Swift, Black Prophets of Justice (Baton Rouge, LA, and London, 1989)

DAVID E. SWIFT

Corp, Harriet (b. c. 1767; d. Brixton, London, 23 Dec. 1853). Novelist. Little is known about Harriet Corp. Sometime proprietor of a boys' preparatory school in Stoke Newington, London, she was friendly with the cultured Nonconformist Aikin and Barbauld families. *An Antidote to the Miseries of Human Life* (London, 1807) and five other works published between 1805 and 1814 were well received by the evangelical press and helped make religious fiction acceptable to Christians. Her account of a minister, *Coelebs Deceived* (London, 1817), who lived with a woman to whom he was not married, was not so acclaimed. Thereafter Miss Corp appears to have published only articles in annuals and a late book *Travellers in Search of Truth* (London, 1849). The absence of obituaries suggests that she was no longer in the public eye when she died aged 86.

BIBLIOGRAPHY
S. Halkett and J. Laing, *Dictionary of Anonymous and Pseudonymous English Literature*, new edn (Edinburgh, 1926–34)
N&Q, 163 (1932): 314

DOREEN M. ROSMAN

Corrie, Daniel (b. Argyllshire, Scotland, 10 April 1777; d. Madras, India, 5 Feb. 1837). East India Company chaplain and first Bishop of Madras. Corrie was educated at Cambridge, obtaining his LL B in 1805 (LL D 1835). In 1806, under the influence of CHARLES SIMEON, he went to Bengal as a company chaplain, becoming the presidency chaplain in 1819 and Archdeacon of Calcutta in 1823. Corrie combined missionary work with his duties as chaplain and worked closely with HENRY MARTYN and Mrs MARY SHERWOOD in establishing schools and translating the liturgy. His generosity to the destitute made him much loved and respected, and also extremely poor.

After 1814, he helped supervise the CMS missions in Bengal, set up an auxiliary CMS, a corresponding committee and acted as a channel of information and advice for the CMS missionaries. This brought him into tension with Middleton, the first Anglican bishop. Corrie believed that Indians should be ordained and was instrumental in the appointment of ABDUL MASIH as the first CMS reader. Eventually, in 1835, after caretaking the see on the death of three bishops, he was appointed the first Bishop of Madras. Within sixteen months he was dead, a gentle and humble man, of judgement, wisdom and firmness, who was universally loved and regarded. There is manuscript material in both the Institute of Oriental Languages, London, and the CMS archives, Birmingham.

BIBLIOGRAPHY
G. E. Corrie and H. Corrie, *Memoirs of the Right Rev. Daniel Corrie* (London, 1847)
DNB, 12: 251
A. Macnaghten, *Daniel Corrie, His Family and Friends* (London, 1969)

PENELOPE CARSON

Corrie, George Elwes (b. Colsterworth, Lincolnshire, England, 28 April 1793; d. Cambridge, England, 20 Sept. 1885). Anglican clergyman and scholar. Corrie was younger brother to DANIEL CORRIE, first Bishop of Madras, whose *Life and Letters* (1847) he edited together with his other brother, Richard, who was qualified as a doctor and then took orders, becoming rector of Kettering (Northamptonshire). George Corrie entered Catherine Hall, Cambridge (BA 1817; MA 1820; BD 1831; DD 1853), becoming fellow and tutor (1817–49). He was Norrisian professor of divinity (1838–54), master of Jesus College (1849–85) and vice-chancellor of the university (1850). He was the founder and four times president of the Cambridge Antiquarian Society. He was also rector of Newton (Cambridgeshire) (1851–85) and rural dean of Wisbech (1851–78). In addition, he was the acknowledged leader of the Cambridge Conservatives. Corrie was a staunch churchman and he edited *The Homilies* (1850), *Wheatly on Common Prayer* (1858), Burnet's *History of the Reformation* (abridged) (1847), and *Latimer's Sermons* (1844) for the Parker Society.

BIBLIOGRAPHY
Boase I: 723
DNB

ARTHUR POLLARD

Cortis, Hannah (b. Northumberland, England). *Fl.* 1820s. CMS missionary to Ceylon. Cortis was only the sixth female missionary sent out by the CMS. (Previously wives had accompanied their husbands but had not been appointed by the CMS.) She appears to have been a schoolmistress. She may have been sent out on 3 May 1823 to replace JANE KNIGHT in Ceylon following news of her marriage to an American missionary. Cortis, however, never made it to Ceylon. On arrival in Madras she married (20 November 1823) J. A. JETTER, another CMS missionary.

Her case is not unique. Eight of the first ten 'female missionaries' sent out by CMS married on the field, often only a few months after their arrival; of the two who did not marry, one died *en route* and the other shortly after her arrival. In seven out of the eight cases the women were married within two years of being sent out. In the nineteenth century this high marriage rate was a continuous problem for mission officials (both male and female) who felt that their investment in single female missionaries was not paying the sort of dividends they had anticipated and desired.

BIBLIOGRAPHY
D. T. B[arry], *CMS Register of Missionaries and Native Clergy* (privately printed) (London, 1906)

DONALD M. LEWIS

Cory, Ann (b. probably Morwenstow, Cornwall, England). Bible Christian itinerant. Ann was the sister of Andrew Cory (1794–1833). She probably started itinerant preaching (1819) in the Luxulyan area of

Cornwall. Many in the nearby villages were converted and eventually a chapel was built. Cory was in South Devon 'breaking up fresh ground' (January 1820), but in June was sent with CATHERINE REED to join the Kent Mission where they aroused much curiosity. Ann is reported to have had a good voice, great courage and an impressive preaching manner. Mr Drawbridge of Hartlip was so delighted he built a chapel at his own expense. In 1822 Ann visited Henry Freeman and Catherine Reed in London and was persuaded to stay. The work prospered and a number of societies were formed. After two years in Devon, Cory spent 1824 as a supernumerary – presumably due to illness – before returning to London and Chatham. She retired to Kilkhampton as a supernumerary (1828–30) before 'disappearing', which may mean she married and left the ministry.

BIBLIOGRAPHY
F. W. Bourne, The Bible Christians (London, 1905)
T. Shaw, The Bible Christians 1815–1907 (London, 1965)

E. DOROTHY GRAHAM

Cossart (de St Aubin d'Espiez), Heinrich Friedrich (b. Frankfurt an der Oder, Brandenburg, Germany, 29 April 1714; d. Herrnhut, Saxony, Germany, 7 May 1763). Tutor, Moravian agent in London, and ecumenical representative. Cossart's father (a Huguenot exile, fencing master at the Frankfurt an der Oder Academy) had met his mother (born in England of French parents) in Jersey. Cossart moved to Saxony in 1730 and from 1734 worked as a tutor near Herrnhut. After joining the community that year, Cossart was sent to tutor a Moravian aristocrat's daughters. Returning in 1736 he was 'confirmed' for full-time Moravian service in 1737 and sent to tutor Carl Adolph von Schachmann (1725–89). With Schachmann he joined ZINZENDORF'S Pilgrim Congregation in Berlin in 1738, moving with it to Wetteravia and (having married in Marienborn) Heerendyk (Netherlands).

His first ecumenical journey was in 1739, to Bishop Thomas Wilson. En route to and from the Isle of Man he also contributed to developments in London. After more tutoring in Rotterdam and Bern, in 1741 he joined the Pilgrim Congregation in Geneva and Marienborn. In Berlin he negotiated the establishment of a settlement at Montmirail in (Prussian) Neuchâtel (Switzerland), where he resided from 1742, visiting, preaching and translating Moravian works into French. In 1745 he visited the Waldensians (having failed to reach them in 1744), was ordained deacon and visited Bishop Sitkovius of the Unitas Fratrum in Lissa (Leszno, Poland).

As the Moravian agent in London from 1746 to 1755, Cossart visited bishops and clergy, colonial proprietors, government ministers and peers, cultivating friends for the Moravian Church and raising its profile. In 1748 he visited Ireland and its bishops and (again) Bishop Wilson. Cossart's lobbying culminated in recognition of the Moravians as an 'antient protestant episcopal church' by Act of Parliament in 1749. Thereafter he negotiated grants of colonial land and the purchase of Lindsey House, but also had to seek to counter growing anti-Moravian propaganda.

Resident from 1755 in Herrnhut, Cossart made a 16-month journey to Egypt (1757–9), visiting the Coptic Pope, the Greek Patriarch of Alexandria and two Moravians in Cairo. Returning through Italy, he made contacts which culminated in a private audience with Pope Clement XIII. He had acquired great diplomatic skills since 1739, while retaining a joy in talking with people he met about the Saviour.

BIBLIOGRAPHY
Gemeinnachrichten (1823) I, 143–54
C. J. Podmore, 'The Bishops and the Brethren: Anglican Attitudes to the Moravians in the Mid-Eighteenth Century', JEH, 41 (1990): 622–46
W. Senft, Ceux de Montmirail (Neuchâtel, Switzerland, 1947)
Zinzendorf und die Herrnhuter Brüder, ed. H.-C. Hahn and H. Reichel (Hamburg, 1977)

C. J. PODMORE

Côté, C(yrille) H(ector) O(ctave) (b. Quebec City, Lower Canada, 1809; d. Hinesburgh, VT, USA, 4 Oct. 1850). French Canadian rebel cum Baptist evangelist. Raised in a French Canadian Roman Catholic home, he went on to study medicine and in 1831 began a practice in the rural L'Acadie area south-east of Montreal. Three years later he was elected to represent the region as a member of the Parliament of Lower Canada. He developed a strong antipathy to British rule, and lent his oratorical powers to the radical Patriot cause. When general rebellion broke out in 1837 he was obliged to flee to the USA. From there in 1838 he helped to mount an eventually unsuccessful military expedition back into Canada.

Through the influence of Swiss Baptist missionary LOUIS ROUSSY, Côté was converted in 1841. Following the proclamation of a general amnesty, he returned to French Canada where, amid considerable opposition, he engaged in vigorous and successful evangelistic efforts in connection with the Grande Ligne Mission. He was ordained at St Pie on 28 August 1844. His untimely death six years later, during a fundraising visit to the United States, was a keenly felt loss to the Protestant cause in Francophone Canada.

BIBLIOGRAPHY
N. Cyr, Memoir of the Rev. C. H. O. Cote, M.D. (Philadelphia, no date)

GLEN G. SCORGIE

Cotterill, Henry (b. Blakeney, Norfolk, England, 6 Jan. 1812; d. Edinburgh, 16 April 1886). Anglican bishop and administrator. Cotterill was the son of John Cotterill, a canon of Norwich Cathedral. After a double first at Cambridge he was elected to a fellowship at his college, St John's. However he gave up a potentially brilliant academic career because his deep evangelical faith drew him into missionary service.

He was ordained in 1836 and appointed to an East India Company chaplaincy in Madras. He returned to England because of ill health in 1846 and was appointed to the staff of the new Brighton College. He became principal in 1851. In 1856, probably due to the recommendation of Lord SHAFTESBURY, he was appointed to the bishopric of Grahamstown, South Africa, by the Secretary of State for the Colonies.

Cotterill devoted himself to expanding the Anglican missionary effort among the Xhosa. He emphasized the learning of the language and a concentration upon preaching the Gospel rather than what he considered the legalistic moralizing that had characterized the missionary approach heretofore. He and Gray, the High Church archbishop, were the joint creators of the autonomous Province of South Africa of 1870. Cotterill became the authority on this issue and became, in 1867, secretary of the Lambeth Conference Committee on the constitutions of autonomous Anglican provinces.

In 1872 he became bishop of Edinburgh. He developed the role of the laity and the synodical system in the Episcopal Church in Scotland. He also awoke that church to its missionary responsibilities and linked it with the Church of the Province of South Africa.

BIBLIOGRAPHY
DSAB
C. Lewis and G. E. Edwards, *Historical Records of the Church of the Province of South Africa* (London, 1934)

ANDREW C. ROSS

Cotterill, Thomas (b. Cannock, Staffordshire, England, Dec. 1779; d. Sheffield, Yorkshire, England, 29 Dec. 1823). Anglican clergyman and hymnodist. He was born probably on 4 December (Miller, 1869: 361; Julian: 263; but 1 December, *Alumni Cantabrigienses*). At St John's, Cambridge (BA 1801, fellow 1806–9), he became a friend of HENRY MARTYN, who, however, once threw a knife at him (Sargent, 1985, viii: 7). After ordination he served churches in Staffordshire before becoming Perpetual Curate of St Paul's, Sheffield, in 1817. He died on 29 December 1823 (Miller, *Alumni Cantabrigienses*, and, correcting *Gentlemen's Magazine* 1824, which gave 25 January 1824, Julian).

Cotterill helped Jonathan Stubbs and others to compile *A Selection of Psalms and Hymns for Public and Private Use* (Uttoxeter, 1805). He also compiled *A Selection of Psalms and Hymns for Public Worship* (Newcastle, Staffordshire, 1810). The two issues with differing titles of the eighth edition (Sheffield, 1819) contained 128 Psalm versions, 6 doxologies, and 367 hymns, many by his assistant, JAMES MONTGOMERY. Many of the hymns, usually as altered by the two compilers, are still sung. Some members of St Paul's, resenting Cotterill's evangelicalism, argued

that hymn singing was illegal in the Church of England and arraigned him before the Diocesan Court of York. The case more or less legalized hymn-singing in that the edition was replaced by one with only 152 hymns, each approved by Archbishop Harcourt, to whom the book was dedicated. This ninth edition (London, 1820) was long used in many North of England churches.

BIBLIOGRAPHY
Al. Cant.
Julian: 263–4, 333–3, 1084–5, 1508–9, 1762
J. Miller, *Singers and Songs of the Church*, 2nd edn (London, 1869): 361–2
J. Sargent, *The Life and Letters of Henry Martyn* (Edinburgh, 1985)

JOHN S. ANDREWS

Cottesloe, first Baron. *See* FREEMANTLE, THOMAS FRANCIS

Cottle, Joseph (b. 1770; d. Bristol, England, 7 June 1853). Baptist litterateur and bookseller. One of HANNAH MORE's circle, Cottle became the friend and patron of Coleridge and Southey, showing a particular interest in Coleridge's movement from Unitarianism to orthodoxy, seen in terms of the fall of man, the Divinity of Christ, and redemption through his blood alone: 'to hear these sentiments so explicitly avowed gave me unspeakable pleasure', he writes. A continuation of opium taking, however, led Cottle to urge Coleridge in strong evangelical tones to turn to Christ. He was a benefactor of Bristol Baptist College where he formed close friendships with the classical tutor, JAMES NEWTON, JOHN FOSTER and JOSEPH HUGHES, Newton's successor at the college, and future founder of the Bible Society, who also became a friend and correspondent of Coleridge. Cottle served on the college committee and was a member of ROBERT HALL's Broadmead congregation.

BIBLIOGRAPHY
J. Cottle, *Reminiscences of Coleridge and Southey* (London, 1847)
DNB
S. A. Swaine, *Faithful Men* (London, 1884)

J. H. Y. BRIGGS

Cotton, Richard Lynch (b. Woodcote, Oxfordshire, England, 14 Aug. 1794; d. Oxford, 8 Dec. 1880). Anglican clergyman and provost of Worcester College, Oxford. Son of Henry Calvely Cotton and grandson of Sir Lynch Salusbury Cotton, Baronet, he was cousin of Lord Combermere. Educated at Charterhouse and Worcester College (1811–15). In 1839 he married Charlotte Bouverie (died 1883), by whom he had a daughter. His wife was the sister of the eminent Tractarian, E. B. Pusey.

Even as a child, Cotton was both pious and studious. While an undergraduate at Worcester he was elected to a Holford Exhibition (1812) and became a Clarke scholar

(1815). He studied for a time under Thomas Arnold. After taking his BA (1815), his academic leanings were soon rewarded; he was made a fellow of his college in 1816. This began an unbroken academic career at Worcester College. Cotton filled the offices of tutor (1822) and bursar (1828). He became MA in 1818 and received the degrees of BD and DD in 1839. He was appointed provost of the college in 1839, a post which he held until his death. He also held a number of university positions, being the select preacher in 1840 and vice-chancellor between 1852 and 1856.

Cotton's college also supplied him with his only living, Denchworth, Oxfordshire. He was vicar of this parish from 1823 until his resignation upon becoming Provost in 1839. Despite the divided commitments of academic and pastoral life, Cotton was a conscientious clergyman who lived in his parish during the university vacations. The Earl of St Germans appointed Cotton as his domestic chaplain in 1824.

Burgon was reluctant to consider Cotton an evangelical, preferring to designate him as a 'good Churchman'. This reflects perhaps the prejudice against evangelicalism in late-Victorian Oxford. However, reference to his *The Way of Salvation* removes any doubt as to Cotton's evangelical sympathies. In 1841, Cotton was a vice-president of that most evangelical of bodies, the CMS.

In truth Cotton was both a 'good Churchman' and an evangelical. This was a typical pattern for Anglican evangelicals in the nineteenth century. It was often coupled with a predilection for Conservative politics, as in Cotton's case. It implied a jealous regard for the interests of the Church of England, reflected in Cotton's non-cooperation with the university commissions. Cotton's deeply rooted position within the Anglican tradition can be appreciated by consulting his second book, *Lectures on the Holy Sacrament*. While rejecting most emphatically Roman Catholic teaching, Cotton nevertheless took a high view of the sacrament. In the sixth lecture, he endorsed Hooker's views on the eucharistic presence.

Cotton acted as a Protestant champion in the face of Tractarianism. With his friend the Reverend C. P. Golightly, he was a prime mover in the erection of the Martyrs' Memorial in 1841. Pusey attempted to persuade his brother-in-law to contribute to the *Tracts for the Times*, but Cotton was horrified by the Oxford Movement.

Cotton sought to exercise a quiet influence over the students of Worcester College, presenting undergraduates with a copy of Bishop Wilson's study on the Lord's Supper. His favourite author was the seventeenth-century divine, Archbishop Leighton. He was small in stature, humble, guileless and much revered in Oxford. However, by the time of his death he was clearly out of sympathy with the developments of the age.

SELECT WRITINGS
R. L. Cotton, *The Way of Salvation Plainly and Practically Traced in a Series of Discourses* (Oxford, 1837)

—, *Lectures on the Holy Sacrament of the Lord's Supper* (Oxford, 1849)

BIBLIOGRAPHY
J. W. Burgon, *Lives of Twelve Good Men* (London, 1891)
DNB

I. T. FOSTER

Coughlan, Laurence (*Fl.* Drumsna, Co. Leitrim, Ireland, 1750; d. London 1785). Methodist lay preacher, Anglican priest, SPG missionary to Newfoundland, founder of Newfoundland Methodism and principal preacher in Lady Huntingdon's Connexion. Coughlan, a convert from Roman Catholicism to Wesleyan Methodism in the early 1750s, entered a trial period as lay preacher in Ireland in 1755 and in 1757 left for England, where he served as a lay preacher, notably in Colchester and Whitehaven. His religious enthusiasm, which brought him into contact with the heterodox Methodist THOMAS MAXFIELD in London, and a controversial ordination at the hands of the Greek Orthodox Bishop Erasmus in 1764 led to a separation from the Wesleyan fold and the establishment of a dissenting meeting house in Bermondsey, Surrey. Here Coughlan was contacted by Anglicans and Congregationalists from Conception Bay, Newfoundland, and asked to serve as their minister.

Through the agency of the EARL OF DARTMOUTH, Coughlan was ordained an Anglican priest in 1766 and took up missionary work in Harbour Grace that same summer. Later supported by the SPG, Coughlan quickly experienced the condemnation of his unorthodox Anglicanism – the preaching of the new birth and a religion of the heart – by Harbour Grace merchants. This animosity heightened when he formally organized believers into class meetings. Here lower class inhabitants held important leadership responsibilities and by doing so were removed increasingly from the social control of the merchants. A subsequent revival with dramatic deathbed conversions spread throughout Conception Bay. For the converted their newly found faith helped them endure a precarious island existence. The joint opposition of the local merchants and the governor led to Coughlan's resignation as SPG missionary in 1773.

After the refusal of JOHN WESLEY to readmit Coughlan to the Methodist itinerancy, he served as a prominent but somewhat unsettled preacher in Lady Huntingdon's Connexion, notably in Norwich and London. In 1776 he published his *Account of the Work of God in Newfoundland, North America*, which he dedicated to his benefactress, Lady SELINA HUNTINGDON. From a letter of John Wesley it appears that Coughlan died sometime in 1785.

SELECT WRITINGS
L. Coughlan, *An Account of The Work of God in Newfoundland, North America* (London, 1776)

BIBLIOGRAPHY
DCB
DNLB

ENL

H. Rollmann, 'Laurence Coughlan and the Origins of Methodism in Newfoundland', in *The Contribution of Methodism to Atlantic Canada*, eds Charles H. H. Scobie and John Webster Grant (Montreal and Kingston, 1992): 53–76

HANS ROLLMANN

Couling, Samuel (b. London, 7 Dec. 1815; d. Boxmoor, Hertfordshire, England, 20 Aug. 1890). Baptist minister and temperance advocate. Early employment in a solicitor's office gave him opportunity to read widely. At the age of 24 he became a total abstainer and began upon the pastoral ministry, removing in 1850 to London where he worked with a number of temperance organizations: The Good Samaritan Temperance Society, the Band of Hope Union, the National Temperance Society and the National Temperance League. In 1862 he undertook a temperance mission to Scarborough and stayed in that Yorkshire town for a further eight years. In 1870 he became pastor at Oakengates, Shropshire, removing in 1872 to Chipperfield, Near Watford, Hertfordshire. Couling wrote a number of works on temperance themes, including a *History of the Temperance Movement* published in 1862. In the year of the Great Exhibition he wrote on *Our Labouring Classes* and the means of their improvement, which brought him into contact with Lord SHAFTESBURY and James Silk Buckingham and others. He also wrote an inventory of Baptist worthies interred in the Bunhill Fields Cemetery.

BIBLIOGRAPHY
Boase
Baptist Handbook (1891)

J. H. Y. BRIGGS

Coulthurst, Henry William (b. St Michael's, Barbados, 28 June 1753; d. Heath nr Wakefield, Yorkshire, 11 December 1817). Anglican clergyman. Though born abroad on his family's sugar estate, Coulthurst came of Yorkshire parentage and was educated at Hipperholme and Skipton before proceeding to St John's, Cambridge (scholar 1771; BA 1775; MA 1778; BD 1785; DD 1791), after which he became a fellow of Sidney Sussex (1781–91). During this decade he was also minister of St Sepulchre's, Cambridge (1782–90), a period in which he both did duty for HENRY VENN at Yelling in 1784 and came to know CHARLES SIMEON.

He moved to Halifax (1790–1817), then the largest parish in England, with 14 chapelries. There he joined the Elland Society, of which body he was treasurer from 1795 to his death. He was a notable leader in that considerable and active body of Yorkshire evangelical Anglicans. Coulthurst was extremely short of stature with, according to Simeon, a low but distinct voice. He was distinguished also for his courtesy and even temper and, though, like his fellow Elland member, HAMMOND ROBERSON, in politics a staunch Tory, in every other respect

they must have made a striking contrast with each other. Hole (1896) records that Coulthurst's 'learning, character, West Indian fortune, efficiency in duty, all combined to make him a most popular and influential man'. He was followed both at Halifax and as treasurer of the Elland Society by SAMUEL KNIGHT.

BIBLIOGRAPHY
Al. Cant., II, ii: 151
M. M. Hennell, *John Venn and the Clapham Sect* (London, 1958)
C. Hole, *Early History of CMS* (London, 1896)

ARTHUR POLLARD

Court, James (b. Hamilton, Lanarkshire, Scotland, 1811; d. Glasgow, 14 Feb. 1883). Businessman and co-founder of the French-Canadian Missionary Society. James Court emigrated to Montreal at 18 years of age, eventually establishing himself as an estate manager and accountant with a reputation for scrupulous honesty. He exercised a positive Christian influence on many of his youthful peers, including JOHN DOUGALL. From 1832 onwards, he led a young men's temperance organization, out of which grew the Montreal Temperance Association and its organ the *Canadian Temperance Advocate*. He identified with the Free Church cause at the time of the Disruption, and served as an elder in the Côté Street Presbyterian Church in Montreal. He was the prime mover in the establishment of the French Canadian Missionary Society, and was its virtual manager during its entire 42-year history (1839–81).

BIBLIOGRAPHY
John Dougall, 'James Court', *Montreal Daily Witness* (19 February 1883): 4
Montreal Gazette (15 February 1883)
Presbyterian Record 8.3 (March 1883): 66

GLEN G. SCORGIE

Coussins, Jonathan (b. Reading, Berkshire, England, 2 Jan. 1757; d. 31 Oct. 1805, Diss, Norfolk, England). Methodist preacher. Born to loyal Anglican parents, he and his sister went from Bath into domestic service in Cheltenham where Penelope Newman, a devout member of the Cheltenham Methodist Society, influenced them to join the Methodists. Penelope Newman was herself a class leader, and also gave Christian witness in prayer meetings and public exhortations in the area, in which Wesley encouraged her. Indeed she was the means of conversion first of her own mother, and then of her future husband, Jonathan Coussins, whom she termed her 'son in the gospel'. Later he light-heartedly termed their wedding 'marrying his mother'.

Returning to Bath and Bristol around 1776, Coussins treasured opportunities of hearing JOHN and CHARLES WESLEY preach, and found John Wesley's *Predestination Calmly Considered* (1752) a valuable remedy for the Calvinistic preaching of some acquaintances belonging to

Lady HUNTINGDON's Connexion. He was also reinforced by the advice of Samuel Wells and Penelope Newman. He pondered entering business, but his Cheltenham friends echoed his own call to preach, urged on by JOHN VALTON and by John Wesley himself.

In 1780 he was stationed in the Norwich circuit, and the following year in Salisbury. John Wesley also fostered Jonathan Coussin's diffident but steadily ripening courtship of Penelope Newman, and may well have given strong support by arranging that Coussins should be stationed in Gloucester circuit (of which Cheltenham was a part) in 1782, and again in 1783. The couple were married shortly after the 1782 Conference, and on 1 October 1782, Wesley wrote warning her: 'I have often been concerned at your being cooped up in a corner; now you are likely to have a wider field of action. Only the danger will be, lest, when you have more opportunity, you should have less desire of doing good. This is the case of many pious persons when they marry' (Telford). It proved a short but fruitful joint ministry. Though both man and wife suffered much serious illness, they rejoiced in many religious revivals, and were cherished by many Methodist followers. Jonathan Coussins's first circuit, in Norwich, was destined also to be his last. He began to suffer great physical pain, and after a short-lived recovery and the possibility of their retirement to Bath, he was returned to Diss again, to die there at the age of 49.

BIBLIOGRAPHY
Methodist Magazine (1806): 289–389
Z. Taft, *Biographical Sketches of . . . Holy Women* (London, 1825): 290–95
J. Telford, Ed., *The Letters of John Wesley*, 8 vols (London, 1931) 7: 143

FRANK BAKER

Cowan, Charles (b. Edinburgh, 1801; d. Edinburgh, 29 March 1889). Paper manufacturer and Scottish MP. Educated at Edinburgh High School and the universities of Edinburgh and Geneva, he made his fortune in paper manufacturing in mills on the Esk and Water of Leith.

A member of the National Anti-Excise Association, in July 1847, Cowan was elected on a tax reform platform as Whig member for Edinburgh (to April 1859). In his maiden speech he asserted an 'intimate connection between suffering and sin' (*Parliamentary Debates*, 3rd ser., 96: 1290) and promised to represent the needs of the poor. Twice he seconded Bright – once on a Game Laws motion and once on a bill to abolish the Bible printing monopoly. He seconded LORD ASHLEY on a bill to abolish Sunday postal deliveries. Cowan introduced a bill to make Scottish university appointments non-sectarian (excepting theological chairs). A fairly frequent speaker, he resisted Sunday railway travel, opposed marriage to a deceased wife's sister by appealing to Leviticus 18, supported abolition of Irish tithes, spoke in favour of savings banks, and defended the Free Church and the Westminster Confession. Otherwise, tax matters preoccupied him.

Cowan was an elder in the Established Church, and from 1843 in the Free Church. He was a member of the EA and was on the committee of the Edinburgh Bible Society.

SELECT WRITINGS
C. Cowan, *Reminiscences* (Edinburgh: privately printed, 1878)

BIBLIOGRAPHY
Boase (supplement)
Stenton

JONATHAN BURKE CUTMORE

Cowan, Thomas (Connolly) (b. Dublin, Ireland, *c.* 1776). Secessionist from Church of Ireland. Cowan was educated at Trinity College, Dublin (BA 1798). Around 1815, Cowan came under the influence of the Western Schism, an antinomian secession of High Calvinists from the Church of England in and around the West Country (in south-western England). In July 1817, while serving as Curate of St Thomas's, Bristol, his licence was suspended by his diocesan. Dismayed over the church's indiscipline and its unreformed baptismal service, he then seceded, being rebaptized by GEORGE BARING at Pithay Baptist meeting on 26 November 1817. In 1819, he became minister at Bethesda Chapel, Great George Street, Bristol. Although adhering to the doctrine of particular redemption, he denied the charge of antinomianism.

SELECT WRITINGS
T. C. Cowan, *A Brief Account* (Bristol, England, 1817)

BIBLIOGRAPHY
Al. Dub.

GRAYSON CARTER

Coward, William (b. *c.* 1648; d. Walthamstow, London, 28 April 1738). English Congregational merchant and philanthropist. Coward was a wealthy dissenting merchant of eccentric habit and strict discipline who was concerned to use his wealth for the promotion and defence of evangelical orthodoxy. Successful in business, he came to own considerable estates in Jamaica. In retirement he lived comfortably in Walthamstow where he founded the Independent Chapel. During his lifetime he sponsored a number of series of apologetic lectures, and took a special interest in the education of ministers' children, though the school he planned to found for them in Walthamstow never materialized.

A large part of the £150,000 he left at his death was bequeathed to charity, and in particular the Coward Trust, with Isaac Watts and Daniel Neal the most famous of the first four trustees, was established 'for the education and training up of young men ... between 15 and 22 in order to qualify them for the ministry of the gospel among the protestant dissenters', which for many years supported Doddridge's Academy at Northampton and later at Daventry. Hostility from the trust was occasioned by Doddridge's friendliness to 'methodism' even when found in the person of GEORGE WHITEFIELD, whose theology was beyond reproof but whose ecclesiology was not of their order. Later their donor power secured the dismissal of both Thomas Belsham and John Horsey from the staff for theological error, whilst ROBERT HALL came to describe the whole institution as a 'vortex of unsanctified speculation and debate'. By 1798 there were few students of a theological outlook that the trust could support, thus causing the closure of the institution. In 1799 the trust founded a new college at Wymondley in Hertfordshire with the hopes that it would prove a centre of evangelical teaching, but failing to shake off the taint of Socinianism, the college was unable to secure the support of the churches until in 1832 it was moved to London and renamed Coward College, which in 1850 became part of New College.

BIBLIOGRAPHY
DNB
R. T. Jones, *Congregationalism in England, 1662–1962* (London, 1962)

J. H. Y. BRIGGS

Cowell, John (b. Chatham, Kent, England). CMS missionary to New Zealand. A rope-maker by trade, Cowell was sent to New Zealand by the CMS on 12 December 1819. His wife died in New Zealand on 22 November 1820 and Cowell ended his connection with the CMS in August 1823.

BIBLIOGRAPHY
D. T. B[arry], *CMS Register of Missionaries and Native Clergy* (privately printed) (London, 1906)

DONALD M. LEWIS

Cowie, George (b. Banffshire, Scotland, 1749; d. 4 April 1806). Minister. Ordained in 1771 to the Anti-Burgher congregation of Huntly, Cowie encountered difficulties with his local presbytery, though not with his own congregation which supported him, when he showed a readiness to cooperate in the evangelistic efforts of those outside his own denomination. He acknowledged to his presbytery that he had acted wrongly in listening to the preaching of a minister of the Relief Church in 1782, but he persisted in cooperating with others in missionary societies and supported the HALDANES. He was suspended by his presbytery but most of his congregation followed him. His openness and readiness to cooperate and work with others was not accompanied with tactful dealings with his fellow presbyters.

R. H. CAMPBELL

Cowles, Giles Hooker (b. Farmington, CT, BNA, 26 Aug. 1766; d. Austinburgh, OH, USA, 6 July 1835). Congregational minister and missionary. A graduate of Yale College (1789), Hooker studied theology under JONATHAN EDWARDS JR, and was ordained to the ministry of the Bristol, Connecticut Congregational Church in 1792. When the Second Great Awakening swept through his congregation in 1799–1800, over 100 converts joined the church. The revival, however, did little to win over church society members to his high Calvinism and so by mutual agreement he resigned in 1810. Hooker then pursued home missionary work for the Connecticut Missionary Society in the Western Reserve, where he is credited with organizing most of the Congregational churches in north-eastern Ohio.

BIBLIOGRAPHY
AAP, 2: 330–1
BSGYC, 4: 634–5

DAVID W. KLING

Cowley, Abraham (b. Fairford, Gloucestershire, England, 8 April 1816; d. Dynevor, Manitoba, Canada, 11 Sept. 1887). Anglican clergyman and secretary of CMS North-West America mission. Cowley attended the CMS College at Islington in 1839 and was sent two years later to join the society's mission at Red River, North West America. At Montreal, *en route*, he was ordained deacon. His ordination as priest was intended to follow shortly at Red River but was delayed because the settlement's lawyer challenged the jurisdiction of the Bishop of Montreal in the north-west. He was finally ordained priest in 1844.

At Red River he was assigned to a variety of tasks, including the establishment of a mission at Fairford, Manitoba. He assisted in the development of new agricultural methods at a demonstration farm for the Indians established by WILLIAM COCKRAN of the CMS mission. He translated parts of the *Book of Common Prayer* into the Saulteaux language and served for many years as secretary for the North-West America mission. He was appointed Archdeacon of Cumberland in 1867. Two of his children are noted in the CMS resister of missionaries.

BIBLIOGRAPHY
DCB, 11

KERRY M. ABEL

Cownley, Joseph (b. Leominster, Herefordshire, England, 26 June 1723; d. Newcastle, England, 8 Oct. 1792). Methodist itinerant. WESLEY regarded him as one of the best preachers in England. He received a good education and then worked as a magistrate's clerk. He was in Bath under Wesley's ministry and after returning to Leominster in 1743 joined one of WHITEFIELD's societies. He was called to preach and in 1746 became one of Wesley's assistants. He spent 36 years of his ministry at Newcastle where he preached regularly at the Orphan House and was responsible for founding many societies in the area. He corresponded with Whitefield as well as with the Wesleys. When he was appointed to Edinburgh in 1788 he was ordained as a presbyter by Wesley for Scottish work. After Wesley's death he supported the dissenting Methodists and himself dispensed the Lord's Supper. He ordained KILHAM who became the leader of the MNC.

BIBLIOGRAPHY
AM (1794)

A. SKEVINGTON WOOD

Cowper, William (b. Berkhamsted, Hertfordshire, England, 15 Nov. 1731; d. Dereham, Norfolk, England, 25 April 1800). Poet. Cowper was the son of the Rector of Berkhamsted, and on his mother's side a collateral descendant of the seventeenth-century metaphysical poet and Dean of St Paul's, John Donne. His mother dying when he was barely six, Cowper was sent away to school but subsequently removed after being bullied by another pupil. He entered Westminster when he was ten, and on leaving at the age of 18 took articles in an office where one of his fellow pupils was the future Lord Chancellor, Thurlow. Cowper was called to the Bar as a member of the Middle Temple (1754), but he suffered the first of his prolonged bouts of melancholia shortly thereafter. He did, however, become a commissioner for bankrupts in 1755 and by the interest of a cousin he was offered the clerkship of the journals of the House of Lords in 1763. The prospect of examination for the appointment before a committee of the House so unnerved him that he attempted suicide. He was counselled by his cousin, MARTIN MADAN, unsuccessfully, and a subsequent attack of madness led to his being committed to the care of Dr Nathaniel Cotton at St Albans.

In 1765, with his means depleted and no occupation, Cowper went to live in Huntingdon where he met, and in November of that year joined, the members of the Unwin household, where at one with their religious sympathies he took part in their daily services, prayers, hymn singing and devotional reading. Mr Unwin died in 1767, whereupon his widow, with whom Cowper was to reside for the rest of her life, moved to Olney. There he became helper to the curate, JOHN NEWTON, with whom he was to produce the collection of *Olney Hymns* (1779). During the years at Olney Cowper also for varying periods enjoyed the close friendship of his cousin, Lady Hesketh, and Lady Austen, relationships which Newton, who left Olney in 1779, felt might be too frivolous. It has been suggested that Newton's influence was altogether too weighty for Cowper's fragile personality and that it may have had some part in the return of his madness in 1773–4.

On his recovery Cowper sought recreation in gardening, sketching and keeping hares. He also began to write serious poetry and in 1782 published the collection of *Poems* which includes 'The Progress of Error', 'Truth', 'Table Talk' and 'Expostulation' as well as his vigorous, at times coarse, reply, 'Anti-Thelyphthora', to his cousin Madan's strange defence of polygamy. It was during this period also that Lady Austen encouraged him with what became his major piece, *The Task* (1785) in blank verse, and also his famous comic ballad, 'John Gilpin'. These works established Cowper in the forefront of the poets of his day.

He now undertook the translation of Homer, to be published by subscription and for which Lady Hesketh worked assiduously. This appeared in 1791, after which he turned his attention to Milton. Cowper, however, had suffered another bout of insanity in 1787 and was to do so again in 1794, and, to compound his troubles, Mrs Unwin fell ill and became paralysed. A distant relative of Cowper's, John Johnson, took charge of them and removed them to East Dereham (Norfolk) where Mrs Unwin died in 1796.

In these final years Cowper also enjoyed the friendship of the minor litterateur, William Hayley, but his last days were clouded with renewed melancholia, which expressed itself poignantly in his last original piece, 'The Castaway', in which he compared his own spiritual state to the bodily condition of a drowning sailor:

We perished, each alone,
But I beneath a rougher sea
And whelm'd in deeper gulphs than he.

Norman Nicholson has called these 'the most passionate lines in Cowper' (in Cowper, 1967), and indeed they are unusual in contrast with his customary gentleness. *The Task*, his best-known work, is occupied with 'rural ease and leisure', with the activities of winter evenings, the countryside in its different seasons and the round of rural duties. Even here, however, the attachment to 'rural life and leisure' is considered in terms of its 'friendl[iness] to the cause of piety and virtue' (letter to W. C. Unwin, 10 October 1784). He claimed that he could 'write nothing without aiming at usefulness; it were beneath my years to do it, and still more dishonourable to my religion' (ibid).

He delights in nature and sees God as active within nature, 'There lives and works/A soul in all things, and that soul is God' (Cowper, *The Task* VI 1967: 184–5); but nature is fallen and cannot lead man up to nature's God. Nor can reason. Indeed, Cowper is strongly anti-intellectual at times, asserting, for example, that ' 'Tis Revelation satisfies all doubts,/Explains all mysteries, except her own' (ibid., II: 527–8).

The earlier moral satires had been more directly didactic. In the first of them, 'Truth', Cowper argued for conversion and justification by faith as against justification by works. The sinner feels 'A growing dread of vengeance at his heels . . . [but] Mercy receives him on her peaceful shore'(ibid., II: 258, 276). In a famous phrase Cowper describes himself as 'a stricken deer', but in the same passage he acknowledged that he had also been 'found by one who had himself/Been hurt by th'archers' (ibid., III: 108, 112–13). These lines demonstrate Cowper's tenderness and in some sense make it less surprising that he interpreted Calvinism to his own terrible disadvantage rather than to the fate of others.

Refusing to exalt works, Cowper nevertheless saw life as a probation in the course of which 'A soul redeem'd demands a life of praise'(Cowper, 'Truth', I, 1967: 279). There is in him a strong element of Protestant asceticism with its distrust of worldly pleasures in his work, together also with a vehement and sometimes shrill condemnation of the morals of public life, a phenomenon by no means rare among those who thus rationalise their fear of participation. Against this, however, must be placed Cowper's vision of the moral intensity and radiance of the regenerate life (e.g. Cowper, 'Charity', 1967: 395–400, 422–31). Not surprisingly and possibly under Newton's encouragement, he was among the earliest opponents of slavery.

Cowper is perhaps now best remembered for some of his hymns – 'God moves in a mysterious way', 'Hark, my soul, it is the Lord' and 'O for a closer walk with God'; less so, and inexcusably, for the powerful 'There is a fountain fill'd with blood'. Though these pieces often convey his sense of his separation from God, they also assert God's benevolent purposes and triumphant provision for man. In expression they are lucid and vivid, strong and economical.

BIBLIOGRAPHY
W. Cowper, *William Cowper, Poetical Works*, ed. Norma Russell, 4th edn (London, 1967)
D. Cecil, *The Stricken Deer* (London, 1929)
V. Newey, *Cowper's Poetry* (Liverpool, England, 1982)
N. Nicholson, *William Cowper* (London, 1951)

ARTHUR POLLARD

Cowper, William (b. Whittington, England, 28 Dec. 1778; d. Sydney, Australia, 6 July 1858). Australian Anglican clergyman. Son of Samuel, a farmer, Cowper was working at Hull when he was converted and befriended by the evangelical vicar, THOMAS DYKES. It was Dykes who encouraged Cowper (though without tertiary education) to prepare for the ministry. Ordained for colonial service, Cowper reached Sydney in 1809.

Cowper's principal aim was the religious and moral reformation of his convict, emancipist and immigrant flock. The upper classes disliked his long-winded, simplistic exhortations but respected the preacher. Although placed at the centre of colonial life as minister of St Phillip's, Sydney's first church, Cowper resolutely refused to be drawn into the political controversies that bedevilled the colony. He reserved his public work for missionary and charitable activities.

Cowper outlived most of the early chaplains and found himself with a High Church bishop. He never abated his evangelical position and continued to be its advocate. Yet he became archdeacon in 1848 and administered the diocese during an interregnum. Cowper died, a patriarchal figure still ruling his parish. Survived by his third wife, he had a son who became premier of the colony and another who was first Dean of Sydney and the evangelical leader of the next generation.

BIBLIOGRAPHY
ADB
S. Judd and K. Cable, *Sydney Anglicans* (Sydney, 1987)

KENNETH J. CABLE

Cowper-Temple (né Cowper), **William Francis** [first baron Mount-Temple] (b. Brockett Hall, Hertfordshire, England, 13 Dec. 1811; d. Broadlands, near Romsey, Hampshire, England, 17 Oct. 1888). British MP and peer. A son of the fifth Earl Cowper, he adopted the name Cowper-Temple in 1869 and was created baron Mount-Temple in 1880. His brother-in-law was Lord SHAFTESBURY and his stepfather-in-law was Lord Palmerston, the prime minister. Cowper was MP for Hertford (1835–68) and Hampshire South (1868–80). His most significant appointments were as a Lord of the Admiralty (1846–55), President of the Board of Health (1855–58), and First Commissioner of Works (1860–6). The Cowper-Temple amendment that secularized the 1870 education bill was his.

Having been an admirer of EDWARD IRVING, Cowper settled for a time into a more mainstream evangelicalism. In the early 1850s he was a member of the EA and of other prominent evangelical societies but by the mid-1850s he was a strong admirer of F. D. Maurice, having moved to a much more liberal churchmanship. When Lord Palmerston became prime minister in 1855, Shaftesbury feared that Cowper would exercise undue influence on his appointment of bishops, regarding his brother-in-law as a 'Mephistopheles, who is ever at Palmerston's elbow' (Battiscombe, 1974: 249). In the end, however, Shaftesbury proved much more influential in appointments to the episcopal bench. Some of Cowper's letters are in the British Library.

BIBLIOGRAPHY
G. Battiscombe, *A Biography of the Seventh Earl of Shaftesbury* (London, 1974)
DNB
B. E. Hardman, 'The Evangelical Party in the Church of England 1855–65' (Cambridge Univ. Ph.D. thesis, 1963)
[Lady Mount-Temple], *Memorials* (London, 1890)

JONATHAN BURKE CUTMORE

Cox, Francis Augustus (b. Leighton Buzzard, Bedfordshire, England, 7 March 1783; d. Hackney, London, 5 Sept. 1853). Baptist minister, educationalist, and organizer. Trained at the Bristol Baptist College, he inherited property from his grandfather and continued his studies at Edinburgh and gained an MA. Ordained to Clipstone, Northamptonshire, ANDREW FULLER, JOHN SUTCLIFF and ROBERT HALL all participating in the service, he supplied in Cambridge for a year but was not invited to the pastorate. Instead he had an outstanding pastorate at Mare Street, Hackney, of more than 40 years.

Possessing real talents and immense energy, his mark is to be found everywhere in Baptist life in the first half of the nineteenth century. Skeats and MIALL refer to him as 'the active, busy, zealous worker in all philanthropical and religious movements'. A committee member of the BMS, he became its first historian. He helped launch the *Baptist Magazine*, was part founder of the Baptist Irish Society, was a stalwart supporter of the Baptist Home Missionary Society, and served as part-time tutor at Stepney from 1813 to 1822. For three years secretary to the General Body of Dissenting Ministers, he was one of the founders, office holders and staunchest supporters of the Anti-State Church Association, later the Liberation Society, while it was largely on his initiative that special services were held in London to celebrate the tercentenary anniversary of the Reformation. He played a crucial role in the founding of London University, indeed has been credited with being the first to conceive the idea, and in this was the close confidant of Lord Brougham, who nominated him for the Glasgow LL D. Secretary to the planning committee, he became the new institution's first librarian.

In 1835 he represented the infant Baptist Union on a fraternal visit to the churches of the USA to make inquiries on the twin topics of slave-holding and revivalism. With JAMES HOBY he wrote *The Baptists in America*, a report on this experience, and also *Suggestions Designed to Promote the Revival and Extension of Religion* and himself conducted revivalist services or 'protracted meetings'. The spread of 'Protestant Popery' through the diffusion of the teaching of the Oxford tracts made the promotion of a healthy 'Christian Patriotism' all the more urgent. Cox was three times chairman of the Baptist Union.

BIBLIOGRAPHY

Baptist Manual (1854)

J. H. Y. Briggs, 'Baptists in Higher Education', in *Faith, Life and Witness*, ed. W. H. Brackney and R. Burke (Birmingham, AL, 1990)

R. Carwardine, 'The Evangelist System: Charles Roe, Thomas Pulsford and the Baptist Home Missionary Society', *BQ*, (1980): 209–25

DNB

J. Ivimey, *History of the English Baptists*, IV (London, 1830)

J. H. Y. BRIGGS

Cox, Melville Beveridge   (b. Halowell, ME, USA, 9 Nov. 1799; d. Monrovia, Liberia, 21 July 1833). First American Methodist Episcopal missionary to Africa. Cox spent his early life on a farm and in 1818 was converted, joining the MEC. Licensed to preach in 1821, he was received on trial in 1822 by the New England Conference and appointed to the Exeter Circuit. In 1825 he contracted tuberculosis and due to his fragile health he located in 1828.

He married Ellen Cromwell in Baltimore, Maryland on 7 February 1828, but she died in December of 1830. During this time he worked collecting funds for Wesleyan University and also for a time edited the religious weekly *The Itinerant*. Though he continued in ill health, he wanted to preach and in 1831 transferred to the Virginia Conference, being appointed to Raleigh. However, his health worsened from the strain of preaching, and on the advice of a physician he gave up his position.

Despite this, Cox in the next year applied to be a missionary to South America, but instead Bishops HEDDING and MCKENDREE suggested Liberia in West Africa, to which Cox agreed. Though his friends and family feared for his health, he wrote to his brother that 'whether it be the path of suffering or enjoyment, of life or death, it shall be the joy of my heart to go' (Bangs, 1834, p. 9). He was commissioned in May and set sail from Norfolk on 6 November 1832.

After a stop in Freetown, Sierra Leone, where he was approached concerning valuable property in Monrovia, Liberia abandoned by the Basle Mission, Cox arrived in Monrovia on 8 March 1833. He bought the Basle property, which included three town lots and a house, for $500.

Cox early on engaged in a controversy with black Methodist preachers already resident in Liberia over his move to place them under the supervision and control of the ME Church of America. 'Only after "several meetings, earnest prayer, and the practice of great discretion" did the "coloured preachers" agree to this affiliation'. Cox considered that the gospel would be best communicated in West Africa by black preachers, but he and other white American Methodist missionaries 'simply assumed without question' that this activity would be under white control (*see* Franklin, 1977, p. 154, n. 4).

Cox energetically set up his mission, conducting a camp meeting at Caldwell where twenty-five to thirty persons were converted. He also revitalized local interest in a Sunday School for the Christian education of tribal boys. He planned to establish mission posts at Grand Bassa (with a school), and at Grand Cape Mount and laid the groundwork for a successful endeavour, doing 'an astonishing amount of work' in the short time he lived there. On 12 April 1833 Cox contracted malaria and died three months later. To him have been attributed the famous words, 'Though a thousand fall, let not Africa be given up'.

BIBLIOGRAPHY

AAP 7: 656–661

N. Bangs, 'Sermon on the Death of the Rev. M. B. Cox,' *MMQR* 16, 1 (1834): 1–17

EWM

B. Franklin, 'The White Methodist Image of the American Negro Emigrant to Liberia, West Africa, 1833–1848', *Methodist History* 15 (1977): 147–66

KENNETH N. PEARSON

Cox, Sarah (b. Wishall, England, 6 March 1773; d. Wishall, England). Wesleyan Methodist (WM) preacher. Cox had religious inclinations from an early age and regularly attended the Church of England. At about 18 Sarah heard WM preachers, went to a class meeting and was converted. Very soon she began praying in public and visiting those in need. Then Sarah felt a call to preach, but she was very diffident, however, she responded and preached successfully in Leicestershire and Nottinghamshire. Her health quickly gave way and she retired, but became a class/band leader.

BIBLIOGRAPHY
Z. Taft, *Biographical Sketches of ... Holy Women ...* 1 (London, 1825)

E. DOROTHY GRAHAM

Cox, William (Hayward) (b. 1804; d. 1871). Anglican clergyman. The son of a lieutenant-colonel who served in the Peninsular war, Cox was educated at Rugby and, beginning a lifelong association with Oxford, at Pembroke College. He graduated BA in 1825 with high honours, and BD in 1841. He was Michael fellow at Queen's 1828–33 and Rector of Carfax, Oxford 1839–52.

In 1836 he was made vice-president of St Mary's Hall, Oxford, through the influence of the then president R. D. Hampden (later Bishop of Hereford), whose 1832 Bampton lecturers had brought accusations of latitudinarianism. Hampden was Cox's lifelong mentor, appointing him in 1848 as his examining chaplain, and in 1854 as Rector of Eaton Bishop. Cox, for his part, in an 1847 pamphlet defended Hampden against the Tractarians in their attempt to keep him off the episcopal bench.

Despite this association, and despite his taking no leading role in the evangelical party, Cox appears to have identified with the evangelical movement. William Tuckwell in his *Reminiscences of Oxford* (1901) speaks of him as 'low Church'. In 1851 J. D. MACBRIDE supported Cox's bid for the principalship of St Edmund Hall. Cox was a contributor to *North British* and the *Church of England Quarterly* reviews, as well as the evangelical *Christian Observer*.

There are four of Cox's autograph letters at the British Library, and two at Lambeth Palace.

BIBLIOGRAPHY
J. S. Reynolds, *Evangelicals at Oxford* (London, 1953): 165
G. H. Townsend, ed., *Men of the Time*, 7th edn (London, 1868)

JONATHAN BURKE CUTMORE

Crabb, James (b. Wilton, Wiltshire, England 13 April 1774; d. Southampton, England, 17 Sept. 1851). Wesleyan and later Independent minister. Converted in his early teens, without any sort of human appointment he began to preach in the open air at the age of 18, often walking from ten to thirty miles a day. He was accepted for the Wesleyan ministry in 1794, being appointed to the widespread Portsmouth circuit, where he remained two years, and in 1796 was sent to Salisbury. But his prodigal use of his strength in travelling great distances on foot and in all weathers undermined his health and he was compelled to desist from the itinerant ministry in 1797.

But he still could not help preaching; and in more than one place he built a chapel to contain his converts, the first of these in Wilton in 1798; and to his evangelical labours he added the task of collecting money to defray the costs. This activity he continued through most of his life. Successively the needs of various groups proved irresistible: prostitutes, sailors, gipsies, the most degraded; for these he provided 'female penitentiaries', chapels and schools. In 1822 he offered again for the Wesleyan ministry with the aim of working in Southampton, but his desire to remain at the one place caused his rejection.

In 1824 he built Zion Chapel in the town, filling it every Sunday. Though he always regarded himself as a Wesleyan, his chapel was designedly undenominational, as were his other establishments, so that by the end of his life he was highly regarded by all, including the town's corporation. He achieved amazing success among many sections of the poorest of the population. His spirituality was marked by constant prayer from his youth upward, of which his diary gives abundant evidence. His most noteworthy convert was ELIZABETH WALLBRIDGE.

BIBLIOGRAPHY
J. B. Dyson, *Methodism in the Isle of Wight* (Ventnor, England, 1865): 177–226
J. Rudall, *Life of the Rev. James Crabb* (London, 1854)
Various tracts

OLIVER A. BECKERLEGGE

Cracroft, George (b. Louth, Lincolnshire, England, 1795; d. Northampton, England, 1 May 1845). Anglican clergyman. Son of Bernard (Rector of Rippingale) and Mary Cracroft, George attended Magdalen College School (chorister), Oxford, 1805–12. Matriculating in 1812, he became scholar of Lincoln College, Oxford, 1815–21, and was fellow 1820 till death. Ordained in 1818 (Bishop Pretyman Tomline's register, Lincoln) while Curate of Marsh Gibbon, Buckinghamshire, 1821–8 (parish registers), his 'views experienced a great change' in an evangelical direction *circa* 1823, according to FREDERICK GAMBIER. But he remained shiftless [A. Clark's manuscript collections (1907) for a Lincoln College register], and his fellowship was sequestrated to pay his creditors. He apparently took to the roads, eventually dying in a workhouse, a member of one of the oldest Lincolnshire families.

BIBLIOGRAPHY
V. H. H. Green, *Commonwealth of Lincoln College* (Oxford, 1979)
A. R. Maddison, *Lincolnshire Pedigrees*, 1 (London, 1902)
J. S. Reynolds, *Evangelicals at Oxford* (Oxford, 1953; Appleford, England, 1975)

J. S. REYNOLDS

Craik, Henry (b. Prestonpans, East Lothian, Scotland, 8 Aug. 1805; d. Bristol, 1866). Scholar and Brethren leader. Educated at St Andrews University, and Edinburgh, he became a Hebrew scholar of repute and was twice offered an honorary doctorate. He attributed his evangelical conversion to the influence of a fellow student, John Urquhart. He served as tutor in the household of ANTHONY NORRIS GROVES at Exeter (1826–8) and later became Baptist minister at Shaldon, Devonshire. There he met GEORGE MÜLLER with whom he formed a lifelong friendship.

In 1832 he was called to the pastorate of Gideon Chapel, Bristol, where he was soon joined by Müller. No fixed pastoral relationship was contracted, and the order and worship of the church became recognizably Brethren. Additionally, a large chapel – Bethesda – was taken over and a new church fellowship formed 'without any rules, desiring only to act as the Lord shall be pleased to give us light through his word' (Müller, *Narrative*, I.97). For the remainder of his life, Craik served as fellow elder with Müller and others. Despite ill health, his sermons and writings were influential, and he made important contributions to the study of Hebrew.

SELECT WRITINGS

H. Craik, *The Hebrew Language* (London, 1860)
—, *New Testament Church Order* (Bristol, England, 1863)
—, *Principia Hebraica* (Bristol, England, revised edn, 1864)

BIBLIOGRAPHY

W. E. Taylor, ed., *Passages from the Diary and Letters of Henry Craik* (Bristol, England, 1866)

HAROLD H. ROWDON

Cramp, John Mockett (b. St Peters, England, 25 July 1796; d. Wolfville, Nova Scotia, Canada, 6 Dec. 1881). Baptist pastor, educator and author. Born to Reverend Thomas and Rebecca (Gouger) Cramp, John was educated at Canterbury, Margate, and Stepney College (Regents Park) 1814–18. He was pastor of Dean Street Chapel, Southwark 1818–25, assisted his father at St Peters Baptist Chapel 1827–42 and became pastor of Wellington Square Baptist Chapel, Hastings 1842–4. He was editor of the *Baptist Magazine* 1825–8, president of the English Baptist Union 1837–8 and served the BFBS 1820–44. The Baptist Colonial Missionary Society sent him as the last president of Canada Baptist College in Montreal 1844–9. Appointed as president of Acadia College, Wolfville in 1851, he revived its failing fortunes before retiring in 1869.

He published 35 historical and theological works, numerous periodical articles, and was influential among Canadian and British Baptists on theological and social issues. An authority on the Roman Catholic Church, he was strongly antipapal. His *Baptist History From the Foundation of the Christian Church to the Close of the Eighteenth Century* made him the most widely read Canadian Baptist author of the nineteenth century.

BIBLIOGRAPHY
DCB

ROBERT S. WILSON

Cran, George (b. Scotland; d. Chicacole, India, 8 Jan. 1809). LMS missionary in south India. Cran was brought up in the Church of Scotland and ordained in the Scotch Church, London (1804) but attended the LMS seminary in Gosport. In 1805 he and AUGUSTUS DES GRANGES were sent by the LMS to India where they started the first Protestant mission to the Telugus. They chose Vishakapatnam, a large coastal trading centre north of Madras, where they soon made influential friends among the British military. This led to their being granted allowances for their religious services to the troops. Cran and Des Granges founded several schools and itinerated in the neighbouring countryside. The schools were successful but baptisms were few, perhaps because they would not allow caste differences. Cran translated tracts and the English liturgy into Telugu. He died in 1809 of a bilious fever. His letters to the LMS can be found in the CWM archives, School of Oriental and African Studies, London.

BIBLIOGRAPHY
J. Hough, *History of Christianity in India*, 4 (London, 1845–60): 254–66

PENELOPE CARSON

Cranfield, Thomas (b. London, 12 March 1758; d. London, 26 Nov. 1838). Pioneer of ragged and Sunday schools. Cranfield, a Congregationalist, whose whole life was lived on the borders of poverty, shares with John Pounds, a Unitarian, the distinction of founding the first ragged school, for children who could not be absorbed by an ordinary Sunday school. While there is more continuity between Pounds' work and later ragged schools, Cranfield's South London School has an earlier foundation date in 1810. Cranfield, 'whose early life was indeed filled with the excess which pious books like to attribute to the unconverted', was the son of a baker. Although during his first apprenticeship he was required to attend church with the family, he ran away from this religious household, and subsequently escaped from a tyrannous master into the army, serving in Gibraltar, returning to London in 1783 to become a journeyman tailor.

On returning to England he was converted under the ministry of WILLIAM ROMAINE, and immediately turned to open-air preaching. Supported in this and in benevolent work among the poor by JOSEPH REYNER, he encountered popular violence stirred up by antagonistic clergy. He opened his own home in Kingsland as a chapel and school in 1791, followed later by other schools in Stoke Newington, Rotherhithe, Southwark, Tottenham and Croydon. The Rotherhithe Sunday school, established in an area where men and animals often lived together in the same room, led him into other activities such as providing clothing for his poor scholars. However, his membership of the London Corresponding Society in the 1790s was at the expense of his spiritual vitality and soon repented of.

With ROWLAND HILL, whose church he had joined, he was the inspiration behind the founding of the Southwark Sunday School Society in 1799, and became a founding member of the Sunday School Union in 1803. He opened a school in the King's Bench Prison for the debtors' children. Involved in 1817 in establishing a sweeps' Sunday school, though this became primarily the work of a former colleague named Kesterton, he believed that he had taken Christian education into 'the very heart of Satan's dominions'. He also engaged in prison visiting, advocating clemency in cases he deemed worthy, and established services in lodging houses in the densely populated area to the south of Southwark Bridge. In this same area he undertook a mission of poor visiting, the supplying of bread and soup, blankets and clothing, and special services for the poor. This was especially intense during the cholera epidemic of 1833.

He had little patience with Hyper-Calvinism: 'To talk of converting sinners by preaching only to saints is an absurdity'. Whereas middle-class concern for the poor was widespread in evangelical Christendom, Cranfield exemplifies the concern of the poor for the poor, often providing for them from his own home or table in the hope that his own needs would be met by Christian friends, so that his own condition was often little different from those to whom he ministered and among whom he deliberately chose to live.

BIBLIOGRAPHY
C. Binfield, *George Williams and the YMCA* (London, 1973)
P. B. Cliff, *The Rise and Development of the Sunday School Movement* (London, 1986)
R. Cranfield, *Memoir of Thomas Cranfield, By His Son*, 1st edn (London, 1840) [*The Useful Christian* (a later RTS title of a latter edition)]
J. Sherman, *The Privilege of Sanctified Poverty* [funeral oration for T. Cranfield] (London, *c.* 1838)

J. H. Y. BRIGGS

Craufurd, James [Lord Ardmillan] (b. Havant, Hampshire, England, 1805; d. Edinburgh, 7 Sept. 1876). Scottish law lord. Craufurd (sometimes spelled 'Crawfurd') was educated at the universities of Glasgow and Edinburgh and became an advocate in 1829. He was appointed Solicitor-General for Scotland in 1853. In 1855 he was made a lord of session and of justiciary, with the judicial title of Lord Ardmillan. He held these positions for life. Craufurd was an elder in the Free Church and a member of the Bible Society. He wrote *The Disruption of the Scottish Church-Establishment* (1843).

BIBLIOGRAPHY
Boase
Oliver and Boyd, *Edinburgh Almanac* (1858)

JONATHAN BURKE CUTMORE

Craufurd, William Howieson (b. 27 Nov. 1781; d. 17 Sept. 1871). Landowner. Educated at the High School and at the University of Glasgow, he succeeded to the estates of Braehead in Midlothian and Craufurdland in Ayrshire. He lived chiefly in Ayrshire and he was a typical small landowner of his day, a Justice of the Peace and a Deputy-Lieutenant for Ayrshire, and much engaged in the round of county business. An active Conservative, he supported Peel. He joined the FCS and helped established it locally in Kilmarnock and nationally. He was also active in the affairs of the Bible Society.

R. H. CAMPBELL

Crawfoot, James (b. Stapleford, Cheshire, England, *c.* 1758; d. Tarvin, Cheshire, England, 23 Jan. 1839). Primitive Methodist mystic. Converted in 1783, Crawfoot's career, even with the Forest or Magic Methodists, a short-lived group which he led, was spent in and around the Delamere Forest. His early spiritual experiences reflected the balance between the spirit and nature. He was a Wesleyan local preacher in the Northwich circuit (Cheshire) until 1809, when he was censured for preaching to the outlawed independent Methodist groups in the Cheshire area, as well as for holding his own monthly Saturday evening prayer meetings at his cottage, where visions, trances and faintings occurred. Impressed by his dynamic enthusiasm, charismatic style and aged wisdom, and aware of Crawfoot's temporal difficulties, the future leaders of the Primitive Methodist Connexion appointed Crawfoot in 1809 as a travelling preacher. Crawfoot was mysteriously taken off the circuit plan in 1813, following a dispute involving Crawfoot's marriage to Hannah Mountford, HUGH BOURNE'S domestic servant.

Renowned for his lack of discipline, Crawfoot believed in freedom of the spirit: he sought Christians not denominationalists, evangelism, not church government. He had an intuitive sense of faith and an ability to communicate and share spiritual suffering. Rather than refined oratory, what Crawfoot offered was clear emphasis upon faith and the mysticism of silent prayer, the significance of dreams, and the importance of healing, together with the descending presence of God. Crawfoot was best with a handful of people, with whom he would quietly sit and engage in intimate 'conversation preaching'.

Known as the 'old man of the forest', for his patriarchal authority, Crawfoot was a holy, rustic man, uncouth and uneducated. Because of his almost mystical faith, Crawfoot's influence on Primitive Methodism has been marginalized, even minimalized. He has been criticized for his defective judgment and lack of Christian humility. Yet according to Hugh Bourne, Crawfoot was his spiritual sage, who, 'brought forth the work of religion' beyond anything he had ever before experienced. His influence in early mainstream Primitive Methodism was crucial. He was always a man to suffer temporally; after his marriage in 1814, his house burnt down. He died in poverty.

BIBLIOGRAPHY
G. Herod, *Historical and Biographical Sketches* (London, 1851)
PM Mag (1902)

WAYNE J. JOHNSON

Crawford, Alexander (b. Arran, Argyllshire, Scotland, c. 1785; d. Tryon, Prince Edward Island, BNA, 15 May 1828). Baptist church planter. Crawford was converted in a meeting conducted by ROBERT and JAMES HALDANE about 1800; he studied at their seminary in Edinburgh in 1805. After an evangelistic tour of the Highlands, he joined the Haldanes in Baptist beliefs in 1808. Alexander and Jane Crawford emigrated to Yarmouth, Nova Scotia in 1810. He taught school but found little fellowship among the local Baptists led by HARRIS HARDING. During his first visit to Prince Edward Island in 1812, Crawford performed the first adult believer's baptism there and founded the church at Three Rivers (Montague). In 1815, he taught school in Charlottetown before settling on a farm at Tryon. He helped found churches at Tryon, East Point, Lot Forty-Eight, Cross Roads and Belfast. He did not join any of them because he believed that prayer, praise, reading of the Scriptures, salutation, breaking of bread, offering, exhortation, and discipline should be observed every Sunday in the company of believers only. Baptists and Disciples of Christ revere him as their founding father on Prince Edward Island.

ROBERT S. WILSON

Crawford, James (b. North Berwick, East Lothian, Scotland, Dec. 1808; d. Nov. 1863). Scottish lawyer. He was a native of North Berwick, where he took his early education, afterwards entering upon the study of law in Edinburgh. He attained considerable eminence in the legal profession, and was a key member of the Church's Law Society which prepared the Church of Scotland's *Book of Styles*. A keen churchman, he was one of the founders of the *Presbyterian Review* in 1831, a publication which exerted a considerable influence upon the affairs of the Scottish Church at the time. He also took part in editing the *Acts of the General Assembly*. His legal knowledge was of great assistance to the FCS, to which he transferred his allegiance in 1843. The quality of his evangelicalism may be judged from his fondness for the *Letters of Samuel Rutherford*, and it was largely due to his action that the 1863 two-volume edition of this work was produced.

BIBLIOGRAPHY
J. A. Wylie, ed., *Disruption Worthies* (Edinburgh, 1881)

DONALD M. LEWIS

Crawford, Thomas Jackson (b. St Andrews, Fife, Scotland, 1812; d. Genoa, Italy, 11 Oct. 1875). Church of Scotland minister. He was the son of William Crawford, a professor of moral philosophy at St Andrews. He was

educated there (BA 1831) and was ordained at the parish of Cults. In 1838 Lord Strathmore presented him to Glamis. In 1843, upon the Disruption, he published his *Reasons of Adherence to the Church of Scotland*. From 1844 Crawford was minister at St Andrew's church, Edinburgh, until his appointment in 1859 as professor of divinity at Edinburgh, a position he held for life. He was moderator of the General Assembly in 1867, was chaplain-in-ordinary to the Queen, and dean of the chapel royal. Crawford was a member of the Scottish Reformation Society.

An orthodox Calvinist theologian of some note, in the *Fatherhood of God* (1866) and *Doctrine of the Holy Scripture* (1871) he interprets the Atonement objectively, as a propitiation; he sees the Atonement as unlimited, salvation as conditional, and takes pains to maintain the unity of the Godhead.

BIBLIOGRAPHY
Boase
DNB

JONATHAN BURKE CUTMORE

Creighton, James (b. Co. Cavan, Ireland, 1739; d. London, 26 Dec. 1819). Anglican clergyman and Methodist preacher. Born of Scots-Irish parents at Moyn Hall and reared by a devout mother, he graduated BA from Trinity College, Dublin, and was ordained (deacon 1764, priest 1765). Appointed curate in the cathedral church, the Bishop of Kilmore advised him 'to say nothing at all about *faith* in his sermons'. Creighton, however, became troubled about his personal religion. When in the spring of 1773 JOHN WESLEY made his biennial tour of Ireland, passing through Creighton's parish of Swanlinbar, Creighton pondered preaching against Methodism, but decided first to direct a series of ten queries to Wesley. Wesley replied swiftly and succinctly in a communication dated 24 May. He claimed, 'The Methodists observe more of the Articles, Rubrics, and Canons of the Church than any other people in the three kingdoms;' and stated, 'They maintain that no man can be saved by a faith which is without works;' gave a hearty prayer-book blessing, 'May God enable *you* perfectly to love him, and worthily magnify his Holy Name!' Wesley added the bonus of his *Earnest Appeal*, though apologizing, 'I could not here procure any other copy of the *Appeal* than this dirty one.' Needless to say, Creighton did not preach against the Methodists, especially as his own brother Robert was a practising Methodist himself.

In 1776 Creighton underwent a conversion experience and began to mingle with his brother's Methodist friends, held divine service, preached, and administered communion in a barn in a distant part of his parish, preached to groups in the open air, and to Methodist gatherings such as their quarterly meetings at Enniskillen and Clones, and even made preaching tours among distant Methodists. He became very friendly with promising young Methodist preachers such as ANDREW BLAIR and WILLIAM MYLES.

Creighton's vicar was becoming restless about his unconventional curate, and threatened to complain to his bishop, whereon Creighton replied, 'I never saw any fruit of my labours until I became irregular.' It became more obvious that John Wesley himself might eventually wish to transplant Creighton to England, from the evidence of his letters of 23 December 1777, 12 July 1778, and especially a direct invitation on 29 September 1779: 'If you are inclined to remove to England, I think you have a very fair opportunity.' (Wesley furnished attractive details, as that a curate for JOHN W. FLETCHER of Madeley was needed, though Wesley was also pondering the idea of Dr THOMAS COKE's temporarily helping Fletcher out, while Creighton might serve Wesley himself as a kind of curate in Bristol or London.) Buzzing around still in Wesley's mind was the idea of building up a team of junior clerics at City Road, London, to anchor Methodism more firmly in the Church of England.

Creighton's devout humility as well as his perplexity about his life's work is obvious from a letter which he wrote on 26 October 1778, from Belturbet to Wesley:

Could I once open a door here for the Methodist preachers, I should willingly go to any part of the globe that God should call me to . . . I thought, if I could do any good, poor Ireland wanted it most; and especially the miserable, dark, benighted region where I am at present: therefore I had resolved to continue here after I should be discharged from my curacy. But I am now inclined to go to England or anywhere else, if God will give me utterance. Were I near you I should be too happy; but O my weakness, my ignorance and inability to fill the place of your assistant! . . . . We must lament the want of discipline in our Church . . . And though I admire the economy of the Methodists, so far as I know it; yet I entirely agree with you that they ought not to leave the church. So long as they mingle with the members of it, they may be a means of bringing them in; but if they separate, they will thereby stop the ears and eyes of thousands: these have been my sentiments long before I heard that they were yours.
(*AM*, 1788)

Such were the kind of sentiments for which Wesley longed in his potential preachers.

During 1781 and 1782 James Creighton, as an Irish clergyman with a vocation for Methodism, was engaged in a continual evangelical tour: 'I preached occasionally in seven different counties, and rode and walked about four thousand miles during that time.' In May 1783 he was twice invited to England by Wesley. After some months' deliberation, and tearful farewells on 28 September with his parishioners, on 1 October he penned a farewell poem to Ireland, 'The Parting Scene', and set out braving the weather, the financial scarcities, a wife more timid than he, and two schoolboys, and launched himself into his new sphere of ministry.

They arrived in London on 14 October. Speedily he was embroiled in the political problems of British Methodism. He was named immediately after the two Wesleys and Thomas Coke as a constituent founding member of the Methodist Conference set out in Wesley's Deed of Declaration of 28 February 1784. Later that same year, as a presbyter, he was an essential element in the ordination of Thomas Coke and those Methodist preachers who were to accompany him to America; indeed Creighton inscribed Coke's Letters of Orders for Wesley to sign, and shared with Coke the preparation of several others. He also warned Wesley to be more cautious in ordaining, especially in ordaining preachers for service in Scotland, as Wesley did from 1785 onwards. It was Creighton who recorded that late in life Wesley continued to regret that he had probably gone too far, so that eventually his preachers were 'too powerful' for him.

On 8 August 1789 Creighton performed another valuable kind of service for the ageing Wesley; he put his printing of the *Arminian Magazine* on a securer footing, rescuing it from what Wesley termed 'the unsufferable errata' of THOMAS OLIVERS, though indeed much of the trouble (as Creighton informed his sister in Ireland) was Wesley's own failing eyesight – 'he can see little by candlelight'.

Wesley's City Road Chapel, however, remained Creighton's realm after Wesley's death in 1791, after he had resigned the 'drudgery' of editing the magazine. He was happy to relax without political tensions, with the composing of a few sermons, a few books, a few poems, such as elegies to Charles Wesley and to John Wesley. For the rest he was a diligent pastor from his home in Hoxton Square, preaching and administering the Lord's Supper to most of the central London Methodists, especially the poor. He strove to ensure worshipful decorum in City Road Chapel, in conformity with his sermon preached there on 28 July 1793, in which he listed nine distressing local customs. He was one who long continued the ministerial practice of leading a choral funeral procession through Finsbury Square to City Road Chapel, accompanied on occasion by a revered local preacher and physician, Dr JAMES HAMILTON, of Finsbury Square. Creighton himself died in 1819, at 81, and was buried with his wife in his own family grave in Hackney.

SELECT WRITINGS
J. Creighton, 'A short account of the experience of the Rev. James Creighton, BA. (Written by himself.)' *Arminian Magazine* (1785): 241–4, 297–302, 354–9, 398–403.

BIBLIOGRAPHY
AM, XI (November 1788): 608–10.
F. Baker, *John Wesley and the Church of England* (London, 1970)
G. J. Stevenson, *City Road Chapel, London, and its Associations* (London, 1872): especially 145–4, 282–3, 587

FRANK BAKER

Crewdson, Isaac (b. Kendal, Westmoreland, England, 6 June 1780; d. Bowness, Westmoreland, England, 8 May

1844). Quaker Seceder. Brought up in 'all the strictness of external Quakerism' he moved when 14 years old from Kendal to Manchester where he prospered as a textile manufacturer. As a minister among Friends in Manchester he was at this time fully committed to Quaker usages and his many family links with Friends were further extended by his marriage (*circa* 1803) to Elizabeth Jowitt of Leeds. His discovery of evangelical truth occurred in middle age after a dangerous illness. He now began assiduously to read the Puritan classics some of which he abridged for publication. He also publicly abandoned his former quietism for a more vigorous, evangelical theology which emphasized the doctrine of atonement.

His *Beacon to the Society of Friends* (1835) maintained that the Quaker rejection of baptism and the Lord's Supper was unscriptural, that Friends placed the authority of the 'Inner Light' of the Holy Spirit above that of scripture and that the movement was tainted with the errors of the American Quaker Elias Hicks, even though the latter's teachings had been condemned by the yearly meeting in London in 1829. Crewdson was supported at the yearly meeting by men like J. J. GURNEY but more local opposition led Crewdson and 53 sympathizers to resign in 1836 and establish a separate assembly of Friends who met in a chapel in Grosvenor Street where there was public reading of scripture and celebration of the sacraments. However Isaac Crewdson was effectively the meeting's focal point of identity and in 1844 shortly after his death the Chapel was sold to the Baptists.

The ecclesiological crisis among Friends which Crewdson's pamphlet had provoked pushed into the background for the time being, the other issues which divided 'Gay' and Strict Quakers. Once the 'Beaconites' (as they came to be called) realized that they could not claim to be either the historic or the prevailing voice of Quakerdom they joined other communities usually those of Anglicans or Plymouth Brethren. Crewdson's death marked the end of a Quaker era though an important evangelical element remained within the Friends' community.

BIBLIOGRAPHY

D. W. Bebbington, *Evangelicalism in Modern Britain* (London, 1989): 155
DNB
M. Grubb, 'The Beacon Separation' *JFHS* 60 (1977): 190–8
E. Isichei, *Victorian Quakers* (Oxford, 1970): 45–51
R. M. Jones, *The Later Periods of Quakerism* 1 (London, 1921): 490–2, 505–8
T. C. F. Stunt, *Early Brethren and the Society of Friends* (Pinner, England, 1970): 6–7, 14
W. R. Ward, *Religion and Society in England 1790–1850* (London, 1972): 68

TIMOTHY C. F. STUNT

Crewdson, William (Dillworth)   (b. Kendal, Westmoreland, England, 26 Dec. 1774; d. 2 April 1851). Quaker banker and Seceder. His parents were Quakers and he became a respected figure in the Kendal Society of Friends. He sent his son and namesake to JOSIAH FORSTER'S school in Southgate and was himself clerk of the yearly meeting from 1815 to 1819. His son married into the Fox family of Plymouth and his daughter Maria married JOHN ELIOT HOWARD of Tottenham. In the wake of the Beaconite controversy initiated by his cousin ISAAC CREWDSON, William followed his children, resigning Quaker membership on 23 April 1840 and henceforth was associated with Brethren, though, unlike the Howards, he maintained good relations with Friends.

BIBLIOGRAPHY

W. Beck, W. F. Wells and H. G. Chalkley, *Biographical Catalogue* (London, 1888): 145–7
A. P. F. Sell, *Church Planting, a Study in Westmoreland Nonconformity* (Worthing, England, 1986)
T. C. F. Stunt, *Early Brethren and the Society of Friends* (Pinner, England, 1970): 11–18

TIMOTHY C. F. STUNT

Crichton, David Maitland Makgill   (b. Rankeilour, Scotland, 4 March 1801; d. Rankeilour, 11 July 1851). Advocate, landowner, and leading FCS layman. Descended from Scottish nobility, he was influenced spiritually by what he saw of Christ in his first wife during her afflictions. He began in 1834 to speak publicly on behalf of THOMAS CHALMERS's church extension schemes. He narrowly failed to be returned as MP for St Andrews, but used his means as landowner and his skill as advocate to promote the cause of spiritual independence, the reform of church–state relations, and the supply of cheap Bibles. Under pressure of work, travel, and abuse in the press, he suffered paralysis in 1844, but though he did not fully recover and was left rather irritable and severe, he continued his efforts on behalf of the FCS and causes which lay near his heart, and encouraged by his hospitality those in the forefront of battle, such as THOMAS GUTHRIE, ROBERT S. CANDLISH, HUGH MILLER and JAMES BEGG. He impoverished the family estate and his statue at Cupar is inscribed 'The Poor Man's Friend'.

BIBLIOGRAPHY

J. W. Taylor, *A Memoir of the late D. M. M. Crichton* (Edinburgh, 1853)
J. W. Taylor, in *Disruption Worthies*, ed. J. A. Wylie (Edinburgh, no date)

HUGH M. CARTWRIGHT

Crisp, Thomas Steffe   (b. Suffolk, England, 1788; d. Bristol, England, 16 June 1868). English Baptist minister and educator. From a Suffolk Congregational family, Crisp was trained at the Wymondley Academy and at Glasgow University (1808–9). He served for eight years as minister of St Ives' Congregational Church, but became increasingly worried about baptizing infants. He consulted JOSEPH KINGHORN on this subject and was baptized by him as a believer in 1817, though he maintained friendly contact with Paedo-Baptists especially JOHN BURDER and WILLIAM JAY of Bath. Soon after this he became assistant minister at Broadmead, Bristol (serving with both JOHN RYLAND and ROBERT HALL) and tutor at the college. When he became president of the college in 1825, his appointment at Broadmead ceased, but so greatly respected was he that the church still looked upon him as their minister, especially during interregnums. Serving as principal until 1868, his views were distinctively evangelical and Calvinistic. A humble man he was a painstaking, but not an exciting, tutor, but greatly loved by his students for his gentlemanly Christian discipleship. 'Never willingly a public man', he was a strong opponent of slavery.

BIBLIOGRAPHY
N. S. Moon, *Education for Ministry* (London, 1979)
S. A. Swaine, *Faithful Men* (London, 1884)
F. W. Trestrail, *Reminiscences . . .* (London, 1879)

J. H. Y. BRIGGS

Cronin, Edward (b. Cork, Ireland, 1801; d. Brixton, England, 1882). Brethren missionary and leader. Brought up a Roman Catholic, he became a Protestant. While a medical student in Dublin he was appalled by the refusal of Independent churches to admit him to communion unless he became a member of one of them in Dublin. With others, meetings were held in the home of Edward Wilson, assistant secretary of the Bible Society in Dublin, at which the Lord's Supper was observed. This small group coalesced with a similar one meeting in the home of FRANCIS HUTCHINSON, and thus entered the mainstream of the emerging Brethren movement.

Cronin served as a missionary with ANTHONY NORRIS GROVES and others in Baghdad and India (1832–7). He then settled in London where he played a prominent part among those Brethren who sided with JOHN NELSON DARBY. He fell foul of Darby in connection with a dispute among the Brethren in Ryde and was excommunicated in 1879, though the two men were personally reconciled before Cronin died.

BIBLIOGRAPHY
Pickering

HAROLD H. ROWDON

Cronyn, Benjamin (b. Kilkenny, Ireland, 11 July 1802; d. London, Ontario, Canada, 22 Sept. 1871). First Bishop of Huron. Educated at Kilkenny College and Trinity College, Dublin (BA 1822, divinity prizeman 1824, MA 1825, DD 1855) Cronyn was ordained priest in 1827 by the Bishop of Tuam. He emigrated to Upper Canada in 1832, settling at London, where he remained for the rest of his life. In 1857 he was elected Bishop of Huron by the clergy and laity of the diocesan synod (the first such election in the British Empire), defeating A. N.

Bethune, the preferred candidate of Bishop John Strachan of Toronto. While in Britain for his consecration Cronyn visited Dr Fleury's Bible class in Ireland where he made an appeal for men for Canada. This resulted in the emigration of Edward Sullivan, James Carmichael, and John Philip DuMoulin, all future bishops in the Canadian church.

Perhaps Cronyn's most intense controversy was that concerning Trinity College, Toronto, and in particular the teaching of its provost, George Whitaker, whose views Cronyn regarded as 'unsound and un-Protestant'. Failing to have Whitaker's views censured, Cronyn took steps towards establishing a theological college in his own diocese. With the help of his colleague ISAAC HELLMUTH, funds were secured for Huron College (chartered 1863) – notably an endowment for a chair in divinity from the Reverend ALFRED PEACHE, who also endowed Peache's College (later St John's, Highbury). The Cronyn family (including the Blakes of Toronto – see W. H. BLAKE) were mainstays of Anglican evangelicalism in Ontario throughout the nineteenth century.

BIBLIOGRAPHY
A. H. Crowfoot, *Benjamin Cronyn* (London, Canada, 1957)
DCB, X

RICHARD W. VAUDRY

Crook, Henry (b. St Kitts, 1708; d. Hunslet, Yorkshire, England, 6 Nov. 1770). Anglican clergyman. Crook was not ordained until 1740 and served five years before being priested. He was Curate of Huddersfield, Kirk Sandal and Kippax before becoming Vicar of Hunslet (1745–70), in the course of which time he offered a title to JOHN NEWTON, who appears, however, to have been unable to take it up probably through objection from the Archbishop of York. Encouraged by his friend, Archdeacon William Bassett of Glentworth, Crook boldly preached justification by faith as set forth not only in scripture but also in the prayer-book and the articles.

He met JOHN WESLEY in 1755, and both he and CHARLES WESLEY preached for Crook, John finally doing so on 30 July 1769. Crook, however, always saw the importance of church order and objected to the increasing exclusiveness of Methodist connexions and to Wesley's encouragement of lay preachers. He had a tight system of activity within his parish, with two services per Sunday, Monday and Tuesday spent in visiting, a special weekly meeting for converted colliers each Thursday, another at one of his neighbour's houses on Fridays and a Saturday service as well. He regularly catechized the children and prepared for confirmation and, in addition, held evening meetings in his kitchen. He was strict in his Sabbatarianism and, censorious and even short-tempered in manner, he even went so far as to reprove Kershaw, the Vicar of Leeds, for attending balls and assemblies.

BIBLIOGRAPHY
L. E. Elliott-Binns, *The Early Evangelicals* (London, 1953)
J. Walsh, 'Yorkshire Evangelicals in the Eighteenth Century' (Cambridge Univ. Ph.D. thesis, 1956)

ARTHUR POLLARD

Crook, John (b. 1742, near Leigh, Lancashire, England; d. Scarborough, Yorkshire, England, 27 Dec. 1805). Methodist itinerant. 'The Apostle of Methodism in the Isle of Man'. Son of a physician, Crook had a good classical education. His father's extravagance, however, brought financial ruin and he went to sea, where he lost his life. John joined the army in Ireland, where he was converted about 1770 under a Methodist sermon in Limerick. He married a religious woman in Cork; his release from the army was secured by an uncle, and he settled in Liverpool, where he became a Methodist class leader and a local preacher. A Liverpool Methodist who had lived in the Isle of Man raised funds to send Crook there as a freelance missionary. There were no Roman Catholics or Dissenters amongst the Isle's 30,000 inhabitants, and apparently no Methodist had ever preached there.

In March 1775 Crook preached to a large crowd in the open air in Douglas and encountered some raucous opposition, then moved on to Ramsey. At Castletown his audience included the Lieutenant-Governor as well as some ministers and gentry. His preaching was plain and simple, though challenging.

After six months's itinerant preaching Crook returned to Liverpool leaving a Methodist society of 53 members at Castletown, and a vigorous class meeting at Peel, where the church communicants had risen to 300. The Leeds Conference admitted him on trial in August 1775. Originally intended for Lincolnshire, Wesley made a private rearrangement that JOHN MASON would oversee the Isle of Man as well as Whitehaven, while Wesley also reassured some Manx laymen that Crook's services would be continued. In October Crook was greeted by great crowds 'of poor, simple, loving people' waiting for him from three miles outside Peel. At other townships which he visited in the following summer he was able to greet healthy new societies organized by John Mason on Crook's behalf while he served part-time in England.

Anti-Methodist persecution was arising, however. Crook secured support from the governor, and Wesley extended Crook's time in 1776. In the streets of Douglas, although the Lieutenant-Governor would not allow any outright persecution, clerical opposition was strong in spite of the fact that Crook encouraged faithful church attendance.

Crook was received into full connexion in 1776 and was sent into normal circuit work for a year, in charge of the Dales circuit, while three preachers in Whitehaven looked after the Isle of Man. Wesley then assigned two more itinerants to Man and went there himself on 30 May 1777, returning 3 June, preaching in Castletown, Peel and Douglas. Although recognizing its uniqueness,

he hesitated about what to do. Full clarity did not come until after his second visit, in June 1781.

In 1778 Wesley sent Crook back to the island for three years, a solid recognition of the incomparable affinity between the man and the island. This was also signalized by the birth of the Isle of Man as an independent new circuit. John Crook was the assistant in charge of the circuit, teamed up in turn with one of three different helpers, none of them remarkable preachers.

Some estimate of the success of Wesley's bold experiment may be gauged from the membership statistics of that and succeeding years. The pooled memberships for Whitehaven and the Isle of Man for 1778 were 933, which implied (on the previous history of Whitehaven) about 600 for the island. In 1779 it was 1,051, in 1780, 1,486 – one of the 12 largest circuits in the nation. The statistics for the following decade were even more astounding. From 1,597 in 1781 to 2,500 in 1791 the membership of the Isle of Man increased fairly steadily, though with a few setbacks, to become the largest but London in the country; and in 1798 an extraordinary increase brought the island's figure to 4,847, while London's remained 3,114 – when surely the Isle of Man was over-ripe for dividing into two circuits.

Actually Crook's most fruitful tours of ministry, from 1781 onwards, were in Ireland, with a refreshed course in the Isle of Man for two years, 1786–7, and another in 1798. In effect, however, his pioneer work in the Isle of Man had been completed by 1781, although its full development was not realized until after his death. In Ireland he was greatly beloved, and greatly respected. In 1784 Crook was named among the 'Legal Hundred' and it was agreed that he should be seen as representing Ireland, with whose circuits he showed an affinity similar to that which he had displayed for the men of Man. He continued to serve as the assistant of varied Irish circuits, usually for two successive years at a time, except that his last station as supernumerary was in Scarborough in Yorkshire.

He had left behind a solid mark of piety and acumen in Ireland. Crook presided over the first Irish conference in 1791. THOMAS COKE, following his return from America, presided over the 1792 Irish Conference, and Crook was appointed secretary. These two occupied these same offices in 1793, 1794, 1795 and 1797. Clearly the standing of Crook among Irish Methodists could hardly be higher. Yet so solidly had Crook laid his foundations as the apostle of Methodism in the Isle of Man that when his firm superintending hand had been removed from the helm in 1781 there was not the slightest disruption, and the membership statistics continued to soar out of all rational understanding.

In one matter Wesley and Crook never agreed. Wesley could never dissuade Crook from fostering the Manx language. Wesley told one of Crook's successors as assistant of the Isle of Man, George Holder, on 20 November 1789, 'I exceedingly disapprove of your publishing anything in the Manx language. On the contrary, we should do everything in our power to abolish it from the earth, and persuade every member of our Society to learn and talk English.'

BIBLIOGRAPHY
'A Memoir of Mr John Crook', *Methodist Magazine* (1808): 3–10, 40–57, 97–105, 145–151, 193–204.
Minutes of the Methodist Conferences, 1 [1744–98] (London, 1862)

FRANK BAKER

Crook, William Pascoe (b. Dartmouth, Devon, England, 1755; d. Melbourne, Australia, 14 June 1846). LMS Missionary on the Society Islands. Crook sailed with the first LMS missionaries for the South Seas on board the *Duff* in 1796. He served in isolation from the Tahitian mission on the Marquesas, first at Tahuata between June 1797 and June 1798 and at Nukuhiva until January 1799. Upon his return to England he married Hannah (née Dare). Before 1804 he and his wife returned to New South Wales. Indecision delayed his return to the islands until 8 May 1816. Crook served at Papetoai until removing to Afareaitu in 1817. In April 1818 he settled at Papeete on Tahiti, and from October 1823 until his retirement in 1830 to Melbourne, Australia, he served at Taiarabu.

BIBLIOGRAPHY
N. Gunson, *Messengers of Grace* (Melbourne, 1978)
R. Lovett, *The History of the London Missionary Society 1795–1895* (London, 1899)
RMD, 4th edn (London, 1923)

R. WATCYN JAMES

Crosbie, Andrew (b. 1733; d. Edinburgh, 25 Feb. 1785). Scottish advocate. In the period 1760 to 1785 Crosbie was the most respectable and powerful lay leader in the Scottish Church General Assembly. A member of the Popular party, in *Thoughts . . . Concerning Patronage and Presentation* (1769) he countered 'Jupiter' Carlyle's call for a politely learned clergy, saying that ministers needed only 'plain sense, a sincere heart, and a sufficient knowledge of practical divinity'. Against his party, however, he supported toleration by drafting the Scottish Catholic Relief Bill of 1779. Extraordinarily gifted in powers of conversation, during Dr SAMUEL JOHNSON's visit to Edinburgh he was, Boswell tells us, Johnson's 'truly learned and philosophical friend'.

Crosbie was called to the Scottish bar in 1757 and became an influential and wealthy advocate. Late in life his fortune failed with the collapse of a provincial bank. His widow was supported by the generosity of the Faculty of Advocates, of which he had been for a time vice-dean. Crosbie may have been the model for Councillor Pleydell in Scott's *Guy Mannering*.

BIBLIOGRAPHY
DNB
J. Irving, *The Book of Scotsmen* (Paisley, Scotland, 1881): 85

R. Sher, *Church and University* (Edinburgh, 1985): 124–27, 158, 281
T. Somerville, *My Own Life and Times* (Edinburgh 1861): 98

JONATHAN BURKE CUTMORE

Crosby, Sarah (b. Leeds, Yorkshire, England, *c.* 1729; d. Leeds, Yorkshire, England, 4 Oct. 1804). Wesleyan Methodist preacher. Crosby had Calvinistic leanings, but she was greatly influenced by JOHN WESLEY's sermon on Christian perfection and converted, becoming a class leader (1752). Deserted by her husband (1757) she went to London, and then joined Mary Bosanquet [FLETCHER, Mrs MARY] and SARAH RYAN in Leytonstone where they started a Christian community. In 1761 Crosby moved to Derby. Here her class increased to 200, and she had to give an exhortation. She was very concerned about female preaching and wrote to Wesley about it, receiving a qualified approval. They corresponded extensively. Soon Crosby received other invitations and travelled from place to place preaching, plus leading her classes, for nearly forty years.

BIBLIOGRAPHY
AM (1806)
L. F. Church, *More About the Early Methodist People* (London, 1949)
Z. Taft, *Biographical Sketches of . . . Holy Women . . .*, 2 (London, 1828)

E. DOROTHY GRAHAM

Crosley, David (b. near Todmorden, Lancashire, England, *c.* 1669; d. Goodshaw, Lancashire, Aug./Sept. 1744). Early Baptist evangelist. The importance of Crosley is in linking the evangelical revival to earlier evangelical movements of the late Puritan period. Brought up by a pious aunt, he worked as a stonemason, preaching at nights. Initially Presbyterian in persuasion by the Spring of 1690 he was in touch with Midland Independents and the Baptists in particular. In 1691 he preached for John Bunyan's congregation in Bedford and published a sermon preached in a meeting house in Spitalfields. In the same year a chapel was built in Bacup, Lancashire, for his ministry and that of his cousin, William Mitchell. Baptized at Bromsgrove in Worcestershire, he was formally called to an itinerant Baptist ministry in August 1692, ministering first in Bacup, then at Barnoldswick, Yorkshire, and from 1695 at Tottlebank, though in the same year he is a signatory to a church covenant at Barnoldswick. Between 1692 and 1705, Crosley and Mitchell rode through the Calder, Aire and Wharfe valleys and further afield, often in appalling weather conditions, planting Baptist congregations, all initially part of the 'Church in Rossendale', but after 1705 organized as separate congregations.

In 1705 Crosley was called to the pastorate of Currier's Hall, London, but was soon to leave the capital in disgrace because of sexual misdemeanours, the story of which spread into Lancashire and Yorkshire causing the churches there initially to refuse him renewal of fellowship. He therefore founded his own churches at Gildersome and Bacup, and even a rival association which did not endear him to his former colleagues. Regrettably Crosley's sexual indiscretions seem not to have been isolated to a single occasion, and he does not seem to have been a good team worker but rather a flamboyant individualist. However, he still won for himself the title, 'Evangelist on the Pennines', and when he resettled at Goodshaw as a schoolmaster, fellowship was renewed. As late as 1736 he was instrumental in establishing a new church in Blackburn. In 1744 he republished his 1691 sermon on 'Samson' with a preface from GEORGE WHITEFIELD with whom he had been in correspondence for some years. A big man of over twenty stones, he preached without difficulty to some 4,000 people in the open air when 72 years of age.

BIBLIOGRAPHY
DNB
C. E. Shipley, ed., *The Baptists of Yorkshire* (London, 1912)
W. T. Whitley, *The Baptists of North West England* (London, 1913)

J. H. Y. BRIGGS

Cross, William (b. Cirencester, Gloucestershire, England, 22 July 1797; d. Somosomo, Fiji, 15 Oct. 1842). Wesleyan missionary in Tonga and Fiji. Born into a Church of England family, William joined the Wesleyan Society in 1820. Having offered for service as a missionary, in 1827 he was appointed by the WMMS to the New Zealand mission and was ordained in London. However, while passing through Sydney he was diverted by the New South Wales District Committee to the Friendly Islands (Tonga) mission, which urgently needed reinforcement. There he worked with NATHANIEL TURNER at Nuku'alofa. His first wife, Elizabeth, whom he had married in 1818, was drowned in Tonga in 1832. Visiting Sydney in 1833, he married Augusta Smith. In October 1835, with DAVID CARGILL, he began a Wesleyan mission in Fiji, where he worked for the remainder of his life. Small in stature and with limited education, William was not a commanding figure, but he was respected by his colleagues as a diligent and devoted missionary.

BIBLIOGRAPHY
J. Hunt, *Memoir of the Rev. William Cross* (London, 1846)

DAVID HILLIARD

Crosse, John (b. London, 1739; d. Bradford, Yorkshire, England, 17 June 1816). Anglican clergyman. Crosse was the son of Hammond Crosse, esquire, of Kensington and educated at Hadley, Hertfordshire. He appears to have been converted in London through the Methodist preacher Alexander Coates and joined a Methodist class

meeting (Stamp, 1844: 6). He matriculated at St Edmund Hall, Oxford on 21 October 1762, took orders and acted as a curate in Wiltshire and the Lock Hospital in London. In 1765–8 he toured the Continent with John Thornton, cousin of JOHN THORNTON of Clapham, meeting Voltaire and taking special note of the evils of 'popery'. He graduated BA only in 1768 and incorporated BA and MA at King's College, Cambridge in 1776. From 1768 he was minister of the chapelries of Todmorden in the parish of Rochdale and Cross-Stone in the parish of Halifax.

In 1774 he became minister of White Chapel near Leeds. He was appointed Vicar of Bradford in 1784, his father having purchased the living. Here Crosse became a model evangelical parish priest, indefatigable in preaching, catechizing, visiting, conducting devotional meetings as well as supporting charitable and missionary societies. Blindness in his later years did not greatly hinder his ministry. Crosse was, unusually, an Arminian in theology, was friendly to the Methodists and once considered leaving the Establishment to assist JOHN WESLEY in London because of opposition in his parish. He secured a permanent evangelical presence in Bradford.

BIBLIOGRAPHY
DNB
W. Morgan, *The Parish Priest* (London, 1841)
W. W. Stamp, *Memoir of Rev. John Crosse* (London, 1844)

H. D. RACK

Crossley, Sir Francis (b. Halifax, Yorkshire, England, 26 Oct. 1817; d. Halifax, Yorkshire, England, 5 Jan. 1872). Congregational carpet manufacturer, philanthropist, and MP. Even as a schoolboy his father made his pocket money dependent on work undertaken, setting up a special loom for his use in the factory. Thus he early learnt to participate in his father's business, which at his death already ranked fourth largest in the country. Through the successful exploitation of tapestry carpeting and the early application of steam power, with his brothers, he developed the company to become one of the largest carpet enterprises in the world, employing over 5,000. In the 1860s he instituted an early share-purchase scheme, offering loans to his employees for them to purchase an interest in the company in which they worked.

Elected Liberal MP for Halifax in 1852 (until 1859), he subsequently sat for the county until his death, speaking in the house in favour of Nonconformist and temperance concerns. His first major gift to Halifax, of which he was mayor in 1849 and 1850, was in 1855 when he endowed 21 almshouses complete with six shillings a week pension, which was followed in 1857 by the endowed gift of a People's Park, laid out by Paxton. This part repaid a vow undertaken by his mother that if God prospered the Crossley enterprise, they would share their prosperity with the poor but also implemented his belief, as a teetotaller, that the working classes be provided with alternative recreational facilities to the public house. Among other local charities, with his brothers, he built and endowed an orphanage on Skircoat Moor. His family, once called the Medici of Halifax, were largely responsible for the building of the magnificent Square Congregational Church (1855–7) of which Enoch Mellor was minister. Known donations include £20,000 to the LMS and £10,000 each to funds for the support of retired Congregational ministers and of ministers' widows. In recognition of his philanthropy he was created a baronet in 1863.

BIBLIOGRAPHY
D. J. Jeremy, ed., *Dictionary of Business Biography*, 5 vols, 1 (London, 1984–6)
DNB
R. Bretton, 'The Crossleys of Dean Clough', *Trans. of the Halifax Antiquarian Society*, 3 (Halifax, England, 1950–2)

J. H. Y. BRIGGS

Croswell, Andrew (b. Charlestown, MA, BNA, 30 Jan. 1709; d. Boston, MA, USA, 12 April 1785). New England Congregational minister. A graduate of Harvard College (BA 1728; MA 1731), he was ordained to serve the Second Church of Groton, Connecticut, in October, 1736. His first step into public attention occurred with his publication in 1741 of a defence of GEORGE WHITE-FIELD and the Great Awakening, after Whitefield's first preaching tour of New England. At almost the same time, he also published a defence of JAMES DAVENPORT, the most radical 'New Light' imitator of Whitefield, and in February 1742, Croswell joined Davenport as an itinerant evangelist in Connecticut and Massachusetts. In May 1743, he resumed his parish ministry in Groton, and in addition to occasional itineration, turned to publishing controversial tracts lauding Davenport and attacking unsympathetic 'Old Light' Congregationalists. He eventually tempered his praise for the confrontational tactics of the itinerant evangelists, but in his more than twenty published works, he continued to attack 'Old Light' ecclesiology.

He warmly advocated immediatism in conversion, and in his sensational *What Is Christ To Me If He Is Not Mine?* (1746) pushed over into a virtually antinomian understanding of justification. In August 1746, he asked for a dismissal from his Groton parish (which they were reluctant to grant) and the following October assumed the leadership of the Eleventh Church in Boston, a Separate Congregationalist church. The occupation of Boston during the American Revolution scattered many of Croswell's followers, and the church dissolved after his death.

BIBLIOGRAPHY
C. C. Goen, *Revivalism and Separatism in New England, 1740–1800* (New Haven, CT, 1962)
L. E. Schmidt, '"A Second and More Glorious Reformation": The New Light Extremism of Andrew Croswell' in *William and Mary Quarterly*, 43 (April 1986): 214–44

C. K. Shipton, ed., *Sibley's Harvard Graduates*, 8 (Boston, MA, 1951)

ALLEN C. GUELZO

Crouch, Isaac (b. Bradford-on-Avon, Wiltshire, England, 25 April 1756; d. Narborough rectory, Leicestershire, England, 30 Oct. 1835). Oxford tutor and Anglican clergyman. Son of Isaac, 'plebeius', and Elizabeth Crouch (ordination papers, Worcester). Bishop DANIEL WILSON and E. SIDNEY (*Life of Rowland Hill*, 1833), perhaps relying on W. Jay, *Memoirs of Cornelius Winter* (1808), were apparently incorrect in stating that Isaac Jr was educated by EDWARD SPENCER, since: a) Spencer certified in April 1780 that he had personally known Crouch for (only) 18 months (ordination papers, Salisbury); b) Spencer's school did not open until 1783 or later. But Isaac is said to have become a Christian early in life, possibly due to that revival recorded at Bradford-on-Avon, under Edward Spencer, during his boyhood. He went up to St Edmund Hall, Oxford in 1774, was made a scholar, was actively identified with such Oxford contemporaries as NATHANIEL BRIDGES and THOMAS CHARLES, and took his bachelor's degree in 1777.

Ordained deacon in 1778 at Oxford (letters dimissory, Worcester; ordination papers, Oxford), he became curate of St Martin's, Worcester, to Prebendary JAMES STILL-INGFLEET, 1778–9. He served as Curate of Winkfield, Wiltshire, to E. Spencer 1779–81 (parish registers), being ordained priest in 1780 at Oxford (letters dimissory, Salisbury). Perhaps for health reasons, he moved to be Curate of Billericay, Essex, to P. D'Aranda, Rector of Great Burstead from 1781/3. [A curate of similar name (Crowch) at Fisherton Delamere, Wiltshire, 1781, was almost certainly J(ohn) Crouch, an older man.] In any case, Crouch derived from Stillingfleet and Spencer virtually continuous personal traditions of evangelical work at Oxford from 1747/8.

Crouch was appointed (by Principal Dixon, who was already inclined to countenance evangelicals), vice-principal and bursar of St Edmund Hall 1783 [battel book; not 1778, as CO (Wilson) and Hole]. From 1783 to 1797 he served also as curate to Dr J. W. Peers (another evangelical), at Chiselhampton and Stadhampton, Oxfordshire, as chaplain of Merton College 1796–1817, and as a city lecturer, St Martin's, Carfax, Oxford, from 1805. In the university, several times a pro-proctor ('most firm, and yet most conciliatory'), he also acted as a substitute preacher of university sermons, when he was 'always listened to with great respect' (L. S. Sutherland and L. G. Mitchell, eds, *History of the University of Oxford*, 5, 1986). Poor health caused him to resign as sole tutor (in favour of DANIEL WILSON) in 1804, and in 1807, as soon as Wilson could succeed, as vice-principal also.

A founder of the Bristol Clerical Education Society in 1795 (*EM*, 1796), in 1799 he was a founder of the CMS and an original country committee member, as well as a member of the EcS. In 1814, with some hesitation on health grounds, Crouch became Rector of Narborough, Leicestershire, remaining, however, partly resident in Oxford till 1820. Though liable to be incapacitated during his last 25 years by 'depression of spirits', and in 1832 suffering a second stroke, he survived, assisted by curates, to hold the incumbency for 21 years, bequeathing property and money for parish schools at Narborough.

Crouch was instrumental in establishing a lasting evangelical tradition (1783–1854) in one of the larger academical halls at Oxford, succeeding principals being content to leave all teaching and administration in the vice-principal's hands. Diligent and unassuming, he prepared the way for wider toleration and acceptance of the evangelical school in the university as a whole, his influence comparable, though different, to that of CHARLES SIMEON at Cambridge. Dr Kelly considers him more influential as regards the hall than either Wilson or Hill. Young men of evangelical persuasion were attracted to it, and Crouch gave them, as in a large family, a thorough grounding in scriptural and secular learning. He had a good library, and was widely read, especially in church history. (His lectures were delivered from carefully prepared manuscript.) Men afterwards well known, such as D. WILSON, senior, W. MARSH, J. PRATT, and J. HILL (1806–7) were taught and encouraged by him, Wilson (1807–12) and Hill (1812–51) succeeding him as vice-principal.

His obituary by Wilson (CO) speaks of Crouch's 'Wisdom, quietness, sweetness of natural temper', while, though small in physical stature, a 'firm disciplinarian', who himself seldom worked less than 12 hours a day during term, starting at 5 a.m., anxious to promote the spiritual and intellectual interests of his pupils at all times. The latter were entertained once a term to meals at his house in Holywell, and young evangelical undergraduates of other societies likewise, who often arrived in Oxford with letters of introduction to him. On Sunday evenings he held family readings of theological authors with six or eight pupils. Together he and his wife 'constituted a bright pattern of domestic piety . . .' Having no children of their own, they ministered effectively to his young charges. Wilson wrote of Crouch's consistency, and continuing growth in grace, 'always the same, always the man of God, always the meek and affectionate friend, always the diligent steward of his Master's talents'. Dr Green takes a more detached view.

Crouch married (1) 1784 Jane [surname unknown] (1756–1828 GM); (2) c. 1830, Mary Anne Hancock, widow (1780–1866), who was buried in St Peter's churchyard, adjoining St Edmund Hall (tombstone destroyed c. 1970). His portrait is in St Edmund Hall.

BIBLIOGRAPHY
CO (1837)
V. H. H. Green, *Religion at Oxford and Cambridge* (London, 1964)
Information from Dr O. R. Barclay, Leicester, and Dr D. D. Aldridge
J. N. D. Kelly, *St Edmund Hall* (Oxford, 1989)

J. S. Reynolds, *Evangelicals at Oxford* (Oxford, 1953; Appleford, England, 1975)

J. S. REYNOLDS

Crowther, Jonathan (b. Northowram, near Halifax, Yorkshire, England, 1759; d. Warrington, England, 8 June 1824). Methodist preacher. Two of Crowther's brothers were Methodist preachers, Timothy (1757–1829) and Robert (1762–1833). In February 1779 he and Timothy were greatly impressed by the open-air evangelical preaching of Reverend BRIAN BURY COLLINS. Crowther was admitted into the Methodist Society at Bradford in September 1779, and was soon converted under the preaching of ALEXANDER MATHER.

Crowther was somewhat daunted by the arduous conditions during his first decade as an itinerant preacher, beginning in the Yorkshire Dales in 1784, and by its constant changes, sometimes (in emergencies) after a few weeks. He served for a few months in 1786 in the Isle of Man. Sent to Inverness in 1787, Crowther candidly wrote to JOHN WESLEY that the town 'was fit for no man unless his flesh were brass, his bones iron, and his heart more unfeeling than a stoic's'. Wesley's homily of 25 September 1787 was supplemented by financial aid which atoned for the stinginess of the Inverness stewards.

The difficult life of the itinerancy appears to have delayed his marriage (to Mary Jones) until 1795, when he was 36. Together they raised 11 children, their lot easing a little in the new century. From 1797 onwards they sometimes stayed two years in a circuit.

Crowther had managed to accumulate some theological knowledge as well as experience of Methodist discipline, especially the solution of financial problems. He was involved in the many controversies between trustees and preachers about church order and the administration of the sacraments which followed Wesley's death, especially in Bristol. From 1794 onwards, indeed, he managed to write a handful of funeral sermons, and some pamphlets on Methodist politics and controversies, and then began to try his pen on larger works, such as *The Scripture Gazetteer* (1810).

In 1810 came a more important work: *The Methodist Manual*, which was a useful handbook, but it was almost immediately enlarged as a political weapon aimed at Lord Sidmouth's 1811 bill designed to undermine Methodist preaching, which raised such an outcry that it was thrown out by the Lords. This 356-page volume added 'the lives and characters of divers of their ministers' and 'a defence of Methodism, containing remarks on toleration, etc.' The second edition changed the title to *A True and Complete Portraiture of Methodism* (1811). This undoubtedly made Crowther's name. It was reprinted in New York in 1813, and by Crowther himself in London in a second edition 'enlarged and improved', with 512 pages, and what became its 'standard' title, *A Portraiture of Methodism* (1815), reprinted on both sides of the Atlantic. The *Portraiture* was matched the very same year by the first full-scale biography of THOMAS

COKE. The authorship of these works undoubtedly contributed to Crowther's election as president of the Wesleyan Methodist Conference in 1819, which carried with it the task of presiding over the Irish Conference in 1820. Sadly his latter years were marked by a paralytic ailment. After his death, his remains were taken for burial in the Chapel-yard at Halifax. His widow Molly died after 45 years of widowhood, still a charming and vivacious class leader in her nineties.

Extracts from Luke Tyerman's biography of Crowther and Crowther's own autobiography, together with notes on the Crowther family, are in the Baker Collection at Duke University, Durham, North Carolina.

SELECT WRITINGS
J. Crowther, *The Methodist Manual* (London, 1810)
—, *The Life of the Rev. Thomas Coke* (Leeds, England, 1815)

FRANK BAKER

Crowther, Samuel (b. New Boswell Court, London [not Yorks., as Hole: cp. ordination papers], 9 Jan. 1769; d. London, 29 Sept. 1829). Anglican clergyman. Son of Richard Crowther, surgeon, and Sarah (daughter of Samuel Richardson, novelist, *DNB*), Samuel was educated first at Croydon free school, becoming scholar of Winchester College. At Brasenose College, Oxford, he was supported by the Elland Society, 1787. While scholar and fellow (1788–1804) of New College, he set out for New South Wales, sponsored by WILLIAM WILBERFORCE, probably to assist RICHARD JOHNSON, but was shipwrecked (1789–90). Ordained at Oxford in 1792, he became curate of East Bergholt, Suffolk; then curate (1795) of Bocking, Essex. From 1800 till death he was Vicar of Christ Church, Newgate, with St Leonard's, Foster Lane, London, and from 1801 alternate Sunday lecturer at St Botolph's, Bishopsgate. He attended the Eclectic Society meetings 1801–14, and was president of Sion College in 1819.

The *Christian Observer* says that Crowther gradually adopted evangelical views after ordination, which is not consistent with some facts above. Certainly he became an excellent preacher, firmly upholding evangelical truth, while personally humble and loving. A diligent pastor, he evangelized from house to house. Nevertheless for most of his incumbency he was a sick man, latterly affected by a stroke. A monument spoke of his 'suavity of manners, and sanctity of life'. He was one of an increasing number of evangelical incumbents in the city of London during the earlier years of the nineteenth century.

Crowther married (1804) a daughter of Reverend Dr H. Ware of Dublin. One of his daughters married his able curate (from 1825) WILLIAM GOODE, Dean of Ripon 1860–8. S. A. CROWTHER, African bishop, was named after him. His portrait is in New College, Oxford; a portrait and bust in Christ Church, Newgate, were destroyed during the Second World War.

BIBLIOGRAPHY
CO (1829) obituary
E. H. Pearce, *Sion College* (Cambridge, 1913)
J. H. Pratt, ed., *Eclectic Notes 1798–1814*, 2nd edn (London, 1865)
J. S. Reynolds, *Evangelicals at Oxford* (Oxford, 1953; Appleford, England, 1975)
W. Thornbury, *Old and New London*, 2 (London, 1881)
R. Wilberforce and I. Wilberforce, *Life of Wilberforce*, 1 (London, 1838)
D. Wilson, funeral *Sermon* (London, 1829)

J. S. REYNOLDS

Crowther, Samuel Ajayi (b. Osogun [modern Nigeria], c. 1806; d. Lagos, 31 Dec. 1891). Missionary bishop and linguist. Kidnapped as a boy in 1822 during the wars in the Yoruba country, he was sold on board a Brazilian slave-ship which was then captured by a British naval ship. Liberated in Freetown, he was sent to one of the nearby villages, learnt to read the New Testament in six months, and was taken on a brief visit to England, as a servant, by THOMAS DAVEY, a CMS missionary. He was one of the first students at the CMS Christian Institution (later Fourah Bay College), leaving to marry another Yoruba recaptive, Susan Asano Thompson. Both worked as teachers. He continued his studies, learnt Greek, and helped missionaries with their linguistic research.

He was chosen to accompany J. F. SCHÖN on the ill-fated Niger Expedition of 1841 to study the languages of the Niger peoples. The intellectual ability, sound judgment and tactful ease in his relations with others which he displayed on the expedition, and in his journal (published with Schön's) impressed the CMS authorities. He was brought to London for further study, and ordained in 1843.

The high European mortality on the 1841 expedition impressed on the CMS secretary, HENRY VENN, that Christianity could only be disseminated through West Africa by native agency. Crowther was sent with an English missionary, HENRY TOWNSEND, to start a mission to his own Yoruba people. In 1846 they established themselves in Abeokuta where, as if echoing the story of Joseph and his brethren, he found his mother and sisters. Yoruba-speaking teachers and catechists were recruited in Sierra Leone. Crowther put teaching before preaching, his aim being to train educated African Christians. He also continued his linguistic studies, publishing Yoruba Bible translations, and a Yoruba grammar and dictionary.

He went on the Niger Expeditions of 1854 and 1857, accompanied in 1857 by JOHN C. TAYLOR, of Igbo origin, to start a mission to the Igbo. These two successful expeditions opened up the Niger to trade. Christian African traders from Sierra Leone moved up the river, settling round the mission stations. In 1864 Crowther was consecrated bishop of those parts of Western Africa not under British rule (in practice, the Niger area). Based ostensibly on Lagos, he was a peripatetic bishop, moving constantly round his diocese, establishing friendly relations with African rulers, and extending his mission – most spectacularly into the Niger Delta region where thousands became Christians. He also acted as a virtual British consul, corresponding with the Foreign Office in London.

In 1873 Venn died and the CMS came under the influence of young missionaries imbued with the racial views that were becoming increasingly prevalent in the British Empire. Their contempt for native agency was shared by the white traders in the Niger country who publicized the shortcomings of the mission agents over whom the kindly old bishop with his far-flung diocese had little control. The CMS constituted a finance committee with a white majority to supervise the mission. At a meeting in 1890 they rounded on Crowther, denouncing his agents, and insulting him to his face, forcing him to resign from the committee.

The news of this public humiliation enraged African Christians. In the Niger Delta it was proposed the churches break away and form a pastorate of their own. Crowther agreed to take charge. But in July 1891 he suffered a stroke and in the last hour of the year died. The Delta Pastorate then seceded under his son Archdeacon Dandeson Crowther, and the rest of the Anglican Church passed under white control.

BIBLIOGRAPHY
J. F. A. Ajayi, *Christian Missions in Nigeria, 1841–91* (London, 1965)
E. A. Ayandele, *The Missionary Impact on Modern Nigeria* (London, 1966)
P. D. Curtin, *Africa Remembered* (Madison, WI, 1968): 289–315
J. F. Schön and S. Crowther, *Journal of an Expedition up the Niger in 1841* (London, 1843)

CHRISTOPHER FYFE

Crummell, Alexander (b. New York, 1819; d. Point Pleasant, NJ, USA, 10 Sept. 1898). African-American Episcopal clergyman and scholar. Born free, he was ordained into the Protestant Episcopal Church in 1844. He visited Britain, preaching in the antislavery cause, and then studied at Queens' College, Cambridge. Originally an opponent of colonization, he changed his views and emigrated to Liberia with his family in 1853, as pastor of a church in Monrovia. He moved to the Protestant Episcopal mission at Cape Palmas, but ministered chiefly to the settler population. When Liberia College was founded he was appointed a professor, but quarrelled with the trustees who dismissed him after three years. He moved into the countryside, farming, and organizing churches for impoverished rural Americo-Liberian communities. In 1872 he was caught up in the political disturbances surrounding the death of President Roye and returned to the United States. From 1874 to 1894 he had a parish in Washington, DC. His *The Future of Africa*, published 1862, has been taken as one of the early documents of Pan-Africanism.

BIBLIOGRAPHY
W. J. Moses, *Alexander Crummell* (Oxford, 1989)

CHRISTOPHER FYFE

Cubitt, George (b. Norwich, Norfolk, England, 1791; d. 13 Oct. 1850). Methodist minister and author. Moving to Sheffield, Carver Street Chapel, in his boyhood, he joined the Methodist Society in 1808, and soon showed his abilities by introducing a system of tract distribution by loan. He became an itinerant in 1813 and was soon sent to Newfoundland where he spent a very successful three years. Returning to England in 1819, he was stationed in several important circuits; his reverence for the Word of God, his ability as an expositor of the Scriptures, and his wide knowledge, were combined with an awareness of the relation between reason and revelation, and of the contentiousness of much contemporary speculation.

These gifts naturally led him to constant authorship; he published various volumes of sermons, theology, etc., a series of biographies of explorers such as Columbus and Cortes, and a defence of the conference in the WARREN controversy. His appointment as connexional editor in 1842 (assistant from 1836) was a natural consequence, though those duties and an ineptitude for everyday business tended to make him into a recluse. He died of a stroke.

BIBLIOGRAPHY
EWM
Minutes (1851): 12–15
G. Osborn, *Outlines of Wesleyan Bibliography* (London, 1869)

OLIVER A. BECKERLEGGE

Cudworth, William (b. London, 1717 or 1718; d. Brentwood, Staffordshire, England, 10 June 1763). Methodist antinomian preacher. Cudworth was an English Presbyterian, converted at the age of twenty, who was drawn among the Calvinist Methodists through contact with JOHN CENNICK in 1743, becoming a teacher at The Tabernacle school, preacher in a chapel in Spitalfields, and a regular preacher at The Tabernacle. By October 1744 there were disputes about his antinomian theology, which was discussed at the English Calvinist Methodist Association meeting in March 1745, to which he replied in pamphlet form. Later that year he published a pamphlet in which he advocated a congregationalist form of church government, and after deep disputes about these issues left the association.

His church continued in Leicester Fields and later in Margaret Street, and he attracted a number of preachers, including William Collins, STEPHEN DIXON and WILLIAM KENDRICK. Cudworth was essentially a controversialist, and engaged in pamphlet warfare with ANNE DUTTON, JAMES RELLY, ROBERT SANDEMAN, and JOHN WESLEY (who wrote two *Dialogues between an Antinomian and a Friend* refuting him). He planned an evangelical library, an abridgement of the Scottish reformed and puritan writers who inspired him. In the 1750s his influence troubled the divided society at Norwich and its renegade Wesleyan preacher James Wheatley. About 1755 he became friendly with JAMES HERVEY, and encouraged him to criticize Wesley in *Thereon and Aspasio*. After Hervey's death he issued letters Hervey wrote to him, highlighting their attack on Wesley.

Cudworth was a 'speculative antinomian', who insisted that justification could not be 'earned' by repentance or righteous action, and that the experience of assurance was a spiritual revelation not based upon changed behaviour. These views were promoted in a blunt and unvarnished style which distressed other evangelicals. HOWEL HARRIS, his most charitable critic, declared: 'I believe Bro' Cudworth's spirit ye most still and selfish and incorrigible yet I believe his Light was originally from the Holy Spirit, and his own wisdom stop'd in secretly' (Harris to Thomas Adams, 5 November 1745, Trevecka Manuscripts Letter 1367). After Cudworth's death his small connexion fell apart, although a chapel in Margaret Street, Westminster survived to the end of the eighteenth century.

SELECT WRITINGS
W. Cudworth, *A Short Account of the Dealings of God, in the Experience of William Cudworth* (London, 1754)
—, *A Second Part of the Experience of William Cudworth, Being an Account of his Trials and Sufferings After He Had Received Jesus Christ* (London, 1754)

BIBLIOGRAPHY
J. C. Whitebrook, *William Cudworth and His Connexion* (London, 1818)

PETER L. LINEHAM

Cuffe, Paul (b. Cuttyhunk, MA, BNA, 17 Jan. 1759; d. Westport, MA, 27 Aug. 1817). African-American trader and shipowner. The son of a freed slave and a Native American mother, he started trading in a small boat, then built up a substantial maritime trade. He joined a Quaker meeting and became concerned to bring Christianity to Africa. In 1810 he sailed in his own ship, with an all-black crew, to Sierra Leone to organize African-American settlement, going on to London to get support from WILLIAM ALLEN, a Quaker businessman. On his voyage back to Sierra Leone he took the first party of Wesleyan Missionary Society missionaries. He returned to the US hoping to come back regularly, but his plans were delayed by war. In 1816 he returned to Sierra Leone with settlers and went back with African produce. But he died the following year and his enterprise died with him.

BIBLIOGRAPHY
C. Fyfe, *A History of Sierra Leone* (London, 1962)
L. D. Thomas, *Rise to be a People* (Chicago, IL, 1986)

CHRISTOPHER FYFE

Cullen, George Downie (b. Doune, near Stirling, Scotland, Oct. 1799; d. 1 Oct. 1891). Scottish Congregational minister. Educated at Glasgow (MA 1820) he served from 1822 as Congregational minister at Leith, for almost seventy years. He was a co-founder of the Edinburgh Medical Missionary Society (1841), and in 1860 was secretary of the Liverpool Conference on missions. His National Bible Society, founded in 1860, was immediately absorbed into the Edinburgh Bible Society (EBS) and in the same year he was made chairman of the EBS; he was its vice-president from 1876. Cullen was also a member of the Scottish Reformation Society and of the EA. He was chairman of the Scottish Congregational Union in 1875.

BIBLIOGRAPHY
Boase
Oliver and Boyd, *Edinburgh Almanac* (1853)

JONATHAN BURKE CUTMORE

Cumming, Alexander (b. Freehold, NJ, BNA, *c.* 1726; d. Boston, MA, BNA, 25 Aug. 1763). Presbyterian minister. Cumming, the son of a Scottish merchant, studied under WILLIAM TENNENT and Cumming's uncle, SAMUEL BLAIR, and earned two degrees at Harvard (BA 1747, MA 1761). Licensed by the presbytery of New Brunswick (*c.* 1747), he was called to the Presbyterian church in New York City in 1750. After a controversy over psalm-singing set the parish's Scots-Irish and New England-English factions against each other, and because of poor health, he asked for dismissal in October, 1753. He became co-pastor with JOSEPH SEWALL at Boston's Old South Church on 25 February 1761, but died two and a half years later at age 37. He published a pamphlet in 1763 that attacked the 'New Light' comment of ANDREW CROSWELL that a damning God was not the object of love.

BIBLIOGRAPHY
AAP, I: 462–4
SGH, XII: 120–5

CHRISTOPHER GRASSO

Cummins, James John (b. Cork, Ireland, 5 May 1795; d. Buckland, Surrey, England, 23 Nov. 1867). Banker and hymn-writer. The son of a merchant, Cummins moved to London in 1834 and served as a director of the Union Bank of Australia. An early supporter of the interdenominational LCM (founded 1835), he was also a founding member of the Anglican 'Scripture Readers' Society' (1844). Cummins was a key figure in the Christian Influence Society, a lobby group which included leading Anglican evangelicals like R. B. SEELEY and LORD ASHLEY (Lewis, 1986: 151–64). He was known as well for his premillennialism, Sabbatarianism and staunch anti-Catholicism.

Cummins' enduring legacy, however, is his hymns.

His *Seals of the Covenant Opened in the Sacraments* (1839) included several hymns and poems and was originally prepared for his children to use in preparation for confirmation. The work was expanded and republished in 1849 as *Lyra Evangelica*. His best known hymns are 'Jesus, Lord of life and glory' and 'Shall hymns of grateful love'.

BIBLIOGRAPHY
D. M. Lewis, *Lighten Their Darkness* (Westport, CT, 1986)
Julian
Record (22 March 1847)

DONALD M. LEWIS

Cunningham, Francis (b. Paddington, London, 1785; d. Lowestoft, Suffolk, England, 8 Aug. 1863). Anglican clergyman. The brother of J. W. CUNNINGHAM, in 1816 he married Richenda Gurney, a sister of ELIZABETH FRY. He was tutored by HENRY JOWETT at Little Dunham, Norfolk, and went up to Queens' College, Cambridge (BA 1812; MA 1815) where he was active in the CMS auxiliary.

Ordained priest (1813) he was, successively, curate to his brother at Harrow, rector of Pakefield, Suffolk (1814–30), and Vicar of Lowestoft, Suffolk (1830–62). At Lowestoft he held weekly prayer meetings, encouraged family and sacramental devotions, and organized charity and Sunday schools. Under his guidance, in 1832 a new chapel was built with 1,215 sittings (900 of them free).

With a few other devoted CMS men he established the Suffolk Church Missionary Union. In the 1830s he twice spoke at annual LSPCJ meetings. He was also an advocate of female education, and in 1820 visited the Protestant Vaudois in Piedmont (*Christian Observer* [December 1826]: 768).

BIBLIOGRAPHY
Al. Cant.
E. Stock, *Church Missionary Society* (London, 1899): I, 141, 233, 274; III, 63
A. Suckling, *History . . . of Suffolk*, 2 vols (London, 1846): II, 73, 89–93, 112

JONATHAN BURKE CUTMORE

Cunningham, Sir Henry Stewart (b. Harrow-on-the-Hill, Middlesex, England, *c.* 1833; d. 1920). Lawyer and novelist. The third son of JOHN 'Velvet' CUNNINGHAM of Harrow, Cunningham was educated at Harrow and Trinity College, Oxford and was admitted to the Inner Temple in April, 1855. Like another impecunious lawyer Cunningham took to supplementing his income by literary work. His first attempts as journalist and novelist drew upon his family heritage, taking the form of an article on Irish Church establishment in *Fraser's Magazine* (1864) and a novel *Wheat and Tares* (1861) in which he presented a clerical household commonly

recognized to be closely based upon that of his paternal uncle, FRANCIS CUNNINGHAM, Vicar of Lowestoft (1830–62) and married to the former Richenda Gurney. The novel-writing continued despite Cunningham's decision in the early 1870s to pursue his legal career in India. *Wheat and Tares* provides a revealing, if satirical, account of the hold evangelicalism could attain in fashionable watering-places, especially in the hands of a powerful and well-connected woman.

BIBLIOGRAPHY
Al. Ox.
J. Foster, *Men at the Bar* (London, 1885)
E. Stock, *My Recollections* (London, 1909): 59–62
WWW

ELISABETH JAY

Cunningham, John William (b. London, 3 Jan. 1780; d. Harrow, Middlesex, England, 30 Sept. 1861). Anglican clergyman, Vicar of Harrow. The son of a hatter and hosier, Cunningham studied under HENRY JOWETT, at Little Dunham. Admitted to St John's College, Cambridge, in 1798, he was 5th wrangler in 1802, and became an MA and fellow in 1805. Ordained deacon in May and priest in December 1803 to the curacies of Send and Ripley in Surrey, he was soon given sole charge of nearby Ockham. He served as curate to JOHN VENN at Clapham between 1809 and 1811, and held the living of Harrow from 1811 until his death.

Cunningham regarded his Harrow pulpit as 'stormy': the public school boys were disruptive and masters openly hostile; the Vicar disagreed with Dr Wordsworth, headmaster between 1836 and 1844; he antagonized Lord Byron, although he named a daughter after him, and was outrageously caricatured by a parishioner, Mrs Trollope (mother of Anthony, the novelist) in her novel *The Vicar of Wrexhill* (London, 1837). At times anxious for preferment to an easier, more remunerative cure, Cunningham, an urbane but zealous man, achieved much. An influential governor of the public school, he founded National and Sunday schools, raised money for one of two new churches built in the parish, and by 1851 could attract a congregation of 1,500. The poor flocked to his first wife's funeral; shops were shut and the parish presented a memorial lychgate when he died.

Unwilling though he was to be absent from his pulpit, Cunningham's influence extended far beyond Harrow. A committee member and speaker for several societies, he was life governor of the CMS and the BFBS and travelled for both. He was the CMS's most frequent anniversary speaker and in 1822 was invited to be BFBS secretary, a post he declined. Correspondence is preserved in both societies' archives. He wrote for periodicals and edited the *Christian Observer* from 1850 to 1858. His own publications were varied: sermons, collections of psalms and hymns, religious controversy, works on missions, friendly societies and politics. Possessing a vivid imagination, he wrote poetry and three religious novels of considerable originality. In the most famous, a *Velvet*

Cushion describes its checkered experiences in pulpits of different denominations: to the annoyance of Dissenters, Cunningham, a staunch churchman, upheld Anglicanism as the ecclesiastical ideal.

Cunningham married first (30 July 1805) Sophia (died 1821), daughter of Robert Williams of Moor Park, Hertfordshire, future MP for Dorchester, and secondly (24 July 1827) Mary Calvert, sister of Sir HARRY VERNEY. One of his 15 children became Lieutenant-Governor of St Kitts and Anguilla, another Secretary of King's College, London, and a third a Bengalee High Court Judge. A daughter married Sir James Fitzjames Stephen. His diaries are lodged in the Dorset County Record Office, and other papers can be found in the Hertfordshire Record Office, the Greater London Record Office, Lambeth Palace Library, and at Sandon Hall, Stafford. Letters among the Peel and Aberdeen papers in the British Library show that he had contact with the eminent. Criticized in *The Times* and other papers for supporting the government in the Queen Caroline affair, he was depicted by cartoonists as a time-server, 'the Cunning Man of Harrow', who hated Roman Catholicism yet supported Catholic emancipation. (This stance was not uncommon at the time.) Sufficiently prominent to attract dislike and opposition, Cunningham received the praise and affection of many.

SELECT WRITINGS
J. W. Cunningham, *A World without Souls* (London, 1805)
—, *The Velvet Cushion*, 2nd edn (London, 1814)
—, *De Rancé, a poem* (London, 1815)
—, *Sancho, or the Proverbialist* (London, 1816)
—, *Cautions to Continental Travellers* (London, 1818)
—, *On the Practical Tendency of Popery* (London, 1828)

BIBLIOGAPHY
Al. Cant.
Boase
Byron, *Letters and Journals*, ed. R. E. Prothero (London, 1898) 6: 29–72; ed. L. A. Marchand (London, 1973–82) 3: 189–90; 10: 65
CO, 61 (1861): 878–85
DNB
M. D. George, *Catalogue of Prints and Drawings in the British Museum Political and Personal Satires*, 10 (London, 1952), no 15392
M. M. Hennell, *John Venn and the Clapham Sect* (London, 1958): 131–3
J. W., *Harrow on the Hill* (London, 1821)
E. Jay, *The Religion of the Heart* (Oxford, 1979): 13–5, 204
Julian
T. F. May, 'A Study of Harrow School in its Relationship to its Neighbourhood' (London Univ. M. Phil. thesis, 1969)
POBC
D. M. Rosman, *Evangelicals and Culture* (London, 1984): 81–4, 148, 200
The Times (18 September 1820, 4 October 1861)
A. L. Wyatt, 'Cunningham of Harrow' (typescript *c.* 1956, Lambeth Palace Library, MS 2238)

DOREEN M. ROSMAN

Cunningham, William (b. Hamilton, Lanarkshire, Scotland, 1805; d. Edinburgh, 14 Dec. 1861). Outstanding theologian of the FCS. Cunningham commenced attendance at Edinburgh University in 1820, and was converted under the preaching of ROBERT GORDON in 1823. Entering the Church of Scotland ministry, he became assistant minister in the Middle Parish, Greenock, in 1830, and minister of Trinity College Church, Edinburgh, in 1834. He played a prominent role in the events leading to the founding of the FCS in 1843, and became its first professor of theology in 1844. In 1845 he was transferred to the church history chair. He became principal of the college in 1847, and was moderator of the Free Church general assembly in 1859.

Cunningham wrote little for publication during his lifetime, but several volumes were published posthumously: *Historical Theology* (Edinburgh, 1862), *The Reformers and the Theology of the Reformation* (Edinburgh, 1862), *Theological Lectures* (Edinburgh, 1878) and *Discussions on Church Principles* (Edinburgh, 1863). A magisterial exposition of the plenary verbal inspiration of scripture is to be found in the *Theological Lectures*, which also offers perceptive treatments of the principles of textual criticism and hermeneutics. His most important work, however, was his *Historical Theology*, which despite the title is virtually a systematic theology.

Cunningham was fundamentally loyal to the scholastic Calvinism of the seventeenth century, and presented it anew for his own generation. His knowledge both of the history of Christian thought and the specific corpus of classical Reformed theology was immense. Cunningham evinced a particular determination to root theology in Biblical exegesis and never to confuse it with philosophical constructs. A notable instance was his repudiation of the attempt to forge an organic link between philosophical determinism and the Reformed doctrines of the divine and human will. He also insisted on the need to see the various Christian doctrines in a graded perspective of significance. While Arminianism, he argued, was an error, it was a mild error in comparison with Roman Catholic theology, and even Romanism palled before the ultimate heresies of Socianianism, rejecting as it did Christ's divinity and substitutionary atonement. His cumbersome literary style has probably prevented the recognition Cunningham merits as Scotland's greatest Reformed theologian of the nineteenth century.

BIBLIOGRAPHY
DNB
N. R. Needham, *The Doctrine of Holy Scripture in the Free Church* (Edinburgh, 1991)
R. Rainy and J. Mackenzie, *Life of William Cunningham* (London 1871)

N. R. NEEDHAM

Currie, John (d. 22 September 1765). Minister of Kinglassie, Scotland (1705–65), opponent of the Secession from the Church of Scotland in 1733, participant in the Cambuslang revival of 1742. He supported RALPH and EBENEZER ERSKINE's efforts against patronage but wrote several works opposing the Secession. He assisted GEORGE WHITEFIELD and WILLIAM MCCULLOCH at the Communion of August 1742 during the Cambuslang revival in defence of which he wrote his *New Testimony and Vindication* (1743).

BIBLIOGRAPHY
Fasti, 5
A. Fawcett, *The Cambuslang Revival* (London, 1971)

JOHN R. MCINTOSH

Cust, Robert Needham (b. Cockayne-Hatley, Bedfordshire, England, 24 Feb. 1821; d. London, 28 Oct. 1909). Member of the Indian Civil Service, rugged Victorian individualist, missiologist, and Christian 'freethinker'. Intellectually, Cust outshone many at Eton and Haileybury, the East India Company College north of London. As a member of the Brownlow-Cust family, he was appointed to the Punjab by Lord Ellenborough in 1843. He served with distinction as district collector, held commissionerships in the Punjab (1858), and for a brief time advised Viceroy JOHN LAWRENCE (1864). His career as an administrator was cut short in 1868 by tragic family circumstances and health considerations.

He began his long writing career in India, making his mark in the pages of the *Calcutta Review*. All told, he published over 1,000 articles, many of review length. Many reviews, missionary policy suggestions, criticisms and provocations, often directed at his own CMS Board, were republished in volume form, most notably eight volumes of *Linguistic and Oriental Essays* (1880–1904), and *Notes on Missionary Subjects* (1889–1896). He also published two volumes of poems (1887, 1897).

Robert first realized the meaning of evangelical faith while serving as Collector of Banda (1852–5) under JAMES THOMASON and JOHN R. COLVIN (Penner, 1987: 173–7). Though always critical, he had a further conversion experience in the Punjab about 1863 (Penner, 1987: 290).

In retirement, following years of stimulating contributions to linguistic questions, he devoted himself to the CMS, at least until 1896. In that year he withdrew when his colleagues would not accept his suggestion that women should be added to the committee of the CMS.

SELECT WRITINGS
R. N. Cust, *R. N. Cust Journals (1842–1909)*, 17 vols, British Library, London, Add, manuscripts
—, *R. N. Cust Manuscript Letters (1828–1861)*, Royal Commonwealth Society Library, London
—, *Linguistic and Oriental Essays*, 7 series, 8 vols (1880–1904)

BIBLIOGRAPHY
P. Penner, *Robert Needham Cust, 1821–1909* (Lewiston, NY, 1987)
E. Stock, 'Dr Cust on Missions and Missionaries', *CM Intelligencer* (February 1895): 103–10

PETER PENNER

Custis, Mary Lee ['Molly'] [née **Fitzhugh**] (b. 22 April 1788, Stafford County, VA, USA; d. Arlington County, VA, USA, 23 April 1853). Liberian colonization advocate and Episcopal spiritual adviser. She was the daughter of William Fitzhugh of 'Chatham' and Ann Randolph. On 7 July 1804 she married George Washington Parke Custis, the adopted son of President George Washington. This couple lived at 'Arlington', a plantation across the Potomac River from Washington, DC, now the National Cemetery. ROBERT E. LEE, who later became General-in-Chief of the Confederate Army, wed her daughter Mary Anna Randolph Custis on 30 June 1831.

A member of Christ Episcopal Church, Alexandria, Virginia and one of the early evangelicals in her denomination, she gave spiritual advice to her cousin, WILLIAM MEADE. Fearing that he did not perceive his inability to save himself apart from divine grace, she persuaded him to study theology under Walter Dulaney Addison, an evangelical Episcopalian. Consequently Meade was converted and became chief architect of the evangelical revival in the diocese of Virginia. Meade referred to her as a 'mother' and 'monitor' in the faith to him. Recognizing her expertise in works of practical religion, Meade family members came to study books under supervision.

A strong advocate of the American Colonization Society like her husband, she housed Ralph Gurley, the society's secretary at 'Arlington', and corresponded with her cousin ANN RANDOLPH PAGE on slavery reform. Deeply religious, she believed her first duty towards slaves was to lead them to faith. She held morning and evening prayer services for their benefit. In order to prepare them for freedom, for which her husband's will provided, she taught them reading and writing and wherever possible a trade so they would be able to earn a living once emancipated.

BIBLIOGRAPHY
E. L. Templeman, *Arlington Heritage* (Alexandria, VA, 1959)
A. D. Thomas, Jr, *The Second Great Awakening in Virginia and Slavery Reform* (Richmond, VA, 1981)

ARTHUR DICKEN THOMAS, JR

Cuthbert, Edward (bapt. Bulphan, Essex, England, 15 Aug. 1746; d. Hatton Garden, London, 18 Dec. 1803). Anglican clergyman. Son of Joseph (Rector of Bulphan) and Elizabeth Cuthbert, Edward was educated at St Paul's School, London, and at St John's College, Cambridge, where he may have been influenced by ROWLAND HILL. Ordained in 1768, he became Curate of Worlingworth, Suffolk. He was rector of Stifford, Essex, 1772–84. From 1780 till death he assisted HENRY FOSTER, as a joint minister of Longacre Chapel, London, in 1799 succeeding his father as Rector of Bulphan and becoming a founder of the CMS. He remains somewhat unknown, though linked with evangelical leaders of his time. Cuthbert married, in 1800, Miss Clark of Norwich. A son by a previous wife is recorded.

BIBLIOGRAPHY
Al. Cant.
C. Hole, *Early History of CMS* (London, 1896)
A. C. H. Seymour, *Life of Selina Countess of Huntingdon,* 1 (London, 1844)

J. S. REYNOLDS

Cuthbert, George Goring (b. Ireland, *c.* 1812; d. Ireland, 22 Oct. 1861). CMS Mission administrator in India. A former schoolmaster educated at Trinity College, Dublin, Cuthbert abandoned prospects of preferment in a teaching career and travelled to Calcutta in 1845. He was sent to the CMS mission in Krishnagur to learn Bengali, and then, in 1847, he began working with the secretary of the CMS Corresponding Committee in Calcutta, a post he held until 1860. During this period he made frequent visits to Krishnagur, and accompanied Bishop DANIEL WILSON on his 1856 tour of North India. His correspondence with HENRY VENN (the CMS archives contain 613 of his letters) gives a complete picture of the development of the CMS fields during this crucial period of expansion and stabilisation. A cautious and shrewd administrator, he tried to improve service conditions and bring better recruits out from London. Cuthbert edited the *Calcutta Christian Intelligencer.* In 1861, after touring Ceylon and Travancore, he returned to Ireland. His wife, E. Cuppaige, died in Ireland 12 years later.

E. M. JACKSON

Cutler, Ann [Nanny] (b. Preston, Lancashire, England, *c.* 1759; d. Macclesfield, Cheshire, England, 29 Dec. 1794). Wesleyan Methodist prayer leader. Cutler was a very serious-minded and moral girl who was converted when the Wesleyan Methodists visited her area. In spite of opposition she started to pray in public and was in great demand to pray with people in trouble. Cutler began to travel further afield to join in prayer meetings for the revival of religion, her prayers were answered, and many were converted. Hers was a life of prayer, both private and public.

BIBLIOGRAPHY
W. Bramwell, *A Short Account of ... Ann Cutler* (Leeds, England, 1798)
Z. Taft, *Biographical Sketches of ... Holy Women ...,* 1 (London, 1825)

E. DOROTHY GRAHAM

Cutler, Benjamin Clarke (b. Roxbury, MA, USA, 6 Feb. 1798; d. Brooklyn, NY, USA. 10 Feb. 1863). Protestant Episcopal clergyman. The son of Benjamin and Sarah Cutler, both sides of his family were Anglican. The younger Cutler was confirmed by Bishop A. V. GRISWOLD at age 16. He enrolled at Brown University in 1818 and, upon graduating in 1822, married Harriet Bancroft.

Having firsthand experience of a religious revival in Providence while in college, Cutler entered the ministry, and was ordained presbyter by Bishop Griswold in 1825. Soon after, he accepted a call by the New York Protestant Episcopal City Mission, taking charge of a mission parish, the Church of the Holy Evangelists, in 1831. In 1833, he was chosen Rector of St Anne's church, Brooklyn where he served for the remainder of his life.

Cutler is best remembered for his long and fervent evangelical ministry at St Anne's. He has been characterized as a moderate evangelical who, though rarely partisan in spirit, was a strong critic of Tractarianism and a champion of the Thirty-Nine Articles.

BIBLIOGRAPHY
J. G. Wilson and J. Firke, eds, *Appleton's Cyclopedia of American Biography,* 6 vols (New York, 1888–9)
H. Gray, *Memoirs of the Reverend Benjamin C. Cutler, D.D.* (New York, 1865)

GILLIS HARP

Cutler, Manasseh (b. Killingly, Windham Co., CT, BNA, 13 May 1742; d. 28 July 1823). Congregational minister, botanist, physician, educator, legislator, and colonizer. Cutler was born of a farming family that descended from John Cutler, who migrated to Watertown, Massachusetts, in 1634. Educated at Yale College (AB 1765; AM 1768; LL D 1781), Cutler's only pastorate was the Congregational church in Ipswich Hamlet (now Hamilton), Massachusetts, where he was ordained and served from 1771 to 1823.

Of inquiring and organized mind, the Reverend Cutler pursued wide correspondence and belonged to the American Philosophical Society (1784), the Philadelphia Linnaean Society (1809), the American Antiquarian Society (1813), the New England Linnaean Society (1815) and was an honorary fellow of the Massachusetts Medical Society. In addition to astronomical observations, Cutler published one of the first systematic surveys of New England flora.

For decades Cutler operated a small preparatory boarding school in his household. He also practised medicine, being especially engaged in the treatment for small pox. A supporter of the American Revolution, he was a chaplain to several Massachusetts military units during the war with England.

A civic leader, Cutler served in the Massachusetts General Court (1800) and two terms in the US Congress (1801–4). After the Revolution he was one of five organizers and a lobbyist for the Ohio Company to plant settlements in the Ohio River Valley. An opponent of slavery, he influenced the passage of the slavery prohibiting Northwest Ordinance of 1787 by the Articles of Confederation Congress. In December, 1787, he sent off the first pioneers to settle Marietta, Ohio, and visited there in 1788.

Theologically he was consistently orthodox throughout his ministry and friendly to awakening impulses. He decried the rise of Unitarianism in New England. An eighteenth-century man who lived well into the nineteenth, he was courtly in manner, curious of mind and pious of spirit without being sanctimonious.

BIBLIOGRAPHY

W. P. and J. P. Cutler, *Life, Journals and Correspondence of Rev. Manasseh Cutler* (Cincinnati, OH, 1888)

N. S. Cutler, *A Cutler Memorial and General History* (Greenfield, MA, 1889)

DAB

F. B. Dexter, *Biographical Sketches of the Graduates of Yale College*, 6 vols (New York, 1885–1912)

J. G. Pulsifer, 'The Cutlers of Hamilton', *Essex Institute Historical Collections*, 107, 4 (October 1971): 335–408

THOMAS A. ASKEW

Cyr, Narcisse (b. Napierville, Lower Canada, 1823; d. Springfield, MA, USA, 18 March 1894). Baptist editor. Cyr converted from Catholicism about 1841. He became the first evangelically trained French Canadian (at l'Oratoire, Geneva), then joined the Grande Ligne mission. In Montreal he founded a French congregation and began the first French Protestant newspaper, the *Semeur Canadien* (1851–62). Cyr wrote the first French Protestant history and backed the anticlerical Institut Canadien. After pioneering French Baptist missions in New England (1869–73), he taught in Boston and published. His long-term Unitarian affiliation seems have been due to non-theological causes. Cyr died a Baptist.

BIBLIOGRAPHY

L'Aurore, Montreal, obituary

K. RICHARD LOUGHEED

Dabney, Robert Lewis (b. Louis Co., VA, USA, 5 March 1820; d. Victoria, TX, USA, 3 Jan. 1898). Presbyterian theologian and educator in Virginia and Texas. A descendent of eighteenth-century French Protestant immigrants, Dabney grew up one of eight children on a modest Virginia plantation. He attended Hampden-Sidney College from 1836 to 1837, and after teaching for a year, completed his college education at the University of Virginia, graduating in 1842. After studying at Richmond's Union Theological Seminary (1844–6), Dabney served as missionary and pastor in the Shenandoah Valley. In 1853 he joined the faculty of his seminary Alma Mater and for thirty years taught church history, polity and theology. Though offered a professorship at Princeton Seminary and the pastorate of New York's Fifth Avenue Presbyterian Church, he declined such invitations because of his ardent allegiance to the South. During the Civil War he was a major on the staff of General T. J. ('Stonewall') JACKSON and served as a chaplain in the Confederate army. Health considerations which demanded a warmer climate prompted Dabney in 1883 to move to the University of Texas where he became professor of philosophy. While in Texas Dabney worked to establish the Austin School of Theology. Though he spent the last four years of his life totally blind and increasingly infirm, he remained a vigorous and productive proponent of strict Calvinism and the Southern way of life.

Dabney resisted change in all aspects of life. In his *Systematic and Polemic Theology* (1871) Dabney propounded the Calvinistic theology commonly associated with Old School Presbyterianism. Dabney's best known work, *Life and Campaigns of Lieutenant-General Thomas J. Jackson* (1866), celebrated the accomplishments of his friend and champion, Stonewall Jackson, and defended the Old South's cultural and spiritual way of life as he also did in *A Defense of Virginia and Through Her the South* (1867). For a time after the Civil War, he had even advocated the emigration of Southerners to Brazil or Australia in order to preserve the South. In *Sensualistic Philosophy of the Nineteenth Century Examined* (1875) Dabney opposed all positivistic and materialistic philosophies, taking particular aim at the implications of Darwinism. Though the course of events went contrary to Dabney's views, his attention to the cultural ramifications of ideas gave insight to his unyielding conservatism.

SELECT WRITINGS
R. L. Dabney, *Systematic and Polemic Theology* (1871)

—, *Life and Campaigns of Lieutenant-General Thomas J. Jackson* (1866)
—, *A Defense of Virginia and Through Her the South* (1867)
—, *Sensualistic Philosophy of the Nineteenth Century Examined* (1875)

BIBLIOGRAPHY
T. C. Johnson, *The Life and Letters of Robert Lewis Dabney* (Richmond, VA, 1903)
D. H. Overy, 'Robert Lewis Dabney: Apostle of the Old South' (Univ. of Wisconsin Ph.D. dissertation, 1967)

D. G. HART

DaCosta, Isaac (b. Amsterdam, 14 Jan. 1798; d. Amsterdam, 28 April 1860). Dutch author and educator. Son of Daniel DaCosta and Rebecca Ricardo, he was a precocious child, joining the literary society *Concordia Crescimus* at age 14. He studied at the University of Leiden, earning doctorates in law (1818) and in literature/philosophy (1821). In 1821 he married his cousin Hanna Belmonte (1800–67). Initially he worked as a lawyer, later as a freelance lecturer, teacher, essayist, poet and author of many books.

DaCosta's Jewish parents could afford Willem Bilderdijk as private tutor by having him share class time and expenses with a distant slightly older relative, ABRAHAM CAPADOSE. A lifelong friendship developed, resulting also in Isaac's and Abraham's conversion to Christianity which was shared by Isaac's wife Hanna (1822). DaCosta remained constantly interested in the Jews about whom he wrote extensively. *Israel en de Volkeren* is one of his major works that was translated into both English and German.

Inspired by Bilderdijk's opposition to the 'spirit of the age', and eager to do battle against the evils of the French revolution, DaCosta published a fiery brochure under the title *Bezwaren tegen de Geest der Eeuw*. This pamphlet caused a flood of protests especially from Enlightenment critics. As he matured, DaCosta modified his intensely conservative and reactionary views, accepting that God in the incarnation had subjected himself to history in which progress and regress would take place on the way to the complete separation of good and evil at the end of time. Thus DaCosta's God of Israel and Christianity lost his static condition of the past. Therefore it was not sinful to abolish slavery, parliaments were no longer pathways to hell, and vaccination against smallpox – in spite of Capadose's strenuous objections – did not constitute a denial of God's design for mankind. DaCosta believed not in human formulations but rather in divine revelation and so he refused, in 1834, to join the Secession from the Dutch Reformed Church with its insistence on confessions of the past.

Always the educator, DaCosta never tired of expounding on the significance of Israel at the core of God's revelation, fully expecting the return of the Jews to their ancient lands. As a popular speaker, DaCosta had many opportunities to explain his views in homilies at the weekly reunions that typified the *Réveil* movement in Europe.

In 1817–18, LEWIS WAY travelled through Germany, Russia, and Holland as the representative of the LSPCJ. As a result, Benjamin Nehemia Solomon, earlier a rabbi in Galicia, came as the society's first missionary to Rotterdam, joined there by the converted Dutch Jew Erasmus H. Simon. But the largest concentration of Jews in Holland lived then at Amsterdam. In 1820, Way succeeded in having the Reverend A. S. THELWALL, the rector of the English Episcopal Church at Amsterdam, assume the added responsibility for the mission to Jews. In 1824 Thelwall became a household name in Holland because of his brochure *Keert U tot Hem Die Slaat* (Turn to Him Who Smites), calling the nation to repentance. Ill health caused Thelwall to return to England in 1826, but contact continued with Capadose and DaCosta, both of whom had frequented his church. Thelwall had several successors but none of them stayed very long. The vacancy of 1835 would last till 1844.

Capadose wrote to DaCosta on 9 July 1842 that the Church of Scotland might be interested in missions among the Jews. On 25 May 1846, Capadose addressed the General Synod of the FCS. He stressed the one dogma that the Free Church was still lacking in its confession: 'in which the restoration of Israel in its hereditary land and the personal reign of King Jesus in glory preceding the day of judgement is acknowledged' (*Eene Rede*, 1849). This event had no immediate results except that it established strong contacts with Scotland. It caused Capadose to try and mobilize the 'Christian Friends' of the *Réveil* in a Society of Dutch Friends of Israel. Similar societies operated already in England, Scotland, France, Switzerland and Germany. But the Dutch government was reluctant to grant legal status to a nationwide society and therefore the local societies remained independent of each other and quite isolated.

CARL SCHWARTZ, a Polish Jew who had been sent to Berlin for his rabbinical training, was converted to Christianity while there. He studied theology at Berlin and Halle before being employed by the LSPCJ at Constantinople. He accepted a call from the FCS which sent him to Berlin, and later to Prague, before he was assigned to Amsterdam where DaCosta and the Amsterdam Committee of Israel's Friends had requested his services.

Schwartz became a very popular preacher. The 'Persian Church' became too small. The French Comedy was rebuilt as the 'Scottish Church' (1856) where attendance sometimes reached 1,400 per Sunday. The FCS

invited *Israel's Friends at Amsterdam* to collaborate in establishing a 'Theological Seminary for Domestic and Foreign Evangelisation'. DaCosta, Schwartz, and J. J. Teding van Berkhout were instrumental in getting both funds and a building in which the seminary could start. In the fall of 1852 the first courses were offered. The seminary envisioned more than training missionaries to the Jews. It wanted also to spread the Gospel among Roman Catholics and work toward reviving the Dutch Reformed Church. DaCosta taught the theology courses and was 'the soul of the institution'.

The seminary did not last long. DaCosta died on 18 April 1860. Two weeks later J. A. Wormser, a strong lay supporter of the seminary, wrote to Carl Schwartz that he was 'of the opinion that the Seminary will soon join DaCosta in the grave' (Brummelkamp, 1910: 391). Indeed, the FCS closed the seminary on 1 October 1861. Dr Schwartz did continue the mission to the Jews as he presided over the Amsterdam Friends of Israel and edited their publication *De Vriend Israels*. In 1864 he accepted a call to London where he died in 1870.

SELECT WRITINGS
I. DaCosta, *Israel and the Nations* (London, 1850; and New York, 1855)
—, *Dichtwerken*, 6 vols (Haarlem, Netherlands, 1856–59)
—, *De Mensch en Dichter Bilderdijk* (Haarlem, Netherlands, 1859)
—, *Bijbellezingen* (1862–75)

BIBLIOGRAPHY
A. Brummelkamp, *Levensbeschrijving van wijlen Prof. A. Brummelkamp* (Kampen, Netherlands, 1910)
A. Capadose, *Eene Rede in de hoogste Kerk-vergadering der Vrije Kerk in Schotland* (s'-Gravenhage, Netherlands, 1849)
—, *Ter Nagedachtenis aan Dr Carl Schwartz* (Amsterdam, 1871)
G. M. den Hartogh, *Het Christelijk Gereformeerd Seminary te Amsterdam* (Delft, no date)
W. T. Gidney, *The History of the London Society for the Promotion of Christianity Amongst the Jews from 1809 to 1908* (London, 1908)
J. Meyer, *Isaac DaCosta's Weg naar het Christendom* (Amsterdam, 1946)
—, *Martelgang of Cirkelgang* (Suriname, 1954)
J. C. Rullmann, *Keert U tot Hem Die Slaat* (Amsterdam, 1925)
A. R. Zalman-Marda, *Van een Engelse Plant in Hollandsche Bodem* (s'-Gravenhage, Netherlands, no date)

GERRIT J. TENZYTHOFF

Dagg, John Leadley (b. Middleburg, VA, USA, 13 Feb. 1794; d. Hayneville, AL, USA, 11 June 1884). American Baptist pastor, educator, and theologian. The oldest of eight children born to Robert and Sarah Davis Dagg, John was unable to attain more than a few years of formal schooling. Nevertheless he taught himself Greek, Hebrew, Latin, and advanced mathematics. He studied medicine, fought in the War of 1812, was ordained a Baptist minister in 1817, and served a number of small congregations in Virginia before becoming pastor of the Fifth Baptist Church of Philadelphia in 1825. After nine years in that post, he had to step down due to a throat ailment.

Dagg devoted the rest of his life to education and writing. In 1834 he became president and professor of theology at Haddington Institute near Philadelphia, then in 1836 became principal of the Alabama Female Atheneum in Tuscaloosa. From 1844 to 1856 he served Mercer University, then in Penfield, Georgia, as president and professor of theology and wrote a number of works on the Bible and Baptist ordinances. After retirement he published his most important books: *A Manual of Theology* (1857), *A Treatise on Church Order* (1858), *Elements of Moral Science* (1860), and *Evidences of Christianity* (1869), which together comprise the first attempt to provide American Baptists with a complete ethical and theological system. Theologically, Dagg espoused a moderate Calvinism and before the Civil War defended slavery on biblical grounds. He was also actively involved in a number of Baptist missionary associations and played a role in the founding of the Southern Baptist Convention (1845).

BIBLIOGRAPHY
DAB
R. G. Gardner, 'John Leadley Dagg', *Review and Expositor*, 54 (1957): 245–63

TIMOTHY P. WEBER

Dale, David (b. Stewarton, Ayrshire, Scotland, 6 Jan. 1739; d. Glasgow, 17 March 1806). Merchant and Independent pastor. David Dale moved in his boyhood to Paisley, where he became a weaver, and thence to Glasgow. In that city he prospered as an importer of linen yarns, and in the manufacture of cotton goods. In 1786, in partnership with Arkwright, he opened the New Lanark Mills and model Industrial Village, later managed by his son-in-law Robert Owen. His prosperity enabled him to be generous to many Christian charities. He was a founder of the Glasgow Bible Society. From 1769 until his death Dale was a joint pastor of the Old Scots Independent Church in Greyfriars Wynd, guiding it through many divisions, occasioned often by 'Glasite' tendencies, and leaving it in a prosperous condition. While polity was strongly influenced by JOHN GLAS and ROBERT SANDEMAN, the Old Scots Independents showed a more evangelistic and cooperative spirit, and Dale exemplified this.

BIBLIOGRAPHY
H. Escott, *A History of Scottish Congregationalism* (Glasgow, 1960)
T. Thomson, ed., *Biographical Dictionary of Eminent Scotsmen* revised edn, 5 vols, 8 (Glasgow, 1855)

DEREK B. MURRAY

Dale, Thomas (b. Pentonville, London, 22 Aug. 1797; d. London, 14 May 1870). Anglican clergyman and scholar. Educated at Christ's Hospital and Corpus Christi, Cambridge (BA 1822; MA 1826; DD 1870), Dale established himself as a writer of verse, translator of Sophocles and successful private schoolmaster. He became first professor of English at University College, London (1828–30), an unusual choice of an evangelical clergyman in the 'godless Institution' of Gower Street, and later, more predictably, at King's College, London (1836–9). He was a very successful preacher, being successively curate of St Michael's, Cornhill (1822–5), of St Bride's, Fleet Street (1826–8), to which he returned as vicar (1835–43) after two other lectureships. He became a Residentiary Canon of St Paul's in 1843, Vicar of St Pancras (1846–61), Rector of Therfield, Hertfordshire (1861–70) and Dean of Rochester (1870). He was a prolific writer and is described by *DNB* as 'an old-fashioned high church evangelical'. One of his sons became a Roman Catholic and another (Thomas P.) spent some time in prison (1880–1) for introducing ritualism at St Vedast's, Foster Lane.

BIBLIOGRAPHY
Al. Cant., II.ii: 214
DNB

ARTHUR POLLARD

Dalhousie, the eleventh Earl. *See* MAULE, FOX

Dallas, Alexander (Robert Charles) (b. Colchester, Essex, England, 29 March 1791; d. Blackheath, London, 12 Dec. 1869). English Anglican clergyman and founder of Irish Church Missions. The son of R. C. Dallas, the historian and litterateur, he became a Treasury clerk and then a commissariat officer in the Peninsular War at Waterloo. Retired on half pay, with encouragement from his father's literary friends, including Southey and Byron, he drew on his continental experiences to write novels, plays and translations. Marriage and family responsibilities led him to seek a profession; he began to study law, but abandoned it to read for orders. After less than a year at Worcester College, Oxford, he was ordained deacon in 1821. His evangelical views developed slowly, helped from 1821 by the friendship of J. B. SUMNER. He held a number of curacies, and a vicarage, before becoming Rector of Wonston, Hampshire, which living he held until his death. He was domestic chaplain to Sumner when the latter became Bishop of Winchester, and received a Lambeth MA by his offices.

An energetic parish minister, he was also a prolific writer, and had his own Wonston printing press. Preaching tours in Ireland led him to deep concern for Irish evangelization, and in 1843 he founded the Society for Irish Church Missions of which he was secretary for 21 years. The society became one of the most conspicuously successful evangelistic agencies among Roman Catholics. Dallas developed elaborate schemes of mass literature distribution planned like military operations, and by

1853 it was reported that the society covered 21 counties and 500 parishes, with 23 separate missions, 70 stations, and 69 schools; and a staff of 37 missionary clergymen, 29 lay agents, 221 scripture readers, 98 schoolteachers, hundreds of teachers of Irish, and many visitors. Intensive visiting was carried out in Dublin, but it was western Galway, or Connemara, which was most thoroughly affected. The work of four years there saw the confirmation of nearly 2,000 converts and the consecration of eight new churches. The society operated strictly within the framework of the Church of Ireland, each missionary clergyman having charge of a district under the bishop's sanction.

So spectacular, indeed, were the successes of this society, founded by an Englishman and drawing its main financial support from England, that the conviction grew among English Anglican evangelicals that the landlords and clergy of Ireland had neglected the spiritual interests of the Roman Catholic population. Irish churchmen later saw in the wide acceptance of this myth a contributory factor in the decision to disestablish their church. In fact, however, the church in Ireland had both maintained the controversy with Rome and sustained the work of evangelism long before Dallas set foot in Ireland. Evangelistic agencies, founded and supported by Irish landlords and clergy, like the Irish Society (1818), the Scripture Readers' Society (1822) and the Island and Coast Society (1833) had seen successes as spectacular as that of the Irish Church Mission in Connemara. The new society, moreover, often entered into the labours of these indigenous societies, and its actual work depended wholly on Irish Churchmen like Hyacinth D'Arcy of Clifden. In his later years Dallas, who spoke Spanish fluently, was much occupied with projects for the evangelization of Spain and the relief of Spanish Protestants.

BIBLIOGRAPHY
CE(D) (1853): 95; (1865): 87–8
A. B. Dallas, *Incidents in the Life and Ministry of the Rev. Alex R.C. Dallas, A.M.* (London 1872): includes autobiographical fragment
DNB

ALAN R. ACHESON

Dalton, William (b. probably Dublin, 1805; d. London, 13 May 1880). Anglican clergyman and anti-Catholic leader. The son of George Forster Dalton of Dublin, he was educated at Trinity College, Dublin (BA 1823, MA 1832). In March 1830 he was appointed travelling clerical secretary to the British Reformation Society and in May 1831, together with NICHOLAS ARMSTRONG, provoked uproar in Exeter Hall by forthright denunciation of the Roman Catholic Church at a meeting convened to discuss famine relief in Ireland. Also in 1831 Dalton married Sarah (née Fereday) of Wolverhampton and became perpetual curate of St Jude, West Derby, Liverpool. In 1835 he was appointed incumbent of St Paul, Wolverhampton, and settled in that town for the

remainder of his ministry. In 1859 he moved to St Philip, holding the latter incumbency until his death, having also become a prebendary of Lichfield in 1856.

Dalton was the leading evangelical clergyman in Wolverhampton during the first half of Victoria's reign, with an influence underpinned by his wife's financial resources and her local social standing. He was active in prompting church extension and home missionary endeavour while continuing staunchly anti-Catholic and anti-Tractarian. A prolific writer, he published pastoral and catechetical works. Although Dalton was a vigorous advocate for the Church of England, both with tongue and pen, it was nevertheless possible for Anglicans and Nonconformists in Wolverhampton to cooperate in common evangelical concerns.

BIBLIOGRAPHY
Boase
J. D. Walters, 'The impact of Anglican Evangelicalism on the Religious Life of Wolverhampton and its locality in the period 1830–1860' (CNAA, Wolverhampton Polytechnic, M.Phil. thesis, 1983)
J. Wolffe, *The Protestant Crusade in Great Britain, 1829–1860* (Oxford, 1991)

JOHN WOLFFE

Daly, Robert (b. Dunsandle, County Galway, Ireland, 8 June 1783; d. Waterford, Ireland, 16 Feb. 1872). Bishop of Cashel and controversialist. The second son of the Right Honourable Denis Daly, a contemporary greatly admired by Henry Grattan, he was – like Bishop JAMES O'BRIEN – of one of Ireland's most ancient families. He inherited his father's eloquence and energies, but owed much also to his mother, Lady Harriet (Maxwell), only daughter of the first Earl of Farnham, a descendant of the kings of Scotland. Ordained (deacon 1807, priest 1808) his preferments were due to her family connection with Euseby Cleaver, successively Bishop of Ferns and Archbishop of Dublin. Daly held a living first in Ferns, and then from 1814 to 1843 was Rector of Powerscourt in the diocese of Glendalough, part of the archdiocese of Dublin. He was converted after ordination, but before he went to Powerscourt.

His family background illustrates the progress of the evangelical revival among the Irish upper classes. The Maxwells identified with it in County Cavan, as did his uncle and cousin, Judge St George Daly of Dublin and his son, James, Warden of Galway from the age of 19. His sister married an evangelical, Horace Newman, later Dean of Cork, while his elder brother, James, became Lord Dunsandle in the year that he became Bishop of Cashel. (He himself was a bachelor.) Naturally he enjoyed much influence among the numerous aristocracy and gentry of county Wicklow at large – the Howards, Probyns and Parnells – in addition to such among his parishioners as the families of Lord POWERSCOURT, Lord Rathdowne and Colonel Howard. In the Wingfield family itself, his converts included Richard, fifth Viscount POWERSCOURT, his first and second [Lady

THEODOSIA POWERSCOURT] wives, and his brother, Edward, who in 1821 was appointed to the living of St James's, Dublin, by his uncle, the Earl of Meath. George IV came among these Wicklow evangelicals when he dined at Powerscourt House in 1821.

A man of boundless energy, he threw himself into all the activity of the revival. In his parish, he began Sunday schools, held weekly classes for the young, gave a midweek lecture during summer and autumn, published a Powerscourt hymn-book, formed agencies to provide for the needs of the poor – and was a good visitor among his 2,000-strong yeomen parishioners. He was a leader in the diocese, active in the local branches of the evangelical societies and in the Glendalough Clerical Society. Centrally, he spoke at the April meetings in the Rotunda, preached charity sermons in the Dublin churches, and – a born controversialist – was an antagonist during the 1820s both of the bishops in the Bible Society controversy, and of Roman Catholic priests in public debates about doctrine. He published much, including (under the initials 'RD') regular articles in the *Christian Examiner.* A fluent Irish speaker, he was co-founder in 1818 of the Irish Society, and from 1825 spent part of each spring in England on its behalf. In 1832 he published an edition of O'Brien's *Focaloir Gaoidhilge-Sax-Bhéarlar*, or *Irish-English Dictionary.*

In the neighbouring parish of Delgany, his kinsman William Cleaver (a son of Archbishop Cleaver) was one of the revival's gentle saints. In 1842 a visitor from Oxford arrived among the Glendalough Anglicans as the guest of Delgany rectory – James Anthony Froude. In his later account of his visit, his allusion to Daly and his characteristically robust opinions on order and doctrine, is unmistakable. Influenced by his experience (of a year's duration) among 'clergymen of weight and learning', Froude's perceptions changed significantly: 'Evangelicalism had been represented to me as weak and illiterate. I had found it in harmony with reason and experience, and recommended as it was by personal holiness in its professors, and general beauty of mind and character, I concluded that Protestantism had more to say for itself than my Oxford teachers had allowed.' (Froude, 1891, IV: 299–300).

Daly's appointment as Bishop of Cashel in 1843 was made by a Conservative viceroy, the Earl de Grey, soon after he had been declared Dean of St Patrick's, Dublin, following a disputed election. He found many evangelical clergy in the united dioceses, presided at meetings of their clerical societies, and ordained men recommended to him by Dr J. H. SINGER in Trinity College, Dublin. As a result of the church's missionary work in the southwest, he consecrated churches in parishes which had known no Protestant worship since the Reformation, and confirmed hundreds of converts. The tone of his episcopate was ruggedly Reformed. (A portrait of Luther in his study was often taken for that of Daly himself.) In a published correspondence with one of its bishops, he declared that the Scottish Episcopal Church, by what he saw as its essential departure from Reformation principles, was no valid part of the historic Anglican Communion. His episcopal charges dealt with such current issues as the progress of Tractarian principles, the baptismal controversy (at the time of the Gorham case), and the demands for prayer-book revision. The essential emphasis in the long ministry of a doughty champion in the reformed Church of Ireland was, however, indicated by his clergy in the words, 'We preach Christ crucified', on the memorial pulpit which they erected in Waterford Cathedral.

BIBLIOGRAPHY
DNB
J. A. Froude, *Short Studies on Great Subjects*, 4 vols, new edn, IV (London, 1891): 293–302
H. Madden, *Memoir of the Right Rev. Robert Daly* (London, 1875)

ALAN R. ACHESON

Dana, James Dwight (b. Utica, NY, USA, 12 Feb. 1813; d. New Haven, CT, USA, 14 April 1895). Geologist, mineralogist and college professor. Dana was the oldest of ten children born to Congregationalist merchant James Dana and his wife Harriet. He entered Yale in 1830 where he developed his interest in geology under BENJAMIN SILLIMAN. After a brief stint as a naval instructor, Dana returned to Yale as Silliman's assistant and soon completed his comprehensive *System of Mineralogy*. Dana than participated as the geologist on the US Exploring Expedition (1838–42) to the Pacific. Again he returned to Yale, succeeded Silliman as editor of *American Journal of Science*, married Silliman's daughter in 1849, and upon Silliman's retirement in 1849 was appointed Silliman professor of natural history. Despite much ill health, Dana was acknowledged as North America's premier geologist with expertise in volcanism, coral reefs and islands, the structure of continents and oceans, crustaceans, the theory of mountain building, and, of course, mineralogy.

Dana's entire life was marked by humble Christian piety and character. He was concerned to place his science within a Christian context and like many other geologists of the era sought to find a way of harmonizing Genesis with geological history. Dana found great satisfaction in the day-age scheme developed by his close friend ARNOLD GUYOT and endorsed Guyot's view in his own *Manual of Geology*. Dana also participated in a famous exchange with TAYLER LEWIS over the appropriate exegesis of Genesis 1 and the role of science in interpreting scripture.

BIBLIOGRAPHY
D. C. Gilman, *The Life of James Dwight Dana* (New York, 1899)
M. L. Prendergast, 'James Dwight Dana: the Life and Thought of an American Scientist' (Univ. California Los Angeles Ph.D. thesis, 1978)

DAVIS A. YOUNG

Danforth, Clarissa (b. Wethersfield, VT, USA, 1792). Freewill Baptist itinerant preacher. She was converted by the Freewill Baptist evangelist John Colby in 1815 when she was 23. The Freewill Baptists did not permit women to be ordained, but they allowed them to perform all ministerial duties except administering the sacraments. By 1817, she was preaching in both Vermont and New Hampshire. She became well-known in Rhode Island, where she led a revival in 1819 in the vicinity of Smithfield and Providence that lasted 16 months. Because she was so popular, her activities were widely reported in the Freewill Baptist press, particularly the *Religious Informer*. In 1822, she married a man identified only as Mr Richmond, a merchant from Pomfret, Connecticut. They moved to western New York and she preached only occasionally. Little is known about her life between 1822 and 1834, when she briefly came out of retirement to travel to Pennsylvania, New York, and New Jersey. There is no record that she ever preached again.

BIBLIOGRAPHY

I. D. Stewart, *History of the Freewill Baptists* (Dover, NH, 1862): 300, 318, 366, 389, 391

Christian Palladium (Union Mills, NY), III, 12 (15 Oct. 1834): 191

CATHERINE A. BREKUS

Daniell, Georgina (b. *c.* 1834; d. Aldershot, Hampshire, England, 24 June 1894). Christian worker among soldiers. Her father was a captain in the 18th Madras Native Infantry and her mother an evangelical philanthropist who in 1857 had established the Mrs Daniell's Village Missions which were later incorporated with the Country Towns Mission. Like her mother, Louisa, she was committed to soldiers' welfare and carried on with the help of other ladies the seven institutes the first of which had been founded in Aldershot in 1862 by her mother (who died in Malvern 20 September 1871, worn out by her philanthropy at the age of sixty) on the suggestion of Mr Wilson, the secretary of the Country Towns Mission and confirmed by the Reverend WILLIAM PENNE-FATHER, whose advice she sought. Miss Daniell enjoyed the goodwill of leading evangelicals, chaplains and others in developing the work.

The Miss Daniell's Soldiers' Home in Aldershot was constructed in an attractive Elizabethan style and provided recreational, dining, educational and hostel facilities and a take-away food service, Mrs Daniell's clear intention being that it should serve as 'a public house without drink'. Lord SHAFTESBURY laid the foundation stone in February 1863. Miss Daniell's assistant Miss Robinson worked among the women of the area, running for a while a small rescue home for them. In 1863 Mrs Daniell formed both the Mrs Daniell's Total Abstinence Society for soldiers and the Aldershot Soldiers' Wives Aid Association, which led on to the formation of the Soldiers' and Sailors' Family Association in 1885.

SELECT WRITINGS

G. Daniell, *A Record of Mrs Daniell's Work Among Soldiers* (London, 1879)

BIBLIOGRAPHY

K. Heasman, *Evangelicals in Action* (London, 1962)

J. H. Y. BRIGGS

Daniell, Louisa. *See* DANIELL, GEORGINA

Darby, John Nelson (b. London, 18 Nov. 1800; d. Bournemouth, England, 29 April 1882). Seceder and Brethren leader. The youngest son of John Darby of Markly, Sussex, and later of Leap Castle, King's County, he attended Westminster School (1812–15) and Trinity College, Dublin (1815–19) graduating as classical gold medallist. Admitted to Lincoln's Inn (1819) he soon abandoned the law, and by December 1824 had a clergyman's gown. Deaconed in August 1825, he worked among the peasants of Calary which was not yet a parish and therefore an ideal field for Darby's missionary zeal. In December 1826 he was injured in a riding accident and spent about a year convalescing in the home of his sister Susan Pennefather in Delgany and Dublin (*see* EDWARD PENNEFATHER). His experience here, to which he often referred in later years, was not a conversion but a realization of deliverance from bondage and a discovery of union with Christ. Like many Irish Anglican evangelicals he had previously been an exact churchman emphasizing sacramental grace. During this time he was also instrumental in the conversion of JOSEPH CHARLES PHILPOT, and greatly impressed FRANCIS W. NEWMAN, whose letters also underline the important influence of Susan Pennefather.

Earlier Darby had criticized Archbishop Magee's Erastianism but now his anxieties were increased. In 1828 he published privately his *Considerations on the Nature and Unity of the Church* emphasizing the unity of believers, the role of the Holy Spirit and the imminent Second Coming, and resigned his curacy to engage in itinerant mission work. He had not yet seceded and still wore his clerical robes but his connection with the Establishment was looser, as he was now in touch with men like ANTHONY NORRIS GROVES, JOHN G. BELLETT, and EDWARD CRONIN who by 1829 had begun informally to 'break bread'. Accounts are divided about the extent of Darby's involvement in this innovation.

In 1830, the cool reception given to him at Cambridge by CHARLES SIMEON (*CW*, 10: 133–4) contrasted with the favourable response to Darby at Oxford in May and June from younger men like JOHN HILL, HENRY B. BULTEEL, GEORGE V. WIGRAM, and BENJAMIN W. NEWTON the last of whom encouraged him to investigate the manifestations of glossolalia near Port Glasgow and then in December to visit Plymouth. In 1831 he revisited Oxford just after Bulteel's University sermon, and published a lengthy though anonymous reply to Bulteel's chief critic.

The foundation in Ireland of the National Board of Education now evoked from Darby (back in Dublin by April 1832) a spirited attack on Archbishop Whately (one of the commissioners) and this may have caused his more decisively separatist position at the Powerscourt prophetic conference in September. This attitude was further intensified by the suppression of the Irish Home Mission in 1833. By now he was closely identified with the 'Brethren' assembly at Plymouth which 'has altered the face of Christianity for me' (*Letters*, 3: 230). His preaching in Ireland in the following years encouraged secession and the foundation of Brethren meetings on the Plymouth pattern. Several clergy followed his lead but by 1837 his Irish activity was limited by his notoriety.

Fascinated by the *Reveil*, Darby had visited Switzerland in 1835 (when he had unsuccessfully sought contact with ALEXANDRE VINET), and again in 1837 at the invitation of Charles de Rodt. At Geneva in 1839 the *dissidents* whose assembly was divided ecclesiologically, welcomed Darby who at this stage emphasized unity rather than separation. Likewise at Lausanne in 1840 they appreciated him as an ally against growing Methodist activity. He also attracted a following in the state church where there was disillusionment with the Erastianism of the new ecclesiastical constitution (to become effective in 1841). Many were impressed by his lectures on *The Hopes of the Church of God* (originally delivered in a private home in Lausanne and containing, in embryo at least, Darby's distinctive teaching that the church is in ruins) and began to 'break bread' with him. When some of the *dissidents* questioned Darby's ecclesiology in 1841 he called for separation from *all* existing churches in favour of 'non sectarian groups of believers' – groups known thenceforth as 'assemblées Darbistes'.

This was but the first of several ruptures arising from his teaching. In 1845 at Plymouth he clashed with B. W. NEWTON over eschatology and over Newton's dominant position in the assembly, from which Darby withdrew in October to break bread elsewhere. In 1847 some Christologically heterodox writings of Newton led Darby to insist that all of Newton's associates *and* any assemblies who received such people (e.g. Bethesda, Bristol, [G. MÜLLER]) should be excluded from Communion. The result was a permanent schism between Open and Exclusive Brethren, the latter of whom treated Darby as their undisputed leader.

Darby's evangelism continued, extending to Germany (1854 invited by J. von Poseck and CARL BROCKHAUS), Canada (1862 building on R. Evans's work), Italy (1871) and New Zealand (1875). His work in the USA (several visits between 1862 and 1877) was at first only among emigrant Brethren but later he was well received in St Louis, Chicago, New York and Boston among non-Brethren. Darby's teaching had considerable impact and his dispensationalism – an interesting corollary of his belief in the ruin of the church – was widely welcomed, though only a few seceded from their denominations. On both sides of the Atlantic much of his writing (e.g. *Synopsis of the Books of the Bible*) was valued outside Brethren

circles. His translations of the Bible into English, French and German, were appreciated as literally accurate but were in regular use only among Brethren. Meanwhile his written polemics continued with Brethren and non-Brethren. Former companions like PERCY F. HALL and WILLIAM H. DORMAN withdrew from him in 1866, charging him with heresy, while another division in 1881 separated him from his former friends EDWARD CRONIN and WILLIAM KELLY. To the end he continued to publish apologetic works defending the authenticity of the Bible against 'Higher Criticism'.

SELECT WRITINGS

W. Kelly, ed., *The Collected Writings of J. N. Darby*, 34 vols (London, no date). There are two undated editions
—, *Letters of J. N. D.*, 3 vols (London, no date)
Le Messager évangélique (Vevey, Switzerland, since 1860) contains many letters which are not included in the English edition

BIBLIOGRAPHY

P. Bovet, [ed.], *Alexandre Vinet; Lettres*, 2 (Lausanne, Switzerland, 1947): 383
J. Cart, *Histoire du Mouvement Religieux et Ecclésiastique dans le Canton de Vaud Pendant la Première Moitié du XIXe Siècle*, 5 (Lausanne, Switzerland, 1870): 340–68
F. R. Coad, *A History of the Brethren Movement* (Exeter, England, 1968)
F. C[uendet], *Souvenez-vous de vos conducteurs* (Vevey, Switzerland, 1966 [1935]): 9–95
DNB
H. de Goltz, *Genève Religieuse au Dix-Neuvième Siècle* (Geneva, 1862): 437–55
E. Guers, *Le Premier Réveil et la Première Église Indépendante à Genève* (Geneva, 1871): 331–42
G. Ischebeck, *John Nelson Darby, son Temps et son Oeuvre* (Yverdon, Switzerland, 1937)
Julian
POBC, 21
E. Rambert, *Alexandre Vinet, Histoire de sa Vie et de ses Ouvrages* (Lausanne, Switzerland, 1875): 301–2
H. H. Rowdon, *Origins of the Brethren 1825–1850* (London, 1967)
E. R. Sandeen, *The Roots of Fundamentalism* (Chicago, IL, 1970): 31–41, 59–80
T. C. F. Stunt 'John Henry Newman and the Evangelicals', *JEH*, 21, (1970): 72
M. Weremchak, *John Nelson Darby* (Neptune, NJ, 1992)

TIMOTHY C. F. STUNT

Darling, David (b. 1790; d. Sydney, Australia, 6 Dec. 1867). LMS Missionary who served in the Pacific region. David Darling was ordained 30 September 1816 and arrived at Moorea in November 1817. He served the mission at Moorea until 1819, at Tahiti between 1819 and 1834, at Tahuata in the Marquesas between 1834 and 1835 and from 1835 to 1859 at Tahiti. Darling's varied career involved a failed attempt to manufacture sugar as well as undertaking some printing. He was sufficiently proficient to be able to preach and translate portions of scripture into the Marquesan dialect. Darling observed at first hand the beliefs of the millenarian 'Mamaia' sect and reported early cases of backsliding. He was a continuous smoker. Darling's determination enabled him to continue to work on Tahiti even when the island had become a French Protectorate. He was highly critical of GEORGE PRITCHARD. Infirmity forced his retirement to Sydney in 1859.

BIBLIOGRAPHY
N. Gunson, *Messengers of Grace* (Melbourne, 1978)
R. Lovett, *The History of the London Missionary Society 1795–1895* (London 1899)
RMD, 4th edn (London, 1923)

R. WATCYN JAMES

Darling, Elizabeth (b. West Bromwich, England, 10 Nov. 1798; d. Colman's Hatch, East Sussex, England, 3 Sept. 1868). Governor's wife and colonial benefactress. The fourth of six children born to Ann and Colonel John Dumaresq, descendent of a leading Jersey family, Elizabeth married General Ralph Darling at Cheltenham on 3 October 1817, subsequently accompanying him to Mauritius and in 1826 to New South Wales. A deep Christian with a strong social conscience, she helped improve the lot of women convicts and female orphans and did much to help her husband govern the penal colony. She painted, wrote and acted as a gracious hostess at Government House. After returning to England in 1831 she devoted herself to her husband and six children and engaged in philanthropic work.

BIBLIOGRAPHY
B. Fletcher, 'Elizabeth Darling: Colonial Benefactress and Governor's Lady', *Journal of the Royal Australian Historical Society*, 67, pt 4 (March 1982)

BRIAN FLETCHER

Darney, William (b. Scotland, *c*. 1684/5; d. Newchurch, Lancashire, England, 30 Nov. 1774). Methodist pedlar and preacher. Darney is said to have been converted by JAMES ROBE during the Scottish awakening of 1741, and felt called to preach in October 1741 (Methodist Church Archives, MARC manuscript MAB B1320. E. Chapman, *William Darney, Pedlar-Evangelist*: 1). By 1743–4 'Scotch Will' was peddling and preaching on the borders of Yorkshire and Lancashire where he founded religious societies and influenced WILLIAM GRIMSHAW's evangelistic methods. His societies came under JOHN WESLEY's control in 1747. Although the Wesleys criticized and periodically expelled him for his Calvinism, 'nonsensical' hymns and eccentricities, they nevertheless employed him frequently as a local or travelling preacher until 1768. Darney's *Collection of Hymns* and *Foundation Doctrines of the Gospel* were designed to appeal to the uncultured with whom he had considerable success.

BIBLIOGRAPHY
C. Atmore, *The Methodist Memorial* (Bristol, England, 1801): 100–1
F. Baker, *William Grimshaw* (London, 1963): 94–8, 101

HENRY D. RACK

Dart, Elizabeth [Eynon, Mrs John H.] (b. April 1792, Marhamchurch, Cornwall, England; d. Little Britain, Canada West, 13 Jan. 1857). Bible Christian itinerant. Raised a nominal Anglican, Dart joined the Wesleyan Methodists in 1811; in 1815 she was one of the founders of the Bible Christian Church and in 1816 became an itinerant under WILLIAM O'BRYAN. Despite strong opposition she travelled in Wales, Devon and Cornwall.

On 18 March 1833 she married John Hicks Enyon (1801–1888) (for whom see *DCB*) who had been converted through her ministry in Wales in 1824. Together they emigrated to Upper Canda where they both exercised considerable influence in establishing the Bible Christian denomination, which consisted almost entirely of West Country immigrants. Elizabeth gave birth to a daughter, who died at birth.

BIBLIOGRAPHY
DCB
F. W. Bourne, *The Bible Christians: Their Origin and History* (London, 1905)
Z. Taft, *Biographical Sketches of Holy Women*, 2 (London, 1828)

DONALD M. LEWIS and E. DOROTHY GRAHAM

Dartmouth, (second) Earl of [**Legge, William**] (b. London, 20 June 1731; d. Blackheath, Kent, England, 15 July 1801). Peer and statesman. He was the younger son of George Legge, Viscount Lewisham, and Elizabeth, daughter and heiress of Sir Arthur Kaye, baronet, of Woodsome, Yorkshire, and grandson of William Legge, first Earl of Dartmouth, whom he succeeded on 15 Dec. 1750. He was educated at Westminster School and Trinity College, Oxford (MA 21 March 1751, DCL 28 April 1756). Legge married, on 11 June 1755, Frances Catherine (died 1805), only daughter and heiress of Sir Charles Gunter Nicholl, KB, by whom he had eight sons and one daughter.

Legge began his political career as a 'Rockingham' Whig, then became a member of Lord North's cabinet, joined the Coalition in 1783, and, after voting with the Foxites for several years, finally came over to Pitt. He served as President of the Board of Trade (1765–6), Lord Privy Seal (1755–82), and Lord Steward (1783). Lord North appointed him Secretary of State for the Colonies (1772–5); his probity, correct conscience, and courteous manner made him a valuable acquisition to the ministry. Although Bute rejected him as Lord of the Bedchamber, 'lest so sanctimonious a man should gain too far on his majesty's piety', Legge nevertheless became a favourite of George III. He was appointed Recorder of Lichfield in

1757, Acting-Lieutenant of Alice Holt and Wolmer forests in 1773, Governor of the Charterhouse in 1781, and was elected a Fellow of the Society of Antiquaries in 1784.

Dartmouth, who spoke rarely in the Lords, did not hold public office after 1783. In 1786 Lord North appointed him steward of Oxford University. He also served as president of the trustees of Dr Wheeler's school for native Americans at Lebanon, Connecticut; in 1769, Wheeler named Dartmouth College in recognition of Legge's zealous support for the school back in England.

A man of real piety and most amiable disposition, he was converted to 'serious religion' through Selina Hastings, Countess of HUNTINGDON, around 1755. She in turn introduced him to many leading evangelicals, including the WESLEYS, GEORGE WHITEFIELD and WILLIAM ROMAINE. It was to the cause of Calvinistic Methodism that he devoted the bulk of his resources and spiritual energies. During Lady Huntingdon's serious illness in 1767, he was selected as 'the fittest person' to continue her work in the event of her demise.

Dartmouth helped to secure ordination for several early evangelicals, such as JOHN NEWTON; he also purchased the advowsons of nearly a dozen livings which he subsequently presented to leading evangelicals. Among those who benefited from his patronage, influence, or financial assistance, besides Newton at Olney, were HENRY VENN at Huddersfield, THOMAS ROBINSON at Leicester, JAMES STILLINGFLEET at Hotham, MATTHEW POWLEY at Dewsbury, and SAMUEL WALKER at Truro. He was also president of the Locke Hospital and the Society for the Suppression of Vice.

Dartmouth's evangelical attachments obtained for him the nickname of 'Psalm-singer'. COWPER alluded to him in 'Truth' as 'one who wears a coronet and prays'. Newton addressed to him the 'Twenty-six Letters to a Nobleman', which were subsequently published in 'Cardiphonia' (1781). Horace Walpole described Legge as 'extremely conscientious and delicate in his honour'. He is, Benjamin Franklin wrote in 1773, 'a truly good man, and wishes sincerely a good understanding with the colonies, but does not seem to have strength equal to his wishes'. His influence upon the development of the English evangelicalism, however, was considerable.

BIBLIOGRAPHY
Al. Ox.
Annual Register (1801) Chronicle: 85
B. D. Bargar, Lord Dartmouth and the American Revolution (Columbia, SC, 1965)
British Library, London, Darmouth Manuscripts
DNB
GEC
GM, 2 (1801); 768, 792
Patshull House, Wolverhampton, Dartmouth Manuscripts
Morning Herald (6 August 1782)
A. C. H. Seymour, The Life and Times of Selina, Countess of Huntingdon, 2 vols, 6th edn (London, 1844)
J. S. Watson, The Reign of George III 1760–1815 (Oxford, 1960)

GRAYSON CARTER

Davenport, James (b. Stamford, CT, BNA, 1716; d. Hopewell, NJ, BNA, 10 Nov. 1757). Controversial revivalist preacher. James Davenport, great-grandson of New Haven's founding minister, John Davenport, was born in 1716. In 1729 he entered Yale College at the age of 13 and graduated in 1732 at the top of his class. At Yale, Davenport associated with a group of pious students who would later play leading roles in the Great Awakening. During this period he determined to become an evangelist and restore New England's waning piety.

In 1738 Davenport accepted a call to the Congregational church at Southold, Long Island, a prosperous community linked by trade and family with New London, Connecticut, the leading Connecticut port. It was at Southold in 1740 that Davenport, stirred by an inspirational sermon from the famed itinerant GEORGE WHITEFIELD, determined to be an itinerant preacher. He conducted revivals in New York and Connecticut and soon became noted for sermons and demonstration which, for sheer energy and popular enthusiasm, exceeded even Whitefield.

Throughout 1741 and 1742 Davenport itinerated in ever-wider circles, achieving ever wilder results. In June 1742, he was arrested in Stratford, Connecticut for disturbing the peace and deported back to Long Island. Undeterred, Davenport moved on to Boston where he was again arrested for rallying large popular audiences in opposition to the settled pastors, and expelled on the grounds that he was 'non compos mentis' – out of his mind.

On March 6, 1743 in New London, Davenport joined with a local Separate congregation he had helped found to stage a demonstration against the local church and its minister Eliphalet Adams. Under Davenport's fevered leadership the rally quickly raged out of control as the group built a bonfire and cast into it a veritable library of Puritan classics including such writers as Matthew Henry, Richard Sibbes, Increase Mather, and BENJAMIN COLMAN. The bonfire incident became the cause célèbre of the Great Awakening and the undoing of Davenport's itinerancy. Called before a church council, Davenport repented of his schismatic behaviour and issued a public retraction of his actions.

From 1747 until his death in 1757, a chastened Davenport lived out the rest of his career a model pastor, serving a small Presbyterian church in Hopewell, New Jersey, and working with local American Indians.

BIBLIOGRAPHY
DAB
E. S. Gaustad, The Great Awakening in New England (New York, 1957)
H. S. Stout and P. Onuf, 'James Davenport and The Great Awakening in New London', Journal of American History 70 (1983): 556–78

HARRY S. STOUT

Davey, Thomas (b. London, c. 1794; d. probably Freetown, Sierra Leone, 14 Aug. 1831). CMS missionary to

Sierra Leone. Davey trained as a schoolmaster at the Central School of the National School Society. He and JAMES NORMAN were sent to Sierra Leone by the CMS on 20 December 1820; Davey served in Leopold. Unlike many early CMS missionaries to Sierra Leone, Davey managed to survive there for five years before returning to England on 13 June 1826. He was ordained (deacon 1826, priest 1827) by the Bishop of London and returned to work in Freetown until he withdrew from CMS on 9 December 1830 (probably for health reasons) and died eight months later. Among his charges in Sierra Leone was SAMUEL CROWTHER.

Davey married Phoebe Goodwin who remarried H. GRAHAM, and following his death, Bishop J. W. WEEKS, both CMS missionaries in Sierra Leone. Samuel Crowther always spoke of her as his 'mother' and claimed a place for her near him at his consecration in Canterbury Cathedral in 1864.

BIBLIOGRAPHY
D. T. B[arry], *CMS Register of Missionaries and Native Clergy* (privately printed) (London, 1906)

DONALD M. LEWIS

David, Christian (b. Senftleben, Moravia, 31 Dec. 1690; d. Herrnhut, Saxony, 3 Feb. 1751). Pioneer Moravian. A Catholic shepherd and then a mercenary soldier in the Prussian army, David read the Bible, and after 1715, working in Görlitz, Upper Lusatia, he found assurance through the ministry of the local Lutheran pastor, Melchior Schäffer and married Anna Elisabeth Ludwig from Niederwiesa. He became a lay emissary of Protestantism in his home territory, and came into contact with the Neisser family (*see* F. W. NEISSER), who were among the remnant of the Utraquist Hussites. David explained their need for a religious refuge to Count ZINZENDORF, and in May 1722 led ten members of the family to Saxony, and they were permitted to settle at Berthelsdorf, the count's estate. David named the settlement Herrnhut, and welcomed other religious refugees there.

In 1727 although he was evangelizing in Hungary at the time and had been misled by an apocalyptic movement in the previous year, he was elected one of the four chief elders of the re-formed United Brethren. From 1733 to 1735 he served as a pioneer missionary to Greenland. He was a founder member of the Pilgrim Congregation, helped to organize the Brethren work in Holland, and visited North America. JOHN WESLEY had close contact with David on his visit to Germany in 1738, and David was an opponent of the quietist Moravian theology of the 1740s. He composed a number of popular Moravian hymns. Zinzendorf described him as one of the apostles who stood out among his generation.

BIBLIOGRAPHY
K. Bosl, G. Franz and H. H. Hofmann, eds, *Biographisches Wörtsbuch zur Deutschen Geschichte*, 1 (Müncher, 1975)

J. T. Hamilton and K. G. Hamilton, *History of the Moravian Church*, 2nd edn (Bethlehem, PA, 1983)
Neue Deutsche Biographie, 16 vols (Berlin, 1953–) 3: 534–5

PETER J. LINEHAM

Davidson, Alexander Dyce (b. Aberdeen, Scotland, 8 May 1807; d. 27 April 1872). Presbyterian minister. Davidson was educated at Marischal College, licensed by the presbytery of Aberdeen on 31 March 1830 and inducted to the South Parish Church of Aberdeen in 1832. He was translated in 1836 to the West Parish Church of the same city. A greatly esteemed, popular and earnest evangelical preacher he, in company with all the Established Church ministers in Aberdeen, adhered to the Free Church; he thus became the first minister of the West Free Church of Aberdeen.

SELECT WRITINGS
A. D. Davidson, *Lectures on Esther* (Edinburgh, 1859)
—, *Sermons and Lectures* (posthumous) (Aberdeen, Scotland, 1872)

BIBLIOGRAPHY
J. Wylie, *Disruption Worthies* (Edinburgh, 1881)
W. Ewing, ed., *Annals of the Free Church of Scotland, 1834–1900* (Edinburgh, Scotland, 1914)
Fasti

ALASDAIR BOTHWELL GORDON

Davidson, Sir David (b. Haddington, East Lothian, Scotland, 1811; d. Edinburgh, 18 May 1900). Bombay army officer and inventor. Son of Henry Davidson, senior sheriff-clerk of Scotland, his early circumstances placed him in proximity to future religious and literary lights, to EDWARD IRVING, mathematical master at the local burgh school that Davidson attended, and to Jane Welsh, the future wife of Thomas Carlyle. (Sixteen letters from Jane, and a few from Thomas Carlyle, are preserved in Davidson's *Memories*.)

His childhood nurse exercised a religious influence on him and as a youth he heard sermons by LEGH RICHMOND and EBENEZER BROWN. However, it was not until 1834 that he underwent a religious conversion in India. Lieutenant St Clair Jameson then introduced him to the works of ABRAHAM BOOTH, PHILIP DODDRIDGE, and WILLIAM ROMAINE, and especially to Doddridge's *The Life of Colonel Gardiner* (1747), which Davidson found particularly affecting. He then worked with Jameson and others in an attempt to introduce Christian religious education into Indian schools. In 1837 he was made superintendent of survey for Bombay and Scinde; in 1844 he was promoted to the rank of captain. He retired from India in 1851.

Davidson was best known as an inventor of military ordnance, of an elongated rifle bullet, and of the telescopic rifle sight, in recognition of which he was made Companion of the Order of the Bath in 1881 and was knighted in 1897. A few of his letters are deposited in the National Library of Scotland.

A member of the Free Church, he was very active in its Foreign Missions Committee. A member of the Scottish Reformation Society, and a founding member of the EA, he was a vice-president of their Edinburgh auxiliaries.

SELECT WRITINGS
D. Davidson, *Memories of a Long Life* (Edinburgh, 1890)

BIBLIOGRAPHY
Boase

JONATHAN BURKE CUTMORE

Davidson, Henry (b. Eckford, Roxburghshire, Scotland, 1687; d. Galashiels, Selkirkshire, Scotland, 24 Oct 1756). Church of Scotland minister. Educated at the University of Edinburgh, he was ordained to the parish of Galashiels in 1714. In 1721 he was one of the ministers who petitioned the General Assembly of the Church of Scotland against its condemnation of *The Marrow of Modern Divinity*. Davidson was a controversial figure. He ceased observing Communion in his own parish and joined with a nearby congregation and, though he offered to resign his charge, the presbytery allowed him to carry out only those duties he felt his conscience permitted.

SELECT WRITINGS
H. Davidson, *The Fulness of the Godhead* [a printed sermon] (Alnick, Scotland, c. 1720)
—, *Letters to Christian Friends* (Edinburgh, 1811) contains a memoir

R. H. CAMPBELL

Davidson, Margaret (eighteenth century, Ireland). Methodist female preacher. Born into a poor family, she was blinded as a result of a smallpox attack at the age of two. She received no formal education, owing her religious conversion to a Methodist testimony heard while suffering acute anxiety over her state of sinfulness. Her subsequent emotional excitement was interpreted as madness by her family, and she was subjected to considerable personal persecution before finding support in a local Methodist society. Her faith was strengthened on hearing JOHN WESLEY preach in 1765, and she began to pray and plead the cause of religion among her family and neighbours. Local Methodist revivals in the 1770s gave her the opportunity to extend her sphere of usefulness and her public appearances were said to have resulted in many conversions. In this most vibrant period of Irish Methodism, Margaret Davidson's blindness and intense emotion, as well as her gender, proved a novel and effective combination.

BIBLIOGRAPHY
C. H. Crookshank, *Memorable Women of Irish Methodism in the Last Century* (London, 1882)
E. Smyth, *The Extraordinary Life and Experience of Margaret Davidson* (Dublin, 1782)

MYRTLE HILL

Davies, Benjamin (b. St Clears, Carmarthenshire, Wales, 26 Feb. 1814; d. Frome, Somerset, England, 19 July 1875). Baptist biblical scholar. Converted early in life, he preached his first sermon at the age of 16 but never became a pastor giving himself instead to research and teaching. He entered Bristol College in 1830, excelling in Hebrew and Old Testament studies. Further work at Trinity College, Dublin and Glasgow led on to study in Germany where he worked with Professors Ewald and THOLUCK, securing a Ph.D. from Leipzig in 1838, to which he later added an honorary LL D from Trinity College, Dublin. His academic career was spent between Canada and England; from 1838 to 1844 he headed the new Baptist College in Montreal; from 1844 to 1847 he was president of Stepney, a post he had been reluctant to accept and which did not work out well, for Davies was neither an administrator nor a disciplinarian, as well as being under suspicion for having worked in Germany. He wisely returned to Canada to a chair at McGill University (1847–57), but then readily responded to Angus' invitation to become Old Testament Tutor at Regent's Park College where he served for 18 years, and was described by one student as 'a great, rolling, lovable, elephantine figure of a man, like Samuel Johnson', for whom every student would readily 'have laid down his life'. He worked on Hebrew grammars and lexicons, was appointed to the panel revising the translation of the Old Testament, and produced biblical commentaries for the RTS.

BIBLIOGRAPHY
R. E. Cooper, *From Stepney to St Giles* (London, 1960)
DNB
S. A. Swaine, *Faithful Men* (London, 1884): 319–22

J. H. Y. BRIGGS

Davies, Daniel (b. Moelfre, Carmarthenshire, Wales, 15 Nov. 1797; d. 19 Feb. 1876). Blind Baptist preacher. Davies became blind at the age of six as a result of smallpox. After five years at work in the Dowlais Works crushing blacking for the foundry, he was admitted to the Liverpool Institute for the Blind in 1815 and taught English and various handicrafts. In 1817 he returned to Wales and began to preach among the Methodists but in 1821 was baptized as a believer and became minister of a Welsh Baptist congregation in London. Five years later he was appointed to one of the key Baptist pulpits in Swansea from whence he exercised much influence amongst Welsh Baptist churches.

He campaigned against dissenting disabilities, was a

firm Protestant, and anxious for political reform. He arranged for Baptist missionaries to visit South Wales to speak about the evils of Jamaican slavery, and was a member of the Swansea and Neath Peace Society. He believed that schools receiving government grants should confine their syllabuses to secular instruction, leaving religious education to Sunday schools, campaigning for the supply of good materials in Welsh for their use. He stayed at Swansea until 1858, after which he undertook pastorates in Cardigan and Aberavon. First president of the Welsh Baptist Union in 1866, he had been awarded an honorary doctorate by Madison University in 1859.

BIBLIOGRAPHY
T. M. Bassett, *The Welsh Baptists* (Swansea, 1977)
DWB

J. H. Y. BRIGGS

Davies, David (b. Llangeler, Dyfed, Wales, 12 June 1763; d. Swansea, Wales, 26 Dec. 1816). Congregational minister. Apart from a short period at a local school, he was self-educated. He married Jane Evans, 1783. He joined the Dissenting church at Pen-rhiw, Dyfed, but since he objected to the Arianism of the minister, David Davies (1745–1827), he moved to the Calvinistic congregation at Pencader. He was ordained, 1790, assistant minister at Dre-fach near his home, moved to Mynydd-bach, Swansea, in 1795, but in 1808 confined his ministry to Ebenezer, Swansea. His career marks the full impact of the evangelical revival on the Congregationalists of west Wales. He was a preacher of extraordinary power and received over 2,000 new members into Communion during his ministry. He founded several new churches and inspired a substantial number of young ministers imbued with the enthusiasm of the evangelical revival both in their preaching and their pastoral work.

BIBLIOGRAPHY
DWB
T. Rees and J. Thomas, *Hanes Eglwysi Annibynol*, 2 (Liverpool, England, 1872): 55

R. TUDUR JONES

Davies, Evan (b. parish of Lledrod, Dyfed, Wales, 1805; d. Hornsey, London, 18 June 1864). Congregational minister, missionary and author. He studied at Neuadd-lwyd and the Western Academy, Exeter. He was ordained at Great Torrington, Devon, but after a short stay he was commissioned on 29 April 1835 at Wycliffe Church, London, for service with the LMS in Penang, Malaya. He married Miss Sweetland, from Sidmouth. They arrived 11 September 1835, but after five years he had to return to England on account of ill health. In 1842 he was appointed superintendent of the Boys' Mission School, Walthamstow and in 1844 was inducted

minister in Richmond, Surrey. In 1857 he moved to Heywood, Manchester, but in 1859 retired to London on account of failing health. His published works are listed by G. Penar Griffith in his *Cenhadon Cymreig* (Cardiff, 1897) and include a memoir of SAMUEL DYER (London, 1846).

BIBLIOGRAPHY
T. Rees and J. Thomas, *Hanes Eglwysi Annibynol Cymru*, 2 (Liverpool, England, 1872)
LMS Register of Missionaries 1796–1923, 4th edn (London, 1923)

IEUAN S. JONES

Davies, Henry (b. *c.* 1680 in Carmarthenshire, Wales but exact date and place uncertain; d. in the Rhondda, Wales, 28 July 1766, aged 86). Congregational minister. He was educated at Carmarthen Academy and ordained at Blaengwrach, near Neath about 1718. About 1740 he moved to serve the church he had gathered at Cymer in the Rhondda Valley. He engaged in evangelistic campaigns before the coming of the evangelical revival. He was a warm admirer of HOWEL HARRIS. His first letter to him is dated 9 June 1738 and the last, 25 January 1766. They reveal his unwavering support for the revival, his high opinion of Harris, as well as the spiritual joy which impressed his contemporaries. He met his death by drowning in the River Rhondda.

BIBLIOGRAPHY
DWB
T. Rees and J. Thomas, *Hanes Eglwysi Annibynol*, 4 vols, 2 (Liverpool, England, 1871–5): 111, 347–8
J. Rufus Williams, *Hen Lyfr Henry Davies* (Llangollen, Wales, 1840)
Selections from his letters in *Y Cofiadur* (1935) and (1957)

R. TUDUR JONES

Davies, Howell (b. possibly Monmouthshire, Wales, *c.* 1716; d. Parke, Pembrokeshire, Wales, 13 Jan. 1770). Methodist Anglican clergyman. Davies first appears as a schoolmaster at Talgarth, Breconshire, in 1737 when he was converted under the ministry of HOWELL HARRIS. Ordained deacon in 1739 and priested in 1740, he became curate to GRIFFITH JONES at Llandeilo Abercywyn in Carmarthenshire, but moved to Llys-y-fran, Pembrokeshire, in 1741. He married twice; in 1744 to Catherine Poyer (died 1745), and in 1748 to Elizabeth White.

An early champion of itinerant preaching, and himself a powerful preacher, he confined himself during his later years to Pembrokeshire, probably due to ill health. From his conversion to his death he was one of the recognized leaders of Welsh Methodism. He was critical of JOHN WESLEY's doctrine, but was highly respected by GEORGE WHITEFIELD and others of the Calvinist branch.

BIBLIOGRAPHY
DWB
R. Griffiths, 'Howel Davies', *CCH*, 11 (1987): 2–14

GERAINT TUDUR

Davies, James (b. in parish of Llanedi, Dyfed, Wales, no date; d. at Merthyr Tydfil, Wales, April, 1760). Congregational minister. He was educated at Carmarthen Academy and ordained minister at Troedrhiwdalar and Llanwrtyd, Powys. In 1724 he moved to the joint pastorate of Cwm-y-glo, Merthyr Tydfil, and Cefnarthen, Dyfed. He was a precursor of the Evangelical Revival in Glamorgan and Gwent and on 13 January 1739 invited HOWEL HARRIS to preach in the area. Davies had a tempestuous ministry because his Calvinism was unacceptable to his Arminian fellow ministers and church members. He preserved his ardent piety to the end and, according to EDMUND JONES (1702–93) had 'an incomparable gift' in prayer. His son, Samuel (died 1781), minister at Kingswood, Wiltshire, and later at Merthyr, was an Arminian.

BIBLIOGRAPHY
Journal of Hist. Soc. of Presbyterian Church of Wales, LI, 3: 42
T. Rees and J. Thomas, *Hanes Eglwysi Annibynol*, 4 vols, 2 (Liverpool, England, 1871–5): 256–7
Y Cofiadur, 12 (1935)

R. TUDUR JONES

Davies, John (b. Llanfihangel-yng-Ngwynfa, Montgomeryshire, Wales, 11 July 1772; d. Papara, Tahiti, 19 Aug. 1855). Welsh Calvinistic Methodist missionary (LMS) to Society Islands. According to tradition Davies was born on a small farm called Pendugwm in the parish of Llanfihangel yng Ngwynfa, and was nurtured in a pious home by his parents David and Martha Davies, together with his sister Ann and brother David. During his youth a friendship with his most regular Welsh correspondent, JOHN HUGHES, was forged. Davies probably received a short period of education at one of BRIDGET BEVAN's charity schools and it is likely that he later received further tuition from THOMAS CHARLES prior to his employment as a teacher in Charles's circulating schools. Davies served at Llanrhaeadr-ym-Mochnant (1797), Machynlleth (1798), and Llanwyddelan (1799).

On 27 May 1800 Davies and his compatriots sailed from Britain on the *Royal Admiral*, arriving in Tahiti on 10 July 1801. Thereafter Davies's career and the mission were inextricably bound. He laboured at Matavai, Huahine, Sydney (New South Wales) then on Eimeo at Papetoai and Afareaitu, followed by another short period at Huahine; from 1820 until his death he served at Papara.

Davies's contribution to the mission was remarkable. He established the first regular day school at Matavai, and similar educational work was undertaken at every station at which he served. He was, arguably, responsible for the formulation of the Tahitian alphabet and grammar. He translated most of the New Testament and all the Psalms; he composed the first Tahitian hymns and published Tahiti's first magazine. Davies was also instrumental in establishing auxiliary missionary societies on many of the islands and a temperance society at Papara.

Manuscript material on Davies may be found in the LMS Archives, SOAS; The Mitchell Library, Sydney, Australia; The National Library of Wales, Aberystwyth, Dyfed, UK; and The University College of North Wales Library, Bangor, UK.

SELECT WRITINGS
J. Davies, *The History of the Tahitian Mission (1799–1830)*, ed. C. W. Newbury (Cambridge, England, 1961)

BIBLIOGRAPHY
DWB
O. M. Edwards, *Gwaith Ann Griffiths* (Conway, Wales, 1905)
R. L. Griffiths, *Y Bara Gwell* (London, 1955)
R. W. James, 'John Davies, Tahiti; an example of the missionary awareness of the early Welsh Calvinistic Methodists' (University of Wales, Ph.D. thesis, 1986)
R. Williams, 'Montgomeryshire Worthies', *The Montgomeryshire Collections* (1894)

R. WATCYN JAMES

Davies, John (b. Rock, Stourport, Worcestershire, England, 1788; d. Worcester, 12 July 1858). Anglican clergyman. Educated at Rock Grammar School, Dr Simpson's Academy, Worcester and Worcester College, Oxford, on being ordained he was curate of Neen Sollars and Milson, Worcestershire, and from 1816 was Rector of St Clement's, Worcester. Davies was converted while visiting Clapham Parish Church. He rebuilt St Clement's and preached at its consecration in 1823, and was active in the city. He was chaplain of Berkley Chapel, ministered in the infirmary and goal, was involved in education, was an active Sabbatarian and wrote and distributed tracts.

Davies became aware of the spiritual needs of the 4,000 boatmen and their families who worked on the River Severn and nearby canals and his ministry to them gained him the title 'the apostle of the watermen'. In Worcester he provided a floating chapel. 'Some of the very lowest of the people . . . occasionally frequented the Watermen's Church, such as scavengers, the inmates of filthy lodging-houses, dustmen, ostlers, cads, match-sellers and now and then a sweep or a gipsy' (CPAS, 1852 *Report*). He supported the erection of the Mariner's Chapel, Gloucester and three churches on the banks of the River Weaver, in Cheshire. Between 1838 and 1840 Davies's biographer was in charge of St Clement's, while he ministered to watermen at Holy Trinity, Runcorn.

BIBLIOGRAPHY
Seventeenth report of the CPAS (May 1852): 39
G. Lea, *Memoir of Rev John Davies* (London, 1873)

ALAN FREDERICK MUNDEN

Davies, Richard (d. 6 Feb. 1854). Anglican clergyman and secretary of CMS. Davies was the son of the curate of Rhuddlan, Flintshire, Wales, and educated locally (he was bilingual from early years), and at Corpus Christi College, Cambridge (BA 1835; MA 1838).

He became his father's curate at St David's, Liverpool. Always active for the CMS, he became association secretary for the Eastern Counties (based in Cambridge) and in 1841 clerical secretary, editing the society's journals. In 1846 he was nominated Bishop of Rupert's Land, but before the endowment was arranged his health deteriorated, and he became instead Vicar of Brenchley, Kent in 1848. He died after a long illness.

BIBLIOGRAPHY
Al. Cant., II, 2: 243
R. Davies, *Sermons* (with preface by HENRY VENN) (London, 1854)

A. F. WALLS

Davies, Samuel (b. New Castle, DE, BNA, 3 Nov. 1723; d. Princeton, NJ, BNA, 4 Feb. 1761). Presbyterian minister in Virginia and president of the College of New Jersey. The son of Welsh Baptist parents, whose mother forsook this tradition for the Presbyterians, Davies was a product of the religious pluralism of the middle colonies. He was educated at SAMUEL BLAIR's New Light academy, Fagg's Manor in Chester County, Pennsylvania between 1739 and 1746 with funds contributed by Hanover County Virginia admirers of the Pennsylvania itinerant, WILLIAM ROBINSON. Davies entered the ministry in 1746 as a New Light evangelist in Pennsylvania, New Jersey, and Maryland. Though recovering from severe illness and grieving over the death of his bride, he moved to Virginia in 1748 where Lieutenant-Governor William Gooch gave him a licence to preach and observed that Davies was 'tall, slim, well-formed, . . . pale and wasted by disease, dignified and courteous in manner' (Pilcher, 1971: 34).

In Virginia he quickly remarried, choosing Jane Holt, daughter of a prominent Williamsburg family. The couple had six children, five of whom lived to maturity. During his 12-year ministry in Virginia, Davies became a prolific poet and hymn-writer. A trip to Britain in 1753–5 gained him entry into the transatlantic evangelical network of clergymen, religious writers, printers, and financial contributors, who created a loose-knit association from later Puritanism in the seventeenth century until abolitionism in the nineteenth. These contacts enabled him to publish many of his poems, hymns, sermons, and letters and, in turn, gain respectability for religious dissent in Virginia.

His most notable achievement in Virginia was to persuade the colonial government to extend toleration to Dissenters. He skilfully argued that if the English Toleration Act did not extend to Virginia, then neither did the Uniformity Act, on which the Anglican establishment depended. He sought repeatedly in the early 1750s to secure extension of his licence to cross county lines, citing a 1711 British law relaxing restrictions on itinerancy, but the Anglican commissary, William Dawson,

and the Bishop of London stubbornly resisted Davies' claim to preach wherever he pleased. His trip to Great Britain did raise funds for the Presbyterian College of New Jersey, but did little to diminish Anglican opposition to religious liberty in Virginia.

Probably more helpful in preparing the way for unlicensed Baptists and Methodists to evangelize Virginia in the 1760s and 70s, and in drawing Presbyterians into positions of political leadership, was Davies' powerful preaching in support of the British cause in the Seven Years' War (1756–63) in which he summoned Virginians to arms 'lest Indian savages and French Papists, infamous all the world over for treachery and tyranny, should rule Protestants and Britons with a rod of iron' (Morgan, 1975: 3).

After declining the presidency of the College of New Jersey he finally accepted it, taking office 26 July 1759; however, his tenure was cut short by pneumonia which led to his death 18 months later.

BIBLIOGRAPHY
E. S. Morgan, *American Slavery, American Freedom* (New York, 1975)
G. W. Pilcher, *Samuel Davies* (Knoxville, TN, 1971)

ROBERT CALHOON

Davies, William (b. Llanfynydd, Carmarthenshire, Wales, *c.* 1727; d. Neath, Glamorganshire, Wales, 17 Aug. 1787). Anglican clergyman and supporter of Methodism. It is believed that he was ordained deacon on 13 August 1758, and priested on 17 August 1760. He was given the cure of Pentyrch, Glamorganshire, but by 1762 had moved to Neath. In 1768 he became curate of Llanfihangel-ynys-Afan, Glamorganshire, and served in the same capacity at Llan-giwg from 1771 to 1775. Throughout this time he was involved with the Methodist movement and was known throughout Wales as a powerful preacher.

BIBLIOGRAPHY
DWB
G. M. Roberts, 'William Davies, Castell-Nedd (*c.* 1727–87)', in *CCH*, LVI (1971): 77

GERAINT TUDUR

Davies, William (b. Wales, *c.* 1787; d. 1842). WMS missionary, Sierra Leone. In 1805, at the age of 18, he became a travelling preacher in Wales. In 1815 he went to Sierra Leone for the Wesleyan Missionary Society (WMS) to take charge of the Wesleyan congregation in Freetown. He was accompanied by his wife, Jennet Jane, the first woman Wesleyan missionary in West Africa, who died within a year. The congregation, founded originally in Nova Scotia by its own preachers, had, a few years earlier, established links with the Wesleyans in England who, at their request sent out white missionaries. But there was constant friction between the two.

The church leaders resented particularly that Davies became the protege of the governor of the colony, Charles MacCarthy. Eventually they refused to let him preach, saying he was too proud. He left Freetown, and took charge, as a government employee, of one of the villages MacCarthy was founding for recaptives liberated from the slave-ships. He was also Mayor of Freetown. In 1818 his health broke down and he returned to Britain.

SELECT WRITING

W. Davies, *Extracts from the Journal of the Reverend William Davies* (Llandidloes, Wales, no date [1835])

CHRISTOPHER FYFE

Davis, Charles (b. Piddletrenthide, Dorset, England, *c.* 1800; at sea, 1829). CMS missionary in New Zealand. Davis, a carpenter, was sent to New Zealand by the CMS on 22 November 1823 along with RICHARD DAVIS (apparently his older brother). In 1828 he returned to England where he married in 1829. Later that year he and his wife were lost at sea on a voyage to New Zealand.

BIBLIOGRAPHY

D. T. B[arry], *CMS Register of Missionaries and Native Clergy* (privately printed) (London, 1906)

DONALD M. LEWIS

Davis, James (b. Margate, Kent, England, 1 June 1812; d. Mortlake, London, 11 June 1894). Independent minister and administrator. From relatively humble origins, Davis had a limited private education. In 1839 he left a business career and entered Cheshunt College to prepare for the Congregational ministry. Subsequently he served undistinguished pastorates in Denton, Norfolk; Pimlico, London; and Rochester, Kent.

In 1846 he was one of the delegates at the international conference which inaugurated the EA. In 1859 he was appointed as general secretary of its British organization, a position which he occupied with distinction for 19 years. Possessing a high degree of entrepreneurial skills, Davis pioneered membership recruitment and extended the EA's activities in the field of religious liberty. The Matamoros case in Spain, the persecution of Nestorian Christians, the oppression of Christians in the Baltic Provinces, all evinced a strong and effective response from Davis. He visited the EA's continental branches, attended its International Conference and gained access to a variety of international leaders, including Bismarck.

Davis supervised the evangelistic and apologetic programme of the Salle Evangelique at the Paris Exhibition in 1878. He suffered a stroke and was compelled into an early retirement. His successors inherited a burgeoning movement embodying the principles of evangelical unity.

BIBLIOGRAPHY

J. W. Ewing, *Goodly Fellowship* (London, 1946)

CLIVE CALVER

Davis, Jefferson (Finis) (b. Christian City, KY, USA, 3 June 1808; d. New Orleans, LA, USA, 6 Dec. 1889). US Congressman, Senator, and Confederate president. Although raised as a 'Hard-Shell Baptist' and for a time educated in a Catholic school, Davis in his early career found little time for public pronouncements of formal religion. Before the Civil War he had served his adopted state of Mississippi as both congressman and senator, commanded a regiment of state troops during the Mexican War and served as President Franklin Pierce's Secretary of War.

During the Civil War, however, he turned frequently to his faith. Soon after his arrival in the Confederate capital of Richmond he joined a prominent Episcopal church, devoted considerable time to the religious welfare of the southern armies, and issued the first of a series of calls for public prayer, thanksgiving and fasting. 'We feel,' he wrote in April 1861, 'that our cause is just and holy.' His ardent religious inclinations in time became a matter of public comment. The Richmond *Examiner*, for example, fretted that the president was too often 'in a corner telling his beads, and relying on a miracle to save the country'.

As late as March 1865, with defeat imminent, Davis still found time to mourn that the Confederate constitution 'should have not merely a religious but a Christian basis; but such is not its character'. Imprisoned at Fort Monroe, Virginia, for two years, Davis became a revered Christian martyr to the Lost Cause, in the extreme regarded as a redeemer. So firm was the image that by 1916 ten southern states had designated his birthday as a ritual Confederate Memorial Day.

BIBLIOGRAPHY

DAB

W. C. Davis, *Jefferson Davis: The Man and His Hour* (New York, 1991)

W. E. Dodd, *Jefferson Davis* (Philadelphia, PA, 1907)

—, *Statesmen of the Old South* (New York, 1929)

A. Tate, *Jefferson Davis* (New York, 1929)

EDWARD D. C. CAMPBELL

Davis, John (b. Pennepek, PA, BNA, 10 Sept. 1721; d. Winter Run, Hartford, MD, USA, 1809). Baptist minister. John Davis was ordained in 1756 as a Particular Baptist minister. He established the Hartford Baptist Church which became the mother church of Baptist churches in Maryland. Davis continued in that pastorate for 53 years. He also established First Baltimore (1795), Taney Town, Gunpowder, and Sater's as churches. He was a founding member of the Baltimore Association, 10–12 August 1793, and endured significant persecution for his Baptist beliefs.

BIBLIOGRAPHY
AAP
W. Cathcart, *Baptist Encyclopedia* (Philadelphia, PA, 1881)
C. B. Hassell and S. Hassell, *History of the Church of God* (Middletown, NY, 1886): 897–8

WADE A. HORTON

Davis, John (b. Northumberland Co., VA, USA, 30 Oct. 1787; d. Hillsborough, VA, USA, 13 Aug. 1853). Methodist minister. He was converted at age 19 and joined the Baltimore Conference in 1810. He was an extraordinary preacher, with more than a 1,000 conversions to his credit in a single year.

He was known for his keen intellect and interest in education, serving as a trustee of Dickinson College. He was also a respected presiding elder, known for his ability as a counsellor, and a delegate to every General Conference between 1816 and his death.

BIBLIOGRAPHY
CM

STEVE HARPER

Davis, Richard (b. Chatham, Kent, England, 9 March 1768; d. Walworth, London, 1832). Baptist minister. The son of a widow of a Baptist minister at Chatham, his first employment was in the dockyard. Converted about the age of twenty and accepted into membership in the church at Chatham, he early became convinced of a call to the ministry, but an early marriage to Sarah Tamsett of Rye, where he had gone to practise his ministerial gifts, together with the nine sons and five daughters she quickly bore him, prevented formal ministerial training. Wrestling with the writings of JONATHAN EDWARDS, he came to adopt a Fullerite position. In 1793 he abandoned the Dockyard for the ministry, supplying at Portsea, Hampshire (6 months), Lyme, Dorset (12 months), Thorn, Bedfordshire (3 years) and Little Wilde Street (9 months). Formal ordination, at the hands of JOHN FAWCETT, seems to have awaited his succession to SAMUEL MEDLEY's pulpit at Byrom Street, Liverpool, where he exercised a fruitful ministry for some ten years until his congregation became unsettled by the antinomian teaching of another Liverpool minister. His ministry at Trowbridge, which led to chapel extension, was followed by a pastorate at Plymouth Dock (Devonport).

Keen on the closest of fellowship with other evangelical Christians (except at the Lord's Table, for he was an ardent strict communionist), in his final pastorate at East Street, Walworth, during which six young men including three of his own sons were sent into the ministry, he exercised a wider ministry within and beyond the denomination, frequently preaching at Whitefield Tabernacle, Tottenham Road Chapel and Surrey Chapel. He was a keen supporter of the BMS for which he frequently undertook preaching tours as also on behalf of the Moravian Missions.

BIBLIOGRAPHY
Bapt Mag (1832)
J. Davis [son], *A Brief Memoir of the Late Rev Richard Davis of Walworth* (London, 1883)

T. E. DOWLEY AND J. H. Y. BRIGGS

Davis, Richard (b. Piddletrenthide, Dorset, England, *c.* 1790; Waimate, New Zealand, 28 May 1863). CMS missionary in New Zealand. Davis, a farmer, was sent to New Zealand by the CMS on 22 November 1823 along with CHARLES DAVIS (apparently his younger brother) and arrived at Paihia on 15 August 1824. Accompanying Davis were his two daughters, Serena and Mary Ann who both later served with the CMS. On 14 April 1831 he was stationed at Waimate. Davis was ordained (deacon 1843, priest 1852) by the Bishop of New Zealand and served for over 40 years with the CMS.

Details of his first marriage are unknown. He then married: Mary Crocker on 11 February 1822 who died 1 February 1837; Mrs Anne Iselton on 18 September 1838 who died 7 April 1854; and finally Jane King (daughter of JOHN KING) in September 1855, who died 5 December 1894.

BIBLIOGRAPHY
D. T. B[arry], *CMS Register of Missionaries and Native Clergy* (privately printed) (London, 1906)

DONALD M. LEWIS

Davis, Stephen (b. Andover, Hampshire, England, 30 Oct. 1783; d. London, 3 Feb. 1856). Baptist minister and missionary in Ireland. Of a clerical family – his grandmother was sister to BENJAMIN FRANCIS – his parents were members of the Little Wild Street Church in London. Davis was converted through the preaching of SAMUEL PEARCE, a conversion confirmed under the ministry of JOHN RIPPON. He was baptized by Thomas Thomas at Devonshire Square where he entered into membership in 1802. Responding to a call to the ministry he was inhibited from college training by an early marriage and instead engaged in pulpit supply until accepted for service with the Baptist Irish Society to which work he was ordained at Carter Lane in 1816. After brief initial service in Dublin he was stationed for seven years at Clonmel, only returning to England in 1823 to raise funds, for which purpose he also visited the USA in 1832–3. From 1837 to 1845 he served as travelling agent of the Irish Society until ill health forced his retirement. A close communionist, he was active in the Baptist Tract Society.

BIBLIOGRAPHY
Baptist Manual (1856)

J. H. Y. BRIGGS

Davison, John (b. Tynemouth, Northumberland, England, 23 Nov. 1799; d. Toronto, Upper Canada, 1

March 1844). Transatlantic Primitive Methodist minister. Davison was apprenticed, aged 14, to a ship-carpenter, after receiving a basic education. Narrowly escaping drowning in the Tyne, Davison became religiously aware. He was convicted of sin during a prayer meeting and converted through conversation with the Primitive Methodist, William Morris. Davison gave his first sermon in 1823, and subsequently engaged in powerful open-air preaching to the fishermen and sailors of the north-east. Sent to 17 stations in 24 years, Davison endured great hardship. In 1847, Davison agreed to a request by the Missionary Committee to go to Toronto (where he lived until his death). He was appointed general missionary secretary in 1857. Davison edited WILLIAM CLOWES' journals (1840) (Davison had married Clowes' step-daughter in 1825), wrote a biography of Clowes (1854), established the journal, *The Evangelist*, and edited the *Christian Journal*. In 1863 he was appointed to the senate of the University of Toronto.

BIBLIOGRAPHY
PM Mag (1884)

WAYNE J. JOHNSON

Davy, William (b. Tavistock, Devon, England, 4 March 1743; d. Winkleigh, Devon, 13 June 1826). Anglican clergyman. From Exeter Grammar School Davy proceeded to Balliol College, Oxford (BA 1764). He returned to his native county as Curate of Moretonhampstead and then of Drewsteignton, where he was reported to the Bishop for preaching against common vices. The Bishop, however, supported Davy, who became Curate of Lustleigh (1785–1825) and finally Vicar of Winkleigh (1825–6). Of a mechanical bent, Davy constructed his own printing press which he used for publishing his detailed system of divinity (26 vols, 1787–1807), followed by 'improved Extracts'.

BIBLIOGRAPHY
CO, xxvii: 65

ARTHUR POLLARD

Davys, George (b. Loughborough, Leicestershire, England, 1 Oct. 1780; d. Peterborough, England, 18 April 1864). Anglican bishop. Davys entered Christ's College, Cambridge in 1799 (BA 1803; MA 1806; fellow 1806–14; DD 1831). He became Curate of Littlebury (Essex) in 1806, then of Chesterford to 1817 and afterwards of Swaffham Priory. He was also Vicar of Willoughby-on-the-Wolds (Lincolnshire) (1811–29), followed by the Crown appointment to All Hallows-on-the-Wall, London (1829–40) as a consequence of his having become by the influence of the Duchess of Kent's confidant, Sir John Conroy, tutor to the future Queen Victoria (1827–37). Davys was responsible for geography, history, French, law and classics, most of which she regarded as 'dry' subjects and in the last he regretfully

recorded that she was making 'little progress'. The future queen, however, was and remained deeply attached to him. He became Dean of Chester (1831–9), after which he was made Bishop of Peterborough (1839–64). He appears to have managed his diocese peaceably but quite unremarkably.

Although a convinced evangelical, Davys played no part in the religious controversies of the time nor in the politics of the period. He published a number of simple educational volumes of 'village conversations' dealing with various aspects of Anglican practice and worship.

BIBLIOGRAPHY
DNB
C. Woodham-Smith, *Queen Victoria*, 1 (1819–61) (London, 1972)

ARTHUR POLLARD

Dawes, William (b. 1762; d. Antigua, 1836). Governor of Sierra Leone. Commissioned in the Royal Marines, he took part in the first British settlement of convicts at Botany Bay, New South Wales, in 1787. A man of strong religious principles, he was dismissed for objecting to being made to take part in an attack on Aborigines (he had already had discussions with an Aborigine woman about their respective religions). He was then recruited by the directors of the Sierra Leone Company, to whom his principles were a recommendation, for their settlement in Sierra Leone where in 1793 he was promoted governor. His rigid style antagonized the black settlers who sent a deputation of protest to London, but the directors supported him, and eventually he worked more harmoniously with them. In 1796 he resigned and became a schoolmaster in England, but returned in 1801. By then the Company's government had antagonized the ruler of the nearby Temne chiefdom who attacked Freetown. Dawes led a final victorious charge and was severely wounded. In 1803 he returned to England and started a missionary seminary for the CMS.

When Sierra Leone became a British colony in 1808 he was sent as a commissioner to report on West Africa, and recommended the British navy be deployed to suppress the slave trade along the entire West African coast, not just part of it. His recommendation was adopted. In 1813 he emigrated to Antigua, where he was an agent for the CMS, and remained for the rest of his life.

BIBLIOGRAPHY
A. Currer-Jones, *William Dawes R.M., 1762–1836* (Torquay, England, 1930)
M. B. Eldershaw, *Phillip of Australia* (London, 1938)
C. Fyfe *A History of Sierra Leone* (London, 1962)

CHRISTOPHER FYFE

Dawson, (John) William (b. Pictou, Nova Scotia, BNA 13 Oct. 1820; d. Montreal, Quebec, Canada, 19 Nov. 1899). Geologist and principal of McGill University.

Regarded as Victorian Canada's foremost natural scientist, Dawson was educated at Pictou Academy and the University of Edinburgh. He was appointed principal of McGill in 1855, a position he held until 1893.

Dawson was known, not only as an outstanding geologist in his own right, but also as one of the most outspoken critics of Darwinism in the Anglo-American world. In 1878, because of this reputation, he was offered the chair of geology at Princeton (a position to be combined with a special lectureship at Princeton Seminary on the relationship of religion and science). Dawson declined this offer, however, in order to remain in Montreal and defend Protestantism against the perceived threat from Ultramontanism. He was a proponent of the day-age theory of creation and was committed to a Baconian/inductive scientific methodology. Active in various church affairs, he also served as president of the Dominion Evangelical Alliance.

BIBLIOGRAPHY
DCB, VII
A. B. Mckillop, *A Disciplined Intelligence* (Montreal, 1979)
C. F. O'Brien, *Sir William Dawson* (Philadelphia, PA, 1971)

RICHARD W. VAUDRY

Dawson, Thomas (b. Wakefield, Yorkshire, England, *c.* 1779; d. Goldsborough, Yorkshire, 6 Feb. 1828). CMS missionary to south India. Dawson studied for two years (1812–14) as a probationer missionary under THOMAS SCOTT and then for a further year under Reverend J. Buckworth, Vicar of Dewsbury. He was ordained (deacon 6 August 1815 and priest 17 December 1815) by the Archbishop of York to the curacy of Wetherby, Yorkshire. Like WILLIAM GREENWOOD, THOMAS NORTON, BENJAMIN BAILEY before him (and JOSEPH FENN after him), Dawson could not obtain ordination even from a sympathetic bishop in England without serving an English curacy. This practice seems to have ended after 1818.

On 6 April 1816 Dawson married Sarah Archer Bailey (sister of Benjamin and JOSEPH BAILEY) and on 4 May 1816 he was sent by the CMS to Cochin in south India. (It almost seems to have been an early CMS policy that male missionaries should marry a few weeks before going overseas.) In April of 1818 he returned to England for health reasons. His wife died in 1824 and he four years later. Dawson wrote a work *Christian Astronomer* and compiled an (unpublished) English, Portuguese, and Malayalim grammar.

BIBLIOGRAPHY
D. T. B[arry], *CMS Register of Missionaries and Native Clergy* (privately printed) (London, 1906)

DONALD M. LEWIS

Dawson, William (b. Garforth, Leeds, England, 30 March 1773; d. Colne, Lancashire, England, 4 July 1841). Farmer and Methodist local preacher. Dawson was the son of a steward to a colliery proprietor, and the eldest of ten children. He received a good education and was brought up in the Church of England, where he was converted in 1791 at a celebration of the Lord's Supper. Experiencing a call to preach, he joined the Wesleyans in 1800 in order to have more scope for preaching, was accepted as a local preacher in 1801 and was recommended as a candidate for the Wesleyan ministry in 1802. Arrangements for his dependants did not materialize, however, and he remained a layman. His vivid sermons spread his reputation across northern England and he was soon in great demand as a preacher on special occasions: chapel openings, missionary meetings and funerals – 10,000 attended his sermon on WILLIAM BRAMWELL.

He was prominent in the first Wesleyan Missionary Meetings in Leeds in 1813. He supported conference in the Leeds Organ Case (1827) and the Warrenite controversy (1834), and always argued strongly against total abstinence. In 1836 an attempt was made to raise 4,000 guineas to enable him to leave his farm and devote himself to preaching, principally for overseas missions. A sum of £3,000 was raised but he served in this way for less than two years before his death.

BIBLIOGRAPHY
W. D. Lawson, *Wesleyan Local Preachers* (Newcastle-upon-Tyne, England, 1874): 64–109

E. ALAN ROSE

Day, Jeremiah (b. Colchester, CT, BNA, 25 Jan. 1737; d. Litchfield County, CT, USA, 12 Sept. 1806). Congregational minister. A descendent of Robert Day who settled first at Cambridge, Massachusetts in 1634, Day studied at Yale from where he was graduated in 1756. He taught school interspersed with a year of theological study with JOSEPH BELLAMY of Bethlehem. He inherited his brother's farm at Sharon in 1763 and turned to farming. Day returned to theological studies with COTTON MATHER SMITH; was ordained and became pastor in New Preston in 1770. Having lost both his first and second wife, he married Abigail Noble in 1772, and they had five children.

Day made two missionary tours, one into western Vermont and another into New York and Pennsylvania. He spoke at Commencement at Yale in 1791 on the subject, 'The Eternal Pre-existence of the World'. He wrote an extended poem 'celebrating the pleasures of a country life', and published a number of individual sermons as well as *Sermons Collected*. He was an editor of the *Connecticut Evangelical Magazine* from its founding in 1800 to 1806.

BIBLIOGRAPHY
AAP
J. G. Wilson and J. Fiske, eds, *Appleton's Cyclopedia of American Biography* (New York, 1888)

DIETRICH G. BUSS

Day, John (b. NC, USA, 1797; d. Monrovia, 1859) African-American Baptist missionary and Chief Justice of Liberia. Apparently born free, a cabinet-maker by trade, he was converted as a young man and officiated as a Baptist minister. In 1830 he emigrated to Liberia with his wife and four children, and became superintendent of the Southern Baptist Board mission, teaching theology at the Baptist seminary in Monrovia. In the transitional period before Liberia became independent he was a member of the Legislative Council. In 1847 he was a delegate to the National Convention and a signatory of the Declaration of Independence. Subsequently he served as Chief Justice of the Supreme Court of Liberia.

BIBLIOGRAPHY
G. W. Hervey, *The Story of the Baptist Missions in Foreign Lands* (St Louis, MI, 1886)
B. I. Wiley, *Slaves No More* (Kentucky, 1980): 330

CHRISTOPHER FYFE

Day, Samuel (Stearns) (b. Bastard Township, County of Leeds, Upper Canada, 13 May 1808; d. Homer, NY, USA, 17 September 1871). First Canadian to serve as a Baptist missionary. A schoolteacher 1827–30, Day studied for the ministry in Hamilton, New York 1831–5. He was appointed by American Baptists as missionary to the Telegus of India on 3 August 1835. Married to Roenna Clark on 22 August 1835, he was ordained to the ministry at Cortland Village, New York the next day.

The Days arrived in Calcutta on 5 February 1836 and proceeded to Chicacole. In 1837 he was formally appointed to work in Madras where he founded a Baptist church. In February 1840 he moved to Nellore. Three converts were baptized in August 1843; and on 12 October a church was organized. Ill health forced him to return to the United States in 1845. Returning to Nellore in 1849, he was again forced by ill health to America in 1853. From 1855 to 1859 he served as a missionary agent for the American Baptist Missionary Union. His final years were spent in interim ministries.

BIBLIOGRAPHY
Baptist Missionary Magazine (Boston, MA, 1836–72)
Southern Baptist Historical Collection, Nashville, TN, 'Samuel Stearns Day Collection', Accession Number 143

JUDITH COLWELL

Day, William (b. probably Bristol, England, *c.* 1766; d. Bristol, 2 Sept. 1832). Anglican clergyman. Day was educated at St Edmund Hall, Oxford, under ISAAC CROUCH (BA 1786; MA 1789). From *c.* 1793 to 1803 he was Curate-in-Charge of Bengeworth in Worcestershire, a living controlled by T. T. BIDDULPH of Bristol who was both its incumbent and patron. After 1803 Day ministered in Bristol and in 1807 the corporation appointed him chaplain of the gaols and in 1810 Vicar of St Philip and St Jacob. He apparently maintained cordial relations with Nonconformist ministers during a time of strained denominational feelings.

BIBLIOGRAPHY
C. Hole, *Early History of the Church Missionary Society* (London, 1896): 626

DONALD M. LEWIS

Dayton, Amos Cooper (b. Plainfield, NJ, USA, 4 April 1813; d. Perry, GA, USA, 11 June 1865). Baptist author and editor. Dayton graduated from medical college in 1834 and, because of frail health, moved to the South, where he lectured on phrenology and other subjects. From 1839 to 1852, he practised dentistry in Vicksburg, Mississippi.

Though raise a Presbyterian, Dayton became a Baptist in 1852. After accepting the Landmarkist views of J. R. GRAVES, he began contributing articles to the *Tennessee Baptist*. He was corresponding secretary for the Southern Baptist Bible Board in 1854 and helped organize the Southern Baptist Sunday School Union in 1857, the same year he and J. M. PENDLETON became associate editors of the *Tennessee Baptist*. In 1859 he served as moderator of the Baptist General Association of Tennessee and North Carolina, and in 1863 became the president of the Houston Female Institute in Perry, Georgia.

Dayton's Landmarkist views led him to oppose all missionary work by conventions or boards and 'alien baptism'. His support of Graves in the Graves-Howell controversy led to his expulsion on grounds of schism from the First Baptist Church of Nashville, Tennessee in 1859.

BIBLIOGRAPHY
J. H. Borum, *Biographical Sketches of Tennessee Baptist Ministers* (Memphis, TN, 1880)
ESB

TIMOTHY P. WEBER

Deacon, John (b. Battersea, London, England, *c.* 1825; d. 1901). Banker. The son of John Deacon, esquire, of Battersea, a friend of WILBERFORCE, he was educated at Oriel College, Oxford, before becoming a very successful London banker. Deeply dedicated to evangelicalism in the Church of England he presented E. H. Carr to the living at Bidborough, near his country home at Mabledon, near Tonbridge in Kent, and discussions between the two men helped shape the idea of creating evangelical theological schools in Oxford and Cambridge. He served as one of the four trustees of Wycliffe and Ridley Halls from their commencement, was treasurer of their joint council and gave an initial gift of £1,000 towards their erection. When the councils were separated in 1893 he remained on the Ridley Council despite his Oxford education. His son Frank succeeded him as treasurer after his death. He married Lucy Katharine, the daughter of Francis Pym esquire.

BIBLIOGRAPHY
F. W. G. Bullock, *The History of Ridley Hall* (Cambridge, 1941)

PETER J. LINEHAM

Deacon, Samuel (b. 1714; d. Barton Fabis, Leicestershire, England, 19 March 1812). Baptist minister. A convert of one of the Countess of HUNTINGDON's preachers, Samuel Deacon, a wool-comber from Ratby in Leicestershire, soon joined with other earnest Christians to form a society along Methodist lines at Barton Fabis where they built themselves a small chapel. Notwithstanding violent opposition, the movement soon spread to such towns as Hinckley, Loughborough and Melbourne in Derbyshire. Moving first to immersion as the mode of baptism they subsequently deduced from their reading of the New Testament that only believers were the proper subjects of the rite. Unable, because of their Arminianism, to secure such baptism from any Baptist minister, in November 1755, two of their ministers first baptized one another and then over sixty of the members. Some, however, remained members who had not undergone the rite. Deacon, non-stipendiary pastor at Ratby, spent an incredible amount of time on the road walking to his preaching engagements; most Sundays this would involve twenty to forty miles and three or four services, with occasional visits to more distant locations, while many a week night saw him on the road after work to visit congregations. By 1760 their numbers had so increased and the distances between congregations being considerable, they divided into five independent churches.

In June 1770 together with DAN TAYLOR's Yorkshire following and such General Baptist churches that had remained orthodox in Christology, they formed the New Connexion of General Baptists embracing non-Calvinist Baptist churches of an evangelical outlook. Samuel's sons, Samuel Junior (1740–1816) and John (1757–1821) were both ordained ministers. Samuel, his father's colleague and successor at Barton, was a considerable devotional writer, hymn-writer and collector (see his *Barton Hymns*, 'full of gospel fervour', 1785); his half-brother, John, trained by Dan Taylor, and pastor in Leicester from 1782 also edited a denominational hymn-book.

BIBLIOGRAPHY
Julian
A. Taylor, *The History of the English General Baptists*, II (London, 1818)
A. C. Underwood, *A History of the English Baptists* (London, 1947)

J. H. Y. BRIGGS

Dealtry, Thomas (b. Knottingley, Yorkshire, England, 1795; d. Madras, India, 4 March 1861). East India Company chaplain and Anglican bishop. Son of James Dealtry (who though poor was apparently of an established family, of Lofthouse Hall, near Wakefield), and self-taught, Thomas became first an usher at Doncaster, then a private tutor. Of Rotherhithe, Kent, when he went up to St Catherine Hall, Cambridge, 1826, he took a first class in law, 1828, becoming LL B in 1829.

Ordained at Ely in 1828, Dealtry assisted at St Peter's and at St Mary-the-Less, Cambridge. Impressed by his preaching, CHARLES SIMEON persuaded him to allow his name to go forward as a chaplain for Bengal, where he was minister of the Old Church, Calcutta, 1829–48. Rarely absent, even for a day, 'the influence which he gained as a pastor has never been surpassed, even if equalled ... Many of the most influential inhabitants of Calcutta were members of his congregation. The average number of his communicants was from three to four hundred' (Higginbotham, 1874: 106). Dealtry's zeal and success were appreciated by Bishop DANIEL WILSON, who made him Archdeacon of Calcutta (1835–48), where for some years he acted as honorary secretary for the CMS.

Dealtry resigned, on health grounds, in 1848, and for about a year, as a temporary measure (following the secession of the Honourable B. W. NOEL) was minister of St John's Bedford Row, London, where Bishop Wilson had served earlier. Consecrated third bishop of Madras in 1849, and made DD by Archbishop Howley, the *Illustrated London News* published not only a likeness of Dealtry, but a second engraving, showing his consecration at Lambeth with two other bishops. (This is a rare portrayal of such a service before Anglo-Catholic influence had appreciably altered, in some respects, the historic Anglican externals, and as such an important liturgical record.) Dealtry's 'liberal and genial disposition won for him widespread esteem and affection'. He set a hardworking example to his clergy, and in 1856 undertook visitation of the diocese of Calcutta for the now aged and infirm Bishop Wilson. Followed shortly by the Indian Mutiny, the knowledge of death and desolation among Christians and others where he had lately ministered, as well as the destruction of several churches he had consecrated, weighed upon him for some time. Responsible himself 'for much church building,' while a convinced evangelical churchman, he was sympathetic to all Christian endeavours.

Bishop Stephen Neill acknowledges that 'His administration was excellent, considerate to all, but firm in essentials.' Ordinands increased appreciably in numbers. Without being specific, but with normal probability, Neill adds that Dealtry had his weaknesses. Yet 'there is no reason to doubt that his influence ... extended to all classes of the Christian community, European and native, official and non-official, in whose estimation he was constantly rising till the day of his death' (*Bombay Times*). Early in 1861, while on visitation Dealtry accidentally damaged his foot. He returned to Madras but the injury deteriorated and led to his death.

Dealtry married, 1819, a pupil's sister, who soon died; and married again, 1824. Archdeacon Thomas Dealtry of Madras was his son. To WILLIAM DEALTRY (1775–

1847), Archdeacon of Surrey, he was apparently unrelated. But George Howson (*DNB*) was his great-grandson. Dealtry's portrait is in the *Illustrated London News*, 15 (1849)

BIBLIOGRAPHY
Al.Cant.
Boase, 1
DNB
J. J. Higginbotham, *Men Whom India Has Known* (2nd edn, Madras, India, 1874)
S. Neill, *A History of Christianity in India*, 2 (Cambridge, 1985)

J. S. REYNOLDS

Dealtry, William (b. Whitgift, Yorkshire, England, 20 July 1775; d. Brighton, Sussex, England, 15 Oct. 1847). Anglican clergyman and mathematician. After early education in the village of Swinefleet, Dealtry spent two years under JOSEPH MILNER at Hull before going on to St Catherine's Hall, Cambridge, in 1792 and transferring a year later to Trinity College (BA 1796; fellow 1798; MA 1799; BD 1812; DD 1829), where he acted as tutor (1801–6), a role he also fulfilled with the sons of CHARLES GRANT of Clapham, the future Sir ROBERT GRANT and Lord Glenelg (CHARLES GRANT) (1798–1800). It was there that he met other members of the 'Clapham Sect', whose rector he would become on the recommendation of his predecessor, JOHN VENN, and sanctioned by CHARLES SIMEON, in 1813. Before that, however, he was curate to ROBERT JARRATT at Wellington (Somerset) (1799–1800), returning to Cambridge as moderator of examinations (1801–6), after which he was professor of mathematics at Haileybury (1806–13) where he published a textbook on Fluxions (1810) and became an FRS in the same year. Besides being Rector of Clapham (1813–43) Dealtry was also Rector of Hatfield Broadoak (1814–16) and of Watton and Clothall (1816–30). He became chancellor of Winchester (1830–45) and Archdeacon of Surrey (1845–7). Dealtry was much influenced by Simeon and preached at Holy Trinity, Cambridge, after the latter's death.

Dealtry was a fervent supporter of the BFBS and during the Cambridge controversy of 1810–12 wrote responses to Wordsworth (the Archbishop of Canterbury's chaplain), Marsh (Lady Margaret professor of divinity) and Norris (Curate of St John's, Hackney). He likewise supported the CMS, and his anniversary sermon at the time of the renewal of the East India Charter by Parliament in 1813 was influential in gaining the admission of missionaries, in addition to and distinct from the company's chaplains, to the subcontinent. He appears to have been diligent and unassuming in his administrative duties as chancellor and archdeacon, and particular mention is made of his kindness and concern for curates. It is recorded that 'as a preacher he was distinguished for clear statements of scriptural truth, for great beauty of style, and for the eloquence of his exhortations rather than for searching appeals to the conscience, or lively delineations of spiritual life in the soul' (*CO*, xlvii: 135).

BIBLIOGRAPHY
Al. Cant, II, ii: 263
CO, xlvii (1848): 64–5, 133–40

ARTHUR POLLARD

Dear, Richard Edward (b. Hampshire, England, 13 May 1809; d. Hobart, Tasmania, Australia, 27 May 1880). Businessman and missionary. Son of a wealthy farmer, Dear was educated at St Nicholas's School. He entered business in London first as a chemist and then as a manufacturing stationer. Converted in Dr HENRY TOWNLEY's church, he became a Sunday school organizer. Soon diversifying, he learning the blind alphabet in order to teach blind children to read the Bible, and for many tears conducted a young man's Bible class. Dear was DAVID NASMITH's first firm supporter and patron in forming the London City Mission, acting as treasurer and also as examiner of the mission's first agents. In 1854, restless for life on the land and aspiring to missionary adventure, Dear emigrated to Tasmania. Shortly after, he was ordained by the Tasmanian Congregational Union, becoming its missionary in country districts, and also travelling agent of the Tasmanian auxiliary of the BFBS. He soon was a familiar horseback traveller in Tasmanian country districts, offering advice on manure and farm chemicals as well as religious matters.

BIBLIOGRAPHY
J. Campbell, *Memoirs of David Nasmith* (London, 1844)
Mercury ([Hobart], 27 May 1880)

RICHARD ELY

De Bruyn (b. Bengal, India, *c.* 1790; d. outside Chittagong, India, March 1817). Baptist missionary in India. 'Country born', De Bruyn spoke both Portuguese and Bengali fluently. This helped him lead a successful mission in Chittagong (beginning in 1812) among the culturally mixed and lapsed Roman Catholics. De Bruyn also created a church among the Mugh (Arakanese) tribal people outside Chittagong, becoming known as 'The Apostle to the Mughs'. Although this church did not thrive, the Mughs transmitted the Gospel on to other tribes. A strong Baptist church still survives in the Chittagong Hill Tracts. De Bruyn's emphasis on self-support undoubtedly helped the much persecuted church to survive without European missionaries. His Burmese converts joined the American Baptist Mission.

On his deathbed – after being attacked by a youth he had adopted as a son and employed as an interpreter – De Bruyn wrote to the local magistrate stating that he had forgiven his murderer, and that he hoped the judge would do likewise.

BIBLIOGRAPHY
Periodical Accounts Relative to the BMS, 33 (Bristol 1817): 265
J. C. Marshman, *The Life and times of Carey, Marshman and Ward*, II (London, 1859): 153 f

E. M. JACKSON

Deck, James George (b. Bury St Edmunds, Suffolk, England, 1 Nov. 1807; d. Motueka, near Nelson, New Zealand, 14 Aug. 1884). Brethren hymn-writer. The eldest son of John Deck, he was born in 1807 (so Pickering: 36, *pace* Julian: 285). After training for the army he went to India in 1824 and was commissioned in the 14th Madras Regiment. When on leave in England he was converted after hearing a sermon given by an Anglican clergyman. In 1829 be married Alicia Feild, daughter of an evangelical Anglican clergyman, Samuel Feild. She died in 1853.

In India Deck met the pioneer Brethren missionary, A. N. GROVES. In 1835 Deck resigned his commission and soon associated with Brethren in the UK, especially in the West Country. Owing to failing health in 1852 he emigrated to New Zealand. He wrote nearly a hundred hymns, often on the human experiences of Christ and the devotional meaning of the resurrection. They included such fine compositions as 'Lamb of God, our souls adore Thee', 'Lord Jesus, are we one with Thee?', and 'O Lord, when we the path retrace'. They were published in *Hymns and Sacred Songs* (Melbourne, 1876; London, 1905).

Deck's sister, MARY JANE WALKER, sister-in-law, MARY ANN SANDERSON DECK, and nephew, H. L. R. Deck (1858–1910) also wrote hymns. A living descendant, Luci Shaw of Regent College, Vancouver, is an American poet.

BIBLIOGRAPHY
J. S. Andrews, 'Brethren Hymnology', *EQ*, 28 (1956): 208–29
Boase
E. E. Cornwall, *Songs of Pilgrimage and Glory*, 1 (London, [1932]): 76–89
DNZB
Julian: 285–6, 1231, 1509, 1628, 1723, 1763
P. J. Lineham, 'The Significance of J. G. Deck 1807–1884', *Christian Brethren Research Fellowship (NZ) Journal*, 107 (November 1986): 13–34
Pickering

JOHN S. ANDREWS

Deck, Mary Ann Sanderson [née **Gibson**] (b. Hull, Yorkshire, England, 1813; d. Wolverhampton, Staffordshire, England, 26 June 1903). Anglican hymn-writer. In 1845 she married John Deck, brother of J. G. DECK and Vicar of St Stephen's, Hull. 'There is a city bright' was written for a children's service at the church, the first verse by her daughter, Amy Catherine, the others by herself. Amy, the future Mrs O[ctavius] F[rank] Walton, wrote her children's story, *Christie's Old Organ* (London, 1874), to illustrate the hymn, which is still sung. Mrs Deck moved to live with her daughter, now in Wolverhampton, where she died in 1903, not 1902 (Hayden and Newton, 1977, *pace* Moffatt, 1927: 317). On the widespread confusion over her daughter's and her son-in-law's Christian names see Cutt (1979: 156–8, but cf. 215!).

BIBLIOGRAPHY
M. N. Cutt, *Ministering Angels* (Wormley, Herts, England, 1979): 155–70, 215–16
A. J. Hayden and R. F. Newton, *British Hymn Writers and Composers* (Croydon, England, 1977)
J. Moffatt, ed., *Handbook to 'The Church Hymnary'* (London, 1927): 163, 317

JOHN S. ANDREWS

Deck, Mary Jane [Mrs Edward Walker]. *See* WALKER, MARY JANE [née Deck]

Decker, Charles Henry (b. Germany). CMS missionary in Sierra Leone. Decker trained at the Berlin Mission Seminary under Professor JOHANNES JÄNICKE and responded to the request from the CMS for German missionaries in the absence of English recruits. He was ordained to Lutheran orders but received further training as a probationer missionary under Reverend A. Westoby, of Emberton, Buckinghamshire. On 19 November 1817 he was sent to Wilberforce, but withdrew from CMS service in 1822.

BIBLIOGRAPHY
D. T. B[arry], *CMS Register of Missionaries and Native Clergy* (privately printed) (London, 1906)

DONALD M. LEWIS

De Courcy, Richard (b. southern Ireland, *c.* 1743; d. Shrewsbury, Shropshire, England, 4 Nov. 1803). Calvinistic Methodist clergyman. He entered Trinity College, Dublin, as a pensioner on 8 July 1764, and graduated MA, BD. After being ordained a deacon he became curate to WALTER SHIRLEY at Loughrea. He was refused priest's orders and inhibited by the Archbishop of Dublin, so went to England about 1768. There he preached at the London Tabernacle and other Methodist meetings. On 23 July 1769 he read the service at the opening of Lady HUNTINGDON's Tunbridge Wells chapel.

He was Curate of Shawbury (Shropshire) for a few months in 1770 and was ordained priest, but soon went north as Lady GLENORCHY's chaplain. In 1774 he received the Crown living of St Alkmund, Shrewsbury which he retained until his death. There he rebuilt the church, wrote many religious works and engaged in controversy with the local Baptists. John Byng, who heard him preach in 1793, commented on his Irish brogue and the length of his sermon. His sermons were published in 1805.

BIBLIOGRAPHY
R. F. Skinner, *Nonconformity in Shropshire* (Shrewsbury, England, 1964)

EDWIN WELCH

Deerr, William James (b. Kaltenwestern [now Neckarwestheim], Württemberg, Germany, 21 Nov. 1791;

d. Marbach, Württemberg, Germany, 26 March 1862). Missionary to India. Born Wilhelm Dürr and trained as a weaver, he enrolled at the Basel Seminary on 9 July 1816. As its first student he received Lutheran ordination two years later. He was then accepted by the CMS, the first person from Basel to serve, and went to England. After spending a few months at the National School of the Central Society, he sailed for Calcutta on 17 April 1819. Together with his Basel classmate J. A. JETTER, he opened a station at Burdwan in Bengal, North India. After five years his colleague returned home, but Deerr expanded the work to Culna and then to Krishnagar, where he started a vernacular school. During the next decade numerous conversions occurred, the most spectacular being in 1838 when the leading men in ten villages simultaneously embraced Christianity: after a period of instruction, Deerr baptized 500 people. In 1825 he married Mary White of the Calcutta Female Orphan Asylum staff, but she died in 1833. He returned to Europe in 1842, spent some time in the USA, and finally settled in Germany where he died in 1862.

BIBLIOGRAPHY
D. T. B[arry], *CMS Register of Missionaries and Native Clergy* (privately printed) (London, 1906)
E. Stock, *History of the CMS* (London, 1899)

R. V. PIERARD

De Fleury, Maria (d. *c.* 1794). Baptist author and hymn-writer. An intimate friend of the younger JOHN RYLAND, and resident for many years in Cripplegate, London, she enjoyed controversial writing (e.g. *Unrighteous Abuses Detected*, 1781; and *Antinomianism Unmasked*, 1791), which were republished in the USA. More particularly she penned a series of papers, some with Ryland, attacking WILLIAM HUNTINGTON. She also wrote a number of hymns which enjoyed quite wide usage, exhibiting as they did the new missionary theology of the end of the century. One collection was of hymns particularly for use at services of Believers' Baptism.

BIBLIOGRAPHY
British Library Catalogue
Julian
W. T. Whitley, *History of British Baptists* (London, 1923): 231
—, *Baptist Bibliography* (London, 1922)

J. H. Y. BRIGGS

de Graft, William (b. Cape Coast, Gold Coast, *c.* 1810) African Wesleyan Missionary Society (WMS) missionary, Gold Coast. Born in the Gold Coast (modern Ghana) into a Fante chiefly family, he and other young men formed a society to study the Bible. Through contact with an English ship's captain, he persuaded the WMS to send out their first missionary to West Africa. He became a local preacher and in 1840 THOMAS FREEMAN, who had

charge of the mission, took him to England, where they went round addressing meetings, to raise money. He had already produced a primer of the Twi language, and in England compiled a Fante-English vocabulary. In 1842 he accompanied Freeman to Badagry to start a Wesleyan mission, remaining in charge until 1844. An article he wrote for a missionary magazine inspired the American missionary T. J. BOWEN to come to Africa. Hence, having brought the English Wesleyans to the Gold Coast, he was also indirectly responsible for bringing the American Baptists to what became Nigeria.

BIBLIOGRAPHY
J. F. A. Ajayi, *Christian Missions in Nigeria, 1841–1891* (London, 1965)
F. L. Bartels, *The Roots of Ghana Methodism* (London, 1965)
J. Beecham, *Ashantee and the Gold Coast* (London, 1841)

CHRISTOPHER FYFE

Deininger, Theophilus Christopher (b. Bernstein, Würtemberg, Germany, *c.* 1799; d. Malta, 22 April 1824). CMS missionary to Malta. Deininger studied at Basel Seminary, was ordained in Lutheran orders and then studied the National School system in England. On 24 September 1822 he was sent by the CMS to join WILLIAM JOWETT in Malta where he died after one and a half years of service.

BIBLIOGRAPHY
D. T. B[arry], *CMS Register of Missionaries and Native Clergy* (privately printed) (London, 1906)

DONALD M. LEWIS

Delamotte, Charles (b. *c.* 1714; d. Aylesbury, Lincolnshire, England, 14 April 1786). Early Methodist and Moravian. The eldest son of a wealthy London sugar merchant and Middlesex magistrate whose home was Blendon Hall near Bexley in Kent, Delamotte volunteered to accompany JOHN WESLEY to Georgia early in October 1735, desiring to 'leave the world and give himself up entirely to God' (Ingham, *Journal*, cited in Wesley, ed. N. Curnock, London, 1831, 8: 253) and as a consequence was excluded by his father from his inheritance. He shared a cabin with BENJAMIN INGHAM on the voyage, learning Greek on the way. Wesley's constant companion and adviser in Georgia, he remained in Georgia after Wesley departed, and met GEORGE WHITEFIELD on his arrival but left Savannah in June 1738. Many of his family had been converted through the ministry of Ingham and CHARLES WESLEY while he was away, and Whitefield later proposed to his sister. He met John Wesley again in Oxford on 23–7 November 1738, and was very critical of Wesley's spiritual state. He was deeply involved in the Fetter Lane Society in 1738–9, but although he chose the Moravian side in the breach, he did not join the Moravians at this time.

He settled in Hull and assisted Ingham's work in Yorkshire, although he possibly fell out of contact with the movement until in 1761 he joined the Moravian Brethren. He retained a warm sympathy for the work of Wesley, meeting him in 1759 and 1782. In the 1770s he moved to Barrow-on-Humber.

BIBLIOGRAPHY
L. Tyerman, *The Life of the Rev. George Whitefield* (London, 1876)

PETER J. LINEHAM

Delamotte, William (b. England, *c.* 1718; d. London, 22 Feb. 1743). Moravian preacher. William Delamotte's father, Thomas, was a sugar merchant and magistrate of Fresh Wharf, London, and Blendon Hall, near Bexley, Kent; his elder brother CHARLES DELAMOTTE was the WESLEYS' companion in Georgia. Delamotte matriculated as a sizar of St Catherine's College, Cambridge on 18 May 1736. During a serious illness he resolved to lead a better life, and while at home during the summer vacation in 1737, was strengthened in his resolve ('struck to the heart' in CHARLES WESLEY's words) by BENJAMIN INGHAM and Charles Wesley. Back in Cambridge he began a fellowship group, whose members were already 'stigmatised for being Methodists' by January 1738. Delamotte did not meet the Moravians whose visit to London in 1738 encouraged a new emphasis on justification by faith, and opponents prejudiced him against it. He therefore resisted at first when Charles Wesley expounded it at Blendon, but on 29 June he experienced the gift of the Spirit for himself.

At some point Delamotte's Cambridge group coalesced with another centred on FRANCIS OKELY, an undergraduate at St John's. Visiting Cambridge in December 1738, Benjamin Ingham found a vigorous group of five students and a society for townspeople. Accompanying Ingham to Bedford, Delamotte supplemented his preaching by expounding the Scriptures in private houses. Delamotte may have continued to visit and advise the society formed as a result. In 1739 he preached to huge crowds in London, but the Moravians advised him to accompany JOHANN TÖLTSCHIG to Yorkshire to assist Ingham. Three or four days a week they went out among the societies, and Delamotte's preaching, a major factor in many conversions, was long remembered. By the summer, however, he had given up preaching, and in September he was back at Blendon Hall. Returning to Cambridge after a year's absence, he had to sell his books and college furniture to meet debts. His exposition of the Scriptures three times a week to the town society led to an explosion of interest; on 27 October he reported an attendance of over thirty and by 2 November this had risen to 200. The student group, however, was depleted. Of the five, two had left and one had withdrawn because Delamotte expounded although only a layman.

Perhaps because of the vacuum caused by the Wesleys' withdrawal from the Fetter Lane Society, at the end of October Töltschig asked Delamotte to return to London. He was reluctant to leave his successful work amongst the townspeople, but other undergraduates had

begun to disrupt his meetings, and he felt isolated in his college. With the same post came his father's permission to remove his name from the college books. By the end of December, however, illness had intervened. Delamotte was in Blendon, prevented from going to London by a swelling (a recurrence of his earlier illness?), which did not respond to treatment; by April he was very ill. In May he looked for a room near the Fetter Lane Chapel, where there were plans to provide a high stool from which he might preach, but by June he was expected to die, and although he was better in July, Ingham observed, 'his outward Man decays'. In August he was able to return to London and the improvement seemed to continue.

In June Delamotte had been received into the Moravian Church's first English congregation, founded to take over Ingham's work in Yorkshire. In August he travelled north to live with the Moravian community in Smith House, in the area where he had preached two years before. He preached once more, and copied and translated, helping with the 1743 *Watchwords* for publication. His running sore, however, though staunched with rags, refused to heal. In January 1743 Delamotte returned to London, where he died.

BIBLIOGRAPHY
J. D. Walsh, 'The Cambridge Methodists' in *Christian Spirituality*, ed. P. N. Brooks (London, 1975)

C. J. PODMORE

Deluc, Jean André (b. Geneva, Switzerland, 8 Feb. 1727; d. Windsor, Berkshire, England, 7 Nov. 1817). Geologist, meteorologist, and natural philosopher. Born and bred in Calvinist Geneva he made his living in commerce and participated in various political activities. In 1768 he went to Paris on an embassy to the Duke of Choiseul and became a member of the Council of Two Hundred in 1770. After a commercial failure in 1773 he made his home in England. He became a fellow of the Royal Society the same year and was appointed as reader to Queen Charlotte, which gave him an adequate income.

Deluc travelled widely and made many scientific excursions to the Swiss Alps. He explained the formation of the earth's geological features as the result of two distinct eras: an older antediluvian period that corresponded to the six days (interpreted as long periods of time) of Genesis, and a newer or diluvian period which began when cavities in the interior of the earth collapsed and filled with water to expose land. Deluc vigorously attacked the uniformitarian doctrines of JAMES HUTTON and John Playfair.

BIBLIOGRAPHY
DNB
DSB

ARIE LEEGWATER

Denny, Sir **Edward** (b. Dublin, 2 Oct. 1796; d. London, 13 June 1889). MP and Brethren hymn-writer. Educated at Eton and Exeter College, Oxford, he was the MP (1818–19) and Sheriff (1827) for Tralee, Kerry, Ireland. On succeeding his father as fourth baronet in 1831 he inherited almost the whole town with an annual rental income of about £13,000. He was a considerate and popular landlord. His rents were fixed at so fair a figure that he was almost alone in escaping reductions by the Land Commissioners. He himself lived mostly in a cottage at Islington in London, giving liberally to poor relations and to religious work. He remained single.

From the early 1830s he associated with the Brethren. Besides several works on prophecy, including charts, he published from 1839 onwards over forty hymns of adoration. Pathos and meditation characterize many of them. Most, except for 'Light of the lonely pilgrim's heart' and 'What grace, O Lord, and beauty shone', are unknown outside Brethren circles. Some might have come into more common use but for their millenarian sentiments. All Christians could profitably sing 'O wondrous hour! when Jesus Thou,/Co-equal with th'eternal God', 'Sweet feast of love divine' and 'To Calvary, Lord, in spirit now'. The fourth edition of his *Hymns and Poems* (London, 1889) is definitive.

BIBLIOGRAPHY
J. S. Andrews, 'Brethren Hymnology', *EQ*, 28 (1956): 208–29
Boase
F. R. Coad, *History of the Brethren Movement*, 2nd edn (Exeter, England, 1976): 75, 84, 110, 237, 238–40
E. E. Cornwall, *Songs of Pilgrimage and Glory*, 1 (London, [1932]): 25–34
Julian: 287–8, 898–9, 1509, 1559
Pickering

JOHN S. ANDREWS

Dent, Caroline (b. Milton, near Northampton, England, 14 Aug. 1815; d. after 1886). Baptist poet, hymn-writer, and editor. A descendant of the Rylands, with her sister, Mrs Trestrail (*see* F. TRESTRAIL), she wrote a number of tracts, hymns and poems and a religious fiction and edited works for the Sunday School Union.

BIBLIOGRAPHY
British Library Catalogue
Julian

J. H. Y. BRIGGS

Des Granges, Augustus (b. 1780; d. Vishakapatnam, India, 12 July 1810). LMS missionary. Des Granges was educated in Gosport. In 1805, he and GEORGE CRAN followed NATHANAEL FORSYTH to India where they founded the first Protestant Telugu mission. They chose Vishakapatnam, a large coastal trading centre north of Madras which was also a British military station. There they soon made influential friends. The allowances they were given for performing divine service, plus the private contributions they were so successful in eliciting, helped finance their missionary and charitable work. Cran and Des Granges founded several schools but Des Granges considered his great work to be the translation of the Scriptures into Telugu. He was a prayerful man, much esteemed by both English and Indians and his death was considered a great loss to the community. His letters to the LMS can be found in the CWM archives, SOAS.

BIBLIOGRAPHY
J. Hough, *History of Christianity in India*, 4 (London, 1845–60): 254–66

PENELOPE CARSON

Devasaghayam, John (b. Tranquebar, India, 1786, d. Kadachapuram, India, 30 Jan. 1864). Pioneer Indian evangelist and pastor. A third generation Christian from Tranquebar, Devasaghayam was baptized in infancy by Dr John of the Royal Danish Mission, and was a student of C. F. SCHWARTZ. He joined the CMS in 1815 and became superintendent of J. C. SCHNARRE's schools. He later worked with G. T. BÄRENBRUCK at Mayavaram, Tirunelveli District.

Devasaghayam was with C. T. E. RHENIUS when the latter resigned, but decided not to follow P. P. SCHAFFTER, J. M. LECHLER, and J. MÜLLER into the serious schism. GEORGE PETTITT (arrived 1833), Edward Dent, and EDWARD SARGENT from the CMS joined Devasaghayam. Bishop DANIEL CORRIE, came to investigate and ordained Devasaghayam as a priest in Palamcottah. In taking Anglican rather than Lutheran orders, he firmly rejected the caste system. He and his wife were persecuted in consequence. In 1842 Devasaghayam was given full missionary status, and placed in charge of Sattankulam district. He was later transferred to Kadachapuram in 1844. A highly significant missionary, he did a wide range of evangelistic work in Tirunelveli.

Devasaghayam successively married two granddaughters of Aaron, the first Tamil (Lutheran) minister to be ordained (Tranquebar, 1733). Two of his sons became priests, while his daughter Anne married Reverend W. T. SATHIYANADAN.

BIBLIOGRAPHY
R. Caldwell, *Early History of the Tinnevelly Mission* (Madras, 1881)

E. M. JACKSON

Dewar, Alexander (b. Lochtayside, Perthshire, Scotland, 1785; d. Avoch, Ross-shire, Scotland, 1849). Itinerant preacher and pastor with the Independents. Brother of JAMES DEWAR. Dewar was trained at a HALDANE class, and was active in Breadalbane before 1808. He founded the Independent church at Avoch, and was pastor from 1808 to 1849. Supported by the Society in Paisley and its Vicinity for Gaelic Missions to the Highlands and Islands, he itinerated in Inverness-shire, Ross-shire, Sutherland and Caithness.

BIBLIOGRAPHY
D. E. Meek, 'The Independent and Baptist Churches of Highland
Perthshire and Strathspey', *Transactions of the Gaelic Society
of Inverness*, 56 (1988–90): 281, 316

DONALD E. MEEK

Dewar, James (b. Lochtayside, Perthshire, Scotland,
1780; d. Nairn, Nairnshire, Scotland, 1843). Itinerant
preacher and pastor with the Independents. He was a
brother of ALEXANDER DEWAR. Trained at a HALDANE
class, Dewar was active as a missionary in Perthshire
and Argyll before 1804. Moving to Nairn in 1804, he
established an Independent church there, and became
its pastor from 1806 to 1843. Supported by the Society
in Paisley and its Vicinity for Gaelic Missions to the Highlands and Islands, he travelled extensively from Loch-
aber to Cape Wrath, and was active in Mull and Skye
in 1827.

BIBLIOGRAPHY
D. E. Meek, 'The Independent and Baptist Churches of Highland
Perthshire and Strathspey', *Transactions of the Gaelic Society
of Inverness*, 56 (1988–90): 281, 316

DONALD E. MEEK

Dibdin, Robert William (b. London, *c.* 1805; d. London,
23 July 1887). Anglican clergyman. He was the son of
Charles Dibdin, esquire, of London and educated at St
John's College, Cambridge (matriculated 1825; BA
1834; MA 1838). He was minister of West Street
Chapel, St Giles' in the Fields, London (apparently from
the mid-1830s till his death) and clearly was an influential evangelical in London by the mid-1840s. Active in
the RTS and the Scripture Readers' Society, he was one
of the few Anglican clergy to support the formation of
the EA in 1845. The reporters for the *Times* of London
informed their editor in 1844 that he 'has considerable
influence with some of the very low church laity by
whom his chapel is principally supported. Extremely low
church. Prepared to take any step.'

BIBLIOGRAPHY
Al. Cant.
D. M. Lewis, *Lighten Their Darkness* (Westport, CT, 1986)
Bodleian Library, Oxford, 'The Principal Clergy of London . . .
prepared for Mr Delane, Edtr. of *The Times*' (1844) Add.
Manuscript *c.*290

DONALD M. LEWIS

Dibrell, Anthony (b. Buckingham Co., VA, USA, 19
Aug. 1805; d. Norfolk, VA, USA, 1 Sept. 1855). Methodist minister and organizer of MEC, So. He was a descendant of a Huguenot family who pursued a law degree at
the University of North Carolina, being admitted to the
bar in Lynchburg, Virginia. Converted in 1828, he soon
became an ordained Methodist Episcopal minister, being
admitted on trial to the Virginia Conference in 1830. He
served prominent appointments and as presiding elder.
He was a member of the Louisville Convention in 1845
that organized the MEC, So and served as a leader in it
until his death.

BIBLIOGRAPHY
CM

STEVE HARPER

Dick, John (b. Aberdeen, Scotland, 10 Oct. 1764;
d. Glasgow, Scotland, 25 Oct. 1833). Professor of theology. After studying at King's College, Aberdeen, and
under JOHN BROWN at Haddington, he became in 1786
Associate (Burgher) Secession minister at Slateford, near
Edinburgh, and in 1801 colleague – in 1810, successor – to Alexander Pirie at Shuttle Street (later
Greyfriars), Glasgow, a leading Secession congregation.
From 1820 he was also the Associate Synod's (from
1821 the United Secession's) professor of theology,
unaided until 1825.

The College of New Jersey's DD (1815) acknowledged
Dick's distinction. ARCHIBALD ALEXANDER reckoned his
Lectures on Theology (4 vols, Glasgow, 1834) the best systematics in English. Other works, including *Essay on the
Inspiration of the Scriptures* (Edinburgh, 1800), partly
reflected Secession divisions – Dick sided with the New
Lights in 1799. A wide reader, Dick preached elegantly
with rare brevity. Doubts about lay preaching tempered
his support for missions.

BIBLIOGRAPHY
A. C. Dick, ed., *Lectures on Theology by the Late Rev. John Dick*,
4 vols, 1 (Edinburgh, 1834): ix–liv
DNB
J. R. Lee, *Greyfriars Glasgow* (Glasgow, 1938)

D. F. WRIGHT

Dickens, Fanny *See* BURNETT, (FRANCES) 'FANNY'
(ELIZABETH) [née **Dickens**]

Dickenson, Elizabeth (b. England, *c.* 1773; d. Staveley,
Yorkshire, England, 17 June 1793). Wesleyan Methodist
preacher. Dickenson lived 'a worldly life', but she was
unhappy; however, she was converted and 'received
wonderful revelations'. She felt it was her duty to preach, often referring to her dreams or visions. Some
people could not accept this, but many came from considerable distances to listen to her so that she could
hardly get any rest. Wherever Elizabeth went great
crowds thronged her and many were converted. She out-
ran her strength, but continued her ministry to the end.

BIBLIOGRAPHY
Z. Taft, *Biographical Sketches of . . . Holy Women . . .*, 1
(London, 1825)

E. DOROTHY GRAHAM

Dickerson, Philip (b. Bucklesham, Suffolk, England, 29 Jan. 1795; d. London, 22 Oct. 1882). Baptist minister in Suffolk and London. Dickerson was a ploughboy when converted in 1811. He became a Baptist and preached in a house-church at Newbourne (1815–17) then at Beccles (July 1817–19) and Rattlesden (1819–32). On 16 April 1832 he became co-pastor with William Shenston (1774–1833) of Little Alie Street, London and then was sole pastor from 3 September 1833 to June 1870. Dickerson served as a committee member of Baptist Evangelical Society and of the Baptist Tract Society, 1844–7 and 1863–7. A strict communionist, he was known as a faithful Gospel preacher.

BIBLIOGRAPHY
Autobiography in *The Gospel Herald* (January 1880–August 1881)
The Baptist Handbook (1883): 260–1
The Earthern Vessel, 38 (1882): 362–5

GEOFFREY RALPH BREED

Dickins, John (b. London, 24 Aug. 1747; d. Philadelphia, PA, USA, 27 Sept. 1798). American Methodist preacher, publisher, and pioneer leader. Educated in England, Dickins emigrated to America *c.* 1774. He was converted in Virginia and became a travelling preacher in 1777. He was most active in Virginia and North Carolina until 1781 when he temporarily suspended his preaching work, perhaps to spend more time with his family.

In April 1783 FRANCIS ASBURY prevailed on Dickins to re-enter the ranks of the itinerants and to move to New York City where he expected Dickins to be a useful Methodist leader. In June Dickins moved his family to his new appointment as pastor of Wesley Chapel (now John Street United Methodist Church). He was one of the first American Methodist preachers to move into a parsonage. Methodist work grew significantly under his ministry.

Dickins was an intimate friend of Francis Asbury. He was also one of the first American Methodists to meet THOMAS COKE, one of JOHN WESLEY's designated superintendents, when Coke arrived in America in November 1784. Dickins may have been the first American Methodist to learn of Wesley's plan for the establishment of a new American church. Coke wrote in his journal: 'I have opened Mr. Wesley's plan to Brother *Dickins*, the travelling preacher stationed in this place, and he highly approves of it, says that all the preachers most earnestly long for such a regulation, and that Mr. Asbury he is sure will agree to it. He presses me earnestly to make it public . . .' (Pilkington, 1968: 70).

When the famous Christmas Conference of 1784 was held in Baltimore at which the Methodists formally organized their church, Dickins was a prominent participant. He was ordained a deacon at this gathering; he was not made an elder until 1786. Dickins is given credit for proposing the name for the new denomination, the MEC, at the Christmas Conference. At the same meeting

the preachers also voted to organize a school for the new church to be named Cokesbury College in honour of their leaders Thomas Coke and Francis Asbury. They used a plan which Dickins had devised a few years earlier as the basis for the new institution.

Dickins returned to preaching in North Carolina for a short time in 1786 and while serving the Bertie circuit, he prepared for publication the third *Discipline* of the MEC. The form which he gave this book became a guide for its many subsequent editions.

The Dickins family moved back to New York in 1786 and he was stationed at the John Street Church where he served as pastor for the next three years. In 1789 when the MEC officially formed the Book Concern, its publishing operation, Dickins was chosen to be its leader as book steward. He moved his family to Philadelphia where he took up his new duties and served as the pastor of St George's MEC. He even offered his personal savings to help start the publishing enterprise.

During Dickins' administration the Book Concern printed and distributed a large number of books written by John Wesley, hymnals, *Disciplines*, and other religious literature. It also produced the church's first periodical, the *Arminian Magazine*. His careful management kept the Book Concern solvent during some of the most precarious times of its earliest years.

Dickins fell ill in Philadelphia during the yellow fever epidemic of 1798. It claimed the life of one of his daughters as well as his own. In a letter to Francis Asbury, Dickins' wife Betsy described his being taken ill:

> On the first day of his sickness . . . he called me to his bedside – 'My dear,' said he, 'I am very ill; but I entreat you, in the most earnest manner, not to be the least discomposed or uneasy. Tell the children, I beg of them not to be uneasy, for *Divine Wisdom cannot err*. Glory be to God, I can rejoice in his will, whether for life or death; I know all is well . . .'
> (Pilkington, 1968: 115).

BIBLIOGRAPHY
DAB
EWM
J. P. Pilkington, *The Methodist Publishing House*, 1 (Nashville, TN, 1968)

CHARLES YRIGOYEN, JR

Dickinson, Jonathan (b. Hatfield, MA, BNA, 22 April 1688; d. Elizabeth Town, NJ, BNA, 7 Oct. 1747). Presbyterian minister and first president of the College of New Jersey. Dickinson, the son of Hezekiah and Abigail (Blackman), was graduated from Yale College in 1706 and received his A.M. shortly thereafter. He was ordained a Congregational minister by the clergy of Fairfield County, Connecticut, on 29 September 1708, to serve Elizabeth Town, New Jersey. In 1709 he married Joanna Melyne (died 20 April 1745).

Dickinson drifted toward Presbyterianism, and in

1717 he and his church became full members of the Presbytery of Philadelphia. In 1724 he wrote a series of essays defending Presbyterian ordination, although he opposed subscription to the Westminster Confession. Influenced by GEORGE WHITEFIELD, he led the New York Presbytery into New Light support. When schism occurred, he was instrumental in the formation of the Synod of New York (1745), and elected its first moderator.

An evangelical, Dickinson opposed enthusiasm and excess. He remained a Calvinist theologian, never abandoning the emphasis on discipline prior to conversion. Evangelists might awaken a sinner, but conversion was not instantaneous. The only proof of conversion was a sanctified life.

He wrote approximately thirty books and pamphlets. Elected president of the College of New Jersey (Princeton) in early 1747, Dickinson died suddenly from pleurisy in October. He was survived by his wife Mary (Crane), whom he had married in April.

BIBLIOGRAPHY
DAB
K. J. Hardman, 'Jonathan Dickinson and the Course of American Presbyterianism' (University of Pennsylvania Ph.D. thesis, 1976)
L. J. Trinterud, The Forming of An American Tradition (Philadelphia, PA, 1949)

SALLY SCHWARTZ

Dickinson, Peard (b. Topsham, Devon, England, 16 Nov. 1758; d. London, 15 May 1802). Anglican clergyman and reader at Wesley's Chapel, London. Educated at Taunton School and intended for a business career, he lodged in Bristol with a Methodist family and was converted. He met WESLEY and proceeded to Oxford where he read classics, graduating BA (1783) and MA (1785). Ordained in 1783, he served as curate to the ageing VINCENT PERRONET at Shoreham, Kent, and married his granddaughter. On Perronet's death parishioners tried unsuccessfully to secure the living for him. After curacies in Nottinghamshire and Lincolnshire he accepted Wesley's invitation to City Road Chapel. Here he preached and administered the sacraments along with other clergy. He assisted Wesley in the ordination of Mather, Moore and Rankin in 1788. Joseph Benson refers to his determination to avoid disputes and concentrate on the word of God and prayer.

BIBLIOGRAPHY
J. Benson, ed., Memoirs (London, 1803)
MM (1802)

A. SKEVINGTON WOOD

Dickson, David (b. Libberton, Lanarkshire, Scotland, 1780; d. Edinburgh, 28 July 1842). Church of Scotland minister. The son of David Dickson (1754–1820), he was educated at Edinburgh University (DD 1824) and entered the ministry in 1801. In 1803 he was made assistant minister to Sir HENRY MONCRIEFF at St Cuthbert's, Edinburgh. Dickson made no great impression at the Church General Assembly, but he was much admired for the learning and eloquence of his sermons. He succeeded Moncrieff in 1827 and in 1832 conducted Sir Walter Scott's funeral service at Abbotsford. He was a director of the Scottish Bible Society and the Edinburgh SPCK, gave long service as secretary to the Scottish Missionary Society, and was a committee member for the Edinburgh auxiliary of the Irish Evangelical Society.

BIBLIOGRAPHY
DNB
Oliver and Boyd, Edinburgh Almanac (Edinburgh, 1828)

JONATHAN BURKE CUTMORE

Dillon, Robert (Crawford) (b. Lothbury, London, England, 22 May 1795; d. Spitalfields, London, 8 Nov. 1847). Anglican clergyman. Dillon was educated at St Edmund Hall, Oxford (BA 1817, MA 1820, BD and DD 1836) and ordained (deacon 20 December 1818, priest 1819). He served as Curate of Poorstock and West Milton, Dorsetshire; then from 1819 to 1824, as assistant minister, St John's, Bedford Row, London; from 1824 to 1825 as Curate of Willesden and Kingsbury; and in 1825 as Curate of St James, Clerkenwell. In 1826, he was Curate of St Matthews, Denmark Hill; in 1828–9, morning preacher at the Female Orphan Asylum; and in 1829–37, early morning lecturer at St Swithin's, London Stone, where he attracted large congregations.

In 1839, Dillon became a candidate for Rector of St James's, Clerkenwell. During the ensuing contest, he was publicly disgraced by revelations of personal immorality. When news of this reached Bishop Blomfield, Dillon's licence to officiate was revoked on 29 February 1840. Soon afterwards, he seceded, establishing a 'reformed English Church' in Friar Street, Blackfriars, later removing to a large building in White's Row, Spitalfields, where he appointed himself first bishop of the new body and ordained ministers to serve branch congregations in various parts of London.

Although his personal life remained tainted by immorality, Dillon remained a popular preacher. He died prematurely on the eve of establishing a nationwide network of branch congregations in his new Church.

BIBLIOGRAPHY
DNB

GRAYSON CARTER

Ditcher, Joseph (b. 1803; d. South Brent, Somerset, England, 28 Nov. 1875). Anglican clergyman. Ditcher was ordained as a literate in 1818 and registered as 'a ten-year man' at Queens' College, Cambridge in 1825, but he received a Lambeth MA in 1837. He was chaplain to HM Superintendent and Commandant, Honduras (1819–21), Perpetual Curate of Holy Trinity, Bitton (Gloucestershire) (1821–35), Curate of Hutton (1835–6), principal acting surrogate and judge of the Episcopal Court of Bath and Wells (1836–41) and Vicar of South Brent (1841–75). His judicial experience rendered him well placed in the legal action he took against G. A. Denison, his clerical neighbour at East Brent and Archdeacon of Taunton, for asserting the objective real presence in the elements at Holy Communion. The case ran for three years (1855–8) before being rejected without a decision by the Judicial Committee of the Privy Council. Reference is made to it in Mrs Arabin's support of an appeal [by Denison] at the end of Trollope's *Barchester Towers*. Ditcher was a keen supporter of the London College of Divinity from its beginnings.

BIBLIOGRAPHY

S. Ditcher, *A Brief Memorial of the Rev. Joseph Ditcher* (London, [1876])
DNB (under Denison, George Anthony)
W. Walsh, *History of the Romeward Movement in the Church of England* (London, 1900)

ARTHUR POLLARD

Dixon, John B. (b. Edinburgh, *c.* 1800; d. Aurungabad, India, 7 Jan. 1846). CMS missionary to India. Dixon was trained at the CMS school at Islington (London) in 1825 and ordained (deacon 1827, priest 1828) by the Bishop of London. On 13 February 1829 he accompanied C. P. FARRAR to Bombay and then to Nasik in western India. During his 17 years of service he translated the Old Testament and much of the Prayer Book into Marathi.

BIBLIOGRAPHY

D. T. B[arry], *CMS Register of Missionaries and Native Clergy* (privately printed) (London, 1906)

DONALD M. LEWIS

Dixon, Stephen (b. Leicestershire, England; *Fl.* 1743–52). East Midlands preacher. A fellow pupil of BENJAMIN INGHAM and JACOB ROGERS at Batley Grammar School, Yorkshire, Dixon became the school's usher, and in March 1739 went to London to seek ordination from the Bishop of Chester, Ingham asking JAMES HUTTON to find him lodgings with a member of the Fetter Lane Society and introduce him to CHARLES WESLEY and WESTLEY HALL. It is assumed that this was the same Stephen Dixon who in 1742 joined DAVID TAYLOR in preaching in Leicestershire. Nothing is known of his activities in the intervening period; he does not seem to have been ordained. By the autumn of 1743 Dixon had founded societies in Leicestershire, Nottinghamshire and Derbyshire (which were the basis of the future New Connexion of the General Baptists (Cook, 1888: 2–3) and in December 1743 he requested Moravian supervision. He

moved to the Moravians' Yorkshire community, a Moravian taking over his societies, but soon returned. He was received into membership in August 1744, despite warnings of his 'indecent behaviour'.

That December Dixon's youth, inexperience and ignorance of Moravian practice led JOHANN TÖLTSCHIG to order him to Germany, fearing his 'being alone and caress'd by every Body and so many young women who belong to his Societys'. Dixon was reluctant, but was recalled and replaced. In January, having left for Leicestershire without permission, he was repudiated. WILLIAM HOLLAND reported his confession that he was 'sometimes a Slave to the lust of the Flesh'. WILLIAM KENDRICK, who supported Dixon, was expelled with him in April 1745. Richard Bell from London joined them when Töltschig apologized for alleging that Dixon had propositioned him three years earlier but refused to retract in writing.

Dixon and Kendrick moved to Barton in the Beans, Leicestershire and formed a church, building a Moravian-style meeting house. Meanwhile, Dixon's evangelistic work extended to visiting societies in Staffordshire. Dixon and Kendrick formed an alliance with WILLIAM CUDWORTH and adopted his doctrinal position, although Dixon told Howel Harris in September 1746 that he regarded himself as within the Calvinistic Methodist Association. Dixon subsequently embraced the doctrine of universal restoration and was expelled from the Barton church, moving to Annesley Woodhouse. In 1752 he repented of leaving the Moravians and attacking them, but they refused his request for renewed supervision of his societies.

BIBLIOGRAPHY

[T. Cook], *Preacher, Pastor, Mechanic* (Leicester, England, 1888)

C. J. PODMORE

Dober, (Johann) Leonhard (b. Mönchsroth, Franconia, 7 March 1706; d. Herrnhut, Saxony, Germany, 1 April 1766). Moravian leader and first missionary. J. MARTIN (1703–48), J. Leonhard and Andreas (1708–96) Dober were Swabian potters. Among early Herrnhut's most important non-Moravians (1725–7, 1730–2), Dober was chosen assistant single brethren's elder in 1731 and (general) elder in 1733. In 1732 he went to St Thomas, West Indies, as the first Moravian missionary, returning in 1735. From 1738 to 1739 he lived in Amsterdam's Jewish quarter, hoping for conversions.

Christ's recognition as general elder (1741) followed Dober's resignation, having failed to resolve disputes in Pilgerruh, Holstein, which led to that congregation's dissolution. Thereafter Dober led the Dutch and English provinces (1741–5, 1745–6) and the Marienborn school (1746–7). Consecrated as a bishop in 1747, he worked in Latvia (1747–9) and led the Moravians in Silesia (1751–8) and Barby (near Magdeburg) (1758–62). Dober, who had chaired a crisis conference in 1753 and conducted ZINZENDORF's second marriage, served on the ten-member Select Conference (1762–4) and eight-member Directory (1764–6).

DOBER, (JOHANN) MARTIN

BIBLIOGRAPHY
Gemeinnachrichten (1832): 416–37
L. Schneider, *Johann Leonhard Dober* (Herrnhut, Germany, 1906)

C. J. PODMORE

Dober, (Johann) Martin (b. Mönchsroth, Franconia, 23 Nov. 1703; d. Herrnhaag, Wetteravia, 9 Dec. 1748). Potter and Moravian leader. Martin Dober, who met N. L. VON ZINZENDORF while living in Dresden with his uncle, built a house in Herrnhut in 1724. Zinzendorf's right-hand man from 1727, the Swabian potter became the community's foremost spiritual guide and teacher, reading the Bible in its original languages.

In 1736 Dober's role in abortive negotiations to establish Pilgerruh (Holstein) initiated a growing divergence from Zinzendorf. Summoned to oversee Moravian affairs in Wetteravia from 1737, in 1738 he declined posting to Pennsylvania and Latvia. Back in Herrnhut in Spring 1742, Dober's addresses, reflecting the sober piety of Herrnhut's Moravian founders, contradicted the new spirituality Johannes Langguth (*see* J. L. VON WATTEVILLE) brought from Herrnhaag.

The Moravian Church's establishment in Silesia (1742–3) displeased Zinzendorf. Dober had taken the lead, and his appointment as Moravian leader in England in 1744 (after consecration as an auxiliary bishop) may have been a deliberate removal from influence at the centre. In England Dober introduced the latest continental practices, but in founding the Bedford congregation (1745) again went against Zinzendorf's ideal of work within the local church.

Recalled in 1745, Dober, by now the leading opponent of the developing 'Sifting Time' spirituality, was appointed warden of its centre, Herrnhaag. After initial conflict Dober submitted, giving addresses in the new style in Herrnhaag and in Upper Lusatia. Zinzendorf attributed Dober's death at the end of 1748 to physical exhaustion combined with inner sorrow. Despite their differences, Dober had retained Zinzendorf's respect. In the intelligent, capable, independently minded but ultimately loyal potter Zinzendorf recognized one who could himself have led the Moravian Church.

C. J. PODMORE

Dock, Christopher (b. *c.* 1698; d. Montgomery Co., PA, BNA, 1771). Mennonite schoolmaster. Little is known about Dock's early life, but he apparently moved to Pennsylvania sometime between 1710 and 1714. Before 1720 he opened a school in Montgomery County, and taught there for ten years. He turned to farming, staying there until 1738, then returned to schoolmastering, remaining in that career until his death. His fame as a teacher spread and he was persuaded to write several articles for the *Geistlishes Magazien* in 1764. Earlier he had refused to be drawn into publishing details about his methods, but through an indirect manner he answered questions about school matters submitted to him by a friend, with the provision that his answers not be published before his death. The result was the *Schulordnung*, one of the earliest books on schoolkeeping in America, initially published a year before his death. The best known sections of the book prescribed 100 rules of conduct for children and 100 Christian rules for children. Central to his methods was gentle persuasion rather than harsh discipline, and simplicity and directness in instruction.

BIBLIOGRAPHY
DAB

WILLIAM G. TRAVIS

Docton, William (b. Padstow, Cornwall, England, 1810; d. St Ives, Cornwall, England, 6 March 1879). Founder of Teetotal Wesleyan Methodists. Docton was one of 16 children born to Anglican parents. Converted at the age of twenty, he joined the Padstow Wesleyans, eventually becoming a local preacher. A tailor, he moved to St Ives, Cornwall, in 1835, where he was converted to teetotalism by the lecturer, James Teare, in 1838. He became a prominent advocate of total abstinence and as secretary of the influential St Ives teetotal society, he clashed with the local Wesleyan ministers in 1841 and led a secession of some 400 teetotallers in the area who formed the Teetotal Wesleyan Connexion. The bulk of these societies joined the MNC in 1860, in order to obtain a settled ministry. A man of great force of character, Docton was Liberal Mayor of St Ives in 1876.

BIBLIOGRAPHY
M. S. Edwards, 'The Teetotal Wesleyan Methodists' in *PWHS*, 33: 63–70

E. ALAN ROSE

Doddridge, Philip (b. London, 26 June 1702; d. Lisbon, 26 Oct. 1751). Independent minister and author. His grandfathers were a rector of Shepperton ejected in 1662 and a minister who had fled from persecution in Bohemia. After the death of his parents (1711, 1715) he spent four years with the minister at St Albans, Samuel Clark, and four at Kibworth Beauchamp, Leicestershire, being trained for the ministry by John Jennings. In 1723, after Jennings' removal and death, he accepted charge of the congregation, and later of a few pupils. In 1729 he and his pupils moved to Northampton, where on 19 March 1730 he was ordained as minister of Castle Hill church, and where he remained for the rest of his life. His influence spread steadily throughout the country and more widely, as preacher, pastor and tutor of what became a large and noted dissenting academy, and also as the writer of many books and innumerable letters. In 1736–7 an honorary doctorate of divinity was conferred on him by the two university colleges of Aberdeen. He died in Lisbon, where he is buried. On 22 December

1730 he married Mercy Maris (1709–90), of a Worcester family. Of their three sons and six daughters only one son and three daughters survived infancy or early childhood.

In his lifetime four works brought Doddridge eminence: his most ambitious intellectual piece, a threefold *Answer* (1742–3) to a deist tract, in which he offered a convincing defence of Christianity on rational grounds; *The Rise and Progress of Religion in the Soul* (1745), an adaptation of the spiritual phenomenology characteristic of Puritanism, which led to the conversion of WILLIAM WILBERFORCE; a *Life* (1747) of Colonel JAMES GARDINER, which likewise mediated Puritan hagiography in a vein soon familiar in the revival and has a sure place in the literature of conversion; and *The Family Expositor* (5 vols, 1738–56), which he justly regarded as his *magnum opus*. His books were studied in New England, where he had contacts with Yale and Princeton; several were translated into Dutch, German, and French. In the century after his death his most influential work was probably his *Course of Lectures* (1763), which often served as the basis for lectures delivered in later academies. Today he is remembered for his hymns, which did much to keep orthodox Dissenters within the ambit of the revival. His friends and correspondents included JOHN WESLEY, WHITEFIELD (whom he allowed to speak from his pulpit), Lady HUNTINGDON, Count ZINZENDORF and other leaders of the revival, as well as scholars at both the universities and a number of bishops. His letters reveal a warm, impulsive, devout personality, not without a touch of playfulness.

Doddridge had a passion for mission and evangelism which never left him. In 1741 he presided over a meeting in Norfolk 'concerning the Methods to be taken for the Revival of Religion'. Ten years later, shortly before his death, he helped to found, in Suffolk, a 'Scheme for the Propagation of the Gospel'. Wherever it might be, in Scotland, in Holland or across the Atlantic, he welcomed news of 'spreading the life of Christianity'.

BIBLIOGRAPHY

J. van den Berg and G. F. Nuttall, *Philip Doddridge (1702–1751) and the Netherlands* (Leiden, Netherlands, 1987)

M. Deacon, *Philip Doddridge of Northampton 1702–51* (Northampton, England, 1980)

DNB

G. F. Nuttall, ed., *Philip Doddridge 1702–51* (London, 1951)

—, *Richard Baxter and Philip Doddridge* (London, 1951)

—, ed., *Calendar of the Correspondence of Philip Doddridge, D.D. (1702–1751)* (London, 1979)

GEOFFREY F. NUTTALL

Dodgson, Jonathan (b. Elland, Yorkshire, England, 8 July 1820; d. 7 March 1909). Lay preacher. His father was a Wesleyan local preacher who set up as a dyer in Elland in 1832. Jonathan was converted at the Leeds Wesleyan Conference prayer meeting in 1837 and began preaching in 1841. Although largely self-taught, his commanding appearance and resonant voice meant that he was in great demand as a preacher and he preached an average of six times a week during the decade 1844–54. He entered the family business and developed it successfully. With his father he joined the Wesley Reformers in 1850 and for twenty years they acted as pastors of the Elland congregation. Severe illness curtailed his activities after 1854 but he remained active in Christian work throughout his long life.

BIBLIOGRAPHY

D. Whiteley, ed., *Illustrious Local Preachers* (Bradford, England, 1891), ch. xx

E. ALAN ROSE

Dodson, John (b. *c.* 1805). *Fl.* 1830–50. Anglican clergyman. Dodson was educated at Giggleswick school, Yorkshire and at Trinity College, Cambridge (BA 1831; MA 1835). He was ordained (deacon 1831, priest 1832), becoming Curate of Barfreystone, Kent (1831) and Vicar of Cockerham, Lancashire (1845–9). In 1849, alarmed at the progress of the Gorham affair and influenced by BAPTIST NOEL's *Essay on the Union of Church and State* (1848), Dodson seceded from the Church of England and became a Baptist. In his *apologia*, he objected to the Anglican formularies and to the principle of establishment, and stated his determined support for voluntarism.

BIBLIOGRAPHY

Al. Cant.

J. Dodson, *Brief Reasons for Leaving the English Establishment* (London, 1849)

Index Ecclesiasticsus: 53

Nonconformist (4 April 1849): 260; (26 December 1849): 1018

GRAYSON CARTER

Dodsworth, William (b. Kirk Ella, Yorkshire, England, 1798; d. London, England, 10 Dec. 1861). Anglican clergyman and writer. Dodsworth was educated at Richmond School, Yorkshire and Trinity College, Cambridge (BA 1820, MA 1823). He was ordained curate (1829) at Margaret's Street Chapel, Cavendish Square, London, where he became a popular preacher and introduced the special observance of saints' days.

Although at first an adherent of evangelical doctrines, during the late 1820s he was attracted increasingly to High Churchmanship. He was appointed, 1 August 1827, Perpetual Curate of Christ Church, St Pancras, where he aided E. B. Pusey in supervising the Sisters of Mercy (the first revived Anglican convent), and became an outspoken advocate of Tractarianism. In 1847, he accompanied H. E. MANNING on his travels to Scotland and the Continent. In December 1850, dismayed over the final decision in the Gorham affair, he was received into the Church of Rome.

Dodsworth published a number of works defending Catholic doctrines. One of the few Cambridge men to support the Tracts, he was described by Manning as possessing 'a strong clear but dry head, without imagination or fertility, but accurate and logical'.

BIBLIOGRAPHY
Al. Cant.
DNB

GRAYSON CARTER

Dohne, Jacob Ludwig (b. Zierenberg, Germany, 9 Nov. 1811; d. Fort Pine, Natal, South Africa, 2 June 1879). German Pietist missionary and linguist. A young saddler in Berlin, he was converted and trained for the service of the Berlin Missionary Society. He was ordained, 1 August 1835 and sent to the Cape Colony, South Africa. There he settled to work among the Rarabe Xhosa and soon learned the language and published several works in Xhosa.

In 1847 he went to Natal to work among the Zulu. After a brief stay with the Voortrekkers as their pastor he returned to work among the Zulu as a servant of the ABCFM in 1850. He published a number of Zulu translations of books of the Bible but his most important work was his long standard *A Zulu-Kafir Dictionary* (Cape Town, 1857). His often erratic behaviour led the Berlin Society, which he had rejoined, to dismiss him in 1870. He died during the Zulu war while minister to a congregation of the Nederduits Gereformeerde Kerk (NGK).

BIBLIOGRAPHY
DSAB

ANDREW C. ROSS

Dolben, Sir **William** (b. 1727; d. 1814). Third baronet of Finedon and British MP. William was the only son of Reverend Sir John Dolben, second Baronet and Elizabeth, daughter of fifth Baron Digby. Descended from archbishops of both Canterbury and York, Dolben epitomized the political, religious and protestant sympathies of the gentry, and in 1768 he entered parliament for Oxford, to secure the Old Interest until the general election (3 February to 11 March 1768). He then became MP for Northamptonshire (1768–77). He returned, now an independent supporter of the Court, in 1780 (as MP for Oxford University). He advocated parliamentary reform in 1783 and 1785; upheld WILLIAM WILBERFORCE's moral reform and antislave trade crusades; and in 1788 carried a bill to protect negroes being transported. He resigned his seat in 1806. He married (1) 1758, Judith, daughter of Somerset English, who died 1771 and (2) 1789, Charlotte, daughter of Gilbert Affleck, MP of Dalton Hall, Suffolk. His papers are at the Northamptonshire County Record Office.

BIBLIOGRAPHY
Sir Lewis Namier and John Brooke, *The House of Commons 1754–90*, 2 (London, 1964)

W. R. Ward, *Georgian Oxford* (Oxford, 1958)
—, *Victorian Oxford* (London, 1965)

W. R. WARD

Dole, Charlotte Knapp [née **Close**] (b. Greenwich, CT, USA, 26 May 1813; d. Honolulu, HI, USA, 5 July 1874). Teacher and missionary to Hawaii. Charlotte accompanied her first husband Horton Owen Knapp to Hawaii with the eighth missionary company. Widowed, she married American missionary Daniel Dole in 1846, Dole's first wife having died, leaving him with two young sons, George and Sanford Ballard. Accomplished in Hebrew, Greek and Latin, Charlotte assisted her second husband with management of Punahou school where he served as the school's first principal 1841–55, and thereafter until her death at a school for Caucasian children at Koloa, Kauai. The pious home environment she provided her stepsons typifies the upbringing of the 'mission boys' who, allied with commercial interests, overthrew the Hawaiian government in 1893. Her stepson Sanford Ballard Dole became President of the Republic of Hawaii and later, Hawaii's first territorial governor.

NANCY J. MORRIS

Doncaster, Mary [Ride, Mrs John] (b. England, c. 1806; d. Brighton, South Australia, 12 Nov. 1875). Primitive Methodist (PM) itinerant preacher. Doncaster was converted in Derbyshire at the age of nine through a Sunday school teacher. She began to preach at 17 and became an itinerant in 1822. She ministered in the Tunstall, Darlaston, Ramsor and Oakengates circuits, before marrying JOHN RIDE, a fellow itinerant (18 March 1824) as his second wife. Together they endured many hardships common to the early PM missionaries. Many of the references to the work of the Rides indicate that Mary worked equally with John wherever they were stationed which was especially in missionary situations. In 1849 they sailed as missionaries to Victoria, Australia. John superannuated in 1852 and they located at Benalla. Mary was widowed in 1862. She died at her son-in-law's home.

BIBLIOGRAPHY
PMMag (1822–3; 1835; 1839; 1862; 1875)

E. DOROTHY GRAHAM

Doolittle, Justus (b. Rutland, NY, USA, 23 June 1823; d. Clinton, NY, USA, 15 June 1880). ABCFM China missionary. The son of a poor farmer, he was converted in a revival and joined the Presbyterian church in 1834. After some years in Indiana he returned to Rutland and joined the Congregational church. With benefit of his wages as a colporteur and charity grants, he was educated at Hamilton College and Auburn Theological Seminary. Already accepted by the ABCFM, he was ordained on the day of his seminary graduation in 1849; he arrived in Foochow in May 1850 and within the year was able to preach in Chinese. Plagued by chronic throat infections he turned to schoolteaching and writing tracts in Chinese. In 1864 illness forced him home to the USA, where he wrote his oft-cited *Social Life of the Chinese* (New York, 1865; London, 1868).

He was at the ABCFM missions in Tientsin and Foochow until 1870, when he became an interpreter with a commercial firm and simultaneously editor of the *Chinese Recorder*. In 1872 he joined the American Presbyterian mission in Shanghai but left China the next year and retired in Clinton, New York.

BIBLIOGRAPHY
S. W. Barnett and J. K. Fairbank, eds, *Christianity and China* (Cambridge, MA, 1985): 107–20

SUZANNE WILSON BARNETT

Doran, John William (b. Ireland, c. 1800; d. London, 30 Dec. 1862). CMS missionary to south India. Doran was educated at Trinity College, Dublin (BA) and ordained (deacon 19 Dec. 1824, priest 29 May 1825) by the Bishop of London. On 31 May 1825 the CMS sent him to Cottayam, Travancore in south India to be principal of the CMS college. His ship was shipwrecked at Table Bay on 3 September but Doran survived and served for over five years before returning to England on 10 November 1830 whereupon he closed his connection with the CMS. He was given an honorary LL D from Trinity College, Dublin, and served from 1834 to 1846 as the CMS association secretary. In 1854 he became rector of Beeston St Lawrence in Norfolk. His wife died in 1864.

BIBLIOGRAPHY
D. T. B[arry], *CMS Register of Missionaries and Native Clergy* (privately printed) (London, 1906)

DONALD M. LEWIS

Dorchester, Daniel (b. Duxbury, MA, USA, 11 March 1827; d. 13 March 1907). Methodist minister and politician. Dorchester was the son of the Reverend Daniel and Mary Otis Dorchester. He was educated at Norwich Academy and Wesleyan University. He served several charges and as presiding elder in the Southern New England and the New England Conferences of the MEC. In 1884 and in 1888 he was a member of the General Conference, the legislative body, of the MEC.

In 1855 he was elected to the Connecticut State Senate. In 1882 he was elected to the Massachusetts legislature and in 1889 he was appointed by President Harrison superintendent of Indian Schools of the United States. He was instrumental in withdrawing government appropriations for sectarian native American schools.

Dorchester was also a prolific writer. He was keenly interested in the intersection of evangelical faith with social problems. He wrote on temperance issues as well as on social reform. His *History of Christianity in the United States* was considered his best-known work.

BIBLIOGRAPHY
S. Ahlstrom, *A Religious History of the American People* (New Haven, CT, 1972)
DAB
DCA

L. DALE PATTERSON

Dore, James (b. Newport, Isle of Wight, England, 1763/4; d. South London, 20 March 1825). Baptist minister. Dore, with two of his brothers, who were brought to evangelical views through the ministry of Sir HARRY TRELAWNY, deliberately converted from his Anglican upbringing to the Baptist position, provoked in James's case by a tract entitled, 'Reasons to Favour Episcopacy', given to him by an aunt. He entered the Bristol Academy in 1779 and in 1783 succeeded Benjamin Wallin as minister of the historic Maze Pond Church, Southwark. ROBERT ROBINSON participating in his ordination stressed that neither church nor minister was bound by historic creeds but rather were free to make their own confession of faith under the authority of 'the New Testament of our Lord and Saviour Jesus Christ'. Dore, a confirmed closed communionist who was distressed by deviation from this principle, exercised a faithful and irenic ministry at Maze Pond for more than thirty years, confessing that 'the grace manifested in the atonement' had been the central point of his ministry. In 1788, he published an influential sermon *On the African Slave Trade* which his congregation backed up with an appropriate collection which was presented to GRANVILLE SHARP. He received an Honorary AM in 1793. An ailment of the throat caused his resignation form his pastorate in 1815.

BIBLIOGRAPHY
J. Ivimey, *History of the English Baptists*, II and IV (London, 1830)
S. A. Swaine, *Faithful Men* (London, 1884)

J. H. Y. BRIGGS

Doremus, Sarah Platt [née Haines] (b. New York, 3 Aug. 1802; d. New York, 29 Jan. 1877). Organizer of foreign missionary and charitable societies. Doremus's parents Elias and Mary Ogden Haines were Presbyterians involved in charitable work. On 11 September 1821 she married Thomas Doremus, a wealthy merchant. They had one son and eight daughters.

A member of the Reformed Church, Doremus became a leader in charitable organizations – the Women's Prison Association, the Isaac T. Hopper House for female ex-convicts, the New York House and School of Industry for poor women, the Nursery and Child's Hospital, the Presbyterian Home for Aged Women, the City Mission and Tract Society, the City Bible Society, and the Woman's Hospital.

Her interest in foreign missions began in childhood at prayer meetings with ISABELLA GRAHAM and JOANNA BETHUNE. Spurred by DAVID ABEEL, missionary from the Orient, she helped found the Woman's Union Missionary Society in 1860, the first women's agency to send women missionaries. A gifted organizer and administrator, she was also well known for her personal acts of charity.

BIBLIOGRAPHY
NAW

NANCY A. HARDESTY

Dorman, William Henry (b. 1802; d. 1878). Congregational minister and Brethren leader. A man of humble parentage, Dorman was converted early in life, became a Congregational minister, holding pastorates at Zion Chapel, Stafford (c. 1829–35), and Union Chapel, Islington (1835–8). In 1838 he published a book, *Principles of Truth*, in which he announced his conversion to Brethren views of the church. He played a leading role in the development of Brethren groups, first in London, then in Stafford, and also in Reading and Bristol.

He remained loyal to JOHN NELSON DARBY – see his *Review of Certain Evils* (London, 1849) until 1866, when he opposed Darby's bizarre views on the sufferings of Christ. His *High Church Claims of the Exclusive Brethren* (London, 1868–9) is a vigorous repudiation of the disciplinary system developed by Darby and his followers.

BIBLIOGRAPHY
H. Pickering, *Chief Men Among the Brethren* (London, 1931)

HAROLD H. ROWDON

Dorsey, Dennis B. (b. Baltimore County, MD, USA, 28 Dec. 1799; d. Fairmont, VA, USA, 18 March 1860). Preacher, physician, and Methodist Protestant reformer. Dorsey and other reformers were expelled from the conference for advocating lay representation and opposing episcopal authority. He helped organize the Associated Methodist Churches, which in 1830 became the MPC. He edited *The Mutual Rights and Christian Intelligencer* from 1830 to 1832.

Dorsey graduated from the Washington Medical College of Baltimore in 1831 and in 1832 he gave up his ministerial work for a medical practice, although he retained close ties to the MPC, serving as president of the Pittsburgh Conference in 1834 and as a pastor in Cincinnati in 1854. In 1857 he started *The Independent Press* in Martinsville, Ohio. He died at his son's home in Virginia, and was buried there.

BIBLIOGRAPHY
N. B. Harmon, ed., *Encyclopedia of World Methodism* (Nashville, TN, 1974)
M. Simpson, *Cyclopaedia of Methodism* (New York, 1856)

SUSAN E. WARRICK

Dorsius, Peter Henry (b. Holland, c. 1710; d. Holland, c.1757). Dutch Reformed educator and minister. After graduating from Groningen University in 1734 and Leyden University in 1736, he went to America in 1737. For the next 11 years he pastored two Dutch Reformed congregations in Bucks County, Pennsylvania, served as a liaison between his denomination and the German Reformed in that colony, and helped to train men for the ministry, including two of THEODORUS JACOBUS FRELINGHUYSEN's sons. Through his tutoring he provided a rigorous religious education similar to that of WILLIAM TENNENT's nearby Log College. Dorsius became embroiled in controversy in 1741 when he, along with Frelinghuysen and Presbyterian GILBERT TENNENT, ordained JOHN HENRY GOETSCHIUS to serve as a minister on Long Island. The Classis of Amsterdam's concerns about proper ecclesiastical authority (the ordination was conducted without its prior approval) and evangelical piety and preaching (like that of Frelinghuysen in the Raritan Valley of New Jersey) led the Classis to reject this ordination. In 1748 Dorsius returned to the Netherlands after being suspended from the ministry because of continued drunkenness, offensive conduct, and deserting his wife and children.

BIBLIOGRAPHY
C. H. Glatfelter, *Pastors and People* (Breinigsville, PA, 1981)
J. I. Good, *History of the Reformed Church in the United States* (Reading, PA, 1899): 190–2
J. R. Tanis, *Dutch Calvinistic Pietism in the Middle Colonies* (The Hague, 1967): 70–2

GARY SCOTT SMITH

Doudiet, J(ean) Frédéric (b. Basel, Switzerland, 1802; d. Montreal, Canada, 22 July 1867). Pastor to French-Canadians. Doudiet studied and painted in Switzerland. In 1829 he was ordained in Basel (Reformed) and also married to Louise Batifolier. While a missionary in France, Doudiet's most notable convert was future evangelist Léon Pilatte. After a Swiss military chaplaincy, the French Canadian Missionary Society recruited Doudiet. From 1844 he pastored their rural Quebec parishes, especially Belle Rivière. Doudiet retired to Montreal in 1860. One son Charles became a Canadian pastor.

BIBLIOGRAPHY
National Archives of Canada, Ottawa, J. Trant (Picture Division), Doudiet research.

K. RICHARD LOUGHEED

Dougall, John (b. Paisley, Renfrewshire, Scotland, 8 July 1808; d. Flushing, NY, USA, 19 Aug. 1886). Religious newspaper publisher and editor. Raised in a Scottish home where literature was prized, Dougall emigrated to Montreal in 1826, and initially made a living selling Paisley shawls. He gravitated to journalism, and edited the *Canada Temperance Advocate* from 1835 to

1845. In 1845 he launched his own weekly religious newspaper, *The Witness*. Through these media he became Canada's foremost temperance advocate, and persuaded thousands to sign the pledge.

Hoping to extend his religious influence, he launched *The Witness* on a daily basis in 1860, and attempted the same in New York in 1870 with *The New York Witness*. After a great struggle to keep the latter financially viable, Dougall closed it the year before his death. The original *Witness*, however, continued even after Dougall's death to exert significant influence in Canada. Dougall for many years was deacon in Montreal's Zion Congregational Church, and a founding and long-term member of the French Canadian Missionary Society. He married Elizabeth Redpath, daughter of wealthy Montreal businessman JOHN REDPATH. His own daughter, Lily Dougall, became a significant Canadian novelist.

BIBLIOGRAPHY
Canadian Congregational Year Book (no place, 1887–8)
Montreal Daily Witness (19 August 1886): 4, 8

GLEN G. SCORGIE

Dougharty, George (b. SC, BNA, *c.* 1772; d. Wilmington, NC, USA, 23 March 1807). Methodist minister. He was accepted as an itinerant preacher in the South Carolina Conference of the MEC in December, 1798. He was appointed to many posts during his nine-year ministry, these included Santee and Oconee. He also held the position of presiding elder of the Seleuda and the Camden districts.

Dougharty was highly regarded as a preacher, and respected for his intellectual capabilities. He had a strong and clear voice, serving him well in assemblies and camp meetings. Dougharty was a pioneer in denominational education. In 1803 he started a Methodist academy in South Carolina but it did not survive long.

In Charleston, Dougharty was attacked by a mob for speaking on slavery. Some women rescued him while the mob was holding him under a pump and attempting to strangle him. Dougharty attempted a trip to the West Indies. When the ship was delayed, his sick condition worsened and he went home where he died. He was buried in the African Church in Wilmington.

BIBLIOGRAPHY
AAP, 7: 290–6

RICHARD E. MCEDWARD

Doughty, Samuel (b. Philadelphia, PA, USA, Jan. 1794; d. Wilmington, DE, USA, 17 Sept. 1828). Methodist minister. He was converted in 1816 and was received as a member of the Philadelphia Conference in 1823. He soon became one of the most popular preachers of the day, with sermons published in the *Methodist Magazine*. He was especially interested in the Sunday school and

benevolent institutions of the church. His life and ministry were brief, but influential.

BIBLIOGRAPHY
CM

STEVE HARPER

Douglas, David (b. Edinburgh, 1789; d. Hamsterley, Durham, England, 1849). Baptist pastor and author. Douglas was a member of the Church at Richmond Court, Edinburgh, under the pastorate of CHRISTOPHER ANDERSON. He studied for the ministry at Bradford College, and began work in 1821 in Falkirk. This proved hard and in 1822 he went to his life's work in Hamsterley.

SELECT WRITINGS
D. Douglas, *History of the Baptist Churches of the North of England, 1648–1845* (London, 1846)

BIBLIOGRAPHY
H. Anderson, *Life and Letters of Christopher Anderson* (Edinburgh, 1854)

DEREK B. MURRAY

Douglas, Neil (b. Glendaruel, Argyll, Scotland, *c.* 1750; d. 9 Jan. 1823). Minister of the Relief Church and radical politician; latterly a Universalist and eccentric. Douglas trained as a Relief Church minister, with charges at Cupar (1785–92) and Dundee (1793–8). About 1784 he and another Relief preacher were dispatched to Luing and Seil, Argyll, where they attempted to participate in the revival which had begun under the Reverend John Smith. With DANIEL MCNAUGHT he preached throughout Kintyre, the Lochgilphead district and Cowal in 1797, and published an account in *Journal of a Mission to Part of the Highlands of Scotland* (Edinburgh, 1799). Spiced with acerbic comments on ministers of other denominations, the journal provides a picture of the early years of dissenting evangelicalism in Argyll, and shows that Douglas was somewhat outspoken, taking a strong stance against patronage, and sympathizing with the French Revolution. Allegedly associated with the Friends of the People, a radical political organization, he left the Relief Church about 1800 and espoused the cause of universalism. He preached latterly in the Andersonian Institution, Glasgow, where he gained a reputation as 'a most extraordinary character . . . in his huge brown wig, and ancient habiliments'.

In his sensational lectures on 'Prophecies of Daniel', he identified the deranged George III with Nebuchadnezzar. As a result he stood trial for sedition before the High Court of Justiciary, Edinburgh, but was acquitted (J. Dow, *Trial of Niel Douglas*, Edinburgh, 1817). Now regarded as a precursor of the Unitarians, Douglas also championed abolitionism, publishing pamphlets under the pseudonym of *Brutus*.

BIBLIOGRAPHY

D. E. Meek, 'Evangelical Missionaries in the Early Nineteenth-Century Highlands', *Scottish Studies*, 28 (1987): 13, 20, 22

L. B. Short, *Pioneers of Scottish Unitarianism* (Narberth, Wales, 1963): 58–64

G. Struthers, *The History of the Rise, Progress and Principles of the Relief Church* (Glasgow, 1843), 396–400

F. Worsdall, *A Glasgow Keek Show* (Glasgow, 1981): 160–3

DONALD E. MEEK

Douglas, Thomas Logan (b. Person Co., NC, USA, 8 July 1781; d. nr Franklin, TN, USA, 9 April 1843). Methodist minister. He was converted at age 17 and received into the Virginia Conference in 1801. For 12 years he ministered in the Virginia Conference in a variety of appointments and in 1813 he transferred to the Tennessee Conference where he served as pastor and superintendent. He was best known for his preaching, but he also served the church as a delegate to three General Conferences. He was a man of deep piety and is said to have influenced the character of the Tennessee Conference more than any other person. Many were converted and entered the ministry because of him.

BIBLIOGRAPHY
CM

STEVE HARPER

Dove, Thomas (b. probably England; d. 15 Dec 1859). Wesleyan Missionary Society (WMS) missionary, The Gambia and Sierra Leone. He was ordained a Wesleyan minister in 1833 and sent by the WMS to The Gambia to found a mission to the Fula. It never got started, and in 1837 he took charge of the Sierra Leone mission. His predecessor there had been engaged in continual strife. He restored order, opened new mission stations, had churches rebuilt and a substantial stone-built building bought for a training institution. He printed the first privately owned newspaper in Sierra Leone on the mission press.

Freetown was full of small shopkeepers who could, he perceived, with overseas credit facilities, turn themselves into import-export merchants. So he took one of his local preachers, John Ezzidio, to England and introduced him to business acquaintances. Set off by this example, a flourishing import-export trade grew up. Dove also took two young men, Charles Knight and Joseph Wright, to London to train as missionaries. He left Sierra Leone in 1846, having transformed the mission and initiated the transformation of the business community.

BIBLIOGRAPHY

W. Fox, *A Brief History of the Wesleyan Missions on the Western Coast of Africa* (London, 1851)

C. Fyfe, *A History of Sierra Leone* (London, 1962)

CHRISTOPHER FYFE

Dow, Lorenzo (b. Coventry, CT, USA, 16 Oct. 1777; d. Georgetown, DC, USA, 2 Feb. 1834). Transatlantic revivalist. Until recently, accounts of nineteenth-century revivalism in Britain and America have often failed to emphasize the transatlantic nature of the movement. One who represented the early generic link in the transatlantic trade in evangelicalism was the impressive but eccentric Connecticut evangelist, Lorenzo Dow, a gaunt, unkempt and effeminate figure, with his long hair, wiry features and sickly countenance. A victim of asthma and epilepsy, Dow's mind was often susceptible to strange, yet vivid spiritual impressions; at the age of four Dow 'suddenly fell into a muse about God and those places called heaven and hell'. Constantly dreaming of God, Jesus, Gabriel, the prophet Nathan, and JOHN WESLEY, when he was 18, Dow saw 'all mankind in the air, suspended by a brittle thread over hell'. Indeed, there was a perpetual struggle in his soul, waged between the powers of good and evil, as he sensed himself influenced in his daily life by divine providence or tempted by Satan. This relationship between all three persisted throughout his life, as he was guided by inward lights and voices. Thus, Dow's faith displayed all the characteristics of a folk legacy rather than any intellectual antecedence, containing heavy doses of the supernatural, with his visions and miracles. Guided by inner lights, visions and voices (he was known as Crazy Dow), he had no academic mentor, only the figures in his dreams.

Converted during adolescence, Dow experienced self-despair and guilt, then repentance towards God, followed by an assurance of God's forgiveness and mercy. Although his burden was lifted, he believed that he continually battled with Satan throughout his life. Admitted on trial by the Methodist Conference in 1798, Dow was never allowed by the Methodists to be officially one of them, because of his rough manner, his ungracious and emotional presentation, and his tendency to follow his own soul rather than the dictates of conference. This did not stop him itinerating under the Methodist banner a revivalism which embraced an unusual mixture of spiritual spontaneity and a traditional use of outdoor preaching, his raw sermons inserting themselves like knives into the hearts and souls of American frontiers-people. The passion that he infused into his audiences, accompanied by hysterics and falling on the ground, ensured his notoriety and fame. Prolific author of numerous works on theology and moral philosophy, as well as the aptly titled two volumes of personal journals, *The Dealings of God, Man and the Devil* (1854), Dow also commented on antislavery, matrimony and cursing.

Dow travelled widely, and was the first itinerant Protestant to preach in many of the wilderness frontier regions of the western United States in the early nineteenth century, often accompanied by his wife, Peggy. It has been suggested that Dow travelled nearly a quarter of a million miles throughout America, Canada, the West Indies and Europe (10,000 miles in 1805 alone), attending between 500 and 800 meetings in any year, preaching the gospel to as many people as had GEORGE WHITEFIELD and Wesley.

Renowned for his political passion, Dow often extolled the virtues of republicanism and the evils of slavery, risking and often suffering imprisonment and physical abuse. He first landed in England in 1805. His impact was intensified by his own accounts of incidents of American revivalism, such as the introduction of the frontier camp meetings in the clearings of the backwoods areas of Kentucky. He also provided descriptions of his visits to Warrington, the home of the Quaker Methodists, and the Delamere Forest, sanctuary of the Magic Methodists. Dow prompted among the Primitive Methodists the demand for a new, more emotional form of worship, which neither Wesleyan Methodism nor the Established Church could either comprehend or supply, but the Primitive Methodist movement was as much influenced by Dow's exemplary emphasis on congregational as against conference ministry.

Dow's influence on the nineteenth century was both cathartic and extensive. In many ways, he acted as a spiritual pioneer; on the American frontier he opened up new regions for the Gospel. In England he served as a catalyst, by his innovative introduction of camp meetings, and in the forming of the earthy Primitive Methodists, the largest denomination to form in England since the birth of Methodism. A firm believer in providence, Dow was convinced that God was at work in the world, that there was no such thing as chance, and that people were guided by divine intervention. It was that message that he preached with his peculiar brand of revivalism. Dow was never in the centre of American revivalism, but remained a marginal figure. As a result, he has been neglected, for the most part banished to antiquarian articles, although Eudora Welty of the American South wrote a worthy short story about this remarkable, colourful and eccentric preacher, who was perhaps the most widely known man in America at his death. Indeed, Dow was one of the most important itinerant revivalists of his generation, certainly amongst those engaged in the transatlantic route. His neglect has mainly been due to his persona, because of his true nonconformity, and his hatred of temporal authority. Dow was a pure peripatetic, an itinerant revivalist in all manner of the word, a free-ranging spirit, a pilgrim on earth.

SELECT WRITINGS
L. Dow, *The Life, Travels, Labours, and Writings of Lorenzo Dow* (New York and Auburn, ME, 1856)

BIBLIOGRAPHY
B. Brawley, 'Lorenzo Dow', *Methodist Review* (1916)
DAB
DCA
N. Hatch, *The Democratization of American Christianity* (New Haven, CT, 1989)
G. Herod, *Biographical Sketches of . . . Early Primitive Methodist Preachers* (London, 1855)
J. Kent, *Holding the Fort* (London, 1978)
C. G. Sellers, *Lorenzo Dow, The Bearer of the Word* (New York, 1928)

WAYNE J. JOHNSON

Downes, John (b. England, *c.* 1722; d. London, 6 Nov. 1774). Methodist itinerant. No details survive relating to his early life and conversion. At the age of 21 he emerges at Horsley, Northumberland, as a member of an infant society first visited by WESLEY in 1742. Encouraged by GRACE MURRAY, he began to preach and was quickly enlisted as an itinerant, joining JOHN WESLEY and JOHN NELSON on a tour to Cornwall. There he was mistaken for the Pretender at a time when Jacobite rumours were rife. In 1744 he was press-ganged for the army and imprisoned in Lincoln Castle but eventually released. He was one of four lay itinerants attending the first Conference. His health gave some concern and in 1751 Wesley invited him to London to manage the printing office responsible for Methodist publications. Wesley had a high appreciation of his capabilities as a mathematician and an engraver.

A. SKEVINGTON WOOD

Dowson, Henry (b. Nottingham, England, 7 March 1812; d. Manchester, England, 23 Nov. 1884). Baptist minister. Dowson grew up in a Baptist family. As a youth he was apprenticed to the printing business of his father, Ralph Dowson. At 19, Dowson experienced a call into ministry. He trained at Horton College (later Rawdon) and at the University of Edinburgh. From 1834 to 1865 he served as pastor at Westgate, Bradford, and in retirement he founded the Crouch Hill Baptist Church. Dowson took a strong interest in theological education, serving Bradford-Horton as secretary (1840–64). From 1865 to 1874 he served as tutor and president of the Strict-Communion Baptist College at Bury, securing its removal to purpose-built facilities in Manchester in 1874, and continuing as president for a further three years. Active in the Baptist Continental Aid Society, Henry travelled in 1840 to Denmark to present a memorial to the King on behalf of persecuted Baptists. He also helped organize a Protestant Chapel in Brussels, Belgium. During a number of addresses as president of the Baptist Union in 1881, he highlighted themes which characterized his career: evangelism, religious liberty, the spiritual life and theological orthodoxy.

BIBLIOGRAPHY
Baptist Handbook (1886)
J. O. Barrett, *A Short History of Rawdon College* (London, 1954)

P. R. DEKAR

Doxsey, Isaac (b. 7 May 1816; d. South London, 13 Dec. 1898). Baptist minister and temperance advocate. Doxsey is described in his obituary as a 'sturdy radical' and 'reformer of the past', and certainly he lived a life of social engagement: serving as a Poor Law guardian, refusing to pay church rate, crusading against compulsory vaccination and against British involvement in the Opium Wars, and acting as a school manager.

At the age of 14 he joined Pickfords, the railway carriers, but subsequently trained for the ministry in Dublin. Here he acted as a prison chaplain and became acquainted with the work of Father Matthew, the Roman Catholic temperance worker whom he accompanied on one of his temperance missions. Doxsey himself had been converted to the temperance cause by listening to a sermon by the Reverend BAPTIST NOEL at a meeting where Silk Buckingham was presiding. Taking the pledge against the use of 'ardent spirits', he embraced both the anti-spirit and the anti-tobacco causes. His first pastorate was at Marsh Gibbon in Oxfordshire from whence he removed to Thame in the same county. He later became secretary of the National Temperance Society, residing in Brixton, where his goods were on one occasion seized on account of his refusal to pay church rate. He also served as editor of the *National Temperance Chronicle*. Towards the end of his career he returned to the pastorate with charge of the church at Lower Edmonton in North London and later at Camberwell. In retirement he was particulary attached to the mission work associated with the Lambeth Baths.

BIBLIOGRAPHY
Baptist Handbook (1900)

J. H. Y. BRIGGS

Drachart, Christian Larsen (b. Skaelskør, near Copenhagen, Denmark, 23 June 1711; d. Nain, Labrador, 18 Sept. 1778). Lutheran minister and Moravian missionary to Greenland and Labrador. Drachart, reared by an uncle who was a Lutheran pastor, studied theology in Copenhagen and became an ordained Lutheran minister in 1739. While serving as a missionary near New Herrnhut, Greenland, he established contact with Moravian missionaries. The experiential religion of the Moravians was congenial to Drachart's own religious inclinations but led to great tensions with Lutheran church authorities. After marrying a Moravian he became a member of his wife's church in November of 1751. After the death of his wife and a subsequent stay at the Moravian headquarters in Herrnhut, Saxony, he participated in JENS HAVEN's exploratory journey to Labrador in 1765. Drachart returned to Labrador two more times, first in 1770, when he preached to the Inuit and made preparations for a more permanent mission, and, finally, when the missionary party under the leadership of CHRISTOPH BRASEN established Nain. He died there seven years later. Manuscript material on Drachart and the Moravian missionaries to Labrador is available in the Moravian archives at Herrnhut, Germany; London, England; and Bethlehem, Pennsylvania; as well as in the British colonial records.

BIBLIOGRAPHY
Public Archives of Canada, Ottawa, 'Catalogus der Missionare in Labrador', Records of the Moravian Mission in Labrador [1764–1944], microfilm 511, reels 11–12, fol. 15195–6

DCB
Kölbing

MARCELLA ROLLMANN

Drake, Benjamin (Michael) (b. Robeson County, NC, USA, 11 Sept. 1800; d. Fayette District, MS, USA, 8 May 1860). Leader and educator in Southern Methodism. He was converted on 22 May 1818, received his licence to exhort on 7 June 1819, and his licence to preach on 19 September 1819. He was married to Susan Priscilla Hawkins Magruder in 1827, a marriage that lasted 35 years.

Drake was admitted on trial in the Kentucky Conference in 1820 and appointed to the Fountainhead circuit and then numerous other appointments in the Mississippi Conference. He was ordained deacon in full connection in 1822 and was ordained elder on 22 December 1824. In 1852 he received an honorary DD from Centenary College. His leadership in the church can be seen in his regular service as a delegate to General Conference. He was also a delegate to the first General Conference for the MEC, So.

Drake had few educational opportunities as a youth, but was an avid student. His interest in education continued through his presidency of the first Methodist school in Mississippi, the Elizabeth Female Academy. He was also acting-president of the newly founded Centenary College for one year. Two of his lasting contributions to Methodism are his promotion of a Course of Study for Methodist preachers and his active insistence that churches provide parsonage homes for pastors regardless of the size of the circuit.

BIBLIOGRAPHY
EWM
R. Holder, *The Mississippi Methodists, 1793–1983* (Jackson, MI, 1984)
H. G. Hawkins, *Methodism in Natchez* (Nashville, TN, 1937)
MQR
MR
M. Simpson, ed., *Cyclopedia of Methodism* (Philadelphia, PA, 1882)

SONDRA H. MATTHAEI

Draper, Bourne Hall (b. Cumnor, Oxfordshire, England, 1778; d. Southampton, Hampshire, England, 12 Oct. 1843). Baptist minister. Educated Christ Church, Oxford, Draper then worked as apprentice at the Clarendon Press. He was converted 1797 under JAMES HINTON's ministry at Oxford and entered Bristol Academy 1802. In 1804 he became pastor at Chipping Norton, subsequently moving to Coseley (1809) and Southampton (1820) where he ministered until his death. Draper was a prolific author, writing about 36 works in all, some being translated into other European languages. A keen advocate for the emancipation of slaves (*Baptist Magazine*, 1821: 450–1), he also gave generously of his time to many Christian organizations such as the Sunday school movement and the Bible Society. Deeply interested in children's and youth work, several of his writings (especially Bible stories and poetry) had young readers specially in mind. He was a frequent contributor to the *Baptist Magazine*.

BIBLIOGRAPHY
BaptMag (1844): 117–21

RAYMOND BROWN

Draper, Daniel James (b. Wickham, Hampshire, England, 28 Aug. 1810; d. at sea, 11 Jan. 1866). Methodist minister. Draper was brought up as an Anglican but, after a spiritual awakening at the age of 17, he joined the Methodist chapel at Fareham in Hampshire. In 1833 he moved to Brecon in Wales where he worked as a carpenter and was active in the Methodist church as a local (lay) preacher. In 1834 he was received by the Wesleyan Conference as a minister on probation. After a year in a circuit he was ordained and appointed to Australia. He and his wife, whom he had shortly before married, sailed from England in October 1835, expressing in a letter the hope that he might convey 'in some humble manner the light of life to the ends of the earth'. The couple arrived in Hobart in Tasmania in February 1836.

Draper spent thirty years in the ministry in the colonies of New South Wales, South Australia and Victoria: roughly ten years in each. It was a period of rapid growth in population, especially during the goldrushes of the early 1850s. By his evangelical preaching, constant pastoral care and sagacious leadership he extended the influence of Methodism in the areas in which he served. He is remembered as a builder of churches (some of which survive) in towns and new settlements. He was chairman of his church in both South Australia and Victoria and in 1859 was elected president of the Australasian Wesleyan Methodist Conference.

In 1865 Draper went to England to represent the autonomous Australian church at the British Wesleyan Conference. He spent a year visiting churches, speaking about the work in Australia and encouraging the emigration of ministers. On 5 January 1866 Draper and his wife boarded the *London* for their return to Australia. A few days later, the ship was caught in a storm in the Bay of Biscay and sank with only 17 survivors out of 263 on board. They told of Draper leading a prayer meeting and exhorting people to accept Christ in the final hours before the vessel was submerged. A verse from CHARLES WESLEY, which friends recalled as being from one of his favourite hymns, became for Draper a tragic reality in the heaving waters off the coast of France:

Happy if with my latest breath
I may but gasp His name;
Preach Him to all and cry in death,
Behold, behold the Lamb.

BIBLIOGRAPHY
ADB, 1
J. C. Symons, *Life of Daniel James Draper* (London, 1870)

ARNOLD D. HUNT

Draper, William Henry (b. near London, England, 11 March 1801; d. Yorkville (Toronto), Ontario, Canada, 3 Nov. 1877). Lawyer, politician, and judge. The son of an evangelical Church of England clergyman, Draper received his early education privately and at age 15 ran away to sea, serving as a cadet aboard an East-Indiaman. In 1820 he emigrated to Upper Canada, settling first at Port Hope. There he taught school for a short period of time and took up the study of law. He was called to the bar of Upper Canada in 1828. Draper moved in the circles of prominent Tory 'Family Compact' members like John Beverley Robinson and Christopher Hagerman. Under Robinson's influence he entered politics, serving successively as Solicitor-General, Attorney-General and ultimately as leader of the Conservatives and in effect, prime minister from 1844 to 1847.

In 1847 he abandoned politics for the bench – always his ultimate career goal. Over the course of the next thirty years he held a variety of judicial positions: puisne judge of the Court of Queen's Bench, Chief Justice of the Court of Common Pleas, Chief Justice of the Court of Queen's Bench, presiding judge and then Chief Justice of the Court of Error and Appeal of Ontario.

Regarded as the 'elder statesman' of Anglican evangelicals in nineteenth-century Ontario, Draper played a prominent role in the controversies between high churchmen and evangelicals. He served as first president of the Church Association, formed in 1873 to do battle with the High Church phalanx which was firmly entrenched in the diocese of Toronto. In its early years the Church Association published a series of occasional papers promoting evangelical views and in 1876 established a paper, the *Evangelical Churchman*. It also took a firm stand against Trinity College (Toronto) and accordingly took steps towards establishing the Protestant Episcopal Divinity School (established 1877 and subsequently renamed Wycliffe College).

BIBLIOGRAPHY
DCB, X
A. L. Hayes, 'The Struggle for the Rights of the Laity in the Diocese of Toronto 1850–1879', *JCCHS*, XXVI (1984), 5–17
D. C. Masters, 'The Anglican Evangelicals in Toronto 1870–1900' *JCCHS*, XX (1978), 51–66

RICHARD W. VAUDRY

Dreisbach, John (b. Buffalo Valley, Union County, PA, USA, 5 June 1789; d. 20 Aug. 1871). American preacher and leader of the Evangelical Association. Dreisbach's parents, Martin and Sabina Fredrica Dreisbach, were among the first people west of the Susquehanna River in Pennsylvania to make their home available for the preaching of JACOB ALBRIGHT, the founder of the

Evangelical Association. John experienced the new birth in 1806 during a meeting held by Albright in his parents' home.

In 1807 Dreisbach was licensed to preach by Albright. Later that year he attended the first annual conference of the Evangelical Association held in the home of Samuel Becker near Kleinfeltersville, Pennsylvania. He was appointed pastor of the Schuylkill circuit, an appointment he shared with his friend George Miller. In 1808 Dreisbach and Miller were appointed to the Northumberland circuit, a territory which encompassed nine counties in central Pennsylvania. Miller's sudden death in 1808 left him in sole charge of the work. The following year he was ordained elder in the church.

Dreisbach was a very important figure in the development of the Evangelical Association. He served as secretary of the church and in 1814 became its first presiding elder (district superintendent). He presided at the dedication of the denomination's first church building and was instrumental in the establishment of the church's first printing operation at New Berlin, Pennsylvania, in 1816. He was responsible for organizing new Evangelical congregations west of the Allegheny Mountains. In 1810 Dreisbach and FRANCIS ASBURY met and discussed the union of the Evangelicals with the MEC, but they could not reach agreement on this matter.

Among Dreisbach's contributions to his church were his talents as an editor and author. He published a German catechism for it in 1809. With Henry Niebel he prepared and published its first authorized hymn-book. He also served as editor of the *Evangelical Messenger*, the church's official English periodical from 1854 to 1857. He was the author of numerous articles, poems and hymns.

Dreisbach was also an advocate of higher education. He was especially interested in having an educated ministry for the church. At the 1847 General Conference of the church he introduced a resolution to establish an educational institution which resulted in the formation of a college.

BIBLIOGRAPHY

J. B. Behney and P. H. Eller, *The History of the Evangelical United Brethren Church* (Nashville, TN, 1979)

CHARLES YRIGOYEN, JR

Drew, Samuel (b. St Austell, Cornwall, England, 6 March 1765; d. Helston, Cornwall, England, 29 March 1833). 'The metaphysical shoemaker', was born of Methodist parents. His father was a small farmer and carrier. His mother died when he was nine and his father remarried. Drew left St Austell School at ten, and, after working at a mill, was apprenticed to a shoemaker. He absconded, and had several other situations, all more or less unsatisfactory, enlivened by poaching and smuggling forays. He was converted through the ministry of ADAM CLARKE in the St Austell society in 1785. The event revolutionized his intellectual life: previously careless of education, he now turned every leisure moment

to reading – theology, philosophy (Locke influenced him most), poetry and grammar, besides the Bible and *Pilgrim's Progress*. He became a class leader and local preacher (suffering a temporary suspension for suspected Calvinism), and wrote some rather indifferent verse. Frequent discussions with a deist surgeon who had lent him *The Age of Reason* led to his first published essay: a pamphlet in reply to Paine. By 1802 he had produced a more substantial treatise on the human soul which went through many editions and was translated into French.

All this time, Drew was conducting his own trade, and writing at night in his kitchen, 'amidst the cries and cradles of my children', but from 1805 onwards he was primarily, engaged in literature. He became literary agent for THOMAS COKE and, through ADAM CLARKE, a reviewer for the *Eclectic Review*. He wrote essays on the resurrection of the body, the Atonement, the divinity of Christ, and on natural theology; he took over and completed a massive *History of Cornwall* (substantially his own work, despite the title page), and compiled the 'official' biography of Coke. In 1819 he undertook the editorship of *The Imperial Magazine*, published by the Caxton Press, which he superintended at Liverpool and then in London.

Despite his early disabilities and the narrowness of his education (he did not travel beyond Cornwall and Devon until he was fifty), Drew gained recognition as a metaphysician and a writer. Marischal College, Aberdeen, awarded him the MA degree in 1824, and there was a move to appoint him to the chair of moral philosophy at London in 1830. In 1833, tired and ill, he left London for his native Cornwall, and died at Helston. His wife, Honour, whom he had married in 1788, had died there of cholera in 1828.

Drew is a remarkable evangelical example of the type of versatile litterateur characteristic of the period. He had many close friendships outside Methodism (he twice declined proposals that he should be ordained in the Church of England), even with those, like Richard Polwhele, whom he combated in print.

BIBLIOGRAPHY

Bibliotheca Cornubiensis: 119–121, 126, 300 ff, 382, 510, 515, 535, 700, 869, 872, 1161 (for list of writings)

Collectanea Cornubiensis (col. 215)

DNB

T. Rowe, 'The Writings of Samuel Drew', *Country Town* (1947–8)

J. T. Wilkinson, *Samuel Drew 1765–1833* (Cornish Methodist Historical Association, 1963)

A. F. WALLS

Drew, Thomas (b. Limerick, Ireland, 26 Oct. 1800; d. County Down, Ireland, 26 Oct. 1870). Anglican clergyman. Educated at Trinity College, Dublin, he served a curacy in Broughshane before being nominated as the first minister of Christ Church, consecrated by Bishop Mant in 1832. This new 'Free Church' was badly needed in Belfast. The market town had begun its transformation into an industrial city, and its population –

37,000 in 1823 – was increasing by 3,000 annually. An unchurched multitude lived within the district assigned to the new church. Drew visited ceaselessly among his people; began Sunday schools for both adults and children, and day schools which, by 1837, had 1,000 children in attendance; held weekly lectures in the church, and regular baptisms, catechizing and confirmation classes; recruited scripture readers to help in visitation; and launched such parochial institutions as a clothing club, a dispensary, singing classes and libraries. He also founded Houses of Prayer in selected parts of his vast district, and was responsible for the foundation of the Magdalene Asylum and chapel. Each of these extensions later became a separate parish.

Despite his efforts, however, the population continued to outgrow the provision of church ministrations, and in his pamphlet, *The Church in Belfast* (1838), he pointed out that a nominal Established Church population of more than 20,000 had but three churches, with total accommodation for 4,000, and the services of only four clergy. To meet these needs, he was instrumental in initiating in the diocese of Down and Connor both the Clergy-Aid Society and the Church Accommodation Society. The latter was launched at a public meeting held in Christ Church, and attended by many Belfast merchants and gentry of counties Antrim and Down. He had done the necessary groundwork, the meeting was a conspicuous success, and substantial funds were pledged for church extension. The two societies were of general benefit to the diocese (of the needs of which he was apprised through his fact-finding tours with Archdeacon Walter Mant), but Belfast gained most, and by 1858 had 16 churches and 18 clergy. The majority were evangelicals, including Theophilus Campbell of Trinity Church, Ballysillan (1843), and Charles Seaver of St John's, Laganbank (1853).

During the 1840s he was chaplain to two (Conservative) Lords-Lieutenant of Ireland, and received an honorary DD from Trinity College, Dublin. He was a regular speaker at the April meetings in Rotunda. He valued Protestant unity, was a leader in the Orange Society, and enjoyed the friendship of the Presbyterian evangelicals, Dr Stewart (in Broughshane), Dr HENRY COOKE, and JAMES MORGAN. The combined influence of his teaching, both in church and cottage meeting, and his pastoral ministry, together with his dominance among the Orangemen, gave him a powerful hold on the working class population of Belfast. Like HUGH MCNEILE in Liverpool and HUGH STOWELL in Manchester, he left his stamp on the character of an industrial city.

His lasting achievement was to ensure that the pace of church extension and the progress of evangelical principles, within the established Church in Belfast, were commensurate with the city's rapid growth. Worn out by his ceaseless exertions over 27 years, he was in 1859 appointed by Bishop Robert Knox to the precentorship of Down Cathedral and a country living, where he spent his remaining years.

BIBLIOGRAPHY
A. Dawson, 'The Annals of Christ Church, Belfast, from its Foundation in 1831' (typescript, 1858)
Representative Church Body Library, Braemor Park, Dublin 14, Report of the Great Meeting of the Diocese of Down and Connor for Church Extension, Belfast 1838
Wills, IV: 536–9

ALAN R. ACHESON

Droese, Ernest (b. Thorn, Prussia, 1817; d. Landour, India, 19 April 1891). Missionary in India. Little is known of his childhood, but he studied four years at the seminary of the Berlin Missionary Society, was ordained in 1842, and left the following year to open a new field at Gazipur, North India. He also assisted the LMS at Varanasi (Benares), remaining there after several workers left due to health problems. In 1849 he married Johanna Schubert. When the Berlin board closed its Indian work, Droese transferred to the CMS, received Anglican orders, and settled in Bhagalpur, Bengal in 1850. There he built the mission house, church, and other structures for the Christian community.

His major achievement was the mastering and reducing to writing Malto, the Dravidian tongue of the Pahari and Santhal people in the Rajmahal Hill Country. He produced a grammar and dictionary of the language and translated the Gospels, Psalms, *Book of Common Prayer*, and Bible stories. As more missionaries came to reinforce the Bhagalpur Station, he spent increasing time in literary labours. Poor health forced his retirement in 1885; but he remained in India doing translation work with his daughter Mary's assistance and died at Landour near Mussooree.

BIBLIOGRAPHY
D. T. B[arry], *CMS Register of Missionaries and Native Clergy* (privately printed) (London, 1906)
CMI (1891): 462
E. Droese, *Indian Gems for the Master's Crown* (London, 1892)
—, *Introduction to the Malto Language* (Agra, 1884)
E. Stock, *History of the CMS* (London, 1899)
M. E. Weitbrecht, *Missionary Sketches in North India* (London, 1858)

R. V. PIERARD

Dromgoole, Edward (b. Sligo, Ireland, *c.* 1751; d. Brunswick County, VA, USA, 1835). Methodist preacher. Dromgoole came to America in 1770. He began preaching as one of the many preachers influenced by ROBERT STRAWBRIDGE. He served under conference appointment from 1774 to 1786 in Maryland, Virginia, and North Carolina.

In 1777 Dromgoole was one of five selected to supervise Methodism should all the British missionaries depart. In 1780 he was in FRANCIS ASBURY's negotiating party during the ordination and sacraments controversy. He was probably a member of the 1784 Christmas Conference which established the MEC. Dromgoole continued an active local ministry after 1786. Francis

Asbury ordained him elder in 1815. Edward married Rebecca Walton and their son George Coke was in his sixth term as a Congressman from Virginia at the time of his death in 1847.

BIBLIOGRAPHY
EWM
NCAB
A. Stevens, *History of the Methodist Episcopal Church* (New York, 1864)

CHARLES W. BROCKWELL, JR

Drummond, David Thomas Kerr (b. Edinburgh, 25 Aug. 1805; d. Pitlochry, Scotland, 9 June 1877). Author and clergyman (deacon 1830, priest 1831). Educated at Edinburgh University and Worcester College Oxford, he was minister of Trinity Episcopal Church, Edinburgh 1838–43. He then resigned from the Scottish Episcopal Church because the Bishop of Edinburgh claimed that the Bible studies he held in Clyde Street Hall were public meetings and canon law required that the Liturgy be used. He admonished Drummond for this omission. A great controversy ensued and all compromise failed. Drummond felt the Gospel was under attack and the Bishop defended the authority of his office. Drummond resigned and with some members of Trinity founded St Thomas's English Episcopal Church, which is his main claim to fame. St Thomas's and St Silas, Glasgow have maintained the evangelical episcopal tradition in Scotland but initially independent of the Scottish Episcopal Church. Drummond defended the evangelical position by his writings and through the founding of St Thomas's.

BIBLIOGRAPHY
Boase

GEOFFREY E. W. SCOBIE

Drummond, Henry (b. the Grange, Northington, Hampshire, England, 5 Dec. 1786; d. Albury, Surrey, England, 20 Feb. 1860). MP and founder of the Catholic Apostolic Church. Drummond was the eldest son of Henry, banker, and Anne, daughter of Henry Dundas, first Viscount Melville. He was educated at Harrow and Christ Church, Oxford. Drummond's father died in 1794; around 1802, his mother remarried and moved to India, leaving him under the care of Lord Melville. This provided Drummond with direct access to the inner circles of the Tory party, and he became a favourite of Pitt. In 1807, he married Lady Henrietta Hay, eldest daughter of the ninth Earl of Kinnoul, by whom he had three sons and two daughters. He was MP for Plympton Earls, 1810–12, and for West Surrey, 1847–60.

After resigning from Parliament due to ill health in 1812, Drummond embarked on an erratic spiritual trajectory. Through the influence of the BARINGS he became involved in the Western Schism of 1815. 'Satiated by the empty frivolities of the fashionable world,

and pressed by the address of our Lord to the rich young man,' he broke up his hunting establishment and sold the Grange. Then, in 1817, he departed on an extended tour of the Holy Land; diverted *en route* to Geneva, he offered his services to ROBERT HALDANE then engaged in evangelism among local students. Drummond, wealthy and dogmatic, quickly provoked the Geneva authorities. Facing arrest, he instead fled to France from where he continued the work, later returning to England to co-found (in 1819, with Haldane and Sir THOMAS BARING) the Continental Society. In 1825, he endowed the Drummond chair in political economy at Oxford.

In 1826, introduced to the study of biblical prophecy by the evangelist LEWIS WAY, Drummond became an early fixture of the English prophetic movement, rejecting mainstream 'Claphamite' evangelicalism as having capitulated to liberalism. In politics Drummond was an 'old-school Tory', although he always voted independently. Alarmed by the 'constitutional revolution' of 1828–32, he withdrew further into pessimistic millennialism.

In late 1825, Drummond vigorously pursued a friendship with EDWARD IRVING, introducing him to the burgeoning prophetic movement – an interest which was advanced by their mutual involvement in the LSPCJ. Drummond subsequently organized the celebrated Albury conferences for the study of prophecy at his Surrey home between November 1826 and July 1830, when, coinciding with the outbreak of the 'gifts' in Scotland, they were moved to Irving's church at Regent Square, London.

On 26 December 1832, Drummond was ordained as angel for the small body which gathered for worship at his Albury home, and which would soon be known as the Catholic Apostolic Church. On 25 September 1833, he became apostle in the new body. He later financed the construction of the Church's cathedral and chapter house at Albury (cost £16,000), and its church in Gordon Square, London (cost £30,000).

Carlyle described Drummond as 'a singular mixture of all things – of the saint, the wit, the philosopher – swimming . . . in an element of dandyism'. Kinglake wrote that he was 'gifted with a piercing cleverness' and possessed of 'a keen lively wit, and a natural devoid of fear'. Drummond forcibly expressed traditional notions of social hierarchy, of organic links uniting the strata in the hierarchy, and of society as a religious phenomenon. With his active, unsettled spirit – fuelled by disquiet over social and political reform – he became one of the most influential theological innovators of the nineteenth century.

BIBLIOGRAPHY
Northumberland Manuscripts, Drummond Papers, Alnwick Castle
H. Bolitho and D. Peel, *The Drummonds of Charing Cross* (London, 1967): 129–44
G. Carter, 'Evangelical Seceders from the Church of England, *c.* 1800–1850' (Oxford University D. Phil. thesis, 1990): 219–71
DNB

W. H. Oliver, *Prophets and Millennialists* (Auckland and Oxford, 1978)

G. L. Standring, *Albury and the Catholic Apostolic Church* (Albury, England, 1985)

GRAYSON CARTER

Duché, Jacob   (b. Philadelphia, PA, BNA, 1 Feb. 1737; d. Philadelphia, 3 Jan. 1798). Anglican clergyman and Swedenborgian. The Duché family were prominent Pennsylvanian Anglicans. Jacob studied at Clare College, Cambridge and was assistant minister of Christ Church and St Peter's, Philadelphia, and in 1776 was appointed rector. He was a popular preacher, and a supporter of GEORGE WHITEFIELD. As political tensions grew Duché led prayers at the meeting of the Continental Congress and was appointed its chaplain, but when the British invaded Philadelphia he denounced the revolutionaries, and in 1778 went into exile in Britain. Duché used the language of evangelical spirituality, but privately he was deeply influenced by the writings of William Law and the German mystic Jacob Boehme. In London he came in contact with a circle of mystical readers, and while drawing crowds from July 1782 to his Sunday services as chaplain of the Asylum for Female Orphans in Lambeth, he was attracted like many other mystical readers to the writings of Emanuel Swedenborg, although he did not support the formation of the New Jerusalem sect. He retired to Philadelphia in 1793. Duché's life reflects a frustration with the outward forms of evangelicalism, in which he was not unique.

BIBLIOGRAPHY
DcAmB, 3
C. Garrett, 'The Spiritual Odyssey of Jacob Duché', *Proceedings of the American Philosophical Society*, 119 (1975): 143–155.
C. Higham, 'The Rev. Jacob Duché, MA', *New Church Review*, 22 (1915): 210–225; 404–420.

PETER J. LINEHAM

Ducie, Second Earl of.   *See* MORETON, HENRY (GEORGE FRANCIS REYNOLDS)

Dudley, Ambrose   (b. Spottsylvania, VA, BNA, 1750; d. Bryan's Station, KY, USA, 27 Jan. 1825). Baptist minister. Ambrose Dudley came to the Christian faith while serving as a captain in the Revolutionary War. Upon his return to Spottsylvania, he entered the ministry, pastored, and was ordained in his home church. In 1785 he removed to the frontier of Kentucky and settled near Lexington. He was highly effective as an evangelist during the Kentucky revivals of 1803. He once baptized 126 persons within a two-week period at Bryan's Station and Dave's Fork, only six miles distant. Dudley ministered to the churches of the Elkhorn Association as their moderator and disciplinarian for many years. In matters of doctrine he was an uncompromising Calvinist who opposed auxiliary church societies of any kind, including sabbath schools and 'moneyed missionaries'. He had eleven sons and three daughters, and is reckoned the patriarch of longstanding Primitive Baptist tradition in Kentucky.

BIBLIOGRAPHY
AAP
R. H. Pittman, *Biographical History* (Indianapolis, IN, 1909): 94
J. B. Taylor, *Virginia Baptist Ministers* (Philadelphia, PA, 1859): 221–3

WADE A. HORTON

Dudley, Charles Stokes   (b. Clonmel, Ireland, 1780; d. 4 Nov. 1862). Merchant, insurance broker and BFBS domestic secretary. The eldest son of Robert and MARY DUDLEY (a Quaker minister), Dudley became a merchant and insurance broker in Bristol in 1798. In London from 1807, he became committed to the BFBS, promoting his 'System' of selling Bibles to the poor by penny-a-week subscriptions. Joining the staff in 1819, he published *An Analysis of the System of the Bible Society* (1821), explaining how to organize local associations. However it was Dudley's rhetoric and passion that were most in demand, and he travelled widely (an estimated 300,000 miles and 8,000 meetings). He married in 1824 and began to attend the Church of England; he retired in 1857. The Bible Society's Archives hold Dudley's correspondence.

BIBLIOGRAPHY
G. T. Edwards, 'Old Friends of the Bible Society,' *Bible Society Monthly Reporter* (1892)

LESLIE HOWSAM

Dudley, Mary   [née **Stokes**] (b. Bristol, England, 1750; d. Peckham, London, 24 Sept. 1823). Quaker traveller. Born of Anglican parents, Stokes joined the Methodists in her late teens, but to JOHN WESLEY's distress, became a Friend about 1773. In 1777 she married Robert Dudley and settled at Clonmel, County Tipperary, Ireland, being recorded a minister about this time. Following her husband's death (1807) she moved to London in 1810.

In 1787, when the youngest of her seven was only ten weeks old, she accompanied Sarah (Tuke) Grubb (1756–90) on a religious visit to Holland, Germany and France. In 1792 she visited Dunkirk and Guernsey. Her other ministerial journeys, though numerous, were all within the British Isles.

While her earlier ministry had emphasized the universality of grace and had been anti-predestinarian, her emphasis after 1800 or so was more markedly evangelical – partly, perhaps, as a result of her association with the evangelical American Quaker DAVID SANDS during his Irish travels, and partly as a reaction to the Irish Quaker 'New Lights' of the 1790s.

BIBLIOGRAPHY
E. Dudley, ed., *The Life of Mary Dudley* (London, 1825)

EDWARD H. MILLIGAN

Duff, Alexander (b. Moulin, Perthshire, Scotland, 25 April 1806; d. Sidmouth, Devonshire, England, 12 Feb. 1878). Missionary and educator. Alexander Duff, pioneer of Christian higher education in India, was born on a farm near Pitlochry in Scotland. His parents, James and Jean (née Rattray) Duff, were evangelicals, deeply influenced by CHARLES SIMEON, who had visited the area in 1796. After primary education locally, in 1821 Duff enrolled at the University of St Andrews, where he remained until 1829. At the end of 1823 the celebrated THOMAS CHALMERS became professor of moral philosophy there, and over the next four years did much to help turn Duff's thought in a missionary direction, and to give it content. The missionary tradition was not strong in the Church of Scotland at the time; and although in 1827 Duff had begun to consider becoming a missionary following the tragic early death of a close friend, John Urquhart (who had been planning a missionary career in China), the door was not yet open. That he was sent two years later to India was the result of a (non-evangelical) proposal for the Church of Scotland to begin educational missionary work in Bengal. Duff was appointed to the post by the Assembly of 1829, was ordained, married Anne Scott Drysdale of Edinburgh, and left for India in October of the same year. He was still only 24 years old.

The Duffs did not arrive in Calcutta for another eight months, having been shipwrecked twice *en route*, once off Cape Town (on which occasion Duff lost the whole of his educational library) and again in the Hooghly estuary. They came ashore on 27 May 1830. The Assembly had instructed him to move inland from Calcutta; but this instruction he wisely chose to ignore. Other missionaries in the area were at first suspicious of his educational enterprise, and were unhelpful; but the great WILLIAM CAREY was encouraging, and gave Duff his blessing. Duff's initial progress was however due very largely to the help of the Brahman reformer Rammohun Roy, who helped him set up his first school and supplied most of his first pupils.

Duff's faith was evangelical to the core; his educational policy, learned primarily from Chalmers, was advanced. His opposition to unreformed 'Hinduism' was passionate; and he believed that every item of sound knowledge he was able to teach would help dislodge some part of its foundations. In opting for the English language as his medium of instruction he was only being practical. In both cases he was however making a cultural, as well as an educational and religious decision. Within five years the Government of India, with the approval of Hindu reformers, settled on the English language as the medium of higher education, reinforcing Duff's original choice.

Duff's first four years in India were not free from controversy, brought about chiefly by those who saw his activities as contravening the East India Company's policy of strict non-interference in matters of religion. Nor did he receive unqualified support in Scotland. The years 1834–9, therefore, he spent in Britain, explaining what he had done thus far and what he planned for the future,

his General Assembly address of 1835 being especially illuminating as a policy statement; and in recruiting colleagues. Not long after his return to India there took place 'the glory and the catastrophe of the modern Scottish Church', the Disruption of 1843. Declaring that where the issue of spiritual independence was concerned, he had neither 'the crossing of a doubt' nor 'the shadow of a suspicion', Duff, like all other missionaries, went over to the Free Church.

During the first twenty or so years of his work in Calcutta, there had been a small number of high-caste Hindu converts. The most important of these was perhaps KRISHNA MOHUN BANERJEA, an able Paleyan-style apologist who afterward became an Anglican. But in the 1840s and 1850s Indian government policy had the double effect of increasing the quantity of English-language education in India and decreasing its quality by making higher ranks of civil service employment conditional upon a knowledge of English. Explicit Christian content decreased, and with it the number of conversions. Duff was out of India again in the early 1850s. In 1851 he was elected moderator of the Free Church General Assembly; and in 1854 paid his one and only visit to North America, enduring a frantic speaking programme and a level of hospitality he called 'absolutely oppressive'. Also in 1854 Wood's 'Education Dispatch' brought into being, at least in principle, the University of Calcutta (together with those of Bombay and Madras). Duff might have become Calcutta's first vice-chancellor had he so desired.

Duff's third and last tour of missionary duty in India lasted from February 1856 to December 1863. During the Sepoy Rebellion ('Mutiny') of 1857–8 he wrote long and detailed letters, afterward published in book form, from the relative safety of Calcutta. By this time he was beginning to be old beyond his years. He still had 14 years left to him between his leaving India amid extravagant though well-deserved compliments late in 1863, and his passing early in 1878. These were busy 'elder statesman' years; but they were not altogether happy. Never a man to use two words when two dozen would do, Duff's was a 'narrative old age'. In 1867 he was elected professor of evangelistic theology at New College, Edinburgh (a post he had been instrumental in creating), and duly lectured in Edinburgh, Glasgow and Aberdeen. The professorship was an excellent idea, but most agreed that, at the age of over sixty, Duff was entirely the wrong man to fill it.

Far more significant was the contribution he was able to make to the missionary administration of his church from his post as missions superintendent. He helped in the creation of a Gond mission in Central India, supported William Miller in the recasting of the Free Church's Madras college on ecumenical lines into the Madras Christian College (1874). Beyond India, he was instrumental in helping to set up new missions in the Lebanon and southern Africa.

Duff's permanent achievement, however, had been accomplished before he was forty years old. In the 1830s and 1840s he had been the best known, best hated and best loved man in Calcutta. He was a man of deep evangelical principle (though his favourite author was the radical Thomas Carlyle), coupled with a flexible educational practice. Apparently without a sense of humour, he had a sense of duty and obligation, and a Highlander's romantic love of place to soften duty's sternness. A country dominie of heroic proportions, Alexander Duff helped to change the educational face of India. He died in his seventy-second year and was buried in Edinburgh. A monument was later erected at Pitlochry, close to his birthplace.

SELECT WRITINGS
A. Duff, *Missionary Addresses* (Edinburgh, 1850)
—, *The Indian Rebellion* (London, 1858)

BIBLIOGRAPHY
W. P. Duff, *Memoirs of Alexander Duff* (London, 1890)
M. A. Laird, *Missionaries and Education in Bengal 1793–1837* (Oxford, 1972): 202–62
W. Paton, *Alexander Duff* (London, 1923)
G. Smith, *The Life of Alexander Duff*, 2 vols (London, 1879)

ERIC J. SHARPE

Duffield, George (b. Pequa township, PA, BNA, 7 Oct. 1732; d. Philadelphia, PA, USA, 2 Feb. 1790). Presbyterian minister in Pennsylvania. Of French Huguenot descent, Duffield's parents migrated in the late 1720s from the north of Ireland to Lancaster County (Pennsylvania). He studied at the Academy of Newark and later at the College of New Jersey, graduating in 1752. After preparing for the ministry with Robert Smith, Duffield was a tutor at the College of New Jersey from 1754 to 1756, at which time he was licensed to preach. He served in several pastorates in Pennsylvania and along the way suffered Old Side opposition to his explicit New Side views. His most prominent position came in 1772 when he accepted the call of Philadelphia's Third Church (Pine Street), though the Old Side and Tories opposed his appointment. Duffield zealously promoted American independence and served as chaplain to the Continental Congress as well as the Pennsylvania militia. Indeed, his chief contribution was his ardent patriotic preaching which, for good or ill, fused the cause of Christ with the struggle for American independence.

BIBLIOGRAPHY
DAB

D. G. HART

Dugdale, R. Bennett (b. Dublin, 1756; d. Dublin, 10 Jan. 1826). Printer and bookseller, Irish Methodist layman and local preacher. As a young apprentice printer he was converted in Dublin under the preaching of PETER JACO. He soon became a leader in the Dublin Methodist Society, an acceptable preacher and an exceedingly hospitable host to JOHN WESLEY on his visits to Ireland. When Irish Methodism in 1817 divided into those who wished to retain connection with the Church of Ireland and those who did not, he joined the former group called the 'Wesleyan Primitive Methodists' (to be distinguished from the Primitive Methodists) and was a leader among them.

His permanent Memorial is his *Diary*, three volumes of which, handwritten, are preserved in the Methodist Archives. The volumes cover the years 1777 to 1815; the volume which deals with the years 1782 to 1786 is unfortunately missing. The *Diary* describes Dugdale's spiritual experiences, and contains lively accounts of the author's travels with John Wesley.

He also wrote, and published, in 1783, *The Experience of the Most Eminent Methodist Preachers*, a copy of which is in John Wesley's Chapel (The New Room) in Bristol, and which contains much valuable historical material. It is clear from his writings that he strongly favoured Wesley's emphasis on a 'Catholic Spirit'.

BIBLIOGRAPHY
J. C. Bowmer, 'The Diaries of R. Bennett Dugdale', *PWHS*, 38, 3 (1971): 89–92

RUPERT E. DAVIES

Dugmore, William (b. Swaffham, Norfolk, England, 1800, d. 1 July 1872). Recordite lawyer. Dugmore, the son of John Dugmore, trained in law, becoming a member of Lincoln's Inn in 1828 and practised as a conveyancer. He became a Queen's Counsel in 1861. One of several lawyers associated with the *Record* newspaper (see NADIR BAXTER, JOHN BRIDGES, G. R. CLARKE, ALEXANDER GORDON and ALEXANDER HALDANE), Dugmore was especially active in the CMS and on the founding committee of the CPAS (1836). He also helped to found the Open-Air Mission in 1856.

BIBLIOGRAPHY
Boase
D. M. Lewis, *Lighten Their Darkness* (Westport, CT, 1986)

DONALD M. LEWIS

Duke, William (b. Petapsco Neck, MD, BNA, 15 Sept. 1757; d. Elkton, MD, USA, 1840). Pioneer Methodist and Episcopalian clergyman, educator, and writer. Duke was converted under the ministry of Methodists and in 1774, at 16 years of age, was received on trial as an itinerant minister. A self-educated man, he was competent in Latin, Greek, Hebrew, rhetoric, and logic. As early as 1775, he recorded his desire for 'human learning' in his journal (which is preserved, with other papers, in the Diocesan Collection of the Maryland Historical Society). When American Methodists separated from their English brethren in 1784, Duke, considering himself a loyal member of the Church of England, felt constrained to break from the Methodists and align himself with the Protestant Episcopal Church. He was ordained to the episcopal ministry by Bishop Seabury in 1785 and served several churches. On 25 May 1793, Duke married Hetty Coudon, who died less than two years later. Duke was professor of classical languages at St John's College, Anapolis, from 1803 until 1806. The next six years he led an academy at Elkton, moving in 1812 to Charlotte Hall School in St Mary's County as principal. He returned to the academy at Elkton in 1818 and later opened a classical school in his home.

Duke ministered for 65 years. His pastoral ministry, teaching and writing – including theological and devotional works as well as textbooks – influenced many in his time. The journal kept during his circuit-riding days and his *Minutes of the American Conferences, 1774–77*, covering Methodist meetings, are valuable sources for those who would understand pioneer Methodism.

BIBLIOGRAPHY
AAP
EWM
Minutes
A. Stevens, *History of the Methodist Episcopal Church* (New York, 1866)

RICK D. RAILSBACK

Dukinfield, Sir **Henry Robert** (b. Sulham, Berkshire, England, 1 Jan. 1791; d. London, 24 Jan. 1858). Anglican clergyman. Dukinfield was educated at Rugby, Eton and Christ Church, Oxford (student, 1809–16; BA 1813; MA 1816). He became Perpetual Curate of Ruscombe (Berkshire) (1814–16) and then Vicar of Waltham St Lawrence (Berkshire) and St Giles, Reading (1816–34) being also a Prebendary of Salisbury (1832–56). His most notable ministry, however, was as Vicar of St Martin-in-the-Fields (1834–48), where he exercised a very considerable influence. He succeeded his brother in the family baronetcy in 1836.

BIBLIOGRAPHY
Boase, I: 927

ARTHUR POLLARD

Dunbar, Sir **William** (b. London, 16 May 1804; d. Dummer, Hampshire, England, 27 Nov. 1881). Anglican clergyman. Sixth baronet in the line of Dunbar of Durn, Banffshire, he was educated at Magdalen Hall, Oxford (1828–30), and was student of civil laws (1830). In 1836 he married Anne Stephen (died 1889), by whom he had two sons and three daughters.

Dunbar was ordained (deacon 1831, priest 1832) and served as curate in the parish of Upton, Somerset (1831–2). He moved to Stoke-on-Trent in 1832, serving as curate there for seven years. He subsequently produced *Pulpit Recollections*, a collection of sermons from his time at Stoke. In 1839, he moved to London, becoming minister of the Floating Church and chaplain to the Sailors' Home.

In 1842, Dunbar accepted the call to become minister of St Paul's Chapel, Aberdeen. Formerly independent, St Paul's was an 'English Episcopal Chapel' practising a form of congregational government. However, in 1841 the church had entered into a 'Deed of Union' with the Scottish Episcopal Church. The deed insisted upon the right of the congregation to select their own clergyman, to manage their own finances and to preserve the usage of the English Liturgy. A promise to pay 'all spiritual obedience' to the Bishop of Aberdeen was so hedged around with qualifications that conflict was perhaps inevitable.

Soon after his arrival in Aberdeen, Dunbar was in dispute with Bishop Skinner and he became embroiled in a bitter ecclesiastical controversy. The occasion was an ordination service held at St Andrew's Chapel in Aberdeen. Dunbar complied, but would not stay for the celebration of the Eucharist, being unwilling to embrace the Scottish liturgy which reflected belief in the real presence. There was also a dispute concerning collections for the Scottish Episcopal Church Society, an ecclesiastical charity with four avowed objectives, only one of which Dunbar felt in conscience able to support. Dunbar further objected to the ecclesiastical independence enjoyed by the unestablished Episcopal Church. In his view, Scottish bishops changed canons at will, whereas the Church of England's canons were regulated by parliamentary statute.

Supported by the congregation of St Paul's Chapel, Dunbar withdrew from association with the Scottish Episcopal Church. On 13 August 1843, Bishop Skinner excommunicated Dunbar. To justify his stance before his fellow evangelicals, Dunbar published his correspondence with Skinner in the *Record* (21 August 1843). In 1845, Dunbar began a libel action against Skinner, claiming that in publishing the order of excommunication the Bishop had seriously damaged his chances of preferment. The case dragged on inconclusively until 1851, when an out-of-court settlement was reached.

Dunbar unsuccessfully attempted to form a 'Church of England in Scotland', in conjunction with the Reverend D. T. K. DRUMMOND, minister of St Thomas's Chapel, Edinburgh. Dunbar remained Minister of St Paul's Chapel until 1854. In 1855, he was Minister of St Paul's, Camden Town. In 1856, Dunbar became Curate with sole charge of Kew. Upon Dunbar's return to London, Bishop Blomfield refused institution until the excommunication had been removed. Dunbar was thus forced to apologize to Skinner.

Dunbar finally became rector in 1862, when he was presented to the living of Walwyn's Castle, Pembrokeshire. He remained there until 1875, when he was presented in turn to the rectory of Dummer, near Basingstoke. During his latter years Dunbar was a faithful country clergyman, eschewing controversy.

SELECT WRITINGS
W. Dunbar, *Pulpit Recollections* (London, 1841)
—, ed., *The Rev. Sir William Dunbar versus the Right Rev. Wm Skinner D.D.* (Edinburgh, 1849)

I. T. FOSTER

Duncan, [Viscount] **Adam** (b. Lundie, Angus, Scotland, 1731; d. Cornhill, Banff, Scotland, 4 Aug. 1804). British admiral, victor at the battle of Camperdown 1797. A captain during the Seven Years War and American Revolution, he became rear admiral in 1787 and commander-in-chief of the North Sea fleet in 1795. When mutiny spread from the Nore anchorage to his ships, he misled the Dutch over the size of his force and for a while maintained his blockade of the Texel with only two ships – in both of which he had quelled insurrection by his humour, popularity and imposing presence. After the Nore mutiny collapsed, Duncan led the recently disaffected fleet to victory over the Dutch at Camperdown. Having pressed for reforms before the disturbances, he characteristically obtained pardon for Nore mutineers still under punishment after his triumph.

Publicly professing his 'trust in a crucified Redeemer', Duncan earned his men's devotion by humanity as much as daring. His correspondence is in the National Maritime Museum, Greenwich (NMM/DUN); Nore Mutiny papers are in PRO. Duncan was the maternal uncle of ROBERT HALDANE (1762–1842).

BIBLIOGRAPHY
DNB
Earl of Camperdown, *Admiral Duncan* (London 1898)

RICHARD C. BLAKE

Duncan, Henry (b. Lochrutton, Scotland, 8 Oct. 1774; d. Ruthwell, Dumfriesshire, Scotland, 19 Feb. 1846). Church of Scotland minister and pioneer of savings banks movement. Son of George Duncan, minister of Lochrutton, he was educated at the universities of St Andrews, Glasgow and Edinburgh. After working in Hayward's Bank in Liverpool, Duncan entered the ministry of the Church of Scotland and was ordained to the parish of Ruthwell in Dumfriesshire in 1799. He remained there for the rest of his life. He was moderator of the General Assembly of the Church of Scotland in 1839 but entered the FCS in 1843.

Duncan was a conscientious parish minister who displayed a diversity of talents for which he is widely remembered, though his wider achievements did not detract from his services to the parish in which he ministered for so long. He had literary interests which included the founding, and editing for seven years, of the *Dumfries and Galloway Courier*, the writing of several cheap and popular tracts, and the publication in 1826 of *William Douglas* or *The Scottish Exiles*, in which he attempted to counter some of Sir Walter Scott's views of the Scottish covenanters in *Old Mortality*. Duncan's antiquarian interests are remembered through his rescue of the eighth-century Ruthwell Cross, the most important Anglian cross in Scotland. Most widely known of all, however, are Duncan's various efforts to improve the lot of his parishioners, which led him to start a parochial friendly society and to open a savings bank in 1810. The latter proved to be such a success that it has been recognized as the pioneer of the entire savings bank movement.

SELECT WRITINGS
H. Duncan, *Memoirs of Rev. Henry Duncan, D.D., of Ruthwell* (Edinburgh, 1848)

R. H. CAMPBELL

Duncan, James (b. Glasgow, 1738; d. Glasgow, 1811). Bookbinder. Glasite, and then Scotch Baptist elder. Duncan was an elder of the Glasgow Glasite Church in 1771, when he wrote to JOHN GLAS protesting about his interference in the affairs of the Church. By 1775 he was chosen elder of the Glasgow Scotch Baptist Church, along with Robert Moncrieff. Duncan had entered the family firm of bookbinders, becoming burgess and guild brother in Glasgow in 1782. His eldest son was a leader in the strict Scotch Baptist party in Glasgow, and was printer to the university.

DEREK B. MURRAY

Duncan, John (b. Aberdeen, Scotland, 1796; d. Edinburgh, Scotland, 26 Feb. 1870). Missionary to Jews and Old Testament scholar. His parents were poor but deeply religious. A small bursary enabled him to attend the University of Aberdeen, but he was an undistinguished student. However, he was studious in the fields of languages, literature and philosophy. At this time he was a self-confessed atheist, but he enrolled as a student in divinity, first in the Secession Church, then in the Church of Scotland. Gradually he progressed from atheism to theism to Christianity and finally to faith in Christ. Subsequently, after a loss of personal assurance he experienced what he described as his 'second conversion'.

He was now 32 years of age; preaching regularly; devoting his spare hours to much miscellaneous study; but his passion for languages, especially classical and rabbinical Hebrew, predominated. The Hebrew Old Testament was the focal point of his studies; hence his sobriquet, 'Rabbi'.

After a probationary period lasting ten months, he was ordained and inducted to the congregation of Milton, Glasgow, in 1836. While there he applied for the chair of Hebrew and semitic languages at Glasgow University. He was unsuccessful but his Alma Mater conferred on him the degree of LL B.

In 1840 Dr Duncan was appointed to be the first ordained missionary of the Church of Scotland to the Jews, and was sent to Pesth (Budapest). His vast learning and character attracted many pastors of Hungary's Reformed Church. Among the converts from Judaism the most prominent were Dr Edersheim and Dr Adolph Saphir, later of the Church of England, and of the English Presbyterian Church, respectively.

When, in 1843, the Disruption of the Church of Scotland occurred Dr Duncan was unanimously elected to the Free Church chair of Hebrew, which he held until his death 27 years later. However, those who knew him most intimately doubted the wisdom of the appointment. True, his knowledge of classical and oriental languages was unrivalled; he had great competence in philology, philosophy and theology; he was deeply versed in the Holy Scriptures which he exegeted masterfully; he was a Christ-centred man whose root principle was the law of a holy God; he loved to teach. Yet it was as a teacher that Dr Duncan was ineffective. He seldom had written material with him when lecturing; and an inherent weakness of purpose, a notorious absent-mindedness and an inability to impart knowledge of the fundamentals of Hebrew, contributed to a considerable degree of student dissatisfaction, and prevented his incredible potential from coming to full flowering. Notwithstanding, Dr Duncan's spiritual character, prayerfulness, child-like piety and humility, exerted a powerful, ineffaceable influence on the students, and of the Church at large.

Dr Duncan wrote very little, but his conversations and many of his striking aphorisms were collected and published by one of his former students, Professor Knight of St Andrews, under the title, *Colloquia Peripatetica* 1870, which conveys impressions of his immense learning, mental ability and precision of language. In the Free Church tradition the celebration of the Lord's Supper is observed with deep devotion. On the many occasions when Dr Duncan officiated at these worship services his preaching ministry, in content and spiritual quality, was outstanding. Shortly after his death a volume of his sermons was edited and published.

BIBLIOGRAPHY
D. Brown, *Life of the Late John Duncan* (Edinburgh, 1872)
—, ed. *In the Pulpit and at the Communion Table*, biographical supplement (Edinburgh, 1874)
A. M. Stuart, *Recollections of the Late John Duncan* (Edinburgh, 1872)

JAMES G. S. S. THOMSON

Duncan, Peter (b. Dundee, Scotland, 1798; d. Devonport, England, 1862). Missionary of the WMMS in Jamaica, British West Indies. Embarking for Jamaica in 1819, Duncan began a missionary career that spanned the final years of British colonial slavery and that provided the basis for his 1849 *A Narrative of the Wesleyan Mission to Jamaica*. In his book and letters, he noted the allegiance of free people of colour to Methodism and the severe restrictions on evangelization imposed by the Anglican plantocracy. He chronicled the 1831–2 slave rebellion and the ensuing persecution of sectarians by the proslavery Colonial Church Union. In 1832, he pleaded for abolition before the Lords' and Commons' select committees on slavery, departing from the previously maintained Methodist neutrality on the slavery question. Duncan defended free blacks and coloureds against white prejudices, and was outspoken in his praise for the 'state of civilization' achieved by the slaves as superior to that of the plantocracy and the contemporary European peasantry. Exhausted by the difficulties of missionary work in a slave society, Duncan left Jamaica for good before emancipation in 1834. He continued as a Methodist minister in Britain until his death in 1862.

SELECT WRITINGS
P. Duncan, *A Narrative of the Wesleyan Mission to Jamaica* (London, 1849)

BIBLIOGRAPHY
Minutes of the British Wesleyan Conference 1862 for the Rev. Peter Duncan: 22–4
M. Turner, *Slaves and Missionaries* (Urbana, IL, 1982)

ROBERT STEWART

Duncan, Robert Bick (b. Scotland, 1821; d. 1883). United Secession minister. He was the youngest of six sons of Professor Duncan of Mid-Calder, all of whom were ministers of the United Secession Church. After ministering briefly in Girvan and Montrose, he was called as the second minister of Wishart Church, Dundee, and ordained on 19 February 1845. During his three-and-a-half year ministry there the congregation trebled in size. From 1848 to 1865 he was minister in Bread Street (now Viewforth) in Edinburgh. Subsequently he joined the Church of England and served for six years as curate at St Mark's, Whitechapel, and then was chaplain of St George's in the East.

SELECT WRITINGS
R. B. Duncan, *Sanctuary at Home* (London, 1862)

BIBLIOGRAPHY
R. Small, *History of the Congregations of the U.P. Church, 1733–1900* (Edinburgh, 1904)

DONALD M. LEWIS

Dunlop, Alexander Colquhoun Stirling Murray (b. Greenock, Scotland, 27 December 1798; d. 1 September 1870). Church lawyer, MP and social reformer. Educated at Edinburgh University, he was called to the Scottish Bar in 1820. The affairs of the Church of Scotland engrossed his interest in the 1830s, when he threw himself fully into the evangelicals' struggle against the abuses of patronage. Dunlop's tireless support by speech and pamphlet of the 'non-intrusion' cause in the conflicts between church and civil courts in 1833–43 helped destroy his chances of advancement in the legal profession. He was principally responsible for drafting the two great non-intrusion documents: the Claim of Right (1842), which expounded the historic relations between Church and State in Scotland and the former's legal rights, and the Protest and Deed of Demission (1843), which heralded and justified the Disruption, when most evangelicals left the established Church of Scotland to form the Free Church. Dunlop was the Free Church's legal adviser until his death.

In 1852 Dunlop was elected Liberal MP for Greenock, and served in this capacity for 15 years. Initially a Tory, he had by this time converted to a zealous Liberalism, and devoted his parliamentary career to securing legal and social reforms. His two central achievements were 'Dunlop's Act', which provided state funding for 'ragged schools', i.e. schools which offered education and vocational training to deprived children, and an act which provided for the building of houses for Britain's working classes. Dunlop's parliamentary conduct was also striking in its exhibition of courageous, conscientious independence, notable his indignant opposition to the Liberal government's handling of the British war with China in 1857, and to its falsification of dispatches from Sir Alexander Burnes in the Afghan war of 1838–42.

BIBLIOGRAPHY
J. A. Wylie, ed., *Disruption Worthies*, 2 vols (Edinburgh, 1881): 237–44
DNB

N. R. NEEDHAM

Dunlop, Henry (b. Linwood, Renfrewshire, Scotland, 7 June 1799; d. Edinburgh, 10 May 1867). Cotton spinner and manufacturer. A cotton spinner and manufacturer at Glasgow, Dunlop was Lord Provost of his city from 1837 to 1840. He was a director of the Glasgow Merchants' House from 1837, and chairman in 1841, 1859, and 1862. He was also a member of the Glasgow Chamber of Commerce. In the Merchants' House he cooperated in drafting the following petitions to parliament: deploring the King's refusal to support the reform bill (1832); begging for repeal of the cotton tariff (1836); and deploring the effect of antislavery legislation on cotton prices (1847). He was author of *The Cotton Trade* (1862).

Dunlop was a member of the EA, a vice president of the Scottish Reformation Society in 1858, and president of the Glasgow Bible Society from 1850 to 1861. A member of the Church of Scotland, he joined the Free Church and was active in its affairs.

BIBLIOGRAPHY
Boase
Lord Provosts of Glasgow from 1833 to 1902 (Glasgow, 1902)

JONATHAN BURKE CUTMORE

Dunlop, John (b. Greenock, Renfrewshire, Scotland, 2 Aug. 1789; d. Kilburn, London, 12 Dec. 1868). British temperance reformer. Dunlop, who 'has the best right to be acclaimed the founder of the temperance movement in Great Britain' was a graduate of Glasgow (residing for his period of study with STEVENSON MACGILL, the evangelical minister of the Tron Church) and Edinburgh

in arts and law. Practising as a solicitor in Greenock (1810–38) where he was ordained an elder in the Church of Scotland, he was a devoted Sunday school teacher and a keen supporter of missions. He became a Justice of the Peace, secretary of the Greenock Infirmary, and also of the Chamber of Commerce, as well as lending support to the Savings Bank movement and to that seeking adult education for artisans.

An overseas visit in 1828 created his temperance conscience which made him more fully aware of the costs of Scottish intemperance; a family inheritance in 1838 enabled him to move to London to pursue his temperance interests, which were further formed by information he received about temperance work in the USA. In exploring what instruments were best designed to serve his concerns, Dunlop was aided by fellow evangelical, WILLIAM COLLINS, an elder of THOMAS CHALMERS' church and founder of the publishing house that bears his name, who was the same age as Dunlop. In November 1829, after a hesitant start, the Glasgow and West of Scotland Temperance Society was formed and in June 1830 Collins produced the first number of *The Temperance Record*. Dunlop particularly attacked the widespread contemporary drink usages in industrial and social life (see his *Philosophy of Compulsory and Artificial Drink Usage*, 1839), as also the payment of wages in public houses; he also eagerly sought medical opinion as to the evils of excessive drinking. By the end of 1830 a hundred temperance societies had been founded in Scotland but thereafter the movement began to split over the issue of total abstinence rather than simply the rejection of spirit-drinking with those in the higher ranks of society very reluctant to adopt the wider prohibition. Initially he found the clergy slow to commit themselves but by 1859 he could report that 800 ministers of the gospel were pledged.

BIBLIOGRAPHY
S. Mechie, *The Church and Scottish Social Development, 1780–1870* (London, 1960)

J. H. Y. BRIGGS

Dunn, Henry (b. 1800; d. Brighton, Sussex, England, 16 March 1878). Quaker educational reformer. In the period 1835–47 Dunn was secretary of the BFSS (successor organization to the Royal Lancastrian Association). Under its auspices he wrote pamphlets calling for a non-denominational school system and, in *National Education* (1838), argued that the Bible should be used in schools as the basic pedagogical instrument. His experience as a teacher, and as secretary of the London Borough Road (Lancastrian) school, qualified him to write *Suggestions . . . for School Teachers* (1837), and *Principles of Teaching* (c. 1860). Dunn was editor from 1870 of *Sunday Morning Magazine*. He also wrote expository commentaries on *Ecclesiastes* and *Revelation* and a few works of speculative theology, all of them negligible.

He is now remembered for his *Guatimala in 1827–8*

[*sic*] (1828; recently reprinted). It was the first account of that region based on personal observation to appear in English since the seventeenth century. In this work (and also in two later books on Italian Protestantism) Dunn reveals a strong anti-Catholic bias.

BIBLIOGRAPHY
Boase

JONATHAN BURKE CUTMORE

Dunn, Samuel (b. Mevagissey, Cornwall, England, 13 Feb. 1797; d. Hastings, England, 24 Jan. 1882). Methodist evangelist and reformer. His father was a sea-captain who had earlier been a smuggler, but had become an active Methodist. Under the influence of Dr ADAM CLARKE young Samuel entered the Wesleyan ministry in 1819 and three years later volunteered to open missionary work in the Shetland Islands. He met with amazing success and was able to report 235 new members after only two years; four years later there were over 1,200 members in the newly formed district.

This amazing evangelistic effort and success was continued after his return to the mainland, especially in Camborne, where many new chapels were erected. But he early came into conflict with JABEZ BUNTING, originally as he shared Adam Clarke's views, condemned by Conference, on the eternal Sonship of Christ. The clash with Bunting reached its climax in the 'Fly Sheets' controversy of the late 1840s, and he was expelled in 1849 because he refused to cease publication of the *Wesley Banner and Revival Record*. After travelling the country in support of reform, he served as minister of a Free Methodist Church in Camborne from 1855 to 1865, during which time he published his *Hymns for Pastor and People*. Then he went to America, but after three years returned to England, thenceforward serving in a freelance capacity among all the branches of Methodism in Cornwall.

He was a most voluminous author, writing pamphlets, sermons, memoirs and selections from the theological writings of Adam Clarke, Puritan divines, and others and a life of Clarke (who offered him the task of republishing his commentary).

BIBLIOGRAPHY
Bibliotheca Cornubiensis: 124–7, 1163–4
DNB
J. D. Dinnick, *The Transfiguration, and Other Sermons, With a Biographical Sketch* (London, [1890])
T. R. Harris, *Samuel Dunn, Reformer* (Cornish Methodist Historical Assoc. Occ. Pub., Truro, England, 1963)
G. Osborn, *Outlines of Wesleyan Bibliography* (London, 1869)

OLIVER A. BECKERLEGGE

Dunn, Thomas (b. York Co., PA, USA, 1782; d. Louisiana, USA, 1852). Minister of the MPC. Although educated for the profession of medicine, he devoted himself to the ministry. He was received into the Philadelphia Conference in 1803. He preached until 1813 when he located and practised medicine for twenty years. In 1837 he became a member of the Maryland Conference, but later moved to Louisiana where he died.

BIBLIOGRAPHY
CM

STEVE HARPER

Dunnell, Mary (b. England). Wesleyan Methodist evangelist. Dunnell is noteworthy as the first female preacher of the Camp Meeting Community, before the establishment of Primitive Methodism. She fell foul of the WM Conference ruling about women preachers, but she was accepted by HUGH BOURNE. Her abilities as a preacher and missioner were considerable, but she caused trouble in the Derbyshire Mission. Hugh Bourne was forced to disown her and she disappeared from the PM scene.

BIBLIOGRAPHY
H. Bourne, manuscript papers, Methodist Church Archives MARC
H. B. Kendall, *The Origin and History of the PM Church*, 1 (London, 1904)
J. Walford, *Life and Labours of ... Hugh Bourne*, 1 (London, 1855)

E. DOROTHY GRAHAM

Dunwell, Joseph Rhodes (b. Pool, Yorkshire, England, *c.* 1807; d. Cape Coast, Gold Coast, 24 June 1835). Wesleyan Missionary Society (WMS) missionary, Gold Coast. As a young man, turned out of his Yorkshire home by his father for associating with the Wesleyans, he walked to London where he became a tea-dealer and Wesleyan local preacher. In 1834 the WMS received an urgent call for a missionary from a group of young African Christians in the Gold Coast (modern Ghana), and he volunteered to go. He was warmly received by the small Christian meeting (though coldly by the resident Europeans), and formed a church with regular worship, class meetings and a study group. But, never robust in his health, he fell ill, and died after less than six months in Africa.

BIBLIOGRAPHY
F. L. Bartels, *The Roots of Ghana Methodism* (Cambridge, 1965)
W. Fox, *A Brief History of the Wesleyan Missions on the Western Coast of Africa* (London, 1851)

CHRISTOPHER FYFE

Dunwoody, Samuel (b. Chester Co., PA, USA, 3 Aug. 1780; d. 8 July 1854). Methodist minister. He was received into the South Carolina Conference in 1806 and founded the first Methodist Church in Savannah, Georgia. He was known for his preaching and for establishing new churches in the South. He also served as a presiding elder and delegate to General Conference. In 1844 at General Conference he championed the cause of the South on the slavery question and joined the MEC So, on its formation. He ministered until two years before his death when his fellow clergy placed him on superannuation.

BIBLIOGRAPHY
CM
EWM

STEVE HARPER

Düring, W. Henry (b. Hanover, Germany, c. 1786; d. at sea, Sept. 1823). CMS missionary in Sierra Leone. Düring underwent a conversion experience after hearing CARL STEINKOPF preach. He joined the German Church at the Savoy and was introduced to the CMS through Steinkopf. He travelled out to Sierra Leone in 1816; his wife (née Mary Watson) delivered a son on the journey. Düring took charge at the CMS Christian Institution on Leicester Mountain before moving to the newly formed village of Gloucester. He and his wife were on government salaries as school teachers. Düring acted as superintendent and witnessed scenes of conversion among his recaptive population similar to that which W. A. B. JOHNSON was experiencing at Regent. He noted how on Sundays and weekdays he was followed by people in distress of spirit. Düring organized the building of the church, the parsonage, the girls' school; he oversaw the planting and harvesting of crops and cared for many of the newly arrived recaptives. In 1819 Düring received Lutheran ordination in Sierra Leone.

He suffered from bronchitis, rheumatism, and cholera, which threatened an imminent return to Britain on more than one occasion. On 3 May 1822 he returned to England but went back to Africa on 10 November. His people expressed their fear that their beloved pastor might go back permanently, but, in 1823, he set sail after the diagnosis that he was 'Labouring under a dropsical affection of the abdomen together with a generally diseased state of the viscera of that cavity' (Nylander 17 August 1823). The ship that he and his wife were on left Sierra Leone 31 Aug 1823 and was never heard of again.

BIBLIOGRAPHY
D. T. B[arry], CMS Register of Missionaries And Native Clergy from 1804 to 1904 (privately printed) (London, 1906)
CMS Archives, s.v. Sierra Leone, University of Birmingham

ELIZABETH GRANT

Dutton, Anne (b. Northampton, Northamptonshire, England, 1692; d. Great Gransden, Huntingdonshire, England, 18 Nov. 1765). Calvinist writer. Born in a centre of Dissent, she joined a Calvinist church, and on marrying in London she remained loyal to that tradition. In 1732 her second husband Benjamin (1691–1747) became pastor of the Congregational church in Great Gransden. Benjamin wrote *Superaboundings of the Exceeding Riches of God's Free Grace* (1743), while Anne penned a number of works about assurance of salvation which anticipated themes of the evangelical revival. By 1740 she had met the leaders of the revival, regularly corresponded with GEORGE WHITEFIELD, and encouraged converts on both sides of the Atlantic. Some of her 25 tracts were devotional, but others urged Calvinist evangelicals to contend against the doctrinal evil of JOHN WESLEY and WILLIAM CUDWORTH. Her husband drowned on a ship returning from America. She influenced her church towards a Strict Baptist emphasis, and before her death was a legend.

SELECT WRITINGS
A. Dutton, *Selections from Letters on Spiritual Subjects addressed to Relatives and Friends*, ed. J. Knight (London, 1884)

BIBLIOGRAPHY
G. F. Nuttall, 'Northamptonshire and *The Modern Question*: A Turning Point in Eighteenth-century Dissent', *Journal of Theological Studies*, new series 16 (1965): 119–20

PETER J. LINEHAM

Dwight, Louis (b. Stockbridge, MA, USA, 25 March 1793; d. Boston, MA, USA, 12 July 1854). Prison reformer. A graduate of Yale College (1813) and of Andover Seminary (1819), he was employed from 1819 to 1821 as the first general agent of the New England (later American) Tract Society, from 1821 to 1824 as agent of the American Education Society, and from 1825 to 1854 as secretary and manager of the Prison Discipline Society (PDS) (Boston). Ordained 27 November 1822, he married Louisa Willis, 30 May 1824.

Later in 1824, in the course of visiting prisons on behalf of the ABS, he was appalled at the inhumane conditions. As a result, he led in the formation of the PDS 30 June 1825. Until his death in 1854 he wrote the society's lengthy annual reports, which constitute valuable primary sources on prison reform and on early nineteenth-century evangelicalism. In his initial report he emphasized the recently developed Auburn system of cell blocks and group labour, which gradually replaced the Pennsylvania system of solitary confinement and solitary labour, partly due to PDS efforts. In 1846 he visited European prisons in the cause of reform. Dwight and the PDS exemplify the tendency to organize for reform across a wide range of social problems, the interlocking leadership of the reform societies, and the close ties of evangelical faith with social reform that marked that era.

BIBLIOGRAPHY
AAP
Annual Report of the Board of Managers of the Prison Discipline Society, Boston, 1–29, 1826–1854 (Boston, MA, 1830–54)

NORRIS A. MAGNUSON

Dwight, Sereno Edwards (b. Greenfield Hill, CT, USA, 18 May 1786; d. Philadelphia, PA, USA, 30 Nov. 1850).

New England Congregational minister. Fifth son of TIM-OTHY DWIGHT, the president of Yale College, and great-grandson of JONATHAN EDWARDS, he graduated from Yale College in 1803. He served as a tutor at Yale from 1806 until 1810 while studying law, and practised law in New Haven for the following five years. Converted in a revival under NATHANIEL WILLIAM TAYLOR at New Haven's First Church, Dwight at once prepared to enter the Congregational ministry, and was licensed to preach on 8 October 1816, by the New Haven West Association. His legal and family connections secured his appointment as chaplain of the United States Senate, but in 1817, he left to assume the pastorate of the Park Street Church in Boston. Ill health forced his resignation in 1826, and he returned to New Haven to organize an unsuccessful German-style *gymnasium*. In 1833, he was invited to become president of Hamilton College, but resigned in 1835 after disagreements with the college trustees. He served briefly as an agent for the Pennsylvania Colonization Society, but mounting illness forced his retirement in 1838. Although Dwight published relatively little, his principal monument turned out to be his biography and ten-volume edition of the works of Jonathan Edwards (1829), where Edwards' scientific and philosophical notebooks were edited and published for the first time.

BIBLIOGRAPHY
AAP, 2
F. B. Dexter, *Biographical Notices of Graduates of Yale College* (New Haven, CT, 1913)

ALLEN C. GUELZO

Dwight, Timothy (b. Northampton, MA, BNA, 14 May 1752; d. New Haven, CT, USA, 11 Jan. 1817). Congregational minister and theologian, revivalist, educator, eighth president of Yale. Born the maternal grandson of the great American theologian and revivalist JONATHAN EDWARDS, Timothy Dwight was educated at home by his mother in much the same way she had been educated earlier by her illustrious father. Dwight proved remarkably precocious. He could read and write by age four, and by age six was found preaching directly from the Bible to Indian men and women, something he had often seen his grandfather do in the wilderness outpost at Stockbridge.

Dwight entered Yale in 1764, not yet 13 years old. He received his degree in 1769, and was subsequently elected college tutor, a position he held from 1771 to 1777. Dwight delivered his first public address, 'A Dissertation on the History, Eloquence, and Poetry of the Bible', at Yale's commencement ceremony in 1771. During his tenure as tutor, Dwight made various attempts to introduce lectures on *belles-lettres* and classics into the curriculum. Along with John Trumbull, David Humphreys, and Joel Barlow, Dwight was a member of a small coterie of literary devotees called the Connecticut Wits. They were determined to develop a distinctly American literature and prosody, much as had been done earlier for England by the Areopagus, a group of English Renaissance scholars that included Sir Philip Sidney, Edmund Spenser, Edward Dyer, and Fulke Greville. Dwight's literary project met with its greatest success years later when he became the college's president, as did his own poetry, chief among which are his *The Conquest of Canaan, a Poem in Eleven Books* (Hartford, 1785) and *Greenfield Hill, a Poem in Seven Parts* (New York, 1794).

In 1777, Dwight became military chaplain to the colonial forces in the Revolutionary War. After only a year as chaplain, however, Dwight was called home to Northampton to fill the place left by the recent death of his father. Then, for the next five years, Dwight immersed himself in the study of theology, a course he pursued under the tutelage of his uncle, JONATHAN EDWARDS (JR). In 1783, Dwight accepted a call to become pastor of the Congregational Church in Greenfield, Connecticut, where he laboured for 12 years. During that time, he also served as headmaster of Greenfield's co-educational academy, the reputation of which soon began to rival even that of nearby Yale. In 1795, Dwight was named the eighth president of Yale, a position he occupied for the rest of his life. In addition to his administrative duties, Dwight also served as chaplain and professor of theology, *belle-lettres*, and oratory.

Dwight rose to prominence as a theologian and an evangelist during his years as Yale's president, years in which the anti-religious animus of the Enlightenment continued to increase in America. Determined to stave off such influences at Yale, Dwight delivered a series of 173 sermons (published posthumously in 1818 as *Theology Explained and Defended*), in which he both spelled out a system of moderate Calvinism and conducted a head-on assault against what he perceived to be the anti-Christian bias of the Enlightenment and its chief proponents, Paine, Hume, Diderot, and Voltaire. In these sermons, Dwight employed the traditional Puritan 'plain style' and his own natural wit and broad learning to great effect. Along with his refutation of Enlightenment errors, Dwight coupled compelling calls to repentance, which helped create several student revivals at Yale. The first of these revivals, which began in 1799 and lasted until 1802, stands at the very beginning of what became the Second Great Awakening. In short, Dwight chose to combat deism by learning and by individual conversion.

Serving as the chief academic officer of what was perhaps the chief religious institution in America enabled Dwight to exercise extensive influence as an evangelical theologian. His weekly lectures were eagerly attended and helped to shape the theology and subsequent career of hundreds of the most prominent American ecclesiastical figures for decades to come. Dwight's significance for evangelicalism, therefore, rests primarily upon the influence he exerted on its theology and its practice. Theologically, Dwight helped to establish what one of his biographers labelled 'evangelical orthodoxy', which differed from the Edwardsianism of the day by de-emphasizing the metaphysical presuppositions and implications of theology and reasserting the practical aspects of personal religion. According to Dwight, religious revivals depended upon, and underscored, the common-sense notion of human freedom: we can choose; we do choose; we must choose. To Dwight, the fact of human volition contravened the metaphysical sophistries that denied it.

This rejection of the soaring metaphysics of determinism made room for what became Dwight's chief influence upon evangelical practice – the belief that religious revival was often the humanly devised product of humanly administered religious practices, such as preaching, counselling, and education. Thus, against the New Divinity school's emphasis on divine omnipotence in salvation, and against its belief that regeneration was a fundamentally unmediated intervention by God himself, Dwight stressed the importance of human agency in the conversion process. This theological emphasis and the practices to which it leads were picked up directly by Dwight's two most prominent students, LYMAN BEECHER and NATHANIEL W. TAYLOR, as well as indirectly by the greatest revivalist of the nineteenth Century, CHARLES GRANDISON FINNEY.

BIBLIOGRAPHY
S. Berk, *Calvinism versus Democracy* (Hamden, CT, 1974)
C. Cuningham, *Timothy Dwight* (New York, 1942)
C. Keller, *The Second Great Awakening in Connecticut* (New Haven, CT, 1942)
A. Wenzke, *Timothy Dwight* (Lewiston, ID, 1989)

MICHAEL BAUMAN

Dyer, Heman (b. Shaftesbury, VT, USA, 24 Sept. 1810; d. New York City, 29 July 1900). Episcopal clergyman. A descendant of the seventeenth-century Quaker martyr, Mary Dyer, he was raised a Congregationalist, but was confirmed in a relative's Episcopal parish in Granville, New York, by Bishop J. H. Hobart in 1826. He graduated from Kenyon College in 1833, and after ordination in 1834 by Bishop C. P. MCILVAINE, he took charge of Kenyon's preparatory school. In 1840, he opened a boys' Latin school in Pittsburgh, but when it failed in 1843, he was unexpectedly rescued by election to a professorship in Greek at Western University of Pennsylvania, and in 1844 became principal of the University. In April, 1849, he was invited to assume the secretaryship of the ASSU in Philadelphia, and undertook extensive preaching tours across the nation on behalf of the ASSU. He served briefly as Rector of the Church of the Mediator, Philadelphia, and in 1854, became secretary and general manager of the Protestant Episcopal Society for the Promotion of Evangelical Knowledge (EKS), as well as editor of the *Episcopal Quarterly Review*. In 1859, he was chosen corresponding secretary for the American Church Missionary Society (ACMS). His involvement with both the EKS and the ACMS brought Dyer into the leadership of evangelical Episcopalian opposition to the influence of the Oxford Movement in the Episcopal Church, and his strategic positions in these organizations gave him the reputation

of being the 'bishop-maker'. Dyer himself was elected Bishop of Kansas in 1862, but declined; in 1874, he was instrumental, under ACMS auspices, in organizing an Episcopal diocese in Mexico.

During the 1860s, the ACMS was viewed as an agency for promoting and supplying evangelical clergymen for vacant pulpits, and aroused the hostility of High-Church and Anglo-Catholic bishops. The defection of several prominent evangelicals to form the Reformed Episcopal Church in 1873 disheartened the evangelical cause in the Episcopal Church, and in 1877, the ACMS was absorbed into the Episcopal Church's Board of Missions. Dyer had felt that the Reformed Episcopal movement was inevitable, but declined to join it himself. In 1878, he was crippled by the loss of the sight of his right eye, and in 1880, after suffering a stroke while preaching, he retired from active ministry. In 1886, he published a biography which remains invaluable for its personal recollections of individuals and institutions of the Episcopal Church.

SELECT WRITINGS
H. Dyer, *Records of an Active Life* (New York, 1886)

BIBLIOGRAPHY
E. C. Chorley, *Men and Movements in the American Episcopal Church* (New York, 1950)

ALLEN C. GUELZO

Dyer, John (b. Devizes, Wiltshire, England, 7 Jan. 1783; d. London, 22 July 1841). Baptist minister and first full-time secretary of the BMS. As a teenager, he was greatly indebted to the pastoral leadership of the Reverend WILLIAM STEADMAN, both at Broughton and Plymouth. Finding business life uncongenial, he became a Baptist pastor, first in Plymouth and then in Reading. He became a keen supporter of the BMS and was elected to its committee in 1812.

After ANDREW FULLER passed away in 1815, the BMS had great difficulty in appointing a successor. Three years later, it invited Dyer to become its full-time secretary, based in London. Bureaucratic changes then occurred in the society's system of management which rankled with the Serampore Trio. Over a decade, misunderstanding and distrust grew between London and Serampore until a formal split occurred in 1827. Unfortunately, Dyer never visited any of the BMS's mission fields. He saw things seriously from a pre-Victorian, metropolitan perspective. After losing his first wife in 1826, life became very hard for him. He died by drowning in 1841.

BIBLIOGRAPHY
[Anon.], 'Memoir of the Reverend John Dyer', *BaptMag*, 33 (September 1841): 433–40
E. A. Payne, 'The Diaries of John Dyer', *BQ*, 13, 6 (1950): 253–9
—, *The First Generation* (London, 1936): 121–6

A. CHRISTOPHER SMITH

Dyer, Samuel (b. Greenwich, England, 20 Jan. 1804; d. Macao, Oct. 1843). LMS missionary to Malaya and China. Dyer was the son of a devout Congregationalist, John Dyer, for a time the secretary of the Royal Hospital for Seamen at Greenwich and who in 1820 became chief clerk to the Admiralty. Samuel was educated at Woolwich and Trinity College, Cambridge where he read classics, mathematics and law; however, because he was a Congregationalist and not an Anglican, he could not take a degree.   His father's friend, ROBERT MORRISON, stimulated his interest in foreign missions and in June 1824 he offered himself to the LMS, then trained at Gosport under DAVID BOGUE, at Homerton under JOHN PYE SMITH and for a short period at the Missionary College, Hoxton. He was ordained in London in February, 1827 and later that year married Maria. Dyer was first sent to Malacca, but was instead placed in Penang where he took up the study of Hokkein and also began developing moveable metal type for Chinese script. This new type was an important contribution to Chinese printing. It reduced the Chinese Bible from six volumes to one, and the New Testament to eighty pages.

In 1835 he returned to Malacca where he worked·at Robert Morrison's Anglo-Chinese College. Dyer's contribution to the college was greatest through his work with the printing press. The press helped the prestige and scholarly work of the college during the late 1830s through 1842 when the college was at its peak. With the closure of the LMS work in south-east Asia in 1842 and the removal of all missionaries to Hong Kong, Dyer's work was ended. Being very supportive of the removal of all Ultra Ganges missionaries to China, he moved to Hong Kong, participated in the organizational meeting of the LMS work in China (26 August 1843) and died two months later. His widow later married J. G. Bausum, a Congregational missionary in Penang. His daughter Maria Jane, born in Penang in 1837, was later to marry J. HUDSON TAYLOR.

BIBLIOGRAPHY

A. J. Broomhall, *Hudson Taylor and China's Open Century*, 1 (London, 1981)

E. Evans, *Memoir* (London, 1846)

I. bin Ismail, 'Samuel Dyer and his contributions to Chinese typography', *The Library Quarterly*, 54, 2, April 1984: 157–69

SCOTT W. SUNQUIST

Dykes, Thomas (b. Ipswich, Suffolk, England, 21 Dec. 1761; d. Cottingham, Yorkshire, England, 23 Aug. 1847). Anglican clergyman. After boarding-school near Ipswich and a spell in his father's business Dykes experienced an evangelical conversion in the course of an illness, as a result of which he sought the advice of JOSEPH MILNER, headmaster of Hull Grammar School, and placed himself under the tutelage of Edmund Garwood, one-time Curate of St Mary's, Hull, and later Vicar of Hessle. Dykes proceeded to Magdalene College, Cambridge, and there became acquainted with such well-known evangelicals as WILLIAM FARISH, HENRY JOWETT and JOHN VENN, but he established a particular friendship with ROBERT JARRATT.

Dykes became Curate of Cottingham in 1788 and married Mary, daughter of the Leeds evangelical surgeon, WILLIAM HEY, in 1789. His friend Jarrett was at nearby Hotham as Curate to JAMES STILLINGFLEET and was to become Dykes's brother-in-law some ten years later on marrying Margaret Hey. Dykes moved to Barwick-in-Elmet (West Yorkshire) as Curate from 1789 to 1791. He had inherited considerable property from a maiden aunt and as early as 1788 he had sought to build a new church in Hull. This was opposed by the corporation as patrons of Holy Trinity, the parish church, but their failure to pursue plans of erecting a church themselves led to Dykes's scheme going forward. St John's Church was consecrated on 30 August 1791 and opened on 13 May 1792. It had 1,000 sittings, but Dykes never realized from pew-rents his full outlay. He also lamented that, though in some cases individuals had purchased as many as six pews, they did not use them and some even left them locked (Letter to Jarratt, 31 July 1792).

Dykes played a notable part in church extension in Hull, where Christ Church (1821) and St James (1829) were offshoots of St John's. The enlargement of Drypool and the establishment of St Stephen's and St Paul's owed much to his efforts and beneficence. He likewise gave of his own and influenced others to give in raising £3,685 under the leadership of another Hull evangelical, JOHN KING of Christ Church, for the purchase of the advowson of the ancient parish church of the city, Holy Trinity, from the Corporation in 1836 and its conveyance to a self-perpetuating body of evangelical trustees who also appoint to North Ferriby.

In 1815 Dykes, urged by his father-in-law and others in Leeds, sought appointment as vicar of the parish church of that city. Failing to secure this, he remained in Hull for the rest of his life, adding to his cures the mastership of the Charterhouse in 1833 and the vicarage of North Ferriby in 1834 on the death of JOHN SCOTT. This latter was served by the existing curate, Charles Rose, who was followed by Dykes's grandson, Charles Wawn and who himself succeeded his grandfather as vicar. Dykes's own curates at St John's formed a notable succession. They included Lorenzo Grainger, usher at the Grammar School under JOSEPH MILNER and the latter's successor as Vicar of North Ferriby; JOHN FAWCETT, curate to Stillingfleet at Hotham, another of Milner's ushers and then, no doubt through the influence of ISAAC MILNER as dean of Carlisle, for over fifty years incumbent of St Cuthbert's in that city; Thomas Sowerby, formerly one of Simeon's curates at Holy Trinity, Cambridge; John Scott; RICHARD JOHNSON, first chaplain at Botany Bay; WALTER SHIRLEY, father of Bishop Shirley; William Knight, later of St James, Hull, and editor of Dykes's sermons; Barrett, who followed EDWARD BURN at Birmingham in 1837; John Deck, first Vicar of St Stephen's, Hull in 1840; and W. H. Kemp, Dykes's successor both at St John's and the Charterhouse.

Other local activity by Dykes included a prominent part in the establishment of branches of the BFBS (1811) and CMS (1814) and an appeal for a female penitentiary (1811). In April and May 1817 he was in Ireland on behalf of the Missionary Society. He was a determined opponent of Roman Catholic relief from as early as 1807 and he spoke strongly against it at the time of emancipation in 1829. He quickly discerned the Romish tendencies of the Tractarians, recognizing the self-aggrandizement which they offered to clergy, preaching 'not Christ, but themselves and the Church'. His own loyalty to the Church of England was such, however, that he refused in 1846 to join the EA because of the Dissenters' antagonism to church and state. Politically Dykes was a conservative and theologically a moderate Calvinist, accepting the doctrine of election but not that of personal reprobation. Of the three great Hull divines Dykes's biographer, John King, said that as preachers 'Milner excelled in *power*, Dykes in *persuasiveness*, Scott in *argument*'.

BIBLIOGRAPHY

J. King, *Memoir of the Reverend Thomas Dykes, LL.B . . .*, ed. W. Knight (London, 1849)

ARTHUR POLLARD

E

Eadie, John (b. Alva, Stirlingshire, Scotland, 9 May 1810; d. Glasgow, 3 June 1876). United Secession exegete and minister. He was the son of John Eadie and Janet Morrison. It was his mother's intelligence, wit, omnivorous reading and retentive memory which were reflected in the son and it was she who introduced him to the Protestant religious classics. From the Alva Grammar School he proceeded in 1826 to study at Glasgow University where he met his close friend, GEORGE GIL-FILLAN.

In 1835 he was licensed to preach and was called by the recently established Cambridge Street church in Glasgow where he ministered for 28 years and saw the congregation increase from 18 to 1,000. In 1863 he established a church in Landsdowne Street where he stayed until his death, similarly increasing his number of congregants. He was moderator of his denomination for 1857. Eadie's popularity depended not upon his preaching but upon the fame he achieved in other spheres.

A harbinger of popular, liberal causes, he gained notoriety in his early twenties as a provincial platform speaker and newspaper letter writer who supported temperance, Chartism and voluntarism. He further extended his influence through many contributions to periodicals. However, Eadie became best known for his immensely successful exegetical and biblical reference works. These included contributions to various Bible dictionaries, an abridged *Cruden's Concordance*, his own analytical concordance, a family bible, a *Biblical Cyclopaedia*, and collected sermons.

In 1838 he was appointed instructor in Hebrew at Anderson's College, Glasgow, and from 1843 to his death was professor of biblical literature in his denomination's seminary. Glasgow conferred the LL D upon him in 1844, and St Andrews the DD in 1850. A genuine scholar, his textual commentaries led to his participation on the 1870 New Testament revision committee. Eadie was also an antiquarian who accumulated a remarkable book collection.

BIBLIOGRAPHY
J. Brown, *Life of John Eadie* (London, 1878)
T. Cooper, ed., *Men of the Time*, 9th edn (London, 1875)
DNB

JONATHAN BURKE CUTMORE

Eagar, Edward (b. Killarney, Ireland, 1787; d. London, 2 Nov. 1866). Lawyer, merchant, and convict. The son of an Anglo-Irish landowner, Eagar became an attorney in Dublin. Sentenced to death for forgery, he was converted in gaol and his new-found piety led to a commutation to life transportation to New South Wales. Reaching Sydney in 1811, he worked for ROBERT CARTWRIGHT and taught scripture. Soon he was preaching and assisting the work of the new Methodist missionary. Emancipated in 1818, he helped the Bible Society and local charitable and mission organizations. Eagar was a striking example of a convict returning to respectability through evangelical religion.

Eagar's convict origins told against him in his efforts to practise law and to trade. Stung by this injustice, he became a fervent propagandist for local and emancipist liberties. He continued this campaign after returning to Britain in 1821, often to the detriment of his finances. By the time of his death in London, however, he had regained prosperity and social status. Eagar married in the colony and had four children. His wife did not accompany him to London. He had ten children by a woman in England.

Eagar's religious zeal did his career no harm and, later, he directed his enthusiasm into politics, albeit in a good cause. In this, again, he was by no means unique in early Australian history.

BIBLIOGRAPHY
ADB

KENNETH J. CABLE

Eardley, Sir Culling [né **Eardley-Smith**] (b. London, 21 April 1805; d. Hatfield, Hertfordshire, England, 21 May 1863). Baronet, philanthropist, and MP. The son of Sir Culling Smith and Charlotte Elizabeth Eardley, he was educated at Eton and Oriel College, Oxford. On his father's death in 1829 he succeeded to the baronetcy and, in 1847 when his cousin, Lord Saye and Sele, died, he inherited the Eardley estates, dropping the surname Smith and assuming that of Eardley. He was MP for Pontefract 1830–1 and later contested the parliamentary seats at Pontefract 1837, Edinburgh 1846, and the West Riding of Yorkshire 1848, as a Liberal, consistently refusing to bribe voters, as was conventional. After leaving Oxford he became a convinced evangelical when such views were unpopular among his class. Although inclined to Nonconformity he never aligned himself with any denomination, attending the parish church where the clergyman espoused evangelicalism. He favoured the disestablishment of the Church of England. In 1846 he was among the founders of the EA which aimed to provide a form of union among Protestants and to promote worldwide religious freedom. From then on he concentrated his energy on EA affairs, serving as its first chairman and president, and also as treasurer. He was the treasurer of the LMS 1844–63 and also of the fund established to relieve the Lebanese Christians after the 1861 massacres there. He tolerated but disliked Roman Catholicism.

During his presidency the EA held congresses in several European cities. He secured toleration for Protestants in mainly Roman Catholic countries in Europe, persuaded the King of Prussia to tolerate the Baptists and other Dissenters among his subjects, and successfully appealed in Turkey to reverse the policy whereby Muslim converts to Christianity were sentenced to death. Yet he intervened in Sweden on behalf of Roman Catholics. His other work included the vigorous campaign for the release from captivity of the Spanish Protestants, and especially Matameros who was freed on the day Eardley died. He was very interested in matters concerning the Jews.

He was treasurer 1842–5 of the Hertfordshire Union of Baptist and Independent churches, encouraged open-air preaching, and worked with the Voluntary Church Society. He was instrumental in the building of two churches, one at Marychurch, near Torquay, Devon, whose costs he partly met, and one near Erith, Kent.

BIBLIOGRAPHY
DNB
J. W. Ewing, *Goodly Fellowship* (London, 1946)

ALAN ARGENT

East, David Jonathan (b. London, 1816; d. Highgate, London, 3 Feb. 1903). Baptist minister and theological educator in Jamaica. Having 'experienced the great change' as a boy, he entered Stepney College to train for the ministry at the age of 18. After college, in whose well-being he maintained an interest to the end of his life, he had pastorates at Leamington, Arlington and Waltham Abbey. At the invitation of the BMS he took up the principalship of Calabar College in Jamaica in 1852, when all the inhabitants of the island were under threat from Asiatic cholera and more general distress. During forty years' residence in Jamaica he trained some sixty ministers and missionaries who served not only in Jamaica but many other islands of the Caribbean, as well as in Africa and the USA. He not only raised the funds for the successful removal of the college to better buildings in Kingston, but set up alongside the theological college a normal school for the training of schoolteachers. East also undertook the pastorate of several churches during this period including that of the historic East Queen Street Church in Kingston. He participated in the revival of the 1860s which saw some 4,000 members added to the church. He was a tower of strength

to Jamaican Baptists during the troubled months of the Morant Bay rising and was personally acquainted with the unfortunate GEORGE GORDON whose execution was subsequently declared judicial murder by the Lord Chief Justice of England. He returned to England in 1892 and was for a number of years a deacon of the Beechen Grove Church, Watford, but later moved to Highgate to live with his widowed daughter, whose husband, the Reverend J. B. Balfour, had been a tutor at Calabar. He was not only a wise adviser to the BMS but his counsel was also sought by government on the funding of Jamaican education. His preaching was 'thoughtful, earnest and thoroughly evangelical.'

BIBLIOGRAPHY
Baptist Handbook (1904)

J. H. Y. BRIGGS

Eastburn, James Wallis (b. London, 26 Sept. 1797; d. at sea, 2 Dec. 1819). Episcopal clergyman and hymn-writer. Eastburn's family emigrated to New York in 1803. He graduated from Columbia College in 1816, and then studied theology under Bishop ALEXANDER V. GRISWOLD at Bristol, Rhode Island. On 21 October 1818 he was ordained deacon by Bishop John Henry Hobart of New York. Shortly after this he transferred to the diocese of Virginia, and on 10 January 1819 he began his work as minister of St George's Parish, Accomac County. With Robert V. Sands he wrote the narrative poem *Yamoyden*, a tale of the wars of King Philip, the Indian leader. He also wrote 'Mountains of Israel' and 'Strangers No More We Wildly Rove'. His evangelical theology is clearly expressed in the Trinity-tide hymn, 'O Holy, Holy, Holy Lord', especially verse two:

O Jesus! Lamb once crucified
To take our load of sins away,
Thine be the hymn that rolls its tide
Along the realms of upper day.

His brother, MANTON EASTBURN was the fourth Bishop of Massachusetts.

BIBLIOGRAPHY
DAB
C. Robinson, *Annotations Upon Popular Hymns* (Cleveland, OH, 1893)

DONALD SMITH ARMENTROUT

Eastburn, Manton (b. Leeds, England, 9 Feb. 1801; d. Boston, MA, USA, 11 Sept. 1872). Episcopal bishop. Eastburn emigrated with his family to the US when two years old, and entered Columbia College at 13. Graduating in 1817, he entered General Theological Seminary, New York City, with its first class in May, 1819. He left before taking his degree in order to be ordained deacon on 17 May 1822 by Bishop John Henry Hobart. He served as assistant rector of Christ Church, New York

City, from 1822 to 1827, and then became Rector of the Church of the Ascension, New York City, until 1842. In that year, he was elected assistant bishop to Bishop ALEXANDER VIETS GRISWOLD (New England). Unhappily, the diocese could not afford a salary for an assistant bishop, and so Eastburn took charge of Trinity Church, Boston, where he remained as rector until relinquishing that post in 1858 to Philips Brooks. In the meantime, the sudden death of Bishop Griswold on Eastburn's own doorstep on 15 February 1843 placed upon his shoulders the responsibilities of the entire diocese as well.

A more difficult trial confronted Eastburn over the introduction of Anglo-Catholicism into General Theological Seminary (GTS), and into his own diocese as well. Eastburn, standing in the forefront of the evangelical bishops of the Episcopal Church, attacked 'the Tractarian movement' as 'the work of Satan' which 'if allowed to continue . . . will destroy the evangelical faith and tradition'. In 1844, accusations levelled at a GTS student, Arthur Carey, led to a call for the GTS trustees to investigate Anglo-Catholic influence at the seminary; and though the trustees incautiously announced that the seminary was in no danger from that quarter, Eastburn joined with six other evangelical trustees in issuing a dissent and a call for further investigation. In that same year, a group of Anglo-Catholic sympathizers in Boston challenged Eastburn by organizing the Church of the Advent, and calling Dr William Croswell as its rector. Eastburn strongly disapproved of Croswell's ritualistic innovations, and in 1846, announced the suspension of episcopal visitation of the parish. Only Croswell's death in 1851, and adoption of a new canon on episcopal visitation in 1856, compelled Eastburn to resume those visitations.

As a preacher, Eastburn was dry and pedantic, although as a bishop he was affable and deeply personal in his care for his clergy and his fellow bishops. Typical of the evangelical Episcopalians, he strongly supported the work of the non-denominational Bible societies, as well as the evangelical societies within the Episcopal Church. By temperament and training, he was a classicist and a linguist, and published several minor translations of German theological literature, and a series of *Lectures, Explanatory and Practical, on the Epistle of St Paul to the Philippians* (1833). Most of his thirty other publications, however, were only occasional sermons, charges, and tracts; his letters concerning his struggle with the Church of the Advent were published in *Correspondence between the Right Reverend the Bishop of Massachusetts and the Rector of the Parish of the Advent, 1845–56* (1856).

BIBLIOGRAPHY
E. C. Chorley, *Men and Movements in the American Episcopal Church* (New York, 1950)
W. S. Perry, *History of the American Episcopal Church, 1587–1883*, 2 (Boston, MA, 1885)
H. C. Potter, *Reminiscences of Bishops and Archbishops* (New York, 1906)

ALLEN C. GUELZO

Easterbrook, Joseph (b. Gloucestershire, England, c. 1751; d. Bristol, England, 21 Jan. 1791). Anglican clergyman; Vicar of Holy Cross (Temple) Church, Bristol. Son of a bellman, he was educated at Kingswood School and Emmanuel College, Cambridge. Prior to entering the university in 1774 to prepare for ordination he taught briefly at Trevecka College and began to preach. He took his living in 1779 and WESLEY often occupied his pulpit. He regarded the Methodists as useful auxiliaries to the Establishment and attached his converts to classes. He occasionally performed exorcisms aided by Wesley's preachers. He was described as a father to the poor and succeeded JAMES ROUQUET as chaplain of Newgate prison. He corresponded with HOWEL HARRIS and at times relieved J. W. FLETCHER at Madeley. Wesley regarded him as a prime example of what an evangelical minister should be. It was claimed that he preached in every house in his parish.

A. SKEVINGTON WOOD

Ebury, Lord. *See* GROSVENOR, ROBERT

Eckett, Robert (b. Scarborough, England, 26 Nov. 1797; d. Clevedon, Somerset, England, 28 July 1862). Methodist reformer. Eckett was born of Methodist parents, who moved to London soon after his birth. After a very basic education, he was apprenticed to a stonemason at the age of 11 and ultimately became a successful builder. He was converted in adolescence and began to preach in his late teens. He achieved public recognition in 1828 by issuing a circular letter in support of the Leeds Protestant Methodists and in 1835 his attendance at the Wesleyan Association delegate meeting in Manchester led to his expulsion from Wesleyan Methodism in the following year. His energy, organizational ability and skill in debate soon made him the leading figure in the fledgling Wesleyan Methodist Association (WMA) especially after the departure of SAMUEL WARREN in 1837. In 1839 he entered the WMA ministry, although he never left London. He was a vigorous advocate of circuit independence and free representation in the Annual Assembly and was instrumental in seeing these principles enshrined in the Foundation Deed of 1840. It was these principles which prevented an early union with the MNC.

During the 1840s Eckett had an unassailable position in the denomination: he was President for three years, secretary for five years and connexional editor for the whole period so that he has been seen as a 'Warrenite Bunting'. Despite his antipathy to JAMES EVERETT he shared in the creation of the United Methodist Free Churches, a fusion of the WMA and many Wesleyan Reformers in 1857 and was elected the second United Methodist Free Churches' President in 1858. His capacity for cogent reasoning is demonstrated in a string of polemical pamphlets produced between 1828 and 1853.

BIBLIOGRAPHY
M. Baxter, *Memorials of the United Methodist Free Churches* . . .
(London, 1865)

E. ALAN ROSE

Eden, Robert *See* HENLEY, second Baron

Edgar, John (b. Ballynahinch, Ireland, 13 June 1798;
d. Rathgar, Ireland, 26 Aug. 1866). Presbyterian theologian, philanthropist and temperance pioneer. The son
of Samuel Edgar, DD, Secession minister, he was educated in Glasgow and Belfast and ordained minister of a
small Belfast congregation in November 1820. He succeeded his father as professor of theology in 1826 and
was actively involved in many of the major areas of
evangelical concern, both in Belfast and in rural Ireland.
He founded the Belfast Religious Tract and Book Society
and instigated the building of a house for fallen women
in the town. While his own congregation grew rapidly,
he also engaged in schemes for both the practical and
spiritual relief of famine victims in the west of Ireland,
setting up industrial schools, undertaking a fund-raising
tour of America, establishing a mission in Connaught
and promoting scriptural education. But it is as founder
of the temperance movement in Ulster that he is best
remembered. His initial act of pouring whisky from his
dining-room window into the gutter was followed by a
public campaign which won considerable support
throughout Britain. While he was opposed to the more
radical teetotalism of Father Mathew's movement, which
he regarded as unscriptural, the rapid spread of temperance societies throughout the country indicates his
importance in the nineteenth-century evangelical campaign for moral reformation. He was moderator of the
Synod of Ulster in 1842 and in 1848 resigned his congregation to devote more time to mission work. His *Selected Works* testify to the energy and enthusiasm he
devoted to philanthropic causes.

BIBLIOGRAPHY
DNB
J. B. Killen, *Memoir of John Edgar* (Belfast, 1867)

MYRTLE HILL

Edkins, Joseph (b. Gloucestershire, England, 19 Dec.
1823; d. Shanghai, 23 April 1905). Evangelist, linguist,
translator, philologist and expert on Chinese Buddhism.
Edkins was educated at the University of London and at
Coward Congregational College. A missionary with the
LMS, he arrived in Hong Kong on 3 July 1848 and
became part of a missionary team which included
WALTER MEDHURST, WILLIAM LOCKHART, WILLIAM
MILNE, WILLIAM MUIRHEAD, ALEXANDER WYLIE, and,
somewhat later, Griffith John. With his colleagues he
engaged in evangelism, participated in a training school
for pastors, researched into Chinese language and culture, and began to produce scholarly books for the work
of missions in China.

Some of these were in Chinese, such as several works
on the errors of Buddhism and the *Chinese and Foreign
Concord Almanac*. His writings in English included three
books on Chinese grammar and conversation and one
entitled *The Religious Condition of the Chinese*. During his
years in Shanghai he made several contacts in Suzhou,
Hankow, and Nanjing with the leaders of the Taiping
Heavenly Kingdom. On one of these trips he and Griffith
John prepared a theological statement which they presented to the leaders in an effort to ascertain their precise
doctrinal beliefs.

In 1860 he and his family surveyed the possibility for
missions in north China and eventually settled in Chefoo
for a short period and then Tianjin. In 1863 he became
one of the first Protestant missionaries to live in Beijing,
where he was based for thirty years. In 1866 he visited
Mongolia. During these years, in addition to evangelism
and nurture, he joined with others in producing a Man-
darin Chinese version of the New Testament. Always the
scholar, he was an active member of the China Branch
of the Royal Asiatic Society and the North-China Branch
of the same society. He is most noted for two of his later
books on Chinese religion: *Religion in China* (1880) and
Chinese Buddhism (1880). In these he claimed that
missionaries needed to see that Buddhism, particularly
in its eschatology, was a preparation for Christianity.

Edkins received the honorary DD from the University
of Edinburgh in 1875. He retired from the LMS in 1880,
but remained in Beijing with the Imperial Maritime Customs. He continued his writing until his death on Easter
Sunday, 1905.

BIBLIOGRAPHY
A. J. Broomhall, *Hudson Taylor and China's Open Century: Book
Four* (London, 1984): 445–6
A. Wylie, *Memorials of Protestant Missionaries to the Chinese*
(Shanghai, 1867): 187–91

RALPH R. COVELL

Edwardes, Herbert Benjamin KCSI (b. Frodesley, Shropshire, England, 12 Nov. 1819; d. London, 23 Dec.
1868). Famous soldier in the Northwest Frontier of
India, commissioner of Peshawar, called 'a Christian
Knight', and retired major-general. Educated at Richmond and King's College, London, he received a cadet-
ship in the Bengal Army and served with HENRY M.
LAWRENCE in the Punjab. He helped to put down Mulraj
of Multan (1848) and held Peshawar quiet during the
Mutiny (1857).

Though not as well liked by Lord Dalhousie (1848–
56) as by Henry Lawrence (Penner, 1986: 281, 304),
Edwardes' reputation as a 'Titan of the Punjab' and as
a Christian zealot grew until John Ruskin proclaimed
him a 'modern military Bishop' (Ruskin, 1885: 1–2). No
one was more outspoken in the post-mutiny period in
denouncing the policy of official indifference to the proclamation of the Gospel in India.

SELECT WRITINGS
H. B. Edwardes, 'Prospects of the Triumph of Christianity in India', in *Tracts on Christian Missions* (1866)

BIBLIOGRAPHY
DIB
DNB
E. Edwardes, *Memorials of the Life and Letters of Maj.-Gen. H. B. Edwardes* (1886)
P. Penner, *The Patronage Bureaucracy in North India* (Delhi, 1986)
J. Ruskin, *A Knight's Faith* (London, 1885)

PETER PENNER

Edwards, Bela Bates (b. South Hampton, MA, USA, 4 July 1802; d. Athens, GA, USA, 20 April 1852). American Congregational minister, editor, and professor at Andover Seminary. After graduating from Amherst College and Andover Seminary, he became assistant secretary to the American Education Society and the ABCFM. In 1837 he was ordained in Meathuen, Massachusetts. He married Jerusah Billings Edwards. For 23 years he edited scholarly publications including *Bibliotheca Sacra* (1844–52). In 1837 he was appointed professor of Hebrew and in 1848 professor of biblical literature at Andover Seminary. He published several books including *The Missionary Gazetteer* (Boston, 1832–3), the most complete study of missions to that date.

BIBLIOGRAPHY
AAP
DAB

LELAND EDWARD WILSHIRE

Edwards, Edward (b. Clenchwarton, Norfolk, England, 1766/67; d. King's Lynn, Norfolk, England, 15 March 1849). Anglican clergyman. The son of John Edwards of Clenchwarton, Norfolk, Edwards received his early education at North Walsham and then moved to Trinity College, Cambridge, but quickly transferred to Corpus Christi (scholar 1785; BA 1787; fellow, 1788–96; MA 1790). While in Cambridge he experienced an evangelical conversion through his association with CHARLES SIMEON. In 1799 he became Rector of St Edmund's, King's Lynn (in the patronage of SAMUEL THORNTON) and, concurrently, lecturer at St Margaret's Church and St Nicholas Chapel in the same town. From 1841 he was canon of Norwich.

Edwards was one of Norfolk's most prominent clergymen, his reputation stemming partly from contributions to his county's cultural life. He contributed to the Anglican evangelicals' educational programme through his active promotion of a national school system and by founding and fostering a number of public schools at Lynn. He was also a charity trustee under the Municipal Reform Act (1835).

From 1808 he was the familiar of ELIZABETH FRY and her brother, JOSEPH JOHN GURNEY, and in the capacity of spiritual counsellor guided them into a 'more decided religious course'. In 1811 he made the acquaintance of Fry's brother-in-law, the Quaker abolitionist THOMAS FOWELL BUXTON, whom he directed to Wheeler Chapel, London, under JOSIAH PRATT, where Buxton became an Anglican evangelical.

He was also the boon companion of two members of the Clapham Sect, JOHN VENN of Clapham, and Charles Simeon. At Cambridge together in the 1780s, this impressive evangelical troika developed an intense and sometimes jealously intimate association. In later years he remained one of Simeon's 'beloved and honoured friends'. Their relationship, however, did not sustain the level of affection that Edwards continued to share with Venn.

He published a number of works based on his parochial sermons, as well as *Some Account of the Chapel of St Nicholas* (Lynn, no date). He was also an occasional correspondent with the *Christian Observer* and one of its original subscribers. Letters of Edwards' are preserved in R. E. Cresswell, *Memoir of . . . Elizabeth Fry* (1847), and in W. Carus, *Memoirs of . . . Charles Simeon* (1848). There are two letters from Edwards to Fry in the British Library and a portrait of Edwards is in the Bodleian Library, Oxford (Western manuscripts 28,109).

BIBLIOGRAPHY
Al. Cant.
J. C. Hare, *Gurneys of Earlham*, 2 vols (London, 1895)
M. Hennell, *John Venn and the Clapham Sect* (London, 1958)

JONATHAN BURKE CUTMORE

Edwards, Edward James Justinian George (b. Harrow, England, 1811; d. London, 27 Nov. 1884). Anglican clergyman. Edwards was educated at Shrewsbury and Balliol College, Oxford (BA 1835; MA 1836), where he was Kennicott Hebrew scholar in 1835. He spent his whole ministerial career at Trentham (near Stoke-on-Trent), first as curate (1836–41), then perpetual curate (1841–68) and finally vicar (1868–84), being also Prebendary of Lichfield (1859–84), for which diocese he also served as proctor in convocation (1868, 1874, 1880). He is credited with the introduction of diocesan calendars.

BIBLIOGRAPHY
Boase, V: 202
Al. Ox: I. 410

ARTHUR POLLARD

Edwards, George (b. Yeovil, Somerset, England, 28 June 1785; d. Baverstock, Gloucestershire, England, 10 March 1818). Anglican clergyman. Edwards began his career as a chemist in Bristol where he sat under the ministry of T. T. BIDDULPH, who perhaps influenced him to seek admission to the evangelical St Edmund Hall, Oxford. He served only a brief ministerial career as curate of Baverstock and Bowerchurch (1813–18) where he is said to have been assiduous in his work with the sick and with children.

BIBLIOGRAPHY
CO, XVII: 415

ARTHUR POLLARD

Edwards, John (b. Shrewsbury, England, probably 1714; d. Leeds, England, 17 Feb. 1785). English Independent minister. Converted by GEORGE WHITEFIELD in Ireland, he served initially as a Wesleyan minister there, incurring considerable persecution during his itinerancy. He was later invited by a secession from the Wesleyan society in Leeds to become their pastor. He served this Independent congregation which congregated in the White Chapel, in Queen's Street, Leeds from 1755 until his death in 1785. More Calvinist than the generality of his brethren, he was nevertheless firmly opposed to Antinomianism, for which distortion of Christian doctrine he was not afraid to secure the exclusion of some twenty members of his congregation in 1758. He entertained 'clear views of the great doctrines of the Gospel and evangelical warmth of soul', keeping his 'rational powers and religious passions in happy harmony'. The *Evangelical Magazine* scolded him for destroying his personal papers: 'as a child of many mercies, he was the common property of the church beyond the confines of his mortality.'

BIBLIOGRAPHY
EM (1793)

J. H. Y. BRIGGS

Edwards, Jonathan (b. East Windsor, CT, BNA, 5 Oct., 1703; d. Princeton, NJ, BNA, 22 March, 1758). Congregational pastor and theologian. Jonathan's father, TIMOTHY EDWARDS, was the pastor of the Congregationalist church in East Windsor, Connecticut and his mother was a daughter of Solomon Stoddard, Congregationalist pastor in Northampton, Massachusetts. Stoddard was sometimes referred to as the 'Pope' of the Connecticut Valley, because of his influence in that frontier region of western Massachusetts and Connecticut. Jonathan was the only boy in a family of 11 children. Graduating from Yale College at age 17 in 1720, he stayed there two years studying theology and privately developing his philosophical interests. He was licensed to preach in 1722 and served as acting pastor of a Presbyterian Church in New York until 1723. In 1724 he returned to Yale where he served as tutor for two years. In 1726 he was called to be assistant pastor to his grandfather in Northampton where, upon Stoddard's death in 1729, he became the sole pastor. In 1727 Edwards married Sarah Pierrepont, daughter of a prominent New Haven pastor. Jonathan considered Sarah a model of piety both before and during their marriage. They raised 11 children.

In 1734 and 1735 Edwards's preaching precipitated a remarkable revival in the Northampton church and surrounding community. Earlier spiritual awakenings had occurred under Stoddard, but this event was unprecedented in its magnitude. Within a six month period 300 members were added to Edwards' congregation. In 1737 Edwards published *A Faithful Narrative of the Surprising Work of God*, detailing the revival and thus contributing to the excitements of those on both sides of the Atlantic who were noticing increasing signs of spiritual quickening. GEORGE WHITEFIELD visited Edwards in 1740 during Whitefield's tour of New England. Whitefield's preaching throughout the colonies was sparking widespread revivals that eventually became known as the Great Awakening. During the exciting months that followed, Edwards participated in the further revivals both in Northampton and in surrounding communities. In 1741 he preached in Enfield, Connecticut what became the best known sermon of the revival, 'Sinners in the Hands of an Angry God'. This sermon graphically depicted God's gracious restraint in not immediately releasing his rebellious and unloving creatures to the awful punishments they deserved. It subsequently became a favourite of anthologies that thereby tagged Edwards as primarily a hell-fire preacher, although that was not typical of most of his preaching or thought.

Edwards himself became deeply concerned about occasional excesses accompanying the intense awakenings that followed Whitefield's visits. Such excesses were being used by critics of the revivals, of whom there were many even in the churches of New England, to discredit the awakening. During the subsequent years, Edwards published several analyses that both defended the revivals and attempted to distinguish what was truly the work of the Holy Spirit from what was not. These culminated in his first major work, *A Treatise Concerning Religious Affections* (1746).

By this time the revival and the spiritual let-down that inevitably followed it were generating an intense controversy that threatened Edwards's ministry in Northampton. Making a sharp distinction between the converted and the unconverted, Edwards believed that his congregation should return to the earlier Puritan practice of making conversion a condition for communicant church membership. Solomon Stoddard, however, had taken the view that the Lord's Supper could be a converting ordinance and had introduced the practice of allowing full membership to upright persons who lacked a conversion experience. Edwards's proposal thus aroused bitter opposition since it would have altered long established practice and kept some respectable townspeople out of full membership in the church. Edwards also had alienated some town folk by attempting to enforce strict mores, particularly in condemning teenagers for circulating a book on midwifery. After a prolonged controversy, the congregation voted to dismiss Edwards from his church in 1750. In 1751 he accepted a call to be pastor of a local church and missionary to the Indians at Stockbridge, Massachusetts.

There he wrote several major theological and philosophical treatises, *Freedom of the Will* (1754), *The Great Christian Doctrine of Original Sin Defended* (1758), and *The Nature of True Virtue* (1765). In 1757 he was chosen to be president of the College of New Jersey (Princeton), succeeding his late son-in-law, AARON BURR (father of the future US Vice-President). Shortly after assuming office Edwards died from smallpox contracted from an inoculation.

Edwards is remembered principally for four aspects of his life and work. First, as recounted above, he was a leading figure and preacher in the Great Awakening. Second, he was noted for his intense, almost mystical piety. In his *Personal Narrative*, he described an intense deepening of his religious experience which took place at about age twenty. In it he spoke of his 'sweet delight in God and divine things', especially his sense of the glory of God perceived through nature. In 'A Divine and Supernatural Light', a sermon preached in 1734, Edwards expounded this wonderful sense of God's excellence and beauty revealed not only in nature, but especially in the revelation of his saving work in Christ.

Third, Edwards is remembered as a Calvinist theologian. All his work was written in the framework of the Puritan theological heritage of New England. While he amplified that heritage in original ways, his overriding concern was to defend Reformed theology, especially its uncompromising emphasis on the sovereignty of God. He defended this doctrine against those modern innovations, which he designated broadly as 'Arminian', that placed greater trust in human goodness or abilities. His treatises on freewill, original sin, and true virtue were all focused on popular eighteenth-century philosophical challenges to Reformed views of God and humans. These treatises also established the fourth aspect of Edwards' reputation, that as America's first major philosopher. Though working in frontier conditions with limited libraries and even sometimes a scarcity of writing paper, Edwards produced some of the most powerful philosophical critiques of the era.

For Edwards these aspects of his life and thought were all of one piece. Everything focused around the sovereignty of God. Edwards was particularly concerned about 'the Justice of God in the Damnation of Sinners' as the title of a early published sermon put it. Edwards confessed that in his younger days he had found this doctrine repugnant, but that his youthful deepening of spirituality was sparked by a sense of delight in divine sovereignty and God's infinite goodness, love and beauty. God's justice had to be understood in that context. Some of Edwards' most effective revival sermons focused on this theme as well.

In Edwards' view God's sovereignty was not an abstraction, but a description of God's active love. In his *Dissertation Concerning the End for which God Created the World* (written 1755, published 1765), for instance, he described how God's creation was an ongoing communication of his beauty and his love. Throughout Edwards's works he reiterated how rebellious humans, loving themselves, have refused to see this love. Conversion,

then, is being given by the Holy Spirit new eyes to see; but the seeing is not just an intellectual apprehension. Rather it was an experiencing of the overwhelming beauty of the love of God, manifested in its most immediately transforming aspects in the sacrificial redemptive work of Christ. To recognize the beauty of this love is to have one's heart drawn to it. The transforming work is all God's doing, but it is not against one's will, since we are drawn to beauty voluntarily, even if we can not help being so compelled by it. Edwards explicates such an understanding of freedom of the will, as being free to do what one wants, even though we cannot ultimately control our most essential dispositions.

The essence of true religion then is the affections, or one's loves, as Edwards elaborates in *Religious Affections*. The job of the preacher is to awaken truly godly affections. Excesses are to be avoided by following scriptural guidelines for assessing the fruits of true spirituality.

In *The Nature of True Virtue*, Edwards argued against eighteenth-century optimism about human natural moral abilities. He argued that human loves that were not motivated by love to God were essentially defective since they refused love to the being most deserving of it. Hence humans could not be safely guided by a natural innate 'moral sense' but needed the transforming illumination of God's love.

When called to Princeton, Edwards was working on a *History of the Work of Redemption*, which he never completed. He was, however, influential in introducing postmillennial views, based on his belief that the recent awakening, combined with the decline of the Papacy (in his view, the anti-Christ), were signs of a new age of spiritual transformation that would complete the world's history.

BIBLIOGRAPHY

N. O. Hatch and H. S. Stout, eds, *Jonathan Edwards and The American Experience* (NY, 1988).

D. Levin, ed. *Jonathan Edwards* (New York, 1969)

P. Ramsey, P. Miller and J. E. Smith, gen. eds. *The Works of Jonathan Edwards*, 13 vols (New Haven, CT, 1957 and ongoing)

H. P. Simonson, *Jonathan Edwards* (Grand Rapids, MI, 1974)

O. E. Winslow, *Jonathan Edwards* (New York, 1940)

GEORGE M. MARSDEN

Edwards, Jonathan (Jr) (b. Northampton, MA, BNA, 26 May 1745; d. 1 Aug. 1801). Congregational theologian and president of Union College. The ninth child and namesake of colonial New England's most brilliant theologian, he graduated from the College of New Jersey (Princeton) in 1745. He studied theology with his father's closest clerical followers in New England, and was licensed to preach in 1766. After serving as a tutor at the College of New Jersey, he accepted a call to the White Haven Church in New Haven, Connecticut, and was ordained in 1769. Edwards remained in New Haven until 1795, when a series of disputes over theological and ecclesiastical issues led to his dismissal from the

White Haven Church. Within several months he was installed in a new pastorate in Colebrook, Connecticut. From this small western Connecticut town he was summoned to the presidency of Union College in Schenectady, New York, in 1799.

Edwards' clerical career followed the model that his father and his New Divinity teachers provided for him. He published theological treatises and essays dealing with the doctrinal and ecclesiastical problems that preoccupied Congregational ministers of his day. He was also actively involved in reform efforts, speaking out and writing in opposition to slavery and the slave trade. He was also committed to missionary work, and he was the individual chiefly responsible for the famous Plan of Union (1801) – a cooperative missionary endeavour between New England Congregationalists and Mid-Atlantic Presbyterians that was designed to bring Christianity to the rapidly developing western frontier.

BIBLIOGRAPHY
R. L. Ferm, *Jonathan Edwards the Younger, 1745–1801* (Grand Rapids, MI, 1976)

JOSEPH CONFORTI

Edwards, Justin (b. Westhampton, MA, USA, 25 Apr. 1787; d. Bath Alum Springs, VA, USA, 23 July 1853). Congregationalist minister and reformer. After graduating from Williams College in 1810 as valedictorian and teaching school at Athens, New York, he began studies at Andover Theological Seminary in 1811. Before completing his degree, however, he became the pastor of Congregationalist South Church in Andover, whose 2000 parishioners included many seminary faculty and students. As much as any other American, Edwards promoted the primary concerns of the 'benevolent empire' which proponents of the Second Great Awakening sought to build during the years between 1815 and 1850. While pastoring South Church from 1812 to 1827, he helped to organize the New England Tract Society in 1814, which in 1825 became the ATS, headquartered in New York City. Edwards supplied much of the leadership and management of the society and wrote some of its most widely circulated tracts.

From 1827 until 1836 (except for one and a half years when he pastored the Salem Street church in Boston) he served as the agent for the American Temperance Society which he helped to establish. Due in large part to his extensive travelling and publishing of hundreds of thousands of copies of temperance tracts, 7,000 temperance societies were formed by 1837 with a combined membership of more than 1,250,000. Edwards was a trustee of Andover Theological Seminary from 1820 until 1853, the president of the institution from 1836 until 1842, and chairman of the board of trustees from 1850 until 1853. In 1842 he became the secretary of the American and Foreign Sabbath Union. He travelled nearly 50,000 miles representing the union and prepared the *Permanent Sabbath Doctrines*, of which more

than 600,000 copies were printed. Edwards spent the last four years of his life writing a brief commentary on the Bible for the ATS, completing the New Testament and about half of the Old Testament. The ATS circulated more of his pamphlets than of any other author.

BIBLIOGRAPHY
AAP
DAB
C. H. Foster, *An Errand of Mercy* (Chapel Hill, NC, 1960)
NCAB
W. A. Hallock, *Light and Love . . .* (New York, 1855)

GARY SCOTT SMITH

Edwards, Lewis (b. Pwllcenawon, Pen-llwyn, Dyfed, Wales, 27 Oct. 1809; d. Bala, Gwynedd, Wales, 19 July 1887). Calvinistic Methodist minister and college principal. He was the son of Lewis and Margaret Edward. He began his education at local schools and then worked as a schoolmaster in various places. His insatiable desire for knowledge took him for a year to the University of London and then, in 1833, he entered the University of Edinburgh and graduated MA. On 30 December 1836 he married Jane Charles, granddaughter of THOMAS CHARLES of Bala. In 1837, together with his brother-in-law, David Charles (1812–78), he opened a preparatory school for ministers at Bala and it became the denominational seminary at which Calvinistic Methodist ministers were trained. He was its principal for fifty years.

Edwards was the most potent intellectual influence in his denomination in the Victorian era. He well understood the value of the printed word. Through *Y Traethodydd*, which first appeared in 1845, he sought to emulate the intellectual pattern set by such quarterlies as the *Edinburgh Review*. He made Welsh readers aware as never before of contemporary developments in theology, science, literature and history. His own articles revealed the acuteness of his mind and his broad interests. He published books on the Atonement and the Person of Christ and in his articles he sought to move away from the controversies on recondite topics that had taken up the energies of his predecessors. He himself did not wander far from the Calvinism of his denomination but his work inevitably paved the way for the later liberal theology. In denominational affairs similarly he was an immensely powerful influence. Of his children, Thomas Charles Edwards (1837–1900), a graduate of the University of London and a scholar of Lincoln College, Oxford, was the author of commentaries on I Corinthians (1885) and Hebrews (Expositor's Bible, 1888). He was the first principal of the University College of Wales, Aberystwyth (1872–91), and then of Bala Theological College in succession to his father. His contribution as biblical scholar and educationist was outstanding.

BIBLIOGRAPHY
DNB
DWB
T. C. Edwards, *Bywyd . . . Lewis Edwards* (Liverpool, 1901)

T. Lloyd Evans, *Lewis Edwards* (Swansea, Wales, 1967)
J. Vyrnwy Morgan, *Welsh Religious Leaders of the Victorian Era* (London, 1905)

R. TUDUR JONES

Edwards, Mary [Turner, Mrs Sampson] (b. Turnditch, Derbyshire, England, 27 March 1802; d. Sunderland, Durham, England, 20 Nov. 1875). Primitive Methodist (PM) itinerant preacher. Her parents, farmers, Robert and Mary, took her to church from an early age, but she joined the PMs at 18, suffering much persecution from family and friends. Edwards soon felt a call to preach and left home to become an itinerant. One of the earliest PM preachers, she worked chiefly in the Tunstall area as extracts from her journal show. In 1824 she married a fellow itinerant, and reverted to local preacher status. They settled in Sunderland when he superannuated.

BIBLIOGRAPHY
PMMag (1822–3)

E. DOROTHY GRAHAM

Edwards, Morgan (b. Trevethin, Wales, 9 May 1722; d. Pencader, DE, USA, 28 Jan. 1795). Baptist preacher, church historian, and educator. Reared by Anglican parents, Edwards became a Baptist at 16, studied at the Baptist College at Bristol (1742–4), and was eventually ordained (1757), firmly committed to the Particular Baptist London Confession of 1689. He served churches in Lincolnshire (1744–51); Cork, Ireland (1751–60); and Sussex (1760–1). Upon JOHN GILL's recommendation, he moved to America in 1761 and became the pastor of the Baptist Church in Philadelphia, which he served with great distinction for a decade.

After leaving the pastorate because of recurring problems with alcohol, Edwards moved to Newark, Delaware, but maintained close ties to the Philadelphia Baptist Association. He travelled on its behalf as a evangelist and a lecturer on religious topics. Along with JAMES MANNING and HEZEKIAH SMITH, he founded Rhode Island College (later Brown University) in the mid-1760s for the training of American Baptist clergy, and travelled extensively in America and Britain to raise funds and collect books for the new enterprise. He also gathered data concerning Baptist history and development in the colonies and published them as *Materials Towards a History of the Baptists* (2 vols, 1770–92), thereby becoming the first Baptist church historian in America.

During the Revolution, Edward's support of the Tories brought him travel restrictions and severe criticism from fellow Baptists who nearly all favoured the patriot cause. In 1774 he joined with James Manning and ISAAC BACKUS in petitioning the Massachusetts delegates to the Continental Congress in favour of the separation of church and state.

BIBLIOGRAPHY
DAB
T. B. McKibbens and K. L. Smith, *The Life and Works of Morgan Edwards* (New York, 1980)

TIMOTHY P. WEBER

Edwards, Roger (b. Bala, Merionethshire, Wales, 26 Jan. 1811; d. Mold, Flintshire, Wales, 2 July 1886). Welsh Calvinistic Methodist minister, author and editor. Following an early and unsuccessful attempt to earn his living as a shop assistant at Bala, and brief periods of further schooling in Liverpool and Wrexham, Edwards established himself as a schoolteacher in Dolgellau in 1830 and in the same year began to preach. In 1835 he moved to Mold to become an editor and proofreader in a local printing firm. On his arrival he was invited to exercise an unofficial pastoral oversight of Bethesda Church, Mold, and although ordained to the ministry in 1843, he was not officially appointed pastor of the church until 1878.

Regarded as a gifted and popular preacher, his main contribution lay in his formative denominational leadership, his influential literary activity and his advocacy of political radicalism. Appointed clerk of the North Wales Calvinistic Methodist Association in 1840, a position he held for almost 35 years, he guided his denomination towards a more fully developed Presbyterian polity. A staunch advocate of theological education, he supported his friend LEWIS EDWARDS, whose academy at Bala was officially adopted by the Calvinistic Methodists as a college for the training of ministers, and became secretary and examiner to the college. He was twice elected moderator of the North Wales Association (1870 and 1886), and was elected moderator of the General Assembly in 1872.

His literary contribution lay chiefly in his work as editor of *Y Drysorfa* (1847–86), the monthly periodical of the Calvinistic Methodists, in which he encouraged promising young writers, including the renowned Welsh author Daniel Owen, who first published his novels in serial form in *Y Drysorfa*, thus overcoming the early Methodist prejudice against novels as false and unedifying fables. Edwards also composed a number of hymns, the best of which retain their popularity with Welsh congregations. With Dr LEWIS EDWARDS he was co-founder and co-editor of the substantial literary and theological journal, *Y Traethodydd*. Previously he had edited the first Welsh political magazine, *Cronicl yr Oes* (1835–9), in which he advocated a radical political stance in opposition to the High Toryism which typified early nineteenth-century Calvinistic Methodism. Although his views brought him into conflict with the foremost Calvinistic Methodist leader of his day, the politically reactionary JOHN ELIAS of Anglesey, he laid the foundations of the later political Liberalism of Welsh Methodism and of Nonconformity as a whole. He also opposed JOHN ELIAS's High Calvinism and pioneered the more moderate Calvinism of a later generation. His eldest son, Ellis

Edwards (1844–1915), became a tutor and later principal of Bala Theological College.

BIBLIOGRAPHY

T. M. Jones, *Cofiant y Parch Roger Edwards* (Wrexham, Wales, 1908)

E. AP NEFYDD ROBERTS

Edwards, Sarah [née Pierpont, Pierrepont] (b. New Haven, CT, BNA, 9 Jan. 1710; d. Philadelphia, PA, BNA, 2 Oct. 1758). Puritan mystic and wife of JONATHAN EDWARDS. Born to James and Mary (Hooker) Pierpont, Sarah's early upbringing prepared her for her duties as the wife of a notable clergyman. Her father was pastor of the First Church of New Haven, and her mother came from a ministerial family.

Sarah's reputation as a youthful mystic had reached Jonathan Edwards prior to their meeting. Edwards recorded in his diary reports of her religious character and experiences. The couple married on 20 July 1727. Guests at their homes in Northampton and Stockbridge, Massachusetts, praised Sarah's ability as a mother of 11 children, homemaker, hostess, and woman of wit, culture, and faith. She maintained her deep piety throughout her life. Portions of her diary published in *The Works of President Edwards* record her spiritual ecstasies and support of the Northampton revivals through prayer, hospitality, and religious conversation. Her daughter, Esther Edwards Burr, who shared her spiritual concerns, left one of the fullest eighteenth-century diaries by an American woman.

BIBLIOGRAPHY

J. Edwards, *The Works of President Edwards*, ed. S. Dwight, 10 vols (New York, 1830)

C. F. Karlsen and L. Crumpacker, eds, *The Diary of Esther Edwards Burr, 1754–1757* (New Haven, CT, 1984)

NAW

O. E. Winslow, *Jonathan Edwards* (New York, 1940)

ESTHER BYLE BRULAND

Edwards, Timothy (b. Hartford, CT, BNA, 14 May 1669; d. East Windsor, CT, BNA, 27 Jan. 1758). Congregational minister. Edwards received the AB and AM from Harvard College in 1691. In 1694 he was ordained and installed as pastor of the parish church in East Windsor, Connecticut. A formidable preacher, Edwards nurtured his congregation through frequent spiritual awakenings that culminated with the Great Awakening itself. Undercutting his ministry were petty quarrels with parishioners and his own attempt to take responsibility for church discipline. By his wife Esther, Solomon Stoddard's daughter, Edwards fathered the theologian JONATHAN EDWARDS.

BIBLIOGRAPHY

AAP

SGH

GEORGE W. HARPER

Edwards, William (b. probably England, *c.* 1816; d. Petworth, England, 3 Dec. 1890). Collector in the Indian Civil Service and judge in the High Court, Allahabad. Edwards left the East India Company College at Haileybury for India in 1836. Following several assistantships, he served as secretary to JAMES THOMASON at Agra, as well as to Lord Ellenborough. As collector at Budaon, he was caught by the Mutiny of 1857 and had to flee for his life. This experience led him to the conviction that the dispossession of the talukdars under WILLIAM BENTINCK's land settlement of 1833 had been a mistake. After a brief tenure at the High Court in Allahabad (1863–7), he retired to England.

JOHN W. KAYE described Edwards as a 'prayerful, God-fearing man, . . . a Christian of Christians, with native converts clustering around him . . . in his own house, ...' In retirement he published a collection of readings, indicative of his evangelical concerns: man's lost condition, 'profession and practice', and walking with God 'in ordinances as well as providences'.

SELECT WRITINGS

W. Edwards, *Narrative of the Escape of William Edwards, BCS, from Budaon to Cawnpore* (Private, 1857)

—, *Reminiscences of a Bengal Civilian* (London, 1866)

—, *Morning Bible Readings* (London, 1878)

BIBLIOGRAPHY

J. W. Kaye, *The History of the Sepoy War in India, 1857–8* (London, 1864–76)

P. Penner, *The Patronage Bureaucracy in North India* (Delhi, 1986)

PETER PENNER

Egerton (né Leveson-Gower), Francis [first Earl of Ellesmere; Viscount Brackley] (b. London, 1 Jan. 1800; d. London, 18 Feb. 1857). British MP and peer, philanthropist, writer, and patron of artists. The second son of the first Duke of Sutherland, and grandnephew of the third Duke of Bridgewater, in 1833 he took the name of Egerton (the family name of the dukes of Bridgewater, whose vast wealth he inherited). He was educated at Eton and Oxford. An MP for Betchingley, Surrey (1822–6), Sutherlandshire (1826–35), and South Lancashire (1835–46), he was a Canningite liberal Tory and then a Peelite, prominent in his support of free trade, the Maynooth Grant and London University. His only significant appointment was as Chief Secretary to the Lord Lieutenant of Ireland (1828–30). He was created Earl of Ellesmere in 1846.

The friend of John Ruskin, Egerton was a generous patron of artists, he opened the famous Bridgewater art collection to the public, was a minor poet, historian, and translator, contributed articles to the *Quarterly Review*, and recorded historically important reminiscences of the Duke of Wellington (published 1904). He was chairman of the Scripture Readers' Association and, with his wife, Harriet Greville (1800–66), in the vicinity of his Worsley, Lancashire estates unostentatiously provided

349

schools, churches, chapels, savings banks, libraries, and hospitals and worked to suppress Sunday trading. Egerton's papers are preserved at the British Library and there are some letters of his at John Murray (Publishers), London.

BIBLIOGRAPHY
J. Bateman, *Great Landowners of Great Britain and Ireland* (London, 1878)
St V. Beechey, *Two Sermons . . . on the Funeral of Francis Egerton* (Manchester, England, 1857)
DNB

JONATHAN BURKE CUTMORE
DONALD M. LEWIS

Ekin, George (b. Newton-Stuart, Tyrone County, Ireland, 22 May 1782; d. Abingdon, VA, USA, 2 August 1856). Methodist minister. His association with Methodism began in Ireland as a youth when he joined a class meeting as a religious seeker. At 15 years of age he was converted and soon became a class leader and local preacher. His Presbyterian family was not pleased about his conversion to Methodism. He emigrated to America in 1810 and was licensed to preach in the MEC. He joined the Western Conference in 1811 and was appointed to a circuit. He travelled as an itinerant for over forty years and by his own account preached at least one sermon a day during his ministry, and thousands were converted and brought into the MEC. He strongly opposed the southern position in the 1844 conflict over slavery and protested the formation of the MEC, So.

BIBLIOGRAPHY
EWM
I. P. Martin, *Methodism in Holston* (Knoxville, TN, 1945): 47–8
Minutes
R. N. Price, *Holston Methodism*, II (Nashville, TN, 1906): 421–50

ROBERTA J. STEWART

Eland, Sarah [also **Healand**] [de Putron, Mrs John] (b. Hutton Rudby, North Yorkshire, England). *Fl.* 1820. Female revivalist. From a Wesleyan Methodist family, converted at the Covenant service (1802), Eland exercised considerable influence for good. Visiting Hull she met Mr and Mrs Woolhouse, Wesleyan Methodist class leaders. After Mr Woolhouse encountered the Primitive Methodists in Nottingham his wife and Sarah went to hear them (1817). They became involved in the revival and returned full of enthusiasm. Sarah met ANN CARR at Waltham Street Wesleyan Chapel, Hull, band meeting (1818). Sarah agreed to go with her to Market Rasen, where they contributed to a revival, however, they were attracted to Primitive Methodism because it readily accepted women preachers. Probably influenced by reports of SARAH KIRKLAND's work they visited Nottingham (1818). By now they and the Woolhouses had become Primitive Methodists.

When the Leeds Circuit was formed (June 1821) Sarah, Ann Carr and MARTHA WILLIAMS, went there, probably as revivalists. Although they were very popular, they quickly became involved in controversy because they would not accept circuit discipline. Soon they left and set up their own church. Sarah married a Wesleyan Methodist minister (1824), and they worked in the Channel Islands.

BIBLIOGRAPHY
Z. Taft, *Biographical Sketches of . . . Holy Women . . .*, 2 (Leeds, England, 1828)

E. DOROTHY GRAHAM

Elaw, Zilpha (b. Pennsylvania, USA, *c.* 1790; d. *c.* 1850). Methodist evangelist. Elaw was born to free black parents and joined a Methodist society near Philadelphia in 1808. She married Joseph Elaw in 1810, and they moved to Burlington, New Jersey. Their daughter was born in 1812. At a camp meeting in 1817, Zilpha fell into a 'trance of ecstasy' and then prayed in public for the first time. Two years later, she preached to another camp meeting crowd. After Joseph's death in 1823, Zilpha could no longer ignore her call to preach. She placed her daughter with a relative and began her evangelistic career. In 1828 Zilpha travelled in the South at great personal risk, preaching to black and white audiences. Eighteen months later, she returned north, and continued her itinerating. Her calling then took her to England, where she preached from 1840 to 1845. As of 1845, she planned to return to the United States, but her activities after that date are unknown.

BIBLIOGRAPHY
W. Andrews, *Sisters of the Spirit* (Bloomington, IL, 1986)
Z. Elaw, *Memoirs* (London, 1846)

SUSAN E. WARRICK

Elias, John (b. Abererch, near Pwllheli, Wales, 6 May 1774; d. Llangefni, Ynys Môn, Wales, 8 June 1841). Usually considered the greatest Welsh preacher of the nineteenth century. Elias was the son of Elias Jones, a small farmer. He early came under the influence of his grandfather with whom the family lived, John Cadwaladr, a devout churchman. Cadwaladr taught his grandson to read and to develop a taste for spiritual matters, although Elias received no formal education. Elias read in his youth Welsh translations of works by Cole, and Edward Fisher's *Marrow of Modern Divinity* and early revealed a strong appetite for scriptural spirituality. After wrestling with his conviction of sin for several years he was enabled to place his trust in the Lord, particularly after hearing a sermon on Mark 8: 38.

He belonged to what is considered the third generation of Welsh evangelists since the pioneers of the eighteenth-century revival, HOWEL HARRIS, DANIEL ROWLAND and WILLIAM WILLIAMS being the leaders of the first, the second consisting of men such as THOMAS CHARLES, THOMAS JONES, and ROBERT ROBERTS. Elias joined the Methodists in 1793, and drifted through various stages of public prayer, catechizing and exhorting, into the task of preaching, though not officially until 25 December 1794.

After moving to Anglesey in 1799, marrying Elizabeth Broadhead, Elias together with his first wife maintained themselves and their four children by keeping a shop. Despite great initial antagonism, he soon transformed the island with his preaching. Two volumes of his sermons from shorthand copies were published in 1846 and 1849, apart from numerous other individual sermons. A fair number remain in manuscript. Although his printed work – including his volume *Golygiad Ysgrythyrol ar Gyfiawnhad Pechadur*, 1821 (A Scriptural View of the Sinner's Justification) – is impressive, Elias was primarily renowned for his oratorical imagination, and his biographers have given graphic accounts of some of his sermons and particularly of the dramatic effects he had, as for instance in addressing the people in Rhuddlan in 1802 on the occasion of the market day and hiring fair, and then again in the open air in Holyhead in 1824 when a number of drunks tried to disrupt a meeting.

His wife died in 1828, and in 1830 Elias married Ann, the widow of Sir John Bulkeley of Presaddfed. The foremost Welsh playwright, Saunders Lewis, has based one of his dramas *Dwy Briodas Ann* (Ann's two marriages) on her life. By this time, and since 1820, he had entered into what can be considered his second major contribution to Calvinistic Methodism, the first being his popular evangelical preaching. He was now the foremost statesman of his denomination, and one of the prime instigators in forming the 1823 Confession of Faith, to which he himself contributed articles on the Covenant of Works, the Election of Grace and the Person of Christ the Mediator, and the Eternal Covenant. This Confession enunciated the official theology of the connexion for several generations, a Federal or Covenant Theology that had already received an eloquent affirmation in William William's long poem *Golwg ar Deyrnas Crist* (A View of Christ's Kingdom) and in the prolific works of Thomas Charles and Thomas Jones. Elias was firmly anchored in this main stream of Welsh Calvinism which was propagated by the main Nonconformist denominations in the country (viz. the Independents, the Baptists and the Calvinistic Methodists apart from the evangelical party in the Established Church), and opposed both High Calvinism on the one hand and Arminianism on the other. Such works formed the basis of his reading, as too in English (or in translation) he delighted in the treatises of John Owen and fellow Puritans.

Despite his immense personal influence on other preachers of his generation, both through his charming manner and because of the leadership he provided in committee, undoubtedly the thrust of his theological impact was mainly through his sermons. One of the most well known of such sermons, one which had little negative content, but which was consciously calculated to combat the inhibiting High Calvinist view that the Gospel message was not offered to all, was preached in the farmyard at Mathafarn on the text John 1: 29. It turned around the rallying cry 'The family is too small for the Lamb'.

Despite his affectionate sensitivity and his undoubted humility, John Elias's occasional rigidity led him to be seriously influenced by a bias that was, as Professor R. Tudur Jones has pointed out, sometimes politically reactionary, morally legalistic and tending rapidly towards dividing the evangelicals along narrow denominational lines.

During the last year of his life John Elias wrote a brief autobiography of 71 pages. It was not published in reliable form until 1974, edited by G. P. Owen. His remains were accompanied to Llan-faes churchyard by a procession of 10,000 people of all classes, a reflection of his continuing immense popularity, and the fact that he was widely considered by his contemporaries as certainly the finest orator in Wales in his time, if not of all time, and a staunch defender of evangelical Calvinism and of nationwide influence.

BIBLIOGRAPHY

R. T. Jones, *John Elias* (Bridgend, Wales, 1974)
E. Morgan, *John Elias* (London, 1973)
G. P. Owen, *Hunangofiant John Elias*, (Bridgend, Wales, 1974)
W. Pritchard, *John Elias a'i Oes* (Caernarfon, Wales, 1911)
J. Roberts and J. Jones, *Cofiant y Parchedig John Elias o Fôn* (Liverpool, 1850)
O. Thomas, *Cofiant John Jones Talsarn* (Wrexham, Wales, 1874)

R. M. JONES

Eliot, George (née Evans, Mary Ann or Marian; Cross, Mrs M.) (b. Chilvers Coton, Warwickshire, England, 22 Nov. 1819; d. London, 22 Dec. 1880). Novelist and critic. Mary Ann Evans, younger daughter of Robert and Christiana Evans, was educated at schools in Attleborough (Warwickshire) and Nuneaton, at the latter her evangelical inclinations being fostered by one of the teachers, MARIA LEWIS. Mary Ann took charge of the family household on her mother's death in 1836. She read voraciously and wrote verse, her first publications appearing in *CO* (Jan. 1840). She moved with her father to Coventry in March 1841, and there met the Brays and Sara Hennell, who led her into freethinking. She translated Strauss's *Leben Jesu* (1846), followed by Feuerbach's humanistic *Essence of Christianity* (1854), at which time she also began her lifelong liaison with the critic George Henry Lewes. She now turned to fiction and under her pseudonym published *Scenes of Clerical Life* (1858), which included such evangelical characters as Amos Barton and Edgar Tryan. *Adam Bede* (1859) had the Methodist woman preacher, Dinah Morris, based on one of the author's relatives (see ELIZABETH EVANS), and *Silas Marner* (1861) portrayed the dissenting community of Lantern Yard, while *Middlemarch* (1872) contains two unsympathetic portraits of Anglican evangelicals in the parson Tyke and the hypocritical banker,

Bulstrode. Her other works included *The Mill on the Floss* (1860), *Felix Holt* (1866) (see FRANCIS FRANKLIN), and *Daniel Deronda* (1874–6). Her early evangelical leaning may have contributed to the solemnly moral and didactic tone in some of her work.

BIBLIOGRAPHY
DNB
G. S. Haight, ed., *Letters*, 9 vols (London, 1954–78)
G. S. Haight, *George Eliot* (London, 1968)
B. Hardy, *The Novels of George Eliot* (London, 1969)
M. Maison, *Search Your Soul, Eustace* (London, 1961) [Published in the USA as *The Victorian Vision*]
R. L. Woolf, *Gains and Losses* (London, 1977)

ARTHUR POLLARD

Elizabeth (b. Maryland, BNA, 1766; d. Philadelphia, USA, 11 June 1866). African-American Methodist itinerant preacher. Elizabeth's last name is unknown. Born a slave, she was raised in Maryland by Methodist parents. She was freed at the age of thirty by a Presbyterian who did not believe in holding slaves for life. She first felt called to preach when she was only 13, during an ecstatic and visionary conversion experience. However, she was barely literate, and she did not find the courage to begin speaking in public until she turned 42. She believed that God had directly inspired her; indeed, she claimed to have received direct revelations through voices, visions and dreams. Courageously, she journeyed to Virginia and spoke against slavery, facing angry crowds who 'would not believe that a coloured woman could preach' (*Elizabeth*, 1889: 10). She also travelled throughout Maryland and Canada, and she established a school for 'coloured orphans' in Michigan that she led for four years. Throughout her career, she commonly encountered hostile clergymen who questioned her authority to preach. However, she did not stop speaking in public until she retired to Philadelphia at the age of 87. She died at the age of 100.

BIBLIOGRAPHY
Anon., *Elizabeth, A Colored Minister of the Gospel* (Philadelphia, PA, 1889)
J. Humez, ed., *Gifts of Power* (Amherst, MA, 1981): 316–21

CATHERINE A. BREKUS

Elizabeth, Charlotte *See* TONNA, CHARLOTTE ELIZABETH

Elliot, Anthony (b. Dartmouth, Nova Scotia, BNA, *c.* 1784; d. Freetown, Sierra Leone, 30 Sept. 1856). African-Canadian-born pastor and pilot in Sierra Leone. His father, a black Loyalist solder in the American War of Independence, was settled in Nova Scotia after the war, and emigrated with his family to Sierra Leone in 1792. He was converted as a member of the Countess of Huntingdon's Church, to which his family belonged, then an independent church without contact with the Huntingdonians in England. In 1839 he became pastor of Zion,

the main Huntingdon church in Freetown. Under his unpaid superintendence, the church opened branches in the villages round Freetown. He also established contact with the English Huntingdonians who at his earnest request, sent out a minister in 1853 to take charge. He was licensed as a pilot to conduct ships into Freetown harbour, a responsible post which he held until he retired in 1854, officiating as a pilot of ships as well as souls – and sometimes needlessly alarming ships' captains who found themselves under the command of a black pilot.

BIBLIOGRAPHY
C. Fyfe, *A History of Sierra Leone* (London, 1962)

CHRISTOPHER FYFE

Elliot, Henry Meirs KCB (b. probably England, 1 March 1808; d. Cape of Good Hope, 20 Dec. 1853). Indian Civil Service secretary, diplomat, and historian. A very talented person, he was educated at Winchester and was appointed in 1826 directly to the East India Company's service. During a very demanding career he found time to collect documents, write history, and make significant contributions to the formation of a glossary of judicial and revenue terms.

Before he became foreign secretary to both Sir Henry Hardinge and Lord DALHOUSIE, he worked as secretary to ROBERT M. BIRD in the application of the land settlement of 1833. He was wholly in agreement with Dalhousie's policy of annexation. His writings reflected this attitude. He is said to have perpetuated 'the [James] Mill tradition in writing on Indian history' (Philips, 1961: 226).

Never overtly evangelical, nevertheless, a critical evaluation by a successor at the revenue board, Francis H. Robinson, brings out a negative aspect of evangelicalism. Robinson stated in 1863 that he recognized evangelicalism in the 'resumption of religious endowments, the levelling of the Sikh nation by militant Christians . . ., and the "crimination" of great Indians . . . by historians such as H. M. Elliot . . .'. (Penner, 1986: 243). At Agra, Elliot supported the founding of St John's College under the ardent evangelical THOMAS VALPY FRENCH.

SELECT WRITINGS
H. M. Elliot, *The History of India, as Told by Its Own Historians* (posthumously edited by John Dowson) (London, 1867–77)
—, *Memoirs of the History, Folklore, and Distribution of the Races of the North Western Provinces of India* (posthumously edited by John Beames) 2 vols (London, 1869)

BIBLIOGRAPHY
DIB
P. Penner, *The Patronage Bureaucracy in North India* (Delhi, 1986)
C. H. Philips, ed., *Historians of India, Pakistan, and Ceylon* (London, 1961): 132, 226

PETER PENNER

Elliot, Robert James (d. c. 1849). British naval officer and philanthropist. Elliot joined the navy and reached the rank of commander in 1814. Thereafter he saw little of the sea but devoted himself and his fortune to the cause of sailors. He was much involved with the Episcopal Floating Church Society on the Thames in 1825, and with G. C. ('Boatswain') SMITH's outreach to sailors at Wellclose Square in conjunction with GEORGE CORNISH GAMBIER another half-pay captain. Elliot and Gambier assumed the directorship of the Destitute Sailors Asylum in 1828 and Elliot remained with the work despite the withdrawal of Smith – and a temporary breach between the two captains – until 1849. The work began with Smith's vision, but Elliot's practical sense and financial generosity turned the scheme into reality. He was joint honorary secretary of the Thames Church Mission in 1844 and keenly supported the opening of St Paul's Church for seamen in Dock Street, London in 1847.

BIBLIOGRAPHY
R. Kverndal, *Seamen's Missions* (Pasadena, CA, 1986)
Naval and Military Bible Society Annual Reports
New Sailors Magazine, ed. 'Boatswain' Smith
W. R. O'Byrne, *A Naval Biographical Dictionary* (London, 1849)

RICHARD C. BLAKE

Elliott, Charles (b. England, 12 June 1751; d. 15 Oct. 1832). Upholsterer. Elliott married Sarah Anne Sherman (daughter of the Reverend Dr Sherman), by whom he had four surviving children. On 10 December 1785 he married Eling Venn, daughter of HENRY VENN. Owner of a prosperous London upholstery business, he was a prominent evangelical Anglican layman and a close friend of BASIL WOODD, apparently attending Bentinck Chapel, Marylebone where Woodd ministered from 1785 to 1831. In 1793 he established a country home in Clapham and became a close associate of WILLIAM WILBERFORCE. He also maintained a seaside home in Brighton and founded St Mary's Chapel there. Although he was a strong lay supporter of the CMS, he is best remembered for his progeny: his daughter CHARLOTTE ELLIOTT became known for her hymns; one son, HENRY VENN ELLIOTT was a leading Anglican cleric, and another son, EDWARD BISHOP ELLIOTT, was an influential theological writer.

BIBLIOGRAPHY
C. Hole, *Early History of the Church Missionary Society* (London, 1896): 626–7

DONALD M. LEWIS

Elliott, Charles (b. Greenconway, County Donegal, Ireland, 16 May 1792; d. Mount Pleasant, IA, USA, c. 6 Jan. 1869). Methodist minister, author, and editor. He was converted in 1811 and was involved in the Methodist Church in Ireland. He studied theology under the tutelage of private scholars after being denied admission to the University of Dublin and received his preaching licence in 1813. He emigrated to America in 1815 and moved to Western Pennsylvania where he joined the Ohio Conference of the MEC in 1818. After serving as a circuit preacher he was appointed the superintendent of missions for the Wyandotte Indians in Upper Sandusky, Ohio in 1822. He served as presiding elder of several districts in the Midwest and was professor of languages at Madison College in Uniontown, Pennsylvania from 1827 to 1831 and professor of biblical literature from 1856 to 1858 and president, from 1858 to 1860, of Iowa Wesleyan University.

A good portion of his career was dedicated to the publishing of religious periodicals. He was editor of the *Pittsburgh Conference Journal*, the *Western Christian Advocate* and from 1860 to 1864 the *Central Christian Advocate* where he became well known for his strong opposition to slavery and his ardent support of the Union. He was elected a delegate to General Conference nine times including the 1844 session with its debate over slavery and was subsequently commissioned by the MEC to write a history of the separation of the church and the formation of the MEC South.

A prolific author, he wrote over a dozen books including *The Bible and Slavery, Delineation of Roman Catholicism, Duties of Americans in Regard to Slavery, History of the Great Secession*, and *Sinfulness of American Slavery*.

BIBLIOGRAPHY
EWM
M. Simpson, *Cyclopedia of Methodism* (Philadelphia, PA, 1881)
J. G. Wilson and J. Fiske, eds, *Appleton's Cyclopedia of American Biography* (New York, 1887)

ROBERTA J. STEWART

Elliott, Charles John (b. 7 July 1818; d. Winkfield, Berkshire, England, 11 May 1881). Anglican clergyman and scholar. Elliott, who was nephew to H. V. ELLIOTT, E. B. ELLIOTT and CHARLOTTE ELLIOTT, graduated from St Catherine's College, Cambridge (BA 1840; MA 1843). He was Crosse scholar in 1840 and Tyrwhitt scholar in 1842. He served as Curate of St John's, Holloway (London) (1842–4), becoming Vicar of Winkfield (1844–81) and Canon of Christ Church, Oxford (1873–81). He was select preacher at Cambridge (1877) and a member of the Old Testament Revision Committee for the Revised Version of the Bible. He also published an *Enquiry into the Doctrine of the Church of England on Private Confession and Absolution* (1859) at a time when High Church practices of this nature were spreading.

BIBLIOGRAPHY
Boase. I: 980
Al. Cant., II, ii: 405

ARTHUR POLLARD

Elliott, Charlotte (b. Clapham, Surrey, England, 18 March 1789; d. Brighton, Sussex, England, 22 Sept.

1871). Hymn-writer. Charlotte Elliott was the daughter of CHARLES ELLIOTT, one of the so-called Clapham Sect and an associate therefore of the Thorntons, Wilberforce and other influential evangelical Anglican families. Her mother was Eling Venn, daughter of HENRY VENN of Huddersfield and Yelling, and sister of JOHN VENN, Rector of Clapham. Her brothers were HENRY VENN ELLIOTT and EDWARD BISHOP ELLIOTT. She was an accomplished versifier with a good singing voice and a talent for drawing, gifts which ensured that she was appreciated in cultivated society. She chose, however, to abandon secular pursuits following her conversion after meeting HENRI-ABRAHAM CÉSAR MALAN in Geneva in May 1822. Thereafter, mainly by correspondence, Malan became her spiritual adviser.

Shortly before meeting him, Elliott experienced the first signs of a breakdown in health, followed in 1829 by complete collapse. The rest of her long life was mainly a succession of winter illnesses followed by summer visits to recover her health. In 1823 with her brother Henry, she visited St Remy, the Normandy estate of the Waddingtons (Maria Waddington, a particular friend, later married WALTER AUGUSTUS SHIRLEY). In 1830 under medical advice she visited Scotland. She was ill again in 1837 and afterwards undertook a continental journey down the Rhine valley and into Switzerland. Another bout of illness in 1843, following a series of family bereavements, led to a stay in Devon, while two years later a projected stay in Italy through the summer and over the winter of 1846 was cut short by renewed illness and a return home.

After many years in what had become the parental home in Brighton, Charlotte removed on her father's death to another house in the same town, but on medical advice she transferred to Torquay in 1845, returning, however, to Brighton in 1857. She left home for the last time on a visit to Keymer in 1867 and spent her final years bedridden.

In 1834 Charlotte met Harriet Kiernan who was in the last stages of tuberculosis. She was inspired by her to assume the editorship of *The Christian Remembrancer Pocket Book*, an annual collection of daily readings in prose and verse. She continued this work until 1859. She contributed hymns to her brother Henry's *Psalms and Hymns* (1835), and in the previous year she had published *The Invalid's Hymn Book* which contained 23 of her own compositions. In subsequent editions this number increased until there were 112. Her other collections were *Hours of Sorrow Cheered and Comforted* (1836) and *Thoughts in Verse on Sacred Subjects* (1869).

She is remembered nowadays for only two of her hymns – 'Christian, seek not yet repose' and, supremely, 'Just as I am' which appeared in the first edition of *The Invalid's Hymn Book*. This piece speaks movingly of personal penitence and response to Christ's invitation to come to Him, with each verse beautifully balanced between the opening words, 'Just as I am' and her characteristically short concluding line, full of gratitude and eagerness, 'O Lamb of God, I come'.

SELECT WRITINGS
C. Elliott, *Selections from the Poems of Charlotte Elliott – With a Memoir by her Sister E[leanor] B[abington]* (London, no date)

BIBLIOGRAPHY
DNB
J. Julian, *A Dictionary of Hymnology* (London, 1907)

ARTHUR POLLARD

Elliott, Edward Bishop (b. Clapham, Surrey, England, 24 Jan. 1793; d. Brighton, Sussex, England, 30 July 1875). Anglican clergyman and author. He was the younger brother of HENRY VENN ELLIOTT and CHARLOTTE ELLIOTT. He was privately educated and entered Trinity College, Cambridge in 1812 (BA 1816; MA 1819; fellow 1817–24). From 1817 to 1819 he toured Italy and Greece with his brother Henry whom he met at Rome. For a brief while he was Curate of Bidborough (Kent) and then he became Vicar of Tuxford (Nottinghamshire) (1824–37). While there he was influenced by J. W. Brooks (of East Retford, and later St Mary's, Nottingham), as a result of which his interest in prophecy developed. He retired to Torquay to write his *Horae Apocalypticae* (1844). In 1853 he was appointed prebendary of Heytesbury (Wiltshire) and in the same year became incumbent of St Mark's, Kemptown, Brighton, which had been built four years before largely through the efforts of his brother. His achievements there included the establishment of Bible classes, a branch of the CMS and, chiefly, schools for over 400 children.

Elliott's fame rests upon *Horae Apocalypticae*, a work, according to the *Christian Observer* (1875: 789), 'read wherever the English language is known'. Sir James Stephen's praise, though less fulsome, was still quite considerable, when he described it as 'a work of profound learning, singular ingenuity and bewitching interest' ('The Clapham Sect', *Essays in Ecclesiastical Biography*). Elliott saw Revelation as a consecutive prophecy of history from the time of Domitian to the end of all things, which he expected to happen before the end of the nineteenth century. It is not surprising in one who always insisted on speaking of 'the Protestant Reformed Church of England' that he saw the beast and Babylon as Rome and the Pope as the 'man of sin' of Thessalonians. The two witnesses of Revelation 10 and 11 are the faithful ones raised up in the western and eastern churches to protest against papal error and are considered to be those slain at the Council of Lateran and raised up three and a half years later when Luther posted his theses at Wittenberg. The seven-horned monster is the Roman Empire in its last stages under the papal yoke for 1,260 years of Antichrist. Elliott sought to establish exact dates. Thus the great earthquake at the time of the French Revolution is identified with the sound of the seventh trumpet and by an addition to the 1260 years of Antichrist he predicted the second coming when Christ would destroy the Antichrist and establish the millennium on earth to take place in 1886. In the same context he considers the three unclean spirits of the sixth vial to be infidelity, popery and sacerdotalism. While his speculations might appear a strange amalgam of literalism and fantasy, his interpretation held great attraction for many Victorian evangelicals.

Other works associated with his prophetic studies included *The Question, 'What is the Beast?' Answered* (1838), *The Downfall of Despotism* (1853) and two replies to the critics of the *Horae*, *Vindiciae Horariae* (to Dr Keith) (1848) and *Apocalypsis Alfordiana* (to Dean Alford). In addition, Elliott published *The Delusion of the Tractarian Clergy* (1856) on the validity of orders, and *Sermons* (1836). He won the Seatonian prize for poetry at Cambridge in 1821 and 1822 and he also edited the *Memoir of Lord Haddo, Fifth Earl of Aberdeen* (1867).

BIBLIOGRAPHY
Al. Cant., II.ii: 405
CO, 74 (1875)
DNB

ARTHUR POLLARD

Elliott, Henry Venn (b. Clapham, Surrey, England, 17 Jan. 1792; d. Brighton, Sussex, England, 24 Jan. 1865). Anglican clergyman. Elliott was the eldest son of CHARLES ELLIOTT, a member of the so-called Clapham Sect, and his wife Eling Venn, and thus a grandson of HENRY VENN of Huddersfield and Yelling, and nephew of JOHN VENN, Rector of Clapham. EDWARD BISHOP ELLIOTT was his brother and CHARLOTTE ELLIOTT his sister. He was educated first at Hammersmith under Elwell, and then prepared for university with a well-known evangelical tutor, HENRY JOWETT of Little Dunham (Norfolk). Elliott entered Trinity College, Cambridge in 1810 (scholar 1811; BA 1814; fellow 1816; MA 1817). After Cambridge he toured the Continent with Scott Moncrieff and (Sir) JOHN KENNAWAY, taking in Brussels, Waterloo, Namur, Aix-la-Chapelle, and Cologne and thence to Zurich and the Swiss lakes via the St Bernard Pass, seeing Mont Blanc, and on to Rome and Naples, thence to Corfu, Athens and several cities of Asia Minor, reaching Jerusalem by Whitsuntide 1819 and touring the Holy Land where the cheap exploitation of the holy places disgusted him, returning home by August 1820.

At Cambridge, Elliott was welcomed by CHARLES SIMEON and came to admire WILLIAM FARISH. With Babington (later to be his brother-in-law) and the Wilsons he took a prominent part in the controversial formation of the Cambridge auxiliary of the BFBS in 1811. It was the zeal of these young men that stimulated their sympathetic seniors into action. In addition, Elliott was active as a Sunday school teacher, mainly at nearby Waterbeach; and on a minor scale he seems to have emulated Simeon by running Sunday-evening gatherings for young men in his rooms, studying sermons of well-regarded divines both for current edification and as preparation for future ministry.

Nevertheless, Elliott himself delayed his own ordination until he was absolutely assured of his calling. Others, like his brother and Babington preceded him to holy orders, but, though he was offered curacies by J. W. CUNNINGHAM at Harrow, ROGER CARUS WILSON at Preston, and Archdeacon HOARE at Godstone, he chose not to accept any of these. After ordination in November 1823, he became curate in the estate village of Lord GEORGE CALTHORPE at Ampton (Suffolk) (1823–5) as well as serving nearby Fakenham. He also took pupils, some of whom included the sons of such well-known evangelical laymen as Sir SAMUEL HOARE, Lord Aberdeen and Lord HARROWBY. After a breakdown in health Elliott returned to Cambridge in November 1825.

His father meanwhile had retired to Brighton, where he built the proprietary chapel of St Mary's, consecrated in January 1827, and to which Elliott was appointed preacher (1827–65). He inherited the chapel on his father's death in 1832. He also extensively assisted his friend, the Marquess of Bristol, in establishing St Mark's Kemp Town, Brighton in 1849. Visiting preachers at St Mary's between 1828 and 1830 included not only such prominent evangelicals as Simeon, BASIL WOODD and JOSIAH PRATT, but also Robert Wilberforce and J. H. NEWMAN, the last named preaching on Isaiah 53: 2 on 27 July 1828.

Elliott married on 31 October 1833 Julia Anne, daughter of John Marshall of Hallsteads, Ullswater, who had visited Brighton to recover his health in 1827. Marshall was a Leeds businessman, whose wife's friendship with Dorothy Wordsworth inspired their move to the Lake District, where he bought the living of Crosthwaite and then within its parish built St John's Church, Keswick. Elliott and his wife had five children. She died of scarlet fever on 3 November 1841, an event which evoked a letter from Edward Pusey among others.

Elliott seems to have maintained an irenical attitude about differences of churchmanship during the Tractarian controversy. Speaking of his select preachership at Cambridge in 1850 and of subsequent visitation and ordination sermons, he expressed the wish 'to avoid the bitterness and strife of theological differences, but to insist on the fundamental points of the Gospel of Christ in a spirit of kindness' (Letter to Archdeacon Hare, May 1852). He was not impressed, however, by the informality and 'the irreverence of appearing almost to inform God, as he would inform his congregation' which he found in the services of the famous evangelical Dissenter, WILLIAM JAY of Bath (Letter to his wife, February 1836), adding that he was 'thankful above all for the Liturgy'.

However tolerant Elliott tried to be about theological differences within the Church of England, and much as he had been impressed by the services in the Sistine Chapel during his stay in Rome during Holy Week, 1818, he had serious differences with Roman Catholicism. He tells of argument with a priest about mariolatry while he was in Rome; and in later life he resolutely opposed the Maynooth Grant in 1845, and was vehement in the fight for 'Protestant truth' at the time of the Papal Aggression in 1850–1.

In February 1851, he preached the funeral sermon of his old friend, WILLIAM CARUS WILSON, the consecration of whose church at Casterton he had attended in 1833. On that visit he also saw the Clergy Daughters' School, which became the model for his own St Mary's Hall at Brighton, opened in 1836. Elliott was helped in this venture by Lord Bristol, but he himself contributed £2,500 and in his will left to the school £1,000, together with land valued at £2,500 and 1,000 books. The roll reached its limit of 100 in 1841. Despite problems – 'incompetent governesses, unreasonable parents, curious visitors, and defaulting subscribers' (Bateman, 1868: 155) – the school prospered and pupils spoke well of it.

Elliott maintained an active interest in many evangelical societies, notably CMS, the Jews' Society, and the Scripture Readers. He was a firm but not narrow Sabbatarian, noting the ways in which proper observance of Sunday provided rest and refreshment for the body and soul, the opportunity for family and more general social intercourse and, above all, occasion for worship. He did, however, oppose the Sunday opening of the Crystal Palace in 1852. Elliott issued his own hymn-book in 1834. It passed through many editions and included some of his own pieces and some by his wife, but none has remained in general use.

BIBLIOGRAPHY
Al. Cant., II.ii: 405
J. Bateman, *The Life of the Rev. Henry Venn Elliott* (London, 1868)
DNB

ARTHUR POLLARD

Ellis, Robert [Cynddelw] (b. Llanrhaeadr, Powys, North Wales, 3 Feb. 1812; d. Llangedwyn, Powys, Wales, 19 Aug. 1875). Welsh Baptist minister. The youngest son of Robert and Elizabeth Ellis, he inherited his mother's literary interest. During his early years he cultivated his poetic ability which led to later fame at eisteddfodau. After conversion and baptism he proceeded to the ministerial school at Llansilin and was ordained 5 May 1836 at Llanelian, Clwyd. His subsequent pastorates were Glyn Ceiriog, Clwyd, 1838–47, Sirhowy, Gwent, South Wales, 1847–62, and Caernarfon, North Wales, 1862–75. Cynddelw's wide interests included poetry, publishing, journalism, history and public lecturing, though his influence within the Welsh Baptist movement coincided with an increasing imprecision in doctrinal matters. He was elected president of the Welsh Baptist Union in 1873.

BIBLIOGRAPHY
DWB

D. DENSIL MORGAN

Ellis, William (b. County Down, Northern Ireland, 1780; d. Harbour Grace, Newfoundland, BNA, 21 September 1837). Methodist missionary and first chairman of the Methodist district of Newfoundland 1816–17. Born into a Methodist family, Ellis – after first serving as a class leader and local preacher – was ordained in 1808 and sent as an itinerant missionary to Conception and Trinity Bay harbours. Later he held pastorates in Brigus, Port de Grave, and Harbour Grace. He was buried in the latter community.

BIBLIOGRAPHY
DNLB
ENL
W. Wilson, *Newfoundland and its Missionaries* (Cambridge, MA, 1866): 181–2

HANS ROLLMANN

Ellis, William (b. London, 29 Aug. 1794; d. Hoddesdon, Hertfordshire, England, 9 June 1872). LMS missionary to the South Seas and Madagascar, and author. Born into modest economic and intellectual circumstances, Ellis led an extraordinarily productive and adventurous life. A gardener in early life, in 1815 he successfully applied for and was ordained as a candidate for the LMS. He left England 23 August 1816 bound for Tahiti. Ellis had studied as a printer in England and while on the island of Moorea, he produced a Tahitian speller (the first work printed on a Pacific island) followed by a catechism and a Tahitian version of the Book of Luke. Ellis is also credited with the conception and printing of a legal code in 1822 for the island of Huahine, protecting that island against undue domination by Pomare II of Tahiti.

Ellis left the Society Islands in 1822 for a visit to Hawaii. His knowledge of Tahitian enabled him to learn Hawaiian quickly and he was the first foreigner to preach to Hawaiians in their own language. Welcoming his abilities, ABCFM missionaries in Hawaii invited him to remain permanently. Ellis found himself informally adopted by Hawaiian royalty and served as a counsellor to Kamehameha II and as intermediary between foreigners and Hawaiians. In 1823 Ellis was a member of a pioneering missionary reconnaissance party to the island of Hawaii. The group conducted a month-long circuit of Hawaii and were the first foreigners to ascend the active volcano of Kilauea. The health of Ellis's wife Mary Mercy failed and with his family he returned to England. In 1829 he published the two volume work, *Polynesian Researches*, a classic among early ethnological studies of the Pacific Islands.

His first wife having died in 1835, Ellis in 1837 married Sarah Stickney, a woman whose literary achievements were significant in their own right. Ellis accepted the important post of foreign secretary to the LMS, and days of high drama in the active mission field, this time in Madagascar, were yet to come. Under the hostile regime of Queen Ranavalona, Malagasy Christians were persecuted and LMS missionaries who had gained a foothold in Madagascar were expelled. In a series of visits to

Madagascar from 1852 to 1865, Ellis succeeded in re-installing the LMS and in re-establishing English influence. For his contributions, Ellis was named a fellow of the Royal Geographical Society. He published four books on Madagascar: *History of Madagascar* (1838), *Three Visits to Madagascar* (1858), *Madagascar Revisited* (1867), and *The Martyr Church of Madagascar* (1870).

BIBLIOGRAPHY
DNB
J. Ellis, *Life of William Ellis* (London, 1873)

NANCY J. MORRIS

Ellis, William Webb (b. Manchester, England, Nov. 1807; d. 24 Jan. 1872). Anglican clergyman. Ellis was the second son of James Ellis of Manchester and was educated at Rugby and Brasenose College, Oxford (matriculated 1825; BA 1829, MA 1831). Ellis was minister of St George's Albemarle Chapel in London from 1836 to 1855 and in 1843 was presented by the Marquess of Exeter to the rectorship of St Clement Danes, the Strand, London (which he held until 1855). The reporters for *The Times* informed their editor in 1844 that he was 'a very influential and popular clergyman. Albemarle Chapel has a most powerful congregation from the neighbourhood of Berkeley Square, and Mr Ellis is held in great repute by them. In St Clement Danes he has shewn himself a most active parochial minister. V. Low Church – Abhors Tractarian heresy.' From 1855 until his death he was Rector of Laver Magdalen, Essex. Ellis wrote on biblical prophecy and on what he perceived were the errors of Roman Catholicism.

BIBLIOGRAPHY
Al. Ox.
W. W. Ellis, *A Concise View of Prophecy Which Relates to the Messiah* (London, 1832)
—, *Sermons* (London, 1838)
—, *Dangerous Errors of Romanism* (London, 1853)
Bodleian Library, Oxford, 'The Principal Clergy of London . . . prepared for Mr Delane, edtr. of *The Times*', 1844, Add. manuscript *c*.290

DONALD M. LEWIS

Elton, Sir Abraham (b. Bristol, England, 23 March 1755; d. Clevedon, Somerset, England, 23 Feb 1842). Clergyman and mine owner. He was the son of Abraham Isaac Elton, Baronet, of Clevedon Court, Somerset. Elton was educated at Eton and Queen's College, Oxford (BA 1775) and at Christ's College, Cambridge (MA 1778). He studied law and was admitted to the Middle Temple in London on 9 December 1771. He succeeded to the baronetcy on 5 February 1790. He married: (1) Elizabeth (died 1822), the eldest daughter of Sir John Durbin, Mayor of Bristol on 7 November 1776; (2) Mary, daughter of Lord Fortrose on 29 March 1823.

He was ordained about 1783 and served as curate to THOMAS ROBINSON at Leicester. He later served as lecturer at West Bromwich, Staffordshire and was chairman of the Somerset Quarter Sessions. In 1800 he became entangled in the 'Blagdon controversy', publishing several impassioned attacks on Mr Bere and defending HANNAH MORE. In turn, he was attacked by the *Anti-Jacobin Review*. Elton was, according to one account, 'admirable in rank and wealth but a man of some timidity who had to be whipped on'.

BIBLIOGRAPHY
Al. Cant.
Al. Ox.
F. K. Brown, *Fathers of the Victorians* (Cambridge, 1961)
Clergy List (1841)
Eton College Register
Complete Baronetage

GRAYSON CARTER

Elven, Cornelius (b. Bury St Edmunds, Suffolk, England, 12 Feb. 1797; d. Bury St Edmunds, England, 10 Aug. 1873). Baptist minister. Brought up an Independent, Elven became a Baptist through reading the New Testament. In 1823 he became pastor of the Baptist congregation in his home town, remaining till he died and increasing the membership from 40 to 600. The huge preacher with his homely, practical sermons was also popular in the Suffolk villages as an evangelist. He wrote the hymn 'With broken heart and contrite sigh'. Elven stood firmly in the evangelical Calvinist tradition of ANDREW FULLER and became the leader of 'open communion' Baptists in Suffolk. C. H. SPURGEON was among his friends. When he died, he was mourned by Christians beyond his own denomination.

BIBLIOGRAPHY
The Baptist Handbook (1874)
A. J. Klaiber, *The Story of the Suffolk Baptists* (London, 1931)
POBC (1988)
The Freeman (22 August 1873)

E. F. CLIPSHAM

Embury, Philip (b. Co. Limerick, Ballingrane, Ireland, 1728; d. Salem, Albany Co., NY, BNA, 1773). Irish pioneer of American Methodism. Philip was a carpenter who, after his conversion in 1752, became a class leader and local preacher. He married into a local Palatine family and emigrated with them to America in 1760. In New York he became a schoolteacher. In October 1766 his cousin, BARBARA HECK, alarmed by the increasing worldliness of their family and neighbours, persuaded him to resume his preaching. This led to the founding of the John Street society. Early in the 1770s the Hecks and Emburys left the city and settled on a farm in Albany County on the Hudson River. From there Philip established societies in Albany and Washington Counties. He died suddenly of pleurisy in 1773.

BIBLIOGRAPHY

F. Baker, *From Wesley to Asbury* (Durham, NC, 1976)

E. S. Bucke, ed., *A History of American Methodism*, 3 vols (Nashville, TN, 1963)

JOHN A. VICKERS

Emmons, Nathanael (b. East Haddam, CT, BNA, 20 April 1745; d. Franklin, MA, USA, 23 Sept. 1840). New England Congregational minister and theologian. After graduating from Yale College in 1767, Emmons studied theology with NATHAN STRONG and JOHN SMALLEY, two Connecticut New Divinity ministers. Licensed to preach in 1769, he spent four years as an itinerant minister in New York and New Hampshire and then became pastor in Wrentham (later Franklin), Massachusetts, in 1773. He served the church until 1827, when poor health required him to retire.

During his long pastorate he achieved an impressive record as a teacher, revivalist, missionary advocate, and theologian. He trained nearly ninety students for the ministry and led revivals of religion in his church in 1784, 1794, and 1809. He was a founder of the Massachusetts Missionary Society (1799), serving as its first president for 12 years and editing the *Massachusetts Missionary Magazine* between 1803 and 1808.

But it was in his novel extension of the New Divinity, or Consistent Calvinist theology, of late eighteenth- and early nineteenth-century New England that Emmons had his greatest influence. He attempted to reconcile moral depravity and free will through the so-called 'Exercise Scheme'. He stressed that sin was not a natural inheritance from Adam but an act of will, based on the exercise of freedom of choice. Though he acknowledged that God influenced the heart in producing volitions, Emmons held that the individual was still free to exercise the will and make moral choices. In fact, regeneration became an ongoing process of 'moral exercises' as the individual continually, and freely, chose good over evil.

BIBLIOGRAPHY

E. A. Park, *Memoirs of Nathanael Emmons* (Boston, MA, 1861)

JOSEPH CONFORTI

Emory, John (b. Spaniard's Neck, Queen Annes County, MD, USA, 11 April 1789; d. nr Reisterstown, MD, USA, 16 December 1835). Methodist bishop. Emory's parents were Robert and Frances Thomas Emory. This strongly Methodist family hosted Methodist worship services and circuit riders. Nevertheless, when Emory left the law (his father's chosen profession for him), his father opposed the change with all his might, even refusing all communication for two years.

Emory attended local schools until he was ten, when, much to his mother's pain, his father placed him in schools away from home. At the close of 1803 he transferred to Washington College, graduating in 1804. The next year he began to read law under Richard Tilghman

Earle of Centreville, Maryland. Emory was admitted to the Bar in July, 1808. Since 1806 he had been a deeply committed Christian and was licensed to preach sometime between 1808 and 1810. He decided in October 1809 to leave law practice and was received into the Philadelphia Conference on trial in April, 1810.

Emory travelled circuits for only three years. Then for ten years he served station (single church) appointments. He was still a deacon when appointed to the first of these, Academy (later Union), Philadelphia. In 1818 he was transferred to the Baltimore Conference and was appointed to Foundry Church, Washington, DC. From the beginning his health stood in the way of full-time, long-term service in the rigours of itinerancy. In 1823–4 he was in the supernumerary relationship because of health.

Emory did not return to pastoral work. The 1824 General Conference elected him assistant agent of the Book Concern, the church's book publishing and marketing agency. In 1828 he was promoted to general book agent. Four years later he was elected bishop. He also edited *Methodist Quarterly Review* from 1830 to 1832.

Recognition of Emory's leadership was early and sustained. Except for 1824 he was a delegate to every General Conference from 1816 to 1832. Though not serving in a full-time, paid position he was named general corresponding secretary for general missions and for the establishment of schools among native American tribes by the 1820 General Conference. This conference also sent him as the official Methodist Episcopal representative to the 1820 Wesleyan Methodist Conference in Britain. Despite his non-delegate status, the 1824 General Conference, which he served as secretary, came within six votes of electing him bishop before he withdrew his name after the second ballot, and did elect him assistant book agent. He declined offers of the presidency of four educational institutions: the soon to be opened Wesleyan Seminary in New York City (1816); Madison College; Allegheny College; and Randolph Macon College (all around 1831). He was instrumental in the organization of Wesleyan University and New York University.

Emory was prominent in the major Methodist Episcopal controversies of his quarter century ministry. As pastor in Philadelphia in 1814 he notified the African Methodist congregation he could no longer serve them because they would not abide by the *Discipline* with regard to pastoral appointments and authority.

His failure to be elected to the 1824 General Conference was owing to his support of one of the major reforms being called for by the later Methodist Protestants. He was on the special committee of the 1820 Conference which devised a plan of episcopal nomination and annual conference election of presiding elders. Two years later at the Baltimore Annual Conference he rebutted Bishop WILLIAM MCKENDREE's address opposing this idea. He did not, however, approve lay delegation to annual and general Conferences. He was the church's chief literary defender of episcopacy in the latter 1820s. On the great human issue of the day Emory opposed both slavery and abolitionism. He wanted slavery to be ended by constitutional means and in a Christian spirit.

His published works centred on controversies of doctrine and polity. First came (1817) 'A Reply' and 'A Further Reply' to Episcopal Presiding Bishop William White's *Objections Against the Position of a Personal Assurance of the Pardon of Sin, by a Direct Communication of the Holy Spirit*. A decade later the major writing of his career was in response to ALEXANDER MCCAINE's Methodist Protestant manifesto *The History and Mystery of Methodist Episcopacy*. Emory's *Defence of Our Fathers, and of the Original Organization of the Methodist Episcopal Church* was entered on the syllabus for men preparing for Methodist ordination. In 1829 McCaine carried the debate further with *A Defence of the Truth*. Emory's 'Reply' appeared in several issues of the *Methodist Quarterly Review* in 1830. After the Annual Conferences of 1835 Emory began a tract, 'The Episcopal Controversy Reviewed'. Intended as an apology for USA Methodism's episcopal polity on the bases of scripture and ancient tradition, it was unfinished at his death and was published by his son in 1838. He also edited the first American complete and standard edition of the *Works* of JOHN WESLEY (7 vols, 1833).

Emory married twice. Caroline Sellers whom he wed on 12 October 1813, died in March, 1816, not yet twenty years old. They had no children. On 12 May 1818 he married Ann Wright. She and five of their six children survived him. At the time of Emory's death the eldest of these was just of age and the youngest but a few weeks old.

Emory was the first Methodist Episcopal bishop since THOMAS COKE to hold an earned academic degree. While the Methodists valued a trained ministry, their model was apprenticeship in itinerant evangelism, not formal academic preparation for ordained ministry in long tenure pastorates. Ironically, had he not been educated for the law Emory would have missed the intellectual formation that won him such rapid advancement in the Methodist connexion. In 1822 St John's College, Maryland, gave him an honorary MA. His *alma mater* Washington College made him DD *honoris causa* in 1823. Emory's fields of scholarly expertise were as follows: Hebrew, Greek, Latin, and some French; natural, international, common, and ecclesiastical law; history; literature; logic; moral philosophy; theology, and the Bible. While living in Baltimore he attended medical lectures, but science and mathematics were not his areas of accomplishment.

In the episcopacy Emory's chief concern was for qualified and consistent leadership. He promoted training for class leaders, local (non-itinerating) preachers, and itinerants. For the latter he stressed the church's course of study designed by the bishops. He worked for uniform administration of the *Discipline* by the bishops, and proposed they gather annually to coordinate their ministry of general superintendency.

Emory died in the evening of 16 December 1835 from a skull fracture suffered that morning when his carriage went off the road between his home and Baltimore. Otherwise, he might have been expected to live well into the middle decades of the century. If so, he would have had a major influence on subsequent USA Methodist history. His leadership ability in service to his strong-willed advancement of church order and ministerial training would have brought the tradition of a learned ministry more rapidly into acceptance in USA Methodism.

BIBLIOGRAPHY
AAP
DAB
R. E. Emory, *The Life of the Rev. John Emory, DD* (New York, 1841)

CHARLES W. BROCKWELL, JR

Emory, Robert (b. Philadelphia, PA, USA, 29 July 1814; d. Baltimore, MD, USA, 18 May 1848). American Methodist Episcopal minister and academic. The eldest son of MEC Bishop JOHN EMORY, he from an early age displayed an inquisitive and disciplined mind. With the patient encouragement of his father he worked to attain a place at Columbia College (later Columbia University) in New York City. Emory graduated at the top of his class in 1831 at the age of seventeen; he then apprenticed in a Baltimore law firm. His conversion occurred in response to an altar call at a Quarterly Meeting on the Montgomery Methodist circuit.

In 1834, at only twenty years of age, he was made Professor of Languages at Dickinson College. Yet even during these years, as a former student recalled, Emory shared that he was having 'most bitter spiritual experiences', and only 'long after he had become a member of the Church . . . found himself able to come out of the shadow into the sun' (*AAP* 7: 830). This event evidently happened around 1839, for in that year he resigned his position to enter the ministry, being appointed on trial to the Harford circuit, Baltimore Conference. Between 1839 and 1845 he served two stations in Baltimore (he was officially admitted as a member of the conference in 1841), becoming Presiding Elder of the Carlisle District in 1845.

During this time he was not only active in ministry but was also in touch with the academic world, serving as Acting President of Dickinson College from 1842–44 while its president, Dr Durbin, was in Europe. In 1841 he wrote what is still the standard biography of his father, *The Life of Reverend John Emory*. He also did much valuble historical work in producing *The History of the Discipline* (1843), a collation and organization of Methodist law which was much better indexed and arranged than its predecessors. In July 1845 he returned to the academic world on a full-time basis when he was elected President of Dickinson College. The following year he was granted a DD degree by Columbia, and was a delegate to the EA conference held in London. His fruitful career was cut short by his untimely death from tuberculosis in 1848. He left a wife and two young children. Emory insisted on his deathbed that the true measure of the religious character was found not in what one said at death, but what one *did* in life.

Emory was extremely well-respected for what he did in ministry and in academia. His scholarship was exceptional, and his leadership of Dickinson was praised. In the words of a contemporary, he was a 'sure friend, a wise counsellor, a thorough teacher, an earnest and instructive preacher, a faithful pastor, he was everywhere the same steady, reliable man' (AAP 7: 831). His colleague at Dickinson, JOHN MCCLINTOCK, spoke of him as 'the purest and best of all the men I have yet known on earth'.

BIBLIOGRAPHY
AAP 7: 828–831
EWM

KENNETH N. PEARSON

Entwisle, Joseph (b. Manchester, England, 15 April 1767; d. Tadcaster, England, 6 Nov. 1841). Wesleyan minister. Entwisle came of Presbyterian and High Church stock. In his early years he several times attempted to run away to sea. He began preaching at 16 and following correspondence with JOHN WESLEY his name appeared on the 1784 stations; but because of an apprenticeship he did not become an itinerant until 1787. Two sons by his first marriage, Joseph and William, also became ministers.

He was appointed secretary of the first Missionary Committee in 1804, was twice president of the Wesleyan Conference (1812 and 1825), and in 1834 became first house governor of the Theological Institution at Hoxton, resigning in 1839 because of ill health. His publications included a memoir of JOHN PAWSON (prefixed to Pawson's *Sermons*, Leeds, 1809) and works on inspiration and prayer.

BIBLIOGRAPHY
DNB
J. Entwisle, *Memoir of the Rev. Joseph Entwisle by his son* (London, 1848)

JOHN A. VICKERS

Equiano, Olaudah (b. Benin, West Africa, 1745; d. London, 1797). African Christian and early abolitionist. Kidnapped into slavery at age 11, Equiano was renamed Gustavus Vassa by a ship's captain. Buying his freedom in 1766, he travelled the Atlantic and was the first black to explore the Arctic. He was baptized at St Margaret's Church, Westminster, in February 1759, but it was not until 1774 that he had an evangelical conversion meditating on Acts 4: 12.

In 1779 he tried unsuccessfully through the Bishop of London to become a missionary to Africa. Six years later he travelled from England formally to thank Quakers of America for their antislavery witness and education of Africans. He was temporarily commissary of stores for a resettlement expedition to Sierra Leone in 1787. Two years later he published his autobiography, which influenced JOHN WESLEY, WILLIAM WILBERFORCE and GRANVILLE SHARP, and which stands as a prototype for slave narratives. Equiano's *Life* went through 36 editions in English, Dutch, Russian and German by 1857. Following a death bed visit from Granville Sharp, Equiano died, leaving his widow, Susanna, and one surviving daughter.

BIBLIOGRAPHY
A. Bontemps, ed, *Great Slave Narratives* (Boston, MA, 1969)
A. Costanzo, *Surprizing Narrative* (New York, 1987)
M. W. Starling, *The Slave Narrative* (Boston, MA, 1981)
C. T. Davis and H. L. Gates, Jr, eds, *The Slave's Narrative* (New York, 1985)

JEANNE KNEPPER AND WILL GRAVELY

Erhardt, Johann Christian (b. Wismar, Mecklenburg, Sweden [now Germany], 24 Oct. 1718; d. Labrador, 1752). Moravian missionary and trading agent to Labrador. Erhardt was a German sailor who became a Moravian after contact with Moravian missionaries in the West Indies. He set sail from London in 1752 to establish a trade and mission post in Labrador. His trade with the Inuit was initially successful, but on one final trading expedition from his mission post at Nisbet's Harbour (probably near what is now Makkovik) to Davis Inlet before returning to England for the winter, Erhardt and six crewmen were murdered.

Erhardt, who had acquired some Inuit words from missionaries to Greenland, was probably unable to make his intentions for the mission clear to the Inuit. They regarded him as other European traders, whom they often plundered. JENS HAVEN's subsequent attempt to establish a mission in Labrador succeeded because he could communicate fluently with the Inuit and was not involved with the trade.

BIBLIOGRAPHY
DCB
Kölbing
M. Rollmann, 'The Role of Language in the Moravian Mission, to Eighteenth Century Labrador', *Unitas Fratrum*, 34 (1993): 49–64

MARCELLA ROLLMANN

Erhardt, John James (b. Bonningheim, Württemburg, Germany, *c.* 1821; d. *c.* 1904). CMS missionary in East Africa and India. After training at the Basel Seminary and from 1846 at the CMS college at Islington, Erhardt received Anglican orders (deacon 1847, priest 1848). In December 1848 he was sent with Johannes Wagner to Rabai in East Africa in response to a call from J. L. KRAPF in 1848. Wagner soon died of fever. Erhardt survived and opened a large station at Rabai. He then travelled with Krapf. As a result of information about Lake Nyassa, gained from traders, and work in Usambaru 1853–5 (when ill health drove him home), through his colleague JOHANNES REBMANN, he published a map of East and Central Africa (Calver Missionsblatt, 1 October 1855; reproduced in the *History of the Church Missionary Society*, II: 136). This led to Speke and Buxton's historic exploration in 1857, which opened up central Africa. Erhardt's great inland sea was what is now known as Lake Victoria and Lake Tanganyika. Speke followed the map into Uganda and found the source of the Nile.

In August 1856 Erhardt married Maria Sophia Deerr (daughter of W. J. DEERR) who died 8 April 1891. In September 1856 Erhardt was sent to India and from 1857 he was stationed at Bhagulpur, from 1860 at Benares, and from 1865 at Lucknow. He then spent two years in England (February 1867 to November 1869) before returning to rebuild the orphanage at Sekundra (from 1870). He revived the famous Bhagalpur press, though it was less profitable than formerly. He also did exemplary service during the famines of 1874 and 1877. He looked after the famous 'wolf boy' 1877–95, though he could not teach him to speak. The episode is thought to have inspired Kipling's Mowgli stories.

BIBLIOGRAPHY

D. T. B[arry], *CMS Register of Missionaries and Native Clergy* (privately printed) (London, 1906)
M. E. Gibbs, *The Anglican Church in India* (Delhi, 1972)
E. Stock, *The History of the Church Missionary Society*, II (London, 1899)

E. M. JACKSON AND DONALD M. LEWIS

Erskine, Lady Anne Agnes (b. 1739; d. London, 5 Oct. 1804). Patron. The eldest daughter of HENRY DAVID ERSKINE, tenth earl of Buchan, she was the older sister of HENRY ERSKINE, Lord Advocate of Scotland. As a young woman she moved with her father to Bath, England, for his health. There they attended the newly opened chapel of Lady HUNTINGDON (1765), and were converted to Methodism. After the earl's death in 1767, Lady Anne spent increasingly longer periods with Lady Huntingdon. For the last few years of the Countess's life, they lived together in Spa Fields chapel house in London. At that time she wrote letters on behalf of the Countess.

In a will made a few months before her death Lady Huntingdon devised all her chapels in trust to the Reverend THOMAS HAWEIS and his wife, Lady Anne, and JOHN LLOYD of Swansea. The Countess had failed to make any permanent provision for her Connexion, and made these arrangements (which could have been overturned by her surviving daughter) as an expedient for its continuation. The four trustees decided that Lady Anne should live at the chapel house and undertake the responsibility of providing itinerant ministers for the chapels.

Lady Anne had little income of her own, and Lady Huntingdon's had died with her. She did not travel to the other chapels as Lady Huntingdon had done for most of her life, and she was dependent on grants of money, principally from the Spa Fields Committee, for the maintenance of ministers. As a result of these changes some congregations chose to leave the Connexion, and Lady Anne's principal task was to find supplies for the larger chapels. Despite this the Connexion probably continued to flourish in most places.

Despite a long and painful illness Lady Anne tried to fill her friend's place, and spent many hours writing letters and meeting people. She was buried at Bunhill Fields, and succeeded as principal trustee of the Connexion by Reverend Dr JOHN FORD. It was not until after his death in 1807 that a legal trust was created for the Connexion.

BIBLIOGRAPHY

Cheshunt College archives, Cambridge, and the National Library of Wales, original letters
Deeds of Trust and Like Documents relating to the Countess of Huntingdon's Connexion (London, 1874)
A. Fergusson, *The Honourable Henry Erskine, Lord Advocate for Scotland* (Edinburgh, 1822)
E. Welch, ed., *Cheshunt College* (Hertfordshire Records Society, 1990)

EDWIN WELCH

Erskine, Ebenezer (b. Dryburgh, Scotland, 22 June 1680; d. Stirling, Scotland, 2 June 1754). Father of Scottish Secession Church. The fourth son of the Reverend Henry Erskine (Areskine) by Margaret Halcro, he graduated MA from Edinburgh University in 1697, then became chaplain and tutor for the family of John, Earl of Rothes. He was licensed by Kirkcaldy presbytery in February and ordained at Portmoak 22 September 1703. The spiritual distress of his wife, Alison Turpie, was instrumental in his conversion about four years later, and his ministry acquired a more evangelical tone. After Alison died, he married Grace, sister of ALEXANDER WEBSTER of Edinburgh (1724). In 1731 he moved to the influential church at Stirling.

Erskine figured in several public controversies. In 1712 ministers in Scotland were required to sign the Oath of Abjuration against the Stuart 'pretender'. The oath provided that the monarch must belong to the Church of England. Since that implied that episcopacy was scriptural, a third of the clergy, including Erskine, abstained, but he conspicuously demonstrated his loyalty to the house of Hanover in the rebellions of 1715 and 1745.

When the General Assembly compromised the free offer of the gospel in 1717, James Hog responded by reprinting *The Marrow of Modern Divinity* (E. Fisher, 1646). The *Marrow* was condemned in 1720, so in 1721 Erskine authored the final draft of a protest. This 'Representation' was signed by several ministers who were then censured by the Assembly in 1722.

Erskine opposed patronage when it was restored by Parliament in 1712, and initially few ministers were settled without popular consent. When the General

Assembly entirely removed congregational participation in the selection of ministers (1732), Erskine decried the act in a sermon before the Synod of Stirling. He was rebuked by the synod, and by order of the assembly he was deposed in 1733 along with three supporters (WILLIAM WILSON, ALEXANDER MONCRIEFF, James Fisher). On 6 December the four constituted themselves a seceding presbytery. In 1734 the Assembly revoked the act and reinstated the Seceders, but Erskine refused reconciliation without a change in the Assembly's principles, so in 1740 the seceding ministers (then eight) were finally deposed. Numerous requests for an evangelical ministry caused the Secession to grow rapidly. It joined the Relief church in 1847 (see THOMAS GILLESPIE).

Unfortunately, the young denomination was rent by strife over the revised Burgess Oath. In 1744 burgesses in Edinburgh, Glasgow and Perth were required to pledge support for the true religion as authorized by the laws of the realm. (Only burgesses could exercise the franchise and certain other privileges.) Erskine and his brother RALPH ERSKINE maintained that they had seceded from the church courts, but not from the church itself. Moncrieff and about half of the secession opposed the oath, withdrew to form the 'anti-burgher synod' (1747), and excommunicated the Erskines and their supporters. The opposition included a son-in-law of Ebenezer and a son of Ralph. The breach was not healed until 1820.

Though not as numerous as Ralph's, Ebenezer's valuable sermons have been frequently reprinted. In an age when Enlightenment-influenced 'Moderatism' threatened the vibrancy of faith in the Church of Scotland, the secession of the Erskines helped to preserve evangelical life both in their own synod and in the national church.

SELECT WRITINGS

E. Erskine, *The Whole Works . . . [with a] Memoir of the Author by D. Fraser* 3 vols (Edinburgh, 1826)

BIBLIOGRAPHY

DNB

Fasti, 4

D. Fraser, *The Life and Diary of the Reverend Ebenezer Erskine* (Edinburgh, 1831)

J. Harper, J. Eadie, and W. Lindsay, *Lives of Ebenezer Erskine, William Wilson, and Thomas Gillespie* (Edinburgh, 1849)

J. Ker, *The Erskines* (Edinburgh, 1881)

A. R. MacEwen, *The Erskines* (Edinburgh, 1900)

JOHN K. LA SHELL

Erskine, Henry (b. Edinburgh, 1 Nov. 1746; d. Ammondell, Scotland, 8 Oct. 1817). Lord Advocate of Scotland and MP. Of Covenanting stock, Erskine was born into an especially pious and illustrious family. He was the second son of HENRY DAVID ERSKINE, the tenth earl of Buchan (who for a time employed HENRY VENN as his chaplain), and of Agnes Steuart, daughter of a Solicitor-General for Scotland. His grandfather was David Erskine, the ninth

Earl of Buchan (and fourth Baron Cardross), whose great-aunt was the wife of Colonel JAMES GARDINER. David Erskine was an aficionado at Bath of GEORGE WHITEFIELD and Selina, the Countess of HUNTINGTON. Henry Erskine's sister, Lady ANNE ERSKINE, was Lady Huntington's executrix and successor as 'the female bishop'.

Educated at Edinburgh and Glasgow universities, Erskine studied law, and in 1768 was called to the Scottish Bar. Influenced by his family's English connection, he had entertained an early ambition to be ordained in the Church of England. This he set aside yet remained privately devoted to the English prayer-book.

In his day Erskine was the pre-eminent leader of the Scottish Whig party, as Lord Advocate (1783, 1806), and dean of the Faculty of Advocates (1785–95). He was briefly MP for Haddington (1806) and for Dumfries (1806–7). Because of his refusal to countenance treason and sedition bills, he lost re-election as dean of the Faculty of Advocates. It was an episode celebrated in Whig history, his few supporters in the election becoming immortalized as the 'thirty-eight'.

Reflecting the close identification in Scotland of church and state, and of Whiggism with Church of Scotland evangelicalism, Erskine played a considerable role in church councils. A man gifted with a striking physical presence and extraordinary debating skills, he made an early mark at the Church General Assembly. In 1779 his association with the 'Highflyers' or 'Wildmen' (evangelicals) cost him the church procuratorship in an assembly dominated by the Moderate party.

For the many years of the eighteenth century when the Whigs were out of power their cause in Scotland was kept alive by a small band of advocates and leading members of the evangelical party in the Church of Scotland. As the acknowledged head of the former, and the most generally respected layman in the latter, Erskine's influence extended far beyond what his relatively meagre official accomplishments might imply. Prior to the advent of THOMAS CHALMERS, no other Scottish evangelical, besides Sir HENRY MONCRIEFF, was as widely respected or more generally influential in Scottish public life. For generations of Scots he stood as a model of political rectitude and exemplary piety that in no small measure contributed to Scottish evangelicalism's intellectual and social respectability.

BIBLIOGRAPHY

DNB

A. Fergusson, *The Honourable Henry Erskine, Lord Advocate for Scotland* (Edinburgh, 1822)

G. W. T. Omond, *The Lord Advocates of Scotland*, 2 vols, I (Edinburgh, 1882): 163–74

JONATHAN BURKE CUTMORE

Erskine, Henry David (b. Edinburgh, 17 April 1710 (Old Style); d. Walcot, near Bath, Somerset, England, 1 Dec. 1767). Scottish nobleman. He was the tenth earl of Buchan, son of David Erskine, the ninth earl and Lord

Cardross, by Francis Fairfax. In 1739 he married Agnes Steuart, an accomplished lady who tutored her own children. He served as Grand Master of the freemasons in Scotland (1745–6). Because of declining health, he moved to Walcot near Bath with his daughter Lady ANNE ERSKINE, where the Countess of HUNTINGDON soon opened a chapel (1765). He joined her circle and under the preaching of GEORGE WHITEFIELD and his associates, was converted.

He made two notable contributions to the evangelical cause. First he was a forthright witness to his evangelical conversion and his funeral service was conducted on a Sunday by George Whitefield at Lady Huntingdon's chapel. Nearly 300 of the nobility and gentry received tickets to be admitted and a number of them dated their conversion to this event. Public services and preaching continued twice a day during the following week through Friday morning. Second, the earl benefited the evangelical cause through his offspring, Lady ANNE, and HENRY ERSKINE.

BIBLIOGRAPHY
A. Fergusson, *The Honourable Henry Erskine, Lord Advocate for Scotland* (Edinburgh, 1822)
Peerage
[A. C. H. Seymour], *The Life and Times of Selina, Countess of Huntingdon* (London, 1840–1)

JOHN K. LA SHELL

Erskine, Colonel John (b. Cardross, Perthshire, Scotland, 30 March 1662; d. Edinburgh, Scotland, 13 Jan. 1743). MP and lay leader in the Church of Scotland. He was the third son by his second wife of David Erskine, second Lord (Baron) Cardross. He studied law at London and Glasgow, but fled in 1685 to Holland where he studied at Utrecht and entered the service of the Prince of Orange. After the revolution he was appointed Lieutenant-Governor of Stirling Castle and attained the rank of Lieutenant-Colonel. In 1700 he purchased Cardross (thereafter Carnock). He was MP for Stirling (1702–7) and in the first Parliament of the United Kingdom (1707–8). He supported the evangelical party in the Church of Scotland, representing Dunfermline as an elder in the General Assembly (1704–42). He actively opposed the religious clause in the 1712 Oath of Abjuration. In 1735 he was appointed, along with two previous moderators of the General Assembly, to request Parliament to repeal patronage. For other evangelical connections *see* RALPH ERSKINE, THOMAS GILLESPIE, his grandson, JOHN ERSKINE, DD and his great grandson, THOMAS ERSKINE (1788–1870). His brother, Henry Erskine, third Lord Cardross, was the grandfather of HENRY DAVID ERSKINE, tenth Earl of Buchan, who in turn had three other offspring included in this volume.

BIBLIOGRAPHY
J. Erskine, *Journal of the Hon. John Erskine of Carnock, 1683–1687*, ed. Walter Macleod (Edinburgh, 1893)

JOHN K. LA SHELL

Erskine [of Carnock], **John** (b. Scotland, 2 June 1721; d. Edinburgh, 19 Jan. 1803). Leading eighteenth-century Scottish theologian. He was grandson of Colonel JOHN ERSKINE and the eldest son of John Erskine of Carnock, professor of Scots law, University of Edinburgh. A strong supporter and defender of the Cambuslang and Kilsyth revivals of 1742, he became a leader of the evangelical wing of the Church of Scotland and of the anti-patronage Popular party at the General Assembly. He was minister of Kirkintilloch (1744–53), Culross (1753–8), Edinburgh (New Greyfriars) (1758–67), and Edinburgh (Old Greyfriars) (1767–1803). In his last charge, Old Greyfriars, which was a collegiate parish, he was the colleague of principal William Robertson, the leader of the Moderate party which supported patronage and whose theology was much influenced by the ideals of Christian Stoic philosophy. Despite their different theological and ecclesiastical positions, the two remained on amicable terms. He corresponded with JONATHAN EDWARDS of New England, and was a leading member of the international evangelical letter-writing network involving Edwards, PHILIP DODDRIDGE, JOHN GILLIES of Glasgow, and others. He also actively propagated the cause of foreign and home missions.

Throughout his life, Erskine maintained a stream of publications, in addition to numerous sermons the most important being *Theological Dissertations* (Edinburgh, 1765 and 1808), which included his *Dissertation on the Nature of Christian Faith*; *Discourses on Several Occasions* (Edinburgh, 1798–1804). He also edited at least twenty publications, chiefly the works of Jonathan Edwards and other American divines.

In his *Dissertation on the Nature of Christian Faith*, Erskine used contemporary ideas about the nature of knowledge and the operation of the will to resolve problems posed by earlier writers who defined faith in terms which looked suspiciously like a mere intellectual assent. He defined clearly and precisely the role of the intellect, the senses, and the will. He differentiated, for the first time in the Scotland of his time, between a faith requiring an intellectual assent and one which was a 'saving faith'. This perception was perhaps the most essential prerequisite for the development of the fully-fledged evangelicalism which was to be the hallmark of the nineteenth-century Scottish Evangelical revival.

BIBLIOGRAPHY
DNB
Fasti, 1
J. MacLeod, *Scottish Theology in Relation to Church History Since the Reformation* (Edinburgh, 1946 and 1974)
S. O'Brien, 'A Transatlantic Community of Saints: the Great Awakening and the First Evangelical Network, 1735–55', *AHR* 91, 4 (1986): 811–32
Scots Magazine, 4–65 (1742–1803)

JOHN R. MCINTOSH

Erskine, Ralph (b. Monilaws, Scotland, 15 March 1685; d. Dunfermline, Fife, Scotland, 6 November

1752). Scottish seceding minister. The fifth son of the Reverend Henry Erskine (1624–96) by his second wife, Margaret Halcro, Ralph dated his conversion to the dying exhortations of his father. He graduated from the University of Edinburgh MA in 1704, then served as tutor to the children of Colonel JOHN ERSKINE (1705–11). He was licensed to preach in 1709 and ordained to the second charge at Dunfermline on 7 August 1711. On the death of his colleague (1716), Erskine transferred to the first charge. After considerable difficulty, the congregation prevailed over the heritors, and James Wardlaw received the second charge in 1718.

Erskine figured in several public controversies. He refused the Oath of Abjuration; opposed the patronage system; and was condemned by the General Assembly during the *Marrow* controversy. When his brother EBENEZER ERSKINE, and three others were deposed in 1733, Ralph continued to hold Communion with them. After much soul-searching he joined the associate presbytery on 16 February 1737 and shared their final deposition in 1740. Erskine's adherents erected a new meeting house, but he preached once each sabbath in his old place. Wardlaw, who never joined the Secession, cooperated, but when he died in 1742, the presbytery forced Erskine to vacate the parish church.

Two controversies marred Erskine's last decade. His correspondence brought GEORGE WHITEFIELD to Scotland (summer 1741), but their harmony was disrupted when Whitefield would not acknowledge Presbyterianism as the only scriptural form of church government and refused to confine his labours to the Associate Presbytery. Extremist Seceders published highly inflammatory tracts. Erskine, though more moderate, harshly denounced the visions and emotionalism associated with the revival in his longest theological treatise, *Faith No Fancy* (Edinburgh, 1745). His final trial was excommunication by the 'anti-burgher' party of the Secession (including his son, John) for his taking the Burgess Oath. He was a fervent preacher and author of several controversial tracts. His collected sermons and his *Gospel Sonnets* have frequently been reprinted. For further details and bibliography see EBENEZER ERSKINE.

SELECT WRITINGS

R. Erskine, *The Sermons and Other Practical Works ... [with] an Account of the Author's Life*, 7 vols (London, 1863); reprint of vols 1–6 (Glasgow, 1991)

BIBLIOGRAPHY
DNB
Fasti, 5
D. Fraser, *The Life and Diary of the Reverend Ralph Erskine* (Edinburgh, 1834)

JOHN K. LA SHELL

Erskine, Thomas (b. London, 12 March 1788; d. Bournemouth, Hampshire, England, 9 Nov. 1864). Lawyer and judge. The fourth son (by his first wife) of Thomas Erskine, the first Lord Erskine, he was also the grandson of HENRY ERSKINE, MP and Lord Advocate for Scotland. He was educated at Harrow and entered Trinity College, Cambridge graduating as a peer's son in 1811 without residence or examination. In 1807 he entered Lincoln's Inn and was called to the Bar in 1813. He was commissioner for the Duchy of Cornwall, chief judge of the Bankruptcy Court (1831–42), and judge in the Court of Common pleas (1839–44).

In the early 1830s he joined the small body of relatively young evangelical Anglicans who were agitating for a test to exclude Unitarians from the BFBS. The unsuccessful agitators formed the Trinitarian Bible Society (TBS), which was almost wrecked by the conflict over Irvingism among its members. Those who remained with the society represented the non-charismatic wing, who nonetheless upheld much of the rest of EDWARD IRVING's pre-1830 agenda, namely Calvinism, the verbal inspiration of the Bible, Britain as a covenant nation, anti-Catholicism, sharp criticism of the older Claphamite leadership of Anglican evangelicalism and, in many cases, premillennialism. Erskine was made president of the TBS in 1832 and occupied this office until 1840.

In 1844 he resigned his judgeship because of ill health and lived for another twenty years as a virtual invalid. From 1852 he resided at Fir Grove, Eversley where his strong support of the rector, Charles Kingsley, would seem to indicate a move away from evangelicalism.

BIBLIOGRAPHY
A. J. Brown, *The Word of God Among all Nations* (London, 1981)
DNB

IAN S. RENNIE AND DONALD M. LEWIS

Erskine, Thomas (b. Linlathen, near Dundee, Scotland, 13 October 1788; d. Edinburgh, 20 March 1870). Scottish theological writer. The nephew of the leading Church of Scotland evangelical, JOHN ERSKINE and thus a distant cousin of THOMAS ERSKINE (1788–1864), he was brought up in the Scottish Episcopal Church, but his adult connections were chiefly with Scottish Congregationalism and the Church of Scotland. He trained as a lawyer at Edinburgh University, where JOHN FOSTER'S *Essays* effected his spiritual awakening. He then practised at the Bar for a few years, but in 1816 succeeded to the country estate of Linlathen, where self-sufficiency enabled him to devote his leisure to theology.

Erskine's first publication, *Remarks on the Internal Evidence for the Truth of Revealed Religion* (Edinburgh, 1820), was a work of apologetics, reflecting his own experience of religious doubt as a lawyer. The *Remarks* argued that Christianity's truth was demonstrated by its fulfilment of man's deepest moral needs. Its theology was that of a moderate Calvinist, and it proved very popular. His next full-length book, however, *The Unconditional Freeness of the Gospel* (Edinburgh, 1828) provoked widespread criticism for its doctrine of universal pardon – that all are in a state of forgiveness through Christ's death. Erskine became a close friend of JOHN MCLEOD CAMPBELL in 1828, and supported him during Campbell's trial and deposition from the Church of Scotland. Campbell's later

Christology is germinally present in Erskine's *The Brazen Serpent* (Edinburgh, 1831).

Erskine encountered EDWARD IRVING at this point, embracing his views on premillennialism, the gifts of the Spirit and Christ's fallen humanity. Erskine initially wrote in support of the 'Irvingite' charismatic movement, but abandoned it as a delusion in 1834. In 1837 he made a final break with Calvinism in his *The Doctrine of Election*. Erskine's later theology revolved around conscience as the touchstone of truth. He taught that God is the universal Father, who is educating all men into a filial relationship with Himself. From *c*. 1840, Erskine regarded the ultimate salvation of all as the essential gospel.

Erskine's influence was considerable. His circle of friends and admirers included J. McLeod Campbell, F. D. Maurice, Benjamin Jowett, Dean Stanley and ALEXANDER SCOTT. A man of rare charm and piety, Erskine's early writings (nothing was published in his lifetime after 1837) and personal influence contributed substantially to the liberalizing of nineteenth-century British theology. He is a classic case study in the evolution of a nineteenth-century British evangelical into a religious liberal.

BIBLIOGRAPHY
DNB
W. Hanna, *Letters of Thomas Erskine of Linlathen*, 2 vols (Edinburgh, 1877)
N. R. Needham, *Thomas Erskine of Linlathen* (Edinburgh, 1990)
J. Tulloch, *Movements of Religious Thought in Britain during the Nineteenth Century* (London, 1885)

N. R. NEEDHAM

Eskridge, Vernon (b. Westmoreland Co., VA, USA, 26 Oct. 1803; d. Portsmouth, VA, USA, 11 Sept. 1855). Leader of the Virginia Conference of the MEC. He united with the MEC in 1820 and soon became a class leader. In 1823 he received his exhorter's licence and in 1827 his licence to preach. Falling prey to ill health in 1851, he had to leave the itineracy, but became a successful navy chaplain on board the frigate *Cumberland* sailing in the Mediterranean. After three years in this ministry, he returned to Virginia where he died of yellow fever.

BIBLIOGRAPHY
CM

STEVE HARPER

Esson, Henry (b. Deeside, Scotland, 1793; d. Toronto, Canada West, 11 May 1853). Presbyterian minister in British North America and educator. The son of an Aberdeenshire farmer, Esson was baptized 7 March 1793. He was educated at Marischal College, Aberdeen (MA 1811) and ordained in 1817 by the presbytery of Aberdeen for service in the St Gabriel Street Church, Montreal. His early ministry in Montreal was distinctly non-evangelical and some have ascribed the formation of a Unitarian

Congregation in that city to the influence of his preaching. However, sometime in the late 1830s or early 1840s Esson became an evangelical and in 1843–4 played an important role in the formation of the Free Church in Canada. In 1844 he was appointed professor of literature and philosophy in the Free Church seminary in Toronto where he remained until his death.

BIBLIOGRAPHY
DCB, VIII
R. W. Vaudry, *The Free Church in Victorian Canada, 1844–1861* (Waterloo, Canada, 1989)

RICHARD W. VAUDRY

Eteson, Ralph (b. Knaresborough, Yorkshire, England, *c*. 1800). *Fl*. 1820s. CMS missionary to India. Eteson trained at the newly opened CMS school at Islington (London) in 1825 and was ordained (deacon 1826, priest 1827) by the Bishop of London. On 11 April 1828 he was sent with CHARLES FRIEND to Chunar in north India. In November 1830 he withdrew from the CMS to become East India Company chaplain to invalids at Chunar. He married Sarah Williams, who died in India on 29 October 1833.

BIBLIOGRAPHY
D. T. B[arry], *CMS Register of Missionaries and Native Clergy* (privately printed) (London, 1906)

DONALD M. LEWIS

Etheridge, John Wesley (b. Youngwoods, near Newport, Isle of Wight, 24 Feb. 1804; d. Camborne, England, 24 May 1866). Wesleyan minister and scholar. Of a studious disposition, he was privately educated. Like his father, whose literary and linguistic interests he shared, he became a Wesleyan local preacher and in 1827 was accepted for the ministry. His first appointment was to Hull circuit as assistant to Dr BEAUMONT, who was ill. Poor health forced him to superannuate in 1838 and he spent the next eight years on the European continent, especially in Caen and Paris. He was particularly proficient in Hebrew and Syriac and his studies in biblical and rabbinic literature brought him an honorary doctorate from Heidelberg in 1847.

Resuming his circuit work in 1846 he served in London, Bristol, Leeds, and several Cornish circuits, before dying while still in the active work at Camborne. His publications include standard biographies of ADAM CLARKE (London, 1858) and THOMAS COKE (1860) and several linguistic studies: *Horae Aramaicae* (pt 1 only, London, 1843); *Jerusalem and Tiberias . . . a survey of the Religious and Scholastic Learning of the Jews* (London, 1856); *The Targums of Onkelos and Jonathan ben Uzziel on the Pentateuch* (London, 1862, 1865); *Outline Lectures on the History of the Patriarchs* (London, 1871).

BIBLIOGRAPHY
DNB
J. Harris, *A Tear and a Floweret* (Truro, England, 1871)
T. Hughes, *Faithful Endurance and High Aim* (London, 1867)
Minutes of the Wesleyan Conference (1866)
T. Smith, 'Memoir' in *Outline Lectures on the History of the Patriarchs* (London, 1871)

JOHN A. VICKERS

Ettwein, John (b. Freudenstadt, Würtemberg, Germany, 29 June 1721; d. Bethlehem, PA, USA, 2 Jan. 1802). Moravian missionary and Bishop of Moravian Church in North America. As the child of two persecuted families, John Ettwein came from humble circumstances and was converted to the Moravian cause in 1739. In 1746 Ettwein was ordained a deacon and appointed to churches in Germany, Holland, and England. Having learned English, he was thought qualified to serve in America and was sent in 1754.

In America, Ettwein served as an itinerant evangelist throughout the colonies and in 1763 was placed in general charge of the Moravian settlements in North Carolina. In 1766, Ettwein was made assistant to Bishop N. Seidel of Bethlehem, Pennsylvania, and while in this capacity, was intimately involved with Indian mission work. Ettwein was leader of the migration of Christian Indians who were later massacred at Gnadenhutten during the Revolutionary War by patriot partisans. An outspoken loyalist, he was arrested and imprisoned, but later served as a chaplain at the Continental hospital at Bethlehem, and represented Moravian interests to the Continental Congress.

In 1787 Ettwein was instrumental in reviving the Society of United Brethren for Propagating the Gospel Among the Heathen and became its president. In 1784 he was elevated to the episcopacy and presided over the Moravian Church in America until 1801. An outspoken man, Ettwein was a dynamic leader who helped shape and guide the Moravians of America through the colonial and early republican periods.

BIBLIOGRAPHY
DAB
NCAB (1907)
WhAmHS

WADE A. HORTON

Evans, Benjamin (b. Meline, Pembrokeshire, Wales, 23 Feb. 1740; d. Dre-wen, Bryngwyn parish, Cardiganshire, Wales, 2 March 1821). Congregational minister and hymn-writer. His father, Daniel Evans, was a Baptist deacon and Benjamin was not baptized until he became a church member in 1764. He was educated at home and at a school in Haverfordwest. He started preaching in 1765 and was ordained at the Congregational Church at Llanuwchllyn, Merionethshire, in 1769. In 1777 he moved to Albany Chapel, Haverfordwest, and in June 1779 to Dre-wen where he remained until his death. He was a pioneer advocate of the Sunday school, a diligent minister who founded several churches. In his early days he was a High Calvinist but moderated his views later. Amongst his publications were sermons, catechisms, hymns and a partial translation of Mathias Maurice's 'Social Religion' (1797).

BIBLIOGRAPHY
J. Bulmer, *Memoirs* (Haverfordwest, Wales, 1826)
DWB
T. Rees and J. Thomas, *Hanes Eglwysi Annibynol*, 4 vols, IV (Liverpool, England, 1871–5): 171–4

R. TUDUR JONES

Evans, Benjamin (b. Bilston, Staffordshire, England, 13 May 1803; d. Scarborough, Yorkshire, England, 6 April 1871). Baptist minister, leader, and historian. A student at Horton College, Bradford, Yorkshire from 1823 to 1825, he served as Baptist minister at Scarborough, Yorkshire, from 1825 to 1862. As well as being a zealous evangelist, he was also an active supporter of the Anti-Corn-Law League, the Anti-State Church Association, and the Parliamentary Reform Association, and was a founder of the Scarborough Mechanics Institute. He was co-founder and editor of *The Freeman*, a weekly Baptist newspaper (1855), and was involved with radical journalism in Yorkshire. He became chairman of the Baptist Union (1858). In his work he sought to promote the BMS and the British and Irish Home Mission.

A closed communionist, he helped found in 1866 a Baptist college in Bury, Lancashire (later Manchester) and lectured there. He wrote for many denominational magazines including *The Primitive Church Magazine* and *The Baptist Magazine*. He edited *The Northern Baptist* (1838–45), *The Church* (1846–c.68), *The Appeal* (1848–c. 68) and was author of *Early English Baptists*, 2 vols (1862, 1864).

BIBLIOGRAPHY
Baptist Handbook (1872): 213–8
BaptMag (1872): 24–36, 105
K. R. Short, 'Benjamin Evans and the Radical Press', *BQ*, XIX (1962): 243–53

GEOFFREY RALPH BREED

Evans, Caleb (b. Bristol, England, 12 Nov. 1737; d. Bristol, England, 4 Aug. 1791). Particular Baptist minister and theologian. Son of HUGH EVANS, he was baptized at Little Wild Street, London, on 29 November 1753. He was assistant to Josiah Thompson at Unicorn Yard, London, from 15 September 1758, then assistant at Broadmead, Bristol, from 12 August 1759. He was ordained co-pastor 18 August 1767. He also shared in the work of the Baptist Academy in Bristol, acting as its principal from 1779 to 1791. His ordination statement indicated his evangelical Calvinism. He had read classics,

Puritans, and JONATHAN EDWARDS whose *Freedom of the Will* he commended to students. ANDREW FULLER in *The Gospel Worthy of All Acceptation* (1785: 183–5), quoted from Caleb Evans' *An Address to the Serious and Candid Professors of Christianity* (1772: 11–13). The link between Evans and Fuller was via the friendship of both with JOHN SUTCLIFF, trained by Evans at Bristol, and afterwards founder, with Fuller and JOHN RYLAND, of the BMS (1792). Active in founding the Bristol Education Society (1770) with his father, Caleb himself engaged with students in missionary tours to Cornwall. His preaching was evangelical, experimental and practical.

He edited a *Collection of Hymns Adapted to Public Worship* (1769) with JOHN ASH. The best compositions, varied in subject and orderly in presentation, were helpful to both congregations and families. Evans had personal friendship with ANNE STEELE and inspired JOHN RIPPON, whose *Selection* (1787), was the foundation of all future Baptist hymn-books. Evans was both a Hanoverian loyalist, for his *Constitutional Liberty* was an attack on American ideas of republicanism, and a political radical, who penned *A Letter to Mr Wesley*, under the pseudonym of 'Americanus', taking the Methodist leader to task for defending the taxation of the American colonists. In opposing the slave trade, however, the two men were agreed.

BIBLIOGRAPHY
N. S. Moon, 'Caleb Evans, Founder of the British Education Society', *BQ*, XXIV (1971): 175–90
—, *Education for Ministry* (London, 1979)
S. A. Swaine, *Faithful Men* (London, 1884)

ROGER HAYDEN

Evans, Christmas (b. Esgair-Waun, Llandysul, Cardiganshire, Wales, 25 Dec. 1766; d. Swansea, Wales, 19 July 1838). Baptist minister. Son of Samuel Evans, a cobbler, Christmas Evans had an extremely unhappy childhood and no formal education. When he was nine years of age his father died and he was left in the care of a harsh, heavy-drinking relative. His earliest work was as a farm-labourer in Carmarthenshire. Hardly able to read, he was helped intellectually by David Davis of Castellhywel, a well-known Presbyterian preacher, schoolteacher, and distinguished bard, with Unitarian views. Evans was converted in 1783, baptized 1788 in the River Duar, Llanybyther, and became a member of Aberduar Baptist Church. 1789 was specially significant for him in that he attended the Baptist Association meetings that year in Maesyberllan, near Brecon, and heard of the need for preachers in North Wales. Also that year he was ordained at Salem, Tynydonnen, and married Catherine Jones, one of his church members. He journeyed throughout Caernarvonshire as itinerant Baptist preacher making extensive tours on foot and preaching at every opportunity. In 1792 he undertook pastoral responsibility for about ten Anglesey Baptist churches. During this time, under the influence of the gifted and arrogant orator, JOHN RICHARD JONES of Ramoth

(1765–1822), he adopted Sandemanian (or Glassite) views which, says Evans, afflicted him 'so far as to drive away the spirit of prayer for the conversion of sinners . . . I had been robbed to a great degree of the spirit of prayer and the spirit of preaching'. After a spiritual crisis he abandoned these ideas and returned to a more orthodox faith. 'I felt as if I had removed from the cold and sterile regions of spiritual frost into the verdant fields of divine promises'.

At this time he made a personal covenant with God (similar to the Puritans and early Methodists) which contains 13 separate prayers and reflects his deep piety (Hood, 1881: 78–81). In 1823 his wife died. By the time he left Anglesey the ten Baptist churches had increased to twenty. For a brief period (1826–8) he was minister at Caerphilly, Glamorgan, during which time the membership increased from 65 to 200 (Evans' letter to J. T. Rowland, *BQ*, 7: 176). During his time at Caerphilly he married his second wife, Mary Jones of Anglesey. He moved to pastoral charges in Cardiff (Tabernacle) 1828 and Caernarvon (Caersalem) 1832. He travelled widely throughout the Principality enjoying considerable fame as one of their most outstanding preachers and was familiarly known as 'the Welsh apostle' or 'the Bunyan of Wales'.

He had a rather ungainly physique, had suffered the loss of his right eye in early life, and was often plagued by ill health. His eye trouble gave him intense pain and at times he was in danger of becoming blind, but his astonishing preaching ability more than compensated for his other limitations. His remarkable memory, copious vocabulary, keen sense of drama, infectious humour, and vivid imagination, all combined to make him a preacher of rare eloquence with deep evangelistic concern. As a young man his preaching method and style was modelled on that of the Calvinistic Methodist preacher, ROBERT ROBERTS (1762–1802) of Capel Uchaf, Clynnog, who was himself influenced, albeit indirectly, by GEORGE WHITEFIELD. Such a forceful and persuasive orator obviously did not escape criticism; his churches occasionally found him overbearing and dictatorial. He did not take kindly to independent judgements in his Anglesey churches during the first thirty years of his ministry, and was particularly annoyed when any congregation took important decisions without consulting him.

During his lifetime he published many booklets and a large number of tracts, expositions, and sermons, some of which were translated into English. He was a prolific letter writer and also wrote hymns. Evans died while on an extensive preaching tour collecting money to clear a heavy chapel debt at Caersalem. ROBERT HALL described Evans as the tallest, the stoutest, and the greatest man he ever saw. The story of his remarkable career was an immense spiritual stimulus to D. L. Moody.

BIBLIOGRAPHY
T. M. Bassett, *The Welsh Baptists* (Swansea, 1977)
BQ, 9: 194–204
DNB
DWB

D. M. Evans, *Christmas Evans, with selections from his sermons* (London, 1863)

EM, 16 (1838), new series: 437

E. P. Hood, *Christmas Evans* (London, 1881)

E. E. Rees, *Christmas Evans* (London, 1936)

RAYMOND BROWN

Evans, Elizabeth [née Tomlinson] (b. Newbold, Leicestershire, England, *c.* 1776; d. Wirksworth, Derbyshire, England, 9 Nov. 1849). Wesleyan Methodist preacher. Evans came from a Christian family. Her conversion at 21 occurred after several years of struggle; soon she felt it her 'duty to call sinners to repentance'. After some heart-searching about female preaching she began to take public services. Elizabeth travelled from place to place preaching in face of much opposition. Elizabeth married Seth Evans, a preacher who approved of her preaching, and they worked together. They made their home in Wirksworth where Elizabeth continued to preach and started class meetings. Elizabeth Evans is probably best known as GEORGE ELIOT's aunt and the model for her Dinah Morris in *Adam Bede*.

BIBLIOGRAPHY

L. F. Church, *More About the Early Methodist People* (London, 1949)

Z. Taft, *Biographical Sketches of . . . Holy Women . . .*, 1 (London, 1825)

E. DOROTHY GRAHAM

Evans, Evan [Ieuan Glan Geirionydd] (b. 20 April 1795, Trefriw, Gwynedd, Wales; d. Rhyl, Clwyd, Wales, 21 Jan. 1855). Welsh Anglican clergyman. He was the son of Robert and Elizabeth Evans, both Calvinistic Methodists. He was educated at Llanrwst Free School and after further instruction from Thomas Richards (1785–1855), the evangelical incumbent of Berriew, Powys, he went to St Bees College and was ordained by the Bishop of Chester, 19 February 1826. He was first licensed to read the Welsh services at St Martin's, Chester, and subsequently served as curate at Christleton, Ince (1843–52) and Rhyl. He is best known in Wales as a poet of distinction and some of his hymns have maintained their popularity. As a theologian he began life as an exponent of Strict Calvinism but later became one of the committed supporters of Moderate Calvinism as expounded by Dr EDWARD WILLIAMS.

BIBLIOGRAPHY

DNB

DWB

W. J. Roberts, *Geirionydd* (Ruthin, Wales, no date)

R. TUDUR JONES

Evans, Henry (b. VA, USA; d. Fayetteville, NC, USA, *c.* 1810). Black pastor and founder of the Methodist Church in Fayetteville, North Carolina. Probably free from birth, Henry Evans was a Methodist and a licensed preacher who made his living as a shoemaker. On his way to South Carolina, the 'profanity and lewdness' (Wightman, 1858: 124–9) of blacks in Fayetteville, North Carolina, made him decide to stay to minister to them. He was forced to preach clandestinely in the countryside for a time, because distrustful Fayetteville whites, fearing that he would incite other blacks to violence, sought to prevent him from preaching. The eloquent Evans won black converts who, in the opinion of the community, had been made 'wonderfully better' (Wightman, 1858: 124–9), and seeing these results, the whites allowed Evans to preach in town.

Evans's church was only the second in Fayetteville and the first Methodist one. In 1805, FRANCIS ASBURY preached there, finding the church 'plain', yet 'it is our duty to condescend to men of low estate' (Asbury, 1958: entry for 15 January 1805). Evans reserved some front-row seats for whites at his services, but as his fame spread, whites began to occupy seats in the rear of the church also, crowding out the blacks. The problem became acute after a successful 1808 revival, and even after the church was enlarged by removing side walls and building sheds to seat black congregants, it remained crowded. A white minister replaced Evans, but the latter remained an assistant in the church he had founded. Just before his death in 1810, Evans recalled his early vicissitudes, but stated that 'if in my last hour I could trust to that or to any thing else but Christ crucified, for my salvation, all should be lost and my soul perish forever' (Wightman, 1858: 124–9). After a funeral attended by more people than any previously held in Fayetteville, Evans was buried in the church. Bishop WILLIAM CAPERS wrote that he had known few preachers 'more conversant with the Scriptures than Evans, or whose conversation was more instructive as to things of God' (Wightman, 1858: 124). While he was obliged to observe the South's rigid caste rules, the evangelical preaching of Evans and many other black preachers contained an implicit egalitarianism, that all are equal in the sight of God. He was an excellent example of the ante-bellum South's many black ministers who accomplished much in the face of daunting obstacles.

BIBLIOGRAPHY

F. Asbury, *Journal*, 2 (Nashville, TN, and London, 1958)

J. S. Bassett, *Slavery in the State of North Carolina* (Baltimore, MD, 1899): 363–75

H. V. Richardson, *Dark Salvation* (Garden City, NY, 1976): 176–9

W. Wightman, *The Life of William Capers, D.D. . . . Including an Autobiography* (Nashville, TN, 1858): 124–9

STEPHEN W. ANGELL

Evans, Hugh (b. Wales, 1712; d. Bristol, England, 28 March 1781). Particular Baptist minister and educator. Son of Caleb Evans (1676–1739, *DWB*), he went to Bristol in 1729 and was baptized at Broadmead church on

13 September 1730 by BERNARD FOSKETT. He was called to assist Foskett on 17 March 1733/4 and was ordained co-pastor on 7 February 1739/40 becoming senior pastor and president of the Baptist Academy, 1758–81. He possessed Welsh as a spoken language and retained the academy's strong links with Welsh Baptist churches. With his son CALEB EVANS he originated the Bristol Education Society (1770) with the objective of broadening denominational financial support to provide educated, able, evangelical ministers for the church's mission. His noted paternalism towards students was positive, creative, pastoral and continued throughout their ministry. He published three addresses, all in 1773; and two Western Baptist Association Letters in 1754 and 1770.

BIBLIOGRAPHY
DWB
N. S. Moon, *Education for Ministry* (London, 1979)
S. A. Swaine, *Faithful Men* (London, 1884)

ROGER HAYDEN

Evans, James (b. Kingston-upon-Hull, Yorkshire, England, 18 Jan. 1801; d. Keelby, Lincolnshire, England, 23 Nov. 1846). Methodist missionary and developer of the Cree syllabic system. Evans was apprenticed as a boy to a grocer who was an active Wesleyan Methodist. He experienced a spiritual awakening at a meeting addressed by Irish preacher GIDEON OUSELEY and spent some time as a local preacher before moving to London and apparently losing interest in religion. When his parents emigrated to Canada in 1820, he decided to follow them two years later and obtained a teaching post in L'Orignal, Upper Canada. Here he met and married Mary Blythe Smith.

In 1826, Evans attended a Methodist camp meeting at which he re-committed himself to the church. He was sent to Rice Lake where the Methodists were operating a school for Ojibwa children and then in 1830 he was accepted on a probationary appointment for the Methodist ministry. After three years as a circuit rider, he was ordained in 1833 and sent to the St Clair mission where he experimented with a system for writing the Ojibwa language.

Evans became interested in extending the Ojibwa mission by the mid-1830s and undertook two mission tours north of lakes Huron and Superior. In 1839 he negotiated an agreement with the Hudson's Bay Company (HBC) for the establishment of Methodist missions in Rupert's Land. The following year, Peter Jacobs and Henry Steinhauer from Upper Canada and British Wesleyans George Barnley, William Mason and ROBERT RUNDLE accompanied Evans to their new posts. Evans was designated superintendent and established his headquarters at Rossville Mission near Norway House. Building on his earlier work with the Ojibwa language, he developed a method for writing the Cree language in syllabics and even built his own simple printing press to commence publication of religious literature.

Like so many other missionaries in the HBC territories, Evans soon found himself in conflict with HBC officials over such issues as Sunday work. His final years in the mission were clouded by other controversies as well. On a mission trip in 1844, he shot and killed his interpreter in what he insisted was an accident. Soon afterward, the Indians at Rossville complained to the HBC that he had raped one of the Indian girls living at his house. A subsequent local trial decided he was not guilty, but Evans felt compelled to travel to London in 1846 to tell his side of the story to the Methodist Missionary Society. He died there suddenly of a heart attack. The Wesleyan Methodist missions in the north never really recovered from the loss. Nevertheless, his syllabic system was adopted by Roman Catholic and Anglican missionaries throughout the Canadian north and a variant of it remains in use today among speakers of Inuktitut in the arctic.

BIBLIOGRAPHY
DCB, 7
J. McLean, *James Evans, Inventor of the Syllabic System of the Cree Language* (Toronto, 1890)
L. Pierce, *James Evans* (Toronto, 1926)
N. Shipley, *The James Evans Story* (Toronto, 1966)

KERRY M. ABEL

Evans, James Harington (b. Salisbury, Wiltshire, England, 15 April 1785; d. Stonehaven, Kincardineshire, Scotland, 18 Dec. 1849). The only son of Dr Evans, prebend of Salisbury Cathedral and master of the Grammar School there, Evans was educated for the ministry of the Church of England and became first a fellow of Wadham College, Oxford. He served a number of curacies in the Church of England, the last at Milford in Hampshire from which he was given notice to quit because of his evangelical preaching which upset some of the local gentry to the extent that they conspicuously left the church before the sermon began. One of the so-called 'Western Schism' of ministers seceding from the Church of England circa 1815, because they believed that their Calvinism could no longer be accommodated in it, they also objected to infant baptism, the union of church and state and the indiscipline that arose from this. After leaving the church the group were together baptized as believers. In his *Dialogues of 1819* Evans adopted a Sabellian position, but in 1826 he published a retraction of this aberration. In 1830 IVIMEY writes that he 'is now a useful and much respected baptized minister' though he did 'not consider himself or his congregation as belonging to our denomination'.

In 1816 he had started preaching in London in the Swiss Church but this soon proved too small; in the chapel in John Street built for him in 1818 at the personal expense of HENRY DRUMMOND, the charismatic banker, a baptistry for the immersion of believers was installed. Evans preached there for thirty years an evangelical Calvinism, more concerned to address the heart than the head, ever exalting faith at the expense of works. The church, to which he early sought to introduce the principle of an eldership as well as a diaconate, seems to have drifted into the Baptist denomination: in 1824 it was reformulated but still retained an eclectic open membership; but in 1837 Evans published a sermon preached on behalf of the Baptist Missionary Society. A supporter of the work of the LCM, at John Street he established schools, and Sick Visiting and Christian Instruction Societies. On Evans's retirement, BAPTIST NOEL, following his baptism as a believer and renunciation of his Anglican orders, became pastor of John Street.

BIBLIOGRAPHY
BapMag (1852)
The Baptist Reporter (1850): 58
D. W. Bebbington, *Evangelicalism in Modern Britain* (London, 1989): 78
J. J. Evans, *Memoir and Remains of the Reverend James Harington Evans, MA*, 2nd edn (London, 1855)
J. Ivimey, *The History of the English Baptists*, IV (1830): 179–80

J. H. Y. BRIGGS

Evans, John (b. Glanrafon, Wrexham, Denbighshire, Wales, 30 Oct. 1723; d. Bala, Merionethshire, Wales, 12 Aug. 1817). Weaver, bookbinder, candle-maker, and Welsh Calvinistic Methodist exhorter. Having spent his early years in the Wrexham area, John moved to Bala in 1742 where he set up trade as a weaver, then as a bookbinder and later in life as a candle-maker. At Bala he joined the newly established Calvinistic Methodist society and travelled the neighbouring districts as a lay exhorter, although he did not gain official recognition as a preacher until 1765. He came to be regarded as a pioneer and leader of Methodism in North Wales. Renowned for his eloquence, originality and wisdom, he figured prominently in meetings of the North Wales Association of the Calvinistic Methodists. Later in life he became a staunch supporter and friend of THOMAS CHARLES who settled in Bala in 1783. Such was the regard in which he was held that, even as a lay exhorter, he was invited to take a leading part in the ordination of the first Calvinistic Methodist ministers in 1811.

BIBLIOGRAPHY
DWB
J. M. Jones and W. Morgan, *Y Tadau Methodistaidd*, 2 (Swansea, 1897): ch. 2

E. AP NEFYDD ROBERTS

Evans, Marian. *See* ELIOT, GEORGE

Evans, William (b. 17 Jan. 1788; d. Allestree Hall, near Derby, England, 8 April 1856). MP, banker, and industrialist. Evans was the elder son of a large landowner, William Evans of Darley Abbey near Derby, and of Elizabeth Strutt, daughter of the partner of Richard Arkwright (inventor of the spinning frame). The Evans family, exceedingly wealthy, had interests in cotton, paper,

copper, red lead, and banking. Upon succeeding his father, he became a model paternalist employer.

Evans was MP for East Retford (1818–26), for Leicester (1830–5), and for North Derbyshire (1837–53). As a 'Saint' in Parliament he was the ally of fellow Anglicans, WILLIAM WILBERFORCE and THOMAS FOWELL BUXTON, and worked closely with his brother-in-law and fellow moderate Radical, THOMAS GISBORNE. Despite being, according to the *Christian Observer*, an 'Established Constitution in Church and State man,' he supported motions for the removal of civil disabilities against Dissenters, Roman Catholics, and Jews, and in the late 1820s he was an enemy of 'no-popery'. He was long active in the affairs of his county as magistrate, deputy-lieutenant, sheriff, and alderman of Derby.

Evans was a generous contributor to the prominent evangelical societies, a member of the LDOS, and, indicative of his liberal sympathy for Dissent, of the EA. Contemporaries underscored his honesty and integrity as a politician and civic leader.

BIBLIOGRAPHY
Boase
CO (June 1856): 430–2
GM (May 1856): 526
Stenton
R. G. Thorne, ed., *The House of Commons 1790–1820* (London, 1986)

JONATHAN BURKE CUTMORE

Everett, James (b. Alnwick, Northumberland, England, 16 May 1784; d. Sunderland, Northumberland, England, 10 May 1872). Methodist preacher, author, and reformer. James Everett's maternal grandfather was one of the first Alnwick Methodists and built its first chapel, and it was to his mother that Everett owed his religious upbringing and it was no doubt she who was responsible for his meeting JOHN WESLEY a year before the old man's death and feeling his hand laid in blessing on his head. To this we can no doubt attribute his life-long veneration of Wesley.

As a lad he was apprenticed to a flax-dresser and grocer, and in January 1803 was awakened to a conviction of sin through a local preacher's sermon. Eventually CHARLES WESLEY's words 'Who did for every sinner die, Hath surely died for me' 'were applied with inexpressible joy' to his heart. A familiar pattern followed; he heard the call to preach the same year and moving to Sunderland he was received on full plan the following year.

Visiting Alnwick in 1806 he met the brothers Thomas and Jacob Stanley who encouraged him to enter the ministry, and in October Jacob Stanley told him his name had been proposed and that he must hold himself in readiness. Hesitating, he conferred with his superintendent who requested him to fill the place of the junior minister who was ill. In due course the quarterly meeting recommended him; in effect then, Sunderland was his first circuit in 1806. He should have been received into full connexion in 1810 but the hesitation that had marked his earlier steps as local preacher and as itinerant, again caused him to hold back, so that he was not received until 1811.

At that time he was stationed at Barnsley and there met the poet JAMES MONTGOMERY with whom he became a close friend. Moving to Sheffield in 1819 the friendship ripened, and these two, with Ebenezer Elliott and John Holland, became known as the 'Sheffield poets'. But he had already begun writing, ten years earlier, when he replied to a sermon by a Unitarian minister, submitting his reply for criticism to (*inter alia*) JABEZ BUNTING. In view of their later relationship, his early – and much later – respect for Bunting is interesting. While *en route* for Belper in 1808 he had taken the opportunity of hearing him and walking with him to Sheffield; and a few years later supplied for Bunting on a number of occasions.

In 1821, however, his health broke down – he was subject to severe bronchitis for the rest of his life – and for the next 13 years he was a supernumerary in Sheffield, London and Manchester. While in London he was asked to help at the Bookroom and here he became critical of Bunting, though not so much to prevent the latter as late as 1838 inviting him to join in a holiday in the Lake District. While in Sheffield and Manchester he helped to maintain himself by setting up as a bookseller – and a writer. He was a compulsive writer, composing valuable histories of Methodism in both places, writing sermons, tracts, defences of Methodism, biographies, and hymns, one of his biographies, *The Village Blacksmith*, being reprinted as late as the 1890s. He rendered great service to the connexion when he acted to prevent the pirating of book room publications, including the hymn-book, and when he served on the committee to consider the celebration of the centenary of Methodism.

But the gathering storms in Methodism involved Everett to the hilt. He had written at the time of the Warrenite controversy; the *Wesleyan Takings, or Centenary Sketches*, in which he was joint author, were heavily criticized and condemned, though it is hard to see why. But in the 1840s a series of *Fly Sheets* appeared, anonymously, criticizing centralization and cliquism, the Conference platform, the Stationing Committee and the Mission House, and in all areas Bunting appeared in an unfavourable light. Instead, however, of answering the criticisms, all the attention was directed to trying to discover the authors. GEORGE OSBORN circulated a declaration among the whole of the ministry inviting them to confirm their innocence of authorship. Many refused to sign and at the 1849 Conference Everett was summoned to face questioning. He refused to answer unless evidence was brought against him, and for this 'contumacy' was expelled.

Thereafter he with his colleagues SAMUEL DUNN and WILLIAM GRIFFITH conducted a campaign throughout the country in favour of reform; and much of his writing was concerned with the same theme. But he edited a hymn-book for the Reformers and was the first president of the United Methodist Free Churches in 1857. He finally died full of years and honours in 1872.

A man of immense energy and wide interests, he was far more than a stormy petrel or even a reformer. His intense veneration for Wesley led to his forming one of the finest collections of Wesleyana ever assembled; it was ironic that he and THOMAS JACKSON, the president who pronounced his expulsion, should have jointly been responsible for the hobby of Wesleyana collecting. He was a preacher of no mean ability – Bunting said he could have any circuit he wished, and when stationed in Manchester, 800 were added to church membership in two years. He was generous in the assistance he gave to others, from unknown colleagues to the great ADAM CLARKE, with whom he formed a close friendship; generous in his travelling to advocate Methodism, in some years covering eight or nine thousand miles; generous in his appreciations, even of Jabez Bunting. And he should be remembered for his part in suggesting the theme of H. P. Parker's centenary picture of Wesley's escape from the Epworth fire.

SELECT WRITINGS
J. Everett, *Adam Clarke Portrayed*, 3 vols (London, 1843–9)
—, *Historical Sketches of Wesleyan Methodism in Sheffield*, 2 vols (only 1 pub.) (Sheffield, England, 1823)
—, *Memoirs of the Life, Character, and Ministry of William Dawson* (London, 1842)
—, *Methodism As It Is* (London, 1863–5)
—, *The Village Blacksmith* (London, 1831)
—, *Wesleyan Methodism in Manchester* (Manchester, England, 1827)
—, (with J. Beaumont) *Wesleyan Takings*, 2 vols (London, 1840)

BIBLIOGRAPHY
EWM
O. A. Beckerlegge, *Bibliography of the WMA etc.* (Westcliff on Sea, England, 1988)
—, 'James Everett 1784–1984', in *PWHS*, XLIV: 135–44
—, *The UMFC* (London, 1957): 30–7
—, *United Methodist Ministers and Their Circuits* (London, 1968)
R. Chew, *James Everett, a Biography* (London, 1875)
B. Gregory, *Sidelights on the Conflicts of Methodism* (London, 1898)
G. Osborn, *Outlines of Wesleyan Bibliography* (London, 1869)
D. W. Riley, *Tegg v. Everett*, PWHS, XLIV: 145–50
E. G. Rupp, *Thomas Jackson, Methodist Patriarch* (London, 1854): 18–19, 33–6
G. J. Stevenson, *Methodist Worthies VI* (London, 1886): 913–21

OLIVER A. BECKERLEGGE

Everett, Joseph (b. Queen Anne's County, MD, BNA, 17 June 1732; d. Cambridge, MD, USA, 16 Oct. 1809). Pioneer Methodist minister. Born in a nominal Anglican home, Everett had no exposure to evangelical religion until adulthood. Through the 'New Light' Presbyterians, he was converted in 1763. In time, however, he grew spiritually careless. Then in 1778 he heard FRANCIS ASBURY preach, read works by JOHN WESLEY and J. W. FLETCHER, and soon faith was rekindled, though now Arminian doctrine replaced his former Calvinism. He became a Methodist itinerant on the Dorchester circuit,

Maryland, in 1780 and was admitted on trial to the travelling connexion in 1781. Everett became a deacon in 1786 and an elder in 1788, being appointed presiding elder over 11 circuits in 1789, retaining the position through 1803. He appears in the Minutes of 1805 as one of the 'superannuated' preachers. He was among those preachers at the Christmas Conference of 1784, when American Methodists severed organizational ties with their British brethren. An autobiographical sketch in the *Arminian Magazine* of 1788 shows his rough-hewn style. In 1794 he was appointed chaplain to Cokesbury College in Abingdon, Maryland, a position he held for some years.

BIBLIOGRAPHY
AAP
AM
EWM
Minutes (1805)

RICK D. RAILSBACK

Ewart, David (b. Alyth, Perthshire, Scotland; d. Calcutta, India, 1860). Presbyterian missionary. Raised in Perthshire and educated at St Andrews University and the Divinity Hall, Edinburgh, he followed his friend ALEXANDER DUFF to Calcutta. He arrived 13 December 1834, just after Duff returned to Britain. Although not so academically talented, he was patient with the slower boys and very good humoured.

Ewart, like Duff, was influential with the early high caste converts, offering them refuge in his home and fighting for them in the courts. He was not afraid to criticize Duff's policies, and was an invaluable administrator at General Assembly of the Church of Scotland's Institution (known popularly as the 'General Assembly's Institution'). He acted as conciliator in the 1856 dispute over catechists' pay and voting rights. Like all the Scottish missionaries except Miss Laing, he joined the FCS after 1843, when the mission lost all its premises and assets.

When a new Bengali church associated with the FCS was formed in October 1848, Ewart became its first pastor. He also served intermittently as secretary of the Calcutta Missionary Council, and as editor of the *Calcutta Christian Observer*. Returning to Calcutta in November 1858 after a forced furlough, Ewart died suddenly of cholera – a devastating blow for the mission. Mrs Ewart, a missionary nurse, made a pioneering approach to Armenian and Jewish girls, starting a Calcutta school for them. This was adopted by the FCS mission in 1846.

BIBLIOGRAPHY
Bishop's College Library, Calcutta, Free Church of Scotland records
Union Chapel, Dharamtolla, Calcutta, Calcutta Mission Council Minutes

E. M. JACKSON

Ewing, Greville (b. Edinburgh, 27 April 1767; d. Glasgow, 2 Aug. 1841). Primary architect of Scottish Congregationalism. Ewing left an apprenticeship to train for the ministry in Edinburgh University. Ordained in the Church of Scotland in 1793, he became colleague to Thomas Snell Jones, minister of Lady Glenorchy's Chapel, Edinburgh. In 1796 he served as the first secretary of the Edinburgh Missionary Society and began to edit the *Missionary Monthly*, the first Scots missionary journal.

Now moving in the circle of ROBERT and JAMES HALDANE, he supported the brothers' Society for the Propagation of the Gospel at Home, which sent itinerant evangelists throughout Scotland. Severing his links with the Church of Scotland in December 1798, he became preacher at the Haldanite tabernacle, Glasgow, and tutor to students being prepared for itineration at Robert Haldane's expense. The demise of the Haldane connexion in 1808, brought on by the brothers' propagation of restorationist and baptist views, moved Ewing and associate, RALPH WARDLAW, to organize both the Glasgow Theological Academy (1809) and the Congregational Union of Scotland (1812). Princeton awarded him the DD in 1821.

BIBLIOGRAPHY
H. Escott, *A History of Scottish Congregationalism* (Glasgow, 1960)
N. Gray, 'Greville Ewing', (Edinburgh Univ. Ph.D. thesis, 1962)
J. J. Matheson, *A Memoir of Greville Ewing* (London, 1843)

KENNETH J. STEWART

Ewing, John (b. East Nottingham, Cecil County, MD, BNA, 22 June 1732; d. Norristown, PA, USA, 8 Sept. 1802). Educator and Presbyterian minister in Pennsylvania. John Ewing was educated at the academy run by Reverend Francis Alison at New London, Pennsylvania and then at the College of New Jersey, where he received his BA in 1754 and then served as a tutor until 1758. Licensed in 1758 by the presbytery of New Castle, Delaware, he was engaged to teach moral philosophy in the College of Philadelphia. In 1759 he was called to be pastor of the First Presbyterian Church of Philadelphia, and, appointed professor of natural philosophy at the College of Philadelphia in 1762, he continued in both pastoral and academic roles for the rest of his life.

In 1773 he was commissioned to solicit contributions in Great Britain for the Academy in Newark in Delaware. He received the degree DD from the University of Edinburgh in 1773 before returning to America in 1775. In 1779 the state legislature transformed the College of Philadelphia into the University of Pennsylvania and named Ewing its first provost. From 1767 until 1779 he was president, and from then until 1801 treasurer, of an insurance organization for relief of ministers and their widows, later known as The Presbyterian Ministers'

Fund. His favourite theological writer in the English language was PHILIP DODDRIDGE.

BIBLIOGRAPHY
AAP, 3: 216–19
Princetonians

WILLIAM S. BARKER

Eyre, John (b. Bodmin, Cornwall, England, 1754; d. London, 1803). Anglican clergyman. He was converted by ANDREW KINSMAN when apprenticed to a Tavistock clothier, and disowned by his father. He was sent to Trevecka College by Lady HUNTINGDON, but his stay there was interrupted by itinerant preaching in Cornwall between 1774 and 1778. He was ordained deacon and priest with the title of Curate of Weston in 1779, and later held curacies at Lewes (Sussex), Reading and Chelsea. In 1785 he was appointed minister of the Episcopal chapel at Homerton (Middlesex) where he remained until his death. He was a founder member of the LMS and the Village Itinerancy, and also edited the *Evangelical Magazine*.

BIBLIOGRAPHY
Cheshunt College archives, Cambridge, original letters
Surman's index of Congregational ministers (Dr Williams' Library, London)

EDWIN WELCH

Eyre, John (b. London 1768; d. 1854). LMS missionary on Tahiti. Before he was ordained on 26 July 1796, Eyre had been a blockmaker. He was among the first group of LMS missionaries to travel to Tahiti and served between 1797 and 1808 on Tahiti, and at Huahine between 1808 and 1809. His activities included some preaching and teaching. In 1809 Eyre returned to the colony whereupon he severed his connection with the mission. Thereafter he served as a teacher at Paramatta in New South Wales.

BIBLIOGRAPHY
N. Gunson, *Messengers of Grace* (Melbourne, 1978)
R. Lovett, *The History of the London Missionary Society 1795–1895* (London, 1899)
RMD, 4th edn (London, 1923)

R. WATCYN JAMES

F

Faaruea (b. Moorea, Tahiti, 1786; d. Oneata, Fiji, 1846). Missionary to Fiji. Faaruea was one of three missionaries the LMS missionary JOHN DAVIES sent from Tahiti, by way of Tonga, to Fiji. Not receiving an anticipated welcome from Lakeba's high chief, he and his companion HATAI went southward to Oneata. Living at a place called Siloama (Siloam), they married and left descendants, being honoured as forerunners of WILLIAM CROSS and DAVID CARGILL of the WMMS, who worked with them from 1835 onward.

BIBLIOGRAPHY
J. Garrett, *To Live Among the Stars* (Geneva and Suva, 1982)

JOHN GARRETT

Faber, George Stanley (b. Calverley, Yorkshire, England, 25 Oct. 1773; d. Sherburn, Co. Durham, England, 27 Jan. 1854). Anglican clergyman and writer. Faber was educated at Hipperholme Grammar School and University College, Oxford (scholar 1790; BA 1793; MA 1796; BD 1803), and on graduating became fellow and tutor of Lincoln College, Oxford (1793–1803) and served in 1801 as junior proctor and as Bampton lecturer, the first evangelical to be chosen for that honour. Taking the Pentateuch for his subject, his *Horae Mosaicae* defended scripture against contemporary speculation arising from geological discoveries. He left Oxford on his marriage and served as his father's curate at Calverley and Bramley (1803–5), thereafter becoming successively Vicar of Stockton-on-Tees (1805–9), Rector of Redmarshall (1805–11) and of Long Newton (1811–32), after which he became master of Sherburn Hospital (1832–54), whose finances and estates he re-organized. In 1830 he became also a Prebendary of Salisbury.

Faber was a prolific writer. Besides other works on early scriptural history such as *The Origin of Pagan Idolatry* (1816), which he linked to the tower of Babel, and *A Treatise on the Genius and Object of the Patriarchal, the Levitical and the Christian dispensations* (1823), he published *The Difficulties of Infidelity* (1824) and *The Difficulties of Romanism* (1826), which was translated into French and Italian.

Faber occupied an interesting position during the Tractarian years. He placed much emphasis on the practice and belief of the early church in such works as *The Apostolicity of Trinitarianism* (1832), *The Primitive Doctrine of Election* (1834) and *The Primitive Doctrine of Justification* (1837), so much so that there were some who dubbed him an evangelical High Churchman.

In the last-named book Faber suggested that the views of the Irish High Church layman, Alexander Knox, verged on the Romanist, and neither with them nor with the Calvinist ideas of JOSEPH MILNER would he have any truck. The appearance of Faber's book on justification immediately preceded J. H. NEWMAN's lectures on the subject, in consequence of which a correspondence took place between the two men and Faber even visited Newman to try to convince him of the error of his position. Faber subsequently added two appendices to the second edition of his work, arguing that it was impossible to make sense of Newman's contrary principles. Indeed, relating to another contemporary controversy, that over baptism, Faber would not allow any automatic efficacy in the sacrament, saying that 'the Inward grace of Baptism does not ALWAYS attend upon the outward sign'. Faber later published *Letters on the Tractarian Secessions* (1846), of which that of his nephew, F. W. Faber, was one; and in 1851 at the time of the 'papal aggression', *Papal Infallibility*.

Faber wrote several works on prophecy, not only tracing the history of the Christian era but also many contemporary events in the foreshadowings of Revelation. Thus *Prophecies Relative to the Period of 1260 Years, the Papal and Mahomedan Apostasies, The Reign of the Anti-Christ and the Restoration of the Jews* (1807) and *A View of the Prophecies Relative to the Conversion of Israel and Judah* (1808) both applied to the increasingly popular concern with ministry to the Jews. Yet other books related to the French and to Napoleon – *Remarks on the Fifth Apocalyptic Vial and the Restoration of the Imperial Government in France* (1815) and, identifying Napoleon I as the seventh beast of the apocalypse, *The Revival of the French Emperorship* (1853). Likewise, the unstable condition of the Ottoman Empire led to latterday speculation on the return of the Jews to Palestine in *The Predicted Downfall of the Turkish Power, the Preparation for the Return of the Ten Tribes* (1853). In *The Many Mansions of the House of the Father* (1854) Faber sought 'to discover from scripture the precise locality of the future Heaven of the blessed'. Faber was noted for his personal generosity, not least in the augmentation of livings in his gift, but he was said also to have been possessed of a hasty and irritable temperament.

SELECT WRITINGS
G. S. Faber, *The Many Mansions in the House of the Father*, with a prefatory memoir by F. A. Faber (London, 1854)

BIBLIOGRAPHY
DNB
P. Toon, *Evangelical Theology, 1833–1856* (London, 1979)

ARTHUR POLLARD

Fabricius, Johann Philipp (b. Kleeburg, Germany, 22 Jan. 1711; d. Madras, India, 23 Jan. 1791). Missionary to India and Bible translator. The son of a civil servant in Hesse, as a teenager Fabricius had an emotional conversion experience. After studying law at Giessen and working as a tutor, in 1736 he decided to enter missionary service and went to Halle to study theology and serve as a teacher at Francke's Institution. In 1739 he was ordained in Copenhagen and appointed to the Danish mission in Tranquebar, South India. Arriving in 1740, his linguistic talent was such that he preached his first Tamil sermon within a half-year. In 1742 he moved to Madras where he lived for fifty years, never marrying or returning home. Although he now served under the auspices of the British SPCK, he remained a Lutheran and most of his support continued to come from Halle. His ministry was often interrupted by warfare. Due to ineptness in the handling of money, he was constantly short of funds.

Fabricius was a caring pastor and teacher. His firm emphasis on prayer and religion of the heart made him a leading Pietist mystic. His primary contributions (and significance), however, lay in literary endeavors. His tract 'First Milk' (1756) was designed for catechumens and his 'The Mirror of the Papacy' (1774) aimed at winning local Tamil Catholics. His Tamil 'Hymnbook' (1774) was widely used even in the nineteenth century. Although his Tamil grammar (1778) and dictionary (1779) were seminal works (with the latter still in print in the twentieth century), Fabricus is most remembered for his work in Bible translation. Soon after going to Madras, he started re-working the Ziegenbalg New Testament. The completed revised version was printed in 1758 and a further revised edition appeared in 1772. His method was always to work with an Indian teacher. When a portion was completed, he would have his catechist read it to others so as to find out how the text could be further improved. Then he began the translating of the Old Testament: the manuscript of this was finished before his death and was published in 1796. His 'Golden Version', a shaping influence among the Tamil Lutheran congregations, was analogous to that of Luther's Bible in Germany.

BIBLIOGRAPHY
J. F. Fenger, *History of the Tranquebar Mission* (Tranquebar, India, 1863)
W. Germann, *Johann Philipp Fabricius* (Erlangen, Germany, 1865)
J. Hough, *The History of Christianity in India*, 3 (London, 1845)
A. Lehmann, *Es Begann in Tranquebar* (Berlin, 1955)
F. Penny, *The Church in Madras*, 1 (London, 1904)
H. Victor, 'Tamil Translations of the Bible by the Danish-Halle during the Eighteenth Century', *ICHR*, 16 (June 1982): 72–85

A. Westcott, *Our Oldest Indian Mission* (Madras, India, 1847)

R. V. PIERARD

Fairbairn, Patrick (b. Hallyburton, Berwickshire, Scotland, 28 Jan. 1805; d. Glasgow, 6. Aug. 1874). Presbyterian minister and theologian. Born the son of a farmer, he was educated locally and entered the University of Edinburgh in 1818, thereafter becoming tutor to the family of the Reverend Thomas Johnstone, Dalry, Ayrshire. Following studies for the ministry of the Church of Scotland, he tutored the family of Captain Balfour, an Orkney landowner. Licensed as a preacher in 1826 by the presbytery of Duns, in 1830 he was presented by the Crown as first minister of the parliamentary parish of the island of North Ronaldsay, Orkney. Although his parishioners had a reputation as 'wreckers', his ministry contributed to spiritual and moral transformation. While in the Orkneys he married (Margaret Pitcairn, daughter of the first clerk of the General Assembly of the FCS), meanwhile engaging in intensive private study. He translated V. Steiger's work on 1 Peter and F. G. Lisco's on the parables (he was later to translate Hengstenberg's works on the Psalms and Revelation).

In 1837 Fairbairn was translated to Bridgeton, now part of Glasgow, to a church extension charge erected under the scheme of THOMAS CHALMERS. In 1840 he moved again, to Saltoun, East Lothian. Committed to the cause of the evangelical party in the church, at the Disruption in 1843 he abandoned his living, bringing with him into the Free Church some 600 of the local population of 800.

His first study in biblical hermeneutics, *The Typology of Scripture*, appeared in two volumes (Edinburgh 1845, 1847), and was soon followed by his commentaries on *Jonah* (Edinburgh, 1849) and *Ezekiel* (Edinburgh, 1851). In 1852 (a year marked by the sadness of his wife's death soon after the birth of their fourth child) he became assistant to Dr McLagan at the Free Church College, Aberdeen. The following year he was appointed professor of divinity, but moved in 1856 to become first professor in the new Free Church College in Glasgow (of which in the following year he became principal). The following year he also published his major work *The Interpretation of Prophecy* (Edinburgh, 1856), a study of biblical hermeneutics which included an exposition of his revised understanding of some strands of biblical prophecy (he now saw Old Testament promises about the land as fulfilled in Christ). His *Hermeneutical Manual* followed in 1858.

Fairbairn remarried in 1861 (Frances [Fanny] Turnbull, sister of the Reverend John Turnbull of Eyemouth) and in 1865 was elected to be moderator of the General Assembly of the Free Church. His labours in editing *The Imperial Bible Dictionary* bore fruit with its publication, in two volumes (London, 1866). His own unsigned articles included those on atonement, covenant, decalogue and inspiration. When appointed to give the third series of Cunningham lectures in 1868 he returned to the discussion of fundamental hermeneutical questions. The lectures were published as *The Revelation of the Law in Scripture* (Edinburgh, 1869). His commentary on the *Pastoral Epistles* (Edinburgh, 1874) and his *Pastoral Theology* (Edinburgh, 1875) followed in due course. He served as a member of the Committee for the Revision of the Old Testament of the Authorized Version. Deeply concerned for evangelism, he gave his support to the work of Moody and Sankey and presided over a number of meetings at which Moody spoke. In April 1874, he became ill and died on 6 August. He is buried in Grange Cemetery, Edinburgh (as are Thomas Chalmers, WILLIAM CUNNINGHAM and THOMAS GUTHRIE).

Fairbairn's chief contributions lay in his careful exegetical study of scripture (once well described as Germanic in character, but not in conclusion), and in his work in biblical hermeneutics (commonly described by reviewers as 'sober'), an area in which his books are still of value.

BIBLIOGRAPHY
DNB
J. Dodds, *Biographical Sketch* in *Pastoral Theology* (Edinburgh, 1875)

SINCLAIR B. FERGUSON

Fairfax, John (b. Warwick, Warwickshire, England, 25 Oct. 1804: d. Sydney, Australia, 16 June 1877). Congregationalist deacon, bookseller, librarian, printer, newspaper proprietor, merchant, and philanthropist. Son of William Fairfax and Elizabeth Jesson of Warwickshire, he was strongly influenced by his mother's independency, the 'spiritual expression of free enterprise'. He was apprenticed at the age of 12 to a bookseller-printer. After two years as typesetter with the London *Morning Chronicle*, he set up business in Leamington Pryors as a printer, bookseller and stationer, married his childhood friend from Chapel, Sarah Reading, commencing his first newspaper, the *Leamington Spa Sketch Book*, in 1828. His political principles leant towards reformist conservatism.

Ruined in a series of libel cases (of which he was acquitted) Fairfax and family emigrated to Australia in 1838, taking up positions as typesetter, and later librarian. Deacon of the Pitt Street Congregational church with other merchants such as David Jones, this close network of energetic Nonconformist businessmen, associated through chapel and company, grew together in wealth and influence, called by their opponents a 'Venetian oligarchy'. In February 1841 he and Charles Kemp bought the *Sydney Herald* for the huge price of £10,000. By 1856, the (now *Sydney Morning*) *Herald* had the third largest circulation in the Empire. In 1853 he bought Kemp out, in 1856 bringing his son James into partnership, setting up a dynasty which lasted 134 years. The *Herald* became the benchmark for Australian newspapers. On its strength, Fairfax branched out into all forms of business, some of which were to become huge conglomerates in their own right.

Renowned for religious tolerance, Fairfax was active in public life and in interdenominational Christian work including the YMCA. He remained senior deacon of Pitt Street until death, assisting in the foundation of Camden Theological College. Serious and energetic, Fairfax represented that class of Christian businessmen who sought to spread moral enlightenment through the institutions of civil society. He was the self-made man who put his fortune down to hard work and faith in God: his favourite motto being 'Pray without ceasing'.

BIBLIOGRAPHY
ADB
J. F. Fairfax, *The Story of John Fairfax* (Sydney, 1941)

MARK HUTCHINSON

Fanch, James (b. Hemel Hempstead, Hertfordshire, England; *fl.* 1704; d. 1767). English Baptist minister. Fanch lived in Hertfordshire until he moved with his sister, Ann, and brother-in-law DANIEL TURNER to Reading in 1741. In 1743, he was called out to preach by the congregation at Reading. He served the congregation at Whitchurch in Hampshire for one year and then served the congregations at Romsey and Lockerly. A hymnwriter and author, he wrote, *Free Thoughts On Practical Religion* (1761), *A Paraphrase of the Psalms of David from Latin* (1761), and *A Compendium of the Principles of Religion* (1769), according to Daniel Turner, was published posthumously with the assistance of JOHN GILL. (Exactly how much assistance Gill may have offered is unknown).

KAREN SMITH

Fancourt, Thomas (b. *c.* 1771; d. London, 2 May 1857). Anglican clergyman. Fancourt appears to be the son of William Fancourt, rector of Bletsoe, and the younger brother of WILLIAM J. L. FANCOURT. He was admitted to Queens' College, Cambridge in 1789 (BA 1793) and was ordained (deacon 1793, priest 1795) by the Bishop of Peterborough. He was Rector of Lowick, Northamptonshire, 1795–7. Little is known of his career except that he resided in London from 1807 to 1813 and actively supported the CMS and the RTS (serving on its committee in 1808). Much later he was assistant minister of the Jews' Episcopal Chapel in Bethnal Green, London, from 1845 to 1857. His son, William Joseph, followed in his father's footsteps in attending Cambridge and in entering the Anglican ministry.

BIBLIOGRAPHY
Al. Cant.
C. Hole, *Early History of the Church Missionary Society* (London, 1896): 627

DONALD M. LEWIS

Fancourt, William John Lowfield (b. *c.* 1767; d. London, 13 May 1840). Anglican clergyman and headmaster. Fancourt was the son of William Fancourt, Curate of

Woodford, Northamptonshire. THOMAS FANCOURT appears to have been his younger brother. William was educated at Eton and Clare Hall, Cambridge (matriculated 1785; BA 1789; MA 1800; DD 1823) and was ordained (deacon 1789) for the curacy of father's parish of Bletsoe and then served as headmaster of St Saviour's Grammar School, Southwark, 1793–1823 which he is said to have rescued from collapse. It appears that during much of his time in Southwark he was Curate of St Olave's. In 1823 he was made Prebendary of Lincoln Cathedral and in June 1828 the Vicar of St Mary's, Leicester and then in November 1828 Vicar of St Leonard's, Leicester (1828–1840). Like his brother, he was an early supporter of the CMS.

BIBLIOGRAPHY
Al. Cant.
C. Hole, *Early History of the Church Missionary Society* (London, 1896): 627

DONALD M. LEWIS

Fanning, Tolbert (b. Cannon Co., TN, USA, 10 May 1810; d. Nashville, TN, USA, 3 May 1874). Disciples of Christ preacher, educator, and publisher. After early contact with the Baptists through his mother, Fanning accepted at age 17 the plea of a religious movement then new in the American West. Denominated the Restoration Movement or the Stone-Campbell Movement, Fanning followed the rational emphasis espoused by ALEXANDER CAMPBELL. Throughout life he would oppose the emotional, camp meeting religion of BARTON STONE.

His first attempts at preaching in Alabama, where he was baptized, were failures. He was a tall (6 feet 6 inches), gangly young man who had difficulty holding the attention of his audiences, which is remarkable in view of his later spell-binding oratory. He moved to Nashville, Tennessee in 1831 to continue his education at the University of Nashville. Here he came under the influence of Philip Lindsey and Gerard Troost. While a student, he preached throughout the region, forming numerous congregations after the order of the Restoration plea.

Following graduation from the University of Nashville in 1835, he came under the direct influence of Alexander Campbell. In the year of his graduation, he travelled with Campbell from Nashville through Kentucky as Campbell returned home. During the next year, Fanning journeyed with Campbell throughout New England and into Canada. Many of the theological positions Fanning would hold for life were formed on these trips. Beyond the personal encounters, Fanning had read Campbell's *Christian Baptist* and the *Millennial Harbinger*. Both men were strongly influenced by Scottish common-sense philosophy.

Fanning and his wife, Charlotte Fall Fanning, were both interested in education. She operated girls' schools on several occasions. Fanning founded Elm Crag School in 1844 to teach manual labour, with special emphasis on agriculture. Besides his interest in religion and preaching, he was a leader in scientific agriculture in Tennessee. He was an editor of *The Agriculturalist*, the official journal of the state agricultural society. In 1845, he renamed his school Franklin College, in honour of Benjamin Franklin. All students studied agriculture along with the standard courses then required in colleges. Chapel and Bible readings were required of all students. Although not a Bible college, the school did graduate young men who preached. The school continued, with the exception of the Civil War years, until 1865 when its buildings were destroyed by fire.

Fanning's theological positions evolved into a very conservative (some would say legalistic) position because of a number of influences. The emotionalism of the Stoneites and the spiritualism of Jesse Ferguson, who preached for the Nashville Christian Church, reaffirmed his position held since the early years of his *Christian Review*. He believed firmly that God's complete revelation is found in the Bible. When Theodore Parker and his associates espoused 'higher lawism' to justify not following the laws of the United States, Fanning became even more adamant in his strong biblical stance.

The religious journal became a major vehicle of Fanning's ideas. In addition to the *Christian Review*, he edited *The Naturalist*, a scientific magazine. These journals were not long lived. His most enduring editorial comment came through *The Gospel Advocate*, a journal begun in 1855. Through this magazine he opposed 'higher lawism', the residue of Ferguson's ideas, and the formation of the American Christian Missionary Society, an event of 1849. In 1857, Fanning and Robert Richardson of the *Millennial Harbinger* and a close associate of Alexander Campbell, indicated the division then in progress within the Disciples of Christ. Richardson deplored Fanning's legalism; Fanning feared Richardson's acceptance of an erroneous view of the Holy Spirit.

The American Civil War would have an impact on Fanning. He strongly condemned the American Christian Missionary Society when it voted, although in recess, its support for the Union in the Civil War. In fact, Fanning was quite southern in his views, although he had been a pacifist since the Mexican War.

Because of his economic losses and the religious division coming as a result of the Civil War, Fanning became rather bitter. He did share with his student, David Lipscomb, the burden of reviving *The Gospel Advocate* in 1866, but his heart was never fully in its mission as a voice to southern Disciples of Christ. He was not associated with the journal after 1869.

Fanning would attempt one additional publishing venture, a journal called *The Historian* in 1872. It would not have a long life as Fanning died in 1874 as a result of a wound suffered when gored by a bull.

David Lipscomb said of his mentor that he was the finest preacher he had ever heard. He could hold spellbound an audience for two hours. His influence lived through *The Gospel Advocate* and its editor David Lipscomb. American Churches of Christ are a part of Tolbert Fanning's religious lineage.

BIBLIOGRAPHY
J. R. Wilburn, *Hazard of the Die* (Austin, TX, 1969)

ROBERT E. HOOPER

Faraday, Michael (b. Newington, Surrey, England, 22 Sept. 1791; d. Hampton Court, Middlesex, England, 25 Aug. 1867). Leading British scientist. The son of a blacksmith, with little formal education, Faraday was apprenticed to a London bookbinder in whose service he came across encyclopedia articles on scientific subjects. Captivated by these and the Royal Institution lectures of Humphry Davy, he secured an introduction and became Davy's assistant. At first little more than a manservant, accompanying Davy on his continental tours, Faraday became a trusted associate and (as has been said) Davy's greatest discovery. The Royal Institution was to become his home and centre of scientific activity. In 1821 he became superintendent of the house and in 1825 director of the laboratory, starting the famous Friday evening discourses and the juvenile Christmas lectures in 1826. Failing health led eventually to retirement and a house near Hampton Court provided by Queen Victoria.

At first Faraday worked in chemistry, discovering benzene and much else. Being convinced (unusually for his time) of the unity of all natural forces he moved effortlessly across traditional boundaries separating chemistry, electricity, magnetism and light. He was thus led to formulate his own laws of electrolysis. Thence he came to electricity and magnetism and in 1831 discovered electromagnetic induction (by which electric currents can be generated by moving magnets). From this work came the invention of the dynamo and a dawning realization that an electric current could be understood, not as a flowing liquid, but in terms of vibrations within a conductor. And so Faraday came to his most lasting achievement: the classical field theory that viewed chemical, electrical, magnetic and optical phenomena in terms of forces between molecules. J. C. MAXWELL was later to develop this even further.

Faraday was a very private person, uninterested in politics and seemed solely devoted to science. But his whole life, including his science, can only be adequately comprehended in terms of his theology. He was a member of the Sandemanian church in London, a small Nonconformist sect of evangelical doctrine and practical piety. He regularly attended their services on Sundays, becoming an elder of the meeting. His faith expressed itself in a nobility of character that even his materialist friends admired, and in a serenity that survived personal tragedy and misfortune and can only be seen in his private correspondence.

His science at first seems detached from his religion. He doubted whether God could be found by reasoning from natural phenomena and stressed the priority of faith. Only then would enlightened eyes perceive the 'evidences' embedded in creation. Equally, he declined to treat scripture as a scientific text and therefore to engage in 'harmonizing' exercises. He appears to have been untroubled by debates on the age of the earth or evolution.

However, he was profoundly convinced of the role of God in creation. It has been convincingly argued that 'his deepest intuitions about the physical world sprang from this religious faith in the Divine origin of nature' (Williams, 1965). A famous manuscript of 1844, a private memorandum to himself, argued the concept of atoms as point-centres of force, rather than the 'billiard-ball' models of the chemists. Yet it contains three explicit references to God, giving a rare insight into Faraday's mind and suggesting that his whole unified field theory (of which point-atoms were an important part) stemmed from the unified world-picture of his Sandemanian faith.

BIBLIOGRAPHY
G. N. Cantor, *Faraday Rediscovered*, eds D. Gooding and F. A. J. L. James (Basingstoke, England, 1985): ch. 4
—, *Michael Faraday* (London, 1991)
DNB
DSB
T. H. Levere, *British Journal for the History of Science*, 4 (1968): 95–107
C. A. Russell, *Cross-Currents* (Leicester, England, 1985)
L. P. Williams, *Michael Faraday* (London, 1965)

COLIN A. RUSSELL

Farish, William (b. Carlisle, Cumberland, England, 1759; d. Little Stonham, Suffolk, England, 12 Jan. 1837). University professor and Anglican clergyman. Farish, son of the Rector of Stanwix, was educated at Carlisle Grammar School and Magdalene College, Cambridge (BA 1778; MA 1781). He was senior wrangler and became fellow and tutor of Magdalene, and thereby played an important part in making the college pre- eminently evangelical. In 1794 he was appointed professor of chemistry and did much to establish cross-links with engineering and mechanics and to promote industrial applications. In 1813 he succeeded to the Jacksonian chair of natural philosophy. His evidence to an early parliamentary committee on railways in which he expressed the opinion that trains might run at sixty miles an hour led to his being considered by the members as of unsound mind!

After being Vicar of North Clifton (Nottinghamshire) (1797–1802), Farish became Rector of St Giles, Cambridge in 1800 and during the years of CHARLES SIMEON's indisposition he undertook the main role in the care of students, enlarging his church to meet this need. He was always prominent in supporting younger members of the university, most notably in their campaign to set up a Cambridge auxiliary of BFBS in 1811, even when Simeon himself was somewhat hesitant. Farish also supported CMS and opposed slavery and the slave trade. He upheld the church-and-state relationship and objected to the removal of Roman Catholic disabilities. He was Rector of Little Stonham only for the last months of his life.

He was a man of simple character, open temperament

and reserved manner. He was also perspicacious enough to recognize (in 1820) that 'We have now far more clergymen than formerly, preaching justification by faith only; but on regeneration and sanctification I cannot say so much.'

BIBLIOGRAPHY
Al. Cant., II ii: 459
CO, xxxvi
DNB

ARTHUR POLLARD

Farmer, Thomas (b. London, 7 June 1790; d. Acton, England, 11 May 1861). Wesleyan industrialist and philanthropist. Farmer was born in his father's house near Kennington Common, London. Following his mother's death in 1794 he and his brother were brought up by their father who worshipped with both the Independents and the Wesleyan Methodists. After being articled to a solicitor Farmer left to join his father's chemical manufactory and carried out a course of self-education and religious study. In 1809 he was converted, took Communion with the Wesleyans and joined a class. In 1810 he became a Sunday school teacher for the Independents.

In 1817 JABEZ BUNTING persuaded him to become a class leader and in 1818 to join the committee of the WMMS. In 1826 he became one of its treasurers and in 1851 offered £1,000 to extend its work in Hong Kong and Canton. In 1820 he joined the committee of the BFBS and in 1859 was made a vice-president; he and his family contributing £4,469 to its funds by 1869. He was also treasurer to the Wesleyan Theological Institution, the EA and the Strangers' Friends Society; besides supporting the RTS. In character he was very cautious, three times refusing requests to stand for Parliament, and was given to deep spiritual introspection and self-examination. He died in his home, Gunnersbury House, Acton, leaving a widow and five daughters.

BIBLIOGRAPHY
J. Hannah, *The Path of the Just* (London, 1861)
H. J. Townsend, *A New History of Methodism*, 2 (London, 1909): 315.
W. Canton, *History of the British and Foreign Bible Society*, 3 (London, 1910): 64

DONALD M. LEWIS

Farnham, eighth Baron. *See* MAXWELL, SOMERSET RICHARD

Farquhar, Sir **Walter Rocliffe** (b. London, 4 June 1810; d. near Dorking, Surrey, England, 15 July 1900). Banker. Educated at Eton, he was the elder son of Thomas Harvie Farquhar, second Baronet, whom he succeeded in 1836. Farquhar was senior partner in an a wealthy St James Street bank (from 1846) and served

as Deputy-Lieutenant and Justice of the Peace for Middlesex county. His letters to W. E. GLADSTONE are deposited in the British Library.

A strong Protestant Tory, Farquhar was treasurer from 1884 of the Liberty and Property Defense League, a private enterprise association. He was also involved in the work of the church as vice-president of the CPAS from its foundation, as a member of the Scripture Readers' Association, and as an executive member of the Home Episcopate Society (1872–4). He was also a key figure in the establishment of the Colonial Church Society in 1835. In 1857 he originated – with Lord SHAFTESBURY and C. M. Sawell – popular special services for the poor that were held in theatres around the metropolis.

BIBLIOGRAPHY
Boase
N. Pope, *Dickens and Charity* (New York, 1978): 143, 273

JONATHAN BURKE CUTMORE

Farquharson, Alexander (b. Strathardle, Perthshire, Scotland, 1793; d. Cape Breton, Nova Scotia, BNA, 1858). Church of Scotland minister and architect of the original Presbyterian parish structure of Cape Breton. Farquharson and his brother, ARCHIBALD FARQUHARSON, were both influenced by the evangelical movement in their district. He trained for ministry with the Church of Scotland, and, supported by the Edinburgh Ladies' Association, was sent to Cape Breton Island in 1833. Cape Breton had by then become the home of many settlers from the Scottish Highlands, but formal religious provision was extremely poor; the island had a 'bad name', and missionaries were very reluctant to serve there. Farquharson settled eventually at Middle River, and, although he found more spiritual interest than had been reported, he itinerated extensively throughout the island, enduring 'many inconveniences . . . which people in Scotland have no idea of'. He submitted to the Ladies' Association a plan for ten parishes, and the society worked to implement it. Their efforts bore fruit, as the first presbytery of Cape Breton was constituted in 1836, and the number of ministers increased slowly. Strongly evangelical, the émigré ministers led their congregations effortlessly into the FCS.

BIBLIOGRAPHY
L. Stanley, *The Well-Watered Garden* (Sydney, Cape Breton, Canada, 1984)

DONALD E. MEEK

Farquharson, Archibald (b. Strathardle, Perthshire, Scotland, 1800; d. Tiree, Argyllshire, Scotland, 1878). Brother of ALEXANDER FARQUHARSON. Pastor and itinerant preacher with the Congregational Union of Scotland, polemicist, and hymn-writer. Farquharson entered Congregational Hall in 1829, and was posted to Tiree in

1832, where he established an Independent church, of which he became pastor in 1835. An ardent evangelist of strongly paedobaptist persuasion, Farquharson lived in creative tension with the local Baptists (*see* DUNCAN MACDOUGALL), and published pamphlets critical of the Baptist position. Some of his own converts became Baptists, and several became Baptist preachers. His perceptive appreciation of the problems caused to Highland mission by doctrinal disagreement, resulting in the division of churches and resources, led him latterly to advocate 'The Unsectarian Gaelic Mission for Highlanders' (pamphlet title, Glasgow, 1872). An enthusiast for the Gaelic language, he wrote several pamphlets in its defence, but is best remembered as the prolific composer of Gaelic hymns, often set to jaunty song-tunes which ensured them a wide currency in the community. Farquharson itinerated extensively, from the Outer Hebrides to his native Perthshire. His church in Tiree, which experienced several revival movements, was severely reduced by periodic waves of emigration and defections to the Baptist cause, and the charge was not filled after his death.

BIBLIOGRAPHY
D. E. Meek, 'Evangelical Missionaries in the Early Nineteenth-Century Highlands', *Scottish Studies*, 28 (1987): 17

DONALD E. MEEK

Farquharson, John (b. Glen Tilt, Perthshire, Scotland; d. Nova Scotia, BNA, *c.* 1820). Pioneer itinerant evangelist with the Independents in Perthshire. Farquharson trained briefly at a HALDANE class in Dundee, but left after six months because he was ill-suited to study. Dispatched to Breadalbane in 1800 as a scripture reader, he displayed a devotion to Christ which deeply influenced the district. A powerful awakening was evident by 1802, and Independent congregations were formed by him at Killin and Acharn, Lochtayside. He was pastor of the Acharn church from 1802 to 1804. Briefly imprisoned in Aberdeen for his preaching in Braemar, Farquharson emigrated afterwards (*c.* 1806) to Nova Scotia. At some point (perhaps *en route* to Canada), he arrived in Skye, preached in the north end of the island, and was instrumental in the conversion of Donald Munro, a blind catechist who later became a major local evangelical leader.

BIBLIOGRAPHY
W. J. Couper, *Scottish Revivals* (Dundee, Scotland, 1918): 96–7, 100–2
A. Haldane, *Memoirs of the Lives of Robert Haldane of Airthrey, and of his brother, James Alexander Haldane* (London, 1852): 316–7
D. E. Meek, 'The Independent and Baptist Churches of Highland Perthshire and Strathspey', *Transactions of the Gaelic Society of Inverness*, 56 (1988–90): 269–343

DONALD E. MEEK

Farrar, Charles Pinhorn (b. London, *c.* 1798; d. 25 June 1877). CMS missionary to India. Farrar was trained at the CMS school at Islington (London) in 1826 and ordained (deacon 1827, priest 1828) by the Bishop of London. On 13 February 1829 he was sent to Bombay and then to Nasik in western India. He returned to England on 1 November 1838 and went out again on 29 October 1841. He left India on 29 May 1847 because of ill health and ended his association with the CMS. Appaji Bapuji, a Brahmin convert and later a CMS worker, attributed his first impressions of Christianity to Farrar's influence. In 1861 Farrar became the incumbent of Sidcup, Kent. His wife (née Turner) had an effective ministry with Indian women. His son, Frederick William Farrar (1831–1903), was a broad churchman who became Dean of Canterbury.

BIBLIOGRAPHY
D. T. B[arry], *CMS Register of Missionaries and Native Clergy* (privately printed) (London, 1906)

DONALD M. LEWIS

Farrar, John (b. Alnwick, Northumberland, England, 29 June 1802; d. Leeds, England, 19 Nov. 1884). Wesleyan educator. The son of a Wesleyan minister, Farrar was among the first seminarians at Woodhouse Grove School, Yorkshire. He was second master there from 1822 to 1826, and returned in 1858 as governor and chaplain. In the meantime, from 1827 to 1839, he was a highly successful minister in a number of locations, including London, until his appointment as classical tutor and governor of Abney House seminary, London. Then, from 1843 to 1857, he was classical tutor at Richmond College, Surrey, and, finally, governor of Headly College, Leeds from 1868 to 1876. A prolific author of biblical reference books, he produced a widely distributed theological dictionary (1851), and his most respected work, a dictionary of sects (1854). He was rewarded for these services by being twice elected president of conference, a rare honour (Birmingham, 1854; Burslem, 1870). He was vice-president (1870) of the Central Association for Stopping the Sale of Intoxicating Liquors on Sunday.

BIBLIOGRAPHY
Anon, *Wesley and His Successors* (London, 1891)
T. Cooper, ed., *Men of the Time*, 10th edn (London, 1879)
DNB
H. L. Malchow, *Agitators and Promoters in the Age of Gladstone and Disraeli* (New York, 1983)

JONATHAN BURKE CUTMORE

Farrer, John (b. 1735; d. Carlisle, Cumberland, England, 23 Nov. 1808). Anglican evangelical minister and schoolmaster. Farrer was baptized at Orton, Westmorland, 22 December 1735. He was educated at Appleby Grammar School and taught in schools before being ordained. In 1759 he became Curate of Escomb and master of Bishop Auckland Grammar School after which he was, for 28 years, Perpetual Curate of Witton le Wear where he ran a successful private school. Farrer was offered preferment as Rector of Sunderland, but resigned through ill health. From 1795 he was Vicar of Stanwix and minor canon of Carlisle cathedral.

He supported The Association of Protestant Schoolmasters and superintended charity and Sunday schools in the Carlisle area. He did much to pioneer evangelical Anglicanism in Cumberland before the work of ISAAC MILNER.

SELECT WRITINGS
J. Farrer, *Memoir of the late Rev John Farrer* (Newcastle-upon-Tyne, England, 1844)

ALAN FREDERICK MUNDEN

Faught, George Steers (b. Ireland, *c.* 1802). *Fl.* 1825–36. CMS missionary to Ceylon. Faught entered the first class of students at the newly established CMS college at Islington (London) in 1825 and was ordained (deacon and priest 1826) by the Bishop of London. He was sent to Ceylon on 9 April 1827 where he served for ten years until failing health forced his return (12 November 1836). He later served as curate of Bradfield, St Clare, Suffolk. Faught married Anne Le Clerc.

BIBLIOGRAPHY
D. T. B[arry], *CMS Register of Missionaries and Native Clergy* (privately printed) (London, 1906)

DONALD M. LEWIS

Fawcett, James (b. Leeds, Yorkshire, England, 1752; d. Great Snoring, Norfolk, England, 10 April 1831). Anglican clergyman and scholar. Fawcett was a member of a well-known evangelical clerical family in Leeds, his brothers being JOHN and RICHARD FAWCETT. Like the MILNERS, he was educated at Leeds Grammar School, whence he proceeded to St John's College, Cambridge (BA 1774; MA 1777; BD 1785; fellow 1777–1803). After a brief curacy with his father at St John's, Leeds (1776) he spent the greater part of his career in Cambridge, being Vicar of St Sepulchre's (the Round Church) (1791–1822) and Norrisian professor of divinity (1795–1815). On resigning St Sepulchre's he moved to Norfolk to his rectory of Great Snoring and Thursford (1801–31). His lectures have been described as ineffective as a result of 'a certain thickness of speech, an awkwardness of manner, a want of energy and an easiness of temper'!

BIBLIOGRAPHY
Al. Cant., II ii: 468
DNB

ARTHUR POLLARD

Fawcett, John (b. Bradford, Yorkshire, England, 6 Jan. 1740; d. Hebden Bridge, Yorkshire, England, 25 July 1817). Baptist minister and hymn-writer. Converted as a teenager through a sermon on John 3.14, preached by GEORGE WHITEFIELD, he became a Methodist, before joining the Baptist church in his home town. He was ordained when he was 24 and became minister of the church at Wainsgate. In 1777 the congregation moved to nearby Hebden Bridge. Twice he was invited to influential spheres outside Yorkshire – in 1772, to the pastorate of Carter Lane, London, and in 1792, to the presidency of Bristol Academy. He declined both 'calls'.

Though entirely self-educated, he was a man of culture. No one did more than he did to encourage and work for an educated ministry within his denomination in the north of England. He himself played a prominent part in the founding of Horton Academy (later Rawdon College). His *Essay on Anger* impressed George III, who would have honoured him had he not declined any personal favour. Instead, Fawcett pleaded for the life of a man awaiting execution. He kept a private academy, JOHN FOSTER, the essayist, being among his students. His friends included HENRY VENN, HENRY FOSTER and DAN TAYLOR.

He encouraged spiritual growth among the Baptists of Yorkshire and Lancashire and actively supported the BMS and the Bible Society. He wrote a number of hymns, including 'Blest be the tie that binds' and 'Lord, dismiss us with thy blessing'. Among his other published works was a two-volume devotional commentary on the Bible, completed in 1811, which achieved a wide popularity. His pastoral practicality is seen in the way he concluded each chapter with 'a devotional exercise or aspiration'. It is not surprising that Fawcett was a key figure in the spiritual revival among Baptists. He spent a great deal of time in prayer and meditation. Theological controversy, so much enjoyed by the Hyper-Calvinists, he shunned not only because he disliked it but because it was spiritually unproductive. It has been said that he 'never preached against Hyper-Calvinism; he simply lived it down.' In his *The Constitution and Order of a Gospel Church* (1797) he argued a cogent case for the congregational ordering of Christian churches defending both the divine initiative in bringing them into being through the faith of their members, and the responsibility of those so gathered in carrying out their evangelistic task.

BIBLIOGRAPHY
J. Fawcett (son), *An Account of the Life, Ministry and Writings of the Late Rev John Fawcett D.D.* (London, 1818)
J. Ivimey, *History of the English Baptists*, 4 (London, 1830)
Whitley, *BB*

E. F. CLIPSHAM

Fawcett, John (b. Leeds, Yorkshire, England, 30 Nov. 1769; d. Carlisle, Cumberland, England, 4 Dec. 1851). Anglican clergyman. Fawcett was educated at Leeds Grammar School and Magdalene College, Cambridge. After ordination (deacon 1793, priest 1794) he was curate to JAMES STILLINGFLEET, Rector of Hotham, then assistant master to JOSEPH MILNER at Hull Grammar

School. Through ISAAC MILNER, Fawcett became the headmaster of Carlisle Grammar School in 1796 and shortly afterwards became curate of St Cuthbert's church. In 1801 the dean and chapter appointed him as Vicar of the parish.

Like other evangelicals Fawcett experienced opposition from his congregation and SIMEON helped fend off opposition from Methodists. He held 'Fawcett parties' based on the Simeonite model and was an early advocate of the temperance cause. His ministry at Carlisle was marked by his support for the CMS and in the erection of schools and two churches. Fawcett sustained an evangelical ministry in Carlisle between the death of Dean Isaac Milner and the appointment of Dean FRANCIS CLOSE.

BIBLIOGRAPHY
C. Hole, *The Early History of the Church Missionary Society* (London, 1896)

ALAN FREDERICK MUNDEN

Fawcett, Richard (b. Leeds, Yorkshire, England, 6 Feb. 1760; d. Leeds, England, 22 Jan. 1837). Anglican clergyman. Like his brother JAMES FAWCETT, Richard was educated at Leeds Grammar School and St John's College, Cambridge (BA 1781; MA 1784), and also like his brother he served a curacy with his father at St John's, Leeds (1782). He was subsequently Perpetual Curate of Armley, Leeds (1792–1815) and Vicar of Leeds (1815–37). JOHN FAWCETT was a younger brother.

BIBLIOGRAPHY
Al. Cant., II ii: 468

ARTHUR POLLARD

Fearon, Devey (b. probably London, *c.* 1769; d. Ore, near Hastings, Sussex, England, 28 July 1847). Anglican doctor and minister. Fearon was the son of Daniel Fearon, Esquire, of London and was educated at Trinity College, Cambridge (BA 1791; MA 1794) where he came under the influence of CHARLES SIMEON. He trained as a physician and practised medicine until 1807 when he decided to seek ordination. He was ordained and became the Curate of Betchworth, near Dorking in Surrey. In 1815 he was instituted as the Rector of Ore where he remained until his death. A friend of RICHARD CECIL, he ministered to him on his deathbed.

BIBLIOGRAPHY
C. Hole, *Early History of the Church Missionary Society* (London, 1896): 627

DONALD M. LEWIS

Feilding, William Basil Percy [seventh Earl of Denbigh] (b. Berwick House, Shropshire, England, 25 March 1796; d. Hampstead, England, 25 June 1865). Peer. He was the son of William Robert, Viscount Feilding, MP, who died in 1799. At the age of four, he succeeded his grandfather (Basil, sixth Earl of Feilding) to become the seventh Earl of Denbigh. Feilding was educated at Eton and admitted to Trinity College, Cambridge in 1814 as a nobleman (MA 1816). He became Lord of the Bedchamber to King William IV (1830–3) and was Lord Chamberlain to Queen Adelaide from 1833 until her death in 1849. He was made a Privy Counsellor in 1833. In 1822 he married Mary Elizabeth Kitty Moreton, sister of HENRY MORETON, second Earl of Ducie.

It is possible that Feilding was influenced in an evangelical direction while an undergraduate at Trinity when CHARLES SIMEON's influence was at its height. Evidence of his involvement in evangelical societies can be found from the mid-1840s when he served on the founding committee of the Anglican 'Scripture Readers' Association' and from 1848 as a vice-patron of the CPAS. He appears to have been a friend of Reverend JOHN H. GURNEY who wrote a memorial of Feilding's wife following her death in 1842. His eldest son and heir, Rudolph William Basil Feilding, was received into the Church of Rome in 1850.

BIBLIOGRAPHY
Al. Cant.
Al. Ox.
Boase
J. H. Gurney, *Funeral Sermon for the Countess of Denbigh* (London, 1843)

DONALD M. LEWIS

Feller, Henriette [née Odin] (b. Montagny, Vaud, Switzerland, 2 April 1800; d. Grande Ligne, Quebec, Canada, 29 March 1868). Pioneer Baptist missionary to francophone Canada. Henriette Odin was raised in a respected Lausanne family. At age 21 she married Louis Feller, a prominent businessman and superintendent of police. In 1827 her husband died, leaving her with three adolescent stepchildren. Meanwhile, she had come under the influence of the *Réveil* and circa 1825 had a significant conversion experience. To the consternation of her social circle, she identified with the persecuted independents, and for a number of years served as a deaconess in their church.

In 1835, she responded to an invitation to join Lausanne missionaries HENRI OLIVIER and his wife in Lower Canada (Quebec), and when the Oliviers returned to Switzerland in 1836, chose to remain in Canada. With the assistance of LOUIS ROUSSY, she established herself in the rural community of Grande Ligne, some sixty kilometres south of Montreal, where she was instrumental in the formation of the first francophone Protestant church in Canada in 1837. An impressive mission house, erected with support largely from interdenominational agencies in the United States, became a centre for educational, Bible colportage and evangelistic preaching efforts on the south shore of the St Lawrence

River. In 1845, Feller led the 'Swiss Mission' into formal affiliation with the Canadian Baptist Missionary Society.

Feller displayed considerable financial, administrative and medical skills, and combined these with personal charisma, culture and spirituality. Without offending contemporary conventions regarding the role of women, she managed to exercise virtual control of the mission operation. Upon her death in 1868, the Grande Ligne Mission had established nine churches, six stations and a number of residential and day schools, and employed seven ordained ministers among its full-time workers. It has proved the most enduring of all nineteenth-century efforts in French-Canadian evangelization, and continues today as the *Union d'Eglises baptistes francaises au Canada*.

BIBLIOGRAPHY
J. M. Cramp, *A Memoir of Madame Feller* (London, no date)
W. N. Wyeth, *Henrietta Feller and the Grande Ligne Mission* (Philadelphia, PA, 1898)

GLEN G. SCORGIE

Fenn, Joseph (b. London, 1789 or 1790; d. Blackheath, England, 10 Jan. 1878). Noted CMS missionary and committee member. After a very promising legal career, he determined to become a missionary in India through the influence of Dr CLAUDIUS BUCHANAN. Like WILLIAM GREENWOOD and THOMAS NORTON before him, Fenn could not find a bishop willing to ordain him as a missionary and thus had first to serve an English curacy before going abroad. He was ordained (deacon and priest 1816) to the curacy of Pakefield and left under CMS auspices in December 1817, arriving early in 1818 in Travancore (Cottayam), south India and worked with the Syrian Church. This he did very imaginatively helping to restore its 'ancient and primitive worship and discipline', and deliberately eschewing any attempt to impose 'the liturgy and discipline of the English Church'. A very able missionary, he mastered Syriac and Sanskrit. Unfortunately ill health forced him to return to England in 1826. He became minister of Blackheath Park Chapel and was a greatly respected member of the CMS Committee (1830–75).

BIBLIOGRAPHY
D. T. B[arry], *CMS Register of Missionaries And Native Clergy from 1804 to 1904* (privately printed) (London, 1906)

C. PETER WILLIAMS

Fenn, Joseph Finch (b. Travancore, India, 3 Oct. 1819; d. Cheltenham, Gloucestershire, England, 22 July 1884). Anglican clergyman. Fenn was educated at Blackheath, London and Trinity College, Cambridge. He became a college fellow and was ordained. Following a brief curacy at Ware, Hertfordshire, he became Vicar of Stotfold, Bedfordshire, and from 1860 to 1884 was Vicar of Christ Church, Cheltenham.

Charles Bell of Cheltenham described Fenn as 'a scholar and a gentleman'. He was awarded a BD in 1877 but published little. Fenn was an effective platform speaker and an able, thoughtful preacher. He was much involved in philanthropic work and charitable work in Cheltenham where he was active in the formation of the public library. In his latter years he became an advocate of total abstinence. 'He was generally regarded as an Evangelical, but was not a party man' (DNB) and avoided theological controversy. He supported the SPG and the CMS, and was sympathetic towards the old High Church party. He was chaplain to Bishop C. J. Ellicott, became an honorary canon of Gloucester and proctor in convocation.

BIBLIOGRAPHY
B. H. Blackler, ed., *Gloucestershire Notes and Queries* (1879–June 1905) 3: 580–2
Cheltenham Examiner (23 and 30 July 1884)
DNB

ALAN FREDERICK MUNDEN

Ferguson, Angus (b. Ross of Mull, Inner Hebrides, Scotland, c. 1810; d. Skye, Inner Hebrides, Scotland, 1842). Baptist itinerant preacher and pastor. Brother of DUNCAN FERGUSON, Angus assisted with evangelization in Mull, and was appointed as pastor of the Baptist church at Uig, Skye, in 1836. Through his ministry in the period 1836–8, the Uig church, which had been seriously depleted by emigration, experienced a revival which boosted its declining membership. While itinerating in Skye, Ferguson caught a chill which resulted in his early death.

BIBLIOGRAPHY
D. E. Meek, *Sunshine and Shadow* (Edinburgh, 1991)
—, 'The Independent and Baptist Churches of Highland Perthshire and Strathspey', *Transactions of the Gaelic Society of Inverness*, 56 (1988–90): Appendix C

DONALD E. MEEK

Ferguson, Duncan (b. Ross of Mull, Inner Hebrides, Scotland, 1800; d. 1882). Baptist itinerant preacher and pastor. Ferguson belonged to a crofting family at Tiraghoill (three miles west of Bunessan). Brought to faith in 1820 partly through the preaching of DUGALD SINCLAIR, he went with Sinclair to be baptized in Colonsay in 1821. He was the first native-born Baptist in Mull, and played a key part in the development of Baptist witness there. By 1822 he had become a charity-school teacher, and was stationed in Ardnamurchan. Returning to Mull, he was appointed one of the two elders (pastors) of the Baptist church at Ardalanish (moved to Bunessan, 1891) when it was constituted in 1835 (*see* DUNCAN MCINTRYE, and CHARLES MACQUARIE). Supported by the Baptist Home Missionary Society for Scotland, he travelled extensively throughout Mull, chiefly in southern and western districts, complementing the labours of ALEXANDER GRANT on the northern side. He retired in 1877, having witnessed major decline, through emigration, in the size of his congregations.

BIBLIOGRAPHY
D. E. Meek, *Sunshine and Shadow* (Edinburgh, 1991)

DONALD E. MEEK

Fernandez, Ignatius (b. Macao, 31 July 1757; d. Bengal, India, 27 Dec. 1830). Baptist evangelist and pastor in India. Of Portuguese (Goan) extraction, Fernandez was educated for the Roman Catholic priesthood but became disillusioned and arrived in Bengal as a merchant in 1774. He received a Bible in 1795, was converted after approaching JOHN THOMAS and becoming friends with JOHN FOUNTAIN and WILLIAM WARD. He was baptized 18 January 1801 and ordained 17 January 1804.

On his indigo plantation Fernandez built a church and schools, and was a very benevolent employer. Evenings and Sundays he preached and conducted worship. Although the churches at Dinapore and Sadamahal were important to the Serampore Mission outreach, they decayed when Fernandez's death removed his sensitive, fatherly personality. He left his entire estate to the mission, but it proved difficult to manage from Serampore. The church was eventually revived by an influx of tribal Christians.

BIBLIOGRAPHY
Circular letters of the Serampore Mission 1808–1816
J. C. Marshman, *The Life and Times of Carey, Marshman and Ward* (London, 1858)
Periodical Accounts relative to the Baptist Missionary Society

E. M. JACKSON

Ferrers, seventh Earl [né Robert Shirley] (b. Ratcliffe, Leicestershire, England, 21 Sept. 1756; d. 2 May 1827). Peer. Ferrers succeeded his father on 17 April 1787. The Shirley family had been early supporters of the evangelical revival and Ferrers continued that tradition: his great-aunt was Lady Frances Shirley, the correspondent of JAMES HERVEY; his father's first cousin was Selina Shirley, the Countess of HUNTINGDON; his father's brother was WALTER SHIRLEY (1725–86), a supporter of the Countess and the father of another WALTER SHIRLEY (1768–1830). Earl Ferrers appointed his cousin to be the Vicar of Shirley, Derbyshire, and in 1828 when Walter Shirley resigned from the living, his son WALTER AUGUSTUS SHIRLEY (later Bishop Shirley) was appointed to the living by Earl Ferrers. W. A. Shirley had long been treated as a son by Earl Ferrers. Earl Ferrers was a country neighbour of another leading evangelical Anglican laymen, THOMAS BABINGTON. Like Babington, Ferrers was an early supporter of the CMS.

BIBLIOGRAPHY
C. Hole, *Early History of the Church Missionary Society* (London, 1896): 627–8

DONALD M. LEWIS

Few, Ignatius (Alphonso) (b. Columbia County, GA, USA, April 1791; d. Athens, GA, USA, 21 Nov. 1845). Scholar, lawyer, minister, educator, and first president of Emory College (later Emory University). His father, Ignatius Few Sr, fought in the American Revolution and after the war became a judge, a senator, and one of the delegates that drew up the Constitution of the United States. In his early teens, Ignatius was sent to the North to stay with his uncle, William Few, so that he could secure a better education. He attended school at Bergen, New Jersey, Princeton, and New York. Upon his return to Georgia, he studied law with General Thomas Flourney of Augusta. In 1811, Few married Selina Carr and settled down to the life of a plantation owner. When the War of 1812 began, he served as a colonel in command of a regiment. After that conflict ended he returned home, but financial reverses led him to move to Augusta in 1823 where he built a successful law practice. Once again circumstances intervened, and he was forced to leave his profession because of ill health.

Before his physical problems, he had taken a sceptical attitude toward religious faith, but when his career was interrupted, he began to think more seriously about God. In 1827 while reading the *Appeal to Matter of Fact and Common Sense* by JOHN W. FLETCHER, he was converted to the Christian faith. He joined the MEC in Augusta, and in 1828 was admitted to the ministry by the South Carolina Conference. Few became a charter member of the Georgia Methodist Conference in 1831 and served churches in Savannah (1831), Columbus (1832), and Macon (1834). After 1835 he was put on a pension and allowed to work on a part-time basis because of failing health.

It was during this period of his life that he became involved in a number of educational projects, including the establishment of a manual labour school and a college. Inspired by the example of Randolph-Macon College in Virginia, he began to plan for an educational institution for Methodists in Georgia. With conference support he secured donors who gave several hundred acres of land on which a manual labour school could be established. The institution was to admit boys as young as twelve years old, who would learn agricultural and mechanical skills by working the land along with their studies of literature, classical languages, science and religion. His egalitarian vision led to the acceptance of both the rich and the poor as students. As he stated, '. . . the indigent will be able to acquire an education, by them generally unattainable; the rich will form habits of industry, and self-dependence, more valuable than gold or silver, both may have vigorous and cultivated intellects in sound and healthy bodies . . .' Despite the fact that the school was in dire financial straits, Few encouraged his colleagues to expand the work into a college.

With a charter from the state and support from the Georgia Conference the new institution named for Bishop JOHN EMORY was established at Oxford, Georgia. Few served as the first president of the college from 1837 to 1840.

After his retirement from Emory, he became involved in some of the bitter regional strife over slavery that led to division in the Methodist Church. At the General Conference in 1840, he sponsored a resolution that denied African Americans the right to testify against white persons in church trials in any state where they were not allowed to testify in the civil courts. Although he was not a member of the General Conference of 1844, which divided the church, his last recorded public activity was composing a report supporting the church split, which was adopted by the Georgia Conference in 1845. A beloved leader of early Georgia Methodism, he is remembered for his scholarship and piety by his church and the University that he founded.

BIBLIOGRAPHY

E. S. Bucke, ed., *The History of American Methodism*, 1 (Nashville, TN, 1964)

H. M. Bullock, *A History of Emory University* (Nashville, TN, 1936)

DAB

EWM

ROBERT G. CLOUSE

Figgins, John Leighton (b. *c.* 1810; d. Blackley, England, 1874). Anglican clergyman. Figgins was a member of Queens' College, Cambridge (BA 1832; MA 1870). After a perpetual curacy at Linthwaite (Yorkshire) (1833–5) and a further curacy at Lymm (Cheshire) (1836–7) he exercised a notable city ministry over nearly forty years, being first curate of St Matthew's, Liverpool (1837–43) and thereafter successively Perpetual Curate of St Clement's, Manchester (1843–66), Rector of St James's, Manchester (1866–9) and of St Peter's, Blackley (Manchester) (1869–74).

BIBLIOGRAPHY

Al. Cant., II, ii: 439

ARTHUR POLLARD

Finch, George (b. Hammersmith, England, 1794; d. London, 29 June 1870). Landowner, MP, and anti-Catholic leader. The illegitimate son of George Finch, ninth Earl of Winchilsea and fourth Earl of Nottingham, he was educated at Harrow and Trinity College, Cambridge. He was twice married, first in 1819 to Jane, daughter of Admiral JOHN TOLLEMACHE of Helmingham Hall, Suffolk, and sister of John, later first Baron Tollemache of Helmingham. She died in 1821, and on 22 October 1832 Finch married, second, Lady Louisa Somerset, daughter of Henry Charles, sixth Duke of Beaufort, and his wife Charlotte Sophia (*see* BEAUFORT).

Through these two marriages Finch was related to numerous other aristocratic evangelicals.

On his father's death in 1826 Finch inherited estates centred on Burley-on-the-Hill in Rutland, while the titles and other estates passed to his cousin George William Finch-Hatton, tenth Earl of Winchilsea, also a prominent anti-Catholic, but manifesting little sign of evangelical religious sentiments. Finch himself however, depressed by the successive deaths of his first wife and his father, found deeper spiritual resources in an increasingly strong identification with evangelicalism.

Finch was a leading member of the committee of the British (later Protestant) Reformation Society from its foundation in 1827. Together with JAMES EDWARD GORDON and FREDERICK EDWARD VERNON HARCOURT he took part in controversial tours of Ireland in the late 1820s. When, in later years, financial crises at various times threatened the survival of the society Finch's substantial donations helped to keep it solvent. He also played a significant part in the extraparliamentary anti-Catholic campaign of 1834–6 which led to the formation of the Protestant Association, and was the author of various tracts and compilations of documents on the controversy with Rome.

Finch served as MP for Stamford (1832–7) and Rutland (1846–7). He was a Tory and a Protectionist, but did not make much impact in the Commons. He was also a Justice of the Peace and a deputy-lieutenant. A small collection of transcripts from his papers survives in the hands of the family.

BIBLIOGRAPHY

Al. Cant.

Burke's

Stenton

J. Wolffe, *The Protestant Crusade in Great Britain, 1829–1860* (Oxford, 1991)

JOHN WOLFFE

Finch, Titus (b. New Haven, CT, BNA, 1756; d. Lobo, Ontario, Canada, 12 April 1834). Pastor and founder of Baptist churches in Ontario. He served in the American Revolutionary War 1776–83 as a sergeant in the Prince of Wales's American Regiment. When peace was declared, Finch was granted land in the Nashwaak Valley (Upper Maugerville), New Brunswick. His land grant was too small for his growing family, so they moved to a 600 acre grant in Charlotteville Township, Upper Canada in 1798.

While in New Brunswick Finch was among those who petitioned Governor Carleton for civil and religious privileges. Upon his arrival in Charlotteville, he began to preach. He was baptized, with his congregation, by missionaries from New York state in 1803. He was ordained in 1805 and licensed to conduct marriages 1807. Until 1827 he was pastor of this congregation which encouraged him to travel as local missionary. After 1827 he became pastor for short periods at the First Oxford Church, at Zorra, and lastly, at Lobo.

BIBLIOGRAPHY
Canadian Baptist Archives (CBA), minutes/files of the following churches: Charlotteville (now Vittoria), Boston, Zorra, Lobo, Aylmer
CBA Titus Finch biographical file
S. Ivison and F. Rosser, *The Baptists in Upper and Lower Canada before 1820* (Toronto, 1956)

JUDITH COLWELL

Fink, J. C. (b. Island of Ternate, 10 Nov. 1794). Serampore Mission Baptist missionary. Born in Batavia, of German extraction, Fink was baptized at Serampore. He completed an apprenticeship there, and, upon the death of Domingo Rebeiro, was sent to Chittagong where he built on the foundations laid by DE BRUYN. Later he went to Dhaka with Mugh Christian refugees from Cox's Bazaar. After the Burmese wars (1822–4), he built up the church in Arrakan using both Burmese and Bengali, and developed a circuit of native preachers and small churches. Based on the border in Akyab, he worked zealously among Buddhist priests, baptizing the first Manipuri Christian (a former Buddhist) on 10 May 1830. His schools failed due to competition from the monasteries, but an English school was more successful. During the Mughs Revolt against East India Company taxes, Fink was sympathetic; but his Christian Mughs did no fighting.

Despite having two sons and five daughters, Fink accepted a one-third salary reduction when the Serampore Mission faced bankruptcy after the 1832 Calcutta bank crash. His sons were baptized at Serampore by John Leechman on 29 December 1833, and Charles Fink took over the school, allowing J. C. Fink to concentrate on preaching. Fink returned to Calcutta for health reasons, and in 1851 was active in the Calcutta Mission Council.

E. M. JACKSON

Finlayson, William (b. Glasgow, Scotland, 30 Nov. 1813; d. Mitcham, South Australia, 19 Dec. 1897). City missionary and Independent pastor. Son of Robert (a Burgess of Glasgow), he commenced work at the age of 11 and at 14 entered the warehousing trade. His father was a member of the Independent Church, but William claimed to have not received conversion until he reached twenty. At this time he was fired with a zeal to follow in the steps of South Seas' missionaries. However, the LMS would not accept his application and he had no success in an approach to Sir THOMAS FOWELL BUXTON. He then became a city missionary with the LCM.

It was while in London that he read of the formation of the colony of South Australia, where he felt something of his ministry to the 'heathen savage' could be worked out. He married Helen (née Harvey) before emigration and arrived in South Australia in 1837. Finlayson farmed for a time and then developed some of his land into a village. While his missionary venture came to nothing he was one of the main founders of the Independent Christian Church in South Australia. He was a

pastor at their Pulteney Street and Stepney churches and saw this independent movement flourish.

BIBLIOGRAPHY
Finlayson Book Committee, *Finlayson* (Adelaide, 1987)
G. E. Loyau, *Notable South Australians* (Adelaide, 1885)

ROB LINN

Finley, James Bradley (b. NC, USA, 1 July 1781; d. Eaton, OH, USA, 6 Sept. 1856). Methodist minister, missionary to the Wyandott Indians, prison chaplain, and author. He was the son of Rebecca (née Bradley) and Robert W. Finley, a Princeton-educated Presbyterian. The father personally educated his sons (three became Methodist preachers). In 1790 the Finleys moved to Cane Ridge, Kentucky, where Robert pastored two Presbyterian churches and began a school. Robert Finley adopted strong antislavery convictions in the early 1790s possibly because evangelicals like W. WILBERFORCE were by then spearheading the antislavery movement in the United Kingdom. Finley freed his family's slaves and persuaded most of the members of both his congregations to leave Kentucky in 1796 for the slave-free North-Western Territory and to settle near what is now Chillicothe, Ohio.

For a time the young Finley studied medicine but preferred the life of a backwoodsman, working the land and hunting. In March 1801 he married Hannah Strane. In August 1801, however, Finley returned to Cane Ridge where his father had pastored and witnessed the remarkable events of the now-famous Cane Ridge revival. Finley was converted upon his return home; his wife soon followed. For several years Finley was devout and anxious to preach but was discouraged by a Presbyterian minister who insisted that he needed three years of theological training before doing so. For three years Finley backslid; in 1808 a hunting accident triggered an overwhelming sense of guilt and in deep depression he considered suicide. Instead he returned to his former faith and made contact with Methodists who encouraged him in his desire to preach.

In 1809 he was admitted on trial by the Western Conference and in 1812 was received into full connexion. For the next seven years he served on the large pioneer circuits in Ohio and from 1816 to 1845 devoted much energy to the role of Presiding Elder of districts. For a time he served the Detroit area where he proved exceedingly popular.

From 1821 to 1827 he served as missionary to the Wyandott Indians (Hurons) near the present Upper Sandusky, Ohio, where the colourful JOHN STEWART had begun such a successful work in 1816. In 1840 the MEC published Finley's *History of the Wyandott Mission* which is an important source for contemporary historians. Following his missionary work, he served numerous circuits both as preacher and Presiding Elder.

Elected eight times to the General Conference, the highest legislative body of the MEC, in 1844 he played a key role in one of the most divisive debates in American Methodist history. Finley had been born and raised in a slave-owning family in the South which had later repudiated slavery; it was his resolution in General Conference which sought the deposition of Bishop J. O. ANDREW. Andrew disliked slavery too, but was considered by some a slave-holder (see the entry on Andrew to appreciate the complicated nature of the case). Thus Finley played a leading part in an incident which contributed to the 1846 withdrawal of many Methodists to form the MEC, South.

Finley was also a key player in drawing up the Plan of Separation, serving with NATHAN BANGS and GEORGE PECK and an equal number of representatives from the Southern Church to appraise the equity the secessionists had in the Book Concern. The issue was eventually decided in court.

Finley became chaplain of the Ohio Penitentiary in April 1846 and served for over three years, and authoured a book about his experiences (*Memorials of Prison Life* [1850]). His 1853 autobiography presents in graphic detail life on the western frontier. He also wrote an invaluable book on Methodist history entitled *Sketches of Western Methodism*. His eminently readable narrative style made him a popular writer in his day and his works provide important details of life on the American frontier and of American Methodism in its greatest period of expansion.

SELECT WRITINGS
J. B. Finley, *Autobiography of Rev. James B. Finley or, Pioneer Life in the West*, ed. W. P. Strickland (Cincinnati, 1853)
—, *History of the Wyandott Mission* (Cincinnati, 1840)
—, *Life Among the Indians*, ed. D. W. Clark (Cincinnati, 1860)
—, *Memorials of Prison Life*, ed. B. F. Tefft (Cincinnati, 1850)
—, *Sketches of Western Methodism*, ed. W. B. Strickland (Cincinnati, 1855)

BIBLIOGRAPHY
DCA

DONALD M. LEWIS

Finley, Robert (b. Princeton, NJ, BNA, 15 Feb. 1772; d. Athens, GA, USA, 3 Oct. 1817). Presbyterian minister, educator, and organizer of the American Colonization Society. Finley was the son of James and Angres Finley, who emigrated from Glasgow at the encouragement of JOHN WITHERSPOON. Finley graduated from the College of New Jersey and held several teaching positions in New Jersey and Charleston before returning to Princeton in 1792 to study theology under Witherspoon. He was ordained in the Basking Ridge Presbyterian Church (1795), and three years later he married Esther Caldwell, daughter of 'soldier parson' JAMES CALDWELL.

While labouring for 22 successful years at Basking Ridge, Finley established a nationally recognized school for boys. His pamphlet 'Thoughts on the Colonization of Free Blacks' (1816), attracted attention from national leaders. On 1 January 1817 the American Colonization Society elected Bushrod Washington president and Finley one of the vice-presidents. Receiving a call to be

president at the University of Georgia in April 1817, Finley resigned his pastorate and moved to Athens, Georgia. He died soon thereafter from a fever contracted while raising funds for the university.

BIBLIOGRAPHY
AAP
A. Alexander, *A History of Colonization on the Western Coast of Africa* (Philadelphia, PA, 1846)
I. V. Brown, *Memoirs of the Rev. Robert Finley, D.D.* (New Brunswick, NJ, 1819)
DAB

W. ANDREW HOFFECKER

Finley, Robert W. (b. Bucks County, PA, BNA, 9 June 1750; d. Germantown, OH, USA, 8 Dec. 1840). Presbyterian minister and Methodist preacher. Educated at the College of New Jersey [Princeton], Finley was first a licensed Presbyterian preacher. Between 1777 and 1788 he served in Georgia, the Carolinas, Virginia, and Ohio. Finley married Rebecca Bradley in 1780. In 1788 they moved to Cane Ridge, Kentucky. Continuing to serve two Presbyterian congregations, he also opened a classical school. At least nine of his pupils became Presbyterian ministers. Finley moved to near Chillicothe, Ohio in 1796. He became a Methodist in 1808 and was received into the Western Conference in 1812. In 1824 he retired from the itinerancy. Three of Robert and Rebecca's sons, JAMES B. FINLEY, John P. and William P. Finley were also Methodist Episcopal ministers.

BIBLIOGRAPHY
AAP
J. B. Finley, *Autobiography* (Cincinnati, OH, 1854)
A. H. Redford, *The History of Methodism in Kentucky*, 3 (Nashville, TN, 1870)
M. Simpson, ed., *Cyclopedia of Methodism* (Philadelphia, PA, 1880)

CHARLES W. BROCKWELL, JR

Finley, Samuel (b. Co. of Armagh, Ireland, 1715; d. Philadelphia, PA, BNA, 17 July 1766). Presbyterian minister and college president. Born and educated in Ulster, Finley came as a Scots-Irish immigrant to Philadelphia in 1734. Intent on pursuing the ministry, he soon came under the influence of the Tennent family, probably studying at WILLIAM TENNENT senior's 'Log College' at Neshaminy, Pennsylvania. The Tennent-inspired presbytery of New Brunswick licensed him to preach in 1740 and ordained him in 1742.

As a member of the Tennent circle, Finley became an important figure in the Great Awakening in the middle colonies. He carried on a successful itinerant ministry in New Jersey and Pennsylvania before encountering legal opposition in Connecticut in 1743 and being thrown out of the colony as a vagrant. His contributions to the Presbyterian 'New Side' included published attacks upon 'unconverted ministers'. Strongly Edwardsian in his theological sympathies, Finley considered a gracious soul rather than academic achievement as the most important ministerial qualification.

In 1744 he accepted a call to the Presbyterian church in Nottingham, Maryland and remained there for 17 years. Beyond his normal pastoral duties, he established a school for ministerial candidates where he gained a reputation as a kind and courteous tutor. During the 1750s, he published several more sermons, served on the board of trustees of the College of New Jersey, and corresponded extensively with clergymen abroad.

As a seasoned leader of colonial Presbyterianism, Finley was a natural choice for the presidency of the College of New Jersey in 1761. Unfortunately, death ended his tenure prematurely in 1766 but not before he had received the DD from the University of Glasgow in 1763.

BIBLIOGRAPHY
A. Alexander, *Biographical Sketches of the Founder and Principal Alumni of the Log College* (Princeton, NJ, 1845)
DAB
DCA

RICHARD W. POINTER

Finney, Charles Grandison (b. Warren, CT, USA, 29 Aug. 1792; d. Oberlin, OH, USA, 16 Aug. 1875). Revivalist, theologian, author, pastor, college professor, and reformer. In 1794 the Finney family moved from Connecticut to New York state where Charles spent his early youth. The family eventually settled at Henderson, near Lake Ontario, and it was there that Finney lived out his adolescent period. Finney decided to study law and began to do so in the office of a local lawyer, Benjamin Wright. In addition, he was an amateur musician with some skill as a cello player, and apparently directed the choir at the local Presbyterian church pastored by the Reverend GEORGE W. GALE. The account of his dramatic conversion is found in his *Memoirs*, which were written some fifty years after the incident. The event was so moving that it changed the course of his life and career. The morning after this conversion a client came to the law office expecting assistance from Finney in a pending case, but the convert announced his attention to give up his study of law so that he might pursue a career as a preacher of the Gospel. He was licensed to preach by the St Lawrence presbytery in December 1823, and subsequently was commissioned a missionary in the local area by the Female Missionary Society of Western New York.

The fledging evangelist preached in the frontier communities of upstate New York with mixed results. His thrust was different from many of the local ministers, with an obvious attempt to break away from traditional Calvinism. He married Lydia Andrews of Whitestown in October 1824, and found his career at a new turn when the two of them went to visit Lydia's parents. On the way they stayed with George W. Gale and his family in the town of Western, New York. Gale asked Finney to preach and the results were dramatic with numerous

people coming to hear the young preacher. Similar results were evident in the nearby towns of Rome and Utica. Indeed, the newly commissioned evangelist became a well-known figure in the area known by historians as the 'Burned-Over District'. These meetings stirred the Oneida presbytery and gave Finney some notice in East Coast newspapers.

Finney's modifications of Calvinism not only caused controversy, but they also led to 'New Measures' in the conduct of his meetings. These New Measures included the use of an anxious bench (a special area for souls under conviction), protracted meetings, the allowing of women to pray in mixed public meetings, and the hasty admission of new converts to church membership. Opposition to the New Measures led to a series of meetings in July of 1828 at New Lebanon, New York. There Presbyterian and Congregational ministers discussed Finney and the New Measures, pro and con, and the result was a partial vindication of Finney and his methods. He became a national figure as a result of the publicity surrounding these meetings. The opposition to Finney by now was clear, emanating from the Old School Presbyterians led by ASAHEL NETTLETON, the revivalistic Congregationalists led by LYMAN BEECHER, and the Unitarians and Universalists, who were offended by what they perceived as the use of scare tactics. The revivalist had his supporters as well, with George W. Gale, THEODORE DWIGHT WELD, NATHAN S. S. BEMAN, JOSHUA LEAVITT, and the philanthropist merchants from New York City, ARTHUR and LEWIS TAPPAN. Eventually, Lyman Beecher invited Finney to preach in New England, but the two were never entirely pleased with each others' positions.

The high point of Finney's revival career was reached at Rochester, New York, during his 1830–1 meetings. Shopkeepers closed their businesses and the whole city seemed to centre on the revivalist. The crude frontier style was gone, and one contemporary observer claimed that Finney appeared to be a lawyer arguing a case before a jury. Finney boasted that many of his hearers were lawyers, merchants, and those from a higher income and professional status.

Finney's career now changed again when he accepted an appointment as pastor of the Chatham Street Chapel in New York City. It was here that Finney delivered a series of sermons published as *Lectures on Revivals of Religion* (1835). The opening statement in this book said that a revival was not a miracle, but rather the right use of means. This added to the controversy surrounding Finney, resulting in an appeal call from CHARLES HODGE of Princeton Seminary that he leave the denomination, and established Finney as the leader of New School thought. His friends, including the Tappan brothers, built the Broadway Tabernacle for him, and he also became one of the leading proponents of the Free Church (or non-denominational) movement.

Events in the West now had a part in determining another move by the revivalist. Students at Lane Seminary in Cincinnati, many of whom were converts from Finney's revivals in the 'Burned-Over District', insisted on debating the topic of slavery even after being forbidden to do so by the seminary's trustees. The students, led by Theodore Weld, left Lane Seminary and travelled to Oberlin, a fledgling school struggling to survive. Their move to Oberlin was made on the condition that Finney also go there as their mentor, a move that was facilitated when the Tappan brothers agreed to underwrite the costs. Now Finney settled in as a theology professor, travelling east each year to meetings, and writing for the *Oberlin Evangelist* so that his New School views became widely known. Finney became involved in an evangelistic network, known by historians as a 'benevolent empire', through which he involved Oberlin in many of the leading reform movements of the Jacksonian era. Finney's postmillennial optimism caused him to believe that the United States could be entirely changed by such reforms as the temperance movement, manual labour education, sabbath observance and antislavery activities. Although he was primarily a revivalist, Finney succeeded in linking evangelical religion to these reforms as a duty required of all Christians. Indeed, he would not allow slave-owners to observe Communion while he was pastor of Broadway Tabernacle.

Further controversy occurred when Finney and ASA MAHAN, president of Oberlin College, formulated a doctrine of Christian perfection. The stigma increased when a connection was made between Oberlin perfectionism and the perfectionism practised by the Oneida Community in New York state under the leadership of John Humphrey Noyes. When not embroiled in controversy, Finney taught his class in pastoral theology, tended to domestic tasks, founded and pastored the First Congregational Church in Oberlin, conducted revivals in Boston, Rochester and other sites of his earlier triumphs. The death of his wife, Lydia, in December 1847 affected him deeply. He was left a widower with five children. Not long after, he married Elizabeth Ford Atkins of Rochester, New York, who would be a major assistant in another part of his career.

Charles and Elizabeth made two trips to Great Britain during their years together. The first was from 1849 to 1851, when Finney used essentially the same methods which had been successful during his career in the United States. Elizabeth maintained a low profile during this first visit, although she did begin holding meetings for women. The second trip to England, from 1859 to 1860, was taken partially at the insistence of Elizabeth who conducted highly successful women's meetings wherever they travelled. Finney's success in England was tempered by the fact that he was invited to some churches affiliated with the Evangelical Union. On the whole, however, he became a part of the bridge established from America to England by nineteenth-century revivalists, a path that was subsequently travelled by Dwight L. Moody.

His later years were spent teaching at Oberlin, serving as its president, writing a harsh indictment of freemasonry, and working extensively on a narrative of his early revivals, later published as his *Memoirs*. After Elizabeth died in 1863, he married Rebecca Rayl, principal of a female department at Oberlin.

Finney's mark on American religious history is well established. Called the father of modern revivalism by one historian, he democratized Calvinism at a time (the Jacksonian era) when society was ripe for the idea. Indeed, historian Whitney Cross has stated that, while Finney did not deliberately try to make Presbyterianism palatable to the common folk, his conclusions achieved that result. He was an evangelistic path-breaker who was followed by a line of revivalists from Moody to Billy Graham. Finney's reform endeavours affected such movements as revivalism, feminism, the Graham (or wheat germ) diet, perfectionism, Sabbatarianism and abolitionism. His writings perhaps made the greatest impact, especially the *Lectures on Revivals*. In fact, many of his writings are still in print. The power of the man is indicated by the fact that some of his critics still refer to a 'Finney Cult' in America which they claim is responsible for some of the more controversial techniques employed in modern mass evangelism.

BIBLIOGRAPHY

R. Carwardine, *Trans-Atlantic Revivalism* (Westpoint, CT and London, 1978)
W. R. Cross, *The Burned-Over District* (Ithaca, NY, 1950)
R. Dupuis and G. Rosell, eds, *The Memoirs of Charles G. Finney* (Grand Rapids, MI, 1989)
K. J. Hardman, *Charles Grandison Finney, Revivalist and Reformer* (Syracuse, NY, 1987)
W. G. McLoughlin, *Modern Revivalism* (New York, 1959)
L. I. Sweet, ed., *The Evangelical Tradition in America* (Macon, GA, 1984)
G. F. Wright, *Charles Grandison Finney* (Boston, MA, 1891)

JAMES E. JOHNSON

Firth, Thomas (b. Sheffield, England, 21 June 1821; d. Sheffield, England, 20 March 1860). Industrialist. The son of a steel smelter, Thomas, with his elder brother Mark, founded a steel works in Sheffield in 1842, beginning with just six pothole furnaces. The brothers were soon joined by their father and Thomas Firth & Sons grew to become a large and prosperous concern making high-grade steels for cutlery and tools. The family were members of the MNC, one of the smaller Methodist bodies and Thomas had a lifelong concern for ministerial education. In the period before a theological college was established, his gifts made it possible for ministerial students to lodge with leading ministers for theological and practical training. His bequest of £5,000 to the connexion was the catalyst which led to the establishment of Ranmoor College, Sheffield, opened in 1864 for the training of New Connexion ministers.

BIBLIOGRAPHY
Methodist New Connexion Magazine (1860): 409

E. ALAN ROSE

Fish, Henry Clay (b. Halifax, VT, USA, 27 Jan. 1820; d. Newark, NJ, USA, 2 Oct. 1877). Baptist minister in New Jersey. Converted at the age of 15, Fish followed in his father's footsteps by entering the Baptist ministry. In 1845, he graduated from Union Theological Seminary and was ordained pastor of Somerville Baptist Church (New Jersey). Fish's next church was First Baptist Church, Newark, where he served for 27 years (1851–77). He promoted an educated ministry, serving as secretary of the New Jersey Baptist Education Society.

Fish was a prolific author, writing a book a year for twenty years. His writings, especially *Primitive Piety Revisited* (1857) reveal the mid-nineteenth century evangelical tendency to combine evangelism and social reform. His call for a return to Pentecostal piety and the gift of sanctification helped usher in the Holiness revival of 1858. Like other northern evangelicals, he attacked slavery and wrote *Freedom or Despotism* (1856).

BIBLIOGRAPHY
T. Smith, *Revivalism and Social Reform* (Gloucester, MS, 1976)

C. DOUGLAS WEAVER

Fishbourne, Edmund Gardiner (b. 1811; d. Kensington, London, 12 May 1887). British naval officer and supporter of mission. He entered the navy in 1824. As a lieutenant he joined the disastrous Niger Expedition under HENRY TROTTER and took command of one of the ships involved on the death of her captain. Subsequent naval service included participation in the Kaffir War of 1852–3, a visit to China, promotion to captain and the award of the CB. He left the navy in March 1866 but reached admiral's rank on the retired list in August 1879.

Fishbourne supported a wide-ranging interest in evangelism. For years he was honorary secretary of the Naval and Military Bible Society and of the Royal Navy Patriotic Fund, and was a founder-member of the Naval Prayer Union. Other concerns included CMS, the Loo-Choo Naval Mission, and the evangelistic enterprises of Lord SHAFTESBURY in London and JAMES HUDSON TAYLOR in China.

BIBLIOGRAPHY
Annual Register (1887)
Anon., 'Narrative of the Niger Expedition 1841–42 complied from Official Documents', in *United Service Journal* (London, 1842): ii: 40; iii: 223–4, 376–84, 591–8
DNB
Navy List
E. Stock, *The History of the Church Missionary Society*, 3 vols (London, 1899)

RICHARD C. BLAKE

Fisher, Henry (b. England, *c.* 1772; d. Masuri, India, 5 March 1845). East India Company chaplain. Fisher was educated at Cambridge University and entered the Anglican ministry in 1795, becoming a curate in Yorkshire.

In 1815 CLAUDIUS BUCHANAN persuaded him to go to India. Although he was a company chaplain, Henry believed that he had to be a missionary too. This was to lead to conflict with company officials. Native Christians flocked to his rooms to read the Scriptures and he set up schools for them. His first baptism in 1816 of a Brahmin, a *naik* in the native infantry, caused a great stir. The Company intervened and the naik was dismissed from the service. Henry was not deterred by the opposition and later baptized a Sikh guru. Fortunately these baptisms did not result in his expulsion; in 1832 he was appointed presidency chaplain. Henry was helpful to dissenting missionaries at a time when there was considerable church/Dissent rivalry.

BIBLIOGRAPHY
British Library, 'Biographical Notes on the East India Company's Chaplains to 1858', India Office Records (1976)

PENELOPE CARSON

Fisher, Peter (dates of birth and death unknown). Early preacher with the Independents and later with the Baptists in Perthshire. Apparently trained by the HALDANES, Fisher comes on record as an Independent preacher at Aberfeldy in 1805. He had become a Baptist by 1808, and baptized WILLIAM TULLOCH. Supported latterly by the Baptist Highland Mission, he was based at Ardeonaig, Lochtayside, by 1822. He engaged in itinerant preaching in Perthshire, Argyllshire, Skye and other islands. He is not known to have held pastoral charge.

BIBLIOGRAPHY
D. E. Meek, 'The Independent and Baptist Churches of Highland Perthshire and Strathspey', *Transactions of the Gaelic Society of Inverness*, 56 (1988–90): 269–343
Report of the Baptist Highland Mission (probably Glasgow, 1822–3)

DONALD E. MEEK

Fisk, George (b. 1810; d. Kempsey, near Worcester, England, 31 Aug. 1872). Anglican clergyman. Educated at Corpus Christi, Cambridge (LL B 1835), Fisk was ordained in 1832. He became Curate of St Botolph's, Cambridge (1832–5), Rector of Darlaston, Staffordshire (1835–7), and was later Vicar of Walsall, near Birmingham (1837–45). A prebendary of Lichfield from 1843, he spent his most productive years as Perpetual Curate of Christ Chapel, Maida Hill, London (1845–56). For reasons unknown, he retired from London in 1856 to become Vicar of Great Malvern, a spa town in Worcestershire.

Fisk rode the crest of certain English evangelical preoccupations: science and religion; no popery and antiritualism; philo-Semitism and foreign missions. He attracted notice with a timely edition of Payley's *Evidences* (1836) that took advantage of the rage in natural theology recently fanned by the *Bridgewater Treatises*

(1833–6). The volume, with 'examination questions', was reprinted throughout the century.

In the 1840s and 1850s he demonstrated a capacity for effective, if bigoted, anti-Catholic pamphleteering. He also tried his hand at sentimental verse in *An Orphan Tale, Told in Rhyme* (1852). In *Twelve Aspects of Christ, Preparatory to the Monthly Communion* (1853) he attempted to rescue personal devotions from the stigma of Anglo-Catholicism. His lecture, 'The Moral Influence of the Commercial Spirit of the Day' (1848), one of three lectures he contributed to the YMCA Exeter Hall series, thoughtfully strove to redeem business as a Christian vocation.

A millennialist interest in Jewish missions led to years of active service in the LSPCJ and to an 1842 visit to the Middle East. His observant and lively record of that visit, *A Pastor's Memorial of Egypt . . . and . . . the Holy Land* (1843; 6th edn 1865), was well received. These pursuits inspired a friendship with the Bishop of Jerusalem, SAMUEL GOBAT, that proved useful during the 1856 uproar over Gobat's proselytizing of local Orthodox Christians. Under Fisk's tutelage, the Maida Hill proprietary chapel, whose congregation was one of London's most active supporters of the CMS, became a centre of metropolitan evangelical life.

BIBLIOGRAPHY
Al. Cant.
Boase
W. T. Gidney, *History of the London Society for Promoting Christianity Amongst the Jews* (London, 1908): 270, 271

JONATHAN BURKE CUTMORE

Fisk, Wilbur (b. Brattleboro, VT, USA, 31 Aug. 1792; d. Middletown, CT, USA, 22 Feb. 1839). American Methodist preacher, educator, and leader. Born to Isaiah and Hannah Bacon Fisk, Wilbur became one of the most notable figures in the MEC in the early nineteenth century. He graduated from Brown University, Providence, Rhode Island in 1815. He studied law for a short time following his graduation, but soon turned to the ministry. On 14 March 1818 he was licensed to preach at Lyndon, Vermont. In June 1818 he joined the New England Annual Conference.

Fisk was pastor of the Craftsbury circuit in Vermont for one year. In 1819 he was appointed pastor at Charlestown, Massachusetts. He was forced to suspend his ministry in November 1820 due to illness. When he returned to good heath he married Ruth Peck of Providence, Rhode Island, 6 June 1823. His pastoral work included a three-year term as superintendent of the Methodist Episcopal work in Vermont.

Fisk was especially known for his educational leadership among the Methodists. From 1826 to 1830 he was principal of Wesleyan Academy, Wilbraham, Massachusetts, a school which he had helped to found. In 1830 he became the first president of Wesleyan University, Middletown, Connecticut, a school whose founding he

had also assisted. He served the university with great distinction until the time of his death.

Among his most important activities were his roles in advocating temperance, promoting missions, supporting the colonization of slaves, and defending Methodist principles and doctrines. He was particularly involved in encounters with universalism, Unitarianism, and Calvinism.

Fisk published two sermons on what he considered the errors of universalism. Both of them produced controversial replies from universalist clergy. He also published an assault on Unitarian views on Christology and the Atonement. His published attacks on New England Calvinism, however, created more extensive theological argument. He was convinced that the doctrinal integrity of New England Methodism meant a confrontation with the Calvinistic ideas about predestination and election. 'This doctrine of predestination destroys human free agency and accountability,' he wrote. Calvinistic 'election annihilates human free agency and moral responsibility in man, doctrines of which the Holy Scriptures and the human conscience are full' (Prentice, 1890: 116, 118). Fisk believed that public revulsion against the 'horrible decrees' of Calvinism was the principal cause of the popularity of Unitarianism and universalism. By contrast, he wrote:

> Had Methodism been as well known in New England fifty years ago, as it now is, it is doubtful whether Universalism or Unitarianism would have gained much influence in this country. Late as it was introduced, and much as it was opposed, it is believed to have done much toward checking the progress of those sentiments.
> (Bucke, 1964: 351)

Fisk was elected a bishop in 1828 and 1836. On both occasions he declined the position, possibly for reasons of health. In 1835 Wesleyan University sent him to Europe for rest and study. Upon his return he published his impressions of this trip under the title, *Travels in Europe* (1838).

BIBLIOGRAPHY
E. S. Bucke, ed., *The History of American Methodism* (Nashville, TN, 1964)
DAB
EWM
G. Prentice, *Wilbur Fisk* (Boston, MA, 1890)

CHARLES YRIGOYEN, JR

Fjellstedt, Peter (b. Sillerūd, Värmland, Sweden, 17 Sept. 1802; d. Uppsala, Sweden, 4 Jan. 1881). Missionary and educator. Born into an impoverished farm family, he was a precocious youth who studied first at Karlstad (1819) and then Lund (1823) where he mastered several languages. A devout upbringing instilled in him a living faith and as a student he became a lay preacher. After a deeply spiritual experience in 1824, he committed himself to missionary service. But he then dropped out of the university for a year because of financial problems and taught languages at the Moravian school in Göteborg. Finally, after graduating from Lund in 1828, he was ordained in the Church of Sweden. After spending some months at the Basel missionary seminary, he was appointed by the CMS in 1831 to the Tinnevelly (Tirūnelvelī) Mission in south India. After marrying a German, Christiana Schweizerbart, he left immediately for India. There he spent three years working with c. t. e. rhenius as a teacher of Bible and languages at the teacher training school in Pallamcotta (Palāyancottai). Ill health forced them to leave India in 1835. The CMS later reassigned him to Smyrna, in Turkey, to work among Muslim and Greek Orthodox peoples. While there he translated the *Book of Common Prayer* into Turkish. Bitter opposition from the Greek Orthodox Church stymied his ministry. In 1840 he returned to England and left the CMS service.

From 1841 to 1851 Fjellstedt served as a roving preacher for the Basel society, stimulating missionary interest in northern Europe. Partly due to his influence, the Swedish Missionary Society had been founded in 1835, and in 1846 he became director of the new missionary training institute which opened at Lund. In 1859, this institute was moved to Uppsala and later renamed the Fjellstedt School. Besides teaching he edited two missionary newspapers, made new translations of Luther's *Shorter Catechism* and the *Book of Concord*, and travelled with his close friend C. O. Rosenius promoting revival within the Swedish church. He also was closely involved in shaping the Swedish immigrant Augustana Lutheran Church in America, but poor health prevented him from accepting the invitation to travel there. After leaving the school in 1861, he became a parish pastor, continuing his itinerant preaching and writing. In 1872 he retired to his wife's home in Germany but went back to Sweden after her death four years later. In 1881 he died of pneumonia contracted while preaching in an unheated church.

SELECT WRITINGS

P. Fjellstadt, *Dr. P. Fjellstedts Samlade Skrifter i Ordnadt Urwal* (Stockholm, 1883–4)

BIBLIOGRAPHY

C. Anshelm, *Peter Fjellstedt* (Stockholm, 1930–57)
D. T. B[arry], *CMS Register of Missionaries and Native Clergy* (privately printed) (London, 1906)
E. E. Eklund, *Peter Fjellstedt* (Rock Island, IL, 1983)

R. V. PIERARD

Fleming, John (b. Kirkroads, Scotland, 10 Jan. 1785; d. Edinburgh, 18 Nov. 1857). Minister and naturalist. Son of a tenant farmer, Fleming studied at Edinburgh University. A Church of Scotland minister from 1806 to 1834, he also achieved renown as a zoologist. He became professor of natural philosophy (i.e. science) at Kings College, Aberdeen (1834). In 1843 many Scottish evangelicals left the established church to form the Free

Church. Fleming was among them, becoming professor of natural science at their New College in Edinburgh in 1845, and enjoying the friendship of other leaders.

From 1824 to 1826 (during which time Charles Lyell was still a catastrophist), Fleming attacked the Cuverian model of English geologists Buckland and adam sedgwick who thought Noah's was the last of a series of cataclysmic floods. Fleming, Sedgwick, and other evangelical scientists, shared the widespread Baconian view that scientific theory should be independent of theology, but Fleming argued that a violent Noarchic flood was both unscriptural and unscientific. Later both Sedgwick (in 1831) and Buckland (1836) abandoned their multiple-flood catastrophism. Fleming wrote to Sedgwick (15 and 23 December 1831) complaining that he had been given insufficient credit for priority in some of the 'uniformitarian' ideas of Lyell. An eminent evangelical naturalist, Fleming advocated in works of 1828 and 1859 the 'gap theory' of fellow Free Church leader thomas chalmers, accepted orthodox geology but rejected evolution.

BIBLIOGRAPHY
DSB

V. PAUL MARSTON

Fleming, John (b. Mifflin County, PA, USA, 17 April 1807; d. Ayr, NE, USA, 27 Oct. 1894). Missionary and linguist among the American Indians. He attended Jefferson College in Canonsburg, Pennsylvania, and graduated from Princeton Theological Seminary. He was ordained as a Presbyterian minister in October 1832. In 1833, Fleming was commissioned by the ABCFM to work among the Creek tribe in the Indian Territory. His most significant achievements included reducing the Creek or Muskogee language to writing and publishing portions of scripture and other materials. After the Creek mission closed due to opposition from tribal leaders, Fleming moved to the Wea Mission in Kansas, operated by the Presbyterian Board of Foreign Missions. He arrived there in August 1837, but the mission closed the following year due to its proximity to a Methodist station. Fleming then transferred to a mission among the Chippewa and Ottawa Indians, on Grand Traverse Bay, Michigan. Shortly after his wife died in May 1839, he retired from missionary service. Later, he served pastorates in Pennsylvania, Illinois, and Nebraska.

BIBLIOGRAPHY
Annual Reports, Board of Foreign Missions, Presbyterian Church (1837–9)
DAB
Reports, ABCFM (1833–7)

MARK S. JOY

Flesher, John (b. Otley, Suffolk, England, 3 Dec. 1801; d. 16 July 1874). Primitive Methodist minister. Originally brought up a Wesleyan he became involved in the camp meeting movement in 1821 and entered the Primitive ministry in 1822. He served with great success in the Tadcaster, Darlington, Whitehaven, Alston, Westgate, Barnard Castle, Barton, Driffield and Patrington branches of the vast Hull circuit. During the difficult transitional period of denominational development after 1830, Flesher, known as 'the silver-tongued pacificator', settled troubles at Edinburgh (1830), London (1835–7) where he saw to the erection of the first permanent Primitive chapel, and Kent and Hull (1841). He was responsible for the founding of the General Missionary Committee (1841), the transfer of the bookroom from Bemersley to London (1843, the year he became connexional editor) and in general the extension of evangelism from the countryside to the towns. A friend and admirer of WILLIAM CLOWES he vigorously championed the latter to the discomfiture of the BOURNE brothers in the 1840s. He edited a new connexional hymn-book in 1853: an eccentric compilation, its appearance provoked controversy but this was caught up in a general assault on the oligarchic character of the conference which had approved it. The hymn-book was revised and reissued and the conference gradually became more open. A great orator, Flesher was known as the Primitives' Chrysostom. He developed a throat affliction about 1842 and retired ten years later.

BIBLIOGRAPHY

Anon., *Earnest Men, Sketches of Eminent Primitive Methodists* (London, 1872)

F. Baker, 'Samuel Bourne and the Bermersley Book Room', *PWHS*, 30 (Leicester, England, 1957)

Obituary, *Minutes of the P.M. Conference* (Bemersley, England, 1875)

G. Herod, *Biographical Sketches* (London, 1855)

IAN SELLERS

Fletcher, John William [de la Fléchère, Jean Guillaume] (b. Nyon, Switzerland, perhaps 11 Sept. 1729; baptized 19 Sept. 1729; d. Madeley, Shropshire, England, 14 Aug. 1785). Anglican clergyman, designated successor of John Wesley, and saint of Methodism. Born the youngest of eight children in a family of the lower gentry, Fletcher studied classics at Geneva, but never undertook theological studies. Before the age of 19, he had left Geneva, tried to start a military career and finally arrived in England in 1750. In autumn 1751, he became tutor to the two sons of Thomas Hill, Esquire, MP for Shropshire. Two years later, he got to know the Methodists and among them CHARLES WESLEY with whom he developed a close friendship. During winter 1753–4, he went through a deep religious crisis. After experiencing much weakness in his new faith in Christ, he concluded a detailed covenant with God in August 1754. For many years, Thomas Hill urged him to take holy orders, which Fletcher accepted finally in spring 1757, after having asked the advice of JOHN WESLEY. By 1757, Fletcher was already known in Methodist circles. He made the

acquaintance of GEORGE WHITEFIELD and was introduced to Lady HUNTINGDON in spring 1758. His contribution to the conversion of Sir RICHARD HILL strengthened the fear of the 'pest of the Methodists' in the related family of Thomas Hill. In the late 1750s, Fletcher was highly esteemed by Methodists, but almost driven to despair by his own high standards of Christian life. He was closely linked in correspondence and friendship to Charles Wesley.

In 1760, Fletcher agreed to become vicar of Madeley, to the indignation of John Wesley who had hoped to find an Anglican clergyman willing to assist him. For 25 years, Fletcher was engaged in a parish ministry. Madeley was, at the time, an important centre of industrial progress. During the first decade of his ministry in Madeley, Fletcher kept contact with Wesleyan and Calvinistic Methodists. He had become one of the chaplains of Lady Huntingdon and, in his desire to promote union, started a regional association of evangelical clergymen. In the 1760s, he was engaged in theological discussions with friends on the question of Christian perfection (for a while, he tried to mediate between John Wesley and THOMAS MAXFIELD) and on the Sandemanian controversy which had brought confusion into the societies of BENJAMIN INGHAM in Yorkshire.

Several times, Fletcher was asked by John or Charles Wesley to work with them among the Methodists. The first offer came before going to Madeley. In 1761, John Wesley even proposed that he take over the leadership of the Methodist movement. By the end of the 1760s, Fletcher thought of becoming a helper to Wesley, but finally accepted to the presidency of Trevecka College, a new theological seminary founded by Lady Huntingdon. There he hoped to promote union between the Methodists. After two and a half years, Fletcher resigned because of the outbreak of the Calvinistic controversy. This controversy on Antinomianism and predestination caused him to side with John Wesley – to the surprise of Calvinistic Methodists. Fletcher wrote his voluminous *Checks to Antinomianism*. What started as a defence of Wesley's conference minutes of 1770 became a theological search for reconciliation between the moderate exponents on both sides. He proposed a 'Society to promote unity and tolerance among Christians', but he was worn out by his untiring efforts. His friend JAMES IRELAND brought him to France and Switzerland (as in 1770), where Fletcher stayed from 1778–81 to cure his consumption. Restless as he was, he talked of God to everyone he met on his journey and wrote religious and philosophical poems in French.

In the midst of the Calvinistic controversy, Fletcher was asked again by John Wesley to become his successor, but declined. In 1776, he accompanied John Wesley on one of his tours and in 1783 agreed to see the Dublin Methodists. By this time, Fletcher had married Mary Bosanquet (*see* MARY FLETCHER) after having shrunk back from doing so in the early 1760s. In his last years, Fletcher's health was feeble, but he kept on his pastoral work and showed more readiness to support John Wesley.

In 1775, Fletcher redrafted a proposal by JOSEPH BENSON to organize the Methodists as the 'Methodist Church of England', a daughter of her holy mother. When Wesley legally settled the future of his 'United Societies' in the Deed of Declaration in 1784, it was Fletcher who overcame the opposition at conference by his fervent speech and prayers. In the 1780s, Fletcher started to reflect on questions of Christology and of the Trinity. Some of his ideas were enlarged for posthumous publication by JOSEPH BENSON. Fletcher died in 1785 and was buried in Madeley.

In his pastoral work, Fletcher had to overcome opposition and suspicion because of his high standards of Christian faith. But his profound love shown towards his parishioners was convincing. He went to them, in their homes and their coal pits. He helped to start day schools and Sunday schools. He reminded the owners of their social responsibility towards the poor in times of crisis. His social engagement was sincere but never challenged the traditional structures. His life as a Christian was a model for many eye-witnesses. Some weeks before his marriage, he professed himself completely filled with the love of God and having attained Christian perfection. In his last years, he neither repeated nor revoked his testimony, but insisted on continual and never-ending growth in the knowledge and love of God. He kept humble to the end. John Wesley compared Fletcher to Gregory Lopez and Monsieur de Renty, one of the reasons why he was called 'the Saint' by Methodists.

In his theological work, Fletcher tried to explain the doctrines of John Wesley. Here as well, he was a man of the second generation. He took over what he had learnt from John and Charles Wesley, and sought to demonstrate it with new and expansive arguments. He tried to bring system into what had been full of the tensions of Christian experience in the revival. His mediating character influenced his writing. He sought a 'via media' and finally discovered that different theological structures of thinking (Calvinistic or Arminian) might – under some conditions – express the same evangelical truth. He explained the doctrines of election within a scheme of dispensations in history which John Wesley found very helpful. When Fletcher talked, however, of a baptism of the Spirit, he linked it with Christian perfection and so smoothed the way to Pentecostal interpretations. Influenced in his youth by theologians of the early Enlightenment, he discovered through the Methodists the Pauline meaning of sin and grace, but continued to esteem reason as second authority after scripture, complemented by experience and tradition. His *Checks* had probably even more influence on American than in English Methodism. There is no complete edition of his works.

SELECT WRITINGS

J. W. Fletcher, *Essai sur la Paix de 1783* (London, 1784)

—, *Discours sur la régénération* (London, 1759)

—, *La Grâce et la Nature* (London, 1785)

—, *La Louange* (Nyon, Switzerland, 1781)

—, *Posthumous Pieces*, ed. W. Horne (London, 1791)

—, *The Works of the Rev. John Fletcher*, 8 vols, 1: Biography by J. Benson (London, 1806–8)

—, *Sermons* (Brussels, 1836)

—, *The Works of the Rev. John Fletcher*, 9 vols (London, 1877)

BIBLIOGRAPHY

F. W. Macdonald, *Fletcher of Madeley* (London, 1885)

Manuscript in Methodist Church Archives, MARC, and other archives

P. Ph. Streiff, *Jean Guillaume de la Fléchère*, in German with lists of published and unpublished material (P. Lang, Bern, 1984)

L. Tyerman, *Wesley's Designated Successor* (London, 1882)

PATRICK PH. STREIFF

Fletcher, Mary [née Bosanquet] (b. Leytonstone, England, 1 Sept. 1739; d. Madeley, Shropshire, England, 9 Dec. 1815). Wesleyan Methodist preacher. Fletcher was brought up in a well-to-do family and at an early age became religiously inclined. She faced much opposition from the family and at 22 left home. She took lodgings in London, joining the Wesleyan Methodists and became involved with the great London Methodist revival of 1761–2. In 1762 Mary went to live in her own house in Leytonstone, where she was joined by SARAH CROSBY and SARAH RYAN to establish a Christian community, and here she began to 'exhort, and to read, and expound the scriptures'. In June 1768 the community was in financial difficulties so they moved to Cross Hall, near Leeds. Fletcher exchanged letters with JOHN WESLEY and in particular consulted him about her call to preach, as Wesleyan Methodism did not permit women preachers and he admitted she had an 'extraordinary call', but neither of them would go so far as agreeing that she be an itinerant preacher.

On 12 November 1781 Mary married JOHN W. FLETCHER, Vicar of Madeley, Shropshire, and they pursued a virtually joint ministry. In order not to offend local people Mary spoke regularly in the tithe-barn and invited Methodist itinerants to preach there. After John's death in 1785 Mary carried on with her work in Madeley almost acting as curate.

BIBLIOGRAPHY

H. Moore, *Life of Mrs. Mary Fletcher ...* (London, 1824)

Z. Taft, *Biographical Sketches of ... Holy Women ...*, 1 (London, 1825)

E. DOROTHY GRAHAM

Fletcher, Samuel (b. Compton, nr Wolverhampton, Staffordshire, England, 1785; d. Broomfield, nr Manchester, Lancashire, England, 13 Oct. 1863). Merchant and philanthropist. Fletcher was the ninth of ten children born to the daughter of a dissenting minister and an Anglican freeholder of Compton in Staffordshire. Between 1785 and 1799 he studied the classics at Wolverhampton Grammar School and was then apprenticed in the town. In 1805 he moved to Manchester and in 1806 joined Grosvenor Street Independent Chapel under the Reverend WILLIAM ROBY, becoming a Sunday school teacher, a lay preacher and, in 1818, a deacon. In 1811 he set up a business in the textile trades, prospered, and subsequently gave away 40 per cent of his annual income to good causes. He founded the Manchester City Mission, paid the salary of a missionary, and supported the EA, the BFBS, the LMS, and the RTS.

In 1836 he promoted plans to found a local college for the education of the middle classes; in 1849 was named a trustee in JOHN OWEN's will and in 1851 helped supervise the foundation of Owen's College, later endowing two scholarships. In 1838 he persuaded the Manchester Chamber of Commerce to petition Parliament for repeal of the Corn Laws, in 1839 championed a direct rail link between Manchester and London and in 1845 gave £500 to the Anti-Corn Law League. He became a city magistrate but refused to stand for Parliament, having neither political nor social ambition. In character he was calm, self-controlled and self-possessed, absorbing even the shock of his daughter and son-in-law's murder by Greek bandits. In religion he valued piety and family devotion, writing two hymns which were included in the *New Congregational Hymn Book* of 1855, and deprecated intolerance and controversy, taking no part in disputes between the Established and dissenting churches. Indeed, during the 1840s he began to worship with the Anglicans as well as the Independents and after his death was buried in St Lukes' Church, Manchester by James Prince Lee, first Anglican Bishop of the city.

BIBLIOGRAPHY
Boase, 5 (1965): 312
J. Millar, *Singers and Songs of the Church*, 2nd edn (London, 1869): 392–3
B. Nightingale, *Lancashire Nonconformity*, 18 (Manchester, England, 1893): 134–6, 200, 224
H. Rogers, 'The Late Samuel Fletcher Esq.' *Good Works* 5 (July 1864): 520–9
J. Thompson, *The Owen's College* (Manchester, 1886): 92–7

DONALD M. LEWIS

Fliedner, Theodor (b. Eppstein, Germany, 21 Jan. 1800; d. Kaiserwerth, Germany, 4 Oct. 1864). Lutheran pastor, social reformer, founder of the modern deaconess movement, and 'higher life' advocate. Son of a Lutheran pastor, Fliedner studied theology in Giessen and Göttingen, worked with the Cologne Bible Society (1820–2), and pastored Kaiserswerth Church near Düsseldorf (1822–64). To relieve social problems there, Fliedner raised money in The Netherlands (1823) and Britain (1824). He returned with funds and three goals: (1) a return to a biblical theology; (2) to emulate British evangelical prison and general social reform; and (3) to encourage liturgical renewal [*Liturgische Mitteilungen aus Holland und England, mit Bezug auf die Neue Preussische Agende* (Essen, 1825)]. In The Netherlands he established contacts with leaders of 'Het Réveil' (a revivalist tradition with Wesleyan as well as reformed roots) and in England

with many evangelical reformers [*Collectenreise nach Holland und England, Nebst Einer Ausführlichen Darstellung des Kirchen-Schul-, Armen- und Gefängnisswesens Beider Länder* (Essen, 1831)], most notably ELIZABETH FRY.

As a result Fliedner developed prison and social ministries and, in 1836, together with his wife Friederike (born 25 January 1800; died 22 April 1842), opened a deaconess hospital. The Kaiserwerth deaconess work served as model throughout Germany, for WILLIAM PENNEFATHER's Mildmay, the Salvation Army, Anglican and Methodist deaconess ministries, and D. L. Moody's work in Chicago. He also had a profound effect on Florence Nightingale, the pioneer of nursing in the English-speaking world. (She in fact spent several months at Kaiserwerth in 1851.) Another person influenced by his example was ELLEN RANYARD who pioneered the employment of Bible women and Bible nurses in Britain. He wrote of his methods in *Some Account of the Deaconess Work in the Christian Church* (Kaiserwerth, 1840), and edited (1849–59) the reform periodical, *Der Armen- und Kranken-Freund, eine Zeitschrift für die Diakonie*. Kaiserwerth became an international centre for 'Higher Christian Life' activity. Fliedner received an honorary doctorate from the University of Bonn (1855).

BIBLIOGRAPHY
G. Fliedner, *Theodor Fliedner, Durch Gottes Gnaden Erneuer des Apostolischen Diakonissenamtes in der Evangelischen Kirche* (Kaiserwerth, Germany, 1908–12)
D. M. Lewis, *Lighten Their Darkness* (Westport, CT, 1986): 220–3
F. Nightingale (anon.), *The Institution at Kaiserwerth on the Rhine for the Practical Training of Deaconesses* (London, 1851)
A. Sticker, *Friederike Fliedner und die Angfänge der Frauendiakonie* (Neuenkirchen, Germany, 1965)

DAVID BUNDY

Flint, Abel (b. Windham, CT, BNA, 6 Aug. 1766; d. Hartford, CT, USA, 7 March 1825). Congregational minister. Flint graduated from Yale (1785), tutored at Brown University from 1786 to 1790, and then was ordained to the Hartford Second (South) Church in 1791 where he remained for the duration of his ministerial career. An ardent Calvinist, Flint's preaching sparked the flames of the Second Great Awakening as revivals broke out at South Church in 1799, 1806 and 1820. He played an important role in the institutional side of the Awakening, serving as an officer in several Hartford-based evangelical societies, including secretary to the Board of Trustees for the Connecticut Missionary Society from its inception in 1798 until 1822. He also edited the *Connecticut Evangelical Magazine* and assisted in the compilation the *Hartford Selection of Hymns* (1799), a work intended for both personal and corporate worship – especially in times of religious awakening.

BIBLIOGRAPHY
AAP, 2: 273–5
BSGYC, 4: 404–7
T. Robbins, *A Sermon on the death of the Rev. Abel Flint* (Hartford, CT, 1825)

R. Shiels, 'The Connecticut Clergy in the Second Great Awakening' (Boston Univ. Ph.D. thesis, 1976)

DAVID W. KLING

Flowerdew, Alice (b. 1759; d. Ipswich, Suffolk, England, 23 Sept. 1830). Baptist poet and schoolmistress. Her husband, Daniel, was for some years in government service in Jamaica. Mrs Flowerdew ran a girls' boarding-school in Islington and was a member of the Worship Street General Baptist congregation. Subsequently she was a member of the 'Glasshouse' congregation in Bury St Edmunds, Suffolk. Some volumes of her published poetry remain extant.

BIBLIOGRAPHY
Julian

J. H. Y. BRIGGS

Fonnereau, Charles William (Thornhaugh, Northamptonshire, England, baptized 18 June 1764; d. 9 Jan. 1840). Anglican clergyman. He was the second son of William Fonnereau, clerk, of Ipswich. He was educated at Charterhouse and Trinity College, Cambridge (matriculated 1791; LL B 1793). As a young man he served in the navy during the American War as a lieutenant on the *Conqueror* and saw action. He was ordained (deacon 1791, priest 1792) by the Bishop of Peterborough. In 1793 he became Perpetual Curate of St Peter's, Ipswich; Vicar of Tuddenham, 1796–1840; Rector of Hargrave, Northamptonshire, 1797–1805 and Perpetual Curate of St Margaret's, Ipswich, 1805. In 1817 he succeeded his father at Christ Church Park, Ipswich.

BIBLIOGRAPHY
Al. Cant.

DONALD M. LEWIS

Foote, William Henry (b. Colchester, CT, USA, 20 Dec. 1792; d. Romney, [West] VA, USA, 22 November 1869). Presbyterian minister and church historian. He received the AB degree from Yale College in 1816 and afterwards became an assistant in the school of WILLIAM HILL in Winchester, Virginia. In 1818 he commenced studies at Princeton Theological Seminary. He was licensed to preach on 30 October 1819 and performed missionary work in Virginia, after which he organized and became pastor of the Presbyterian Church of Woodstock and assumed care of the congregation at Stoverstown [now Strasburg], Virginia. In September 1824 Foote commenced pastorates at Mount Bethel, Springfield, and Romney, [West] Virginia where he had a male and female academy. From 1838 to 1845 he served as agent of the Central Board of Foreign Missions and travelled throughout Virginia and North Carolina during

which time he gathered materials to include in his three historical works: *Sketches of Virginia Historical and Biographical* first series (1850) and second series (1855) and *Sketches of North Carolina Historical and Biographical* (1846). These works provide important data on the rise of evangelicalism during the First and Second Great Awakenings in the Presbyterian Church. In a lively style he preserved accounts of the conversion, piety, conflicts, denominational politics and preaching of the revival leaders and college educators in these two states.

BIBLIOGRAPHY
A. Nevin, ed., *Encyclopedia of the Presbyterian Church in the United States of America* (Philadelphia, PA, 1884) *s.v.* 'Foote, William,': 243–4

ARTHUR DICKEN THOMAS, JR

Forbes, Gordon East India Company servant 1798–1824. Forbes joined the East India Company as a writer. In 1809 he was appointed superintendent of Chandernagore and commissioner for Chinsurah and Serampore. In this capacity he came into contact with LMS and Baptist missionaries. Although on the Calcutta Diocesan Committee of the SPCK, Forbes did not hesitate to help the dissenting missionaries in Bengal. His testimony helped prevent the expulsion of the LMS missionary, ROBERT MAY, from India. Forbes used his influence to persuade the Bengal government to subsidize May's elementary schools – the first case of government funding to missionary schools in India. He was also instrumental in forwarding May's idea of a school society to provide free books for Indian elementary schools. This resulted in the formation of the Calcutta School Society in 1818. He was appointed judge of the Calcutta Court of Appeal in 1818.

BIBLIOGRAPHY
R. Doss, *Register of Hòn. East India Company's Bengal Civil Servants 1790–1842* (Calcutta, 1844)
M. A. Laird, *Missionaries and Education in Bengal, 1793–1837* (Calcutta, 1972)

PENELOPE CARSON

Forbes, James (b. Leochel-Cushnie, Aberdeenshire, Scotland, 4 April 1813; d. Melbourne, Victoria, Australia, 12 Aug. 1851). Presbyterian minister in Melbourne. Forbes was educated at the local parish school and Aberdeen University. On 29 June 1837 he was ordained by the presbytery of Glasgow. At the invitation of JOHN DUNMORE LANG he arrived in Sydney in December 1837 and in January 1838 moved to Port Phillip. In June 1839 he became the founding minister of Scots Church. When the presbytery of Melbourne was constituted in June 1844 he was elected moderator. On receiving news of the Disruption, Forbes sided with the Free Church and resigned his charge. He founded Knox Church, and with it the Free Church of Australia Felix was born. He was a leader in education, commencing three schools, including Melbourne Academy (later Scotch College) in 1851. He was also owner of the *Port Phillip Christian Herald* and an ardent promoter of missions to the Aborigines.

BIBLIOGRAPHY
ADB

STEWART D. GILL

Forbes, John (b. Moulin, Scotland, 1800; d. Glasgow, Scotland, 1874). Church of Scotland minister. Forbes was educated at the University of St Andrews, of which he became a DD. In early life he taught mathematics in Perth Academy, which led later to his publication of *The Differential and Integral Calculus*. Ordained in 1826 to Hope Park Chapel, Edinburgh, he moved to the Outer High Church in Glasgow in 1828. He joined the FCS in 1843. He was awarded an LL D by the University of Glasgow.

R. H. CAMPBELL

Ford, John (b. Worcester, England, 21 March 1801; d. York, England, 16 Aug. 1875). Quaker schoolmaster. He was (1829–65) superintendent of the Quaker Boys' School at York (from 1846, Bootham): 670 boys passed under his care. He saw in Stanley's *Life and Correspondence of Thomas Arnold* (1844) a man whose educational principles were broadly in tune with his own. Ford, who promoted the study of natural history, was active in the Friends' Educational Society (1837) and his papers 'Influence and Authority' (1853) and 'The Duties and Difficulties of Young Teachers' (1856) illustrate his combination of idealism and realism.

He was recorded a minister in 1859, the year of his wife's death. In retirement he took an active interest in the York Bluecoat School, the School for the Blind, and the Castle Howard Reformatory. He warmly supported the Bible Society. His ministry laid emphasis on the love of Christ for us and he did not attempt to expound elaborate doctrinal argument nor to erect theological structures.

BIBLIOGRAPHY
Annual Monitor (1876): 67–78
W. Robinson, ed., *Friends of a Half Century* (London and Ashford, England, 1891): 109–13
S. Thompson, *Memorials of John Ford* (London and York, 1877)

EDWARD H. MILLIGAN

Ford, Reuben (b. probably Goochland Co., VA, BNA, 1742; d. 1823). Baptist minister in Virginia. A convert of GEORGE WHITEFIELD at the age of twenty, Ford was a lay exhorter for seven years before being baptized by James Read in 1769. As a member of JOHN WALLER's Lower Spotsylvania Church, Ford was a delegate to the formation of the General Association of Separate Baptists in Virginia in 1771. The same year he helped found and was called as pastor of Goochland Church. His ministry helped give birth to five other churches.

Beyond the local church, he spoke against the office of Apostle, a Baptist bishopric that the Separates quickly abandoned. He served as clerk of the Dover Association for over thirty years and also served as clerk of the Separate Baptists General Committee, the influential advocate for separation of church and state in Anglican Virginia. Ford was the one Baptist leader who most often presented petitions to the General Assembly of the Colony. In the union of Regular and Separate Baptists (1787), he was a leading figure.

BIBLIOGRAPHY
G. Ryland, *The Baptist of Virginia* (Richmond, VA, 1955)

C. DOUGLAS WEAVER

Fordyce, Alexander (Dingwall) (b. Aberdeen, Scotland, 4 Mar. 1800; d. Aberdeen, Scotland, 16 July 1864). British naval officer and MP. Born into an eminent and ancient Aberdeenshire family, Fordyce was educated at the Aberdeen grammar school. He entered the navy in 1813 as a midshipman, was promoted lieutenant in 1826, and commander in 1841, at which time he was put on half pay. He retired in 1857 at the rank of captain. Fordyce was the author of *Outlines of Naval Routine* (1837).

Deputy-Lieutenant of his county, he was MP in the Whig interest for Aberdeen from 1847 to 1852, at which time he retired. Having been supported in his candidacy by his fellow Free Churchmen, he used his parliamentary position to argue against state support of religious establishments. Fordyce was a member of the EA and attended its fourth General Conference at Geneva in 1862.

BIBLIOGRAPHY
Boase
Stenton

JONATHAN BURKE CUTMORE

Forester, Orlando (Watkin Weld) [fourth Baron Forester] (b. London, 18 April 1813; d. York, England, 22 June 1894). Anglican clergyman. He was from a line of wealthy Shropshire landowners whose lineage is traceable to the reign of Stephen. His father died in 1828 and his mother a year later. Forester was educated at Westminster and at Trinity College, Cambridge (MA 1835). Ordained deacon 1837 and priest 1839, he was Curate of Dunton, Buckinghamshire (1836–41), Rector of Broseley (1841–59), Prebendary of Bullinghope in Hereford Cathedral (1847–74), Vicar of Doveridge (1859–67), Rector of Gelding, near Nottingham (1867–87), Rural Dean of Nottingham (1874–87), and Canon and Chancellor of York Cathedral (from 1874). He succeeded to the barony in 1886.

By his own testimony, he experienced a conversion in 1840 (see his *Extracts from Letters to a Brother*, 1853). He contributed published works on the Gorham and Hampden controversies. Despite his Anglicanism Forester was a member of the EA. In 1883 he was founding vice-president of the Central Vigilance Committee for the Repression of Immorality (to suppress prostitution). His son, Orlando, was a CMS missionary.

BIBLIOGRAPHY
J. Bateman, *Great Landowners of Great Britain and Ireland* (London, 1883): 172
Boase
M. B. Young, *Robert Wilton* (London, 1967)

JONATHAN BURKE CUTMORE

Forman, Charles William (b. Washington, KY, USA, 3 March 1821, d. 1894). Presbyterian missionary and educational pioneer in India. Orphaned at 15, Forman was converted after buying a Bible at age twenty. He was baptized and returned to his family estates (his father had been a prosperous farmer). There he unsuccessfully tried to organize education for slave children. He then trained at Central College, Kentucky, and Princeton Theological Seminary, before sailing for India (after ordination).

In his 1882 essay 'Who are the Sikhs?', Forman showed a sympathetic view of the Sikh religion and its founder, and a considerable respect for the Sikh people. Yet his Presbyterian Mission directed most of its polemic against Islam. Forman preached in the Lahore bazaar and contributed to the educational system in the Punjab. He created the Anglo-Vernacular College in Lahore which now bears his name. Though fee-paying, the Presbyterian schools and colleges remained more popular and respected than the government colleges. He served on virtually every committee set up in the Punjab during his long domicile: the Textbook Committee, the University of the Punjab Committee, etc.

Like ALEXANDER DUFF in Calcutta and JOHN ANDERSON of Madras, Forman worked with several teenage high caste converts whose teenage baptisms caused an uproar. His attitude to converts was paternalistic, allowing for little freedom of expression. He married Margaret Newton in Lahore in 1855.

BIBLIOGRAPHY
J. C. B. Webster, *The Christian Community and Change in 19th Century North India* (Delhi, 1976)

E. M. JACKSON

Forrest, Sir James (b. probably at Edinburgh, 16 Oct. 1780; d. Plymouth, Devon, England, 5 April 1860). Lord Provost of Edinburgh. The son of James Forrest of Edinburgh (1744–1820), a Writer to the Signet, he was made an advocate in 1803 and Lord Provost of Edinburgh in 1838. In that year he was created a baronet. Forrest, who had been very active in the councils of the Church of Scotland, upon the Disruption of 1843 became one of the most prominent lay leaders to secede to the Free Church. A strong Protestant, he was Grand Master of the Scottish freemasons and was a member of the EA.

BIBLIOGRAPHY
Boase
Evangelical Christendom (1847): 65

JONATHAN BURKE CUTMORE

Forster, Josiah (b. Tottenham, England, 2 July 1782; d. Tottenham, England, 27 June 1870). Quaker schoolmaster and philanthropist. Beginning in 1805 Forster operated a boarding-school for the sons of wealthy Friends, at Southgate and later at Tottenham where Grove House School opened in 1828. He eventually retired from school teaching to devote himself to philanthropy and scholarship.

Clerk of the yearly meeting of the Society of Friends for 12 years, he was a friend and associate of THOMAS CLARKSON and ZACHARY MACAULAY, and was also much influenced by J. G. BEVAN (whose *Memoirs* he authored). He also wrote the memoirs of William Grover and volume 11 of *Piety Promoted*, an influential series of brief memoirs. Forster was active in the Antislavery and Bible societies, travelling abroad for both organizations.

BIBLIOGRAPHY
Bible Society Monthly Reporter (1 August 1870)

LESLIE HOWSAM

Forster, Robert (b. Tottenham, London, 13 Dec. 1791; d. Tottenham, 11 Oct. 1873). Quaker businessman and philanthropist. Tottenham in the late eighteenth and early nineteenth centuries had a large (and wealthy) Quaker community in which Forster grew up and spent his whole life. Less well-known than his brother JOSIAH FORSTER he was nevertheless a supporter of causes dear to the hearts of evangelicals, including the Bible Society and the Anti-Slavery Society. His main interest, however, was the BFSS, on whose committee he sat for 56 years, from 1817 until his death.

Within the Society of Friends he served as an elder and he was for many years a member of Meeting for Sufferings (the standing representative committee of British Quakers). Perhaps his most notable service was as a member of deputations to present to European governments 'A Plea for Liberty and Conscience' drawn up by British Quakers in 1856. He travelled to Paris in July 1856, to Holland and Germany in August 1857, and to Russia and Northern Europe in July 1858.

BIBLIOGRAPHY
Annual Monitor (1875): 53–9

EDWARD H. MILLIGAN

BIBLIOGRAPHY
W. H. Carey, ed., *Oriental Christian Biographies*, 1 (Calcutta, 1850): 173–80

PENELOPE CARSON

Forster, William (b. Tottenham, Middlesex, England, 23 March 1784; d. Louis's Ferry, TN, USA, 27 Jan. 1854). Quaker minister. He was the son of a Quaker land agent. In 1817 he married Anna Buxton, sister of Sir T. F. BUXTON. From 1815 he enjoyed the friendship of J. J. GURNEY. Both men gave Quakerism a marked evangelical character in faith and action.

Forster was recognized as a Quaker minister in August 1805 and travelled widely in this service in the British Isles, Europe, and the United States of America. His ministry deeply affected JOSEPH STURGE's career after 1813. Forster supported the work of the BFBS and the BFSS.

He cared much for the less fortunate, undertaking much charitable work, particularly in Norwich where he lived from 1837. With STEPHEN GRELLET he encouraged ELIZABETH FRY to begin her prison work in 1813. He made an important investigative journey in Ireland between November 1846 and April 1847 to arouse public awareness and assist Quaker famine relief efforts. In 1849, with Quaker support, he tried to arouse the active interest of European rulers in the abolition of slavery. He undertook a similar mission to President Pierce and the governors of the Southern and Western United States between October 1853 and January 1854, when he fell fatally ill with pleurisy.

BIBLIOGRAPHY
The British Friend, 12: 96–8 (Glasgow, 1854)
The Friend, XII: 49, 81–2, 99–101, 119–20, 182–5, 197–200 (London, 1854)
—, XIII: 41–3 (London, 1855)
B. Seebohm, ed., *Memoirs of W. Forster*, 2 vols (London, 1865)

HOWARD F. GREGG

Forsyth, Nathanael (b. Dumfriesshire, Scotland, 1769; d. Chandernagore, India, 14 Feb. 1816). First LMS missionary to India. Forsyth was more highly educated than usual, having studied at Glasgow University. He arrived in Calcutta in 1798 and decided that his mission was to the Europeans in Calcutta, Chinsurah and Bandel. He set up a number of schools in the area but these do not appear to have born fruit. Forsyth was fiercely independent, supporting himself and living in spartan simplicity. His life was one of self-denial, his favourite maxim being 'Freely you have received freely give'. He tended the sick and gave virtually all to the poor. Forsyth was a man of prayer and visions who could seldom be induced to socialize. His conscientiousness and deep and powerful convictions made him irascible and earnest, altogether an uncomfortable prophet. His letters are in the CWM archives, School of Oriental and African Studies, London.

Fortescue, Hugh [Viscount Ebrington, second Earl Fortescue] (b. Castle Hill, nr Filleigh, Devon, England, 13 Feb. 1783; d. Exeter, Devon, 14 Sept. 1861). British MP and peer. The eldest son of the first Earl Fortescue, he was educated at Eton and Brasenose College, Oxford (BA 1803). In 1817 he married Susan Ryder, the eldest daughter of Dudley Ryder, the first EARL OF HARROWBY. Fortescue was MP for Barnstaple (1804–7) and St Mawes (1807–9). In 1808 he abandoned his seat to fight under Wellesley in the Peninsula. He resumed his parliamentary career in 1812 as MP for Buckingham (to 1817), and then for Devon (1818–20), Tavistock (1820–30), Devon (1830–2), and North Devon (1832–9). Summoned to the Lords in 1839, he was made Lord Lieutenant of Ireland (1839–41), Lord Steward of the Household (1846–50), and in 1847 parliamentary secretary to the Poor Law Board. A Grenvillite in his early career, he exhibited daring independence. Later, with CHARLES GRANT, Henry Parnell, and others, he was one of the third generation of Whigs notable for their piety and commitment to reform (Wasson, 1976). He supported slave trade abolition, parliamentary reform and Catholic emancipation. He succeeded his father as second earl in 1841 and was knighted in 1856.

BIBLIOGRAPHY
GM, 56 (Oct. 1861): 440–1
R. G. Thorne ed., *The House of Commons 1790–1820* (London, 1986)
E. Wasson, 'The Young Whigs' (Cambridge Univ. Ph.D. thesis, 1976)

JONATHAN BURKE CUTMORE

Foskett, Bernard (b. Crawley, Buckinghamshire, England, 10 March 1685; d. Bristol, England, 17 Sept. 1758). Particular Baptist minister and educator. Foskett trained as doctor in London but accepted a call to Baptist ministry and started as assistant to John Beddome, at Henley-in-Arden, Warwickshire, 29 April 1711. On 7 October 1720 he became assistant pastor at Broadmead Baptist church, Bristol, with special responsibility for teaching student ministers. He succeeded Peter Kitterel (died 1724) as senior pastor at Broadmead, remaining tutor of the Baptist Academy established by Edward Terrill's deed of gift in 1679. HUGH EVANS, a Broadmead member, became his assistant and co-tutor from 1734 to 1758. An increasing number of students were trained after 1730. Between 1720 and 1758, 37 English students from 21 churches, and 37 Welsh students from 14 churches, completed training. Students were members in 'transient communion' at Broadmead, boarding with the ministers while studying for about three years. Students were involved in village preaching. Bristol was the only denominational theological training academy for British Baptists in the eighteenth century.

Foskett was deeply influenced by the 1689 Particular Baptist Confession of Faith and was responsible for making it the basis for the re-organized Western Baptist Association in 1732, thereby excluding General Baptists. He was an active participant in association life as preacher, moderator, author of the 1744 Association Letter to churches, he introduced the catechizing of children (1724), encouraged congregational hymn-singing and wrote hymns to follow his sermons. He was the principal Baptist exponent of evangelical Calvinism in the west of England, keeping evangelical faith alive in the provinces at a time when Brine and GILL's Hyper-Calvinism dominated London Baptists to the detriment of the mission of the church.

BIBLIOGRAPHY
N. S. Moon, *Education for Ministry* (London, 1979)
S. A. Swaine, *Faithful Men* (London, 1884)

ROGER HAYDEN

Foster, George F. (b. Sabden, Lancashire, England, 20 March 1796; d. Sabden, Lancashire, England, 11 April 1882). Baptist layman and calico printer. Foster's claim to fame is as Richard Cobden's partner at Sabden, near Blackburn, Lancashire. The factory there had been founded by Richard Fort, a Baptist entrepreneur of an earlier generation. Fort had moved the Oakenshaw church to Accrington when he relocated his works there in 1765, one of the few examples of close integration of chapel and factory. Cobden came to Manchester in 1828 to establish himself in business, beginning by selling printed calico for Fort on commission. In 1831, at a moment when the removal of duty made trade more buoyant, he determined to become a manufacturer, taking over Fort's works at Sabden, with which there had also been associated James Bury [1817], the generous first treasurer of the Baptists' Northern Education Society. George Foster, hitherto manager, in 1831 became partner in charge of an enterprise which in the year following had 600 wage earners. John Morley (1879) notes 'A diminutive Baptist chapel, irregularly served, was the only agency for bringing so far as it did bring, the great religious traditions of the western world within reach of this isolated flock'. Foster, Morley called, 'a Liberal of the finest and most enlightened type, with a clear head and a strong intelligence and the good old-fashioned faith in freedom, justice and progress'. He is said to have led the Sabden voters to Clitheroe to vote in the first election after the Reform Act, taking good care to get them away from Clitheroe before the attractions of its taverns and ale-houses became apparent, to be refreshed by the unintoxicating springs of the Pennine hills! Foster had a great interest in education, early giving support to the Northern Education Society and its academy at Horton, later becoming treasurer to JOSEPH

HARBOTTLE's academy in Accrington. In 1844 he convoked a special conference of Northern Baptist Churches to consider the implications of the newly emerging educational opportunities. A committee was established to collect funds and to supervise educational work, encouraging the churches to establish day schools, but not to accept any aid which was conditional upon control being diverted from the local church, and not to accept any arrangement which disallowed the use of schools as preaching stations on Sundays. Foster declined the moderator's chair of the Lancashire and Cheshire Association in the 1870s on the grounds of ill health.

BIBLIOGRAPHY
BQ, 5 (1930)
BQ, 23 (1969)
Burnley Express, Accrington Times (April 1882)
J. Morley, *Life of Richard Cobden* 2 vols (London, 1879)
W. T. Whitley, *The Baptists of North West England* (London, 1913)

J. H. Y. BRIGGS

Foster, Henry (b. Wadsworth, Yorkshire, England, c. 1745; d. Clerkenwell, London, 26 May 1814). Anglican clergyman. Baptized 17 March 1745, the son of a shalloon manufacturer, he entered Queen's College, Oxford, in 1764 and graduated BA in 1767. Ordained deacon (1767) and priested (1769), he was curate to WILLIAM ROMAINE at St Anne's, Blackfriars. For over twenty years he held a lectureship in the parish as well as others in London. From 1780 he was minister of Long Acre proprietary chapel. A new building was consecrated by Beilby Porteus, Bishop of London, in 1792. JOHN THORNTON thought highly of Foster and left instructions in his will that if Clapham became vacant it was to be offered to him. Foster was unwilling to leave Long Acre and JOHN VENN went instead. In 1807, however, he was instituted to Clerkenwell on the nomination of the parishioners. An outstanding preacher, admired by WILLIAM WILBERFORCE, he was co-founder of the EcS and pioneer of the CMS.

A. SKEVINGTON WOOD

Foster, John (b. Halifax, Yorkshire, England, 17 Sept. 1770; d. Downend, Bristol, England, 15 Oct. 1843). Essayist. John Foster's father, a farmer who supplemented his income by weaving, was a Baptist and avid reader of theological works. His elder son inherited his studiousness. He joined the church in 1787 and was encouraged to enter the ministry, studying under his pastor, Dr JOHN FAWCETT, before attending Bristol Baptist College for a year from 1791 to 1792.

As a minister Foster was a failure: he served in Newcastle-on-Tyne for three months at the end of 1792, moving in 1793 to Dublin, where his small congregation dwindled to nothing. He ran an unsuccessful school and tried his hand at business and at literature before finally returning to England in 1796. The following year he was invited to minister to the General Baptist congregation at Chichester. He stayed for two and a half years, and then moved to Battersea, lodging for a few months with JOSEPH HUGHES, with whom he had formed a lasting friendship at Bristol. Here he took charge of a group of Sierra Leonese boys brought to London for an English education. In 1800 he became stated preacher at Downend Chapel near Bristol, and in 1804 on ROBERT HALL's recommendation was appointed pastor at Frome in Somerset, a charge he resigned in 1806 on grounds of ill health: thyroid trouble had made regular preaching impossible. After some years' residence at Bourton-on-the-Water in Gloucestershire his throat gradually improved and he resumed preaching but with no more success. He served for a further six months at Downend in 1817 but resigned, unable to interest the people. In 1821 he moved to Stapleton, near Bristol, and a year later agreed to lecture on a regular basis in Broadmead Chapel. Once Robert Hall accepted the pastorate Foster felt that his efforts were unnecessary and he gave up lecturing altogether.

While at Frome Foster published *Essays in a Series of Letters to a Friend*, a book which opened the way to a much more successful career as a writer. In 1805 the *Eclectic Review* was founded and Foster soon became a major contributor. A slow and procrastinating writer, he published nothing under his own name for many years, but between 1819 and his death produced further original essays. Regular reviewing enabled him to support a family, and his long-delayed marriage to Maria Snooke, the original recipient of the 'letters', took place in 1808: she bore him five children, but two did not survive infancy and their remaining son died in 1826.

One of the most intellectually able evangelicals of his generation, Foster was a thoughtful and logical writer and a discriminating reviewer. Widely read and eclectic in his interests, he appreciated the skill of authors antagonistic to Christianity such as the historian Gibbon. Like many evangelicals, however, he had some difficulty in reconciling his enthusiasm for secular literature with his faith: he concluded that Christians living in a civilized society had no option but to read classical works which would to some degree harm as well as inform and polish their minds.

The essay in which he worked out these ideas, 'On Some of the Causes by which Evangelical Religion has been rendered less acceptable to Persons of Cultivated Taste', was a damning indictment of his fellow evangelicals. He objected to preachers' pseudo-biblical jargon and grotesque gestures and to the complacent ignorance of many of their hearers. In a later essay on *Popular Ignorance* he argued that some intellectual aptitude was a prerequisite for conversion. Unable to conceive of a non-intellectual approach to life and ready to ask difficult questions himself, he could not understand those who did not want to probe and analyse the mysteries of faith, hence in part his failure as a pastor.

Foster disliked institutional religion. Although he served for many years on the governing body of the Baptist College, he tried to avoid the busy round of committees and meetings in which many evangelicals engaged. A naturally reclusive man, he inclined to isolated living and was always happier mixing with a small number of congenial people than in communal gatherings. Characteristically he worked out his theology for himself. At the time of his Chichester ministry he inclined towards Arianism, but subsequently came to adopt a moderate Calvinist faith. However, he rejected the doctrine of eternal punishment, refused to administer baptism and tended not to attend communion services.

Foster regarded freedom to think for oneself as a central tenet of the dissenting heritage. In 1809 he lambasted the editors of the *Eclectic Review* for their unwillingness to speak out on issues over which Anglicans and Dissenters differed: 'all systems, institutions, and practices, as being merely of human authority, are fully open to the exercise of human reason' (Ryland, 1846, 1: 377). He was highly critical of the Church of England, believing that an established church was inevitably subject to secular machinations which got in the way of its evangelistic task. He also objected to priestly authority, religious ceremonial and corporate institutions, and protested when Dissenters appeared to adopt these. In 1829 he refused to take part in a dissenting ordination, and he devoted much time to defending the Serampore missionaries in their fight against the controlling BMS committee.

Foster's belief in liberty had political as well as religious implications. He was opposed to war in which the interests of individuals were subordinated to those of states and also objected to censorship. He had republican sympathies and in Ireland associated with those whom he described as 'violent democrats' (Ryland, 1846, 1: 38). He was exultant when a measure of parliamentary reform was passed in 1832. He supported popular education, believing that it would discourage unquestioning deference and enable working people to think and question for themselves.

His own independence of mind enabled him to make an unusual contribution to the church of his day. The *Eclectic Review*, which owed much to him, flourished, and his own works were regularly reprinted. His cultured and critical approach to life and faith may have had a wider appeal than he always recognised.

SELECT WRITINGS

J. Foster, *Essays in a Series of Letters to a Friend* (London, 1805)
—, *Discourse . . . Delivered at the AGM of the Baptist Missionary Society* (London, 1819)
—, *An Essay on the Evils of Popular Ignorance* (London, 1820)
—, Introductory essay to P. Doddridge's *The Rise and Progress of Religion in the Soul* (Glasgow, 1825 edn)
—, 'Observations on Mr Hall's Character as a Preacher' in *The Works of Robert Hall* (London, 1832)
—, *The Established Church* (London, 1834)
—, *Critical Essays Contributed to the Eclectic Review*, ed. J. E. Ryland, 2 vols (London, 1856)
—, *Fosteriana, Consisting of Thoughts, Reflections and Criticisms* ed. H. G. Bohn (London, 1858)

—, *An Essay on the Improvement of Time and Other Literary Remains*, ed. J. E. Ryland (London, 1863)

BIBLIOGRAPHY
Alli
T. Crisp, *On Seeing Him Who Is Invisible, a Sermon Occasioned By the Death of the Rev John Foster* (London, 1843)
DNB
P. Kaufman, 'John Foster's Pioneer Interpretation of the Romantic', *Modern Language Notes*, 38 (1923): 1–14
W. Landels, *Baptist Worthies* (London, 1883): 271–306
A. G. Newell, 'A Christian Approach to Literature', *EQ*, 32 (1960): 79–106
D. M. Rosman, *Evangelicals and Culture* (London, 1984)
J. E. Ryland, ed., *Life and Correspondence of John Foster*, 2 vols (London, 1846)

DOREEN M. ROSMAN

Foster, Randolph Sinks (b. Williamsburg, Clermont County, OH, USA, 22 Feb. 1829; d. Newton Centre, MA, USA, 1 May 1903). MEC bishop in the USA. Foster was the son of Israel and Polly (Kain) Foster. The family moved to Kentucky where the young Foster attended Augusta College. He proved to be a gifted young preacher and several friends encouraged him to abandon his education in his sophomore year to enter the ministry, which he did in 1837. He joined the Ohio Annual Conference of the MEC, being ordained a deacon in 1839 and an elder in 1841. In July, 1840, he married Sarah A. Miley of Cincinnati; she died in 1871. He became well known as a preacher and as an apologist for evangelical Methodism. In 1849 he published *Objections to Calvinism*, which reflected the continuing dialogue in American evangelicalism between its constituent parts. In 1850 Foster transferred to the New York Annual Conference and served in the New York City area for the next 18 years, except for three years (1857–60) when he served as president of Northwestern University in Evanston, Illinois. In 1868 he became professor of systematic theology at the newly created Drew Theological Seminary in Madison, New Jersey, and served as president, 1870–2.

Foster was a delegate to the General Conference, the legislative body of the church, in 1864, 1868, and 1872. In 1872 he was elected bishop and served in that capacity for the next 24 years, retiring in 1896. As bishop he visited all of the mission fields of the church in Europe, Asia, and South America.

As both pastor and bishop Foster had an important influence on the Methodist denomination and in the church at large. Although a 'college dropout', Foster continued to study and came to realize the importance and necessity of education for the minister in the changing world of late nineteenth-century America. In 1855 he wrote *A Treatise on the Need of the Methodist Episcopal Church with Respect to Her Ministry*. The book was important in the debate over the merits of a seminary education in preparation for the ministry. But Foster was also interested in spiritual formation and added to the growing literature of Methodist spirituality. In 1851 he wrote the *Nature and Blessedness of Christian Purity*. The book was so well received that Foster revised and enlarged the work in 1869 and retitled it *Christian Purity or the Heritage of Faith*. Under the later title it was placed on the course of study from 1872 until 1892 and again in 1900 until 1904. The course of study was a list of required texts that ministerial candidates of the MEC read. The text discussed the Methodist understanding of the doctrine of perfection. Foster was attempting to be irenic as there were developing two schools of thought concerning the doctrine in that church. His book was not only an attempt to heal the rift, but also to the expound the moral character and quality of Christian holiness. Foster also wrote other works on heaven and the realities of the invisible world. In addition to his spiritual works, he also wrote a six volume work on theology, *Studies in Theology* (1889–99). Only one of these was used on the course of study, *The Supernatural Book*, from 1892 until 1908.

Foster's work was varied and busy: pastor, teacher, educator, administrator, spiritual guide, theologian. In an age and era which tended to emphasize the freedom of the human will in relationship to salvation, Foster emphasized the action and activity of the Holy Spirit in the life of the believer. In this respect Foster's work made an important contribution to mid-nineteenth-century American Methodist theological and spiritual tradition. In the ensuing years of the holiness controversy his work was claimed by both sides.

SELECT WRITINGS
R. S. Foster, *Objections to Calvinism as it is, in a Series of Letters Addressed to N. L. Rice* (Cincinnati, OH, 1849)
—, *Nature and Blessedness of Christian Purity* (New York, 1851)
—, *A Treatise on the Need of the Methodist Episcopal Church with Respect to Her Ministry* (New York, 1855)
—, *Christian Purity* (New York, 1869)
—, *Beyond the Grave* (New York, 1879)
—, *Studies in Theology*, 6 vols (New York, 1889–99)

BIBLIOGRAPHY
DAB
J. E. Earl, 'Foster, Randolph Sinks', *Encyclopedia of World Methodism*, ed. N. B. Harmon (Nashville, TN, 1974)
EWM
F. D. Leete, *Methodist Bishops*, (Nashville, TN, 1948)

L. DALE PATTERSON

Fountain, John (b. Rutland Co., England, 1767; d. Dingepore, India, 20 Aug. 1800). Pioneer Baptist missionary in India. From an Anglican family, Fountain was converted in his teens and baptized in London. There he became engaged to Miss Tidd of Oakham Chapel. Fountain arrived unannounced in Mudnabatty (1796) to join WILLIAM CAREY. Since his was the only musical talent among the missionaries, he soon began composing hymns. Fountain's radical political views, indiscreetly expressed in his letters and journal, scandalized ANDREW FULLER and alarmed Carey. (Carey was a pacifist and republican.)

Fountain began preaching in fluent Bengali in July 1799. He helped Carey to proofread the New Testament's first translation into Bengali. He died from dysentery while helping FERNANDEZ with the indigo crop at Dingepore. Married to Miss Tidd in Calcutta on 7 November 1799, his son, born posthumously, was adopted by WILLIAM WARD and died in Serampore on 25 October 1836. Important letters and an account of his death are found in JOHN RIPPON's *Baptist Annual Register* (II: 410 f).

E. M. JACKSON

Fowler, Joseph (b. Bradford, Yorkshire, England, 1791; d. Wesley's House, London, 17 March 1851). Methodist minister and historiographer. Converted through the influence of an evangelical vicar, Fowler became a local preacher in 1810, and entered the ministry in 1811, under Joseph Sutcliffe. He always set apart the anniversary of his conversion. He spent most of his ministry in the North of England, in some circuits enjoying distinguished colleagueship.

One of the leaders of opposition to the rule of JABEZ BUNTING (though in circuit he followed Bunting's dictum to be not merely a chairman, but a pastor in charge), from 1827 to 1849 he kept a journal of the conference debates, acknowledged to be accurate and impartial. Regarded as 'the soul of truthfulness and honour', he was the standard bearer of freedom of speech. Accused by Bunting of complicity with the 'Fly Sheets', he refused to sign GEORGE OSBORNE's declaration in 1849. His circuit work was marked by earnestness and kindliness; he had a racy sense of humour, kept carefully in check; was a pattern of pastoral visitation and gave three hours a day to sick visiting; he preferred a sustained ministerial efficiency to extraordinary agencies and preached with freedom and feeling. When in London he was chairman of the district and became secretary of Conference in 1848, though that was not followed by the presidency the following year. His son H. H. Fowler became the first Methodist peer, as Lord Wolverhampton.

BIBLIOGRAPHY
EWM
B. Gregory, *Sidelights on the Conflicts of Methodism* (London, 1898): 6–47
WMM (1852): 742–6

OLIVER A. BECKERLEGGE

Fowler, Littleton (b. Smith City, TN, USA, 12 Sept. 1802; d. San Augustine, TX, USA, 19 Jan. 1846). Methodist minister and evangelist. Converted at a camp meeting in Caldwell County, Kentucky, Fowler joined the MEC in 1819. In 1826, he was licensed to preach in the Kentucky Conference. After a successful pastorate in Louisville, Kentucky, Fowler joined the Tennessee Conference in 1832. From 1833 to 1837 he served as financial agent for La Grange College, Tuscumbia, Alabama. In 1837, Fowler was appointed as a missionary to the Republic of Texas. He organized and served as a presiding elder of six different districts. Following his marriage to Missouri M. Porter in 1838, Fowler settled on a farm near San Augustine, Texas, although he continued to serve regular pastoral appointments until his death. Fowler was a delegate to the MEC's General Conference of 1844, and was also a delegate to the convention held in Louisville in 1845 which resulted in the organization of the MEC,So. Noted as a powerful preacher, Fowler left a deep legacy in Texas Methodism. A diary kept by Fowler is an important source for the history of early Methodism in Texas. Fowler's personal papers are located at Southern Methodist University, Dallas, Texas.

BIBLIOGRAPHY
EWM, 1: 870
M. Phelan, *A History of Early Methodism in Texas* (Nashville, TN, 1924): 255–8

WILLIAM KOSTLEVY

Fox, Henry (Watson) (b. Westoe, Co. Durham, England, 1 Oct. 1817; d. Durham, England, 14 Oct. 1848). CMS missionary in India. Fifth son of George Townsend Fox, and Ann (Stott), Henry was educated at Durham Grammar School (1828–30), and Rugby (Bonamy Price's house 1831–6), where he was converted. In 1836 he went up to Wadham College, Oxford, then under Warden SYMONS. Spiritually immature, however, he was initially attracted by worldly ways; growth in grace encouraged him to teach in St Ebbe's Sunday schools under W. W. CHAMPNEYS. E. P. HATHAWAY, was among his friends. Elected Goodridge university exhibitioner (1837), he took his degree in 1839. In that year, influenced by H. V. ELLIOTT, he responded to an appeal by J. TUCKER, from Madras. Accepted by the CMS on 21 December 1840 he was made deacon 'for the colonies' (ordination papers, London). On 30 December he married, at Bagborough, Somerset, Elizabeth James of Wolverhampton.

Appointed a missionary to the Telagu, in July 1841, Fox, with his wife, reached Madras. In conjunction with R. T. NOBLE, and aided by his own linguistic gift, he worked in the Masulipatam neighbourhood 1841–3, where he laid the foundations of the Village Mission, which in later years 'gathered thousands of souls'. With declining health, insufficiently improved by living in hill country 1843–4, Fox visited England 1845–6, his ailing wife and third child having died on board ship before leaving Madras. At Oxford especially, and still with youthful impetus, he made moving appeals for more missionaries. T. V. FRENCH, afterwards Bishop of Lahore, was one of those attracted. Fox's Oxford visit, influencing juniors, coincided nearly with that of Bishop DANIEL WILSON, from Calcutta, a corresponding influence among seniors. While in England, Fox wrote incisively in

Chapters on Missions in South India, eventually published before his death two years later.

Returning to India, Fox's health failed again. At home once more, in 1848 he was appointed assistant secretary of the CMS; but he overworked, and died in the autumn, not before he had composed a moving hymn for the CMS jubilee services the following month. In his memory an annual missionary sermon was endowed at Rugby, in aid of a schoolmastership in South India. Fox was remarkable for his deep spirituality. Like HENRY MARTYN, whose biography he read at school, Fox's example stimulated considerable concern for evangelism abroad. Two children survived, one Prebendary H. E. Fox, becoming honorary secretary of the CMS, 1895–1910, and a founder of the Bible Churchmen's Missionary Society (1922). H. W. Fox's brother, Sir William Fox (*DNB*), became Prime Minister of New Zealand.

BIBLIOGRAPHY

G. T. Fox (brother), *Memoir of Henry Watson Fox*, 4th edn (London, 1854)

Hole manuscripts, Birmingham University

J. S. Reynolds, *Evangelicals at Oxford* (Oxford, 1953; Appleford, England, 1975)

E. Stock, *History of the CMS*, 1 (London, 1899)

J. Tucker, memorial *Sermon* (London, 1849)

J. S. REYNOLDS

Fox, Joseph (b. London, 1776; d. London, 11 April 1816). Surgeon, dentist, and Baptist educator. A distinguished surgeon and dentist, and lecturer at Guy's hospital, he was a member of RIPPON's Carter Lane Church in Southwark (not a Quaker passe Ford K. Brown, *Father of the Victorians*: 351). His generosity in terms of a benefaction of more than £2,000 rescued the Lancasterian system of education when it looked as if the debt of the founder and general lack of finance might kill it. Convinced of its usefulness, and 'humbly relying on redeeming love', he did all he could, including published replies to its opponents, to promote it, not only at home but worldwide, becoming one of the secretaries of the BFSS. He was also the founding secretary, from 1808, of the LSPCJ until Dissenters were excluded from the administration in 1815.

BIBLIOGRAPHY

Baptist Magazine (1811, 1816)

EM (1816)

J. H. Y. BRIGGS

Fox, William (b. Clapton, Gloucestershire, England, 14 Feb. 1736; d. Cirencester, Gloucestershire, England, 1 April 1826). Businessman and Baptist philanthropist. From BENJAMIN BEDDOME's church at Bourton he was apprenticed to a draper and mercer in Oxford. Inheriting this business enabled him to move to London and set up business in a very considerable way in Leadenhall Street, becoming at the same time one of ABRAHAM BOOTH's deacons at Prescot Street. A friend of GRANVILLE SHARP and WILLIAM WILBERFORCE, in 1785, after correspondence with ROBERT RAIKES, and already convinced of the need of a system of universal education for the betterment of the poor, he established the interdenominational Sunday School Society, which within two years had more than 7,000 children enrolled in schools. With a committee of 12 Episcopalians and 12 Dissenters, it was one of the first organizations to unite both interests in common action. Fox was also first treasurer to the Baptist Home Missionary Society.

BIBLIOGRAPHY

J. Ivimey, *Memoir of William Fox, Esq.* (London, 1831)

J. H. Y. BRIGGS

Foxall, Henry (b. Monmouthshire, Wales, 24 May 1758; d. Handsworth, England, 11 Dec. 1823). Methodist lay minister and foundryman. The son of devout Methodists, Henry worked as an iron-moulder in Birmingham until 1794. He emigrated to the United States in 1797 and started Eagle Iron Works in partnership with Robert Morris, Jr. In 1800, he relocated to Georgetown, DC, and established the Columbian Foundry. He manufactured guns for the United States government until 1815 when he sold the foundry. In recognition for his acts of charity, he was elected to elders orders by the Baltimore Conference of the MEC in 1814. FRANCIS ASBURY, who had served as a blacksmith's apprentice to Foxall's father, was a frequent guest in the Foxall home.

BIBLIOGRAPHY

DAB

EWM, 2: 870–1

WILLIAM KOSTLEVY

Foxcroft, Thomas (b. Boston, MA, BNA, 26 Feb. 1697; d. Boston, MA, BNA, 18 June 1769). Congregational minister. Born into a wealthy Boston family and graduating from Harvard College in 1714, Foxcroft served for a period as a schoolteacher in nearby Roxbury before his ordination and installation in 1717 as Benjamin Wadsworth's colleague at Boston's First Parish Church. After Wadsworth's death, Foxcroft was joined there in 1727 by Charles Chauncy. While Wadsworth and Chauncy were both theological liberals, Foxcroft was a centrist whose soundness was sometimes doubted by liberals and conservatives alike. On the one hand, he lent timely support to the controversial Robert Breck, an Arminian who crossed swords with JONATHAN EDWARDS; on the other, he championed the Great Awakening, writing in defence of GEORGE WHITEFIELD and in 1745 taking his place among New Light clergy soliciting the evangelist's return to Boston. A stroke that felled

Foxcroft in 1736 left him in frail health, unable to function as a counterbalance to Chauncy during a critical era in the history of First Church.

BIBLIOGRAPHY
SGH

GEORGE W. HARPER

Francis, Benjamin (b. Newcastle Emlyn, Dyfed, South Wales, *c.* July 1734; d. Shortwood, Gloucestershire, England, 14 Dec. 1799). Baptist minister and hymnist. The youngest son of Enoch Francis, the most influential Baptist pastor in South-West Wales, he was brought up in Swansea, Glamorganshire, where he was baptized in 1749 before proceeding to the ministerial school at Trosnant, Gwent, *c.* 1752, and to the Bristol academy in 1753. After supplying the church at Chipping Sodbury, Gloucestershire, for two years, he was ordained minister at Shortwood (or Horsley) on 12 September 1758. This church flourished, becoming one of the foremost Baptist causes in England outside of London. Francis also gained a reputation as an effective itinerant evangelist, both in the surrounding localities and as far abroad as Cornwall, London, and Ireland, demonstrating the ongoing commitment of Bristol-trained Baptists to evangelical outreach while Socinianism and Hyper-Calvinism stultified the church's mission in many places. He refused an invitation to succeed Dr JOHN GILL as pastor of the prestigious Carter Lane church in Southwark. An accomplished poet and hymnist in both English and Welsh, it was as a preacher that he was principally revered by his contemporaries. His manuscript correspondence with his compatriot JOSHUA THOMAS affords a fascinating glimpse of eighteenth-century dissenting life.

BIBLIOGRAPHY
DWB
T. Flint, *Sketch of the Life of Benjamin Francis* (London, 1799)
T. L. Jenkins, 'Bywyd, Gwaith a Chyfraniad Benjamin Francis yr Emynydd (1734–1799)', (Univ. of Wales M. Phil. thesis, 1989)
G. F. Nuttall, '"Questions and Answers": an Eighteenth Century Correspondence', *BQ*, 27 (April 1977): 83–90
N. Moon, *Education for Ministry* (London, 1979)

D. DENSIL MORGAN

Franklin, Benjamin (b. Belmont County, OH, USA, 1 Feb. 1812: d. Anderson, IN, USA, 22 Oct. 1878). A leading second generation evangelist, debater, and editor in the American Restoration Movement. Franklin was a descendent of John, brother of the famous Benjamin Franklin of Philadelphia (1706–90). Franklin's parents were Methodists, but along with young Benjamin, were baptized (1834) by Samuel Rogers who had been influenced by BARTON W. STONE and ALEXANDER CAMPBELL. Franklin commenced to preach shortly thereafter. He grew in demand as an evangelist, preaching in meetings from Pennsylvania to Missouri. According to estimates he converted over 8,000 persons. He held about thirty religious debates and was involved in editing five popular religious periodicals beginning in 1845 with the *Reformer*. Other journals were the *Western Reformer*, *The Gospel Proclamation*, *Proclamation and Reformer*, and *The American Christian Review* (1856). The latter under Franklin's editorship attained the widest circulation of any journal in the Restorationist movement. He was a moderate at first, supporting mission societies, but opposing instrumental music. He denounced both slavery and the Civil War. After the war he identified with conservatives, and opposed the mission societies. His legacy has been preserved in the Christian Churches (Independent) and the Churches of Christ.

BIBLIOGRAPHY
O. L. Castleberry, *They Heard Him Gladly* (Rosemead, CA, 1963)
DAB
J. Franklin and J. A. Headington, *The Life and Times of Benjamin Franklin* (St Louis, MO, 1879)
J. F. Rowe and G. W. Rice, *Biographical Sketches and Writings of Elder Benjamin Franklin* (Cincinnati, OH, 1892)

THOMAS H. OLBRICHT

Franklin, Francis (b. Mursley, Buckinghamshire, England, 1772; d. Coventry, England, 12 Nov. 1852). Particular Baptist minister. Apprenticed to a relative in Oxford, he came under the influence of JAMES HINTON of Oxford, who baptized him in 1793 at Abingdon and encouraged him to train for the ministry at Bristol Academy under JOHN RYLAND. In 1796–7 he itinerated with WILLIAM STEADMAN in Cornwall under the aegis of the BMS. Ordained to Cow Lane Baptist Chapel, Coventry, he remained there until his death. He had a great interest in missionary work – JOHN DYER, secretary of the BMS, was his brother-in-law, and one of his daughters served in Jamaica. Franklin also helped to foster the Baptist cause in a number of places, including Rugby and Kenilworth. Preaching and praying were his delight, and he is reputed to have preached more than 10,000 sermons.

Two of Franklin's daughters, Mary and Rebecca, kept what became a celebrated school at Hertford House. The school's most notable pupil, Marian Evans (GEORGE ELIOT) later used Francis Franklin as the prototype of 'Rufus Lyon' in *Felix Holt*.

BIBLIOGRAPHY
Annual Reports of the Baptist Denomination, 3 (1853)
C. Binfield, *Pastors and People* (Coventry, England, 1984)
Coventry Herald (19 November 1852, 26 November 1852)
Coventry Standard (19 November 1852)
G. Eliot, *Felix Holt* (Edinburgh and London, 1866)
D. Lovegrove, *Established Church, Sectarian People* (London, 1988)
I. Morris, *Three Hundred Years of Baptist Life in Coventry* (Coventry, England, 1925)

NIGEL SCOTLAND

Franklin, Sir **John** (b. Spilsby, Lincolnshire, England, 1786; d. in the Arctic, 11 June 1847). Captain Royal Navy and polar explorer. He fought at Copenhagen and Trafalgar in early career, and accompanied Matthew Flinders on his Australian survey. His first expedition to the Canadian Arctic (1819–22) explored 500 miles of coast from the Coppermine River by canoe; the party nearly perished from starvation during their overland return. His second expedition (1825–7) explored the coast westwards from the Mackenzie River and eastward to link up with his earlier discoveries. He was knighted for these achievements and given command of a frigate before going to Van Diemen's Land (Tasmania) as Lieutenant-Governor in 1836. Although a kindly and conscientious administrator he was recalled in 1843 on the basis of malicious reports circulated by a factious executive and a vituperative local press. These frustrations made him anxious to return to exploration.

In May 1845 the ships *Erebus* and *Terror* with 129 men under Franklin's command set out to search for the north-west passage. The expedition became ice-bound off King William Island before Franklin died aboard ship on 11 June 1847. The ships were abandoned in April 1848, but lacking tents, sleighs or suitable techniques for survival the entire party perished in their efforts to reach safety.

He was a staunch supporter of the Naval and Military Bible Society and a key figure in the establishment of the 'Western Australia Missionary Society' (1835) which in 1837 became known as the Colonial Church Society. He wrote: *Narrative of a Journey to the Shores of the Polar Sea* (London, 1823); *Narrative of a Second Expedition to the Polar Sea* (London, 1828); *Narrative of Some Passages in the History of Van Diemen's Land* (London, 1845).

BIBLIOGRAPHY
R. J. Cyriax, *Sir John Franklin's Last Arctic Expedition* (London, 1939)
K. Fitzgerald, *Sir John Franklin in Tasmania* (Melbourne, 1949)
G. F. Lamb, *Franklin – Happy Voyager* (London, 1956)
F. L. McClintock, *The Voyage of the Fox in the Arctic Seas* (London, 1859)
H. A. Seegmiller, 'The Colonial and Continental Church Society in Eastern Canada', (Unpublished D.D. thesis for the General Synod, Windsor, Nova Scotia, Canada, 1966): 45
H. D. Traill, *Life of Sir John Franklin, RN* (London, 1896)

RICHARD C. BLAKE

Franks, **James** (b. Loughborough, Leicestershire, England, 1760; d. Chelsea, London, 1829). Anglican clergyman. Franks was educated at Magdalene College, Cambridge (scholar 1784; BA 1787; MA 1791). He began his career as Curate of Haddenham (Cambridgeshire) (1787) and was subsequently minister of the English chapel at Glasgow and curate to H. W. COULTHURST at Halifax before becoming Perpetual Curate of Sowerby Bridge (near Halifax) (1802–29). He was a member of the ElS and father of JAMES CLARKE FRANKS of Huddersfield.

BIBLIOGRAPHY
Al. Cant., II, ii: 567

ARTHUR POLLARD

Franks, **James Clarke** (b. Halifax, Yorkshire, England, 1793; d. Huddersfield, Yorkshire, England, 18 April 1867). Anglican clergyman. The son of an evangelical, JAMES FRANKS of Sowerby Bridge, J. C. Franks was educated at Halifax and Trinity College, Cambridge which he entered in 1810 (scholar 1814; BA 1815; MA 1818; BD 1855). He won the Hulsean Prize in 1813 and the Norrisian in 1814, 1816, 1817 and 1818. He became chaplain of Trinity in 1819, was select preacher before the university in 1819 and 1820 and Hulsean lecturer in 1821 and 1823, on the first occasion discoursing on the evidences of Christianity and on the second on the apostolic preaching as it is displayed in the Acts of the Apostles and the Epistles of Peter and to the Hebrews. He returned to his native Yorkshire as Vicar of Huddersfield (1823–40) where he knew PATRICK BRONTË and married Charlotte's godmother, Elizabeth Firth. He served subsequently as Curate of Whittlesey (Cambridgeshire) (1844–54) and Rector of St Margaret's, Canterbury (1859–63).

BIBLIOGRAPHY
Al. Cant., II. ii: 567

ARTHUR POLLARD

Fraser, **Edward** (b. Barbados, West Indies, 1798; d. Jamaica, West Indies, 1872). Methodist preacher. Edward, born a slave, was a model Methodist preacher, greatly admired for his sanctified intellect and splendid Christian life. In 1818, his owner took him to Bermuda, and coming under the Christian influence of Enoch Matson and James Dunbar, he became a class leader. He and James Cox built the Methodist Chapel at Warwick in 1827, the year of his liberation. Bermudan Methodism was held in high regard because of his remarkable Christian influence. He humbly declined to become a colonial bishop and entered the Methodist ministry. He served in Dominica and later in Jamaica as superintendent of the Morant Bay circuit and was district secretary for 18 successive years. In 1846 he successfully met the formidable task of visiting the Methodist churches in England and challenging them to raise funds to meet the needs of the missionaries and build Wesleyan West Indian Schools.

BIBLIOGRAPHY
G. G. Findlay and W. W. Holdsworth, *The History of the Wesleyan Methodist Missionary Society*, 2 (London, 1921): 252–373
Minutes (London, 1872): 41–3

LESLEY G. ANDERSON

Fraser, **William** (b. Strathspey, Scotland, 1801; d. Bruce Co., Ontario, 1883). Baptist itinerant preacher in Scotland and in Canada. Fraser was converted through the preaching of PETER GRANT, and later became a member of the Baptist church at Grantown-on-Spey. Trained at ROBERT HALDANE's seminary, he began itinerant preaching in 1825, and was active in Lewis. He settled a year later in Uig, Skye, where he was given charge of the local Baptist church. He was formally ordained to the pastorate in July 1828.

In response to a plea for Baptist leaders for the Canadian churches, Fraser emigrated to Ontario in 1831, and became the pastor of Breadalbane Baptist Church, Lochiel Township, Glengarry County, where he remained until 1850. While at Breadalbane, he sustained an itinerant ministry in eastern Ontario and southern Quebec, and served as superintendent of public schools in the counties of Glengarry, Stormont and Dundas. In 1850 he moved west to Bruce County, Ontario, where he founded the Baptist church at Tiverton. This church grew rapidly as emigrants from the Hebrides settled in the area. A gifted preacher, leader and planter of churches, Fraser travelled to Manitoba in 1881 in the hope of gathering another congregation of Highland emigrants.

BIBLIOGRAPHY
J. Dempsey, 'William Fraser', The McMaster University Monthly (March 1899): 244–5
D. E. Meek, 'Evangelicalism and Emigration: Some Aspects of the Role of Dissenting Evangelicalism in Highland Emigration to Canada', in Proceedings of the First North American Congress of Celtic Studies, ed. G. MacLennan (Ottawa, 1988): 29–31

DONALD E. MEEK

Frech, Theobald (b Breitenbach, Upper Alsace, Germany, 1 Feb. 1740; d. Okak, Labrador, Canada, 13 June 1792). Moravian deacon and missionary to the Labrador Inuit. Frech, a carpenter, was a Lutheran before he became a member of the Moravian Church on 22 November 1767. He helped establish the mission at Nain, Labrador in 1771 and was ordained deacon in 1786.

BIBLIOGRAPHY
Public Archives of Canada, Ottawa, 'Catalogus der Missionare in Labrador', Records of the Moravian Mission in Labrador [1764–1944], Microfilm 511, Reels 11–12, fol. 15195–6
Kölbing

MARCELLA ROLLMANN

Freeman, Thomas Birch (b. Twyford, Hampshire, England, 6 Dec. 1809; d. Accra, Ghana, 12 Aug. 1890). African-English Wesleyan Missionary Society (WMS) missionary, Gold Coast. Born in England, the son of an African father and an English mother, he was introduced to Methodism as a boy. He worked as a gardener on a large estate, gaining a serious knowledge of botany, until his employer told him to choose between his job and Methodism. He left, and was taken on by the WMS which sent him to Cape Coast, Gold Coast (modern Ghana). Immediately he began to invigorate the ailing mission – acquired new premises, had a church built, and began training young Fante men for the ministry. He himself never learnt Fante and tended, being light-skinned, to be regarded by Africans as a white man.

He determined to expand the mission, started new stations along the coast, visited the kingdom of Asante, and tried over the years, though never with any lasting success, to open a mission there. In 1840 he took WILLIAM DE GRAFT, one of his Fante catechists to England to raise money. They preached all round the country and raised nearly £5,000. On a subsequent visit he raised a similar sum.

With such resources he was inspired to even wider outreach. Recaptives from Sierra Leone were now beginning to move back to their homelands in the Yoruba country. Freeman visited Badagry, the seaport they were using, taking de Graft and his wife, and established a mission there – 'the effective beginning', as the Nigerian historian Jacob Ajayi put it, 'of missionary enterprise in Nigeria'. At this period the inland country was torn by wars between the rival kingdoms of Abeokuta and Dahomey. Having visited Abeokuta (where the CMS were to settle) he went in 1843 to visit King Gezo of Dahomey, publishing an account of his experiences on his return. Over the next few years he paid two more visits to Dahomey, returning from one visit on foot, some 300 miles from Badagry to Cape Coast.

Meanwhile he persuaded the mission to buy a large, well-stocked plantation near Cape Coast, renaming it Beulah, which was then laid out as a Christian village community, with a boarding-school and agricultural training centre. He also had six new churches built. All these projects, and his constant travels, demanded heavy expenditure. Year after year the WMS committee in London found itself in debt, sometimes into thousands of pounds. In 1856 there was an enquiry into his finances. He was cleared of any dishonesty, but was found to have kept no proper accounts, or distinguished between expenditure on the mission and on himself. He therefore resigned, undertaking to repay his debts over the years.

He had regularly worked in friendly association with the colonial government, and sometimes undertaken official assignments. So in 1857, to support him, and to help pay off his debts, the governor appointed him civil commandant of the Accra district. He administered the district, and mediated successfully in a war between neighbouring peoples. But once again his muddled accounts made it impossible for him to remain in the public service for more than a few years. He had already bought land near Accra, and here he settled, farming it efficiently, and returning to the botanical studies of his early years, corresponding regularly with the botanical authorities at Kew Gardens. He also published a novel entitled Missionary Enterprise no Fiction. In 1873 he was persuaded to return to the mission, and worked as a village pastor until he retired in 1885. Two successive English wives had died soon after their marriage. His third (Fante) wife outlived him.

BIBLIOGRAPHY
J. F. A. Ajayi, *Christian Missions in Nigeria, 1841–1961* (London, 1965)
F. L. Bartels, *The Roots of Ghana Methodism* (Cambridge, 1965)
D. Kimble, *A Political History of Ghana* (Oxford, 1963)
L. H. Ofosu-Appiah, ed., *Encyclopaedia Africana, Directory of African Biography*, I, Freeman (New York, 1977)

CHRISTOPHER FYFE

Frelinghuysen, Theodorus Jacobus (b. Wolfenbuettel, East Friesland, The Netherlands, 1691, bapt. 6 Nov. 1692; d. New Jersey, *c.* 1747). Dutch Reformed minister in New Jersey. When Frelinghuysen arrived in New York in 1720, his contumacious behaviour toward his Dutch Reformed colleagues signalled trouble for the Dutch Reformed Church in the Middle Colonies. Frelinghuysen refused to cooperate with the established Dutch clergy because he regarded them as dead formalists and found them wanting in piety. Frelinghuysen, however, enjoyed considerable success among the Dutch in the Raritan Valley of New Jersey, many of whom also felt alienated from the imperious Dutch clergy of New York. Frelinghuysen flouted ecclesiastical conventions and excoriated the Dutch Reformed hierarchy in Amsterdam for refusing to send more Pietist ministers to the New World. His pietistic scruples demanded the exclusion of the unworthy from the Lord's Table, but his opponents charged that he enforced that discipline arbitrarily in order to taunt his ecclesiastical enemies. Frelinghuysen's own character was called into question when unrefuted allegations of homosexuality were levelled against him.

Frelinghuysen's evangelical fervour and his itinerancy contributed substantially to the Great Awakening in the Middle Colonies. GILBERT TENNENT acknowledged that Frelinghuysen had taught him much about piety and revival, and both GEORGE WHITEFIELD and JONATHAN EDWARDS admired Frelinghuysen's ministry. Plagued through much of his career with recurrent, debilitating bouts of mental illness, Frelinghuysen's final years are shrouded in mystery, but by the time of his death, about 1747, he had pushed the Dutch Reformed Church in America toward a more pietistic spirituality.

BIBLIOGRAPHY
DcAmReB
R. Balmer, *A Perfect Babel of Confusion* (New York, 1989)
J. R. Tanis, *Dutch Calvinistic Pietism in the Middle Colonies* (The Hague, 1967)

RANDALL BALMER

Fremantle, Sir **Thomas Francis** [first Baron Cottesloe] (b. London, 11 March 1798; d. Swanbourne, Buckinghamshire, England, 3 Dec. 1890). MP and peer. Fremantle, the son of one of Nelson's admirals, was created a baronet in 1819 in recognition of his father's achievements. His younger brother was WILLIAM ROBERT FREMANTLE. He was educated at Oriel College, Oxford (BA 1819) and entered Parliament as Conservative member

for Buckingham (1830–46). He held office under Peel as a secretary of the Treasury (1834, 1841–4), Secretary at war (1844) and Chief Secretary for Ireland (1845–6), in which latter office he defended the grant to the Roman Catholic college at Maynooth. He left Parliament to become deputy chairman and then chairman of the Board of Customs (1846–73), after which he was created Baron Cottesloe. His most notable effort in the House of Lords was his attempt to limit the creation of new bishoprics in 1875, but he also sat on the select committee on intemperance. He celebrated his ninetieth birthday by inviting his oldest friends to Holy Communion at St Michael's, Chester Square. He supported the CPAS and was a generous patron of the CMS. One of his sons was William Henry Fremantle, later Dean of Ripon.

BIBLIOGRAPHY
DNB

ARTHUR POLLARD

Fremantle, William (Robert) (b. Swanbourne, Buckinghamshire, England, 30 Aug. 1807; d. Inglewood, Atterbury Road, Wimbledon, England, 8 March 1895). Anglican clergyman. Fourth son of Vice-Admiral Sir Thomas Fremantle, Bt, and Elizabeth (Wynne), William was educated at Westminster School (1818–25), where he was minor canon (1821), and captain of oppidans (1825), and at Christ Church, Oxford (Fell exhibitioner, 1826) 1825–9. In 1829 he was cox in the first university crew versus Cambridge, with T. GARNIER. A page at William IV's coronation, he became fellow of Magdalen 1831–5 (with H. LINTON), proceeding DD in 1876.

Fremantle was ordained at Oxford 1831 (Bishop's register), becoming Curate of Swanbourne (also experiencing a brief curacy at Godalming, and later a short evangelistic ministry at West Street Chapel, Seven Dials, London), 'greatly esteemed for his piety and earnest work'. Pitchcott, Buckinghamshire, where he was rector 1832–41, 'became a centre of blessing under the manly, handsome young Fellow of Magdalen'. He was Vicar of Steeple Claydon, Buckinghamshire, 1841–68, and Rector of Middle Claydon with East Claydon, and the first Rural Dean, 1841–76, promoting the first ruridecanal conference in Oxford diocese, acting successfully as secretary of the new Diocesan Conference, and becoming honorary canon of Christ Church 1869–76. Always remarkable for sturdy independence of character (and as a staunch Protestant), when *Essays and Reviews* (1860) received a favourable legal judgement, Fremantle organized 11,000 signatures affirming Biblical inspiration and contemporary orthodoxy.

With his first wife's active cooperation he worked the Claydon parishes vigorously. Annual meetings of the Oxford Union for Private Prayer were held at Claydon vicarage. Already president of the Prophetical Society, in 1875 Fremantle founded the Navvy Mission (amalgamated to form the Industrial Christian Fellowship, 1918). From 1876 till death he was Dean of Ripon, where he maintained the strongly evangelical tone already prevailing, and provided a meal for 'all the country people' attending parish services at the Minster on Sundays. He was an original member of the council of Wycliffe Hall, Oxford, 1877–87. Altogether his influence among evangelicals 'was very great'. Brother of Sir Thomas Francis Fremantle, the first Lord Cottesloe, and uncle of the Hon. W. H. Fremantle, his successor at Ripon, Fremantle married (1) 1835 Emily Caroline Calvert (died 1877); (2) 1879 Caroline Leslie-Melville (died 1926). J. W. CUNNINGHAM, and H. Wright, honorary secretary of the CMS, were his brothers-in-law.

BIBLIOGRAPHY
Boase, 5
Burke's
Hole manuscripts, Birmingham University
ILN (London, 16 and 23 March, 1 June 1895) obituary
Record (London, 15 March 1895) obituary
Photograph, Church Portrait Journal, 3 (London, 1879)
J. S. Reynolds, Evangelicals at Oxford (Oxford, 1953; Appleford, England, 1975)

J. S. REYNOLDS

French, John (b. Goochland Co., VA, BNA, probably 1772; d. Holladay's Point, VA, USA, probably 13 Oct. 1839). Prominent leader in the MPC. Educated for medical practice, he gave himself to this profession and to lay preaching in the MEC. In 1828 he retired from medicine to devote himself full time to the ministry. He joined the Reform movement in Methodism and was one of the organizers of the MPC. From 1830 onward he laboured to establish this new denomination along the eastern seaboard, being known especially for the church in Norfolk. Chief Justice John Marshall called him, 'one of the ablest preachers' in America.

BIBLIOGRAPHY
CM
EWM

STEVE HARPER

French, Thomas Valpy (b. Abbey, Burton-on-Trent, Staffordshire, England, 1 Jan. 1825; d. Muscat, Oman, 14 May 1891). Distinguished CMS missionary in India; linguist, administrator, and evangelist; the first Bishop of Lahore. French was the son of Peter French, Vicar of Holy Trinity, Burton-on-Trent. Educated at Rugby under Thomas Arnold, he read 'Greats' at University College, Oxford, won the chancellor's Latin essay prize (Piggin, 1984: 201) and was elected a fellow in 1848.

Following his ordination, he offered his services to the CMS. His first assignment in April 1850 made him principal of St John's College in Agra, where evangelicals in the Indian Civil Service, headed by JAMES THOMASON, had pledged their support for this project. In 1854, with K. G. PFANDER of the CMS, French debated with Muslim theologians in an Agra chapel built by the evangelical chaplain DANIEL CORRIE (DIB) some years earlier [CMI (November 1854): 254]. From this followed several notable conversions among leading Muslims. During the mutiny, when all the Agra civilians took shelter in Akbar's fortress, it was only at French's insistence that all Indian Christians associated with the CMS Mission at nearby Sikander were also sheltered there (Gibbs, 1972: 199).

While still in Agra Fort and following the death of JOHN RUSSELL COLVIN there on 9 September 1857, French pleaded with his fellow Englishmen to refrain from further vengeance-taking on rebellious India: 'There is a point where *vengeance* is satisfied, and ceases to cry for blood; though it must be long ... before our *grief* can be soothed. Yet grief is not like vengeance, a destructive principle' (French, 1859: 123). Unsparing of himself, he usually worked ten hours during the hot weather, and 'after that I am fit for nothing' (Gibbs, 1972: 283–4). Following a furlough, 1858–61, he returned to India to found the Derajat Mission, named after Reynell Taylor, on the north-west frontier. Back in England again in 1863, he was appointed vicar of St Paul's, Cheltenham, from 1865 to 1869. His third stint in India took him to the Punjab, where he established the Lahore Divinity School.

When he left India in 1874 he took incumbencies at Erith, Kent, and St. Ebbe's, Oxford. In 1877 he received a honorary doctorate from Oxford University and was consecrated Bishop of Lahore (21 December) in Westminster Abbey. His administration and visitations in his jurisdiction of Sind and the Punjab included Simla during the tenure of Viceroys Lytton and Ripon. His rather puritanical standards proved irksome to some (Gibbs, 1972: 283–4). He resigned his see in 1887 when the burden became too much for him. Even then his career was not over. In the fortieth year of his missionary service (1890), he went to Muscat where he overtaxed his waning strength and died. He was known widely as the 'seven-tongued man', for his linguistic achievements and for his publications in several south Asian languages.

SELECT WRITINGS
T. V. French, Sermons Commemorative of the War, Pestilence, and the Mutiny, preached in the Years 1852 to 1858, chiefly to the Civil and Military Congregation in Agra (Calcutta, 1859)
—, Injil i Daud (The Gospel According to David, or the Messianic prophecies of the Psalms)

BIBLIOGRAPHY
DIB
DNB Supplement, 2
D. T. B[arry] CMS Register of Missionaries and Native Clergy (1804–1904) (privately printed) (London, 1906)
'Movements Among Mohammedans', CMI (November 1854): 251–63
H. Birks, The Life and Correspondence of T. V. French, 2 vols (London, 1895)
M. E. Gibbs, The Anglican Church in India, 1600–1970 (Delhi, 1972)
J. P. Haythornthwaite, St. John's College, Agra 1850–1930 (London, 1932)

S. Piggin, *Making Evangelical Missionaries, 1789–1858* (Sutton Courtenay, England, 1984)

PETER PENNER

Frere, James Hatley (b. 6 Feb. 1799; d. Shillington, Bedfordshire, England, 8 Dec. 1866). Writer on prophecy. Frere was the son of John (1740–1807), antiquary, of Roydon Hall, Norfolk, and Finnington, Suffolk; and Jane, daughter and heiress of John Hookham of London. In June 1809 he married Merian, the second daughter of Matthew Martin, of Poet's Corner, Westminster, by whom he had five sons.

Frere was one of the most prominent advocates of prophetic study in early nineteenth-century England, influencing, among others, EDWARD IRVING and HENRY DRUMMOND. In 1826, he co-founded (with Irving and LEWIS WAY) the Society for the Investigation of Prophecy. After initial meetings in London, the society transferred its gatherings to Drummond's luxurious country home at Albury, Surrey, where, between November 1826 and July 1830, the five celebrated Albury conferences were convened. These attracted, besides Frere, many prominent evangelicals.

Frere became obsessed with the restoration of the Jews to Palestine and with Napoleon, whom he denounced (*Combined View*, 1815) as Antichrist. He regarded Britain as God's favoured nation, but warned that its 'sacred character' had been tarnished by its 'infidel amalgamation with the Papacy'. Although less pessimistic than Irving or Drummond, Frere nevertheless regarded Catholic emancipation (and Napoleon's predicted restoration at Rome) as preludes to Armageddon and hence to Britain's ultimate undoing. Frere was a moderate in a body of extreme millennialists. His numerous writings on prophecy were immensely influential upon the Irvingites and other like-minded nineteenth-century religious movements.

BIBLIOGRAPHY
Burke's
DNB
W. H. Oliver, *Prophets and Millennialists* (Auckland and Oxford, 1978)

GRAYSON CARTER

Freshfield, James William (b. Windsor, Berkshire, England, 1775; d. London, 27 June 1864). Lawyer and MP. Freshfield was admitted as a solicitor in 1795 and served the Bank of England, the East and West India Dock Company, and the Globe Insurance Company. He was a member of the BFBS Committee eight times between 1814 and 1824, and published controversial pamphlets defending the formation of an auxiliary society in Hackney in 1812–14. He went to Cambridge in 1827, being admitted as a pensioner at Peterhouse. Freshfield was elected MP for Penryn and Falmouth for 1830–2, again in 1835–41 and 1852–7, and MP for

Boston in 1851–2. He was made a fellow of the Royal Society in 1834 and called to the bar at Gray's Inn in 1842.

BIBLIOGRAPHY
Al. Cant.
L. Howsam, 'The Bible Transaction' (York Univ. Ph.D. thesis, 1988)

LESLIE HOWSAM

Frewen Turner (né **Frewen**), **John** (b. 1 Aug. 1755; d. Cold Overton, near Oakham, Leicestershire, England, 1 Feb. 1829). British MP and landowner. A descendent of Accepted Frewen, Archbishop of York, his father, the Reverend Thomas Frewen, in the 1770s adopted the name of Turner as a condition of inheritance. Frewen Turner was educated at Rugby, Queen's College, Oxford, and at the Middle Temple. In 1791 he inherited ancient estates at Cold Overton, Leicestershire, and Brickwell, Sussex and later purchased estates at Siggeston and Winton, Yorkshire. Frewen Turner was Tory MP for the borough of Athlone (1807–12). He seldom voted and is not known to have spoken in debate. In 1808 he married Eleanor Clarke (born 1786, died 1879), a fellow evangelical. Together they supported foreign missions and slave-trade abolition, and, very substantially, local charitable work. She established Knossington National School in 1855. Their son Thomas (1811–70) married a daughter of WILSON CARUS WILSON.

BIBLIOGRAPHY
GM, 99 pt I (February 1829): 182
M. Lesser, *Clarkey* (London, 1984)
R. G. Thorne, ed., *The House of Commons 1790–1820* (London, 1986)

JONATHAN BURKE CUTMORE

Frey, Joseph Samuel Christian Frederick [né **Levi, Joseph Samuel**] (b. Mainstockheim, Germany, 21 Sept. 1771; d. Pontiac, MI, USA, 5 June 1850). Missionary to the Jewish people. Born into a German Jewish family, Frey worked in trade while studying for the rabbinate. A Lutheran merchant converted him to Christianity in 1798. Quickly convinced of a missionary vocation, Frey accepted an appointment with the LMS. DAVID BOGUE tutored the young man, who began preaching to London's Jewish community.

Frey soon became dissatisfied with contemporary mission methods. He encouraged instead the establishment of a 'house of industry' to train Jewish immigrants for employment with Christian industrialists. He also proposed a boarding-school where children could be raised outside the influence of Judaism. When the LMS resisted these innovations, Frey resigned to help found the LSPCJ in 1809. This agency proved amenable to his ideas, instituting with mixed success a free school, boarding-school, and the house of industry. Frey, however, left with other

Dissenters in 1815 when the LSPCJ became an Anglican society.

On 23 July 1816, Frey sailed for the United States. Letters of introduction from England enabled him to take a Congregational Church in New York City, though he retained a concern for the Jewish people. Accordingly he helped organize the American Society for Meliorating the Condition of the Jews in 1820. Given the country's small Jewish population, Frey envisioned not conversion but the settling of converts in America. In 1823 he became the society's general agent, holding that position intermittently through 1837. In this capacity, he travelled 50,000 miles, lecturing Americans on Jewish history and customs, and crusading against European anti-Semitism. He also publicized his autobiography, *The Converted Jew*, which eventually ran through 17 editions. Still, the American Society attracted few converts to its community which closed in 1826. Attempts to refocus on Jewish conversion failed, and Frey resigned to accept a Baptist pastorate on Long Island. In 1844 he moved to Michigan where he taught Hebrew at the University of Michigan until his death.

In an age when few Americans understood or had contact with Jewish people, Frey acquainted Christians of all denominations with them. While unsuccessful as a missionary, he consistently encouraged Americans to resist anti-Semitism, and aid the cause of Jewish emancipation in Europe.

BIBLIOGRAPHY
L. Friedman, *The American Society for Meliorating the Condition of the Jews* (Boston, MA, 1925)
R. Martin, *Evangelicals United* (Metuchen, NJ, 1983)
L. Ratner, 'Conversion of the Jews and pre-Civil War Reform', *American Quarterly*, 13 (1961): 43–53

JAMES WARNOCK

Friend, Charles (b. London, *c.* 1799; d. Chunar, India, 12 June 1829). CMS missionary to India. Friend trained at the newly opened CMS training school at Islington (London) in 1825 and was ordained (deacon 1826, priest 1827) by the Bishop of London. On 11 April 1828 he was sent with RALPH ETESON to north India but died within a year of his arrival in India. He appears to have been single.

BIBLIOGRAPHY
D. T. B[arry], *CMS Register of Missionaries and Native Clergy* (privately printed) (London, 1906)

DONALD M. LEWIS

Frothingham, Ebenezer (b. Charlestown, MA, BNA, *c.* 1717; d. Middletown, CT, USA, 30 Nov. 1798). Separate (Strict Congregational) minister and apologist. Baptized in Charlestown on 9 June 1717, and joining that town's First Congregational Church in 1734, Frothingham became a Separate while living in Wethersfield, Connecticut, *circa* 1741, and pastor of the Separate church there on 7 January 1747. He moved with the church to Middletown in 1754, served as its minister until 1788, and died a decade later. Frothingham and other Separates were repeatedly fined and imprisoned for refusing to pay taxes to support a 'hireling' Congregational ministry filled, they feared, with many unconverted ministers. He was a leading spokesman for the Separate movement; his *Articles of Faith and Practice* (1750) and *A Key to Unlock the Door* (1767) emphasized the conversion experience and the chasm between the regenerate church and the corrupt world.

BIBLIOGRAPHY
R. Frothingham, 'Ebenezer Frothingham', *American Writers Before 1800* (Westport, CT, 1983): 617–20
C. C. Goen, *Revivalism and Separatism in New England, 1740–1800* (New Haven, CT, 1962): 126–36

CHRISTOPHER GRASSO

Fry, Elizabeth (b. Earlham, Norfolk, England, 21 May 1780; d. Ramsgate, Kent, England, 12 Oct. 1845). Quaker philanthropist and prison reformer. Born into the important Quaker family of Norfolk Gurneys, sister to JOSEPH JOHN GURNEY, at the age of 17 under the influence of an American preacher named William Savery she underwent a conversion experience, which was subsequently developed by more domestic influences including that of the female Quaker preacher, Deborah Darby. Her family's Quakerism had been accommodating to the prosperous society in which, as banking gentry, the family mixed; while conversion for Elizabeth reinforced her consciousness of Quaker distinctiveness, it also committed her to social action. In August 1800 she married Joseph Fry, a wealthy London merchant from a rather stricter Quaker family, and rapidly became mother to a large family. However, from before her marriage she had been testing out whether she had a call to ministry: that conviction seems to have come to maturity on the death of her father in 1809 which apparently released in her the capacity for public participation. For her the essence of ministry, in which she was formally confirmed by the society in 1811, was obedience to the conviction that she was called to speak what God wanted to be heard, first within the Society of Friends and then as a natural extension of this in the prisons of England.

Though her first visit to Newgate had been in 1813, domestic responsibilities delayed sustained work until 1817, when the prisons of Britain were facing the problems of a postwar boom in crime. The cause of crime she explained in terms of the lower orders aping the self-indulgence and dishonesty of their social superiors. As over against the Benthamite remedy of administrative tidiness, Elizabeth Fry offered an evangelical humanitarianism. Remedies were to be found in education, the encouragement of Bible reading and the cultivation of rational recreation; indeed, she was committed to reforming the prisoner by work rather than punishing him by labour.

In her involvement she was influenced by an essay penned by her brother-in-law, THOMAS FOWELL BUXTON, in 1818, entitled, *An Enquiry Whether Crime and Misery are Produced or Prevented By Our Present System of Prison Discipline*, in which he identified, in particular, the incarceration of those not yet tried alongside hardened criminals, while others were imprisoned for debt or such generalized complaints as the idleness charged by a master against his 17-year-old employee. Buxton praised his sister-in-law's work which also fed into J. J. Gurney's, *Notes of a Visit Made to Some of the Prisons in Scotland and the North of England in company with Elizabeth Fry*, which described the evils of a lack of segregation, lack of useful employment, gross overcrowding and insanitary conditions.

At Newgate she began by organizing a school for the prisoners' children, which also admitted some of the younger women prisoners, with a prisoner as the first schoolmistress. A committee of 12 women, almost exclusively Quakers, called 'An Association for the Improvement of the Female Prisoners in Newgate' sought, with their consent, to provide clothing, basic education, instruction in 'order, sobriety and industry', employment, and Bible reading. What she was offering the prisoners was an ordered prison, informed by Christian conscience in place of the mostly unsuperintended chaos of the *status quo*. She drew up rules which provided for regular employment, the exclusion of unhelpful pastimes, the adoption of the monitorial system to prison life, and daily Bible reading. Under this discipline, with appropriate rewards and occasional punishments, the women agreed to live, and to be superintended by a matron whose salary was initially largely financed by the Ladies Committee, which also provided a significant mechanism for the liberation of at least some women into social utility. It was also suggested that a good report from the Ladies Committee could be an influential factor securing an early pardon, as in fact occurred in the case of her first schoolmistress.

The evidence is that it was not only her system that brought relief to Newgate but also Elizabeth Fry's own personality, especially as focused in her reading of the Scriptures amongst the women prisoners, nor was her influence wholly confined to the women. It is significant that as a successful woman she provoked Lord SHAFTESBURY's disapproval. She also campaigned for better conditions on the ships which transported women to Australia, but failed to get the Newgate Rules adopted on board once the ships had left England and the scrutiny of the Ladies' Committees.

Her experience meant that she was able to appear before the Select Committee of 1818 and the Parliamentary Committee of 1831, as a uniquely well-informed witness. Her evidence to the House of Lords Committee in 1835 was less well received at a time when official minds were turning to devising mechanisms for more effective punishment. There was, in fact, a deliberate and coordinated attempt by the prison inspectors of the time to discredit her evidence. Edwin Chadwick, well known for his views on less eligible workhouses, went so far as

to maintain that 'because of the HOWARDS and Frys the prisons had been so reformed by "narrow sentiment and blind zeal" as actually to attract vagrants and others who preferred their comfort to labour'. For her part, Elizabeth Fry was prepared to go so far as to label some aspects of the new system quite deliberately 'cruelty', which she believed was growing in the prisons of the 1830s, especially in protesting against the use of solitary confinement in dark cells and the coupling of dietary reductions with hard labour.

Her Quaker convictions led Elizabeth Fry to oppose the death penalty, which at the time was compromised by all-too-frequent reprieves, so that its deterrent value was nullified. These convictions are to be found in her *Observations on the Visiting, Superintendence and Government of Female Prisoners*, published in 1827 but expressing long-held views. She interested herself in foreign prisons and corresponded and lobbied foreign royalty on the prisoners' behalf. Elizabeth also engaged in local charities, organized libraries for coastguards, and helped found a night shelter for the London homeless. Her private life suffered considerable embarrassment from her husband's business failure in 1828, for bankruptcy normally involved expulsion from the Society of Friends, as also from her failure to bring up her children as Quakers.

SELECT WRITINGS
E. Fry, *Memoir of Elizabeth Fry*. ed. by two of her daughters (London, 1847)

BIBLIOGRAPHY
DNB
J. Kent, *Elizabeth Fry* (London, 1962)
J. Rose, *Elizabeth Fry* (London, 1980)
J. Whitney, *Quaker Heroine* (London, 1937)

J. H. Y. BRIGGS

Fry, Thomas (b. Compton Bishop House, Axbridge, Somerset, England, 10 Dec. 1774 (ord. pprs., Oxford); d. Emberton House, Bath, Somerset, 22 March 1860). College tutor and Anglican clergyman. Eldest son of Peter Fry, armiger (Treasurer of Somerset), of Quaker descent, and Elizabeth (Homfray), Thomas entered Oriel College, Oxford, in 1792, becoming (Somerset) fellow of Lincoln College 1796–1803 (with G. S. FABER and W. Yeadon), and 'having some reputation for scholarship', though 'disliked'. 'Father' (H. MORE) to a group of evangelical undergraduates, he was an early supporter of ISAAC CROUCH whom, following ordination, he succeeded as curate to Dr J. W. Peers, at Chiselhampton, Oxfordshire, in 1797. In 1799 he was a founder of the CMS. Vicar of Radley, Berkshire, 1801–2, he became chaplain of the Lock Hospital, London, 1803–12, succeeding THOMAS SCOTT. He acted as honorary secretary (1810–14), and trustee, of the newly founded LSPCJ. His (non-conformist) co-secretary (1812–14) was Dr W. B. COLLYER. They translated the New Testament from Greek to Hebrew, then a long unprecedented advance in evangelism. Published anonymously in 1813, their version was reprinted at intervals; a related Judaeo-German text appeared posthumously in 1872. Anonymity has helped to obscure this phase of Fry's career, and thus an important element in his *oeuvre*.

Having acquired the patronage of Emberton, Buckinghamshire, Fry was rector 1804–60. By 1808 however he had made himself responsible also for Toot Baldon, Oxfordshire, a neglected parish near Oxford which by 1814 he was serving altogether by deputy, but did not resign as perpetual curate until 1858. E. G. MARSH was curate 1811–13. George Porter, curate 1816–31, fellow of Queen's College, Oxford, 1815–30, attracted large congregations, including sometimes the undergraduate W. E. GLADSTONE who, accompanied by F. D. Maurice, noticed him as 'a calvinist independent of the *clique*,' 'a wild but splendid preacher,' and, jointly, as 'a man of remarkable power'. His only publication, *Inward Songs*, is dated from Baldon (1823). Porter was followed later by an able fellow of Balliol, A. C. Tait (afterwards Archbishop of Canterbury) 1836–7, succeeded by C. P. Golightly of Oriel College (*DNB*) 1837–45, remembered for his moral mnemonics for village children. Fry initiated an appeal for a better parsonage (built 1860) and bequeathed £25 per annum towards the scarcely endowed benefice. A modest stained glass window (1873) in the chancel recalls him as a benefactor.

More than one authority refers to Bishop Samuel Wilberforce (from 1845 Fry's diocesan) having been among his pupils at Emberton rectory. Thomas Fry's long ministry at Emberton – at intervals his large church was repaired inexpensively but unperceptively -- where he initiated a (well-documented) school of industry (1821–32) and other schemes to help poorer parishioners – was not without opposition to his teaching and conduct of affairs, although admirers moved from London to live there. Small in stature but with a strong, dominant character, financially acute (in 1797 he had already published *The Guardian of Public Credit*), he was known as an unquestionably able preacher. A staunch friend to his neighbours LEGH RICHMOND, Rector of Turvey, and HENRY GAUNTLETT, Vicar of Olney, he preached at the latter's funeral (1833) a sermon which, with two others (1805, 1832), is preserved in print. Altogether Fry published at least ten works, some substantial, several (including *Heraesius Mastrix*, 1821) anonymously, and consequently, like his Hebrew New Testament, later unrecognized or incorrectly attributed. Thus an (anonymous) *Domestic Portraiture* (1833) is a valuable supplement by him to Grimshawe's *Life of Richmond* (1828), the latter however confusingly ascribed to Fry by J. Bateman (*Life of Bishop D. Wilson*). In 1847, bereft of second wife and two promising sons, and having made an unpopular third marriage, Fry arranged for a curate-in-charge (C. B. A. G. Hulton) for his lifetime, who would succeed as rector, and retired to Bath, where he continued to preach. Canon Overton rightly drew attention to him as 'a man of some eminence' but already (1894) 'forgotten'.

Fry married (1) 1802 Anne (died 1811), a friend of HANNAH MORE and daughter of Thomas Cresswell, MP,

of Bibury, Gloucestershire. In her memory Fry founded (1844) a Hebrew scholarship at St John's College, Cambridge. (2) *c*. 1813 Margaret Henrietta Middleton (a competent Hebrew and Greek scholar, protegée of W. WILBERFORCE) from Chapel-en-le-Frith, Derbyshire (*c*. 1782–1845). In her memory Fry built the village clock tower, Emberton. Their son, Thomas Osmond, Fry's curate and intended successor, much beloved at Emberton, died 1846, another son, Charles Simeon, having died previously (cp. *A Father's Reasons for Repose*, [T. Fry], 1839). (3) 1846 (*GM*) Mary Anne Foster, née Bagshawe (living 1860), daughter of Sir W. C. D. Bagshawe of The Oaks, Derbyshire. T. C. Fry, Dean of Lincoln 1910–30 (*DNB*) was Fry's grandson. His portrait is in Emberton church.

BIBLIOGRAPHY
Boase, 5
Information from Mrs C. Ellis, Emberton
Manuscript Memories, T. C. Fry. 1928
W. T. Gidney, *History L.S.P.C.J.* (London, 1908)
V. H. H. Green, *Religion at Oxford and Cambridge* (Oxford, 1964)
—, *Commonwealth of Lincoln College* (Oxford, 1975)
Hole manuscripts, Birmingham University
M. D. Lobel, ed. *A History of the County of Oxford* (The Victoria History of the Counties of England) 5 (London, 1957)
J. S. Reynolds, *Evangelicals at Oxford* (Oxford, 1953; Appleford, England, 1975)

J. S. REYNOLDS

Frye, Christopher (b. Winchester, VA, USA, 13 Feb. 1778; d. Leesburg, VA, USA, 18 Sept. 1835). Minister in the MEC. He was converted in 1796, joined the MEC, and was admitted into the Baltimore Conference in 1802. Up to that time, he had been a farmer. For thirty years he served the Baltimore Conference as pastor and presiding elder of the Baltimore, Greenbrier, Monongahela, and Potomoc districts. After taking a superannuated relationship, he returned to farming in Leesburg, Virginia. He died shortly after an accident in which a threshing machine crushed his leg. He is known for remarkable calm in facing his death.

BIBLIOGRAPHY
CM
EWM

STEVE HARPER

Frye, Joseph (b. Winchester, VA, USA, 1786; d. Baltimore, MD, USA, May 1845). Methodist minister. Though his parents were devout Lutherans who raised him in the faith he experienced a personal conversion through the preaching of Methodist ministers. He preached briefly on the local level before joining the Baltimore Conference of the MEC in 1809 as an itinerant minister. He travelled various circuits throughout the conference and subsequently served as presiding elder of several districts. Well mannered and highly respected with a propensity for emotional preaching, his biblically based sermons 'were never lacking in substantial evangelical truth'. It was reported that President Jackson while attending a service in Washington was moved to tears by the persuasive nature of his preaching.

BIBLIOGRAPHY
AAP
Minutes

ROBERTA J. STEWART

Fuller, Andrew (b. Wicken, Cambridgeshire, England, 6 Feb. 1754; d. Kettering, Northamptonshire, England, 7 May 1815). Baptist theologian and first secretary of the BMS. He attended the village school at Soham and, as a youth, worked on the land. At the age of 16, after several years under conviction of sin, he found spiritual peace and was baptized at the local Baptist church. Soon afterwards, one of the members, guilty of drinking to excess, excused himself by claiming that he could not keep himself from evil. The incident forced the young Fuller to think out for himself the relationship between human responsibility and divine sovereignty. It also led to controversy, as a result of which the Hyper-Calvinist pastor left the church and Fuller took his place.

His study of the Bible and his reading, particularly of JONATHAN EDWARDS, convinced him of the falsity of Hyper-Calvinism, then widespread among Particular Baptists. Such a system, he believed, obscured the great evangelical truths of Christianity and led to the abandonment of evangelism and the general deterioration of vital religion. In order to clarify his thinking he set out his views in writing. This was the manuscript he was to publish, in 1785, as *The Gospel Worthy of All Acceptation*. Its scope and overriding concern are indicated by the subtitle: 'The duty of sinners to believe in Jesus Christ'. Three years before its publication Fuller left Soham for Kettering, where he ministered till his death. Within the Northamptonshire association he came into contact with other ministers, like the elder ROBERT HALL, JOHN SUTCLIFF and JOHN RYLAND, whose thinking was tending in the same direction as his own. He played a leading part in the prayer movement of the 1780s, which prepared Baptists for WILLIAM CAREY's missionary challenge, and, when the BMS was formed in October 1792, he became the first secretary of the mission.

Fuller gave himself unsparingly to the support of the BMS. Though not a great administrator, his keen critical judgement, his firm grasp of missionary principles and his ability to understand both the missionaries and the religious public, enabled him to give the mission the kind of leadership it needed in its early years. To Fuller his position was a sacred trust arising from a 'vow' to Carey to 'hold the rope' while Carey penetrated what was compared to a deep, unexplored gold mine. Though supported by able ministers and laymen, the main burden of responsibility fell on him. He preached throughout the country on behalf of the mission, corresponded with the missionaries and pleaded their cause in high places. The position of the BMS was, in the early years, extremely delicate. Not only did the missionaries have to work without the approval of the East India Company, but an influential body of opinion in England was opposed to the spread of evangelical Christianity in British territories overseas. Fuller's *Apology for the Late Christian Missions to India* was written, in 1807–8, at a particularly critical time. When Parliament renewed the East India Company's charter, in 1813, his efforts to obtain permission for non-episcopal missionaries to serve in India were rewarded.

He was above all a theologian. His interpretation of Calvinism, which admitted the reality of human freedom without doing violence to divine sovereignty, liberated his denomination from the tyranny of Hyper-Calvinism, thus providing a theological basis for home and foreign missions. The best statement of 'Fullerism' is that contained in *The Gospel Worthy of All Acceptation*. Its main thesis was that faith in Christ is the duty of all who hear, or have the opportunity to hear, the Gospel. Every sinner, whatever his character, is 'completely *warranted* to trust in the Lord Jesus Christ for the salvation of his soul'. The only thing preventing him from doing so (or indeed from obeying the law), is 'moral slavery', i.e. sheer unwillingness – a want not of *ability* but of *inclination*. Man is free in the sense that he is 'at liberty to act according to his choice, without compulsion or restraint'. In his later writings he expounded and worked out the implications of his 'leading principles', defending them against the attacks of Hyper-Calvinists like William Button on one hand and Arminians like DAN TAYLOR on the other. He was also an able champion of Christian orthodoxy, his most outstanding work of Christian defence being *The Gospel its Own Witness* (1799), occasioned by Paine's *Age of Reason*. He published several anti-Socinian works, notably *The Calvinistic and Socinian Systems Examined and Compared as to their Moral Tendency* (1793), and opposed the universalism of William Vidler.

Fuller never forgot that he was a pastor. He regarded his church as a family, showing special concern for the poor. At the time of his death he had 174 members and a congregation of nearly 1,000. His preaching was both textual and topical, practical and evangelical. Moreover, he had a powerful voice and was blessed with the ability to express himself clearly. He possessed a remarkable store of physical and mental energy which enabled him to work at his desk ten hours a day, though rarely free of headaches. Slow and deliberate in his thinking, with a Fenman's independence of judgement, he was thorough and accurate in all he did. He had a shrewd understanding of men and situations, and an intimate knowledge of affairs in the religious world. Closely in touch with influential persons in business and in Parliament, he was no stranger to the group of evangelical churchmen at Clapham which included WILBERFORCE, the THORNTON brothers, ZACHARY MACAULAY and CHARLES GRANT.

Despite his severe, forbidding manner, he had a deep

concern for people, his personal sorrows helping to mellow him. He lost his first wife and 11 of his 17 children, while his eldest son, Robert, caused him considerable grief by his wild behaviour. Andrew Fuller was a man of remarkable achievement. His contribution to theology was recognized by the award of a DD by New Jersey in 1798, and by Yale in 1805, though characteristically he declined to use the title 'Doctor'. Worn out by his labours, he died 'as a penitent sinner at the foot of the cross'. Fuller was one of the outstanding evangelical leaders of his day.

SELECT WRITINGS

A. Fuller, *The Complete Works of the Rev. Andrew Fuller*, 5 vols, with a memoir by A. G. Fuller (London, 1831–2)

BIBLIOGRAPHY

E. F. Clipsham, 'Andrew Fuller and Fullerism', *BQ*, 20, 3–6 (1963–4)

—, 'Andrew Fuller and the Baptist Mission', *Foundations*, 10, 1 (Jan.–March 1967)

DNB

A. G. Fuller, *Andrew Fuller* (London, 1882)

T .E. Fuller, *A Memoir of the Life and Writings of Andrew Fuller* (London, 1863)

A. H. Kirkby, 'Andrew Fuller – Evangelical Calvinist', *BQ*, 15, 5 (January 1954)

G. Laws, *Andrew Fuller, Pastor, Theologian, Ropeholder* (London, 1942)

J. W. Morris, *Memoirs of the Life and Writings of the Rev Andrew Fuller*, corrected and enlarged edn (London, 1826)

E. A. Payne, 'Andrew Fuller as Letter Writer', *BQ*, 15, 7 (July 1954)

POBC

J. Ryland, *The Work of Faith, the Labour of Love, and the Patience of Hope Illustrated in the Life and Death of the Rev Andrew Fuller* (London, 1816)

W. Ward, *A Sketch of the Character of the late Rev. Andrew Fuller* (Bristol, England, 1817)

Whitley, *BB*

E. F. CLIPSHAM

Fuller, Andrew Gunton (b. Soham, Cambridgeshire, England, 26 Jan. 1799; d. Wolverhampton, Staffordshire, England, 22 Jan. 1884). Baptist minister and biographer. The son of ANDREW FULLER, he was educated at a boarding-school and then at Kettering Grammar School. After ten years in business, he became at the age of 25 the founding minister of the church at West Drayton, Middlesex. Subsequent pastorates were at Blockley, Worcestershire; Old Ford, London; Evesham, Worcestershire and Cardiff. He retired in 1855 after 'plodding earnest work as both preacher and pastor'. His claim to fame is as the biographer and editor of his father's *Collected Works*.

BIBLIOGRAPHY

Baptist Handbook (1885)

J. H. Y. BRIGGS

Fuller, Joseph (Jackson) (b. Jamaica, 29 June 1825; d. England, 11 Dec. 1905). Black Jamaican missionary to West Africa. Born a slave, Fuller was among 42 Jamaicans who sailed for Fernando Po on the *Chilmark* to establish a Baptist witness under the auspices of the BMS and the Jamaican Baptist Missionary Society. His father Alexander preceded him and his brother Samuel accompanied him. His work was centred on Fernando Po between 1844 and 1858 but tensions between England and Spain forced Protestants from the island. Settling on the mainland he helped to plan and build a new settlement, Victoria. Collaborating with ALFRED SAKER he produced the Dualla Bible and a translation of *Pilgrim's Progress*. However, he did not get much encouragement due to differences between Saker and the other missionaries. His knowledge of local languages led to a developed national consciousness which in turn led to abandonment of the slave trade. Upon the partition of Africa between European powers, he helped to arrange treaties between local rulers and the naval squadrons posted to the region, thus averting much loss of life. Twice married, his second wife was the widow of a former English missionary, Joseph Diboll. He retired to England where he died.

SELECT WRITINGS

J. Fuller, 'Autobiography', unpublished manuscripts (1902) BMS Archives

—, 'Journal' 4 pages in note form, BMS Archive

—, 'The West African Mission of the BMS from its beginning to 1887', manuscripts, no date

BIBLIOGRAPHY

Baptist Handbook 1909 (Miss. Her., February 1909)

HORACE O. RUSSELL

Fuller, Richard (b. Beaufort, SC, USA, 22 April 1804; d. Baltimore, MD, USA, 20 October 20, 1876). Baptist pastor and denominationalist. Known for his eloquent preaching and writing, Fuller was a leader in both the Triennial and Southern Baptist conventions. Born in Beaufort, South Carolina, and educated for the bar at Harvard (1824), he was converted in a revival and was ordained to the Baptist ministry in 1832. For 15 years he pastored his home town Baptist congregation, which by his departure numbered 200 white and 2,400 slave members. In 1847 he became pastor of the Seventh Baptist Church in Baltimore, Maryland. His reputation as a pulpiteer grew, though at times bringing him criticism for being an extempore speaker.

In the 1840s Fuller, a slave-holder, defended slavery most prominently in an exchange of letters with Brown University president, FRANCIS WAYLAND. This debate was published in 1847 under the title, *Domestic Slavery Considered as a Scriptural Institution*. Along with individual and collected sermons, his other publications included *Baptism and the Terms of Communion* (1860), and he co-authored a supplement to *The Psalmist*, the first denominational hymnal published in America.

BIBLIOGRAPHY
T. Armitage, *History of the Baptists* (Philadelphia, PA, 1887)
W. Cathcart, *The Baptist Encyclopedia* (Philadelphia, PA, 1881)
H. L. McBeth, *The Baptist Heritage* (Nashville, TN, 1989)

ANDREW MANIS

Fulton, Henry (b. probably Lisburn, County Antrim, Ireland, 1765; d. Castlereagh, New South Wales, Australia, 17 Nov. 1840). Convict and colonial clergyman. Probably a Lisburn Fulton, he entered Trinity College, Dublin, as a pensioner in 1788, graduated BA in 1792 and was ordained by Bishop Knox of Killaloe in September 1794. He married Anne Walker, daughter of James Walker, a rector in Killaloe, in January 1795. (JOHN WALKER, chaplain of Dublin's Bethesda until his secession, was her brother.) He became Curate of the Kilmore Union and Vicar of Monsea, in County Tipperary. [*ADB* places him, wrongly, at St. Cronan's, Roscrea.] In 1797 his name appeared, as of Silvermines, on a list of 29 'principal names' of evangelical clergy supplied by a Dublin bookseller, Johnston. It appeared next on the Minerva's convict list in 1799. [From his age, as given here, he was born in 1765: *ADB* has 1761].

Fulton's admiration for Wolfe Tone had involved him in the Society of United Irishmen. Whatever the idealism that motivated him, he was convicted of 'seditious practices' at Tipperary in 1799, in the aftermath of the '98 Rebellion, and transported for life. He arrived in Sydney on 11 January 1800, his wife accompanying him as a free settler. He was conditionally pardoned – his absolute pardon being granted later – and free to resume his ministry. For some time he was the only clergyman in the colony. He worked in the Hawkesbury area, then on Norfolk Island. The long arm of William Knox (now Bishop of Derry) procured a Crown chaplaincy for him and – to SAMUEL MARSDEN's chagrin – a share in the principal chaplain's salary. He settled finally in the Nepean region, serving Richmond and Penrith, and residing at Castlereagh. Anne Fulton died in 1836. She had been the ideal partner for a pioneer, matching at once his toughness and his gentle spirit.

Marjorie Quarton's researches have established that the Irish records for him were destroyed, presumably at the instigation of his family. Her novel has a footnote, 'Henry Fulton – The Historical Facts': 308–10. Her conclusion as to his situation in Killaloe is (*pace ADB*) corroborated by the cryptic information in the 1797 list.

BIBLIOGRAPHY
ADB
M. C. Motherwell, *A Memoir of the late Albert Blest* (Dublin, 1843): 64 (for the clergy list of 1797)
M. Quarton, *Renegade* (London, 1991)

ALAN R. ACHESON

Furley, Samuel (b. West Ham, Essex, England, 17 Oct. 1732; d. Roche, Cornwall, England, 6 Aug. 1795). Anglican clergyman. Entering Queens' College, Cambridge, in 1753 and befriended by HENRY VENN, he graduated BA in 1758. After ordination, he spent some months in London before moving to Lakenheath, Sussex. He then assisted HENRY CROOK at Kippax, Yorkshire, where he met Lady HUNTINGDON who took an interest in his ministry, as had JOHN WESLEY with whom he regularly corresponded. By 1762 he was perpetual curate of Slaithwaite, appointed through Venn. He gathered large congregations, necessitating an extension to the church. In 1766 he was presented by JOHN THORNTON to the living of Roche where he joined a group of evangelical incumbents in Cornwall. He lectured in midweek as well as preaching twice each Sunday. His style was said to be that of a Boanerges rather than a Barnabas. Latterly his sight failed and then a fatal cancer struck.

BIBLIOGRAPHY
EM (1797)

A. SKEVINGTON WOOD

Furman, Richard (b. Esopus, NY, BNA, 9 Oct. 1755; d. SC, USA, 25 Aug. 1825). Baptist pastor, educator, and denominational leader. Born in New York to Wood and Rachel Furman, Richard grew up in South Carolina. His intellectual gifts were evident early in his life. With little formal education, he mastered the classics of language and literature, and developed an extensive knowledge of medicine. Converted in 1771, Furman began preaching as a teenager, his theology shaped by the Calvinism of the Regular and Separate Baptists present in the Carolinas. Throughout his life he was a popular revivalist, well known throughout the region. Ordained in 1774, he served as pastor of High Hills Baptist church (1774–87), and Charleston Baptist Church (1787–1825). From the Charleston pulpit he exercised extensive influence among Baptists in America.

During the Revolutionary War, Furman was an outspoken supporter of the American cause and a leader in the call for religious liberty and church/state separation. His concern for Christian education led Furman to develop numerous programmes for promoting ministerial training. His educational endeavours led to the establishment of Columbian college (later George Washington University). Furman University, organized in 1827, now located in Greenville, SC, was named in his honour.

A strong supporter of Southern racial attitudes, in 1822 he set forth one of the best known 'biblical' defences for slavery. An advocate of denominational cooperation on the local, state and national levels, Furman was elected first president of the Triennial Convention (1814), the first national alliance of Baptists.

BIBLIOGRAPHY
ESB

BILL J. LEONARD

Furneaux, Philip (b. Totnes, Devonshire, England, Dec. 1726; d. 27 Nov. 1783). Congregational minister. Furneaux studied under the direction of David Jennings at the academy at Wellclose Square from 1742 or 1743 until 1749, perhaps assisting Jennings for part of that time. After his ordination in 1749, he was assistant to Henry Read, minister of the Presbyterian congregation at St Thomas's, Southwark. In 1752, he became one of the two lecturers to preach on Sunday evenings at Salter's Hall. In 1753, he became pastor of the Independent congregation at Clapham. He was awarded the DD in 1767 from the Marischal College in Aberdeen. He was a member of the Coward trust and he served as a trustee of Dr Williams's foundations. He was outspoken in his stand for the rights of Nonconformists, especially in the area of relief from doctrinal subscription. In particular, he was associated with the 'sheriff's case' in 1754–67. In 1777, he was taken ill with what has been described as 'hereditary insanity' and remained ill until his death. Prior to his illness, he published a number of sermons and treatises.

BIBLIOGRAPHY
DNB

KAREN E. SMITH

Furz, John (b. Wilton, Wiltshire, England, 26 Dec. 1717; d. Bath, England, 1800). Methodist itinerant. Brought up as a nominal Anglican and educated at the Free School, he was led to vital faith after hearing WESTLEY HALL at a Presbyterian meeting. He began to preach in his own home and in a private house licensed for dissenting worship. His mother and then his wife were converted through his message. The Earl of Pembroke and the local mayor supported him when attempts were made to restrain his preaching. For five years he carried on a fruitful ministry at Sarum after Hall had left. Stationed from 1758, he served mainly in the west of England and in Wales, superannuating in 1780, a victim of mental illness. His obituary in the Minutes

refers to him as 'a zealous defender of our purest doctrines'.

BIBLIOGRAPHY
AM (1782)
MM (1800)

A. SKEVINGTON WOOD

Fyfe, Robert Alexander (b. Laprairie, Lower Canada, 20 Oct. 1816; d. Woodstock, Ontario, Canada, 29 Aug. 1878). Baptist pastor, educator, and leader. Educated at Canada Baptist College, Montreal, and Newton Theological Institute, Fyfe was the first Baptist pastor to make inroads into the crucial city of Toronto. He twice pastored what would later become Jarvis St Church; from 1844–8, and then from 1855 to 1860. Deeply committed to uniting the disparate Baptist groups, he spent six years in self-imposed exile in the United States being frustrated over continuing theological battles.

Remembered primarily as an educator, Fyfe began his teaching career in 1843–4 as principal of Canada Baptist College. He later served as the guiding force behind the Canadian Literary Institute, Woodstock, acting as president from its opening in 1860, until his death. Fyfe also drew Baptists out of their narrow isolationism. While in Montreal he began to champion such political causes as non-sectarian universities and public schools. This slowly brought Baptists into the national arena. He also possessed a tremendous sense of mission, spearheading efforts into western Canada, as well as the 1870 formation of the Regular Baptist Foreign Missionary Society of Canada. To promote this vision he recognized a denominational paper was necessary. So, in 1859 he formed a group to assume control of the 'Christian Messenger' (subsequently renamed 'The Canadian Baptist'). He served briefly as its editor.

BIBLIOGRAPHY
T. T. Gibson, *Robert Alexander Fyfe* (Burlington, Canada, 1988)
J. A. Wells, *Life and Labours of Robert Alexander Fyfe, D.D.* (Toronto, 1885)

DONALD A. GOERTZ

G

Gadsby, William (b. Attleborough, near Nuneaton, Warwickshire, England, 3 Jan. 1773; d. Manchester, Lancashire, England, 27 June 1844). Strict Baptist pastor. Gadsby was the ninth child of a poor road worker. He attended Nuneaton Church School and was apprenticed to a ribbon weaver at the age of 13. A wild and dissolute youth, he was converted after attending a triple public hanging and began to attend Bedworth Independent and Cow Lane Baptist Chapel, Coventry. He was baptized in 1793, and in 1796 moved to Hinckley where he worshipped in a barn in Hogg Lane, set up as a stocking-weaver and married Elizabeth Marvin.

He preached for the first time in a room in Bedworth in 1798. His sermons, though coarse and vulgar to refined tastes, were powerful and soul-searching and at once attracted large congregations. New chapels were built for him at Desford in 1800 and Hinckley in 1802. While on a fund-raising tour for these causes in the north-west in 1803 he preached at the chapel in Back Lane, otherwise St George's Road, later Rochdale Road, Manchester, and was called to the pulpit there.

A remarkable 39-year-long ministry began in 1805. As well as feeding his own constantly growing flock, Gadsby was tireless in missionary travels around Manchester. He calculated that he preached in all 12,000 sermons, travelled 60,000 miles and planted about forty new churches. Two men whom he baptized, JOHN KERSHAW and JOHN WARBURTON, are with him regarded as the three founders of the Gadsbyite wing of the English Strict and Particular Baptists. As a bond of union for this grouping he founded in 1835 the *Gospel Standard Magazine*; he only edited it for a short time but thereafter wrote the annual address and contributed articles under the noms de plume 'A Lover of Zion' and 'An Old Soldier'. ['A Nazarene's' contributions to the *Evangelical Magazine* were likewise Gadsby's.]

Exalting the Gospel above the law, he injected into Strict Baptist life an introspective or 'experimental' piety which is more properly to be described as very High rather than Hyper-Calvinist – the latter like the epithet antinomian, often without any justification hurled at him, being a pejorative term. No mean controversialist he assailed ANDREW FULLER's 'invitation system' and fellow Strict Baptist James Stephens' suspect Christology, as well as Arminians and Sandemanians. His first selection of hymns appeared in 1814; new editions, incorporating his own and the whole corpus of JOSEPH HART's hymnody and other High Calvinist religious verse, appeared regularly thereafter. 'Gadsby's Selection'

remains in use to this day. Gadsby had an intense sympathy for the poor. He was always busy with fund-raising and charitable giving, and, unusually for a Strict Baptist, would appear on political platforms, to press for temperance reforms, the abolition of the Corn Laws or the rights of Dissenters: his oratory could hold an audience of 8,000 in the Free Trade Hall, Manchester, spellbound. The last years of his ministry were clouded by the insanity of his wife. His pamphlets were reprinted by his son, John, a master printer, in two volumes (1851) as was a collection of his sermons in 1884.

BIBLIOGRAPHY
DNB
J. Gadsby, *Memoir of William Gadsby* (Manchester, England, 1844)
J. C. Philpot, *A Tribute of High Esteem and Love* (London, 1844)
B. A. Ramsbottom, *A History of the Gospel Standard Magazine* (Carshalton, England, 1985)

IAN SELLERS

Gainsborough, (first) Earl of [Noel, Charles] (b. Catmore, Rutland, England, 2 Oct. 1781; d. London, 10 June 1866). MP and peer. Noel was the eldest son of Sir Gerard Noel-Noel, Baronet, and Diana, BARONESS BARHAM, and brother of FRANCIS, GERARD and BAPTIST NOEL. He was educated at Langley School, Kent, and Trinity College, Cambridge (but it is doubtful if he resided or took a degree). He was admitted at Lincoln's Inn, 12 December 1803, and served as MP (1808–14), magistrate and Deputy-Lieutenant for Rutland. In politics, he was a Whig of the old school. On 12 April 1823, he succeeded his mother as third Baron Barham, and, on 25 February 1838, his father as second baronet. He was created Earl of Gainsborough and Viscount Campden on 16 August 1841.

Noel married, on 1 July 1809, Elizabeth (died 1811), daughter of Thomas Welman; on 13 May 1817, Elizabeth (died 1818), sister of the Honourable Sir GEORGE GREY, by whom he had one son and one daughter. He died from an attack of bronchitis at his home in London, and was buried at Teston, Kent.

Noel was a great benefactor of the poor on his estates, as well as to a number of evangelical causes. On one occasion he was fined £40 by a local magistrate for holding conventicles at Barham Court, Kent. Upon the death of Lady Barham he became leader of her Calvinistic connexion in Wales.

BIBLIOGRAPHY
Al. Cant.
R. H. Carne, *Reasons for Withdrawing from the National Establishment* (London, 1820)
C. Gilmore, *A Reply to . . . Baptist Noel's Essay on the Union of Church and State* (London, 1849)
GM, 2 (1866): 123
A. N. Jones, *Gower Memories of William Griffiths* (Aberayron, Wales, 1957)
Leicestershire County Record Office, Noel manuscript
Peerage

GRAYSON CARTER

Gale, Alexander (b. Logie Coldstone, Scotland, 1800; d. Albion Mills, Canada West, 6 April 1854). Presbyterian minister in British North America. Educator. Gale was baptized 18 December 1800, educated at Marischal College, Aberdeen (MA 1819) and licensed by the presbytery of Kincardine O'Neil in the Church of Scotland. He emigrated to British North America in 1827 and served variously as schoolmaster, missionary and minister before being called to the pastoral charge of Hamilton in 1833. He joined the Free Church in 1844 and served as first editor of *The Ecclesiastical and Missionary Record*. He was Principal of the Free Church's grammar school, Toronto Academy, and professor of classical literature in Knox College, Toronto, joining his uncle HENRY ESSON on the faculty. He was elected moderator of the Free Church Synod in 1853.

BIBLIOGRAPHY
DCB, VIII
R. W. Vaudry, *The Free Church in Victorian Canada, 1844–1861* (Waterloo, Canada, 1989)

RICHARD W. VAUDRY

Gale, George W. (b. Stanford, NY, USA, 3 Dec. 1789; d. Galesburg, IL, USA, 13 Sept. 1861). Presbyterian minister, reformer, and founder of Knox College, Galesburg, Illinois. Gale graduated from Union College in 1814, and after an interruption due to ill health, completed a course of study at Princeton Theological Seminary in 1819. He was called to pastor a church in Adams, New York, and served there from 1819 to 1824. While at Adams, he met CHARLES G. FINNEY, and after Finney's dramatic conversion, became his theological tutor. The two differed dramatically in their theological views, but remained lifelong friends nevertheless.

Another bout of ill health caused him to resign from the church at Adams in 1824, and he moved his family to a farm in Western, Oneida County, New York. Convinced that many qualified young men lacked the necessary means to obtain an education, he developed a plan to remedy the situation. He took several young men into his family, and provided them with instruction and books in return for a few hours of manual labour each day. The result of this experiment was the founding of the Oneida Institute at Whitesboro, New York, which Gale headed from 1827 to 1834. Gale was re-united with Charles G. Finney at Western, where Finney preached extensively and continued his meteoric rise to fame.

Gale moved west in 1836, founding a Christian colony named Galesburg, and then drew up plans for a Christian college based on the manual labour principle. To facilitate his plan, he had visited Oberlin in 1835 to learn about both their manual labour organization as well as their experiment in co-education. The school was chartered in 1837 as Knox Manual Labour College, but the manual labour experiment did not do well, and in time the name was changed to Knox College. Gale was the first pastor of the local church in Galesburg, a trustee of the college, president of the board, and a professor of languages and moral philosophy. In earlier years, Finney had characterized his theology as Hyper-Calvinistic, but his earnestness was never questioned regarding his concern for the spiritual welfare of those around him.

SELECT WRITINGS
G. W. Gale, *A Brief History of Knox College* (Cincinnati, OH, 1845)
—, *Autobiography of George Washington Gale, Founder of Galesburg, Illinois and Knox College* (NY, privately printed, 1964)

BIBLIOGRAPHY
W. Lamb, 'George Washington Gale, Theologian and Educator' (Syracuse University, ed. D. diss., 1949)
Princeton Theological Seminary Biographical Catalog (Trenton, NJ, 1909)
M. F. Webster, *The Story of Knox College* (Galesburg, IL, 1912)

JAMES E. JOHNSON

Galland, Antoine Jean Louis (b. Geneva, *c.* 1792; d. Neuveville, Switzerland, *c.* 1862). Early preacher of the Swiss *Réveil*. Galland was a member of a pietist circle while a theological student at Geneva. Ordained there in 1815, he subsequently served a francophone congregation in the canton of Berne. He was known for his preaching about the new birth prior to his seminal meeting with the Scot, ROBERT HALDANE, in late 1816. Galland promoted foreign missions in Switzerland and served the Paris Missionary Society as director 1824–6. By 1831, he was again at Geneva, supporting the foundation of the Geneva Evangelical Society. His involvement as lecturer in homiletics in that society's Evangelical School of Theology provoked the Geneva Company of Pastors to dismiss him as a minister in 1832. In this, he shared the lot of F.-S.-R. L. GAUSSEN and J. H. MERLE D'AUBIGNÉ. After 1838, Galland served congregations of the French Reformed Church.

BIBLIOGRAPHY
E. Guers, *Le Premier Réveil et le Premier Eglise Independent à Genève* (Geneva, 1872)
A. Haldane, *Lives of Robert and James Haldane* (Edinburgh, 1852)
H. Heyer, *L'Eglise de Genève* (Geneva, 1909)

KENNETH J. STEWART

Galland, Thomas (b. Hull, England, 1794; d. Hull, England, 12 May 1843). Methodist minister. Converted at the age of 15, his Anglican parents sent him to Cambridge in preparation for the Anglican ministry; but he retained his Methodist membership, examining and comparing doctrines and ecclesiastical systems and finding Methodism in harmony with New Testament teaching and example. Consequently this Cambridge MA entered the Methodist ministry in 1816, choosing to spend his life in the self-denying duties of a laborious ministry, when he was in possession of considerable affluence; this he looked upon as a trust from God.

His education furnished him with stores of biblical and classical learning, and he was a great preacher and scholar. But at a time when official Methodism was largely Tory, Galland was a Whig, and consequently in frequent conflict with JABEZ BUNTING, notably in the affair of J. R. STEPHENS. He excelled in feeding the flock; faithful to discipline when necessary, he was possessed of a sound judgement and powers of discrimination, so that he exercised great tenderness, forbearance and charity, distinguishing between error of judgement and perversion of the truth. But in time of agitation he threw himself on the side of order so as to preserve the unity and institutions of Methodism; he diligently applied himself to supporting Methodist institutions, especially the WMMS. His publications included sermons, letters, etc.; but his life was cut short when he was seized with paralysis when preaching at the age of 49.

BIBLIOGRAPHY
EWM
Minutes (1844): 15–18
G. Osborn, *Outlines of Wesleyan Bibliography* (London, 1869)

OLIVER A. BECKERLEGGE

Gallaudet, Thomas Hopkins (b. Philadelphia, PA, USA, 10 Dec. 1787; d. Hartford, CT, USA, 10 Sept. 1851). Educator and social reformer. Descendant of a Huguenot family, he graduated from Yale in 1805 and then studied law and English literature. In 1808 he became a tutor at Yale for two years; in 1811 he entered Andover Seminary. His precarious state of health kept him out of the ministry following graduation, but his interests led him to work with a deaf and mute girl, Alice Cogswell, of Hartford. At that time, a group of Hartford citizens sent Gallaudet to Europe to study the latest methods of teaching deaf mutes. Gallaudet's plans to study the oral methods of the (John) Braidwood school in England were frustrated, and he proceeded to Paris where Abbé Sicard, director of the Institut des Sourds-Muets, accorded him a warm welcome. These experiences led to Gallaudet establishing the sign method at the Connecticut (later American) Asylum for the Education of Deaf-Mutes which he founded in 1817. Laurent Clerc, one of the Sicard's outstanding students returned with Gallaudet and became a staunch apologist for the sign method. Gallaudet steadily developed the Asylum, in part through a land grant from Congress, and advanced the cause of the deaf and mute through legislation in New England, the Middle States and in Congress until 1830, when he stepped down as director.

His wife, Sophia Fowler, a deaf mute was one of his students. They had eight children and of them, Edward Miner Gallaudet (1837–1917) succeeded his father as director, and was instrumental in founding the Columbia Institution for the Deaf and Dumb in Washington, DC, now named Gallaudet College, in honour of Thomas Gallaudet.

After 1830, Gallaudet wrote extensively on themes related to Christian education and gave service to a variety of volunteer societies including the American Peace Society, American Colonization Society and the Connecticut branch of the ATS, which he served as president. He held the position of chaplain with the Connecticut Retreat for the Insane for 13 years. He was honoured with the LL D from Western Reserve College in 1851.

BIBLIOGRAPHY
AAP
J. G. Wilson and J. Fiske, eds, *Appleton's Cyclopedia of American Biography* (New York, 1888)
H. Humphrey, *The Life and Labors of the Rev. Thomas H. Gallaudet* (New York, 1877)
Webster's
R. Winefield, *Never the Twain Shall Meet* (Washington, DC, 1987)

DIETRICH G. BUSS

Gallienne, Matthew (b. Le Bordage, St Peter Port, Guernsey, UK, 28 Aug. 1812; d. St Peter Port, UK, 10 Oct. 1900). Methodist missionary in France. Matthew was the son of Matthew Gallienne, lawyer and Methodist local preacher. The call to work in France came through a Guernsey friend, James Hocart. Beginning in 1836 under CHARLES COOK near Nîmes, Matthew also served in the Drôme, the French Alps, and Switzerland. He was assisted by his wife Catherine. In 1844, he initiated at Nîmes a *pensionnat évangélique* for young ladies. In 1859, he was president of the French Methodist Conference. He then retired to the Channel Islands apart from service in England during the 1870s. He was editor of *Les Archives du Méthodisme* in the mid-1850s and *Le Magasin Méthodiste des Iles de la Manche* in later years. He exemplified the dictum of Matthew Lelièvre: 'The Methodist Church of France is an offspring of Channel Islands Methodism'.

BIBLIOGRAPHY
M. Morley, *And Are We Yet Alive* (Jersey, UK, 1987)
J. Waller, *A Methodist Pilgrimage in France* (Loughborough, England, 1989)

JOHN WALLER

Galusha, Elon (b. Shaftsbury, VT, USA, 1790; d. Lockport, NY, USA, 6 Jan. 1856). Baptist abolitionist and early Adventist leader. Elon Galusha was the son of

Jonas Galusha, a governor of Vermont. He had a fine classical education and studied to be a lawyer but, due to an earlier evangelical conversion, decided instead to be a preacher. Galusha pastored various Baptist churches throughout the 'burned-over district' of central and western New York from 1816 to 1844. Known as an eloquent speaker, he was president of the Baptist Missionary Convention and several antislavery societies. He was also an avid promoter of the abolitionist Liberty Party. In 1843, while pastoring in Lockport, New York, Galusha became enamoured with the premillennialist apocalypticism of WILLIAM MILLER, and soon was convinced that the second advent of Christ was imminent. He resigned his pastorate in 1844 and became a full-time itinerant, preaching Miller's Adventist teachings. After the so-called 'great disappointment', when Christ did not return as predicted by Miller, Galusha was a leader in organizing the scattered and disillusioned Adventists.

BIBLIOGRAPHY
D. L. Rowe, 'Elon Galusha and the Millerite Movement', *Foundations* (July–September 1975)

DOUGLAS M. STRONG

Gambier, Frederick (b. 1797; d. 1870). Anglican clergyman. Gambier was the nephew of the admiral and peer of that name who was first president of the CMS. He entered Merton College, Oxford, in 1814 (BA 1818; MA 1822) and was subsequently a fellow of All Souls (1818–39). He was curate at Steeple Claydon (Buckinghamshire) where the squire was Sir HARRY VERNEY. Gambier was subsequently Rector of Barford St Martin (Wiltshire) (1837–44).

BIBLIOGRAPHY
J. S. Reynolds, *The Evangelicals at Oxford* (Abingdon, England, 1975)

ARTHUR POLLARD

Gambier, George Cornish (d. 1879). British naval officer and philanthropist. A nephew of Lord GAMBIER he entered the navy in 1806, was commissioned lieutenant in 1815, and had extensive service in Biscay, the Mediterranean and the East Indies before obtaining his own command in 1819. Promoted captain in June 1821, he commanded the *Dauntless* until the end of 1823. Thereafter he had no service afloat but became rear-admiral on the retired list in 1852 (and admiral April 1863).

From 1828 he and Captain R. J. ELLIOT gave practical effect to G. C. ('Boatswain') SMITH's idea of providing respectable lodgings for discharged sailors in the Port of London, although for a while his 'Irvingite' theological opinions caused a breach of fellowship with his collaborators.

BIBLIOGRAPHY
R. Kverndal, *Seamen's Missions* (Pasadena, CA, 1986)
Navy List
W. R O'Byrne, *A Naval Biographical Dictionary* (London, 1849)

RICHARD C. BLAKE

Gambier, James [Baron Gambier] (b. New Providence, Bahamas, 13 Oct. 1756; d. Iver Grove, Buckinghamshire, England, 19 April 1833). British Admiral of the Fleet, naval administrator and patron of evangelistic and charitable causes. Of a French refugee family, he was a younger son of Samuel Gambier, the Lieutenant-Governor of the Bahamas. He was greatly influenced by his aunt Margaret Gambier who married CHARLES MIDDLETON, a future Comptroller of the Navy and First Lord of the Admiralty. With such powerful patronage he rose quickly in naval rank despite restricted service afloat.

When in command of the *Defence* (1793–5) he employed controversial and unpopular measures – strictly lawful but long dormant in the service – against profanity and immorality. He earned a high reputation for his courageous action at the Glorious First of June (1794) when his ship was the first to break the French line and suffered heavy damage and casualties. Made rear-admiral on 1 June 1795, he served as one of the Lords of the Admiralty until 1801, went to Newfoundland as Governor in 1802, but returned to the Admiralty Board in 1804 for another two years. During part of this period his uncle, now Lord Barham, was First Lord. As a naval administrator, Gambier was particularly concerned with improvements in ship construction, development of the signalling system and revision of General Instructions for the guidance of officers in the ordering of their ship's companies.

In 1807 he was awarded a peerage for his seizure of the Danish fleet after bombarding Copenhagen. Commander of the channel fleet from 1808 until 1811, he incurred such criticism for his handling of the Basque Roads action (April 1809) that he demanded a court martial on his own conduct. Captain Lord Cochrane had led a fire-ship attack on a French squadron at the mouth of the Charente; in spite of the stranding of the enemy warships Gambier took little action and only four were destroyed. Although Cochrane denounced the caution and even lethargy of his Admiral, the court martial was well disposed towards Gambier who was 'most honourably acquitted'.

Gambier helped negotiate peace with the USA in 1814; he was made Knight Grand Cross of the Order of the Bath (GCB) in June 1815, and rose by seniority to become Admiral of the Fleet on 22 July 1830.

As captain and admiral he had distributed tracts to sailors in his ships; he remained a strong supporter of the Naval and Military Bible Society, seamen's charities and other evangelical causes. He was the first president of the CMS. Although his naval career was attended by controversy, he deserves credit for his work at the Admiralty, his resolution at the Glorious First of June and at Copenhagen, his evangelistic efforts among seamen and the use he made of his title and position to advance many worthy Christian charities.

Surprisingly no adequate biography exists, Lady Chatterton's 2-volume work being largely uninformative. Cochrane's autobiography is critical; Dillon, one of his officers, gives a detailed picture of his conduct as a captain. Some of his correspondence may be found in the various manuscript collections in the National Maritime Museum, Greenwich.

One of his nephews was FREDERICK GAMBIER, a fellow of All Soul's, Oxford. Another nephew, GEORGE CORNISH GAMBIER (captain 1821, ashore from 1823, but vice-admiral by seniority on the retired list in 1857) and Captain R. J. ELLIOT together opened a Destitute Sailors' Asylum in London on 8 January 1828, largely at their own expense, thus furthering the scheme pioneered by 'Bo'sun' GEORGE CHARLES SMITH.

BIBLIOGRAPHY
DNB
H. G. Chatterton (Lady), Memorials Personal and Historical of Admiral Lord Gambier (London, 1861)
T. Cochrane (Dundonald, Earl of), Autobiography of a Seaman (London, 1860)
H. B. Gurney, Minutes of a Court Martial (Portsmouth, England, 1809)
R. Kverndal, Seamen's Missions (Pasadena, California, 1986)
M. A. Lewis, ed., Dillon's Narrative (London, 1953)

RICHARD C. BLAKE

Gambold, Anna (Rosina) [née Kliest] (b. 1 May 1762; d. Springplace, GA, USA, 19 Feb. 1821). Missionary and educator to the Cherokees, and pioneer of American botany. A Moravian schoolteacher who gained recognition at the Seminary for Young Ladies, Bethlehem, Pennsylvania, her marriage was arranged to JOHN GAMBOLD, superintendent of the Moravian mission and school at Springplace, Georgia. Anna Gambold was a gifted teacher who was well loved by her students. She was an accomplished botanist who in her spare time, collected over 1,400 samples of plants, minerals, and aboriginal manufactures from the surrounding territory. This was instrumental in founding the scientific study of botany in North America. An accomplished poet and musician, she is credited with the introduction of the formal studies of music and the fine arts to the Cherokee nation. Anna Gambold was one of the few married women of the post revolutionary era who attained academic excellence, scientific respect, and the status of an intellectual.

BIBLIOGRAPHY
C. Mauleshagen, Translation of the Springplace Diary (no date, typescript)
E. Schwarze, History of Moravian Missions (Bethlehem, PA, 1923)

WADE A. HORTON

Gambold, John (b. Puncheston, Pembrokeshire, Wales, 21 April 1711; d. Haverfordwest, Pembrokeshire, Wales, 13 Sept. 1771). First English Moravian bishop. Gambold went up to Christ Church, Oxford, in 1726. In 1730 he met CHARLES WESLEY and became one of the Oxford Methodists. He was ordained in September 1733 and became Vicar of Stanton Harcourt (near Oxford), where he was looked after by his sister Martha and, for about two years, Keziah Wesley.

Gambold had been affected profoundly by the death of his father William, a clergyman, in 1728. Before meeting the Oxford Methodists he 'was in a despairing mood and totally neglected all care of his person and clothes'. He performed his parochial duties conscientiously, but otherwise shut himself away, devoting himself to the Greek fathers, philosophical speculation and mysticism. By October 1738 he had even given up the fathers, and described himself as 'almost swallowed up with melancholy' and 'peevish ... by an hypochondriac constitution, and an internal religion ending in despondency'.

Gambold had met PETER BÖHLER when he visited Oxford earlier in 1738, and in 1739 met ZINZENDORF in London. In December 1740 his brother Hector gave him an attractive account of his life in London with members of the Fetter Lane Society, and as a result Gambold was drawn into the Moravian circle, breaking with the Wesleys by July 1741. Despite occasional meetings, the friendship was never restored. The Moravians' emphasis on faith, their spirituality and community life were the answer to Gambold's depression, and in October 1742 he finally resigned his living and moved to London, where he was received into the new Moravian congregation on 11 November.

Gambold became a teacher at the Moravian boarding school at Broakoaks (Essex), where he married Elizabeth Walker in May 1743. In the autumn they moved to Haverfordwest, where he kept a school and preached in local churches. Gambold had felt happy in the gentle but intense atmosphere of the Moravian school, describing himself in April 1743 as 'at peace', but was not suited to schoolmastering. By his own admission, he had never loved children, found their concerns trivial and preferred silent solitude. In Haverfordwest he was 'too feeble' to keep order, and unwilling to punish. The venture failed.

In November 1744 Gambold returned to London. It helped the Moravians' image to have a learned Anglican priest as preacher at the Fetter Lane Chapel, where Gambold remained until 1768. In the autumn of 1746 he was ZINZENDORF's intermediary in abortive negotiations with Archbishop Potter for recognition of the Moravians as a society within the Church of England under Potter's personal oversight, helping to develop the proposals. A visit to the Moravian centre Herrnhaag (Wetteravia) for the 1747 General Synod served to seal his commitment to the existing Moravian spirituality and community life.

Beginning with Acta Fratrum Unitatis in Anglia (1749), Gambold became the chief translator and editor of a series of books designed to promote the Moravians' image in England, including Zinzendorf's Maxims (1751). Assisted by JAMES HUTTON, he was responsible for most of the literary defence mounted when they came under attack between 1753 and 1755. He also played a considerable part in the preparation of the Moravians' *Londoner Gesancbuch* of 1754 and edited their English hymnbooks of 1754 and 1769 and (assisted by LUDOLF ERNST SCHLICHT) the 1759 *Litany Book*.

In November 1754 Gambold was consecrated the first English Moravian bishop. As such he consecrated several new chapels, attended the constitutive General Synod of 1764, and made a visitation to Ireland in 1765. When his health failed in 1768 Gambold returned to Haverfordwest as minister of the Moravian congregation.

SELECT WRITINGS
J. Gambold, *Works of the late Rev. John Gambold*, ed. B. La Trobe (Bath, England, 1789)

BIBLIOGRAPHY
D. Benham, *Life and Labours of the Rev. John Gambold* (London, 1865)
DNB
DWB
Gemeinnachrichten (1863) I: 286–305
L. Tyerman, *The Oxford Methodists* (London, 1873)

C. J. PODMORE

Gambold, John (b. Shechem, NY, BNA, 16 June 1760; d. Oothcalaga, GA, USA, 7 Dec. 1827). Moravian missionary to the Cherokee nation in Georgia. A Moravian minister, married to ANNA ROSINA GAMBOLD, and superintendent of the Springplace mission, he was also founder of the Oothcalaga mission near New Echota, Georgia. He pioneered mission works within the Cherokee nation and was affectionately known to Cherokees and other missionaries alike as 'Father Gambold'. His advice was often sought by other denominations, missionaries, and ministers who wished to start mission stations and schools. John Gambold, and his successors, took an apolitical stance that eventually discredited the Moravian voice among the Cherokees, but he and his wife were directly responsible for the education of many young Cherokee chiefs and headmen who led the opposition against removal. Chief John Hicks was converted under his ministry and became an advocate of Christianity in the Cherokee nation.

BIBLIOGRAPHY
C. Mauleshagen, *Translation of the Oothcalaga Diary* (no date, typescript)
E. Schwarze, *History of Moravian Missions* (Bethlehem, PA, 1923)

WADE A. HORTON

Gano, John (b. Hopewell, NJ, BNA, 22 July 1727; d. Lexington, KY, USA, 10 Aug. 1804). Baptist pastor, missionary, and denominationalist. A descendant of French Huguenots, he was probably the most prominent Baptist leader in New York during his life time. Educated by Baptist ministers and also at Princeton, he became

convinced of believers' baptism and was ordained as a Baptist on 29 May 1754, after participating in a preaching mission to the South. The Philadelphia Association immediately commissioned him to begin another Southern mission. As a result, he became pastor of the Baptist church in Jersey, North Carolina from 1758 to 1760. After Cherokee invasions precipitated his removal, he was eventually called to be pastor of the newly formed (1762) First Baptist Church in New York City.

A staunch patriot during the Revolutionary War, Gano served in General De Witt Clintons' New York Brigade as a chaplain. Though expected to remain behind lines with the surgeons, he occasionally exhibited exemplary bravery at the front. Such service prompted George Washington to remark that 'Baptist Chaplains were the most prominent and useful in the army'. After the war, the First Baptist Church New York (whose building had been used as a stable by the British) was reduced to 37 of its prewar 200 members. Gano rebuilt the membership to over 300 by his departure in 1787–8. Because of his low salary, he migrated to Kentucky settling near Lexington, where he pastored the Town Fork Baptist Church, which was famous in part for its black membership. Calvinist in doctrine but ecumenical in spirit, Gano was highly respected for his preaching, which, according to ISAAC BACKUS, was 'as much admired as [George] Whitefield's'. His work as a denominationalist strengthened churches and associations throughout the Middle and Southern states.

BIBLIOGRAPHY
AAP
T. Armitage, *History of the Baptists* (New York, 1887)
D. Benedict, *A General History of the Baptist Denomination in America* (New York, 1848)
W. Cathcart, *The Baptist Encyclopedia* (Philadelphia, PA, 1881)
W. G. McLoughlin, ed., *The Diary of Isaac Backus* (Providence, RI, 1979)

ANDREW MANIS

Garbett, Edward (b. Hereford, England, 10 Dec. 1817; d. Lewes, Sussex, England, 11 Oct. 1886). Anglican clergyman and scholar. Garbett's education matched that of his brother (*see* JAMES GARBETT) by taking him to Hereford Cathedral School and Brasenose College, Oxford in 1837 (BA 1841; MA 1847). He became curate to his father at Upton Bishop (1841–2) but then moved to his cousin JOHN GARBETT, who supported the CMS and was fiercely anti-Roman and anti-Unitarian, at St George's, Birmingham, subsequently becoming Vicar of St Stephen's before moving to London at St Bartholomew's, Grays Inn Road (1854–63), after which he was Vicar of Christ Church, Surbiton (1863–77) and Barcombe (Sussex) (1877–86). He declined more influential cures such as St Martin's, Birmingham and St Paul's, Onslow Square, but he was active on a national scale as editor of *The Record* (1853–67) and for some time of *The Christian Advocate* as well as speaking regularly at Church Congresses (1866, 1870–4 and 1879).

He delivered the Boyle lectures on *The Bible and its Critics* (1861), which were directed against *Essays and Reviews*, and *The Divine Plan of Revelation* (1863). His Bampton lectures were on *The Dogmatic Faith* (1867), while his Church Association lectures considered *The Doctrine of the Lord's Supper the Keynote of the English Reformation* (1869). In 1862 he replied to Colenso in *The Pentateuch in its Relation to the Other Scriptures and to the Scheme of Christianity*.

BIBLIOGRAPHY
British Library Catalogue
DNB

ARTHUR POLLARD

Garbett, James (b. Hereford, England, *c*. 1802; d. Brighton, Sussex, England, 26 March 1879). Anglican clergyman and scholar. Garbett was the eldest of the seven sons of James Garbett (1792–1857), prebendary of Hereford, of whom others were EDWARD GARBETT, George (1811–65, vicar of St. James, Accrington) and Charles (1815–?) Vicar of Tongham, Hampshire and father of Cyril Garbett, Archbishop of York). All of them were educated at Hereford school and Brasenose College, Oxford, James entering this latter in 1819 (BA 1822; MA 1825; fellow 1825–36. He was also fellow of Queen's (1824–5), Hulmeian lecturer in divinity (1828), Bampton lecturer (1842) and professor of poetry (1842–52). He is said to have declined the Ireland professorship of biblical exegesis in 1847. He held the college living of Clayton-cum-Keymer (Sussex) (1835–79), became Prebendary of Chichester (1843–79) and followed H. E. MANNING as archdeacon (1851–79) on the latter's secession to Rome. Not surprisingly his 1851 charge distinguished the Church of England from Rome, a view reiterated in 1857, and to some degree, with the Tractarians in mind, dealt with in the Bampton lectures on *Christ as Prophet, Priest and King, Being a Vindication of the Church of England from Theological Novelties*, where he rejected sacerdotalism both by what the New Testament does say and also *ex silentio*.

BIBLIOGRAPHY
Al. Ox. II. 506
DNB

ARTHUR POLLARD

Garbett, John (b. 1791; d. Harborne, Staffordshire, England, 23 Aug. 1858). Anglican clergyman. The son of Thomas Garbett of Hereford and younger brother of Thomas Garbett, the master of Peterborough Grammar School, he was educated at Hereford Cathedral School and All Souls' College, Oxford (matriculated 1814, Bible clerk 1814–18, BA 1818; MA 1821). He was ordained (deacon 1817, priest 1818) to the curacy of Cardington and Cople, Bedfordshire (1817–22). He moved to Birmingham to become Curate of St Bartholomew's in 1822, and incumbent of the newly erected St George's from 1822 to 1851 (he was rector from 1830). As first Rural Dean of Birmingham (1835–51), he was responsible for the Ten Churches building scheme and became fully involved with town life, being a governor of King Edward's School for 24 years, a member of the hospital board and library committee, and a conscientious pastor.

His brusque and lofty manner concealed a kind heart and a wise judgement that made him valuable as a counsellor and able to cooperate with men of different outlooks. His evangelicalism was moderate, and he inclined towards men like Francis Jeune. Garbett declined the offer by the Simeon Trust of the vicarage of Bradford, but failing health led him to accept Archdeacon HODSON's offer in 1851 of the vicarage of Harborne, Staffordshire, a residential village just outside Birmingham. His cousin EDWARD GARBETT was for a time his curate and was presented by him to the daughter-parish of St Stephen's, Birmingham.

BIBLIOGRAPHY
Al. Ox., 3 (1715–1886): 507
Aris's Birmingham Gazette (27 September 1830, 27 May 1839, 13 October 1851, 30 August 1858)
Clergy List
Crockford

D. E. H. MOLE

Gardiner, Allen Francis (b. Basildon, Berkshire, England, 28 June 1794; d. Picton Island, Tierra del Fuego, 6 or 7 Sept. 1851). British naval officer and pioneer South American missionary. The fourth son of Samuel Gardiner of Coombe Lodge, Oxfordshire, he entered the Royal Naval College, Portsmouth, in May 1808, serving first as a volunteer on board HMS *Fortune* and then as a midshipman on HMS *Phoebe* (under the command of JAMES HILLYAR) on which he earned distinction for his role in the capture of the American frigate, *Essex*, off Valparaiso in March 1813. Made a lieutenant in 1814 he saw naval service in many parts of the world before in 1826 leaving the service with the rank of commander.

During the course of his naval service while he was serving with the *Dauntless* on the South American station, he became interested in the local aboriginal tribes and decided to devote his life to Christian missionary work. He went first to Africa where from 1834 to 1838 he worked among the Zulus. With the permission of the Zulu king, Dingaan, he set up a mission station at Hambanarti, and a Hambanarti Church Missionary Association was formed in 1838 to support the work; but incursions by the Boers, destabilizing the country, made any permanent achievement impossible.

Gardiner withdrew with his second wife, Elizabeth Marsh (daughter of E. G. MARSH), whom he married in 1836 two years after the death of his first wife Susanna Reade, to Chile where he intended to preach the Gospel to the Araucanian Indians, but circumstances were not propitious. A further attempt to undertake missionary work in New Guinea was also frustrated, partly as a result of the hostile attitude of the Dutch. He turned his attention again to South America and in March 1842 made a first visit to Tierra del Fuego; and in 1844 with ROBERT HUNT as catechist went as a missionary on behalf of the Patagonian Missionary Society (now the South American Missionary Society) which he helped to found in 1844 to forward missionary work in South America. The first attempt was unsuccessful but in September 1845, accompanied by a Spanish Protestant, Federico Gonzalez, he distributed Bibles among the Indians in the Gran Chaco, an activity which was greeted with hostility by the local Roman Catholics. In 1847 he again visited Tierra del Fuego, intending to set up a mission station, but he failed to win the support of the missionary societies, and personally suffered hardship. He did, however, win the support of an English benefactor, a lady from Cheltenham, Gloucestershire, and was able to organize a further expedition which in 1850 landed at Picton Island, Tierra del Fuego. But the natives proved hostile, supplies of food failed and after much suffering Gardiner and his companions died of starvation; in the last entry of the journal which he kept on 5 September 1851 he commented that he had been without food and water for the last four days. When HMS *Dido* arrived off Picton Island on 6 January 1851 the vessel could only ensure that the bodies were properly interred and bring back Gardiner's journal. News of the disaster spurred on others to take up the challenge, leading to the eventual formation of the South American Missionary Society.

Gardiner published *A Narrative of a Journey to the Zoolu Country in South Africa . . . Undertaken in 1835* (London, 1836); *A Visit to the Indians on the Frontiers of Chili* (London, 1840), and *A Voice from South America* (London, 1847). His son, Allen Weare, educated at Magdalen College, Oxford, went as a missionary to Patagonia in 1856.

BIBLIOGRAPHY
DNB
GM
R. Hough, *The Blind Horn's Hate* (London, 1971)
A. W. Marsh and A. W. Stirling, *Story of Commander A. Gardiner* (London, 1867)
P. Thompson, *An Unquenchable Flame, the Story of A. Gardiner* (London, 1983)

V. H. H. GREEN

Gardiner, James (b. Carriden, Linlithgowshire, Scotland, 11 Jan. 1688; d. Tranent, near Edinburgh, 21 Sept. 1745). Soldier. The son of a professional soldier, he was himself by age 14 a mercenary for the Dutch. He transferred his allegiance to the English sovereign and served with distinction under Marlborough. He was wounded at Blenheim in 1704. Gardiner saw other action and became invaluable as aide-de-camp under the Earl of Stair. He met his death heroically in the 1745 Scottish rebellion as a colonel in the light dragoons.

Though twice wounded, he attempted to rally his deserting troops, but was finally brought down at Prestonpans, having suffered five wounds in all.

According to his own testimony, on the Continent Gardiner had lived a rakish life. But one day, while reading Watson's *The Christian Soldier*, he had a vision of Christ and was in an instant converted. He then became intensely pious; he would pray for hours before battle and would exhort his soldiers with words from scripture. Colonel Gardiner's witness, especially as related in PHILIP DODDRIDGE's *The Christian Warrior* (1747), inspired many early evangelical leaders, including JOHN NEWTON, WILLIAM WILBERFORCE and THOMAS M'CRIE.

BIBLIOGRAPHY
DNB and texts mentioned *supra*

JONATHAN BURKE CUTMORE

Gardner, John (b. Great Coggeshall, Essex, England, 1804; d. London, 14 Nov. 1880). Medical lecturer and apologist. Licensed to practise medicine from 1824, Gardner first came into prominence in 1844 as co-founder of the Royal College of Chemistry. He was then secretary to the college until 1846, and for some time thereafter was professor of chemistry at the General Apothecaries school.

Gardner, a member of the EA, published works in support of the argument from design, *The Wonders of the Heavens* (no date), and *The Great Physician* (1843). His *Hymns for the Sick and Convalescent* warranted a second edition in 1879. Two of his letters are in the British Library.

BIBLIOGRAPHY
Boase
DNB

JONATHAN BURKE CUTMORE

Garner, John (b. Kegworth, Leicestershire, England, 13 Feb. 1800; d. Epworth, Lincolnshire, England, 12 Feb. 1856). Primitive Methodist minister. Raised a Baptist, with a strong sense of values and decent behaviour, Garner was apprenticed, aged 14, to a shoemaker. Converted in 1818, after hearing a Primitive Methodist speak (he was affected by their zeal), he joined the Primitive Methodist Connexion, becoming an itinerant preacher in 1819, travelling widely through Staffordshire, Yorkshire and Nottinghamshire. He converted his brother, WILLIAM GARNER, in 1821. He was known for his eloquent, musical preaching and his intelligent, business mind. When the connexional offices and the organizational centre of Primitive Methodism was transferred from Bemersley to London, Garner was appointed the first general missionary secretary. He was a frequent president of the conference. From 1842 onwards, he was a victim of asthma, which led to a withering of his physical strength. In 1848 he retired, moving to Burnham, near Epworth. His name is one of only four to be recorded on the 1830 Deed Poll of the Primitive Methodists enrolled in the Court of Chancery.

BIBLIOGRAPHY
PM Mag (1856)

WAYNE J. JOHNSON

Garner, William (b. Kegworth, Leicestershire, England, 8 April 1802; d. Hull, Yorkshire, England, 27 Jan. 1881). Primitive Methodist minister. Born to poor parents, Garner enjoyed the elements of education at Sunday school. A stocking-weaver by trade, he supported his widowed mother and 13 brothers and sisters (his father died when William was 15). Going to a Primitive Methodist camp meeting in Nottingham, and to a subsequent prayer meeting at his mother's cottage, Garner was converted in 1821 through the instrumentality of his brother, JOHN GARNER; he then became a travelling preacher in the Hull circuit. A product of 'self-improvement', Garner carried a small batch of books (including works by Paley), which he read, studied and prayed over during his long rides and walks over the Yorkshire Wolds. A quiet preacher of clear sermons, Garner developed an intellectual reputation, compiling the Primitive Methodist *Almanac*, and writing a life of WILLIAM CLOWES. A keen denominational administrator, Garner was twice elected president of the conference, as well as being appointed general missionary (1848) and conference secretary for seven years.

BIBLIOGRAPHY
PM Mag (1881)

WAYNE J. JOHNSON

Garnet, Henry (Highland) (b. Kent County, MD, USA, 1815; d. Liberia, 12 Feb. 1882). Black Presbyterian minister and political activist. Born a slave, Garnet escaped with his parents at age nine. He attended New York City's African Free School. After a narrow family escape from slave catchers, Garnet began to worship at The First Coloured Presbyterian Church where THEODORE S. WRIGHT was minister. Powerfully influenced by Wright, Garnet decided to enter the Presbyterian ministry and enrolled at the biracial Oneida Theological Institute, in upper New York State. During his years there he emerged as an electrifying public speaker. He was the first former slave to give a major address to the largely white American Anti-Slavery Society. In it he declared that the true heroes of America were the blacks who had laboured on southern plantations, fought and died in the United States' wars, and given birth to the most powerful American religion, the black church. Only the prayers of African-Americans, he insisted, had held in check God's fiery vengeance upon both the North and South for their collusion with slavery. In the early 1840s, now pastor of the black Presbyterian church in Troy,

New York, Garnet joined the black editor CHARLES RAY in trying to arouse the state's blacks to political activism. At annual black conventions and through petition campaigns, African-Americans pressed the legislature for restoration of the vote to blacks. Yet such re-enfranchisement was not to be won until after the Civil War. In 1840 Garnet strongly supported the formation of the national Liberty party committed to ending slavery. And at a 'National Negro Convention' in 1843 he issued a stirring call to slaves to stage a massive revolt.

After missionary service in Jamaica in the early 1850s, Garnet succeeded JAMES W. C. PENNINGTON as pastor of New York city's black Prince Street Presbyterian Church. Early in the Civil War Garnet urged Lincoln to authorize enlistment of African-American troops. In 1881, having had a long-standing interest in the progress of African nations, Garnet was appointed United States minister to Liberia. He died there the following year.

BIBLIOGRAPHY
E. Ofari, *Let Your Motto Be Resistance* (Boston, MA, 1972)
J. Schor, *Henry Highland Garnet* (Westport, CT, 1977)
D. E. Swift, *Black Prophets of Justice* (Baton Rouge, LA, and London, 1989)

DAVID E. SWIFT

Garnier, John (b. Bishopstoke, Hampshire, England, 26 April 1813; d. Merton College, Oxford, England, 26 March 1838). Anglican clergyman. Third son of Thomas (Rector of Bishopstoke, *DNB*) and Mary Garnier, and brother of THOMAS GARNIER, John was educated at Winchester College, and Exeter College, Oxford. At cricket he represented Oxford University against Marylebone Cricket Club, 1832, and, until 1835, Hampshire. From the latter year till death he was a fellow of Merton College. Ordained in 1836, he became Curate-in-charge of St Ebbe's, Oxford, late in 1837. 'He was of manly and vigorous intellect, open and affable in manner, eloquent and zealous in his preaching, as well as affectionate and unwearied . . .' After three months, during a smallpox epidemic, baptizing two infected infants proved fatal. His memorial in St Ebbe's was erected by parishioners.

BIBLIOGRAPHY
A. E. Garnier, *The Garniers of Hampshire* (Norwich, England, 1900)
Jackson's Oxford Journal (30 March 1838), obituary
J. S. Reynolds, *Evangelicals at Oxford* (Oxford 1953; Appleford, England, 1975)

J. S. REYNOLDS

Garnier, Thomas (b. Bishopstoke rectory, Hampshire, England, 15 April 1809; d. Deanery, Lincoln, England, 7 Dec. 1863). Anglican clergyman. Second son of Thomas Garnier (afterwards Dean of Winchester [*DNB*]), by Mary (Parry, sister of Rear-Admiral Sir EDWARD PARRY, Arctic navigator), brother of J. GARNIER, Thomas was educated at Winchester College and (1827–30) at Worcester College, Oxford. A prominent cricketer and athlete, he rowed in the first university crew versus Cambridge (1829), with W. R. FREMANTLE. He became fellow of All Souls College 1830–5, proceeding BCL in 1833.

Ordained 1833 at Oxford (ordination papers missing), after a curacy at Old Alresford, Hampshire, Garnier was Vicar of Lewknor, Oxfordshire, 1835–40, where he not only initiated parish schools, but reclaimed many evangelical nonconformists, including their minister. 'Kindest of husbands and fathers', his 'great animal spirits' were especially appreciated by children. From 1840 to 1849 Garnier was Rector of Longford, Derbyshire, where he built school and parsonage. Preacher at the Lock Hospital and Speaker's chaplain (House of Commons), he became Rector of Holy Trinity, Marylebone, 1850–9, where he continued to word hard. An able preacher, appointed Dean of Ripon (1859), in 1860 he was made Dean of Lincoln. A 'winning manner displayed to all alike . . . was one source of the great popularity which attended him through life', while 'the distinguishing feature of his character was humility of mind,' devoid of narrowness. After a fall in 1855, partly the effect of overwork, Garnier's health deteriorated. Following a second fall in 1861, spinal injury induced a fatal decline.

Garnier married (1835) Lady Caroline Keppel, by whom he was father of Canon T. P. Garnier (Boase, 5). A portrait can be found in the *Illustrated News of the World*, volume 9 (London, 1862).

BIBLIOGRAPHY
Anon., *Some Account of T. Garnier* (Winchester, England, 1863)
Boase, 1
A. E. Garnier, *The Garniers of Hampshire* (Norwich, England, 1900)
J. S. Reynolds, *Evangelicals at Oxford* (Oxford, 1953; Appleford, England, 1975)

J. S. REYNOLDS

Garratt, Samuel (b. 20 Feb. 1817; d. Ipswich, Suffolk, England, 21 March 1906). Anglican clergyman and author. Garratt was a grandson of JAMES STEPHEN of the Clapham Sect, and son of WILLIAM A. GARRATT, a barrister-member of the committee of the CMS. Educated at Trinity College, Cambridge, where he graduated in 1839, and ordained priest in 1841, Samuel served curacies in Islington and at Grappenhall in Cheshire, and incumbencies at Holy Trinity, Waltham Cross (1845–50) and Trinity Church, St Giles's (1851–67), where he ministered to the poor in the slums around his church, and founded the English Church Missions to proselytize Irish Roman Catholic immigrants in England (1853–7). Despite his vigorous polemics against Roman Catholics and High Churchmen, he was later to attack the Church Association and the Kensitite preachers for opposing spiritual error by an unspiritual persecution. As a book reviewer for the *Record* from 1858, he defended the inerrancy of scripture against the higher criticism and

welcomed the 1859 revival as reproclamation of true Protestant principle. Like his grandfather a strong opponent of slavery, he championed the northern side in the American Civil War, encouraged the importation of Indian free-grown cotton, and was honorary clerical secretary to the Freedman's Aid Society for the education of American blacks. From 1867 to 1895 he was Vicar of St Margaret's, Ipswich, and was an honorary canon of Norwich from 1881. An enthusiastic millenarian from his early years, he wrote a number of works on Biblical prophecy, most notably *A Commentary on the Revelation of St John* (1866), and was president (1900–5) of the Prophecy Investigation Society, to which he devoted his retirement.

SELECT WRITINGS
Samuel Garratt, 'Personal Recollections' in *Life and Personal Recollections of Samuel Garratt* (London, 1908)

BIBLIOGRAPHY
Evelyn R. Garratt, 'A Memoir', in *Life and Personal Recollections of Samuel Garratt* (London, 1908)

SHERIDAN GILLEY

Garratt, William Albin (b. London, 19 April 1782; d. Brighton, Sussex, England, 1858). Lawyer. The son and heir of Francis, a London merchant, he was educated at Woodford, Essex, and entered Trinity College, Cambridge in 1800 (BA 1804; MA 1807; fellow 1805). He was called to the Bar at Lincoln's Inn. Garratt established strong links with the Clapham Sect by marrying Ann, the daughter of JAMES STEPHEN, and became an exceptionally influential member of the CMS Committee. He also had particularly cordial relations with his brother-in-law, Sir JAMES STEPHEN. Garratt contributed to many benevolent causes. He also laboured to resist the threat of forces that were challenging the Protestant constitution. These included theological liberalism, constitutional secularism, renascent Roman Catholicism and Tractarianism. He was on the committee of the Reformation Society which sought to counter Roman Catholicism, while in 1846 writing *An Inquiry into the Scriptural View of the Constitution of a Christian Church*. SAMUEL GARRATT was his son.

BIBLIOGRAPHY
Al. Cant.
S. Garratt, 'Personal Recollections' in *Life and Personal Recollections of Samuel Garratt* (London, 1908)

IAN S. RENNIE AND DONALD M. LEWIS

Garrettson, Catherine [née Livingston] (b. New York City, 14 Oct. 1752; d. Rhinebeck, NY, USA, 13 July 1849). Methodist mystic and spiritual counsellor. Born into a family of immense wealth and political prominence, she astonished the moderately Calvinist Livingstons when she became a fervent Methodist at age

35. Her family's tolerant dismay turned into utter horror when she fell in love with the Methodist preacher FREEBORN GARRETTSON. The aristocratic slaveholding Livingstons strenuously battled her relationship with the middle-class abolitionist Garrettson, but Catherine's obstinacy proved stronger than familial opposition, and they married in 1793.

Her four difficult years of clandestine courtship with Garrettson were marked by a richly textured spirituality. Disciplined practices of prayer, introspection, and meditation on scripture precipitated breathtaking visions of Christ and experiences of union with God. These experiences ceased upon marriage, when energies once directed inward were channelled into different arenas. As a woman bound by cultural assumptions, she could not exercise her capabilities in public church leadership, so she used her formidable talents in domestic spheres. She evangelized privately and extensively among friends and family, and served as spiritual mentor to other women. Her most public domestic ministry flourished in 'Traveler's Rest', her home in Rhinebeck, which became a retreat centre for hundreds of exhausted Methodist preachers and other travelling Christians. Here she presided, prayed, taught, and counselled, providing a ministry of hospitality until her death at 96.

The meticulous records of her spiritual life – over 2,000 pages of diaries and letters – are held in the Methodist Archives in Madison, New Jersey.

BIBLIOGRAPHY
C. W. Buoy, *Representative Women of Methodism* (New York, 1893)
A. Stevens, *The Women of Methodism* (New York, 1866)

DIANE H. LOBODY

Garrettson, Freeborn (b. Harford City, MD, BNA, 15 Aug. 1752; d. New York City, 26 Sept. 1827). Methodist itinerant evangelist in the United States and Canada. Garrettson was first drawn to Methodist ways through the preaching of ROBERT STRAWBRIDGE. By 1775 he had decided to enter the ministry, and the following year, he was admitted 'on trial' to the Methodist Conference meeting in Baltimore. For the next six years, Garrettson was an untiring itinerant, carrying the Methodist evangel into Maryland, Delaware, Virginia, and both Carolinas.

Garrettson's ministry thus began while the American War for Independence was under way. The struggle with Britain rendered American Methodists suspect because of their links with British evangelicalism and because JOHN WESLEY opposed the independence movement. In Garrettson's case, that suspicion was more pronounced since he was personally a committed pacifist. That pacifism led him to refuse to take a required oath in Maryland to bear arms and also in 1777 to refuse to take an oath of allegiance to the revolutionary government in Virginia. These actions convinced detractors that Garrettson was a Tory, if not a British spy, and resulted in his being imprisoned at one point, being stoned several times by angry mobs, and enduring other acts of violence until the war ended. But such opposition and hardship did not deter his commitment to carry the Methodist message wherever he could gain a hearing. His determination and his success in gaining converts to the Methodist cause quickly earned him the respect of Methodist leaders THOMAS COKE and FRANCIS ASBURY; for several years he was a confidante of Asbury. The physical abuses Garrettson endured were also widely known, and he documented them all in a journal he kept. Wesley urged Garrettson to publish his journal so that it might become a source of inspiration for other itinerants; Garrettson sent part of the journal to Wesley for publication in Britain, but the manuscript was lost at sea. However, much of Garrettson's journal from 1752 through 1826 has survived and is available at the Methodist Archives at Drew University.

Another controversy also marked Garrettson's early ministry. Garrettson's father was a man of some wealth who left his son a considerable number of slaves as part of his inheritance. At first, Garrettson did not question the legitimacy of chattel slavery, but he soon became convinced that it was morally wrong for some human beings to hold other human beings in bondage. Consequently he freed his own slaves and became an increasingly vocal advocate of the gradual emancipation of all slaves. Never a radical, Garrettson endorsed calls for legislation that would require the government to pay slave-holders reparations to compensate for their presumed monetary loss in manumitting slaves. But this opposition to slavery made Garrettson suspect in the Southern states where he ministered and where the overwhelming majority of Methodist adherents were found in the revolutionary era; it may well have been as significant as his pacifism in making him the subject of much violent opposition. Garrettson maintained a continuing interest in the religious life of African-Americans and attended the organizing conference of the African Methodist Episcopal Zion Church in 1821.

Following the war in 1784, when Methodist leaders prepared to call the now famous Christmas Conference to organize the American denomination, Garrettson was dispatched to summon itinerants to the Baltimore meeting. There it was decided to send him to Canada as a missionary. For three years he itinerated in Nova Scotia, Newfoundland, and New Brunswick, again exemplifying the ideal of the travelling evangelist. At the 1787 Methodist Conference, Garrettson anticipated being designated as the general superintendent for Methodist labours in Nova Scotia and Antigua, largely because it was widely known that Wesley supported such a move. But delegates to the conference rankled at the thought that Wesley was still attempting to dictate the direction American Methodism should take and instead named Garrettson the presiding elder over Methodist work on the Delmarva peninsula.

Because Methodist strength remained concentrated in the Southern states, Asbury was particularly anxious to expand the Methodist presence in the North. Hence in 1788, he appointed Garrettson as presiding elder over much of New York State. Working with a handful of other itinerants, Garrettson traversed much of the state from Westchester County north to the Canadian border and westward through the Mohawk River valley. Many congregations in upstate New York owe their genesis to Garrettson's evangelizing activity, and later interpreters credit Garrettson as being the single most influential figure in bringing Methodism to central and western New York. But Garrettson also remained deeply involved in issues facing Methodism at large in the new nation. By 1792, American Methodism was facing internal controversy over its hierarchical polity. JAMES O'KELLY was the most prominent of those who wished to see Methodism adopt a more democratic structure. While Garrettson personally thought a congregationally-based organization would allow for more effective ministry and hence greater Methodist expansion, he nevertheless threw wholehearted support behind the decision of the 1792 General Conference (and subsequent conferences) to maintain an episcopal, hierarchical polity because he was convinced that divisiveness would seriously endanger Methodist expansion. Within the Methodist connexion, Garrettson became known as a peacemaker who insisted on placing higher priority on a united ministry than on individual preferences about how ministry could best be carried out.

In 1793, Garrettson married CATHERINE [GAR-RETTSON] LIVINGSTON, whose brother Robert was a signer of the American Declaration of Independence. Their home in Rhinebeck, New York, along the Hudson River, quickly became such a favourite gathering place for Methodist itinerants and for other evangelical preachers that it was soon dubbed 'Traveler's Rest'. From the time of his marriage, Garrettson made Rhinebeck the base of his ministerial work. From 1793 to 1803, he served as presiding elder in New York City and Philadelphia, at one point including Methodist work in New Jersey in his purview. There followed two years as pastor of the Methodist church in Rhinebeck, three again as a missionary for the conference, and then two as a pastor in New York City. In 1811, Garrettson began another three-year tenure as presiding elder over Methodist work in New York City. But by 1815, ill health required him to curtail his labours, and he was not appointed that year, nor again in 1817. By 1819, he was well enough again to be appointed as missionary of the conference and also to work with NATHAN BANGS in founding the Methodist Missionary Society. He retained appointment as an itinerant evangelist/missionary until his death.

It is difficult to underestimate Garrettson's role in early Methodist expansion in the United States. Nathan Bangs, who wrote an early biography of Garrettson, portrays him as virtually second in influence only to Asbury in Methodism's success in the early republic. That appraisal may well be accurate, for Garrettson was the archetypal Methodist itinerant whose unswerving commitment to preaching the gospel helped make Methodism the largest Protestant denomination in the United States in the first half of the nineteenth century.

SELECT WRITINGS
F. Garrettson, *A Dialogue Between Do-Justice and Professing-Christian* (Wilmington, DE, 1812)
—, *The Experience and Travels of Mr. Freeborn Garrettson* (Philadelphia, PA, 1791)
—, *American Methodist Pioneer*, ed. R. Simpson (Rutland, VT, 1984)

BIBLIOGRAPHY
AAP, 7: 54–63
N. Bangs, *The Life of the Rev. Freeborn Garrettson* (New York, 1829)
DAB
DCA
DcAmReB
EWM
NCAB: 480–1
E. S. Tipple, *Freeborn Garrettson* (New York, 1910)

CHARLES H. LIPPY

Garrison, Nicholas (b. Staten Island, New York, 1701: d. Bethlehem, Pennsylvania, 24 Sept. 1781). Moravian sea captain. Garrison, a seaman since the age of 12 and religiously minded, was invited by ZINZENDORF in 1743 to captain the Moravians' first 'congregation ship'. After reception into membership at Marienborn, Wetteravia, he purchased the *Little Strength* in London and became elder of the 132-strong 'Second Sea Congregation', comprising the crew (all Moravians except three) and colonists destined for Bethlehem, Pennsylvania. After the *Little Strength*'s capture on its return voyage, Garrison commissioned a purpose-built replacement, the *Irene*, completed in 1748. He captained it until 1756, retiring to Niesky, Saxony (1757–63) and Bethlehem (1763–81).

BIBLIOGRAPHY
Gemeinnachrichten (1837) I, 321–37

C. J. PODMORE

Garry, Nicholas (b. England *c.* 1782; d. Claygate, Surrey, England, 24 Dec. 1856). Deputy governor of the Hudson's Bay Company. Garry was the son of Isabella Garry. His father was probably Nicholas Langley, a London merchant, but he was raised by Nicholas's brother, Thomas, who became a director of the Hudson's Bay Company (HBC) in 1807. Garry followed his guardian into the company as a director in 1817. By this time he was a committed evangelical and devoted his energies to the spiritual well-being of the company's servants in Rupert's Land, North America. Together with BENJAMIN HARRISON, he convinced the CMS to provide £200 toward the establishment of a mission at the growing Red River settlement where a Roman Catholic mission was just being formed. In 1821, Garry volunteered to travel to North America to facilitate the business merger of the HBC and its rival, the North West Company. He visited the Red River settlement where he met with the prominent native leader, Peguis. With the cooperation of

HBC chaplain JOHN WEST, Garry founded the first Bible society in the north-west at York Factory. The diary which Garry kept during this voyage has become something of a classic description of fur trade society.

In 1822, Garry was appointed deputy governor of the HBC. In that position he took particular interest in the development of the Russian and Chinese trade as well as pursuing his religious goals. He married Phoebe Vesey on 4 August 1829. He was declared 'of unsound mind' in 1835 and relieved of his position with the HBC, apparently never recovering. Fort Garry (later upper Fort Garry) at Red River, Garry Lake and Garry Bay in the Canadian arctic were named in his honour.

BIBLIOGRAPHY
DCB

KERRY M. ABEL

Garwood, John A. (b. c. 1805; d. Kilburn, London, 6 Dec. 1889). Anglican clergyman and author. An Oxford graduate (matriculated October 1828 aged 23; BA 1832), Garwood was Perpetual Curate of St Mary's, Spital Square from 1832 to 1846. One of the first Anglican clergy to support the formation of the LCM in 1835, he was the first to invite it to place a 'city missionary' in his parish to work under his superintendence. In 1836 he was involved in a dispute with Bishop Blomfield, the Bishop of London, who objected to the LCM's use of lay agents and to its interdenominational character. Garwood obeyed what he understood to be Blomfield's order to withdraw from the LCM in 1836. When the religious press got hold of the story Blomfield denied any order to withdraw; Garwood rejoined the LCM in his former capacity and was again reprimanded by Blomfield. Garwood then resigned as clerical secretary but not from his membership in the LCM. Blomfield eventually moderated his position and from 1844 to 1876 Garwood served as LCM clerical secretary and as editor of the *London City Mission Magazine*, continuing as an active member of the committee until his death. Among other writings commending its work, he published in 1853 his analysis of the religious needs of London under the title, *The Million Peopled City*.

BIBLIOGRAPHY
Boase
D. M. Lewis, *Lighten Their Darkness* (Westport, CT, 1986): 61
J. M. Weylland, *Round the Tower, or the Story of the LCM* (London, 1885)

J. H. Y. BRIGGS

Gary, George (b. Middlefield, NY, USA, 8 Dec. 1793; d. NY, USA, 25 March 1855). Methodist minister. One of the youngest itinerant ministers in the history of the Methodist church, Gary was ordained by FRANCIS ASBURY at the age of 15. After serving in the New England Conference for four years, he transferred to the Genesee Conference in central New York where his

father resided. Though reticent and unemotional, Gary was widely respected. Thus, in 1818, he became a presiding elder, a position he held for much of the remainder of his life.

In 1843, Gary received a four-year appointment as superintendent of the struggling Oregon Mission, superseding JASON LEE, the founder. In accord with his instructions, Gary liquidated much of the missionary establishment in Oregon, thus effectively ending the Methodist work among the Indians there. Upon return to New York, he resumed his work in the Black River Conference. Liver disease, however, developed in 1854 and made Gary unable to continue active ministry. His exceedingly 'happy termination of life' is recorded in the writing of Z. Paddock.

BIBLIOGRAPHY
E. S. Bucke, ed., *The History of American Methodism* (New York, 1964)
EWM
Z. Paddock, *Memoir of Rev. Benjamin G. Paddock* (New York, 1875)

LYDIA H. HOYLE

Gatch, Philip (b. MD, BNA, 2 March 1751; d. 28 Dec. 1835). Early American Methodist preacher and leader. Born to Conduce and Priscilla Gatch on their farm six miles north-east of Baltimore, Philip became one of the most significant personalities in American Methodism. His conversion took place in January 1772 under the ministry of Nathan Perigau, one of ROBERT STRAWBRIDGE's local preachers. Shortly thereafter he felt compelled to become an itinerant Methodist preacher. He was present for the first annual meeting of the American preachers called by THOMAS RANKIN in Philadelphia in 1773. Gatch was especially active organizing Methodist work in New Jersey, Maryland, and Pennsylvania.

Although Gatch was responsible for attracting many people to Methodism, he did suffer opposition and persecution in his labours. He described one confrontation with a mob in Maryland who attacked him and covered him with tar as follows:

> If I ever felt for the souls of men I did for theirs; when I got to my appointment the Spirit of the Lord so overpowered me that I fell prostrate in prayer before him for my enemies. The Lord no doubt granted my request, for the man who put on the tar and several others of the party were afterwards converted.
> (Maser, 1965: 68)

On another occasion Gatch was seized by two men who

> caught hold of my arms and turned them in opposite directions with such violence that it thought my shoulders were dislocated, and it caused me the severest pain I ever felt. The torture, I concluded, must resemble that of the rack.

My shoulders were so bruised that they turned black, and it was considerable time before I recovered the use of them.
(Maser: 1965: 69)

Gatch concluded the first phase of his travelling ministry in 1778. For sometime thereafter he was a successful planter and local preacher in Virginia. He was one of the leaders of the Methodist preachers in 1779 who set about to ordain each other so they could administer the sacraments to their people. This issue threatened to divide Methodism. After considerable dispute FRANCIS ASBURY was able to get Gatch and the others who favoured ordination to suspend their action for a year. This effectively ended their plan to secure ordination in an 'irregular' manner.

Although Gatch travelled occasionally during the settled phase of his ministry in Virginia, in 1798 he moved into Ohio where he was the pastor of a circuit. It is believed that he spent the last years of his life cultivating the Methodist work in that area.

BIBLIOGRAPHY
EWM
F. B. Maser, *The Dramatic Story of Early American Methodism* (Nashville, TN, 1965)
J. McLean, *Sketch of Rev. Philip Gatch* (Cincinnati, OH, 1854)

CHARLES YRIGOYEN, JR.

Gatesman, Frederick (b. Gosport, Hampshire, England, c. 1804; d. Freetown, Sierra Leone, 23 April 1827). CMS missionary to Sierra Leone. Gatesman trained briefly at the newly opened CMS training school at Islington (London) in 1825 before being sent to Sierra Leone with the CMS. He (and apparently his wife) were sent to Leopold on 16 October 1826 but Gatesman lasted only six months. It is not known what became of his wife. Their willingness to serve in Sierra Leone is remarkable in view of the fate of other early CMS couples (*see* M. RENNER, P. HARTWIG, J. G. PRASSE, J. C. BARNETH, J. QUAST, C. H. MEISSNER, H. MEYER, J. H. SCHULZE and C. JOST).

BIBLIOGRAPHY
D. T. B[arry], *CMS Register of Missionaries and Native Clergy* (privately printed) (London, 1906)

DONALD M. LEWIS

Gauntlett, Henry (b. Market Lavington, Wiltshire, England, 15 March 1762; d. Olney, Buckinghamshire, England, 27 March 1834). Anglican clergyman. Gauntlett was educated privately and was ordained 1786 (deacon 24 September, priest 22 October) as Curate of Tilshead and Imber, Wiltshire. In 1800 he married Arabella Jenkinson. Between 1800 and 1804 he served as Curate of Botley, Hampshire. In April 1804 Sir RICHARD HILL appointed him Curate of Wellington, Shropshire. In the following March, objecting to the Anglican baptismal service, he considered seceding. Instead, in October

1805, he became Minister of Castle Street 'Anglican' Chapel in Reading. In 1807 he became Curate of Nettlebed and Pishill, Oxfordshire and in January 1811 Curate (Vicar in 1815) of Olney, Buckinghamshire, where he remained until his death.

Although Gauntlett was a respected clergyman within evangelical Anglican circles he remained somewhat restless throughout his career. He was particularly vocal in his opposition to the prophetic speculations of LEWIS WAY. Between 1818 and 1823 he was responsible for educating five probationer-missionaries for the CMS, including MICHAEL WILKINSON, JOHN RABAN, DAVID T. JONES and ISAAC WILSON, taking over a role which THOMAS SCOTT had relinquished in 1814 and which was rendered obsolete with the founding of the CMS College at Islington in 1825.

BIBLIOGRAPHY
H. Allon, *Memoir of the Rev. James Sherman* (London, 1863)
Annual Register (1834)
D. T. B[arry], *CMS Register of Missionaries And Native Clergy from 1804 to 1904* (privately printed) (London, 1906)
C. T. Gauntlett, ed., *Sermons* 2 vols (London, 1835)
Index Ecclesiasticus

GRAYSON CARTER AND DONALD M. LEWIS

Gaussen, (François-Samuel-Robert) Louis (b. Geneva, 25 Aug. 1790; d. Geneva, 18 June 1863). Genevan Reformed pastor and professor of theology. After completing a degree in theology Gaussen was ordained (1814) in the Church of Geneva. In 1816 he married Caroline-Philippine Lullin, but a year later she had an untimely death; he never remarried. At the same time he attended the Bible teachings of the travelling Scot, ROBERT HALDANE. Convinced of the need to return to an orthodox Calvinism, Gaussen laboured to reform the Church of Geneva from within. For 12 years, 1816–28, Gaussen was a pastor in Satigny (Geneva). In 1819 he co-edited, with the elder orthodox pastor J. I. S. Cellérier, the 1566 *Second Helvetic Confession*, stressing the need and utility of a confession of faith. Another project he hoped would reform the church was the 'Society of Missions' which he helped to establish in 1821. By 1825, however, Gaussen came into greater conflict with the Socinian leadership in the church, which eventually led to his dimission as a preacher in 1832, together with GALLAND and MERLE D'AUBIGNÉ.

Gaussen's greatest achievement came in 1831 with the founding of the 'Evangelical Society of Geneva'. With the support of prominent Genevans and international groups, especially through the *Réveil* (Awakening), he established an important organization which was to become one of the key supports of the evangelical movement on the continent. The society, under the direction of Gaussen and Merle d'Aubigné, opened an 'Evangelical School of Theology' in 1832 – Gaussen taught there from 1834 to 1863. European-wide interest for this school can be demonstrated by the monetary gifts, especially from English-speaking evangelicals (over 70,000 francs).

Gaussen became known to many English-speaking evangelicals with the publication of his defence of biblical inerrancy, *Theopneustia* (Paris, 1840; London, 1841 – with numerous editions), and *The Canon of the Holy Scriptures Examined in the Light of History*, 2 vols (Lausanne, 1860; London, 1862). In addition, over 25 of his discourses and sermons have been translated into English. He is also known for his prophetic studies and his interest in catechism and the Sunday school movement; e.g. *The Prophet Daniel, Considered in a Series of Lessons, for a Sunday-School* (London, 1840). He supported the Anti-papal movement with *Geneva and Rome* (Edinburgh, London, New York, 1844).

BIBLIOGRAPHY
L. Froom, *The Prophetic Faith of Our Fathers* (Washington, DC, 1946–54)
H. de Goltz, *Genève Religieuse* (Geneva, 1862)
G. Mützenberg, 'L. Gaussen,' in *Genève Protestante*, ed. O. Fatio (Geneva, 1983): 67–89

JOHN BURTON RONEY

Gavin, (Abram) Daniel (b. Brenles, Switzerland, 8 April 1805; d. Sabrevois, Quebec, 18 April 1855). Missionary and teacher. Converted in the HALDANE revivals, he trained as a medical missionary and worked among the Sioux. He was 'much esteemed and beloved' because of his pains to learn the Sioux and Dakotah language and culture. In June 1839 at Wisconsin he married LUCY CORNELIA [GAVIN] STEVENS, a missionary teacher, and in July 1840 at Quincy he was ordained by Congregationalist ministers. Proceeding to Canada in 1846, he taught at Grande Ligne but soon disagreed with Mme FELLER's transfer to the Baptists. He valued 'wholesome tradition', and was received by the Anglicans in 1847; AMELIA M. CHRISTIE guaranteed the French mission's expenses at Sabrevois.

Gavin believed that people were best won to faith by example, and freely invited them into his life. His Bible classes were well attended and the mission grew around its fine schools. He authored some tracts which have not survived. After his death, his widow was the focus of unity for some years.

BIBLIOGRAPHY
R. M. Black, 'A Crippled Crusade ... 1835–1868,' (Univ. of Toronto, unpublished Th.D. thesis, 1989)

ROBERT MERRILL BLACK

Gavin, (Lucy) Cornelia [née Stevens, Lucy; Sister Cornelia SGS] (b. Peterboro, NY, USA, *c.* 1818; d. Baltimore, MD, USA, 8 Sept. 1872). Missionary and teacher. Follower of GERRIT SMITH, at 16 she left the 'burned over district' of New York for labour in Wisconsin; she married ABRAM DANIEL GAVIN, a Swiss missionary. Her health failed while teaching, nursing, and assisting in production of a Dakotah dictionary. Coming to French

Canada, the family adhered to the Anglican church in 1847. She shared her husband's ministry at Sabrevois; their groups of young people were models of Christian equality. Her influence continued after his death. Moving to Virginia in 1861, she opened a school which failed during the war. Impoverished, she was won to an Episcopalian nursing order, the Good Shepherd sisters.

Gavin believed that conversion required a simple decision, followed by good works. She rejected any gap between rhetoric and righteous behaviour, and represents an early and hard-won feminism seeking to maintain evangelicalism's radical self-sacrifice. When her order moved to St Louis her remains were reinterred there.

BIBLIOGRAPHY
R. M. Black 'A Crippled Crusade ... 1835–1868' (Univ. of Toronto, unpublished Th.D. thesis 1989)

ROBERT MERRILL BLACK

Geddie, John (b. Banff, Scotland, 10 April 1815; d. Geelong, Australia, 14 Dec. 1872). Canadian Presbyterian to New Hebrides. His father, John Geddie, clockmaker, was influenced by the HALDANES. His mother, Mary Menzies, was of Secession stock. The family emigrated to Pictou, Nova Scotia, 1816, and joined Prince Street Presbyterian Church where Geddie made his profession of faith on 22 June 1834. He studied in Pictou Academy, then took theological training. Restored from illness, he resolved to become a missionary. The Presbyterian Church of the Lower Provinces of British North America stemmed from the United Secession Church of Scotland which had dealings with the LMS. Geddie was licensed by the presbytery of Pictou, 2 May 1837 and ordained and inducted to Cavendish, Prince Edward Island, 13 March 1838. On 21 September he married Miss Charlotte McDonald, daughter of Dr Alexander McDonald of Antigonish.

Fired by LMS reports, Geddie roused his denomination to a concern for foreign missions. In 1845 the church selected West Polynesia as its field. Geddie was appointed the first missionary and sailed with his family in a whaler from Halifax on 30 November 1846, via Cape Horn. Geddie had learned printing, building, plastering and rudiments of medicine. Seven months with the LMS in Samoa enabled him to learn Samoan and observe missionary methods in Polynesia. He sought LMS advice on his field. The *John Williams* sailed for New Caledonia but adverse winds brought her to Aneityum, southernmost island in the New Hebrides, where they landed on 29 July 1848. A French Roman Catholic mission preceded them, but left in 1852. LMS teachers had been on Aneityum since 1841. Aneityum then had about 4,000 people, speaking one language, scattered along the 35 miles of coastline and in the mountains, and given to 'all the abominations of heathenism ... May the time to favour this dark island soon arrive' (Geddie's first journal entry, 29 July 1848).

Geddie's principles were biblical, indigenous and far-sighted. He moved modestly among the islanders, respected their *tapus* and won their respect. He survived malaria, murder-plots, and hurricanes, and the church was born on 13 May 1852 when 13 'well-known and long-tried natives' were baptized with the concurrence of the LMS. Geddie worked towards a self-governing church, nourished with literacy aids, Bible translations and other helps. JOHN INGLIS's arrival in 1852 proved decisive. The first case of discipline was dealt with by the church in 1853, first deacons were elected in 1856, the authority of the traditional chiefs gained church recognition in 1854. They ruled that no more women be hired to trading crews. In 1859 the population was 3,513 with 297 communicants, 56 village schools and 11 area churches. These were self-supporting. In 1860 the first elders were ordained after popular election. Geddie asked for permission to form a presbytery of the southern islands, but the home churches in Canada and Scotland demurred. His policy of indigenization, receiving this setback, waned after his death. Mission control took its place.

Geddie and Inglis trained the converts for leadership and office. A passion to go out to the unevangelized islands gripped the converts. Some were martyred. All were married men of note. By 1860 23 couples were away as missionaries. The Geddies took furlough in Canada, 1863–6. He received the DD of Queen's College, Kingston. He was grieved that JOHN G. PATON had sought British naval help in redressing injuries to the mission. After 1866 he devoted his energies to pushing the frontiers of the mission further north. Two daughters married missionaries, Neilson of Tanna and Macdonald of Efate. Geddie suffered a stroke on Aneityum on 12 June 1872 and died in December. The Mission Synod spoke of him as 'the venerable father of the mission,' and the Presbyterian Church of Vanuatu today sees him as its founder. The epitaph in the stone church at Anelgauhat, Aneityum, read: 'When he landed in 1848 there were no Christians here; when he left in 1872 there were no heathens'. Mrs Geddie died in Melbourne in 1916 aged 93.

BIBLIOGRAPHY
J. Inglis, *In the New Hebrides* (London, 1887)
J. G. Miller, *Live, A History of the Church Planting in the New Hebrides*, 1–3 (Sydney, 1978–85)
R. S. Miller, *Misi Gete, John Geddie, Pioneer Missionary to the New Hebrides* (Launceston, Tasmania, 1975)
G. Patterson, *Missionary Life Among the Cannibals* (Toronto, 1882)

J. GRAHAM MILLER

Geden, John Drury (b. Hastings, Sussex, England, 4 May 1822; d. Didsbury, Lancashire, England, ʻ9 March 1886). Wesleyan minister and periodical editor. His father, John, a Wesleyan minister, sent him to Kingswood grammar school near Bristol (1830–6). After an interim of private study he attended the Wesleyan theological college at Richmond, Surrey (1844–7). He was then made assistant tutor of sacred and classical languages (1847–51). In 1856 he was appointed professor of Hebrew and classics at Didsbury, Lancashire, from which position he retired in 1883. St Andrews University awarded him an honorary DD in 1885.

Between his appointments at Richmond and Didsbury, Geden was active in the ministry, in 1851 as a colleague of W. M. Punshon at Newcastle-upon-Tyne, then for one year on the neighbouring circuit of Durham, and finally three on the Manchester (Oxford Road) circuit.

An occasional contributor to the Methodist literary periodical, *London Quarterly Review*, in the period 1857–62 he was assistant editor. The Wesleyan Conference saw fit to publish his 'Doctrine of a Future Life' (1874) in which he defended the Old Testament as a source of doctrine. His *Didsbury Sermons* (1878), delivered at the college chapel, were also published. He was elected into the Wesleyan executive Legal Hundred (1868), was a member of the 1870 Old Testament revision committee, and of the EA. Widely respected as a Methodist scholar and writer, Geden's broad range of interests included oriental literature, philology, philosophy, and natural science.

BIBLIOGRAPHY
Boase
DNB
T. Cooper, ed., *Men of the Time* 10th edn (London, 1879)
WI, IV

PAUL PERONE AND JONATHAN BURKE
CUTMORE

Gedge, Sydney (b. probably Bury St Edmunds, Suffolk, England, 3 April 1802; d. Cromer, Norfolk, England, 29 Aug. 1883). Anglican clergyman and noted CMS supporter. He was the third son of Peter Gedge who began the *Bury Post* and wad educated at King Edward's School, Bury St Edmunds and at St Catherine's College, Cambridge (BA 1824; MA 1827; fellow 1825–7). After Cambridge he abandoned the legal profession and was ordained (deacon and priest 1826). He served for many years as second master of the famous King Edward's School, Birmingham (1835–59). He then became Vicar of All Saints, Northampton (1859–75). In his retirement he moved nearer to Dorking and was able to be even more involved in CMS affairs. A daughter, Mary, became a CMS missionary while a son, Sydney, was a Liberal MP and also a long-serving CMS committee member.

BIBLIOGRAPHY
Al. Cant.
DNB

C. PETER WILLIAMS

Geeting, George Adam (b. Nieder Schelden, Prussia, 6 Feb. 1741; d. near Baltimore, MD, USA, 28 June 1812). Early leader of the United Brethren in Christ. Geeting was second in importance only to MARTIN BOEHM as a colleague of PHILIP WILLIAM OTTERBEIN in the formation of the Church of the United Brethren in Christ, the largest denomination that developed from the flames of German-American evangelicalism.

Geeting was reared as the youngest child in a family that adhered to the faith of the German Reformed church. He migrated to Maryland as an 18-year-old labourer, and lived the rest of his life in a small community of German immigrants on the Antietam River (Washington County). Having received a modest education in Germany, Geeting now assumed the role of the village schoolmaster, in addition to quarrying stone and digging wells.

The village had frequently been visited by German Reformed pastors from nearby Frederick, among whom was Otterbein, who met Geeting during his preaching visits here that began in 1760. Being converted under Otterbein's ministry, Geeting became beloved to Otterbein as Timothy was to St Paul. After Otterbein moved to York, Pennsylvania, in 1765, there was a cessation of the visits to the Antietam by Reformed pastors. As a consequence, Geeting was invited in 1772 to read sermons from books of homilies by Reformed pastors, such as those that were to be published by Otterbein's brothers who remained as pastors in Germany. Otterbein, upon hearing about his efforts, directed that the brethren should discreetly take the book of homilies from him on the next sabbath, in order that his sermon might take the form of an extemporary witness. The deed was done and, after a momentary hesitation, Geeting proceeded to give an impressive, heartfelt exhortation.

After serving during the next decade as the informal leader of the Antietam church, that remained nondenominational despite its German Reformed leaning, Geeting was informally consecrated to the ministry on Pentecost, 1783, by Otterbein and a pastoral colleague, William Hendel. Five years later Geeting received formal ordination by the Reformed Coetus (synod).

In his person, Geeting was hearty in constitution, neat in dress, sensitive toward the spiritual condition of his hearers, studious, and in his preaching he was regarded as earnest and inspiring. Lacking Otterbein's European theological training, he was more exclusively a product of the frontier revivals that preceded the Second Great Awakening in America. He accompanied Otterbein on numerous preaching journeys and 'big meetings', during which they shared intimately in prayer and conversation. These trips required frequent partings from his wife and ten children.

The first meeting house of the Otterbein-Boehm movement was built on Geeting's property on the Antietam before 1774. The log structure, that became known as the Geeting meeting house, was the centre of informal religious society for whom Geeting served *ad hoc* as pastor, although his ministry remained largely itinerant.

Due to their increasing involvement with the budding United Brethren movement that had its roots in the Otterbein-Boehm meeting of 1767 and had received new impetus after the Revolutionary War, Geeting and Otterbein were irregular in their attendance of the annual sessions of the Reformed Synod in the 1790s. Geeting was one of the few Reformed pastors who remained active in the Otterbein-Boehm movement after the war, and he emerged as a leader of this movement at its meeting that was held at Otterbein's Baltimore parsonage in 1789. As a consequence, Geeting, who also had not received formal theological training, was expelled 'without delay' from the Reformed Synod in 1804.

Geeting's efforts on behalf of the United Brethren were untiring, and his zeal for souls was unwavering, despite the opposition he encountered. There is an unsubstantiated tradition that he was elected to be the third bishop of the United Brethren in Christ in 1812. His death occurred in 1812 during a trip that he had made with his wife to visit Otterbein, his revered mentor. When Methodist Bishop FRANCIS ASBURY learned of his death, the bishop exclaimed that Geeting was 'the most splendid orator among the United Brethren in Christ'.

BIBLIOGRAPHY

A. W. Drury, *History of the Church of the United Brethren in Christ* (Dayton, OH, 1924)

P. E. Holdcraft, *History of the Pennsylvania Conference of the United Brethren in Christ* (Fayetteville, PA, 1938)

J. Lawrence, *The History of the Church of the United Brethren in Christ* (Dayton, OH, 1868)

J. STEVEN O'MALLEY

Gell, Philip (b. Hopton, Derbyshire, England, 1783; d. Duffield, Derbyshire, England, 7 Jan. 1870). Anglican clergyman. Gell came of a Derbyshire squirearchical family and was educated under Heyrick at Leicester before proceeding to Trinity College, Cambridge in 1800 (scholar 1802; BA 1805; MA 1808). He was Curate of Matlock and then Perpetual Curate of Rocester (Staffordshire) from 1812 to around 1820, and of St John's, Derby from 1829 to 1846. He assisted W. A. SHIRLEY at All Saints', Derby in 1836 and was assistant lecturer there from 1850 to 1852. He was a leading member of Matlock Bath Clerical Society. He sent his sons to Rugby under Arnold, one – Frederick (1820–1902) – being for 38 years Bishop of Madras and the other – John Philip (1816–98) – serving in Tasmania before taking up a living in England in 1854.

Gell published a popular *Church Hymn Book* (1826) which reached its seventeenth edition by 1860. In that year he also published his *Thoughts on the Liturgy*, seeking revision based largely on his discontent with some of the expressions in the service of baptism. He contributed *The Second Coming and the Millennial Reign of the Saints* (1853) to the millennialist controversies and he also wrote *The Revelation of the Second Coming of Jesus Christ* (1854). Gell was an accomplished classicist and Hebraist.

BIBLIOGRAPHY
Al. Cant., II, iii: 32
Boase, V: 305
British Library Catalogue

ARTHUR POLLARD

Genähr, Ferdinand (d. near Hong Kong, 6 August 1864). China missionary. Genähr was one of the first missionaries to live in China outside of the five treaty ports. He served in China from 1847 to 1864 as a pioneer missionary under the Rhenish Missionary Society, and for a time also in association with KARL GÜTZLAFF. Aware of Gützlaff's limitations he adopted Chinese dress and worked in one place to train Chinese preachers. He evangelized and established schools in several small, rural villages near Canton, except from 1856 to 1858 when he was interrupted by Great Britain's war with China. He and two sons died from cholera contracted from a sick woman he took into his home.

BIBLIOGRAPHY
A. Wylie, *Memorials of Protestant Missionaries to the Chinese* (Shanghai, 1867): 161–3

RALPH R. COVELL

George, David (b. Essex county, VA, BNA, 1743; d. Sierra Leone, 1810). African-American Baptist missionary. Escaping Virginian slavery to live among Indians, George was resold into slavery to George Galphin in South Carolina. GEORGE LIELE's sermon on Matthew 11: 28 converted him. White Baptist preacher Wait Palmer baptized him into the Silver Bluff Church just before the American Revolution. When the British occupied Savannah, Georgia, George took about fifty slaves into loyalist lines and reconnected with Liele. With the British evacuation of Charleston, South Carolina, George and his wife Phillis moved to Nova Scotia where he formed seven Baptist churches. Migrating to Sierra Leone in January 1792, he travelled with the organizer of the African expedition, JOHN CLARKSON, to England. There he dictated his memoirs to JOHN RIPPON. After his return, George held minor civil posts and served a Baptist congregation in Sierra Leone.

BIBLIOGRAPHY
S. R. Frey, *Water for the Rock* (Princeton, NJ, 1991)
G. Gordon, *From Slavery to Freedom* (Hantsport, NS, 1992)
J. Rippon, ed., *The Baptist Annual Register* (1792): 473–84
E. G. Wilson, *The Loyal Blacks* (New York, 1976)

LINDA GLENN AND WILL GRAVELY

George, Enoch (b. Lancaster Co., VA, BNA, 1767 or 1768; d. Staunton, VA, USA, 23 Aug. 1828). American Methodist Episcopal Bishop. Although his father was 'wordly and irreligious', George's family apparently attended DEVEREAUX JARRETT's Anglican parish church in Dinwiddie county, Virginia, before moving to North Carolina when Enoch was still a boy. In North Carolina he became disillusioned with Christianity because of an allegedly immoral minister. Later, however, he was converted through John Easter, a Methodist preacher. George was licensed to preach by Bishop ASBURY (*c.* 1788/9) who sent him to help establish a circuit on the Catawba and Broad Rivers in North Carolina. He was tempted to withdraw from such a difficult assignment but Asbury spurred him on by letter; in 1790 he was admitted on trial to preach in the Pamlico circuit in North Carolina.

In 1792 he was ordained a Deacon and admitted into full connexion, serving on several circuits in the Carolinas until 1798 when his health forced him to locate. He opened a school until he recovered his strength, then rejoined the preaching circuit; in 1800 he was made Presiding Elder of the large Patomic District but within a year he located again. He married and had several children but in 1803 he yet again returned to the itineracy and served for a dozen years as Presiding Elder of several districts.

The death of his wife in 1816 devastated him, but later that year he was elected delegate to the General Conference, the highest legislative body of the church. Enoch George was one of two men elected Bishop by the General Conference (Bishop Asbury died shortly before the conference, and Bishop MCKENDREE was in poor health). George proved to be an able and competent bishop. A good administrator, he was also a disarming preacher.

George served the rest of his life as a bishop, touring a wide range of districts. He died while on a tour of the Southern Conferences.

BIBLIOGRAPHY
AAP
EWM

KENNETH N. PEARSON

Gerber, John (b. Berne, Switzerland). *Fl.* 1820s. CMS missionary to Sierra Leone. Gerber studied at Basel Seminary and was ordained as a Lutheran minister. He then studied at the National School system in England and on 8 November 1822 was sent by the CMS to Sierra Leone with C. W. BECKHAUER and two other couples (*see* W. H. SCHEMEL and J. BUNYER), serving successively at Kissey, Bathurst and Bananas. His first wife, Magdalena Haug of Tübingen, died in Sierra Leone in May of 1825. (Apart from her husband, she was the last of the original seven to die.) In 1827 Gerber returned to Europe for nine months and married Maria Wagner who died in December 1828. Gerber left Sierra Leone for good in February 1832 and ended his association with the CMS in 1833. His third wife was Eleanora Sessing. The Gerbers' willingness to serve in Sierra Leone is remarkable in light of the fate of earlier CMS missionary couples (*see* M. RENNER, P. HARTWIG, J. G. PRASSE, J. C. BARNETH, J.

GERICKE, CHRISTIAN WILHELM

QUAST, C. H. MEISSNER, H. MEYER, J. H. SCHULZE and C. JOST).

BIBLIOGRAPHY
D. T. B[arry], CMS Register of Missionaries and Native Clergy (privately printed) (London, 1906)

DONALD M. LEWIS

Gericke, Christian Wilhelm (b. Colberg, Pomerania, 5 April 1742; d. Vellore, India, 3 Oct. 1803). Missionary to India. Little is known about his background. But, in 1760, he began theological studies at Halle University and then worked at the Francke girls' school as a teacher and inspector. Called by the SPCK to serve in its Indian mission, he went to London in 1766; and, after a perilous voyage, reached his post in Cuddalore the following year. The French occupation had left the mission in a shambles. Only one European worker, G. H. C. Hüttemann, remained. Gericke helped him start a new church and married Hüttemann's daughter Anna Sophia. At the same time he began a fruitful itinerant ministry, with some success in winning Roman Catholics.

However, drought and famine followed by an attack by the combined forces of the French and Hyder Ali in 1781 again devastated the work at Cuddalore. During these trying times Gericke functioned both as a diplomat and pastor to people of various nationalities. In 1787 he was instrumental in opening an 'asylum' (home) for orphan girls at Madras. The next year he took charge of the Vepery Mission in Madras, due to the deteriorating health of its leader J. P. FABRICIUS. But he continued visiting the other stations in the region. Incessant travelling, coupled with trauma resulting from deaths of his two children and his mentor C. F. SCHWARTZ (who had made him the trustee of the Tanjore and Tinnevelly missions), left him broken in body and spirit. Still he pressed on with his preaching and teaching of converts until he died at Vellore in 1803. Besides his work as an itinerant missionary, Gericke derived income from his position as an East India Company chaplain, as secretary of the girls' home, and as pastor of European congregations. His modest estate was left as an endowment for the Vepery Mission. He spent 37 years without a home leave. His passing marked the ending of an era when Germans from Halle served with the SPCK in India.

SELECT WRITINGS
C. W. Gericke, Hrn. Missionarii Gerickens merkwürdige Seereise von London nach Ceylon und Cudelur in den Jahren 1766 und 1767 (Halle, 1773)

BIBLIOGRAPHY
Anon., Lives of Missionaries, Southern India (London, 1863)
J. F. Fenger, History of the Tranquebar Mission (Tranquebar, India, 1863)
J. Hough, The History of Christianity in India, 3 (London, 1845)
F. Penny, The Church in Madras, 1 (London, 1904)
R. Vornbaum, Evangelische Missionsgeschichte in Biographien (Düsseldorf, 1852)

A. Westcott, Our Oldest Indian Mission (Madras, India, 1847)

R. V. PIERARD

Gibbs, Michael (b. London, 1812; d. London, 19 Jan. 1882). Anglican clergyman. Gibbs was the son of Michael Gibbs of Walworth, Surrey. He was admitted to Caius College, Cambridge in 1830 (scholar 1832–4; prizeman; BA [tenth wrangler] 1835; MA 1838; fellow 1837–43). He was ordained (deacon 1836; priest 1837) and served as Curate of Barrington, Cambridgeshire from 1836 to 1838 and lecturer of All Saints', Cambridge, 1837–9 and of St Andrew-by-the-Wardrobe, London, and St Anne's, Blackfriars, 1843. From 1842 to 1882 he was Vicar of Christ Church, Newgate Street, London, and was chaplain to his father when he served as Lord Mayor of London in 1844/5.

The reporters for The Times described Gibbs to their editor in 1844 as follows: 'A son of the Lord Mayor. V[ery] much esteemed by his brother clergy, but rather shunned by the influential laity by the bad odour of his name. Is decidedly an active, zealous clergyman & v. "low church" in his opinions. Abhors Tractarian heresy.' Gibbs was a strong supporter of the Young Men's Society for Aiding Missions.

BIBLIOGRAPHY
Al. Cant.
Boase
Bodleian Library, Oxford, 'The Principal Clergy of London . . . prepared for Mr. Delane, Edtr. of The Times', (1844) Add. manuscript c. 290

DONALD M. LEWIS

Gibson, David (b. Irvine, Ayrshire, Scotland, 24 Aug. 1777; d. Auchencairn, Kirkcudbrightshire, Scotland, 22 Oct. 1853). Baptist home missionary. Gibson was one of the men from GEORGE BARCLAY's congregation who was sent out by the Baptist Itinerant Society at its formation in 1808. He settled in the south-west, and eventually found a centre for his activities in the village of Auchencairn, where a chapel was built in 1822, although the church was not formed until 1839. From 1824 he was aided by the Baptist Home Missionary Society. He itinerated widely in Galloway, and his diary shows a keen interest in such events as the Disruption. The church ceased on his death.

BIBLIOGRAPHY
G. Yuille, History of the Baptists in Scotland (Glasgow, 1926)

DEREK B. MURRAY

Gibson, James (b. London, 1786; d. Worlington rectory, Suffolk, England, 4 Oct. 1850). College tutor and Anglican clergyman. Son of James Gibson (gentleman), he was admitted to Wadham College, Oxford, in 1803. Hody exhibitioner 1804–9, he was fellow of Wadham

1812–19, serving college offices 1813–17. Thus he shared in the rise of the college as an evangelical stronghold in Oxford. Ordained in 1812 he was appointed a chaplain of the Lock Hospital, London, succeeding THOMAS FRY. Vacating his fellowship by marriage in 1818, he became also Rector of Worlington, a small Suffolk village, holding the living till death. He continued to serve at the Lock till 1838, when the congregation moved to an episcopal chapel nearby, where Gibson continued to minister till 1846.

SELECT WRITINGS
J. Gibson, *Sermons* (London, 1851)

BIBLIOGRAPHY
GM, new series, 34 (1850)
J. S. Reynolds, *Evangelicals at Oxford* (Oxford, 1953; Appleford, England, 1975)

J. S. REYNOLDS

Gibson, Mary Ann Sanderson. *See* DECK, MARY ANN SANDERSON

Gibson, Timothy (b. *c.* 1793; d. London, 2 Feb. 1864). Anglican clergyman. Gibson was ordained (deacon 1836, priest 1837) and in 1837 was instituted Perpetual Curate of Ash, near Whitchurch, Shropshire in 1838. Four years later he moved to the capital to become Senior Curate and afternoon lecturer of St Matthew's, Bethnal Green. In the absence of the non-resident rector, he had the immediate charge of some 8,000 souls. The contemporary manuscript 'Principal Clergy of London Classified . . . prepared for . . . *The Times*' (1844, Bodleian Library, Oxford) identifies him as 'decidedly evangelical' and a 'very popular preacher'. He was at various times also lecturer at St George's, Southwark and at Allhallows, Lombard Street. In 1861 he was instituted as Rector of St Matthew's, and the *Clergy List* for 1862 records him as a DD. He published several of his sermons and a defence of conformity.

BIBLIOGRAPHY
Crockford (1860)

D. B. HINDMARSH

Gibson, Tobias (b. on Great Pee Dee River, SC, BNA, 10 November 1771; d. Warren County, MS, USA, 5 April 1804). Methodist preacher. Gibson's known history begins with his admission on trial to the South Carolina Conference of the MEC in 1792. He travelled circuits in this state, North Carolina, and Tennessee. In January, 1799 Bishop FRANCIS ASBURY appointed him to the Natchez Country in Mississippi.

From his starting point in South Carolina to Nashville, Tennessee was some 600 miles. There he sold his horse and purchased a canoe. The rest of the journey to his mission appointment was by river, down the Cumberland to the Ohio and on to the Mississippi, another 600 to 800 miles. Nearly all of his river travel was unaccompanied. He landed at Natchez about the last of March.

Gibson had no colleagues in this Natchez Mission, but several Gibson families, relatives of his from South Carolina, were already in the region, near Washington and Natchez. He travelled the territory from the thirty-first parallel latitude to just above the present city of Vicksburg. In October he performed a wedding in a home some 12 miles from Natchez. At the close of 1799 he reported sixty members. He could count eighty at the end of 1800 and 100 in his final report to South Carolina.

From 1799 to 1802 Gibson's Natchez Mission was attached to the Georgia district of the South Carolina Conference. The Georgia district presiding elder never visited him and Gibson continued to work alone. When in 1802 the work was named the Natchez circuit and put in the Cumberland district of the Western Conference, Gibson was able once more to attend annual conference sessions each October. He was present for the 1802 and 1803 meetings of the Western Conference, near Gallatin, Tennessee (Strother's meeting house) and near Cynthiana, Kentucky (Mount Gerizim Church) respectively. Even the reduced distance to annual conference was formidable; 600 miles one way, much of it through territory feared to be unsafe for whites.

Moses Floyd volunteered to go with Gibson to the Natchez country from the 1802 Western Conference, and the following year Bishop Asbury sent two more preachers, Hezekiah Harriman and Abraham Amos. Gibson had reported only 87 members at the close of 1802, but 1803 was a year of significant emigration into the territory.

Gibson's personal life was dominated by struggle against ill health. This enemy reduced his effectiveness in ministry, cost him his opportunity for marriage, and ended his life while he was still young. His health suffered from the exposure of itinerant life even before 1799. When Floyd joined him, Gibson agreed to be a supernumerary and to take the junior status on the circuit. He refused to superannuate and be left without appointment.

Gibson fell in love with Sarah Griffing, a daughter of one of the first families to entertain him and to join one of his small societies. It seems that sometime in late 1803 they made a commitment to marriage, but Gibson's rapidly deteriorating condition fatally intervened. An unrelated but poignant footnote to this story is that Sarah too died later in 1804.

Gibson died at the residence of his sister-in-law, the widow of his brother Nathaniel, on Big Bayou in Warren County, Mississippi. The site of his burial, about six miles south-west of Vicksburg, was forgotten and nearly lost forever. In 1856, however, owing to the assistance of the African-American man who had dug the missionary's grave, Gibson family descendants identified it and erected a monument.

Gibson inherited some slaves, whom he emancipated. So far as we know, he did not challenge the institution of slavery as part of his evangelistic proclamation. Like Methodism generally in the new USA, the Natchez mission was biracial. There may be a cryptic message in some of the membership returns during and just after Gibson's service. The first time he gave membership statistics by racial category was in 1802 when the membership had dropped from 100 to 87. Of the 87, two were African-American. Then in 1804 the mission gained 60 African-American members and lost 26 whites.

Gibson is a primary example of the youthful Methodist Episcopal preachers of the period of the new nation in USA history. Hundreds of them gave the best years of their young adulthood to establish Christian communities in the scattered and thinly populated outposts of white settlement. It cannot be denied that Gibson consciously laid down his life in response to this vocation. When his South Carolina colleagues learned of his death some of them said that Gibson preached, professed, possessed and practised Christian perfection.

BIBLIOGRAPHY
AAP
J. G. Jones, and E. R, Williams, Jr, *A Complete History of Methodism as Connected with the Mississippi Conference of the Methodist Episcopal Church, South, Vols. I & II, 1799–1845* (Baton Rouge, LA, 1966)
Minutes

CHARLES W. BROCKWELL, JR

Gifford, Andrew (b. Bristol, England, 17 Aug. 1700; d. London, 19 June 1784). Baptist minister, numismatist and antiquary. After pastoral service in Nottingham and Bristol he moved to Little Wild St, London, in 1730. A division in the church led to the formation of a new church at Eagle Street, in 1736, where he remained till his death. He was a forceful, evangelical preacher, loved by his congregation. He was not popular among his fellow ministers, however. He had links with the evangelical movement through his friendship with WHITEFIELD and HOWELL HARRIS.

A man of wide interests, Gifford was known for his collection of coins and books. He bequeathed a Tyndale New Testament to Bristol Baptist College. He was a freeman of Edinburgh, a DD of Aberdeen and a sublibrarian of the British Museum.

BIBLIOGRAPHY
DNB
L. G. Champion, *Farthing Rushlight* (London, 1961)

E. F. CLIPSHAM

Gilbee, Earle (b. Southwark, London, 1764; d. Barby, Northamptonshire, England, 3 Oct. 1813). Anglican clergyman. Gilbee was a member of University College, Oxford (BA 1786; MA 1797; BD and DD 1800), who became Vicar of Barby (1795–1813). He is said to have been noted for his 'manly, simple and impressive sermons'. He was a supporter of the CMS and preached its anniversary sermon in 1812.

BIBLIOGRAPHY
Al. Ox. II, 525
Evangelical Magazine, XXI (1813): 422

ARTHUR POLLARD

Gilbert, Ann (b. Cornwall, England, c. 1735; d. Cornwall, England, 18 July 1790). Preacher, class/band leader. Although converted under the preaching of Mr Williams (1743) Ann was not 'fully awakened' till 1760. She found great blessing in her class meetings and then in 1771 she went to the preaching in a neighbouring village. However, as the preacher did not arrive Gilbert gave out a hymn, led the people in prayer and then felt 'constrained to entreat and beseech them to repent and turn to the Lord'. Many were converted. After this Gilbert quite often exhorted in services with considerable effect. At one stage she consulted JOHN WESLEY about her ministry and he gave her his blessing, 'Sister do all the good you can'. Gilbert did not have an easy life and lost several of her children. She dictated her experience, having been blind for several years.

BIBLIOGRAPHY
AM (1795)
Z. Taft, *Biographical Sketches of ... Holy Women ... ,* 1 (London, 1825)

E. DOROTHY GRAHAM

Gilbert, Jeremiah (b. Cauton, Nottinghamshire, England, 1789; d. Chesterfield, Derbyshire, England, 30 Dec. 1852). Primitive Methodist pioneer. Gilbert was brought up a Wesleyan but, after attending a camp meeting, joined the Primitive Methodists and began to preach for them in 1819. He is best known as the instigator of the work in Sheffield, where he suffered much persecution but where a circuit was formed in 1820. He later missioned Chesterfield, Bolsover, Rotherham and Doncaster, and served in North Shields with much success (1823–5). His later ministry was spent mainly in the North East and the East Midlands. He retired to Chesterfield in 1847.

BIBLIOGRAPHY
Obituary, *Minutes of the Primitive Methodist Conference* (1853)
Primitive Methodist Magazine (1899): 923

IAN SELLERS

Gilbert, Joseph (b. Wrangle, Lincolnshire, England, 20 March 1779; d. Nottingham, England, 12 Dec. 1852). Independent minister. And **Ann** (née Taylor) (b. London, 30 Jan. 1782; d. Nottingham, England, 20 Dec. 1866).

Writer. The son of a staunch churchman converted by JOHN WESLEY, Joseph Gilbert read widely in controversial divinity while an apprentice, his faith gradually deepening. He worked as a shop assistant and proprietor in East Retford, Nottinghamshire, but gave up his business in 1806, training for the Independent ministry under EDWARD WILLIAMS at Rotherham College. While still a student he was commissioned to produce a defence of Williams's views and he later wrote his official biography. After an 18-month ministry in Southend, Essex, he returned to Rotherham in 1810 as classical tutor.

The eldest daughter of ISAAC TAYLOR of Ongar, Ann published well-received volumes of children's verse with her sister JANE TAYLOR and contributed to the *Eclectic Review*. Her writing so impressed Gilbert that, following the death of his first wife, he proposed even before they met. In December 1813 they married and he was ordained to a Sheffield pastorate, a post he combined with his tutorship. They moved to Hull in 1817 but Gilbert resigned his charge in 1825 on account of ill health, accepting a co-pastorate in Nottingham. Here they were actively involved in civic life, combating Anglican dominance and campaigning for municipal reform and the repeal of the Corn Laws. She was much involved in philanthropic activity and he gave public lectures defending Christianity. A separate chapel was erected for him in 1828 which he served until he retired in 1851.

Gilbert was an indefatigable and able student and respected minister: he chaired the first Annual General Meeting of the Congregational Union and in 1835 delivered the third course of Congregational lectures. His wife's reputation rests on works published before her marriage. The demands of eight children and numerous pupil boarders precluded much further writing, although she retained an active mind, travelling with enthusiasm in her seventies. Her letters are preserved in the Nottinghamshire Archives Office and some early diaries in the Alexander Turnbull Library, Wellington, New Zealand.

SELECT WRITINGS
A. Gilbert, *A Biographical Sketch of the Rev. Joseph Gilbert* (London, 1853)
A. Gilbert, *Autobiography and Other Memorials of Mrs Gilbert*, ed. J. Gilbert (London, 1874)

BIBLIOGRAPHY
Congregational Yearbook (1854): 229
DNB
Gentleman's Magazine, ii series 39 (1853): 213–4; iv series 3 (1867): 247–8
Julian

DOREEN M. ROSMAN

Gilbert, Nathaniel (Honourable) (b. Antigua, West Indies, c. 1721; d. Antigua, West Indies, 20 April 1774). Methodist evangelist, planter, and politician. Nathaniel was a descendant of the distinguished navigator, Sir Humphrey Gilbert, and Jonathan Gilbert, of Hartford,

Connecticut, who was Marshall of the Colony. He was the eldest son of Nathaniel Gilbert (*circa* 1697–1761) by his first wife. Gilbert entered Gray's Inn (29 July 1741) and was called to the Bar (6 February 1746). In 1747 he took his father's seat in the Antiguan Assembly and was appointed to the Governor's Council (1750).

His younger brother, Francis, had emigrated to England, joined the Methodists, and sent Methodist literature back to Nathaniel, including JOHN WESLEY's *Appeals to Men of Reason and Religion*. Studying these, Gilbert determined to seek out the English Methodists. On 3 February 1757 he resigned his seat in the Antiguan Assembly, and after the baptism of his fourth daughter a few days later set out for England with his wife, their four daughters, and three house-slaves. He settled in Wandsworth, south of London. On 17 January 1758 John Wesley preach in his new home, and on 29 December 1758 baptized two of the slaves (perhaps this was also the occasion when Wesley baptized the fifth daughter, Elizabeth). Now thoroughly converted, and anxious to bring more of his slaves into the Christian fold, Gilbert returned to Antigua, apparently early in 1759. His brother Francis followed him, sharing with Nathaniel the leadership of the racially mixed Methodist society.

In 1761 their father died, still unreconciled to Francis, but sufficiently tolerant of Nathaniel's quixotic visit to England to bequeath to him the large plantation and its hundreds of slaves. Nathaniel did not emancipate those slaves, however, as Wesley had urged, but did instruct them in Christianity and led them in Methodist worship, aided by Mary Leadbetter, a young Methodist widow who travelled back with them, and who later married Francis. (The emancipation of the slaves did not come about until 1835, at the hands of Nathaniel's son, another NATHANIEL GILBERT.)

In 1763 Nathaniel Gilbert was elected Speaker of the House and resigned both his seat and the chair in 1769. Francis stayed for a time in Antigua, but then restlessly shuttled backwards and forwards between Antigua and England, where he died in 1779.

BIBLIOGRAPHY
F. Baker, 'The Origins of Methodism in the West Indies: The Story of the Gilbert Family', *London Quarterly Review* (January 1960): 9–17
W. Blackman, *Methodism* (Barbados, 1988): 2–3, 70
E. W. Thompson, *Nathaniel Gilbert – Lawyer and Evangelist* (London, 1960)

LESLEY G. ANDERSON AND FRANK BAKER

Gilbert, Nathaniel [Jr] (b. Antigua, West Indies, 1761; d. England, 18 Nov. 1807). Gilbert was the son of NATHANIEL GILBERT, Speaker of Antigua, and related by marriage to Captain THOMAS WEBB. Like his cousin MELVILLE HORNE he was curate to JOHN W. FLETCHER at Madeley, and in 1792 became the Sierra Leone Company's first chaplain in the Christian settlement of freed slaves in West Africa (where Horne soon joined him).

His evangelical convictions, West Indian background and evident tact must have been his qualifications for this task; he remained in Sierra Leone, however, less than two years.

He became incumbent of Bledlow, Buckinghamshire in 1798. When the CMS planned a training centre for its West African missionaries, it was proposed to locate it at Bledlow, where Gilbert might help with tuition: his untimely death prevented further developments.

Gilbert married Sarah Ford, 1784. Their son, Nathaniel, a missionary, married Grace, daughter of Melvill Horne, and their daughter, Euphemia, married the son of his neighbour THOMAS SCOTT, the commentator; Sir George Gilbert Scott, the architect, was their son.

BIBLIOGRAPHY
C. Evans, *PWHS*, 34 (1964): 49–50, 192
A. M. Falconbridge, *Two Voyages to Sierra Leone* (London, 1794)
C. Hole, *Early History of the Church Missionary Society* (London, 1896): 116ff
A. F. Walls, *PWHS*, 34 (1964): 151

A. F. WALLS

Giles, John Eustace (b. Dartmouth, Devon, England, 20 April 1805; d. London, 24 June 1875). Baptist minister. John's father, WILLIAM GILES, had been a Wesleyan missionary but on returning from Sierra Leone entered the Baptist ministry. Part of John's education was at his brother's school at Chatham where Charles Dickens also studied. Trained at Bristol Baptist College, he spent six years building up a congregation in the recently re-opened Salters' Hall meeting house in London. Ten distinguished years at South Parade, Leeds followed. His chapel was twice enlarged as he drew influential people and also became known as the working man's friend. He sympathized with Chartism but vehemently attacked Robert Owen. He took issue with, and defeated, the famous Dr Hook, Vicar of Leeds, over church rates. They were again antagonists concerning the education clauses of Graham's Factory Bill. The Anti-Corn Law League and Liberation Society had his support and twice he went to the Continent successfully to plead for persecuted Baptists in Hamburg and Denmark (his account of the meeting with the King of Denmark was published in the *Baptist Magazine*, December 1841). Several sermons and lectures were published. Leaving Leeds in 1846 he was minister of Broadmead, Bristol, for a year before locating in Sheffield for 15 years, where he wrote articles for the *Eclectic Review*. After a brief pastorate in Dublin he ministered for 13 years at Clapham Common, London, until his death.

BIBLIOGRAPHY
Baptist Handbook 1876: 252–5
F. Beckwith, *BQ*, 21, 2 (1965): 7
I. Sellers, ed., *Our Heritage* (Leeds, 1987): 35–6
E. C. Starr, ed., *A Baptist Bibliography*, 25 vols (New York, 1947–76)

DAVID B. MILNER

Giles, William (b. Tavistock, Devon, England, 1 May 1771; d. Ashton-under-Lyne, Lancashire, England, 25 Jan. 1845). Baptist minister. Of Anglican parentage and converted amongst the Independents, he joined the Methodists and was selected to serve with the Methodist Missionary Society in Africa, going out to Sierra Leone on the same boat as the new governor, ZACHARY MACAULAY. Association with Baptist missionaries led him to adopt Baptist views and on his return to England he was baptized by ISAIAH BIRT. During WILLIAM WINTERBOTHAM's imprisonment, he assisted George Gibbs in Plymouth before removing to Dartmouth where his itinerant ministry in the surrounding villages sometimes provoked violent reaction. His next pastorate was at Lymington where his village work again encountered difficulties. He entered into controversy over Anglican evangelicals' apparent espousal of Baptismal Regeneration and was in this respect one of the influences effecting JAMES HARRINGTON EVANS' secession from the Church of England. In 1817 he removed to Chatham where he attacked the position of the Unitarians. His church was rebuilt for him in 1821 but soon thereafter suffered schism. In 1832 he removed to Preston where once more his preaching required an enlargement of the chapel; here he engaged in controversy with the Mormons. He resigned in 1842, but after a few years of itinerant preaching accepted the pastorate at Ashton-under-Lyne, 1843–5. It was not this William Giles, but his son of the same name, that taught Charles Dickens. He defended the close-communion position and wrote on Baptismal Regeneration and on Antinomianism.

BIBLIOGRAPHY
BaptMag (1846)

J. H. Y. BRIGGS

Gilfillan, George (b. Comrie, Perthshire, Scotland, 30 Jan. 1813; d. Brechin, Angus, Scotland, 13 Aug. 1878). Literary biographer and poetaster. A brother of JAMES GILFILLAN, he was the eleventh child of the Reverend Samuel Gilfillan (*DNB*), and of Rachel Barias, a great beauty. Educated at Glasgow, he also studied theology at Edinburgh where he was an intimate of De Quincey and Carlyle.

Gilfillan's fame rests on his *Gallery of Literary Portraits* (1845), a series of encomiums on the Romantic poets. Sentimental and dogmatic, coated in a feverish, misty, religious veneer, the *Gallery* and an avalanche of similar essays exercised unparalleled influence on mid-nineteenth-century popular taste. His long poem, *Night*, inexplicably admired by Emerson, qualified him for membership in the so-called 'Spasmodic School'.

Gilfillan was Secession minister at the School-Wynd Church, Dundee (1836–78). Though otherwise orthodox, he was censured by presbytery for his meliorist view of eternal damnation. He was also a premillennialist. A liberal in his political and social ideas, Gilfillan gave notable support to city missions, mechanic's institutes, and popular lectures (including the YMCA Exeter Hall series); he sympathized with the European nationalists Garibaldi and Kossuth, and with the American slaves.

BIBLIOGRAPHY
DNB
W. R. Nicholl, *Gilfillan's Literary Portraits* (London, 1909)
E. S. Watson, *George Gilfillan, Letters and Journals* (London, 1892)

JONATHAN BURKE CUTMORE

Gilfillan, James (b. Comrie, Perthshire, Scotland, 11 May 1797; d. Portobello, near Edinburgh, 28 Jan. 1874). United Secession minister. James, brother of GEORGE GILFILLAN, was educated at Glasgow College (1808–14), and then at the Anti-Burgher seminary, Edinburgh. He was minister of the United Secession Church, Stirling, from December 1822 to 1869. His ambitious *The Sabbath Viewed in the Light of Reason, Revelation, and History* (1861) was the work of twenty years. Authoritative, though predictable, it was well received in evangelical circles as a source-book of information and orthodox arguments, in recognition of which Glasgow granted him the DD in 1866.

BIBLIOGRAPHY
Boase
DNB

JONATHAN BURKE CUTMORE

Gill, John (b. Kettering, Northamptonshire, 23 Nov. 1697; d. Camberwell, London, 14 Oct. 1771). Baptist minister and theologian. Although his parents were poor, he spent a short time at the Kettering Grammar School, and subsequently became an excellent Hebraist, studying with John Skepp, a major figure in the promotion of High Calvinism amongst eighteenth-century Baptists, an overreaction to prerevival Arminianism and potential Pelagianism. Starting to preach shortly after his baptism in November 1716, Gill was ordained at Higham Ferrers, Northants in 1718 where he studied with the minister, John Davis. Helped in his training by a book grant from the Particular Baptist Fund, he was for over fifty years a manager of that fund.

In 1719 he moved to the historic Horsleydown Church in Southwark, where for half a century, alongside his contemporary, John Brine of the Cripplegate Church, he expounded High Calvinism. Indeed Gill was almost unique amongst eighteenth-century Baptists as a doughty protestant scholastic willing to take on board the problems of systematic theology.

However, his nineteenth-century successor, C. H. SPURGEON, while affirming his own Calvinism, said that Gill in his 'method of address to sinners cramped himself, and was therefore straitened when there was no scriptural reason for being so', 'the non-invitation, non-application scheme' as IVIMEY (1823) called it. While, therefore, Brine and Gill were able defenders of Trinitarian

orthodoxy against the inroads of Socinianism, and while Gill defended his theology against antinomian deduction, it has recently been said of them, that the effect of their teaching was to divert the thinking of many Particular Baptist ministers into patterns of abstruse Hyper-Calvinism which 'caused the good news to be a matter for arid debate rather than confident proclamation, "chilling"', in Spurgeon's words 'many churches to their very soul'.

The problem was only partly in Gill's work; worse was the enthusiasm of some disciples who exaggerated certain tendencies with disastrous consequences for the missionary impact of the life of the churches. It is against this background that the theological work of ANDREW FULLER for the renewal of Baptist missionary consciousness becomes so important.

ROBERT HALL, JR, doubtless overreacted in calling Gill's voluminous works 'a continent of mud', for his biblical commentaries were widely resorted to, because Gill had developed a considerable expertise in oriental languages, and his biblical work derived considerable benefit from a mastery of rabbinic sources. His three-volume *Body of Doctrinal Divinity* was an able exposition of the Calvinistic theology of this period, 'his honest and learned defence of the true sense of the Holy Scriptures, against the profane attacks of deists and infidels' being recognized by the award of an Aberdeen DD in 1748. It can, however, be argued that the attractions of Socinianism and rationalism needed not only the cerebral exposition of high doctrine, but also the warm fire of revival experience to which this volume provides ample testimony.

BIBLIOGRAPHY
R. Brown, *The English Baptists of the Eighteenth Century* (London, 1986)
E. F. Clipsham, 'Andrew Fuller and Fullerism', *BQ*, XX [1963]: 101ff
DNB
T. George, 'John Gill' in T. George and D. S. Dockery, *Baptist Theologians* (Nashville, TN, 1990)
J. Ivimey, *History of the English Baptists*, III (London, 1823)

J. H. Y. BRIGGS

Gill, Silas (b. Beckley, Sussex, England, 1 Feb. 1807; d. Kempsey, New South Wales, Australia, 10 Sept. 1875). Wesleyan Methodist local preacher. Son of a farmer, he was converted during the ministry of the Reverend Thomas Collins (1832–4) in the Sandhurst Wesleyan Methodist circuit. Seeing Silas make his way up the aisle in response to his appeal Collins remarked of this big-framed young man, 'Here comes a giant for Jesus'. Such he became in Christian witness and service. A farm labourer he immediately began witnessing for Christ in Sussex.

He and his family emigrated on the *Augusta Jessie* and arrived in Sydney, New South Wales, on 11 October 1837. He worked on farms successively at Cobbitty (near Camden), Woodville and Sugarloaf (both places on the Hunter River), Wauchope and Kempsey (towns on the central north coast). In Kempsey and other centres he inaugurated preaching services, encouraged people to build churches, and maintained a Christian witness for four years prior to the arrival of the first Methodist minister in 1864. Poor in this world's goods, he was rich in faith and strong in character. His exuberant Christian faith constantly found expression in song. Five hundred attending his funeral testified to his gracious influence in their lives. His tombstone bears these words: 'For 38 years he followed Christ, Doing Good and Turning many to Righteousness. His preaching and his life proved him a Man Full of Faith and of the Holy Ghost.'

BIBLIOGRAPHY
E. G. Clancy, *A Giant for Jesus* (Waitara, Australia, 1972)

ERIC G. CLANCY

Gillespie, Thomas (b. Clearburn, 1708; d. Dunfermline, Fife, Scotland, 19 July 1774). Founder of Scottish Relief Church. His father, a farmer and brewer, died early. When he was about twenty his godly mother introduced him to Thomas Boston, the elder, whose exhortations proved effective for his conversion. He studied for the ministry at Edinburgh University, but left in his last year. He visited WILLIAM WILSON, professor of theology for the Seceders, but being dissatisfied with their principles, he transferred to the academy of PHILIP DODDRIDGE in Northampton. He was ordained in January 1741 by Doddridge and a group of Independent ministers. That spring he was presented to the parish of Carnock by Colonel JOHN ERSKINE. His Independent ordination was accepted by the presbytery of Dunfermline even though he took exception to the Confession's endorsement of the ecclesiastical powers of the magistrate. Gillespie supported the revivals in Cambuslang and Kilsyth (1741), and he became an admirer of GEORGE WHITEFIELD and a correspondent of JONATHAN EDWARDS.

In 1749 Andrew Richardson was presented to the parish of Inverkeithing, in the presbytery of Dunfermline. The people objected, so the presbytery refused to induct him. The usual practice in such cases was to appoint a 'riding committee' to perform the ceremony, but the General Assembly was controlled by 'moderates' who wished to crush the opposition. In 1752 the assembly resolved that one of the six objecting ministers be deposed. Gillespie alone read a further defence, so he was selected. He replied, 'I desire to receive this sentence of the General Assembly ... pronounced against me, with real concern, and awful impressions of the divine conduct in it: but I rejoice that to me it is given in behalf of Christ, not only to believe on him, but also to suffer for his sake' (Struthers, 1843: 92). Gillespie preached in the fields until fall, then moved to Dunfermline. Amid rising sympathy, the 'popular' party sent a majority to the General Assembly of 1753. They elected an evangelical, ALEXANDER WEBSTER, as moderator, but attempts to have Gillespie reponed were squelched by the Royal Commissioner – 'the *throne* was higher than the moderator's chair' (Struthers, 1843:118).

Gillespie's labours were intense. At communion seasons (Thursday through Monday) he preached nine sermons and seven or eight table addresses from complete manuscripts. THOMAS BOSTON, the younger, of Jedburgh joined him in 1758. Then on 22 October 1761 Gillespie and Boston ordained THOMAS COLIER at Colinsburgh, and the three congregations formed themselves into the presbytery of Relief (i.e. for oppressed Christians). The Relief increased and in 1847 merged with the Secession to form the United Presbyterian Church (*see* EBENEZER ERSKINE).

Only two of Gillespie's works were printed. His significance lies in the principles which his firm stand helped to establish. Against the Established Church he insisted that ministers must not be intruded on a congregation against its will and that the civil powers have no rightful authority in ecclesiastical affairs. In contrast to the Seceders he maintained 'communion with all that visibly hold the Head' (Struthers, 1843: 123).

SELECT WRITINGS
T. Gillespie, *An Essay on the Continuance of Immediate Revelations of Facts and Future Events in the Christian Church* (Edinburgh, 1771)
—, *A Treatise on Temptation* (Edinburgh, 1774)
—, Correspondence between Gillespie and Edwards in Dwight's 'Memoirs' of Edwards in *The Works of Jonathan Edwards*, ed. by Hickman (1834; reprinted Edinburgh, 1974)

BIBLIOGRAPHY
DNB
Fasti, 5
J. Harper, J. Eadie, and W. Lindsay, *Lives of Ebenezer Erskine, William Wilson, and Thomas Gillespie* (Edinburgh, 1849).
G. Struthers, *The History of the Rise, Progress, and Principles of the Relief Church* (Glasgow, 1843)

JOHN K. LA SHELL

Gillett, Alexander (b. Granby, CT, BNA, 14 Aug. 1749; d. Torrington, CT, USA, 19 Jan. 1826). Congregational minister. A 1770 graduate of Yale, Gillett attributed his conversion to reading the works of JONATHAN EDWARDS. He was ordained at Farmingbury, Connecticut in 1773. Typical of his generation, Gillett spent long hours in the study of Edwardsian Calvinism. Also typical of the Edwardseans or 'New Divinity' men, Gillett endured a stormy relationship with the church society over his objections to the Half-Way Covenant. By mutual consent he resigned in 1791. Gillett then accepted a call to the congregation at Torrington in 1792. During a tenure which lasted until his death, Gillett witnessed several revivals among his people, and also made numerous tours on behalf of the Connecticut Missionary Society.

BIBLIOGRAPHY
AAP, 2: 68–71
BSGYC, 3
L. Hart, *A Sermon, Delivered at the Funeral of Rev. Alexander Gillett* (New Haven, CT, 1826)

DAVID W. KLING

Gillette, Daniel Holbrook (b. Cambridge, NY, USA, 25 March 1813; d. Mobile, AL, USA, 9 Feb. 1845). Baptist pastor in the Middle and Southern states. Baptized into the Baptist congregation in Hague, New York, in 1832, he quickly determined to enter the ministry. He was educated by his minister brother, PHILANDER DUNHAM GILLETTE, and at Hamilton Institute. By his graduation he had developed a reputation as a strong preacher. He became pastor of the Baptist church in Rahway, New Jersey in 1840. Illness soon struck him and curtailed his preaching ministry. He journeyed to the South, seeking better climate, preaching along the way and entertaining requests to become pastor in Charlottesville, Virginia, Mobile, Alabama, and Columbus, Mississippi. He moved intermittently between North and South until establishing residence in Mobile in 1844, where he succumbed to illness after two years.

BIBLIOGRAPHY
AAP

ANDREW MANIS

Gillette, Philander Dunham (b. Piscataway, NJ, USA, 8 Jan. 1793; d. Elmira, NY, USA, 28 March 1845). Baptist pastor in New Jersey and New York. Though in feeble health, at age 17 Gillette was elected teacher of the school in Cambridge, New York. He fought in the War of 1812, after which he studied divinity with a minister in Philadelphia. Ordained in 1822, he pastored several churches in upstate New York and Philadelphia. He performed his ministry without remuneration for most of his career and served for many years as the moderator of the Chemung (Elmira, New York) Baptist Association.

BIBLIOGRAPHY
AAP

ANDREW MANIS

Gillies, John (b. Scotland, 1712 or 1713; d. Glasgow, 29 March 1796). Minister of Glasgow Blackfriars (1742–96). Evangelical publicist and leading member of the Popular party in the General Assembly of the Church of Scotland. Gillies was an important member of the international letter-writing network involving JONATHAN EDWARDS, PHILIP DODDRIDGE, JOHN ERSKINE and others. He was also one of the leaders of the campaign against repeal of the laws against Roman Catholics at the General Assembly of 1778, but protected in his own house the family of a Glasgow Roman Catholic manufacturer whose property had been destroyed by a mob.

Perhaps one of the greatest works of evangelical history to that date was Gillies' *Historical Collections Relating to Remarkable Periods of the Success of the Gospel* (Glasgow, 1754). Gillies incorporated passages from WESLEY's *Journals*, and also from his *Christian Library*. Included in his supplement of 1761 was material gleaned from WILLIAM GRIMSHAW, Wesley's right-hand man in Yorkshire and the north of England. Immediately after the death of GEORGE WHITEFIELD, his friend Gillies not only published his biography, but preceded this by six volumes of his works, which remains the major source for his voluminous letters.

JOHN WESLEY was surprised in 1753 to receive an invitation from Gillies to stay in his home and preach from his pulpit. He accepted, however, and reciprocated by inviting Gillies to preach to the Methodists at Newcastle two years later. They remained good friends for life.

BIBLIOGRAPHY
DNB
J. Erskine, *A Supplement to Gillies' 'Historical Collections'* (Edinburgh, 1798)
Fasti, 3
S. O'Brien, 'A Transatlantic Community of Saints: the Great Awakening and the First Evangelical Network, 1735–55', *AHR*, 91, 4 (1986)
Scots Magazine, 17–58 (1746–96)

JOHN R. MCINTOSH AND FRANK BAKER

Gillon, Alexander [of Wallhouse] (*fl.* 1752). Presbyterian elder. Gillon was one of the 'elders of considerable Rank and Distinction' who assisted at the celebration of the second Communion at the Cambuslang revival of 1742.

Earlier, on 17 March 1742, he had written to THOMAS MCCULLOCH asking for definite news of the revival and expressing the hope that God would visit every corner of the land with 'a like plentiful effusion of his spirit'.

BIBLIOGRAPHY
Edinburgh Christian Instructor (1838): 219
A. Fawcett, *The Cambuslang Revival* (London, 1971): 119–24

JOHN R. MCINTOSH

Gilly, William Stephen (b. Hawkendon, Suffolk, England, 28 Jan. 1789; d. Norham, Northumberland, England, 10 Sept. 1855). Anglican clergyman and Canon of Durham. The son of William Gilly, a wealthy 'high and dry' churchman, the rector of Wanstead, Essex, and of Hawkendon, Suffolk, he was educated at Christ's Hospital, London, and St Catharine's, Cambridge (BA 1812; MA 1817; DD 1833). Ordained in 1812 as his father's curate at Hawkendon, he served in a St Pancras district church until 1817. Due to his father's influence in Ultra Tory circles, Gilly benefited from the patronage of Lord Chancellor Eldon by being appointed Rector of North Fambridge, Essex.

In 1823 Gilly made his first of numerous visits to the Vaudois in Italy (a persecuted Protestant sect, the Vaudois were historically the focus of English anti-Catholic propaganda, most famously in Milton's poem 'On the Late Massacre in Piedmont') and on the basis of that visit published his *Narrative of an Excursion to the . . . Vaudois* (1824), a timely work appearing as it did during the lead-up to Catholic emancipation. The book inspired a relief subscription headed by the King and Barrington, Bishop of Durham, and, buttressed by further visits, published sequels, and platform addresses, it made Gilly a leading anti-Catholic polemicist. By the 1830s he was well positioned, then, to take a role in resisting the Oxford Movement, which he did in sermons and in print. With Bishop Barrington's support Gilly was made Prebendary of Durham (from 1826); later he was appointed Perpetual Curate of St Margaret's, Durham (1827–51), Vicar of Norham, Northumberland (from 1831), and finally Canon of Durham (from 1853).

Typical of Anglican evangelicals of his generation, Gilly inherited his father's Tory paternalist approach to social and economic issues, an approach reflected in his *Peasantry of the Border* (1841) in which he chastised landed aristocrats over conditions suffered by Northumberland agricultural workers.

Contemporary evangelicals applauded Gilly as a man of learning and culture; he supported popular religious education and called for a better-educated clergy. In 1837 he founded a school and library at La Tour, Piedmont, which he endowed with a grant of £5,000. At Christ's Hospital Gilly befriended the Romantic writer Leigh Hunt, and through Hunt met Lord Byron in Genoa in 1823 (an episode discussed in *Review of English Studies* new series, 29, 114 [1978]: 185–90). There are a few of Gilly's letters at Lambeth Palace, the British Library, and the National Library of Scotland.

BIBLIOGRAPHY
Al. Cant.
CO (1855): 859–61
DNB
GM (October 1855): 437–39

JONATHAN BURKE CUTMORE

Gilmour, Jannet [née Walker] (b. Irvine, Ayrshire, Scotland, 1789; d. Peterborough, Upper Canada, Canada, 22 March 1852). Co-founder of Baptist churches in Scotland and Canada, poetess. Converted and baptized in 1803, she became a charter member of the Baptist Church in Kilwinning, Ayrshire. After her marriage to JOHN GILMOUR, June 1822 she joined him in his new church in Aberdeen. She bore a son in 1823. The family remained in Aberdeen until 1830. They sailed to Montreal where she was one of the company who formed a Baptist Church in 1831. In 1835 the Gilmours moved to Clarence and then settled in Peterborough in 1837. Jannet was a founding member of the churches at Smith Township and Peterborough.

Throughout her life she suffered greatly from frequent extreme headaches. Begrudging herself any luxury, she gave faithfully to the care of the sick and of immigrants to Canada who she visited as often as her health allowed. Her faith was expressed in poetry. Some of her poems were published, posthumously, in *The Christian Observer* (1852–3).

BIBLIOGRAPHY
Canadian Baptist Archives, diaries and journals of John Gilmour
The Christian Observer (Toronto, 1852–3)

JUDITH COLWELL

Gilmour, John (b. Ayr, Scotland, 4 Aug. 1792; d. Peterborough, Ontario 22 May 1869). Baptist minister and missionary. Raised a Presbyterian and apprenticed as a merchant mariner, Gilmour was captured and imprisoned from 1809 to 1814 in France. Returning to Scotland, Gilmour was influenced by GEORGE BARCLAY of Irvine to adopt Baptist convictions and was baptized in 1814. He trained at Horton College, Bradford and served as pastor from 1820 to 1821 in Greenock. In 1821 Barclay and JOHN ANDERSON sent him to gather a church in Aberdeen where he served from 1821 to 1830. In 1822, he married Jannet Walker; they had one son. In 1830, the Gilmours sailed to Montreal where Gilmour served as pastor of St Helen Street Baptist Church, later renamed First Baptist Church. In 1835, Gilmour moved to Clarence, near Ottawa, where he served as assistant to JOHN EDWARDS. In 1837, Gilmour settled in Peterborough.

In 1836, Gilmour participated in a revival in the Ottawa River valley. Modelled upon the work of JAMES and ROBERT HALDANE in Scotland, the revival resulted in many conversions, start of a home missionary society and formation of the Ottawa Valley Baptist Association. Gilmour returned to the United Kingdom in 1836 where he founded the Baptist Canadian Missionary Society and raised funds for missionaries to serve in Canada and for creation of a theological college to train pastors in Canada. Returning to Canada, he helped establish Canada Baptist College, Montreal; the Grande Ligne Mission; the Regular Baptist Missionary Convention of Canada West; and *The Canada Baptist Magazine and Missionary Register*.

A powerful preacher and an advocate of open communion, Gilmour was the dominant Baptist evangelist of the period. He was not narrowly Baptist. From 1837 to 1868, he served as agent of the non-denominational New England Company, which pioneered work among First Nations peoples. He collaborated with Presbyterians through the Canada Education and Home Missionary Society.

BIBLIOGRAPHY
P. R. Dekar, 'The Gilmours: Four Generations of Baptist Service,' in P. R. Dekar and M. J. S. Ford, eds., *Celebrating the Canadian Baptist Heritage* (Hamilton, Canada, 1984)
J. L. Gilmour, 'John Gilmour,' *McMaster University Monthly*, 4 (November 1894): 49–59

PAUL R. DEKAR

Girdlestone, Charles (b. Bream's Buildings, Chancery Lane, London (ordination papers, Oxford), 6 March 1797; d. Holywell House, Somerset, England, 28 April 1881). College tutor and Anglican clergyman. Son of

Samuel Rainbow Girdlestone (Middle Temple, chancery barrister), armiger, and Caroline Roberts (Powell), Charles was educated at Tonbridge School and (like his father) at Wadham College, Oxford, 1814–18 (Goodridge exhibitioner 1815; Hebrew and botany exhibitioner 1815–19; Hody Greek exhibitioner 1816–18), where (with C. G. ROUND) he took a first in *literae humaniores*. A college historian, Warden Wells, cites him as an example of the earlier evangelicalism of Wadham. Greenhill (*DNB*) says he became an evangelical later. Not least in view of his second curacy with a known evangelical incumbent, the former is more likely. Certainly Tuckwell reproduces his adverse reply (1833) to a letter from his erstwhile friend JOHN HENRY NEWMAN. From 1818 to 1826 he was a fellow of Balliol College, serving as lecturer in Latin, mathematics and logic. In the university he was classical examiner 1825, 1826, and select preacher 1826, 1830 (not 1825, 1829, as *Al. Ox.*, Gardiner). With two other first-class men recently elected fellows (one, C. A. Ogilvie, apparently much influenced by HANNAH MORE), he is said to have raised Balliol's reputation.

But Girdlestone's heart was in pastoral work, though he continued writing. Ordained at Oxford in 1820, he became tutor to the twin sons of Sir John Stanley; then served as Curate of Hastings, Sussex, 1822–4, and of North Hinksey, Oxford (to E. G. MARSH), 1824–6. Resigning his fellowship on marriage, he was appointed (by Sir John Stanley, who became Lord Stanley of Alderley), as vicar of the large parish of Sedgley, Staffordshire, 1826–37. Declining health required removal to a less demanding sphere. Girdlestone became Rector of Alderley, Cheshire (another Stanley living), 1837–47, where his stand about his and his successors' rightful dues alienated his patron; and (circumstances thus dictating), by a friendly cousin of Sir John, Lord Ward, afterward Earl of Dudley, was nominated Rector of Kingswinford, Staffordshire, 1847–77. At Sedgley he erected several district churches, and other parochial buildings. Bad outbreaks of cholera in 1832 and 1849 gave him additional interest in social conditions. His own health eventually giving way, at eighty he resigned, having already retired to live at Weston-super-Mare. Author of some sixty publications, the most notable was his *Bible Commentary* for family use (1832–5, 1842) re-issued by him subsequently (1873) with more explicitly Protestant perceptions, which may incidentally have given the impression recorded by Greenhill. Always an 'evangelistic and enlivening preacher', Girdlestone however perhaps became an increasingly thoroughgoing evangelical as life went on.

He married (1826) Anne Elizabeth (1804–82), daughter of Baker Morrell, solicitor to the University of Oxford. Thus their children were cousins of the (evangelical) brewing branch of the Morrell family at Headington Hill Hall, Oxford. Among them was Canon R. B. Girdlestone, first principal of Wycliffe Hall (1877–89). Canon EDWARD GIRDLESTONE, 'the agricultural labourers' friend', was Charles's brother.

BIBLIOGRAPHY
Boase, 1
C. Girdlestone, *Farewell Sermons*, preface (London, 1837)
R. B. Girdlestone, *Genealogical Notes on the Girdlestone Family* (privately printed, 1904)
J. Jones, *Balliol College* (Oxford, 1988)
J. S. Reynolds, *Evangelicals at Oxford*, (Oxford, 1953; Appleford, England, 1975)

J. S. REYNOLDS

Girdlestone, Edward (b. London, 6 Sept. 1805; d. Bristol, England 4 Dec. 1884). Anglican clergyman, education and rural labour advocate. A younger brother of CHARLES GIRDLESTONE, he was educated at Balliol College, Oxford (BA 1826; MA 1829). He became Curate (1828) and then Vicar of Deane, Lancashire (1830–54). In the early 1850s, as an active member of the National School Society, he advocated compulsory education and opposed clerical control of the proposed state educational system. In support of these opinions he co-founded the Church of England Education Society. Probably in recognition of this work, he was made Canon of Bristol (1854–8) and Vicar of St Nicholas, Bristol (1855–8). From there he moved to Wapley, Gloucestershire as vicar, and was later Vicar of Halberton, Devonshire (1862), and of Olveston, Gloucestershire (1872).

In a sermon delivered in 1865 he drew attention to conditions suffered by agricultural labourers. Thus began an agitation that carried him around the country from platform to platform, gaining him national fame and the appellation 'the agricultural labourers' friend'. The remedies he proposed included transplanting workers to more prosperous parishes. He himself uprooted 500 or so families, most of whom he sent to the industrial north. He supported the idea of labour unions, but because he opposed strikes, in the 1870s his influence was eclipsed by more radical leaders.

Besides numerous works on educational and doctrinal subjects, he also published anti-Tractarian literature. Though vigorous and even bigoted in his arguments, he at least avoided *ad hominems*. In 1871 he described himself as a doctrinal liberal, and indeed by that time he had set aside his earlier belief in verbal inspiration and had perhaps come to embrace a form of universalism. However, in his *Remarks* (1860) he responded negatively to *Essays and Reviews*.

BIBLIOGRAPHY
Boase
DNB
P. J. Perry, 'Edward Girdlestone 1805–84: A Forgotten Evangelical', *Journal of Religious History*, 9 (1977): 292–301
T. H. Ward, ed., *Men of the Time*, 12th edn (London and New York, 1886)

JONATHAN BURKE CUTMORE

Gisborne, Thomas (b. Yoxall, Staffordshire, England, 31 Oct. 1758; d. Yoxall, 24 March 1846). Country gentleman, writer, and Anglican clergyman. Gisborne's family were the hereditary squires of Yoxall, and after private education, at Harrow and St John's College, Cambridge which he entered in 1776 (BA 1780 – sixth wrangler) he settled there in 1783 on the death of his father, having refused the chance of a seat in Parliament and taken orders to become Perpetual Curate of Barton-under-Needwood nearby, a living which he retained until 1820 when he was succeeded by his son, James. He was a prebendary of Durham and Vicar of Croxall (Derbyshire) (1838–46).

Gisborne married Mary Babington of Rothley Temple in 1784, herself of a family related by marriage to the Macaulays, while Gisborne himself was a close friend of WILLIAM WILBERFORCE, who delighted to spend time at Yoxall and Rothley. Gisborne was a man of quiet, civilized demeanour with a high sense of social responsibility. He drew attention to the plight of factory children as early as 1794, but he is important principally for his moral writings in which he opposed his own ethical absolutism to the expediency of Paley. At this time Wilberforce was publishing his *Practical View* (1797) and it is not extravagant to think that there may have been some interplay between this work and Gisborne's *Principles of Moral Philosophy* (1789), and his more important *Inquiry into the Duties of Men in the Higher Ranks and Middle Classes* (1794) with its chapters on politics, the civil service, the army, the law, medicine, the church and business, all the time stressing honesty, integrity and responsibility. Gisborne also published sermons and a collected edition of his works in nine volumes in 1813.

He had six sons and two daughters, one of the latter being Lydia, wife of Edward Robinson, later Lady Scott, with whom Branwell Brontë, tutor to her son, may have had an affair. His son Thomas was an MP.

BIBLIOGRAPHY
Al. Cant., II, iii: 60
I. Bradley, *The Call to Seriousness* (London, 1976)
DNB

ARTHUR POLLARD

Gladstone, Sir John, Bart. (b. Leith, Scotland, 11 Dec. 1764; d. Fasque, Kincardineshire, Scotland, 7 Dec. 1851). Merchant and MP. John was the son of Thomas Gladstones, a corn merchant who had prospered in Leith, the port of Edinburgh. On leaving school at 13, John was apprenticed to an Edinburgh rope manufacturer for three years and then joined his father's business. Already by the age of twenty he was travelling for his father to the Baltic ports of north Germany. In 1787 John decided to move to Liverpool in order to enter a partnership in the corn trade, at the same time dropping the 's' from his surname. His great energy and acute business sense brought him success. In 1789–90 he travelled to the United States in order to open fresh trading links and averted a potential financial disaster by skilful purchases. He diversified into tobacco and

insurance and by 1801, when his partnership ended, his fortune had reached over £40,000. He then formed a new 14-year partnership with his younger brother Robert. He had already sponsored all five of his other brothers in their early mercantile careers. John was becoming one of the most prosperous men in Liverpool.

John's father, who was to die in 1809, frequently warned him not to let 'the affairs of this life so occupy your attention as to shut out a serious concern for the more important interests of another life' (Checkland, 1971: 18). When he first came to Liverpool, John naturally worshipped at the main Presbyterian meeting house in Benn's Garden. The ministry there, though not overtly Unitarian until 1811, was distinctly Arian. In 1792, however, a group of Scottish adherents including Gladstone decided to form a separate congregation and erected a building in Oldham Street. In the same year he married Jane Hall, the daughter of another Liverpool merchant, and in 1793 they moved into a new home, designed by John, in Rodney Street. Jane suffered from chronic ill health and died childless only six years after their marriage.

In 1800 John married a second time. His wife was Anne Mackenzie Robertson, daughter of the provost of Dingwall, a leading lawyer of the Highland town. The religious traditions of the family were Episcopalian and the town was noted for its warm evangelicalism. Anne, herself an evangelical by conviction, was dissatisfied with Oldham Street and in 1804 John purchased two seats in the new St Mark's Church. In the undenominational spirit of the time Anne was subsequently pleased to attend the ministries of the Independents P. S. Charrier at Bethesda Chapel (from 1809) and THOMAS RAFFLES at Great George Street Chapel (from 1812). Nevertheless it was largely at Anne's urging that in 1815 John erected two new Anglican churches, St Andrew's in Renshaw Street and St Thomas's at Seaforth, and arranged for evangelical incumbents. She regularly subscribed to the BFBS, the CMS and the Jews' Society, and she bought tracts for binding and lending. In later years, like Jane before her, Anne experienced poor health that restricted her activities, but her devotional spirit shone through her infirmity.

John's business interests continued to expand. He played an increasing part in the East India trade and by 1809 was chairman of the Liverpool West India Association. He dealt in sugar and cotton, and acquired plantations in Demarara. Although he had never participated in the slave trade, he experienced no personal qualms about being a slave-owner. By 1828 he was worth over £500,000. Gladstone was able to display his wealth by erecting, in 1811, a large new home, Seaforth House, five miles outside Liverpool. In the following year he threw his formidable energy into politics. In 1806 and 1807 he had supported the reforming Whig candidate for Liverpool, but now he acted as campaign manager for George Canning whose liberal brand of Toryism attracted him. Contact with Canning whetted his appetite for public life, and he became MP for Lancaster 1818–20, Woodstock in Oxfordshire 1820–6 and

Berwick-upon-Tweed 1826–7. Nevertheless there is no record of his speaking in his first Parliament. He was too immersed in business to concentrate on a political career.

Gladstone's West Indian interests declined after slave emancipation in 1833, but he continued to develop commercial relations with India and China. His oldest child, Anne, who shared her mother's evangelical faith, died in 1829 at the age of 26, and his wife herself died after prolonged weakness six years later. From 1832 he lived as a landed proprietor at Fasque in Kincardineshire and in 1846 he was granted a baronetcy. After returning to Scotland, he was content to worship in the local Presbyterian congregation, but in the 1840s he was harried by his son William into giving generously towards Trinity College, Glenalmond, a seminary and school for Scottish Episcopalians, and into building St Andrew's Episcopal Church on his estate. He never warmed to his son's Anglo-Catholicism. William was dismayed when in his closing hours his father refused Holy Communion but called for a plate of porridge. Although he had joined his wife in supporting evangelical causes, John cannot be regarded as a wholehearted evangelical either. He described himself as no party man in religion. He retained his thrusting, argumentative characteristics almost until his death at the age of 86. He left five surviving children, among them WILLIAM EWART GLADSTONE, the Liberal Prime Minister. The Glynne-Gladstone Papers at the Clwyd County Record Office contain the family correspondence.

BIBLIOGRAPHY
D. W. Bebbington, *William Ewart Gladstone* (Grand Rapids, MI, 1992)
P. Butler, *Gladstone* (Oxford, 1982)
S. G. Checkland, *The Gladstones* (Cambridge, 1971)

DAVID WILLIAM BEBBINGTON

Gladstone, John Hall (b. Hackney, London, England, 7 March 1827; d. London, 6 Oct. 1902). Chemist. Despite a wish to enter the Christian ministry Gladstone was dissuaded by his father, a London draper, and instead studied chemistry at University College, London, and then Giessen. A lecturer at St Thomas's Hospital in 1850–2, he became financially independent but continued work on reactions in solution and spectrochemistry. He was made FRS, professor of chemistry at the Royal Institution, and president of the Physical (1874) and Chemical (1874) Societies. He taught in a Congregational Sunday school and (later) in a young men's Bible class, being also associated with the YMCA. On the day of his death he presided at a meeting of the Christian Evidence Society. He published books on spelling reform, theology and science, miracles, and a biography of MICHAEL FARADAY.

BIBLIOGRAPHY
DNB
DSB

W. A. Tilden, *Journal of the Chemical Society*, 87 (1905): 591–7

COLIN A. RUSSELL

Gladstone, William Ewart (b. Liverpool, England, 29 Dec. 1809; d. Hawarden, Flintshire, Wales, 19 May 1898). MP and British Prime Minister. The youngest son of JOHN GLADSTONE and his second wife, Anne, he imbibed an evangelical faith from his mother. In 1818 or 1819 she wrote that she believed her son to have been truly converted to God. From the age of 11 he was at Eton, where religion was a formality but where his confirmation and first Communion stirred his devotion. At Christ Church, Oxford, he was partly drawn into the circle of undergraduates clustering round the High Calvinist HENRY BULTEEL, but private examination of a range of theological authorities convinced Gladstone that the Church of England taught baptismal regeneration.

As a student he was attracted by a clerical career, but opposition from his father and the Reform crisis of 1831–2 turned him toward politics. During the 1830s, in parallel with the Oxford Movement, the young MP developed an Anglo-Catholic understanding of apostolic succession and the eucharist. He expounded his mature religious opinions in *Church Principles considered in their Results* (London, 1840). Although he continued to believe that evangelicalism had represented a true revival of religion, he now held a much higher churchmanship. The essentials of his religious position were unchanged when he was four times Liberal Prime Minister between 1868 and 1894.

The Glynne-Gladstone Papers at the Clwyd County Record Office contain the family correspondence. The Gladstone Papers in the British Library reflect Gladstone's public work.

BIBLIOGRAPHY
D. W. Bebbington, *William Ewart Gladstone* (Grand Rapids, MI, 1992)
P. Butler, *Gladstone* (Oxford, 1982)
S. G. Checkland, *The Gladstones* (Cambridge, 1971)

DAVID WILLIAM BEBBINGTON

Glas, John (b. Auchtermuchty, Fife, Scotland, 21 Sept. 1695; d. Dundee, Angus, Scotland, 2 Nov. 1771). Minister and writer. Glas, who had the distinction of having a sect named after him, was born in a clerical succession, graduated from St Andrews University in 1713, was licensed in 1717 and appointed *jure devoluto* to the parish of Tealing outside Dundee in 1719. Opposing Covenanting views in his parish, he was forced to examine the constitution of the Christian church, and he came to the reluctant conclusion that the Kingdom of Christ is purely spiritual. He gathered 74 members of his congregation into a society for prayer discipline and a monthly celebration of the Lord's supper. For his energy in propounding his new views he was prosecuted at presbytery and at length deposed from the ministry of the Church of Scotland at the General Assembly of 1730.

Glas removed to Dundee, where Bailie George Lyon had been one of his chief supporters. In a church list of 1746 Glas is described as the 'teaching bishop'. John Baxter, founder of a famous textile firm in Dundee, moved from Tealing with Glas. Gradually the little church developed its views of worship and theology within the Calvinist tradition. Communion was celebrated each Sabbath afternoon, and between services an agape was held, obligatory for members. Complete unanimity was required in all church decisions, and 'primitive practices' such as the pedilavium and the kiss of charity were enjoined on occasion. Uneducated elder-preachers, an innovation in Scotland, were introduced, and the first edition of a hymn-book in Scotland was published. An intellectualist view of faith developed, and infant baptism was maintained.

Although the Glasite churches were strictly non-evangelistic in emphasis, holding that the apostolic commission had been confined to the original 12, the ideas of Glas spread, to Perth in 1733, Edinburgh in 1734, Arbroath, Dunkeld and Montrose in the 1730s, Galashiels in 1738, and Glasgow in 1762. Glas energetically visited the churches, which, although nominally independent, were held closely together by their founder and by his son-in-law, ROBERT SANDEMAN, from whom they took their English and American name of Sandemanian.

A number of Independent ministers in London, such as Samuel Pike, were strongly influenced by Glas's writings, and a London church established. JOHN WESLEY's friend, BENJAMIN INGHAM, for a time adopted the Glasite scheme in the north of England, and Sandeman was instrumental in planting a few churches in New England. In the 1760s a new interest in Glas's works led to the establishment of two small denominations, the Old Scots Independents and the Scotch Baptists, both of which perpetuated in a modified form Glasite church order and theology. Subsequently the HALDANE brothers, and ALEXANDER CAMPBELL who was instrumental in the early days of the Churches of Christ were influenced by Glas's ecclesiology and his intellectualist view of faith.

Glas himself outlived all his children, and continued to write, expound scripture and build up a strong church in Dundee until his death. He is characterized as a man of friendly and cheerful disposition, and his works exhibit no small measure of patristic and Puritan learning. Despite his lack of evangelical tenets, and his ultimately isolating view of the church, his influence is to be found beyond the little communities that took his name.

SELECT WRITINGS

J. Glas, *Works*, 2nd edn (Perth, Scotland, 1782–3)

BIBLIOGRAPHY

G. Cantor, *Michael Faraday, Scientist and Sandemanian* (London, 1991)

D. B. Murray, 'The Social and Theological Origins of Scottish Non-Presbyterian Protestant Dissent, 1730–1800, (St Andrews, unpublished thesis, 1977)

DEREK B. MURRAY

Glascott, Cradock (b. Cardiff, Wales, *c.* 1743; d. Hatherleigh, Devon, England, 11 Aug. 1831). Anglican clergyman. The son of Thomas Glascott of Cardiff, he was educated at Jesus College, Oxford (BA 1763, MA 1767). The date of his ordination is unknown, and there is little further information about him until he began to preach for Lady HUNTINGDON in 1766. He continued to do so until 1781.

He was one of the ministers at Spa Fields who were prosecuted in the Court of Arches at the promotion of the Reverend William Sellon, and was considering secession with Lady Huntingdon and her other ministers, when he was offered the benefice of Hatherleigh. He thereupon left the Connexion, but was able to retain his friendship with the Countess.

During his fifty years as Vicar of Hatherleigh he preached occasionally in Lady Huntingdon's chapels. He retained his Calvinistic Methodist sympathies, but objected to the Bible Christian chapel at Hatherleigh because it was Arminian. He examined candidates for Cheshunt (Trevecka) College when in London and continued to be interested in the work of the Connexion.

BIBLIOGRAPHY

Al. Ox.

Cheshunt College archives, Cambridge, original letters

E. Welch, ed., *Cheshunt College* (Hertfordshire Record Society, 1990)

EDWIN WELCH

Glazebrook, James (b. Madeley, Shropshire, England, 11 Oct. 1744; d. Belton, Leicestershire, England, 1 July 1803). Glazebrook was a collier when he was converted under the ministry of J. W. FLETCHER at Madeley. Fletcher nominated him in 1768 to be one of the first students at Trevecca College. Provision was made for his mother's support and he spent three years in training. Lacking a university education, he was nonetheless ordained deacon by the Bishop of Lichfield in 1771. His title was to the donative of Smisby (then in Derbyshire, now Leicestershire) in the gift of Lady HUNTINGDON's son. While at Smisby he preached in the area and was able to open a chapel for the Ashby-de-la-Zouch society on his Lordship's property.

In 1773 he became curate of the chapel of ease at Rowley Regis (Staffordshire), but was refused ordination as priest by a new bishop of Lichfield because of his evangelistic activities. It was not until 1777 and a new curacy that the Bishop of Worcester priested him. In 1779 he took charge of the chapel of ease newly opened at Latchford, near Warrington (Lancashire). Although he had already ceased to preach for the Countess of Huntingdon, he managed to combine Latchford with curacies in various benefices belonging to the Hastings family. On 11 February 1796 the Earl of Moira, Lady Huntingdon's grandson, who had inherited most of the Hastings estates, presented him to the vicarage of Belton in Leicestershire. He retained his Latchford cure in addition to the benefice until his death.

Despite his close links in early life with Fletcher, Glazebrook chose the Calvinist side in the disputes of 1770 and 1771. As a consequence he encountered some opposition from the Arminians and believed that JOHN WESLEY had preached against him at Ashby de la Zouch. He also engaged in a controversial exchange on baptism with Gilbert Wakefield who had resigned Anglican orders and moved to the dissenting Warrington Academy.

In later life he appears to have given up itinerant preaching and confined his evangelism to his own cures. THOMAS WHITAKER, in a brief biography added to the posthumous edition of Glazebrook's sermons, entirely ignores his early career and emphasizes his complete loyalty to the Anglican Church. Besides his *Letters on Infant Baptism* (1781), Glazebrook also published *The Sacrifice of Thanksgiving* (1789) and (posthumously) *Sermons* (1805), together also with an anonymous essay in defence of extempore preaching. Of a nervous temperament, Glazebrook was subject to extremes of spirits, 'being alternately much exalted and then as suddenly depressed' (Beaumont, 1889: 146).

BIBLIOGRAPHY
W. Beaumont, *History of Latchford* (Warrington, England, 1889)
Cheshunt College archives, Cambridge, original Fletcher letters
Methodist Archives, Manchester, copies of Fletcher's letters
(A. C. H. Seymour), *Life and Times of the Countess of Huntingdon* (London, 1844)
E. Welch, 'Lady Huntingdon's Chapel at Ashby', *Transactions of the Leicester Archaeological and Historical Society* (Leicester, England, 1992)
T. D. Whitaker (ed), *Sermons on Various Important Subjects* (Warrington, England, 1805)

ARTHUR POLLARD AND EDWIN WELCH

Gleed, George (b. Reading, England, c. 1779; d. Chalfont St Peter vicarage, Buckinghamshire, England, 6 June 1863). College tutor and Anglican clergyman. Son of Thomas Gleed (gentleman), George was educated at Reading School under Dr Valpy. In 1797 he matriculated from St John's College, Oxford, as fellow, becoming one of a circle of evangelical undergraduates of whom DANIEL WILSON was a leader. With JOHN NATT and three younger fellows, SAMUEL ARNOTT, CHARLES MAYO and JOHN BALL, he apparently assisted a growing evangelical influence at St John's *circa* 1800–30, holding various college and university offices. Ordained in 1804, he was Curate of Hanborough, Oxfordshire 1813–15 (parish registers), and Perpetual Curate of Northmoor, Oxfordshire, 1823–7. Appointed Vicar of Chalfont St Peter, Buckinghamshire, in 1830, he assisted materially in restoring the church *circa* 1854, and bequeathed funds to build a chapel of ease.

BIBLIOGRAPHY
GM (London, 1863)
J. S. Reynolds, *Evangelicals at Oxford* (Oxford, 1953; Appleford, England, 1975)

V. Sillery, *St John's College Biographical Register 1775–1875* (Oxford, 1987)

J. S. REYNOLDS

Glendinning, William (b. Moffatt, Dumfriesshire, Scotland, Oct. 1747; d. Raleigh, NC, USA, 28 June 1816). Methodist preacher. When Glendinning was 13 his father died and the boy was apprenticed to a tailor. Upon his mother's death six years later, and with his apprenticeship completed, Glendinning immigrated to America, arriving at Alexandria, Virginia in June 1767.

In Scotland and England Glendinning's religious association was largely with Presbyterians. He became acquainted with the Methodists in America. He was a Methodist travelling preacher for about ten years, until 1785. Glendinning enjoyed some prominence in the movement. In 1777 he was on the committee of five empowered to serve as an executive secretariat in case the general assistant appointed by JOHN WESLEY to supervise the American mission should return home before the next conference. He was a member of the 1784 Christmas Conference which established the MEC, but ceased travelling in June, 1785. He had been bitterly disappointed at not being selected for ordination at the Christmas Conference.

Glendinning had trouble with Bishops THOMAS COKE and FRANCIS ASBURY owing to sharing his unusual psychological experiences in his sermons. He was visited by apparitions, and experienced grotesque mood swings in his spiritual life. Another problem was that he wanted to travel at large and responsibility for a specific circuit was odious to him. Glendinning left the MEC after 1792 in support of the Republican Methodist movement led by JAMES O'KELLY.

SELECT WRITINGS
W. Glendinning, *The Life of William Glendinning, Preacher of the Gospel* (Philadelphia, PA, 1795).

BIBLIOGRAPHY
EWM
R. K. Lile (Unpublished genealogical research notes, 1991)
A. Stevens, *History of the Methodist Episcopal Church*, 4 vols (New York, 1864)

CHARLES W. BROCKWELL

Glenorchy, Lord. (*See* BREADALBANE, second Marquess and fifth Earl of.) [Campbell, John.]

Glenorchy, Lady Willielma [née Maxwell] (b. Preston, Scotland, 2 Sept. 1741; d. Edinburgh, Scotland, 17 July 1786). Willielma was the daughter of William, a wealthy medical man, and Elizabeth. Her father died before she was born, so she and her sister lived with their mother and step-father, till their marriages. She married on 26 September 1761 and her father-in-law, Lord Breadalbane, gave the Glenorchys almost complete control of his estates. Although a society lady Glenorchy was not content, and, becoming friends with ROWLAND HILL and family, she was influenced by evangelical thought which led to her conversion. She kept an introspective diary and corresponded with Jane Hill. Lady Glenorchy remained a convinced Calvinist, attached to the Church of Scotland and although she met and respected JOHN WESLEY she could not agree with his Arminianism. On her husband's death in 1771 Glenorchy became a very wealthy woman. She made plans to build a chapel in Edinburgh, which was opened in 1774. During 1776–86 Lady Glenorchy, often with Lady HENRIETTA HOPE, travelled to different parts of England and usually set up a chapel in her stopping places, especially if she felt the town was lacking in 'suitable' religious provision. Thus she opened chapels in Exmouth, Buxton, Carlisle, Matlock, Bristol Hot-Wells, Newton Burhill, Devonshire, and Workington. Lady DARCY MAXWELL was appointed her executrix.

BIBLIOGRAPHY
E. D. Graham, 'The Contribution of Lady Glenorchy and her Circle to the Evangelical Revival' (Leeds Univ. BD thesis, 1965)
T. S. Jones, *The Life of Willielma, Viscountess Glenorchy* (Edinburgh and London, 1822)

E. DOROTHY GRAHAM

Glyn, Sir **George Carr** [first Baron Wolverton] (b. London, 1797; d. 24 July 1873). British MP and banker. The fourth son of Sir Richard Carr Glyn, MP, a vice-president of the Royal Humane Society, he was the elder brother of the Reverend JOHN CARR GLYN, and a cousin of JOHN PEMBERTON PLUMPTRE (1791–1864), MP. Glyn inherited his father's prosperous banking firm, Glyn, Halifax and Company, and had interests as well in railways and shipping. Whig MP for Kendal (1847–68), he supported the ballot and the abolition of church rates. He was created first Baron Wolverton in 1869.

Glyn was on the original committee of the evangelical Scripture Readers' Association (1844) and is said to have taken a high moral tone in his business dealings. In 1869 he attended the EA General Conference at Geneva. In 1823 he married Marianne Grenfell, a daughter of Pascoe Grenfell, MP. Glyn's son, George Grenfell Glyn, the second Baron Wolverton (*DNB*, 1824–87), was a Liberal politician of some note.

BIBLIOGRAPHY
Evangelical Christendom (1869): 39
Record (4 March 1844)
Stenton

JONATHAN BURKE CUTMORE AND DONALD M. LEWIS

Glyn, John Carr (b. 1 July 1799; d. Witchampton, Dorsetshire, England, 25 Oct. 1896). Anglican clergyman.

He was the son of Sir Richard Carr Glyn (1755–1838), a Whig MP and sometime Lord Mayor of London (see *DNB*), and younger brother of GEORGE CARR GLYN, MP (first Baron Wolverton from 1869) and an exeedingly wealthy banker. John Carr Glyn was educated at Westminster and Christ Church, Oxford (BA 1821; MA 1827), becoming Rector of Standbridge (or Little Hinton) and Witchampton, where he spent the rest of his life in a remarkably long incumbency (1830–96). He was a member of the Dorset Clerical Meeting and came to know HENRY MOULE and to be godfather of Moule's youngest son, Handley Carr Glyn Moule, subsequently Bishop of Durham. From 1839 he served on the board of the LCM, at a time when few Anglican ministers would countenance such interdenominational cooperation. Glyn founded the Girls' Industrial Home at Poole and built St John's Church, Wimborne (1876) as well as two church schools. He was CMS secretary for Dorsetshire (1848–50 and 1867–96) and active nationally with the Bible Society.

BIBLIOGRAPHY

Boase
J. S. Reynolds, *The Evangelicals at Oxford 1835–71* (Abingdon, England, 1975) Additional Contents: 105

ARTHUR POLLARD

Gobat, Samuel (b. Berne, 26 Jan. 1799; d. Jerusalem, 11 May 1879). CMS missionary and second Anglican bishop in Jerusalem. Gobat was born when Berne was a part of France, with French rather than German as his mother tongue. Gobat grew up Swiss in a comfortable Christian home, and was converted under pietistic influences. He studied at the Basel Seminary and in Paris before his Lutheran ordination in 1826. In the same year he went to the CMS Institute (Islington, London), and was sent to Egypt by the CMS in the hope that he might reach Abyssinia (Ethiopia). He was able to study Amharic, and with a companion (who died in an accident) reached Gondar in 1829. Apart from some leave in Europe, he remained in Abyssinia, at Shoa, until 1841. He had married in 1834 and his wife bore several children (and lost two) in that period. Other CMS missionaries joined him; their relations with the ancient Coptic church, though friendly, did not lead to reforms. The Galla they met, not yet Christian or Muslim, showed more hope for mission.

In 1841 Gobat left Ethiopia for health reasons, and resigned from CMS. He was teaching in Malta, and already an Anglican deacon, when he received an invitation from the King of Prussia to succeed MICHAEL ALEXANDER as Bishop in Jerusalem. He was priested and consecrated at Lambeth, as second Anglican bishop in Jerusalem, in 1846, and at Christmas he reached Jerusalem. His appointment did not change the hostility shown to such an episcopate by High Church Anglicans, Lutherans and Roman Catholics, as well from the Orthodox hierarchy and Muslim authorities. Gobat also refused to direct his energies to the aims of those Christians who wished to see a return of Jews (without their conversion) to the Holy Land. He received support from the British archbishops, and while avoiding proselytism among Orthodox Christians, he encouraged scripture distribution and reserved the right to accept individuals excommunicated by their own priests.

Linguistically well prepared for his new role, he was active from the beginning. Christ Church on Mount Zion was completed and consecrated in 1849. He started schools and dispensaries for different communities in and around Jerusalem, and recruited some missionaries through CMS. Many of these were Basel-trained German or Swiss, who served for long periods, such as Frederick Klein, 52 years in Palestine and Egypt. The Crimean War (1854–6) was seen as bringing new opportunities, with a decree granting religious liberty throughout the Turkish empire, and K. G. PFANDER, S. W. KOELLE and others began a witness in Constantinople, which continued till 1864. The missionaries were then expelled, Bibles seized and converts imprisoned. This was the end of the mission, though Koelle continued to live in Constantinople.

Gobat remained as bishop in Jerusalem until his death in 1879. He transferred to the CMS the institutions he had established, such as the hospitals in Nazareth and Nablus, and from 1876 the number of missionaries sent from Britain increased considerably. His work in establishing schools, appropriate for the community they would serve, was a much appreciated feature of his episcopate. His successor as bishop in Jerusalem, Barclay, did not live long, and the episcopacy was suspended for a number of years.

His wife died just three months after his death. Of their seven surviving children, two of his daughters married CMS missionaries who served under him (Zeller and J. T. WOLTERS). His grandson, the Reverend Theodore Gobat, was present in Jerusalem in 1899 when the jubilee of Christ Church was celebrated.

BIBLIOGRAPHY

Anon., Memoir: Samuel Gobat, Bishop of Jerusalem, drawn chiefly from his own journals (London, 1884)

M. A. Gidney, The History of the London Society for Promoting Christianity Among the Jews from 1809 to 1908 (London, 1908)

S. Gobat, Journal of a Three Year's Residence in Ethiopia (London, 1834)

JOCELYN MURRAY

Goddard, Kingston (b. Philadelphia, PA, USA, 20 Oct. 1813; d. Richmond, Staten Island, NY, USA, 24 Oct. 1875). Episcopal clergyman. He graduated from the General Theological Seminary and was ordained (deacon 3 July 1836, priest 25 April 1838) by Bishop Benjamin T. Onderdonk. He was Rector of Christ Church, Brooklyn, 1838–43, Emmanuel Church, Brooklyn, 1843–6, and St John's Church, Clifton, 1846–7, all in New York. From 1847 to 1859 he was the first Rector of the Church of the Atonement, Philadelphia. He was Rector of Christ Church, Cincinnati, 1859–62, Rector of St Paul's Church, Philadelphia, 1862–6, and finished his ministry as Rector of St Andrew's Church, Richmond, New York. He belonged to numerous evangelical associations and defended the secessionist evangelicals who formed the Reformed Episcopal Church but did not join them.

DONALD SMITH ARMENTROUT

Godet, Frédéric (b. Neuchâtel, Switzerland, 25 Oct. 1812; d. Neuchâtel, Switzerland, 29 Oct. 1900). Reformed theologian, pastor, professor, and author. Godet, a native of Switzerland, was an ordained clergyman and theologian for the Eglise Evangélique Indépendante. He served as professor of Old and New Testament at the University of Neuchâtel (1873–87). Deeply concerned at the incursions of critical biblical studies methods into the church and their use in the universities against structures of biblical authority, he sought to use the tools of historical and critical research to bolster the revelational authority of the biblical text in the church and society. To that end he engaged in an extensive publishing programme. In 1863 he published the first volume of his massive commentary on the Gospel of John: Commentaire sur l'Evangile de Saint Jean (Paris, 1863, 1865). This was accompanied by a small volume which responded to critical questions raised by contemporary research on the Gospel of John: Examen des Principals Questions Critiques Soulevées de Nos Jours au Sujet du Quatrième Evangile . . . avec un Chapitre Nouveau sur la Certitude de l'Histoire Évangélique (Paris, 1865); an essay which was supplemented by an analysis of recent scholarship on the early witnesses to the Gospel of John [Compte Rendu des Discussions Récentes Relatives aux Témoignages Ecclésiastiques sur le Quatrième Evangile (Paris, 1869)]. He also published a defence of the authenticity of the miracles reported in the Gospel narratives: Les Miracles de Jésus-Christ (Neuchâtel, 1867).

Commentaries on Romans, I Corinthians and Luke soon followed: Commentaire sur l'Epître aux Romains (Paris, 1879, 1880), Commentaire sur la Premiere Epître aux Corinthiens (Paris, no date) and Commentaire sur l'Evangile de Saint Luc (Neuchâtel, 1871). In addition to the commentaries, an introduction to the New Testament was provided: Introduction au Nouveau Testament (Neuchatel, 1893, 1894); this to supplement Etudes Bibliques (2nd edn, Paris, 1873, 1874).

A committed churchman, he also became an apologist in the public arena. He published his response to the liberal theologian Colani [M. Colani et le Protestantisme Évangélique, Réponse à une Conférence Libérale Tenue dans Plusieurs Églises du Midi (Paris, 1893)] and Conférences Apologétiques (Paris, no date) translated as Lectures in Defence of the Christian Faith (Edinburgh, 1881).

Because of his approach to critical biblical studies, Godet's works were translated into German. His theories, methods and conclusions, framed in his massively erudite and comprehensive analysis, provided an intellectual biblical framework for the Free Churches and *Gemeinschaftsbewegung* in Germany. He continues to influence conservative German churches through such instruments as the Wuppertal *Studiebibel* which builds on his work. His works were translated in English, German, Italian, Spanish and Swedish. In England and North America, his work was translated and transmitted through numerous editions and printings. The commentaries and apologetic approaches significantly influenced all branches of American evangelicalism.

BIBLIOGRAPHY
P. Godet, *Frédéric Godet (1812–1900) d'Après sa Correspondence et d'Autres Documents Inédits* (Neuchâtel, Paris, 1913)
—, *Souvenirs de Jeunesse* (Neuchâtel, Paris, 1923)
G. Hörster, 'Godet, Frédéric', *Evangelisches Gemeindelexikon* hrsq. E. Geldbach, *et al.* (Wuppertal, Germany, 1978)

DAVID BUNDY

Godfrey, Henry (b. London, 1781; d. Cambridge, England, 16 Oct. 1832). Anglican clergyman and scholar. Godfrey was educated at St Paul's and Queens' College, Cambridge (BA 1802; MA 1805; BD 1813; DD 1822), of which he became a fellow (1803) during the presidency of ISAAC MILNER, whom he succeeded in that office (1820–32), thus maintaining the evangelical character of the college. He also served as Vice-Chancellor of the university (1822) and was an active supporter of the CMS.

BIBLIOGRAPHY
Al. Cant., II, iii: 71

ARTHUR POLLARD

Godwin, Benjamin (b. Bath, Somerset, England, 10 Oct. 1785; d. Bradford, Yorkshire, England, 20 Feb. 1871). Baptist minister. Godwin ran away to sea at the age of 15 and saw action in the Napoleonic wars. Largely self-educated he engaged in pioneer evangelism in the Forest of Dean and Cornwall. After ministries at Dartmouth and Great Missenden he was appointed classical tutor at the Horton Academy, Bradford, and pastor of Sion Chapel. In this fastest growing Victorian industrial town he quickly became part of a very influential Nonconformist Liberal elite. He was prominent in many causes such as, the antislavery movement and opposition to the teaching of Robert Owen. Lectures on these two themes were delivered to packed audiences and subsequently published, both series were republished in America resulting in the University of Columbia conferring on him the degree of DD. He was also active in general election campaigns, the Mechanics' Institute, Peace Movement, debates on the Roman Catholic controversy, the founding of the *Bradford Observer* (which was Bradford's leading newspaper for the rest of the century), the BFBS, and in the Yorkshire Baptist Association.

In 1836 he moved to Liverpool on becoming the secretary of the Serampore Mission. He worked hard for two years for the reconciliation of the mission and the BMS in 1842. From 1838 he was minister of the New Road Church, Oxford. In 1843 he published an *Examination of the Principles and Tendencies of Dr. Pusey's sermon on the Eucharist*. Failing health caused retirement in 1845 and he moved back to Bradford where he soon resumed his involvement in local affairs including discussions on the 'Secular' question with Holyoake. A very lengthy manuscript autobiography, written for his son, is in the Angus Library of Regent's Park College, Oxford and an edited transcription in Bradford City Library. Bradford Archives department hold unpublished lecture notes and essays. Godwin's son became Mayor of Bradford and his grandson the first Lord Mayor.

BIBLIOGRAPHY
Baptist Handbook 1872: 220–22
E. C. Starr, ed., *A Baptist Bibliography*, 25 vols (New York, 1947–76)

DAVID B. MILNER

Goetschius, John Henry (b. Berneck, Switzerland, 8 March 1717; d. Schraalenburgh, NJ, BNA, 14 Nov. 1774). Dutch Reformed minister in the Middle Colonies. Upon his arrival in Pennsylvania in 1735, Goetschius, then 17 years old, began preaching in various churches in the Delaware Valley. When the presbytery of Philadelphia denied him ordination because of his lack of learning, Goetschius studied in the 'kitchen seminary' of PETER HENRY DORSIUS in Bucks County and was later ordained by Dorsius, THEODORUS JACOBUS FRELINGHUYSEN, and GILBERT TENNENT.

The Classis of Amsterdam and most of the Dutch Reformed ministers in the Middle Colonies refused to recognize Goetschius's ordination because of his pietistic leanings and his schismatic tendencies. In 1740, however, amid the ferment of the Great Awakening, Goetschius secured an appointment among the pietistic Dutch on Long Island, where his tenure was marked by bitter recriminations between supporters and opponents of the revival. His adversaries haled him before an ecclesiastical commission, where he met with questions about his personal probity and his practice of barring opponents from Holy Communion. Goetschius initially refused to cooperate in the investigation, denying the ecclesiastical authority of both the Classis of Amsterdam and the New York clergy and calling his accusers 'plainly godless people'. At the insistence of the Classis of Amsterdam, however, Goetschius finally submitted to an ordination examination and transferred to the Dutch Church at Hackensack, New Jersey, where he served until his death in 1774.

BIBLIOGRAPHY
DAB
R. Balmer, *A Perfect Babel of Confusion* (New York, 1989): 123–7
—, 'John Henry Goetschius and *The Unknown God*: Eighteenth-Century Pietism in the Middle Colonies', *Pennsylvania Magazine of History and Biography*, 113 (1989): 575–608

RANDALL BALMER

Gogerly, George   (b. London, 10 Nov. 1794; d. London, 11 Feb. 1877). LMS missionary in India. Converted after the death of his baby son (the first of four boys lost), he began street preaching and studying theology with JAMES HILL, but there was considerable opposition to his ordination. Six months after his arrival in Calcutta in April 1819, he was described as 'inadequate in all respects'. A printer by trade, he was incapable of managing the under-resourced LMS press.

From 1822 onwards Gogerly was constantly ill with dysentery and hepatitis. Accused of altering the minutes while district secretary, Gogerly's health completely broke down after the Union chapel controversy of 1836–7. An 1838 furlough did not improve his health, and he sailed home after acting as LMS treasurer from 1839 to 1841. His first wife died in April 1823. Agnes Ferris, whom he married in 1824, campaigned for girls' schools, raising funds in Britain. She died 23 November 1877. Gogerly's book, *Pioneers of the Bengal Mission* (1871), is wild and inaccurate.

E. M. JACKSON

Going, Jonathan   (b. Reading, VT, USA, 7 March 1786; d. Granville, OH, USA, 9 Nov. 1844). Baptist pastor, educator, and mission executive. He was descended from Robert Gowing of Edinburgh. Converted as a freshman at Brown University, he was licensed to preach before his graduation in 1809. His parents and siblings made a profession of faith in response to his preaching, and his three brothers followed him into the Baptist ministry. He served as pastor in Cavendish, Vermont (1811–15) and Worcester, Massachusetts (1815–32). Influenced by several years' correspondence with JOHN MASON PECK and a tour of the Midwest in 1831, he became chief organizer and first corresponding secretary of the American Baptist Home Missionary Society (1832–7) and president and professor of theology at Granville (Ohio) Literary and Theological Institution, now Denison University (1837–44). He held honorary degrees from the University of Vermont (AM 1812) and Waterville (Maine) College (DD 1832). His leadership skills and generous spirit were enhanced by an iron constitution and a ready wit. True to his name, he was always 'going', tirelessly promoting Sunday schools, ministerial education, temperance reforms, and 'revivals of religion'.

BIBLIOGRAPHY
AAP
DAB

NCAB
WhAmHS

F. CALVIN PARKER

Golak Nath   (b. India, 1816, d. India). Indian Presbyterian minister. A convert from a high caste Bengali family based in the Punjab, Golak Nath was baptized while at college in Ludhiana. He joined the Presbyterian mission and espoused the Princeton theology. Golak Nath single-handedly ran the American Presbyterian station at Jullundur from its inception in 1846 until the first European missionaries arrived in 1886, shepherding a mass movement and organizing a school programme.

When American missionaries tried to make him a permanent consultative member of the mission, and then a full member (a status he held 1857–67), they were overruled by the Home Board. His eminent son-in-law, K. C. Chatterji, received similar treatment. Golak Nath saw racial motivations in these decisions. Not unsurprisingly, his son Charles was present at the founding of the Indian National Congress, and was a member of its steering committee in 1888, 1893, and 1900.

Golak Nath was the patriarch of a family dedicated to public service: his son Henry was a Princeton-trained pioneer missionary; John, a judge; Charles, the Principal of Lahore Law College; and William, a distinguished civil servant, was awarded an MBE. One of Golak Nath's granddaughters, Raj Kumari Amrit Kaur, was Minister of Health in the first independent government of India.

BIBLIOGRAPHY
H. Golaknath, *Golak the Hero* (Bombay, 1932)
J. C. Webster, *The Christian Community and Change in Nineteenth Century North India* (Delhi, 1976)

E. M. JACKSON

Goldie, Hugh   (b. probably Scotland; d. Old Calabar [eastern Nigeria], 18 Aug. 1895). Scottish missionary of the United Presbyterian Church in Jamaica and Old Calabar. He went as a catechist in 1840 from a congregation in Stirling, Scotland, to the United Presbyterian Church Mission in Jamaica where he and his wife worked for six years at Negril. In 1847 he was ordained and they moved to the Old Calabar mission, founded in 1846 by HOPE WADDELL, where he was to remain for 48 years. The religious instruction he gave was based on close expositions of the Bible, reinforced by constant catechizing. His converts too had to catechize the members of their households regularly. A scholarly linguist, he worked systematically on the Efik language, published an Efik translation of the New Testament in 1852, and subsequently Efik grammars and an Efik dictionary. He also printed many religious tracts in Efik, and wrote 300 Efik hymns, mostly translated from the Psalms.

SELECT WRITINGS
H. Goldie, *Calabar and its Mission* (Edinburgh, 1901)

BIBLIOGRAPHY
D. M. Macfarlan, *Calabar* (London, 1957)

CHRISTOPHER FYFE

Gollmer, Charles Andrew (b. Kircheim, Wurtemburg, Germany, 30 Nov. 1812; d. Margate, England, 23 December 1886). CMS missionary in Sierra Leone and Yorubaland. Like many of the early CMS missionaries, Gollmer was born in Germany, and, after experiencing a conversion, was educated at the Basel Mission College, and the CMS College, Islington. He was ordained (deacon and priest 1841) and sent to Sierra Leone. There he prepared for his future assignment in the Yoruba country by learning Yoruba, and by building two large portable wooden houses for the mission. He took charge of the mission at Badagry in 1845, moving to Lagos in 1851, and in 1857 to Ikija where he remained until he retired in 1862. He translated religious tracts into Yoruba, and circulated them round the mission. During his retirement he revised the Yoruba version of the Bible. Two of his successive wives died in West Africa, the third, by whom he had four children, survived and returned home with him.

BIBLIOGRAPHY
J. F. A. Ajayi, *Christian Missions in Nigeria, 1841–1941* (London, 1965)
C. H. V. Gollmer, *Charles Andrew Gollmer, his Life and Missionary Labours in Africa* (London, 1889)

CHRISTOPHER FYFE

Good, John Mason (b. Epping, Essex, England, 25 May 1764; d. Shepperton, Middlesex, England, 2 Jan. 1827). English author and medical practitioner. He was the son of a Congregational minister who was his first tutor. At the age of 15 he was apprenticed to a medical practitioner and in 1784 went to London to study at Guy's Hospital. In 1793 he was admitted to the College of Surgeons and two years later won a prize for an essay on diseases in workhouses. In 1794 he had become active in the General Pharmaceutic Association, for whom he wrote his *History of Medicine as it Relates to the Profession of the Apothecary* (1795). At this point his professional career seems to have taken off.

At the same time he was also much engaged in translating classical verse and mastering a wide variety of languages. From 1804 to 1812 he was much engaged with his friend and biographer, OLINTHUS GREGORY, in preparing his *Pantologia*, an encyclopedia in 12 volumes, many of the articles written by himself. In 1805 he was elected an FRS and in 1820 secured his MD, while two years later he became a licentiate of the Royal College of Physicians. In 1812 he published a series of lectures entitled, *A Book of Nature*, and in 1822 a well received *Study of Medicine* in four volumes. Essentially, however, he was a conscientious rather than a creative scholar.

At the beginning of the 1790s he had become a Unitarian but in 1807 he withdrew from them because he believed that their teachings were leading people into scepticism, becoming thereafter an evangelical Anglican, supporting the work of the CMS, giving introductory medical instruction to future missionaries. He also published poetry and biblical translations. J. M. Neale, the Cambridge ecclesiologist, was his grandson.

BIBLIOGRAPHY
DNB
O. Gregory, *Memoir* (London, 1828)

J. H. Y. BRIGGS

Goode, Francis (b. 1797 or 8; d. Clapham, Surrey, England, 19 Nov. 1842). Anglican clergyman and missionary. He was the son of WILLIAM GOODE (1762–1816), who had succeeded WILLIAM ROMAINE as the Rector of St Andrews-by-the-Wardrobe and St Anne's, Blackfriars, by his wife, Rebecca, daughter of Abraham Coles, silk manufacturer of London, and was the elder brother of WILLIAM GOODE (1801–68), one of the leading Anglican evangelicals of the Victorian period. He was educated at St Paul's School, London, of which he was captain in 1815, and at Trinity College, Cambridge, where he was awarded the Bell University scholarship in 1817 and became Perry exhibitioner in 1821. He was elected to a fellowship after graduating as seventh wrangler in 1820. After ordination he went to India in the service of the CMS. On his return he was made evening lecturer of Clapham, Surrey and in 1834 morning preacher at the Female Orphan Asylum, London. He published a number of sermons of which a collection *The Better Covenant* (1833) reached its fifth edition in 1848.

BIBLIOGRAPHY
GM
DNB

VIVIAN H. H. GREEN

Goode, William (Sr) (b. Buckingham, Buckinghamshire, England, 2 April 1762; d. Stockwell, Surrey, England, 15 April 1816). Anglican clergyman. After early schooling in his home town Goode passed under the tuition of two evangelicals, first Bull at Newport Pagnell and then Thomas Clarke at Chesham Bois. He experienced an early evangelical conversion at the age of 13. Under Clarke he was a fellow pupil with EDWARD BURN (later of St Mary's and St James's, Birmingham) and BASIL WOODD (later of Bentinck Chapel, London). He entered Magdalen Hall, Oxford in 1780 (BA 1784; MA 1787). He became Curate of Abbots Langley (1784–6), adding King's Langley in 1785. He then joined WILLIAM ROMAINE as Curate of St Andrew-by-the-Wardrobe and St Anne's, Blackfriars in 1786, adding the Sunday afternoon lectureship at St Anne's (1789–96) and the Tuesday evening lectureship at St Lawrence Jewry in 1793. He followed Romaine as Rector of St Andrew's and St Anne's (1795–1816) on the death of the latter.

Resigning the lectureship at St Anne's, he became Sunday afternoon lecturer at St John's, Wapping (1796–1816), Sunday evening lecturer at Christ Church, Spitalfields (1807–10) and Wednesday morning lecturer at Blackfriars in 1810. It will be seen that he was a diligent and frequent preacher.

Goode was also active in the formation and development of various societies. He was present at the famous Castle and Falcon Hotel meeting which saw the first suggestions of CMS, and the committee met in his study till 1812. He also travelled extensively on its behalf, undertaking tours, for example, to Derbyshire, North Cheshire and Shrewsbury in the autumn of 1813 and to Norwich and Ipswich in the following year, this latter with JOSIAH PRATT. Goode supported the BFBS at its establishment and was president of the Blackfriars auxiliary. He also helped the Naval and Military Bible Society and in 1809 he was among the early members of the Jews Society.

Goode was a firm Churchman, his candidature for St Michael, Wood Street, in 1792 recording that 'The Articles of the Church he firmly believes, without *limitation* or *reserve*; and the whole of its services he glories in, as most conformable to the word of God.' He continued Romaine's practice in holding a weekly Communion. Like contemporary and later Evangelicals he was against 'the theatre and almost all places of public resort for the *mere* purpose of pleasure' (Goode, 1828: 94) and against card-playing for its associations with gambling. These antagonisms may have had something to do with Goode's own retiring disposition, for the same writer alleges that 'his piety was of the most cheerful and rational kind, and quite free also from anything of a narrow or self-opinionated nature' (ibid.: 83).

His series of 156 *Essays on All the Scriptural Names and Titles of Christ* was published posthumously (1822), but he had earlier published *An Entire New Version of the Book of Psalms* (1811), said to embody 'closeness of interpretation, simplicity of diction and an adaptation to New Testament views' (Goode, 1828: 121). He sent the whole print run of the second edition to SAMUEL MARSDEN in New South Wales but the Colonial Office forbade its issue as an unauthorized version.

The son describes Goode's theology as 'comprehensive, moderate and scriptural' and not 'a religion of feelings and impulses' and classifies him as 'a moderate Calvinist' (ibid.: 164–6). Among his sons were his biographer WILLIAM GOODE (1801–68) who became Dean of Ripon and FRANCIS GOODE (1797–1842), CMS missionary to India and on his return evening lecturer at Clapham.

BIBLIOGRAPHY
Al. Ox.: II. 537
DNB
W. Goode, ed., *Memoir of the Late Rev. William Goode*, (London, 1828)

ARTHUR POLLARD

Goode, William (b. London, 10 Nov. 1801; d. Ripon, Yorkshire, England, 13 Aug. 1868). Anglican clergyman and theological writer. Goode was the second son of the Reverend WILLIAM GOODE and the younger brother of FRANCIS GOODE. He was educated at St Paul's School, London, at Trinity College, Cambridge (BA 1825; MA 1828), and at Peterhouse, Cambridge (DD 1860). He was ordained in 1825 (deacon 19 June; priest 18 December), and served as Curate of Christchurch, Newgate Street, London, under SAMUEL CROWTHER. In 1835, he was appointed by Lord Melbourne, the Prime Minister, to the rectory of St Antholin, Watling Street, London. He was presented, in 1849, by J. B. SUMNER to the rectory of All Hallows the Great with All Hallows the Less, Thames Street, London. Between 1853 and 1857, Goode was Warburtonian lecturer. On the death of Archdeacon Hollinsworth in 1856, he was presented by Lord Chancellor Cronworth (as a reward for his labours, particularly in the Gorham case) to the wealthy living of St Margaret, Lothbury, St Christopher le Stocks, Threadneedle Street, and St Bartholomew-by-the-Exchange, Bartholomew Lane, London. In 1860, upon the recommendation of Lord SHAFTESBURY (who, sensitive to the charge of doctrinal partisanship, misleadingly described Goode as 'Moderate High Church'), he was elevated by Lord Palmerston to the deanery of Ripon. He was married to Katherine Isabella, daughter of the Hon. William Cust, but seems to have died childless.

For several years Goode served as editor of the *Christian Observer*, the mouthpiece of the moderate wing of the evangelical party. In this capacity, he championed a number of causes, most especially its opposition to the more extreme doctrines advanced by the leaders of the Oxford Movement.

Goode's opposition to the advancement of Tractarianism reached something of a climax in the celebrated Gorham affair, which occurred during the late 1840s and early 1850s, and which chiefly concerned the doctrine of baptismal regeneration. He took a most active part in this prolonged – and embittered – debate, serving as one of G. C. GORHAM's most loyal and articulate supporters, and publishing a series of pamphlets in support of his cause: *The Doctrine of the Church of England as to the Effects of Baptism in the Case of Infants* (1849); *A Letter to the Bishop of Exeter* (1850); *The case of Archdeacon Wilberforce Compared With That of Mr. Gorham* (1854).

In the course of the debate, Goode argued that regeneration could occur in baptism, but insisted upon the conditions of faith and repentance for the efficacy of the sacrament, albeit not denying that infants might receive grace through it. As a concession to his doctrinal opponents, he conceded that, in some cases, regeneration and adoption are 'formally made over, and in that sense given, in and by baptism'. Such a position was broadly representative of that held by the moderate wing of the evangelical party, and was not inconsistent with that advanced by Gorham during the course of his examination before Bishop Phillpotts and his chaplain William Maskell. Despite his willingness to appear conciliatory, Goode warned Phillpotts that if the doctrine of baptismal regeneration were to be made authoritative by the Judicial Committee of the Privy Council, a large evangelical schism out of the Church of England could not be avoided. Phillpotts, no doubt, anticipated this.

Goode was a learned divine and a zealous supporter of scriptural and Protestant principles. Regarded by contemporaries as the *facil princeps* of the evangelical party, he left his mark on many aspects of English Church life. He was theologically moderate, decidedly loyal to the Church of England and its Protestant heritage, and suspicious of theological innovation such as premillennialism, High Calvinism, and prayer-book reform (which he feared would undermine its Protestant character). Besides editing the *Christian Observer*, he also published a large number of books, tracts, and pamphlets (which alone fill seven columns in the British Library Catalogue), addressing a remarkable range of spiritual subjects. His work, *The Divine Rule of Faith and Practice* (1842), a systematic exposition of the leading doctrines of Protestant theology, was particularly influential. Goode's scholarship, second to none within the 'gospel party', bore comparison with that of any English divine. His contribution to the evangelical cause in England is difficult to overestimate.

BIBLIOGRAPHY
Al. Cant.
Anon., Obituary, reprinted from the *Clerical Journal* (London, 1833)
Anon., *Men of the Time*, 1 (London, 1865): 357–8
Boase, 1: 1172–3
CO (September 1868): 701–2
DNB
Guardian (19 August 1868)
ILN, III, 187 (1868)
J. C. S. Nias, *Gorham and the Bishop of Exeter* (London, 1951)
Record (14 August 1868)
P. Toon, *Evangelical Theology 1833–1856* (London, 1979)

GRAYSON CARTER

Goodell, William (b. Coventry, NY, USA, 25 Oct. 1792; d. Janesville, WI, USA, 14 Feb. 1878). Editor, social reformer, and political abolitionist. After an early career in business, Goodell became an editor of a temperance paper. In 1833, he was one of the organizers of the American Anti-Slavery Society. He published the society's organ, the *Emancipator*, and then edited another abolitionist paper, *The Friend of Man*. In the 1840s, he was one of the founders of the Liberty Party, an avowedly Christian antislavery political party. When a large portion of the Liberty Party merged into the more moderate Free Soil Party in 1848 (and later into the Republican Party), Goodell was the leader of a faction that continued to propose a thoroughgoing reformist platform. Eventually this faction became the Radical Abolitionist Party; Goodell became editor of its paper, the *Radical Abolitionist*, later called the *Principia*. Goodell was also committed to ecclesiastical reform on the basis of 'Christian union', whereby sanctified persons would secede from corrupt, proslavery churches and unite together into democratically congregational 'Union churches'. Toward this end, he established and pastored a model non-sectarian abolitionist church in Honeoye, New York, and edited a Unionist paper, the *Christian Investigator* from 1842 to 1848.

BIBLIOGRAPHY
DAB

DOUGLAS M. STRONG

Goodman, Sir **George** (b. 1792; d. Roundhay, Leeds, Yorkshire, England, 13 Oct. 1859). Baptist, mayor, and MP. The first mayor of the reformed Leeds corporation, Goodman, a wool-stapler, became mayor on three further occasions (1847, 1850, 1851), advocating the municipal provision of services for the health and welfare of the people. A convinced free-trader, he supported the initiative called 'Leeds New Move', an early group advocating household suffrage. The Leeds representative to the Great Exhibition and so knighted in 1852, he served as MP for Leeds from 1852 to 1857. Although brought up in the South Parade Baptist Church, and laying the foundation stone of the future open-membership Blenheim Chapel in 1849 which he had helped to gather, he did not become a member until 1850 after being baptized in his own house. A generous supporter of Leeds charities, he also gave freely to the building of Baptist chapels and to the support of the Yorkshire College.

BIBLIOGRAPHY
Boase
D. W. Bebbington, *BQ*, (1981): 12
D. Fraser, *Urban Politics in Victorian England* (London, 1976)
E. P. Hennock, *Fit and Proper Persons* (London, 1973)
C. E. Shipley, in *The Baptists of Yorkshire* (London, 1912): 149

J. H. Y. BRIGGS

Gopi Nath Nandi (b. Calcutta, India, 1807; d. 16 March 1861). Indian Presbyterian minister. Gopi Nath Nandi entered the General Assembly of the Church of Scotland's Institution at its 1830 opening, and was influenced there by ALEXANDER DUFF's lectures. After being baptized, he and DANIEL CORRIE went to Futtehpur and started a school for orphans. Financial support for this school declined as the American Presbyterian Mission expanded from its base at Allahabad.

He was licensed as an evangelist and then ordained. He helped organize the first synod in November 1845 and developed a wide-ranging ministry, including superintending village schools, running a jail ministry, and itinerating. His bungalow was a meeting place for Christians of all denominations.

When Gopi Nath's European friends were murdered during the Mutiny, he and his wife acted with great courage to save orphans. He was captured and imprisoned, and given three days to recant. Major Brazier rescued him in time, but his health was shattered and he died on the operating table.

BIBLIOGRAPHY
D. Corrie, *Memoirs of the Rt Revd Daniel Corrie Compiled By His Brothers* (London, 1847): 536–7
National Library of Scotland, Edinburgh, Alexander Duff's correspondence: 164f
M. A. Sherring, *The Indian Church in the Great Rebellion* (London, 1859): 184–6
G. Smith, *A Life of Alexander Duff*, I: 169f

E. M. JACKSON

Gordon, Adam (b. Ireland, *c.* 1770; d. Serampore, India, 17 July 1834). Baptist gaoler. One of the Serampore Trio's oldest friends, Gordon ensured that his prisoners in Calcutta received pastoral visits and were treated humanely. He also supported Bengali evangelists with money and friendship. Reports of his work appeared regularly in the *Periodical Accounts* of the BMS from 1809 onwards. During 'the Controversy', Gordon supported Serampore. He died in the same epidemic that claimed his old friend WILLIAM CAREY.

BIBLIOGRAPHY
BMS archives, London, W. Ward, Journal

E. M. JACKSON

Gordon, Alexander (b. Scotland; d. 1857) Lawyer and financier. Gordon was one of a number of expatriate Scots among the lawyers and businessmen who provided so much lay leadership for Anglican evangelicalism in the second quarter of the nineteenth century. According to Ford K. Brown's *Fathers of the Victorians*, he contributed to at least 33 societies, was vice-president of two, treasurer of two, committee member of one and governor of eight.

When the newly founded *Record* newspaper began to flounder in 1828, he was one of the three who guaranteed its financial stability as an evangelical mouthpiece, and secured the active involvement of ALEXANDER HALDANE. Haldane would set his powerful and unmistakable stamp upon the *Record* for over half a century, and would make it by far the largest of the religious press. If there was any task which Haldane set himself, it was the defence of the United Kingdom as a Christian nation, and there was no policy which Gordon supported more strongly or sought to implement more actively. He was the dominant figure in the Christian Influence Society, which brought THOMAS CHALMERS to London in 1838 to give his highly popular lectures on church establishments, arguing primarily from pragmatic considerations, and then brought HUGH MCNEILE in 1840 to give the biblical basis. Gordon was instrumental in the organization of the Established Church Society, LDOS, the Christian Electors' Committee, and the Anti-Maynooth Committee which sought to protect Protestant Britain from

supporting the education of the Irish Roman Catholic priesthood. He was also involved with the LCM from its inception in 1835, believing not only in missionary work overseas and at home, but also convinced that the Christian nation could not continue without the evangelization of the urban proletariat.

BIBLIOGRAPHY
D. M. Lewis, *Lighten Their Darkness* (Westport, CT, 1986)

IAN S. RENNIE

Gordon, Lady **Elizabeth** [the fifth Duchess of Gordon]. *See* BRODIE, ELISABETH

Gordon, George William (b. Kingston, Jamaica, 1820; d. Morant Bay, 1865). Political and Creole Baptist leader. Gordon was the illegitimate son of a wealthy Scottish planter and his servant of African descent. He developed into an astute businessman with a deep concern for the poor, which led him into politics. After 1834 he became one of an increasing number of coloured members of the House of Assembly. He acted as deputy mayor of Kingston during Edward Jordan's long term of office. He was a Justice of the Peace until he was forced out of office. His political and social ire was directed at the Governor Edward John Eyre, bringing him into direct conflict with the authorities. His politics were encouraged and stimulated by the native Baptist Church which was now coming into being. A damning letter sent by E. B. UNDERHILL, secretary of the BMS to the Colonial Secretary E. Cardwell, and the poverty and neglect on the island, exploded into a revolt in Morant Bay 1865, led by one of Gordon's deacons. Eyre blamed Gordon entirely, and illegally brought him from Kingston to Morant Bay to stand trial and be hanged, under martial law. Political tension resulted in Jamaica becoming a Crown Colony. The modern parliamentary meeting place in Jamaica is called Gordon House, indicating Gordon's place in their history.

BIBLIOGRAPHY
G. A. Catherall, 'George William Gordon: Saint or Sinner?', *BQ*, 27 (October 1977)
B. Semmell, *The Governor Eyre Controversy* (London, 1962)

GORDON A. CATHERALL

Gordon, James Edward (b. Aberdeen, Scotland, *c.* 1790; d. 1862). MP and Protestant propagandist. Gordon entered the Royal Navy in 1804, soon becoming a midshipman. He was made lieutenant in 1811, commanding the schooner *St Lawrence* in 1814, from which he gained some validity for calling himself 'Captain'. Captured in that year by an American privateer, he left the navy in 1815. A person of private means, he engaged in evangelistic and philanthropic work with THOMAS CHALMERS in Glasgow for several years, where he met EDWARD IRVING and members of ALEXANDER

HALDANE's family. Making his way to London, he was touched by the plight of discharged sailors, and on applying to the Admiralty for assistance in meeting this need, he was refused. He went ahead and raised £20,000, and in 1819 founded the Floating Seamen's Hospital, making a name for himself with the evangelical Anglicans, and became involved in the life of the voluntary societies.

Gordon's closest friend was Alexander Haldane of the *Record*, and he eagerly shared Haldane's fears, convictions, attitudes and agenda. He feared liberal theology, resurgent Roman Catholicism, and the non-confessional state. As a romantic he tended to find truth in the extreme, garbed with intensity and emotion. He was a strong Calvinist, a believer in the verbal inspiration of the Bible, a defender of the Established Church and the Protestant Constitution. He deplored what he conceived to be the pragmatic strategy of the previous generation of evangelical Anglican leaders, modifying many positions in order to make evangelicalism successful. He rather chose to enunciate what he conceived to be the truth as clearly and vehemently as possible, trusting God to bless such faithfulness. Like Haldane, although there is no evidence of his becoming a premillenarian, he adopted a more sombre view of the future fortunes of church and state.

Travelling in Ireland in the mid-1820s as an agent of the London Hibernian Society, he was captivated by the New or Second Reformation. This movement, traced to the primary charge of Archbishop Magee of Dublin in 1822, urged the Anglican clergy to evangelize Roman Catholics. By 1824 this policy led to highly charged debates between Anglican and Catholic orators. Back in England, Gordon in 1827 organized the PRS to support the New Reformation and to convene similar meetings in England in the hope of converting Roman Catholics, persuading Protestants of the evils of Roman Catholicism, and making them more militant in their Protestant convictions. This society became a pillar of the Recordite evangelicals (i.e. those associated with the *Record* newspaper).

In 1831 Gordon saw his opportunity to be the political leader of the Recordites when he was offered Lord RODEN's Irish pocket borough of Dundalk. He knew that most Anglican evangelicals opposed Catholic emancipation and a non-confessional system of education in Ireland and sought to represent such views. In the House of Commons he was continually on the attack, but by the time his seat disappeared due to the Reform Bill of 1832, his violence had caused most Anglican evangelicals to be happy to see him go. But he was given something of a second chance. The appropriation clause in the Whigs' Irish Church Bill of 1834–5 raised evangelical and Protestant fears afresh. Gordon was in the forefront of the great No Popery crusade which emerged, and which found its institutional expression in the Protestant Association.

Gordon had a part in the growth of political conservatism in England in the 1830s and in the defence of the Established Church. Of more importance was the heritage which he and his associates bequeathed to a segment of evangelical Anglicanism of a paranoid anti-Catholicism and an alliance with the most extreme forms of cultural and political conservatism.

In 1836 Gordon married a daughter of Samuel Smith, the wealthy banker, but was soon felled by a stroke which largely confined him to his home at Hadlow House, near Tonbridge. His son became a CMS missionary in the Punjab, where his career was characterized by devotion, heroism and sacrifice.

BIBLIOGRAPHY
D. Bowen, *The Protestant Crusade in Ireland 1800–70* (Dublin, 1978)
J. E. Gordon, *Original Reflections and Conversational Remarks* (London, 1854)
G. I. T. Machin, *Politics and the Church in Great Britain 1832–1868* (Oxford, 1977)
W. R. O'Byrne, *A Naval Biographical Dictionary* (London, 1849)

IAN S. RENNIE

Gordon, John (Brown) (b. Upson City, GA, USA, 6 Feb. 1832; d. Miami, FL, USA, 9 Jan. 1904). Confederate general. A lawyer and mining operator before the Civil War, Gordon as a skilled combat officer rose quickly in the esteem of his Confederate commanders and was promoted to brigadier-general in November 1862 and to major-general in May 1864. From his new positions of command he regularly took the opportunity to instill in his troops a degree of religious fervour.

Gordon's camp revivals in which 'with eloquent words and tearful eyes' he made 'powerful appeals to his men to come to Christ' became legendary. Concerned for the soldiers' welfare he repeatedly requested more 'missionaries' to serve within the ranks and lamented that so many brigades lacked chaplains. A non-sectarian, he had been a Baptist as a child, a Methodist upon his marriage, and later a Presbyterian elder. He often prayed in public, led his men in religious meetings, and was sometimes even seen with some wayward private discussing salvation. Proud of his charges, he declared they were 'more eager to listen to the Gospel than are the people at home' and years afterward recollected that their camp-side revivals formed 'a most remarkable and impressive chapter of war history'.

In the postwar years Gordon served as a United States senator, Governor of Georgia, first Commander-in-Chief of the United Confederate Veterans, and Grand Dragon of the Georgia Ku Klux Klan, an organization he, like many, perceived as a Christian bulwark of the Lost Cause.

BIBLIOGRAPHY
DAB

EDWARD D. C. CAMPBELL

Gordon, Robert (b. Glencairn, Dumfriesshire, Scotland, 5 May 1786; d. Edinburgh, Scotland, 21 Oct. 1853).

Church of Scotland minister. Educated at the universities of Edinburgh and Aberdeen, he became a DD of the latter in 1823. He taught mathematics in Perth Academy and contributed articles on mathematical subjects to the *Edinburgh Encyclopaedia*. In 1816 he was ordained to the parish of Kinfauns and held other charges before moving to Edinburgh in 1830. He was moderator of the General Assembly of the Church of Scotland in 1841 and after the Disruption of the church in 1843 became minister of the Free High Church in Edinburgh.

SELECT WRITINGS
G. Robert, *Christ as Made Known to the Ancient Church*, 4 vols (Edinburgh, 1854)

R. H. CAMPBELL

Gorham, George Cornelius (b. St Neots, Huntingdonshire England, 21 Aug. 1787; d. Brampford Speke, Devon, England, 19 June 1857). Anglican clergyman, theologian and antiquary. George Cornelius was the son of George James Gorham, a merchant banker. He was educated under Thomas Laundy, a Quaker, and entered Queens' College, Cambridge in 1805 where he graduated BA in 1808, MA in 1812 and BD in 1820. In 1811 Gorham was elected a fellow of his college, a position which he held until his marriage in 1827. Dr Thomas Dampier, Bishop of Ely, raised questions about his understanding of baptismal regeneration but eventually consented to his ordination in 1811. For a while Gorham resided in Queens' College taking private pupils. He then served several curacies at Beckenham, Clapham, Maidenhead, and Fawley near Henley-on-Thames before Lord Lyndhurst presented him with the valuable living of St Just-in-Penwith, Cornwall.

On 2 November 1847 Lord Chancellor Cottenham presented him with the less demanding parish of Brampford Speke near Exeter. Bishop Phillpotts whose hackles had already been aroused by Gorham having advertised the previous year for a curate 'free of tractarian error', first demanded to examine him on the matter of baptismal regeneration. This took place on 17–18, 21–2 December 1847 and 10 March 1848. The examination brought the Church of England's teaching on baptismal regeneration into the public view. High Churchmen, such as Phillpotts asserted that the baptized infant was regenerate whereas evangelicals maintained that such regeneration was conditional on the subsequent faith of the child. Gorham's views were strongly Calvinist and did not exactly fit with either party. He contended that regeneration might be given before baptism or subsequently. The bishop based his arguments largely on the language of the prayer-book services while Gorham took his stand on the Articles of Religion. Phillpotts found Gorham an able theologian but nevertheless refused to institute him. After losing his case in the ecclesiastical Court of Arches, Gorham appealed to the Judicial Committee of the Privy Council who reversed the decision in his favour.

The dispute aroused intense excitement and was widely discussed in the religious and national press. It considerably increased the tension between the evangelicals and the Tractarians led by John Keble and Edward Pusey who questioned the right of a civil court to legislate on a matter of Christian doctrine. It strongly influenced HENRY MANNING, Robert Wilberforce and others to become Roman Catholics.

SELECT WRITINGS
G. C. Gorham, *Extracts From the Writings of Martyr and Bullinger on the Effects of Baptism* (London, 1850)

BIBLIOGRAPHY
G. R. Balleine, *A History of the Evangelical Party in the Church of England* (London and New York, 1908)
O. Chadwick, *The Victorian Church*, 2nd edn (London, 1972): 1
DNB
J. C. S. Nias, *Gorham and the Bishop of Exeter* (London, 1951)

NIGEL SCOTLAND

Gosford, (second) Earl of [**Acheson, Sir Archibald**] (b. 1 Aug. 1776; d. Markekhill, Co. Armagh, Ireland, 27 March 1849). Irish MP, peer, and colonial governor. An Oxonian, he served during the 1798 rebellion as a lieutenant colonel in the militia of County Armagh. He was MP for the county until he succeeded his father in 1807, and a representative peer for Ireland from 1811. His seat was Gosford Castle, Markethill. He married Mary, only daughter of Robert Sparrow, of Worlingham Hall, Suffolk. Most of his generation identified with the evangelical revival. Of his sisters, Lady Olivia Acheson married Brigadier-General Bernard Sparrow of Brampton Park, Huntingdonshire (*see* Lady OLIVIA SPARROW), and Lady Mary Acheson, Lord WILLIAM BENTINCK, Governor-General of India (1827–35).

While he supported the evangelical societies – he was a vice-patron of Hibernian Church Missionary Society from its formation – in public life he was a liberal, in contrast with both the majority of his peers and with most, but by no means all, Irish evangelicals. Thus he opposed the Act of Union in 1800, supported Catholic emancipation in 1829, and consistently supported the Irish policies of the Whigs in the 1830s, including their reforms of the Irish Church and magistracy. Again, as His Majesty's Lieutenant for County Armagh, he pursued a policy of conciliation during periods of sectarian tension.

On 1 July 1835 he was appointed Governor-in-Chief of British North America (and created Baron Worlingham in the peerage of the United Kingdom). Here he extended his conciliatory approach to the intractable problems of Lower Canada. Despite his administrative ability and political sensitivity, however, he failed to prevent the French Canadian rebellion of 1837. Although he was able to limit its severity, he nonetheless tendered his resignation in November 1837. Lord Durham's harsh judgment of him at the time is now considered undeserved.

BIBLIOGRAPHY
DCB
DNB (supplement)

ALAN R. ACHESON

Gosse, Emily [née Bowes] (b. London, 10 Nov. 1806; d. London, 10 Feb. 1857). Tract writer. Her parents, as children of Loyalists, were brought to England in 1778. Her childhood was spent near Llanelltyd, Wales, and Exmouth, Devon. She was governess to the family of the Reverend John Hawkins in Berkshire, 1824 to 1838, and similarly in Brighton to five orphan girls, 1838 to 1841. On returning to her parents' home in north London she associated with Brethren. At Tottenham she married P. H. GOSSE on 22 November 1848.

In Berkshire she wrote many religious poems and in later years more than sixty evangelistic tracts and many articles for religious periodicals. In 1855 her major work, *Abraham and his Children*, was published by JAMES NISBET, giving lessons on parental duties. The considerable influence of her example in faith and prayer is well described in Anna Shipton's *Tell Jesus* (London, 1863).

BIBLIOGRAPHY
E. B[owes], *Hymns and Sacred Poems* (Bath, England, 1832)
—, *Hymns and Sacred Poems, Second Series* (Bath, England, 1834)
P. H. Gosse, *Memorial of . . . Emily Gosse* (London, 1857)

ROBERT BOYD

Gosse, Philip Henry (b. Worcester, England, 6 April 1810; d. Torquay, Devon, England, 23 Aug. 1888). Naturalist. From 1825 to 1839 he worked successively as a trading clerk in Poole, England and Carbonear, Newfoundland, as farmer in Quebec and teacher in Alabama. During these years in North America, as his interest in natural history developed, he occupied his leisure time observing, recording and making many careful drawings of flora and fauna.

On his return to England his first major work, *The Canadian Naturalist*, was published in 1840, to be followed within twenty years by more than thirty others. Among these were detailed accounts of his personal observation in Canada, Alabama, Devon and Jamaica, with many of his own fine illustrations. He was a successful popularizer of the marine aquarium and supplied many of the earliest specimens for London's first public aquarium at Regent's Park in 1853. In middle life he delivered popular lectures in London and other centres throughout Britain. His classes on the shore at Tenby, Wales (1854, 1866) and Ilfracombe, England (1855) demonstrated his ability to spread the popularity of these studies. From his pen came over 140 articles for scientific journals. His work was acknowledged by admission to the Royal Society (1856) and several other scientific bodies. Among his most lasting works have been his *Birds of Jamaica* (1847), *Actinologia Britannica* (1860) and *The Rotifera* (1886) which was jointly written with C. T. Hudson.

Brought up by devout parents and sitting under the ministry of the Reverend T. Durant at Skinner Street Independent Chapel, Poole, a basis of evangelical belief was laid which shaped his thought and behaviour into adult life. After leaving Poole his connection was with Methodists until at Hackney in 1843 he associated with Brethren. On moving to Devon he took a leading part in the Brethren assembly at St Marychurch. His religious writings included six Gospel tracts, many devotional and expository articles for Christian periodicals, several pamphlets and five fuller works. He was a founder member and vice-president of the Victoria Institute. The reading of Habershon's *Dissertation on the Prophetic Scriptures* in 1842 created an interest in Bible prophecy which was frequently expressed in his expository writing and preaching.

He entered the debate on creation by publishing his own views in *Omphalos: an Attempt to Untie the Geological Knot* (1857). He argued that since all newly created organic species would have shown signs of unaccountable 'previous existence', it was at least possible that this was also true of the inorganic matter in the earth's crust. It followed, then, that geologists' conclusions on the age of the world could well be mistaken. Gosse's views received little acceptance.

He married Emily Bowes in 1848 (see EMILY GOSSE) and Eliza Brightwen in 1860. Until recent years most published biographical material has come directly or indirectly from the writings of his son, Sir Edmund Gosse (1849–1928), whose vivid account of family life, *Father and Son* (1907), has gone through numerous editions. Recent researchers have shown that this 'study of two temperaments' is unreliable. Gosse earned lasting respect as a meticulously accurate observer of nature, a brilliant artist in that field, a lucid writer, prodigious worker, and devout Christian.

BIBLIOGRAPHY
E. Charteris, *The Life and Letters of Sir Edmund Gosse* (London, 1931)
R. B. Freeman and D. Wertheimer, *Philip Henry Gosse, a Bibliography* (Folkestone, England, 1979)
E. W. Gosse, *The Life of Philip Henry Gosse* (London, 1890)
F. Gosse, *The Gosses* (Canberra, 1981)
P. H. and E. Gosse, *Narrative Tracts* (London, 1864)
D. L. Wertheimer, 'Philip Henry Gosse: Science and Revelation in the Crucible' (Univ. Toronto Ph.D. thesis, 1977)

ROBERT BOYD

Gossner, Johannes Evangelista (b. Hausen bei Augsburg, Germany, 14 Dec. 1773; d. Berlin, 20 March 1858). German evangelical; founder of the Gossner Mission. Born into a Roman Catholic family, Gossner attended the St Salvator-Gymnasium in Augsburg before enrolling at the universities of Dillingen (1792) and Ingolstadt (1793–6). He was ordained priest in Dillingen on 9 October 1796. After his ordination he experienced an evangelical conversion and was assigned as pastor at Dirlewang. Here he came into contact with the Deutschen Christenthumsgesellschaft of C. F. SPITTLER in Basel where he spent a number of months in 1811. Assigned to Munich (1812–19) he promoted revivalism (the 'Erweckungsbewegung') and published a translation of the New Testament, with the assistance of the BFBS, and a devotional book, *Herzbuchlein* (Munich, 1812) which was translated into 26 languages.

In 1820, Gossner was invited by the Tsar to St Petersburg where he worked to unite the various revivalist groups into one church and established an Erweckungsbewegung in Finland. Forced to leave because of political exigencies, he pastored revivalist communities in Hamburg, Leipzig and finally Berlin. In 1826 he completed his translation to the Lutheran Church and was appointed pastor (1829) of the Bethlehemgemeinde in Berlin. There he established a programme of home and foreign mission which evolved into the Gossner Mission (1836). It sent out 141 foreign missionaries before 1858. This organization was especially active in the USA and in India where it developed into the Evangelical Lutheran Gossner Church of India. In addition to a children's educational programme (Kindergarten), Gossner founded the deaconess centre and hospital, the Elizabeth-Diakonissen-und Krankenhaus (1837). To promote this ministry, he edited the mission periodical *Die Biene auf dem Missionsfelde* (1834–58) and *Der christliche Hausfreund* (1847–57). He was a prolific author and his books were translated into many foreign languages.

BIBLIOGRAPHY
H. Dalton, *Johannes Gossner*, 3. aufl. (Berlin, 1898)
W. Holston, *Johannes Evangelista Gossner* (Göttingen, Germany, 1949)
—, 'Gossner, Johannes Evangelista', *Neue Deutsche Biographie* 6 (Berlin, 1958): 652–3
H. Lokies, 'Gossner, Johannes Evangelista', *Evangelisches Gemeinde Lexikon* (Wuppertal, Germany, 1978): 228

DAVID BUNDY

Gotch, Frederick William (b. Kettering, Northamptonshire, England, 1808; d. Bristol, 17 May 1890). English Baptist minister and educator. The son of a wealthy Kettering Baptist, Gotch trained for the ministry at Bristol Baptist College (1832–4) and at Trinity College, Dublin, where he graduated MA in 1836 and was later made an LL D. In 1836 he became minister at Boxmoor, Hertfordshire, three years later addressing the association on 'The Duty devolving on every Christian of making Personal Efforts for the Promotion of the Cause of Christ'. In 1841 he added the duties of tutor in philosophy and natural science at Stepney College to his pastoral responsibilities, which prepared for his moving back to a tutorship at Bristol in 1845.

Here he proved himself an accomplished theologian and Hebraist of great precision. As a tutor he both upheld the principle of free enquiry and warned against its misuse, the latter including any divergence from absolute submission of the heart to God. Academic excellence always needed to be undergirded with spiritual depth. In 1851 he addressed the Bristol association on *The Inspiration of the Holy Scriptures*, warning against theories of inspiration, preferring to affirm: 'We have a revelation from God – an inspired word given to us by inspired men. Is that not enough? Ought we to desire more?' In 1868 he both became president of Bristol College (until 1883) – because of CRISP's age and health he had *de facto* acted as principal since 1860 – and president of the Baptist Union. He was a determined voluntaryist, believing that Baptists ought not to fear the charge of sectarianism if the principles they sought to uphold were true. His second presidential address was entitled 'Christ at the Centre', which if properly guarded gave scope for reverent criticism. Granted that principle he enquired, 'Will our faith be in vain if it is proved that the first book of the Bible is compiled from several records or if we attribute to Isaiah or Zechariah not two authors but one?' 'Christ at the Centre' for him lead him to affirm, 'The power of Christianity resides not in the example of Christ, but in his work of reconciling us to God, His life and His death, as Mediator between God and man.'

Shortly thereafter he was invited to join the panel of revisers of the Old Testament. He also translated the Pentateuch for JOSEPH GURNEY's *Revised English Bible* (1877) and contributed numerous articles to Biblical Dictionaries and Encyclopedias. His writings were less than they might have been had he not undertaken the heavy duties of college leadership; accordingly his influence was not so much through the written word but on the lives of the men whom he sought to prepare for ministry. He served on the Bristol School Board, the council of the University College and that of the local hospital, and was an examiner for the University of London.

BIBLIOGRAPHY
BaptMag, (1890)
N. S. Moon, *Education for Ministry* (London, 1979)

J. H. Y. BRIGGS

Gottwald, John Daniel (b. Westhofen near Strassburg, Germany, 9 August 1726; d. Neusalz, Germany, 20 August 1805). Minister and missionary of the Moravian Church. The son of a Lutheran clergyman, Gottwald joined the Moravian church in 1743. He became manager of the bookbinding business run by the Church at Neusalz, serving also in Zeist (Holland), Bedford (England) and N. Ireland and was ordained in 1766. While minister at Gracehill near Ballymena the settlement was attacked during the 'Hearts of Steel' uprising. Gottwald confronted the raiders with great courage, persuading them to leave without harming any of the residents.

He was called to begin a mission in St Kitts where he arrived 13 June 1777. There seems to have been less opposition than in most other islands and his work among the slaves proved fruitful. He enjoyed the friendship of the Reverend JAMES RAMSAY who, it is said, 'began the public debate about the slave trade which was only closed by its abolition.' Gottwald returned to Europe in 1788 to continue his ministry until he retired in 1797.

BIBLIOGRAPHY
Anon., memoir in *Periodical Accounts Relating to the Missions of the Church of the United Brethren*, 34 vols, 19 (London, 1790–1889) 1ff

FRED LINYARD

Gould, George (b. Bristol, England, 20 Sept. 1818; d. Norwich, Norfolk, England, 13 Feb. 1882). English Baptist minister. The son of a deacon of the Couterslip (Bristol) Chapel, he was baptized at the age of 19 and preached his first sermon a month later. He worked first for a wine merchant and then for an accountant. He explored the possibility of entering the ministry of the Established Church but found for himself conscientious objection. After training at Bristol College, he had pastorates in Dublin 1841–6 and Exeter 1846–9, where in 1848 some of his chattels were sold against his refusal to pay the church rate. In 1849 he succeeded the Reverend WILLIAM BROCK at St Mary's Chapel, Norwich, where he continued until his death 33 years later. 'The wealth, enterprise and culture of Norwich' it has been said, 'were nowhere better represented than in his congregation', which was also conspicuous for its liberality and spiritual depth. In 1860 he ably negotiated the St Mary's Chapel Case, successfully upholding that any congregation was free to decide whether to practise open or closed Communion, the case for which he prepared so expertly as to receive high praise from his counsel, Lord Cairns, subsequently Lord Chancellor, and is of great value to the historian in terms of the case histories recorded. Under his guidance the whole administration of the poor rate in Norwich was revised with a consequent reduction in pauperism, but he was equally interested in ensuring that the poor had adequate housing and education which he sought as a governor of the grammar and commercial schools and later as chairman of the School Board.

A member of the founding committee of the Liberation Society, he worked tirelessly for the resolution of dissenting grievances: the abolition of church rate, access to the ancient universities, the opening of the graveyards of the kingdom to all citizens; he drafted the text of Sir SAMUEL MORTON PETO's Burials Bill, the first such bill to be presented to the Commons. He was a committee member of the BMS and an advocate of its interests. In 1879 he was elected to the chair of the Baptist Union on the proposition of C. H. SPURGEON. He frequently delivered evangelistic addresses and was the major promoter of the United Evangelistic Services held in St Andrew's Hall in Norwich. His son and biographer became principal of Regent's Park College.

BIBLIOGRAPHY
Baptist Handbook, (1883)
G. P. Gould, *Memoir* (London, 1883)

J. H. Y. BRIGGS

Govett, Robert (b. Staines, Middlesex, England, 1813; d. Norwich, 1901). Seceder and dissenting minister. Govett was the grandson of WILLIAM ROMAINE. He was educated at Worcester College, Oxford (BA 1834; MA 1837; fellow 1835–44). He was ordained in 1837, becoming Curate of Bexley, Kent and later Curate of St Stephen's, Norwich, where, in 1844, he seceded over objections to baptismal service. Afterwards, he preached at Victoria Hall, Norwich; in 1854, he built Surrey Road Chapel, Norwich, along Baptist/Brethren lines, where he remained until his death. Govett was one of the foremost millennialist writers of the nineteenth century.

BIBLIOGRAPHY
Al. Ox.
E. J. Poole-Connor, *Evangelical Unity* (London, 1941): 152–5
E. C. Starr, ed., *A Baptist Bibliography*, 25 vols (Chester, PA, 1952)

GRAYSON CARTER

Gowring, John William (b. London, 1810; d. London, 31 Aug. 1880). Anglican clergyman. Gowring entered Gonville and Caius College, Cambridge but migrated to Trinity College (BA 1833). He served curacies at St Matthew's, Liverpool and Witton near Northwich (Cheshire), after which he moved to other curacies, first at Harewood (Yorkshire) (1841–3) and then to Brixton and St Mark's Kennington, London (1843–64). He was also lecturer at St John's, Horsley Down (1860–74) and St Giles, Cripplegate (1865–80).

BIBLIOGRAPHY
Al. Cant., II, iii: 105

ARTHUR POLLARD

Grace, Thomas (Samuel) (b. Liverpool, 16 Feb. 1815; d. Tauranga, New Zealand 30 April 1879). CMS missionary in New Zealand. Trained at St Bee's College, deaconed 1848 and priested 1849, Grace sailed to New Zealand in 1850. He was stationed at Turanga, Poverty Bay 1850–3, Auckland 1854, Pukawa (Taupo) 1855–65, based in Auckland 1863–72, at Tauranga 1872–9. Grace identified with Maori aspirations, encouraging their commercial pursuits, opposing both the sale of their land to settlers and CMS support for racial amalgamation. He regularly itinerated around Maori settlements, renewing contact after the disastrous impact on the mission of the wars of the 1860s. He advocated Maori leadership in their church affairs.

BIBLIOGRAPHY
S. J. Brittan, G. F., C. W. & A. V. Grace, eds, *T. S. Grace* (Palmerson North, 1928)
DNZB

ALLAN K. DAVIDSON

Grafe, Hermann Heinrich (b. Palsterkamp, Germany, 3 Feb. 1818; d. Elberfeld, Germany, 25 Nov. 1869). Teacher, pastor, and promoter of the EA. Grafe experienced a conversion to evangelical Christianity as a teacher in Duisberg in 1834. While in Lyon, France, for education in spirituality (1840–1), he became acquainted with A. MONOD and was grounded in French Reformed Church ideas. After his return to Elberfeld, he joined the Reformed Church. After serious conflict in the Elberfeld church in 1849, he, together with others including C. BROCKHAUS founded (1850) the Evangelisches Brüderverein. He resisted the growing influence of J. N. DARBY and Darbyist exclusivism in the congregation and sought an alternative with the Baptists. However, on 22 November 1854, Grafe and five others founded the 'Freie Evangelische Gemeinde' in Elberfeld, which related in matters of creed to the Eglise Evangélique Libre in Geneva. As a committed ecumenist and as an elder in this congregation, he participated nationally in the development of the EA and was a formative influence in German ecumenism.

BIBLIOGRAPHY
H. Hermes, *Hermann Heinrich Grafe und Seine Zeit* (1933)
H. Lenhard, *Die Einheit der Kinder Gottes* (1977)

DAVID BUNDY

Graham, Charles (b. Sligo, Ireland, 20 Aug. 1750; d. Athlone, Ireland, 23 April 1824). Methodist itinerant preacher. His family were of Scottish Presbyterian descent but his parents conformed to the Church of Ireland. Graham was converted at a Methodist service in Sligo, became a local preacher and then had a spectacular career as an itinerant evangelist in the troubled decade of the 1790s. Known as 'the apostle of Kerry' he achieved notable success in south-western Ireland in the early stages of his itinerant ministry.

After the rebellion of the United Irishmen in 1798 the Methodist conference appointed a small team of Irish-speaking evangelists as missionaries at large in Ireland. Graham and GIDEON OUSELEY in particular were associated with remarkable bursts of Methodist revivalism in the border counties of Ulster in the immediate post-rebellion period. Lively descriptions of these events by Graham and Ouseley survive in the Methodist Missionary Society archives in the School of Oriental and African Studies, London, and in the Methodist collections held by the Northern Ireland Public Records Office. An Irish-speaking outdoor preacher of formidable vigour, Graham made an important contribution to the growth of Methodism in Ireland in the first generation after the death of JOHN WESLEY.

BIBLIOGRAPHY
W. G. Campbell, 'The Apostle of Kerry', *The Life of the Rev. Charles Graham* (Dublin, 1868)
D. N. Hempton, 'Methodism in Irish Society 1770–1830', *TRHS*, 5th series, 36 (London, 1986): 117–42

DAVID N. HEMPTON

Graham, Henry (b. Oxford, England, *c.* 1804; d. probably Sierra Leone, before 1840). *Fl.* 1830s. First CMS medical missionary. Graham studied medicine under a Dr Whiting and trained at the CMS training school at Islington in 1827. On 29 October 1829 he went to Sierra Leone as the CMS's first medical missionary. His wife, Susannah (née Pharaoh), died in Africa on 31 March 1831 and his own health seems to have forced his withdrawal from CMS in February 1832. His second wife, Phoebe (née Goodwin), was the widow of THOMAS DAVEY, another CMS missionary. She outlived him and married J. W. WEEKS, later Bishop of Sierra Leone.

BIBLIOGRAPHY
D. T. B[arry], *CMS Register of Missionaries and Native Clergy* (privately printed) (London, 1906)

DONALD M. LEWIS

Graham, Isabella [née Marshall] (b. Lanarkshire, Scotland, 29 July 1742; d. New York, 27 July 1814). Teacher and early organizer of charitable societies. Daughter of John and Janet Hamilton Marshall, a staunch Scottish Presbyterian family, Isabella married army surgeon John Graham of Paisley in 1765. They went to Canada in 1767 and had five children before John's death in 1773 in Antigua. Returning to Scotland, Isabella supported her children by opening a school. Moving to Edinburgh, she served as almoner to Lady GLENORCHY, a patron of her school, and organized the Society for the Relief of the Destitute Sick.

In 1789 she moved to New York and established a girls' school. In 1797 she founded the Society for the Relief of Poor Widows with Small Children, the earliest such charitable association. Graham and daughter JOANNA BETHUNE organized the first Orphan Asylum Society in 1806 and taught in its Lancastrian school. They also established some of the first American sabbath schools. Graham headed the Ladies Board of the Magdalen Society.

BIBLIOGRAPHY
D. Bethune and J. Bethune, *The Power of Faith* (New York, 1816)
NAW

NANCY A. HARDESTY

Graham, John (b. 21 Oct. 1765; d. York, Yorkshire, England, 6 Jan. 1844). Anglican clergyman. Graham was educated at St Bees and ordained in 1788. By the influence of WILLIAM WILBERFORCE he was presented with the livings of St Saviour and St Mary, Bishophill Senior, York, which were in the gift of the Lord Chancellor (1796–1844). In addition, he was chaplain of the York County Asylum. Graham exercised an influential ministry at York. He was a staunch supporter of the CMS and preached the annual sermon in 1831. He was also a member of the ElS from 1794. His son, JOHN BAINES GRAHAM, succeeded him as Rector of St Saviour's.

BIBLIOGRAPHY
C. Hole, *Early History of CMS* (London, 1896)

ARTHUR POLLARD

Graham, John Baines (b. York, Yorkshire, England, 23 Feb. 1794; d. Felkirk, Yorkshire, 15 June 1860). Anglican clergyman. Son of JOHN GRAHAM, J. B. Graham was educated at Queens' College, Cambridge (BA 1814; MA 1817) where he was a fellow from 1817 to 1822. He became an MA of Oxford by *ad eundem* arrangement in 1829. He became curate to his father at St Saviour's, York (1816), and was Vicar of Holy Trinity, Micklegate York (1822–60). He was also master of Hemsworth Grammar School (1832–7), Rector of Burnsall (Yorkshire) (1832–8) and Vicar of Felkirk (1837–60).

BIBLIOGRAPHY
Al.Cant., II, iii: 109

ARTHUR POLLARD

Graham, Sylvester (b. West Suffield, CT, USA, 5 July 1794; d. Northampton, MA, USA, 11 Sept. 1851). Presbyterian minister and health reformer. Soon after his ordination as a Presbyterian minister in 1828, Graham began studying physiology and nutrition, seeking medical grounds to vindicate his temperance convictions. Graham came to believe that the violation of physical laws was an offence against God and that sexual excesses both before and during marriage weakened the constitution. He foreswore all tobacco, liquor, caffeine, and most condiments; he believed in chastity, cold showers, fresh air, and firm mattresses as part of what he called 'the science of human life'.

Graham's lectures on temperance, sexual moderation, and vegetarianism stirred controversy throughout the Atlantic seaboard. He railed against the millers who, when grinding grain for flour, bolted out much of the bran and thereby lost the grain's vitamins and minerals. In his *Treatise on Bread and Breadmaking*, published in 1837, he attacked commercial bakers by insisting that bread should be made of whole grain, coarsely ground, and that it should be baked at home by the wife and mother of the household.

Although Ralph Waldo Emerson derided Graham as the 'poet of bran bread and pumpkins', Graham numbered such luminaries as Horace Greeley, ARTHUR TAPPAN, and William Lloyd Garrison among his admirers.

Students at Oberlin College, Wesleyan University, and Williams College lived by Graham's brown-bread doctrine. Graham hotels and boarding-houses were established in many towns and cities; the Graham cracker became a staple of many nineteenth-century households.

After 1840, Graham turned his attention to publishing his biblical lectures, although failing health allowed him to complete only one of a projected four volumes. He died in 1851 at his home in Northampton, after taking a dose of Congress water and a tepid bath.

BIBLIOGRAPHY
Gerald Carson, 'Graham: The Man Who Made the Cracker Famous', *New-England Galaxy*, 10 (1969): 3–8
DAB

RANDALL BALMER

Grane, William (*fl.* 1830–50). Recordite lawyer. One of the many members of the London legal profession who assumed an influential position within evangelical Anglicanism during the second quarter of the nineteenth century, and who were most prominently represented by such figures as ALEXANDER HALDANE, JOHN BRIDGES and CHARLES BRODRICK. His involvement in the hereditary mainstream of evangelicalism was demonstrated by his long-term and active membership in the CMS Committee. He was also partial to the movement which sought to retain England as a Christian nation, thus being legal adviser to the LDOS. He was secretary of the governing committee of Exeter Hall, the cavernous assembly room on the Strand, where the power and interests of evangelicalism were publicly on display, and there he maintained his professional office.

IAN S. RENNIE

Grant, Alexander (b. Duthil, Inverness-shire, Scotland, 1784; d. Tobermory, Mull, Inner Hebrides, Scotland, 23 May 1874). Pioneer Baptist missionary in the Inner Hebrides. Grant was initially a schoolmaster with the Edinburgh Society for the Support of Gaelic Schools. He served in the island of Shuna (in the parish of Kilbrandon and Kilchattan) from 1819 to 1821, when he was removed for preaching in the parish in opposition to the Established Church minister. Supported by JAMES HALDANE, he moved to Mull, where he operated as a Baptist missionary. He established a Baptist church at Tobermory in 1830, and contributed substantially to the formation of another in the Ross of Mull in 1835. Ordained at Tobermory in 1832, Grant encouraged the growth of Baptist work in the surrounding islands (especially Tiree) and adjacent mainland. He maintained a remarkably consistent and faithful ministry at a time of major social dislocation, when the churches that he founded were almost destroyed by successive waves of emigration.

BIBLIOGRAPHY

Annual Reports of the Edinburgh Society for the Support of Gaelic Schools, 8 (1819): 62; 10 (1821): 65

D. E. Meek, *Sunshine and Shadow* (Edinburgh, 1991)

Obituary in the *Oban Times* (30 May 1874)

Reports of the Baptist Home Missionary Society for Scotland, 1831: 11–12; 1833: 14–15

G. Yuille, ed., *History of the Baptists in Scotland* (Glasgow, 1926): 119–20

DONALD E. MEEK

Grant, Charles (b. Glen Urquhart, Scotland, March, 1746; d. London, 31 Oct. 1823). Director and chairman of the East India Company, MP, and Clapham 'Saint'. Grant was a director and chairman of the East India Company, and as a Member of Parliament, was instrumental in bringing evangelical principles to bear on British India by opening it to missionary work, appointing evangelical chaplains, urging the creation of an episcopal see of the Church of England, encouraging the introduction of English education, and, in general, insisting that, as a Christian government, Great Britain must rule India according to Christian principles.

Grant went to India in 1767 in the service of the East India Company, which at that time was establishing British control over vast territories in the Indian subcontinent. While he made money, he lived beyond his means, lost heavily at gambling, and then two of his children died of smallpox. In his letters he says that this convinced him that he had become 'an object of the just displeasure of God', and that his mind was 'a habitation of horror' until he had an experience that brought him to 'a trust in free salvation' (Embree, 1962: 51).

As a result of his conversion experience, Grant became convinced that as the new rulers of India, the British had an obligation to spread the Gospel there. This was not, however, a position shared by many people in Great Britain, and the East India Company expressly forbade the entry of missionaries into its territories in India, fearing that the Indians, seeing this as an interference in their religious beliefs, would revolt. A long letter he wrote in 1787 urging government support for a Protestant mission in India is probably the earliest explicit proposal for such work. This document seems to have had considerable influence among evangelicals but JOHN WESLEY was said to have opposed the proposal as unlikely to further true evangelism.

After a successful career in India, including being an adviser to Lord Cornwallis, the Governor-General, and having made a considerable fortune, Grant returned to England in 1792. He became a dominant figure in all aspects of the management of the East India Company's affairs, and he was an especially bitter opponent of the great expansion of British power in India that took place when Lord Wellesley was Governor-General. He believed that such conquest was both morally wrong as well as placing too great a burden on Great Britain. Since the conquests had been made, and there was no likelihood of relinquishing them, the great passion of his life was to get the British to carry out what he considered the duty of a Christian government towards its non-Christian subjects, namely, to give them good government based on Christian principles. These views found expression in 1792 in a very influential tract, *Observations of the State of Society among the Asiatic Subjects of Great Britain, Particularly with Respect to Morals, and the Means of Improving It*. His thesis, spelled out in great detail, was that Indian society was utterly corrupt because of a false, idolatrous religion that degraded humanity, and that it was the duty of the British to alleviate this situation through the 'introduction of light', by which he meant both the preaching of the Gospel and the use of English as the language of government. The Hindus erred, he believed, not because of any racial inferiority, but because they had never had the truth fairly laid before them. Grant differed from many Europeans, including churchmen, who believed that it was useless to preach the Gospel to Indians since they were incapable of receiving its truths. Despite his denunciations of Hinduism, Grant was not a racist, but believed that the Gospel could transform the Indian people and their social order.

Grant found a very influential ally in WILLIAM WILBERFORCE, and they, with other members of the Clapham group, made the 'Christianizing of India', as they put it, a major concern of evangelicals in the Church of England, the Church of Scotland, and in the dissenting churches in England. Aside from the movement for the abolition of slavery, no other cause so united British evangelicals. Grant's arguments aroused antagonism, however, among his associates in the East India Company, in Parliament, and in the Established Church. A measure of victory came for Grant's evangelical proposals in 1813 as a result of the mobilization of evangelical public opinion throughout the country in support of what was known as the 'Missionary Clause', when the East India Company's charter was being renewed. Missionaries were finally allowed to work in India, a bishop of the Established Church was appointed to Calcutta, and the first modest grant of £10,000 was made for education.

The East India Company had long sent chaplains to India to look after the needs of its British employees, but Grant, recalling those he had known when he lived in India, considered many of them a disgrace to their calling. One of his concerns, therefore, was to send out evangelical clergy who would help in the great work of spreading the Gospel. Among those he had appointed were CLAUDIUS BUCHANAN, whose books on the evils of Hinduism were widely read in evangelical circles, and HENRY MARTYN, whose special mission was the conversion of Muslims. Both of them angered the British officials and traders in India when they castigated them, as well as the Indians, for their immoral lives.

One of the great controversies in evangelical circles concerned the involvement of the British officials in India with the management of Hindu temples and the collection of what was known as the 'Pilgrim Tax' for the regulation of the vast crowds that attended Hindu festivals. Even though the British were only following the example of previous governments, whether Hindu or Muslim, Grant denounced this involvement on the grounds that a Christian government was actively encouraging what he regarded as the licentious abominations of Hinduism. Again, there was very strenuous objection to Grant's position, and although it was widely supported by evangelicals, it was only after this death that the government involvement he deplored was abandoned. Among those who took a leading part in this struggle were two of his sons, CHARLES GRANT (Lord Glenelg) and Sir ROBERT GRANT, both well known for their evangelical views. (Sir Robert, who became Governor of Bombay, was the author of the hymn, 'O, worship the King, all glorious above'.)

Charles Grant's strongly held views, rooted in his evangelical faith, that the British government should transform Indian society through Christianity, were never accepted as official policy. By the middle of the nineteenth century, however, a remarkable change had taken place in the attitudes of British officials in India, with many army officers as well as civilian leaders, being fervent supporters of the very evangelical principles for which their predecessors had condemned Charles Grant. While this reflects broad changes that had taken place in British religious life, there is little doubt that Grant, more than anyone else, was responsible for the evangelical interest in Great Britain for 'Christianizing India'.

SELECT WRITINGS
C. Grant, *Observations on the State of Society in Asia* (London, 1813)

BIBLIOGRAPHY
A. T. Embree, *Charles Grant and British Rule in India* (New York, 1962)
H. Morris, *The Life of Charles Grant* (London, 1904)

AINSLIE T. EMBREE

Grant, Charles [first Baron Glenelg] (b. Kidderpore, Bengal, 26 Oct. 1778; d. Cannes, France, 23 April 1866). MP and peer. Grant was the eldest son of CHARLES GRANT and in 1802 became a fellow of Magdalene College, Cambridge, a stronghold of late eighteenth-century evangelicalism. He was MP for Inverness Burghs (1811–18) before succeeding his father as MP for the county, which he represented until he was made a peer in 1835. After holding minor office he succeeded Peel as Chief Secretary for Ireland (1818–23), where he instituted a conciliatory regime, suppressing Orange demonstrations, promoting Catholic education, and proposing reforms of police and magistracy. Grant's policies proved far-sighted, but the fact that they coincided with an upsurge in agrarian violence (due to adverse economic conditions) discredited both them and him.

As Vice-President of the Board of Trade (1823–7), Grant grew close to Canning, and was president of the board in the Canning, Goderich, and Wellington administrations before resigning with the other 'Canningites' in June 1828. Like several other 'liberal' Tories, he joined Grey's nominally Whig government in 1830 as President of the Board of Control (1830–4), and was responsible for renewing the East India Company's charter in 1833. Later he served under Melbourne as Secretary of State for War and Colonies (1835–9) when – as in Ireland – his conciliatory approach to colonial subjects was attacked by hard-line imperialists for its tendency to promote disaffection. Moreover, his 'ambiguous, dilatory, and irresolute' response to a succession of problems in Cape Colony, New South Wales, Van Diemen's Land, and above all the Canadas, led to a motion of censure in the Commons and the loss of his colleagues' confidence. Grant eventually resigned in bitterness and withdrew almost entirely from public life.

Of all those politicians who were formally linked to the Clapham Sect, Grant achieved the highest office. His evangelical piety was of that 'moderate' or 'natural law' variety which was typical of Clapham, and which one of its evangelical opponents (HENRY DRUMMOND) called 'Evangelical liberalism . . . that spurious theology which has pervaded the land.' In other words, Grant passionately supported free trade and Catholic emancipation (whereas 'extreme' evangelicals like Drummond detested the new political economy and regarded any concession to Catholics as tantamount to supping with the devil). In the 1830s Grant combined with two others 'sons of Clapham' – JAMES STEPHEN (Permanent Under-Secretary of the Colonial Office 1836–47) and T. B. Macaulay – to re-orientate the course of British imperial policy. Grant and Stephen drafted the Act of 1833 which, besides opening up the company's monopoly of the China trade, appointed commissioners to draft a uniform law code for India. Together with Macaulay's Education Minute of 1835, directing the use of the English language in Indian schools, this marked an attempt to promote Christianity and other western values in India after long years of company indifference to the cultural side of empire. Grant also insisted on establishing bishoprics at Bombay and Madras, and on abandoning the Pilgrim Tax (the proceeds of which had helped to maintain Hindu temples). As Colonial Secretary he completed the abolition of slavery in the British empire by ending the apprenticeship system. According to one historian, Grant's 'period of office was significant in that it saw a real attempt to base an imperial policy on moral considerations' (Hyam, 1976: 44–6), and it may well be that his failure had less to do with his notorious 'languor and slowness' than with the inherent difficulty of trying to govern an essentially materialist structure like the British empire according to the dictates of a 'humanitarian impulse'. At all events, Grant's resignation in 1839 brought this brief moralistic phase of imperial policy to an end.

BIBLIOGRAPHY
DNB
D. R. Fisher, *The House of Commons 1790–1820*, ed. R. G. Thorne, 5 vols (London, 1986)

R. Hyam, *Britain's Imperial Century 1815–1914* (London, 1976)

BOYD HILTON

Grant, Daniel (b. Backcharn, Strathspey, Scotland, 1811; d. Tullymet, Perthshire, Scotland, 1887). Baptist pastor and itinerant preacher in Perthshire. Nurtured initially in PETER GRANT's church at Grantown-on-Spey, Grant trained as a city missionary in Aberdeen about 1837. While pastor of the Baptist church at Tullymet from 1839 until 1884, he maintained a vigorous programme of itinerant preaching in Perthshire and adjacent districts, sometimes covering more than 2,000 miles in a year. Involved in several revival movements, Grant composed Gaelic hymns which were particularly popular at times of revival. His volume, *Laoidhean Spioradail* ('Spiritual Hymns'), was published in 1842 (reprinted Perth, 1862). The hymns reflect the influence of Peter Grant, and explore themes such as conversion, consolation and encouragement in the Christian life.

BIBLIOGRAPHY
D. E. Meek, 'The Independent and Baptist Churches of Highland Perthshire and Strathspey', *Transactions of the Gaelic Society of Inverness*, 56 (1988–90): 269–343
Obituary of D. Grant, *Scottish Baptist Magazine* (1887): 16–18
Report of the Baptist Home Missionary Society for Scotland (1857): 18

DONALD E. MEEK

Grant, James (b. Elgin, Morayshire, Scotland, 1802; d. London, 23 May 1879). Journalist. Beginning at age 19 Grant became one of the century's most active journalists. He was founder and first editor of the Elgin *Courier*, was editor of the London *Morning Advertiser* (1850–71), and of the *London Saturday Journal* (from 1839), of *Grant's London Journal* (from 1840), and then of the *Christian Standard* (from 1872). He is now remembered chiefly for his *Random Recollections of the House of Commons* (1836), *The Great Metropolis* (1837), and *The Newspaper Press* (1871–2), each of which provides useful anecdotal information. Also valuable is his *Memoir* (1870) of the evangelical MP Sir GEORGE SINCLAIR.

Grant was equally prolific in his production of religious monographs, some thirty in all. In *The Metropolitan Pulpit* (1839), over fifty London preachers fell under his purview, most of them evangelicals. He attacked extreme evangelicalism in *The Plymouth Brethren* (1875), and premillennialism in *The End of All Things* (1866). In 1859 he investigated Irish revivalism for the *Metropolitan Advertiser*. He declared it a delusion. A Calvinist, Grant was undoubtedly a member of one of the London Presbyterian congregations.

BIBLIOGRAPHY
T. Cooper, ed., *Men of the Time*, 10th edn (London, 1879)
DNB

JONATHAN BURKE CUTMORE

Grant, Johnson (b. Edinburgh, Scotland, 1774; d. London, 4 Dec. 1844). Anglican clergyman. Grant was a member of St John's College, Oxford (BA 1799; MA 1805). After a first curacy under Edward Owen at Warrington he accepted the incumbency of Latchford nearby, succeeding JAMES GLAZEBROOK and himself being succeeded by SOLOMON PIGGOTT in 1809 when he moved to Binbrook, Lincolnshire (1809–22). His next move was to Kentish Town, London (1822–44), where he remained for the rest of his life. He revived the Sunday school at Latchford and was a voluminous writer not only of lectures, tracts and sermons but also of a *History of the English Church and of the Saints Who Have Departed From Her Communion*.

BIBLIOGRAPHY
Al. Ox. II. 550
W. Beaumont, *History of Latchford* (Warrington, England, 1889)

ARTHUR POLLARD

Grant, Peter (b. Ballentua, Strathspey, Scotland, 1783; d. 1867). Baptist pastor and celebrated Gaelic evangelical poet. Born of small-farming stock, Grant became the precentor in the local parish church when the HALDANE movement was beginning to affect certain parts of the Highlands. He was later converted through the preaching of LACHLAN MACKINTOSH, the founder and first pastor of the Baptist church at Grantown-on-Spey. He then became an itinerant missionary. When Mackintosh left Grantown in 1826, Grant succeeded him as pastor of the church, and was formally ordained in 1829. He possessed considerable evangelistic gifts. Under his ministry and that of his son, William, the church achieved a membership of almost 300, and experienced intermittent revivals.

Grant's hymns owe some themes to DUGALD BUCHANAN, but are noticeably different in style and content. Their main focus is the 'pilgrim's progress' in the life of faith. The Christian pilgrimage is followed from conversion until the believer's arrival in heaven. Grant extols the efficacy of Christ's blood, emphasises the inevitability of death, and anticipates the joy of the eternal home. The world is depicted as a cold place, a vale of tears; the Christian Hope compensates for the sorrow of believer's parting with loved ones. The experiential emphasis is reminiscent of Methodist hymnology. Set to well-known tunes, Grant's compositions became extremely popular in the Highlands, and helped establish an enduring trend in Gaelic hymnology.

BIBLIOGRAPHY
H. MacDougall, ed., *Spiritual Songs by Rev. Peter Grant* (Glasgow, 1926)
D. E. Meek, 'The Independent and Baptist Churches of Highland Perthshire and Strathspey', *Transactions of the Gaelic Society of Inverness*, 56 (1988–90): 269–343
—, 'Images of the Natural World in the Hymns of Dugald Buchanan and Peter Grant', *Scottish Gaelic Studies* (forthcoming)

DONALD E. MEEK

Grant, Sir **Robert** (b. Kidderpore, Bengal, 15 Jan. 1780; d. Dalpoorie, western India, 9 July 1838). Governor of Bombay and periodical writer. The second son of CHARLES GRANT, he was tutored by JOHN VENN and HENRY JOWETT, and went up to Magdalene, Cambridge in 1795 (Craven scholar 1799; BA 1801, third wrangler, second chancellor's medalist; fellow 1802; MA 1804). He was called to the Bar at Lincoln's Inn in 1807.

Grant's earliest success was as a writer for the influential *Edinburgh* and *Quarterly* reviews. His six articles in the liberal *Edinburgh Review*, all on India (between 1805 and 1810), echo his father's views. In 1809 his friends JOHN THORNTON and Reginald Heber convinced him to contribute to the newly founded *Quarterly Review*, a Canningite journal more amenable to his political temperament. In great secrecy, Grant offered accomplished articles on the Whig and Tory mandarins, Fox and Pitt, and on political, foreign and economic policy. The 1810 article on Pitt was a landmark – the *Quarterly*'s editor called it 'our manifesto' and it established the journal's reputation for literary brilliance. He was offered the editorship in 1824 but declined it.

Through family influence, Grant became an MP for Elgin Burghs (1818–20) and subsequently for Inverness Burghs (1826–30), Norwich (1830–2) and Finsbury (1832–4). He was the quintessential liberal Tory. Like Canning and Huskisson, his mentors, in the early 1820s he advocated limited constitutional adjustments. In 1828, in defending Catholic emancipation, he saw no principle of religious exclusion in the constitution and criticized 'out-of-doors' evangelical opposition to the measure (*Parliamentary Debates* 2nd ser., 20: 1222). Though initially hostile to parliamentary reform (see his uncharacteristically vituperative 'State of Public Affairs,' *Quarterly Review*, 22 [1820]: 492), in 1832 he supported it as 'a restorative and conservative measure' (*PD* 3rd ser., 7: 398). Grant also favoured repeal of the Test and Corporation Acts, liberalized trade, the abolition of flogging in the navy and liberalized divorce laws. Speaking in favour of criminal law reform, he called the number of capital crimes 'disgraceful' (*PD* 2nd ser., 23: 541). Somewhat surprising, given his general support of tolerance, in 1833 he voted in favour of sabbath observance legislation. A member of the LSPCJ and the Philo-Judean Society, his philo-Semitism partly motivated his sponsorship in 1830–4 of Jewish Emancipation bills. This was a task which his brother had refused and which he took on at some risk to his career.

All of his appointments were of sub-Cabinet rank: he was a Commissioner of Bankrupts (*circa* 1814–30); Serjeant-at-Law, Duchy of Lancaster (1827–30); Privy Councillor (from 1830); Judge Advocate-General (1830–4); and a commissioner of the Board of Control (December 1830–June 1834). He was appointed Governor of Bombay in 1834 and was knighted in the same year. His governorship awaits close investigation; but he seems to have been a sound and energetic administrator, responsive to local sensitivities. Upon his death, the *Bombay Courier* spoke of his 'unostentatious piety'. The Grant Medical College at Bombay (established 1845 and still in operation), was erected to his memory.

Materials concerning his governorship, holograph copies of a number of his sermons (delivered as governor), and manuscript drafts of his *Quarterly Review* Pitt article, are preserved at the India Office library, London. Other correspondence and papers, few in number, can be found at the British Library, the Bodleian Library, and the national libraries of Scotland and Wales.

Grant supported the great evangelical societies, in particular the CMS and the LSPCJ, and he briefly co-edited the *Christian Observer*. His sermons, mentioned above, are models of evangelical exhortation. His hymn, 'O worship the King all-glorious above', appeared in a posthumous volume of his poems and hymns edited by his brother.

BIBLIOGRAPHY
DNB
T. M. Endelman, *The Jews of Georgian England* (Philadelphia, PA, 1979)
H. Morris, *Charles Grant* (London, 1904)

JONATHAN BURKE CUTMORE

Grantham, **Thomas** (bapt. Ashby, Lincolnshire, England, 13 May 1794; d. Bramber rectory, Sussex, England, 18 April 1864.) College tutor and Anglican clergyman. Son of John (Rector of Ashby-cum-Fenby, Lincolnshire) and Elizabeth Grantham (ordination papers, Oxford), Thomas was a chorister of Magdalen College, Oxford, 1803–9, attending Magdalen College school (where he was a senior contemporary of GEORGE CRACROFT). His brother George was usher of the school 1801–40. As a demy of Magdalen Thomas matriculated in 1809, and in 1813 took a first class in *literae humaniores*, becoming a fellow 1813–31, and proceeding BD 1823. He served as junior dean of arts in 1821, senior dean of arts and bursar 1822, tutor 1827–31, and dean of divinity, 1828. In the university he was master of the schools (1818–20), and public examiner, 1822–4.

Ordained deacon in Kildare in 1817, he was chaplain to Dr Charles Lindsay, last Bishop of Kildare, till the latter's death in 1846. Ordained priest at Oxford in 1818, in 1830 he took the college living of Bramber-cum-Botolph's, Sussex, remaining rector till death. A memorial there says that he was 'the humble-minded, self-denying, and beloved Minister of this Parish'.

In 1847 Grantham had the distinction of being the last editor of JOSEPH and ISAAC MILNER's *History of the Church of Christ*, which since 1794 had been the received church history among English evangelicals and beyond, exerting a wide and deep influence. By the mid-nineteenth century, however, standards of historical scholarship had overtaken the Milners' work (neither of them, though learned men, were other than amateur historians), and tractarian and liberal theology accorded with its underlying spiritual assumptions even less than earlier schools of thought. It was therefore a courageous and determinedly Protestant step, taken by another highly qualified man (but still in days before academic qualifications in history had been introduced), to revise a standard work, extremely influential in its day, but already to some extent overtaken by scholarly activity essentially unrelated to its spiritual flavour. Grantham's was a 'greatly improved' edition (*DNB*, J. Milner). Sixteen or more sermons and essays, one on the claims of the CMS were published by Grantham in *The Church of England Magazine*. Grantham married Lucy (1793–1868).

BIBLIOGRAPHY
Al. Ox.
J. R. Bloxham, *Magdalen College Register*, 1, 3 and 7 (Oxford, 1853, 1863, 1881)
Crockford (1860)
J. D. Walsh, 'Joseph Milner's Evangelical Church History', *JEH*, 10 (1959)

J. S. REYNOLDS

Grasett, Henry James (b. Gibraltar, Spain, 18 June 1808; d. Toronto, Ontario, Canada, 20 March 1882). Anglican clergyman. The son of a regimental surgeon, Grasett was educated at the Royal Grammar School of Quebec, studied theology under Bishop Charles James Stewart and then proceeded to St John's College, Cambridge (BA 1834; MA 1842; BD 1853; Hon. DD 1877). Ordained deacon (1834) and priest (1835) by Bishop Stewart, he was appointed curate to John Strachan, the Rector of St James, Toronto. He was appointed as Bishop Strachan's domestic and examining chaplain in 1839; rector and chaplain to the garrison in 1847 and dean of the cathedral in 1867.

Grasett was the most prominent evangelical clergyman in the diocese of Toronto and he led the campaign against the High Church party and the Ritualists. He supported Bishop BENJAMIN CRONYN's efforts to have the teaching of Trinity College censured in the early 1860s. He served as president of the Evangelical Association (established 1869) and as vice-president of the Church Association of the diocese of Toronto which replaced it in 1873. Accordingly he actively supported the establishment of the *Evangelical Churchman* newspaper and an evangelical seminary, Wycliffe College, in which he taught pastoral theology.

BIBLIOGRAPHY
DCB, XI
H. E. Turner, 'Protestantism and Progress: The Church Association of the Diocese of Toronto 1873–9', *JCCHS*, XXII (April 1980), 1–28

RICHARD W. VAUDRY

Gratrix, James (b. Stockport, Cheshire, England; d. Leamington, Warwickshire, England, 21 Feb. 1881). Anglican clergyman. Gratrix was educated at St John's College, Cambridge (scholar, 1827; BA 1828; MA 1831) and acted as curate successively at Hayfield (Derbyshire),

Great Snoring (Norfolk) (to HENRY GODFREY) and Halifax. He then became Perpetual Curate of St James's Halifax (1834–54), at which time he also joined the ElS. He moved to be Vicar of Kemsworth (Hertfordshire) (1854–62), but returned to Yorkshire as Vicar of Armitage Bridge (1862–72).

BIBLIOGRAPHY
Al. Cant., II, iii: 117

ARTHUR POLLARD

Graves, Charles Caspar (b. Mickleton, Gloucestershire, England, 1717; d. 1787). Oxford Methodist and Anglican clergyman. The son of a Gloucestershire antiquary, Graves was educated at Magdalen College, Oxford, 1736–41, where he became friendly with the Wesleys, and spent three months with CHARLES WESLEY in Stanton Harcourt, Oxfordshire, in 1737. But two years after the Wesleys sailed for Georgia his friends removed him from College, believing him 'stark mad', and prevailed on him in 1740 to sign a paper renouncing Methodism, but not before he had proved to be a zealous outdoor preacher. In 1742 he accompanied Charles Wesley to Donnington Park and later JOHN NELSON found him a tower of strength in the Leeds area, preaching effectively.

But he seems to have been most unstable, and while in 1742 he wrote to the fellows of Magdalen advising them that he would not be bound by anything he had written in the paper 'so unchristianly imposed upon him', and as Vicar of Ocbrook, Derbyshire, welcomed JOHN WESLEY to his church in 1746 and 1747, he soon after 'proclaimed open war'. Wesley's comment on that occasion sums up his character, 'Oh poor head and honest heart'.

OLIVER A. BECKERLEGGE

Graves, James Robinson (b. Chester, VT, USA, 10 April 1820; d. Memphis, TN, USA, 26 June 1893). Southern Baptist author, journalist, and controversial founder of Landmarkism. Though reared in a Congregationalist home, Graves became a Baptist at 15, then four years later moved with his widowed mother and sister to northern Ohio. Though uneducated himself, Graves taught school in Ohio and Kentucky, where he was also ordained a Baptist minister. After moving to Nashville, Tennessee, in 1845 to teach, he joined First Baptist Church, where personal contacts enabled him to become editor of the *Tennessee Baptist* (1848), which eventually became the most widely read religious newspaper among Southern Baptists. He also established his own publishing company, which supplied religious literature throughout the South.

For thirty years Graves used his position as editor and author to foment controversy among Southern Baptists. In 1851 at a meeting in Cotton Grove, Tennessee, Graves gave shape to Landmarkism, which taught that only Baptist churches were authentic New Testament churches whose unbroken line could be traced to apostolic times. He published his views in *Old Landmarkism* (Memphis, TN, 1880). With the assistance of J. M. PENDLETON and A. C. DAYTON, he used this sectarian ecclesiology to deny the validity of missionary societies beyond the local church, open communion, any immersions not performed in Baptist churches. His sentiments also led him to oppose other Southern Baptist Sunday school and publishing organizations. Despite his vituperative and divisive style, many people consider him the most influential Southern Baptist in the nineteenth century.

BIBLIOGRAPHY
DAB
O. L. Hailey, *J. R. Graves* (Nashville, TN, 1929)
H. Wamble, 'Landmarkism: Doctrinaire Ecclesiology among Baptists,' *Church History*, 33 (1964): 429–47

TIMOTHY P. WEBER

Gray, Andrew   (b. Aberdeen, Scotland, 2 Nov. 1805; d. Perth, Scotland, 10 March 1861). Minister. Educated at Marischal College, Aberdeen, he was ordained in Aberdeen in 1831 and moved to the West Church, Perth, in 1836. He was a noted controversialist who wrote a popular pamphlet supporting the claims of the non-intrusionists before the Disruption of the Church of Scotland in 1843 and afterwards he compiled a catechism for the young to instruct them on the claims of the new FCS. The same controversial interests were evident in other published works, including disputes with the Duke of Argyll on the claims of presbytery and a critical work on *The Mary-Worship of Rome*.

R. H. CAMPBELL

Gray, Asa   (b. Sauquoit, NY, USA, 18 Nov. 1810; d. Cambridge, MA, USA, 30 Jan. 1888). Botanist. Although Gray began professional life as a medical practitioner, due largely to the influence of James Hadley and other peripatetic medical teachers whom he encountered at Fairfield's College of Physicians and Surgeons, his interests in botany were stimulated by his association with John Torrey with whom he collaborated on the *Flora of North America*. In the early 1830s he abandoned his dying medical practice and over the following years took up a number of teaching positions prior to his appointment to the Fischer professorship of natural history at Harvard in 1842. By the 1850s Gray was regarded as America's leading botanist with a worldwide reputation in botanical taxonomy.

One of a close circle of confidants with whom Darwin shared the essentials of his theory of natural selection prior to the publication of *The Origin of Species* in 1859, Gray became one of Darwin's leading American defenders. Not only did he mobilize Darwin's theory in his own accounts of the biogeographical distribution of plants in eastern Asia and eastern North America, but he vigorously debated evolution theory with America's leading anti-Darwinian, Louis Agassiz. Since he had been converted to Christianity in 1835 and had espoused a modified Calvinism burnished with the reinterpretative impulses of New School Presbyterianism, he undertook (along with George Frederick Wright) the task of interpreting Darwinism in a way compatible with the argument from design in nature. The essays drawn together in *Darwiniana* (1876) and his later lectures at the Yale Divinity School in 1881, published as *Natural Science and Religion*, confirmed his reputation as a leading reconciler of evolutionary science and Christian theology in post-Darwinian America.

BIBLIOGRAPHY
DSB
H. Dupree, *Asa Gray* (Cambridge, MA, 1959)

DAVID N. LIVINGSTONE

Gray, J[ohn] W[illiam] D[ering]   (b. Preston, Nova Scotia, Canada, 23 July 1797; d. Halifax, Nova Scotia, Canada, 1 Feb. 1868). Church of England minister and controversialist. Gray arrived in Saint John, New Brunswick, in 1826 as curate to his father, whom he succeeded as rector of the leading Anglican church in 1840. Together, the two Grays were the most influential clergymen in the city for over forty years. Both were earnest evangelicals, active in the BFBS, RTS, sabbath observance and temperance efforts, where they lead the common Protestant cause.

In the 1840, however, as J. W. D. Gray became rector, this Protestant leadership was challenged on both flanks. Newly arrived Presbyterian and Congregationalist ministers from Ireland and England shattered Saint John's evangelical united front by establishing an evangelical union, a leading tenet of which was abolishing residual vestiges of Anglican establishment. Even more alarming was an upsurge of Romanism, as the Roman Catholics established their bishopric in Saint John and Anglican bishops sympathetic to the Oxford Movement were installed in both New Brunswick and Nova Scotia. Gray focused the rest of his career as the leader of Maritime evangelical Anglicans in resisting the spread of Catholic tendencies in doctrine, music and architecture. In addition to a number of anti-Catholic pamphlets he founded the weekly *Church Witness*. While Gray lived his campaign against the Anglo-Catholic leadership of his bishop was largely successful and, especially in Saint John, its influence endured well into the twentieth century.

BIBLIOGRAPHY
T. W. Acheson, *Saint John* (Toronto, 1985): ch. 6

D. G. BELL

Greaves, Richard   (b. *c.* 1794; d. Cheltenham, Gloucestershire, 28 March 1870). Anglican clergyman. One of the many sons of Charles Greaves of London, he studied at Wadham College, Oxford (1813–16). For a while Curate of Lutterworth, he was in Switzerland in 1821 for health reasons. He married the daughter of William Wilson of Worton, Oxfordshire, who may have secured his appointment as Vicar of Deddington in 1822. For a while he was an important figure in the circle around JOHN HILL with whom he cooperated in BFBS and CMS work. The CMS made use of his ability in German and of his Swiss contacts when their relations with the Basel Mission Institute were strained. By 1836 his opinions had changed, to the distress of the orthodox Hill and he left Deddington. He was later in South Wales where Hill visited him in 1840. One account suggests that he became a Unitarian.

BIBLIOGRAPHY
Al. Ox.
Crockford (1865)
T. C. F. Stunt, 'The Greaves Family', Notes and Queries (1981): 406

TIMOTHY C. F. STUNT

Green, Ashbel (b. Hanover, NJ, BNA, 6 July 1762; d. Philadelphia, PA, USA, 19 May 1848). Presbyterian minister and educator. Green entered Princeton College in 1782, where he quickly won the attention of president JOHN WITHERSPOON who, after Green had graduated, appointed him tutor and then professor of mathematics at the college. With SAMUEL STANHOPE SMITH, who succeeded Witherspoon as president of Princeton, Green contended for Witherspoon's influential legacy in the Presbyterian church. Where Smith continued Witherspoon's work as a promoter of the Enlightenment side of eighteenth-century Scottish and American Presbyterianism, Green was a doughty defender of its confessional Calvinism. In 1787, Green became a minister in Philadelphia's Second Presbyterian Church. From 1790 to 1803 he was the stated clerk of the Presbyterian General Assembly, and from 1792 to 1800 one of two chaplains to the United States Congress.

During the first decade of the new century Green sought to change the direction of Princeton College and also provide an alternative place for training Presbyterian ministers. Both efforts came to fruition in 1812 when Green replaced Smith as president of the college and also became the founding board president of Princeton Theological Seminary. After leaving Princeton in 1822, Green served as an editor, published catechetical materials, and ardently defended Old School views in the controversies that led up to the Presbyterian schism of 1837. While Green's great capacities as an organizer made him invaluable to countless Presbyterian ventures of his day, a fragile, unbending personality prevented him from winning the affection of his students and peers.

SELECT WRITINGS
A. Green, The Life of Ashbel Green, Begun to Be Written By Himself (New York, 1849)

BIBLIOGRAPHY
AAP
M. A. Noll, Princeton and the Republic, 1768–1822 (Princeton, NJ, 1989)
Princetonians

MARK A. NOLL

Green, Beriah (b. Preston, CT, USA, 24 March 1795; d. Whitesboro, NY, USA, 4 April 1874). Political abolitionist and social reform educator. Educated at Middlebury College and Andover Seminary, Green pastored several Congregational churches before becoming, in 1830, a professor at Western Reserve College in Hudson, Ohio. While there, Green spoke out forcefully in support of the immediate abolition of slavery – resulting in his dismissal. From 1833 to 1843, Green was president of Oneida Institute in Whitesboro (near Utica), New York. Under his direction, Oneida Institute became known as a training ground for perfectionist evangelical social reforms of every kind. Green was particularly supportive of political abolitionism and the organization of independent antislavery churches. The school was also the first institution in the United States to educate African-Americans and native Americans as equals with European-Americans. This experiment in interracial education stirred up considerable opposition, and helped to cause the financial demise of Oneida Institute. In the latter decades of his life, Green became increasingly idiosyncratic in his political and religious views.

BIBLIOGRAPHY
DAB
M. C. Sernett, Abolition's Axe (Syracuse, NY, 1986)

DOUGLAS M. STRONG

Green, Jacob (b. Malden, MA, BNA, 2 Feb. 1722; d. Morris Co., NJ, USA, 24 May 1790). Presbyterian minister and patriot. Jacob Green was a student at Harvard College when he was 'awakened' by the ministry of revivalist GILBERT TENNENT. After his graduation in 1744 he was called to the Hanover Presbyterian Church in Morris County, New Jersey. During the American Revolution Green published an effective plea for independence, served on influential state committees, and assisted General Washington's troops during the winter encampment of 1777–8. But while he supported the patriots, he vigorously attacked the continuation of slavery in the United States. Green was a strong advocate of JONATHAN EDWARDS' conviction that church membership should be reserved for the professedly regenerate. When the Presbyterian General Assembly was established in 1789, Green protested by forming a decentralized 'associate presbytery'. Although his son, ASHBEL GREEN, said he never saw his father smile, Jacob Green also published a number of effective satirical essays, including A Vision of Hell (1767 and many editions thereafter).

BIBLIOGRAPHY
M. A. Noll, 'Observations on the Reconciliation of Politics and Religion in Revolutionary New Jersey: The Case of Jacob Green', *JPH* 54 (1976): 217–37
C. K. Shipton, *Sibley's Harvard Graduates*, XI (Boston, MA, 1960)

MARK A. NOLL

Green-Armytage, Joseph North (b. Meltham, Yorkshire, England, 2 Apr. 1805; d. Clevedon, Somerset, England, 16 Feb. 1873). Anglican clergyman. Green-Armytage was educated at Leeds Grammar School and St John's College, Cambridge (BA 1830; MA 1834). He began his ministry at Almondbury and Slaithwaite (Yorkshire) but quickly moved to St Thomas, Lancaster, where he remained until 1847 when he became secretary of the CPAS first in the South-East and then in the south Midlands. He was Rector of Flax Bourton (Somerset) (1866–70). His son became an extreme High Churchman.

BIBLIOGRAPHY
Al. Cant., II, iii: 132

ARTHUR POLLARD

Greenfield, William (b. London, 1 April 1799; d. London, 5 Nov. 1831). Scriptural translator and editor. Greenfield's background was Scottish; his widowed mother took her two-year-old son to Roxburghshire, returning to London in 1809. A Congregationalist and follower of ALEXANDER WAUGH, Greenfield discovered his gift for languages while apprenticing as a bookbinder. He learned to read the scriptures in Greek, Hebrew and Chaldee, then began to study modern languages. He was employed by the publisher SAMUEL BAGSTER in 1824 to prepare scriptural translations. Greenfield's *Comprehensive Bible* (1827), with variant readings and philological and explanatory notes, was popular with Unitarians but regarded as heretical by Recordites and others. In 1830 he joined the BFBS staff as editorial superintendent, learning four new languages and working with 21 others in the 19 months before his sudden death of 'brain fever'. Greenfield's competence as linguist and translator was crucial to the BFBS in a period when new and accurate versions were much in demand.

BIBLIOGRAPHY
CO (November 1831)
CM (December 1831)
DNB

LESLIE HOWSAM

Greenway, William (b. probably India, 24 March 1807; d. Kanpur, India, June 1857). Baptist evangelist. Sent to England for secondary education, Greenway completed his studies in Serampore College and was ordained by WILLIAM CAREY, JOHN MACK and GOTTLOB BRUCKNER. He then operated his mother's printing press in Kanpur and worked with Hossein Bakus, CMS evangelist. He also itinerated throughout the 1830s. He visited the great Hindu *melas* (festivals) with other Baptist, CMS, and LMS evangelists. Greenway learned Hebrew but failed as a translator; his talents lay in street preaching and in pastoral care. Many of these were European soldiers and their Indian wives.

The Greenway family business (wine and general provisions) prospered and sustained the church of which Greenway was pastor after the collapse of the Serampore Mission. Curiously, the first temperance society in India seems to have been formed in his church. In the Mutiny, Mrs Edward Greenway, an Eurasian who wore saris, negotiated the surrender of the besieged Europeans to Nana Sahib. Following this, the entire family except one brother (who was running the Calcutta office of the business) was massacred. The three Greenway brothers and their families are commemorated on the martyrs' memorial in St John's Church, Kanpur.

BIBLIOGRAPHY
Periodical Accounts of the Serampore Mission. European Series 1827–33 and 'New Series' January 1827 onwards, ed. by J. C. Marshman

E. M. JACKSON

Greenwood, William (b. Dewsbury, Yorkshire, England, 1780). CMS missionary to India. With THOMAS NORTON, Greenwood was the first English missionary of the CMS to arrive in India. (Germans, such as C. T. E. RHENIUS, had already gone out under the CMS; and East India Company chaplains had unofficially served the CMS in India.) A cloth and blanket-maker by trade, Greenwood grew up in Dewsbury, Yorkshire. He trained for missionary service under THOMAS SCOTT, and was ordained (deacon 13 June 1813) by the Bishop of Salisbury, but was never priested. In Calcutta, where he arrived in 1815, and in Chunar he worked as a pastor and teacher. Appointed headmaster of Calcutta Grammar School in 1827, Greenwood withdrew from CMS on 4 February 1828.

BIBLIOGRAPHY
D. T. B[arry], *CMS Register of Missionaries and Native Clergy* (privately printed) (London, 1906)
E. Stock, *The History of the Church Missionary Society* (London, 1899)

STUART PIGGIN

Gregg, John (b. Cappa, near Ennis, County Clare, Ireland, 4 Aug. 1798; d. Cork, Ireland, 26 May 1878). Anglican bishop. Gregg described himself as 'the orphan child of the only Protestant family in one of the obscurest parishes in the most neglected county in Ireland' (Gregg, 1879: 15). Although the Methodist itinerant, GIDEON OUSELEY, had spoken to him early about personal religion, he was converted under the preaching of B. W. MATHIAS when a scholar of Trinity College, Dublin. He was ordained in 1826 for the French Church, Portarlington, and in 1828 appointed to the Crown living of Killsallaghan in north County Dublin.

His gifts as a preacher were widely used. On regular tours for the Church Home Mission (founded in 1828), he preached in all 32 counties, in the native tongue wherever it was understood. Archbishop TRENCH welcomed him to Tuam, and he preached in Irish to a congregation of 1,500 Roman Catholics in St Nicholas's, Galway. Although an active controversialist and a rugged Protestant, he was devoid of all personal bitterness towards Roman Catholics, and this fact, allied to his fluency in the Irish tongue, his Celtic humour, his intimate knowledge of the customs of Ireland, and his friendliness, meant that Irish peasants heard him attentively, and as incumbent of a country living he always received his tithes.

In 1836 the trustees of the Bethesda offered him the chaplaincy in succession to Mathias. His ministry in Dublin spanned 26 years (the last five as Archdeacon of Kildare) until in 1862 he became Bishop of Cork. So vast were the crowds attending his early preaching, however, that in 1839 a new church was built to accommodate them – Trinity Church in Lower Gardiner Street, near the Custom House, with a parochial district allocated from St Thomas's parish. With its business affairs in the hands of a lay committee, he was free for spiritual ministry. He preached to congregations of over 2,000, many of them Trinity College, Dublin, students who stood in the aisles (the church seated 1,800). Pastoral care of the poor was also his forte, and was extended when Trinity rescued the struggling Swift's Alley church. Again, the surplus of the fund that had built Trinity – donated by a Mr Vance – had been entrusted to him, and was applied to church building: Trinity Church, Killiney, was thus built as late as 1859.

Dublin in the mid-nineteenth century, though no longer a parliamentary capital, was yet the capital of a nation and a commercial centre of wealth and magnificence. Much of its business, and some 40 per cent of its population, was Protestant. Church extension in the expanding suburbs of south Dublin was largely the achievement of evangelical Church of Ireland clergy. In central Dublin few of the older parishes came into their hands before the 1850s, and their strength remained in their proprietary chapels. Among their ministers were some remarkable men: HENRY IRWIN and W. Pakenham Walsh in Sandford Chapel; Hamilton Verschoyle in the Episcopal Chapel, Baggot Street; Charles Fleury, tenth in a succession of Huguenot pastors, in the Molyneux Asylum; Maurice Day in St Matthias's, and Gregg in Trinity. Of these six, four became bishops – two before disestablishment, and two afterwards. Gregg was pre-eminent among them. He was an extempore preacher of extraordinary power. A natural orator, he prepared his sermons through intense concentration of mind and spirit. He was esteemed, too, for the purity and simplicity of

his personal life, and for his unremitting pastoral work in the lanes of the teeming inner city.

In 1862 he was appointed Bishop of Cork, Cloyne, and Ross by the Earl of Carlisle. It was the era of 'Palmerstonian bishops' – and Lord Palmerston, having heard him preach in Dublin, had earlier offered Gregg the living of All Souls', Marylebone (which he declined). But his influence is not apparent here. Lord Carlisle attended Trinity Church and knew Gregg's worth at first hand. He announced his appointment in person at a public meeting in Dublin. The ensuing enthusiasm was stilled by the bishop-elect's declaring, characteristically: 'I shall be John Gregg still – a humble and laborious minister of the Gospel' (Gregg, 1879 : 191).

Gregg's tenure of the see of Cork was noted for his extensive confirmation tours; for the emphasis in his charges on preaching Christ; for his being the first Irish-speaking bishop since Bedell, more than two centuries earlier; for his part in the work of reorganization and moderate prayer-book revision after disestablishment; and for the fact that his son, Robert Samuel, joined him on the bench in 1874 as Bishop of Ossory. He also built the beautiful St Fin Barre's Cathedral in Cork, and erected there stained-glass windows in memory of fellow evangelicals (including Carlisle); and brought Achilles Daunt, the outstanding preacher in Dublin in the early 1870s, to the deanery of Cork in 1874.

But supremely, it was 'the spark that set my soul on fire', caught from Mathias, that burned on unquenchably in Gregg. The future primate, Charles F. D'Arcy, heard him preach in Cork when he was a boy: 'He was then an old man, but the wonderful fire of his eloquence must have been as bright as ever, for I can never forget the effect he produced' (Seaver, 1963: 17).

BIBLIOGRAPHY
DNB
R. S. Gregg, *Memorials of the Right Rev. John Gregg DD* (Dublin, 1879)
G. Seaver, *John Allen Fitzgerald Gregg* (London and Dublin, 1963)

ALAN R. ACHESON

Gregory, Olinthus Gilbert (b. Yaxley, Huntingdonshire, England, 29 Jan. 1774; d. Woolwich, London, England, 2 Feb. 1841). Applied mathematician and editor. Born the son of humble parents, he attended the local schools and was privately tutored in mathematics and astronomy by Richard Weston, a Leicester botanist. In 1793, at 19, he published a small volume, *Lessons Astronomical and Philosophical*. After moving to Cambridge in 1796 Gregory was a sub-editor for the *Cambridge Intelligencer* and opened a bookshop. In 1803 he was appointed instructor of mathematics at the Royal Military Academy at Woolwich through the influence of Professor Charles Hutton. When Hutton resigned in 1807 Gregory succeeded him as the Academy's mathematics professor. His scientific publications include *A Treatise of Mechanics*

(London, 1806), which treated pure and applied mechanics, and a useful book for civil engineers, *Mathematics for Practical Man.* He also carried out experimental research on the velocity of sound. Gregory edited the *Gentleman's Diary* from 1802 to 1819 and the *Ladies' Diary* from 1819 to 1840.

Gregory made several important contributions to the evangelical cause. His *Letters on the Evidences of Christianity* (1815) was reprinted several times and was published in abridged form by the RTS in 1853. He also wrote an influential biography of ROBERT HALL, a Calvinistic Baptist preacher, in 1833. Gregory, recognized as a prominent scientist and religious Dissenter, was one of the founders of London University (now University College) the first non-denominational university in England.

BIBLIOGRAPHY
DNB
DSB

ARIE LEEGWATER

Gregson, William (b. Liverpool, 1790; d. Liverpool, Feb. 1863). Civil servant. A graduate of Brasenose College, Oxford (BA 1810, MA 1813), in 1815 he was called to the Bar at Lincoln's Inn and served as a barrister on the northern circuit. Gregson became 'invaluable' as a legal adviser to Robert Peel who from 1822 employed him as counsel to the Home Office. He continued in that capacity until 1833, having drafted much of Peel's reform legislation and Earl Grey's parliamentary reform bills of 1831–2. Henry Goulburn appointed him Under-Secretary of State for the Home Office (January to April 1835). He was then very briefly private secretary to Peel when Prime Minister.

Deeply concerned for the welfare of the underclasses, Gregson was a prison visitor and a supporter of the ragged school movement. He was a committee member of the CPAS (1844–54). He also co-founded Marlborough College (1843) and a training college at Highbury. Letters of his to Robert Peel and George Bentham are in the British Library.

BIBLIOGRAPHY
Boase
GM (1863): 666
N. Gash, *Mr Secretary Peel* (London, 1961): 330, 480–2, 495
J. C. Sainty, *Home Office Officials 1782–1870* (London, 1975): 14, 41

JONATHAN BURKE CUTMORE

Greig, George (b. Edinburgh, Scotland, 1778; d. *c.* 1831). Minister. Educated at the University of St Andrews, he and his wife sailed for service with the LMS. They were captured by a French privateer, landed in South America, and returned to Scotland with great difficulty. In 1805 while in London he preached in Crown

Court Church of Scotland and was ordained to the charge later in the year. He started the first Sunday school at Crown Court in 1814.

R. H. CAMPBELL

Greig, John (b. London, 1771; d. Worcester, England, 28 May 1819). Anglican clergyman. Son of John (gentleman) of Newgate Street, London, Greig studied at St Edmund Hall, Oxford 1795–8, where he was one of DANIEL WILSON'S undergraduate circle. Ordained in 1798 (ordination papers, Salisbury), he became curate to EDWARD VANSITTART NEALE at Shottesbrooke and White Waltham, Berkshire. By 1806 he had moved to Worcester, where by 1808 he was Curate of St Nicholas. His excellent preaching filled an empty church. Local disregard of Christianity was greatly lessened. At 48 he died 'much regretted'. Bateman (*Daniel Wilson*, 1, 1860) is incorrect in saying that Greig was a fellow of St John's College, Oxford. That he had married a sister of NICHOLAS VANSITTART (afterwards Lord Bexley) appears to be unsubstantiated. He left part of his fortune to the CMS.

BIBLIOGRAPHY
Berrows' Worcester Journal (3 June 1819)
C. Bullock, *Memorials of W. H. Havergal* (London, 1870)
EM (1819)
G. Lea, *Memoir of Rev. John Davies* (London, 1859)
J. S. Reynolds, *Evangelicals at Oxford* (Oxford, 1953; Appleford, England, 1975)

J. S. REYNOLDS

Greig [also **Grieg**], **Peter** (b. 1775; d. 1800). Early missionary martyr. A gardener on the Earl of Moray's Donibristle estate, Greig was a member of Ebenezer Brown's Secession congregation in Inverkeithing, Fife, Scotland. He was accepted by the Edinburgh Missionary Society in 1796, and sailed in 1798 with HENRY BRUNTON for Sierra Leone, whence they were directed to Susu territory to the north. Soon after the first modest signs of success he was murdered for his possessions by Fulani traders in January 1800, one of the earliest martyrs of the modern missionary movement.

BIBLIOGRAPHY
W. Brown, *History of the Propagation of Christianity*, 2 (London, 1814): 415 ff
G. Smith, *Twelve Pioneer Missionaries* (London, 1900): 122ff

A. F. WALLS

Grellet, Stephen [de Grellet du Mabillier, Etienne] (b. Limoges, France, 2 Nov. 1773; d. Burlington, NJ, USA, 16 November 1855). Quaker minister and humanitarian. Son of a French manufacturer of porcelain, Grellet served in the royalist army during the French Revolution. Taken prisoner of war, Grellet managed to escape to New York via Dutch Guiana. Having read William Penn's *No Cross, No Crown* with the aid of a dictionary, and inspired by the ministry of English Quaker Deborah Darby, he joined the Society of Friends in 1796 and was recorded as a minister two years later. His religious travels over the next forty years were very extensive, as he journeyed through most of the United States and Canada, and visited nearly every European country, presenting his concerns to many heads of state during his four tours of that continent. He was deeply concerned about all manner of human suffering, caring for the sick during yellow fever epidemics, preaching against slavery, and visiting prisons and asylums in nearly every country to which he travelled. He was largely responsible for English Quaker ELIZABETH FRY embarking on her career as a prison visitor and reformer. Grellet was a moving preacher, combining deep mystical experience with fervent evangelical testimony to Christ's 'eternal Divinity and God-head [and] his meritorious sacrifice for the sins of the world' (Seebohm, 1864: 71). Poor health limited his activities after 1842, and he died peacefully at home.

BIBLIOGRAPHY
H. Barbour and J. W. Frost, *The Quakers* (New York, 1988): 321–2
DAB
DCA
B. Seebohm, ed., *Memoirs of the Life and Gospel Labors of Stephen Grellet* (Philadelphia, PA, 1864)

STEPHEN W. ANGELL

Greville, Robert Kaye (b. Bishop Auckland, Durham, England, 13 Dec. 1794; d. Murrayfield, near Edinburgh, 4 June 1866). Botanical collector and illustrator. Gaining an inheritance in the 1810s allowed him to set aside medical training in favour of a life devoted to private botanical study. He became a most energetic and successful collector and illustrator of plants, insects and marine invertebrate. In collaboration with other important botanists, in the 1820s and 1830s he published numerous botanical works illustrated by himself. The British Museum and the universities of Edinburgh and Glasgow purchased his collections.

A member of the EA, Greville was also active in many evangelical causes, including temperance, foreign missions, ragged schools, antislavery and Sabbatarianism. He was vice-president of the Anti-Slavery Convention (1840), was a secretary of the Sabbath Alliance, and in 1850 issued a pamphlet against Sunday postal deliveries. He also published *The Drama Brought to the Test of Scripture and Found Wanting* (1830). A Scottish episcopalian, with D. T. K. DRUMMOND he compiled the *Church of England Hymn-Book* (1838).

BIBLIOGRAPHY
DNB (that incorrectly states he was an MP)

JONATHAN BURKE CUTMORE

Grey, (Sir) **George** (b. Gibraltar, 11 May 1795; d. Fallodon, Northumberland, England, 9 Sept. 1882).

MP and Colonial Secretary. Grey's mother was a strongly religious woman and a friend of WILLIAM WILBERFORCE. Her son was educated privately and then at Oriel College, Oxford (BA 1821; MA 1824). Grey intended to take holy orders but felt himself unfitted by temperament to do so and therefore entered Lincoln's Inn. to read for the Bar. In 1827 he married Anna Sophia, daughter of HENRY RYDER, the first evangelical bishop. He entered Parliament in 1832 as member for Devonport, which he held until he changed to his native Northumberland in 1847. After a brief period out of Parliament he moved to Morpeth (1853–74).

Between 1834 and 1839 he acted as Under-Secretary for the Colonies under CHARLES GRANT [Lord Glenelg], moving first to be Judge-Advocate-General in 1839 and then for a few months Chancellor of the Duchy of Lancaster. After 1846, apart from a brief period as Colonial Secretary in 1854, Grey was mainly at the Home Office, where his work was largely concerned with civil order (not least the Chartists) and Ireland. He was held in high regard for his administrative ability and his moral character. His grandson was Lord Grey of Fallodon, Foreign Secretary at the outbreak of the 1914–18 war.

BIBLIOGRAPHY
DNB

ARTHUR POLLARD

Grey, Henry (b. Alnwick, England, 11 Feb. 1778; d. Edinburgh, 13 Jan. 1859). Minister of the Church of Scotland and the FCS. Born the only child of English parents, Grey was brought up by his mother after his father, a Morpeth doctor, left her. After schooling locally and in Newcastle she escorted him in 1793 to Edinburgh University to prepare for the Church of Scotland ministry. (He graduated MA in 1818.) Influenced evangelically by his mother and HENRY MONCRIEFF, he was Church of Scotland minister in East Lothian at Stenton (1801–13) and in Edinburgh at St Cuthbert's chapel of ease (1813–21), New North (1821–5) and St Mary's (1825–43). After the Disruption he served Free St Mary's (1843–59). Moderator of the Free Church's third assembly (1844), he fostered conciliation, displaying a cultivated refinement and catholicity of sympathy rare among evangelicals. Against ANDREW M. THOMSON he favoured using Bibles containing the Apocrypha to reach Roman Catholics. He advocated more frequent Communion, and his sermon on 'the Macedonian Cry' moved ALEXANDER DUFF. New York University made him a DD (1845), and friends endowed a Grey scholarship at New College, Edinburgh, which has a bust by Patric Park.

In 1808 he married his cousin Margaretta who bore three sons and three daughters. C. M. BIRRELL, a Baptist minister, was his son-in-law, and his grandson, Augustine Birrell, became a well known MP and man of letters.

BIBLIOGRAPHY
[John Anderson], *Sketches of Edinburgh Clergy* (Edinburgh, 1832): 64–9

C. M. Birrell, ed., *Thoughts in the Evening of Life* . . . (London, [1871])

Fasti, 1: 112–13

D. F. WRIGHT

Grey, Henry (b. Chester, Cheshire, England, 1784; d. Babbacombe, Devon, England, 25 March 1860). Anglican clergyman. A scion of the Stamford family, Grey was educated at Eton and Brasenose College, Oxford (BA 1806). He was curate at Hodnet (Shropshire) where he knew the Heber family and the Hill family of Hawkstone nearby. He was Vicar of Knutsford (1809–24), where his zeal extended to clearing the public houses by nine each evening and disapproving of card-playing by the local squirearchy. He speaks of 'bitter trials [and] vast mercies' with numerous conversions. He welcomed Nonconformists to the Lord's table. One of his curates was WILLIAM GREENWOOD, an early volunteer from Dewsbury for the CMS in India. His rough Yorkshire accent and unrefined manner did not commend itself to some of the Knutsford parishioners. In the period 1810 onwards Grey preached assiduously for CMS in Cheshire and neighbouring areas. He suffered severe illness in 1813 which left him epileptic for over twenty years. He retained his living 'for the Gospel's sake', arranging for it to be cared for by godly curates. He spent much time for his health's sake in Clifton (1813–17) and then in Frenchay and Babbacombe in later years. As a result of local opposition the Bishop of Chester deprived him of his living in 1824 on the grounds of non-residence. It has to be said that his autobiography is nauseatingly pietistic.

SELECT WRITINGS

H. Grey, *Autobiography of the Rev. Henry Grey* (London, 1861)

ARTHUR POLLARD

Grey, Thomas (b. Llangyfelach, Glamorganshire, Wales, 1733; d. 2 June 1810). Independent minister. Baptized 26 December 1733, he began his career as a coal miner. Following his conversion *circa* 1754, he joined an Independent church at Llangyfelach, began preaching, and by 1757 had been accepted as a student at a dissenting academy at Abergavenny, Monmouthshire. In 1762 he was called to minister to the Independent churches of Llwynpiod and Abermeurig in Cardiganshire. Having made his home at Nantcwnlle, he worked alongside DANIEL ROWLAND and preached regularly at Llangeitho and at various Methodist meetings. He also established new Independent churches in Cardiganshire, but on his death these decided to join the Calvinistic Methodists. Grey's involvement with the Methodists led many to be critical of him, but he was an example of how common theology allowed movement across the sectarian boundaries.

BIBLIOGRAPHY

DWB

T. Rees and J. Thomas, *Hanes Eglwysi Annibynnol Cymru*, IV (Liverpool, England, 1875): 210

GERAINT TUDUR

Gribble, Robert (*fl.* Devon, England, *c.* 1800–60). Pioneer Brethren evangelist. Little is known of his background. A draper of Barnstaple, England, he began about 1815 to establish Sunday schools in nearby villages. Needing to preach, he taught himself to do so and built a small chapel in the village of Eastacombe, being appointed pastor of the little church on 27 July 1821. In March 1832, he started itinerant evangelism in the North Devonshire villages, and received believer's baptism at about the same time.

Gribble was by now in touch with R. C. CHAPMAN, who had moved to Barnstaple in 1832, and like Chapman he was adopting views characteristic of the growing Brethren movement. During the next 25 years, living 'by faith' and working among the poorest classes, he saw at least nine churches formed with several hundred converts, a number of whom became full-time Christian workers. The most noted of these was George Beer who in 1836 went with A. N. GROVES to India.

SELECT WRITINGS

R. Gribble, *Recollections of an Evangelist* (London, 1858)

BIBLIOGRAPHY

H. H. Rowdon, *The Origins of the Brethren* (London, 1967)

ROY COAD

Griffin, Edward (Dorr) (b. E. Haddam, CT, BNA, 6 Jan. 1770; d. Newark, NJ, USA, 8 Nov. 1837). Congregational and Presbyterian minister and educator. Following graduation from Yale (1790) and a conversion experience in 1791, Griffin studied New Divinity theology under JONATHAN EDWARDS, (JR). He was licensed in 1792 and ordained in 1795. Typifying a generation of mobile evangelical pastors, Griffin held pastorates in New Hartford, Connecticut (1795–1801), Orange, New Jersey (1801), Newark (1801–9; 1815–21), and at Boston's Park Street Congregational Church (1811–15). He taught homiletics at Andover Seminary (1808–11), and completed his career as president of Williams College (1821–36).

A key figure in the America's Second Great Awakening, Griffin sparked revivals in nearly every church he pastored, as well as at Williams College. He delineated his theology in *Park Street Lectures* (1814), and issued a clarion call for overseas missions in 'The Kingdom of Christ' (1805).

BIBLIOGRAPHY

AAP, 4

P. Cooke, *Recollections of Rev. E. D. Griffin* (Boston, MA, 1855)

DAB, 7

D. Kling, *A Field of Divine Wonder* (University Park, PA, 1993)

W. B. Sprague, *Memoir of the Rev. Edward D. Griffin* (New York, 1839)

DAVID W. KLING

Griffith, John (b. Pencader, Carmarthenshire, Wales, 10 May 1752; d. Caernarfon, Gwynedd, Wales, 18 Feb. 1818). Congregational minister. He was educated at the Carmarthen Presbyterian Academy and ministered at Llanfyllin (1780–2), Caernarfon (1782–4), Abergavenny (1784–96) and Caernarfon again from 1796 until his death. He published a volume of hymns in 1783 and a translation of PHILIP DODDRIDGE's *Rise and Progress of Religion in the Soul* in 1788.

Griffith's eldest son, John (1799–1877) was also a Congregational minister who served successively at Beaumaris, Manchester, Rhayader and Buckley. His second son, William (1801–81), also a Congregational minister, was educated at the Neuadd-lwyd Academy, and the Carmarthen Presbyterian Academy. He was ordained at Holyhead in 1822. His wife, Alicia Evans, was the granddaughter of William Griffith (1719–82) of Drws-y-coed, Gwynedd, the Moravian. William and Alicia were married in the Moravian Chapel at Bristol. William Griffith's ministry at Holyhead was remarkably successful and he himself became one of the most respected leaders of Congregationalism in north Wales.

BIBLIOGRAPHY

DWB

R. T. Jenkins, *The Moravian Brethren in North Wales* (Honourable Society of Cymmrodorion, London, 1938)

J. Lewis, *A Memoir of . . . William Griffith*, 2nd edn, (Caernarfon, Wales, 1934)

R. TUDUR JONES

Griffith, William (b. London, 4 Nov. 1806; d. Derby, England, 7 Dec. 1883). Wesleyan Reformer, the son of a Wesleyan minister of the same name. He entered the Wesleyan ministry in 1828 but in 1849 with JAMES EVERETT and SAMUEL DUNN was expelled because of his suspected activities in connection with periodicals advocating Methodist reform. After joining with Everett and Dunn in Reform meetings up and down the country, he settled down in 1855 as minister of a Wesleyan Reform chapel in Derby where he remained till the end of his life. In 1877 he declined to serve as president of the Annual Assembly of the United Methodist Free Churches.

He was an able preacher, often blessed with conversions, and no one became a member of his Derby church without giving evidence of conversion; and he maintained an extensive and deeply pastoral correspondence. At the same time he was keenly interested in ecclesiastical and national politics; he was an ardent opponent of a state church, a republican and pacifist, and disliked the use of the term 'Reverend'.

BIBLIOGRAPHY

O. A. Beckerlegge, *United Methodist Ministers and their Circuits* (London, 1968)

R. Chew, *William Griffith, Memorials and Letters* (London, 1885)

G. J. Stevenson, *Methodist Worthies*, 6 (Edinburgh, 1896): 929–38

UMFC Minutes (1883): 12

OLIVER A. BECKERLEGGE

Griffiths, Ann [née **Thomas**] (b. Llanfihangel yng Ngwynfa, Montgomeryshire, Wales, April 1766; d. Llanfihangel, Aug. 1805). Hymn-writer. Born in 1776 (*pace DNB*) she was the eldest daughter of John, a farmer, and Jane Thomas. Her parents were churchgoers. Until about her twentieth year she lived an irreligious life but on hearing a sermon by Benjamin Jones (1756–1823), the Independent minister of Pwllheli, a great change came over her. She attached herself to the Independents, then in 1797 joined the Calvinistic Methodists at Pont Robert and corresponded with JOHN HUGHES (1775–1854), a teacher and preacher. She could generally repeat any sermon she heard and is said to have written out several by JOHN ELIAS (1774–1841). In 1804 she married Thomas Griffiths, a Meifod farmer, but died after the birth of their child.

She recited her hymns to her maid, Ruth Evans, who memorized them. When Ruth married JOHN HUGHES, with whom Griffiths had corresponded, Hughes wrote down the hymns. They were first edited and published in 1805, but in their original version not until 1905, when Sir Owen M. Edwards published them in *Gwaith Ann Griffiths*. They were 'characterized by a wealth of scriptural allusion, by deep religious and mystical feeling, and by bold metaphors' (*DWB*). Although mostly written in an anacrustic metre and not intended for congregations, the hymns found their way into most Welsh hymn-books. For the Welsh and English texts see Hodges.

BIBLIOGRAPHY

A. M. Allchin, *Ann Griffiths* (Cardiff, 1986)

H. A. Hodges, ed., *Homage to Ann Griffiths* (Penarth, Wales, 1976)

A. Luff, 'A Strange Hymnological Occasion' *Hymn Society Bulletin*, 8, 12 (1977): 216–8

C. D. Morgan, *Y Ferch O Ddolwar Fach* (London, 1977)

JOHN S. ANDREWS

Griffiths, Benjamin (b. Llanllwyni, Cardiganshire, Wales, 16 Oct. 1688; d. Montgomery County, PA, BNA, 5 Oct. 1768). Baptist minister, pamphleteer, and early 'historian'. Griffiths emigrated to America in 1710, was baptized 12 May 1711, and ordained 23 October 1725. He was appointed the first clerk of the Baptist churches near Philadelphia. Without his diligence and attention to duty, much of the early history of the Baptist denomination in America would be lost. Griffiths also wrote on the subjects of Baptist associations, discipline, and infant baptism.

BIBLIOGRAPHY
AAP
W. Cathcart, *Baptist Encyclopedia* (Philadelphia, PA, 1881)

WADE A. HORTON

Griffiths, David (b. Llanbedr Efelffre, Pembrokeshire, Wales, 1756; d. Newport, Pembrokeshire, Wales, 18 Sept. 1834). Methodist and Anglican clergyman. Educated at Pembroke Grammar School, he was appointed (*circa* 1774) private tutor to the Bowen family of Llwyngwair, Nevern, Pembrokeshire. There he met several of the Methodist leaders and also married the eldest daughter of his patron. Ordained deacon in 1779 and priest in 1780, he became vicar of Nevern in 1783. He opposed the ordination of Methodist ministers in 1811 and left the movement; for the remainder of his life, he confined his activities to his own parish. He was also a trustee of BRIDGET BEVAN'S will.

BIBLIOGRAPHY
DWB

GERAINT TUDUR

Griffiths, David (b. Gwynfe, Dyfed, Wales, 20 Dec. 1792; d. Machynlleth, Powys, Wales, 21 March 1863). LMS missionary and scholar. He was trained for the ministry at Neuadd-lwyd, Wrexham and Gosport. He married Miss Mary Griffiths, at Machynlleth, 20 May 1820. On 27 July he was ordained at Gwynfe and sailed for Madagascar on 25 October 1820, arriving at the capital (Antananarivo) on 30 May 1821. He worked with DAVID JONES, with the support of King Radama, to establish schools. Together the two reduced the Malagasy language to writing and translated the Bible, later with the help of DAVID JOHNS. Following the death of Radama, Queen Ranavalona outlawed Christianity in 1835. David Griffiths returned to Wales and ministered in Hay-on-Wye, South Wales. He continued his literary work in Malagasy, English and Welsh. His other chief works were *A History of the Martyrs of Madagascar*, *Malagasy Grammar*, and *English/Malagasy Dictionary*.

BIBLIOGRAPHY
LMS Register of Missionaries 1796–1923, 4th edn (London, 1923)
T. Rees and J. Thomas, *Hanes Eglwysi Annibynol Cymru*, 4 (Liverpool, England, 1875)

IEUAN S. JONES

Griffiths, John (b. Llanglydwen, Dyfed, Wales, 1731; d. Glandŵr, Dyfed, Wales, 1 Nov. 1811). Schoolmaster and Congregational minister. He entered Carmarthen Presbyterian Academy, October 1754, but his evangelical views led him with others to join the newly founded Abergavenny Academy in 1756. He ordained minister at Glandŵr, 20 June 1759. The school that he conducted gained a high reputation and amongst others Dr GEORGE LEWIS was educated there. He was especially good at teaching Latin. In theology he was a strict Calvinist and inculcated his views by insistent catechizing. He was severely incapacitated by a stroke in 1803 and was assisted thereafter by his son, WILLIAM GRIFFITHS (1777–1825).

BIBLIOGRAPHY
DWB
T. Rees and J. Thomas, *Hanes Eglwysi Annibynot Cymru*, 4 vols, III (Liverpool, England, 1874): 50–1

R. TUDUR JONES

Griffiths, John (b. Rochester, Kent, England, 1806; d. Oxford, 14 Aug. 1885). Anglican clergyman and scholar. Griffiths was educated at Winchester and Wadham College, Oxford (scholar 1824; BA 1827; MA 1833; BD and DD 1872), of which he was a fellow from 1830 to 1854, during which time he was variously classical lecturer (1830–4), tutor (1834–48), divinity lecturer (1848–54) and subwarden (1837–54). He was one of the Four Tutors, including in their number A. C. Tait of Balliol, later Archbishop of Canterbury, who protested against Newman's Tract 90.

Griffiths was essentially a scholar and after resigning from Wadham in 1854 he edited Innet's *Origines Anglicanae* (3 vols, 1855). Earlier he had published editions of Aeschylus' *Prometheus* (1834) and *Septem Contra Thebes* (1835) and a book on *Greek Accents* (1839) which ran into several editions. He returned to Oxford in 1857 as keeper of the archives, in which post he published *An Index of Wills Proved in the Court of the Chancellor of the University of Oxford* (1862) and *Enactments in Parliament Concerning the Universities of Oxford and Cambridge* (1868). He also edited the *Homilies* (1869).

At various times he was select preacher to the university, delegate of the university press, curator of the university chest and member of the hebdomadal council. His career culminated as warden of his college, Wadham (1871–81), but he does not appear to have found the post congenial.

BIBLIOGRAPHY
DNB

ARTHUR POLLARD

Griffiths, Thomas (baptized Bristol, England, 3 March 1794; d. Redland, Bristol, 31 March 1849). College tutor and Anglican clergyman. Son of Dr Thomas and Martha Griffiths, he matriculated from Wadham College, Oxford, in 1811. Scholar of his college 1812–19, he was fellow 1819–38, being subwarden under BENJAMIN SYMONS,

1831–7. Thus he played his part in establishing Wadham as an evangelical stronghold. Ordained in 1829 – when in Bristol he attended T. T. BIDDULPH's ministry (ordination papers, Oxford) – from 1832 to 1834 he was Vicar of St Peter's-in-the-East, Oxford. In 1836 he took the Wadham living of Limington, Somerset, remaining rector till death. Miss Church, in her biography of Dean Church, confuses him with John Griffiths, fellow and subsequently warden of Wadham.

BIBLIOGRAPHY
GM, new series, 31 (1849)
J. S. Reynolds, Evangelicals at Oxford (Oxford, 1953; Appleford, England, 1975)

J. S. REYNOLDS

Griffiths, William (b. Glandŵr, Dyfed, Wales, 1777; d. Glandŵr, Dyfed, Wales, 9 Jan. 1825). Congregational minister. He was the son of JOHN GRIFFITHS (1731–1811), Congregational minister, and Dinah, his wife. He was admitted to Wrexham Academy in February 1795. He was an advocate of Moderate Calvinism and this led to a split in his home church at Glandŵr. He was ordained there in 1803 to assist his father. He himself later suffered from bouts of mental instability but he was greatly admired for his extensive scholarship and winsome personality.

BIBLIOGRAPHY
DWB
Diwygiwr (1865)
T. Rees and J. Thomas, Hanes Eglwysi Annibynol Cymru, 4 vols, III (Liverpool, England, 1874): 52–3

R. TUDUR JONES

Griffiths, William (b. Blaenbrwynen, Clydau, Pembrokeshire [Dyfed], Wales, 21 Dec. 1788; d. Burry Green, Gower [West Glamorgan], Wales, 21 July 1861). Calvinistic Methodist minister; known as the 'Apostle of Gower'. Griffiths was the eldest of six children born to the godly Thomas and Mary Griffiths. William, who was about 19 years of age when he was converted, enlisted in the Carmarthenshire Militia and visited Devonport, Bristol, Sunderland, Newcastle and Manchester.

He commenced preaching in 1814 and in 1816 the Calvinistic Methodist Association at Fishguard decided to send Griffiths to exercise a teaching and preaching ministry on the Gower peninsula. He was ordained in 1824 and was married in 1826. Towards the end of his life his ministry was highly successful. Griffiths was not well known outside his locality even in his own day. He is not remembered for his eloquence but for his piety and his longing for the conversion of unbelievers.

BIBLIOGRAPHY
Anon., 'William Griffiths, Browyr', Y Traethodydd (1870): 176–193
DWB

D. Howells, 'Y Diweddar Barch. William Griffiths, Browyr', Y Drysorfa, (7 July 1862): 241
W. Williams, Memoir of William Griffiths (London/Swansea, 1863)

R. WATCYN JAMES

Grimke, Angelina (Emily) [Angelina Grimke Weld] (b. Charleston, SC, USA, 20 Feb. 1805; d. Hyde Park, MA, USA, 26 Oct. 1879). Abolitionist and woman's rights advocate. Judge John Faucheraud and Mary Smith Grimke were prominent in South Carolina politics and the Episcopal Church. Angelina was the youngest of their 14 children.

She experienced conversion in a Presbyterian revival and then followed her sister SARAH GRIMKE into Quakerism. She moved to Philadelphia in 1829 and joined the Philadelphia Anti-Slavery Society in 1835. After a sympathetic letter to William Lloyd Garrison was printed in the Liberator, she wrote An Appeal to the Christian Women of the South (1836). Angelina and Sarah were among the 'Seventy' groomed as abolition lecturers by THEODORE DWIGHT WELD in 1836. In 1837 she wrote a second pamphlet, Appeal to the Women of the Nominally Free States. In defence of their public speaking, she wrote Letters to Catharine Beecher, in Reply to an Essay on Slavery and Abolition (1838).

Angelina married Weld on 14 May 1838 in Philadelphia. With Sarah, they moved to New Jersey. Three children were a toll on Angelina's health. Actively interested in health, dress, and diet reform, the family lived for a time in the Raitan Bay Union and ran a school. In 1863 they moved to Massachusetts. The sisters' firsthand experience of slavery gave their abolition sentiments force and cogency. Theirs was the first major defence of woman's rights.

BIBLIOGRAPHY
G. H. Barnes and D. L. Dumond, eds, Letters of Theodore Dwight Weld, Angelina Grimke Weld and Sarah Grimke, 1822–1844 (New York, 1934)
G. Lerner, The Grimke Sisters from S.C. (New York, 1967)
K. D. Lumpkin, The Emancipation of Angelina Grimke (Chapel Hill, NC, 1974)
NAW

NANCY A. HARDESTY

Grimke, Sarah (Moore) (b. Charleston, SC, USA, 26 Nov. 1792; d. Hyde Park, MA, USA, 23 Dec. 1873). Abolitionist and woman's rights advocate. Judge John Faucheraud Grimke, was a graduate of Trinity College, Cambridge. Mary Smith's family was prominent in South Carolina politics and the Episcopal Church. Sarah was the sixth of their 14 children.

Sarah was 'deeply stirred' by a Presbyterian revival in 1813. After her father's death in 1819, she found solace in a Methodist revival. Along with her sister ANGELINA GRIMKE, Sarah moved to Philadelphia in 1821 and joined the Quakers 29 May 1823. Discouraged from preaching by Quaker leadership, she and Angelina were among the 'Seventy' instructed as abolitionist lecturers by THEODORE DWIGHT WELD in November 1836. Sarah published *Epistle to the Clergy of the Southern States* (1836), a refutation of biblical arguments favouring slavery.

During the sisters' speaking tour of New England in 1837, men attended their meetings, causing a sensation. Denounced by Congregational clergy in a *Pastoral Letter*, Sarah wrote *Letters on the Equality of the Sexes and the Condition of Woman* (1838), one of the first scriptural defences of woman's rights.

After Angelina married Weld in May 1838, Sarah made her home with them in New Jersey. She cared for the family's three children and taught in several schools they opened. In 1863 they moved to Massachusetts where Sarah continued to write and to campaign for woman's rights.

BIBLIOGRAPHY

G. H. Barnes and D. L. Dumond, eds, *Letters of Theodore Dwight Weld, Angelina Grimke Weld and Sarah Grimke, 1822–1844* (New York, 1934)

G. Lerner, *The Grimke Sisters from S.C.* (New York, 1967)

NAW

NANCY A. HARDESTY

Grimshaw, William (b. Brindle, Lancashire, England, Sept. 3 [New Style Sept. 14], 1708; d. probably Haworth, Yorkshire, probably April 1763). Anglican clergyman and chief architect of the evangelical revival in the north of England, Grimshaw became the unlikely right-hand man of JOHN WESLEY in spite of boisterous behaviour which earned him the nickname, 'Mad Grimshaw'. His parents were poor Lancashire farming stock, and he was the first of three children. He derived a fairly neat legal hand from the headmaster of Blackburn Grammar School, and went for some pre-university training to another Elizabethan foundation, Heskin Free School (now almost forgotten), which possessed a good library. In 1726, at 17, he was admitted as a sizar or poor student to Christ's College, Cambridge. He was 'sober and diligent the first two years', but then learned 'to drink, swear, and what not', though this did not prevent his graduation in 1730. He remained technically in residence until on Passion Sunday, 4 April 1731, he was ordained privately by Samuel Peploe, Bishop of Chester, in Queen Square Chapel, Westminster, 'much affected with a sense of the ministerial office, and the diligence which ought to be used in the discharge of it'. After a brief curacy at Littleborough, in the parish of Rochdale, in September 1731 he was transferred to the much more important St Mary's Chapel, Todmorden. Not until 10 September 1732, however, was he technically authorized to administer the Lord's Supper by his ordination as priest, again by Bishop Peploe, but this time at Chester Cathedral. This had no profound spiritual effect on him, however, and he often visited his parishioners 'in order to drink and be merry with them',

and he gained a reputation for bizarre pranks, such as dressing up as the devil – which had the effect of scaring a reluctant suitor to marry the girl he had seduced.

His spiritual awakening was probably sparked by his failure to comfort a bereaved couple by his advice 'to get into merry company and divert themselves'; the change seems to have occurred during the winter of 1734–5, when for a time his register entries were inscribed, 'in the year of our redemption'. This was simply a beginning, of course. As Grimshaw confided to his manuscript 'Experiences' (p. 59), 'Christians are like apprentices, they must serve Christ seven years before one can confide in them.' His marriage in 1735 to the widowed Sarah Sutcliffe of Ewood seems to have slackened for a time his spiritual development, but the birth of a son, and then a daughter, renewed his religious urge, and in 1738 he embarked on a conscious reformation, beginning a written ledger of spiritual debits and credits, and also a solemn covenant with God. His arduous religious regimen, however, did not bring peace of mind, and the death of his wife on 1 November 1739, plunged him into despair. On one occasion he paused in the middle of a service at Todmorden, and exclaimed, 'My friends, we are all in a damnable state, and I scarcely know how we are to get out of it!' He found some relief in the companionship of his younger brother John, who had become curate of nearby Cross Stone in 1737. Through John's wife Mary Cockcroft he was introduced to Elizabeth Cockcroft of Heptonstall, whom William married in 1741, though she was only able to give his children a few years' motherly care before her own death in 1746.

On Wednesday, 23 June 1742, William Grimshaw accompanied his brother John to York, that both might be admitted to the charge of parishes in that diocese, John to the curacy of Luddenden, William to the perpetual curacy of Haworth in the parish of Bradford. This was a new spiritual as well as ecclesiastical beginning. At Todmorden Grimshaw had made fumbling attempts at preaching salvation by faith; at Haworth he speedily found revivalistic tumult on his hands. As he described it to Dr JOHN GILLIES, the historian of revivals: 'In 1742 . . . our dear Lord was pleased to visit my parish . . . My church began to be crowded, insomuch that many were obliged to stand out of doors . . . It was amazing to hear what weeping, roaring, and agonies many people were seized with at the apprehension of their sinful state, and the wrath of God' (Baker, 1963: 61; cf. 55 n. 4). By the end of the year the parishioners supported him in an appeal to enlarge the church 'for the open and orderly attendance of public service of Almighty God'. York agreed about the need, although it was 1755 before sufficient funds were raised for the purpose, and Grimshaw continued to preach to increasingly huge crowds in the churchyard. Meantime he ran a kind of Methodist circuit, preaching monthly at twelve separate centres in his wide parish, and 'allowing any people of the neighbouring parishes that pleased to attend that exhortation'.

All this was before Grimshaw had any organized contact with Wesley's Methodism, although the surrounding area had been evangelized by BENJAMIN INGHAM of

Ossett, the former Oxford Methodist, and by JOHN NEL-SON, the preaching stonemason of Birstall. Grimshaw's own ministry was quickened by the solemn renewing of his covenant with God on 8 August 1744, followed by a trance accompanied by a vision of Christ on 2 September 1744, which filled him with 'a joyful assurance of the love of Christ'. Although this remained an intimate secret, it stabilized Grimshaw's faith, deepened his devotional life, and irradiated his ministry. He entered into another solemn written covenant with God on 4 December 1752, which he formally renewed on 4 August 1754, and with quarterly fasts from 1760 onwards. He was tormented especially by sexual temptations, though in 1758 he was convinced that it was 'not expedient' for him to enter into a third marriage.

The coming to Haworth in 1744 of WILLIAM DARNEY, a travelling evangelist from Scotland, may possibly have increased Grimshaw's assurance of salvation and enriched his evangelical preaching. At least the saying went around, 'Mad Grimshaw is turned Scotch Will's clerk!' Another lay evangelist taken under Grimshaw's wing was Paul Greenwood of Stanbury. Grimshaw also inaugurated in his parish a kind of Methodist class meeting system to furnish pastoral support and spiritual fellowship for his converts. His successful evangelism could hardly go unnoticed by the Wesleys.

On 2 October 1746, CHARLES WESLEY preached at Keighley and went on to Haworth to meet Grimshaw, 'a faithful minister of Christ', but 'found him and his wife ill of a fever' – a precursor of her death a month later. It was not in the least surprising that the following May JOHN WESLEY himself preached in Haworth Church, and was persuaded to take 'William Darney's Societies' into the Methodist fold, and even the idiosyncratic Darney himself, though only under Grimshaw's supervision. Much more welcome to Wesley as regular itinerant Methodist preachers were two others of 'Mr. Grimshaw's men', Paul Greenwood and Jonathan Maskew. Grimshaw himself often ventured to preach outside the bounds of his own parish, and all his scruples against extraparochial preaching vanished after he had accompanied JOHN BENNET for five days in July 1747 around his societies in Lancashire and Cheshire. It was Grimshaw who conducted the first circuit quarterly meeting in Methodism, at Todmorden Edge, on 18 October 1748. Earlier that same year he had entrusted his two children John and Jane, to Wesley's Kingswood School in Bristol, where the little girl died in January 1750, whereupon the boy was brought home and apprenticed to a Haworth weaver.

His beloved daughter's loss caused no breach with Methodism, however. Grimshaw continued to preach in Methodist buildings and to attend Methodist Conferences as he was able. From 1750 John Wesley named Grimshaw in the trust deeds of Methodist preaching houses as the next in absolute authority – after his own death and that of his brother Charles – to name the preachers who alone should preach therein: for Birstall in 1750, for Bolton and for Manchester in 1751, for Haworth (built by Grimshaw) and for Padiham in 1758, for York in 1759, for Bacup in 1761, and thus printed in Wesley's model deed in the 'Large' *Minutes* of 1763. Grimshaw's death at the age of 54 on 7 April 1763, prevented this designated succession. He had speedily been recognized, however, throughout the northern half of England, and much farther afield, as the primary preacher and pastor in Methodism. In 1758 he had crossed an ecclesiastical Rubicon in seeking evangelical perpetuity in Haworth after his own death by building a Methodist preaching house for his parishioners, of which John and Charles Wesley joined him as trustees, along with four Methodist laymen. On its commemorative tablet, however, he discarded Wesley's favourite term 'preaching house' for 'This Chapel'.

William Grimshaw was also a focal point of vibrant Christianity in general in the north, ecumenical in evangelism and Christian fellowship wherever it could be found, promoted, or encouraged. Although he sympathized with most moderate elements of Calvinist theology, he had no taste for doctrinal controversy, restricting himself to the positive aspects of Christian evangelism and nurture. His own preaching was the means of renewing the declining causes of Dissent, especially among the Baptists; indeed he remarked ruefully on one occasion, referring to the defections among his own converts, 'So many of my chickens turn ducks!'

Although he welcomed lay Dissenters and the Methodist lay itinerants alike when they preached a simple gospel, he found it repugnant when Charles Wesley informed him in 1760 that a group of Methodist itinerants in Norwich contemplated licensing themselves as Dissenters in order to administer Communion. This was to him, as to Charles, *undermining the Church*, and he replied in a fiery letter: 'If it be so, to your tents, O Israel! It's time for me to shift for myself, to disown all connection with the Methodists.' He proved to be a major advocate, indeed, in helping Charles to stave off separation from the Church of England for at least a generation.

With all his boisterous ways William Grimshaw remained a High Churchman, with a deep devotion to the sacrament of the Lord's Supper. During his funeral sermon for Grimshaw in Haworth on 10 April 1763, HENRY VENN remarked: 'Which of you ever received with him the Holy Communion without perceiving it was an exquisite feast of joy to his soul?' The 12 regular communicants who welcomed Grimshaw to Haworth in 1742 had increased by 1743 to fifty or sixty, and – as he replied to an interrogation by his new archbishop in 1748 – 'In the winter from four to five hundred, and sometimes in the summer near twelve hundred.' Occasionally he was on duty in his church from 9 a.m. until 5 p.m., and on one occasion when GEORGE WHITE-FIELD assisted him the communicants sipped away almost 35 bottles of wine.

Grimshaw's only printed work was *An Answer to a Sermon Lately Published Against the Methodists by the Rev. Mr. George White, M.A.* (1749). He left a handful of very interesting autobiographical and devotional manuscripts, as well as some correspondence with evangelical leaders, pastoral epistles to Methodist societies, and a series of 33 letters written 1750–62 to the wife of a naturalized Swiss mercenary officer in the Dragoons and the Grenadier Guards. These contain some lengthy sermonizing spiced with the aphorisms which he sprinkled over most of his preaching and writing: 'A reasoning heart is a great impediment to spiritual growth', and 'Rejoice when you can rejoice, and when you cannot, hope; hope is our anchor.'

BIBLIOGRAPHY
F. Baker, *William Grimshaw, 1708–1763* (London, 1963)

FRANK BAKER

Grimshawe, Thomas Shuttleworth (b. Preston, Lancashire, England, 4 May 1777; d. Biddenham, Bedfordshire, England, 17 Feb. 1850). Anglican clergyman. Thomas was a member of the distinguished Preston family of Grimshaw (he adopted the final 'e' in his surname). He was educated at Macclesfield School and Brasenose College, Oxford (BA 1798; MA 1800). He was ordained (deacon 1802, priest 1803) and after serving curacies became Vicar of Biddenham 1808–50, and non-resident Rector of Burton Latimer, Bedfordshire 1809–43.

In the early 1820s he became embroiled in a controversy with Bishop Herbert Marsh over his strictures against evangelical clergy. Grimshawe was a historian, a fellow of the Society of Antiquaries (1837) and biographer of LEGH RICHMOND and WILLIAM COOPER. He was also an opponent of the practise of 'suttee', publishing a work against it in 1825.

Grimshawe supported numerous societies, including the LSPCJ, and in which connection he visited the Holy Land and Egypt. He was a committed premillennialist and in 1844 lectured on the subject as one of H. M. VILLIERS's Lenten speakers.

SELECT WRITINGS
T. S. Grimshawe, *An Earnest Appeal to British Humanity in Behalf of Indian Widows* (London, 1825)

BIBLIOGRAPHY
DNB
Edinburgh Review, 37 (1822): 432–49

ALAN FREDERICK MUNDEN

Grindrod, Edmund (b. Rochdale, Lancashire, England, 1786; d. 1 May 1842). Methodist preacher. Converted in his teens, Grindrod became a local preacher in *circa* 1805 and entered the ministry in the following year. He early distinguished himself by his natural abilities, diligent application and sound judgement; and his acquaintance with the best English divines and Wesleyan theology led to his appointment to many important circuits. While he was elected president in 1837, he is chiefly remembered as having been superintendent of the Leeds circuit in 1827–8 at the time of the Leeds Organ Case, his handling of which was convinced but

incautious. Involving JABEZ BUNTING in the dispute, he found that the affair led to a loss of 1,000 members and of his own health. But there was no doubt of his exemplary piety, his self-control, and great moral courage: 'When placed in circumstances of more than ordinary trial and perplexity, he was enabled to possess his soul in patience and peace'.

SELECT WRITINGS
E. Grindrod, *Compendium of the Laws and Regulations of Wesleyan Methodism* (London, 1842)

BIBLIOGRAPHY
EWM
Minutes (1842): 17–18
G. Osborn, *Outlines of Wesleyan Bibliography* (London, 1869)

OLIVER A. BECKERLEGGE

Griswold, Alexander Viets (b. Simsbury, CT, BNA, 22 April 1766; d. Boston, 15 Feb. 1843). Episcopal clergyman and bishop. Son of Elisha and Eunice Viets Griswold, he was refused admission to Yale College because of his parents' supposed Anglican loyalist sympathies during the American Revolution. He became a farmer and educated himself in both law and theology. In later years, he was awarded honorary degrees from Brown University and Harvard College. In 1794, he presented himself for Episcopal orders, and a year later was ordained a deacon. He served a number of churches in Connecticut from 1795 until 1804. In 1805, he became Rector of St Michael's Church in Bristol, Rhode Island. In 1811, he was elected Bishop of the Eastern Diocese (all of New England except Connecticut) and continued to work as a parish priest as well. In 1830, he moved to St Peter's Church in Salem, Massachusetts. In 1835, he resigned his parish responsibilities and thereafter served only as bishop.

Griswold's early ministry reflected the High Church formalism of the Episcopal Church in Connecticut. His early sermons were mainly moral discourses, and he opposed religious enthusiasm. During his years in Bristol, he began to question the exclusivist tendencies of Episcopal polity and was impressed by the growth of the local Methodist society. He was consecrated as bishop of a languishing diocese on 29 May 1811 at the age of 46. His new responsibilities prompted a religious crisis, and Griswold began to preach more on 'Jesus Christ and him crucified' than on moralism or Episcopal church order. In 1812, his Bristol parish experienced a revival which added more than 100 communicants to the church. He experimented with prayer meetings, special services and inquirers' classes. After this episode, he determined that only through such means would the Episcopal Church ever be revived.

Bristol became a centre for the education of Episcopal clergymen as evangelically minded young men arrived to study under Griswold – the most well known of the group was STEPHEN H. TYNG. Meanwhile, the bishop travelled throughout his diocese preaching, converting and confirming new Episcopalians. The small diocese grew rapidly under his charge. In 1842, MANTON EASTBURN was elected and consecrated as his assistant bishop.

Although Griswold claimed no party allegiance in the developing tensions between High Church and evangelical Episcopalians, the evangelicals clearly regarded him as their leader until his death in 1843. He valued the institutions and forms of the Episcopal Church, but he valued more highly the personal, spiritual experience of life in Christ. As early as 1812, Griswold promoted world missions, corresponded with the CMS and dreamed of a similar American society. In 1820–1, he was instrumental in establishing the Domestic and Foreign Missions Society in the Episcopal Church. He wrote numerous articles which appeared in one of the evangelical party's journals, the *Washington Theological Repertory*. He advocated the use of 'free', or non-liturgical, prayer meetings and deplored any suggestion that revivalism was incompatible with the ministry of the Episcopal Church.

When the influence of Tractarianism began to be felt in America, Griswold was appalled. He responded with his most substantial theological work, *The Reformation* (1843). In it, he delineated his vision of the 'true catholicism' which existed between all members of Christ, attacked the Roman Catholic claims to exclusivity, and outlined the doctrinal position of the English Reformers on issues dividing Protestants and Roman Catholics. Mostly a polemical and anti-Roman work, *The Reformation* nevertheless demonstrated Griswold's deep desire for pan-evangelical unity and his commitment to the Protestant theological heritage of the Episcopal Church.

His greatest achievement, however, was the growth of the Episcopal Church in New England. In 1811, his diocese consisted of 22 churches and 16 clergyman. At the time of his death, there were over 100 Episcopal churches in New England and five bishops were elected to replace him. Through most of the nineteenth century, New England Episcopalianism (with the exception of Connecticut) retained the evangelical ethos which Griswold established in his diocese's early years.

Most of Griswold's published works were convention addresses and sermons. In addition, see his *Discourses on the Most Important Doctrines and Duties of the Christian Religion* (Philadelphia, 1830); *The Reformation* (Boston, 1843); *Remarks on Social Prayer Meetings* (Boston, 1858).

BIBLIOGRAPHY
AAP
DAB
DcAmReB
J. S. Stone, *Memoir of the Life of the Rt Rev. Alexander Viets Griswold* (Philadelphia, PA, 1844)

DIANA HOCHSTEDT BUTLER

Groen van Prinsterer, Guillaume (b. Voorburg, Netherlands, 21 Aug. 1802; d. The Hague, Netherlands, 19 May 1876). Dutch jurist, archivist, and scholar. The son of the medical doctor, Petrus Jacobus Groen van Prinsterer, and Adriana Hendrika Caan, he received a classical education which he capped with a printed essay entitled *M. Tullii Ciceronis Indole Consiliis Factisque Viri Accommodato* (1817). In May 1817, he enrolled at the University of Leiden as a student of law, over against the wishes of his parents who wanted him to study medicine. He passed his candidate's examination in 1819 and in 1823, defended two doctoral dissertations, the one in law [*Disputatio de Juris Justinianei Praestantia ex Eius Rationibus Mainfesta*] (Leiden, 1823)] and the other in classical studies [*Prosopographia Platonica, Sive Expositio Judicii Quod Plato Tulit de Iis, Qui in Scriptus Ipsius aut Loquentes Inducuntur aut Quavis de Causa Commemorantur* (Leiden, 1823)].

After his studies, he began work at the Ministry of Internal Affairs [Binnenlandse Zaken]. In 1827, he was appointed 'Referendarius' to King Willem I and married Maria Magdelena van der Hoop (6 February 1804–14 March 1879). Promoted to Cabinet Secretary in 1829, he founded that same year a periodical publication devoted to political commentary entitled *Nederlandsche Gedachten* which continued through 1832 and was published again from 1869 to 1876. It was also during 1829 that he made his first contact with the *Réveil*, the Swiss-French-Dutch revival tradition which owed a significant debt to JOHN WESLEY and Methodism as well as to Pietism. Particularly influential in his intellectual development were MERLE D'AUBIGNÉ and Willem de Clercq.

Continuing his work in the government, Groen was appointed Archivist of the Royal Dutch Palace Archives. He published several volumes of documents, but most of all the experience made him an expert in the development of Dutch law and history. Many of his juridical and historical publications come from this formative period or were influenced by his reading of these primary documents. In 1840 he began his political career by becoming a member of the 'Double Chamber' [Dubble Kamer] and later of the Second Chamber [Tweede Kamer] representing Hardewijk (1849–50), Zwolle (1850–4), The Hague (1854–6), Leiden (1856–7), Arnhem (1862–6) and Leiden (1866). Between 1857 and 1862 he was occupied with the issues posed by New Guinea as well as the re-organization of the State Council [Raad van State]. He was editor of the daily newspaper, *De Nederlander* from 1850 to 1855.

Education became a major concern. This brought him into conflict with the secularizing influences in Dutch society and he founded the Vereniging voor Christelijk Nationaal Schoolonderwijs on 30 October 1860 to work for retaining Christian values in the educational structures. From this lengthy period of struggle came numerous essays and books making the argument. The writings circulated through Europe (some were written in French) and had an impact upon legal and educational developments in Belgium and France as well as Switzerland. His perspective was denominated the 'Anti-revolutionary and Confessional' party. The volume *Ongeloof en Revolutie* (Leiden, 1847), which went through several editions, became a standard analysis of Dutch law and society as well as the basis for a political agenda, which would come to fulfilment under the influence of his protege, Abraham Kuyper. With the assistance of leading Dutch evangelicals, including P. J. Elout van Soetewoude, J. W. van Loon and A. baron Mackay, a Reformed seminary was established in Amsterdam (1852) as an alternative to the extant clergy educational forums. It was associated closely with the Scottish Presbyterian Church and became also a centre for missions to the Jews.

Throughout the legal and constitutional conflicts, Groen van Prinsterer was sustained by his participation in the Evangelical community. From 1845, he was a participant with the confessional movement, the Vereniging Christelijke Vrienden, related to the *Réveil*, within the Reformed Church. He contributed to the historiography with *Evangelie Prediking op Java* (The Hague, 1844) and the studies of the Paris and Dutch missionary societies: *Het Parijsche Zendlinggenootschap, Werkzaam in Zuid-Afrika* (The Hague, 1847) and *Het Nederlandsche Zendlinggenootschap* (The Hague, 1848). Because of these contacts, Groen became a firm and influential advocate of mission and opponent of slavery. He was active in the international EA and wrote of its influence in The Netherlands: *La Nationalité Religieuse en Rapport Avec la Hollande et l'Alliance Evangelique* (Amsterdam, 1867). In 1874, attracted by the reports of the Moody-Sankey and Robert Pearsall Smith evangelistic campaigns in England, he arranged for several Dutch evangelicals to attend the Oxford and Brighton conventions of Robert Pearsall and Hannah Whitall Smith. Among those he sent to Brighton was Abraham Kuyper. After Brighton, Groen van Prinsterer hosted Robert Pearsall Smith at his home in The Hague and introduced him to the leading political and evangelical leaders who flocked to hear the American evangelist. With encouragement from Groen, Kuyper began to edit a Holiness periodical.

Groen van Prinsterer remains an influence in Dutch law, education, and theology as well as in the wider culture as is evidenced by the essays compiled to celebrate the hundredth anniversary of his death, *Een Staatsman ter Navolging* (The Hague, 1976), which also contains an extensive bibliography of secondary literature on Groen. Unfortunately, very little of Groen's massive *oeuvre* has been translated into English.

SELECT WRITINGS

A. Goslinga, *Briefwisseling van Mr. G. Groen van Prinsterer met Dr. A. Kuyper 1864–1876* (Kampen, Netherlands, 1937)

G. Groen van Prinsterer, *Beidrage Tot Herzeining der Grondwet in Nederlandsche Zin* (Leiden, Netherlands, 1840)

—, *Aan de Hervormde Gemeente in Nederland* (Leiden, Netherlands, 1843)

—, *Handboek der Geschiedenis van het Vaderland* (Amsterdam, 1852)

—, *De Anti-Revolutionnaire en Confessionele Partij in de Nederlands Hervormde Kerk* (Goes, Netherlands, 1954)

—, *La Hollande et l'Influence de Calvin* (The Hague, 1864)

—, *Parlementaire Studien en Schetsen*, 3 vols (The Hague, 1865–1876)

—, *L'Empire Prussien et l'Apocalypse; à Mes Amis de Berlin* (Amsterdam, 1867)

—, *Aan de Conservatieve Partij*, 3 vols (Amsterdam, 1869)

—, *Maurice et Barneveld. Etude Historique* (Utrecht, Netherlands, 1875)

Groen van Prinsterer. Schriftlijke Nalatenschap, uitg. van C. Gerretson en A. Goslinga, 4 vols (The Hague, 1925–1967)

BIBLIOGRAPHY

W. Aalders, *Theocratie of Ideologie* (The Hague, 1977)

R. Kuiper, *Zelfbeeld en Wereldbeeld* (Kampen, Netherlands, 1992)

H. J. W. Mulder, *Groen van Prinsterer, Staatsman en Profeet* (Franeker, Netherlands, 1973)

W. H. de Savorin Lohman, 'Groen van Prinsterer', *Nieuw Nederlandsch Biografisch Woordenboek*, 2 (1912): 507–20

G. J. Vos, *Groen van Prinsterer en zijn Tijd*, 2 vols (Dordrecht, Netherlands, 1886)

T. de Vries, *Mr. G. Groen van Prinsterer. Een Bibliographie* (Leiden, Netherlands, 1908)

J. Zwaan, *Groen van Prinsterer en de Klassieke Oudheid* (Amsterdam, 1973)

DAVID BUNDY

Groser, William [Jr] (b. London, 12 Aug. 1791; d. Islington, London, 6 Aug. 1856). Baptist minister, author, and editor. Brought up in the Baptist manse at Watford, his isolation led him from an early age to read such authors as Matthew Henry, Bunyan and JOHN GILL. This precocious education prepared Groser to become assistant to his father in his newly opened Watford school. In due course he was baptized and in 1811 preached for the first time. After declining several pastoral invitations he settled at Princes Risborough in 1813. Impending marriage and a good command of Puritan literature led him not to enter Stepney College, though he was interviewed by WILLIAM NEWMAN with whom he established cordial relations. The Princes Risborough pastorate provided ample opportunity for itinerating in the surrounding villages. But an extension to the chapel which had to be paid for in the depression years following the coming of peace in 1815, caused problems, and Groser resented having to 'beg' in other churches to remove this debt. By contrast a fraternal with BENJAMIN GODWIN of Great Missenden and the ministers of Haddenham and Tring made for creative mutual improvement.

The death of his only son and the illness of his wife led him to take a temporary pastorate at Battle before settling at Maidstone, 1820–39, in a congregation 'free as any church in the county from what was called Hyper-Calvinism'. While there he argued against the martyrdom of those like Richard Carlile who sold the writings of Tom Paine, as against dissenting principles, simultaneously courting the wrath of some cautious older men like JOSEPH IVIMEY, but establishing his claims upon the intentions of others. In 1826 he began to serve as reviews editor of *The Baptist Magazine*.

In 1839 he resigned the pastorate and removed to London to become secretary to a committee concerned about the East India Company's abuse of its power in pressing the opium trade. For the campaign of this Anti-Opium Society, whose leading force was W. S. Fry, son of ELIZABETH FRY, Groser both penned a number of tracts, and provided LORD ASHLEY with appropriate briefing papers so that he could fight the issue in the Commons.

From 1838 Groser edited *The Baptist Magazine*, which he carried out with great care for detail, though some thought him 'too rigid in his attachment to the "old school"' entertaining a lively suspicion of all 'Germanizing influence'. After serving 11 years on the committee of the Baptist Irish Society, he was summoned to its secretaryship in 1851 to take vigorous action to clear a substantial debt which he achieved within a year, continuing in office until his death. He served the BMS and a number of denominational agencies with great diligence, preaching regularly in the churches around London. He sat on the committee of the RTS, was for 12 years secretary to the Board of Baptist Ministers in London as also to the 'General Body of the ministers of the Three Denominations'. From 1849 he also exercised an evangelistic ministry from a small Baptist chapel in Chelsea. His publications were partly protestant [*Six Lectures on Popery*, RTS, 1825, republished as *Popery Unveiled*, 1839], partly training guides for Sunday schools, partly editions of hymn-books for use both in the United Kingdom and in Jamaica, as well as devotional writings and reviews.

BIBLIOGRAPHY
The Baptist Magazine (September and October 1856)
Boase
Julian

J. H. Y. BRIGGS

Grosvenor, Robert [first Baron Ebury of Ebury Manor, Co. Middlesex] (b. Westminster, London, 24 April 1801; d. Westminster, London, 18 Nov. 1893). MP and peer. Third and youngest son of Robert, first Marquess of Westminster, and Eleanor, daughter of Thomas (Egerton), first Earl of Wilton, he was educated at Westminster School and Christ Church, Oxford, graduating in 1821. He then served as MP for Shaftesbury (1822–6), Chester (1826–47) and Middlesex (1847–57). He was sworn of the Privy Council in 1830; was Comptroller of the Household, 1830–4, Treasurer of the Household, 1846–7, and Groom of the Stole to Prince Albert, 1840–1. He was created a baron in 1857. He married in 1831 Charlotte Arbuthnot, first daughter of Henry (Wellesley) first Baron Cowley of Wellesley by his first wife, Charlotte, daughter of the first Earl Cadogan.

Ebury was a strenuous supporter of the evangelical party in the Church of England, being active in the CPAS and the Scripture Readers' Association. In the House of Lords during the 1860s he made efforts to 'relax the rules of subscription to the Thirty-Nine Articles and the Act of Uniformity, and to effect liturgical revision' [Machin, 1977: 333]. A Royal Commission was appointed, resulting in the Clerical Subscription Act of 1865. Doctrinal purity was thereafter guarded by the incumbent's conscience and the discipline of his bishop. Ebury was also concerned to suppress ritualistic practices and to this end sought, unsuccessfully, a revision of the prayer-book.

BIBLIOGRAPHY
Peerage
G. I. T. Machin, *Politics and the Churches in Great Britain, 1832 to 1868* (Oxford, 1977)
The Times (20 November 1893)

DAVID J. JEREMY

Groves, Anthony Norris (b. Newton, Hampshire, England, 1 Feb. 1795; d. Bristol, 20 May 1853). Brethren leader and missionary pioneer. The third of six children, but the only son, of a Lymington businessman, Groves was educated at schools in Lymington (Hampshire) and Fulham (London). After studying chemistry in London, he learned dentistry with an uncle, and acquired surgical skills in London hospitals, starting practice in Plymouth on his nineteenth birthday. Converted there, he influenced MICHAEL SOLOMON ALEXANDER, then Jewish rabbi, but later first Anglican bishop in Jerusalem, and rescued and educated JOHN KITTO, later celebrated biblical scholar. After marrying his cousin Mary Bethia Thompson in 1816 they moved to Exeter, where (though an Anglican) he came under the spiritual influence of ELIZABETH and Charlotte PAGET, dissenting evangelical ladies who were later to be of considerable influence among (Open) Brethren.

Prospering, Groves and his wife developed strong convictions on Christian stewardship of possessions, which he embodied in a pamphlet *Christian Devotedness* (1825). He offered for missionary service with CMS, and took up external studies at Trinity College, Dublin with a view to ordination. In Dublin he associated with a group who were beginning to develop convictions on liberty of lay ministry, free celebration of the Lord's Supper, and the oneness of Christians that were to produce the Brethren movement. One of these men, J. G. BELLETT, named Groves as a first exponent of these views. In Exeter, Groves engaged as a home tutor a Scottish scholar, HENRY CRAIK, who absorbed his influence and was to become the lifelong colleague of GEORGE MÜLLER in establishing Brethren churches in Bristol and district. Müller was to marry Groves's sister Mary on 7 Oct 1830.

In 1829 Groves received believer's baptism, while disclaiming any sectarian position, and renounced his plans both for ordination and service with CMS. On 12 June 1829, he left Gravesend for St Petersburg for the overland journey to Baghdad, where CMS had no missionary. Kitto was with him, and he was accompanied to St Petersburg by J. V. PARNELL (later Lord Congleton), one of the Dublin group, who returned to assemble a party to join him in Baghdad.

Groves arrived on 6 December, and his skills, which included eye cataract surgery, won him some acceptance; but 15 months later Baghdad was devastated by plague, flood and civil war. Mary Groves dying of plague on 14 May 1831, and their infant daughter on 24 August, Groves was left with their two sons and Kitto, until Parnell, with FRANCIS W. NEWMAN, EDWARD CRONIN and others arrived in June 1832.

A boyhood interest in India was rekindled by a visit by Colonel Cotton of the Madras Engineers, and in May 1833 Groves left with Cotton for Bombay. He spent a year travelling widely throughout India (reaching Jaffna in Ceylon) encouraging and exhorting missionaries, but his support of the Lutheran CHARLES RHENIUS at Tirunelveli in the latter's dispute with CMS led to an estrangement from that body which was to be a source of heartache. In Calcutta he was warmly appreciative of the Anglican leaders, met WILLIAM CAREY in Serampore, and was befriended by ALEXANDER DUFF, whom he attended through a serious illness and with whom he returned to England during the latter half of 1834. Before he left India, he had published a treatise *On the Liberty of Ministry in the Church of Christ* embodying his views.

Groves recruited missionaries for India from Britain and from Germany, which he visited with Müller. The visit also brought him into closer contact with the developing Brethren movement, and he threw his influence strongly against exclusive tendencies which were arising, expressing his convictions in a significant letter of remonstrance to J. N. DARBY on 10 March 1836. He was remarried, to Harriet Baynes, in Malvern, England, on 25 April 1835.

From July 1836 to July 1837 Groves was in Madras, but the opposition caused by his support of Rhenius led him to establish his own work at Chittoor, 96 miles away, where there was no mission. This remained his centre for the remainder of this life, and passed to JOHN SCUDDER's American mission after his death. Groves's strong convictions on simple lifestyle and his increasing antipathy to denominational or society control of indigenous work led him to establish plans for a self-supporting mission. In addition to schools he experimented first with silk farming and then with a sugar factory. Under his influence an Indian disciple, J. C. Aroolappen, who had originally been with Rhenius, established autonomous Indian churches in Madras state which have influenced later indigenous development; while Brethren missions in the Godavari area of India were developed by men who had returned with him in 1836, William Bowden and George Beer. A third son was born in India in 1836.

Groves visited England again briefly in 1848, and supported Müller and Craik in the breach with Darby. He returned to India, but, his health failing, returned to England for the last time in 1852. His remaining eight months enabled him to renew many old friendships, in particular the Tottenham group of Brethren who were nurturing the youthful JAMES HUDSON TAYLOR, and to meet Count GUICCIARDINI from Florence. He died at the home of his brother-in-law, George Müller.

Groves was a man of singular winsomeness and breadth of sympathy. His thought developed and matured, as seen both in his later emphasis on a disciplined structure of authority in the local church, and in his transition from an early dislike of commercial adjuncts to mission to his later experiments in self-sufficiency. His complete dependence on God inspired much of the later faith mission movement, and the extensive worldwide development of Brethren missions in the century following his death, which his son Henry Groves did much to stimulate, is a lasting memorial to his influence. Among Brethren, the large-heartedness of Groves has always been a touchstone for those who have sought to combat the sectarian tendencies endemic in the movement. In his active dislike of divisiveness among Christians, his emphasis on Christian unity of spirit, his strong opposition to what would be seen today as colonialist attitudes affecting mission, his emphasis on simple lifestyle, and his experiments with relevant local economic activity in support of mission, he was outstanding. But the essential mainspring of his life was an unusually wholehearted devotedness to Christ, aptly summed up in his dying exclamation: 'Precious Jesus!'.

BIBLIOGRAPHY

F. R. Coad, *A History of the Brethren Movement*, 2nd edn (Exeter, England, 1976)

H. Groves, ed., *Memoir of the Late Anthony Norris Groves*, 2nd edn (London, 1857)

G. H. Lang, *Anthony Norris Groves* (London, 1949)

W. B. Neatby, *A History of the Plymouth Brethren*, 2nd edn (London, 1902)

H. H. Rowdon, *The Origins of the Brethren* (London, 1967)

ROY COAD

Grubb, Jonathan (b. Clonmel, Co. Tipperary, Ireland, 12 Jan. 1808; d. York, England, 17 June 1894). Quaker evangelist. In 1818 the family (his father Irish, his mother English) settled in England. His mother Sarah (Lynes) Grubb (1773–1842) was a noted and powerful ministering Friend of the Quietist tradition. Jonathan, however, reacted strongly against his upbringing and became a decided evangelical. He was recorded a minister in his thirties.

After some unsuccessful business ventures he and his brother-in-law became managers of the Sudbury branch of Alexander & Co.'s Bank. This in effect freed him for extensive travels in the ministry. He visited nearly every Quaker meeting in the British Isles, including virtually every Friend family in Ireland; he held meetings in dissenting places of worship and church halls; and he visited the Shetland Islands and the protestant communities in the Vaudois valleys of Piedmont.

He was a zealous temperance advocate, a warm supporter of the Salvation Army, and a leader from the 1870s in Quaker home mission work, promoting evangelistic meetings and commending congregational singing and the appointment of financially supported home missioners.

BIBLIOGRAPHY
Annual Monitor (1895): 79–91

EDWARD H. MILLIGAN

Gruber, Jacob   (b. Lancaster Co., PA, USA, 3 Feb. 1778; d. Lewistown, PA, USA, 25 May 1850). American Methodist pioneer preacher. Born of German Lutheran parents, at 15 Gruber was converted and became a Methodist, which resulted in his being disowned although a reconciliation was soon effected. About six years later he was again forced to leave home due to his zealous and outspoken concern for his family and neighbours' spiritual lives, and he set out on foot towards Lancaster, uncertain of his future. A Methodist minister met him on the road and told him of an opening on a nearby circuit. Gruber promptly set off on an itinerant life, gaining formal admittance to the Methodist itinerancy and appointment to the Tioga Circuit in 1800.

Gruber ably served in a variety of positions from 'the lakes to the shores of Chesapeake Bay': thirty-two years of circuit riding, 11 years as Presiding Elder for three districts, and seven years on stations in Philadelphia, Baltimore and Washington, DC. An effective preacher, he was looked upon by contemporaries as a talented and witty, if sometimes gruff and eccentric character: 'candid to abruptness, firm even to obstinacy, and faithful in reproof almost, if not quite, to discourtesy' (Hurst, 1902, II: 621). He had little patience for ostentation or moral laxity, and 'his powers of irony, sarcasm, and ridicule were tremendous'. Even so, he was seen by many as an untiring and beneficent minister of the Gospel. Gruber was also fiercely opposed to slavery as a national sin and was once arrested in Maryland for preaching these views. He was easily acquitted of inciting an insurrection, but it was a sign of the times that as a result of this issue the Baltimore Conference advised him 'to be more cautious in the future and forebear as much as possible from the use of epithets and allusions calculated unnecessarily to irritate' (*EWM*).

He died while on his way to a conference meeting in Alexandria, Virginia – fifty years after he began his career. He had married twice but had no children. Because of his frugality he was able to leave considerable amounts to the Chartered (Pension) Fund, Dickinson College, the church in Lewiston, and the Methodist Missionary Society.

BIBLIOGRAPHY
AAP 7: 341–6
EWM
J. Hurst, *History of Methodism: American Methodism* 2 vols, II (New York, 1902): 620–1

KENNETH N. PEARSON

Grundell, John   (b. Sunderland, England, June 1761; d. North Shields, England, 1 Dec. 1815). Methodist minister. Although blind from early childhood, Grundell became a popular Methodist local preacher. In 1793 he became a pastor of a chapel at Byker, Newcastle-upon-Tyne, where the Lord's Supper was celebrated in opposition to the pro-Anglican trustees of the main Newcastle chapel. In 1797 he was one of the founder ministers of the MNC and was appointed successively to virtually all their circuits. He was president of the conference in 1799.

BIBLIOGRAPHY
H. Smith, *Sketches of Eminent M.N.C. Ministers* (London, c. 1893)

E. ALAN ROSE

Grundy, George (Docker)   (b. Manchester, England, 2 Aug. 1807; d. Oldham, Lancashire, England, 9 Nov. 1901). Anglican clergyman. Educated at Brasenose College, Oxford, where he fell under the influence of two leading Calvinists (JOHN HILL of St Edmund Hall and HENRY BULTEEL of St Ebbes), Grundy graduated in 1829 and was ordained a year later. In 1838, after serving a number of curacies, Grundy was licensed as Perpetual Curate of St John's, Hey, where he remained until his death. In theology a Moderate Calvinist, Grundy in later life developed into what his son termed 'an evangelical high churchman' who introduced full choral services and placed a high value on the sacraments. Grundy's leading characteristic was assiduous devotion to a parish work founded on popular preaching, domiciliary visitation and the development of a broad range of educational institutions. This work bore fruit in large congregations, an extensive communicant roll, and, as time passed, the development of immense local popularity. An estimated 50,000 people, mainly local mill-workers, attended his funeral in 1901.

BIBLIOGRAPHY
S. Andrew, *A History of Hey* (Oldham, England, 1905)

M. A. SMITH

Guers, Emile   (b. Prévessin, near Geneva, 25 March 1794; d. Geneva, 27 Oct. 1882). Swiss dissenting pastor. Son of an *émigré* priest, Guers associated with a Moravian group but studied for the Reformed ministry in the Genevan Academy. Meeting ROBERT HALDANE confirmed his evangelical convictions. Just before his exams in 1817, the Company of Pastors (fearful of the potential divisiveness of the preaching of the *Réveil*) forbad sermons on some basic doctrines and Guers felt he had to secede. He became a founder member, and in 1818, a joint-pastor of the Bourg-de-Four Assembly (later the Pélisserie Assembly), going to London to receive congregational ordination in 1821. In the 1830s his congregation was depleted by the departure of some Irvingites and in 1840 by some forty followers of JOHN NELSON DARBY whom Guers had welcomed in 1837. Years of experience made him less suspicious of clerical structures and in 1849 he became an elder in the Free Evangelical Church of Geneva which resulted from the fusion of his assembly with HENRI-ABRAHAM CÉSAR MALAN's chapel at the Oratory. A charitable man, an able expositor and author, Guers spans the whole gamut of the experience of the Swiss *Réveil*.

BIBLIOGRAPHY
F. Chaponnière, *Pasteurs et Laïques de l'Eglise de Genève au dix-neuvième siècle* (Geneva, 1889): 88–9
E. Guers, *Le premier Réveil et la Première Eglise indépendante à Genève* (Geneva, 1871)
T. C. F. Stunt, 'Geneva and British Evangelicals in the Early 19th Century' *JEH* 32 (1981): 35–46

TIMOTHY C. F. STUNT

Guicciardini, [Count] **Piero** (b. Florence, Italy, 21 July 1808; d. Florence, Italy, 23 March 1886). Italian nobleman, reformer, and evangelical leader. A Florentine nobleman, he came early in contact with a group of liberal reformers, mostly foreign Protestant or freethinkers who were involved in promoting social reforms. Their influence, his own educational work and reading of the Scriptures led to his conversion in 1836. Without neglecting his previous involvement in business and reform, Guicciardini became an active Christian, convinced that Italy was in need of a 'religious regeneration' through non-sectarian missionary work. After 1849, the political repression in Tuscany forced the evangelicals underground and resulted in the arrest of Guicciardini (1851), caught reading the Bible in a private home. Charged with Protestant propaganda and offence to the religion of the state, through the intervention of his family and friends he was freed under condition of going into exile.

After extensive travel, he sought refuge in Britain, settling in Teignmouth, Devon, where he was received as a hero of the evangelical faith. In Teignmouth he associated with the [Plymouth] Brethren and revised the Italian translation of the Bible made by Giovanni Diodati in the seventeenth century. In London, he was instrumental in the conversion of one of the many Italian political exiles, TEODORICO PIETROCOLA-ROSSETTI (cousin of Dante Gabriel Rossetti) – later Guicciardini's closest collaborator. Guicciardini devoted himself to the organization of missionary work in northern Italy, supported by committees in Britain, Nice, and Geneva. A British citizen from 1858, Guicciardini travelled throughout Europe until 1860, when the new liberal government in Tuscany gave him the opportunity to return home.

From his family palace he promoted and administered the churches which Rossetti and others were tirelessly founding throughout Italy (which was progressively being freed from papal and foreign domination). Of these 'Free Evangelical Churches' those which followed a congregational pattern eventually took the name of *Chiese cristiane dei fratelli* (Christian churches of the brethren), akin to the Plymouth (Open) Brethren. Guicciardini continued to provide them with spiritual leadership as well as financial help. Guicciardini devoted his energy and patrimony to collecting ancient Italian Bibles and works on the abortive Italian Reformation. This collection is held by the National Library of Florence, and a new multi-volume catalogue is being published.

BIBLIOGRAPHY
L. Giorgi and M. Rubboli, eds., *Piero Guicciardini (1808–1886)* (Florence, 1988)
S. Jacini, *Un Riformatore Toscano Dell'epoca del Risorgimento* (Florence, 1940)
D. Ronco, *'Per me vivere è Cristo'* (Fondi LT, 1986)

MASSIMO RUBBOLI

Guinness, Arthur (b. Dublin, 12 March 1768; d. Beaumont, county Dublin, 9 June 1855). Irish brewer and philanthropist. He was the second son and business heir of the first Arthur Guinness, who established the family brewery at St James's Gate, Dublin, and the family seat at Beaumont. It was under the sway of the second Arthur, and largely through his example and encouragement, that the lines of expertise for future generations were determined – in banking, philanthropy, and ordained ministry, as well as brewing. He also provided, with patience and prudence – for his charity began at home – for the inevitable misfits in a large family connection, from the black sheep to the merely impecunious.

Guinness was conspicuously successful in expanding the business of the brewery. He was a major employer and contributor to the Irish economy. In point of conscious social policy, he offered at once a more acceptable alternative to the national weakness for whisky, and a more realistic approach than that of a 'Temperance' movement which preached total abstinence. Within the wider mercantile community he was president of the Dublin Chamber of Commerce, and as Governor also of the Bank of Ireland, received George IV at College Green in 1821. He was involved in a host of civic causes: the Farming Society of Ireland, the Dublin Society, the Meath Hospital. He was his own man in politics. He supported the cause of Catholic emancipation, and withdrew his support from O'Connell only when he began his campaign for repeal of the Union. To the Dublin *Freeman's Journal* he was 'our most distinguished citizen', to the vast crowd at his funeral a man of business integrity, high character, and unstinted benevolence.

His elder brother, Hosea, was Rector of St Werburgh's, the Castle parish; his eldest son, William Smyth, became Rector of Rathdrum. He himself attended Bethesda Chapel. That such a quintessential Establishment figure should identify with a proprietary (and until 1825, unlicensed) chapel, needs explanation. Both through his mother and his wife Anne, the daughter of Benjamin Lee of Merrion, he was related to the Bethesda's founder, William Smyth. But more than that, he was at one with him in developing a strong Anglican evangelical tradition in Dublin, while maintaining his formal allegiance to St Catherine's parish. His steadiness during the crisis that befell the chapel in 1805 was crucial to the survival of that tradition and, by extension, of its already considerable influence in the life of the Irish Church. That steadiness marked his support of Bethesda for a further fifty years. He was a generous benefactor of the foundation's charities, an orphanage and penitentiary, and – in conjunction with the philanthropist, Dr Robert Perceval – of medical and other evangelical charities in Dublin. His influence among the Church evangelicals generally may be compared with that of Archbishop TRENCH and Lord RODEN, each in his own sphere.

BIBLIOGRAPHY
P. Lynch and J. Vaizey, *Guinness's Brewery in the Irish Economy 1759–1876* (Cambridge, 1960)
M. Guinness, *The Guinness Legend* (London, 1989)

ALAN R. ACHESON

Guinness, Sir **Benjamin Lee** (b. Dublin, 1 Nov. 1798; d. London, 19 May 1868). Brewer, MP, and restorer of St Patrick's Cathedral, Dublin. The third son of ARTHUR GUINNESS, and his sole successor at the brewery, he developed its export trade substantially and became probably the wealthiest man in Ireland. He also maintained his father's record of involvement in both civic life and evangelical charities. He was elected Lord Mayor of Dublin in 1851 and MP for the city in 1865. An ecclesiastical commissioner for Ireland, he was created a baronet and received an honorary LL D from Trinity College, Dublin.

His greatest public achievement was to restore the twelfth-century St Patrick's Cathedral from virtual ruin, at a personal cost of £150,000. Reopened in 1865, St Patrick's was thus equipped to become the national cathedral of the Church of Ireland after disestablishment in 1871 – an event he did not live to see. Renowned also for his hospitable and humane qualities, he was widely mourned when he died, only 13 years after his father. Bishop JOHN GREGG, himself the builder of St Fin Barre's Cathedral in Cork, preached at his funeral.

He married in 1837 his cousin, Elizabeth ('Bessie') Guinness. Their sons, Sir Arthur Edward (Lord Ardilaun) and Edward Cecil (Lord Iveagh) carried on the family tradition of public benevolence. Their daughter, Anne Lee, married William Conyngham, Lord Plunket, who – as Archbishop of Dublin 1884–97 – was the leader of the Anglican evangelicals until his death.

BIBLIOGRAPHY
DNB
Wills, IV: 40–2

ALAN R. ACHESON

Gulick, Luther Halsey (b. Honolulu, HI, USA, 10 June 1828, d. Springfield, MA, USA, 8 April, 1891). Medical missionary to Micronesia, Spain, Italy, China, and Japan. One of the seven missionary sons of P. J. Gulick, Luther Halsey Gulick was educated at Auburn Academy and received his medical degree from the medical college of the University of the City of New York in 1850. After attending lectures at Union Theological Seminary he was ordained 4 October 1851. *En route* to Micronesia with his wife Louisa, he stopped at his boyhood home, Hawaii, and was chief organizer for the Hawaiian Mission Children's Society whose members were largely composed of Hawaii mission descendants who had pledged to Christianize the Pacific Islands beyond Hawaii. At his station on Ponape in the Caroline Islands (1852–9) and on Ebon in the Marshall Islands (1859–60) Gulick succeeded in establishing not only the Gospel but also a vernacular press. Gulick carried his belief in the power of the printed word to the Far East by representing the ABS in Japan and China, 1876–90. He founded the Bible House in Yokohama, Japan, and is credited with greatly increasing the circulation of Bibles in China. He married Louisa Lewis of New York.

BIBLIOGRAPHY
DAB
F. Jewett, *Luther Halsey Gulick, Missionary in Hawaii, Micronesia, Japan, and China* (Boston, MA, 1895)

NANCY J. MORRIS

Gundert, Hermann (b. Stuttgart, Württemberg, 1814; d. 1893). Scholar, linguist, publisher and missionary. Gundert was raised in a Pietist family and educated at the University of Tübingen where he studied theology and obtained his Ph.D. Attracted for a time to the teachings of D. F. Strauss, his conversion in 1833 moved him a very different theological direction. Gundert's study of philosophy and linguistics eventually enabled him to become a great Tulu and Kannada scholar: he left dictionaries and grammars of permanent value.

Visited by GEORGE MÜLLER in 1834 and by ANTHONY NORRIS GROVES in 1835, he was drawn to consider India as his mission field. In October 1835 Gundert travelled to England where his 'Plymouth Brethren' friends reinforced his reservations about the wisdom of the tradition of German missionaries cooperating with the CMS in India.

In 1836 Gundert joined Groves in Calcutta, and moved with him to Madras, then to Chittoor but found it too difficult to work with him. He briefly considered joining C. T. RHENIUS in Tirunelveli but Rhenius' death in June 1838 caused him to join his friend Dr Hermann Friedrich Mögling (1811–81) in the Basel Mission's Kannada mission in Mangalore in October 1838. He arrived just after a great conflict between SAMUEL HEBICH and the younger brethren who thought that he and they should be living in a more Indian style. Gundert managed to pour oil on troubled waters. He married a Huguenot lady, noble and capable, who was the first woman missionary in Mangalore.

From the early 1840s to 1849 he worked in Tellicherry, south of Mangalore (with a furlough in Germany from December 1845 to February 1847). In 1849 he became the general secretary of the Basel Malabar mission and transferred to the mission station of Chirakkal, north-west of Cananore. Partly the move was due to the Basel Mission's concern for Hebich's health and loneliness. Gundert was the only missionary who ever succeeded in working with Hebich.

Both Gundert and Hebich worked well with the British colonial and military officials in Cananore and received significant support from them. Gundert was often consulted on the translation and manufacture of texts for government schools and in 1857 finally agreed to accept, on a provisional basis, the position of Inspector of schools (whether Catholic, Protestant or Brahman). Ill health forced his return to Germany in 1859.

From 1862 Gundert headed a Pietist publishing house in Calw, 'a firm which was among the most influential Pietist publishing foundations in nineteenth-century Germany' (Brecht, 1990: 136). Gundert remained a key figure in the Basel Mission and played a key role in linking German Pietism with the English-speaking evangelical world. His grandson, another Hermann, shared his interest in India: the Nobel Prize-winning author, Hermann Hesse (1877–1962).

BIBLIOGRAPHY
M. Brecht, 'The Relationship Between Established Protestant Church and Free Church: Hermann Gundert and Britain', trans. D. Meldrum, in K. Robbins, ed., *Protestant Evangelicalism: Britain, Ireland, Germany and America c. 1750–1950* (Oxford, 1990): 135–51
H. Gundert, *Tagebuch aus Malabar 1837–1859* (Stuttgart, Germany, 1983)
—, *Schriften und Berrichte aus Malabar* (Stuttgart, Germany, 1983)
W. Schlätter, *Die Geschichte der Baseler Mission*, 3 vols, III (Basel, 1916)
G. Thomssen, *Samuel Hebich of India, The Master Fisher of Men* (Cuttack, India, 1905)

E. M. JACKSON AND DONALD M. LEWIS

Gunn, Peter (b. Tacher, Wick, Caithness, Scotland, 1812; d. Campbellfield, Victoria, Australia, 2 June 1864). Presbyterian minister. A Presbyterian minister set aside to minister to Gaelic-speaking colonists in Victoria. He was educated at Marischal College, Aberdeen University and then at the University of Edinburgh. On 11 August 1841 he was ordained by the presbytery of Caithness and sent to Port Phillip at the request of JAMES FORBES to minister to the Gaelic speakers.

On 25 February 1842 he arrived in Melbourne. Having no settled ministry he moved around the colony preaching wherever he found Scots and as such he was responsible for the establishing of some 15 to 20 churches. From 1843 to 1845 he was the minister of the Heidelberg Church and from 1845 until his death he pastored a Presbyterian congregation in Campbellfield. He was moderator of the presbytery of Melbourne in 1846, 1848 and 1851, and clerk in 1852. In 1854 he became moderator of the first Synod of Victoria. He was married to Jane Scott and they had five children.

BIBLIOGRAPHY
Fasti
J. Hetherington, *Pillars of Faith* (Melbourne, 1966)

STEWART D. GILL

Gunn, William (b. Caswell Co., NC, USA, 13 March 1797; d. Lexington, KY, USA, 3 Sept. 1853). Minister in the MEC. He was converted as a youth in Tennessee, but later moved to Kentucky where he entered the itineracy in 1819. He was known and respected for his devoted life, evidenced by early rising, reading, and prayer. He served appointments in the Kentucky Conference for 34 years, half that time as presiding elder. He was known for his expository preaching, exhortation, and a strong musical voice. In 1830 he survived being struck by lightning and only lost two months of ministerial service as he recovered. He died 23 years later of typhoid.

BIBLIOGRAPHY
CM
EWM

STEVE HARPER

Gunn, (William) Alphonsus (b. Rotherlithe, Surrey, England, 29 Sept. 1760; d. London, 5 Dec. 1806). Anglican clergyman. The namesake of his father, a gentleman, Gunn matriculated in 1788 at Magdalen Hall, Oxford. He was a 'serious' Christian by the age of ten, and apparently began a curacy at St Andrew's, Farnham, Surrey in 1792. There he gained a reputation as a Calvinist and 'methodist' for which, except among a few of his more wealthy parishioners, he was generally popular. The Rector of Farnham, whom the *Evangelical Magazine* impugned as having been swayed by the double entreaties of jealousy and avarice, dismissed him. Like other church evangelicals in this period, Gunn was at pains to demonstrate his 'sincere attachment to the Church of England' (Gunn, 1807: 383). In 1793 he had an opportunity to do so when he was offered the pastorate of a Lady Glenorchy chapel in Bristol. He declined and three years later was made curate to JOHN NEWTON at St Mary's Woolnoth, London. He also held concurrent lectureships at St Margaret's, Lothbury, at St Mary's, Somerset, and at Broadway Chapel, Westminster. He was buried at St Mary's Woolnoth.

Gunn's sermons, clear and pithy, were thought of as among the evangelicals' best; JOSIAH PRATT, ROBERT HAWKER, and JOHN HATCHARD subscribed to them in published form. He was present at the founding of the CMS in 1799.

BIBLIOGRAPHY
EM (1807): 44–5
GM (December 1806): 1180
W. A. Gunn, *Sermons and Letters* (London, 1807)

JONATHAN BURKE CUTMORE

GRAYSON CARTER

Gunther, James William (b. Nagold, Würtemburg, 12 May 1806; d. Mudgee, Australia, 20 Dec. 1879). CMS missionary and priest. Trained at the Basel Mission Institute, in 1832 Gunther became one of the four Basel graduates annually accepted by CMS. Ordained by the Bishop of London, he was appointed to New South Wales, arriving in 1837. Gunther was the third missionary at CMS's first Australian mission at Wellington.

The Gunthers found the tensions of missionary life difficult. The Wellington missionaries struggled against the Australian climate to demonstrate to Aborigines the supposed 'advantages' of a settled farming life. Gunther learned Wiradjuri, attempting some Bible translation. He had a strict attitude to baptism, refusing to recognize Christian faith unaccompanied by a change to European lifestyle. The mission closed in 1843. Gunther became rector, later Archdeacon, of Mudgee ministering faithfully there for 36 years.

BIBLIOGRAPHY
B. Bridges 'The Church of England and the Aborigines of NSW, 1788–1855' (Univ. of New South Wales, Ph.D. thesis, 1978)
J. Woolmington, 'Early Christian Missions to the Australian Aborigines – A Study in Failure' (Univ. of New England, Ph.D. thesis, 1979)

JOHN HARRIS

Gurdon, Philip (b. Bures, Suffolk, England, 10 Nov. 1746; d. Assington Hall, Suffolk, 7 May 1817). Anglican clergyman and squire. Descended from the puritan John Gurdon, MP (*DNB*), and son of Philip Gurdon (Rector of Bures) by Elizabeth (Pelham), Philip was educated at St Paul's school, London (scholar) 1760–4 (contemporary with E. CUTHBERT), at Queen's College, Oxford (Pauline exhibitioner) 1764, becoming demy (1765–8) and fellow of Magdalen College 1770–8. As an undergraduate, concerned about his soul, and introduced to JAMES STILLINGFLEET's evangelical circle, helped by their converse, their advice on reading, and above all by studying the Bible, Gurdon was converted, *circa* 1766–7. JOHN NEWTON recorded that at Oxford he had 'great hindrances thrown in his way'.

Ordained 1770 (ordination papers, Oxford), Gurdon served as Curate of Cookham, Berkshire, where in 1771 the Vicar, Dr George Berkeley, son of Bishop Berkeley, and Prebendary of Canterbury, became non-resident (*DNB* under [his wife] Eliza Berkeley) and where Gurdon's ministry 'was blessed to the conversion of many'. In 1774 Newton wrote 'he is for judgement and spirit one of the first of the younger ministers'. In 1777 he succeeded to family estates in Suffolk, residing thereafter at Assington Hall. In 1778 Gurdon published *A Sketch ... of the Christian Character*, a forgotten precursor of Wilberforce's *Practical View* (1797). In 1780 he nominated his Oxford friend JOHN HALLWARD, vicar of Assington, with whom he worked in conjunction till death. Well versed in Hebrew, Greek, and Latin authors, Gurdon 'valued none of these accomplishments ... further than as they might contribute to his usefulness,

and the more successful diffusion of the Gospel . . .' RICHARD CECIL refers to him (1798) as 'a sound, solid, and evangelical minister'. His local influence was certainly considerable. He contributed liberally to good causes. A supporter of the CMS as early as 1801, he became a regional vice-president in 1811, though by then ill health prevented attendance at meetings. A memorial in Assington church by J. BACON, JR, (son of J. BACON) has unfortunately become almost illegible.

Gurdon married (1778) Sarah Richardson (1753–1822) of Birmingham. Their daughter Elizabeth married J. A. Stephenson, son of Gurdon's Oxford evangelical contemporary, C. Stephenson.

BIBLIOGRAPHY
J. Bull, *John Newton* (London, 1868)
Burke's
CO, 1817 (London, 1818), obituary
C. Hole, *Early History C.M.S.* (London, 1896)
J. S. Reynolds, *Evangelicals at Oxford* (Oxford, 1953; Appleford, England, 1975)
A. C. H. Seymour, *Countess of Huntingdon*, 2 (London, 1844)

J. S. REYNOLDS

Gurney, John Hampden (b. London, 15 Aug. 1802; d. London, 8 Mar. 1862). Honorary Prebendary of St Paul's Cathedral. The elder son of Sir John Gurney (*DNB*), he was educated at Trinity College, Cambridge (BA 1824; MA 1827), gaining prizes in English and the classics. He studied law, but, inspired by a religious conversion, gave it up in favour of the church. He declined several offers of advancement, satisfied for most of his career to be Curate of Lutterworth (1827–44). He moved only once, to London, as Rector of St Mary's, Bryanston Square (1847–62) and was made Honorary Prebendary of St Pancras in St Paul's Cathedral (1857).

When, in 1834, municipalities were compelled to sell their rights of patronage, Gurney worked with CHARLES SIMEON to purchase advowsons, raising on his own initiative over £10,000. A man of ecumenical temper, he actively supported the CMS, the High Church dominated SPCK, and the non-denominational BFBS. Between his curacy and rectorship, as honorary secretary to the Scripture Readers' Society, he was a pioneer of lay evangelism. He died of typhoid at the height of his career.

Besides sermons, Gurney published some didactic historical sketches (given as lectures in the YMCA Exeter Hall series for 1854–5 and 1860–1); also a pamphlet against Catholicism, and ones in support of the New Poor Law, and the FCS; and two hymn collections. His harvest hymn, 'Fair waved the golden corn', is still known. Two of his autograph letters are in the British Library. He was an intelligent organizer and preacher who made a significant, if secondary, contribution to the evangelical movement at mid-century.

BIBLIOGRAPHY
Boase
CO (April 1862): 313–16

DNB
GM (April 1862): 513, 783

JONATHAN BURKE CUTMORE

Gurney, Joseph (1744–1815). *See* GURNEY, THOMAS

Gurney, Joseph (1804–79). *See* GURNEY, THOMAS

Gurney, Joseph John (b. Norwich, Norfolk, England, 2 Aug. 1788; d. Norwich, Norfolk, England, 4 Jan. 1847). Quaker minister, theologian, banker, and humanitarian. He was the tenth of 11 children born to John Gurney, a prosperous banker and fourth-generation Quaker, and his wife Catherine, who died when Joseph was four years old. From 1796 to 1805, he was sent to study with Anglican ministers in Norwich, Hingham, and Oxford. As a Quaker, he could not obtain an Oxford degree, but he read Latin, Greek, Hebrew, and Italian classics in the original languages and formed intensive study habits. Religious studies consumed his early morning hours for the rest of his life. When his father died in 1809, Joseph John inherited his position in the Norwich Bank and as head of household at the family mansion, Earlham Hall.

Gurney's ecumenical commitments were deep rooted and long lasting. In 1811, he joined other evangelicals, Anglicans and Dissenters, in founding the Norwich Lancastrian school and the Norwich branch of the BFBS. He befriended such leading evangelicals of his time as WILLIAM WILBERFORCE, CHARLES SIMEON, HENRY VENN, THOMAS CHALMERS, and his sister Hannah's husband, THOMAS FOWELL BUXTON. Gurney's commitment to Quakerism came after he had plunged himself into ecumenical activities. His family had brought him up as a 'gay Quaker', not fully conforming to Quaker testimonies in speech and dress. But his Bible study and the sermons he heard from his uncle impelled him to become a 'plain Quaker' by 1812, as he flouted social conventions by entering the parlours of a local squire and the Bishop of Norwich with his hat on.

Gurney's first marriage, in 1817 to Jane Birkbeck, produced much happiness as well as two children, Anna and John Henry. He grieved deeply when in 1822 Jane died of pleurisy and excessive bleeding by her doctors. His second marriage, to Mary Fowler, lasted from 1827 until her death in 1836. Gurney's third wife, Eliza Kirkbride, an American whom he married in 1841, survived him. Both his second and third marriages were childless.

In June 1818, Gurney was recorded as a Quaker minister by the Norwich monthly meeting. His considerable travels within the British Isles over the next 15 years led him (accompanied by his sister, prison reformer ELIZABETH FRY) to examine the state of prisons in Scotland, as well as to deliver thoughtful messages at numerous Quaker meetings. From 1818 onwards, Gurney became well known for his fervent advocacy of strengthening Quaker schools and instituting daily Bible study. He was instrumental in upgrading the quality of education at Ackworth School in Yorkshire, and the foundation of Earlham College in Indiana can be traced to his influence. In the arena of English politics, Gurney identified himself with liberal and reform causes. He seriously considered standing for Parliament in 1832, but admonitions from friends and family helped to persuade him against taking that step.

During the 1820s and early 1830s, he gained a reputation as an author of religious books. He published about fifty books, sermon collections, letters, and tracts. Perhaps Gurney's best loved book was his *Essay on the Habitual Love of God* (1834), a devotional classic which contained moving meditations on the earthly and heavenly existences of Christ. His *Observations on the Religious Peculiarities of Friends* (1824), the first systematic Quaker theology in 148 years, affirmed traditional Quaker principles on an unpaid ministry, silent worship, the disuse of oaths, pacifism, and, albeit with some misgivings, the ministry of women and the disuse of sacraments. This book (and succeeding books such as his *Essay ... on Christianity*) elaborated a controversial view of Christ's atonement which differed from that previously accepted by Friends. Quakers had believed that the 'inner light', or 'light of Christ', within human beings, whether Christian or not, was sufficient to bring them to know and to do what is good. For Gurney, influenced by evangelicals such as SIMEON on this point, the inner light was primarily useful in bringing one to renounce one's sins and to accept Christ. It was barely possible that the inner light might show someone how to be good, but a much surer guide was the illuminations of the Holy Spirit produced by a Christian's thorough acquaintance with God's 'outward revelation', the Bible. Many Quakers rejected his views. American followers of Elias Hicks (Hicksites) equated the inner light with 'the grace of God', and naturally Gurney repudiated them and their theology when they split from orthodox Quakerism in 1827. But even some orthodox Quakers disapproved of Gurney; English Quietist Thomas Shillitoe called him an Episcopalian in Quaker garb.

In 1837, Gurney felt drawn to undertake a ministerial trip to the United States in order to foster Bible study and to assist the antislavery cause. A divided London yearly meeting finally gave him its blessing. Gurney spoke before audiences numbering in the thousands, many of whom were not Quaker, in Philadelphia, Indiana, and New York. In May 1838, he led a worship service in the US House of Representatives attended by President Martin Van Buren and many American Congressmen. He held private meetings with Van Buren, Henry Clay, John C. Calhoun, Daniel Webster and others in order to pray with them, but primarily to urge them to end slavery in the United States and to advocate fair treatment for American Indians.

Gurney visited the West Indies and was pleased by the 'moral and religious improvement, ... the vast extent of elementary and Christian education, ... [the] decided diminution of crime', and the greatly increased productivity that he observed among freed African-Americans there. He returned to the United States, published his findings as *Familiar Letters to Henry Clay* (1840) and revisited Van Buren, Clay and many others in Washington to share the encouraging news with them. Gurney spoke favourably about immediate abolition, but encouraged as a useful first step the abolition of slavery in newly acquired American territories such as Florida. Generally, American officials received him cordially but politely demurred from the reforms he urged upon them. Gurney visited Quaker meetings in New York and New England urging daily Bible study and Sunday schools. One traditional American Quaker, John Wilbur of Rhode Island, was so outraged by Gurney's departures from Quaker orthodoxy that he followed Gurney to protest his innovations. After Gurney's return to England, American orthodox Quakers suffered a schism between a majority of 'Gurneyites', who approved of Gurney's ideas on theology and regular Bible study, and the 'Wilburites', who staunchly opposed these ideas. New England (1845) and Ohio (1855) yearly meetings split apart, and Philadelphia yearly meeting maintained a precarious unity only by taking the drastic step of ceasing correspondence with all other Quaker yearly meetings.

Gurney and Elizabeth Fry travelled to the continent of Europe in 1841 and 1842. They visited prisons in Holland, Denmark, and Germany. Gurney and Fry met with Dutch, Danish, and French royalty, urging them to free the slaves in their West Indies colonies, and advocating that their hosts undertake prison reforms and institute daily scripture instruction in schools. In December 1846, Gurney fell from his horse, and he died from the injuries he sustained in the fall two weeks later. His exemplary evangelical Quakerism, combining forthright public advocacy, a concern for education of youth, and theological integrity, has been justly influential in both Great Britain and America.

BIBLIOGRAPHY
H. Barbour, *Slavery and Theology* (Dublin, IN, 1985): 29–54
S. Bright, 'Joseph John Gurney: a study in Evangelical Quaker Biography' (unpublished MA thesis, University of Keele, 1992)
DCA
DNB
T. D. Hamm, *The Transformation of American Quakerism* (Bloomington, IN, 1988): 15–35
D. E. Swift, *Joseph John Gurney* (Middletown, CT, 1962)

STEPHEN W. ANGELL

Gurney, Thomas (b. Woburn, Bedfordshire, England, 7 March 1705; d. London, 22 June 1770); **Gurney, Joseph** (b. 1744; d. 1815); **Gurney, William Brodie** (b. Stamford Hill, London, 24 Dec. 1777; d. Denmark Hill, London 25, March 1855); **Gurney, Joseph** (b. London, 15 Oct. 1804; d. Wimbledon, London, 12 Aug. 1879). Baptist short-hand reporters and philanthropists. The Baptist Gurneys of Walworth are almost as important as the Quaker Gurneys of Norfolk. Thomas Gurney, a clockmaker and schoolmaster in Newport Pagnell and Luton, purchasing William Mason's shorthand in a combined lot containing a work on astrology he wanted, soon

learnt the system and began to use it to note sermons. In 1737 he came to London and was appointed first shorthand writer to the Old Bailey, practising both there and in other courts and at the House of Commons. He also traded as a clock-maker, and in 1750 published his *Brachygraphy, or, Swift Writing Made Easy to the Meanest Capacity*. His son, Joseph, became a deacon at Maze Pond, and was also connected with Stepney College. Taking over his father's practices, he held appointments at the law courts from 1790, whilst also working for both Houses of Parliament. During the trial of Warren Hastings he was called upon to read back remarks of Edmund Burke, leading to a vote of censure being passed upon him, the first public acknowledgement of the verbal accuracy of shorthand, which also led to the profitable publication of state trials.

William Brodie Gurney, Joseph Gurney's younger son, was baptized as a believer at the Maze Pond Chapel in 1796. Following in the family profession, he became official shorthand writer to the Houses of Parliament. A friend of JOSEPH FOX and a pioneer of Sunday schools in South London, he was one of the founders of the Sunday School Union in 1803, becoming successively secretary, treasurer and president. He was first editor of the Sunday School Union's highly successful *The Youth's Magazine*, the first periodical of its kind. One of the founders of The London Female Penitentiary in 1807, he was one of the lay preachers who frequently conducted services there. Treasurer of Stepney College (1828–44), he also was active in the Bible Society. Like his father he was an active campaigner against slavery. A generous benefactor of the Jamaica Mission, he was treasurer of the BMS from 1835 to 1855, and of the Particular Baptist Fund from 1842 to 1855. Marrying one of the Benhams also of Maze Pond, missionaries often found hospitality in his home; it was to a residence of his in Muswell Hill, subsequently licensed for religious worship, that EUSTACE CAREY retired from India and for four years conducted evening services in the drawing room.

Joseph, his eldest son, whose second wife was Harriet Tritton, continued the family profession, succeeding his father in parliament in 1849. Treasurer of both the RTS and Regent's Park College, of which his brother in law, JOSEPH ANGUS was president, he was keenly interested in Biblical scholarship and published both The Annotated Bible [1850–60] which embraced both texts and notes and on similar lines The Revised English Bible [1877].

BIBLIOGRAPHY
DNB

J. H. Y. BRIGGS

Gurney, William Brodie. *See* GURNEY, THOMAS

Guthrie, Thomas (b. Brechin, Angus, Scotland, 12 July 1803; d. St Leonards on the Sea [Hastings], Sussex, England, 23 Feb. 1873). Disruption worthy and social reformer. The son of a banker, after studies in arts and divinity at Edinburgh University he was licensed as a preacher in 1825. Unwilling to 'sell my liberty' under the patronage system, he spent two years pursuing medical and scientific studies at the Sorbonne. Thereafter (due to the death of his older brother John), he served for two years as manager of the family banking agency, preaching only occasionally.

In 1830 he was inducted to Arbirlot, near Arbroath and married Anne Burns, a cousin of w. c. and i. BURNS. While naturally catholic in his personal friendships, Guthrie became increasingly antagonistic to moderate principles. In 1837 he was called to Old Greyfriars, Edinburgh and went with the intention of developing a genuine parish ministry, an ambition partly fulfilled by the completion in 1840 of St John's Church with its 650 free seats reserved for residents only. Here his hearers and friends included Sir JAMES Y. SIMPSON, Lord Rutherfurd, Henry Cockburn, and HUGH MILLER.

Guthrie's name is inextricably linked with ecclesiastical and social reforms. An opponent of the patronage system which had been restored to the Church of Scotland in 1712 by Queen Anne, he found the Veto Act of 1834 inadequate ('That no person be intruded in any of the offices of the Church contrary to the will of the congregation to which they are appointed'). He believed opposition should be directed against the practice of patronage as such and saw the 'Ten Years Conflict' as a battle for 'the right of Jesus Christ as King to reign within his own Church' (Guthrie, 1874, II: 35). Although not himself a leading spokesman (he deferred to THOMAS CHALMERS and ROBERT S. CANDLISH), after the Disruption he made a vital contribution to the cause by organizing the Free Church Manse Fund which raised £116,370 between May 1845 and June 1846. He was awarded a DD by Edinburgh University in 1849 and elected moderator of the General Assembly of the FCS in 1862.

His major contribution lay in the area of evangelical social and educational reform. While minister at Greyfriars he became concerned about the condition of the local poor, frequently recording the distressing discoveries of parish visitation: 'Taylor's Land – Mother 48 – shake down; pawned gown to help rent!' The realization that 8 in every 10 children in hunger had alcoholic parents led him in 1844 to adopt a position of total abstinence and become a founder of the Free Church Temperance Society. He was active in the pressure for social reform which led to the Forbes Mackenzie Act, reducing opening hours for public houses.

The needs of children motivated Guthrie to create his famous 'ragged schools' in 1847. He spoke frequently in support of them, and is remembered both for his affection for needy children and the effect of the schools: within four years the proportion of prisoners in Edinburgh gaol under 14 years of age had fallen from one in twenty to one in a hundred. His concern was expressed in *The City* (Edinburgh, 1857). His pleas for his great causes were published together in *Seed Time and Harvest of Ragged Schools* (Edinburgh, 1860). Such was

his commitment that he opposed the Free Church Education scheme for church schools in favour of a national education scheme ('what care I for the Free Church, or any Church [i.e. denomination] on earth, in comparison with my desire to save and bless these poor children in the High Street [of Edinburgh]'. His longings came to fruition in the Education Acts of 1872.

In 1864 Guthrie resigned his charge of Free St John's (which stood only fifty yards from his former church) on health grounds (17 years after being told by his physicians that his heart condition would preclude him from ever preaching again!). He became editor of *The Sunday Magazine*, with a monthly circulation of around 90,000. He took a wide interest in evangelical causes at home and abroad, and was a founder of the Waldensian Aid Society and an early supporter of the EA. In 1869 he was elected a fellow of the Royal Society of Edinburgh.

The esteem in which Guthrie was held is indicated by the massive gift of £5,000 given to him as a testimonial in 1865. As a leading figure in the Disruption, he was a preacher rather than a theologian: 'Guthrie was a power, unique in himself . . . He did not venture much in the uncongenial domain, to him, of ecclesiastical polemics . . . But in his own sphere and in his own way, he was to us and to the principles in which we acted, a tower of strength' (Candlish, in his sermon at Guthrie's funeral). As a writer his genre was that of the tract and the edited sermon. In this he had considerable popular success with such works as *The Gospel in Ezekiel* (Edinburgh, 1855), and *Christ in the Inheritance of the Saints* (Edinburgh, 1858). D. L. Moody once commented to his sons, 'I owe more to the writings of your father than to those of any other man.' He is best remembered as a visionary pastor with a passion for the needy.

BIBLIOGRAPHY
DNB
D. K. and C. H. Guthrie, *Autobiography and Memoir* (Edinburgh, 1874)

SINCLAIR B. FERGUSON

Gutteridge, Joseph (b. 1752; d. Denmark Hill, London, 5 May 1844). Baptist layman and philanthropist. Baptized in 1778, he rapidly became 'a pillar of the Baptist denomination', as early success in business allowed him time to give support to a number of benevolent and Christian institutions. The nature of his business is undefined: ambitions to enter banking or the law were preempted by his father's death which committed him to trade and manufacture, which he apparently conducted with impeccable decorum: in later years the extent to which even religious men deployed debt financing of their business activities was a cause of concern to him. A clue to the area in which he operated may be found in a presentation made to him by the tanners for his part in securing the repeal of discriminatory legislation against them. He rejected appointment as a Justice of the Peace which at that time still required occasional conformity.

He was connected with the (Particular) Baptist Fund from 1794 and its treasurer from 1798, witnessing its annual income grow four times during his near half century of office. He became involved in the work of the BMS through the need to press for changes on the renewal of the East India Company Charter in 1813. He persuaded the Dissenting Deputies, whom he served as treasurer, 1805–16, and vice-chairman, 1816–25, to make successful representation to Parliament allowing 'benevolent persons of the various congregations of Christians', intent upon 'the promulgation of our holy religion', to enter India under regulation and work there unmolested. He was also active as a deputy in seeking the repeal of the Test and Corporation Acts. With WILLIAM FOX he was a founder of the Sunday School Society, helped in the founding of Mill Hill School, and also sat on the committee of the Orphan Working School, later declining its presidency because of his age. He was one of those who in 1819, after the death of ANDREW FULLER, pressed the BMS for practical purposes to establish a more orderly form of government including the holding of regular committee meetings in London. For the next twenty years he was regularly called to chair the society's annual public meetings, and was for a time the society's treasurer.

As first treasurer of Stepney College, he secured the initial funding of the college but his responsibilities were more than financial, for it was he who carried out the delicate, and in the end abortive, negotiations to secure JOSEPH KINGHORN as president, arguing that the infant college needed a person to preside 'whose prudence, moderation and good sense would form a connecting link between the higher and lower classes of our Calvinistic friends'. For more than fifty years he was a deacon of ABRAHAM BOOTH's church at Prescot Street, but provided the site for the new Denmark Place Chapel, Camberwell, near to his home, as well as helping to establish the Independent Chapel at Wheathampstead, Hertfordshire, where he had a farm on which he spent much of the summer. At Camberwell he secured the services of EDWARD STEANE for this new open-communion cause, which he defended in these terms: 'Love to the Saviour is the great master principle of Christianity and whenever we see the impress of the Redeemer's image we are ready to exclaim, "Peace be with all who love our Lord Jesus in sincerity"'. (Steane, 1850: 81–6).

BIBLIOGRAPHY
E. Steane, *Memoirs of the Life of Joseph Gutteridge* (London, 1850)

J. H. Y. BRIGGS

Guttridge, John (b. Birmingham, England, 22 Nov. 1819; d. Manchester, England, 22 Mar. 1886). United Methodist Free Churches preacher and president (1863). Guttridge was a Wesleyan by upbringing. He experienced conversion at the age of 12 and he became a local preacher four years later. In 1835 he left the Wesleyans to join the Wesleyan Methodist Association, and he became a full-time preacher in 1838. He was one of the most popular Free Methodist preachers of his generation, renowned for the style as much as the substance of his preaching. Equally at ease in chapel, lecture hall and open-air meeting, he was a vigorous teetotal campaigner, an exponent of liberal political views, and a lecturer on sundry topics. His main publication, *Life Among the Masses*, largely relates his experiences among the working class of Lancashire where he spent much of his ministry.

SELECT WRITINGS
J. Guttridge, *Life Among the Masses* (Manchester, England, 1884)

D. A. GOWLAND

Gützlaff, Karl Friedrich August (b. Pyritz, Prussia, 8 July 1803; d. Hong Kong, 9 Aug. 1851). Independent missionary to China. Son of a tailor, Gützlaff was reared in a pietist family. At municipal school Gützlaff came under Enlightenment influences and his lifelong ambivalence between a simple pietist faith and an insatiable thirst for knowledge began. He also revealed, quite early, a propensity toward being a loner, an impatience with authority and a preference for independence. Gützlaff next apprenticed himself to a girdler in Stettin where he encountered interest in missions. In 1818 after hearing a mission sermon, he decided to become a missionary. Lacking funds, he pursued private studies, but of science and poetry, not the Bible.

Adventurousness and ambition also characterized Gützlaff and King Frederick William III's visit to Stettin in 1820 provided an opportunity to seek social mobility and wider horizons. Gützlaff and a friend presented the king with a poem that so pleased him that he offered to finance their higher education. Gützlaff was directed to Professor JOHANNES JÄNICKE's missionary school in Berlin, a product of the Second Great Awakening having close ties with pietist and Moravian circles. Gützlaff's ambition and avid pursuit of intellectual growth, including study at the University of Berlin, offended Jänicke. Only after intense pressure from the Jänicke community did Gützlaff undergo the desired emotional experience of religious rebirth and return to the non-sectarian, Christocentric faith of Pietism.

In 1823 he went to Rotterdam for three years of training with the Netherlands Missionary Society. During this time he studied Malay and journeyed to London to meet ROBERT MORRISON, first Protestant missionary to China. The challenge of millions of heathen Chinese became irresistible for the ambitious, adventurous Gützlaff. Posted to the Dutch East Indies in 1826, Gützlaff met WALTER MEDHURST in Batavia and accompanied him on itinerations to preach the Gospel and distribute the Word. His heart was set on China, however, and despite protestations by the Netherlands Mission Society, he left his assignment in Sumatra for Chinese communities in south-east Asia. In 1831, after his first wife's death, Gützlaff boarded a junk bound for China, to spend the rest of his life as an independent missionary on the fringes of China.

During this coastal journey, Gützlaff continued the techniques of Medhurst: forays into villages to preach a minimalist doctrine of repentance and salvation, offer simple medical remedies, and distribute religious tracts. Ideally, these efforts would be consolidated by schools and the training of native assistants. Christian evangelism in China had, however, been illegal since 1724. To gain access and secure a livelihood, Gützlaff subsequently took employment as Chinese interpreter on various coastal expeditions: opium smugglers, explorations for the secret of tea culture, and experiments with trading beyond Canton. His travel journals were published, excerpted, and reprinted in many languages and countries. Gützlaff also corresponded with the BFBS, the ABS, and the RTS, and numerous mission societies and magazines. His contention that China was open to enterprising missionaries and that the general populace was receptive to Christianity stimulated Western interest in China. More Protestant missionaries volunteered for China.

In 1834 Gützlaff became Chinese secretary to the British administration in the Canton region, an office he held until his death. During the Opium War of 1839–42, he was guide for British military forces, interpreter in treaty negotiations, and civil administrator of occupied territories. His mission work became confined to weekends and after hours and to the Hong Kong environs. Though Gützlaff's dual role was not unique, Chinese perceptions of linkage between missions and imperialism, opium and Bibles were strengthened.

Gützlaff and Medhurst translated the Bible into Chinese, Gützlaff's revised version being adopted by the Taipings. He composed numerous Chinese Christian tracts and edited a Chinese magazine which discussed Western geography, history, government and commerce along with Christianity. In Western languages, his works include Chinese histories and essays on the Chinese classics, language, religions, folkways and literature.

Frustrated by minimal missionary success in converting Chinese and convinced that only Chinese could Christianize China, in the 1840s Gützlaff founded the Chinese Union. Chinese evangelists would circulate throughout China distributing tracts and preaching the doctrine of salvation while Western missionaries would supervise them. Gützlaff persuaded the Basel and Rhenish missionary societies to send recruits to work with the Chinese Union as the number of local evangelists multiplied rapidly. In 1849–50 he made a triumphal tour of England and Europe to publicize the Chinese Union and establish dozens of non-denominational support societies. Meanwhile, it became apparent that many Chinese Union evangelists were accepting payment without completing assignments. Gützlaff arrived in Hong Kong in January 1851 amid acrimonious controversy. His death in August, 1851 dashed hopes of reviving and reforming the Chinese Union. Support societies withered away.

Despite death under a cloud, Gützlaff left a legacy. He stimulated Western interest in China itself and Protestant missions in particular. A core of Chinese Union evangelists had been nurtured and continued to assist Western missionaries and convert small communities on their own. Though he aroused unrealistic expectations, some societies and missionaries inspired by Gützlaff modified and refined his methodology. Examples are Basel and Rhenish Mission work among the Hakka and the CIM founded by JAMES HUDSON TAYLOR, all of which sponsored initiatives toward an indigenized Christianity.

BIBLIOGRAPHY

A. J. Broomhall, *Hudson Taylor and China's Open Century*; Bk 1, *Barbarians at the Gates* (Sevenoaks, England, 1981); Bk 2, *Over the Treaty Wall* (Sevenoaks, England, 1982)

J. G. Lutz, 'Karl F. A. Gützlaff: Missionary Entrepreneur', in *Christianity in China*, ed. Suzanne W. B. Barnett and J. K. Fairbank (Cambridge, MA, 1985): 61–88

—, 'The Missionary-Diplomat Karl Gützlaff and the Opium War', in *Proceedings of the First International Symposium on Church and State in China*, ed. Li Ch'i-fang (Taipei, 1987)

—, 'The Grand Illusion: Karl Gützlaff and the Popularization of China Missions in the United States during the 1830s', in *United States Attitudes and Policies toward China*, ed. Patricia Neils (Armonk, NY, 1990)

—, 'Karl Gützlaff's Approach to Indigenization: The Chinese Union,' in *Christianity and China, The Eighteenth Century to the Present: Essays in Religious and Social Change*, ed. D. H. Bays (Stanford, CA, 1995)

H. Schlyter, *Karl Gützlaff als Missionar in China* (Lund, Sweden, 1946)

—, *Der China-Missionar Karl Gützlaff und Seine Heimatbasis* (Lund, Sweden, 1976)

JESSIE G. LUTZ

Guyot, Arnold Henri (b. Boudevilliers, Switzerland, 28 Sept. 1807; d. Princeton, NJ, USA, 8 Feb. 1884). Geographer, geologist, and college professor. Guyot was one of 12 children born to Swiss Protestants. After studying in Neuchatel, Metzingen, and Carlsruhe, Guyot went to Berlin in 1829 to prepare for the ministry, but studies with Humboldt and Ritter persuaded him to pursue science instead. He earned his Berlin doctorate in 1835 with a dissertation on the natural classification of lakes. He became professor of history and physical geography at the newly founded Academy of Neuchatel and established himself as a leading authority on glaciers. In 1848, Guyot went to Boston where he taught physical geography at Lowell Institute and published *Earth and Man*. In 1854, Guyot took his final position as professor of physical geography and geology at the College of New Jersey in Princeton where he developed the geology curriculum and natural history museum. He also distinguished himself as one of America's premier scientists by establishing the requirements for meteorological stations throughout the United States and by systematically surveying Appalachian topography. In America Guyot joined the Presbyterian Church which he represented in 1861 at the Evangelical Alliance in Geneva. In 1840 he developed a scheme for harmonizing geology with Genesis 1. Many modifications of his scheme culminated in the issuance of *Creation, or the Biblical Cosmogony in the Light of Modern Science* just prior to his death.

BIBLIOGRAPHY

J. D. Dana, 'Memoir of Arnold Guyot 1807–1884', *National Academy of Sciences Biographical Memoirs*, 2 (1886): 309–47

DAVIS A. YOUNG

Gwalchmai, Humphrey (b. Llanwyddelan, Montgomeryshire, Wales, 14 Jan. 1788; d. Oswestry, England, 29 March 1847). Welsh Calvinistic Methodist minister. Having come early in life under the influence of the Calvinistic Methodist movement, Gwalchmai was invited in 1816 to become the pastor of the Calvinistic Methodists at Llanidloes, Montgomeryshire. His significance lies in the fact that, in a period when Calvinistic Methodist ministers exercised an itinerant preaching ministry only, he was the first to be called to be a pastor of a specific church and thus pioneered the move towards a settled pastoral ministry. Ordained in 1819 he was clerk of the North Wales Association of the Calvinistic Methodists from 1820 to 1830 and played a significant role in the formulation of the Confession of Faith (1823) and the Constitutional Deed (1826) which gave legal recognition to the Welsh Calvinistic Methodist Connexion.

BIBLIOGRAPHY

DWB

T. Mordaf Pierce, *Y Parchedig Humphrey Gwalchmai* (Llanidloes, Wales, 1908)

E. AP NEFYDD ROBERTS

Gwynne, Marmaduke (b. Llanhuan, Co. Brecon, Wales, *c.* 1694; d. April 1769). Landowner and patron of early Welsh Methodism. Gwynne, the son of Howell of Garth, Breconshire, matriculated at Jesus College, Oxford, on 5 May 1710 at the age of 16. However, in 1711 he began studying law, enroling at Lincoln's Inn in London. It is not clear if he practised law. A wealthy landowner Gwynne further consolidated his personal fortune in 1716 through his marriage to Sarah Evans of Ffynnon Bedr, Cardiganshire, who brought with her a dowry of £30,000.

A man of considerable influence in his own locality, a Justice of the Peace and Sheriff of Radnorshire in 1718, he was converted under the ministry of HOWELL HARRIS in 1737. From that time he was deeply interested in the progress of Methodism, extending to both preachers and exhorters his patronage, and intervening on their behalf when they were prosecuted in the courts. Following the marriage of his daughter, Sarah, to CHARLES WESLEY in 1749, Gwynne and his wife moved to Ludlow where they lived for a short time until they finally took up residence in Brecon.

BIBLIOGRAPHY

Al. Ox.

DWB

F. C. Gill, *Charles Wesley* (London, 1964): 125–42

A. H. Williams, *John Wesley in Wales* (Cardiff, 1971): xxiv

GERAINT TUDUR

H

Habersham, James (b. Beverley, Yorkshire, England, 26 Jan. 1712; d. New Brunswick, NJ, USA, 28 Aug. 1778). Calvinistic Methodist and supporter of Bethesda Orphan House. Born the son of a Beverley merchant, he was sent to London to engage in trade. There he encountered GEORGE WHITEFIELD preaching his first sermons in London and was converted to Methodism. By September 1737 he knew Whitefield well enough to persuade him to preach a charity sermon in an Anglican chapel of ease. In December Whitefield was able to persuade him to leave his business and accompany him on his first voyage to Georgia. Habersham did this 'contrary to the sentiments' of all his friends and 'without having any particular design in view'. On arrival at Savannah, Whitefield decided to build an 'orphan house' on the lines of Francke's institution at Halle in Germany. Recognizing Habersham's efficiency he persuaded him to take the responsibility for its erection and operation.

While Whitefield returned to England to collect contributions, Habersham found a suitable site some miles from Savannah and prepared the ground for Bethesda Orphan House. Before the buildings could be completed Whitefield had already collected a group of orphans. By 1742 sufficient progress had been made for 49 children to be moved to Bethesda. There they were given an elementary education and worked to help in their maintenance. Habersham became the business superintendent of the orphan house, and clergymen were employed for the spiritual education of the orphans.

Although Habersham resigned his position in 1744, established a highly successful business and developed rice plantations he remained committed to the care of Bethesda. When Whitefield died in 1770 and committed the orphan house to Lady HUNTINGDON, Habersham filled the gap between his death and the arrival of her team of ministers and students. With the onset of the American Revolution it was Habersham, and later his three sons, who protected Bethesda from the ravages of both sides, and ensured its return to Lady Huntingdon. He held various political offices and from 1771 to 1773 he was acting-governor of the colony, which gave him the necessary authority to do so.

BIBLIOGRAPHY
Cheshunt College Archives, Cambridge, original letters
J. Habersham, 'The Letters of the Hon. James Habersham', *Georgia Historical Society Collections*, 6 (Savannah, GA, 1904)
G. Whitefield, *George Whitefield's Journals* (London, 1960)

EDWIN WELCH

Hadfield, George (b. Sheffield, England, 28 Dec. 1787; d. Manchester, England, 21 Apr. 1879). Attorney and radical Liberal MP. A long-time Manchester attorney, he first gained prominence in the 1830s through his attempt to bar Unitarians from enjoying the benefits of the Hewley charitable trust. The Dissenters' Chapels Act (1844) essentially defeated his cause.

In 1841 he co-founded the Manchester Anti-Corn Law League and in 1852 entered Parliament for Sheffield, a seat he held until 1874. The Qualification for Offices Abolition Act (1866), introduced by him, was an important step toward the separation of church and state. As a Member he also contributed to common law, education and military reform. Hadfield granted £10,000 for the erection of 100 Independent chapels, and £2,000 for a new building for Lancashire Independent college, Whalley Range, which he had co-founded. In the 1870s he was a patron of the Howard Association, a prison reform society that was against capital punishment. He also supported the EA.

BIBLIOGRAPHY
J. O. Baylen, ed. *Biographical Dictionary of Modern British Radicals* (Sussex, England, 1984): II: 226–27
DNB
H. L. Malchow, *Agitators and Promoters* (New York, 1983)

JONATHAN BURKE CUTMORE

Hadfield, Octavius (b. Bonchurch, Isle of Wight, *c.* 6 Oct. 1814; d. Marton, New Zealand, 11 Dec. 1904). CMS missionary to New Zealand and Bishop of Wellington. The tenth child of a silk merchant, Hadfield attended Charterhouse School, and then Pembroke College, Oxford, but asthma meant his education was left incomplete. In October 1837 despite family opposition, the CMS accepted him for missionary service. He became a deacon in Sydney and was the first priest ordained in New Zealand on 6 January 1839. Initially he taught at the Waimate North school, but when in November 1839 the son and the nephew of the notorious West Coast chief Te Rauparaha visited the Bay of Islands and asked for a missionary, he was chosen. A church was erected in Waikanae in 1843, as he won acceptance. Illness forced him to withdraw to Wellington in 1844 for nearly five years, but in 1849 he was appointed Archdeacon of Kapiti and returned to his work. The focus of the mission was now Otaki, and in 1849 the Maori erected the great Rangiatea church there.

Hadfield took his converts' side as European settlers threatened Maori interests, and when the Governor approved a land purchase at Waitara in contravention of Maori custom, Hadfield appealed to British public opinion in several pamphlets including *One of England's Little Wars*. Consequently the anti-European king movement had little impact in his district. In 1857 he declined the offer to become Bishop of Wellington, but in 1870 he became the second bishop. In this role he gave strong leadership to the church, attacking secular education, and in 1889 was elected Primate, retiring to Marton in 1893. He married Catherine (Kate) the daughter of HENRY WILLIAMS on 19 May 1852, and they had ten children. Kate died on 8 January 1902. His temper was terse, his relationships with his colleagues tetchy, and he was a conservative churchman more than an evangelical, but Hadfield was passionately committed to the growth of the gospel and justice for all.

BIBLIOGRAPHY
DNZB
B. MacMorran, *Octavius Hadfield* (Wellington, New Zealand, 1969)

PETER J. LINEHAM

Haeberlin, John [Johannes] (b. Tuttlingen near Singen in Würtemburg, 19 Aug. 1808; d. at sea off Dhaka, Nov. 1849). CMS missionary and translator. Educated in Korntal, Haeberlin spent 1827–30 in the Mission House at Basel before his 1830 move to the CMS College in Islington. He was deaconed by the Bishop of London (18 December 1831) and sailed to Calcutta with Bishop DANIEL WILSON (on 20 June 1832), who priested him (6 January 1833) and sent him to Krishnagur near Burdwan. He quickly learned Bengali, and was soon superintending small congregations despite persecution from the local zamindars (wealthy landholders).

Haeberlin moved to Calcutta in 1836 for health reasons. The CMS being unhappy with Bishop's College, he was put in charge of an institution for training catechists. A group of high caste converts gathered in his house. They soon objected to his elementary, simplistic methods and the lack of any promise of ordination. They accepted KRISHNA MOHUN BANERJEA and Archdeacon THOMAS DEALTRY's invitation to join Bishop's College. Haeberlin, who believed passionately in simple vernacular theological education, was incensed and returned to Basel in June 1837. In January 1838 the CMS seconded him to the Calcutta Bible Society.

After a visit to Simla for health reasons in 1843, Haeberlin started a new, independent mission in Dhaka. Six colleagues arrived from Basel; and in 1848, 26 converts were baptized. The congregation grew to fifty, but local support dwindled. Following his death, the mission's property had to be sold to settle his debts. Three of his colleagues joined the CMS, and the congregation joined WILLIAM ROBINSON's Baptist congregation.

In 1838 Haeberlin married Charlotte Küllner in the same ceremony that his sister Johanna Dorothea married the Basel Missionary Society's director, C. G. BLUMHARDT. His eldest son Karl served the Gossner Mission in India; and his younger son, John, was a merchant. Two other children died in Korntal in 1854. His wife wrote and published his memoirs in 1855.

BIBLIOGRAPHY
D. T. B[arry], *CMS Register of Missionaries and Native Clergy* (privately printed) (London, 1906)
Archives of the Basel Mission, Basel

E. M. JACKSON

Hagerty, John (b. Prince George's Co., MD, BNA, 18 Feb. 1747; d. Baltimore, MD, USA, 4 Sept. 1823). American Methodist minister. Hagerty grew up a pious and religious young man, but following his conversion by JOHN KING in 1771 he esteemed his apparently moral life as 'self-righteousness, while it served to confirm . . . in self-deception'. The following year King made him the leader of the local Society, and henceforth Hagerty gradually developed into an effective preacher, joining the itinerancy in 1779. In 1784 he was made an elder at the organizing 'Christmas Conference' of the MEC, and he served in this and various ministerial positions until the early 1790s, when his wife's illness forced him to locate to the Baltimore area. Though himself afflicted with epilepsy in his later years, Hagerty continued in the fruitful service of others 'at any hour, night or day', until a violent attack took his life.

BIBLIOGRAPHY
AAP 7: 65–8
EWM (incorrect death date)
J. Soule, 'Memoir of the Rev. John Hagerty', *AMMag*, 7 (1824): 209–12

KENNETH N. PEARSON

Haidt, Johann Valentin (b. Danzig, 4 Oct. 1700; d. Bethlehem, PA, USA, 18 Jan. 1780). Leading Moravian painter. Haidt learned drawing at the Berlin Royal Academy, took up his father's goldsmith's trade, working in Dresden (1714–16), Augsburg (1716–18), Northern Italy and Rome, and settled in London in 1724, marrying Catherine Compigni.

Haidt heard H. F. COSSART and A. G. SPANGENBERG preach in 1739, and was visited. He moved to Wetteravia in May 1740, was received into membership in August, began to preach and became warden of Herrnhaag. In 1744 he accompanied JOHANN MARTIN DOBER to England, looking after the infant Bedford Congregation briefly in early 1745. Increasingly unhappy, Haidt was recalled in 1746.

Unwilling to preach in line with the 'Sifting Time' spirituality, Haidt obtained permission to paint the Gospel instead, also painting leading Moravians and symbolic representations of Moravian achievements, e.g. the

'First Fruits' (Herrnhaag, 1747). He moved to Herrnhut in 1748. In London from 1752, he painted for ZINZEN-DORF's Lindsey House, leaving for Pennsylvania in March 1754. Ordained in Gnadenhütten that August, after 14 months in Philadelphia he moved to Bethlehem. Haidt's numerous paintings made a major contribution to the cultural richness of early Moravianism in Germany, England and America.

BIBLIOGRAPHY
Gemeinnachrichten (1885) I, 814–21
V. Nelson, *John Valentine Haidt* (Williamsburg, VA, 1966)

C. J. PODMORE

Haime, John (b. Shaftesbury, Dorset, England, 18 Feb. 1708; d. Whitchurch, Hampshire, England, 18 Aug. 1784). Methodist itinerant. He worked first as a gardener with his father and then learned button-making with an uncle in Blandford. After employment in transport with a tanner he enlisted in 1739 as a dragoon in the Queen's regiment. Bunyan's *Grace Abounding* was instrumental in his conversion. He fought at Dettingen and Fontenoy in the Thirty Years' War. After seeking JOHN WESLEY's advice he began to preach with the permission of his commanding officers. On his discharge from the army he became one of Wesley's helpers and for some time travelled with the evangelist himself. He was regularly stationed only for a comparatively short period. He is rightly recognized as a pioneer of Methodist work in the armed forces. As a preacher he was plain and positive. He persevered with his ministry despite serious physical limitations.

BIBLIOGRAPHY
AM (1780, 1785)

A. SKEVINGTON WOOD

Haldane, Alexander (b. Edinburgh, 15 Oct. 1800; d. London, 19 July 1882). Lawyer and proprietor of the *Record*. Descended from an ancient Perthshire family, and born in Edinburgh, he was the son and nephew of the famous and wealthy Sottish Calvinistic lay evangelists, JAMES ALEXANDER and ROBERT HALDANE. Although the Haldane brothers had found it necessary to leave the Church of Scotland to maintain their itinerant ministry, they still shared much of the ethos of upper-class evangelicals of the Kirk. As a result the Haldanes had an affinity for the evangelicals of the Church of England. Accordingly, Alexander at age 13 was sent to further his education with an evangelical clergyman, Grainger of Wintringham. He matriculated at the University of Edinburgh and in 1820 began legal studies at the Inner Temple in London. In 1822 he married Emma Hardcastle, whose grandparents had been Whitefield converts, and whose father JOSEPH HARDCASTLE had been the first treasurer of the LMS and a close dissenting associate of the Clapham Sect and other Anglican evangelicals.

Assured by his religious and social associations of a welcome by the leading Anglican evangelicals, the characteristics noted by Edwin Hodder helped thrust him into prominence: 'an active, energetic man, strong in body and mind, of great intellectual force and tenacity of purpose, and full of keen warm-hearted sympathies'.

Haldane emerged in the 1820s at a propitious moment for one assured that he was destined for evangelical leadership. The threat of liberal theology, resurgent Catholicism, and a non-confessional view of the state demanded a revamped agenda, while a hiatus of leadership presented an open door. A group of young Anglican evangelicals of good family, and conspicuously non-English, led by Haldane in the press, HUGH MCNEILE among the clergy, and J. E. GORDON in public life, thrust themselves to the fore. Behind them was the *eminence grise* of EDWARD IRVING. They were profoundly influenced by popular Romanticism, thus frequently turning to golden ages of the past for direction, envisioning reality in cataclysmic polarities and presenting their ideas with quasi-prophetic arrogance, intolerance and fire. And many Anglican evangelicals, though by no means all, were prepared to listen. They insisted on a return to robust Calvinism, the verbal rather than the plenary inspiration of the Bible, and a more sombre eschatology and philosophy of history than postmillennialism. They deplored the pragmatic tendency of previous evangelical Anglican leaders to downplay distinctiveness in public for the sake of success, being confident that God would bless the truth when spoken with clarity and force. They struck a particularly responsive chord among Anglican evangelicals when they stressed the need to maintain the state church and England as a Protestant nation. This was as far as Haldane went. Others espoused premillennialism, while some, impressed by Irving's charismatic emphasis, soon found themselves outside the Church of England.

Haldane's voice was the *Record*. Founded in 1828 as a twice-weekly Anglican evangelical family newspaper, it soon fell into financial difficulty, from which it was rescued by HENRY DRUMMOND, the banker and close associate of Irving, who made Haldane the leading writer. In 1830, as Drummond and the more extreme Irvingites were beginning to loosen their ties with the Church of England, Haldane managed to gain control, becoming chief proprietor and editorial writer for the next half century and more. Within a few years it had by far the largest circulation of any religious newspaper, and a sizeable section of Anglican evangelicals were known colloquially as Recordites. In 1855 W. J. Conybeare estimated that among the evangelical clergy they numbered 2,500 out of 5,800.

Although Haldane had little interest in the humanitarian legislation of Lord SHAFTESBURY, they became the closest of friends in the 1850s in opposition to Tractarianism. Through this connection Haldane was actually the force behind the appointment of the evangelical 'Palmerston' bishops.

Haldane's son was R. G. Chinnery-Haldane, a High Church Scottish Episcopal bishop. He was an uncle of the Lord Chancellor, Haldane of Cloan, and as with so many nineteenth-century evangelicals, was related to the emerging intellectual aristocracy.

Haldane helped the Anglican evangelicals retain their faith, their Established Church, and some lineaments of their Christian nation. But he also bequeathed a harsher evangelicalism, which for generations would give the impression of being unable to cope with the contemporary world.

SELECT WRITINGS

A. Haldane, *The Lives of Robert Haldane of Airthrey and His Brother James Alexander Haldane* (Edinburgh, 1855)

BIBLIOGRAPHY

Anon, *A Biographical Sketch of Alexander Haldane* (London, 1882)

J. A. L. Haldane, *The Haldanes of Gleneagles* (Edinburgh, 1929)

IAN S. RENNIE

Haldane, James Alexander (b. Dundee, Angus, Scotland, 14 July 1768; d. Edinburgh, 8 Feb. 1851). Itinerant evangelist, pastor, and theological writer. In 1794 as a young, newly married captain in the East India fleet he sold his command of the vessel in which there was a family interest and retired from the sea to settle in Edinburgh. This decision was related to a process of religious enquiry and conversion initiated by DAVID BOGUE, Independent pastor at Gosport, Hampshire. Though still a member of the Church of Scotland his religious efforts rapidly turned from committee membership of the SSPCK to unauthorized lay preaching. The latter developed from an exploratory journey to the north of Scotland in 1797. Over the following eight summers he undertook extensive preaching tours which encompassed areas as widely separated as Shetland, Argyll and Galloway.

In 1798, appreciating the need for continuity and support, he helped to found the Society for Propagating the Gospel at Home (SPGH), which for more than a decade employed lay catechists and itinerant preachers and encouraged settled ministers to establish Sunday schools and preach in surrounding communities. By disregarding parish boundaries, criticizing existing incumbents and advocating a system of lay agency he contributed to the sense of outrage which induced the 1799 General Assembly of the Church of Scotland to issue a Pastoral Admonition against unqualified teachers and to condemn the SPGH. In contrast he was supported by his elder brother, ROBERT HALDANE, who liberally defrayed the costs of evangelism, erecting 'tabernacles' or preaching houses in several provincial centres, and financing a series of academy classes which provided basic theological training for nearly 300 preachers, a number of whom eventually found their way to the United States and Canada.

In 1799 he accepted ordination as pastor of an Independent congregation which met at the former Circus

building in Edinburgh until a large purpose-built tabernacle was opened in 1801. In discarding Presbyterianism Haldane remained on good terms with the evangelical leadership of the Church of Scotland, although the dual allegiance permitted by the tabernacle created some ill feeling with Edinburgh ministers including Walter Buchanan and JOHN ERSKINE who suffered depletion of their congregations. Similar tensions extended to the independent community in the capital as he introduced such apparent New Testament features as a plurality of elders, weekly Communion, and mutual exhortation by church members during public worship. The willingness to experiment, coupled with personality differences and a decision in 1808 to adopt the practice of believer's baptism, divided the Edinburgh Tabernacle and the wider Haldane evangelistic movement, in the process weakening considerably the nascent forces of Scottish independency of which he was a pioneer.

As a prolific theological writer Haldane produced lengthy expositions of the New Testament understanding of the church and the doctrine of atonement, but his literary output was largely directed at the refutation of what he considered to be contemporary errors. Among these were EDWARD IRVING's belief in the corruptibility of the human nature of Christ and the rejection of the doctrine of limited atonement by his fellow Baptist, JOHN HOWARD HINTON. However, Haldane did not himself give slavish allegiance to existing religious formularies, and by openly rejecting the authority of the Westminster Confession he represented that element in contemporary evangelicalism which emphasized biblical orthodoxy rather than formal Calvinist rectitude. A strong-minded and authoritative individual, his adherence to voluntary religion avoided the erastian predicaments faced by many clerical contemporaries, but it also severely restricted his own sphere of influence.

BIBLIOGRAPHY

A. Haldane, *The Lives of Robert Haldane of Airthrey, and of His Brother, James Alexander Haldane* (London, 1853)

D. W. Lovegrove, 'Unity and separation: contrasting elements in the thought and practice of Robert and James Alexander Haldane', *Studies in Church History: Subsidia 7* (Oxford, 1990): 153–77

DERYCK LOVEGROVE

Haldane, Robert (b. London, 28 Feb. 1764; d. Edinburgh, 12 Dec. 1842). Independent preacher, philanthropist, and controversialist. The oldest of three children of Captain James Haldane, of Gleneagles, Stirlingshire, Robert lost both parents in his first decade. He was thereafter raised in the vicinity of Dundee by his kinfolk. With his brother JAMES HALDANE, he studied at the High School of Edinburgh. Neither completed courses of study begun at Edinburgh University. Robert joined the Royal Navy in 1780 and served aboard the *Monarch* and the *Foudroyant*. He was often ashore at Portsmouth and adjacent Gosport; there he came under the pious influence of DAVID BOGUE, an expatriate Scot serving an Independent congregation and ministerial academy.

His naval career concluded with the peace of 1783; he thereafter turned to additional study at Gosport and Edinburgh University. He travelled the Continent twice, married, and settled at the family estate of Airthrey, Gleneagles; he spent a decade living the life of an energetic country laird. Like many of his countrymen, he initially entertained hopeful views of the revolution in France; he furthermore opposed attempts to raise local militia against the threat of French invasion. However, when his initial optimism about the revolution had given way to dismay, he found that he had gained an unwanted reputation as a republican sympathizer. Yet the very raising and dashing of hopes for the revolution had the effect of moving him toward an evangelical conversion which occurred in 1795.

Haldane now rapidly sought ways in which his very considerable wealth, realized from the sale of his estate, could be utilized for evangelical enterprises. From 1796 to 1804, he joined his friend Bogue as a director of the LMS and heartily supported various society efforts. Even though that society had, from its foundation, countenanced continental mission and pursued this within the constraints imposed by wartime, Haldane was already, by 1803, attempting to personally recruit and finance missionary agents for Italy and Germany. In 1796, he had sought permission from the government and the East India Company to undertake a self-financed mission to Bengal with four friends. The rebuff given this proposed mission was rooted in his assumed republican outlook. At the same period, he financed the education of West African children in Britain.

In 1796, his brother James had begun itinerant preaching in the highlands and islands of Scotland, encouraged by the example of CHARLES SIMEON of Cambridge. Robert Haldane turned his considerable wealth to the promotion of this work through the Society for the Propagation of the Gospel at Home, founded in 1797 with the help of other laymen. In this he relied initially on the assistance of prominent English evangelicals such as Bogue and ROWLAND HILL, who preached extensively in the north. He began as well to assist Scots training in English ministerial academies and to employ them as seasonal missionaries. The upshot of this endeavour was a growing connection of Sunday schools and meeting houses, particularly in the east and south-west of Scotland, all dependent upon the patronage of Haldane. The relation of this connection to the Church of Scotland was unclear; the patron himself still attended the services of this communion. The General Assembly of 1799 forced the issue; reacting against the censorious preaching of James and others, they determined to bar the preaching of English ministers and native laymen.

From January of that year, Haldane financed the education of scores of catechist-preachers in academy-style settings at Glasgow, Edinburgh, Dundee and Elgin. Desirous of reaching the underprivileged classes flocking to industrial centres, he built sizeable tabernacles, free from pew-rents, in major cities. Associates such as GREVILLE EWING desired to see the connection follow the example of many English Independents towards congregational

polity; it is far from clear that Haldane, the patron, desired any such diminution of his own prerogatives. The connection foundered in 1808, when it had reached 85 churches, as a result of doctrinal tensions introduced by the Haldanes themselves.

Both James and Robert had, since 1804, come to embrace forms of restorationism traceable to JOHN GLAS and ROBERT SANDEMAN. They now believed that each well-ordered church must have multiple preachers (elders), give opportunity for weekly lay exhortation, observe the Lord's Supper weekly, and employ the kiss of peace. By 1808, the brothers submitted to (re)baptism by immersion. They spoke, on the one hand, of forbearance in secondary doctrines; they acted, on the other, to disseminate these views in the connection which depended utterly on Robert's patronage. In Edinburgh and elsewhere, division resulted. The Edinburgh Tabernacle, of which James was chief and Robert, briefly, co-pastor, saw its congregation being pulled in eight directions. Many unseemly conflicts arose between Robert, deed-holder, and congregations determined not to accept his innovations. Connection preachers of similarly independent outlook suffered as his patronage was withdrawn. Yet the Haldanes were not easily deterred; their restorationism was even urged on friends and churches south of the Tweed.

It was only a somewhat chastened Robert Haldane who left Edinburgh for the Continent in October, 1816. Ill advised about the proportion of Genevan Christianity he might find orthodox, he proceeded there on the mistaken assumption that nearly all the canton's ministers were apostate. In fact, many were orthodox and pietistic. Haldane's now famous expositions of *Romans*, while the means of the conversion of numerous theological students who subsequently spread evangelical fervour through the Reformed churches of western Europe, were also the means of encouraging or confirming a smaller group in the path of separatism. These Geneva Independents were both tutored by Haldane in establishing their congregation and financed directly by him after his departure. They, not surprisingly, took up several of his restorationist practices and (in part) his baptistic outlook, along with his evangelical Calvinism. A similar posture, though with less polarizing effects, was struck by Haldane in an extended sojourn at Montauban, France from 1817 to 1819.

Haldane was a man of conviction and means; he believed in the indispensability of his own private initiatives. He was consistently among the largest supporters of the Continental Society – founded in London in 1818 with his encouragement from Montauban. Such was his distrust of the relatively orthodox theological faculty at Montauban – then France's only Reformed seminary – that he funded alternate theological training for Independents at Paris from 1824. He helped to lead opposition to the BFBS's policy over the inclusion of the apocrypha in bound scriptures (a policy soon reversed). He was instrumental in the founding of the alternative Trinitarian Bible Society in England and the anti-apocryphal Edinburgh (now National) Bible Society in his own city. His personal wealth was often the means of sustaining his role as pamphleteer and polemicist against the directors of the BFBS and against theologians he deemed unsound. He is said to have expended £60,000 of his wealth in various public and private evangelical initiatives. In old age, he found himself increasingly in affinity with the rising evangelical party of the Church of Scotland. He was buried in Glasgow Cathedral.

BIBLIOGRAPHY
E. Guers, *Le Premier Reveil et le Premier Eglise Independent à Genève* (Geneva, 1872)
A. Haldane, *The Lives of Robert and James Haldane* (Edinburgh, 1852)
R. Kinniburgh, *Fathers of Independency in Scotland* (Edinburgh, 1851)
D. Lovegrove, 'Unity and Separation: Contrasting Elements In the Thought and Practice of R. and J. Haldane', in K. Robbins, ed. *Studies in Church History* (Subsidia 7) (Oxford, 1990)
K. J. Stewart, 'Restoring the Reformation: British Evangelicalism and the Réveil at Geneva, 1789–1849' (Edinburgh Univ. Ph.D. thesis, 1991)

KENNETH J. STEWART

Hale, Jeffrey (b. Quebec City, Lower Canada, 19 April 1803; d. Tunbridge Wells, Kent, England, 13 Nov. 1864). Naval officer and philanthropist. Hale was born into a prominent English family with important connections to both Quebec and India. He was educated in England and served ten years in the Royal Navy, including a brief time in India where his uncle, William Pitt Amherst, was Governor-General, 1823–8. He retired from the Royal Navy with the rank of lieutenant and returned to Quebec where he acted as assistant to his father, John Hale, who was then Receiver-General of Lower Canada. His plans to succeed his father did not materialize and Hale spent the rest of his life involved in religious and philanthropic activities.

One of his chief interests was education. He established the first English Sunday school at Quebec in 1833, was a prominent supporter of the British and Canadian School Society and is reported to have founded several other schools. He was also a founder of the Quebec Provident and Savings Bank and in his will left money to establish a hospital for Protestants at Quebec which still bears his name. He was a warm supporter of a number of Anglican and pan-evangelical societies, including the BFBS, the RTS and the Quebec Mission Society. Hale was also one of the leaders of the evangelical Church of England Lay Association, which in 1858–9 unsuccessfully tried to limit the powers of the bishop over the newly founded synod of the diocese of Quebec.

BIBLIOGRAPHY
DCB IX, X
R. Pierre-Georges, *Fils de Quebec*, III (Lévis, Canada, 1937)

RICHARD W. VAUDRY

Hale, Mathew Blagden (b. Alderley, Gloucester, England, 18 June 1811; d. Bristol, England, 3 April 1895). Missionary and bishop in Australia. Educated at Trinity College, Cambridge, Hale was ordained in 1837, serving in Gloucestershire parishes. Although he keenly supported both CMS and SPG, his family dissuaded him from missionary service.

Hale married Sophie Clode in 1840. Grieving the deaths of his wife and mother in 1845, he lived in semi-retirement with his father. The newly consecrated Bishop of Adelaide, Augustus Short, discovering Hale's missionary interests, invited him to be Archdeacon of Adelaide.

Arriving in December 1847, Hale became an outspoken leader of colonial society. He took immediate interest in the Aborigines, already suffering humiliation and dispossession after a decade of white settlement. 'We profess to admitting them to the privileges of British Subjects, but in reality the only one they enjoy is that of being hanged' (Hale in *SA Church Society Reports*, 1849–50).

Visiting Western Australia in 1848, Hale married Sabina Molloy. At JOHN SMITHIES's Perth Wesleyan Mission, Hale was impressed with the self-sufficient village concept. He planned and opened his Native Institution at Poonindie in 1850, partly financed by his father. Despite deaths from European diseases, Aborigines at Poonindie developed into a confident Christian community, widely admired as a 'successful' mission.

Consecrated in 1857, Hale was Bishop of Perth from 1857 to 1875, and Brisbane from 1875 to 1885. He strove to establish the authority of the Bishop, assist struggling remote parishes, improve clergy welfare, and influence public opinion in community needs such as education and the welfare of Aborigines and Chinese. He found public apathy frustrating, nearly resigning to open another Aboriginal institution. Although never seeking controversy, Hale was confronted by Anglo-Catholic clergy over ritual and his cooperation with 'Dissenters'.

Hale retired to England in 1885. Always more a missionary than an administrator, he is best remembered for his work for Aboriginal people. At Poonindie, against all popular opinion, he gathered dispossessed Aborigines 'into one little community . . . That success is possible . . . no-one who believes the Scriptures can doubt; being men it cannot be impossible that these natives should come to the knowledge of the truth and gain eternal life' (*South Australian Register*, 28 August 1850).

SELECT WRITINGS
M. B. Hale, *The Aborigines of Australia* (London, 1892)

BIBLIOGRAPHY
ADB
J. Harris, *One Blood* (Sutherland, Australia, 1990)
A. deQ. Robin, *Mathew Blagden Hale* (Melbourne, 1976)

JOHN HARRIS

Hale, Warren Stormes (b. Bennington, Hertfordshire, England, 2 Feb. 1791; d. Hampstead, London, 23 Aug.

1872). Lord Mayor of London. Hale was orphaned and in consequence moved to London as apprentice to his brother in the chandler's trade. He himself became highly successful and was elected to the common council of the City of London in 1826, serving as Alderman from 1856 and being Sheriff in 1858/9 and Lord Mayor in 1864/5. He was prominent in applying a corporation charity to the foundation of the City of London School, of which he was chairman from 1837 to his death. He also promoted the Freemen's Orphan School at Brixton in 1854, doubtless recalling his own early years. He was master of the Tallow Chandlers' Company, a friend and supporter of JOSIAH PRATT and a member of the CPAS Committee in the 1840s.

BIBLIOGRAPHY
DNB

ARTHUR POLLARD

Hales, Richard (Cox) (b. Dinapore, Bengal, India, 29 Sept. 1817; d. 27 Cambridge Road, Hove, Sussex, 25 April 1906.) Anglican clergyman. Descended from John Hales, Baron of the Exchequer (died 1539; *DNB* under Sir James Hales), son of Major James Hales, 2nd Bengal Native Infantry, and Frances Charlotte (Blair), Richard was educated at King's College School, London, and (1836–40) at Magdalene College, Cambridge (scholar from 1838). Admitted at Oxford MA *ad eundem* 1847, Hales incorporated at Magdalen Hall (1850), migrating to University College, 1892. One of few Cambridge men (more notably A. M. W. CHRISTOPHER) in those days who moved to Oxford, Hales was immediately drawn in by resident evangelicals, and soon favoured by the city fathers.

Ordained at Winchester in 1841 (ordination papers missing), after a curacy at Itchen Stoke, Hampshire (to Honourable F. Baring) 1841–3, and occasional duty 1843–4, he moved to Brighton, where he is said to have assisted at St Mark's (founded 1849). Hales took charge of St Peter-le-Bailey, Oxford (for non-resident rector) 1847–55, living (1851) at 3 Park Villas (Banbury Road), and becoming in 1848 one of the secretaries of the Oxford Association of the CMS, his name still appearing on its committee in 1897. In 1851 he was appointed by the corporation of Oxford a city lecturer at St Martin's, Carfax; and served as Rector of Carfax ('city rector') 1852–60.

Hales moved to the small parish of Woodmancote, Sussex, where he was Rector 1860–88 (diocesan surrogate 1897–1906), retaining however his lectureship at Oxford till 1872, while becoming a member of the Steyning Board of Guardians. Nairne speaks of an (architecturally) 'disastrous restoration' of Woodmancote church in 1868. (I. Nairne and N. Pevsner, *Sussex*, 1970). Hales' roses frequently won prizes at Sussex shows. Ill health caused him to retire, to Brighton, where however he served on the council of Brighton College and on the committee of Sussex County Hospital.

Hales married (1) 1846 Esther Phillips Williams of Uxbridge, Middlesex (died 1847); (2) 1871 Ada Young Elton (alive 1906).

SELECT WRITINGS
R. C. Hales, 'Brief Notes on the Hales Family', *Archaeologia Cantiana*, 14 (London, 1882)

BIBLIOGRAPHY
Census return (Oxford, 1851)
CMS *Reports*, Oxon. (Oxford 1848, 1856–97)
J. S. Reynolds, *Evangelicals at Oxford* (Oxford, 1953; Appleford, 1975)
Sussex Daily News (26 April 1906), obituary

J. S. REYNOLDS

Hall, Christopher Newman (b. Maidstone, Kent, England, 22 May 1816; d. London, 18 Feb. 1902). Congregational minister. He was the son of John Vine Hall (*DNB*), a printer who authored a famous tract, *The Sinner's Friend*. Setting aside his printer's apprenticeship, in 1837 he commenced studies for the ministry at Highbury College. He obtained the BA from London University in 1841 (LL B 1856) and was ordained in Hull in 1842.

Hall achieved national fame with his tract *Come to Jesus* (1848) that sold in excess of 4 million copies and was translated into many languages. In 1854 he moved to London to succeed JAMES SHERMAN at Surrey Chapel. The same year he delivered one of the YMCA lectures at Exeter Hall and was invited to do so again in 1858 and 1862. In 1859–60, in an attempt to attract the lower working classes to public worship services, Hall cooperated with Lord SHAFTESBURY and the LCM by conducting special religious services at the Britannia Theatre, Hoxton. Guided by Hall, in 1876 the Surrey Chapel congregation built Christ Church in Westminster Bridge Road. He retired in 1892, having been honoured with degrees from Amhurst and Edinburgh universities.

A prominent antislavery advocate, he was vocal in support of the North in the American Civil War. Hall was personally acquainted with W. E. GLADSTONE and in 1870 was consulted by W. E. Forster concerning the education bill. He was a member of the EA.

SELECT WRITINGS
C. N. Hall, *Autobiography* (London, 1898)

BIBLIOGRAPHY
DNB
N. Pope, *Dickens and Charity* (London, 1978): 143–8

JONATHAN BURKE CUTMORE

Hall, Francis (b. London). *Fl.* 1820s. CMS missionary in New Zealand. Hall appears to have been a schoolmaster when he volunteered to go to New Zealand with the CMS. He was sent out on 15 December 1818 with JOHN and SAMUEL BUTLER and JAMES KEMP. Hall returned to

England on 5 December 1822. He resigned his connection with the CMS on 26 June 1824 and was appointed to a position at the Charterhouse School.

BIBLIOGRAPHY
D. T. B[arry], *CMS Register of Missionaries and Native Clergy* (privately printed) (London, 1906)

DONALD M. LEWIS

Hall, Gordon (b. Tolland, MA, USA, 8 April 1784; d. Doorlee-D'hapoor, India, 20 March 1826). Congregational missionary. Hall graduated with highest honours from Williams College in 1808, and was a member of the famed Haystack prayer meeting. Planning for overseas service, he entered Andover Seminary in 1810. Ordained at Salem, Massachusetts, in February 1812 with four other missionary appointees, he sailed for India later that month, under the auspices of the ABCFM, arriving in Calcutta in August. Hampered at first by the opposition of the East India Company, Hall and his companions did not receive formal permission to stay in India until 1815. The following year he married Margaret Lewis, an English woman resident in Bombay, from which place Hall's work was carried out: evangelistic preaching and the distribution of books and tracts in the adjoining region. For health reasons Mrs Hall and the children left for the USA in 1825. In 1821 Hall experienced the first attack of the cholera that led to his eventual death five years later when on one of his gospel tours.

BIBLIOGRAPHY
AAP

WILLIAM G. TRAVIS

Hall, (Captain) **Percy (Francis)** (b. 1804; d. Weston-super-Mare, Somerset, England, 11 Oct. 1884). British naval officer and Brethren leader. The son of C. H. Hall, Regius professor of divinity (1807), Dean of Christ Church (1809), Oxford, and Dean of Durham (1824), Percy Hall was a naval officer in charge of the Plymouth coastguards. Influenced by BENJAMIN WILLS NEWTON and other early Brethren, Captain Hall resigned his commission, publishing his reasons in a celebrated pamphlet, *Discipleship*, which is basically a catena of world-renouncing scriptural quotations.

An enthusiastic preacher, he was active in open-air preaching, first in Plymouth and then in Hereford from 1837. At first he remained loyal to JOHN NELSON DARBY, leading a small secession movement from the Hereford Brethren in his support. Later with WILLIAM H. DORMAN and others, he opposed Darby's views on the sufferings of Christ which came to light in 1866.

BIBLIOGRAPHY
Pickering

HAROLD H. ROWDON

Hall, Peter (b. probably London, 31 Dec. 1803; d. Great Malvern, Worcestershire, England, 10 Sept. 1849). Anglican clergyman, liturgist, and antiquarian. Hall was educated at Winchester College and Brasenose College, Oxford (BA 1825; MA 1830) and ordained in 1828. He became Curate of St Edmund's Salisbury, was converted to evangelical views, and in 1833 dismissed by his Rector for allegedly 'inculcating doctrines inconsistent with the Bible, and with the public interpretations of the Church of England'. However, Hall, who had recently published a vigorous reply to WILLIAM TIPTAFT's arguments against the Church of England, remained an Anglican. In September 1834 he became Rector of Milston-cum-Brigmerston, Wiltshire, but did not reside there for long, pursuing a career as minister of proprietary chapels, first in London, at Tavistock Chapel, Drury Lane (1836–41) and Long Acre Episcopal Chapel (1841–3), and then in Bath, at St Thomas, Walcot from 1843.

Hall published topographical and antiquarian works relating to Dorset, Hampshire and Wiltshire, and produced editions of a number of classic Anglican works, notably John Jewell's *Harmony of the Protestant Confessions* and the collected works of Joseph Hall (1574–1656), Bishop of Exeter and Norwich, from whom he claimed descent. He also compiled documents relating to the liturgy.

While in London, Hall had been one of the earliest Anglican clergy to support the interdenominational LCM (*Record*, 8 February 1838) and in the mid-1840s he worked with the interdenominational Town Missionary Society. However, he published his views opposing the EA in 1845. Staunchly anti-Catholic, he served from 1846 to 1848 as a travelling secretary for the British Reformation Society. According to the *Christian Guardian* he became mentally deranged and died by his own hand.

SELECT WRITINGS
P. Hall, *The Church and the World* (Salisbury, England, 1833), and other works by Hall

BIBLIOGRAPHY
Alli
CG (November 1849): 526–7
DNB
D. M. Lewis, *Lighten Their Darkness* (Westport, CT, 1986)
J. Wolffe, *The Protestant Crusade in Great Britain, 1829–60* (Oxford, 1991)

JOHN WOLFFE

Hall, Robert (b. Black Heddon, Newcastle-upon-Tyne, England, 26 April 1728; d. Arnesby, Leicestershire, England, 13 March 1791). Baptist minister. As a youth he was troubled by a sense of guilt and despair before eventually finding spiritual peace. Coming into contact with Baptists he attempted to refute their views. However, his study of the subject led to his being baptized and joining the Baptist church at Hexham, in 1752. He became pastor at Arnesby, supplementing his annual stipend of £15 by farming. Like FULLER, he was disturbed by the spiritually deadening effects of Hyper-Calvinism and wrestled with the problem of the relationship between divine sovereignty and human responsibility. As a result, he modified his views, setting out his new thinking in 1781, in *Help to Zion's Travellers*.

BIBLIOGRAPHY
G. W. Hughes, 'Robert Hall of Arnesby, 1728–1791', *BQ*, 10, 8 (October 1941)

E. F. CLIPSHAM

Hall, Robert (b. Nottingham, England, 25 Feb. 1754; d. Sneinton, Nottinghamshire, England, 6 Aug. 1827). Master dyer and Methodist layman. From a middle-class family, he joined the Methodists at the age of 17. He went into business as a bleacher and cotton-spinner at Basford, near Nottingham, where in 1793 he built at his own expense a chapel for his employees in the grounds of his home, Basford Hall. He was occasionally host to JOHN WESLEY, whose help he solicited towards the building of Hockley Chapel, Nottingham. In 1797, the greater part of the Nottingham Methodists joined the MNC and Hall became a leading member of the connexion both in Nottingham and countrywide. Between 1797 and 1805 he was seven times a member of the influential Annual Committee and twice acted as secretary of the conference. In 1799 he was principal editor of the first *Life* of ALEXANDER KILHAM. He retired from business in 1815 and suffered a long period of ill health and gradual paralysis.

BIBLIOGRAPHY
Methodist New Connexion Magazine (1828): 1–7, 45–50

E. ALAN ROSE

Hall, Robert (b. Arnesby, Leicestershire, England, 2 May 1764; d. Bristol, England, 21 Feb. 1831). English Baptist theologian and activist. His father, the older ROBERT HALL, was the author of *Help to Zion's Travellers*, 1781, one of the publications which reflected the new evangelical outlook then beginning to characterize the midland Baptists. A spinal defect from birth, which caused him great pain and weakness, may have encouraged his early intellectual development. A precocious boy, who is said to have learned the alphabet from tombstones, and mastered the thought of JONATHAN EDWARDS before he was nine, the younger Robert Hall gave his first public address, mistakenly in his own later judgment, at Kettering at the age of 11. In 1776 he entered Dr RYLAND's boarding-school in Northampton and two years later was baptized as a believer, proceeding almost immediately to Bristol Baptist College before completing his education with four years as an exhibitioner at the University of Aberdeen (1781–5), where he formed a close friendship with the future Whig philosopher and historian, Sir James Mackintosh, graduating MA in March 1785.

By then he had already returned to Bristol to assist CALEB EVANS in the Broadmead Church and at the college in succession to JAMES NEWTON. At this period of his life he seems to have been fascinated by Joseph Priestley, and is reputed to have suggested on a visit to Birmingham that Priestley would escape the judgment of a just God. For this he was severely censured by John Rylands in a letter which speaks forcefully of 'the lusts of the mind', and certainly Hall, himself, in a letter of 1815 is categoric in denying the 'salvability' of Socinians. There was also uneasiness at the Broadmead Church as well as tension with Evans which led to Hall's resignation in November 1790, two months before he succeeded ROBERT ROBINSON in Cambridge. However, he soon became a redoubtable defender of Christian orthodoxy; while attacking the Antinomianism of the Hyper-Calvinists, he equally engaged the insidious dangers of modern Unitarianism, and helped by the force of the arguments he deployed to secure respect for the intellectual integrity of evangelical Dissent. His pastorate at Cambridge lasted from 1791 to 1806. From 1807 to 1826 he was pastor of Harvey Lane, Leicester, when he returned to be pastor of Broadmead, Bristol until his death in 1831.

His own writings, principally sermonic and polemical, do not include the systematic theological exposition he was certainly capable of producing but his sermon 'On the substitution of the innocent for the guilty' which defended substitutionary atonement, the greatest sermon he preached, was still being cited half a century later. The *Quarterly Review*, which judged him an 'absolute master of English' considered that his talents were 'surpassed by those of very few men in his time', while the *British Critic* deemed his published sermons 'of such surpassing splendour and power, that they took at once an elevated station in our standard theological literature, and placed their author beyond all dispute among the great and commanding spirits of the age.'

A keen defender of religious liberty, Hall produced two important defences of freedom in the 1790s, the product of the crisis of those years as much as any inclination to be a political preacher. The first, *Christianity Consistent With a Love of Freedom* (London, 1791), provoked by the advocacy of pietistic abstention from worldly affairs by JOHN CLAYTON, the patrician Independent minister at the King's Weigh-House Church in London, argued in favour of the Christian's civil engagement and, therefore, against dissenting disabilities. 'The devout mind', Hall affirmed of events in Europe in the late 1780s and 1790s 'will behold in these momentous changes the finger of God'; 'That fond attachment to ancient institutions, and blind submission to opinions already received, which has ever checked the growth of improvement, and drawn on the benefactors of mankind danger or neglect, is giving way to a spirit of bold and fearless investigation. Man seems to be becoming more erect and independent.'

The second, *An Apology for The Freedom of the Press and for General Liberty* (London, 1793), arose out of discussions in a Book Society mainly composed of members of Hall's and CHARLES SIMEON's congregations in Cambridge and contains the former's forthright denunciation of the policies of Pitt, 'a veteran in frauds while in the bloom of youth ... falsifying every promise and violating every political engagement', thus entitling 'him to a fatal pre-eminence in guilt'. In fact, the pamphlet offers a substantial argument for equality 'as opposed to feudal oppression and hereditary distinction', advocating reform and the development of democratic institutions, including legal changes, popular education, universal suffrage, the redistribution of parliamentary seats and annual parliaments. The pursuit of such objects rendered revolution unnecessary whilst failure to act in these areas fuelled revolutionary potential. While contemplating 'the crimes and disorders with which it has been stained, with the deepest regret', Hall confessed 'the French revolution has always appeared to me, and does still appear, the most splendid event recorded in the annals of history'. While his biographer affirms that his political principles remained in substance unchanged in later, less critical, years, they were less frequently articulated.

Hall was never frightened of applying his political convictions to practical situations, as for example in his establishment of the Framework Knitters' Fund to deal with the distress among the Leicester stockingers in 1819 which led to controversy with William Cobbett who opposed such a scheme. Hall also proved a keen advocate of the abolition of slavery and of the need to revise the charter of the East India Company to allow missionary access. He vehemently opposed war, 'the most awful scourge that Providence employs for the chastisement of man'.

There was a note of catholicity about Hall's evangelicalism that had important consequences for the Baptist denomination; as early as 1790, he told the church at Broadmead that he would be unprepared to rebaptize by immersion somebody who had been sprinkled as a believer, thus in some measure anticipating his subsequent advocacy of a Communion table open to all believers, and his debate with JOSEPH KINGHORN on the same issue. In 'The Signs of the Times', itself interesting as a sermon preached in 1820 for the benefit of the Anglican National Schools, citing the work of the Bible Society, Hall affirmed 'Even catholics and protestants, influenced by a kindred spirit, can now cordially embrace each other'. 'The union of Christians in the promotion of a common cause', Hall believed to be one of the most propitious of the signs of the times in which he lived; 'is it possible', he asked, 'after mingling thus their counsels, their efforts, their prayers, and standing side by side in the thickest of the conflict ... for them to turn their backs on each other, and refuse to unite at that table which is covered with the memorials of his love and the fruit of his victory?' (Hall, 1858) Unity in mission was the logic that preceded unity at the table. 'No man, or set of men', he argued, 'are entitled to prescribe as an indispensable condition of communion, what the New Testament has not enjoined as a condition of salvation.'

SELECT WRITINGS
R. Hall, *The Works of Robert Hall*, ed. O. Gregory (with a Memoir by the editor and an essay on Hall as preacher by John Foster) 6 vols, (London, 1858)

BIBLIOGRAPHY
DNB
G. W. Hughes, *Robert Hall* (London, 1943)
S. A. Swaine, *Faithful Men* (London, 1884)

J. H. Y. BRIGGS

Hall, Samuel (b. Manchester, England, *c.* 1780; d. London, 21 Oct. 1858). Anglican clergyman. Hall's father and namesake was rector of St Peter's, Manchester and for a time guardian and tutor to Thomas de Quincey. Hall himself was educated at Manchester Grammar School and St John's College, Cambridge (BA 1804; MA 1807; fellow 1806–15). He was Perpetual Curate of Billinge (Lancashire) (1813–33), but resigned because he could not reconcile his extreme Calvinist views with those of the Church of England. He ministered for some years at a small meeting house in Southport, but eventually returned to the church.

BIBLIOGRAPHY
Al. Cant., II, iii: 203

ARTHUR POLLARD

Hall, Westley (b. Salisbury, England, 17 March, 1711; d. Bristol, England, 3 Jan. 1776). Anglican clergyman and early Methodist. The son of Thomas Hall, he matriculated at Lincoln College as a gentleman-commoner on 26 January 1731 and became a pupil of JOHN WESLEY, to whom he was distantly related, and a member of the Holy Club. He became secretly engaged to Wesley's sister Martha, but shortly afterwards proposed marriage to his other sister Keziah. Hall married Martha, conduct which was strongly criticized by CHARLES and Samuel WESLEY. He remained, however, in close relations with the Wesleys, and was described by John Wesley as 'holy, and unblamable in all manner of conversation' and by John's mother as a man of 'extraordinary piety and love to souls'. In practice Hall combined a genuine interest in religion with a meretricious charm and ruthless pursuit of his own interests. He designed with his wife to accompany the Wesleys to Georgia, but instead took a curacy at Wootton Rivers, Wiltshire. In 1739 he moved to London where he supervised the Methodist society there; both Wesley's mother and his sister Keziah lodged with him. Although at first critical of Moravian beliefs, by 1741 he had become a Moravian and denounced Wesley for his management of the society and religious principles. In 1743 he removed to Salisbury where he formed his own congregation which broke from the Church of England. 'You are', Wesley wrote to him, 'a weak, injudicious, fickle, irresolute man, deeply enthusiastic and highly opinionated of yourself

. . . You jilted one of my sisters and married the other . . . Your life has been one blunder ever since' (Baker, 1982: 103).

His views became increasingly idiosyncratic. He defended polygamy and seems to have sought to put it into practice, migrating with his mistress to the West Indies. Besides illegitimate issue, Hall had ten children by his wife. 'Brother Hall's', Samuel Wesley wrote, 'is a black story. There was no great likelihood of his being a favourite with me; his tongue is too smooth for my roughness, and rather inclines me to suspect than believe.' Apparently he showed signs of penitence on his deathbed.

BIBLIOGRAPHY
F. Baker, ed., *The Works of John Wesley*, 26 (Oxford, 1982)

VIVIAN H. H. GREEN

Hall, William (b. Carlisle, Cumbria, England; d. Australia, 28 Oct. 1832). CMS missionary to New Zealand. Hall, a carpenter/joiner, with his first wife Dinah was selected by SAMUEL MARSDEN among the first artisan missionaries for New Zealand. Finally arriving in 1814, they were to introduce European culture to the Maori to facilitate reception of the Christian Gospel. Difficult to work with, Hall built mission houses at Rangihoua and Kerikeri, but also farmed, traded and helped construct the mission schooner *Herald*. In 1825 illness caused his return to Australia where he supervised a CMS aboriginal school and served as catechist.

BIBLIOGRAPHY
ADNZB
J. R. Elder, *Marsden's Lieutenants* (Dunedin, New Zealand, 1934)

BRYAN D. GILLING

Halley, Robert (b. Blackheath, Kent, England, 13 Aug. 1796; d. Batworth Park, Arundel, Sussex, England, 18 Aug. 1876). Congregational minister and historian. He was the son of Robert Halley, nurseryman, and Ann, his first wife. Halley was educated at Maze Hill School, Greenwich, and joined his father's business before entering Homerton Academy, 18 January 1816. He was ordained, 11 June 1822, at St Neot's Congregational Church. He was a tutor at Highbury College, 1826–39, and minister of Mosley Street, Manchester, from 1839 to 1857 (Cavendish Street from June 1848); principal of New College, London, from 1857 to 1872 and then retired to Clapton. He was chairman of the Congregational Union in 1855. In March 1823 he married Rebekah Jacob. His sons, Robert and Jacob John, also became Congregational ministers. Halley is best known as a historian. In 1869 he published *Lancashire: its Puritanism and Nonconformity* in two volumes, with a second edition in 1872, and an admirable study it is. Although it is not packed with detailed local information, it excels in presenting a broad and intelligent interpretation of the historical developments in the county and the whole is composed in a readable prose style.

BIBLIOGRAPHY
DNB
R. Halley (Jr), *A Short Biography* (London, 1879)
S. M. Jackson, ed., *The New Schaff-Herzog Religious Encyclopedia of Religious Knowledge*, 12 vols (New York, 1908–12) 5 (1909): 127

R. TUDUR JONES

Hallock, Jeremiah (b. Brookhaven, NY, BNA, 13 March 1758; d. West Simsbury, CT, USA, 23 June 1826). Congregational minister. Hallock's interest in the ministry was sparked by his conversion in 1779. Ill prepared for Yale College – the traditional training ground for the Connecticut clergy – he compensated by apprenticing himself to five ministers. He was ordained at West Simsbury, Connecticut in 1785. Hallock's church was one of the first to be caught up in the Second Great Awakening in Connecticut when nearly seventy people converted in the autumn and winter of 1798–9. Other revivals followed in 1805, 1812–13, 1816, and 1821. Hallock was a much beloved pastor who made two summer missionary journeys for the Missionary Society of Connecticut.

BIBLIOGRAPHY
AAP, 2: 229–34
C. Yale, *The Godly Pastor* (New York, [1854])

DAVID W. KLING

Hallward, John (b. Worcester, England, 3 Dec. 1749; d. Assington, Suffolk, England, 21 Dec. 1826). Anglican clergyman. The son of Thomas Hallward, gentleman, he was educated at private schools and from 1763 by the Reverend Edward Davies at Bengeworth near Evesham, Worcester, where, aged 15, he was converted. In 1766 he went up to Worcester College, Oxford (scholar 1769; BA 1770; MA 1773; fellow 1775). He was a member of a small group of evangelical undergraduates, which included HENRY FOSTER of Queen's, who met for Bible study and prayer. In 1767 JAMES STILLINGFLEET, fellow of Merton, who had hitherto led it, left Oxford and the leadership passed to Hallward. (A similar society at Cambridge, led by ROWLAND HILL, kept in touch with its Oxford counterpart.) PHILIP GURDON of Magdalen, who became Hallward's lifelong friend, was converted through his connection with members at Oxford. In 1768 six of their associates were expelled from St Edmund Hall, mainly for 'ecclesiastical irregularity'. Hallward and Gurdon, however, both became in due course, and in spite of some persecution, fellows of their colleges, though both moved away to curacies. Foster was perhaps Hallward's friend of whom Hallward wrote in 1826 'His conduct at Oxford made an indelible impression on me . . . .'

Hallward became curate at St Giles, Reading, 1773–5 (being ordained priest at Oxford, on letter dimissory from Salisbury [ordination paper, Oxford) to one of the most striking leaders of the contemporary evangelical revival, w. TALBOT, 'whose faithful labours were greatly blessed in the awakening of sinners', and who ministered to a large congregation. Talbot, however, died in 1774, and the incoming vicar, the Honourable w. B. CADOGAN, dismissed Hallward, in spite of a petition from a substantial number of parishioners. In 1775 Hallward published a sermon prefaced by a brief tribute to Talbot. Cadogan was furious, little realizing that his own conversion was yet to come. By 1780 he was inviting Hallward to return to his old curacy. But Hallward had meanwhile become fellow of Worcester College, Oxford (1775), Vicar of Shawbury, Shropshire (through Sir RICHARD HILL) (1775–80), and chaplain to the Countess of Elgin. In 1779 his friend Gurdon had nominated him Rector of Milden and Vicar of Assington, Suffolk. Together they happily worked the two parishes until Gurdon's death in 1817, Hallward continuing alone until death also came, very suddenly, in 1826. Both were strong supporters of the CMS. Hallward was married, and had two sons at Oxford.

BIBLIOGRAPHY
J. Bickersteth, *Mortality Swallowed Up in Life* (London, 1827)
R. Cecil, *Works*, 1, *Memoirs of Cadogan*, 2nd edn (London, 1816)
C. Hole, *The Early History of the CMS* (London, 1896)
J. S. Reynolds, *Evangelicals at Oxford* (Oxford, 1953; Appleford, England, 1975)
C. H. E. Smyth, *Simeon and Church Order* (Cambridge, 1940)

ARTHUR POLLARD AND J. S. REYNOLDS

Hambleton, John (b. Liverpool, 1820; d. Australia, 8 Dec. 1889). Brethren evangelist. Leaving home at 16, Hambleton travelled as an actor in Australia and then sought his fortune in the California gold-rush of 1849. Returning to England in 1857 he experienced conversion (apparently through the ministry of REGINALD RADCLIFFE) and began preaching in Liverpool and later throughout the British Isles. His racy style could always draw a crowd. Associated (but not exclusively) with Brethren, 'the converted actor' was the means of the conversion of Thomas Barnardo in 1862, and many others. He returned to Australia *circa* 1879.

BIBLIOGRAPHY
Pickering: 101–6
G. Read and D. Jebson, *A Voice in the City* (Liverpool, England, 1979)
G. Wagner, *Barnardo* (London, 1979)

TIMOTHY C. F. STUNT

Hamilton, George (b. Armagh, Ireland, 1783; d. Killermogh, Queen's County, Ireland, 10 Aug. 1830). Anglican clergyman, Hebraist, and author. The fourth son of Dr Hugh Hamilton, Dean of Armagh – afterwards Bishop of Clonfert, and Ossory – a founder of the Royal Irish Academy, he was educated at Trinity College, Dublin, ordained in 1808, and Rector of Killermogh (Ossory) 1809–30. (Leslie is wrong to insinuate nepotism. His father died in 1805).

He was involved in the formation of Hibernian Church Missionary Society in 1814, but – as befitted a Hebrew scholar – his main interest was in the LSPCJ. Among his many extant letters are two series written during tours for the society, in the west of Ireland with LEWIS WAY in 1820, and in England in 1821–2. His letters generally provide detailed information on the burgeoning evangelical revival in the Irish Church, and clarify the significant support given by Archbishop William Magee of Dublin, particularly to scholarly evangelical clergy.

His major publications were *A General Introduction to the Study of the Hebrew Scriptures* (Dublin, 1813), and *Codex Criticus of the Hebrew Bible* (London, 1821) – dedicated to Magee. He also published *A Letter to the Rabbi Herschell* (1824), and contributed papers to *CE(D)*, the *Jewish Expositor*, PETER ROE's *The Evil of Separation from the Church of England* (1815), and *Transactions of the Royal Irish Academy*.

BIBLIOGRAPHY
DNB
J. B. Leslie, *Ossory Clergy and Parishes* (Enniskillen, Ireland, 1933): 37, 298
Public Record Office of Northern Ireland, Belfast. Johnston of Kilmore manuscripts include many of his letters from 1808

ALAN R. ACHESON

Hamilton, James (b. Dunbar, Scotland, *c*. 1 Dec. 1740; d. 21 April 1827). Methodist physician and preacher. Hamilton, a fellow of the Royal College of Physicians of Edinburgh, preserved few papers for posterity. From about 1759 to 1763 he served as surgeon on a British man-of-war; a naval skirmish with a French vessel deepened his religious interests. He left the navy to work as a surgeon and apothecary in Dunbar.

On 30 May 1762 following prolonged conviction of sin, he experienced an evangelical conversion. Although a loyal member of the Church of Scotland, he joined the small Methodist Society in Dunbar which in 1764 built a small Methodist preaching house. By 1770 Hamilton had become a Methodist local preacher and unashamedly mingled prayer and spiritual advice with his medicine. JOHN WESLEY visited Dunbar biennially from 1757, then annually from 1765, and again biennially from 1770. During his 1772 visit Wesley was in great physical pain, and Hamilton treated him and insisted on his consulting two eminent specialists in Edinburgh who confirmed Hamilton's diagnosis. Wesley as well as others believed also in Hamilton as a spiritual healer.

Wesley confided in Hamilton his fears that Methodism might separate from the Church of England. In 1789 Wesley asked Hamilton, a 'mere' local preacher, to address the Methodist preachers assembled in conference. Taking Jeremiah 7: 4 as his text, Hamilton insisted: 'All external religion is of no use any farther than it advances the spiritual kingdom of Christ in the soul. [Therefore] God called a race of men named prophets, . . . what we call laymen, chiefly farmers and shepherds, holy men, men of strong faith, . . . practising the strictest temperance, and clothed in the plainest manner' (Hamilton, 1790: 20). He testified to the Wesleys and WHITEFIELD, who, 'although their brother priests in the Church thrust them from them, . . . they retained a strong and affectionate attachment to . . . the Church, [without which] the Methodists would have long ere this become a distinct body, separate from the Church, . . . sunk into the dead formality of the numerous sects' (Ibid.). He urged the preachers to rouse the people, 'to bring them from resting in external duties to the possession of internal holiness; from an opinion in the head to the love of God in the heart' (Ibid.). He closed with an appeal:

If ever ye set up as a separate people by external distinctions and creeds; if ye substitute a silken gown and sash for rough garments and a leathern girdle, and call one another, Rabbi! Rabbi! then the glory will depart from you, and God will raise up another people; and he will send them to call *you* from opinions and forms, and to sound in *your* ears, 'Trust not unto lying words, saying, The temple of the Lord are these.'
(Ibid.)

He published the sermon with a preface which referred to its 'deep and weighty truths', signed by Wesley.

As a physician Hamilton cared especially for the poor; he was, indeed, always ready to prescribe for the poor – or Methodist preachers – without any fee. Desiring a larger medical practice he moved to Leeds briefly, and then to London after Wesley's death. Here he lived for over thirty years, most of that time in Finsbury Square, close to Wesley's City Road Chapel. He enjoyed almost uninterrupted health, but suffered frequent bereavement, of two wives, and of two sons in the army. He was also frequently requested for funeral sermons for the great (and the small) of Methodism, and a white marble tablet in City Road Chapel spoke of his being 'a local preacher in the Wesleyan Connexion for more than 60 years,' with the text of Luke 9: 6 as his testimonial, 'Preaching the gospel and healing everywhere'.

SELECT WRITINGS
J. Hamilton, *A Sermon Preached at Leeds, July 29th, 1789, Before the Methodist Preachers* (London, 1790)

BIBLIOGRAPHY
G. J. Stevenson, *City Road Chapel, London, and its Associations* (London, 1872): especially 356, 503–4
WMM (1827): 433–49, 505–13 (Memoir by Henry Moore)

FRANK BAKER

Hamilton, James (b. Paisley, Scotland, 17 Nov. 1814; d. London, 24 Nov. 1867). Church of Scotland minister.

The son of a Church of Scotland minister at Strathblane, he graduated from the University of Glasgow in 1835. His first appointments were as assistant minister in 1839 to R. S. CANDLISH at Edinburgh, and during the following two years at Abernyte, Dundee. He was briefly minster at Roxburgh Church, Edinburgh in 1841, but in July of that year transferred permanently to London to become minister of the National Scotch Church, Regent Square (built in 1827 for EDWARD IRVING). Under his ministry, in 1843 Regent Square severed its connection with the Church of Scotland.

Hamilton helped to establish the YMCA Exeter Hall lecture series. In its first season (1845/6) he delivered three of its seven lectures, and in the next two decades five more. He was also a prolific writer of devotional literature and pious biographies, popular in their day. His *Proposed Evangelical Alliance* (1845) illustrates his close involvement in the founding of that organization. He was also much involved in the LSPCJ.

BIBLIOGRAPHY
W. Arnot, *Life of James Hamilton* (London, 1870)
DNB

JONATHAN BURKE CUTMORE

Hamilton, William (b. Longridge, Lanarkshire, Scotland, 4 Feb. 1780; d. Strathblane, Stirlingshire, Scotland, 16 April 1835). Church of Scotland minister. Educated at the University of Edinburgh and ordained at Dundee in 1807, he was translated to the parish of Strathblane in 1809, and was a prominent critic of patronage in the Church of Scotland. He wrote extensively and published on both systematic and pastoral theology and to a lesser extent on some social questions.

BIBLIOGRAPHY
DNB
J. Hamilton (son), *Life and Remains*, 2 vols (Glasgow, 1836)

R. H. CAMPBELL

Hamlin, Cyrus (b. Wateford, ME, USA, 5 Jan. 1811; d. Lexington, MA, USA, 8 Aug. 1900). Missionary and educator. An 1834 graduate of Bowdoin College, Hamlin attended Bangor Theological Seminary in Maine for three years in preparation for missionary work with the ABCFM (Congregational). He arrived in Turkey in 1839, and established a school on the Bosphorus in 1840, most of whose students were Armenian. During the twenty years he directed the school he achieved notoriety by having his students and the community of Armenian Protestants engage in various commercial enterprises, including some connected with the Crimean War. He broke with the American board in 1860 over policy matters, met a wealthy New York merchant named Robert who wished to establish a school in Constantinople, and in 1863 Hamlin established Robert College. He was connected with the school during its growing years, but was fired by Robert in 1877. The following year he began teaching at Bangor Seminary, and published his *Among the Turks*. Three years later he took up the presidency of Middlebury College in Vermont, thoroughly reorganizing the institution, and finally retired from active work in 1885.

BIBLIOGRAPHY
DAB

WILLIAM G. TRAVIS

Hamlin, James (b. Norton-sub-Hamdon, Somerset, England, 2 Sept. 1803; d. Auckland, New Zealand, 15 Nov. 1865). CMS missionary to New Zealand. A flax-dresser and weaver, Hamlin was the first student of the CMS Islington Institution, coming with his wife Elizabeth to New Zealand in 1826 as a CMS missionary catechist at Kerikeri. In 1830 he was one of four selected to found a model mission farm at Waimate. An able linguist, he joined the CMS committee translating the Bible into Maori, and, competent at every task he attempted, became a 'main prop' of the mission.

In 1834, with ALFRED N. BROWN he explored the Waikato and in 1835 moved there, first to Mangapouri with James Stack (1835), then to Moeatoa with ROBERT MAUNSELL (1836–9) and Orua Bay (1839–44), becoming the first European to be told the migration traditions of the Tainui canoe.

Deaconed in 1844, he founded a station at Wairoa where he and his wife taught school and agriculture while raising 12 children. He was priested in 1863, but in 1864 retired after his brother's murder by Kingite Maori.

BIBLIOGRAPHY
ADNŽB
ENZ
H. J. Ryburn, *Te Hemara* (Dunedin, New Zealand, 1979)

BRYAN D. GILLING

Hamline, Leonidas Lent (b. Burlington, CT, USA, 10 May 1797; d. Mount Pleasant, IA, USA, 23 Mar. 1865). Methodist bishop, editor, and philanthropist. Born to parents of French Huguenot descent, Mark and Sarah [Moses] Hamline, Leonidas attended Andover Academy with the intention of preparation for ministry. After an apparent mental breakdown, he studied law in Zanesville, Ohio (1824). He married the wealthy Eliza Price (1825) and was admitted to the Bar (1827). However, he again decided to enter the ministry and was licensed to preach (1829), admitted to the Ohio Conference of the MEC (1832) and ordained (1834). Eliza Hamline died 27 March 1835; Hamline married the widowed Melinda Truesdale (1836).

After short ministry experiences in Cincinnati and Columbus, he was appointed (1836) interim assistant editor of the *Western Christian Advocate* published at Cincinnati,

and elected to that post by the General Conference of 1840. He achieved a reputation as a statesman for his efforts to temper, opponents would say limit, the discussion of slavery issues in the *Advocate*. While working in Cincinnati, he became involved with the developing German Methodist churches and recommended to the Bishops the publication of a German Methodist periodical. Permission was granted with no funding. *Christliche Apologete* (Cincinnati, OH, 1839–1918) began with Hamline on the editorial board, and with subsidies from Hamline. He also gave funds for the building of German Methodist churches throughout the USA. The 1840 General Conference authorized publication of a magazine for women. Hamline was appointed editor of the *Ladies Repository* (January 1841 to December 1876) and remained editor until 1844 when he was elected bishop.

It was on 22 March 1842, in New Albany, Indiana, that Hamline experienced 'sanctification', responding to the challenge of a sermon on 'perfect love' by Methodist Episcopal pastor W. D. Daniels who had experienced the same six years earlier. This brought him into contact with east coast holiness advocates, such as PHOEBE and WALTER C. PALMER, with whom he corresponded frequently and in whose home he was a guest. He also had personal contact with THOMAS C. UPHAM and ASA MAHAN.

Hamline was elected bishop in 1844, partly because of his moderate stand on the slavery issue and his ability, on the floor of the General Conference, to state precisely and decisively the disciplinary and financial issues related to the separation of the church into politically defined regions. After the division of the MEC over slavery, he worked to consolidate the Northern Church. This involved Hamline's suggestion that the Northern MEC accept the national political boundaries between North and South as the boundary between the northern and southern churches. The border states continued, however to present problems. The denominational publishing and distribution centres, the 'Book Concerns', including pension funds, were divided according to a Hamline proposal. Administration of the church's business, during the troubled period proved stressful. Throughout this period, his published correspondence and addresses show him to have been an active advocate of holiness theology and experience. Because of declining health, Hamline resigned from an active and effective bishopric in 1852, provoking a controversy about the nature of episcopal ordination. It was decided that it was actually an ecclesiastical office rather than an order which cannot be relinquished but at death.

He retired to Mount Pleasant, Iowa, where he occasionally preached. He gave funds to Hamline University, Mount Vernon Institute (Iowa), Ohio Wesleyan University, the Methodist Episcopal Mission Society and the Bible Society, as well as other philanthropic causes. He provided counsel and funds to rescue Iowa Wesleyan University from financial ruin between 1860 and 1864. During the last two decades of his life he suffered from heart disease and other ailments. He was first buried in

Mount Pleasant, Iowa, but later at Rose Hill Cemetery in Chicago.

BIBLIOGRAPHY
EWM
F. G. Hibbard, *Biography of Rev. Leonidas L. Hamline, D.D., Late One of the Bishops of the Methodist Episcopal Church* (Cincinnati, OH, and New York, 1880)
—, ed., *Works of Rev. Leonidas L. Hamline* (Cincinnati, OH, 1869–71)
A. Miller, ed., *Experience of German Methodist Preachers*, with an introduction by Charles Elliott and a preliminary discourse by L. L. Hamlime (Cincinnati, OH, 1859)
W. Palmer, *Life and Letters of Leonidas L. Hamline, D.D.* (New York, 1866)

DAVID BUNDY

Hammet(t), William (d. Charleston, SC, USA, 1803). Methodist missionary and a founder of West Indian Methodism. Hammet was adventurous, determined and energetic. He began his ministry in Ireland (1784), and was ordained by JOHN WESLEY (1786). On his way to Newfoundland with THOMAS COKE, a storm blew them off course and they arrived in Antigua, West Indies, on 25 December 1787. On 5 January 1787, he sailed with Coke, JOHN BAXTER and John Clarke to several islands. He ministered in Dominica and pioneered the work in St Kitts, Nevis and Tortola (1787–8). In St Kitts he brought into membership approximately 700 persons, and prepared two candidates for the ministry. He arrived in Kingston, Jamaica, and started the work in August 1789. He laboured well, enduring persecution and dangers, to proclaim the Gospel. He formed the first society class at his manse. He achieved such great success that the Jamaican Grand Jury declared him and his chapel a public nuisance.

When Coke arrived in Jamaica (1791), Hammet was sick and physically burnt out. Coke sent him to America to recuperate. There he accepted an invitation to minister to an independent church in Charleston (South Carolina). He subsequently became embroiled in a dispute with Bishop FRANCIS ASBURY, concerning the itinerant system and centralized power. He resigned from the Methodist ministry, erected Trinity Church and developed what he called the Primitive Methodist Church.

BIBLIOGRAPHY
EWM
G. G. Findlay and W. W. Holdsworth, *The History of the Wesleyan Methodist Missionary Society*, 2 (London, 1921): 27–65, 143–215, 226

LESLEY G. ANDERSON

Hammond, Edward Ranson (b. Brettleham, Bildeston, Suffolk, England, 17 June 1795; d. 9 May 1860). Baptist minister in London and the Home Counties. Hammond was converted at Maze Pond Chapel, Southwark, London and baptized at Zion Baptist Chapel, Chatham, Kent, England. He served as Baptist minister at: Clare, Suffolk, 1832–7; Ilford, Essex, 1837–40 (while there his wife and four children died); Romney Street, Westminster, London, 1841–6; Grafton Street, Soho, London, 1847–8; West Malling, Kent, 1848–58; and Tabernacle, Charles Street, Woolwich, London, 1859–60. He is buried in chapel ground, West Malling.

BIBLIOGRAPHY
Baptist Handbook (1862): 107
BaptMag (1861): 231–2

GEOFFREY RALPH BREED

Hampson, John (b. Chowbent, Lancashire, England; d. Southborough, Kent, England, 1795). Methodist itinerant. Brought up in a dissenting congregation, Hampson joined the Methodists at 17 and, encouraged by JOHN WESLEY though perhaps not officially appointed by him, began preaching to societies in Cheshire and Lancashire. Later he removed, seemingly well circumstanced, to Manchester but seems to have abandoned preaching in the 1760s before being taken 'on trial' in 1777. He travelled for two years in Ireland but withdrew from the connexion in 1785 in protest against the *Deed of Declaration* (1784) which excluded those unordained (such as himself and his son) from the body of men appointed to lead Methodism after John Wesley's death. He retired 'old and infirm' with a Preachers' Fund annuity of ten pounds to Southborough and superintendence of a dissenting assembly.

Hampson's associations with Methodism were never comfortable. In 1760 his belief that unordained preachers should be free to adminster the sacraments led CHARLES WESLEY to think him 'ripe for separation'. In 1764, opposing conference sentiment, he expressed the view that Methodists should be free to preach in parishes served by 'awakened ministers' and, in 1778, was implicitly accused by John Wesley of insubordination and perversity. Finally, before the 1784 Conference he promulgated *An Appeal to the Reverend John and Charles Wesley* (sic!) arguing against what he regarded as authoritarianism which had shackled the growth of Methodism.

C. J. SPITTAL

Hampson, John [Jr] (b. probably Didsbury, Lancashire, England, *c.*1753; d. Sunderland, County Durham, England, 7 Dec. 1819). Methodist preacher and Anglican clergyman. Son of JOHN HAMPSON (died 1795), he was probably baptized at Didsbury, Lancashire on 21 October 1753. Educated at Kingswood School from 1763 to 1765, he was admitted a trial preacher in 1777 and sent to Ireland where suspicion of Methodists brought him under personal attack. From 1780 he served in Britain, finally at Sunderland in 1784, the year of the Deed of Declaration which provoked his withdrawal from Methodism in 1785. Local Anglican clergy then assisted Hampson to Oxford where he graduated MA in 1792. Returning to Sunderland he became first Curate and in 1795 Rector of St John's Chapel and functioned also at the parish church of Holy Trinity.

Though the author of a book on slave emancipation, Hampson is best remembered for his *Memoirs of the late Rev. J. Wesley* (3 vols, 1791) the first biography of its subject and initially the object of much partisan hostility, arising from suspicions of the author's motives. More objective modern scholarship has enabled a re-appraisal of it as a valuable source of contemporary reminiscence.

BIBLIOGRAPHY
DNB

JEFFREY SPITTAL

Hampton, Richard (b. Illogan, Cornwall, England, 4 April 1782; d. Porthtowan, Cornwall, England, 21 April 1858). Eccentric Cornish evangelist known as Foolish Dick. Deformed, and of limited abilities, as a result of fits when a small child, his only schooling was seven months; but there he learnt to read, and all his life he possessed only two books, the Bible and the hymn-book, both of which he knew intimately. Working in the mines and on farms, he was converted in May 1804 when he summed up his experience in Wesley's 'Wrestling Jacob'.

He opened his public work by praying in the class and prayer meetings, becoming a local preacher when he was thirty. His shrewdness as a thinker, his facile expression, and great knowledge, and readiness in apt quotation of the Scriptures, won over many who initially were critical because of his strange appearance. His work was largely in his native West Cornwall where his out-of-door preaching was very fruitful in converts. His remarkably exact memory for names, dates and places was called on when he dictated his memoirs to Thomas Garland.

BIBLIOGRAPHY
S. W. Christophers, *Foolish Dick, an Autobiography of Richard Hampton* (London [1873])

OLIVER A. BECKERLEGGE

Hanbury, Robert (b. Holfield Grange, Essex, England, 2 July 1796; d. Poles, Ware, Hertfordshire, England, 20 Jan. 1884). Anglican brewer and philanthropist. Son of Osgood Hanbury (1762–1852) and cousin of Sir THOMAS FOWELL BUXTON, he represented the important contribution that the Quakers were to make to evangelical Anglicanism in the first half of the nineteenth century. Anglicanism not only seemed appropriate for those who were upwardly mobile socially, but evangelical Anglicanism provided worship, teaching and fellowship for many of the Quakers who were emerging into a more evangelical faith. Hanbury secured his wealth, which he stewarded well, from his partnership in the brewing firm of Truman, Buxton and Company. One of his most active

involvements was with the LCM, in which evangelical Nonconformists and Anglicans worked together, a type of organization in which he might be expected to feel very much at home. Although at times he was hard on the episcopate, he was exceedingly generous to the Church of England in his home area of Hertfordshire, where he built and endowed Thundridge Church and Christ Church, Ware.

BIBLIOGRAPHY
Boase
D. M. Lewis, *Lighten Their Darkness* (London, 1986)

IAN S. RENNIE

Hanby, Thomas (b. Carlisle, England, 16 Dec. 1733; d. Nottingham, England, 29 Dec. 1796). Methodist itinerant. His father was the manager of a woollen factory. When both his parents died he was brought up by an aunt in Barnard Castle. He was episcopally confirmed but it was through a Methodist shoemaker from Leeds that he was first led towards conversion. Employed as a stuff-maker, he began to preach in 1753 and itinerated from the following year. In a lengthy ministry he served in various parts of England as well as notably in Scotland, for which work he was ordained in 1785. When he continued administering the sacraments on his return to England he was reprimanded by JOHN WESLEY but nevertheless felt bound by conscience to respond to congregational requests. He was president of conference in 1794.

BIBLIOGRAPHY
AM (1780)
MM (1797)

A. SKEVINGTON WOOD

Hands, John (b. Roade, Northamptonshire, England, 1780). Pioneer LMS missionary in India. Educated at Gosport under DAVID BOGUE, he arrived at Bellary in 1810. There he learned Kannada and worked on a grammar, a dictionary, and a Kannada version of the Synoptic Gospels. His Kannada version of the New Testament appeared in 1815. A church, a charity school for orphans, and a school for Indians were also founded. The school was so successful that a second school was founded. Although Hands started a Tract Society and made long itinerations in 1815, he did not see his first convert until 1819. In 1824, Hands raised 7,000 rupees to build a church. He established a press in 1826 which printed a number of Kannada works, as well as Telegu books. After furloughs from 1828 to 1832 and 1835 to 1838, from 1838 he worked in Bangalore following a scandal in WILLIAM CAMPBELL's Christian village. Hands left India in 1841.

One of Hands's greatest achievements was to visit Cuddapah every cold season and start a movement of conversions among people of the Mala caste. This movement, fostered by Verappa, a Brahmin convert, and Venkappa, a Sat-Sudra farmer, gathered momentum in the 1860s. Because of this Hands can be considered one of the builders of the Church in India.

E. M. JACKSON

Hankey, Thomson (b. Dalston, near London, 5 June 1805; d. London, 13 Jan. 1893). British MP and banker. The elder son of a prominent West Indian merchant, an evangelical, in 1857 he became senior partner in his father's firm. He made a fortune in shipbuilding. He was a Bank of England director from 1835, acted as its deputy director from 1849 to 1851, and as governor from 1851–3. Hankey was also Liberal MP for Peterborough (1853–68 and 1874–80).

A member of the Political Economy Club (1855–77) and a pamphleteer, he strenuously promoted liberal economic theory and its application, was prominent in the 1844 Bank Act debate, and in the aftermath of the 1866 banking panic. His letters to w. e. gladstone are in the British Library. Hankey was treasurer of the Foreign Sailor's Society and was on the original committee of the District Visiting Society.

BIBLIOGRAPHY
BLC
Boase
DNB
Record (22 May 1852)
The Times (16 January 1893): 10

JONATHAN BURKE CUTMORE
DONALD M. LEWIS

Hankinson, Edward Francis Edwards. *See* HANKINSON, ROBERT EDWARD

Hankinson, Robert (1769–1863). *See* HANKINSON, ROBERT EDWARD (1798–1868)

Hankinson, Robert Edward (b. King's Lynn, Norfolk, England, 3 Dec. 1798; d. North Creake, Norfolk, England, 27 March 1868). Anglican clergyman. He was the eldest son of Robert Hankinson (1769–1863), a Norfolk clergyman closely associated with early leaders of Anglican evangelicalism. He and both his brothers also became ministers. Thomas Edward Hankinson (1805–43) was minister of St Matthew's Chapel, Denmark Hill, Camberwell, and a prolific religious author and prizewinning poet; and Edward Francis Edwards Hankinson (1810–1903) held various charges in Norfolk.

Hankinson took his BA from Corpus Christi College, Cambridge in 1821 and then became Curate of St Stephen's, Walpole in Norfolk under his father. After a brief curacy in Hampshire in 1830, he removed to Pakefield in Norfolk to serve as curate under the zealous evangelical, FRANCIS CUNNINGHAM. From 1833–7 he was a curate and popular lecturer at Norwich. Then, for ten years

he was minister of a proprietary chapel at Hampstead in London before returning to a charge previously held by his father, becoming Rector of King's Lynn, Norfolk (1847–50). He was Rector of Halesworth in Suffolk from 1850–63 and Rector of North Creake in Norfolk from 1863 until his death. Serving for a time as domestic chaplain to the Bishop of Norwich, he was from 1857 also Archdeacon. He published a few sermons, edited a hymnal for his own congregation at Lynn, and edited some of his brother Thomas' writings posthumously. (Boase wrongly credits him with some of his brother's work.) While he advocated evangelical causes and supported the District Visiting Society and CMS, he withdrew from the interdenominational LCM under pressure from his bishop in 1838.

All four Hankinsons were educated at Cambridge, held moderate evangelical views, supported missionary causes and maintained a primary loyalty to the Established Church. Together, they exerted a significant evangelical influence in East Anglia.

BIBLIOGRAPHY
Al. Cant.
T. E. Hankinson, *Sketch of the Life of T. E. Hankinson ... in a Series of His Own Letters and Unpublished Poems* (Norwich, England, 1861)

D. B. HINDMARSH

Hankinson, Thomas Edward. *See* HANKINSON, ROBERT EDWARD

Hanna, Hugh (b. Dromora, Ireland, 1824; d. Belfast, 1892). Irish Presbyterian minister. The son of Peter Hanna, a farmer, he was educated at Old College, Belfast and ordained minister of Berry Street Presbyterian Church in February 1852. Under his leadership this congregation became the largest in Belfast, moving to the newly built and imposing St Enoch's in Carlile Circus in 1872. The flourishing Sunday school attached to the church was composed largely of adults and provided an encouraging example of pastoral success. Hanna's evangelical zeal and ardent anti-Catholicism made him a prominent and controversial figure in Belfast life at a period when sectarian tension was rising. As 'Roaring Hanna', proclaiming the right to preach the Gospel against the tyranny of 'Romish mobs', his street-preaching activities were often the subject of controversy, but they assured his position as a hero of popular Protestant conservatism. He was commissioner for national education between 1880 and 1892, and following his death a bronze statue was erected in Belfast to his memory. Hanna exemplifies a tradition of popular politico-religious leadership which has become an inherent part of the Ulster heritage.

BIBLIOGRAPHY
Presbyterian Historical Society of Ireland, *A History of Congregations in the Presbyterian Church in Ireland 1610–1982* (Belfast, 1982)

J. McConnell, *Presbyterianism in Belfast* (Belfast, 1912)

MYRTLE HILL

Hanna, William (b. Belfast, 26 Nov 1808; d. London, 24 May 1882). Minister and author. Son of Samuel Hanna, an Irish presbyterian minister and professor, and educated at Glasgow and Edinburgh universities, he became parish minister at East Kilbride 1835, and at Skirling, Peebleshire, 1837, leading this congregation into the FCS in 1843. He became colleague of THOMAS GUTHRIE in Free St John's Edinburgh in 1850, engaging in home mission work which resulted in formation of the Pleasance Church. Awarded LL D by Glasgow 1852 and DD by Edinburgh 1864, he resigned his pastoral ministry in 1867. Known mainly for his memoirs of the life and writings of his father-in-law, THOMAS CHALMERS (Edinburgh, 1849–52), he briefly edited the NBR and wrote Biblical, biographical and historical works, including volumes on the life, ministry, passion and resurrection of our Lord, on the martyrs of the Scottish Reformation, and on Wycliffe and the Huguenots. His publication of the letters of THOMAS ERSKINE of Linlathen (1877), friend of JOHN MCLEOD CAMPBELL, indicates his theological stance.

BIBLIOGRAPHY
DNB
W. Ewing, *Annals of the FCS 1843–1900* (Edinburgh, 1914)
Fasti

HUGH M. CARTWRIGHT

Hannah, John Sr (b. Lincoln, England, 3 Nov. 1792; d. Didsbury, England, 29 Dec. 1867). Wesleyan minister and theologian. He showed early ability as a scholar and became a local preacher while still in his teens. His offer to accompany COKE to India in 1813 came to nothing, but he entered the ministry a year later. His outstanding gifts as a preacher won him early recognition. In 1824 and again in 1856 he represented British Wesleyanism in America. He became the first theological tutor of the Theological Institution at Hoxton in 1834, moving to Didsbury when the northern branch was established in 1843. He served twice as secretary of the conference (1840–2 and 1854–8) and was president in 1842 and 1851.

He combined a loyalty to Methodism with wide ecclesiastical sympathies. His publications included an inaugural lecture on *Ministerial Training* (London, 1860) and *Introductory Lectures on the Study of Christian Theology* (London, 1872).

BIBLIOGRAPHY
J. Dixon, *Memorial Sermon* (London, 1868)
DNB
W. B. Pope, memoir prefixed to *Introductory Lectures on the Study of Christian Theology* (London, 1872)

JOHN A. VICKERS

Hänsel, Charles Lewis Frederick (b. Bavaria, *c.* 1797). *Fl.* 1825–37. CMS missionary to Sierra Leone and Jamaica. Hänsel studied at Basel Seminary and trained briefly at the newly opened CMS training school at Islington (London) in 1826 before being ordained (deacon and priest 1826) by the Bishop of London. On 9 January 1827 he was sent by the CMS to Sierra Leone to work at the Christian Institution at Freetown. He served in Sierra Leone until 1834 (with two furloughs in Britain) and then transferred to the CMS work in Jamaica, presumably to work with W. K. BETTS. He left for Jamaica on 23 October 1835 but withdrew from CMS on 5 April 1837. He later served as an Anglican rector in Hamilton, Canada West (now Ontario) and continued to support the CMS financially.

BIBLIOGRAPHY
D. T. B[arry], *CMS Register of Missionaries and Native Clergy* (privately printed) (London, 1906)

DONALD M. LEWIS

Hanson, Thomas (b. Horbury, Yorkshire, England, May 1734; d. Horbury, Yorkshire, England, 18 Oct. 1804). Methodist itinerant. Baptized 2 June 1734, he was attracted by Methodist preachers as an apprentice clothier. On moving to Netherthong he was helped by two local schoolmasters who taught him accountancy and the rudiments of Latin and Greek. Back in Horbury some four years later he was converted by his brother Joseph and read JOHN WESLEY's *Works* and volumes in the *Christian Library*. He began to exhort and then to preach in Ossett. Encouraged by THOMAS OLIVERS he became an itinerant in 1760, starting in York and finishing at Huddersfield. His ministry was unusually productive in terms of converts. He refused to involve himself in unnecessary doctrinal controversies, especially in the area of predestination. He served on the committee of the Preachers' Fund. 'He was a plain, honest, faithful, zealous man', according to the Minutes.

BIBLIOGRAPHY
AM (1780)
MM (1805)

A SKEVINGTON WOOD

Hape (b. Tahiti; d. *c.* 1851). Tahitian missionary to Tonga and Rapa (Society Islands). Hape, trained by JOHN DAVIES of the LMS and intended for Fiji, was detained *en route* in 1826, with his companion Tafeta, by the Chief ALEAMOTU'A on Tongatapu. They taught school and led worship. Tafeta went home in 1827; Hape stayed until 1828, then served for many years on Rapa. Resourceful, faithful – and a hunchback, he prepared Aleamotua's later reception of the WMMS.

BIBLIOGRAPHY
J. Garrett, *To Live Among the Stars* (Geneva and Suva, 1982)

JOHN GARRETT

Harbottle, Joseph (b. Tottlebank, near Ulverston, Lancashire, England, 25 Sept. 1798; d. Accrington, Lancashire, England, 19 Jan. 1864). English Baptist minister. The son of the minister of the Tottlebank church for almost half a century, he was converted at 15 and baptized in 1819, a delay which he subsequently regarded as a sin. A good classical scholar, he soon started lay preaching, before moving to Horton in 1822 to prepare for the ministry under Dr WILLIAM STEADMAN, at the same time undertaking some language teaching for the other students. An advocate of 'the doctrines of the Cross and the free promises of a full redemption in the blood of the Lamb', in 1823 he accepted a call to the church at Accrington and ministered fruitfully to a fast growing congregation until 1846. His personal philanthropy was seen in his hiring a man and a donkey in times of distress in the cotton industry to distribute food and clothing provided by himself from his own limited salary. As secretary of the Lancashire and Yorkshire Association, he sought to moderate its Calvinism. From 1835 to 1839 he was also secretary of the County Home Mission, his 1835 Association Letter being entitled, 'The Means of Revival' and that of 1838, 'The duty of individual effort for the conversion of souls'. Already in his Accrington pastorate he was offering preliminary training to those who sensed a call to the ministry, and in 1841 he began, with David Griffiths, who became his co-pastor, to combine the pastorate with the classical tutorship of a new college established in Accrington, but this came to an end in 1848. In the following year Mr Harbottle began his ministry in Oswaldtwistle, 1849–62 which in 1859 withdrew from the Lancashire and Cheshire Association over the supposed liberalism of an Association Letter written by Charles Williams, joining the close-communion North Western Association when it was founded in 1860. Returning to Accrington in 1862, Harbottle became pastor of a newly established cause in Barnes Street, serving there till his death.

BIBLIOGRAPHY
Baptist Handbook (1865)
T. Taylor, *J. Harbottle* (London, 1866)

J. H. Y. BRIGGS

Harcourt, Francis Vernon (b. Rose Castle near Carlisle, Cumberland, 7 Jan. 1801; d. Buxted Park near Uckfield, Sussex, 23 Apr. 1880). British MP. He was the tenth child of Edward Vernon Harcourt, Archbishop of York, and brother of FREDERICK EDWARD VERNON HARCOURT, and OCTAVIUS HENRY CECIL VERNON HARCOURT. Educated at Sandhurst, he entered the army in 1816, was promoted to captain in 1834, was placed on half pay in 1840, and became a colonel in 1846. Harcourt was Tory MP for the Isle of Wight (1852–7) and served for some time as magistrate and Deputy-Lieutenant of the Isle of Wight and Sheriff of Sussex. In 1837 he married Lady Catherine Julia, the elder daughter of the Earl of Liverpool. Harcourt was active in the CPAS Committee and the LCM from 1837 to 1859.

BIBLIOGRAPHY
Boase
Stenton

JONATHAN BURKE CUTMORE
DONALD M. LEWIS

Harcourt, Frederick Edward Vernon (b. 1790; d. London, 30 April 1883). Naval officer and anti-Catholic leader. The fourth son of the Most Reverend Edward Venables Vernon Harcourt, Archbishop of York, and his wife Anne (née Leveson-Gower), daughter of the first Marquess of Stafford, he entered the Royal Navy as a midshipman in February 1803. He served with distinction, being promoted to lieutenant in 1809, and captain in 1814. Later, although on half pay after the end of the Napoleonic Wars, he attained the rank of admiral. In 1829 he married Martha, daughter of Admiral John Richard Delap Tollemache.

Together with GEORGE FINCH (his wife's brother-in-law) and JAMES EDWARD GORDON, he played a key role in the early development of the British Reformation Society, and remained for many years one of the most active and conscientious members of its committee. In 1853 he wrote to the *Record* forcefully attacking Gordon for the latter's support of the Protestant Association and the English Church Missions to Roman Catholics against the Reformation Society. Also in 1853 he published *The Protestant Missionary's Catechism*, which was used by the society's lay agents.

BIBLIOGRAPHY
D. M. Lewis, *Lighten Their Darkness* (Westport, CT, 1986)
W. R. O'Byrne, *A Naval Biographical Dictionary* (London, 1849)
J. Wolffe, *The Protestant Crusade in Great Britain* (Oxford, 1991)

JOHN WOLFFE

Harcourt, Octavius Henry Cyril Vernon (b. Rose Castle, Cumberland, England, 25 December 1793; d. Swinton Park, Yorkshire, England, 14 August 1863). Naval officer and church builder. Harcourt was the eighth son of the Most Reverend Edward Venables Vernon Harcourt, Archbishop of York, and his wife Anne (née Leveson-Gower), daughter of the first Marquess of Stafford. He entered the Royal Navy as a midshipman in August 1806, served in Egypt, Spain and the West Indies, and attained the rank of captain in 1827. In 1834–6 he surveyed the coast of Central America and California. On half pay from 1836, he eventually, by seniority, attained the rank of vice-admiral.

On 22 February 1836 Harcourt married Anne, widow of William Danby. Through this marriage he acquired Swinton Park, near Masham (Yorkshire). During the 1840s he paid for the building and endowment of St Paul's Church in the neighbouring village of Healey, the first significant work of the evangelical architect E. B. Lamb. He also built a church at Brent Tor (Devon) and restored that at Masham, where he also erected and endowed almshouses. Harcourt was Sheriff of Yorkshire in 1848. An active evangelical layman, he supported the CPAS, the LDOS and the EA.

BIBLIOGRAPHY
Boase
DNB
P. Howell and I. Sutton, *The Faber Guide to Victorian Churches* (London, 1989)
W. R. O'Byrne, *A Naval Biographical Dictionary* (London, 1849)

JOHN WOLFFE

Hardcastle, Charles (b. Yorkshire, England, 22 July 1793; d. Waterford, Ireland, 1 July 1847). Baptist minister. Little is known of Charles's background, but he served for three years as assistant minister of the Baptist church in Dudley, Worcestershire. After a trial period he was called as minister of Waterford Baptist church in Ireland in May 1826. In the following year he married Susannah Williams, who had nine children. Four of them survived their parents, one daughter marrying Charles's successor as minister. With the support of the Baptist Irish Society, Charles undertook evangelistic work around Waterford. He travelled to Dublin and other centres, becoming a leader in the affairs of the Southern Baptist Association during the 1840s. In the famine of 1846–7, he served on the Waterford Relief Committee. His wife died of typhus in March 1847. Charles himself succumbed four months later.

BIBLIOGRAPHY
Waterford Church Book (unpublished)

DAVID WILLIAM BEBBINGTON

Hardcastle, Joseph (b. Leeds, England, 7 Dec. 1752; d. Hatcham House, Surrey, England, 3 March 1819). Methodist cotton importer and shipper. Hardcastle arrived in London at 15 to join an uncle in business. A member of the Bury Street Independent Chapel, he was director of the Sierra Leone Company from 1791, and treasurer of the LMS and the Village Itinerancy Society. In 1802 he travelled to Paris with WILLIAM WILBERFORCE to inquire about starting evangelistic work there; the dearth of Bibles they encountered sparked their interest in the BFBS. Not only was Hardcastle an active evangelical and 'consistent nonconformist' (Morison, 1844: 47), but the counting-house he shared with his partner JOSEPH REYNER, and his later residence at Hatcham, were the settings for many meetings of the LMS, RTS, and BFBS.

BIBLIOGRAPHY
R. H. Martin, *Evangelicals United* (Metuchen, NJ, 1983)
J. Morison, *Fathers and Founders of the LMS* (London, 1844)

LESLIE HOWSAM

Harding, Harris (b. Horton, Nova Scotia, BNA, 10 Oct. 1761; d. Yarmouth, Nova Scotia, BNA, 7 March 1854). New Light evangelist and Baptist minister. A disciple of HENRY ALLINE, Harding was one of the most successful New Light Baptist preachers in early nineteenth-century Nova Scotia; he played a key role in triggering a number of revivals in the Yarmouth region and he was also, largely because of his pastoral skills, directly responsible for ensuring that by the 1850s the Baptists made up well over 50 per cent of the population of Yarmouth County. Though not educated himself, Harding supported the creation of Acadia College in 1838 and he was also very active in the Nova Scotia Temperance movement and the Bible Society.

BIBLIOGRAPHY
DCB
G. A. Rawlyk, 'From New Light to Baptist: Harris Harding and the Second Great Awakening in Nova Scotia, in *Repent and Believe*, ed. B. Moody (Hantsport, 1980): 1–26

GEORGE RAWLYK

Harding, John (b. Bloomsbury, London, 7 Jan. 1805; d. Ore near Hastings, Sussex, England, 18 June 1874). Bishop of Bombay. Son of William Harding, chief clerk in the transport office, he was educated at Westminster School and Worcester College, Oxford (BA 1826; MA 1829; BD and DD 1851). After he was ordained (deacon 1827; priest 1829) and served a curacy in Cambridgeshire, he became minister at Park Chapel, Chelsea in 1834 and Rector of St Andrews-by-the-Wardrobe with St Anne's Blackfriars in London in 1836. This church had long been an stronghold of evangelical Anglicanism (WILLIAM ROMAINE had ministered there). Harding soon became a leader among the evangelical incumbents in the capital whose numbers increased rapidly in the late 1830s and 1840s. He was an honourary secretary of the CPAS and a committee member of the CMS. Archbishop J. B. SUMNER selected Harding as the second Bishop of Bombay in 1851.

Harding supported the 1855 call for further CMS missionaries to be sent to Bombay, but was critical of the SPG, which started in his diocese after the Indian Mutiny (1857). Harding did not shine as a bishop and travelled little outside of the three main centres of his province. In 1867, he returned to England due to ill health and resigned his see in 1869. He lived the rest of his life near Hastings.

BIBLIOGRAPHY
Al. Ox., ii: 604
Annual Register (1874): 156
Boase
DNB

DONALD M. LEWIS

Hardinge, (Sir) Charles (b. Hampton, Middlesex, England, 22 March 1780; d. Tunbridge Wells, Kent, England, 3 Feb. 1864). Anglican clergyman. Hardinge was educated at University College, Oxford (BA 1801; MA 1804) and succeeded his father in the family baronetcy in 1826. He was rector of Crowhurst (Sussex) (1804–64) and also followed his father as vicar of Tonbridge (1809–64). His writings included *A Plain Exposition of the Election of Grace* (1847) and a contribution to the Gorham controversy on *Baptismal Regeneration* (1850). He was a supporter of the CPAS.

BIBLIOGRAPHY
Boase, I: 1328

ARTHUR POLLARD

Hardy, John (b. Parish of Horton, Bradford, Yorkshire, England, *c.* 1773; d. Dunstall, Staffordshire, England, 29 Sept. 1855). Anglican lawyer, MP, and industrialist. In a remarkable way his life centred around Bradford. Born in the town, he returned after his legal training in London, making his home at Odsall. He was the chief owner of the iron works at Low Moor, where he was an active participant in the life of Holy Trinity Parish Church, where Joshua Fawcett, a member of an old West Riding evangelical family, was minister. He was MP for Bradford (1832–7 and 1841–7). He gave large sums of money for church extension, and was known as 'the great Bradford Church builder of that day'.

Although his son-in-law, JOHN WOOD, was the leading woollen manufacturer in the campaign to reduce factory hours, Hardy as a Whig found it difficult publicly to support a movement so aligned with ancient, organic conceptions of the state. But in Parliament he did vote for Lord Ashley's (*see* SHAFTESBURY) legislation. He was married to Isabel, daughter of the Gathornes of Kirkby Lonsdale, and some of their descendants, along with many of those of the Clapham Sect, became key components in the intellectual aristocracy of England.

BIBLIOGRAPHY
Boase

IAN S. RENNIE

Hare, Edward (b. Kingston-upon-Hull, Yorkshire, England, 19 Sept. 1774; d. Exeter, England, 14 March 1818). Methodist minister. His father was a Methodist leader in the city, a ships's chandler by trade, his mother a pious Baptist. He was educated at the Hull Grammar School under the tutelage of JOSEPH MILNER. Understandably in that seaport an experimental sea voyage led to his being bound apprentice in 1788 to a sea captain. In 1793 he returned from a voyage during a revival in the Hull Wesleyan circuit, then led by ALEXANDER MATHER, a good administrator and powerful evangelist, who had been ordained by JOHN WESLEY himself, and who the previous year had been elected president of the conference. Hare was soundly converted, constantly attended prayer meetings in George Yard Chapel and private houses, and came under the personal supervision

and encouragement of Alexander Mather as he ventured to exhort his fellow worshippers.

His apprenticeship not being ended, however, Hare then embarked as chief mate on a voyage to Italy, serving a well-known Methodist captain, Francis Reynolds. They sailed on the *Olive Branch*, bound for Leghorn, on 19 June 1794. Hare gained permission from the captain to begin nightly prayer meetings for the crew in the main cabin, and also to preach to passengers during the captain's Prayer Book Service every Lord's Day. Captain Reynolds later described for Mrs Hare her husband's nervous beginnings but growing confidence throughout the voyage, which ended with their capture by a French squadron of war ships on 7 October 1795 off Cape St Vincent. During his incarceration in the ship's hold, and later in Cadiz, he found support in deep biblical meditation. Eventually he was set ashore on the coast of Cornwall. Thence he walked back to Hull, carrying 'his society-ticket, watch, hymn-book, and Bible, and as much money as he calculated would serve him with bread and water during a journey of 250 miles'. He stopped about every thirty miles to request 'the favour of a lodging in the hay-chamber or some out-building' – almost invariably granted – but never accepted money. He arrived home early in 1796. 'Resolved to go no more to sea', he worked in his father's business, but employed 'every leisure hour in reading such books and pursuing such studies as were calculated to improve his mind, and prepare him for usefulness in the Church of God'.

He was soon taken on to the Hull circuit plan as a local preacher, and on 1 June 1798 JOSEPH BENSON (the assistant that year, and elected president at the conference in July) entered in his diary that in consultation with other local Methodist leaders summoned to the George Yard vestry he had commissioned 'Edward Hare, a promising young man', to fill a ministerial vacancy in the York circuit until the conference. This Hare did to such good effect that at the conference he was accepted as an itinerant preacher on trial, and stationed in the Sunderland circuit. Appointed in 1799 to Ripon – where he fell in love with his future bride, named Hindrie – in 1800 Benson requested him for the London circuit, in which he himself was stationed as assistant, before becoming editor in 1804. As Mather had done before him, Benson took this 'promising young man' under his wing. Hare lodged with the Bensons in 'the chapel house' in City Road, London, and his Hull Grammar School training in the classics was sharpened into a true familiarity with the Greek New Testament during Benson's tuition of his own children. Thus in John Wesley's own former headquarters he came to love Wesley's doctrine and Wesley's discipline, and to regard them as central in his own all too brief ministry.

On 1 August 1801, Hare returned to Ripon to marry his former sweetheart, and took his bride (whose grandmother had been converted under the ministry of WILLIAM GRIMSHAW) to the centre of Grimshaw's early ministry, Todmorden. From here they moved successively to Oldham (1802–3) and Stockport (1804), where (as his wife later wrote to Benson, hinting at some disciplinary problems) he evinced 'his steady attachment to the discipline and rules of Methodism, and on all occasions stood as an iron pillar strong, and steadfast as a wall of brass' (cf. Jeremiah 1: 18). In 1805 they spent a peaceful, 'profitable year' in Nottingham, which was cut short against his and the circuit's wishes by the 1806 Conference decision that he should join a senior preacher, Miles Martindale, in assuaging the severe doctrinal turmoil in Rochdale, to which they were therefore appointed.

Joseph Cooke (1775–1811), had been appointed to Rochdale in 1803 and 1804. Early in 1805 Cooke had introduced controversy by preaching two sermons expressing doubt about two cardinal points in Wesley's teaching, justification by faith and the witness of the Holy Spirit. The conference of 1805 therefore stationed him in Sunderland to cool his heels, under the supervision of Miles Martindale, with the understanding that he should refrain from such teaching for a year, and that then the doctrinal charges against him would be reconsidered. In fact he used the interval to publish the substance of those sermons – in Rochdale! – and the 1806 Conference promptly expelled him. A group of his Rochdale supporters built a new chapel for him there, which constituted the first chapel of the Methodist Unitarian Movement. After Cooke's death the movement fizzled out, though it was important in the 1844 beginnings of the Cooperative Movement in Rochdale. More important from our standpoint, this marked the birth of Edward Hare's ministry in the footsteps of John Wesley and JOHN W. FLETCHER as the defender of the Methodist faith for the following decade.

In 1806 Miles Martindale duly came to stabilize the Rochdale circuit, while Hare set the Methodist theological record straight on 28 October that year by publishing *Remarks on Two Sermons ... Lately Published by Mr. Joseph Cooke, in Five Letters addressed to the Author*. This Cooke contested in 1807 with a major doctrinal attack, *Methodism Condemned by Methodist Preachers*. This Hare countered on 14 April with *Genuine Methodism Acquitted, and Spurious Methodism Condemned*. He nailed the coffin shut on 30 July 1807, with *The Sentence Confirmed*.

Edward Hare was so sensitive about Wesley's teaching that in 1809 he even published two letters to MELVILLE HORNE, one of John Wesley's preachers who followed John Fletcher at Madeley, intimating that he was mistaken in the scriptural doctrine of Christian assurance of salvation. In 1810 Hare also published a letter to Dr William Magee (1766–1831, later Archbishop of Dublin), claiming that in the second edition of his *Discourses on the Scriptural Doctrines of Atonement and Sacrifice* (1809) his charges against Methodism had been false. In 1814 he published a 400-page indexed *Preservative Against the Errors of Socinianism*, castigating John Grundy's Unitarian lectures in Cross Street, Manchester, 'on the principal doctrines of Christianity'. In 1815 he published *The Exclusive Claims of Episcopal Ordination Examined and Rejected, and the Methodist Ministry Vindicated*, and followed this in 1816 with *A Further Vindication of the Methodist Ministry*, as well as *A Caveat Against Antinomianism*, which was itself followed in 1817 by *A Second Caveat Against Antinomianism*. In 1817 also Edward Hare published a large *Treatise on the Scriptural Doctrine of Justification*.

By March 1817, however, Edward Hare was marked for death by overwork and pulmonary consumption, at the age of 42, forbidden not only to preach, but even to engage in conversation, though he struggled to write *An Apology for Continuing in the Steadfast Belief of the Eternal Sonship of our Lord and Saviour Jesus Christ*. This was published posthumously in 1818 by Joseph Benson, who also edited Hare's *Pulpit Remains* from his manuscripts. Hare's lengthy official biography in the *Minutes* of his Church claimed that in addition to a deep love of family and friends, he dedicated himself to 'the great doctrines of Methodism', for which he 'laboured with high reputation and great success', and finally characterized him as 'this great and good man'.

SELECT WRITINGS
E. Hare, *Pulpit Remains ... To Which is Prefixed a Memoir of His Life, by the Rev. Joseph Benson*, ed. J. Benson (London, 1821): xii, 3–39, 40–416

BIBLIOGRAPHY
H. McLachlan, *The Methodist Unitarian Movement* (Manchester England, 1919): xi, 151

FRANK BAKER

Harford, John (Scandrett) (b. Bristol, England, 8 Oct. 1787; d. Blaise Castle, near Bristol, 16 Apr. 1866). Banker, biographer, and connoisseur. The son of a prominent Quaker banker of the same name, Harford was first introduced to evangelicalism at Christ's College, Cambridge. The deaths of three siblings led to a religious conversion and his baptism into the Church of England in 1809. In 1815 he succeeded to his father's property due to the premature death of his elder brother. Until his retirement in 1845 Harford was a partner in a respected Bristol banking firm.

Harford was the close friend of evangelical leaders, W. WILBERFORCE, H. MORE, T. BIDDULPH, Bishop H. RYDER and Archbishop J. B. SUMNER, and was an important early supporter of the CMS and the BFBS. He was the hero of More's *Coelebs in Search of a Wife*, wrote a life of Burgess, and was author of *Recollections of William Wilberforce* (1864). He was also a vociferous opponent of social utopianism, attacking Thomas Paine in print and Robert Owen in debate.

Harford, like his father who commissioned Nash to design the famous Blaise Hamlet workers' cottages, was a notable connoisseur of fine art and architecture. He was the travelling companion of the portraitist Sir Thomas Lawrence, employed John Flaxman to illustrate his monograph on Greek tragedy, owned an important collection of European paintings, and wrote a two-volume life of Michelangelo.

Harford and his wife Louisa spent several years in Italy. So prominent a part did they play in the life of the British community in Rome that Mrs Harford was described by Pope Pius VII as 'the fair heretic'. Harford's brother Abraham, took the name Harford-Battersby in 1815 so as to inherit the property of his uncle William Battersby who died in 1812.

BIBLIOGRAPHY
CO, 66 (July 1866): 489–98·
DNB and corrigenda
A. M. E. Harford, *The Annals of the Harford Family* (London, 1909)
Western Daily Press (17 April 1866)

JONATHAN BURKE CUTMORE

Hargreaves, James (b. Bacup, Lancashire, England, 13 Nov. 1768; d. Waltham Abbey, Essex, England, 16 Sept. 1845). Baptist minister. From age three, Hargreaves was raised by a paternal uncle who compelled him to work in a public house. While he received no formal religious education, Hargreaves began to read the Bible and to preach. Hargreaves adopted Baptist convictions and was called to a succession of pastorates at Bolton (1794), Ogden (1798), where he also taught school, Little Wild Street in London (1822) and Waltham Abbey (1829). Hargreaves espoused several evangelical causes, including the Bible Society and Baptist ministerial education. From 1824 to 1831 he acted as secretary of the Baptist Building Fund, which encouraged church extension. In 1818 he joined the London Peace Society, serving as its secretary for twenty years and speaking frequently on behalf of peace. Hargreaves wrote tracts and addresses on a variety of subjects. His publications included *Universal and Permanent Peace a Desirable Object* (1818), *The Doctrine of Eternal Reprobation Disproved* (1821); *Essays and Letters on Important Theological Subjects* (1833).

BIBLIOGRAPHY
DNB
Herald of Peace, 4, new series (1845): 364
P. J. Saffery, 'Memoir of the Late Rev. James Hargreaves', *BaptMag.* (1847): 196–201, 273–7

P. R. DEKAR

Hargrove, Charles (Frearson) (b. Limerick, Ireland, 1792; d. 1869). Anglican clergyman; Brethren leader. Converted while studying medicine at Edinburgh, he decided to seek ordination in the Church of England. After graduating from Trinity College, Dublin (BA 1819), he became Perpetual Curate of Turlough, Castlebar (1822) and Rector of Kilmena, near Westport (1830), Ireland. He indulged in extraparochial preaching under the auspices of the Irish Church Home Mission, came under the influence of JOHN NELSON DARBY and other Brethren, and began to question the baptismal theology and other aspects of the Church of England. In 1835 he resigned his living, associated with the Brethren, and eventually settled in London.

His pamphlet, *Some Thoughts on Ministry*, was a notable contribution to the Brethren debate on the nature of ministry in the church. Despite his early associations with Darby, Hargrove did not follow him in the division of 1849. Hargrove's son, Charles became first a Roman Catholic then a Unitarian, and is the subject of L. P. Jack's biography, *From Authority to Freedom*.

BIBLIOGRAPHY
J. D'Arcy Sirr, *Westport Darbyism Exposed* (Dublin, 1843)
—, *A Memoir of the Honourable and Most Reverend Power Ie Poer Trench* (Dublin, 1845)

HAROLD H. ROWDON

Harington, John Herbert (b. 1764; d. London, 9 Apr. 1828). East India Company servant and orientalist. Harington joined the East India Company's service as a writer in 1780. In 1783 he became a Persian translator in the revenue department. He was a law specialist at Lord Wellesley's Fort William College, becoming president of the council in 1809. In 1811 he was made Chief Judge of the Sadr Diwani Adalat. In 1822 he became a member of the Supreme Council of Bengal, and by 1825 was its leading member. In 1825 he became president of the Board of Trade. He was the most distinguished Persian scholar of his time. Secretary of the Royal Asiatic Society, vice-president in 1797 and president in 1822, his publications include translations of the Sufi poet Sadi, a Sanskrit-English dictionary and an analysis of Bengal laws and regulations. He discovered the inscriptions on the Nagarjuni caves of Gaya and wrote an article on Buddhist stupas in Ceylon. He was particularly interested in Indian education and presented 'Observations for the Promotion of Science and Literature amongst the Inhabitants in India' to the Bengal government, advocating 'engraftment' of European knowledge on to Indian knowledge as the way to press forward. He was the first president of the Committee of Public Instruction set up in 1823, and chaired the first meeting of the Calcutta School Society. While he was an Oriental scholar with a deep appreciation for the treasures of Indian civilization, he was also a committed Christian. He became president of the Calcutta branch of the BFBS in 1811, and was a member of the BFSS. He was on the committee of the SPCK and the committee of the Calcutta auxiliary of the CMS. He was one of the greatest friends of Calcutta's philanthropic societies. His wholehearted support went to any plan for the amelioration of the miseries of humanity.

BIBLIOGRAPHY
DNB
M. A. Laird, *Missionaries and Education in Bengal 1793–1837* (London, 1972)

PENELOPE CARSON

Harland, William (b. Pickering, Yorkshire, England, 1 Oct. 1801; d. Hull, Yorkshire, c. 1881). Primitive

Methodist minister. After receiving an excellent education by an Anglican clergyman, Harland became a schoolteacher. He joined the Primitive Methodist Connexion after hearing WILLIAM CLOWES preach in the open air at Robin Hood's Bay in Yorkshire. Clowes found Harland to possess considerable education and ability. Becoming a travelling preacher in 1828, Harland spent most of his ministry in the Hull circuit. He was renowned for his clear voice and diction, although he was criticized for giving sermons on topics, such as philosophy, which were found to be too esoteric for his impatient congregation. This gave way to a more practical, simple and plain style. As a result, Harland became immensely popular as a friendly and sympathetic Primitive Methodist, preaching to sailors in the seafaring vernacular and often unrefined humour. Becoming editor of the *Primitive Methodist Magazine* (1862–8); Harland was president of the conference and conference secretary four times.

BIBLIOGRAPHY
Boase
PM Mag (1881)

WAYNE J. JOHNSON

Harms, Georg Ludwig Detlef Theodor (b. 5 May 1808, Walsrode, Germany; d. 14 Nov. 1865, Hermannsburg, Germany). Lutheran theologian and founder of the Hermannsburger Mission. The son of pastor Christian Harms (1773–1848) and Lucie Frieder (1783–1833), Ludwig Harms studied at Gottingen where he had a conversion experience which brought him into the *Erweckungsbewegung*. From 1830 to 1844, he worked as a teacher and preacher in Pietist convents in Lauenberg (Elbe) and Luneberg. With a few friends, he founded (1834) the Lauenberger Missionsverien which merged (1836) with the Norddeutschen Missionsgesellschaft.

Harms was called (1844) as assistant to his father at Hermannsburg and succeeded him as pastor (1849). At the request of his parishioners, Harms founded (1849) a mission organization in Hermannsburg. His involvement in both the *Erweckungsbewegung* and the German Lutheran Confessional movement led to his alienation from the Norddeutschen Missionsgesellschaft and to the further development of his own organization with a special interest in ministry to German emigrants, colonists and native peoples. Missionaries were sent to North and South America, Papua, South Africa (worked among the Zulu) and to the German African colonies. The mission built its own ship, the *Kandace* (1853), and began (1856) the mission periodical *Hermannsburger Missionsblatt*. Harms was succeeded by his brother Theodor Harms who led the Hermannsburg Church and the mission out of the State Lutheran Church.

BIBLIOGRAPHY
H. Bartels, 'Harms, Georg Ludwig Detlef Theodor', *Neue Deutsche Biographie*, 17 (1965): 687–8

—, 'Die theologische Grundlagen der Missionsarbeit bei Ludwig Harms' (Diss. Göttingen, Germany, 1960)
H. Grafe, *Die Volkstumliche Predigt des Ludwig Harms* (Göttingen, Germany, 1965)
T. Harms, *Lebensbeschreibung des Pastors Ludwig Harms* (Hermannsburg, Germany, 1868)
H. Wagenmann, 'Harms, George Ludwig Detlef Theodor', *Allgemeine Deutsche Biographie*, 10 (1879): 612–14

DAVID BUNDY

Harper, James (b. Lanark, Scotland, 23 June 1795; d. 13 Apr. 1879). United Presbyterian minister. As Secession minister at North Leith (1819–79), Harper's preaching was much admired, even by EDWARD IRVING, a lifelong intimate. Temperamentally moderate and liberal-minded, he calmly and effectively opposed ANDREW THOMSON during the Apocrypha controversy in the BFBS, gaining a national reputation that he consolidated as editor of the Secessionist *Edinburgh Theological Magazine* (from 1826), and then of the *United Presbyterian Magazine* (from 1850). In the 1830s he publicly favoured the Reform Bill and campaigned for his friend, the Whig Lord Advocate, John Archibald Murray.

Harper served as professor of pastoral theology in the Secession seminary from 1843, and of systematic theology from 1848 in the United Presbyterian seminary. In 1876 he was made principal. Chairman of the Secession Synod in 1840, he was moderator of the United Presbyterian synod in 1860. He actively promoted presbyterian union by supporting the 1847 Secession and Relief union and in 1873 the attempted union between the United Presbyterian and Free churches. Harper was a co-founder of the EA.

BIBLIOGRAPHY
DNB
A. Thomson, *Memoir of James Harper* (Edinburgh, 1880)

JONATHAN BURKE CUTMORE

Harris, Catherine (b. England, *c.* 1804; d. Medland, England, 9 Jan. 1894). Bible Christian (BC) itinerant preacher. Harris started to itinerate in 1825 and continued in the active ministry till 1852, having had only three years leave as a supernumerary. From 1853 Harris was listed in the *BC Minutes* as a supernumerary till 1874, but she then disappears. It is likely that she remained a supernumerary till her death without her name appearing. Unfortunately there is little record of Harris's time as an itinerant, but through her work societies were revitalized and at least two of her converts became BC itinerants.

BIBLIOGRAPHY
F. W. Bourne, *The Bible Christians* (London, 1905)

E. DOROTHY GRAHAM

Harris, Howell (b. Trevecka, Breconshire, Wales, 14 Jan. 1714; d. Trevecka, Breconshire, Wales, 21 July

1773). Founder of Welsh Methodism. The third son of a carpenter who had migrated from Carmarthenshire to Breconshire, Harris was initially intended for holy orders. He was educated at several local schools, and at Llwyn-llwyd Academy near Hay-on-Wye in Breconshire. While there, the death of his father led to a need for him to secure an income for himself. He therefore began his career as a schoolmaster and kept schools at Llangorse and Llangasty, a few miles from his home.

On Palm Sunday 1735, during a service at Talgarth parish church, he heard the vicar, Pryce Davies, encouraging his parishioners to partake of the sacrament on Easter Sunday. His words signalled the beginning of Harris's conversion, a process which took several weeks. Convinced that his sins were forgiven him, he was filled with a missionary zeal, and following attempts to bring his family and friends to see their duty towards God, he expanded his sphere of activity by embarking on an open-air ministry and visiting neighbouring parishes. Though opposed by many for his 'enthusiastic' behaviour, he met with considerable success; small religious societies were established to nurture the new converts, thus laying the foundation of what was later to become known as the Welsh Methodist movement.

Harris's circumstances during the period 1735–9 accentuated his 'enthusiastic' spirit; his longing for meaningful Christian fellowship led to the possibility of joining the Dissenters and later to his first meeting with GRIFFITH JONES of Llanddowror. Having met an Anglican clergyman who could advise him on how to proceed, he was to suffer a serious setback during one of his visits to Llanddowror, and it was not until 1739 that he was able to overcome the doubts that troubled him. At the same time, he was searching for a theology which would reflect his own spiritual experiences; his criticism of the doctrines preached from the pulpits of the parish churches was often scathing, and he was tempted to look elsewhere for spiritual nourishment. Though the Dissenters were unsuccessful in their attempt to persuade him to leave the church, it was mainly through their influence that Harris became a Calvinist.

Having already met DANIEL ROWLAND in 1737, Harris's meeting with GEORGE WHITEFIELD in 1739 brought him into contact with the English revival. However, Harris was conscious of his responsibility towards his own countrymen, and though he was later to spend much of his time in London, Wales continued to be his main sphere of activity.

With the expansion of his ministry, and a rapid growth in the number of societies under his care, there appeared a need for better organization. Rules were adopted for the societies in 1740, and in the same year Harris attempted to establish a 'Society of Ministers' comprising of all the leaders of the revival in Wales. The eventual collapse of the society led him to reconsider his strategy and later to convene another meeting in January 1742. This time, the meeting was a success, and the gathering was later to become known as the first Methodist association meeting.

Though refused ordination by the Bishop of St Davids in 1736 and 1739, and despite the opposition of many Anglican clergymen to his efforts to promote the work of the Gospel, Harris continued to be a member of the Church of England throughout his life. His attachment to the church was a complex blend of loyalism and dissatisfaction, a fact which the Dissenters repeatedly attempted to use to their advantage in the hope that they would be able, through revival activity, to swell their own ranks. They were, however, to be disappointed; Harris opposed every attempt to undermine the Methodists' attachment to the church.

Despite his marriage to Anne Williams of Erwood, Radnorshire, in 1744, Harris continued with his evangelistic work. Between 1745 and 1750 tension developed between him and the other leaders of the revival in both England and Wales due to his harshness towards the society members, his views on the doctrine of the Trinity and his association with a 'prophetess', Sidney Griffith of Cefnamwlch in Caernarvonshire. This part of his career has always aroused much interest, but the nature of the relationship with Sidney Griffith remains enshrouded in mystery, and much of the comment made in the past regarding the episode has often been based on speculation rather than fact. There is little doubt that by this time Harris was very near, if not actually suffering, a severe nervous breakdown; this would be the only logical explanation for many of his actions at this time.

By the beginning of 1750, he had been totally isolated by the other Methodist leaders, and in June a separation occurred. Harris retired from the work of the revival to establish, with Sidney Griffith, a community at his home in Trevecka; the old house was demolished and new buildings erected to accommodate those who remained faithful to him and wished to make their home with him. Though Sidney Griffith died in 1752, the community survived well into the middle of the nineteenth century.

Harris's retirement lasted until 1759, when he joined the Breconshire Militia to defend Protestantism against the French Catholic threat. When the regiment was disbanded in December 1762, he was invited by the Methodist leaders to return to his former position within the movement, and in 1763 a reunion occurred.

By that time, a new revival had begun in Wales, centring on Llangeitho in Cardiganshire. Following his reinstatement, Harris resumed itinerating, but despite his valiant efforts, it could hardly be said that he was as successful during these years as he had been during the period 1735–50. He was an older man; a new generation had emerged during his absence who had to a certain extent taken the reins of the movement into their own hands, and as Harris moved among them, emphasizing the need for discipline and organization, there was friction. There were also his responsibilities at Trevecka, where the establishment of the Countess of HUNTINGDON's college in 1768 was to add to his burden.

Following the death of his wife in 1770, Harris's own health began to deteriorate. He often complained of agonizing bouts of pain, which restricted his involvement in the revival work. He died at his home on 21 July 1773, aged 59.

Apart from a few hymns, Harris's only literary contribution was a brief autobiography, completed and published by members of the Trevecka community under the title, *A Brief Account of the Life of Howell Harris* (Trevecka, 1792). Following his conversion, Harris began keeping a diary, a discipline which he kept up until his death. Though unpublished in their entirety, extracts have occasionally appeared in *Cylchgrawn Cymdeithas Hanes y Methodistiaid Calfinaidd* and other publications. 294 volumes are extant, and are currently kept at the National Library of Wales at Aberystwyth. They are always difficult to read but are unique in providing an amazingly detailed, frank and unedited account of a revivalist's life during a period of extraordinary religious activity and ferment.

BIBLIOGRAPHY
DWB
H. J. Hughes, *Life of Howell Harris* (Newport, Wales, 1892)
G. F. Nuttall, *Howel Harris* (Cardiff, Wales, 1965)
G. Tudur, 'A Critical Study, based on his own Diaries, of the Life and Work of Howell Harris and his Contribution to the Methodist Revival in Wales between 1735 and 1752' (Oxford Univ. D.Phil. thesis, 1989)

GERAINT TUDUR

Harris, James (Lampen) (b. probably Radford, Plymouth, England, 13 Feb. 1793; d. Weston-super-Mare, England, 9 Oct. 1877). Anglican clergyman and Brethren leader. The fourth son of John Harris, a Plymouth banker, he was educated at Eton and Exeter College, Oxford (1811–15) where he was later a fellow (1815–29). Ordained in 1817 he was Curate of Ringmore, South Devon (1819–26) and Perpetual Curate of Plymstock, Devon (1826–32).

His cousin, HENRY BULTEEL, introduced him to Oxford evangelicals in March 1829 which, BENJAMIN WILLS NEWTON claimed, led to his conversion. In October 1832 he seceded and became associated with Brethren at Plymouth where he played a leading role with Newton. From 1835 he edited *The Christian Witness*, the first Brethren journal, to which he contributed extensively. In 1845, having married LEGH RICHMOND's daughter, he left Plymouth and sided with JOHN NELSON DARBY against Newton. In 1847 his tract *The Sufferings of Christ as Set Forth in a Lecture on Psalm VI* which was critical of Newton, precipitated the disruption of the Brethren movement. He was later identified with Open Brethren.

BIBLIOGRAPHY
C. W. Boase, *Registrum Collegii Exoniensis* (Oxford, 1893): 112
Bodleian, Oxford, Diary of Dr John Hill 7: 37, St Edmund Hall *MSS* 67
Devon Record Office, Exeter, Curates Licence Book 1: 110; Perpetual Curates Licence Book, 29 (manuscripts 92: 78)
Pickering: 18

H. H. Rowdon, *The Origins of the Brethren Movement* (London, 1967)

HAROLD H. ROWDON

TIMOTHY C. F. STUNT

Harris, John (b. Ugborough, Devon, England, 8 March, 1802; d. St John's Wood, London, 21 Dec. 1856). Congregational minister and scholar. The son of a tailor, he secured local fame in the Bristol area as 'the boy preacher', travelling around the village chapels under the auspices of the Bristol Itinerant Society while still in his early 'teens. Trained at Hoxton, he was ordained in 1825 to the Independent congregation at Epsom which grew under his leadership. A remarkable talent for winning prize essays early established him as an author; these included his study of Christian missions published in 1842 under the title of *The Great Commission*. Appointed a tutor at Cheshunt in 1837, in the following year he both assumed the presidency and received a DD from Brown University in the United States of America, where his writings were more influential than in Britain. In 1851, he became the first principal of the amalgamated London Congregational colleges that formed New College. Chairman of the Congregational Union in 1852, he was one of the editors of *The Biblical Review*.

BIBLIOGRAPHY
DNB

J. H. Y. BRIGGS

Harris, Joseph [Gomer] (b. Llantydewi, Dyfed, S. Wales, c. 1773; d. Swansea, Glamorganshire, S. Wales, 10 Aug. 1825). Welsh Baptist minister and publisher. Little is known of his early life apart from his having rejected the religion of the Established Church in favour of that of the Baptists, being baptized at Llangloffan, Pembrokeshire, in 1793. He began preaching three years later and was ordained at the Back Lane Church, Swansea, in 1801 gaining a reputation there as a dependable pastor and stout defender of evangelical trinitarianism. It is as the initiator of Welsh periodical literature, though, that he is chiefly remembered. His *Seren Gomer* (1814–15) was the first Welsh language weekly, becoming by 1818 a monthly topical magazine.

BIBLIOGRAPHY
DWB
G. Williams, 'Gomer', 'Sylfaenydd ein Llenyddiaeth Gyfnodol', *Grym Tafodau Tân* (Llandysul, Wales, 1984): 237–67

D. DENSIL MORGAN

Harris, Richard (b. Leicester, England, Oct. 1777; d. Leicester, 2 Feb. 1854). Hosiery manufacturer, MP, and Baptist deacon. Described as both 'a self-made man and a man of God', Harris was the son of a master stocking-maker, and received his only education at St Mary's Sunday school and night school. An apprenticeship to a Quaker printer, RICHARD PHILIPS, was terminated when Philips was sent to prison for supposedly selling revolutionary literature. Sent to Nottingham to learn fancy weaving and enlisting in the army during the scares of a Napoleonic invasion, serving 1797–1802, he drifted away from his moorings, until a funeral sermon preached by WILLIAM CAREY's successor at Harvey Lane secured his conversion.

He was baptized and joined the church and married Fanny Dove, whose father had been one of Carey's deacons. He set up business on his own and prospered in fancy hosiery, doing well enough to survive the postwar depression after 1815, gaining a reputation as a fair and considerate employer, maintaining, for example, old machines alongside new ones simply to keep in employment his older workers who could not adapt to the demands of the newer technology. He was alone among the manufacturers in supporting ROBERT HALL's efforts for the frame-work knitters, his philanthropy even going so far as to support a working men's cooperative. By 1832 he had a large factory on the banks of the River Soar, employing some 4,000 men and exporting extensively within Europe and to the Americas. A member of the Anti-Corn Law League, and much concerned with Nonconformist disabilities, he was elected to the newly constituted town council in 1837 and was mayor for 1843/4. An alderman and a Justice of the Peace, he was elected MP for Leicester in 1848 as a Liberal but on a purity ticket, insisting that 'not a shilling' should be spent on improper influence. A deacon and lay preacher at Harvey Lane under Robert Hall, and J. P. MURSELL, when described as the church's 'chief supporter', he was a founder, deacon and treasurer of the new cause in Upper Charles Street.

BIBLIOGRAPHY
T. Lomas, *Memoir* (London, 1855)
S. Mitchell, *Not Disobedient* (London, 1984)
A. Temple Patterson, *Radical Leicester* (London, 1975)

J. H. Y. BRIGGS

Harrison, Benjamin (b. West Ham, London, 29 July 1771; d. Clapham Common, England, 18 May 1856). Treasurer of Guy's Hospital and deputy governor of the Hudson's Bay Company. Harrison was the fourth son of Benjamin Harrison, treasurer of Guy's Hospital and grandson of Sir Thomas Harrison, Chamberlain of the City of London. In 1797, Harrison took his father's place as treasurer of Guy's Hospital, a position which he was to hold for fifty years and in which he gained considerable notoriety for his dictatorial manner. He was also an active member of the Clapham Sect.

In 1809, Harrison was appointed to the Governing Committee of the Hudson's Bay Company. He brought his evangelical zeal to the position and promoted an interest in mission work among the directors, hoping to obtain company sponsorship of a mission to the Indians of Rupert's Land and support for religious education for company servants and their families. He developed an extensive plan for the establishment of schools throughout the company's lands in North America although he was able to obtain an initial commitment of just £30 in 1816 to purchase books. When fellow evangelical NICHOLAS GARRY became a director of the company the following year, Harrison was able to obtain a larger commitment which permitted the appointment of JOHN WEST as the first company chaplain. Harrison succeeded Garry as deputy governor of the Hudson's Bay Company in 1835 and served in that capacity for three years. He also served as deputy governor of the South Sea Company, chair of the Exchequer Loan Board and as an appeal commissioner following the introduction of the income tax in London.

Harrison married Mary Le Pelly in 1797. The eldest of their three sons, also Benjamin, was the author of four of the *Tracts for the Times* and later became Archdeacon of Maidstone. A number of geographic features in the Canadian north were named in honour of Harrison, including the Harrison Islands.

BIBLIOGRAPHY
DNB

KERRY M. ABEL

Harrison, Sarah. *See* KIRKLAND, SARAH

Harriss, Samuel (b. Hanover, VA, BNA, 12 Jan. 1724: d. Pittsylvania, VA, USA, 1799). Public official, state legislator, soldier, and Separate Baptist minister. Reared in the Anglican tradition, Harriss served as a public official until his conversion to Baptist thought in 1759. He was baptized by DANIEL MARSHALL in that same year and ordained in 1769. From 1759 to 1770 he served as an itinerant evangelist throughout Virginia and North Carolina, and was persecuted and imprisoned for his beliefs. During the Revolutionary War he served as a chaplain to the Continental forces. He planted 22 churches before his death.

BIBLIOGRAPHY
AAP
W. S. Simpson, *Virginia Baptist Ministers, 1760–90* (Richmond, VA, 1990): 31–9

WADE A. HORTON

Harrowby, (first) Earl of [Ryder, Dudley] (b. London, 22 Dec. 1762; d. Sandon, Staffordshire, England, 26 Dec. 1847). MP, statesman, and church reformer. The eldest son of Nathaniel, first baron Harrowby, he was educated at Harrow where he formed a lasting friendship with SPENCER PERCEVAL, and at St John's College, Cambridge. He married in 1795 Lady Susan Leveson-Gower, daughter of the Marquess of Stafford. He was a brother of Bishop HENRY RYDER.

Ryder's political career began in 1784 when he was returned as MP for his family's pocket borough of Tiverton and became a supporter of Pitt. During the next two decades he held a range of minor government offices and in 1804 was briefly Foreign Secretary. Thereafter he had short spells as Chancellor of the Duchy of Lancaster (1805–6) and President of the Board of Control (1809) before serving as Lord President of the Council from 1812 to 1827. In November 1827 George IV offered him the premiership, but he turned it down on grounds of ill health. Meanwhile he had in 1803 succeeded his father as second Baron Harrowby and had been raised to an earldom in 1809.

Harrowby was a staunch supporter of the Church of England and played an important role in its reform. In 1812 he promoted the Stipendiary Curates Act, passed in the following year, designed, as he put it, to reduce the problem of curates 'galloping about from church to church'. When an incumbent was non-resident, bishops were empowered to appoint a curate and fix a stipend in accordance with a statutory scale, thus reducing substantially the number of parishes without a resident minister. Later, in his old age, he was from 1835 a conscientious member of the Ecclesiastical Commission initially appointed by Sir Robert Peel.

His evangelicalism, like that of many aristocrats of his generation, was one of broad sympathy rather than intense commitment. In later life he regretted what he saw as a misspent youth, but does not appear to have experienced any sharp crisis of conversion. He identified himself with the campaign against the slave trade, and, like other evangelical moderates, was a firm advocate of Catholic emancipation. As a statesman he was distinguished by his conscientious approach to his duties and a striking lack of personal ambition, although he was hampered by indecision, hypochondria and a certain small-mindedness. His career well illustrates both the extent and the limits of the permeation of evangelicalism in early nineteenth-century public life. HUGH FORTESCUE [Viscount Ebrington; second Earl Fortescue] married Harrowby's daughter, Susan.

SELECT WRITINGS
Earl of Harrowby. *Autobiography of Dudley, 1st Earl of Harrowby* (privately printed, 1891)
—, *Family Reminiscences by Dudley, 1st Earl of Harrowby* (privately printed, 1891)

BIBLIOGRAPHY
G. F. A. Best, *Temporal Pillars* (Cambridge, 1964)
DNB
R. G. Thorne, *The House of Commons 1790–1820*, 5 (London, 1986)
The Times (28 December 1847)
P. Virgin, *The Church in a Age of Negligence* (Cambridge, 1989)

JOHN WOLFFE

Harrowby, (second) **Earl of** [Viscount Sandon] [Ryder, Dudley] (b. London, 19 May 1798; d. Sandon, Staffordshire, England, 19 Nov. 1882). MP and philanthropist. The eldest son of the first EARL OF HARROWBY, he was educated privately, and at Christ Church, Oxford, gaining a double first in 1819. In 1823 he married Lady Frances Stuart, daughter of the first Marquess of Bute.

Viscount Sandon (as he was styled during his father's lifetime) was first returned to Parliament for Tiverton in 1819, and represented that constituency until 1831. He was then returned for Liverpool and until 1847 served as a conscientious representative of the business interests of the town. Meanwhile he held junior government office under Liverpool and Grey. A Conservative in general political loyalty, he nevertheless supported Catholic emancipation, the Maynooth Act of 1845, and the repeal of the Corn Laws. In 1847 his father's death raised him to the House of Lords. He was chairman of the Maynooth Commission from 1853 to 1855, and served under Palmerston as Chancellor of the Duchy of Lancaster in 1855 and Lord Privy Seal from 1855 to 1857. In 1869 he was a leader of the resistance in the House of Lords to the disestablishment of the Church of Ireland.

Harrowby was a firm but moderate evangelical, vigorous but not hysterical in opposing ritualism. His liberal political attitudes towards Roman Catholicism exposed him to the hostility of more extreme Protestants. He was a friend of Lord SHAFTESBURY, and himself an active supporter of a range of humanitarian, educational and religious causes. His eldest son, later third earl, continued into a further generation the family tradition of disinterested public service, underscored by evangelical religious conviction.

SELECT WRITINGS
Second Earl of Harrowby, *Reminiscences of Dudley, 2nd Earl of Harrowby* (privately printed, 1891)

BIBLIOGRAPHY
DNB
The Times (21 November 1882)
J. R. Wolffe, *The Protestant Crusade in Great Britain, 1829–1861* (Oxford, 1991)

JOHN WOLFFE

Harry, Miles (b. Bedwellty, Gwent, S. Wales, 1 Jan. 1699; d. Pontypool, Gwent, S. Wales, 1 Nov. 1776). Welsh Baptist minister. Born at Llyswedog Fach, Sirhowy, the son of Henry Williams and Margaret Jenkin, Miles was baptised at Blaenau Gwent on 1 April 1724. His ordination was postponed due to suspicions of unorthodoxy, but early in 1730, after having allayed fears on that score, he became assistant to the minister, John Harry. His name, though, was to become synonymous with the newly established church of Pen-y-garn to which he was inducted on 24 May 1732. As well as preaching, his interests extended to publishing and education. In 1739 he became overseer of the press set up at Abergavenny by the Farley brothers of Bristol, and later was involved in the work of the ministerial school at Trosnant. He also helped ensure that charges of riotous assembly, levelled against HOWELL HARRIS, were dropped. He married twice, first in 1736 to Elizabeth Williams of Llantarnam and then on 20 October 1774 to Hannah Davies of Abergavenny. An able disputant and popular preacher, Harry was perhaps the foremost Welsh Baptist minister of his generation.

BIBLIOGRAPHY
DWB
R. Jones, 'Miles Harri'(sic), *Trafodion Cymdeithas Hanes Bedyddwyr Cymru* (1926): 15–53

D. DENSIL MORGAN

Hart, Hannah (England; d. at sea, Oct. 1829). CMS missionary to New Zealand. Hart was a widow who on 25 April was sent by the CMS to assist Mary Anne [also Marianne] Williams (*see* HENRY WILLIAMS) as a school-teacher in the education of European and Maori children. She left Sydney for New Zealand on 24 October 1829 but the boat apparently was lost at sea. Hart was only the eighth female missionary sent out by the CMS and the first single female directed to New Zealand.

BIBLIOGRAPHY
D. T. B[arry], *CMS Register of Missionaries and Native Clergy* (privately printed) (London, 1906)

DONALD M. LEWIS

Hart, Joseph (b. London, 1712; d. London, 24 May 1768). Hymn-writer. Little is known of his early life except that he seems to have had Christian parents and was well educated. A teacher of languages in a London school, he lapsed into dissolute ways but was conscious of a serious conviction of sin. Occasionally he went to WHITEFIELD's tabernacle; but it was not until Whitsun, 1757, that he was converted after hearing a sermon on Revelation 3: 10 at the Moravian Chapel in Fetter Lane. Two years later he became pastor of Jewin Street Independent Chapel and published for use in the chapel *Hymns Composed on Various Subjects, with the Author's Experience* (London, 1759). A *Supplement* was added in 1762, and an *Appendix* in 1765. He was a popular preacher, strong Calvinist, and a severe critic of JOHN WESLEY. About 20,000 were said to have attended his funeral in Bunhill Fields, where an obelisk was erected to his memory in 1875. After Watts he was the most popular of the eighteenth-century Independent hymn-writers. Many of his 222 hymns were 'marked by great earnestness, and passionate love of the Redeemer' (Julian: 492). The following are the best known: 'Come, Holy Spirit, come, / Let Thy bright beams arise', a fitting celebration of the anniversary of his conversion; the also autobiographical 'Come, ye sinners, poor and wretched'; and the doxology, 'This, this is the God we adore' (or 'How good is the God we adore', both amended centos from his 'No prophet, nor dreamer of dreams').

BIBLIOGRAPHY
Julian: 492–3, 1511, 1764
E. R. Routley, *I'll Praise My Maker* (London, 1951): 243–8, 278

JOHN S. ANDREWS

Hart, Levi (b. Southington, CT, BNA, 10 April 1738; d. Preston, CT, USA, 27 Oct. 1808). Congregational minister. A 1760 graduate of Yale, Hart studied theology with JOSEPH BELLAMY – a devotee of JONATHAN EDWARDS and leader of the emerging New Divinity theological movement in New England. Under Bellamy, Hart embraced the Calvinist Edwardsianism of the New Divinity. In 1762, he was ordained into the ministry of Preston's First Church Congregational, where he remained until his death.

Hart's ministry spanned the tumultuous years of the American Revolution and the early republic. In a sermon (1774) endorsing independence, he employed Edwards's language on the will to define the 'sacred cause of liberty' as an opportunity to act morally by abolishing both black slavery and colonial bondage to the British. Following the Revolution, Hart ardently promoted home missionary efforts to the expanding frontier. He directed the formation of the Connecticut Missionary Society (1798), and was an editor for the *Connecticut Evangelical Magazine* (1800–6).

BIBLIOGRAPHY
AAP, 1
BSGYC, 2
D. Weber, *Rhetoric and History in Revolutionary New England* (New York, 1988)

DAVID W. KLING

Hart, Luther (b. Goshen, CT, USA, July 1783; d. Plymouth, CT, USA, 25 April 1834). Congregationalist minister. Converted at age 16 during a wave of revival which swept through Connecticut, Hart graduated with honours from Yale in 1807. After teaching at the academy at Litchfield, Connecticut and studying theology with Ebenezer Porter, a pastor in Washington, Connecticut. He was a member of the first graduating class of Andover Theological Seminary, established in 1808 near Boston. He was called and ordained by the Congregationalist church at Plymouth, Connecticut where he ministered from 1810 until his death in 1834. About 500 people professed faith in Christ and joined his congregation, many as the result of four periods of revival (1812, 1824, 1827, 1831) which revitalized his church during the Second Great Awakening. In 1818 Hart joined with several other Connecticut clergymen to publish a series of doctrinal tracts to which he contributed 'Plain Reasons for Relying on Presbyterian Ordination'. He also played an important role in founding the *Christian Spectator* and wrote many articles for this periodical. His other publications include a Christmas sermon entitled 'Salvation for Lost Men' (1818), an installation sermon, and two memoirs of clergymen who served nearby congregations.

BIBLIOGRAPHY
AAP

GARY SCOTT SMITH

Hart, Oliver (b. Warminster, PA, BNA, 5 July 1723; d. Hopewell, NJ, USA, 31 Dec. 1795). Baptist minister, author and political activist. Influenced by the preaching of GEORGE WHITEFIELD and the TENNENTS, Hart was licensed to the minister 20 December 1746, and ordained 18 October 1749. He travelled to Charleston, South Carolina, in search of a position, and arrived the same day that Isaac Chanler, the only Baptist minister in that region, was buried. Hart assumed the pastorate of the Ashley River Church (16 February 1750), and was instrumental in the formation of the Charleston Association. Before the Revolutionary War and during its progress, Hart travelled with WILLIAM TENNENT and William Drayton to convince the people of the Carolina interior to support the Continental Congress and its often unwelcome measures. When the British occupied the harbour of Charleston in 1780, Hart fled to the safety of New Jersey. There he accepted an invitation to the pastorate of the Baptist church at Hopewell, New Jersey, in December of that same year. He continued in that post till his death.

BIBLIOGRAPHY
AAP
W. Cathcart, *Baptist Encyclopedia* (Philadelphia, PA, 1881)

WADE A. HORTON

Hart, Richard (b. 15 May 1727; d. Bristol, England, 4 Nov. 1808). Anglican clergyman; Vicar of Kingswood. He was born into a wealthy Bristol mercantile and clerical family with Tory, even Jacobite, affiliations. His tutor at Christ Church, Oxford 1744–9 was JOSEPH JANE, and after study at Cambridge he was curate at Warminster by 1756. In April 1759 Hart became Vicar of St George's Kingswood, the new parish created to offer Anglican care to the coal-mining community which had attracted so much early evangelical preaching. He held this post to his death, reporting by 1766 that Methodism was declining in the parish. In 1801 he published *Dr Gill's Reasons for Separating From the Church of England Clearly Considered in a Letter to a Friend* (Bristol). Yet, together with JAMES BROWN and Samuel Johnson, Perpetual Curate of Cirencester (a relation by marriage), he worked closely with all evangelical groups, often preaching in the countryside and for the Countess of HUNTINGDON. Hart sought evangelical unity in 'apostolical preaching' and willingness to accept that 'whatever doctrine cannot

maintain its ground without the aid of humanly invented words is not of God' (Curnock, 1909–16, 5: 63–4). The primacy of scripture is emphasized in his *The Importance of the Word of God* (Bristol, 1766). Hart thus represents mainstream Anglican evangelicalism, sympathetic to itinerancy but working within the parochial system and promoting adherence to scripture to prevent doctrinal schisms.

BIBLIOGRAPHY
N. Curnock, ed., *John Wesley's Journal*, 8 vols (London, 1909–16)
A. C. H. Seymour, *Life and Times of Selina Countess of Huntingdon*, 2 vols (London, 1844)

JONATHAN BARRY

Hartley, John (b. Bedford, Bedfordshire, England, c. 1796; d. Chambrey, France, 10 June 1843). CMS missionary to Malta. Hartley was the oldest son and namesake of an Anglican minister of the town of Bedford. He was educated at St Edmund's Hall, Oxford (BA 1823; MA 1831) under the sponsorship of the Bristol Clerical Education Society, and was ordained (deacon 1823; priest 1824) to the curacy of St Michael's, Gloucester. On 12 October 1824 the CMS sent him to join WILLIAM JOWETT in Malta. Two earlier recruits, THEOPHILUS DEININGER and HENRY ANDREWS, had died shortly after their arrival. He served there until October 1829 when he returned to England and in February 1831 withdrew from the CMS. He married in 1832 and was re-admitted travelling to Corfu on 6 June 1832 but his wife's health forced their withdrawal in December 1833. Hartley then became an Anglican chaplain in Nice. He authored *Researches in Greece and the Levant.*

BIBLIOGRAPHY
Al. Ox.
D. T. B[arry], *CMS Register of Missionaries and Native Clergy* (privately printed) (London, 1906)

DONALD M. LEWIS

Hartley, Richard (b. Bingley, Yorkshire, England, 1764; d. Bingley, 26 Oct. 1836). Anglican clergyman and schoolmaster. Hartley was a graduate of Christ's College, Cambridge (scholar 1783; BA 1787; MA 1790; DD 1805). Apart from his university years and a brief spell as curate of The Bournes (Kent) (1789), he spent his whole life in his native place, becoming headmaster of the local grammar school (1791–1836) and Vicar of Bingley (1795–1836). He is described as having been 'an excellent classic, a hard-reading man, and of irreproachable character'.

BIBLIOGRAPHY
Al Cant., II, iii: 272

ARTHUR POLLARD

Hartley, Thomas (b. London, *c.* 1709; d. East Malling, Kent, England, 10 Dec. 1784). Anglican clergyman and translator of Swedenborg. Educated at St John's College, Cambridge (1725–8) he was Curate of Chiswick in 1737, becoming Rector of Winwick, Huntingdon in 1744. At first an evangelical through contact with the Countess of HUNTINGDON, he came to appreciate the mystic writers whom he defended against Warburton in *Paradise Restored* (1764). Several times he visited Swedenborg whose *De Commercio Animae et Corporis* he translated in 1769. In 1770 he moved from Winwick while still holding the living. His *Nine Queries* addressed to Swedenborg, concerning the Trinity, were published posthumously.

BIBLIOGRAPHY
A. E. Beilby, *Rev. Thomas Hartley, A.M.* (London, 1931)
DNB

TIMOTHY C. F. STUNT

Hartwig, Peter (b. Prussia, *c.* 1777; d. Freetown, Sierra Leone, 1 March 1815). Pioneer CMS missionary in Sierra Leone. A mechanic, he joined Berlin Seminary on 1 February 1800 and studied under Professor JOHANNES JÄNICKE. He went to England in response to a CMS request to the seminary for missionaries. He learned English and Susu (at the School for Africans in Clapham run by William Greaves) before returning to East Friesland to be ordained as a Lutheran minister in 1803. He married Sarah Windsor, governess to the family of the Reverend JOHN VENN, and they set sail along with MELCHIOR RENNER for Freetown, arriving on 14 April 1804.

His wife fell ill and, unable to attend to the girls' school that she had established, left Freetown to travel back to Europe. Hartwig held joint services with the Nova Scotians in Freetown. He disagreed in policy and attitude with Renner. Many gathered outside the ill-constructed missionary house to listen to arguments between the two men. The Governor, Ludlum, wrote of him, 'The weakest of our Black Settlers have eyes to discern his failings' (Ludlum to Henry Venn, 20 March 1806). After extending his stay in Freetown a year longer than the CMS had advised, he travelled to the Susu country. Here he met with a slave trader, Mrs Williams, an English woman who had lived and traded in the region for over twenty years. Hartwig left the CMS and joined Mrs Williams.

In 1814 he repented for his misdemeanours, and asked to join the CMS again. While he was never reinstated as a missionary he worked as a translator, and soon had produced the first five chapters of the Gospel of John and some elementary textbooks in Susu. His wife rejoined him on 13 February 1815 but he was suffering from dropsy acquired in the Gambier settlement. He died some two weeks later; his wife died on 30 April 1815.

BIBLIOGRAPHY
D. T. B[arry], *CMS Register of Missionaries And Native Clergy from 1804 to 1904* (privately printed) (London, 1906)

CMS Archives, s.v. Sierra Leone, University of Birmingham

ELIZABETH GRANT

Harvey, George Gayton (b. Norfolk, England; d. Hampstead, London, 29 April 1875). Anglican clergyman. Harvey graduated from St John's College, Cambridge (BA 1826) and was subsequently Perpetual Curate of Horton, near Leek (Stratfordshire) (1831–40) and of Winster (Derbyshire) (1840–6), during which period he was also a member of the Matlock Bath Clerical Society. He moved to Hailsham (Sussex) as vicar (1846–72), where he was succeeded by his son, Francis, who held the living for fifty years (1872–1922).

BIBLIOGRAPHY
Al. Cant., II, iii: 276

ARTHUR POLLARD

Harvey, Thomas (b. Barnsley, Yorkshire, England, 15 March 1812; d. Headingley, Leeds, England, 25 Dec. 1884). Quaker pharmacist. After Quaker schooldays ('Though we had valuable Scriptural instruction I do not think I had a real grasp of the Gospel plan of redemption') he was apprenticed to a Quaker firm of chemists in Birmingham. Here he was deeply influenced by the ministry of JOSEPH JOHN GURNEY and experienced conversion. Here, too, he met JOSEPH STURGE; they visited the West Indies to assess, following abolition of slavery, the apprenticeship system, their report *The West Indies in 1837* being a damning indictment of it. Harvey revisited in 1866.

He was a Leeds pharmacist, retiring in 1867. In 1856 he and Sturge visited Finland, administering relief funds to sufferers from British bombardment of civilian property during the Crimean War. In 1867 he visited Mennonites in south Russia and in 1884 was on a deputation to Canadian Quakers. For many years an elder, he was recorded a minister in 1868.

BIBLIOGRAPHY
Annual Monitor (1886): 79–89
S. G. Harvey, *Memorials of Thomas Harvey* (privately printed, 1886)
W. Robinson, ed., *Friends of a Half Century* (London and Ashford, England, 1891): 203–10

EDWARD H. MILLIGAN

Hasell, Samuel (b. UK, *c.* 1819; d. 5 June 1879). CMS schoolmaster and pastor in India. Trained as a schoolmaster, Hasell was stationed in Calcutta (1847–51), Krishnagur (1851–7), and Chapra (1858–60). Soon after arrival Hasell began preaching in Bengali and supervising a circle of schools. He favoured closing English schools except where well established, and was critical of prevailing educational practices, favouring vernacular, technical and crafts education instead.

Nevertheless, in 1855 he helped organize an ecumenical conference on English medium education.

In 1851 Hasell became secretary of the Calcutta Bible Association. His much loved wife died in July 1852; and, in 1859, his letters ended abruptly, and for no apparent reason.

BIBLIOGRAPHY
CMS archives, University of Birmingham, UK

E. M. JACKSON

Haslam, William (b. Sumatra, 1817; d. St Leonard's on Sea, England, 26 Jan. 1905). Anglican clergyman, author and evangelist. He began his ministry, after graduating from Durham University in 1841, in the diocese of Exeter, as a priest committed to Tractarian principles, but is widely remembered as the 'Parson who was converted by his own sermon'. After serving a curacy in the parish of Perranzabuloe in Cornwall, he was appointed the first incumbent of Baldhu, a new 'Peel' parish not far away, one of several which he had planned at the request of the Bishop of Exeter. Here he designed, and had built the church (no longer in use due to the cessation of mining in the area which led to a great shift of population). The building, like others he designed, displays his architectural skill. Many of his parishioners were revivalist Methodists who unsettled him by their accounts of their experiences of conversion. As a result he consulted ROBERT AITKEN, Vicar of Pendeen, another Cornish parish, about this. Aitken convinced him of the absolute necessity of conversion, and returning home Haslam preached the sermon, gaining an assurance of personal salvation in the process and causing a Methodist local preacher in the congregation to exclaim 'The Parson is converted'. This occurred in 1851. He immediately adopted the revivalist methods of evangelism then current with his Methodist neighbours. This was characterized by a great deal of noise and physical phenomena, and brought him the objections not only of his Tractarian friends, but also that of the more traditional evangelicals. Clergy also condemned his conducting open-air preachings in parishes other than his own without their consent.

In 1855, after nine years at Baldhu, Haslam was invited to take charge of a new parish in Plymouth, but this move did not materialize because Bishop Phillpotts of Exeter, after accepting his resignation of Baldhu, refused to allow him to take up the Plymouth post. The Bishop, though, did allow him to become incumbent of Carnmenellis the following year, but he was there for only about 12 months before becoming curate-in-charge of a district in Hayle, Cornwall. Here he continued his revivalist ministry until moving to a similar district in Bath, Somerset. Three years later he moved to Buckenham in Norfolk. Then in 1872, after a year at Little Missendon, he was appointed minister of the Curzon Chapel in Mayfair, London, where he remained until 1878. This was his last parochial charge and from then on his evangelistic ministry was mainly with the Church Parochial Mission Society. Several of those associated with this society were the so-called Catholic evangelicals who combined a thoroughgoing Tractarianism with revivalist evangelism.

Haslam himself retained a few elements of his earlier Tractarianism, particularly in his ideas about church decoration and furnishings, but he accepted and propagated the ideals of the Keswick Convention together with a premillennial dispensationalist eschatology. His books were expositions of these doctrines together with many detailed accounts of individuals' conversions. Of his doctrine of conversion the same could probably be said about it that WALKER of Truro said about WESLEY's view in the eighteenth century:

> I cannot agree with Mr Wesley's definition of faith. It hath had this effect with the most of the Methodists I have conversed with, that they have thought believing to be feeling, and faith by them hath been placed in the affections instead of the heart; the consequence of which hath been doubting, when the stir of the affections hath been less. (E. Sidney quoted in Davies, 1951: 153)

It was no doubt his emphasis on feeling that caused some of his evangelical brethren to have misgivings about his methods.

SELECT WRITINGS
W. Haslam, *The Threefold Gift of God* (London, 1876)
—, *From Death unto Life* (London, 1880)
—, *Yet Not I* (London, 1880)
—, *Full Salvation* (London, 1884)
—, *Leaves from my Notebook* (London, 1889)
—, *Notes from Keswick* (London, 1890)
—, *Praise* (magazine edited by Haslam, 1897 to 1899)
—, *Building from the Top* (London, 1903)

BIBLIOGRAPHY
G. C. B. Davies, *The Early Cornish Evangelicals 1735–1760* (London, 1951)
P. Evans, 'William Haslam', *The Evangelical Library Bulletin* (Autumn, 1986)

A. J. VINCENT

Haslope, Lancelot (b. 1767; d. Selly Hall, Worcester, England, 30 April 1838). Lawyer, judge, Wesleyan missions treasurer. Haslope, a London lawyer, was a Justice of the Peace in London, and in his later years was an acting-magistrate for Middlesex county in which he resided at his Highbury Lodge estate. In the 1830s he was a lay treasurer of the WMMS and a member of the Committee of Privileges.

BIBLIOGRAPHY
GM (1838): 670
W. R. Ward, *Early Victorian Methodism* (London, 1976): 32n

JONATHAN BURKE CUTMORE

Hassall, Rowland (b. Coventry, England, 31 March 1768; d. Parramatta, NSW, Australia, 28 Aug. 1820).

LMS missionary to Tahiti, lay preacher and landowner in NSW. Rowland Hassall joined the pioneer LMS missionary voyage of the *Duff* with his wife Elizabeth (née Hancox), landing in Tahiti 5 March 1797. Hassall worked as a blacksmith with other artisan missionaries. After initial good relationships with the Tahitians, the group found increasing difficulty. When serious confrontation with the Tahitians threatened the work, Hassall fled with others, arriving as refugees in Sydney, New South Wales, in May 1798. Hassall remained in New South Wales, becoming a wealthy landowner. He worked as an itinerant lay preacher, and on many committees with special interest in education. Though he never returned to Tahiti, he 'never lost sight of his original designation as a missionary'.

BIBLIOGRAPHY
Hassall Correspondence (manuscript, Mitchell Library, NSW)
W. Wilson, *A Missionary Voyage . . . 1796–98* (London, 1798)

MARGARET I. REESON

Hassall, Thomas (b. Coventry, England, 29 May 1794; d. Cobbitty, NSW, Australia, 29 Mar. 1868). First Anglican clergyman from colonial Australia. Child of pioneer LMS missionaries to Tahiti, Thomas Hassall grew up in NSW. He received the best education possible in the penal colony, with encouragement from parents and mentor, the Reverend SAMUEL MARSDEN. In 1813, Hassall began the first Sunday school in New South Wales, in his parents' home. He left New South Wales in 1817 to study for the Church of England ministry in England, the first Australian to do so, and was ordained deacon and priest in 1821.

On returning to New South Wales in 1822, he became curate to Marsden and married Marsden's daughter Anne. After brief ministries in Port Macquarie and Bathurst, he began his life work in 1827 and remained in Camden parish till his death forty years later. His parish included much of newly settled south-east New South Wales and he became known as 'the galloping parson', travelling widely to care for his scattered people, until the area was divided into several parishes. He had special care for youth and distribution of Christian literature and was greatly loved, not only by his own people but also by people of other faiths, particularly local Methodists, and no faith. As a landowner, he suffered with his people through economic recession, droughts and floods. Hassall received an MA from the Archbishop of Canterbury through Bishop Broughton in 1843.

BIBLIOGRAPHY
Hassall Correspondence (manuscript, Mitchell Library, NSW)
J. S. Hassall, *In Old Australia* (Brisbane, 1902)

MARGARET I. REESON

Hastings, Lady **Elizabeth** (Betty) (b. 19 Apr. 1683; d. Ledston, Yorkshire, 22 Dec. 1739). Evangelical and educational reformer. She was the daughter of the seventh Earl of Huntingdon by his first wife, Elizabeth Lewis. Her brother George (eighth earl) gave her the Lewis estates in Yorkshire absolutely in exchange for her rights to the Hastings estates, and she settled at Ledston Hall in 1705.

In her youth she lived in and near London where she became well known for her learning, piety and charity. She supported the feminist Mary Astell, and the Anglo-Saxon scholar Elizabeth Elstob. She was praised by Steele in *Tatler* under the pseudonym of Aspasia. After inheriting the Lewis estates she was able to increase her influence. Her friendship with Sir JOHN PHILIPPS brought her to support the SPCK, the SPG and Dr Bray's parochial libraries. She provided bursaries for poor students (including GEORGE WHITEFIELD and possibly BENJAMIN INGHAM) to attend Oxford. By her efforts the parish church of Leeds received an extra endowment and a second church was built in the town. Her friends included William Law, Bishop Wilson of Sodor and Man, and the antiquary Ralph Thoresby.

At Ledston she provided a home for the children of her father's second marriage, including Lady MARGARET INGHAM. Prayers were said four times a day in the household, and visiting clergymen invited to preach. Her interest in missions led her to consult CHARLES WESLEY about a mission to the Indians of Georgia, and she supported both the Tranquebar and the Moravian missionaries.

She died from cancer after a long and very painful illness, leaving part of her estates to found an educational charity in the North of England which still flourishes. Her Ledston property was bequeathed to her nephew Francis (later Earl of Huntingdon) and her library of religious and literary works to his younger brother.

BIBLIOGRAPHY
T. Barnard, *An Historical Character . . . of the Lady Elizabeth Hastings* (Leeds, England, 1742)
Huntington Library and the Leicestershire Record Office, original letters
G. H. Wheler, ed., *The Hastings Wheler Letters*, 1 (London, 1929) and 2 (Wakefield, England, 1935)

EDWIN WELCH

Hastings, John (b. Suffield, CT, BNA, *c.* 1743; d. Suffield, CT, USA, 17 Mar. 1811). Baptist pastor and church planter in Connecticut. John's father was Joseph Hastings, a Congregationalist farmer turned Separatist who became founding pastor of First Baptist Church, Suffield, in 1763. John was a 'contemner' of religion until his marriage to Rachel Remmington. In 1775 he was ordained and became co-pastor with his father. During his first year the Suffield church grew from a membership of 20 to about 200. He became sole pastor at his father's death in 1785 and continued there until his own death. Suffield soon became the premier Baptist church in Connecticut. Travelling widely, Hastings started a number of churches and is reported to have baptized 1100 persons during his 36-year ministry. Becoming 'prematurely an old man', his pulpit was filled by others the last two years of his life.

BIBLIOGRAPHY
I. Backus, *A History of New England*, 2 vols (1777–84, reprinted Newton, MA, 1871)
W. Cathcart, *The Baptist Encyclopedia* (Philadelphia, PA, 1883)

WILLIAM LOYD ALLEN

Hastings, Margaret. *See* INGHAM, MARGARET

Hatai (b. Tahiti, Society Island; d. Oneata, Fiji, 1846). Missionary to Fiji. John Davies of the LMS in Tahiti sent Hatai to Fiji, accompanied by FAARUEA. Their hope of welcome by Lakeba's high chief was disappointed. They settled instead, in 1830, on nearby Oneata, taught and worshipped on a site called *Siloama* (Siloam), married, and both died in the same year (1846). In 1835 they joined WILLIAM CROSS and DAVID CARGILL of the WMMS in their work.

BIBLIOGRAPHY
J. Garrett, *To Live Among the Stars* (Geneva and Suva, 1982)

JOHN GARRETT

Hatchard, John (b. London, 17 Oct. 1768; d. Clapham, Surrey, England, 21 June 1849). Publisher and bookseller. He was the son of Thomas Hatchard and Sarah Clarke. Having served as a printer's apprentice with a bookseller from the age of eight, in 1789 he entered a partnership with a bookseller in Castle Street. In 1797 he opened his own bookshop, moving in 1817 to 187, Piccadilly (where his portrait is still displayed on the ground floor).

He soon began to publish books and pamphlets of a loyal and pious caste, often the work of moderate Tories and evangelicals. He was a friend of WILLIAM WILBERFORCE, was HANNAH MORE's early publisher and bookseller, published the Clapham evangelicals' periodical, the *Christian Observer*, the reports of the Society for Bettering the Condition of the Poor, and those of the African Institution. His store was the haunt of Tory politicians: the Duke of Wellington was a long-standing patron and he was a friend and publisher of George Canning, leader of the moderate Tories.

Hatchard supported numerous evangelical and philanthropic societies, 37 of which received legacies in his will. In 1845 he retired, his son Thomas continuing the firm's evangelical and conservative traditions.

BIBLIOGRAPHY
CO (Aug. 1849): 574–75
DNB
GM (Aug. 1849): 210–11

A. L. Humphrey, *Piccadilly Bookmen* (London, 1893)

JONATHAN BURKE CUTMORE

Hatchard, Thomas. *See* HATCHARD, JOHN

Hatchard, Thomas Goodwyn (b. Chelsea, London, 18 Sept. 1817; d. Mauritius, 28 Feb. 1870). Anglican bishop. Hatchard was the son of Thomas Hatchard, publisher (died 1858), and grandson of JOHN HATCHARD. He was educated at King's College, London and Brasenose College, Oxford (BA 1841; MA 1845; DD 1869). He was Curate of Windlesham (Surrey) (1842–4), domestic chaplain to the Marquess of Conyngham (one time protege of Bishop C. R. SUMNER) (1846–69). He was consecrated Bishop of Mauritius in succession to V. W. RYAN, but died of fever within the year. He was considered to be a moderate evangelical. His wife, a daughter of Bishop MICHAEL SOLOMON ALEXANDER of Jerusalem, was active in the establishment and organization of mothers' meetings.

BIBLIOGRAPHY
DNB

ARTHUR POLLARD

Hathaway, Edward (Penrose) (b. Queen Street, London [ordination papers, London], 16 Dec. 1818; d. 16 Calverley Park, Tunbridge Wells, Kent, 16 May 1897). Lawyer and Anglican clergyman. Third son of William Silas Hathaway, merchant, and Elizabeth his wife, Edward was educated at Sherborne School (head 1834–5) under Dr R. Lyon, an evangelical, and read classics at Queen's College, Oxford (Bridgeman exhibitioner) 1836–9, also attending Pusey's lectures. Among his undergraduate friends were H. W. FOX and A. W. THOROLD. Admitted to Lincoln's Inn 1842, and called to the Bar 1846, he practised as a barrister for 18 years, residing at Harrow, with chambers at 5, Old Square, Lincoln's Inn.

In 1853, Hathaway and a few friends, concerned about theological trends at Oxford, started a fund to augment poor livings there where an evangelical ministry might thus be made available. Thus N. J. MOODY became Rector of St Clement's (1855) and H. LINTON Rector of St Peter-le-Bailey (1856). This initiative led to acquiring patronage. In 1864 Hathaway established a patronage trust, consisting of St Peter-le-Bailey, St Clement's, and St Ebbe's, to which he added Holy Trinity in 1881, and gave Littlegate House (now used as St Aldate's rectory) as a vicarage for Holy Trinity in 1891. In 1859 Hathaway had, in effect, presented A. M. W. CHRISTOPHER to St Aldate's before that advowson, acquired from Pembroke College, was given to Simeon's Trustees. During the next thirty years, W. H. Barlow, T. V. FRENCH, and F. J. Chavasse were among other notable men appointed to these parishes. Every year, Hathaway raised individual augmentations for each of their incumbents. If it had not been for his foresight, it is unlikely that there would have been any continuing evangelical church in central Oxford.

Hathaway was ordained in 1864. He served successively as missioner and Curate of St Giles-in-the-Fields, London, under his friend Thorold; and as Curate of Camberwell 1867–8. From 1868 he was Rector of St Ebbe's, Oxford, where he restored evangelical teaching. He added to the rectory a large room, using it *inter alia* for Greek Testament readings for undergraduates, and enlarged the parochial schools. Following his wife's accidental death (1872), he resigned in 1873 and retired from parish ministry for nine years. By 1877 he was living at Clifton, Bristol.

In 1882 Hathaway became Vicar of St Andrew-the-Less, Clifton. From 1885 to 1892 he was Rector of Holbrook, Suffolk, retiring to Broxbourne, Hertfordshire, then (1894) to Tunbridge Wells. In 1893 he presided at a meeting which founded the (continuing) Oxford Pastorate, to provide additional spiritual guidance for undergraduates attached to local evangelical parishes. One of his curates at St Ebbe's had been H. E. Fox (son of his undergraduate friend), honorary secretary of the CMS from 1895; another, at Clifton, was A. R. Tucker (*DNB*), from 1890 Bishop of Uganda, who regularly consulted him.

A capable administrator, a self-effacing Christian, a devoted pastor, a determined upholder of evangelicalism, Hathaway inclined to remain in the background. Prebendary Fox wrote more strongly:

> Gifted with an intelligence of rare power, and trained in the niceties of legal science, few men have held or preached more clearly and fully the doctrines of Divine grace ... Equally at home in the cottage-lecture and in the Bible-reading for cultured Christians, he left on all who met him the impress of a saintly mind, as exalted as it was humble.
>
> (Hathaway, 1898: Preface)

Hathaway married (1) 1849 Catherine Louisa Legh (1824–72: tablet, St Ebbe's), daughter of Reverend E. D. Legh, granddaughter of Sir Christopher Robinson, judge (*DNB*); (2) 1874 Eleanor Bush Wood (1830–1908), daughter of Captain H. Wood (23rd Regiment) of Littlegate House, St Ebbe's, Oxford. A photograph is reproduced in Reynolds, 1953, 1967, 1975.

SELECT WRITINGS

E. P. Hathaway, *Steps and Stages in the Christian Life*, preface by H. E. Fox (London, 1898)

Article on J. W. Knott, *Churchman* (March 1897, London)

BIBLIOGRAPHY

Anon., ed., *Records of Lincoln's Inn*, 2 (London, 1896)

J. S. Reynolds, *Evangelicals at Oxford* (Oxford 1953; Appleford, England, 1975)

J. S. Reynolds, *Canon Christopher* (Abingdon, England, 1967)

A. P. Shepherd, *Tucker of Uganda* (London, 1929)

J. S. REYNOLDS

Hatley, Thomas (Legerwood) (b. Greenlaw, Berwickshire, Scotland, 1815; d. Edinburgh, 1867). Printer and hymn-writer. Hatley was a printer who exercised his enthusiasm for music as a Church of Scotland precentor, first at North Leith and then at St Mary's Parish Church. Upon the Disruption of 1843 he was almost unique among precentors to join the Free Church. He conducted the choir at the first Free Church General Assembly and was later official precentor of the Free Church Assembly and of the Free High Church. The General Assembly commissioned him in 1851 to tour the congregations in order to raise the standard of denominational worship in music. He then devoted himself to the training of church teachers in music and to editing books, such as the *Free Church Psalmody* (1844) and the *National Psalmody*. He was also a prolific writer of Psalm tunes.

BIBLIOGRAPHY

J. M. Barclay, *Handbook to the Church Hymnary* (London, 1979): 277–8

JONATHAN BURKE CUTMORE

Hatton, George Edward (b. London, 1 Feb. 1840; d. 21 July 1920). Founder and first superintendent of the St Giles's Christian Mission. Hatton was confirmed in his evangelical upbringing by the metropolitan ministries of the Reverend D. F. Jarman, of the Bedford Episcopal Chapel, and by Dr WILLIAM BROCK of the Bloomsbury Chapel. As a schoolteacher there, he was influenced by GEORGE WILSON MCCREE to join with other like-minded young men in 1860 in opening a mission hall, the beginning of the St Giles's Christian Mission to the most notorious slums of West Central London. In 1864, the Bloomsbury Chapel Domestic Mission Committee supported the mission in its move to a building formerly used by the United Free Methodists. Another mission station was established in 1870 first at the coal yard in Drury Lane then at Great Earl Street, Seven Dials. Services were held in 1873–4 in the Oxford Music Hall and in Leicester Square, and in 1874 the Earl of SHAFTESBURY and CHARLES SPURGEON opened a former Baptist Chapel in Little Wild Street as the mission's central headquarters. In 1877, Hatton and his co-worker William Wheatley began their work of reclaiming criminals, with free breakfasts and hostel accommodation for convicts just discharged from gaol, and an agency for finding them regular and immediate employment. His mission also established three large schools for 600 of the poorest children of the district, and employed a nurse and a Visitation Society with fifty members in house-to-house visiting of the 'low lodging houses' in which St Giles's then abounded. He resigned as superintendent in 1892, when he was succeeded by Wheatley. Hatton's charitable and evangelistic methods and message were of the simplest sort, the promise of salvation to all who repent, and practical help and consolation for the poor and distressed; and with some at least of his charges, he enjoyed a remarkable success.

BIBLIOGRAPHY
G. Holden Pike, 'George Hatton in St Giles's', *Pity for the Perishing* (London, 1884): 187–210
—, *Saving to the Uttermost* (London, 1885)
—, *The Story of Thirty Years in St Giles, under the Superintendence of Mr G. Hatton* (London, 1891)
The mission has preserved its Annual Reports from 1877, and an archive (information from the mission's superintendent)

SHERIDAN GILLEY

Haussmann, Johann Gottfried (b. Sonnenwalde, Prussia, 25 Oct. 1811; d. Beenleigh, Australia, 31 Dec. 1901). Lutheran missionary and pastor in Australia. Trained as a 'godly mechanic' by JOHANNES GOSSNER in Berlin, Haussmann was one of 12 Lutheran missionaries sent to Australia at the request of the Presbyterian, JOHN DUNMORE LANG. Under the leadership of Reverends Christopher Eipper and Karl Wilhelm Schmidt, the mission commenced on Moreton Bay at Zion's Hill in 1838. Emphasis on self-sufficiency led to over-concentration on agriculture. The mission was closed in 1845. Haussmann entered Lang's Australian College in 1848 and was ordained, serving Lutheran congregations in Victoria and Queensland. From 1866 to 1883 he ran an Aboriginal mission, 'Bethesda', at Beenleigh, remaining in Beenleigh as pastor until his death.

BIBLIOGRAPHY
J. Nolan, 'Pastor J. G. Haussmann, a Queensland Pioneer, 1838–1901' (Univ. of Queensland BA Hons., 1964)
H. J. J. Sparkes, *Queensland's First Free Settlement, 1838–1938* (Brisbane, 1938)

JOHN HARRIS

Havelock, Sir Henry (b. Bishop Wearmouth, County Durham, England, 5 April 1795; d. Lucknow, India, 24 Nov. 1857). Baptist, major-general, and war hero. His father was a substantial shipbuilder but lost his fortune through unsuccessful speculation, causing his son to abandon his legal training for the army, securing his commission in 1815 at the end of the Napoleonic Wars. Lack of action caused him in 1823 to transfer regiments so as to go to India. On the journey there, a fellow officer, Lieutenant Gardner, seems to have secured his religious conversion, and shortly after arriving in India he made the acquaintance of the Serampore missionaries, marrying HANNAH MARSHMAN in February 1829, and being baptized in 1830. For much of his time in India, notwithstanding his talents, he held only minor rank; in part, it has been suggested, because of his Nonconformity. During the Burmese War of 1824 he gathered together soldiers of religious commitment for nightly services, and it was this group of 'Havelock's saints' that were called upon to deal with a surprise attack when the guard were incapable of so doing through heavy drinking. His carefully disciplined and intelligent soldiering in the Afghan Wars, of the early phases of which he produced a remarkably balanced two-volume account, secured for

him his majority and the award of numerous medals and distinctions including a Companion of the Order of the Bath in 1842.

The discipline of his devotional life was as obvious and rigorous as that which controlled his professional actions. His bravery in the Sikh War of 1845–6 was legendary; on several occasions he had his horse shot from under him. In 1854 he was promoted to colonel and appointed adjutant-general of the Queen's forces in India. Early in 1857, during the Persian War he planned and directed an entirely successful attack upon Mohumra, a fortress on the Euphrates. That action was curtailed by the signing of peace in Paris. Immediately thereafter, he undertook a distinguished role in relieving a number of significant besieged garrisons (Allahabad, Futtepore and Cawnpore), during the mutiny: characteristically he recorded, 'By the help of God I have won Cawnpore'. Granted the climate, his age and the distances involved, all of this action was quite remarkable. He well deserved his promotion to major-general in July 1857. The rescue of Lucknow being launched, he was strategist enough to realize this could not be accomplished without reinforcements. But, with assistance, Lucknow was eventually relieved. This was in progress when news came that Havelock had been made a KCB. Within days, however, dysentery had robbed the nation of its newly acclaimed hero and evangelicalism of one of its soldier-saints.

BIBLIOGRAPHY
DNB
W. Landels, *Baptist Worthies*, II (London, 1884)
J. C. Marshman, *Memoirs of Sir Henry Havelock* (London, 1858)

J. H. Y. BRIGGS

Haven, Gilbert (b. Malden, MA, USA, 19 Sept. 1821; d. Malden, MA, USA, 3 Jan. 1880). Methodist abolitionist, editor, and bishop. Gilbert was the son of Gilbert and Hannah [née Burrill] and cousin of Erastus Otis Haven, later MEC bishop. While attending Wilbraham Academy, he experienced a religious conversion during a revival on 19 October 1839. He graduated from Wesleyan University in 1846, where he was noted for his scholarly abilities and abolitionist convictions. He accepted a position teaching Greek and German in Amenia Seminary, Amenia, New York, and was appointed principal in 1848. He married Mary Ingraham on 17 September 1851.

In spring 1851 he joined the New England Annual Conference of the MEC and subsequently served appointments in Massachusetts at Northampton (1851–3), Wilbraham (1853–5), Westfield (1855–7), Roxbury (1857–9), and Cambridge (1859–61). During this time he became well known within his denomination for his sermons and newspaper articles on slavery, temperance and racial injustice.

Motivated by patriotism, and perhaps by his grief over his wife's death (25 March 1860, after childbirth), Haven volunteered for military service early in the Civil

War. On 18 April 1861, he was commissioned chaplain of the 8th Massachusetts Regiment. His three-month enlistment gave him the opportunity to view slavery in Maryland and Northern Virginia and to report his observations in weekly contributions to the *Zion's Herald* and the *Christian Advocate and Journal*. After his military service was finished, he continued to publish his reflections on slavery and on the war, but with a new awareness of the church's involvement in slave ownership.

After an extended trip to Europe for health, Haven served as pastor of the North Russell Street MEC, Boston 1863–5. On 25 May 1863, he addressed the Church Anti-Slavery Society, arguing that the end of slavery was only the first step toward the ideal of human brotherhood. 'This important address signified the continuity in Haven's abolitionism from prewar protest against slavery to an even more active leadership in the struggle for racial justice after emancipation' (Gravely, 1973: 110). During his Boston years, he wrote numerous articles that called on the nation and the church to develop a new social order based on racial equality and justice, Haven pressed the issue in two articles published in the *Christian Advocate and Journal* in 1865, challenging the leaders of the MEC to adopt an official policy of racial equality for the reconstruction of the church in the South. Possibly in an attempt to silence or discredit him, he was assigned by Bishop Edward R. Ames to serve as a missionary in Vicksburg, Mississippi. The ensuing controversy was debated vigorously in the press by Haven's supporters and detractors. Although obliged as a Methodist minister to obey and prepared to go, Haven maintained that he could not accept the appointment under the church's unequal racial policy for missions. The controversy continued and, as a result, he suffered a physical collapse in March 1866. He retired from the New England Conference because of 'nervous prostrations'. After a year of recuperation and inactivity, Haven was elected editor of *Zion's Herald* in March 1867. During the five years of his editorship, the paper prospered, supporting a large number of ecclesiastical and social reforms including women's suffrage, prohibition, lay representation to the general conferences, and the ordination of women; the primary concern, however, was racial justice.

Haven was one of eight bishops elected in the 1872 MEC General Conference. He was assigned to Atlanta where he attempted to apply his principles on racial equality. His reputation as a radical abolitionist and his continuing efforts to promote racial equality within the denomination and at the national level were causes of frequent controversy during his episcopal years. Although he proved to be an able leader in ecclesiastical affairs, he found few converts to the cause of racial equality in the South or, for that matter, the MEC. He travelled to Mexico in 1873 on behalf of the mission work of the MEC and to Liberia and Spain in 1876. He died in his family home, Malden, Massachusetts, from malaria contracted in Liberia and the effects of several other afflictions.

According to his obituary, 'Bishop Haven was an important factor in the history that was made in this land during the years of his activity. He had opinions concerning every public man and measure, and his opinions were not without force' (*Christian Advocate*, 8 January 1880: 25). Gilbert Haven was one of many voices that spoke against the institution of slavery in the years leading up to and during the Civil War. In the midst of national conflict, however, he was able to look beyond the abolition of slavery to a new social order that treated all humans equally and justly. His vision was based on a deep, biblical faith, belief in a national covenant with God, and a millennial understanding of human brotherhood. His views were perceived as extreme by most whites in the South and by many in the North. Only the freedmen seemed to appreciate his vision and his actions. Ultimately, his concepts had little effect on race relations within the church and postwar society. His calls for racial equality during his later years seemed increasingly shrill against the background of the end of Reconstruction and the imposition of racial barriers within the MEC.

In addition to numerous articles in newspapers and periodicals, he wrote *The Pilgrim's Wallet* (New York, 1866), *National Sermons* (Boston, 1869), *Father Taylor, The Sailor Preacher* with Thomas Russell (New York, 1872), *Our Next Door Neighbour: A Winter in Mexico* (New York, 1875), and *Christus Consolator* (New York, 1893).

His daughter, Mary Michelle Haven (1858–1934), was very active in benevolent causes throughout her life. Most notable was her work in the Women's Home Missionary Society, MEC, where she served as president 1913–26. She married Wilbur Patterson Thirkield (later MEC bishop) in 1881. His son, William Ingraham Haven (1856–1928), was a member of the New England Annual Conference, MEC, (1881–1928); general secretary of the ABS (1899–1928); and a founder of the Epworth League and the Federal Council of Churches.

BIBLIOGRAPHY
DAB
W. H. Daniels, ed, *Memorials of Gilbert Haven* (Boston, MA, 1880)
DeAmReB
EWM
W. B. Gravely, *Gilbert Haven, Methodist Abolitionist* (Nashville, TN, 1973)
G. Prentice, *Life of Gilbert Haven* (New York, 1883)

MICHAEL PAUL BODDY

Haven, Jens (b. Wust, N. Jutland, Denmark, 23 June 1724; d. Herrnhut, Saxony, Germany, 16 April 1796). Moravian missionary to Labrador. The son of a Lutheran farmer, Haven completed an apprenticeship as furniture-maker under a Moravian and on 29 September 1748 was received into the Moravian community at Herrnhut. Prior to this he had been drawn to the pietistic revivalism of the Danish pastor Langaard after a dramatic conversion experience in a thunderstorm. From 1758 to 1763 this somewhat tempestuous Dane served as missionary in Lichtenfels, Greenland, but in 1764 he received permission from the Moravian authorities and from Hugh Palliser, Governor of Newfoundland, to sail for Labrador, for which he had long felt a call to serve. Palliser hoped Haven would pacify the Inuit and reduce any interference with fishing and the Labrador trade by converting them to Christianity. While the first Moravian expedition to Labrador under the leadership of JOHANN CHRISTIAN ERHARDT had resulted in 1752 in the murder of Erhardt and six crewmen, Haven gained the confidence of the Inuit by speaking to them in their own language, which he had learned in Greenland. After an additional exploratory trip with the veteran Greenland missionary CHRISTIAN LARSEN DRACHART in 1765 and successful negotiations between the Society for the Furtherance of the Gospel and the British colonial authorities to secure a land grant in Labrador, he returned there in 1770, chose a mission site, and purchased land from the Inuit.

In 1771 he departed for London, where, on 12 April 1771, he married Mary Butterworth from the Moravian settlement of Fulneck. Together with his new bride and 12 others – under the leadership of the Danish surgeon CHRISTOPH BRASEN – he returned to Labrador, where, in August of the same year, the missionaries erected the first mission house at the present-day location of Nain. In 1776 he established a second mission at Okak and, in 1782, a third at Hopedale. After spending 13 years in Labrador, Haven retired to Herrnhut in 1784, where, blind for many years, he died of complications from diabetes.

In the year of his departure from Labrador, Haven could look back upon a successful missionary and revivalistic activity among the Inuit of Labrador, which had been greatly aided by his ability to communicate with them. Manuscript material on Haven and the Moravian missionaries to Labrador is available in the Moravian archives at Herrnhut, Germany; London, England; and Bethlehem, Pennsylvania; as well as in the British colonial records. The main source for his life is his German autobiography of 1784, published 1844.

BIBLIOGRAPHY
Public Archives of Canada, Ottawa, 'Catalogus der Missionare in Labrador', Records of the Moravian Mission in Labrador [1764–1944], Microfilm 511, Reels 11–12, fol. 15195–6
DCB
Gemeinnachrichten (1844) 900–25
Kölbing
W. H. Whiteley, 'The Establishment of the Moravian Mission in Labrador and British Policy, 1763–83', CanHR, 45, 1 (1964): 29–50

MARCELLA ROLLMANN

Havergal, William Henry (b. High Wycombe, Buckinghamshire, England, 18 Jan. 1793; d. Shareshill, Staffordshire, England, 19 April 1870). Church musician. Havergal was the eldest son of an alderman, and educated at Merchant Taylors and St Edmund Hall, Oxford

(BA 1816; MA 1818) with a view to the ministry. His daughter makes no reference to any specific conversion experience. He was ordained in 1816 to a curacy with T. T. BIDDULPH which principally involved the care of the Somerset parishes of Durston and Lyng which Biddulph held in plurality with St James, Bristol. Pressure by Bishop HENRY RYDER secured him in 1822 a more populous sphere at Coaley, Gloucestershire, which carried a lectureship at Dursley, but the non-resident incumbent removed him in 1822.

Havergal then became Curate of Astley, Worcestershire, and on the death of its sickly incumbent in 1829, held the living in commendam until 1842. His twenty years at Astley left a deep impression on the village. He made preaching tours for the CMS, and in the crisis of 1828 edited a paper opposed to Catholic emancipation, the Protestant Warder. Left again without a cure by the inheritor of the living taking orders, Havergal spent three years in Worcester, principally as a private tutor. In 1845 he became an honorary canon of the Worcester Cathedral, until failing health and eyesight led him to a smaller charge at Shareshill, Staffordshire, which he held till his death.

For most of his life Havergal was primarily an active parish pastor, but church music was always a major concern. A church organist at 14, he was a pioneer of the use of the Seraphine organ and he revolutionized congregational singing in all his charges. At Astley he wrote many hymns, now unregrettably forgotten, but as an editor, composer and arranger of Psalm and hymn tunes he was deeply effective. For him the English Reformation was the golden age of theology, liturgy and church music alike, and convinced of Protestant ascendency in music, he laboured to revive and express a tradition of which he saw Ravenscroft, Handel and Crotch as pillars. He accepted Crotch's maxim 'new church music, but no new style', and urged 'style is an appointment of God in both nature and art. He follows it Himself' (Records: 173). Not unnaturally, he was out of sympathy with Hymns Ancient and Modern, which he held to debase worship both musically and theologically. His convictions were undergirded by a wealth of musicological research. He was well acquainted with the church music of the Continent (which he frequently visited for his health) and his harmonizations of chorales like 'Franconia' and 'Narenza' are in regular use. The hymn tune 'Adoration' is perhaps his best known original composition.

Havergal married in 1816 Jane Head of East Grinstead, who died in 1848. In 1851 he married Caroline Cooke of Gloucester. He had two sons, the Reverend Henry East Havergal, who also published musical works, and the Reverend Francis Tebbs Havergal, Vicar Choral of Hereford Cathedral and antiquary (see DNB) and four daughters, including Jane Miriam (Mrs Crane) his biographer, and Frances Ridley, his amanuensis, the hymn-writer.

His daughter denominates over fifty of her father's published works by opus numbers. Many of his musical publications were issued for specific occasions or charitable causes. The introductions and appendices to this collections embody his musical ideas. *Psalmody* (1871) (prepared by Frances Ridley Havergal), incorporated several of these works and many other of his compositions. A new edition by C. B. Snepp was prepared in 1875 as a companion to *Songs of Grace and Glory*. *Fireside Music* was a posthumous collection of compositions for the periodical *Our Own Fireside*. Havergal also published sermons, notably *Sermons Chiefly on Historical Subjects* (London, 1853) and memorials.

SELECT WRITINGS
W. H. Havergal, *A Selection of Hymns* (London, 1821)
—, *A Collection of Original Airs and Harmonized Tunes* (London, 1825)
—, Ravenscroft, *Whole Booke of Psalms* (London, 1844)
—, *Old Church Psalmody* (London, 1847)
—, *History of the Old Hundredth Psalm Tune with Specimens* (New York, 1854)
—, *Hundred Psalm and Hymn Tunes* (London, 1859)
—, *The Grand Chant in Forty Different Forms* (London, 1867)
—, *Havergal's Psalmnody and Century of Chants* (London, 1871)

BIBLIOGRAPHY
DNB

A. F. WALLS

Haweis, Thomas (b. Redruth, Cornwall, England, 1 Jan. 1734; d. Bath, England, 11 Feb. 1820). Anglican clergyman; rector of All Saints, Aldwincle, Northamptonshire. Chaplain and trustee-executor to Lady HUNTINGDON, and joint-founder of the LMS. He was the son of a solicitor who died when Haweis was a child. Little is known of his earliest years, although he was evidently able to read at a precocious age and learned Latin before he was five. He went to Truro Grammar School where GEORGE CONON was the headmaster. Haweis made rapid progress, distinguishing himself in classics and as a potential orator. Conon represents Haweis's first real contact with evangelicals. 'To his honour I wish to record it that his diligence to make us scholars was equalled by his zeal to make us Christians', Haweis later testified (manuscript Autobiography 7). In normal circumstances he would have proceeded to the university but family finances did not allow this and he was apprenticed to a surgeon-apothecary in Truro.

At this time he confessed that he was 'full of spirits, careless and indifferent about anything holy or heavenly' (manuscript Autobiography 10), but probably early in 1754 he was arrested by the preaching of SAMUEL WALKER at St Mary's and was enrolled as a member of his religious society. It was now, as he put it, that he learned the use of his knees in prayer, studied the Scriptures, and read books by THOMAS BOSTON, Baxter, PHILIP DODDRIDGE, William Law, and the ERSKINES. A call to the ministry soon followed and with his friend GEORGE BURNETT he began to prepare himself for ordination. Walker intended to send him to THOMAS ADAM at Winteringham, but when JOSEPH JANE visited Truro

he advised Haweis to go to Oxford and promised support. Haweis matriculated from Christ Church on 1 December 1755. For a time he associated with a group of Hutchinsonians without sharing all their views but soon parted from them. He formed a more lasting link with the Moravians in the area and found a friend in BENJAMIN LA TROBE. We may trace the germ of Haweis's significant concern for overseas missions to these contacts. While at Oxford he gathered around him a company of like-minded undergraduates who constituted a second Holy Club.

Ordained deacon in 1757, he took a curacy with Jane at St Mary Magdalene, Oxford, where his preaching drew large congregations and aroused considerable opposition. He transferred to Magdalen Hall in an attempt to avoid official censure but, after ordination as priest in 1758, he was eventually compelled to leave Oxford despite the efforts of Jane and other prominent evangelicals. He accepted an appointment as Assistant Chaplain to the Lock Hospital in London under MARTIN MADAN and thus added another evangelical voice in the capital where ROMAINE and THOMAS JONES were already ministering. He was also engaged as chaplain to the Earl of Peterborough and introduced to a circle of aristocratic supporters which included Lord and Lady DARTMOUTH (WILLIAM LEGGE), the HOTHAMS, Sir Sidney Stafford Smythe, and Lady HUNTINGDON. It was at this time too that he was instrumental in securing ordination for JOHN NEWTON, declining the curacy at Olney in his favour. Newton's *Authentic Narrative* originated in letters to Haweis. When Jones died in 1762, Haweis' name was advanced to succeed him at St Saviour's, Southwark, but to no avail, and in the following year he was pressed by WHITEFIELD to respond to a call from St Paul's, Philadelphia, but did not feel led to leave England. After the Dean of Westminster had vetoed a move to appoint him to Broadway Chapel, he was then offered the living at Aldwincle which he held from 1764 until his death. An unscrupulous patron later accused him of obtaining the incumbency under false pretences, a charge he and his evangelical friends were able to refute.

On arrival in his parish he found that the revival message had not yet penetrated this rural area and consequently his preaching carried with it an air of novelty. The church was soon filled with worshippers who travelled in from up to twenty miles away. There were regular conversions and societies were established not only in Aldwincle but also in neighbouring villages. Newton declared that Haweis's preaching sounded throughout the countryside like the report of a canon. Open-air meetings were held, homes were systematically visited, family worship was encouraged, and the poor and sick cared for. In the midst of all these activities he found time to complete an LL B degree at Cambridge in 1772 and to work on his comprehensive Bible commentary which was the best known of his many publications. Haweis had already preached in Lady Huntingdon's chapels, but in 1774 he was officially appointed as one of her chaplains. 'So great a door and it seems effectual was opened', he told Martha Biddulph (manuscript Letter), 'that I am willing, whilst my taper burns, it should be in that candlestick'. He devoted several months each year to itineration, relying on a curate and his evangelical neighbour, Brooke Bridges, Rector of Wadenhoe, to look after his parish in his absence. When the Countess's connexion ceased to be an Anglican society in 1781 Haweis resigned his chaplaincy and on resuming it in 1789 he declined to participate in ordinations. When Lady Huntingdon died he was named as trustee-executor and was in effect responsible for the continuation of her work along with Lady ANNE ERSKINE.

Stirred by reading accounts of South Sea voyages by Wallis and Cook, Haweis broached the possibility of sending missionaries to Tahiti in 1789. Two volunteers from Trevecka College were ready to embark but withdrew when episcopal ordination was refused. Although disappointed, Haweis did not abandon his purpose and in 1794 urged the formation of an interdenominational missionary society. This appeal led to the inauguration in 1795 of the LMS of which he is rightly regarded as a co-founder along with JOHN EYRE and DAVID BOGUE. He preached the first sermon of the society and presided at the valedictory communion service before the *Duff* sailed for Tahiti in 1796 with 30 missionaries on board. He kept in constant touch with those on the field and secured the interest of influential benefactors, including Sir Joseph Banks, president of the Royal Society.

After 44 years at Aldwincle, Haweis retired to Bath but continued to preach despite declining health. He was buried in Bath Abbey where a memorial tablet pays tribute to his achievements. His full importance has only been recognized in comparatively recent years when his manuscript Autobiography and correspondence have been examined. He emerges as a major figure in the development of eighteenth-century evangelicalism and as a pioneer of the missionary awakening. His pastoral care was exemplary in an age of negligence. His preaching, as reflected in his published sermons, was eloquent and soundly biblical. His principal works – his Bible commentary, his New Testament translation, and his Church history – were useful and popular if not outstanding. His defence of theological orthodoxy in controversial writings was firm and well informed. His contribution to the hymnody of the revival was notable. But above all Haweis was a man of action and it is as a tireless advocate of mission at home and abroad that he is best remembered still. His outlook was essentially irenical and while remaining loyal to the Church of England, he readily joined hands with Dissenters in furthering the gospel for which he lived. His manuscript Autobiography and Diary, together with an extensive correspondence, are preserved in the Mitchell Library, Sydney. Other letters are to he found in the Sutro Library, San Francisco, the National Library of Wales and the LMS.

SELECT WRITINGS

T. Haweis, *Evangelical Principles and Practice: Fourteen Sermons* (London, 1762)

—, *The Communicant's Spiritual Companion* (London, 1763)

—, *The Evangelical Expositor*, 2 vols (London, 1765–6)

—, *A Familiar and Practical Improvement of the Church Catechism* (London, 1775)

—, *Carmina Christo, or Hymns to the Saviour* (Bath, England, 1792)

—, *A Translation of the New Testament From the Original Greek* (London, 1795)

—, *A Plea for Peace and Union* (London, 1796)

—, *Missionary Instructions* (London, 1796)

—, *The Life of William Romaine* (London, 1797)

—, *An Impartial and Succinct History of the Rise, Declension, and Revival of the Church of Christ*, 3 vols (London, 1800)

—, *The Church of England Vindicated From Misrepresentation* (London, 1801)

—, *A View of the Present State of Evangelical Religion Throughout the World* (London, 1812)

BIBLIOGRAPHY

Julian

J. Morison, *The Fathers and Founders of the London Missionary Society*, 2 (London, no date): 170–208

A. S. Wood, *Thomas Haweis (1734–1820)* (London, 1957)

A. SKEVINGTON WOOD

Hawker, Robert (b. Exeter, England, 13 April 1753; d. Plymouth, England, 6 April 1827). Anglican clergyman and Calvinistic controversialist. Hawker was the son of Jacob Hawker, surgeon, of Exeter. He was educated at Exeter Grammar School before becoming a pupil of Mr White, surgeon, of Plymouth. In 1772, he married Anne (died 3 April 1817), daughter of Lieutenant (later Captain) Rains, Royal Navy, by whom he had eight children. After an apprenticeship at the London hospitals, he served for about three years as assistant surgeon in the Royal Marines. On 27 May 1778, he matriculated at Magdalen Hall, Oxford, but left without taking a degree. On 20 September 1778, he was ordained Curate of St Martin, near Looe, Cornwall. In the following December, he became curate to John Bedford at Charles, near Plymouth, on whose death, in 1784, he succeeded as vicar. Here he remained for the rest of his life.

On 5 July 1792, Hawker was made DD by diploma by the University of Edinburgh for his work, *Sermons on the Divinity of Christ*. In 1797, he accepted the deputy-chaplaincy of the military garrison at Plymouth. In 1802, he founded The Great Western Society for Dispersing Religious Tracts among the Poor in the western district; he also founded, in 1813, the Corpus Christi Society.

Hawker was a popular extemporary preacher known throughout Britain. For many years he made an annual visit to London where he preached to large crowds (mostly Dissenters) in the principal churches. In doctrine he was a High Calvinist; his detractors considered him a Hyper-Calvinist. Hawker particularly angered the mainstream Claphamite evangelicals by his refusal to preach the need of holiness of life. He informed CHARLES SIMEON that the only reason the Apostles had done so was because of the infant state of the church. Whenever Hawker preached at the Locke Chapel in London, WILLIAM WILBERFORCE avoided the services, anxious as he was to shield his children from what he termed Hawker's 'poison'. Accused by his opponents of Antinomianism, having advanced the doctrine of imputed (or immediate) sanctification, he exercised a considerable influence upon West Country evangelicalism. It was not a coincidence that many of the secessions of evangelical clergy from the Church of England in this period were led by men influenced by Hawker. High Calvinism continued to flourish in the West Country until it was finally dampened down by Bishop Phillpotts during the 1840s and 1850s.

Hawker wrote voluminously on Christian doctrine and discharged a vigorous discipline over his flock. He was also a pioneer in introducing Sunday schools at Plymouth, compiling one of the first children's hymn-books. Despite a reputation for strictness, he was a simple, lovable man and charitable almost to excess. He was grandfather of Robert Stephen Hawker, Vicar of Morwenstow, Cornwall, a very different churchman.

BIBLIOGRAPHY
Al. Ox.
G. C. Boase, *Bibliotheca Cornubiensis, 3 vols* (London, 1874): 219–20, 497, 510, 515, 1116, 1316, 1417
J. Davidson, *Bibliotheca Devoniensis* (Exeter, England, 1852): 146, 167, 168, 200; supplement: 9, 33
J. Dixon, *The Autobiography of a Minister of the Gospel* (London, 1866)
DNB
H. Dowling, *Funeral Discourse* (London, 1827)
D. M. Lewis, *Lighten Their Darkness* (Westport, CT, 1986): 29–30
J. Williams, 'Memoirs of the Rev. Robert Hawker, D.D.', in *The Works of the Rev. Dr. Hawker, D.D.*, 10 vols (London, 1831)

GRAYSON CARTER

Hawksworth, James (b. *c.* 1748; d. 1810). Methodist and Moravian minister. Little is known of James Hawksworth's ancestry. He was one of the earliest students at Trevecka College (founded 1768), and a great favourite with Lady HUNTINGDON, whose letters to him have been preserved. He was sent by her to preach in the West Country in 1771, transferred to Dublin in 1773, and sent to Devon in 1774.

He was ordained at Plymouth, in ANDREW KINSMAN's Tabernacle, in September 1774, and almost immediately returned to Ireland, where Lady Huntingdon considered his services were of most use. With the arrival of other students Hawksworth was able to itinerate in southern Ireland with some success. In 1782 he joined the Moravians, but continued to preach in Dublin. Exceptionally this did not produce a breach with Lady Huntingdon who continued to correspond with him. His Moravian ministry seems to have been particularly obscure, and all that is known of his later life is that he retired to Horsley in Gloucestershire.

BIBLIOGRAPHY
Cheshunt College archives, Cambridge and Dr Williams' Library, original letters

EDWIN WELCH

Hawley, Gideon (b. Bridgeport [Stratfield], CT, BNA, 5 Nov. 1727; d. Marshpee, MA, USA, 3 Oct. 1807). New England Congregational missionary and clergyman. He graduated from Yale College in 1749 with the intention to devote himself to missionary work among the Indians of New England and New York. He was licensed to preach by the Fairfield East Association on 23 May 1750, and installed as the schoolmaster to the Housatunnock (Housatonic) Indians at the mission station at Stockbridge, Massachusetts, operated by the Society in London for Propagating the Gospel in New England (SPGNE). There he came under the influence of the resident missionary, JONATHAN EDWARDS. In 1753, Hawley established a mission of his own to the Iroquois at Oughquauga (Windsor, New York) under the auspices of the Commissioners for Indian Affairs (who acted as agents for the SPGNE), and was ordained for that work in Boston on 31 July 1754. The outbreak of the Seven Years' War (the French and Indian War, 1756–63) disrupted Hawley's mission work, and in June, 1756, he joined a colonial regiment as chaplain. In 1758, the SPGNE installed him as pastor of the Indian congregation at Marshpee, Massachusetts, where he followed a violently anti-Edwardsean pastor, Lemuel Briant. However, Hawley's labours as a preacher and evangelist won him permanent popularity with the congregation, and he remained the pastor at Marshpee until his death.

BIBLIOGRAPHY
AAP
F. B. Dexter, *Biographical Notices of the Graduates of Yale College* (New Haven, CT, 1913)
O. E. Winslow, *Jonathan Edwards* (New York, 1940)

ALLEN C. GUELZO

Hawtrey, Charles (Sleech) (b. 1780; d. 17 July 1831). Anglican clergyman and exponent of prophecy. He attended Oriel College, Oxford (BA 1801; MA 1813) and was Curate of Holyrood, Southampton and Vicar of Wilston, Monmouth. In 1805 he became minister of the episcopal Chapel for the Jews at Bethnal Green (where J. WOLFF attended *circa* 1820). As secretary of the LSPCJ he was editor of the *Jewish Expositor and Friend of Israel* and connected with LEWIS WAY. In 1826 he attended the Albury prophetic conference hosted by HENRY DRUMMOND.

BIBLIOGRAPHY
L. E. Froom, *The Prophetic Faith of our Fathers*, 3 (Washington, DC, 1946): 428–9
A Spiritual Watchman [C.S. Hawtrey], *The Nature of the First Resurrection* (London, 1826)
A. M. W. Stirling, *The Ways of Yesterday ... Chronicles of the Way Family from 1307–1885* (London, 1930)
Travels and Adventures of the Rev. Joseph Wolff (London, 1861): 79–80, 598
C. L. Shadwell, *Registrum Orielense*, 2 (London, 1902): 272

TIMOTHY C. F. STUNT

Haycroft, Nathanael (b. near Exeter, Devon, England, 14 Feb. 1821; d. Leicester, 16 Feb. 1873). English Baptist minister. From a substantial family, he followed a good education in Devon by studying under w. h. murch at Stepney, refusing an invitation to a pastorate in Ipswich in order to continue his studies at Edinburgh and Glasgow. His first pastorate was at Saffron Walden in Essex, removing to Broadmead, Bristol in 1852, where he served for 14 years, where he was active in city life, defending the interests of Protestant Dissent and serving as secretary of the college. He preached finely crafted literary sermons of some intellectual weight, rather rapidly delivered. In 1866 he pioneered new work at Victoria Road, Leicester, where a new church had been built largely at the initiative and beneficence of RICHARD HARRIS, hosiery manufacturer, treasurer of the Charles Street Church. An MA of Glasgow, Haycroft was later awarded that university's DD. He long served on the committee of the BMS, and sat on the first School Board in Leicester, staunchly upholding Nonconformist principles. An active freemason, he published a number of lectures, the last of which was an inaugural discourse given to the Leicester Philosophical Society on whose Council he sat on *The Limits of Scientific Inquiry*.

BIBLIOGRAPHY
BaptMag (March 1873)

J. H. Y. BRIGGS

Haynes, Lemuel (b. West Hartford, CT, BNA, 18 July 1753; d. Granville, NY, USA, 28 Sept. 1833). Congregational preacher. He was a 'New Light' Separate or Strict Congregationalist minister who pastored churches in Connecticut, New York, and, particularly, Rutland, Vermont. The illegitimate child of a white mother and black father, both unknown, he served in the American Revolution both as a minuteman and in the Continental Army. His early writing included a poetic ballad 'The Battle of Lexington' (*circa* 1775), and 'Liberty Further Extended' (*circa* 1776), a militant essay attacking slavery. Haynes' most influential sermon was 'Universal Salvation' (1805), a satiric and witty Calvinist attack on Universalist Hosea Ballou which appeared in some seventy editions. In Manchester, Vermont, Haynes became involved in the Boorn case in which two brothers were tried and convicted of murder on circumstantial evidence. Haynes befriended the brothers, who were later proved innocent, and published 'Mystery Developed' (1820) a narrative account of the case, as well as a sermon 'The Prisoner Released' (1820).

BIBLIOGRAPHY
R. Newman, ed., *Black Preacher to White America* (Brooklyn, NY, 1990)

RICHARD NEWMAN

Hayward, James (b. Tisbury, Wiltshire, England, 1769; d. 1850). LMS Missionary on Tahiti. Hayward arrived on Tahiti in July 1801. He was married twice. Hayward served at Tahiti from 1801 to 1808, at Moorea from 1808 to 1809 and at Huahine and Moorea between 1809 and 1818. Ill health hindered his work and although he returned to Tahiti in April 1821 his wife's infirmities led to his departure from the island in December 1822, whereupon his association with the society ceased.

BIBLIOGRAPHY
N. Gunson, *Messengers of Grace* (Melbourne, 1978)
R. Lovett, *The History of the London Missionary Society 1795–1895* (London 1899)
RMD, 4th edn (London, 1923)

R. WATCYN JAMES

Hazlewood, David (b. Fakenham, Norfolk, England, 8 Jan. 1820; d. Maitland, New South Wales, Australia, 30 Oct. 1855). Wesleyan missionary in Fiji. Hazlewood, who had been brought up in the Church of England, joined the Wesleyan Methodists at the age of 14 and in 1842 migrated to New South Wales, Australia. In Sydney in February 1844 he married Jane McIntyre. Having been a local preacher, he was accepted by the New South Wales district meeting as a missionary to Fiji, where he sailed with his wife in March 1844. He was ordained in Fiji in 1847. As a missionary, Hazlewood became a skilled linguist and scholar of languages. His principal achievement was the compilation of a Fijian grammar and dictionary and a translation of the Old Testament. After the death of Jane in 1849 his faith, he recorded, 'seems to diminish rather than increase' (Williams, 1931: 509). Visiting Sydney in 1851, he married Sarah Webster. Because of ophthalmia and tuberculosis, Hazlewood was compelled to leave the Fiji mission in 1853 and settled in New South Wales. He continued his translation work until his early death.

BIBLIOGRAPHY
W. G. Hazlewood, 'The Hazlewood Story', *Descent*, 2 (Sydney, 1965): 65–7
'Reverend David Hazlewood, 1820–1855', *Australasian Methodist Historical Society Journal*, 69 (October 1955): 931
T. Williams, *The Journal of Thomas Williams, Missionary in Fiji, 1840–1853*, ed. G. C. Henderson (Sydney, 1931)

DAVID HILLIARD

Heald, James (b. Stockport, England, 1 March 1796; d. Parr's Wood, Manchester, 26 Oct. 1873). MP, banker and philanthropist. For a time Heald retired from his father's Portwood spinning business to study for ordination in the Church of England, but returned both to business and to Methodism, becoming treasurer to the Missionary Society, and a leading supporter of the Theological Institution, especially the Didsbury branch, opened in 1842, near his home at Parr's Wood. A Tory who was prepared to see Peel's Government sacrificed to the Protestant cause, he was MP for Stockport, 1847–

52, losing the seat when he accepted the principles of free trade. He did not marry. Heald appears not infrequently in the political columns of the Manchester press in the 1830s and 1840s.

BIBLIOGRAPHY
DNB
W. R. Ward, *Religion and Society in England* (London, 1972)
—, *Early Victorian Methodism* (London, 1976)

W. R. WARD

Heald, William (Margetson) (b. Dewsbury Moor, near Leeds, Yorkshire, England, 1767; d. 11 Jan. 1837). Anglican clergyman; Vicar of Birstall. He was educated at Batley Grammar School and studied medicine in Edinburgh and London. Beginning to practise as a surgeon and apothecary in Wakefield he abandoned the profession and prepared for ordination at Catherine Hall, Cambridge (1790–4). He took a curacy at Balsham, Cambridgeshire, where he also tutored pupils and in 1796 was appointed Curate of Birstall near Leeds, where he became vicar in 1801. On his resignation in 1836 the living was promised to his son by the Archbishop of York.

BIBLIOGRAPHY
DNB
R. V. Taylor, *The Biographia Leodiensis* (London, 1865)

TIMOTHY C. F. STUNT

Healey, John (b. Leicester, Leicestershire, England, 31 Oct. 1764; d. 17 June 1848). Baptist minister and denominational organizer. Raised within the Anglican tradition, Healey became a Baptist and began preaching about 1792, gathering a small group about him. He, along with part of his group, emigrated to Baltimore, Maryland, where they constituted themselves as a church in 1797 and ordained Healey as their pastor in 1798. Healey continued in that post till his death in 1848. Healey was a founding member of the Triennial Convention, formed to support foreign missions on 18 May 1814, and served on its Board of Managers.

BIBLIOGRAPHY
AAP

WADE A. HORTON

Hebich, Samuel (b. Nellingen, Würtemburg, 29 April 1803; d. Korntal, near Stuttgart, 21 May 1868). Pioneer Lutheran missionary. Son of an impoverished Lutheran pastor, Hebich was prospering as an apprentice in business before his conversion on 21 June 1821. After several years as a commercial traveller around the Baltic and as an estate manager he applied to the Basel Mission to serve in India. This following the momentous meeting on 12 February 1834 when the Basel Mission decided to enter India on its own. He was instructed to go to P. P. SCHAFFTER to learn Tamil, find Indian co-workers and then start a Lutheran church in Tamil Nadu. However, English friends persuaded him to go to Malabar.

He landed in Calicut on 14 October 1834 and was met by Judge Nelson who gave him and his two companions hospitality and commended them to the Collector in Manglore. He discovered that nothing was being done for the Tulu-speaking people (the language spoken around Mangalore). Tulu did not even have its own script. Hebich settled in Mangalore and opened a school in May 1838 for Kannada boys, and later a school for high caste boys. The latter did not flourish until English classes were added. The first convert was Abraham Mandshu, a fisherman, who was baptized in September 1837. Four colleagues were sent to reinforce the mission at the end of 1836. There were revivals in 1847 and 1858. Disapproving initially of HERMANN GUNDERT'S European-style theological training for Indian candidates for the ministry, Hebich had four European catechists, former soldiers working with Indians. Two were successful but the experiment was dropped.

In 1849, with a congregation of 27 former Hindus, 5 Anglo-Indians, 2 converts from Islam, and 4 who had left the Roman Catholic Church, a congregation was formed with a proper constitution. Stations were opened at Cannanore (1851), Dharwar and Hubli with 11 minor stations. Following a visit from Inspector Josenhans from Basel, a general conference of the mission met in 1852 and elected Hebich 'Präses', or presiding minister, with his colleague Mögling as secretary.

Hebich itinerated ceaselessly, and preached at all great festivals. He worked especially among the poorest of the poor, the plantation workers, and was in constant danger from assassination by fanatical Muslims. He preached through interpretation but it was his direct conversational approach employed on Europeans and Indians alike which won converts. His English vocabulary was estimated at 530 words but he had unparalleled success among the European forces stationed on the Malabar coast. Hebich is chiefly known for "Hebich's Own', a band of converted army officers to whom he preached a simple evangelical gospel. In October 1858 he was forced to return to Europe. After three years' itineration in Germany and Switzerland he settled near Stuttgart where he finally succumbed to liver disease.

BIBLIOGRAPHY
W. Schlätter, *Die Geschichte der Baseler Mission*, 3 vols, III (Basel, 1916)
G. Thomssen, *Samuel Hebich of India*

E. M. JACKSON

Heck, Barbara [née Ruckle] (b. Rathkeale, Ireland, *c.* 1734; d. Augusta, Upper Canada, *c.* 1804). Methodist leader. Heck's parents, members of the immigrant Palatine community, became Methodists. Barbara, a quiet deep-thinking girl joined the Methodist Society when she was 18, taking part in meetings. In 1760 she married

Paul and they, PHILIP EMBURY, a carpenter, his wife and others, sailed in June for America. In New York many of them drifted into religious indifference, but when a new group of Irish immigrants arrived in 1765, Barbara, concerned by the growing secularism challenged Embury to start a Methodist society. She gathered a congregation together and numbers increased so rapidly that ever larger premises were needed. Soon Barbara was the prime mover in getting a chapel built. A site in John Street was purchased, the building erected with Embury doing some of the carpentry and preaching at the opening in 1768. Tradition says Barbara whitewashed the walls herself.

When Wesley's missionaries arrived the Emburys, Hecks and others went to the Camden Valley (1770) and started another Methodist society. The Hecks moved to Canada when the American War of Independence broke out, going first to Montreal, then to Upper Canada. Here, in Augusta they started the first Methodist class and welcomed Wesleyan Methodist missionaries when they arrived. A widow for 12 years, Barbara died at her youngest son's home. Barbara was pious, unassuming, but determined, often prodding the men into action when they hesitated.

BIBLIOGRAPHY
A. Stevens, *The Women of American Methodism* (London, no date)
N. W. Taggart, *The Irish in World Methodism, 1760–1900* (London, 1986)

E. DOROTHY GRAHAM

Hedding, Elijah (b. Dutchess County, NY, USA, 7 June 1780; d. Poughkeepsie, NY, USA, 9 April 1852). Itinerant preacher, bishop and great interpreter of church law. Elijah was the son of James Hedding, of English ancestry. None of his parents were church members, but his mother was deeply religious and instructed her son in the doctrines and duties of the Christian faith. He began praying in secret at the age of four and did so until he was led to abandon all serious matters by some of his friends. In 1791 the Hedding family moved to Starksborough, Vermont, a sparsely settled frontier area. As he grew up he tried Deism, atheism and universalism, but could not get away from the doctrines he heard BENJAMIN ABBOTT preach in 1789. After some years, a Methodist family moved into the neighbourhood. They gathered their neighbours for religious services on Sundays, usually reading from JOHN WESLEY's sermons or something similar. Hedding was a good reader and was often called upon to read. Through this, and reading books this family lent him, he became well acquainted with the basic Methodist doctrines.

In 1798, the Vesgennes circuit was organized, during a great spiritual revival. After some months, Hedding was greatly moved. He went into a grove, he says, and 'I solemnly made a dedication of myself to God, I laid my all – soul, body, goods and all – for time and for eternity, upon the altar, and I have *never* taken them back'. However, he was still troubled by guilt and anguish. At a class meeting, sensing his great distress of mind, the preacher and the pious cottagers bowed around Hedding and prayed for peace for his soul. He felt the burden of guilt removed, and was filled with joy. On the same day, 24 December 1798, he enrolled as probationer in the MEC. He began to pray and exhort in public. Although resisting the thought, he began to feel a call to preach the Gospel and consented to receive an exhorter's licence, often accompanying the preacher in his appointments. In 1799, the eccentric LORENZO DOW was sent to the Essex circuit. He got the idea he was called to preach in Ireland and left the circuit. Young Hedding was asked to take his place. Great revivals broke out, and he continued with great success. He received a local preacher's licence in 1800, and was admitted on trial in the New York Conference on 16 June 1801; into full connexion and ordained deacon by Bishop RICHARD WHATCOAT in 1803 and elder by Bishop FRANCIS ASBURY in 1805. In 1803 he had an attack of malignant dysentery, and shortly after seized with inflammatory rheumatism, from which he never fully recovered.

Hedding became one of the foremost agents in spreading Methodism in New England. He diligently studied grammar, the English language and theology, often encountering Calvinistic ministers with great success. He was presiding elder over several districts, and a member or bishop in all General Conferences after 1808. In 1808 his influence helped in carrying through the proposal for a delegated General Conference. He at first supported the proposal to make the presiding elders elected by the annual conferences, but changed his mind later. After seeing several circuits, he was elected bishop against his will in 1824. He became a specialist on church law and did much to put the church order on a fair and uniform basis. When the slavery issue became acute in 1844 he supported the antislavery provisions of the *Discipline*, but felt that a division of the church was the worst that could happen. Consequently, many accused him for being positive toward slavery. At the General Conference of 1848, he was relieved from all pastoral and episcopal duties for health reasons.

On 10 January 1810, he married Lucy Blish, of Gilsum, New Hampshire. During Hedding's later years he resided in Poughkeepsie, New York, where he died with 'glory, glory' on his lips, and was buried at a rural graveyard south of Poughkeepsie.

BIBLIOGRAPHY
AAP
D. W. Clark, *Life and Times of Rev. Elijah Hedding* (New York, 1855)
DAB
EWM
MQR
T. L. Flood and J. W. Hamilton, eds., *Lives of Methodist Bishops* (New York, 1882)
M. Simpson, ed., *Cyclopaedia of Methodism* (Philadelphia, PA, 1881)

OLE E. BORGEN

Heighway, Thomas (b. London, *c.* 1793; d. Sierra Leone, 7 Jan. 1828). CMS missionary to Sierra Leone. Heighway studied at the CMS College at Islington from 1826 before being sent with EDMUND BOSTON on 18 November 1827 to Sierra Leone. Heighway died shortly after his arrival in West Africa. His willingness to serve in Sierra Leone is remarkable in view of the high death rate among early CMS missionaries in West Africa. Heighway was married to Sarah Phipps who survived him and married another CMS missionary, JOHN WARBURTON. (She died 21 July 1890.)

BIBLIOGRAPHY
D. T. B[arry], *CMS Register of Missionaries and Native Clergy* (privately printed) (London, 1906)

DONALD M. LEWIS

Hellmuth, Isaac (b. near Warsaw, Poland, 14 Dec. 1817; d. Weston-super-Mare, Somerset, England, 28 May 1901). Anglican clergyman, educator and bishop. Of Jewish parentage, Hellmuth appears to have been converted to Christianity while a student at the University of Breslau. In 1841 he emigrated to England, settling at Liverpool where he came under the influence of HUGH MCNEILE. Three years later he left for British North America, where he was ordained (deacon and priest 1846) and appointed professor of Hebrew in Bishop's College, Lennoxville. He resigned from the college in 1853 and served for nearly a decade as general superintendent of the Colonial and Continental Church Society in BNA. He played an important role in the founding of Huron College in 1863 and was appointed its first principal and professor of divinity. When BENJAMIN CRONYN died in 1871 Hellmuth succeeded him as Bishop of Huron. He held this position until 1883 when he left Canada for England, where he remained until his death. Hellmuth was a determined opponent of Tractarianism and Ritualism and also wrote in response to Bishop Colenso's views on the Pentateuch.

BIBLIOGRAPHY
A. H. Crowfoot, *This Dreamer* (Vancouver, Canada, 1963)
DNB, Second supplement (1901–1911)

RICHARD W. VAUDRY

Hemmenway, Moses (b. Framingham, MA, BNA, 15 Sept. 1735; d. Wells, ME, USA, 5 April 1811). New England Congregational divine. Although converted under the preaching of GEORGE WHITEFIELD in the Great Awakening, he showed little sympathy for the opinions or the excesses of many 'New Light' Congregationalist leaders. Hemmenway hewed firmly to the course of 'Old Calvinism', which sought an evangelical middle ground between the lure of enlightenment deism and unitarianism on the one hand and revivalistic 'enthusiasm' on the other.

Much of his conservatism grew out of his training at Harvard College, where attitudes ran strongly against the Awakening. After he graduated in 1755, Hemmenway taught school and supplied pulpits while awaiting a pastoral call. But it was not until 1 March 1759 that he was finally invited to fill the pulpit of the First Church of Wells, Maine (then a province of Massachusetts) and subsequently ordained on 8 August 1759. Short of stature, careless of dress, peculiar of gait, he was forced by nearsightedness in one eye and blindness in the other to read his sermons from manuscripts which he held close to his face. Nevertheless, his preaching 'was not only decidedly evangelical, but highly practical'. He was invited to deliver the Dudleian lecture at Harvard in 1783, to preach the Massachusetts election sermon in 1784, and to sit in the Massachusetts ratifying convention for the Federal Constitution in 1788.

Although a conventional Calvinist, and in some respects an admirer of JONATHAN EDWARDS, he was utterly out of sympathy with the theological extremism and separatism promoted by Edwards's disciples, the New Divinity Men. Hemmenway's first major publication, *Seven Sermons on the Obligation and Encouragement of the Unregenerate* (1767), was clearly intended as a reply to one of the principal architects of the New Divinity, SAMUEL HOPKINS, and Hopkins's demand in 1765 for immediacy in conversion apart from the 'use of means' by the unregenerate. Hemmenway clashed again with the New Divinity in 1792, when he published *A Discourse Concerning the Church*, which argued again that 'All who credibly profess Christianity are to be considered as belonging to the household of faith'. The *Discourse* touched off another round of controversy for Hemmenway, this time with another New Divinity partisan, NATHANAEL EMMONS of Franklin, Massachusetts, which ran through 1795. Hemmenway ministered continuously in Wells until the end of 1810, when the development of a cancerous tumour near one of his eyes forced his retirement; and, after severe suffering, the cancer resulted in his death less than a year later. In addition to his controversial works, Hemmenway also published a dozen sermons and charges, and received honourary DDs from both Harvard (1785) and Dartmouth (1792).

BIBLIOGRAPHY
AAP
A. C. Guelzo, *Edwards On The Will* (Middletown, CT, 1989)

ALLEN C. GUELZO

Henderson, Ebenezer (b. The Linn, Dunfermline, Scotland, 17 Nov. 1784; Mortlake, England, 16 May 1858). Linguist, translator and BFBS agent. The son of George Henderson, an agricultural labourer, by his wife, Jean Buchanan, he was educated at Dunduff school and then at Dunfermline. He left school at the age of ten to work. From 1803 he studied at ROBERT HALDANE's seminary in Edinburgh. In 1805 he and John Paterson were sent as missionaries to India; they went to Denmark *en route* to the Dutch colony of Serampore, but, finding they could not obtain passage to India, they began preaching in Copenhagen.

In January 1806 Henderson settled as minister at Elsinore in Denmark and supported himself by teaching English. By 1807 he was preaching in Danish. The bombardment of Copenhagen in September forced him to move on to Sweden where he ministered to Danish prisoners. By 1808 he had become competent in Latin, Greek, Hebrew, French, German, Danish and Swedish. He spent part of 1810 in England but in 1811 was in Sweden again where he established the first Swedish Congregational church. In 1812–13 he was in Copenhagen to supervise the translation of Icelandic New Testament and in 1814 he helped found the Danish Bible Society and travelled to Iceland to distribute New Testaments.

In 1816 he went to St Petersburg where, under the patronage of Tsar Alexander, he printed the Bible in a number of different languages and dialects. In 1818 he undertook another journey to Russia. Henderson's strong objections to a Turkish translation of the New Testament caused him to break formally with the BFBS in 1822. He returned to Russia and lived in St Petersburg until 1825 when the Greek Orthodox Church succeeded in securing an imperial edict against the work of the Bible Society.

In July 1825 Henderson returned to Britain and took charge of the missionary students at Gosport and moved with them to Hoxton College. From 1830 to 1850 he was tutor of Highbury College and then he retired. From 1852 to 1853 he was minister of Sheen Vale Independent Chapel in Mortlake, where he died.

BIBLIOGRAPHY
Boase
DNB

DONALD M. LEWIS

Henderson, John (b. Bo'ness, West Lothian, Scotland, 1782; d. Glasgow, 1 May 1867). Scottish Presbyterian layman and philanthropist. A tragic accident in 1842 in which his brother drowned and he but narrowly escaped is said to have changed Henderson into a wholehearted Christian philanthropist who gave away annually thousands of pounds, the profits of his Glasgow drysalting business. The United Presbyterian Church (UPC) in which he was an important figure received much support towards education, outreach and mission but he was no narrow denominationalist. He paid for the FCS kirk at Inchinnan where his country estate was because that was what the locals wanted, and he was active in the formation in 1845 of the EA following his publication of a volume of essays on Christian Union. Protestant work in Europe was underpinned financially by him, and in 1860 he was the first chairman of the National Bible Society of Scotland. A cause that he held dear was that of Sabbath Observance, and to prevent

trains being run on a Sunday he bought shares in Scottish railway companies in order to speak and vote against such operations. This proved an unsuccessful strategy as the majority English shareholders were not sympathetic to any practice that reduced profits. The defenders of the Sabbath, Henderson among them, were capable of provoking endless controversy but not ultimately of imposing their views on a reluctant society.

BIBLIOGRAPHY
Memoirs and Portraits of one Hundred Glasgow Men, 1 (Glasgow, 1886): 159–60
C. J. A. Robertson, 'Early Scottish Railways and the Observance of the Sabbath', *ScHR*, 67 (1978): 143–67

ALASTAIR J. DURIE

Henderson, Richard (b. Scotland; d. 12 Dec. 1769). Minister of Blantyre, Scotland, 1722–69; frequent preacher at Cambuslang before and during the revival of 1742. He was interim-moderator of Cambuslang before the settlement of WILLIAM MCCULLOCH in 1731. He assisted McCulloch at the 1739 Communion and again at the second 1742 Communion at which GEORGE WHITEFIELD was also present.

BIBLIOGRAPHY
A. Fawcett, *The Cambuslang Revival* (London, 1971): 29, 49, 120
Fasti, 3

JOHN R. MCINTOSH

Henkel, David (b. Staunton, VA, USA, 4 May 1795; d. Catawba, County, NC, USA, 15 June 1832). Lutheran pastor and confessional polemicist. The youngest and most brilliant of PAUL HENKEL's six sons, David Henkel was licensed to preach at the age of 17 in South Carolina after studying theology under Godfrey Dreher. The following year he moved to North Carolina where he also obtained his licence. Unsuccessfully seeking ordination in 1817 and 1818, his petition in 1819 coincided with rising tensions within the North Carolina Synod between the Henkel family and the synod secretary, Gottlieb Schober – a former Moravian. Schober and the majority of the pastors in the synod wanted to participate in the formation of the General Synod of American Lutherans, even though this involvement meant changing the constitutionally mandated time of the synod meeting, Trinity Sunday. The Henkels and their supporters held a rump synod meeting on that day, ordained David Henkel, and elected Paul Henkel synod president.

When the two factions bitterly clashed at the 1820 meeting, the Henkelite minority withdrew and created, along with several like-minded churches in eastern Tennessee, the Tennessee Synod. Eventually, the Tennessee Synod included many Lutheran churches in both Carolinas and Virginia. The schism lasted until 1920.

Henkel defended the action in an explosive pamphlet,

The Carolinian Herald of Liberty, Religious and Political (1821). In it, he condemned the creation of a pan-Lutheran body in the United States and the dilution of Lutheran adherence to the Augsburg Confession in America. The new synod was a human creation which would usurp to itself doctrinal authority which alone belonged to the ordained ministeriums. The action of the North Carolina Synod in 1820 in abandoning the doctrine of the real presence of Christ in the Eucharist was, for Henkel, an act of blasphemy. It was in this sense that Henkel regarded himself and the Tennessee Synod as evangelical: 'the doctrine of the real presence . . . is not an invention of my own, nor a novel doctrine. Should anyone think Luther was wrong, let him openly declare it and forsake the Lutheran Church'.

BIBLIOGRAPHY
Socrates Henkel, *History of the Evangelical Lutheran Tennessee Synod* (New Market, VA, 1890)
E. Clifford Nelson, ed., *The Lutherans in North America* (Philadelphia, PA, 1975)

ROBERT CALHOON

Henkel, Paul (b. Dutchman's Creek, Rowan County, NC, BNA, 15 Dec. 1754; d. New Market, VA, USA, 27 Nov. 1825). Lutheran pastor, patriarch of conservative, confessional Lutheranism in the South, and publisher of Lutheran theological and liturgical works. Through numerous pastorates in Virginia and North Carolina, through the work of his six sons who he trained for the ministry, and through the religious press he established in New Market, Virginia, Paul Henkel made conservative, confessional Lutheranism a coherent religious force in the South from the 1790s to the 1820s.

He grew up on the North Carolina and Virginia frontier in danger and hardship. His family fled the Catawba war in 1760 for Augusta County, Virginia where his sister burned to death in an Indian attack. His brother became a convert to Methodism; Paul studied theology under a Lutheran pastor in Fredericksburg, Maryland, was licensed by the Pennsylvania Ministerium in 1783 and ordained in 1792. Called by several Lutheran churches in Rowan County, North Carolina in 1800, he returned to Virginia in 1803, where the retiring Peter Muhlenberg bequeathed Henkel his black silk vestments. New Market was his principal base, from which he served churches from the Shenandoah Valley to Botetourt County. On trips into settlements of Virginians in eastern Tennessee, he encouraged the creation of churches there which would later become the nucleus of the Tennessee Synod, a conservative, confessional Lutheran body created in 1820 under the leadership of Henkel's sons, DAVID and Philip HENKEL. The Henkel Press of New Market, Virginia became a major resource for Tennessee Synod churches in Virginia, Tennessee, and the Carolinas, publishing German and English language liturgies and confessional writings.

BIBLIOGRAPHY
W. E. Eisenberg, *The Lutheran Church in Virginia, 1717–1962* (Roanoke, VA, 1967)

ROBERT CALHOON

Henley, second Baron, of Chardstock [né **Robert Henley Eden**, replacing 'Eden' by 'Henley', 31 March 1831] (b. Dresden, Germany, 3 Sept. 1789; d. London, 3 Feb. 1841). Barrister, church reformer, MP and peer. The grandson of a lord chancellor and son of a diplomat, Robert was educated at Eton and Christ Church, Oxford. He became a barrister, specializing in bankruptcy law, and was appointed a master in chancery in 1826. In 1824 he had married Harriet, the daughter of Sir ROBERT PEEL and sister of Robert Peel, then Home Secretary and later Conservative leader. He sat as Tory MP for Fowey 1826–30 and succeeded his father in his Irish title on 6 December 1830. In 1832 Henley's book *A Plan of Church Reform* created a stir by proposing the endowment of new churches from cathedral funds and the exclusion of bishops from the House of Lords. It occasioned Thomas Arnold's *Principles of Church Reform* (1833) and formed a blueprint for the Ecclesiastical Commission established by Peel in 1835. Henley's Church Reformation Society foundered on his wish for joint action with evangelical Dissenters, of whose Christian Instruction Society he was a patron. He suffered a period of insanity before his death.

BIBLIOGRAPHY
DNB

DAVID WILLIAM BEBBINGTON

Henry, Joseph (b. Albany, NY, USA, 17 Dec. 1797; d. Washington, DC, USA, 13 May 1878). Physicist and first secretary/director of the Smithsonian Institution. Henry was the son of William Henry, a poor day-labourer of Scottish descent. He was baptized as a Presbyterian and professed that faith throughout his life. In 1819 Henry enrolled in the Albany Academy after having become interested in science upon reading Reverend George Gregory's *Popular Lectures on Experimental Philosophy, Astronomy*, and *Chemistry* (London, 1809). Henry remarked that this book 'has, under Providence, exerted a remarkable influence on my life'. For some time after 1822 Henry was occupied as a private tutor and surveyor. His real career as a researcher began with his appointment as professor of mathematics and natural philosophy at Albany Academy in 1825. In 1832 he accepted a chair at the College of New Jersey (now Princeton University).

Henry's major research was in electromagnetism. A consummate experimenter, he developed powerful electromagnets and independently discovered self-induction. He also examined terrestrial magnetism and other geophysical phenomena. He advanced a Newtonian view and did not accept the field concept of his contemporary

MICHAEL FARADAY. In 1846 Henry felt duty bound to become secretary of the Smithsonian Institution. Against many odds he proposed that the Smithsonian support original research and encourage the development of a professional scientific community rather than become involved in applied science or education. Henry was an original member of the National Academy of Sciences, and served as vice-president in 1866, and president from 1868 until he died.

BIBLIOGRAPHY
DNB
DSB

ARIE LEEGWATER

Henry, Patrick (b. Hanover County, VA, BNA, 29 May 1736; d. Prince Edward County, VA, USA, 6 June 1799). Revolutionary statesman and orator. Son of a Scottish Anglican father and an English Presbyterian mother, Patrick was baptized into the Church of England by his uncle, the Reverend Patrick Henry (the local rector) and remained a member of that body throughout his life. Early on, his faith was influenced by the evangelical preaching of SAMUEL DAVIES, Presbyterian pastor in Hanover County. Henry's later oratorical success was largely due to his adaptation of the evangelical extempore sermon for use in the courtroom and on the legislative floor. His rise to prominence in Virginia began with his role as a defence attorney in the Parsons' Cause (1759). His political republicanism and Christian sensibilities made him deeply concerned with fostering Christian virtue in Virginian society during and after the American Revolution. To that end, Henry enthusiastically supported legislative attempts in the 1780s to create a new religious establishment on a multidenominational basis, and the same convictions influenced his opposition to the United States Constitution, where God is not mentioned.

BIBLIOGRAPHY
R. Beeman, *Patrick Henry* (New York, 1974)
T. Buckley, *Church and State in Revolutionary Virginia, 1776–1787* (Charlottesville, VA, 1977)
C. L. Cohen, 'The "Liberty or Death" Speech: A Note on Religion and Revolutionary Rhetoric', *William and Mary Quarterly*, 38 (1981): 702–17
DAB
R. Isaac, *The Transformation of Virginia* (Chapel Hill, NC, 1982)

RICHARD W. POINTER

Hensman, John (b. Bedford, Bedfordshire, England, 22 Sept. 1780; d. Clifton, Bristol, England, 23 April 1864). Anglican clergyman. Hensman was educated at Corpus Christi College, Cambridge (BA 1801; MA 1804), of which he was elected to a fellowship (1801). In the same year he became curate to CHARLES SIMEON at Holy Trinity, but moved to Wraxall (Somerset) (1803–9) to become curate to James Vaughan, whose daughter he married. He was curate-in-charge at Clifton (1809–22) where he was largely responsible for the rebuilding of the parish church. He then became Curate of the Dowry Chapel in the same place (1822–30) until his friends built Holy Trinity, Hotwells, of which he became first incumbent (1830–44), removing to Christ Church, Clifton (1844–7) and finally becoming Rector of Clifton (1847–64), during which time he built St Paul's (1853) and St Peter's (1856), thus establishing what still remains an important evangelical Anglican presence in Clifton. He was also a canon of Bristol (1858–64). He was known as a gentle personality and an uncontroversial preacher, 'one of the wisest and oldest members of the evangelical party' (*DNB*).

BIBLIOGRAPHY
Al. Cant., II, iii: 334
DNB

ARTHUR POLLARD

Hepburn, James (Curtis) (b. Milton, PA, USA, 13 March 1815; d. East Orange, NJ, USA, 21 Sept. 1911). Early medical missionary to China and Japan. Hepburn was associated with the Presbyterian Board of Foreign Missions. After malaria foiled work in Amoy, he became in 1859 the third Protestant missionary in Japan. With others he introduced new techniques to treat eye disorders, developed the definitive Romanization of Japanese which bears his name, published the first English-Japanese dictionary, and translated the Bible. Schools founded by him and his wife became Meiji Gakuin University and Ferris Jogakuin University. His careful husbanding of an elaborate copy of the English Bible for 13 years before it could be presented to the Emperor reflected both his evangelical fervour and his conviction that Japanese Christianity required official recognition. He retired to New Jersey in 1892. An Imperial decoration and Japanese official presence at his funeral publicly recognized his contributions.

BIBLIOGRAPHY
DCA
W. E. Griffis, *Hepburn of Japan and His Wife and Helpmates*, (Philadelphia, PA, 1913)
G. Itasaka, ed., *Encyclopaedia of Japan*, 9 vols (Tokyo and New York, 1983)
M. Takaya, *Hebon* (Hepburn) (Tokyo, 1989) summarizes Takaya's many other studies

JOHN F. HOWES

Hepburn, Thomas (b. Pelton, England, 1795; d. Newcastle, England, Dec. 1864). Primitive Methodist local preacher and Mineworkers' Trade Union leader. Hepburn worked from an early age at Fatfield and Hetton Collieries. At this time boys were working up to 18 hours a day in the mines. In 1830 in an effort to improve conditions, Hepburn formed the miners of Northumberland and Durham into what was the first mineworkers' trade union. For a time Hepburn became their full-time organizer and in March 1831 he coordinated a major strike. Hepburn was always noted for his advocacy of moderation and peace. On one occasion in May 1831 he insisted that Lord Londonderry, the chief pit-owner, kneel in prayer with him for guidance. In his later years Hepburn worked for Mr T. E. Forster at Felling colliery and remained in his employ until 1859.

BIBLIOGRAPHY
Durham Advertiser (16 December 1864)
Durham Chronicle (14 May 1831)
R. Fynes, *The Miners of Northumberland and Durham* (Blyth, England, 1873; Newcastle-upon-Tyne, England, 1986 reprint)
Primitive Methodist Quarterly Review (July 1882)
R. F. Wearmouth, *Methodism and the Working-class Movements in England 1800–50* (Clifton, NJ, 1972)

NIGEL SCOTLAND

Hepworth, Abraham (b. Graffham, Huntingdonshire, England, 25 Feb. 1771; d. Ingoldisthorpe, Norfolk, England, 11 Aug. 1855). Anglican clergyman. Hepworth was a scholar of Corpus Christi College, Cambridge (LL B 1786) and commenced his ministerial career as Curate of Long Preston (Yorkshire) (1798). He performed a long and notable incumbency in Manchester as Vicar of St Luke's, Charlton-on-Medlock (1806–43) and spent his last years as rector of Ingoldisthorpe, where he died.

BIBLIOGRAPHY
Al. Cant., II, iii: 335

ARTHUR POLLARD

Herschell, Ridley Hain (b. Strzelno, Poland, 7 April 1807; d. Brighton, Sussex, England, 14 April 1864). Undenominational minister and missioner to the Jews. The son of devout Jews and much influenced by his rabbi grandfather, Herschell was educated first in a rabbinical school and then at the University of Berlin. His conversion was largely brought about by an independent reading of the New Testament in Paris, but his Jewish instincts revolted against Catholic ritual. On a third visit to London, he was baptized by the Bishop of London in 1830. Working initially for Lady OLIVIA SPARROW in the missions and schools established by her, in 1838 friends helped him to open an undenominational chapel in London, in which churchmen and Dissenters happily united together, moving in 1846 to Trinity Chapel, John Street, Edgware Road. He took the principal part in founding the British Society for the Propagation of the Gospel among the Jews, and engaged in numerous continental visits in connection with the work which also lead to a large number of publications. He also established a home for Jews seriously interested in finding out more about Christianity, and gave much effort to finding employment for converted Jews. He was one of the founders of the EA. His son, the first Lord Herschell (1837–99), an eminent lawyer and politician, became Solicitor-General in 1880 and Lord Chancellor in 1886.

BIBLIOGRAPHY
DNB

J. H. Y. BRIGGS

Hervey, James (b. Hardingstone, Northamptonshire, England, 26 Feb. 1714; d. Weston Favell, Northamptonshire, England, 25 Dec. 1758). Anglican clergyman and author. He was the son of the Rector of Collingtree and grandson of the Rector of Weston Favell, benefices which he was to inherit. He was educated at Northampton Grammar School and Lincoln College, Oxford, where he went in 1731. Hervey had a great interest in science throughout his life, and this led him to religion and Methodism. By 1733 he was a member of the Holy Club, the WESLEYS' religious society for students, and also a friend of PHILIP DODDRIDGE and some of the students at his Northampton Academy.

Hervey obtained his BA in 1736, and was ordained by the Bishop of Oxford on 14 September 1736. He served first as curate to CHARLES KINCHIN at Dummer in Hampshire for a year, and then spent two years as chaplain to Paul Orchard at Stoke Abbey in Devon. From 1740 to 1743 he was curate of Bideford, where he corresponded with GEORGE WHITEFIELD and adopted Calvinist views. During all this time he adopted the Methodist practice of forming religious societies in his own and his father's parishes.

His first published poetry, *Meditations Among the Tombs*, was written at this time, but not published until later. In 1743 he returned to Weston Favell, now his father's parish, to act as curate there and at Collingtree. Between 1746 and 1748 he published almost all of his religious verse, which was extremely popular in evangelical circles for many years.

His father died in 1752, and Hervey was able to succeed to both his parishes with the assistance of George Whitefield, who obtained the position of chaplain to a peer for him, thus permitting the plurality of benefices. He devoted all his time to his parishes and lived in Weston Favell rectory with his mother and sister. He rebuilt the rectory, a building which still exists. Hervey continued to correspond with his evangelical friends, both Anglican and Dissenters, and in 1750 began a long correspondence with Lady Fanny Shirley, who had been Lord Chesterfield's mistress. He acted as her almoner, received gifts of books from her and reported on local events.

In 1752 he published his first prose work, a refutation of Bolingbroke, and in 1755 his famous defence of Calvinism, *Theron and Aspasio*. This is a series of dialogues and letters between Theron, a gentleman interested in science 'chiefly to cultivate the nobler Principles of Religion and Morality,' and Aspasio, a more mild man with similar scientific concerns. It was attacked both by

JOHN WESLEY and ROBERT SANDEMAN, but defended by Hervey's friends.

Hervey suffered from ill health for most of his life. In the winter of 1749 he was persuaded to leave Weston Favell for Middlesex, where he lived for some time in Whitefield's house. Overwork in his two parishes undoubtedly contributed to his death at an early age. Although Hervey was a modest man, consulting his friends before publishing any work and confining his preaching to his own parishes, he was able through his writing and correspondence to exert a great influence on the evangelical movement. He was also ready, though reluctant, to enter into controversy when he thought a stand was required. He is, perhaps, still one of the most attractive of the early Methodists, but has never been the subject of a good biography.

BIBLIOGRAPHY
Anon., *Letters from the late Rev. James Hervey ... to Lady Frances Shirley* (London, 1782)
J. Brown, *Life of the Rev. James Hervey* (Edinburgh, 1809)
J. Cole, *Herveiana, or Graphic & Literary Sketches of Rev. James Hervey*, 2 vols (Scarborough, England, 1822, 1823)
DNB
M. Harrison, *Weston Favell* (Northampton, England, 1984)
G. Lawton, 'The Letters of James Hervey' (Nottingham Univ. Ph.D. thesis, 3 vols, 1970)

EDWIN WELCH

Hervey, Thomas (b. 1741; d. Underbarrow, Westmorland, England, 21 July 1806). Anglican clergyman. Hervey was an early and isolated Anglican evangelical, who was even accused before his bishop of heterodoxy by some of his clerical colleagues. He does not appear to have possessed a university degree. His first curacy was in the chapel of Rampside (in the parish of Dalton-in-Furness), but in his late twenties by the invitation of the freeholders who had the right of nomination he was invited to the perpetual curacy of Underbarrow near Kendal, where he also acted a schoolmaster. Besides a book on shorthand Hervey also published *Elementa Christiana*, a work on the Thirty-Nine Articles.

BIBLIOGRAPHY
CO (September 1806)

ARTHUR POLLARD

Hetherington, William Maxwell (b. near Dumfries, Scotland, 4 June 1803; d. Glasgow, 23 May 1865). Free Church professor. Hetherington was educated at Edinburgh University and was ordained in the Church of Scotland at Torphichen in 1836. A prominent spokesman for the evangelical party during the Non- intrusion Crisis, his *History of the Church of Scotland* (1842) was designed to serve evangelical arguments. Within two months of the Disruption his Free Church adherents at Torphichen had built a new church and manse, the first in the new denomination. Later that year he became Free Church minister at St Andrews and in 1848 of St Paul's, Edinburgh. In 1857 he obtained the professorial chair of apologetics and systematic theology at New College, Edinburgh.

Hetherington contributed 'Coleridge and his Followers' to the 1853 YMCA Exeter Hall lectures, London. The author of many published works, most of them of an anti-Catholic character, he had articles in the *British and Foreign Evangelical Review* and the *North British Review*, and was the founding editor of the *Free Church Magazine* (1844–8). He was a member of the EA.

BIBLIOGRAPHY
T. Brown, *Annals of the Disruption* (Edinburgh, 1892): 338
DNB

JONATHAN BURKE CUTMORE

Heugh, Hugh (b. Stirling, Scotland, 1782; d. Glasgow, 10 June 1846). United Secession minister. Heugh was the son of John Heugh (1731–1810), minister to a burgher Secession congregation at Stirling. In 1806 he was ordained as his father's assistant. As the last moderator (1819) of the Burgher Synod before it reunited with the Anti-Burgher Synod in 1820, Heugh was much involved in the negotiations that led to union. In 1821 he commenced a successful ministry to the United Secession congregation in Regent Place, Glasgow.

He was a keen advocate of home and foreign missions – as is suggested by his *Duty and Privilege of the United Secession Church in Regard to Missions Home and Foreign* (1836). In 1830 he spoke at Surrey Chapel, London, for the LMS. In a number of published works Heugh reflected the Secessionists' adoption of voluntaryism in the 1830s. He was a member of the EA. Nine of his sermons appeared in the *Pulpit*.

BIBLIOGRAPHY
DNB
H. M. Macgill, *Memoir of Dr. Heugh* (Edinburgh, 1850)

JONATHAN BURKE CUTMORE

Heurtley, Charles Abel (b. Bishop Wearmouth, England, 4 Jan. 1806; d. Oxford, 1 May 1895). Anglican clergyman and theologian. Heurtley was born in the north-east of England. His father, Charles Abel Heurtley, a banker in Sunderland, died when he was two months old and his mother, Isabella (née Hunter) when he was ten. Under the guardianship of his mother's family he attended a local school in West Bolton and, from 1817 to 1821, a private school in Witton-le-Wear which at the time 'had a considerable reputation'. In 1822 his guardians pressed him to accept a clerk's position in a timber merchant in Liverpool, but as Heurtley wrote later, 'My own wish had been to go to the university and to be admitted to Holy Orders'. After nine months he returned to school in Louth, Lincolnshire, and in 1823 secured a scholarship (for boys in the diocese of Durham) to Corpus Christi College, Oxford.

At Oxford his academic ability led to a first-class degree in Mathematics in 1827. Unsuccessful in 1828 to gain a fellowship to the then prestigious Common Room at Oriel College, he taught at Brompton from 1828 to 1831. In 1831 he took his MA and was ordained, serving his curacy at Wardington, Oxford from 1831 to 1840. In 1832 he also became fellow and reader in Latin back at Corpus and so began his lifelong career in the university. Though a canon of Worcester Cathedral from 1848 to 1853 and Rector of Fenny Compton, Worcestershire from 1840 to 1872, it was to teaching and preaching in the university that he devoted most of his energies. Select preacher in 1834, 1838 and 1851, and a member of the Hebdomadal Council from 1862 to 1872, he was in 1853 awarded a DD and elected Lady Margaret professor of divinity and Canon of Christ Church, a position he held until his death.

Though by nature moderate in manners and opinions, he was not unaffected by nor uninvolved in the controversies of the university and wider church. His Huguenot roots (cf. his eighteenth-century forebear Charles Abel Heurteleu) inspired strong professional sympathies. In 1845, the year JOHN HENRY NEWMAN seceded to Rome and the first phase of the Oxford Movement ended, it was Heurtley who delivered a countervailing series of Bampton lectures on 'Justification' and withdrew from the panel preparing the *Library of the Fathers*. When in 1856 Archdeacon Denison was arraigned for unsound eucharistic doctrines, Heurtley sat on the panel that adjudged the case. In 1873 he took strong theological exception to bestowing an honorary degree on the free-thinking scientist John Tyndall, and later protested Cardinal Manning's preferential treatment in the jubilee celebrations of the Oxford Union.

Heurtley was, though, neither by character nor conviction a controversialist. William Ince's *Memoir* describes his as 'a man of godly simplicity and profound devoutness of soul', a judgement confirmed by Heurtley's actions and his contemporaries. Generous in his philanthropy (he oversaw establishment of an effective water supply to his parish, Fenny Compton) and in his judgements (he preached a sermon in 1890 repudiating mindless condemnation of 'Higher Criticism'), he exerted a wholesome, scholarly, moderate influence over many years upon the character of Oxford evangelicalism.

Heurtley's scholarly interests were broad but his writings few. Between 1849 and 1868 he published four series of *Parochial Sermons* and in 1864 the first of a number of works on the Creeds, which culminated in 1892 in *A History of the Earlier Formulations of the Western and Eastern Churches*. In addition, he published his university sermons and pamphlets on, among other things, the Eucharist, prayer through Christ, and the Athanasian Creed. A churchman to the core, he combined scholarship and piety in an exemplary Anglican manner.

Heurtley died in Oxford on 1 May 1895 and was buried beside his wife Jane (née Harrison, died 23 Sept.

1893) in Oseney Cemetery. He had one son (Charles Abel, Rector of Ashington, Sussex) and three daughters.

SELECT WRITINGS
C. A. Heurtley, *Wholesome Words ... with a Prefatory Memoir ... by Rev. William Ince, DD* (London, 1856)

BIBLIOGRAPHY
Boase
DNB
J. S. Reynolds, *The Evangelicals at Oxford 1735–1871* (Abingdon, England, 1975)
P. Toon, *Evangelical Theology 1833–1856* (London, 1979)

CHRISTOPHER D. HANCOCK

Hey, Richard (b. Pudsey, Yorkshire, England, 11 Aug. 1745; d. Hertingfordbury, Hertfordshire, England, 7 Dec. 1835). Essayist. Richard, younger brother of WILLIAM HEY, was educated at Leeds Grammar school and Magdalene College, Cambridge (scholar 1765; BA 1768; MA 1771; LL D 1779). He was a fellow of Sidney Sussex College (1768–78) but returned to Magdelene as fellow and tutor (1782–96). He was called to the bar at the Middle Temple (1771) and became an advocate of the Court of Arches (1778) but obtained little practice. In 1783 he published his *Dissertation on the Pernicious Effects of Gaming* (3rd edn, 1812), followed by another on *Duelling* (1784) and on *Suicide* (1785), for all of which he received prizes from the university. He had already published *Observations on the Nature of Civil Liberty and the Principles of Government* (1778), and later he replied to Thomas Paine's *The Rights of Man* with his own *Happiness and Rights* (1792). His final work was *Some Principles of Civilisation with Detached Thoughts on the Promotion of Christianity in India* (1815). He also wrote a tragedy, *The Captive Monarch* (1784) and a novel *Edington* (1786).

BIBLIOGRAPHY
Al. Cant., II, iii: 351
DNB

ARTHUR POLLARD

Hey, Samuel (b. Pudsey, Yorkshire, England, 1745; d. Steeple Aston, Wiltshire, England, 31 Jan. 1828). Anglican clergyman. Hey was educated at Leeds and Magdalene College, Cambridge (BA 1771; MA 1774), of which he became a fellow, and served the university as senior proctor (1782). He was preferred to the vicarage of Steeple Aston (1787–1828), which was in the gift of the college and there he spent the rest of his life.

BIBLIOGRAPHY
Al. Cant., II, iii: 351

ARTHUR POLLARD

Hey, William (b. Pudsey, Yorkshire, England, 23 Aug. 1736; d. Leeds, Yorkshire, England, 23 March 1819).

Surgeon and mayor. Hey is an important lay figure in the history of evangelicalism in Leeds. He was educated at Heath near Wakefield, apprenticed to a surgeon, Dawson, in Leeds, and studied at St George's Hospital, London (1757–9). He was prominent in the establishment of Leeds Infirmary (1767) and was its senior surgeon (1773–1812). He was made a fellow of the Royal Society (1775), partly through the recommendation of his friend, the Unitarian scientist, Joseph Priestley, whose theological views he opposed in a number of tracts. Hey lost an eye at the age of four and was severely crippled in mounting a horse in 1778, but these accidents in no way affected his skill as a doctor. He was responsible for advances in the treatment of hernia, cataract and dislocations as well as for partial amputation of the foot, which last was named 'Hey's operation'. He also proved the transmission of venereal disease to the foetus. He was founder president of the Leeds Literary and Philosophical Society, to which he read many papers, and he gave courses on anatomy at Leeds Infirmary in 1800, 1803, 1806 and 1809, using the bodies of executed criminals.

Hey was a Methodist until 1781 when he transferred to the Church of England. He was Mayor of Leeds in 1787/8 and 1801/2, using his office vigorously to control public behaviour, to the extent even that his effigy was burnt by the mob. By the marriage of his daughter, Mary, he was father-in-law to THOMAS DYKES.

BIBLIOGRAPHY
DNB

ARTHUR POLLARD

Heyer, J(ohn) C(hristian) F(rederick) (b. Helmstedt, Germany, 10 July 1793; d. Philadelphia, PA, USA, 7 Nov. 1873). Lutheran missionary in America and India. Son of a master furrier, Heyer emigrated to America in 1807. In 1810 he began to study theology under J. H. C. Helmuth, senior pastor of Zion Lutheran Church, Philadelphia. He returned to Germany in 1815 and studied at the University of Göttingen for one term. Licensed in 1817 and ordained deacon in 1820, he was involved in active missionary work in the eastern United States until 1840. Later, between 1857 and 1867, he served in Minnesota.

Commissioned as a foreign missionary in 1840, Heyer began the first permanent mission in India for the Lutheran Church in America in 1842. During three terms (1842–5, 1848–57, and 1869–71) he expanded mission work in the Telugu-speaking region of South India, establishing centers at Guntur and Rajahmundry. He is considered the founder of the Andhra Evangelical Lutheran Church.

BIBLIOGRAPHY
E. T. Bachmann, *They Called Him Father* (Muhlenberg, PA, 1942)

PETER L. SCHMITTHENNER

Hibbard, Billy (b. Norwich, CT, BNA, 24 Feb. 1771; d. Canaan, NY, USA, 17 Aug. 1844). American Methodist Episcopal preacher. Born and raised in New England, by the age of twenty Hibbard had chosen Methodism over the Calvinistic doctrines prevalent in his surroundings; throughout his life he engaged in spirited, if generally civil, debate with Calvinists. Though sensitive to his relative lack of education and to his family's needs (he and his wife eventually had ten children), he felt a call to preach. In 1798 he was admitted to the Methodist itinerancy, mainly serving in New York and New England. During the War of 1812 he served as a chaplain in the army, converting 43 soldiers. Hibbard was renowned for his quick wit and eccentricities (the stories of which are plentiful), which helped to make him a very popular preacher and controversialist. He published his *Memoirs*, two pamphlets, and numerous newspaper pieces.

BIBLIOGRAPHY
AAP: 298–306
J. Hurst, *History of Methodism: American Methodism*, 2 vols, II (New York, 1902): 615–20

KENNETH N. PEARSON

Higgins, Charles Longuet (b. Turvey, Bedfordshire, England, 30 Nov. 1806; d. Turvey, 23 Jan 1885). Landed gentleman. Higgins grew up under the ministry of LEGH RICHMOND at Turvey and not surprisingly therefore came also under the influence of CHARLES SIMEON at Cambridge, where he was a member of Trinity College (BA 1830; MA 1834). He wanted to take holy orders, but acceded to his father's wishes and entered Lincoln's Inn, on whose books he remained until 1847 but never sought a call to the Bar. He studied medicine at St Bartholomew's Hospital (1836–8) and practised at Turvey, succeeding to the family property in 1846. Thereafter, apart from a visit to the Holy Land and Egypt in 1848, he concentrated his attention on various improvements in the village, establishing schools (1847), opening a museum (1852), upgrading the condition of the cottages (1849 onwards) and restoring the church (1852–4). He proposed a new hymn-book for universal use in the Church of England and read a paper on hymnology to the Northern Church Congress in 1871.

BIBLIOGRAPHY
Boase, I: 1403
J. W. Burgon, *Lives of Twelve Good Men* (London, 1888)
DNB

ARTHUR POLLARD

Higginson, Henry (b. Pendleford Mills, Wolverhampton, England, 10 Aug. 1805; d. Birmingham, England, 15 March 1871). Primitive Methodist minister. Higginson was the son of a miller and a farmer. He received an extended formal education, in preparation for a medical career. He was converted in 1828 at a Primitive Methodist lovefeast and after a brief spell as a schoolmaster, entered the Primitive Methodist ministry in 1833. He was a successful minister in this pioneering phase of the connexion's development, serving in 23 circuits in all. He experienced some opposition in his early circuits as at Marlborough, Wiltshire, where 17 policemen were sent to prevent his preaching. He was the first Primitive Methodist preacher to visit Swansea and established a successful cause there. Somewhat eccentric in his manner, he had a ready utterance, often humorous, and was the author of a number of hymns, now largely forgotten.

BIBLIOGRAPHY
PMMag (1871)

E. ALAN ROSE

Hill, Alexander   (b. St Andrews, Fife, Scotland, 19 July 1785; d. Ayr, Scotland, Jan. 1867). Church of Scotland minister. He was the son of the eminent George Hill, principal of St Mary's College, St Andrews (*DNB*). After obtaining his undergraduate degree from St Andrews in 1804, and having been licensed to preach in the Church of Scotland in 1806, Hill travelled in England and abroad until 1815 when he was ordained at Colmonell. From 1816 to 1840 he served the parish of Dailly. He was then professor of divinity at Glasgow (to 1862).

Hill remained in the Established Church upon the Disruption of 1843 and, indeed, was moderator two years later. He was greatly admired by contemporaries of every party for his urbanity and catholic temper. Although he was a prominent moderate, he became a member of the EA. Besides editing his father's lectures, he published half a dozen ephemeral works, most of them pastoral in character.

BIBLIOGRAPHY
DNB

JONATHAN BURKE CUTMORE

Hill, Charles   (b. *circa* 1727; d. Tawstock, Devon, England, 13 Feb. 1801). Anglican clergyman. The son of Charles Hill, Vicar of Fremington in Devon, he matriculated at Hertford College, Oxford in March 1748. While at home for the summer vacation that year he heard GEORGE THOMSON of St Gennys in Cornwall preach in his father's pulpit. At the close of the service the junior Hill stood up in his pew and with tears in his eyes testified to his immediate and heartfelt belief in the Atonement, urging the congregation to believe likewise. When he was later plunged into spiritual darkness, however, many rumoured he was mad. But by 1750 he was manifestly restored and had resumed his studies at Oxford, taking his BA and becoming Curate of Fremington under his father in 1752. After four years he

removed a few miles away to Tawstock where he was instituted rector in 1756 and spent the next 36 years. He joined other clergy from the region in meeting with the Countess of HUNTINGDON during her visits to Bath and Bristol. Thomson described his evangelical ministry as effective in the awakening of sinners and comforting of believers.

BIBLIOGRAPHY
Al. Ox.
C. Hole, 'Biographical Sketches', *CO* (1877)

D. B. HINDMARSH

Hill, Green   (b. Franklin County, NC, BNA, 1741; d. near Nashville, TN, USA, 11 Sept. 1826). Methodist local preacher. Hill became associated with the Methodists in the early 1770s and was licensed as a local preacher. He represented his county in the North Carolina colonial assemblies, including the one in 1776 where North Carolina became the first colony to sanction independence from Great Britain. He was a major in the North Carolina militia and in 1781 entered the Continental Army as a chaplain. Hill is also credited with introducing North Carolina's first bill providing care for the indigent.

Green married Mary Seawall in 1773. They and their eight children offered hospitality to Methodist preachers and conferences. Their house at Louisburg, now a Historic Shrine of the United Methodist Church, was the site of conferences in 1785, 1790, 1791, and 1794. The Hills relocated near Nashville, Tennessee in 1796. Here too, in 1808, another Methodist conference convened.

BIBLIOGRAPHY
EWM

CHARLES W. BROCKWELL, JR

Hill, James   (*fl.* 1821). Pioneer LMS missionary in India. Hill arrived in Calcutta in 1821 and became pastor of the Union Chapel, Dharamtolla. An excellent preacher and organizer, he held the congregation and mission together while striving to make both financially self-sufficient. Hill irritated the Serampore Baptists by perpetuating HENRY TOWNLEY's attempts to create a separate 'paedo-baptist' congregation. (Until 1816, both Congregationalists and Baptists worshipped in the Lal Bazaar Chapel.) He also annoyed the Calcutta Baptists by fundraising in 'their' constituency and by publishing a booklet criticizing adult 'believer's' baptism. During the Union Chapel controversy of 1835–6, Hill was accused of accumulating wealth. In reality, he had lost everything in the bank crash of 1832. Previously he had personally covered expenses usually born by the LMS. His health forced his return to England in 1833.

BIBLIOGRAPHY
LMS Calcutta mission archives, CWM archives, School of Oriental and African Studies, London

E. M. JACKSON

Hill, John (b. London, 23 Oct. 1786 [ordination papers, Oxford; not 1787 as Boase, *et al.*]; d. Wyke Regis Rectory, Dorset, England, 22 March 1855 [not February as Boase]). Oxford tutor and Anglican clergyman. Son of John Hill of London, even in 1809–10 John Hill Jr's baptismal record could not be found, and to satisfy ordination requirements an affidavit was necessary, sworn by a clergy widow present at his birth (ordination papers). He was apparently educated first by the Reverend Mr Eden (Hole's *Phelps*, 1, 1871). Since in boyhood Hill sat under T. T. BIDDULPH, at Bristol, this early teacher was perhaps John Eden, Vicar of St. Nicholas, Bristol from 1799 to 1840. Subsequently Hill was a boarder with E. SPENCER, at Winkfield rectory, Wiltshire, 1803–6, and possibly earlier. He then went up to St Edmund Hall, Oxford, where he studied successively under ISAAC CROUCH and DANIEL WILSON, becoming assistant tutor to the latter in 1809, and when only 25 succeeding him as sole tutor and vice-principal, 1812–51, proceeding BD 1844.

Ordained at Oxford in 1809, Hill served as curate (to Dr J. Cobb, Vicar of Charlbury) of Hampton Gay, Oxfordshire from 1809 to 1814, and Perpetual Curate from 1814 to 1851. From 1851 till death he was Rector of Wyke Regis, Dorset, acting also as city lecturer, St Martin's, Carfax, Oxford, from 1851 to 1855. In 1811 he married Sophia Warriner, thereafter living at 65 High Street, Oxford, where eight children were born.

Like Crouch, Hill regarded St Edmund Hall, which they administered on behalf of successive principals, somewhat in the light of an evangelical seminary – teaching, lecturing and ministering to about thirty mostly devoted young men, mainly ordinands, of whom a few became notable, but who usually remained in after life offering devoted ministry in relative obscurity. Nine of his pupils, however, including W. H. HAVERGAL and HUGH STOWELL, appear in the *DNB*. Hill considered that having almost all members living in Hall 'lies at the bottom of our superior discipline' (letter to G. Warriner, Jr, 1820). In term time, like his two immediate predecessors, Hill was kept continually busy, as both his letters, from 1814, and his diary, from 1820, show clearly. By early middle life he had made his mark. 'To young academicians of the *Evangelical* school, whatever their college', wrote FRANCIS W. NEWMAN (younger brother of J. H. NEWMAN), a Worcester undergraduate 1822–6, 'the Rev. Mr. *Hill* was an important standard bearer'. Tuckwell (New College, 1848–52), whose father, a medical practitioner, was a neighbour in High Street, wrote less sympathetically of 'the evening parties of John Hill, vice-principal of St. Edmund's (*sic*) Hall, where prevailed tea and coffee, pietistic Low Church talk, prayer and hymnody of portentous length . . .' HENRY LINTON, fellow of Magdalen, testified more positively. But T. Mozley, fellow of Oriel, wrote less than favourably of St Edmund Hall in Hill's time. Even allowing for tractarian views (and the evangelical convictions of some of his own relations), Mozley's exaggerations render his transparent tendency to vilification more than suspect, whatever underlying value his criticisms may possess. That Hill

was a convinced moderate Calvinist – like many of his evangelical brethren, in line with Article 17 – is undeniable. But though perhaps he found congenial the spiritual understanding of High Calvinists like HENRY BULTEEL, there seems no clear evidence that he shared their distinctive doctrinal beliefs.

In spite of his day-to-day preoccupations, Hill managed to publish, as early as 1816, a version of Aldrich's *Artis Logicae Compendium*, which as a university textbook went through several editions. In 1825 Hill founded an Oxford and Oxfordshire Association of the CMS, of which he continued to act as principal secretary till 1851, and from which J. H. Newman, as an assistant secretary no longer in sympathy with the churchmanship of the parent society, was voted out at a general meeting in 1830. This local association throve increasingly throughout the nineteenth century, and has continued to exist. In 1827 Hill started a similar association for the LSPCJ. When a local branch of the CPAS was founded in 1848–9, Hill was immediately made a vice-president. By then he had, as Dr A. B. Emden wrote, 'faithfully kept the lamp of Evangelical piety alight within the Hall' (H. E. Salter and M. D. Lobel, 1954) for nearly forty years. His wife died in 1849. Undergraduate admissions were dropping. Hill was beginning to feel too old for the work involved. E. A. LITTON, an able theologian, proved a willing successor.

Late in 1851, with long experience of parish work, albeit on a small scale, at Hampton Gay, Hill was able to make a good start at Wyke Regis, which he had been offered by the Bishop of Winchester, Dr C. R. SUMNER; but serious illness overtook him in 1855, and he did not recover. A memorial tablet in Wyke church commemorates his ministry. The Hill vault in St Peter's-in-the-East churchyard, Oxford, has been preserved.

Hill married (1811) Sophia (1788–1849), daughter of George Warriner, linen-draper, of New Bond Street, London, and of Bloxham Grove, Oxfordshire. In 1925 their great-grandson, the Reverend A. T. du B. Hill, presented Hill's surviving diaries to St Edmund Hall. In 1990 some twenty letters written by Hill came to light. These complement the more formal impression of the diaries. His portrait in St Edmund Hall was painted by J. Wood in 1841 to mark the twenty-eighth anniversary of Hill's vice- principalship.

SELECT WRITINGS
J. Hill, Letters 1814–23 (Warriner Papers, Warwick Record Office)
J. Hill, Diaries 1803–6 (mostly notes of sermons); 1820–55 (deposited Bodleian Library, Oxford)

BIBLIOGRAPHY
Boase, 1
DNB, Missing Persons (London, 1993)
J. N. D. Kelly, *St. Edmund Hall* (Oxford, 1989)
J. S. Reynolds, *Evangelicals at Oxford* (Oxford, 1953; Appleford, England, 1975)
H. E. Salter and M. D. Lobel, eds, *Victoria History of Oxford*, 3 (Oxford, 1954)
St. Edmund Hall Magazine, 1, 6 (1925), Aularian Notes by A. B. Emden; 14, 1 (1992), 'New Light on J. Hill' by J. S. Reynolds

M. Warriner, *The Warriner Family* (privately printed, 1975)

J. S. REYNOLDS

Hill, Mary [née Beardsmore] (b. Newcastle under Lyme, England, 1791; d. Calcutta, 1 Sept. 1847). LMS missionary in India. With her husband MICAIAH HILL (married 10 October 1821) she arrived in Tollygunge in 1822. She began learning Bengali and sought to establish girls' schools. In 1831 she also began itinerating with her husband. She concentrated on work with orphans and Indian Christian women.

When she returned from furlough (December 1836 to May 1839), Hill began writing. The LMS published her moving account of a *sati* in March 1845. She also churned out fiery letters to LMS secretaries concerning the unjust treatment of her overworked and debt-laden husband, and of her two sons WILLIAM and SAMUEL HILL, who were without support in England while waiting to be accepted for missionary training. In February 1847 Hill and her husband moved to Calcutta for reasons of health. At the time of her death, four of her five children were active church members, and two were missionaries.

BIBLIOGRAPHY
LMS Calcutta mission papers, CWM archives, School of Oriental and African Studies, London

E. M. JACKSON

Hill, Micaiah (b. Walsall, Staffordshire, England, 1791; d. near Benares, India, 3 Feb. 1849). Pioneer LMS missionary in India. Hill and his wife MARY HILL arrived in India in 1822 and went to Tollygunge, Calcutta where JAMES KEITH had started a school. Under the first known 'comity' agreement, known as the 'Tollygunge Agreement,' the Hills moved to Berhampore in March 1824.

At Berhampore (120 miles from Calcutta and within easy reach of Murshidabad, a declining centre of former Muslim government and culture) the Hills established seven schools, including Mary Hill's school for girls. Although JAMES PATERSON arrived to help in July 1827, the station was chronically short of funding and of trained personnel. Hill faced acute hostility from civil and military authorities, from the Brahmans, the landlords, and from street mobs. By 1837 this hostility had largely disappeared, partly because of his accessibility and his extensive itinerations. After the floods and famine of 1837–8 Hill established a model farm and an orphanage, supported by sericulture, with an 'industrial training school' funded from local sources. When forced to take furlough in 1838, Hill lobbied for the right of dissenting ministers to conduct marriages.

Upon his November 1842 return, he found that funds donated to the station were not getting through. By 1846 Hill became depressed and his health deteriorated. Sent to Union Chapel, Calcutta, to replace THOMAS BOAZ

while he was on furlough (February 1847), his wife's death affected him, and he died alone while travelling upstream to visit his daughter Eliza in Jullunder.

BIBLIOGRAPHY
LMS Berhampore station papers/Calcutta, CWM Archives, School of Oriental and African Studies, London

E. M. JACKSON

Hill, Sir Richard (b. Hawkstone, Shropshire, England, 6 June 1732; d. Hawkstone, Shropshire, England, 20 Nov. 1808). Baronet, author, and MP. Richard was the eldest son of Sir Rowland Hill, and the brother of ROWLAND HILL, and was educated at Westminster School and Magdalen College, Oxford. His own account of his religious experience suggests that, like a number of the early evangelicals, he was tortured by a sense of guilt for years, and only later, meeting a number of like-minded men, owed any allegiance to any particular church view. His conversion he dated from 1759, by which time he was an intimate of a number of prominent evangelicals, including FLETCHER of Madeley, who helped him most. In his turn, Richard gave spiritual help to his younger brothers. Curiously, though Rowland was much persecuted by his father for his evangelical beliefs, Richard's attachment gave little obvious offence.

In 1768 the famous expulsion of six Oxford students took place, and Richard made the ablest contribution to the controversy which followed when he wrote a much quoted tract entitled 'Pietas Oxoniensis'. He was also a contributor to the Calvinistic Controversy which followed WHITEFIELD's death in 1770, retaining a courtesy which most of the disputants spurned, especially brother Rowland and AUGUSTUS M. TOPLADY. Richard's rank perhaps gave him too early prominence in the evangelical world. His promise as a pamphleteer and his fluency as a speaker also encouraged the hope that once he entered the House of Commons the evangelicals would have a worthy representative in a seat of power.

Richard entered Parliament in 1780 as the member for Shropshire. He resolved to be as independent as a man could be. He largely confined himself to what he considered Christian matters. No man could have been more anxious to serve his Christian cause. He had a gift for lucidity, a wit and elegance, and he was entirely fearless. Notwithstanding all these qualities, he must be looked upon as a very great disappointment. In the first place, he flooded every speech with religious sentiment and scriptural quotation and made himself and his cause ludicrous; in the second place, his conduct and manner and mode of life were exactly that of any other country gentleman of rank, and this seemed somehow a world away from the asceticism of WESLEY and Whitefield and most of the early evangelicals; and in the third place, he was most active and long-winded in the House when supporting hopeless causes. Far from advancing the evangelical cause in Parliament, Richard Hill too often made himself and his party a subject of derision. Evangelicals had to await the appearance of WILLIAM WILBERFORCE to have a worthy champion of their ideals, a practical politician as well as a convinced Christian.

Richard succeeded to the baronetcy on the death of his father in 1783, and remained an MP until 1806, when illness compelled him to retire. The little time that remained to him he spent in looking after his beautiful estate in Shropshire. In 26 years of parliamentary life, so much, it seems, might have been done. So little was.

BIBLIOGRAPHY

E. Sidney, *The Life of Sir Richard Hill* (1839)

P. E. SANGSTER

Hill, Richard (b. Helston, Cornwall, England, 23 Dec. 1799; d. Bath or perhaps London, 11 March 1880). Seceder and Brethren teacher. He was educated at Truro Grammar School from which he went in 1818 as an exhibitioner to Exeter College, Oxford. In 1824 he was ordained and appointed as Curate of Grade, Cornwall and in 1829 became curate at West Alvington and South Molton, Devonshire. Soon after, he seceded and met with the first Brethren at Plymouth. He married Henrietta Soltau (sister of H. W. SOLTAU and aunt of Henrietta Soltau of the CIM) and lived at Plymstock. In the Brethren divisions of the 1840s he resisted the Exclusive position of J. N. DARBY as did both of his sons. One of them, Richard, was secretary of the CIM for its first thirty years.

BIBLIOGRAPHY

C. W. Boase, *Registrum Collegii Exoniensis* (Oxford, 1893): 144
M. Cable and F. French, *A Woman who laughed* (London, 1934)
H. Pickering, ed., *Chief Men Among the Brethren* 2nd edn (London, 1931): 17–18

TIMOTHY C. F. STUNT

Hill, Rowland ('Roly') (b. Hawkstone, near Wem, Shropshire, England, 23 Aug. 1744; d. London, 11 Apr. 1833). Anglican clergyman, minister of Surrey Chapel, London. The sixth son of Sir Rowland Hill of Hawkstone Park, he was educated at Shrewsbury and Eton. He was converted through his elder brother RICHARD HILL and at Eton formed a religious society through which some of his friends were converted. Hill entered St John's College, Cambridge in 1764 and formed a religious society of 10–12 friends including CHARLES EDWARD DE COETLOGON, THOMAS PENTYCROSS ('Penty') and DAVID SIMPSON. Like the Holy Club at Oxford before them, the friends read the Greek New Testament, evangelical books and prayed. They also visited the sick and those in prison and Hill preached in Cambridge and in neighbouring villages. GEORGE WHITEFIELD wrote approvingly to 'My dear professor', that 'A preaching, prison-preaching, field-preaching, Esq strikes more than all the black gowns and lawn sleeves in the world' (Sidney, 1861: 54). But

Hill's itinerant ministry angered his parents and brought censure from the university authorities.

After his brother, George Whitefield and JOHN BERRIDGE had a considerable influence over Hill. From them may be traced his Calvinism and determination to preach as a roving evangelist. Had he not fallen out with the Countess of HUNTINGDON, Hill might have gained her patronage and become Whitefield's successor. He might too, have become a chaplain to Lady GLENORCHY and taken Presbyterian orders.

After gaining his BA in 1769 Hill spent four years preaching throughout England and Wales. He said, 'Till I am ordained, I will preach by proxy' (Sidney, 1861: 75). He applied for Anglican orders but because of his irregularities was refused ordination by six bishops. At last in 1773 he was ordained deacon by the Bishop of Bath and Wells to the curacy of Kingston, near Taunton. Though he was diligent in his parish duties, he would not be confined by the parochial system and continued to itinerate. The Bishop of Carlisle had agreed to ordain him priest (on letters dimissory from the Bishop of Bath and Wells) but the Archbishop of York intervened and for the rest of his ministry Hill remained in deacon's orders. In his own words he passed through life 'wearing only one ecclesiastical boot' (Smyth, 1940: 179). Shortly before ordination Hill married Mary Tudway and they settled at Wotton-under-Edge, Gloucestershire. Though they had no family, Hill deeply loved children and wrote them hymns, prayers, books and a catechism.

At Wotton, Hill built his own chapel ('The Tabernacle') in which he used the prayer-book, but opened the pulpit to evangelicals of any denomination. This pattern he repeated at Surrey Chapel, Blackfriars, London (opened 1783), at Cheltenham Chapel (opened 1809) and at Mill Street Chapel, Leamington Spa (opened 1829, bought by Hill 1831). His custom was to spend the summer months in Gloucestershire – including making his 'episcopal visitation' to Cheltenham – and the rest of the year at Surrey Chapel. At his first three chapels he employed assistant ministers to preach in his absence. Throughout the year Hill went on extended preaching tours, and described himself as the 'Rector of Surrey Chapel, Vicar of Wotton-under-Edge and curate of the fields, commons etc. throughout England and Wales' (Sidney, 1861: 215).

Surrey Chapel, which seated 3,000 people, was the centre of Hill's ministry and the focus for missionary and philanthropic work. Attached to it were 13 Sunday schools for over 3,000 children (Hill was the earliest supporter of Sunday schools in London). In addition there was a Dorcas Society for the relief of poor married women, an almshouse for 24 poor women and a school of industry for 24 poor girls. On the nearby River Thames Hill was one of the promoters of a floating chapel.

Hill supported the LMS and raised large sums of money on his preaching tours, and was involved in the formation of the RTS and BFBS. Living in Gloucestershire he met Dr Edward Jenner, and he became keen advocate of vaccination and even published a tract on the subject.

Hill was an outstanding preacher. In his younger days he preached numerous sermons each week and well into his eighties he preached six to seven times a week. His extempory preaching was described by ISAAC MILNER as 'slap-dash preaching', but Richard Sheridan said that 'his ideas come red-hot from the heart' (Sidney, 1861: 140). Like Whitefield, he could attract immense crowds – on one of his Scottish tours he reportedly spoke to between 15–20,000 people. His presence was arresting, his style a combination of humour, pathos and vivid illustration. He wrote or contributed to a number of publications including material on the Calvinist/Arminian controversy. Hill wrote a number of hymns which were improved by WILLIAM COWPER. Hill's most popular work of fiction was his *Village Dialogues* (thirty editions).

Hill was a unique figure in the evangelical revival. He was concerned with order and freedom. He valued the scriptural content of the liturgy, but he would not be restricted by episcopal censure or inhibited by parochial boundaries. He made it clear that he was not a Dissenter – 'The church turned me off, and not I her' (Sidney, 1861: 138). But he could also say, 'See what a churchman I am; I must have it all correct' (Sidney, 1861: 237).

He was deeply committed to promoting evangelical unity, and spoke of lowering the walls between denominations so 'that we may shake hands a little easier over them' (Sidney, 1861: 475). Hill would not countenance any doctrinal restrictions being placed upon the work of the BFBS.

In the fast-growing spa towns of Cheltenham and Leamington his chapels provided an evangelical ministry where none yet existed (in Cheltenham before CHARLES JERVIS and in Leamington before WILLIAM MARSH). When an evangelical incumbent was appointed to Wotton, or when his biographer EDWIN SIDNEY preached, Hill generously closed his chapel and encouraged his congregation to worship at the parish church. Hill was deeply loved and highly regarded by evangelicals in the Established Church and in Dissent. He was buried beneath the pulpit of Surrey Chapel and the funeral sermon was preached by WILLIAM JAY, who referred to 'The preacher once, the witness now' (Sidney, 1861: 497).

BIBLIOGRAPHY
DNB
J. Julian, *A Dictionary of Hymnology* (London, 1915)
P. E. Sangster, *The Life of the Rev Roland Hill (1744–1833) and His Position in the Evangelical Revival* (University of Oxford, D. Phil., 1964)
E. Sidney, *The Life of the Rev Roland Hill* (London, 1834). Quotations from the 5th edn, 1861
C. Smyth, *Simeon and Church Order* (Cambridge, 1940)

ALAN FREDERICK MUNDEN

Hill, Samuel (b. Berhampore, India, Dec. 1825; d. Berhampore, 1891). LMS missionary in India. Son of the LMS missionaries MARY and MICAIAH HILL, he attended Spring Hill College but was not accepted for missionary training by the LMS. He returned to Calcutta and worked as an accountant with an engineering firm while reading theology and preaching in his spare time.

Although fluent in Bengali and Urdu (Hindustani), and very zealous, the LMS was slow to appoint him. He assisted A. F. LACROIX from 1852 to 1853. The LMS finally sent him to strengthen its Berhampore work in November 1853. In the same year he married Miss Miller of Union Chapel, Calcutta. She proved an excellent partner. Following Lacroix's 1858 death, Hill moved back to Calcutta to continue his bazaar preaching. He also superintended the Bhowanipore native church, from 23 April 1860 until his health broke down in 1861. After his recovery he returned in 1864 and worked at Berhampore. There he greatly improved standards in the schools and orphanage. He remained there until his death.

BIBLIOGRAPHY
Annual Reports, Berhampore Mission
CWM Archives, correspondence in LMS papers

E. M. JACKSON

Hill, Thomas (d. Harrogate, Yorkshire, England, 14 Sept. 1875). Anglican clergyman. Hill was educated at Trinity College, Cambridge (BA 1810; MA 1813; BD 1822) and became Vicar of Badgeworth (Gloucestershire) in 1821, but quickly removed to Chesterfield as vicar (1822–46). He was promoted Archdeacon of Derby (1847–73) by Bishop W. A. SHIRLEY, whose *Letters and Memoirs* (1849) he edited. He was Perpetual Curate of Hasland (Derbyshire) (1851–63) and was also a residentiary canon of Lichfield. He published *The Doctrine of the Trinity* (1820).

BIBLIOGRAPHY
Boase, I: 1475

ARTHUR POLLARD

Hill, William (b. Cumberland County, VA, BNA, 3 March 1769; d. Winchester County, VA, USA, 16 Nov. 1852). Presbyterian minister and church historian. The son of Joseph and Joanna [née Read] Hill, he entered Hampden-Sydney College in Virginia in 1785 and found the 80 students to be totally irreligious. His reading of Joseph Alleine's *Alarm to Unconverted Sinners* (1672) brought about his conversion. In 1787 three other students – including CARY ALLEN – joined him for secret religious exercises. When other students objected to their 'carrying on like Methodists,' president JOHN BLAIR SMITH held prayer meetings in his parlour for them. This proved to be the beginning of a revival which engulfed the college and spread to Presbyterian churches in central Virginia in 1787 and to Western Virginia, North Carolina, and Kentucky in 1788 and 1789. Hills' manuscripts were used by one of his own students, the historian WILLIAM HENRY FOOTE, in his *Sketches of Virginia* to chronicle the revival; the manuscripts were published in 1968 and are an important source for the rise of evangelicalism among Presbyterians.

Following graduation in 1788, Hill began his theological studies under Smith and was ordained by Hanover presbytery in 1790. In 1792 he became a Presbyterian pastor in Berkeley County, Virginia. He took charge of the Winchester Church in 1800, and in 1834 of the Briery Church in Prince Edward County. At Briery, Hill's salary was raised by the rental of the congregation's slaves to the highest bidder. When Hill opposed this policy, he met resistance and soon moved back to Winchester.

In 1837 Hill stood with the New School during the Old School-New School schism of the Presbyterian Church USA. As intellectual leader of this party in Virginia, Hill responded to CHARLES HODGE who had published a constitutional history of the church to justify the actions of the Old School in exscinding from the church those synods with objectionable theological and abolitionist views. Hill replied with *A History of the Rise, Progress, Genius, and Character of American Presbyterianism*. Hill found the origins of American Presbyterianism in the more 'experimental' religion of the Puritans and Congregationalists rather than in the rigid subscription to the Westminster Confession as demanded by some of the Scottish founders of colonial Presbyterianism.

SELECT WRITINGS
W. Hill. *Autobiographical Sketches* . . . (Richmond, VA, 1968)

BIBLIOGRAPHY
A. Nevin, ed., *Encyclopedia of the Presbyterian Church*, s.v., 'Hill, William'
A. D. Thomas, Jr, 'Reasonable Revivalism,' *Journal of Presbyterian History*, 61 (Fall, 1983): 316–34.
E. T. Thompson, *Presbyterians in the South*, 3 vols (Richmond, VA, 1963)

ARTHUR DICKEN THOMAS, JR

Hill, William Henry (b. Calcutta, India, 3 June 1822; d. England, post 1876). Second generation LMS missionary. Son of MARY and MICAIAH HILL, educated at Western College Plymouth, Spring Hill and University College, London, his parents could not dissuade him from entering missionary service. Although he failed the LMS admission examination in 1842, he was later accepted, and ordained in 1847. In 1848 he returned to Calcutta to become joint pastor with his father of the LMS chapel in Coolie Bazaar.

The LMS home board criticized Hill for travelling as far as Monghyr with his father on his last journey, and, in 1852, for being 'unfeeling.' Hill's honest reports about the state of south Calcutta's churches, in which he urged the LMS to be more realistic about the possibility of self-support, were particularly resented. Hill held very conservative political views, and was the only dissenter to the indigo planting report (*see* JAMES LONG and H. C. L. KRÜCKEBERG).

Hill married Miss Menzies Sinclair of Union Chapel, Calcutta, his sister-in-law's cousin. In April 1856 she bore him a son, and in 1860 stillborn twins. In 1858 Hill's throat became ulcerated, and he could not speak or preach. He sailed to South Africa in April 1860, and then, when his health did not recover, returned to Britain in 1861. He resigned in 1863 because of his health problems. In 1865 he became pastor of the Congregational chapel in Faversham. In 1876 he resigned as district superintendent of the LMS in Kent.

BIBLIOGRAPHY
CWM archives, School of Oriental and African Studies, London, LMS Calcutta mission papers

E. M. JACKSON

Hillyar, Sir James, (b. 29 Oct. 1769, d. Torpoint, Cornwall, England, 10 July 1843). British naval officer. He entered the navy in 1779, served in the War of American Independence and was commissioned lieutenant in 1794. He fought at Toulon and in the Battle of the Glorious First of June, had service in the Channel and the Mediterranean and in 1801 commanded armed boats on the Nile. Promoted captain in February 1804 he saw more war service in the Baltic, East Indies, Java and Mauritius. In command of the frigate *Phoebe* he engaged the US frigate *Essex* (Captain David Porter) off Valparaiso and captured her in March 1813 after a gallant action. Later he commanded ships of the line, was twice knighted and was promoted rear-admiral in 1837. A committee member of the Naval and Military Bible Society, he was known for his active promotion of Christian and humanitarian causes.

BIBLIOGRAPHY
DNB
W. R. O'Byrne, *A Naval Biographical Dictionary* (London, 1849): 516
United Service Journal, III (London, 1842): 271–85

RICHARD C. BLAKE

Hinderer, Anna and **Hinderer, David** (Anna, née **Martin**, b. Hempnall, Norfolk, England, 19 March 1827; d. Martham, Norfolk, England, 6 June 1870); (David, b. Schorndorf, Württemberg, Germany, *c.* 1817; d. Bournemouth, Hampshire, England, 16 Sept. 1890). CMS missionaries, Yoruba Mission, West Africa. David trained at the Basel Seminary, and from 1846 at the CMS College, Islington, and like many of the early CMS missionaries was German. He was ordained (deacon 1847, priest 1848) by the Bishop of London and on 17 January 1849 went out to the Yoruba Mission. In 1851 he visited Ibadan, an enormous, recently founded, city. On leave in England in 1852 he persuaded the CMS to let him start a mission there. In that year he also married Anna Martin who had been living with the family of FRANCIS CUNNINGHAM.

In December 1852 they went out together to settle in Ibadan. She opened a school and planted a garden, and despite constant illnessess, they both came to love what she called 'this dear place'. David, a kindly, humane man, wisely cultivated the friendship of two of the leading Ibadan families who became pillars of the church. In 1860 war broke out between Ibadan and Ijaye, a neighbouring Yoruba city. Abeokuta, the main CMS base, supported Ijaye but the Ibadan government let the Hinderers stay. However, they were cut off from supplies from Lagos, and even after Ijaye was destroyed, other Yoruba cities maintained the blockade. In 1865 Governor Glover of Lagos (since 1861 a British colony) sent an officer to bring Anna back to Lagos. David remained in Ibadan for a few months to hand over to new missionaries. In 1866, after leave in England, they returned to Ibadan where David translated *The Pilgrim's Progress* into Yoruba. A Hebrew scholar, he also supervised the translation of the Old Testament into Yoruba. In 1867 the CMS missionaries were expelled from Abeokuta but the Hinderers were allowed to stay in Ibadan, to 'go on with your work with a quiet mind'. Eventually in 1869 with over 100 people baptized and attending church, and a new church opened at another station, they left Ibadan.

In 1869 they retired to Martham, Norfolk, where Anna – who had been very ill before leaving Lagos – died. He had charge of the church there but went out again in 1874 to found stations at Leke and Ode Ondo. In 1877 he retired again and involved himself in translation work. *Seventeen Years in the Yoruba Country*, based on her letters, was published posthumously in 1872.

SELECT WRITINGS
A. Hinderer, *Seventeen Years in the Yoruba Country* (London, 1872)

BIBLIOGRAPHY
D. T. B[arry], *CMS Register of Clergy and Lay Missionaries* (privately printed) (London, 1906)
J. F. A. Ajayi, *Christian Missions in Nigeria, 1841–1891* (London, 1965)

CHRISTOPHER FYFE

Hinderer, David. *See* HINDERER, ANNA

Hindley, Charles (b. Fairfield, Worcester, England, 1800; d. London, 1 Dec. 1857). British MP. In 1819 Hindley was a tutor at a Moravian school in Gracehill, Ireland; later he made his fortune in Manchester, in cotton spinning. Hindley was a labour reform and social welfare advocate who in 1825 founded the Aston and Dukinfield mechanic's institute (Manchester). A Whig with Radical tendencies, as MP for the industrial riding of Ashton-under-Lyne (1835–57), he spoke in favour of free trade, an expanded franchise, and labour legislation. In the 1840s and 1850s Hindley was a leader in the LDOS, the Health of Towns Association, the Metropolitan Drapers' Association, the Ragged Schools Union, and

the LCM. He was the father-in-law of Henry Woods (1822–82), MP.

BIBLIOGRAPHY
Boase
GM (January 1858): 115
N. Pope, *Dickens and Charity* (NY, 1978): 61, 205, 275
W. Ward, *Early Victorian Methodism* (London, 1976): 242–5

JONATHAN BURKE CUTMORE
DONALD M. LEWIS

Hindmarsh, Robert (b. Alnwick, Northumberland, England, 8 Nov. 1759; d. London, 2 Jan. 1835). Early Swedenborgian preacher. James, his father, taught at Kingswood school in the 1760s and then served as a Wesleyan itinerant preacher. Robert was converted at the school in 1768, but abandoned Methodism for mystical religion and then the teaching of Emanuel Swedenborg. In 1787 he became secretary of the Swedenborgian Society in London which established the New Jerusalem church. Inactive from 1798 to 1810, he then became a minister of New Church in Salford, and caused a controversy in that sect through his claim that in 1787 he had been directly ordained by God. Thus the tensions of evangelicalism spilt over into the sects.

BIBLIOGRAPHY
DNB
C. T. Odhner, *Robert Hindmarsh, a Biography* (Philadelphia, PA, 1895)

PETER J. LINEHAM

Hinman, Clark Titus (b. Kartwright, NY, USA, 3 Aug. 1819; d. Troy, NY, USA, 21 Oct. 1854). Methodist educator and holiness advocate. Graduated from Wesleyan University, Connecticut, in 1839, Hinman was hired as instructor at Newbury Seminary (1839–46), Newbury, Vermont, where he taught Greek, mathematics and intellectual science. For two years (1844–6) he was principal of the institution as well as instructor. While at Newbury, he married Martha Morse, daughter of one of the trustees of the seminary. He also developed skills as an orator and teacher.

In 1846, Hinman accepted an appointment to Wesleyan College, Albion, Michigan, where he served as the first president of what is now Albion College. On 23 June 1853, Hinman was elected the founding president of Northwestern University, Evanston, Illinois. His role was not only administrative. He also recruited students and raised funds. Soon after the opening of the second academic year, Hinman returned to Newbury, Vermont, raising funds for Northwestern along the way. He died at Troy, New York, and was buried at Newbury, Vermont.

BIBLIOGRAPHY
E. H. Martin, 'Hinman, Clark T.', *The Encyclopedia of World Methodism* (Nashville, TN, 1974): 1, 1127

M. Simpson, 'Hinman, Clark Titus, D.D.', *Cyclopedia of Methodism* (Philadelphia, PA, 1878): 445

DAVID BUNDY

Hinton, James (b. Buckingham, Buckinghamshire, England, 3 Sept. 1761; d. Reading, Berkshire, England, 28 July 1823). Baptist minister. The son of devout parents Hinton was apprenticed to the grocery trade: he was converted at the age of 15 and was baptized at 20 while in the service of his cousin Benjamin at Chesham. He began to preach, entered Bristol Baptist College in 1784 and was called to the Independent/Baptist church in Oxford, then in a low state, in 1788. His ministry was overshadowed by poverty (he was compelled to run a small school), ill health (a succession of assistant pastors was engaged to help him after 1799), and dissensions within his congregation between Baptists, Independents and an antinomian faction. Even so he built up his church from 29 to 200 members, and saw it twice enlarged, in 1798 and 1819 (to hold 800 and with a baptistry in that year: previously Oxford Baptists had had to travel to Abingdon for baptismal services). His evangelical Calvinism, warm heart, wit and transparent piety made him particularly successful among young people. He, and they, were tireless preachers in the villages around Oxford, and raised up new causes in Eynsham and Littlemore.

James had an irenic temper, not uncommon in that period. With other evangelicals, including Anglicans, he conducted a society for promoting Sunday schools in Oxford and district, supported the *Evangelical Magazine* (till 1810), the Oxfordshire auxiliary of the Bible Society, and was friendly with the Wesleyans and the promoters of the CMS. Yet in the bigoted atmosphere of the Oxford of his day he was often attacked and insulted; his services were interrupted by riotous undergraduates, a particularly cruel pamphlet was published against him by Dr Tatham, Rector of Lincoln College, in 1792, and two years later, while preaching at Woodstock, he was attacked and nearly killed by a band of soldiers. Accused of radicalism, he was in effect a very mild Whig, supporting the Oxford Volunteers during the invasion scare of 1798 and having them parade at his chapel, and even adopting a moderately pro-government stance in 1819, the year of Peterloo.

He was very active in denominational affairs, helped to promote the Oxfordshire Baptist Association (1802), supported Bristol College, and the BMS which for a short period (1816–17) he served as joint secretary, and Mill Hill school. It was a powerful sermon of his to the BMS in 1813 which led to the founding of the Baptist Union. In 1790 he married ANN TAYLOR of Deptford, the daughter of the engraver of JOHN HOWARD's books, and two of their sons entered the Baptist ministry. Apart from his *Vindication* in reply to Dr Tatham (1792), James's other most popular and frequently reprinted work was his account of the death of Thomas Davis, a forger, executed at Oxford in 1805, whom he attended

on the scaffold. An interesting manuscript Commonplace Book is in the Baptist Union Library.

BIBLIOGRAPHY
P. Hayden, 'The Baptists in Oxford', *BQ*, 29, 3 (1981): 127
J. H. Hinton, *Biographical Portraiture* (Oxford, 1824)
W. Stevens and W. W. Bottoms, *The Baptists of the New Road, Oxford* (Oxford, 1948)

IAN SELLERS

Hinton, John Howard (b. Oxford, England, 24 March 1791; d. Bristol, England, 17 Dec. 1873). Baptist leader and theologian. Son of JAMES and ANN (of the important Taylor family) HINTON, John Howard (a name given by his mother at the prison reformer's request after the loss of his own son) was trained at Bristol Baptist College and Edinburgh University. After early pastorates in Wales and in Reading, he was pastor at Devonshire Square, London from 1837 to 1863, thereafter returning for a short while to a new church in Reading before retiring to Bristol in 1868. He was secretary of the Baptist Union from 1841 to 1866, and its president in 1837 and 1863. A keen campaigner against slavery he was active in the Christian Instruction Society arguing against Owenism, lectured for the Complete Suffrage Union and helped found the Liberation Society, though with other Baptists he withdrew after 1855, troubled by the aggressiveness of MIALL. He found himself in the ironic position of being a complete individualist seeking to engineer the unity of a group of independent churches. Although he gave ample support to the BMS, writing a memoir of WILLIAM KNIBB, he seemed to be in some confusion as to whether the missionaries or the London committee should determine action. Missionaries should not create dependant churches but seek to move on swiftly to open up new areas, always remembering that much missionary work remained to be done in Europe – he himself visited Holland, Germany and Sweden in the Baptist interest. Ministry was essentially the ministry of the local church with the clerical function never divorced from that of the whole membership.

Against all church establishments, he ardently advocated the principles of the voluntary church, attacking in print the education clauses of Graham's Factory Bill of 1843. Later he became critical of absolute voluntaryism and began to defend intervention through social legislation and the need for the Christian minister to combat class distinctions, arguing that labour and capital were joint partners in the creation of wealth. But sympathetic to evangelical Anglicans, he keenly supported the EA. Full of enthusiasm for JONATHAN EDWARDS and the New Divinity revivalism which he believed Edwards had stimulated he saw the development of church life in the USA as an abundant corroboration of voluntaryism. His own attempts to secure a new synthesis in the Calvinist-Arminian debate is less than satisfying, leading him into unsatisfactory teaching on human responsibility for which the rationalism of his

Edinburgh education must be in part to blame. This notwithstanding he was a strenuous advocate of personal evangelism, while in the 1850s he was seriously worried by the drift from historic orthodoxy amongst the Congregationalists which found in him a strong advocate of historic evangelical doctrine.

SELECT WRITINGS
J. H. Hinton, *Works*, 7 vols (London, 1864–5)

BIBLIOGRAPHY
Baptist Handbook (1875)
DNB
I. Sellers, 'John Howard Hinton, Theologian', *BQ* (1989)
S. A. Swaine, *Faithful Men* (London, 1884)

J. H. Y. BRIGGS

Hislop, Stephen (b. Duns, Berwickshire, Scotland, 8 Sept. 1817; d. Tukalghat, near Nagpur, India, 3 Sept. 1863). Scottish missionary to India. As a young man the writings of ALEXANDER DUFF fired Hislop's imagination, and he determined to go to India as a missionary. He arrived in Nagpur In the Central Provinces in 1844, the year after the Disruption, to establish a mission under the auspices of the FCS. He followed Duff's strategy of giving priority to education as a necessary preparation for the gospel, and established schools, in and about Nagpur, at that time in a Hindu princely state. The most famous of these survives as Hislop College. He made a name for himself as a fearless critic of misgovernment in the native states, and of dilatoriness and corruption on the part of British officials.

Unlike Duff, Hislop did much itinerant preaching in Marathi in towns and villages in the Nagpur region. He became a pioneer anthropologist, publishing studies on the languages and customs of the Gonds, and he was also a recognized authority on the geology and fossils of Central India. He died in a drowning accident in 1863.

BIBLIOGRAPHY
E. G. K. Hewat, *Vision and Achievement* (London, 1960)
G. Smith, *Stephen Hislop*, 2nd edn (London, 1889)

DUNCAN FORRESTER

Hitchcock, Edward (b. Deerfield, MA, USA, 24 May 1793; d. Amherst, MA, USA, 27 Feb. 1864). Congregational minister and geologist. Hitchcock's interest in natural history was stimulated by an encounter with Amos Eaton and a subsequent exchange of letters with the Yale mineralogist, BENJAMIN SILLIMAN in 1817. Besides these scientific pursuits, Hitchcock, having returned to the Congregationalism of his family after a brief flirtation with Unitarianism, studied theology at Yale in the early 1820s prior to taking up his first pastoral duties in Conway, Massachusetts. Subsequently, from 1825 to 1845, he served as professor of chemistry and natural history at Amherst College, and there authored numerous scientific textbooks and works of popular

science alongside technical monographs on geology. At various times during these years he secured appointments as state geologist for Massachusetts and Vermont. An enthusiast for the theories of Werner, Hitchcock only half-heartedly endorsed the new glacial theories of Agassiz, and despite his admiration of Charles Lyell, he continued to adhere to a modified form of catastrophism.

Understandably, Hitchcock felt a special obligation to articulate his faith in both science and religion, and found in the tradition of British natural theology the most appropriate vehicle for fusing scientific and theological convictions. *The Religion of Geology* which he thus published in 1859 presented his mature reflections on the subject, though it revealed the extent to which he had abandoned his earlier attempts to find detailed correspondences between the book of nature and the book of scripture.

BIBLIOGRAPHY
DAB
DSB
S. M. Guralnick, 'Geology and Religion before Darwin: the Case of Edward Hitchcock', *Isis*, 63 (1972): 529–43
P. J. Lawrence, 'Edward Hitchcock: The Christian Geologist', *Proceedings of the American Philosophical Society*, 116 (1972): 21–34

DAVID N. LIVINGSTONE

Hitchcock, Roger (b. Andover, Hampshire, England; d. Budleigh Salterton, Devon, England, 1851). Seceder and Baptist minister. Hitchcock was educated at Queens' College, Cambridge (matriculated, 6 July 1815). He was Curate of Fittleton, Wiltshire, 1822–6, when he seceded from the Church and was baptized at Devizes on 2 January 1827, by Mr Cox, minister of Hosier Street Chapel, Reading. He became minister of the Old Baptist Chapel, Devizes, 1830–3, when he resigned due to ill health. Hitchcock was a successful and popular Calvinistic Baptist minister.

BIBLIOGRAPHY
Al. Cant.
R. W. Oliver, *The Strict Baptist Chapels of England*, 5 vols, (London, 1968) 5: 57, 59
J. H. Philpot, *The Seceders*, 2 vols (London, 1931–2), 1: 182, 341; 2: 93

GRAYSON CARTER

Hitchins, Thomas Martin (b. Merton, Devon, England, 1766; d. Devonport, Devon, 19 Dec. 1830). Anglican clergyman. After Exeter College, Oxford, Hitchins became tutor to the Goulburn children (the future statesman and his brother) at Prinknash Park, Gloucestershire. He acted as Curate of Haresfield nearby, after which he moved successively to curacies at St Hilary, Cornwall and Stoke Damerel, Devon (1794–6). He did not experience an evangelical conversion until 1797, an event to some degree influenced by his brother who was

Curate of Falmouth. St John's, Devonport was built for Hitchins who ministered there until his death (1796–1830). He established a Sunday school and Benevolent Societies for the sick, and strongly supported the Bible Society and the CMS. He was also registrar of the Consistory Court of Exeter.

BIBLIOGRAPHY
Al. Ox. II: 667
CO, XXXI: 247

ARTHUR POLLARD

Hitt, Daniel (b. Fauquier County, VA, BNA, *c.* 1768; d. Washington County, MD, USA, Sept. 1825). Methodist preacher, presiding elder and publisher. Only Hitt's 35 years as a Methodist preacher are historically recoverable. He became an appointed circuit rider in 1790 and for six years served five circuits in Pennsylvania and Ohio. Then for 11 years he was presiding elder over five districts. These districts were great frontier regions west of the Alleghany Mountains as well as more settled areas in Virginia and Maryland. In 1807 he was assigned to be Bishop FRANCIS ASBURY's travelling companion.

The General Conference of 1808 selected him to serve under John Wilson as assistant book agent for the denomination's publishing enterprise, the Book Concern, headquartered in New York. He had a close relationship with the Book Concern dating to his earliest days in the circuits when he was one of the few preachers who promptly remitted money from his sales of Methodist titles. Upon Wilson's death two years later Hitt succeeded to the office of book agent or book steward and was elected to this post in his own right in 1812.

Hitt's era at the Book Concern was not successful. His predecessors had tried to keep the price of most of their publications under $1.00. They did much publishing of brief works for laity. Hitt favoured more expensive titles, including multivolume sets, better suited to the minister's library. His financial reports to General Conference were vague. The oversight committee appointed at the 1812 Conference to receive the book agent's report could not learn from the information he provided exactly where their publishing enterprise stood financially. They assumed the situation was all right, but by 1816 the Book Concern was in crisis. Hitt reported a debt of $22,000, interest on which was consuming all the profits. The modern historian of the Methodist publishing house concluded it was a small miracle that the Book Concern survived the 1812–16 period.

The last nine years of Hitt's career and life were spent as presiding elder over four districts in the Philadelphia and Baltimore annual conferences, plus one year (1822–3) as the travelling companion of Bishop WILLIAM MCKENDREE. Hitt's death was unexpected. He came down with typhus fever on 1 September 1825 at a camp meeting near Greencastle, Pennsylvania. Taken to the home of a physician he responded to treatment and seemed past danger. At his request he was moved to the home of a nephew, also a physician, where he suffered a relapse and died.

Hitt was apparently a man of rigidly conservative personal style. One companion characterized him as 'an old bachelor of the straitest sect'. His bearing was stern. He was uncompromising in his convictions. He continued to dress in the styles of the USA Revolutionary War period and to comb his hair artistically after the fashion of that day. When persons came to the New York office to purchase books Hitt did not engage them in small talk. On the other hand, colleagues remembered him for simplicity, integrity, absolute commitment to duty, sensible preaching, sound judgment on issues, and warmth and uncommon tact among peers.

BIBLIOGRAPHY
AAP
Minutes
J. P. Pilkington, *The Methodist Publishing House*, 1 (Nashville, TN, 1968)

CHARLES W. BROCKWELL, JR

Hoare, Charles James (b. London, 14 July 1781; d. Godstone, Surrey, England, 18 Jan. 1865). Anglican clergyman. Hoare was a member of the banking family of that name, his father HENRY HOARE being among the founders of CMS. After private education he went on to St John's College, Cambridge (BA 1803; MA 1806; fellow 1806–11), where his friends included HENRY MARTYN, J. W. CUNNINGHAM, the GRANT brothers (CHARLES and ROBERT) and WILLIAM DEALTRY. He won the Seaton prize for his poem on *The Shipwreck of St Paul* (1807). He was Curate of Alton (1804–7), Vicar of Blandford Forum (1807–20) and of the family living of Godstone (1820–65), near which WILLIAM WILBERFORCE lived at Marden Park. Hoare was Canon of Winchester (1831–60), Archdeacon of Winchester (1829–47) and, in succession to William Dealtry, of Surrey (1847–65), where he played a large part in church extension work in South London. He held a yearly missionary gathering at Godstone. His writings include works in defence of the Irish Church, in the cause of education, and for the maintenance of cathedral establishments.

BIBLIOGRAPHY
Al. Cant., II. iii: 387
DNB

ARTHUR POLLARD

Hoare, Edward (b. Hampstead, Middlesex, England, 5 June 1812; d. Tunbridge Wells, Kent, England, 7 July 1894). Anglican clergyman. Grandson of London banker SAMUEL HOARE (1751–1825), he graduated from Trinity College, Cambridge in 1834 and was ordained two years later. Following curacies at Pakefield, Suffolk (1836), Richmond, Surrey (1837–46) and St John's Holloway (1846–7), he was incumbent of Christ

Church, Ramsgate (1847–53) and Holy Trinity, Tunbridge Wells (1853–94). Appointed Honorary Canon of Canterbury in 1868, he was a CMS committee stalwart and active in the CPAS and other societies. An important local evangelical leader, he was also a well-known missioner and a significant participant in national church affairs. He spoke out against ritualism and 'holiness' teaching. He was an early premillennialist and a widely read author of doctrinal, eschatological and homiletical works. He married Marie Eliza Brodie (died 1863), daughter of Sir Benjamin Collins Brodie, in 1839 and had 11 children, including two future clergymen.

BIBLIOGRAPHY
Al. Cant.
J. H. Townsend, ed., Edward Hoare . . . a Record of his Life Based Upon a Brief Autobiography (London, 1896)

JOHN OAKES

Hoare, Edward (Newenham) (b. Limerick, Ireland, 1800; d. Waterford, Ireland 1 Feb. 1877). Church of Ireland clergyman. He was the son of John Hoare, of Rathkeale, and of Rachel, daughter of Sir Edward Newenham, two early evangelical families in County Limerick. Educated at Trinity College, Dublin, he was briefly Curate of St John's, Limerick, and (despite Bishop Jebb's opposition) founded Trinity Church, an evangelical trustee chapel attached to a charitable institution, and providing from 1834 accommodation for some 3,000 Protestants in St Michael's parish who were without a church. He was also founding editor of the *Christian Herald*, which expressed the strong interest of the early 1830s in unfulfilled prophecy, but terminated it after five years in disillusionment at what he saw as the extreme tendencies of Irvingites and early 'Plymouth' Brethren. He became Archdeacon of Ardfert, then Dean of Achonry, and finally Dean of Waterford (1850–77) in Bishop DALY's dioceses. His eldest son, John Newenham Hoare, became Vicar of St John's, Keswick.

BIBLIOGRAPHY
J. B. Leslie, Ardfert and Aghadoe Clergy and Parishes (Dublin, 1940)

ALAN R. ACHESON

Hoare, Henry (b. 20 April 1750; d. 15 March 1828). Banker and subscriber to evangelical causes. The only surviving son of William Hoare (died 1753), a London merchant, and great-grandson of Sir Richard Hoare (1648–1718), who founded Hoare's Bank in 1673, he was a career banker, who became partner in Hoare's in 1778 and senior partner in 1787. He retained the latter position until his death and was remembered for his wise and industrious stewardship during a period of significant financial turbulence. In private life, he devoted time and resources to evangelical societies, including the CMS. In 1775, he married Lydia Henrietta Malortie, the

daughter and co-heiress of a London merchant. Among his four sons were William Henry Hoare (1776–1819), a one-time CMS Committee member, and Archdeacon CHARLES JAMES HOARE (1781–1865). His daughter, Lydia Elizabeth Hoare (1786–1856), married Sir THOMAS DYKE ACLAND in 1808.

BIBLIOGRAPHY
Burke's Landed Gentry (London, 1939)
H. P. R. Hoare, Hoare's Bank, A Record, 1672–1955 (London, 1955)
C. Hole, Early History of the Church Missionary Society (London, 1896)

JOHN OAKES

Hoare, Samuel (b. Stoke Newington, London, 9 August 1751; d. Hampstead, London, 14 July 1825). Banker and subscriber to evangelical causes. Second son of Samuel Hoare (1716–96), a Cork merchant who had acquired a significant fortune in London, he was the first Hoare to become partner, in 1772, in the Lombard Street bank later known as Barnett, Hoare and Co. (from 1826). A lifelong Quaker, he was a pioneer abolitionist and a supporter of prison reform and the movement for the establishment of Sunday schools. He was further active in plans for the African settlement of Sierra Leone. His political activities, in which he was followed by his son, Samuel (1783–1847), who was also a career banker, brought him into contact with leading evangelicals of his day, including WILLIAM WILBERFORCE and HANNAH MORE. His grandson, EDWARD HOARE (1812–94), was a leading Church of England clergyman.

BIBLIOGRAPHY
Burke's
F. R. Pryor, ed., Memoirs of Samuel Hoare by his Daughter Sarah and his Widow Hannah . . . (London, 1911)

JOHN OAKES

Hoare, Sir Samuel (1783–1847). *See* HOARE, SAMUEL (1751–1825)

Hoare, William (Deane) (b. Limerick, Ireland, c. 1772; d. Limerick, Ireland, 1823). Church of Ireland clergyman and philanthropist. He was the younger of two clerical – and evangelical – sons of Deane Hoare, Vicar-General of the diocese of Limerick. John Hoare, Rector of Rathkeale, was his elder brother, EDWARD HOARE his nephew. He was Rector of St George's, Limerick, and Vicar-General. Bishop Jebb described him as a man of prayer, and of inner and outward holiness, who preached 'the whole gospel', and was the founder or the principal support of every charitable institution in the city. His wife, Louisa, a sister of ARTHUR GUINNESS, died in 1809, in her twenty-seventh year.

BIBLIOGRAPHY
J. Jebb, *A Sermon Preached at the Funeral of the Rev. W. D. Hoare* (Cork, Ireland, 1823)

ALAN R. ACHESON

Hoare, William Henry. See HOARE, HENRY

Hobbs, John (b. Isle of Thanet, Kent, England, 22 Feb. 1800; d. Auckland, New Zealand, 24 June 1883). WMMS missionary to New Zealand. Converted at 16, Hobbs began preaching three years later and in 1822 arrived in Tasmania. Encouraged by SAMUEL MARSDEN he became an artisan assitant to the WMMS in New Zealand where he helped pioneer mission stations at Whangaroa (1823-7) and Hokianga (1827-55). He was ordained in 1827. From 1833 to 1837 he served in Tonga. Hobbs' skills in building, mechanics, horticulture, medicine, navigation, language and printing were invaluable. He composed hymns in both Maori and Tongan, printed the first books in Fijian and Samoan, was one of the translators of the Maori Bible and acted as interpreter at the Mangungu signing of the Treaty of Waitangi. With JOHN H. BUMBY he circumnavigated the North Island to select sites for the extension of the mission. In 1848, while establishing a mission station on the Wanganui River he was shipwrecked. This brought on an increasing deafness which necessitated his retirement in 1856. He married Jane Broggref in 1827, with whom he had nine children.

BIBLIOGRAPHY
DNZB
T. M. I. Williment, *John Hobbs 1800-1883* (Wellington, New Zealand, 1985)

W. A. CHAMBERS

Hobson, Benjamin (b. Welford, Northamptonshire, England, 2 Jan. 1816; d. Forest Hills, London, England, 16 Feb. 1873). Medical missionary in China. After studying in London, Hobson joined the LMS. Assigned to China, he arrived in Macao in 1839. In 1842, military action on the part of the British government forced open five Chinese ports and made Hong Kong a Crown colony. Along with other members of the LMS, Hobson began a mission there.

Hobson was assigned to open a mission hospital in Canton in 1843-4. Because of hostility and his wife's declining health he travelled to Great Britain but his wife died *en route*. He returned to China and married Mary R. Morrison, daughter of ROBERT MORRISON. In October 1847 he opened a mission hospital at Canton and could claim immediate success in his medical practice. In one year alone, he reported that he had treated some 20,000 Chinese patients. Conversions however, remained low.

While at Canton, Hobson carried out two studies on opium. The first was for the LMS in 1843, while the second was for the British governmental representative, Sir John Bowring. Hobson translated Chinese treatises

on medicine and physiology and made Western medical ideas available in Chinese. Sibree and others refer to him as 'the father of the modern medical literature of China'. In 1859 Hobson retired from the LMS and returned to London where he died in 1873.

BIBLIOGRAPHY
CWM archives, School of Oriental and African Studies, London
ESM
J. Sibree, *A Register of Missionaries, Deputations, Etc.* (LMS, London, 1925)
Wellcome Institute, London, Hobson Correspondence, 'Missionary in China', Box 5

JEAN PAQUETTE

Hobson, William (b. Waterford, Ireland, 25 Sept. 1792; d. Auckland, 10 Sept. 1842). First Governor of New Zealand. Hobson joined the Royal Navy in 1803, rising to commander in 1824. In 1837 he was sent to New Zealand where British subjects were threatened by Maori tribal conflict. His report encouraged CHARLES GRANT (Lord Glenelg) to support limited British involvement in the government of the country. He was appointed Lieutenant-Governor to New Zealand in 1839. With the help of James Busby and CMS missionaries, in particular HENRY WILLIAMS, he secured Maori support for the signing on 6 February 1840 of the Treaty of Waitangi, which recognized British colonial authority.

CMS and WMMS missionaries played a significant part in helping him gain further Maori support throughout the country. Hobson became Governor but was handicapped by ill health, poor advisers, financial difficulties and antagonism from the colonizing New Zealand Company. Friendly towards the missionaries and concerned to safeguard Maori land rights, he appointed CMS missionary GEORGE CLARKE 'protector of aborigines'. A deeply religious man with high ideals and a strong sense of justice, he was also sensitive to criticism, proud and obstinate. A competent naval commander he was unsuccessful as a governor.

BIBLIOGRAPHY
DNZB
G. H Scholefield, *Captain William Hobson, first Governor of New Zealand* (London, 1934)

ALLAN K. DAVIDSON

Hoby, James (b. London, 1788; d. Caterham, Surrey, England, 20 Nov. 1871). Baptist minister. The son of George Hoby, bootmaker to King George III, who was a deacon at the Eagle Street Church, London, he early developed a friendship with its minister, JOSEPH IVIMEY. Trained at Bristol Baptist College, he had pastorates at Maze Pond, London (assistant minister), Weymouth, Birmingham, where as first pastor, he built up a considerable congregation at the Graham Street Church from almost nothing, and Twickenham. A private income enabled him to build up small causes. With FRANCIS A. COX, he formed a delegation to the American churches both to explore their views on revivalism and to make a 'fraternal expostulation' on slave-holding, which JOHN FOSTER thought an absurd project; their report was published as *The Baptists in America* (1836). He subsequently visited Europe in the Baptist interest, undertook a number of special functions for the BMS, and was the author of *An Anti-Popery Lecture*. Hoby was elected to the chair of the Baptist Union, on whose committee he sat for many years, for both 1851 and 1854.

BIBLIOGRAPHY

Baptist Handbook (1872)

E. A. Payne, *The Baptist Union* (London, 1959)

S. A. Swaine, *Faithful Men* (London, 1884): 242

J. H. Y. BRIGGS

Hodge, Charles (b. Philadelphia, PA, USA, 27 Dec. 1797; d. Princeton, NJ, USA, 19 June 1878). Presbyterian theologian. Hodge was the best known confessional Calvinist and one of the most formidable polemical theologians in the United States during the middle third of the nineteenth century. He was the first American to teach theology for more than fifty years, and at the time of his death he had personally instructed more students than had attended any other seminary in the country. Hodge's commanding influence was not, however, a result of simple longevity so much as the product of a tireless pen, forceful theological views and deep personal piety.

Hodge's father, Hugh, a Philadelphia physician with Scotch-Irish ancestry, died from the effects of Yellow Fever seven months after Charles was born. His mother, Mary (née Blanchard), who was descended from New England patriots, provided courageously for Charles and his older brother, saw that they learned the Westminster Catechism and provided them a sound primary education. In 1812 Hodge entered the College of New Jersey (later Princeton University) where the president was the redoubtable confessionalist, ASHBEL GREEN, who had earlier been the family's pastor in Philadelphia. Even more influential than Green, however, was ARCHIBALD ALEXANDER, who also in 1812 had come to Princeton as the first professor at the new Presbyterian theological seminary. Alexander befriended Hodge as a collegiate undergraduate, directed the course of his seminary studies, invited him along on preaching tours in Virginia and then persuaded the seminary directors to hire the young graduate as a temporary professor of biblical languages. From Alexander, Hodge learned the singular combination of commitments that defined his own exposition of 'the Princeton theology' – heartfelt piety, commitment to the inspiration of Scripture, devotion to the Westminster Confession and Catechisms, confidence in the European Calvinism of savants like François Turretin and intuitive reliance upon Scottish common-sense moral philosophy.

Hodge was ordained to the Presbyterian ministry in November 1821, but his entire career was spent as an instructor at the seminary. In May 1822, he was appointed a regular professor of scripture (in 1840 the title would be changed to professor of theology). Also in 1822 he married Sarah Bache, a great-grand-daughter of Benjamin Franklin. The Hodges had eight children, one of whom, Archibald Alexander Hodge, succeeded his father as professor of theology at Princeton. (Three years after Sarah's death in 1849, Hodge married a widow, Mary [Hunter] Stockton, who survived him.)

Early in his career at the seminary, Hodge took a two-year study tour of European universities where he thoroughly enjoyed first-hand exposure to the rigours of German scholarship, but where he also strengthened the wariness he had learned from Alexander against what the Princetonians called 'rationalism', 'mysticism' and 'ritualism'. Upon his return to Princeton in 1829, Hodge resumed his teaching, expanded an already diligent round of reading, entered vigorously into family and church affairs and also transformed the seminary's theological journal (which he had founded in 1825) into the *Biblical Repertory and Princeton Review*. For nearly a half-century thereafter, Hodge poured great energies into this periodical, which he edited along with a shifting cast of associates from Princeton College and Princeton Seminary. It became the major outlet for Hodge's advice to the Presbyterians (almost every year he wrote a comprehensive article for the July number on the deliberations of his denomination's General Assembly), the major vehicle for his searching criticisms of contemporary theological trends in Europe and North America, and the organ through which, especially during the American Civil War, he discussed the momentous political events of the day. In 1871 a writer in the *British Quarterly Review* called this journal 'beyond all question the greatest purely theological Review that has ever been published in the English tongue' (A. A. Hodge, 1880: 257).

Hodge's theological reputation arose from the skill (or, as his opponents would have it, the obduracy) with which he defended confessional Calvinism. In the pages of *The Princeton Review* he chastized NATHANIEL WILLIAM TAYLOR and the 'New Haven' theology for departing from the high Calvinism of JONATHAN EDWARDS. He attacked the revivalism of CHARLES GRANDISON FINNEY for promoting Pelagianism. He called to account the Mercersburg theologians, JOHN WILLIAMSON NEVIN and PHILIP SCHAFF, for wandering into mysticism. In a particularly momentous exchange of learned essays with EDWARDS AMASA PARK of Andover Seminary in 1850 and 1851, Hodge defended the capacity of language to communicate theological truth propositionally. He directed telling shafts at England's Oxford Movement and German neologisms. He defended a high view of the Bible's inspiration against both Roman Catholic arguments for apostolic hierarchy and the first waves of Continental biblical criticism. And he offered encouragement to specifically Calvinist theological movements in other places (especially, after 1843, the Free Church of Scotland) and more generally to expressions of Protestant confessionalism (as in many warm, if not entirely comprehending, commendations of contemporary Lutheranism). In these polemics, Hodge sometimes exploited historical arguments casually; for someone whose thought was extraordinarily sophisticated on other matters, he could be quite naïve on questions of theological method; and he sometimes did not discriminate well between the minor errors of near-by allies and the major problems of theologians at a distance. Yet for all the admitted weaknesses of his polemical writings, they also displayed a breadth of learning, grasp of basic Christian teaching, cohesive understanding of Scripture, forcefulness of prose, and greatness of soul that was rarely, if ever, matched in nineteenth-century evangelicalism.

It is regrettable that Hodge is today known more through his books than through his contributions to the *Princeton Review*, since the latter display the results of piety in league with learning more powerfully than almost any of his separately published works. Yet these too – especially a commentary on the Book of Romans (1835), a winsome catechetical volume written for the American Sunday School Union (1841), a massive systematics (1872–73), and a penetrating critique of Darwinistic naturalism (1874) – were important in their day and have been read with appreciation by considerable numbers since. Hodge once claimed that 'a new idea has never originated in this Seminary', but it was an ambiguous claim. Hodge was correct in describing the intent of his long and influential career, but wrong in shortchanging the freshness of his own defense of Augustinian Protestant orthodoxy.

SELECT WRITINGS
A Commentary on the Epistle to the Romans (Philadelphia, 1835)
The Way of Life (Philadelphia, 1841); modern edition ed. Mark A. Noll (Mahwah, NJ, 1987)
Essays and Reviews: Selected from the Princeton Review (New York, 1857); modern edition ed. Bruce Kuklick (New York, 1987)
Systematic Theology, 3 vols. (New York, 1872–3)
What Is Darwinism? (New York, 1874)

BIBLIOGRAPHY
DAB
DcAmReB
A. A. Hodge, *The Life of Charles Hodge* (New York, 1880)
W. A. Hoffecker, *Piety and the Princeton Theologians* (Grand Rapids, 1981)
M. A. Noll, ed., *The Princeton Theology, 1812–1921* (Grand Rapids, 1983)
D. F. Wells, *Reformed Theology in America* (Grand Rapids, 1985)

MARK A. NOLL

Hodgson, Thomas Laidman (b. Darlington, Co. Durham, England, 12 June 1787; d. Cape Town, 21 June 1850). Methodist missionary. Hodgson was converted in 1807 and was ordained in 1815, six years before he was sent by the WMMS to South Africa.

He insisted that he felt called to go where no other missionary had been, so he, his wife, Anne, and another couple went north beyond the colonial frontier, over the Orange River to work with the Rolong division of the seTswana-speaking peoples. They settled at Maquassi in the present Transvaal in February, 1823. In 1824 the society recalled him to Cape Town but he returned to Maquassi together with JAMES ARCHBELL in 1825 only to find the station had been burned down during a raid by the neighbouring Tau people. Recurrent warfare finally drove Hodgson and the Rolong to migrate and they finally settled near Warrenton in the present Free State in July, 1826.

Hodgson chose in 1828, to leave the Rolong and go to work among the Griqua, where he stayed only two years before returning to England in 1830. In 1831 his wife died and he stayed on in England serving the Methodist church until 1836. That year he and his new wife, Elizabeth, went to Cape Town to succeed BARNABAS SHAW as superintendent of the Cape district. In addition to his work as superintendent, Hodgson worked assiduously for the spread of Christianity among the so-called 'Cape Coloureds'.

BIBLIOGRAPHY
T. Smith, *Memoir of the Reverend Thomas Laidman Hodgson* (London, 1854)

ANDREW C. ROSS

Hodgson, William (b. London, 15 Dec. 1809; d. Clifton, Westmorland, England, 2 Dec. 1869). Anglican evangelical minister. Hodgson was educated at Richmond Grammar School and at Sidney Sussex College, Cambridge. After ordination he became a curate at Whalley, then Perpetual Curate of Colne, Lancashire. From the obscurity of the hamlet of Brathay, where Hodgson was Perpetual Curate (1842–56), his friend Frederick Barker, Bishop of Sydney, invited him to become the first principal of Moore Theological College. In his 11 years as Principal he built up the college from scratch and saw 46 students ordained into the ministry.

Ill health forced him back home and Barker advised Bishop SAMUEL WALDEGRAVE to secure a position for him and in 1868 Hodgson became the Rector of Clifton. The Bishop's intention was that Hodgson would curb the activities of the local branch of the English Church Union, but he died 18 months later.

BIBLIOGRAPHY
M. L. Loane, *A Centenary History of Moore Theological College* (Sydney, 1955)

ALAN FREDERICK MUNDEN

Hodson, George H. (b. 1788; d. Riva, Italy, 13 Aug. 1855). Archdeacon of Stafford. The youngest son of Carlisle merchant George Hodson, he was educated privately by JOHN FAWCETT as well as at Carlisle Grammar School and Trinity College, Cambridge (BA 1810), becoming a fellow of Magdalene College in 1810 (MA 1813). He was ordained (deacon 1811, priest 1812) and became curate at Clifton Old Church (1815), chaplain to LEWIS WAY at Stanstead Park, Sussex (1819), and tutor to the young Samuel Wilberforce. He became a trustee of Simeon's Trust in 1837.

He moved to the diocese of Lichfield and Coventry in 1824 – the same year HENRY RYDER became its bishop – and was incumbent of Christ Church, Birmingham (1824–33), Vicar of Colwich, Staffordshire (1828–51), Archdeacon of Stafford (1829–55), Chancellor of Lichfield Cathedral (1833–55), and Vicar of St Mary's, Lichfield (1851–5).

Hodson married Mary Somersall Stephen (died 1846), the niece of JAMES STEPHEN, in 1815. These family ties reinforced the religious convictions that placed him within the Clapham tradition of Anglican evangelicalism. Hodson's central beliefs in the middle period of his life are evident in his collection of *Twelve Sermons, Illustrative of Some of the Leading Doctrines of the Gospel in Connection with Christian Temper and Experience* (1825). Having preached in July 1855 with emphasis on the final testimony of St Paul (2 Timothy 4: 6–8), he left in good health for a short holiday on the continent, but contracted cholera while staying at Riva on Lake Garda and died within a few hours.

BIBLIOGRAPHY
Al. Cant., 3 (1752–1900): 402
Burke's
R. Gilbert, *Clerical Guide* (London, 1836)
GM (November 1855): 551; (December 1855): 663

D. E. H. MOLE

Hoernle, Christian Theophilus (b. Ludwigsburg, Württemberg, Germany, 24 Nov. 1804; d. Cannstatt, Germany, 7 June 1882). CMS Missionary to India. He was born in Württemberg, raised by a godly uncle in Cannstatt after his father's death at age 11, and after a decisive conversion in 1825, gave his life to missionary service. In 1828 he enrolled at the Basel Missionary Society school, and, after four years' study, was ordained and sent to Shusha in Armenia. In 1835 Armenian Orthodox clerics induced Tsar Nicholas I to order the station closed; and Hoernle relocated in the Kurdish region of Persia where he engaged in translation work. Because the ongoing opposition endangered the missionaries' safety, the Basel mission terminated the Persian work in 1837 and transferred Hoernle to the CMS North Indian mission.

While on home leave in Germany in 1838 he married Emilie Mögling, and five of their children became CMS workers. They organized an orphanage at Secundra near Agra, where he also engaged in printing, teacher training, and evangelistic work. A gifted linguist, he published material in Hindi and Urdu, and was responsible for revising the Urdu New Testament. The work at Secundra was destroyed during the Great Mutiny of 1857, but he restored it. In 1861 he was assigned to lead the Meerut mission, and he obtained Anglican orders since he would be involved in training and commissioning Indian clergy. He retired in 1874 but kept charge of the Christian village at Annfield. In 1881 the Hoernles returned to Germany where he died in 1882 and Emilie died a year later.

BIBLIOGRAPHY
D. T. B[arry], *CMS Register of Missionaries and Native Clergy* (privately printed) (London, 1906)
J. F. D. Hoernle, *Memoir of C.T. Hoernle* (Dorking, England, 1884)
W. Oehler, *Geschichte der Deutschen Evangelischen Mission*, 1 (Baden–Baden, 1949): 153–5

R. V. PIERARD

Hoffman, Cadwallader Colden (b. New York City, 15 Dec. 1819; d. Cape Palmas, West Africa, 25 Nov. 1865). Episcopal missionary. He was the son of Martin Hoffman and his second wife Mary Seaton. He graduated from the Virginia Theological Seminary in 1848, and was ordained deacon by Bishop ALONZO POTTER of Pennsylvania on 30 July 1848, and priest by Potter on 17 September 1848. On 24 February 1848, he and Jacob Rambo, a seminary classmate, sailed for the Episcopal mission in West Africa, which was centred in Cape Palmas, and was under the leadership of John Payne, later (1851) the first missionary Bishop of Cape Palmas, Liberia. He lived and worked in Liberia for 16 years and has been called as a 'very Barnabas to Africa and the Africans'. He was once described as being 'one of the gentlest, loveliest, most devoted, zealous missionaries of the American Episcopal Church'. An editorial in the primary Episcopal missionary publication from 1836 to 1939, stated after his death:

> C. Colden Hoffman may be called the Henry Martyn of our American Church. If his intellectual abilities were not fully equal to those of Henry Martyn, yet his love for the Saviour was as intense, his consecration to his service was as thorough, his delight in making known His truth was as great, and his character altogether was as lovely, as that of him who is considered the most Christ-like missionary of modern times.
> (*The Spirit of Missions*, March 1868: 129)

BIBLIOGRAPHY
G. T. Fox, *A Memoir of the Rev. C. Colden Hoffman, Missionary to Cape Palmas, West Africa* (London, 1868)
The Spirit of Missions, 31, 3 (1868): 129–33

DONALD SMITH ARMENTROUT

Hoffmann, Ludwig Friedrich Wilhelm (b. Leonberg, Germany, 30 Oct. 1806; d. Berlin, 28 Aug. 1873). Second inspector of the Basel Mission, Pietist, and court preacher in Berlin. After studies at the seminaries of

Schorntal and Tübingen, Hoffmann served (1829–34) as rector at Heumaden. From 1834 to 1839 he served as deacon at Winnenden where he worked in the healing work at the Sanitarium. Academic recognition was won by his careful critique of D.F. Strauss' 'Life of Jesus', published as *Das Leben Jesu, Kritisch Bearbeitet von Dr. D. F. Strauss, Geprüft für Theologen und Nichttheologen* (Stuttgart, 1836; 2nd edn, 1839).

He was invited to Basel by C. F. SPITTLER to be inspector (director) of the Basel Mission. From 1839 to 1850, Hoffmann reorganized the Basel Mission and greatly expanded its influence and credibility in Europe as well as the scope of its mission in Africa, Asia and North America. He was active in the Basel churches and taught at the University of Basel. Hoffmann edited the *Basler Missionsmagazin* and published numerous reports and sermons on mission theory and activity. From this period came the impetus for a number of important publications dealing with mission theory, including *Missionsstunden und Vorträge* (3 vols, 1847–53) and *Die Christlicke Litteratur als Werkzeug der Mission* (Berlin, 1855). He reflected on his experience at the Basel Mission in *Elf Jahre in der Mission, ein Abschiedsword an den Kreis der Evangelischen Missionsgesellschaft zu Basel* (Stuttgart, 1853).

From Basel, Hoffmann went to Tübingen as professor and director of the seminary. In 1852, Frederick Wilhelm IV appointed this devout pietist court preacher and eventually general superintendent of the Brandenburg Consistory, a position he held for two decades. In much of the literature and on some of his publications, Hoffmann is referred to as Wilhelm Hoffmann.

BIBLIOGRAPHY
C. H. Hoffmann, *Leben und Wirken des Dr. Ludwig Friedrich Wilhelm Hoffmann*, 2 vols (Berlin, 1878–80)
W. Schlatter, *Geschichte der Basler Mission 1815–1915*, 1 (Basel, 1916): 144–216
RGG, 3rd edn, 3 (1959): 414–15

DAVID BUNDY

Hoge, Moses (b. Cedar Grove, Frederick County, VA, BNA, 15 Feb. 1752; d. Philadelphia, PA, USA, 5 July 1820). Reformed theologian, spiritual director and college educator. Hoge studied at Liberty Hall Academy, fought in the American Revolution, and completed theology under JAMES WADDEL. Ordained in 1782, Hoge served as a Presbyterian pastor in Hampshire County (1782–7) and at Shepherdstown Church, [West] Virginia (1787–1807). He defended Calvinism in *Strictures upon a Pamphlet* (1793) and attacked Thomas Paine's religious infidelity in *Sophist Unmasked* (1797). He married first in 1783 Elizabeth Poage and second in 1803 Susan [née Watkins] Hunt (see SUSAN HOGE).

While he was President of Hampden-Sydney College (1807–20), the Presbyterian Synod of Virginia established there in 1812 Union Theological Seminary in Virginia with Hoge as its first professor. Hoge developed a Pietist approach to education partly modeled · after August Hermann Francke. Believing like Francke that God would provide, Hoge admitted poor students to study free of charge. The Hampden-Sydney College revival of 1814–15 began in praying societies of students meeting in his residence. Hoge also carried on a ministry of spiritual direction beyond the college through correspondence to former parishioners and friends.

Hoge was also concerned for poor slaves in his neighbourhood. In December 1812 some of his students formed a praying society to meet weekly for their benefit. During communion seasons, he welcomed African-American communicants to his house for spiritual advice. He emancipated the slaves which he inherited. Hoge was moderate in his call for emancipation; he favoured the Liberian scheme of the American Colonization Society by which manumitted slaves were given the option of commencing their freedom in this new African colony.

In his practice of spiritual guidance, Hoge encouraged solitary communion with God. In his practice of meditation, Hoge did not limit himself to scripture. He made use of the Puritan practice of 'spiritualizing the creature' by which one pondered spiritual truths that could be derived from meditating upon an object in the natural world.

BIBLIOGRAPHY
DAB
J. B. Hoge, *Sketch of . . . Moses Hoge* (Richmond, VA, 1968)
A. D. Thomas, 'Moses Hoge: Reformed Piety and Spiritual Guidance', *American Presbyterians* (Summer 1993): 95–101
—, *Second Great Awakening in Virginia* (Richmond, VA, 1981)

ARTHUR D. THOMAS JR

Hoge, Moses Drury (b. Hampden Sidney, VA, USA, 17 Sept. 1818; d. Richmond, VA, USA, 9 Jan. 1899). Presbyterian pastor and editor. Hoge was the son of Presbyterian minister, SAMUEL DAVIES HOGE and his wife Elizabeth Rice Lacy, and the grandson of MOSES HOGE, President of Hampden-Sidney College (1807–20), and Drury Lacy, Vice-President and Acting-President of Hampden-Sidney (1789–97). Moses Drury Hoge graduated from that institution in 1839 and then from Union Theological Seminary in Virginia in 1843. He became assistant pastor of the First Presbyterian Church of Richmond, Virginia, the following year. On 20 March 1844, he married Susan Morton Wood. In 1845 he founded the Second Presbyterian Church in Richmond, a church which under Hoge became the largest in the Synod of Virginia and a very influential church in the Presbyterian Church of the United States (which was formed as the southern branch of Presbyterianism after the start of the Civil War).

Hoge served five years as a co-editor of *The Central Presbyterian* (1855–9), and was a member of a committee to prepare a hymnal and directory of worship for the Presbyterian Church of the United States. In 1875 he served as moderator of the Presbyterian General Assembly.

Hoge was a volunteer chaplain to Confederate forces in the Civil War and in 1862–3 successfully ran the Union blockade on a journey to England to secure Bibles and other religious materials for the soldiers. Active in ecumenical endeavours, Hoge served as a delegate to the EA conferences to New York (1873), Copenhagen (1884), and Boston (1889) and the Alliance of Reformed Churches meetings in Edinburgh (1877), London (1888), and Glasgow (1896).

BIBLIOGRAPHY
DcAmB
P. H. Hoge, *Moses Drury Hoge* (Richmond, VA, 1899)

STEPHEN R. GRAHAM

Hoge, Samuel Davies (b. Shepherdstown, VA, USA, April 1792; d. Athens, OH, USA, 24 Dec. 1826). Presbyterian minister and college educator. He graduated from Hampden-Sydney College in Virginia in 1810 where his father MOSES HOGE was president. He continued his study of theology under his father and served as a tutor at the college. He was licensed to preach by Hanover presbytery in 1813. Emulating his namesake, SAMUEL DAVIES, the colonial evangelist to slaves, he instructed slaves in the faith along with other college students. He was ordained in 1815. He married Elizabeth Rice Lacy, the daughter of Drury Lacy. His evangelistic outreach in Culpeper County resulted in the formation of the Cedar Run Meeting House (now Mitchells Presbyterian Church, Mitchells, Virginia).

He left Culpeper in 1817 and moved back to Hampden-Sydney to serve as professor and vice-president to his father. Here his eldest son, MOSES DRURY HOGE, was born. He emancipated his one slave and sent him to Liberia. Discouraged over the evil of slavery, he wrote in 1818, 'my desire to leave the land of slaves is not at all abated, nor is it likely to abate'. In 1820 he left Virginia for Ohio, partly to secure a ministry outside the slave states. He became pastor of the Presbyterian churches at Hillsborough and Rocky Spring, Ohio. In October 1823 he was called as professor of mathematics and natural philosophy in the University of Ohio at Athens.

BIBLIOGRAPHY
P. H. Hoge, *Moses Drury Hoge* (Richmond, VA, 1899)
A. Nevin, ed., *Encyclopedia of the Presbyterian Church* (Philadelphia, PA, 1884)
A. D. Thomas, Jr, *Early Churches of Culpeper* (Culpeper, VA, 1987)

ARTHUR DICKEN THOMAS, JR

Hoge, Susan (b. Charlotte County, VA, BNA, c. 1768; d. probably Charlotte County, VA, USA, 8 April 1848). Presbyterian evangelist. The daughter of Colonel Joel Watkins, she married William P. Hunt, an attorney. Following his death, she married MOSES HOGE in 1803.

They had no children of their own, but she reared those from their first marriages.

She served as a spiritual guide to students and friends throughout her life. From the age of 14 she read the Bible through annually and was widely read in Puritan and evangelical writers. While not permitted to preach, she sought to evangelize all whom she met. Before her marriage, she provided ARCHIBALD ALEXANDER with spiritual counsel that was instrumental in his conversion. She was known for her meditative and contemplative life despite all of the activity of raising a family and of entertaining as the wife of a college president and pastor of a local church.

BIBLIOGRAPHY
T. P. Hunt, *The Life and Thoughts of Rev. Thomas P. Hunt. An Autobiography* (Wilkes Barre, PA, 1901)
A. D. Thomas, Jr, 'Moses Hoge: Reformed Pietism and Spiritual Guidance,' *American Presbyterians* (Spring 1993)

ARTHUR DICKEN THOMAS, JR

Hogg, James Maitland (b. Kirkliston, West Lothian, Scotland, 7 Sept. 1799; d. Edinburgh, Scotland, 31 July 1858). Landowner and advocate. A minor landowner, he was the only one in the county of West Lothian who joined the FCS in 1843. He supported THOMAS CHALMERS in the movement for church extension and accompanied him on tours throughout Scotland to promote interest and raise funds. He was not an aggressive opponent of patronage and hoped for reconciliation between church and state especially under Lord Aberdeen. Hogg left the Church of Scotland only after the breach when the church acknowledged decrees of the civil courts as its own. Subsequently he played a major part in promoting the foundation of bursaries at New College and was chairman of the committee of the Free Church which investigated the refusal of landowners to grant sites for churches. A strong Sabbatarian, he opposed the running of trains on Sundays.

R. H. CAMPBELL

Holcombe, Henry (b. Prince Edward County, VA, BNA, 22 Sept. 1762; d. Philadelphia, PA, USA, 22 May 1824). Baptist minister and social reformer. Seventh child of Grimes and Elizabeth Holcombe, Henry was born in Virginia and raised in South Carolina. His family was Presbyterian. Holcombe received little religious instruction. Fired by the ideals of the War for Independence, Holcombe joined the cause and attained the rank of captain. In 1784, he attended two revival services. After days of emotional soul-searching, he was 'converted to God'. Infused with the 'precepts, life and whole ministry' of Jesus, Holcombe resigned his commission, joined a Baptist church and began to preach. He served pastorates in Pipe Creek, South Carolina (1785–91); Eushaw, South Carolina (1791–5); Beaufort, South Carolina (1795–9); First Baptist Church, Savannah, Georgia (1800–10);

and, after recovery from illness, First Baptist Church, Philadelphia, (1812–24).

Holcombe gained his reputation as a powerful preacher. He also championed political causes and social reform. In 1788 he participated as a representative from the South Carolina lowlands in a convention which ratified the US Constitution. At Savannah, Holcombe's congregation set up a committee for the 'relief of indigent and distressed persons'. With his wife, the former Frances Tanner, Holcombe established a female orphanage. In Philadelphia, they supported a 'Female Hospitable Society for the Relief and Employment of the Poor'. Self-educated, Holcombe promoted higher education. At Eushaw, he helped found, and became president of the Beaufort District Society for the Encouragement of Literature, which became Beaufort College. Holcombe endowed Mount Enon Academy and helped organize the Charleston Baptist Association and the Georgia Baptist Convention. Holcombe was no narrow sectarian. When, in 1802, he launched the *Georgia Analytical Repository*, first religious periodical in the South, he announced it would be non-partisan. Its purposes were to spread religious knowledge, to discuss literature and theology and to further Christian unity.

Holcombe did not avoid controversy. Despite adverse reaction, in 1802 he participated in the ordination of black preachers. That year, his periodical drew attention to the hanging of a thief, John Rice. The case led him to espouse reform of the Georgia penal code. A fruit of this campaign was the elimination of the death penalty for certain crimes. In 1814, the General Convention of the Baptist Denomination in the United States of America for Foreign Missions named Holcombe first vice-president. Differences led to his leaving the post. In 1816, another dispute prompted Holcombe to lead First Baptist Church out of the Philadelphia Baptist Association.

In 1776 and 1812, Holcombe supported the principle of defensive war. Hesitations about Christians taking up arms led to a change of mind. In 1822, he founded the Pennsylvania Peace Society, the African Baptist Peace Society in Philadelphia and a local peace society in Augusta, Georgia. *Advocate of Peace* published three peace sermons. Other publications included his autobiography *The First Fruits* (1812) and *Primitive Theology* (1822).

BIBLIOGRAPHY
AAP, 6: 215–20
J. B. Boles, 'Henry Holcombe, A Southern Baptist Reformer in the Age of Jefferson', *Georgia Historical Quarterly*, 54 (1970): 381–407
W. Cathcart, ed., *The Baptist Encyclopedia* (Philadelphia, PA, 1881): 531–2
DAB
W. D. Thompson, *Philadelphia's First Baptists* (Philadelphia, PA, 1989)

PAUL R. DEKAR

Holland, John M. (b. Williamson County, TN, USA, c. 1803; d. 13 Aug. 1851). Methodist minister. Converted as a young man in 1822 he became a preacher in the Methodist Episcopal Church. He served numerous posts in Tennessee and Mississippi for the duration of his 20 year ministry as an itinerant preacher and Presiding Elder in the Methodist Church. In 1837 he was an agent for La Grange College and in 1839 agent for Holly Springs University. Sources say he was a powerful and skillful preacher and an effective evangelist. He was financially ruined in 1837 due to poor investment advice but continued his ministry despite his economic situation.

BIBLIOGRAPHY
APP

R. J. STEWART

Holland, William (d. London, 23 Feb. 1761). English Moravian. Holland, a painter with relatives in Wales and London, joined a London religious society in 1732 and became a devotee of William Law in 1736. He joined a new society formed by JAMES HUTTON, and heard PETER BÖHLER address it in April 1738, but was out of London when Böhler formed a Moravian-style band. In May Holland showed CHARLES WESLEY Luther's *Commentary on Galatians*, had an experience of liberation as Wesley read the Preface aloud, and joined one of the new bands stemming from Böhler's. Holland has been identified with the 'one' whose reading of Luther's Preface to *Romans* occasioned JOHN WESLEY's 'heartwarming'.

The bands grew into the Fetter Lane Society, and on 26 March 1741 a Moravian group assumed its leadership. Five days later Holland married Elizabeth Delamotte (1710–80), who had refused GEORGE WHITEFIELD the year before. Elected one of two new society stewards in August, he liquidated his large business in September to become a full-time 'labourer', moving from Basinghall Street to a room in the Moravians' headquarters. Holland was chosen elder of the London Moravian Congregation established on 30 October 1742, and in October 1743 replaced the disaffected RICHARD VINEY as warden of the Yorkshire Congregation.

In 1744 Holland became dissatisfied, sympathizing with Viney, and from August led opposition to proposed registration under the Toleration Act as Dissenters, pleading the assurance he had secured in 1742 that Anglicans received into Moravian membership could remain Church of England members. He was relieved of his office in 1745 and summoned to Germany, where he wrote his historical *Account* of Moravian work in England to support his views. After returning to England he attended a General Synod in Holland in May 1746 and was sent on a mission to Wales in November. On his return in March 1747 he was readmitted to the leadership's conference and sent to supervise work in

Wiltshire temporarily. Back in London from July, Holland seems to have attempted to conform to the prevailing Moravian spirituality, but was instructed in October 1747 to cease preaching and resume his trade. In December he withdrew from the Moravian Church.

Holland associated with the Wesleys, but did not join them, taking communion in the Church of England and mainly attending the preaching of its 'awakening ministers'. Elizabeth Holland remained a Moravian, and her mother, who lived with the Hollands at the Rolls Buildings in Fetter Lane, became one. In 1755 Holland supplied information to the Moravians' opponent Henry Rimius, but he later became more friendly towards them again.

C. J. PODMORE

Hollond, Edmund (b. London, 10 Dec. 1801; d. London, 18 March 1884). Anglican clergyman. Hollond was educated at Haileybury and Queens' College, Cambridge (B.A., 1828; M.A., 1831). He came of a wealthy family and succeeded his cousin as lord of the manor of Middleton Austin. His family seat was at Benhall Lodge, Saxmundham, Suffolk. He was patron of eight livings and a Simeon Trustee from 1850 to his death. He contributed to millennialist writings with his *Israel's Premillennial Future* (1875).

BIBLIOGRAPHY
Al. Cant.
Boase

ARTHUR POLLARD

Holloway, Thomas (b. London, 1748; d. near Norwich, Norfolk, England, 22 Feb. 1827). Baptist and Royal engraver. The son of a merchant who was an early follower of JOHN WESLEY, his mother's portrait was painted by the evangelical artist, JOHN RUSSELL. Articled to a seal engraver, Holloway was soon exhibiting engravings and miniatures at the Royal Academy, and producing engravings of various ministers for the religious press. Through a friend he secured access to Windsor and was given the sole right to make engravings of the Raphael cartoons. After examining different religious systems he sought baptism from SAMUEL STENNETT at Little Wild Street alongside his friend, JOSEPH HUGHES. He determinedly promoted the dissenting interest and was an occasional preacher.

BIBLIOGRAPHY
DNB
D. M. Rosman, *Evangelicals and Culture* (London, 1984): 154

J. H. Y. BRIGGS

Holly, Israel (b. Sharon, CT, BNA, 3 April 1728; d. CT, USA, 28 June 1809). Congregationalist minister and polemical pamphleteer. Israel Holly (who also appears as Holley) was an unusually interesting product of the colonial Great Awakening. Little is known of his background or training, except that it did not include college. It is clear from his publications, however, that he promoted 'New Light' revivalism, read JONATHAN EDWARDS with appreciation, and modelled his pulpit oratory on GEORGE WHITEFIELD. From 1763 to 1784, Holly pastored a Separate Congregationalist church in Suffield, Connecticut. Then, for reasons that are not clear, he returned to the established Congregationalist church and was minister in Granby, Connecticut (1784–93), and stated preaching supply in North Cornwall, Connecticut (1795–1801). Holly stood out in his age as a pugnacious writer of considerable theological depth. Whatever his theme – defending the laity and the power of a local congregation to ordain ministers, defending extempore preaching, attacking New England's traditional halfway covenant, defending infant baptism against the Baptists (including ISAAC BACKUS), promoting the cause of American rights at the time of the War for Independence, attacking the innovations of New Divinity theology, or defending historic Calvinism – his work reveals a keen theological wit.

BIBLIOGRAPHY
General Association of Connecticut, *Contributions to the Ecclesiastical History of Connecticut* (New Haven, CT, 1861)

MARK A. NOLL

Holmes, Abiel (b. Woodstock, CT, BNA, 24 Dec. 1763; d. Cambridge, MA, USA, 4 June 1837). Congregational minister. Graduating from Yale College in 1783 and ordained to the ministry two years later, Holmes served a Georgia congregation before coming to Massachusetts in 1792 for the pastorate of Cambridge's First Parish Church. A combatant in the Unitarian-Trinitarian civil war that roiled early nineteenth-century Massachusetts Congregationalism, he joined with JEDIDIAH MORSE and JOHN CODMAN in organizing Boston's Park Street Church as a bastion of orthodoxy. Holmes's Calvinist theology and his refusal to open his pulpit to those of more liberal views combined to ignite a controversy that culminated in 1829 with his dismissal by his Cambridge parishioners. A group of sympathetic members responded by withdrawing to organize a new church, the Shepard Congregational Society, with Holmes as minister. His publications include *The Life of Ezra Stiles* (1798) and *Annals of America* (1805; 2nd edn, 1829). Holmes's first wife was EZRA STILES's daughter; by his second, Sarah Wendell, he fathered the physician and author Oliver Wendell Holmes.

BIBLIOGRAPHY
DAB

GEORGE W. HARPER

Holmes, A(ndrew) F(ernando) (b. Cadiz, Spain, 17 Mar. 1797; d. Montreal, Lower Canada, 9 Oct. 1860). Physician, scientist, and academic. Born of Irish evangelicals during a Napoleonic captivity, Holmes came to Montreal in 1810. He served a medical apprenticeship; a brother was an important politician. After studies in Scotland, Holmes helped establish the first medical school in Canada in 1823 (becoming the medical faculty of McGill University in 1829). His detailed scientific investigations in medicine, chemistry, botany, mineralogy, and geology produced a vigorous tension with his evangelical convictions, rendering him somewhat irascible. His prominence, and disaffection with Trinity Chapel after 1848, inspired many to imitate his transfer to St George's (Anglican) Church.

Holmes' impeccable scientific and social credentials won much 'respectable' support for evangelical causes in Montreal, and he did much to promote Christian unity on an evangelical basis. He often chaired public meetings in Montreal, and was a particular supporter of scriptural education and missions.

BIBLIOGRAPHY
R. M. Black, 'A Crippled Crusade ... 1835–1868,' (University of Toronto, unpublished Th.D. thesis, 1989)
DCB, VIII, 403–5
A. Hall, A Biographical Sketch of the Late A. F. Holmes ... (Montreal, 1860)

ROBERT MERRILL BLACK

Honoré, Abraham (b. Fridericia, Jutland, Denmark, 1 May 1821; d. Foxton, New Zealand, 23 July 1894). Missionary to New Zealand. Honoré was sent to New Zealand by the North German Missionary Society (NGMS) in 1848 to help JOHANN FREIDRICH HEINRICH WOHLERS' work among Maori in the Southland province. In 1868 the NGMS placed the missionaries in the care of the Otago Presbyterian Synod and in 1869 Honoré was ordained. In 1871 he moved to Marton in the North Island where the population was larger, and in 1874 became Maori missioner for the national Presbyterian church. He was supported by gifts from British Plymouth Brethren, since he 'lived by faith'. He had a modest impact among West Coast tribes, and also helped the Norwegian and German settlers in the Manawatu district.

BIBLIOGRAPHY
P. J. Lineham, There we found Brethren: A History of Assemblies of Brethren in New Zealand (Palmerston North, 1977)
S. Natusch, Brother Wohlers (Christchurch, 1969)

PETER LINEHAM

Hooker, Asahel (b. 29 Aug. 1762, Bethlehem, CT; BNA; d. Norwich, CT, USA, 19 April 1813). Congregational minister. Hooker's life illustrates the personal ties among the students of JONATHAN EDWARDS, a group collectively known as the New Divinity. In his youth Hooker sat under the ministry of JOSEPH BELLAMY

(Edwards's protege) in Bethlehem, Connecticut. He graduated from Yale (1798), married Phoebe Edwards (granddaughter of Jonathan Edwards), and was ordained to the pastorate of the Goshen, Connecticut church in 1791.

When the Goshen church was shaken by the Second Great Awakening in 1799, eighty converts were added to the church. Hooker utilized the young men he prepared for the ministry (some thirty men studied in his 'parlor seminary') as assistants in sparking another revival in 1807. Persistent health problems (pleurisy) led to his resignation in 1810. Following several interim pastorates, Hooker briefly resumed his ministerial labours at Norwich, Connecticut in 1812–13.

BIBLIOGRAPHY
AAP, 2: 316–21
BSGYC, 4: 640–3
A. G. Hibbard, History of the Town of Goshen, Connecticut (Hartford, CT, 1897)

DAVID W. KLING

Hoole, Elijah (b. Manchester, England, 3 Feb. 1798; d. London, 17 June 1872). Wesleyan missionary and orientalist. The son of a shoemaker, Elijah joined his father on leaving Manchester Grammar School, but entered the Wesleyan ministry in 1818. In 1820 he was sent out as assistant to THOMAS SQUANCE at Negapatam, India. The Tanjore on which he sailed was wrecked off the coast of Ceylon and he lost all his baggage, including his library. During his service in Bangalore he travelled extensively throughout southern India, achieved a mastery of Tamil and translated into it various works, including a life of JOHN WESLEY and a number of Wesley hymns. In 1822 he was summoned to Madras to help in the work of revising the Bible in Tamil.

By 1828 his health had begun to suffer from his exertions and he returned to England. After service in Ireland as the Missionary Committee's agent for Irish schools, he returned to London in 1834 to become a secretary of the Missionary Society, an office he held for nearly forty years. Despite continuing ill health, he was an efficient administrator with a mastery of detail, but also showed a kindliness and consideration which won him the affection of the missionaries with whom he dealt.

The support his wife gave him earned her the unofficial title of 'Women's Secretary'. She founded the magazine known as The Juvenile Offering and when the Women's Auxiliary was formed in 1858 she became its foreign correspondent.

Hoole interested himself in a wide variety of issues, including the colonization of New Zealand, negro marriage and the treatment of the indigenous people in the British colonies. He served as honorary secretary of the British SPG among the Jews and of the London Home for Asiatics. Besides his Tamil translations he published A Personal Narrative of a Mission to the South of India (London, 1829), The Year Book of Missions (London, 1847) and Oglethorpe and the Wesleys in America

(London, 1863), together with various articles in the *Wesleyan Methodist Magazine* and *The London Quarterly Review*.

BIBLIOGRAPHY
DNB
WMM (1872): 947–8

JOHN A. VICKERS

Hope, Lady **Henrietta** (b. Scotland, *c.* 1750; d. Bristol, England, 1 Jan. 1786). Evangelical supporter. Henrietta, the eldest daughter of John, Earl of Hopetoun, met Lady GLENORCHY soon after her conversion (1772). They became great friends. In 1780 her father allowed Henrietta to join Lady Glenorchy and they visited London, Exmouth, Exeter, Bath and then went to Hawkestone to stay with Jane Hill before returning via Buxton to Scotland. Lord Hopetoun died in 1781 and thereafter Lady Henrietta lived with Lady Glenorchy. Both were keen to promote the cause of religion visiting Lady Glenorchy's churches and starting others. They took up residence in Matlock (summer 1785), and then went on to Bristol Hot-Wells. Here Lady Henrietta's already poor health deteriorated, she became dropsical and suffered terribly before her death. She left £2,500 towards building a chapel near Bristol Hot-Wells, which project Lady Glenorchy started before her own death in July. The chapel was named Hope Chapel by Lady DARCY MAXWELL, Lady Glenorchy's executrix.

BIBLIOGRAPHY
E. D. Graham, 'The Contribution of Lady Glenorchy and her Circle to the Evangelical Revival' (Leeds Univ. BD thesis, 1965)
T. S. Jones, *The Life of Willielma, Viscountess Glenorchy* (Edinburgh and London, 1822)

E. DOROTHY GRAHAM

Hope, Sir **Henry** (b. 1787; d. Holly-Hill, Hampshire, England, 23 Sept. 1863). British naval officer. One in a long line of illustrious naval commanders, Hope entered the navy in 1798 as midshipman and was promoted lieutenant in 1804, commander in 1806, and captain in 1808. He saw a 'variety of hard service throughout the world'. In 1815, commanding the *Endymion*, he captured the American ship *President*, for which he was made Companion of the Order of Bath (Knight Commander, 1855). He retired in 1815 on half pay and according to naval custom, although on the retired list, he proceeded through the ranks to rear-admiral (1846), vice-admiral (1853), and admiral (1858). He was naval aide-de-camp to William IV and to Victoria (1831–46).

Hope left a substantial legacy – £30,000 – much of which was bequeathed to evangelical societies: £4,000 each to the CMS and the BFBS; £2,000 each to the Colonial Church and School Society, the CPAS, and the LSPCJ (he was a committee member from 1839 and vice-president 1861); £1,000 each to the Irish Church Mission and the Sailor's Home, London Docks, with an additional £6,000 to its church; £500 each to a variety of sailors' charitable societies.

BIBLIOGRAPHY
DNB
GM (1863): 662

JONATHAN BURKE CUTMORE

Hope, **John** (b. Dalry, Midlothian, Scotland, 12 May 1807; d. Edinburgh, 25 June 1893) Lawyer and philanthropist. The son of James Hope and his wife Jane (née Walker), he was educated at Edinburgh Royal High School and the University of Edinburgh, and admitted to the Society of Writers to the Signet in 1828. Following a Grand Tour he began a successful career as a solicitor in Edinburgh, which gained him considerable wealth and social influence.

He was converted in 1838 and throughout the rest of his life manifested a searching concern for the spiritual welfare of others, whom he exhorted to pray, study the Bible and observe the Sabbath. In 1843 he was one of the minority of evangelicals who remained loyal to the Established Church at the Disruption. Later in the 1840s Hope developed his particular concern for total abstinence and anti-Catholicism. In 1847 he founded the British League of Juvenile Abstainers and from 1850 developed a similar Protestant movement, centred on Edinburgh but with a presence elsewhere in Scotland. His efforts were concentrated on young people whom he sought to reach by classes, tracts and periodicals. He also worked with the British/Protestant Reformation Society in setting up missions to Roman Catholics in several Scottish towns.

Hope was active in local politics, supporting the electoral endeavours of the Conservative Party, and himself serving on the Edinburgh Town Council from 1857 to 1889. From 1859 he took a leading role in the Volunteer Movement. He died unmarried and left his substantial fortune to endow the Hope Trust to promote total abstinence, the use of unfermented wine at the Lord's Supper and, above all, Protestantism. A substantial collection of his papers survives in the Scottish Record Office in Edinburgh.

BIBLIOGRAPHY
D. Jamie, *John Hope* (Edinburgh, 1900)
J. Wolffe, *The Protestant Crusade in Great Britain, 1829–1860* (Oxford, 1991)

JOHN WOLFFE

Hope, **Samuel** (b. Liverpool, England, 1760; d. Liverpool, England, 15 Oct. 1837). Baptist layman. A prosperous cottonbroker, Hope founded the first Baptist Sunday school in Liverpool in 1801 and the Liverpool Sunday School Union in 1815. The most prominent lay member of SAMUEL MEDLEY's Byrom Street Church, he was for a time treasurer in England of the Serampore Mission and a promoter of non-sectarian education in the mid-1830s. His daughter married SAMUEL MORLEY, the Liberal politician.

BIBLIOGRAPHY
Liverpool City Record Office, Evan Owen Papers

IAN SELLERS

Hopkins, Henry (b. Deptford, England, 16 Aug. 1787; d. Hobart, Australia, 27 Sept. 1870). Congregational philanthropist. Of Nonconformist merchant family, as a young man he entered the English wool trade. Emigrating with modest capital in 1822 to Van Diemen's Land (now Tasmania), by the 1840s he had amassed considerable wealth. An Independent by preference, in 1828 he offered financial assistance to attract an English Independent minister to Hobart. FREDERICK MILLER arrived in 1830, ministering to the first permanent Independent congregation in the Australian colonies. Hopkins was Australia's Congregational Maecenas, contributing extensively to church building. He also made large donations to the LMS, the CMS, Bible societies and other Protestant denominations. For most of his life he was a Sunday school teacher. Avoiding public verbal testimony, his chief religious statements were his works. His wife Sarah (née Rout) mostly confined religious works to the family circle; but after her death in 1849 the publication of her religious 'Memoranda', recounting 32 years of reflection and struggle since 'a poor sinful worm like me' received 'sure hope' of inheriting 'eternal glory', displayed acute sensibility. The 'Memoranda' are intimate expressions of evangelical spirituality.

BIBLIOGRAPHY
ADB
A. Alexander, 'Henry Hopkins and George Clarke: Two Tasmanian Nonconformists' (Univ. of Tasmania M.A., 1983)
G. Clarke, *The Need of Man and the Help of Christ* (Hobart, 1870)
J. West, *The Hope of Life Eternal* (Launceston, 1850)

RICHARD ELY

Hopkins, Samuel (b. Waterbury, CT, BNA, 17 Sept. 1721; d. Newport, RI, USA, 20 Dec. 1803). New England theologian and reformer. He grew up in Waterbury and graduated from Yale in 1741. After studying for the ministry with JONATHAN EDWARDS, he was ordained as the pastor of a newly established church in Housatonic (later Great Barrington), Massachusetts, in 1743. By the late 1750s he began publishing major theological works and came to be identified as the leader of a new hyper-Calvinist movement within New England Congregationalism that was referred to as the New Divinity, Consistent Calvinism or simply Hopkinsianism.

While Hopkins began to win adherents, his own church became dissatisfied with him and he was dismissed in 1769. In 1770, he was installed as the pastor of

the First Congregational Church in Newport, Rhode Island, where he remained for the rest of his life. Hopkins continued to write controversial works that developed the New Divinity. In 1773, he published *An Inquiry into the Nature of True Holiness*, a work that explained his influential doctrine of disinterested benevolence. He defined true holiness as radical selflessness; ultimately he argued that a truly virtuous person ought to be willing to be dammed, if necessary, for the glory of God and the good of mankind. He also began to outline the connection between disinterested benevolence and the antislavery cause. He spoke out early and often against slavery and in 1776 published *A Dialogue Concerning the Slavery of the Africans*, a major antislavery work.

Hopkins continued to oppose slavery and to publish theological works in the 1780s and 1790s. In 1793, he published *System of Doctrines*, a comprehensive two-volume work that attempted to define the New Divinity. Hopkins drew on his own writings, on the work of other Consistent Calvinists and on Jonathan Edwards to explain the distinctive Calvinism of the New Divinity such as the doctrine of disinterested benevolence. As the *System of Doctrines* makes clear, the New Divinity evolved out of Jonathan Edwards' theology and became the first indigenous school of American Calvinism.

Hopkins was the most original theologian in this school, and in the years after the publication of his monumental *System of Doctrines* the New Divinity became increasingly identified as Hopkinsianism. The movement won many clerical followers and came to dominate New England Congregationalism during the first two decades of the nineteenth century. Hopkins's legacy also influenced religious reformers. His doctrine of disinterested benevolence, for example, helped inspire the foreign missionary movement from America.

SELECT WRITINGS
S. Hopkins, *Sin, Thro' Divine Interposition an Advantage To the Universe*, (Boston, MA, 1759)
—, *The True State and Character of the Unregenerate, Stripped of All Misrepresentation and Disguise* (New Haven, CT, 1769)
—, *An Inquiry into the Nature of True Holiness* (Newport, RI, 1773)
—, *A Dialogue Concerning the Slavery of the Africans, Shewing It To Be the Duty and Interest of the American States to Emancipate Their African Slaves* (Norwich, CT, 1776)
—, *The System of Doctrines contained in Divine Revelation Explained and Defended: with A Treatise on the Millennium*, 2 vols (Boston, MA, 1793)

BIBLIOGRAPHY
J. A. Conforti, *Samuel Hopkins and the New Divinity Movement* (Grand Rapids, MI, 1981)
E. A. Park, *Memoir of the Life and Character of Samuel Hopkins* (Boston, MA, 1852)

JOSEPH CONFORTI

Hopper, Christopher (b. Low Coalburn, Co. Durham, England, 25 Dec. 1722; d. Bolton, England, 5 March 1802). Methodist itinerant. JOHN WESLEY regarded him as the apostle of the north. He came from farming stock and was the youngest of nine children. His parents were respectable churchgoers but strangers to vital religion. As a boy he was taught the faith by a devout schoolmaster. He was employed as a waggoner carrying coal from the newly opened pits to the River Tyne. Under the preaching of JONATHAN REEVES he underwent a remarkable and undeniable change. Wesley made him a leader in the Methodist society and he then began to preach. He equipped himself by learning Hebrew and Greek. He turned schoolmaster in 1744 and used his home for preaching services before being accepted as an itinerant. In 1750 he accompanied Wesley through Wales and across to Ireland. The following year he pioneered Methodist work in Scotland and returned later for an extended ministry there from 1759 to 1765. Wesley put him in charge of northern Methodism, anticipating the role of a district chairman. At the conference of 1780 Hopper presided over some sessions when Wesley could not be present. It is a measure of the esteem in which he was held that he was elected by the vote of his fellow itinerants. In 1790 he became a supernumerary but continued to preach. His sermons throughout his long years of activity were reported as being stocked with sound theology. He was regarded as a Boanerges – a son of thunder – to the callous, but as a Barnabas – a son of consolation – to the contrite. At the time of his death he was the oldest of the itinerants.

At an early stage he was inclined to favour separation from the Church of England. He concurred with EDWARD PERRONET's attack on the Establishment in *The Mitre* and evidently had some sympathy with the preachers in Norwich who had administered the sacrament. CHARLES WESLEY considered him ripe for a separation along with JOSEPH COWNLEY and JOHN HAMPSON. In response to a letter from Charles Wesley on the issue, Hopper expressed the view that if matters were brought to a head in the future, Methodist preachers must either be ordained, turn Dissenters, or be altogether abandoned. He himself would resist the temptation to 'locate' if he could obtain episcopal ordination on honourable terms. Charles Wesley was prepared to support him, but such a suggestion was quite impracticable since no bishop was likely to ordain men for Methodist work. In the perfectionist controversy Hopper was commended by Charles Wesley for his stand against the torrent. He later deplored the militancy of Alexander McNab.

On the death of Wesley, Hopper realized that a keen debate would ensue before an acceptable plan for the constitution of Methodism could be drawn up. He believed that the Deed of Declaration and Wesley's will were incompatible and was uncertain what the outcome would be. He feared that too many of the preachers were overambitious but warned his friend and protege JOSEPH BENSON against any premature judgement on such a vital matter. Hopper subscribed to the Halifax Circular which recommended the filling of vacant places in the Legal Hundred according to seniority, the annual appointment of president and secretary of conference, and the setting up of district committees. In 1795 he was

satisfied that the Plan of Pacification had been adopted without undue wrangling. By then he was a venerable father in God, respected by all parties. ADAM CLARKE declared that Hopper was in the strictest sense a great man who, with proper advantages, would have been outstanding in any sphere. The Methodist Church Archives, MARC, hold many of his letters.

BIBLIOGRAPHY
AM (1781)
C. Atmore, ed., *A Brief Memoir of the life and death of Christopher Hopper* (Manchester, England, 1802)

A. SKEVINGTON WOOD

Horne, Melville [formerly **Melvill**] (b. *c.* 1761 [in a pamphlet he says he was active with the Methodists to the age of thirty]; d. The Green, Ashborne [Ashbourne], Derbyshire, England, *c.* 2 April 1841.) Anglican clergyman and early proponent of mission work. He was the fourth son of Edward Horne (died 1766), an Antiguan barrister and planter, and of Mary (Gilbert), the fourth daughter of Nathaniel Gilbert (1697–1761) by his first wife. Horne is said to have been religiously awakened at the age of six, by the preaching of JOHN HAMPSON SR, a preacher who left JOHN WESLEY's connexion when he was not nominated among the first Legal Hundred. Wesley accepted Horne on trial as an itinerant preacher in 1784, and in the following year appointed him to the Chester circuit, of which JOHN W. FLETCHER, the Vicar of Madeley, Shropshire, was superintendent. It was Fletcher's wish to have him as his successor in the vicarage, but when Fletcher died in 1785, the patron appointed his own son. Wesley then recommended Horne as a suitable curate for Madeley, should he be able to obtain ordination. Horne was ordained on Trinity Sunday, 1786, and succeeded to the curacy. He also edited a number of Fletcher's unpublished pieces. In 1787 Wesley appointed him (as he had appointed Fletcher) superintendent of the new Wolverhampton circuit, describing him in the minutes as 'supernumerary' and in one way or another he was appointed to the Wolverhampton circuit till Wesley's death in 1791. In 1792 he became the second chaplain in Sierra Leone, joining his cousin NATHANIEL GILBERT JR. Unable to acclimatize, Horne returned to England in 1793 and in 1794 published his *Letters On Missions* which advocated evangelical involvement in overseas missions. He was an early and prominent advocate of the CMS.

From 23 May 1796 to December 1799, he was Vicar of Olney and then he succeeded DAVID SIMPSON, the founder and first incumbent of Christ Church, Macclesfield, in that living from 1799 to 1811. His connection with Shropshire did not come to an end; in 1813 he reported enthusiastically to the CMS 'that religion begins to flourish in Shropshire, and the number of serious clergy is greatly increased'.

In Macclesfield Horne's Methodist connections were briefly renewed and then finally broken. JABEZ BUNTING, the future star of the Wesleyan ministry, completed his probation in the Macclesfield circuit, 1801–3. The two who engaged in translating classics of the French pulpit into English, were quickly on terms of respect even intimacy, but Bunting's respect for Horne changed rapidly into impatience, which was requited by hostility. Whether this breach owed anything to the firmness with which Bunting rebuffed Horne's efforts to tempt him into the ministry of the Church of England with a view to succeeding to another Macclesfield living is not clear. In 1809 Horne complained, probably unjustly, that 'the Methodists considered him an enemy because for 17 years he had declined preaching in their pulpits', and went on to the attack in *An Investigation of the Definition of Justifying Faith, the Damnatory Clause Under Which It Is Enforced, and the Doctrine of a Direct Witness of the Spirit*, receiving rough polemical treatment in return in pamphlets and the *Methodist Magazine*. Quite apart from personal issues, Horne's career illustrates how hard it had now become to sustain a cross-bench position between Methodism and the Church of England.

From 1811 to March 1814 he was curate in charge of West Thurrock in Essex and then to about 1816 Minister of Marazion in Cornwall. From 25 October 1817 to 1823 he was Curate of St Stephen's, Salford. His later years were apparently affected by ill health.

BIBLIOGRAPHY

F. Baker, 'The Origins of Methodism in the West Indies: The Story of the Gilbert Family', *London Quarterly Review* (Jan. 1960): 9–17

F. K. Brown, *Fathers of the Victorians* (Cambridge, 1961): 271, 277

T. P. Bunting, *The Life of Jabez Bunting*, 2 vols (London, 1859–87)

C. Hole, *Early History of the Church Missionary Society* (London, 1896): 632

Methodist Church Archives, John Rylands Library, University of Manchester. Manuscript Jabez Bunting to George Marsden, June 10, 1803

Methodist Magazine (1810): 11–18, 59–68

J. Telford, ed., *The Letters of John Wesley*, 8 vols, 7 (London, 1931): 294, 324

The Early Correspondence of Jabez Bunting ed. W.R. Ward, Camden fourth series, 11 (London, 1972): 13

W. R. WARD

Horne, Thomas Hartwell (b. London, 20 Oct. 1780; d. London, 27 Jan. 1862). Polymathic bibliographer and biblical scholar. Son of a London barrister's clerk, Horne was one of the most prolific writers of his day on subjects as varied as grazing, topography, psalmody, law, history and biblical criticism. Born in Chancery Lane, he lived, worked and died in the City 'a patriarch in literature ... and loved as a man' as colleagues at the British Museum later described him.

Completing his schooling at Christ's Hospital (1789–95), where the poet Coleridge encouraged his literary interests, Horne followed his father's trade for a while, supplementing his meagre clerk's salary of £20 per annum by publishing *A Brief View of the Necessity and*

Truth of the Christian Revelation (1800) and by assisting Dr Willich in production of *The Domestic Encyclopedia*. Thereafter, joining the Wesleyan Methodists and acting as private clerk to JOSEPH BUTTERWORTH, MP (1806–9), Horne found himself increasingly drawn to bibliography, theology and the ordained ministry.

In the field of bibliography at the British Museum, he rose from part-time cataloguing of the Harleian manuscripts indexes (1808), to work on the *Rotuli Scotiae* (1821), to a senior assistant librarianship (1824–60), with responsibility for cataloguing the library's holdings, and to a fellowship of the Society of Antiquaries and Librarians. As a theologian, publication of his oft-reprinted *An Introduction to the Critical Study and Knowledge of the Holy Scriptures* (3 vols, 1818, 11th edn 1860), which became a standard student text, secured for him widespread academic recognition and honorary degrees from Aberdeen (MA), Pennsylvania (DD), and Cambridge (BD). Ordained by Bishop Howley, he was Curate of Christ Church, Newgate Street (1819–25), and he became Assistant Minister of Welbeck Chapel (1825–33), Rector of St Nicholas Acons, Lombard Street (1833–62), and a Prebend of St Paul's Cathedral (1831–62).

Horne married Sarah (née Millard) in 1812 (died 7 July 1858) and had two daughters. His evangelical love of the Bible prompted tercentenary celebrations of Coverdale's Bible in 1835 and an exemplary life of sacrificial study and scholarly service.

BIBLIOGRAPHY

DNB

Boase

R. Cowtan, *Memories of the British Museum* (London, 1872)

J. B. McCaul, *The Rev. T.H. Horne* (London, 1862)

T. H. Ward, ed. *Men of the Reign* (London and New York, 1885)

CHRISTOPHER D. HANCOCK

Horton, John (b. London). *Fl.* 1810s. CMS missionary to Sierra Leone. Horton trained as a schoolmaster at the Central School of the National Society before volunteering to go to Sierra Leone with the CMS. He was sent to Leicester on 17 March 1816 travelling in a party with W. A. B. JOHNSON, W. H. DÜRING and C. Jost. He withdrew from CMS after two years of service and returned to England where in 1821 he was ordained by the Bishop of London as chaplain at Bathurst, River Gambia. He was later Rector of St George's, Southwark. His wife's maiden name was Neale.

BIBLIOGRAPHY

D. T. B[arry], *CMS Register of Missionaries and Native Clergy* (privately printed) (London, 1906)

DONALD M. LEWIS

Hosier [Hoosier; Hoshur; Hossier], Harry (b. probably near Fayetteville, NC, BNA, *c.* 1750; d. Philadelphia, PA, USA, May 1806). African-American Methodist preacher.

Hosier was born a slave. By the time he was active among the Methodists he was free, but it is not known how this occurred. Hosier is thought to be the first African-American licensed by the Methodists to preach. Although the MEC of his day would ordain African-Americans as deacons (not as elders), Hosier was never ordained.

Hosier travelled and preached from the Carolinas to New England. He was companion, colleague, and servant to a number of itinerants. Among them were Methodism's first three bishops, THOMAS COKE (1784; 1787); FRANCIS ASBURY (1780-1; 1785; 1786; 1787); and RICHARD WHATCOAT (1786-8), and presiding elder FREEBORN GARRETTSON (1789-90). Asbury and Hosier may have met as early as 1773, 1775 or 1776. If, as has been suggested, Hosier belonged to Henry Dorsey and Prudence Ridgeley Gough he would have been present when Asbury was hosted at Perry Hall, their plantation near Baltimore. Asbury's first mention of him is on 29 June 1780 when they were together in North Carolina. Asbury assigned Hosier to guide the newly arrived Coke through the Methodist work in the Delaware-Maryland Peninsula in the weeks prior to the Christmas Conference, 1784. Hosier then attended this conference which established the MEC. Hosier's New England tour with Garrettson was probably the apogee of his career. Soon Hosier's fame went before them. He was the preferred preacher at their stops, sometimes having audiences of more than 1,000. Hosier may even have accompanied Garrettson to Nova Scotia.

The decade of the 1780s is the best documented period of Hosier's life. In 1791 one Sally Lyon brought charges against him. We do not know the nature of the complaint, but the committee which heard the case declared him innocent. Otherwise, he is hardly mentioned in the 1790s, but appears again in 1803 assigned with the preacher on the Trenton circuit (New Jersey). He was in characteristic form at a Maryland camp meeting in 1804 and at St George's MEC, Philadelphia early in 1805. In May, 1805 19 preachers recommended Hosier to Bishops Asbury and Whatcoat, but the document does not state specifically that they were asking for his ordination. Hosier was to live only one more year. He fell victim to alcoholism and for a time was a street person in Philadelphia. However, after a certain all-night vigil he recovered. Though spiritually renewed, Hosier was very sick when visited by one of his old travelling colleagues in March and April, 1806. The date of his death is unrecorded, but his funeral was on 18 May 1806.

Hosier was the greatest preacher of the first generation of the MEC. He was illiterate but possessed high intelligence, a prodigious memory for hymns, scripture and Methodist doctrine, and verbal communication skills which even amazed educated men. Dr BENJAMIN RUSH of Philadelphia called him the greatest orator in America. Bishop Thomas Coke, holder of an Oxford doctorate, wrote, 'I really believe he is one of the best Preachers in the world . . .'. The first time any New York City newspaper mentioned Methodist preaching was in 1786. The

Packet gave a detailed account of Hosier's sermon preached at John Street MEC, his first appearance in the city. Congregations preferred Hosier's preaching to that of his supervisors. Once Freeborn Garrettson gave over the preaching entirely to Hosier because that was who the people had come to hear. One wonders what Hosier might have achieved had he learned to read and write. RICHARD ALLEN wanted to teach him, but Hosier felt that when he tried to read he lost the gift of preaching. He refused to proceed into literacy. One result is that so little of his record survived for Methodists to remember.

Hosier's ministry is characteristic of early USA Methodism among African-Americans. The movement/denomination was biracial from the first. JOHN WESLEY hated slavery. USA Methodism, especially after 1784, compromised with the institution, but never surrendered the apostolate of evangelizing African-Americans. From 1790 to 1810 one of every five members of the young denomination was African-American. African-American preachers were used. Hosier's experience at John Street, New York and St George's, Philadelphia shows they sometimes preached in the major Methodist Episcopal churches as well as in camp meetings and private homes. They could be local preachers and deacons but not elders or voting members of conference. Thus they were employed but always supervised, respected but restricted. As Hosier's biographer Warren T. Smith put it, 'Elevated though he may have been, Hosier never seems to have stood on exactly the same footing with [his white companions]'.

Hosier's story provides an instructive comparison and contrast with that of his colleague RICHARD ALLEN, a man perhaps ten years his junior. Together they were the two African-American Methodist preachers at the Christmas Conference. Asbury ordained Allen deacon in 1799, the first African-American to be ordained in the MEC. In 1816 Allen led the formation of a new denomination, the African MEC and became its first bishop. Thus though Hosier was more famous than Allen during his lifetime, the younger man's learning and institutional leadership ability secured his place in a history from which Hosier was for long nearly forgotten.

BIBLIOGRAPHY
EWM
W. T. Smith, *Harry Hosier* (Nashville, TN, 1981)

CHARLES W. BROCKWELL, JR

Hosken, Charles Heath (b. Hayle, Cornwall, England, 1811; d. Norwich, Northamptonshire, England, 25 March 1892). Baptist minister, evangelist, and controversialist. Educated at Borough Road College, London, he was tested for the ministry by JAMES UPTON's congregation at Blackfriars in 1838, and invited by the church at St Agnes, Cornwall to be its minister. He did not stay long for the same year he went to Clonmel in Ireland as an agent of the Baptist Irish Society, where he rode an average of 4,000 miles a year in the interest of his mission. He followed this by visiting Holland, preaching in

Rotterdam, before being sent by the BMS as a missionary to Honduras in 1841. Problems with the climate led him on to ministry in the USA where he was successively minister at West Troy, New York State and Patterson, New Jersey. In both places enlarged churches had to be provided for the increased congregations attracted by his ministry. At West Troy he replied to Dr Brownlee's strictures on the Baptists and himself wrote a book on baptism, while at Patterson he won an essay prize for a work on slavery. More importantly, a bold abolitionist, his home became a recognized station on the 'underground railway' which aided fugitive slaves on their journey to freedom in Canada.

In 1847 he returned to England to the pastorate at Crayford which he combined with the running of a school in Bexleyheath to which C. H. SPURGEON sent some of his early students for instruction prior to the opening of Pastors' College. His many interests were shown in his writing of a critical study of the relationship of the Septuagint to the New Testament, and by his refusal to pay the church rate, for which some of his goods were distrained and sold at auction, which provoked a public protest meeting under the chairmanship of J. Carvell Williams. In 1858 he removed to the pastorate of Fenny Stratford where he produced the abolitionist tract *The Song of the Lash*, moving on three years later to become pastor of a new Strict Baptist Chapel in Norwich where he ministered for 14 years (1861–75).

BIBLIOGRAPHY
Baptist Handbook (1893)
S. J. Price, *Upton* (London, 1935)
C. H. Spurgeon, *Autobiography*, II (London, 1899)

J. H. Y. BRIGGS

Hoskins, John (b. Stoke Abbas, Dorset, England, 1718; d. after 1788). Methodist schoolmaster and lay preacher in Old Perlican, Trinity Bay, Newfoundland. Hoskins, who experienced religious conversions at the age of 14 and again later while teaching in Bristol, left England for North America in 1774 with his 16-year-old son. Originally, Hoskins had planned to earn enough money in Newfoundland to immigrate to America, where he wanted to combine teaching with missionary work, but he remained in Old Perlican as a lay preacher and teacher. Here he initiated a revival by preaching 'the most essential parts of the religion of the heart', which according to Hoskins consisted of 'repentance, remission of sins, and holiness'. He also insisted upon conversion, a spiritual rebirth with a subsequent life of moral seriousness. Hoskins organized his followers into classes and was recommended by the principal inhabitants of his community to be ordained a priest. When Bishop Lowth of London refused ordination, JOHN WESLEY agitated without avail for Hoskins' ordination. The bishop's persistent refusal became one of the stepping-stones in the eventual separation of the Methodists from the Church of England. Little is known about Hoskins' later life. By the time of WILLIAM BLACK's missionary tour through Newfoundland in 1791, he no longer served in Old Perlican.

BIBLIOGRAPHY
'An Account of Mr. John Hoskins: in a Letter to the Rev. John Wesley', Old Perlican, 15 October 1781, *Arminian Magazine* 8 (1785): 24–7, 85–8, 143–4 (=6): 194–6; 43–4
John Hoskins to Mr. Squire, Old Perlican, 5 Nov. 1784, *Arminian Magazine*, 8 (April 1785): 628–30
ENL

HANS ROLLMANN

Hosmer, William (b. Brimfield, MA, USA, 29 May 1810; d. Auburn, NY, USA, 17 June 1889). Methodist minister, author and publisher. Educated at Franklin Academy, Plattsburg, New York, Hosmer was ordained into the Methodist ministry in 1833. He edited the *Northern Christian Advocate*, official periodical of the Genesee Conference of the MEC from 1848 until his strong abolitionist posture resulted in his being replaced in 1856. From 1856 to 1871, he edited the *Northern Independent* (Auburn, New York), an abolition and temperance periodical. Poor health forced him to retire from public life in 1871. He was the author of several works on slavery including *The Higher Law* (1852) and books on education.

BIBLIOGRAPHY
Auburn Daily Advertiser (17 June 1889)

WILLIAM KOSTLEVY

Hotham, Lady Gertude (b. England, 1697; d. South Dalton, Yorkshire, England, 16 April 1775). Evangelical benefactress. The eldest daughter of Philip Stanhope, third Earl of Chesterfield and sister of the notorious fourth earl, she was named after her maternal grandmother the Marchioness of Halifax. In 1724 she married Sir Charles Hotham (1693–1739), fifth Baronet, a colonel in the Grenadier Guards and from 1727 Groom of the Bedchamber to George II. The Queen was the godmother of their daughter Caroline. After the death of her husband, Lady Gertude was prominent in the aristocratic circle influenced by the revival and supported WHITEFIELD and the WESLEYS. She was a close friend of Lady HUNTINGDON. Her houses in London and Bath were made available for preaching. Horace Walpole declared that she had all the wit of her brother without, of course, his cynical scepticism.

Her son Sir Charles Hotham (1735–1767), sixth Baronet, was also identified with the evangelical cause as was his wife, Clara, a wealthy heiress. Educated at Marylebone and Westminster Schools he served in the courts of George II and George III. He was a friend of HENRY VENN as well as of other revival leaders. MARTIN MADAN's tune set to Charles Wesley's 'Jesu, Lover of my soul' was named after him. St Mary's, South Dalton, near Beverly, close to the family seat, increased the number of its services with his encouragement. He died on October 1767 at Stavelo near Spa in Germany after being thrown from a horse on his way to Nice.

BIBLIOGRAPHY
A. M. W. Stirling, *The Hothams*, 1 (London, 1928): 146–7, 239–80

A. SKEVINGTON WOOD

Hough, James (b. *c.* 1789; d. Hastings, Surrey, England, 2 Nov. 1847). Founder of the CMS Tinnevelly Mission. Hough was from Cumberland and appears to have been ordained before he went to university. According to *Alumni Cantabriensis* he was appointed chaplain by the East India Company in 1815 and based at Palamcottah from 1816 to 1821. It appears that CHARLES SIMEON, whom he had met in 1815, arranged the EIC chaplaincy.

Arriving at Madras with his wife, he was met by friends of the CMS mission. He readily acceded to Lieutenant-Colonel Trotter's request to serve the EIC's military garrison at Palayancottai (Palamcottah). There he found 3,100 Christians in 63 villages. One Indian pastor, Abraham, was struggling with decaying schools, crumbling churches and a lack of books. Hough began to learn Tamil. Another Tamil Christian leader, Viswanathan, who worked at Nazareth, re-organized and revitalized the schools. Since the SPCK could not send missionaries, despite an increase of 482 converts in 1814–17, he turned to the CMS. In 1820 the CMS sent C. T. E. RHENIUS (from Madras) and L. BERNARD E. SCHMID (from Mayaveram). But Hough's health began to fail. A transfer to the garrison at Poonamallee, near Madras, did not help; and he returned to Britain with a chronic liver disease in 1822. In 1824 he returned to India again, this time as chaplain of St George's, Madras. However, he returned to England permanently in 1826. He was then educated at Corpus Christi College, Cambridge (matriculated 1828; BA 1832; MA 1835). From 1832 until his death he served as perpetual curate at St Andrew's, Ham, Surrey.

His *Vade mecum. Instructions to Missionaries* (1832) are still in use, as are his *Commentary on Daniel, Lectures on Genesis* and *Dialogue Between a Protestant and a Roman Catholic*, which he wrote in Tamil. He also wrote a *History of the Church of India* in five volumes (London, 1839–60). Possibly the most important thing he initiated was the establishing of two seminaries for catechists in 1818–19, which ensured the indigenization of the work. His work was carried forward by Rhenius, one of the evangelical giants of Tamil Christianity in Tinnevelly (Tirūnelveli).

BIBLIOGRAPHY
Al. Cant.

E. M. JACKSON

Housman, Robert (b. Skerton, Lancashire, England, 25 Feb. 1759; d. Woodside, Lancashire, England, 22 April 1838). Anglican clergyman. Housman was educated at Lancaster Grammar School and apprenticed to a surgeon. Discovering a clerical vocation, he entered St John's College, Cambridge, as a sizar in 1780 (BA 1784). He was ordained in 1781 and became Curate of Gargrave (Yorkshire). He regarded himself as C. SIMEON's first convert. He was successively curate at St John's Chapel, Lancaster (1785), Langton (Leicestershire) (1786–7), St Mary's, Leicester under T. ROBINSON (1787–8), Markfield (1788–92), afternoon lecturer at St Martin's, Leicester (1792) and Curate of Foston. Housman then returned to Lancaster, where with help from such evangelical benefactors as Simeon, W. WILBERFORCE, JOHN THORNTON and the elder CARUS WILSON he built St Anne's Church of which he became incumbent (1795–1836). He introduced his own hymn-book in the face of opposition in 1803, set up a Benevolent Society (1797) and a Sunday school (1812) and supported the Lancaster auxiliary of BFBS. Of a mild, contemplative and studious nature, he supported the liberation of slaves but refused to oppose Roman Catholic emancipation, being 'too good a Protestant to dread Popery' (Housman, 1841: ccxlii). Doctrinally he was Calvinistic, opposed to perfectionism and to millenarianism.

BIBLIOGRAPHY
Al. Cant., II, iii: 456
DNB
R. F. Housman, *The Life and Remains of the Rev. Robert Housman* (London, 1841)

ARTHUR POLLARD

Howard, Charles Beaumont (b. Dublin, 1807; d. Adelaide, South Australia, 19 July 1843). First Colonial Chaplain of South Australia. Howard graduated BA Trinity College, Dublin 1828 and served two curacies in the diocese of Chester 1832–6. He married Grace Montgomerie Neville 1832. Appointed Colonial Chaplain to South Australia in February 1836, he ministered vigorously to a scattered community in the new, unfamiliar land. He established the first Anglican parish, Holy Trinity, and joined many community committees. He and his parish suffered financially in the colony's bankruptcy of 1841. His death was brought on by overwork and exposure to the weather as he served his flock.

He preached 'Jesus Christ and him crucified' as 'the sole foundation of a sinner's hopes' in moderate, plain style, so forming the evangelical tradition in South Australian Anglicanism. He was a short-lived embodiment of cooperation between Anglicanism and the powerful dissenting component of South Australian society.

BIBLIOGRAPHY
ADB, 1
B. Dickey, *Holy Trinity Adelaide* (Adelaide, 1988)

BRIAN DICKEY

Howard, John (b. Clapton, London, 2 Sept. 1726; d. Kherson, Russia, 20 Jan. 1790). Congregationalist philanthropist. The son of a successful upholsterer and carpet seller, who had bought himself a small estate at Cardington in Bedfordshire, he was a Congregationalist rather than a Baptist, though a regular 'hearer' at SAMUEL STENNETT's Little Wild Street congregation ('No man ever entered more into my religious sentiments or more happily expressed them'). Both a teetotaller and a vegetarian, he was one of the leaders of the Congregationalist secession from Bunyan Meeting in Bedford. Brought up in Bedfordshire and Hertfordshire, but apprenticed to a wholesale grocer in London, he inherited financial security on his father's death in 1742. In 1756, *en route* to Portugal, he was caught by a French privateer and imprisoned in France, thus providing him with firsthand experience of the abuses against which he was to spend his life campaigning. Back in England he built model cottages, a village school, and encouraged domestic industry and sanitary improvements on his estate in Cardington in Bedfordshire.

From 1767 he travelled extensively in Europe. As High Sheriff of Bedfordshire in 1773, an office undertaken despite the Test Acts, and leading to his discovering the widespread abuses of the British prison system, he campaigned successfully against them, giving evidence before the House of Commons in March 1774. He personally paid for copies of the legislation to be posted to the governors of every prison in Britain but the legislation was very largely neglected. Perhaps this is why he virtually appointed himself Inspector of Prisons, Workhouses, and Hospitals, not only in England but throughout Europe. He is said to have spent some £30,000 of private income on the task and to have refused government offers of help. Thus three years of travel and investigation lay behind his *The State of the Prisons* in England and Wales, with *Preliminary Observations* and an *Account of Some Foreign Prisons* (1777). In 1778 he again gave evidence before the House on the perniciousness of the hulk system. Between 1775 and 1785 he made six European tours, investigating the conditions of continental prisons, travelling as far east as Turkey and Russia.

After 1785 he added hospitals to his agenda of concern and lost his life while investigating the health of the Russian army near the Turkish frontier. His statue, the first to be allowed to be erected within St Paul's Cathedral, is by fellow evangelical, JOHN BACON. The motivation for his philanthropy was a compassion born out of intense evangelical conviction.

BIBLIOGRAPHY
DNB
H. H. Scullard, *John Howard* (London, 1911)

J. H. Y. BRIGGS

Howard, John (Eliot) (b. Plaistow, Essex, England, 11 Dec. 1807; d. Tottenham, Middlesex, England, 22 Nov. 1883). Quaker seceder and Brethren scientist. John and his brother Robert Howard were sons of the Quaker, LUKE HOWARD and were both associated with his chemical factory at Stratford. In 1836 and 1839 respectively, in the wake of the Beaconite controversy (led by ISAAC CREWDSON) they left the Society of Friends and in 1838 a Brethren assembly was established at Tottenham. They both opposed DARBY in the 1848 division of the Brethren.

J. E. Howard's fame as a quinologist rested on his purchase in 1858 of Paven's specimens together with Paven's manuscript of his *Nueva Quinologia* which Howard published in 1862. His *Quinology of the East Indian Plantations* appeared in 1869. The government thanked him for this and he was elected a fellow of the Royal Society (1874). His religious writings ranged from biblical exposition and ecclesiastical controversy to apologetics. Many family papers are preserved in the Greater London Record Office.

BIBLIOGRAPHY
F. R. Coad, *A History of the Brethren Movement* (Exeter, England, 1968)
DNB (article by G. S. Boulger omits his secession from Friends)
H. Lloyd, *The Quaker Lloyds and the Industrial Revolution* (London, 1975): 262–5, 287
'Notes on Archives: City Quakers' in *History Today*, 20 (1970): 221–2
H. Pickering, ed., *Chief Men Among the Brethren* (London, 1931): 57–60
T. C. F. Stunt, *Early Brethren and the Society of Friends* (Pinner, England, 1970): 20–2

TIMOTHY C. F. STUNT

Howard, Luke (b. London, 28 Nov. 1772; d. Tottenham, Middlesex, England, 21 March 1864). Meteorologist and Quaker seceder. Son of a wealthy Quaker manufacturer, he was apprenticed at the age of 15, to a Stockport chemist and in 1793 established his own business in London. In 1796 he married John Eliot's daughter, Mariabella through whom the family inherited the Ashmore estates in Dorset. In partnership with W. ALLEN he supervised until 1812 the factory at Plaistow where he also pursued his own researches. The names Cirrus, Cumulus, Stratus and Nimbus were coined in a paper which Howard read to the Askesian Society and later published with his meteorological observations in *The Climate of London* (1820). This work greatly impressed Goethe and appears to have influenced the painting of Constable.

He visited Germany in 1816 to administer relief for victims of the Napoleonic Wars. Other benevolent interests included temperance, antislavery, animal protection, and support for the BFBS and for Quaker missionary work particularly that of HANNAH KILHAM in Sierra Leone. His evangelical convictions are well demonstrated in *The Yorkshireman* which he published from 1833 to 1837. He hoped to mediate in the Beacon controversy (led by ISAAC CREWDSON) but his baptism and taking of communion in JOHN PYE SMITH's Congregational church at Homerton led to his disownment by Friends in 1838.

Since 1812 he had lived at Ackworth, Yorkshire or at Tottenham where his sons cared for him after his wife's death in 1852. From 1839 he was associated with Brethren.

SELECT WRITINGS

[L. Howard], *An Appeal to the Christian Public Against a Sentence of Disownment by the Society of Friends, for Absenting Himself From Their Silent Meetings, and Submitting to the Ordinance of Christ* (London, 1838)

BIBLIOGRAPHY

See Bibliography for Howard, John Eliot

K. Badt, *John Constable's Clouds* (London, 1950)

Brook Street Chapel Archives, Tottenham, Membership Register

T. Compton, *Recollections of Tottenham Friends and the Forster Family* (London, 1893): 55

DNB (article by T. Hodgkin ignores his secession from Friends)

J. O. Greenwood, *Quaker Encounters*, vol 1, *Friends and Relief* (York, England, 1975): 8–16; vol 2, *Vines on the Mountains* (York, 1977): 101, 105, 114–15

L. Hawes, 'Constable's Sky Sketches,' *Journal of the Warburg and Courtauld Institute*, 32 (1969): 344–8

E. Isichei, *Victorian Quakers* (Oxford, 1970): 47–52

D. F. S. Scott ed., *Luke Howard* (York, England, 1976)

TIMOTHY C. F. STUNT

Howard, Robert. See HOWARD, JOHN ELIOT

Howels, William (b. near Cowbridge, Glamorgan, Wales, Sept. 1778; d. Wales, 18 Nov. 1832). Welsh Calvinistic clergyman. He attended Oxford from 1800 to 1803. In 1804 he became curate of Llangan in Wales. Perhaps because of the undeveloped state of evangelical Anglicanism in Wales, his ministry was akin to that of the previous first generation of evangelicals in England. He was a staunch Calvinist and was not strict on church order, being prepared to preach in Nonconformist chapels. In 1812 he came to London as the curate of WILLIAM GOODE SR, at St Anne's Blackfriars, and St Andrew-by-the-Wardrobe, where he continued to maintain the heritage which reached back to WILLIAM ROMAINE in the previous century. In 1817 he became lessee of the proprietary Episcopal Chapel in Long Acre, where his theological, experiential and straightforward Calvinistic sermons attracted many younger people such as ALEXANDER HALDANE, who were becoming increasingly critical of the second generation evangelicals. At the same time, Howels was totally committed to evangelical Anglicanism, leaving his whole estate to the CMS.

SELECT WRITINGS

W. Howels, *Sermons, With a Memoir by Charles Bowdler* (London, 1834)

BIBLIOGRAPHY

DNB (spelled Howells)

E. Morgan, *A Brief Memoir of the Late Rev W. Howels* (London, 1854)

IAN S. RENNIE

Hubbold, Lucy (b. Townsend, England, 14 July 1809; d. Brierley [Hill], Staffordshire, England, 2 Nov. 1860). Primitive Methodist (PM) itinerant preacher. Hubbold's upbringing was strictly moral and she attended both day and Sunday schools. When the PMs visited the village she went, from curiosity, to hear them and was converted. Although feeling a call to preach she was very reluctant, but eventually responded (1835) and quickly became an itinerant. Hubbold itinerated in the Hopton Bank, Ludlow and Longton circuits, but while at Longton she broke a bone in her foot, which caused so much lameness that she was forced to give up itinerating. Hubbold continued as a hired local preacher until her voice gave way under the strain and she had to retire completely. She located at Longton, where, William Belcher bequeathed her (1847), as a token of respect, a house, in which she lived until she developed rheumatic fever; friends then took her in to their home. In retirement, Hubbold remained a local preacher and class leader.

BIBLIOGRAPHY

PMMag (1847, 1861)

E. DOROTHY GRAHAM

Hughes, Hugh (b. near Llandudno, Wales, early 1790; d. Great Malvern, Worcestershire, England, 11 March 1863). Artist and controversialist. He was baptized 20 Feb. 1790 and orphaned early in life. He was brought up by his maternal grandfather and later apprenticed to an engraver in Liverpool, moving on to become a painter in London. He was a radical in both religion and politics and was disciplined by the Calvinistic Methodists for supporting Catholic emancipation, an action which he denounced in *Seren Gomer*. While a later meeting of the Calvinistic Methodists disowned such interference with political conscience, Hughes did not return to their Communion but became an Independent, eventually joining the Plymouth Brethren. He wrote extensively under the pseudonym of 'Cristion' attacking church establishments and the payment of tithes and church rates: he also produced a series of caricatures featuring the Welsh Education Commission of 1846–7. His best known artistic work is his *The Beauties of Cambria* (60 plates published in 1823).

BIBLIOGRAPHY

DNB

DWB

J. H. Y. BRIGGS

Hughes, James (b. Ciliau Aeron, Cardiganshire, Wales, 3 July 1779; d. London, 2 Nov. 1844). Welsh Calvinistic Methodist minister, Bible commentator and hymn-writer. The son of a blacksmith, Hughes underwent a religious conversion at the age of 18 and joined the Calvinistic Methodist church at Llangeitho, Cardiganshire. Moving to London in 1799, he helped to establish a

Welsh congregation in Deptford. He began to preach in 1810, was ordained by the South Wales Calvinistic Methodist Association in 1816, and was invited to minister to the newly built Jewin Crescent Church, London. Known by the bardic name of 'Iago Trichrug', he composed a number of hymns, the best of which are still sung in Welsh congregations. He is best known for his monumental Bible commentary, *Esboniad ar y Beibl*, published after his death, which became the most widely used commentary in the Sunday schools of Wales during the nineteenth century. He died at Rotherhithe and was buried in Bunhill Fields cemetery.

BIBLIOGRAPHY
J. E. Davies, *Cyfrol Goffa James Hughes* (Denbigh, Wales, 1911)
DWB

E. AP NEFYDD ROBERTS

Hughes, John (b. Llanfihangel yng Ngwynfa, Montgomeryshire, Wales, 22 Feb. 1775; d. probably Pontrobert, Montgomeryshire, 3 Aug. 1854). Preacher and hymnodist. Originally a weaver, he heard THOMAS JONES of Llanwynog preach and joined the Calvinistic Methodists in Penyllys. THOMAS CHARLES of Bala engaged him as a teacher in his circulating schools. Hughes began to preach in 1802 and was ordained in 1814. A regular contributor to periodicals, he also wrote memoirs. One, published in 1827, was of JOHN DAVIES, the missionary (1772–1855). Hughes's sermons were published between 1836 and 1838. He was buried at Pontrobert.

'Uncouth in appearance', according to *DWB*, 'and laboured in speech, he yet had a remarkable personality, and his piety was never in doubt.' He and Ruth Evans, whom he married in 1805, preserved the hymns of ANN GRIFFITHS. Ruth, her maid, had memorized them, and John wrote them down. His memoir of Ann appeared in book form in 1854. According to *DWB*, the best of John's own hymns were 'still held in high esteem'. For Luff they were 'so far inferior to those of Ann Griffiths that there [could] be no suspicion of the genuineness of the stanzas' attributed to Ann.

BIBLIOGRAPHY
A. Luff, 'A Strange Hymnological Occasion', *Hymn Society Bulletin*, 8, no. 12 (1977): 216–18

JOHN S. ANDREWS

Hughes, John (b. Brecon, Powys, Wales, 18 May 1776; d. Knutsford, Cheshire, 15 May 1843). Welsh Wesleyan Methodist minister. He was the son of William Hughes, hatter, and Elizabeth his second wife. In 1778 he entered Christ's College, Brecon. He heard JOHN WESLEY preach at the well-to-do religious society at Brecon of which his parents were members and opted to join the Methodist ministry rather than to seek Anglican holy orders. In 1796 he became a Methodist exhorter. In 1800 he was appointed to assist Owen Davies (1752–1830) in pioneering the newly launched Wesleyan mission in Wales. Hughes's work met with considerable success despite his lack of fluency in Welsh and his distaste for the oratory of his more rombustious colleagues. Nor did he find Owen Davies easy to work with. He was a man of scholarly instincts and made it a matter of concern to provide reading material in Welsh for his converts. His work in Wales lasted but a short time and his plans conflicted with those approved by Dr THOMAS COKE (1747–1814). So he was moved to England where, but for a brief respite at Ruthin, he spent the remainder of his ministry. Hughes was also an antiquary of some stature in his own day. His unpublished autobiography is in the National Library of Wales, manuscript 3501.

BIBLIOGRAPHY
DWB
Hugh Jones, *Hanes Wesleyaeth Gymreig* (Bangor, Wales, 1911)
A. H. Williams, *Welsh Wesleyan Methodism* (Bangor, Wales, 1935)
WMM (1847)

R. TUDUR JONES

Hughes, John (b. Llanfihangel Geneu'r Glyn, Cardiganshire, Wales, 8 June 1787; d. Aberystwyth, Cardiganshire, Wales, 1 Nov. 1860). Anglican clergyman. Born and educated in an area much influenced by the Welsh Methodist movement, John was ordained as a literate (i.e. admitted to Anglican orders without having obtained a university degree) at St Asaph Cathedral in 1811. Curacies in that diocese and in England – including Deddington, near Oxford, where his eloquence is said to have attracted many undergraduates, including J. H. NEWMAN – led to his appointment as Perpetual Curate of Aberystwyth in 1827, which he held with the mother church of Llanbadarn Fawr from 1834. Here his ministry rebuilt evangelical church life, and ensured its survival against methodist and tractarian encroachment. One of the most noted Welsh preachers of his day, his work was recognized by his appointment as Archdeacon of Cardigan in 1859.

BIBLIOGRAPHY
J. Ross, *A Light upon the Road* (Aberystwyth, Wales, 1989)

ROGER L. BROWN

Hughes, John (b. Adwy'r Clawdd near Wrexham, Denbighshire, Wales, 11 Feb. 1796; d. Abergele, Denbighshire, 8 Aug. 1860). Welsh Calvinistic Methodist minister and author. The son of Hugh Hughes, a carpenter, he followed his father's trade until age 19. At the age of 12 he began attending a Sunday school and progressed rapidly in his studies. At 14 he joined the Calvinistic Methodist church and at 17 began to preach. In 1815 he opened his own school but in 1817 went to school himself to learn Latin and Greek. In 1819 he began another school at Wrexham which took older students intent on entering the ministry. Here he trained a number of men, including ROGER EDWARDS, who became prominent preachers.

Although a respected preacher, his ordination was delayed until 1829 when he was able to convince the hyper-Calvinists in his presbytery of his orthodoxy. In order chiefly to have greater opportunities to preach, in 1834 he gave up his school and became a shopkeeper at Adwy'r Clawdd and from 1838 in Liverpool where he co-pastored the Calvinistic Methodist churches with HENRY REES.

Hughes authored several books, the most important of which was his history of Welsh Calvinistic Methodism: *Methodistiaeth Cymru* (3 vols, 1851–6). Hughes was also significant in lessening the ecclesiastical and political conservatism of the Welsh Calvinistic connexion.

BIBLIOGRAPHY
DNB
DWB

DONALD M. LEWIS

Hughes, Joseph (b. London, 1 Jan. 1769; d. London, 3 Oct. 1833). 'Father' of the BFBS. Baptized by SAMUEL STENNETT at Little Wild Street, Hughes had the benefit of a varied education which included study at Bristol Baptist Academy, King's College, Aberdeen, and Edinburgh University. At Aberdeen he pioneered in Sunday school work. In 1791, he returned to Bristol as classical tutor, becoming CALEB EVANS's assistant and managing both the church and college after Evans's death during a lengthy interregnum. While there he made a number of friends including S. T. Coleridge and HANNAH MORE. Differences of opinion with JOHN RYLAND, Evans's successor, led to his leaving Bristol for Battersea, then a pleasant Thameside village, where he ministered to the Baptist congregation, from 1797 till his death. Hughes practised 'mixed communion' and had ecumenical sympathies not always appreciated by his fellow Baptists.

He supported various evangelical and educational enterprises, and took a keen interest in the founding of London University. From its commencement in 1799 he was secretary of the RTS for a period of 34 years. At a meeting of this society, in 1802, an appeal from THOMAS CHARLES of Bala for Welsh Bibles led to the formation of the Bible Society, some two years later. Hughes himself was the principal mover, writing a pamphlet in support. He was appointed one of the secretaries, proving a wise counsellor during the society's formative years, years made especially difficult by the death of colleagues, two serious controversies, family grief and personal ill health. At the end of his life there was a conflict between the society of which he was secretary and his fellow Baptists over the BMS missionaries' desire to translate the Greek '*baptizo*' by a word meaning immerse. But Paedo-Baptists of the Bible Society committee rejected this, leading eventually to the setting up of a separate Baptist Society.

The then secretary of the BMS argued he would rather forfeit Bible Society aid than accede because such action would be 'selling the truth for the sack of gold'.

BIBLIOGRAPHY
J. Leifchild, *Memoir of the late Rev. Joseph Hughes, A.M., One of the Secretaries of the British and Foreign Bible Society* (London, 1835)
S. A. Swaine, *Faithful Men* (London, 1884)

E. F. CLIPSHAM

Hughes, Robert (b. London; d. Bathurst, Gambia, Sierra Leone, c. 1821). CMS missionary to Sierra Leone. Hughes trained as a schoolmaster in England and went out with Mr and Mrs J. C. SPERRHACKEN on 5 January 1815 to Sierra Leone under the auspices of the CMS. He worked in Sierra Leone and then in Goree in West Africa. His association with the CMS ended in March 1818. He returned to England and was ordained and then appointed Government Chaplain at Bathurst, Gambia. He had married in 1820 and his wife accompanied him to West Africa where they both died five months after their arrival.

BIBLIOGRAPHY
D. T. B[arry], *CMS Register of Missionaries and Native Clergy* (privately printed) (London, 1906)

DONALD M. LEWIS

Hulbert, Charles (b. Manchester, England, 18 Feb. 1778; d. Hadnall, Shropshire, England, 7 Oct. 1857). Factory owner, publisher, author, and promoter of Sunday schools. Originally intended for the ministry, Hulbert had instead to learn the cotton-weaving trade due to family misfortunes. While a young man working near Manchester, he became an earnest Christian under the influence of neighbouring clergy and his Wesleyan employers. He devoted himself to Sunday school work nearby and his school increased dramatically to some 1,000 scholars. In time he and his brother became the owners of some large cotton factories in Shrewsbury, and he carried on classes and services in one of the large rooms and opened a Sunday school which numbered as many as 600. WILLIAM WILBERFORCE drew on a report on Hulbert's factory in 1808 to rebut the charge in Parliament that all factories were hotbeds of vice.

Five years later, the cotton business suffering, Hulbert moved into the printing and book trade. He himself wrote or edited some two dozen books of religious instruction, biography and local history. His eldest son Charles A. Hulbert (1804–88), who became Honorary Canon of Ripon in 1866, wrote widely on similar themes. The senior Charles Hulbert's religious activism illustrates well the leadership exercised by the laity in early nineteenth-century evangelicalism.

SELECT WRITINGS
C. Hulbert, *Memoirs of Seventy Years of an Eventful Life* (Providence Grove, England, 1848–52)

BIBLIOGRAPHY
C. A. Hulbert, *Obituary of the Late Mr. Charles Hulbert*, 2nd edn (London, 1860)
DNB

D. B. HINDMARSH

Hull, Hope (b. Worcester County, MD, BNA, 13 March 1763; d. Athens, GA, USA, 4 Oct. 1818). Pioneer Methodist preacher and supporter of education. Hull came from the Eastern Shore of Maryland and was apprenticed as a youth to a house carpenter in Baltimore. The date and circumstances of Hull's conversion are not known, but he was received on trial to the travelling connexion of Methodist preachers at the first conference of the MEC, held in Baltimore in June of 1785. In 1795 he took a location, a settled post of ministry. The following year, on 13 March 1796, Hull married Anne Wingfield. During the ten years he travelled – 1785–95 – Hull sought to improve his education, studying English and Latin language and literature. His travels convinced him that educational opportunities were sorely needed; he established a school for all ages in Wilkes County, Georgia, while continuing to preach. During the winter of 1802/3, he moved to Athens, Georgia and soon became involved in the establishment of Franklin College, later to be called the University of Georgia.

After experience on several circuits, Hull was ordained a deacon in 1788 and an elder in 1789. In 1785, while still on trial, he served in Salisbury, North Carolina. The next year his assignment was the Pee Dee circuit in South Carolina, where he and Jeremiah Maston had spectacular success. Dr THOMAS COKE noted in his journal:

> When I was in *America* before, there were but twenty in Society in this circuit . . . But now, chiefly by the means of . . . *Hope Hull* and *Jeremiah Maston*, the Societies consist of eight hundred and twenty-three members.
> (Coke, 1793: 68)

In 1787 Hull's assignment was the Amelia circuit in Virginia. The Washington circuit was newly established in Georgia in 1788, and Hull was sent to people unfamiliar with Methodism, and often ignorant of Christianity. His pioneering work resulted in the conversion of many and the building of a brick academy, the most substantial structure in the area. Hull's task for 1790 was establishing a Methodist society in Savannah. This proved to be the most difficult of all his scenes of labour. Two factors especially militated against his success there. The remembrance and reputation of JOHN WESLEY's ministry in Savannah in the 1730s was negative. Furthermore, it was known that Methodist conferences had passed resolutions against slave-holding. Though at first he had

the freedom to preach in a chair-maker's shop, he soon received mob threats of violence and found himself forced to leave. He remained, however, in Georgia, on the Burke circuit, through 1791. Connecticut was the scene of his labours in 1792, but the following year he returned to Georgia to work on the Savannah circuit. The last full year of his travels was 1794, when he accompanied FRANCIS ASBURY on journeys throughout the country.

A notable service after leaving the travelling connexion was to help establish Franklin College. He became a member of the Board of Trustees and also of the Prudential Committee. Hull was largely in charge of the administration of the lands that constituted the endowment of the college. For a short time, he functioned as the acting-president of the institution.

Hull was known as a powerful and discerning preacher. He was often referred to as the 'Broad Axe preacher' because of the force with which he delivered his sermons. His messages so often penetrated to the precise spiritual problems of his hearers, that he was charged with discovering people's secrets. So effective was his work in Georgia, other than that in the town of Savannah, that Hull has been called the father of Georgia Methodism.

BIBLIOGRAPHY
AAP
J. Atkinson, *Centennial History of American Methodism* (New York, 1884)
T. Coke, *Extracts of the Journals of the Rev. Dr. Coke's Five Visits to America* (London, 1793)
EWM
Minutes
A. M. Shipp, *History of Methodism in South Carolina* (Nashville, TN, 1884)
A. Stevens, *History of the Methodist Episcopal Church* (New York, 1866)

RICK D. RAILSBACK

Hull, William (Winstanley) (b. Blackburn, Lancashire, England, 15 March 1794; d. Hazlewood, Derbyshire, England, 28 Aug. 1873). English barrister and liturgical reformer. The son of a notable physician, John Hull (*DNB*), he was educated at Brasenose College, Oxford (BA 1815; MA 1817; fellow 1816–21). Called to the Bar at Lincoln's Inn (1814), he practised at Chancery from 1820 to 1846, when he retired to the countryside.

A high Tory and Protestant Constitutionalist, he backed Sir ROBERT HARRY INGLIS over Robert Peel in a celebrated contest for the Oxford University parliamentary seat (1829). Against the Tractarians he supported the elevation of Bishop Hampden (1836), but he thought unwise the persecution of the Tractarian, W. G. Ward, for heresy (1845). He is best known as a liturgical reformer. Working with ROBERT GROSVENOR (Lord Ebury) and Edward Berens, his main concern was to suppress the regenerative implications of baptism as outlined in the prayer-book. He also produced two collections of hymns (1833), and a collection of family prayers

(1828). He was married three times, his first two wives dying in childbirth.

BIBLIOGRAPHY
Boase
DNB
J. S. Reynolds, *Evangelicals at Oxford*, 2nd edn (Abingdon, England, 1975) part II: 106

JONATHAN BURKE CUTMORE

Hume, Robert Wilson (b. Stamford, CT, USA, 9 Nov. 1809; d. at sea, 26 Nov. 1854). Congregational missionary. An 1833 graduate of Union College, New York, Hume studied theology at Andover and Princeton, was ordained in 1839 and went that year with the ABCFM to Bombay. Stationed there for 15 years, he held a variety of positions. Annually he made evangelistic tours on the nearby mainland region. An ardent advocate of the temperance cause, he was at times secretary of the local temperance organization and editor of its magazine. For ten years he was secretary of the Bombay Tract and Book Society, bringing to that organization the new concept of paid colporteurs, and generally energizing the work of the society. Shortly after his arrival in India a new magazine in the Marathi language was established, the sole native language Christian journal in western India, and for ten years he was the editor of the publication, writing a great many of the articles, mostly in Marathi. Taken very ill in 1854, he was advised to seek a colder climate, sailed from Bombay, but died at sea within sight of the African coast.

BIBLIOGRAPHY
ESM

WILLIAM G. TRAVIS

Humes, Susan (b. Thompson, CT, USA, 1803 or 1804; d. Providence, RI, USA, 1827 or 1828). Freewill Baptist itinerant preacher. Little is known about her childhood except that she was orphaned when she was only 12. Her uncle became her legal guardian, but disowned her after she experienced conversion at 17. Two years later, she began to travel as an itinerant preacher. She addressed large crowds throughout New York, Rhode Island, and Canada, journeying over 3,000 miles between 1822 and 1826. She was never ordained, but the leadership of the Freewill Baptists gave her a letter commending her as a 'public labourer'. In 1826, she led two revivals, one at a Free Communion Baptist church in Russia, New York, and another in the village of the Swansecut Factory in Scituate, Rhode Island. She preached at many official Freewill Baptist gatherings, including the Holland Purchase yearly meeting in New York in 1824 and the Rhode Island quarterly meeting held in Rehoboth, Massachusetts in 1826. Her preaching career was successful but brief, lasting only four years. She died at the age of 23.

BIBLIOGRAPHY
Freewill Baptist Magazine (Providence, RI), I, 3 (November 1826): 89
I. D. Stewart, *History of the Freewill Baptists* (Dover, NH, 1862): 394
A. Thornton, *The Life of Elder Abel Thornton* (Providence, RI, 1828): 48–9, 126
N. Towle, *Vicissitudes Illustrated* (Portsmouth, NH, 1833): 37–8, 45–6

CATHERINE A. BREKUS

Humphrey, Heman (b. West Simsbury [now Canton], CT, USA, 26 March 1779; d. 3 April 1861). Congregationalist minister and president of Amherst College. Graduating from Yale College in 1805, Humphrey studied theology with Reverend ASAHEL HOOKER of Goshen, Connecticut before his ordination into the ministry in 1807. He served two pastorates: Congregational churches in Fairfield, Connecticut (1807–17) and in Pittsfield, Massachusetts (1817–23). His record of theological orthodoxy, support for temperance, and successful relations with young people in his two pastoral charges led to his call to become President of Amherst college (then known as the Charitable Collegiate Institution) in 1823.

During his 22-year tenure as president, over 400 of the 765 all male graduates of Amherst went on to careers in the ministry. Humphrey was also noted for encouraging his students to take a pledge promising to abstain from the use of alcohol, tobacco or opium.

BIBLIOGRAPHY
DAB
F. B. Dexter, *Biographical Sketches of the Graduates of Yale College*, 5 (New York, 1911)

STEVEN R. POINTER

Humphreys, Joseph (b. Burford, Oxfordshire, England, c. 1720). Methodist exhorter. The son of a dissenting minister in Burford in Oxfordshire he studied at Abraham Taylor's dissenting academy in Deptford from 1733, and was converted through GEORGE WHITEFIELD's preaching. He founded a religious society at Deptford, and at Christmas 1739 was expelled from the academy. He became an intimate friend of the WESLEYS, and preached at the Foundery. However, visiting Bristol in 1740, he was caught up in the Calvinist debate, and in April 1741 became one of Whitefield's itinerants, particularly in rural societies. He returned to Dissent as minister of a Bradford-on-Avon church some time after 1748. Evidently he was later ordained into the Anglican church, for in 1762 he was described as 'fallen asleep' preaching dead morality within the Church of England.

BIBLIOGRAPHY
G. Nuttall, 'George Whitefield's "Curate": Gloucestershire Dissent and the Revival', *JEH*, 27, 4 (1976)

PETER J. LINEHAM

Hunt, Aaron (b. Eastchester, Westchester County, NY, BNA, 28 March 1768; d. Sharon, CT, USA, 25 April 1858). American Methodist preacher. Born into the Protestant Episcopal Church, 19-year-old Hunt heard his first Methodist sermon at John Street Church in New York City. He was converted two years later, and in 1791 was admitted on trial into the New York Conference. Following his ordination by FRANCIS ASBURY in 1793, Hunt preached for thirty years in New York and Connecticut.

Hunt apparently introduced the 'altar call' to the North in 1806 after hearing of its success in southern camp meetings. His resolution to the 1804 General Conference of the MEC established the practice of compulsory time limits on the length of preachers' appointments. Hunt retired in 1823, although he continued to preach as often as his health would permit until his death in 1858 at the age of ninety.

BIBLIOGRAPHY

N. B. Harmon, ed. *Encyclopedia of World Methodism* (Nashville, TN, 1974)

M. Simpson, *Cyclopaedia of Methodism* (New York, 1856)

SUSAN E. WARRICK

Hunt, John (b. near Lincoln, England, 13 June 1812; d. Viwa, Fiji, 4 Oct. 1848). WMMS missionary in Fiji. After a few years of village schooling in Lincolnshire, Hunt worked from the age of ten as a farm labourer. He came to assurance of faith in a Methodist chapel when he was 17 and immediately sought to make up for his lack of education. He became a local preacher and in 1835 was received as a minister on probation and sent to the recently established Wesleyan theological institution at Hoxton in London. Here his mind was opened to a wide range of subjects. He worked assiduously, studied Greek and Hebrew and gave special attention to WESLEY's doctrine of holiness or entire sanctification.

In 1837 the Wesleyan church in England was moved by the plea 'pity poor Fiji' in a letter by JAMES WATKIN. Polynesian teachers from Tahiti had begun work among Fijians in 1830 and two Methodist ministers from Tonga had established a foothold in the eastern part of the island group in 1835, but most of the chiefs and people had still to hear the Gospel. Cannibalism was widespread and this and other baneful aspects of Fijian life lay behind the appeal to the home church. Asked to go to Fiji, Hunt accepted, was married and ordained, and in April 1838 sailed, with two other missionaries, for the Pacific. The party reached Fiji just before Christmas.

After a few months on Rewa, Hunt was appointed to Somosomo but the power of the native religion and intertribal fighting made the soil intractable. In 1842 he went to the island of Viwa where in the next six years he made his major contribution. Like his colleagues Hunt showed a readiness to risk any danger, especially during his three years at Somosomo, and to endure any hardship (he and his wife lost two children) in order to win the Fijian people. Appalled as he was by their cannibal

customs and savagery Hunt, nevertheless, attempted to understand their religion and social life and, above all, to love them and to pray for them.

Hunt was aware of the key role played by chiefs and the influence that their conversion could have on the spread of Christianity. On Viwa it was the conversion of the chief's nephew that provided the breakthrough leading to significant numbers being prepared for baptism. It was the eventual conversion in 1854 of the high chief, Cakobau of Bau, before whom Hunt preached and for whom he prayed, that facilitated the Christianization of the islands.

Other early missionaries had translated portions of the Bible but Hunt's work on Viwa was of lasting significance. Drawing upon the Greek and Hebrew he had learned at Hoxton and choosing the Bauan dialect as his medium he had translated the New Testament, Genesis, Exodus and 46 Psalms by the time of his death.

For Hunt holiness was the goal of the Christian life and from Viwa he wrote a number of letters on this Wesleyan doctrine to a colleague, JAMES CALVERT, on a distant station. After his death these were published and became part of the literature on the subject in Methodist circles.

Hunt shared in laying the foundations of the church in Fiji. The story of his consecrated life and death was often retold and helped to foster an interest in Fiji among Methodists, especially in Australia. He died at the age of 36 with the prayer 'Lord, Save Fiji' on his lips.

SELECT WRITINGS

J. Hunt, *Entire Sanctification* (London, 1853)

BIBLIOGRAPHY

A. Birdwhistle, *In His Armour* (London, 1954)

G. S. Rowe, *The Life of John Hunt, Missionary to the Cannibals of Fiji* (London, 1860)

ARNOLD D. HUNT

Hunt, Robert (b. probably Brighton, Sussex, England, c. 1802; d. England, 27 Aug. 1886). CMS missionary in North-West America. Hunt served as a lay catechist in South America before joining the CMS; he began training at the CMS College, Islington, in 1845. He was ordained (deacon and priest 1848) by the Bishop of London and accompanied DAVID ANDERSON to the North-West America mission on 6 June 1849. He and his wife, A. G. C. Wathen (died 1886), assisted at St Andrew's, Red River then established a mission farm at Lac la Ronge. After two relatively unproductive years, they moved the mission to Stanley which they hoped to use as a base to extend the work of the CMS into the far northern districts of Athabasca and Mackenzie River. The plans never materialized, however, for Hunt returned to England with his family in 1862 after an apparent breakdown in health.

In England Hunt served as curate at Mildmay to WILLIAM PENNEFATHER, the organizer of the Deaconess

Movement, and was first chaplain to the Deaconesses' Home in Mildmay. He also developed of a system of syllabic writing for Indian languages which he considered superior to the system devised by Methodist missionary JAMES EVANS. Hunt's system was never widely used.

BIBLIOGRAPHY
D. T. B[arry], *CMS Register of Missionaries And Native Clergy from 1804 to 1904* (privately printed) (London, 1906)

KERRY M. ABEL

Hunter, Andrew (b. Edinburgh, 15 Feb. 1744; d. Edinburgh, 21 Apr. 1809). Scottish divine. Privileged from birth, he studied at Edinburgh and Utrecht and was ordained to Dumfries (second charge, 1770). In 1779 he married Lord Napier's daughter, received Edinburgh's DD, was translated to New Greyfriars, Edinburgh, and elected colleague (successor, 1787) to the university's professor of divinity. In 1786 he moved to the Tron church, Glasgow.

Hunter was at home in Edinburgh's literary societies, becoming a founding member of its Royal Society (1783). He 'improved' his Barjarg estate (near Thornhill, Dumfriesshire), bought in 1772. A decided Calvinist, he lectured conscientiously on the system of Benedict Pictet of Geneva (11 manuscript vols, University Library). A prominent evangelical and moderator of the Church of Scotland's General Assembly (1793), he won an unblemished reputation by his gracious temper and generosity.

BIBLIOGRAPHY
A. Bower, *History of the University of Edinburgh*, 3 (Edinburgh, 1830): 204–9
DNB
Fasti, 1: 34–5
H. M. Wellwood, *A Sermon . . . the Rev. A. Hunter* (Edinburgh, 1809)

D. F. WRIGHT

Hunter, James (b. VA, BNA, 16 May 1767; d. 5 Dec. 1831). Prominent minister in the MPC. He joined the MEC in 1792, but early became identified with the movement that would become the MPC. He attended the first meeting of the Roanoke Union Society on 6 November 1824 which met at Sampson's Meeting House in Halifax County, North Carolina. Later that month he was elected secretary *protem*. In April 1828 he was brought to trial by MEC authorities for his involvement in the society. In December 1828 he attended the organizational meeting of the North Carolina Conference of the MPC and was assigned to serve the Roanoke circuit.

BIBLIOGRAPHY
EWM

STEVE HARPER

Hunter, James (b. Barnstaple, Devon, England, 25 April 1817; d. London, 12 Feb. 1882). CMS missionary in North-West America. Hunter attended the CMS college at Islington and was ordained deacon in 1843 and priest in 1844. He was sent overseas to the society's North-West America mission and for ten years served alongside HENRY BUDD at The Pas. In 1854 he was named first Archdeacon of Cumberland and transferred to the Red River settlement.

In 1858, Hunter undertook an extensive missionary journey into the Mackenzie River district of the far north to initiate a new field for the CMS work. He was accompanied on the voyage by a representative of the Oblates of Mary Immaculate, the Roman Catholic mission order active in the north-west. The competition of that journey became a deeply rooted part of northern mission work in Canada. In 1865, Hunter returned to England where he remained active in evangelical circles until his death.

Hunter's missionary career involved considerable controversy because of his outspoken manner and firmly held opinions. Nevertheless, he and his wife translated a considerable amount of religious literature into Cree, and the first booklet printed at Red River in 1860 was a copy of his ordination sermon.

BIBLIOGRAPHY
DCB, 11
W. B. Heeney, *Leaders of the Canadian Church: Second Series* (Toronto, 1920)
W. S. Wallace, *The Macmillan Dictionary of Canadian Biography* (Toronto, 1963)

KERRY M. ABEL

Hunter, Robert (fl. 1846–1873). Free Church of Scotland missionary in India. Hunter was ordained in the Free West Church, Aberdeen. He sailed immediately to join the Free Church of Scotland Mission in Nagpur, to assist STEPHEN HISLOP. Initially stationed at Seetabuldee, he became a close friend and invaluable assistant, even sharing Hislop's hobby of geology, and having a stone named after him, 'Hunterite'. Unfortunately his health gave way, and he resigned in September 1857. His brother, Thomas, was murdered in Delhi together with his wife and baby on 9 July 1857 as they were about to start a new mission in Sialkot. Hunter raised £1500 for Hislop's new Institution in 1855–6 and became the chronicler of the mission.

BIBLIOGRAPHY
R. Hunter, *History of the Missions of the Free Church of Scotland in India and Africa* (London, 1873)

E. M. JACKSON

Hunter, William [Sr] (b. *c*. 1730; d. Liverpool, 16 Sept. 1797). Baptist sea captain. The son of pious parents, like his father his whole career was spent as a sea captain. For almost a quarter of a century he was a member of SAMUEL MEDLEY's congregation in Liverpool, where he took a special interest in work amongst the young. After some 50 years at sea he retired *circa*1795 and most unfortunately lost his life in a capsizing accident in a small boat on the Mersey in September 1797.

BIBLIOGRAPHY
EM (1797)

J. H. Y. BRIGGS

Huntingdon, Selina, Countess of [née Shirley] (b. Staunton Harold, Leicestershire, England, 24 Aug. 1707; d. London, 17 June 1791). Calvinist Methodist leader. Born into a noble household as the second of three daughters of Washington Shirley, second Earl Ferrers and his wife Mary (née Levinge), on his death she inherited a third part of his estate and a title. From her youth she was noted for piety, ability and a strong temper. On 3 June 1728 she married Theophilus Hastings, the ninth Earl of Huntingdon (born 1696), and moved to the family seat at Donnington Park, Leicestershire. His family had connections with the court and were warm supporters of Walpole. The couple had four sons, Francis (1729–1789), George (1730–43), Ferdinando (1732–43) and Henry (1741–1759) and three daughters, Elizabeth (1731–), Selina (1735–1735) and Selina (1737–63).

The Countess first heard evangelical teachings from her sister-in-law, Lady Margaret Hastings, who responded to Methodist preaching *circa* 1738. Probably early in 1739 Selina herself accepted the message, although her husband asked the Bishop of Gloucester to dissuade her. She became a member of the Fetter Lane Society, but took the 'Methodist' side in the tensions in the society, and was JOHN WESLEY's closest ally in the split. She had close links with CHARLES WESLEY. The death of her sons George and Ferdinando in 1743, and her husband on 13 October 1746, deepened her Christian commitment. The Hastings' home passed to her eldest son Francis when he came of age, and the Countess moved to a rented house in Ashby-de-la-Zouche, also hiring a London house in the season, and other dwellings in the summer months.

About 1748 her associations and theology switched to the Calvinist Methodists. In 1743 she had denounced predestination, but her attitude may have been affected by John Wesley's lack of sympathy to the rich and GEORGE WHITEFIELD's respect. From the time of her conversion leaders of the social world were invited to hear Methodist exhorting in her London apartment, and later in her Chelsea residence. Various evangelical clergy were invited to speak, but George Whitefield was her favourite and she appointed him as her chaplain. A few aristocrats were converted, including Lord DARTMOUTH and Lady GERTRUDE HOTHAM, but others mocked. Together they decided that she would take control of Whitefield's connexion since he was so often absent in America, but

resistance from his societies prevented the implementation of this plan. The family's associations with Frederick, Prince of Wales and his Leicester House fraternity were used to protect evangelical preachers, and held prospects for Whitefield's advancement, but Frederick's death brought these prospects to an end.

Before 1741 she encouraged her servant DAVID TAYLOR, to go preaching in the north; she urged THOMAS MAXFIELD to become a lay preacher, and introduced JOHN BENNET to the Wesleys. The success of this pioneering ministry and her drawing-room meetings led her to the strategy of appointing large numbers of evangelical clergy as personal chaplains on assignment throughout the south of England. As a peeress she had the right to her own chaplains (no upper limit existed) who might hold Church of England services where she desired. Lady Huntingdon increasingly used this power to sponsor public evangelical Anglican services. Then in 1761 she sold her jewels in order to pay £698 to erect a chapel at Brighton, a popular resort. Further chapels were opened in the vicinity at Oat Hall where she leased a house, at Lewes in 1765, and at Tunbridge Wells in Kent where she purchased a house in 1768. A chapel was opened in Bath in 1765, and others followed in sundry other places in the 1770s.

Her aim seems to have been to provide an evangelical ministry where parish clergy were not sympathetic. The chapels were sometimes only open in the fashionable season, and prominent evangelical Anglican clergy including HENRY VENN and ROWLAND HILL accepted summer assignments to preach in them. Meanwhile she wrote strong letters to the bishops expressing her concern about the condition of the Church of England and purchased advowsons to give evangelical clergy parishes. She used her influence to criticize the Archbishop of Canterbury to the King, to oppose the Feather Tavern petition in 1772, to seek relief for dissenting clergy, and to suppress ungodly behaviour on the stage and in public life.

In 1768, in the wake of the exclusion of evangelicals from Oxford in the St Edmund's Hall incident, she established a training college for evangelicals with a call to the ministry. She wanted evangelicals of all types to make use of the college, and appointed a Wesleyan itinerant, JOSEPH BENSON, as the headmaster, and one of Wesley's Arminian friends, JOHN W. FLETCHER, the Vicar of Madeley, as non-resident president. Unfortunately her own dominating personality and intolerance of what she regarded as deviations from the faith meant that Benson's position soon became impossible, and after his dismissal and Fletcher's consequent resignation the college became restricted to Calvinist Methodists, particularly preachers for her chapels, and the needs of the connexion generally took precedence over their course. Her intense support for the Calvinist cause broadened Benson's dismissal into a debate over Calvinism, in which her intemperate approach (which included abruptly refusing to allow Wesley to speak in her chapels after August 1770) did nothing for harmony.

In 1779 the opening of a huge chapel in Spa Fields

provoked the local vicar, and the consistorial court of the diocese of London rejected her claim to unlimited right to build chapels. Somewhat pre-emptorily she reacted by licensing all her chapels under the Toleration Act, and required her chaplains to become dissenting clergy. Understandably most of those who had priest's orders in the church were reluctant to do so, and thereafter her connexion was much reduced and rather more isolated than previously.

The finances for this remarkable ministry were drawn from her personal fortune, but this was spent all too quickly, and after Whitefield willed her with his orphanage she inherited the debts from its destruction by fire. She thereafter struggled with financial impecunity.

The Countess outlived all her family except her eldest daughter Elizabeth who married Lord Rawdon (Moira) and did not sympathize with her mother's views. The strong, purposeful and somewhat undiplomatic approach which she took made her an effective personal evangelist but a bad leader of her connexion, and many of its preachers sought to escape her control and became Independent ministers. Not until 1790 did she arrange the continuation of her connexion by the formation of an association, and this took place just in time, for her death a year later would otherwise have resulted in her chapels falling into the unsympathetic hands of her heir. Lady ANNE AGNES ERSKINE (along with THOMAS HAWEIS and JOHN LLOYD) took her place as the practical head of the connection.

Manuscript material may be found in the Countess of Huntingdon's Connexion Records, Westminster College, Cambridge University, Cambridge, England and in the Hastings Family Records, Leicester County Record Office, Leicester, England.

BIBLIOGRAPHY
A Member of the Houses of Shirley and Hastings [A. C. H. Seymour], *The Life and Times of Selina Countess of Huntingdon* 2 vols (London, 1844)
F. F. Bretherton, *The Countess of Huntingdon*, WHS Lecture No. 6, (London, 1940)
DNB
M. Francis, 'Selina, Countess of Huntingdon (1707–1791)' (Oxford Univ. B. Litt. thesis, 1958)
C. F. Mullett, ed., *Dr Cheyne's Letters to Countess of Huntingdon* (San Marino, CA, 1940)
A. H. New, *The Coronet and the Cross* (London, 1858)
G. F. Nuttall, 'Howel Harris, and the "Grand Table": a Note on Religion and Politics 1744–50', *JEH*, 39, 4 (1988): 531–44
C. E. Welch, 'Lady Huntingdon's Plans', *Guildhall Studies in London History*, 2, 1 (1975): 31–40
C. E. Welch, *Spiritual Pilgrim: A Reassessment of the Life of the Countess of Huntingdon* (Cardiff, 1995)

PETER J. LINEHAM

Huntington, Joshua (b. Norwich, CT, USA, 31 Jan. 1786; d. Groton, CT, USA, 11 Sept. 1819). American Congregational minister and founder of AES. He was graduated from Yale College in 1804 and stayed to study theology under TIMOTHY DWIGHT, ASAHEL HOOKER and

JEDIDIAH MORSE. He was licensed to preach by the New London, Connecticut, Association in 1806. He was ordained in 1808 upon accepting the call to Old South Church in Boston as collegiate pastor. In 1811, he became the sole pastor of the church which he served until the end of his life. He married Susan Mansfield Huntington in 1809.

He originated early benevolent institutions of the church particularly as the founder of the American Education Society in 1815. He was also president of the Boston Society for the religious and moral instruction of the poor. He died of the typhus fever at age 34.

BIBLIOGRAPHY
AAP
J. G. Wilson and J. Fiske, eds, *Appleton's Cyclopaedia of American Biography* (New York, 1887)

LELAND EDWARD WILSHIRE

Huntington, William (b. Cranbrook, Kent, England, 2 Feb. 1745; d. Tunbridge Wells, Kent, England, 1 July 1813). Calvinist preacher. Born illegitimate, he was baptized and named after his putative father as William Hunt in November 1750. With little formal education, he undertook a wide variety of jobs. Having seduced a young woman in 1769 he moved from the area and changed his name to Huntington apparently to avoid discovery. He then formed an association with Mary Short, who was called Mrs Huntington, though it is unclear as to whether they were formally married. In the midst of poverty, he became convinced of sin and adopted a High-Calvinist theology which was confirmed to him in a vision. He associated with the Calvinistic Methodists in the Kingston area for a time, combining preaching with coal-heaving. He did not disguise his early misdemeanours and used the letters SS after his name, indicating that he was a 'Sinner Saved'.

In 1782 he moved to London and built himself Providence Chapel in Titchfield Street in which he ministered until it was burnt down in July 1810, having by then, it is claimed, gathered a congregation of up to 3,000 hearers securing him an income of £2,000 a year. By this time he was living comfortably in Cricklewood. Although the chapel was uninsured he soon secured sufficient funds (£10,000) to build a larger New Providence Chapel in Gray's Inn Road, indicating that he had attracted a large and affluent body of supporters. Opened in 1811, he ministered there for a further two years. He was, at the beginning of his ministry, to have been baptized as a believer but at the last minute decided against it; however, a considerable part of his London congregation was Baptist and he allowed others to conduct services of believers' baptism in his chapel.

Isolated by other clergy as an Antinomian, he readily entered into controversy with ROWLAND HILL, CALEB EVANS, JOHN RYLAND and others. He was frequently attacked by satirists and by the *Satirist*, a periodical, as well as by Crabbe, Southey, Macaulay and J. M. Rigg, the author of the *Dictionary of National Biography* entry, but received support from WILLIAM ROMAINE, with whom he had some intimacy, Carlyle's friend, John Sterling, J. C. PHILPOT and other High-Calvinist writers, including his biographer. His *God, the Guardian of the Poor and the Bank of Faith* (1784–1803) and *The Kingdom of Heaven Taken by Prayer* (1784) provoked similarly mixed reaction. In August 1808 he married Lady Sanderson, the widow of a former Lord Mayor of London in St Marylebone Parish Church. He wrote his own epitaph: 'Here lies the Coalheaver, beloved of his God, but abhorred of men. The omniscient Judge, at the great assize, shall ratify and confirm this, to the confusion of many thousands: for England and its metropolis shall know there hath been a prophet among them.' The *Evangelical Magazine* produced neither obituary nor memoir but reproduced the *Sussex Weekly Advertiser's* account of his funeral.

BIBLIOGRAPHY
DNB
T. Wright, *The Life of William Huntington, SS* (London, 1909)

J. H. Y. BRIGGS

Hurle, Fanny [Parker, Mrs John] (b. Kingston Deverill, Wiltshire, England, *c.* 1790; d. Longbridge, Deverill, England, 18 April 1858). Primitive Methodist (PM) itinerant preacher. Hurle, a well-brought-up young lady, came from a respectable, bigoted Anglican family. When she was about 25 she visited Wales, attended a Wesleyan chapel, was converted and stayed for a month, chiefly because she was apprehensive about her family's reactions. She persevered in spite of much opposition, becoming a class leader. However, when the PMs visited her area she joined them. Her considerable talents meant that she was quickly asked to preach and became an itinerant. She worked assiduously in Bath and Shefford (Berkshire), but her health was not strong and she was advised to retire. Hurle married (*circa* 1836). Her last illness, dropsy, was long and painful.

BIBLIOGRAPHY
PMMag (1858)

E. DOROTHY GRAHAM

Hutchings, John (b. Woollmiston, Somerset, England, *c.* 1716). Oxford Methodist, Anglican clergyman and Moravian. Hutchings matriculated from Pembroke College, Oxford, on 30 May 1734 at age 18. By 1737 INGHAM described him as a zealous member of the Holy Club. Graduating with a BA in 1738, he was ordained and acted as a curate to CHARLES KINCHIN at Dummer in Hampshire. JOHN WESLEY felt however that his witness was needed back at Oxford. He was present at the crucial lovefeast at Fetter Lane, London at the beginning of 1739, and met with six other evangelical clergy at the first clerical conference at Islington. He preached for GEORGE WHITEFIELD in Bristol but was unable to undertake open-air preaching despite the latter's urging. Wesley found him strong in faith but physically delicate. He eventually joined the Moravians and was enrolled as a 'married brother' at Fulneck as well as in London. Tyerman and others confuse him with Richard Hutchins of Lincoln College.

BIBLIOGRAPHY
PWHS, 5: 151

A. SKEVINGTON WOOD

Hutchins, William (b. Ansley, Warwickshire, England, 26 Nov. 1792; d. Hobart, Tasmania, Australia, 4 June 1841). Anglican clergyman and first Archdeacon of Van Diemen's Land (Tasmania). Son of the Vicar of Ansley, Hutchins was educated at Atherstone Grammar School and Pembroke College, Cambridge, where he graduated ninth wrangler in 1818. Among his friends at Pembroke were HENRY BLUNT and HENRY SIM and also William Broughton, the first Bishop of Australia who was to nominate Hutchins as archdeacon. Ordained (deacon 1821, priest 1822), he served as curate at Huddersfield in 1824 and in 1825 he was licensed as Curate-in-Charge of Wirksworth, Derbyshire, by Bishop HENRY RYDER. In 1829 he moved to Kirk Ireton, where in 1836, he received from Sir GEORGE GREY the invitation to Van Diemen's Land to which he sailed with the new governor, Sir JOHN FRANKLIN. He immediately impressed the colonists as 'a plain and practical man, gentlemanly but without affectation or cant'. He established the *Guardian*, a new church paper, superintended all the government schools and visited all the chaplaincies in the colony four times every year. He had 18 parish churches built and manned in five years. He invigorated the church with a fresh vision of its role in society and did much good for the convicts and Aborigines. His untimely death was deeply mourned and a celebrated Anglican school was named in his honour.

BIBLIOGRAPHY
ADB
D. B. Clarke, *William Hutchins 1792–1841* (Hobart, Australia, 1986)
B. W. Rait, *Official History of the Hutchins School* (Hobart, Australia, 1935)

DUDLEY CLARKE

Hutchinson, Francis (b. Ireland, 18 Jan. 1802; d. 3 Apr. 1833). Early Brethren leader. The son of Sir Samuel Synge, Archdeacon of Killala in the Irish Church, he was one of a number of pious, extreme evangelicals – JOHN NELSON DARBY, JOHN G. BELLETT, EDWARD CRONIN, and ANTHONY NORRIS GROVES – who, disaffected with the Established Church, and enamoured of prophecy and 'primitive' worship, came together to establish the 'Plymouth Brethren'.

It was at his house, 9, Fitzwilliam Square, Dublin, that

the group's earliest meetings were held, in 1828–9. The group moved significantly toward the formation of a sect when in November 1829 Hutchinson, a layman, became the first among them to conduct a communion service independent of the prayer-book.

BIBLIOGRAPHY
W. B. Neatby, *History of the Plymouth Brethren* (London, 1902)
H. Pickering, *Chief Men Among the Brethren* (London, 1918)

JONATHAN BURKE CUTMORE

Hutchinson, George Watson (b. Hagley, Worcester-shire, England, 1783; d. Tutbury, Staffordshire, England, 11 May 1818). Anglican clergyman. Hutchinson was educated at Birmingham and Lincoln College, Oxford. He performed an assiduous ministry at Tutbury, first as curate (1806–12) and then, probably itself a mark of the esteem in which he was held, as rector (1812–18). He established a parish library, a writing school for poor children and a weekly class for adults, as well as a Friday association to help the CMS, the Bible Society and the Jews' Society. On Sundays he conducted a class for children in the local cotton mill at 8 a.m., followed by Sunday school and adult classes with further services at 1.30 p.m. and 5.30 p.m. to 8 p.m. in the evening. He failed, however, to abolish the notoriously dissipated Statute Fair.

BIBLIOGRAPHY
CO, XVII: 482

ARTHUR POLLARD

Hutchinson, Jonathan (b. Gedney, Lincolnshire, England, 7 Feb. 1760; d. Gedney, Lincolnshire, England, 1 April 1835). Quaker farmer. Though inclined to 'speculative unbelief' in early manhood, Hutchinson became a decided Friend and in his late forties was recorded as a minister. JOSEPH JOHN GURNEY, his junior by 27 years, described Hutchinson's ministry as simple, concise and evangelical, claiming friendship with him as 'one of the choicest privileges of my life'.

Hutchinson read widely, reflected deeply, and was an assiduous letter-writer, corresponding with many notable ministering Friends. Frequently at the yearly meeting of British Quakers, he was on its 1814 committee to judge the appeal of the London Friend Thomas Foster against disownment for holding and propagating Unitarian views – a significant episode in promoting evangelical emphasis among British Quakers.

Hutchinson's life is, in one sense, remarkable for its uneventfulness, living as he did in a small village remote from even the main part of Lincolnshire. Yet his influence on J. J. Gurney and on others was considerable and he must be reckoned a significant figure.

BIBLIOGRAPHY
J. Forster, *Extracts from the Letters of J. Hutchinson with some Brief Notices of his Life and Character* (London, 1841)

EDWARD H. MILLIGAN

Hutchison, William (b. Insh, parish of Kingussie and Insh, Inverness-shire, Scotland, 1781; d. 1850). Pioneer preacher with the Independents and later with the Baptists. Hutchison, described as a 'merchant, grocer' in the 1841 Census returns, probably combined his trade with his activities as an itinerant preacher and pastor. Apparently converted about 1801, he became pastor of the Independent church at Kingussie, and later espousing Baptist principles, he served the Baptist church at Kingussie from the time of its foundation in 1808 until his death. He was supported at different stages by various bodies, including the HALDANES' church at Leith Walk, Edinburgh, and from 1819 by the Baptist Highland Mission; later he was employed by the Baptist Home Missionary Society for Scotland. He accompanied WILLIAM TULLOCH and PETER GRANT on preaching tours, and was active in the northern Highlands and Hebrides, including Skye and Tiree. His gravestone at Insh carries the following inscription: 'Here lies Wm Hutchison's remains or dust / His soul in glory now enjoys its rest / By heavenly aid he ran the Christian race / At twenty years he knew the path of peace / For fifty years he served the church below'.

BIBLIOGRAPHY
D. E. Meek, 'The Independent and Baptist Churches of Highland Perthshire and Strathspey', *Transactions of the Gaelic Society of Inverness*, 56 (1989–91): 269–343
Report of the Baptist Highland Mission (1822–3)
Report of the Baptist Home Missionary Society for Scotland (1828)

DONALD E. MEEK

Hutton, James (b. London, 3 Sept. 1715; d. Godstone, Surrey, England, 3 May 1795). Bookseller and founder of the Moravian church in England. He was the son of John Hutton, a non-juring clergyman, and Elizabeth Ayscough, a second cousin of Isaac Newton. The Huttons settled in College Street, Westminster, took Westminster boys in to board and educated their son in the school. As the head usher in the school, 1713–33, was their next door neighbour, the younger Samuel Wesley, as CHARLES WESLEY was educated there and JOHN WESLEY was a frequent visitor, and as the two families had a common interest in the world of religious societies, it is not surprising that Hutton was early introduced to Oxford Methodism. He and his sister were converted at home under the preaching of John Wesley, and, prevented by apprenticeship from accompanying the Wesley brothers to Georgia, he saw them off at Gravesend. The Hutton house gathered correspondence for Georgia, and Hutton received letters from John Wesley, some on business and the supply of books, some edifying and designed to be read at the religious societies. Meanwhile Hutton completed his apprenticeship as a bookseller, and set up on his own at the 'Bible and Sun' near Temple Bar, premises which he opened to the religious societies. When the Wesleys returned, he published many of their early works, and later the journals of GEORGE WHITEFIELD.

The connection with John Wesley was not an easy one. Even after his conversion, he distressed the Hutton parents by doctrinaire and inconsiderate behaviour at a meeting in their house, and he introduced Hutton to representatives of a cause which was to divide them, that of Moravianism. On 7 February 1738 PETER BÖHLER, Schulius, NEISSER and Richter, in effect the fourth Moravian diplomatic mission to London, arrived. The principal task of the first two was to answer a request of the Georgia Trustees for catechists to instruct blacks; but they were also to make contact with Oxford students through John Wesley. He found them lodgings close to the Hutton house where he was staying, and Hutton was soon assisting them at meetings by translating from the Latin. Böhler's success in this work led him to found a new religious society at Fetter Lane, with rules advised by himself. These rules did not include the standard requirement of the religious societies of membership of the Church of England, though the members were mostly Anglican and there were as yet no English members of the *Brudergemeine*. Fetter Lane was an English version of a Moravian band, and among those converted in contact with it, John Wesley had had an application for full membership of the Moravian Unity refused in Georgia, and when he, by no means the first, set out for Herrnhut in the summer of 1738, he was taking a step which commonly led to full membership. Hutton himself followed this route in April 1739, and began what proved to be a voluminous correspondence with ZINZENDORF himself.

It was Wesley who took the new turn. Excluded from Moravian communion on the continent as a *homo perturbatus*, he found increasing difficulty with the Fetter Lane Society on his return. These troubles he ascribed to doctrines of 'stillness' he wrongly attributed to Molther; Hutton, perhaps equally mistakenly, ascribed them to the self-will of the Wesley brothers and their undue influence over susceptible young women. The fact was that a society always under Moravian influence had come to the point of accepting full Moravian fellowship and control, and those to whom this was impossible must withdraw. This the Wesley brothers did, taking with them most of the women in the society and a minority of the men. Of the remainder Hutton was the chief, and as such played a notable part in the diplomacy by which, in the 'forties, Zinzendorf obtained statutory recognition of the Unity as an 'antient episcopal church', and privileges, including exemption from military service, for its members in the American colonies. In 1741 he helped found the Society for the Furtherance of the Gospel, and was for many years an officer. When in the early 'fifties the consequences of chronic over-borrowing, principally on the Dutch money market, came home to roost, Hutton worked strenuously to redeem the catastrophe. The imbroglio seems in no way to have reduced his respect for Zinzendorf, and he continued as a public apologist for the Unity.

His troubles with the Wesleys (with whom he was fully reconciled in the early 'seventies) at Fetter Lane taught Hutton that the work needed female supervision, and, with this in view, on his visit to Marienborn in 1740, he was married by Zinzendorf himself to Louisa Brandt (1709–78), the daughter of a protestant pastor driven from Neuchâtel. She had come to Moravianism via Inspirationism and deism. This connection enabled Zinzendorf to employ him in 1748 and 1756–63 to consolidate the early work of the Unity in Switzerland. A kindly man, Hutton was comforted in his last years by the kindness of two ladies connected with the evangelical Inglis family whom he had met in the course of his own charitable work and who took him into their home.

BIBLIOGRAPHY

D. Benham, *Memoirs of James Hutton* (London, 1856)

H-C. Hahn and H. Reichel, eds, *Zinzendorf und die Herrnhuter Bruder* (Hamburg, Germany, 1977)

Moravian Church House, London, and in the Archiv der Bruder-unitat, Herrnhut, Oberlausitz, Germany, manuscript correspondence of James Hutton

C. J. Podmore, 'The Fetter Lane Society, 1738', *PWHS* 46 (1988): 125–53

C. J. Podmore, 'The Fetter Lane Society', *Ibid.*, 47 (1990): 156–86

Unitas Fratrum 29/30 (1991) [A number devoted to Switzerland]

P. Wernle, *Der Schweizerische Protestantismus im 18. Jahrhundert*, 3 vols (Tubingen, 1923–5)

The *Journal* and *Letters* of John Wesley in both the Standard and Bicentennial Editions

W. R. WARD

Hyde, Alvan (b. Norwich, CT, BNA, 2 Feb. 1768; d. Lee, MA, USA, 4 Dec. 1833). Congregational minister. Born and raised on a farm, Hyde graduated from Dartmouth College (1788), then prepared for the ministry under CHARLES BACKUS and STEPHEN WEST, two Edwardsians of New Divinity theological sympathies. In 1792 Hyde was ordained to the pastoral charge in Lee (Berkshire County), Massachusetts, where he remained throughout his career. Almost immediately after settling at Lee, Hyde's congregation experienced a revival which resulted in the addition of 110 members. Some contemporaries dated this revival as the beginning of the Second Great Awakening in New England.

Hyde prepared between thirty and forty men for the ministry, impressing upon them the high Calvinism of the New Divinity. For over two decades he served nearby Williams College – the birthplace of modern American missions – as a trustee and vice-president. A dedicated and beloved minister, Hyde published nearly twenty sermons, contributed to various evangelical journals, compiled the life of STEPHEN WEST (1819), and wrote an essay on the state of infants (1830).

BIBLIOGRAPHY

AAP, 2: 300–6

R. Birdsall, *Berkshire County* (New Haven, CT, 1959)

A. Hyde, Jr, *Memoir of Rev. Alvan Hyde, D.D. of Lee, Mass.* (Boston, MA, 1835)

DAVID W. KLING

I

Ince, Henry (b. Penzance, Cornwall, England, 1736; d. Gittisham nr Honiton, Devon, England, 10 Sept. 1808). Engineer and Methodist pioneer. A Methodist pioneer and engineer in Gibraltar, he joined the Queen's Regiment in 1754. Drafted to Gibraltar in 1767–8, he entered the Soldier Artificer Company (the first Royal Engineer unit), and in 1782, now sergeant-major, took charge of the building of the famous 'galleries' for the defence of the Rock. He retired as lieutenant in 1803 and died at Gittisham near Honiton.

BIBLIOGRAPHY
JCMHA, 3, 1 (1968): 14 f. and references there

A. F. WALLS

Ingelow, Jean (b. Boston, Lincolnshire, England, 17 March 1820; d. London, 20 July 1897). Poet, novelist, and children's writer. After her father's bank had failed in 1826 Ingelow was educated at home with her brothers. Her evangelical upbringing continued in Suffolk where her father became a manager of a bank in 1834. A family friend, the Curate of Tamworth, Edward Hastie, edited her first publication, *A Rhyming Chronicle of Incidents and Feelings* (1850). *Allerton and Dreux* (1851), a tale of doctrinal dispute between two Anglican clergymen, was the first of her six novels. She edited the evangelically inclined *Youth Magazine* for a year (1857–8) and published her own pseudonymous contributions under the title, *Tales of Orris* (1860). Her poetry, particularly the 1863 collection, proved very successful and gained her the acquaintance of Tennyson, Browning, Christina Rossetti and Edmund Gosse and the close friendship of John Ruskin. Her popularity in America was such that a group of American authors petitioned Queen Victoria to make her poet laureate.

BIBLIOGRAPHY
F. Hays, *Women of the Day* (London, 1885)
M. Peters, *Jean Ingelow: Victorian Poetess* (Ipswich, 1972)

ELISABETH JAY

Ingham, Benjamin (b. Ossett, Yorkshire, England, 11 June 1712; d. Aberford, Yorkshire, 2 Dec. 1772). Anglican clergyman then Moravian minister. Son of William and Susannah Ingham, Benjamin was educated at Batley Grammar School and Queen's College, Oxford where

in 1733 he met JOHN and CHARLES WESLEY, an encounter which led him to become an 'Oxford Methodist' and to adopt a disciplined lifestyle in the pursuit of holiness. As part of this endeavour he began keeping a diary, following a pattern suggested by CHARLES WESLEY. The diary from September 1733 to August 1734 is in the Methodist Church Archives, Manchester and has been published.

He graduated BA in 1734 and returned briefly to Ossett, where he conducted religious meetings in his mother's house and did some teaching. He visited the Wesley family at Epworth, who gave him the nickname 'Nathaniel' (cf. John 1:47). In June 1735 he was ordained at Christ Church, Oxford, and in October he accompanied the Wesley brothers and CHARLES DELAMOTTE to Georgia to preach to the native population. The mission was unsuccessful and early in 1737 Ingham returned to England, but not before he had experienced an evangelical conversion.

While abroad he was much impressed by the Moravians, believing them to be 'more like the Primitive Christians than any other Church now in the world' (*Journal*, quoted in Tyerman, 1873: 68). His visit, along with JOHN WESLEY, to their headquarters at Herrnhut and to Count ZINZENDORF at Marienborn confirmed his attachment to them. By April 1738 his societies in Yorkshire were multiplying and to assist him in the work, Ingham twice requested that JOHANN TÖLTSCHIG, a Moravian whom he had met in Georgia, be allowed to return with him from Germany. Toltschig came to Yorkshire in 1739, to be followed by PETER BÖHLER in 1741.

Meanwhile Ingham was also involved with the growing evangelical network centred on the society at Fetter Lane, London. He visited the 'Cambridge Methodists' in December 1738 and went on to kindle the revival in Bedford. Following the significant Fetter Lane lovefeast on New Year's Day 1739 he returned to Yorkshire and began preaching, at first in the churches and then, as pulpits were closed to him, in houses, barns and open fields, with such success that by mid-August his societies numbered about forty. The 'stillness' crisis in the Fetter Lane society which provoked the withdrawal of the Wesleys in 1740 affected their relations with Ingham, although he had attempted to take up a mediating position in the controversy. The work in the north widened until it embraced much of the West Riding and the neighbouring parts of Lancashire. The fifty societies in this area were placed under Moravian control in July

1742 and in 1744 Ingham gave them land for a settlement at Fulneck, which replaced Smith House as the Moravian headquarters in the north.

His evangelistic work brought Ingham in contact with the family of the Earl of Huntingdon, whose youngest daughter, Lady Margaret Hastings, he married in November in 1741 (MARGARET INGHAM). From this time his home was at Aberford, Yorkshire, from which he continued as an evangelist at large. Little by little he drew away from the Moravians. Zinzendorf's letter to the Archbishop of Canterbury in June 1749 did not include Ingham among the Moravian hierarchy and in 1752 Ingham withdrew his son Ignatius from the Brethren school at Fulneck. The separation was complete by 1754. There were now some 80 congregations of 'Inghamites'. At the Leeds Methodist Conference of 1755, Charles Wesley, always closer to Ingham than John, urged the amalgamation of his societies with those of the Methodists but John Wesley resisted the suggestion. So the Inghamites remained an independent, somewhat loosely organized, 'connexion' extending over Lancashire, Yorkshire and Westmorland. The first chapel was built at Wheatley, Lancashire in 1750 and Ingham ordained his own preachers in 1756.

In 1760 Ingham fell under the influence of the teaching of ROBERT SANDEMAN and JOHN GLAS, who held intellectualist views on faith. He sent his two leading preachers to Scotland to meet Sandeman and Glas and they returned converted to Sandemanian doctrine and discipline. The spread of these views – 'the horrid blast from the north' in the words of WILLIAM ROMAINE – led to embittered controversy within the societies and coupled with the erosion of Ingham's personal authority, chaos was the result. Many of the preachers left and ultimately only 13 societies were left, a handful of which still survive in the Pennines. Ingham never recovered from this blow; he remained an elder of his church at Tadcaster until his death. His Georgia Journal is in Lincoln Cathedral Library. Rylands Library, Manchester, English MSS 1062 is a copy of a manuscript account of Ingham and his work by William Batty.

SELECT WRITINGS

B. Ingham, *A Collection of Hymns for Societies* (Leeds, England, 1748)
—, *A Discourse on the Faith and Hope of the Gospel* (Leeds, England, 1763)

BIBLIOGRAPHY

Al. Ox.
D. F. Clarke, 'Benjamin Ingham (1712–1772), with special reference to His Relations with the Churches ... of His Time' (Leeds Univ. M.Phil. thesis, 1971)
DNB
R. P. Heitzenrater, ed., *Diary of an Oxford Methodist, Benjamin Ingham 1733–1734* (Durham, NC, 1985)
R. W. Thompson, *Benjamin Ingham and the Inghamites* (Kendal, England, 1958)
L. Tyerman, *The Oxford Methodists*, (London, 1873): 57–154

E. ALAN ROSE

Ingham, Lady **Margaret** [née Hastings] (b. Ashby-de-la-Zouch, Leicestershire, England, 1700; d. Aberford, Yorkshire, England, 5 May 1768). Moravian and Methodist supporter. She was the daughter of Theophilus, seventh Earl of Huntingdon, by his second wife, Frances, and thus was the half-sister of the eighth Earl of Huntingdon. After her father's death and her mother's remarriage, she went to live with her half-sister, Lady ELIZABETH HASTINGS at Ledston in Yorkshire. There she met BENJAMIN INGHAM, a protege of Lady Betty, and became very actively involved in obtaining support for the Moravian missions which he brought to her attention. After Lady Betty's death in 1739, her sisters left Ledston, now the property of their nephew, Lord Hastings, and settled at Ashby Place, Ashby-de-la-Zouch. Lady Margaret did not join them, but remained in Yorkshire to be near Ingham.

Despite considerable opposition from relations and friends she married Ingham at Aberford by licence issued the previous day on 12 November 1741. (She was 12 years his senior and greatly above him in social station.) Four years later their only son Ignatius was born. Ingham resented the objections to their marriage, and it was several years before he was reconciled with the Hastings family. After she was widowed, Selina, Countess of HUNTINGDON paid at least one visit to her sister-in-law. Meanwhile Ingham had turned over his Methodist societies in Yorkshire to the Moravians, and assisted in the establishment of Fulneck. When he left the Moravians under Sandemanian influence he formed his own connexion. She seems at various times to have patronized the Moravians and Calvinistic Methodists, although she also appears to have supported her husband on his extensive itinerations. She corresponded with Count ZINZENDORF, and with JOHN BERRIDGE, sending a donation towards clothing his lay preachers.

BIBLIOGRAPHY

Aberford parish register
Leicestershire Record Office, original letters
A. C. H. Seymour, *The Life and Times of Selina, the Countess of Huntingdon* (London, 1844)
L. Tyerman, *The Oxford Methodists* (London, 1873)

EDWIN WELCH AND PETER J. LINEHAM

Ingham, Richard (b. Heptonstall, Yorkshire, England, 1810; d. Halifax, Yorkshire, England, 1 June 1873). Minister in the New Connexion of General Baptists and author. His father was a founder and deacon of the influential hill top church at Heptonstall Slack and his mother belonged to a notable local family, the Gibsons. His uncle, of the same name, was the minister; and another uncle, Jonathan, was also a minister of the same denomination. Richard worked for a while in his father's business of cotton-spinning and manufacture before training for the ministry in the academy at Wisbeach. Subsequently he was the first minister at Tetley Street, Bradford, where he built up a strong church. His subsequent charges were Louth; North Parade, Halifax;

Vale, Todmorden; North Parade; and Infirmary Street, Bradford.

He was a voluminous writer on the subject of baptism. He begins his second volume, *Subjects of Baptism*, 'I feel . . . a tiredness of this controversy. I shall endeavour, however, to unite justice with brevity'. The book is full of lengthy quotations and has 650 pages! In another book *Pre-Millenial Thoughts on the Church* he argued for the plurality of elders and consequently sought to have associate ministers in his churches.

BIBLIOGRAPHY
General Baptist Year Book 1873: 58
E. C. Starr, ed., *A Baptist Bibliography*, 25 vols (New York, 1947–76)

DAVID B. MILNER

Inglis, Henry David (b. Edinburgh, 10 July 1757; d. Edinburgh, 12 May 1806). Advocate and Scotch Baptist elder. Inglis' mother was a daughter of Colonel JAMES GARDINER, defeated at Prestonpans in 1745, whose conversion is recorded by PHILIP DODDRIDGE. She was a granddaughter of the Earl of BUCHAN. In 1757 Inglis was converted and followed legal by divinity studies. Influenced by CHARLES STUART, he joined the Independent Church in 1776, was baptized in 1777, by ARCHIBALD MCLEAN, and was made a co-elder with McLean and WILLIAM BRAIDWOOD in 1784. In addition to his pastoral duties in the Scotch Baptist Church, Inglis preached in the villages around Edinburgh, and in 1794 qualified as an advocate. He was drawn to an evangelistic ministry to prisoners under sentence of death, and his 'Letters to the Public concerning the Execution of James Mills' was still in print in 1850.

SELECT WRITINGS
H. D. Inglis, *Letters, Tracts and Sermons*, with Memoirs (Edinburgh, 1812)

BIBLIOGRAPHY
New Evangelical Magazine, 2 (London, 1816)

DEREK B. MURRAY

Inglis, John (b. Minnyhive, Glencairn, Scotland, 14 July 1808; d. Kirkcowan, Scotland, 18 July 1891). Stonemason and Reformed Presbyterian missionary, New Zealand and New Hebrides, 1844–76. Educated at Glasgow University and the Reformed Presbytery's Divinity Hall, Paisley, Inglis was licensed 14 June 1841. He was ordained and set apart as a missionary to the Maori of New Zealand on 26 September 1843. He married Miss Jessie McClymont 11 April 1844; they sailed on 6 August 1844 and reached New Zealand on 11 January 1845. Initially he assisted Reverend J. Duncan in the Manawatu, then moved to Wellington because there were sufficient missionaries present. His church approved his seeking a field in West Polynesia. JOHN

GEDDIE on Aneityum, New Hebrides, sought his help and he arrived there on 1 July 1852. They made a strong and complementary team. After Geddie's death in 1872 Inglis became the father of the mission, showing 'tact and wisdom, kindliness and firmness, persevering energy and eminent zeal'. By 1860 the population of some 3,500 was under instruction, with indigenous patterns of church life and a vigorous mission to the unevangelized islands. Inglis edited *The Slave Trade in the New Hebrides* (Edinburgh, 1872). He, Geddie, and Copeland translated the Bible into Aneityumese (New Testament, 1863, Old Testament, 1879). He retired in 1876, supervised the printing of Old Testament, wrote a *Dictionary of Aneityumese* (London, 1882) and two valuable accounts of the work: *In the New Hebrides* (London, 1887) and *Bible Illustrations from the New Hebrides* (London, 1890). He was awarded the DD by Glasgow University 1883. Mrs Inglis died in 1885.

BIBLIOGRAPHY
J. G. Miller, *Live! A History of Church Planting in the New Hebrides to 1880*, 1 (Sydney, 1980)

J. GRAHAM MILLER

Inglis, Sir Robert Harry (b. 12 Jan. 1786; d. London, 5 May 1855). MP. Inglis was the son of Sir Hugh Inglis, Bart, chairman of the East India Company and MP (1802–6). Inglis was educated at Winchester, receiving a final year's personal tuition from the warden, Bishop Huntingford, and at Christ Church, Oxford, graduating BA in 1806. He entered Lincoln's Inn in 1806 and was called to the bar in 1808 but did not practise. Through his school-friend Henry Addington he became private secretary to Lord Sidmouth (Home Secretary from 1812) before being appointed commissioner for investigating the debts of the nabobs of the Carnatic district of India (1814–30). On Sidmouth's suggestion, Inglis acted for the government in refusing admission to Queen Caroline at George IV's coronation (1821). Inglis married in 1807, but was childless. In 1815 he and his wife were appointed guardians of the nine children of HENRY THORNTON, whose devotional works Inglis later edited. E. M. Forster presents a sympathetic picture of their life at Battersea Rise in *Marianne Thornton*. Inglis succeeded to the baronetcy in 1820 and became DCL of Oxford in 1826.

From May 1824 to November 1826 Inglis was MP for Dundalk and from February 1828 for Ripon. He opposed the repeal of the Test and Corporation Acts in 1828, and made his reputation by two major speeches against Catholic emancipation. In February 1829 he defeated Robert Peel for the representation of Oxford University on the Catholic question. He became the acknowledged Commons spokesman of the clergy, urbane but intransigent. He denounced parliamentary reform, church reform, Jewish relief and the admission of Dissenters to the ancient universities. He was vehemently anti-Catholic, reacting particularly strongly against the proposal in 1845 to make a permanent endowment to the Irish Catholic seminary at Maynooth. He carried an address condemning the foreign slave trade (1838), supported first MICHAEL T. SADLER and then LORD ASHLEY in the cause of factory reform and demanded parliamentary grants for church extension. He generally acted with Lord Derby's Protectionists from 1846 until his retirement from the Commons in January 1854. Although incapable of eloquence, Inglis gained respect and even affection as a redoubtable champion of the existing constitution in church and state.

Inglis delighted in giving London dinner parties and in undertaking foreign travel. He became fellow (and fellow of the Royal Society, eventually vice-president) of the Society of Antiquaries, a commissioner on the public records, president of the Literary Club, antiquary of the Royal Academy and a trustee of the British Museum. He was a supporter of evangelical societies such as the CMS and the London Clerical Education Society, and equally of wider church societies such as the Clergy Orphan Society and the Society of the Sons of the Clergy. His piety, nourished successively by Percy Chapel, Clapham Parish Church and St George's, Bloomsbury, was distinctly evangelical and yet, like that of his college friend Reginald Heber, marked by a devotion to the forms of the Church of England. Shaftesbury (Lord Ashley) summarized Inglis' character, public and private, as 'Pure-minded, affectionate, true, incorruptible'. There is a collection of Inglis' papers in Canterbury Cathedral Library.

BIBLIOGRAPHY
J. C. Colquoun, *William Wilberforce* (London, 1866): 337–66
E. M. Forster, *Marianne Thornton* (London, 1956)
E. Hodder, *The Life and Work of the Seventh Earl of Shaftesbury, K.G.*, 2 (London 1886): 522

DAVID WILLIAM BEBBINGTON

Ingram, James (b. c. 1719; d. Ludlow, Shropshire, England, 1788). Welsh Methodist exhorter and Independent minister. Little is know of his early days. Ingram first appears in November 1742 when he became HOWELL HARRIS's travelling companion and clerk; at that time he lived at Cwmbrith near Llandrindod in Radnorshire. In 1744 he was press-ganged into the army, but after the intervention of MARMADUKE GWYNNE, the Countess of HUNTINGDON and others, he was released.

Following the controversy that occurred among the Welsh Methodists in 1750, Ingram disappears from view, but it is believed that he joined the Independents at Maesyronnen in Radnorshire. In the 1770s he became minister of the Independent church at Ludlow.

BIBLIOGRAPHY
DWB
G. M. Roberts, ed., *Hanes Methodistiaeth Galfinaidd Cymru*, 1 (Caernarfon, 1973): 287–8

GERAINT TUDUR

Innes, William (b. Gifford, East Lothian, Scotland, 29 March 1770; d. Edinburgh, 3 March 1855). Scottish Baptist pastor. Innes was the son of a Church of Scotland parish minister, and was ordained chaplain to Stirling Castle and third minister of the charge of Stirling in 1793. In 1799, caught up in the HALDANE movement, he resigned his charge, becoming pastor of the tabernacle in Dundee. In 1800 he came to Edinburgh to minister to the group who formed in 1810 Elder Street Open Communion Baptist Church. He carried on business as a bookseller, but became insolvent in 1836. Exonerated by his deacons he continued to be honoured in Edinburgh Christian circles as a prime mover in all religious enterprises. 'Little children loved him.'

BIBLIOGRAPHY
A. M. Baines, *History of Dublin Street Baptist Church* [privately printed] (Edinburgh, 1958)
W. Innes, *Instruction for Young Enquirers* (7th edn, Edinburgh, 1850; Gaelic edn, Edinburgh, 1827; Welsh edn, Merthyr Tydfil, Wales, 1832)
—, *Political Economy of the New Testament* (Edinburgh, 1839)

DEREK B. MURRAY

Inskip, John S(wanel) (b. Huntington, Huntingdonshire, England, 10 Apr. 1816; d. Ocean Grove, NJ, USA, 7 Mar. 1884). Methodist Episcopal pastor, editor, first president of the National Camp Meeting Association, evangelist, and holiness advocate. Inskip emigrated to the United States with his parents at age five, settling at Wilmington, Delaware, and then Marshallton, Pennsylvania. He was converted (1832) within the context of the MEC through the influence of the future Bishop, L. Scott. He was licensed to preach (1835) and began itinerating under the supervision of the presiding elder. In 1836 he was taken into the Philadelphia Conference on trial and appointed to Cecil circuit, Maryland. There he met Martha Jane Foster [Inskip-Bateman] (born Cecil Country, Maryland, 11 August 1819; died Eggleston Heights, Florida, 26 December 1890). They were married 1 November 1836. Together they worked in various appointments. There were large numbers of conversions. He became popular as a revival and camp meeting speaker. An ardent abolitionist, Inskip worked for that cause within and without the church.

Ministerial credentials were transferred to the Ohio Conference (1845) where he served in Cincinnati, Dayton and Urbana. At Urbana, he became involved in the 'promiscuous seating' controversy. His church had decided that families should sit together for worship. He was censored by the Ohio Conference and responded by writing *Methodism Explained and Defended* (Cincinnati, 1851). He also appealed to the 1852 General Conference of the MEC where he delivered a six-hour address on the issue which caused the conference to reverse the decision of the Ohio Conference. Thereafter, Inskip transferred to the New York Conference.

During the early years of the Civil War, Inskip served as a chaplain (May 1861–summer 1862). Martha Inskip accompanied her husband who had to return to civilian life because of illness. Inskip had long sought the experience of sanctification, but without result. After their return to New York, Martha Inskip began to attend the Tuesday meetings of PHOEBE PALMER and then experienced sanctification under the instruction of Sarah Lankford (*see* SARAH PALMER) at the Sing Sing camp meeting (19 August 1864). John Inskip had the same experience on 28 August 1864.

The Inskips continued to pastor (until 1871) but became increasingly involved in the promotion of holiness causes. He joined with William B. Osborn, presiding elder of the South Jersey Conference, to establish (1867) a 'national' Camp Meeting Association of which John Inskip was elected the first president. He established a publishing house for the association, served as evangelist throughout the USA and edited *The Christian Standard and Home Journal*.

In June, 1880, Inskip, William McDonald, J. A. Wood and wives embarked on an around-the-world evangelistic tour. They preached and sang in England, India, Ceylon [now Sri Lanka] and Australia. Returning to Philadelphia, Inskip worked for the association and devoted himself to editorial work. He preached the opening sermon, 'Holiness to the Lord,' at the 1883 National Camp Meeting (Pitman Grove, New Jersey). Soon after he had a stroke, and after a few days, died.

Inskip was not a trained theologian or scholar, but an effective speaker who combined a forceful style with an emotional appeal. Personal papers of John Inskip are preserved at Drew University and Asbury Theological Seminary. A diary of Martha Inskip 11 June 1881 to May 1890 has been preserved and is available on film at Asbury Theological Seminary. An edition is being prepared by K. O. Brown.

BIBLIOGRAPHY

J. E. Ayers, *The Holiness Revival of the Past Century* (Philadelphia, PA, no date)

L. E. Breeze, 'The Inskips: Union in Holiness,' *Methodist History* 13 (1975), 25–45

K. O. Brown, 'Leadership in the National Holiness Association' (Drew Univ. Ph.D. diss., 1988)

DAB
EWM

DAVID BUNDY

Ireland, James (b. Beaminster, Dorset, England, 1724; d. Bristol, England, 9 July 1814). Benefactor. Considered the JOHN THORNTON of the west of England, he was a wealthy Bristol sugar merchant and shipowner who resided at Brislington Hall as the first squire there. JOHN WESLEY, JOHN W. FLETCHER and WILLIAM ROMAINE, among other leading figures, were welcomed to his home and he corresponded with them. He was a magistrate and High Sherriff of Somerset. Concerned to assist the poor both in his own area and elsewhere, he was also generous with time and money to increase the number of evangelical clergy through training ordinands. With his help the Bristol Clerical Education Society was launched in 1795. He was no lover of ideological disputes and maintained firm links with both camps during

the Calvinistic controversy from 1770. Ireland apparently had a second home in the south of France and was able to take Fletcher there to restore his health.

A. SKEVINGTON WOOD

Irons, Joseph (b. Ware, Hertfordshire, England, 5 Nov. 1785; d. Camberwell, London, 3 April 1852). Independent minister and preacher. Described as a popular evangelical preacher, Irons commenced preaching in March 1808 under the auspices of the London Itinerant Society, founded in 1797, after having been converted by WILLIAM A. GUNN, an evangelical Anglican minister who seceded to become a Congregationalist. Irons' first sermon was preached at a blacksmith's shop in Dulwich. Following the pattern of many evangelists, he soon turned to the settled pastorate, and while running a school near Ware served at Wotton nearby, 1810–12, and thereafter at Hoddesdon, 1812–15, Sawston, Cambridgeshire, 1815–18, and at Camberwell until his death.

The initial invitation to Camberwell came to him from the trustees of Camden Chapel (which subsequently became a proprietary chapel within the Church of England where HENRY MELVILL, sometimes called 'the Evangelical Chrysostom', preached to crowded congregations, 1829–43) but the trustees seem to have decided against proceeding. But such was the popular support that an invitation came to him from a significant part of the congregation, and the upper room of a carpenter's shop was fitted up for the purpose of worship and preaching, and a church of 12 members formed. Within 12 months the Grove Chapel, 1819, was erected for him, a Mr Samuel Carter being the principal benefactor in the sum of £2,000, and enlarged twenty years later. During Irons' ministry in Camberwell, though the church discipline at the Grove was of an over-strict order, over 1,200 new members were admitted. While the minister and congregation promoted the Home Missionary Society as vital to evangelism in England at large, in its own area the church ran Sunday schools, a Tract and a Dorcas Society. It supported the Aged Pilgrims' Friend Society and its theology was distinctly both Protestant and Calvinist. Irons' son, William Josiah Irons (1812–83), a graduate of Queen's College, Oxford was ordained into the Church of England, and became a prebendary of St Paul's and Bampton lecturer at Oxford. Though accused of Tractarianism, he also had connections with the Victoria Institute.

BIBLIOGRAPHY

G. Bayfield, *A Memoir of the Rev. J. Irons* (London, 1852)
DNB

J. H. Y. BRIGGS

Ironside, Samuel (b. Sheffield, England, 9 Sept. 1814; d. Hobart, Tasmania, Australia, 24 April 1897). Wesleyan minister in New Zealand and Australia. The brother of Isaac, a political activist and social reformer, Samuel was trained at Hoxton Theological Institution for missionary service, and arrived in New Zealand in 1839. From December 1840 until 1843 he led the Cloudy Bay mission to the Maori of Marlborough, which collapsed after the Wairau massacre in 1843. Thereafter he served European circuits in Wellington, Nelson and New Plymouth.

A trusted mediator between Maori and settler, and sympathetic to working men's aspirations, he was critical of market manipulation, and advocated temperance and government funding of denominational schools. His Protestant sympathies led to his involvement in the formation of an EA in Wellington in 1849. As an evangelist with a strong social conscience, he possessed marked ability in communicating in speech and writing. From 1858 he served in five Australian states where he was active in camp meetings, the founding of the Home Mission Society and the *Wesleyan Methodist Magazine*.

BIBLIOGRAPHY
W. A. Chambers, *Samuel Ironside in New Zealand* (Auckland, 1982)

W. A. CHAMBERS

Irving, Edward (b. Annan, Dumfrieshire, Scotland, 4 Aug. 1792; d. Glasgow, Scotland, 7 Dec. 1834). Scottish preacher and founder of the Catholic Apostolic Church ('the Irvingites'). Irving, second son of Gavin Irving, tanner, of Annan, was educated at Annan Academy and Edinburgh University (MA 1809). In 1810, he commenced a teaching career, first at Haddington where he tutored privately Jane Welsh, future wife of the essayist Thomas Carlyle, and later at Kirkcaldy where he met Carlyle and Isabella Martin, his wife-to-be. In June 1815, he was licensed to preach in the Church of Scotland.

Ambitious and longing for advancement, Irving abandoned teaching in 1818 and moved to Edinburgh to study theology. In July 1819, he was invited by ANDREW THOMSON to preach at St George's, Edinburgh, before the celebrated THOMAS CHALMERS; soon afterwards he was invited to become Chalmers's assistant at St John's, Glasgow – a congregation which could now boast the two most famous preachers in modern Scotland.

Here, as elsewhere, Irving made an instant impression. Tall, handsome, overconfident, and possessing a melodious voice, his noble presence was scarcely at home among the rough-and-tumble atmosphere of the Glaswegian weavers and cotton-spinners. Nor was his relationship with Chalmers entirely congenial: his natural abilities were overshadowed by the older man's, and his extreme conservatism clashed with Chalmers's burgeoning social and economic liberalism. Not surprisingly, in 1822, Irving became minister of the small Scottish chapel at Hatton Garden, London. Prior to departing for England, he was ordained by the Church of Scotland.

Irving's ambitions and abilities were well suited to the greater sphere of influence provided by a metropolitan pulpit. Highly authoritarian and by now a gifted orator, and aided by a compliment paid him by Canning in a parliamentary speech, his chapel was soon thronged with fashionable visitors and sightseers. Within two years, having outgrown its confines, the foundation stone of a much large church was laid at Regent Square. The effects of this rapid success aided Irving's feelings of self-importance and encouraged his belief in his own divine mission. This, in turn, made him a ready prey to flatterers and religious fanatics.

During the mid 1820s, an important development occurred within English evangelicalism. Influenced by the vast upheavals of the French revolutionary era, the Napoleonic wars, and the imminent passage of Catholic emancipation, some evangelicals began to speculate that present tribulations might be a prologue to a new age previously unimagined. In this climate of anxiety arose a new emphasis on premillennialism in which Irving was at the forefront.

In 1825, Irving announced that the church was about to enter 'a series of thick-coming judgements and fearful perplexities' foreshadowing Christ's imminent advent. Later that same year, he became acquainted with the evangelical philanthropist HENRY DRUMMOND, who, in turn, introduced him to the apocalyptic writings of an obscure Chilean Jesuit named Lacunza. So impressed was Irving by Lacunza's *The Coming of the Messiah in Glory and Majesty* that, in 1827, he translated it into English. Irving had also by now become highly critical of the prevailing liberalism of the period. In 1828, he published an emotive tract opposing Catholic emancipation, followed by a highly conservative diatribe on church and state.

One of the strongest influences in the development of Irving's speculative interest in unfulfilled biblical prophecy was the LSPCJ. Conversion of the Jews was seen by many premillennialists as a precursor to Christ's second advent. From the LSPCJ was launched the Society for the Investigation of Prophecy, which subsequently led to the organization of the celebrated Albury conferences beginning in November 1826, in which Irving played a seminal role. In these efforts he was influenced by the more extreme Drummond, whose wealth and fashionable connections entirely captivated the younger man. Without this influence, Irving might have avoided many of the theological entanglements which eventually led to his discrediting and early demise.

Despite public acclaim, Irving's private life remained unfulfilled. Since 1812, he had been engaged to Isabella Martin; over time, however, the prospect of their union became to Irving less attractive. In 1821, he and Jane Welsh fell deeply in love. Appeals to the Martins to release him from his obligation proved unsuccessful, and, in 1823, he reluctantly married Isabella. Although surprisingly congenial as a partner, Isabella was blind to Irving's imperfections and temperamentally unable to protect him from the vicissitudes of life. 'If I had married Irving', Jane Welsh later retorted, 'the tongues would never have been heard'.

In early 1827, the National Scotch Church at Regent Square was opened. Irving's star, however, was now in the descendant. Moreover, speculation arose over his doctrinal soundness; in December 1830 formal charges were brought against him by the presbytery of London on grounds of Trinitarian heterodoxy. (This arose more from Irving's indiscretion and theological indiscipline than from wholesale apostasy.) In response, Irving simply withdrew his church from the jurisdiction of the London presbytery.

In early 1830, manifestations of the 'miraculous gifts' began to appear in the west of Scotland. Premillennialists predicted their imminent arrival in London; Irving became so expectant that he resisted seeking medical treatment for his terminally ill son. The 'prophets' were not to be disappointed. On 30 April 1831, 'speaking in tongues' appeared at a private prayer meeting in London. In early October, manifestations of the 'gifts' occurred in the vestry at Regent Square; on 16 October, and with Irving's tacit approval, outbursts of tongues and prophecy repeatedly interrupted public worship. When Irving refused to suppress the 'gifts' at the insistence of the trustees, they turned against him. On 26 April 1832, Irving was locked out of his church; he had succumbed to indiscretion and vanity, and now faced ostracism and ruin.

Undeterred – and joined by over 800 members of his congregation – Irving began holding services in a large bazaar in Gray's Inn Road, later relocating to a picture gallery in Newman Street. This body soon became known as the Catholic Apostolic Church. Irving's troubles continued, however, for the General Assembly of the Church of Scotland soon initiated action against him on Trinitarian grounds, and, in March 1833, he was deposed from the ministry. Although largely devoid of practical significance, deposition nevertheless inflicted a severe blow upon his emotional and spiritual well-being.

Irving was now technically without status as a Christian minister – a situation which caused no little distress within his London congregation. Never personally favoured with the 'gifts', he was required by conscience to give way to those who had. Therefore, when an 'inspired' voice claimed that Irving – as a layman – must cease from administering the sacraments, he yielded, meekly submitting to men of inferior talent who now seized control of his church. Subsequently, Irving continued to preach and occasionally to undertake missions; however, devoid of his former confidence, his health began to deteriorate. Broken and confused, he died of tuberculosis during a visit to his native Scotland.

Irving's life was full of contradictions. He was one of the most gifted preachers of modern times: passionate, imaginative, and benevolent; yet he remained encumbered by ambition, vanity, and impetuosity. Most importantly, he was a poor judge of character, unable to discriminate between sincere admirers and those who sought his undoing. Nevertheless, he made an important contribution to Victorian evangelicalism, especially in advancing premillennialism and the return of the 'gifts'.

SELECT WRITINGS
E. Irving, *The Collected Writings of Edward Irving*, ed. G. Carlyle, 5 vols (London, 1865)

BIBLIOGRAPHY
DNB
T. Carlyle, *Reminiscences by Thomas Carlyle*, ed. J. A. Froude, 2 vols, 1 (London, 1881): 67–338
M. Oliphant, *The Life of Edward Irving* (London, 1862)
W. H. Oliver, *Prophets and Millennialists* (Oxford, 1978)

GRAYSON CARTER

Irwin, Frederick Chidley   (b. Raphoe, Donegal, Ireland, c. 1793; d. Cheltenham, England, 31 Mar. 1860). Soldier and administrator. Son of Reverend James Irwin, he served in the Peninsular War 1809–14, then in Canada and Ceylon, before being sent in 1829 as captain in charge of a detachment of the 13th Regiment to garrison the new Swan River colony in Western Australia. A staunch Anglican, Irwin organized church parades before the arrival of an ordained minister, and fostered the erection of a rush-thatched church in Perth and a mud church near his own property, Henley Park on the Upper Swan. Acting Governor 1832–3, he returned to England and published *The State of Western Australia* (London 1835). He also lobbied for missionaries to the Aborigines to reduce conflict with the settlers, and in 1835 the West Australian Missionary Society was formed, which eventually developed into the Colonial and Continental Church Society; as a result more Anglican clergy were eventually sent to the colony.

Having married Elizabeth Courthope in 1836 he returned as commandant to Western Australia from 1837 until his retirement in 1852, with the rank of lieutenant-colonel. He encouraged prayer meetings among his troops and promoted a temperance society in Perth. Acting Governor for 18 months in 1847–8, he gave encouragement to the establishment in 1848 of an archdiaconate in Western Australia under the Bishop of Adelaide. Perturbed at the success of the Catholic Church in schooling, in 1847 he established a General Board of Education, its membership Protestant, to subsidize teachers and otherwise to encourage the founding of schools based on broad Christian principles in the major centres of population. This is usually regarded as the genesis of state education in Western Australia. He authorized the experimental introduction of Chinese labour in an unsuccessful bid to prevent convict transportation. A strict moralist, Irwin was respected rather than popular, but when he left Western Australia in 1854 the church was stronger for his presence.

BIBLIOGRAPHY
ADB
C. L. M. Hawtrey, *The Availing Struggle* (Perth, Australia, 1948)

G. C. BOLTON

Irwin, Henry (b. Drogheda, Ireland, 31 Oct. 1773; d. Co. Dublin, 26 Feb. 1858). Church of Ireland clergyman and evangelical leader. Irwin experienced an evangelical conversion while Curate of Castlecomer, 1796–1810. He later moved to Carrigrohane, Co. Cork, 1810–26, and to Sandford, Co. Dublin, 1826–58; he also served as Archdeacon of Emly, 1843–58. Prominent in all the major evangelical organizations of his day, Irwin gained national notoriety on two occasions: in 1824 for public controversies with Catholics about Bible distribution, and in 1838 for a sermon before the Lord Lieutenant in which he denounced the government's pusillanimous pragmatism in failing to uphold Protestantism. However, he probably exerted his greatest influence through the consistent evangelicalism and churchmanship of his long pastoral career. On the sixtieth anniversary of his ministry, almost 1,000 clergymen signed an address thanking him for his leadership 'in awakening the slumbering Church of Ireland to Evangelical truth and life' (Irwin, 1858: 241).

SELECT WRITINGS
H. Irwin, *Remains of the Venerable Henry Irwin*, ed. W. P. Walsh (Dublin, London and Edinburgh, 1858)

JOSEPH CHRISTIAN LIECHTY

Isaac, Daniel (b. Caythorne, Lincolnshire, England, *c.* 1780; d. York, England, 21 March 1834). British Wesleyan minister. He was converted in Nottingham in his nineteenth year. He soon became a local preacher and proved himself so useful that in 1800 he was called upon to supply a vacancy in the Grimsby circuit. He maintained an active ministry for 32 years until, while preaching in Manchester in 1832, he was seized by a stroke from which he never fully recovered. Moving to York the same year, further strokes overcame him, and he lingered in increasing weakness until his death.

He was well read, and his preaching showed marked originality in marshalling his thoughts so as to retain the attention of his hearers. An able expositor, he published many works of a controversial nature which gained him the nickname of 'The Polemic Divine', the name which JAMES EVERETT gave to his biography (London, 1839). His own writings were collected in three volumes by John Burdsall in 1841.

BIBLIOGRAPHY
J. Everett, *The Polemic Divine* (London, 1839)

OLIVER A. BECKERLEGGE

Isles, Samuel (b. Holbeck, near Leeds, Yorkshire, England, 14 April 1723; d. Antigua, 15 Jan. 1764).

Moravian missionary to the Caribbean. Samuel Isles was much influenced by PETER BÖHLER and joined the Moravian Church in England in 1743. After serving the Church in a number of communities in England and Germany, he was called as a lay missionary to St Thomas in the Danish West Indies in 1748. He was ordained as a Moravian minister the following year.

With his wife, Molly, he moved to Antigua to begin work among the slaves in 1756. In a letter home he writes: '(They) … are certainly as lacerated and oppressed a people as ever was.' In spite of the conditions in which the slaves lived and worked, Isles established a church. The first converts were baptized in 1757. One biographer judges that he does not show as much originality or organizational ability as some missionaries, and yet was more resourceful and adaptable than most.

BIBLIOGRAPHY
Transactions of the Moravian Historical Society, 21

FRED LINYARD

Ivimey, Joseph (b. Ringwood, Hampshire, England, 22 May 1773; d. London, 8 Feb. 1834). English Calvinistic Baptist pastor, leader, and historian. Baptized by JOHN SAFFERY at Wimborne, Dorset, he was an itinerant at Portsea before settling as assistant at Wallingford. He soon moved on to become minister of Eagle Street Baptist Church, London (1805–34). He published many writings and especially *The History of the English Baptists* (4 vols, 1811–30). He was a man of immense energy, helping found the Baptist Union in 1812 (which he served as secretary until his death), he virtually directed the Baptist Irish Society, serving on the committee of Stepney Academy (later Regent's Park College), working on the committee of the BMS and editing (1812–34) the *Baptist Magazine*. In 1817–19 he undertook missions to the Channel Islands. Meanwhile, he was apparently a well-loved and effective pastor, an active itinerant preacher and money-raiser for missions and a firm supporter of the antislavery movement while a lifelong strict communionist, believing only those baptized as believers should be admitted to the Lord's Supper. He separated from many other leading Dissenters over his hostility to Catholic emancipation.

BIBLIOGRAPHY
DNB
G. Pritchard, *Memoir of the Life and Writings of the Rev. Joseph Ivimey* (London, 1835)

BARRIE WHITE

J

Jackson, Alvery (b. Sutton in Craven, Yorkshire, England, *c.* 1700; d. Barnoldswick, Yorkshire, 31 Dec. 1763). Baptist minister. Probably belonging to a Quaker family, he was the third of that name, and was converted through the ministry of a Baptist, Thomas Dewhurst, and baptized at Sutton-in-Craven, 21 September 1715. He became a member of the Baptist Church at Heaton and Rawdon. In 1718 he became minister of Barnoldswick Baptist Church. He advocated hymn-singing, once preaching a sermon on the subject with 60 divisions which must have lasted two hours. In 1744 his church drew up a statement of faith and a covenant which was adopted by several churches in Yorkshire, which sought to show the wide agreement on doctrine with other Protestant denominations. Perhaps Jackson's most important influence was in opposing the Hyper-Calvinism of JOHN JOHNSON and John Brine.

BIBLIOGRAPHY
E. R. Lewis, *History of the Bethesda Baptist Church, Barnoldswick, Yorks* (Cwmavon, Wales, 1893): 16–64
C. E. Shipley, ed., *The Baptists of Yorkshire* (Bradford, England, 1912): 89–90
E. C. Starr, ed., *A Baptist Bibliography*, 25 vols (New York, 1947–76)

DAVID B. MILNER

Jackson, Ann [Hammond, Mrs Isaac] (b. Oswestry, Shropshire, England, 10 May 1810; d. England, 8 March *c.* 1876/7). Primitive Methodist itinerant preacher. Jackson's family were Anglicans and 'her parents occupied a respectable position' (unspecified). Her father died when she was 17 and Ann went to live with her aunt, Mrs Edwards, a Primitive Methodist local preacher. She was converted, became a local preacher (*circa* 1825) and an itinerant (*circa* 1830). She was known as 'The Weeping Prophetess'. Around 1832 she married and reverted to local preacher status and also served as a Sunday school teacher. She suffered from a severe illness for about four and a half years.

BIBLIOGRAPHY
PMMag (1851, 1877)

E. DOROTHY GRAHAM

Jackson, John (b. Lastingham, Yorkshire, England, 31 May 1778; d. London, 1 June 1831). Portrait painter. Apprenticed to his father, a tailor, Jackson so impressed noble patrons with his miniature painting that they bought him out of his apprenticeship and paid for his training at the Royal Academy. Affable and courteous, he related well both to his fellow artists and to potential clients, gaining recognition as an academician in 1817. While not at the top of his profession, he made a very adequate livelihood, building up a sizeable clientele and travelling abroad. He also served as official portrait painter to the Wesleyan Conference. Converted in a 1793 revival, he remained a loyal Methodist for the rest of his life, meeting in JOSEPH BUTTERWORTH's class. His papers are held in the North Yorkshire County Record Office.

BIBLIOGRAPHY
DNB
A. Graves, *The Royal Academy of Arts* (London, 1905–6) 4: 226–8
MM, 54 (1831): 511
H. C. Morgan, 'The Life and Works of John Jackson RA' (Leeds Univ. MA thesis, 1956)
D. M. Rosman, *Evangelicals and Culture* (London, 1984): 155–6

DOREEN M. ROSMAN

Jackson, John (b. London, 22 Feb. 1811; d. London, 6 Jan. 1885). Bishop of London. Jackson was educated at Reading School and Pembroke College, Oxford (BA 1833; MA 1836; DD 1853). Ordained in 1836, having been headmaster of Islington Grammar School (1833–46), he held a number of church appointments, including Royal Chaplain (1847–53) and Canon of Bristol (1852–3), before being elevated to the see of Lincoln (1853–9), and then of London (1859–85).

The LCM and the Scripture Readers' Association received his early support. In 1875 he chaired the CMS missionary conference and gave the annual CMS sermon in which he sounded a favourite note by warning against ritualism. His continuing support of evangelical associations, such as the LSPCJ (vice-patron from 1861; annual sermon 1881), indicates no significant falling away from evangelicalism, as has been suggested. He has been called a 'moderate evangelical', by the *Christian Observer* (1853), and a 'pious and tolerant Evangelical', by Ollard and Cross (*Dictionary of English Church History* [1912]: 342). Jackson's papers are at Lambeth Palace and in the British Library.

BIBLIOGRAPHY
CO (April, 1853): 288
DNB
E. Stock, *The History of the Church Missionary Society*, 3 vols, III (London, 1899): 66–67, 295

JONATHAN BURKE CUTMORE
DONALD M. LEWIS

Jackson, Rebecca Cox (b. 1795; d. Philadelphia, PA, 1871). African-American itinerant preacher and Shaker leader. Converted in July, 1830, and sanctified a year later, Jackson refused to join Philadelphia's African Methodist Episcopal Church (AME) in which her brother Joseph Cox, was a minister. She soon moved away from evangelicalism. She and Mary Trusty Peterson (an AME preacher's wife) led weekly covenant meetings composed largely of women. Alert to dreams, visions and a divine inner voice, she already believed that holy living required celibacy before meeting the Shakers. Her belief ended a marriage to Samuel Jackson.

After periods of itinerant preaching, she joined the Shaker community at Watervliet, New York, staying from 1847 to 1851. She left to begin a mission to blacks in Philadelphia. Her Shaker community there was led from 1871 to 1901 by her companion of 35 years, Rebecca Perot.

BIBLIOGRAPHY
J. M. Humez, ed., *Gifts of Power* (Amherst, MA, 1981)

WILL GRAVELY

Jackson, Samuel (b. Sancton, Yorkshire, England, 1786; d. Newcastle-upon-Tyne, England, 1861). Methodist minister. Like his brother THOMAS JACKSON, Samuel was the son of a farm labourer whose talents were developed by his conversion when young. Entering the ministry in 1806, he quickly took a leading part in urging the improvement first, of Methodist day schools and then of the religious instruction of Methodist children. The vigour of his character, combined with his richly evangelical presentation, rendered his sermons weighty and powerful. In difficult situations he showed marked discretion, and his sensitivity meant that on occasion he faltered in debate because he was clearly moved at having to differ from esteemed brethren. He was described by his contemporaries as being 'an example of manly and Christian Virtue, loved and venerated'.

Having been called to various connexional offices, he was elected president in 1847 and the following year began a seven-year period as governor of Richmond College. At the time of the 'Fly-Sheet' controversy, he edited *The Wesleyan Vindicator and Constitutional Methodist*, but his main publications related to the education of youth. Attending the Newcastle Conference, he died of paralysis in the course of its sittings.

BIBLIOGRAPHY
[Anon.], *Samuel Jackson and the Children of Methodism* (London, 1875)
—, *Wesley and His Successors* (London, 1892), 167–8
T. Jackson, ed., *Sermons on Several Important Subjects, with a Memoir . . .* (London, 1863)
G. Osborn, *Outlines of Wesleyan Bibliography* (London, 1869)

OLIVER A. BECKERLEGGE

Jackson, Thomas (b. Sancton, Yorkshire, England, 12 Dec. 1783; d. London, 10 Mar. 1873). Wesleyan Methodist minister and author. Thomas was born into a humble Yorkshire home. His childhood consisted of an inadequate village school education often interrupted by employment on the farm of a relative. His father, a farm labourer, had acquired a small plot of land by marriage to the daughter of the village carpenter. Yet this small-holding was hardly sufficient to support a large family, and at the age of 12 Thomas left home to become a farm labourer. Three years later he was apprenticed to a Shipton carpenter, and he maintained this position until he entered the Wesleyan itinerancy.

During his apprenticeship he attended Methodist meetings, and in July 1801 he experienced conversion through the services of MARY BARRITT, who was one of the most successful and also controversial female evangelists within Methodism at this time. Shortly afterwards he felt the call to preach and began to conduct services in cottage meetings. This new sphere of activity instilled in him a determination to pursue the course of the auto-didact. The standard works of Methodist literature immediately attracted his attention, but his lively enquiring mind quickly demonstrated an eagerness to explore a wider range of sources. His studies had scarcely commenced when the Wesleyan Conference of 1804, short of itinerant preachers, called on his services. He responded positively as he was to do when assigned equally unexpected and major tasks in later years.

In the period 1804–24 Thomas served in ten circuits. First stationed in Spilsby where he had welcome access to the library of ROBERT C. BRACKENBURY of Raithby Hall, his second appointment was Horncastle where he met his future wife. At the end of his next appointment, Lincoln, he was sent to Leeds and then Preston, the birthplace of his son, Thomas, who became an Anglican clergyman. Further travels took him to Sowerby Bridge where he established a friendship with the Wesleyan leader JABEZ BUNTING and where he did not hesitate to distance the Methodist chapels from the Luddite disorders of the time. On this as on so many other public issues, with the notable exceptions of Catholic emancipation and Irish education, he shared Bunting's views. He left Sowerby Bridge for Wakefield and was subsequently stationed at Sheffield, at which point he succeeded Bunting as sub-secretary of the Wesleyan Conference in 1817. In 1818 he was appointed to Manchester, and during this turbulent Peterloo period he had ample opportunities to demonstrate his understanding of and support for Christian Toryism. At the same time he was a source of strength to both colleagues and members who confronted public attacks on and internal disputes within the Wesleyan chapels. The events of these years in the aftermath of revolution and war in Europe served only to strengthen his confidence in the superiority of English political institutions and liberties.

While Thomas easily commanded the attention of congregations as a plain-speaking preacher, his reputation in Wesleyanism at large principally rested on his literary skills. In 1815 he published a spirited defence of Arminianism in the form of four letters to the Reverend John Cockin, a Calvinist dissenting minister. His first major work, a biography of the Puritan divine John Goodwin, appeared in 1822, by which time he had moved to London where he acted as an assistant at the Book Room. Two years later he succeeded Bunting as connexional editor, an appointment which he approached with much trepidation largely on account of the reputation of his predecessors and his lack of formal education.

During the next 18 years a wide variey of publications established Thomas as a Wesleyan apologist, biographer, and historian. Besides his biography of CHARLES WESLEY, a centenary history of Wesleyanism, and *Expository Discourses*, he edited a number of publications including JOHN WESLEY's sermons and works. During the second half of his editorship he wrote several pamphlets which collectively represented the most convincing defence of Wesleyanism during that period. One such pamphlet, *The Church and the Methodists*, was designed to dissociate Wesleyanism from disestablishment politics at a time when JOSEPH RAYNER STEPHENS, a young Wesleyan preacher identified with the disestablishment cause, was at the centre of controversy. Further writings, e.g. *An Answer to the Question, 'Why Are You a Wesleyan Methodist?'*, presented a solid exposition of Wesleyan principles in the face of a growing volume of criticism from High Church quarters.

The final stage of Thomas's lengthy ministry commenced in 1842 when he was appointed theological tutor at the southern branch of the Theological Institution in Richmond. He remained in that post until poor health forced him into retirement in 1861. Throughout this period his vast store of knowledge and his comprehensive understanding of Methodist doctrine, experience and discipline gave a sound basis to this new college. His later publications, orthodox in content, reflected the subject-matter of his college lectures, in particular *The Duties of Christianity*, *The Providence of God*, and *The Institutions of Christianity*.

The Wesleyan Conference recognized Thomas's services when he was twice elected to the presidency in contrasting situations. On the first occasion in 1838 he was an obvious choice to preside over the centenary celebrations of Methodism, especially since none of his colleagues had such an intimate knowledge of Methodist history. His second election occurred in the unpropitious circumstances of 1849 and on the eve of the largest schism in the history of British Methodism. This elevation to office was as much a sign of how the conference

proposed to deal with troublemakers as a token of its regard for personal services. Thomas was called upon to deliver the conference's judgement on the ministerial rebels, JAMES EVERETT, SAMUEL DUNN, and WILLIAM GRIFFITH. The ensuing 12 months proved the most difficult period in a ministry that displayed a mixture of native intelligence, and indefatigable support of Wesleyanism. On his death the *Minutes of Conference* fairly recorded how Thomas had made use of his life, 'Without brilliant parts and without educational advantages he applied himself with all his heart to the improvement of such talents and opportunities as were granted to him, and with the Lord's pound he gained ten pounds'.

SELECT WRITINGS

T. Jackson, *Misrepresentations Exposed, and the Arminians Defended; in Three Letters to the Rev. John Cockin* (Leeds, England, 1815)
—, *A Fourth Letter to the Rev. John Cockin* (Leeds, England, 1815)
—, *The Life of John Goodwin* (London, 1822)
—, ed., *Wesley's Sermons* (London, 1825)
—, ed., *The Works of the Rev. J. Wesley, M.A.*, 14 vols (London, 1829–31)
—, *The Church and the Methodists* (London, 1834)
—, *The Centenary of Wesleyan Methodism* (London, 1839)
—, *Expository Discourses* (London, 1839)
—, *The Life of the Rev. Charles Wesley*, 2 vols (London, 1842)
—, *An Answer to the Question, 'Why Are You a Wesleyan Methodist?'* (London, 1842)
—, *The Life of the Rev. Robert Newton* (London, 1855)
—, *The Duties of Christianity* (London, 1857)
—, *The Providence of God* (London, 1862)
—, *The Institutions of Christianity* (London, 1868)

BIBLIOGRAPHY

B. Frankland, ed., *Recollections of My Own Life and Times by T. Jackson* (London, 1878)
G. Rupp, *Thomas Jackson, Methodist Patriarch* (London, 1954)

D. A. GOWLAND

Jackson, Thomas (b. Derbyshire, England, *c.* 1795; d. England, 6 June 1870). Primitive Methodist pioneer. Thomas was a Derbyshireman and was converted by JOHN BENTON at Belper in 1817. He at once threw himself into evangelistic work in Nottinghamshire, North and West Derbyshire, Leicestershire and Rutland. After suffering severe persecution and hardship he proceeded in 1818–19 to introduce Primitive Methodism to Sandbach, Preston Brook, and using this village as a centre, to the north-west Cheshire area and across the Mersey to Liverpool. From 1821 to 1822 he served in a number of circuits, mainly in Yorkshire, but after two years' ministry in Cambridge (1832–4) he suddenly left the ministry and little more is known about him.

IAN SELLERS

Jackson, Thomas (b. Newcastle-under-Lyme, Staffordshire, England, 1811; d. London, 1879). Primitive Methodist minister. Thomas was apparently converted at the age of nine and while in his early teens began a successful Sunday school in his native town and also became one of the Primitive Methodists' more outstanding 'boy preachers'. He became a circuit minister in 1832 and was appointed by the Sheffield circuit as a pioneer missionary in Reading where he established what was to become a thriving cause. He served for the whole of his ministry in the large Brinkworth district, notably in Brinkworth itself, Witney and Farringdon. He was secretary of the Primitive Methodist Conference in 1866, and retired to London in 1875.

BIBLIOGRAPHY
Obituary, *Minutes of the Primitive Methodist Conference* (1880)

IAN SELLERS

Jackson, Thomas Jonathan ['Stonewall'] (b. Clarksburg, VA, USA, 21 Jan. 1824; d. Chancellorsville, VA, USA, 10 May 1863). Confederate general. Graduated from the US Military Academy in 1846, Jackson fought in the Mexican War, after which he trained cadets at Virginia Military Institute. Participating in the hanging of JOHN BROWN in 1859, he then served as a general in the Confederate Army. At the first battle of Bull Run (21 July 1861), he was lionized for 'standing like a stone wall' against the enemy and became ROBERT E. LEE's most trusted comrade-in-arms. Most pious of all Confederate generals, he called on the Presbyterian General Assembly to send chaplains to the armies. A staunch Calvinist and spiritual descendant of Puritan Oliver Cromwell, he gained renown for his military obedience to Christ as a prophet-warrior. Shot by one of his own soldiers during a victory at Chancellorsville, he later died of pneumonia. His eccentric piety and military genius made him a symbol of belief in divine favour on the Confederacy and installed him as a Confederate saint celebrated in the postwar 'religion of the Lost Cause'.

BIBLIOGRAPHY
J. Bowers, *Stonewall Jackson* (New York, 1989)
R. Dabney, *Life and Campaigns of Lieutenant-General Thomas J. Jackson* (New York, 1886)
G. H. Shattuck, Jr, *A Shield and Hiding Place: The Religious Life of the Civil War Armies* (Macon, GA, 1987)
C. R. Wilson, *Baptized in Blood: The Religion of the Lost Cause, 1865–1920* (Athens, GA, 1980)

ANDREW MANIS

Jac(k)o, Peter (b. Newlyn, Cornwall, England, 1728; d. Margate, England, 6 July 1781). Methodist itinerant. His was the first preacher's life to be published in *AM*. Baptized 4 May 1728 he was employed after schooling in a pilchard fishery. He listened to JOHN WESLEY's open-air preaching in 1746, but it was through a tin miner's sermon that he was awakened to his need and at a sacramental service that he was assured of his acceptance with God. When Wesley came to Cornwall again in 1751, Jaco was appointed to visit several societies. From being an occasional helper he was recognized as an itinerant in 1754 and sent to the then widespread Manchester circuit. He travelled both in England and Ireland, enduring considerable hardship and persecution. At night he was often thankful for a little clean straw, with a canvas sheet to lie on. A commanding presence and a lucid mind reinforced his message.

BIBLIOGRAPHY
AM (1778)

A. SKEVINGTON WOOD

Jacob, Philip (b. 1803; d. Winchester, Hampshire, England, 28 June 1884). Anglican clergyman. Jacob was one in a line of accomplished men, though he was perhaps least among their number. A great-grandfather, his father, a brother, and a son are the subject of entries in the *Dictionary of National Biography*. Educated at Christ Church, Oxford (BA 1825; MA 1828), he was Curate of Newport, Monmouth (1827–31), and Rector of Crawley and Huton, Wiltshire (1831–84). He rose to be Canon of Winchester in 1834 and was archdeacon from June 1860.

BIBLIOGRAPHY
Boase
Foster, *Index Ecclesiasticus* (Oxford, 1890)
J. S. Reynolds, *Evangelicals at Oxford* (Oxford, 1975): 91, 157

JONATHAN BURKE CUTMORE

Jacoby, Ludwig Sigismund (b. Altstrelitz, Mecklenburg, Germany, 21 Oct. 1813; d. St Louis, MO, USA, 20 June 1874). Methodist missionary. Of Jewish parentage, Jacoby worked for mercantile firms in Hamburg and Leipzig. In 1835 he was baptized a Lutheran and three years later emigrated to the United States where he worked as a tutor in Cincinnati. In 1839 he was converted under the ministry of the German-American Methodist leader WILLIAM NAST, who persuaded him to receive ordination. In 1840 he married another German convert to Methodism, Amalie Nuelsen, who bore him eight children. In 1841 he began mission works among German immigrants in St Louis and the upper Mississippi, and in 1849 the American Methodist Episcopal church appointed him as its first missionary to Germany. A gifted preacher and organizer, he formed a congregation in Bremen, dispatched co-workers to start works elsewhere in Germany and Switzerland, founded magazines, a publishing house (Anker-Verlag), and a seminary, and served as 'superintendent' of the entire enterprise. He returned to the US in 1871, where he served as a pastor and presiding elder in St Louis. His major literary works were *Handbuch der Methodismus* (1855), *Geschichte der Methodismus* (1870), and *Letzte Stunden, oder, Die Kraft der Religion Jesu Christi im Tode* (1874).

BIBLIOGRAPHY
W. C. Barclay, *History of Methodist Missions* (New York, 1949)
DAB
EWM
H. Mann, *Ludwig S. Jacoby* (Bremen, Germany, 1892)
F. C. Tucker, *The Methodist Church in Missouri* (Nashville, TN, 1966)
F. Wunderlich, *Methodists Linking Two Continents* (Nashville, TN, 1960)

R. V. PIERARD

Jaggar, Thomas James (b. Cheltenham, Gloucestershire, England, 1814; d. Kaukapakapa, New Zealand, 28 Jan. 1882). Wesleyan missionary in Fiji. The son of an English Wesleyan minister, Thomas was educated at Kingswood School and in January 1837 married Sarah Porter. In the same year he offered to serve the Wesleyan Methodist Missionary Society as a missionary for the South Seas and was appointed as a printer to its newly founded mission in Fiji, where he arrived in December 1838. He was received into full connexion by the British Wesleyan Conference in 1841. Thomas was a diligent printer, but was plagued by isolation and physical illness. In 1848, following allegations of a sexual liaison with a part-Fijian girl, he was suspended from the mission. Having settled with his family in Auckland, New Zealand, he became a Wesleyan class leader. After the death of Sarah he married Mary Martyn in 1866 and spent the last 15 years of his life as a Wesleyan home missionary in a farming community north of Auckland.

BIBLIOGRAPHY
E. Keesing-Styles and W. Keesing-Styles, eds, *Unto the Perfect Day* (Auckland, 1988)
S. J. Paech, 'Thomas Jaggar and the Fiji Mission' (University of Adelaide, BA Hons thesis, 1973)

DAVID HILLIARD

James, John Angell (b. Blandford, Dorset, England, 6 June 1785; d. Birmingham, Warwickshire, England, 1 Oct. 1859). Congregational minister and leader. The son of a draper, he was apprenticed to the same trade before training for the ministry, with a bursary from ROBERT HALDANE, under DAVID BOGUE at Gosport, where he was baptized and admitted into Communion. In 1805, in a five-hour marathon, he was ordained to the pastorate of Carr's Lane Birmingham, where initially he had little success, which only came in 1812–13 when James' congregation moved temporarily to the Old Meeting while changes were undertaken at Carr's Lane. Thereafter, his ministry in Birmingham took off: in 1820 Carr's Lane had to be rebuilt to twice its previous size, with six other chapels planted at the same time.

Nationally he supported the Home Missionary Society and encouraged the Congregationalists to plant and build more churches. Although active in municipal affairs, he opposed the extension of the franchise as also the founding of the Anti-State Church Association. In 1819 he preached the LMS sermon, a lengthy affair of two hours' duration delivered without a note. Active in the foundation of the Congregational Union, he persuaded his fellows to accept a Declaration of Faith as a basis for cooperation. He was chairman of the Board of Education of Spring Hill College from its foundation in 1838 till his death. Interested in promoting a deeper piety amongst Congregationalists and encouraged by the revival movement in the United States of America, he wrote a number of evangelical works the best known being *The Anxious Enquirer after Salvation Directed and Encouraged*.

Very conscious of the inroads of worldliness in the life of the churches, his condemnation of many forms of literary enjoyment, as well as such practices as smoking, extended to oratorios, arguing that Handel's Messiah was a 'profanation of the most serious subjects the human mind can contemplate, by their application to purposes of amusement'. He further argued 'ours is an age of man-worship, the idolatry of genius'. Thus logically, while many universities offered him honorary degrees, he rejected them all. Evangelical religion, he believed, was under threat: 'The battle of the Reformation may yet have to be fought again'. Not surprisingly, he played a major part in the foundation of the EA. At the end of his life he became increasingly concerned at Congregationalism's movement away from Calvinist theology even though his own Calvinism was essentially of a practical kind. From the summer of 1853, he was assisted at Carr's Lane by R. W. Dale.

SELECT WRITINGS
J. A. James, *Autobiography* (London, 1864)
—, ed., *Works* (London, 1860–4)

BIBLIOGRAPHY
R. W. Dale, *The Life and Letters of John Angell James* (London, 1861)
DNB

J. H. Y. BRIGGS

Jameson, William (b. Scotland; d. Old Calabar, West Africa, 5 Aug. 1847). Missionary of the United Presbyterian Church, Jamaica and Old Calabar, West Africa. A great-grandson of Professor WILLIAM WILSON (1690–1741), Jameson was ordained a minister of the United Presbyterian Church in 1836, and sent by an Edinburgh congregation as a missionary to Jamaica where he was stationed at Goshen. When an academy was opened he had charge of teaching catechists training for the ministry. In 1846 he was chosen to go to Africa, to the newly opened mission in Old Calabar. He arrived in January 1847, took charge of the school, and began to learn Efik. Using an Efik vocabulary compiled by HOPE M. WADDELL, he translated the Lord's Prayer, and some Bible passages. But after only seven months in Calabar he had a sudden attack of fever and died.

BIBLIOGRAPHY
J. M'Kerrow, *History of the Foreign Missions of the Secession and United Presbyterian Church* (Edinburgh, 1867)

CHRISTOPHER FYFE

Jamieson, Robert (b. Edinburgh, 3 Jan. 1802; d. Glasgow, 26 Oct. 1880). Church of Scotland minister. The son of an Edinburgh baker, he was educated at the High School and proceeded to the University of Glasgow, where he obtained high honours. He set aside medical ambitions to study divinity and was licensed to preach in 1827. In 1830 he was appointed Church of Scotland minister at Weststruther, in the presentation of the King. He served that charge for seven years, and from 1837 until 1843 was minister of Currie Street, Edinburgh. Although he identified with the church's evangelical party, during the Non-Intrusion Crisis he insisted that differences could be overcome within the establishment. In 1843 he took over permanently the charge of St Paul's, Glasgow when it was deserted by JOHN FORBES.

The author of various works on biblical themes, by far his most important contribution was as co-author with A. R. Faucett and DAVID BROWN of their well-known six-volume *Commentary* (1861–65). Prominent in church affairs, and especially concerned in the education of ministerial candidates, he was elected moderator of the General Assembly in 1872.

BIBLIOGRAPHY
DNB

JONATHAN BURKE CUTMORE

Jane, Joseph (b. Truro, Cornwall, England, 1716; d. Stapleton, Avon, England, 7 Jan. 1795). Anglican clergyman and Oxford tutor. Baptized 21 February 1716 the son of Joseph Jane, Rector of St Mary's, Truro, and master of Truro Grammar School, he was educated at Westminster School and Christ Church, Oxford, proceeding BA (1737), MA (1740) and BD (1748). He became a tutor, censor, and junior proctor. He served as curate at Cowley and then briefly as Vicar of St Thomas, Oxford, before transferring to the parish of St Mary Magdalene where he exercised a significant ministry from 1748 to 1763. His church was the focus of evangelical witness in Oxford. From 1763 to 1788 he was Rector of Iron Acton, Gloucestershire. A substantial bequest of his helped to launch the CMS. He shared WESLEY's brand of Arminianism while maintaining friendships with Calvinists like THOMAS ADAM and SAMUEL WALKER. There is a lengthy biographical entry in the Hole Manuscript in Birmingham University Library.

BIBLIOGRAPHY
J. Reynolds, *Evangelicals at Oxford* (Oxford, 1975): 22–33, 172

A. SKEVINGTON WOOD

Janes, Edmund Storer (b. Sheffield, MA, USA, 27 April 1807; New York City, NY, 18 Sept. 1876). American Methodist bishop. Converted in 1820, Janes became a member of the MEC. For several years he taught school and studied law. He became a member of the bar about 1827. Janes went through a spiritual crisis when his law partner died suddenly. He decided to enter the ordained ministry and became a member of the Philadelphia Annual Conference of the MEC in 1830. He also studied medicine as he prepared for the ministry.

From 1830 to 1840 Janes was pastor of churches in: Elizabeth, New Jersey; Orange, New Jersey; Philadelphia, Pennsylvania; and New York City. His pastoral service was interrupted for one year (1834) when he was the financial agent for Dickinson College, Carlisle, Pennsylvania. He was elected financial secretary of the ABS in 1840, a position he held for four years. At the Methodist Episcopal General Conference of 1844 Janes was elected to the episcopacy. He was the last bishop elected by the church before it divided into northern and southern sections over the slavery issue.

Janes exercised his episcopal duties with vigour in America and overseas. He travelled through much of the USA as well as Great Britain, Germany, Switzerland, France and Ireland. He served as president of the denomination's Missionary Society, Sunday School Union, and Tract Society. He was a manager of the ABS and an elected director of the American Colonization Society. Janes was also a trustee of Wesleyan University, Middletown, Connecticut, and Drew Theological Seminary, Madison, New Jersey. He published a few sermons and pamphlets.

BIBLIOGRAPHY
E. S. Bucke, ed., *The History of American Methodism* (Nashville, TN, 1964)
EWM
F. D. Leete, *Methodist Bishops* (Nashville, TN, 1948)

CHARLES YRIGOYEN, JR

Jänicke, Johannes (b. Berlin, 6 July 1748; d. Berlin, 21 June 1827). Pastor, founder of the first German missions school and founder of the *Berliner Missionsgesellschaft*. Educated first as a schoolteacher, Jänicke became associate pastor (1779) and then head pastor of the *Bohmisch-lutherischen Bethlehemsgemeinde* in Berlin. As part of the revivalistic Pietist Lutheran tradition, he was interested in missions. His younger brother, JOSEPH DANIEL JÄNICKE, went to India as a missionary where he died in 1800. Johannes established a mission training centre which opened in 1800, the first such project in Germany. Due to the lack of mission societies in Germany, he developed relationships with English missionary societies, especially the LMS. In 1823, the *Berliner Missionsgesellschaft* (Berlin Missionary Society) which grew out of his mission training school received a royal charter. Before his death, more than 80 missionaries were sent throughout the world, including K. F. A. GUTZLAFF, pioneer of China missions.

Jänicke also established (1811) a tract society which evolved into the national organization to promote spiritual literature, the *Hauptverein für christliche Erbauungsschriften im preussischen Staate*. He also founded a bible society (*Biblische Gesellschaft*) in 1805 which printed German and Polish Bibles. This led to his involvement in the organization (1814) of the national Bible Society which coordinated regional and local efforts, the *Hauptbibelgesellschaft*. He was also influential in the evolution of the Basel Mission of C. F. SPITTLER.

BIBLIOGRAPHY

R. Gareis, *Geschichte der Evangelischen Heidenmission* (Konstanz, Germany, 1902)

F. Glaue, 'Jänicke, Johannes', *Die Religion in Geschichte und Gegenwart*, 2nd edn, 3 (Tubingen, Germany, 1909–13): 231–2

E. Schick, *Verboten und Bahnbrecker* (Basel, 1943)

E. Geldbach, 'Jänicke, Johannes', *Evangelisches Gemeindelexikon* (Wuppertal, Germany, 1978): 274

DAVID BUNDY

Jänicke [Jaenicke], **Joseph Daniel** (b. Berlin, 27 July 1759; d. Tanjore, 10 May 1800). With SATIYANATHAN and RASA CLORINDA (a wealthy Brahman, converted widow) he was a 'Father of the Church in Tinnevelly' (south India). Of Bohemian origin, the first influences on Jaenicke were Moravian. The younger brother of JOHANNES JÄNICKE (1748–1827), the founder of Mission Seminary in Berlin, he studied in Halle. On 5 March 1788, he sailed from London as a missionary of the SPCK.

Jänicke arrived in Madras on 27 August 1788. Working under CHRISTIAN FRIEDERICH SCHWARTZ at Tanjore (Thanjavur), he learned Tamil and went to Palamcottah in 1791 to join SATHIYANATHAN. While travelling through Ramnad, he met Colonel Martinez, who contributed generously to the development of the mission there, and to the building of a church which Jänicke and CHRISTIAN WILHELM GERICKE consecrated in February 1800. This building was built upon land endowed by the converted Brahman widow, Clorinda.

In Palamcottah, Jänicke found 283 converts, 120 from Roman Catholic backgrounds and 43 new candidates. These were the fruits of Sathiyanathan's labours. Congregations grew steadily, chapels were built or enlarged in a number of villages, and a mass movement among Shanars brought thousands of new converts.

In 1792 Jänicke suffered repeated attacks of 'hill fever'. After ten months he returned to Tanjore because of deteriorating health. He could not visit the Shanar (now Nadar) community's new churches or the special 'sanctuary village' built at Mudalur in his name for those suffering persecution. Instead he sought to restore his health by undertaking a 500-mile evangelistic tour in cooler climes, but died peacefully in Tanjore.

BIBLIOGRAPHY

R. Caldwell, *Early History of the Tinnevelly Mission* (1881)

E. M. JACKSON

Jarratt, Devereux (b. New Kent County, VA, BNA, 17 Jan. 1733; d. Dinwiddie County, VA, USA, 29 Jan. 1801). Protestant Episcopal clergyman and evangelist. He was the son of Robert and Sarah (Bradley) Jarratt and of English and Irish descent. His father was a carpenter who gave his sons religious instruction (including the prayer-book catechism). Losing both parents as a child, Jarratt lived with his eldest brother until age 17 when he moved in with another brother to learn carpentry. Neither sibling was particularly religious and the younger Jarratt became interested in horses and the other amusements of the Tidewater gentry. Largely self-educated, he was invited to pursue a position as tutor in Albemarle County at age 19. As a boarder, Jarratt came under the influence of a pious Presbyterian family where he first encountered a vital Christian faith. A Puritan sermon read by his hostess made him conclude (he later wrote) 'that he was in a state of deep moral darkness, . . . and he resolved deliberately . . . to save his soul'.

After his conversion, he returned to teaching but was encouraged to consider entering the ministry. Tutored by Alexander Martin, Jarratt proved to be a good student and quickly learned Latin and Greek. Most of Jarratt's Christian friends were Presbyterian and he, therefore, first leaned toward Presbyterian orders but decided finally to seek Anglican ordination. With no bishop in the American colonies, he was forced to travel to England where he was examined and ordained to the presbyterate in 1763 by the Bishop of Chester. Returning to Virginia in the summer of the same year, Jarratt obtained the rectorship of Bath parish in Dinwiddie county which he held for the rest of his life. At about this time, he also married Martha Claiborne who became a very effective manager of her husband's affairs during his lengthy absences.

Given his evangelical convictions and the moribund state of the established church in Virginia, it was inevitable that Jarratt would cooperate with the Methodists, then making inroads in the southern colonies. Alone or with Methodist itinerants, he travelled sometimes as far as 600 miles from his home parish. Jarratt was an important support for Methodist evangelist, ROBERT WILLIAMS, during his Virginia trip of 1773. Moreover, he attended Methodist conferences; the Conference of 1782 actually instructed its 'preachers in the south to consult him, and to take his advice in the absence of brother [FRANCIS] ASBURY'. Jarratt worked with Methodists confident that they would remain loyal members of the Church of England but when the formal break finally came in 1784, he became far less sympathetic. Unfortunately for Jarratt, his relations with members of his own denomination were cool at best. Most of his fellow clergy treated him as a fanatic and when he visited a diocesan convention in Williamsburg in 1774, he came away feeling ostracized and insulted. Gradually, however, the climate for evangelicals improved within the now autonomous Episcopal church. By 1791, he was being asked to preach at clerical gatherings and the sermon he delivered at the Richmond convention of 1792 was warmly received. Jarratt remained active until the last year of his life when a painful cancer finally prevented him from carrying out his ministerial duties.

Jarratt was among the most important Anglican evangelicals in eighteenth-century America. For many years, he was a lone evangelical voice in a church notorious for its worldly congregations and sceptical, indifferent clergy. Due primarily to his efforts (and those of his Methodist allies), large portions of Virginia witnessed revival between 1764 and 1772. His teaching regarding human depravity and the need for spiritual rebirth, though unpopular in some circles, helped lay the foundation for the evangelical flowering within southern Episcopalianism in the early nineteenth century.

SELECT WRITINGS

D. Jarratt, *Sermons on Various and Important Subjects*, 3 vols (Philadelphia, PA, 1783–94)
—, *The Life of the Reverend Devereux Jarratt, . . . Written by Himself* (Baltimore, MD, 1806; New York, 1969)
—, *Thoughts on Some Important Subjects in Divinity* (Baltimore, MD, 1806)

BIBLIOGRAPHY
AAP
DAB
DARB

GILLIS HARP

Jarratt, Robert (b. *c.* 1766; d. Leeds, England, 24 Jan. 1843). Anglican clergyman. The son of John Jarratt of Hull, he was educated at the High School there before going up to Trinity College, Cambridge. He matriculated in 1783 and obtained the BA in 1787 (MA 1790). Jarratt was for 52 years Rector of Wellington, Somerset (1791–1843), a charge worth only £15 per annum. Much admired by JOSIAH PRATT, he was also 'justly revered' by his parishioners.

BIBLIOGRAPHY
Clerical Guide (1822)
GM (1841): 440
J. Pratt, *Memoir of the Rev. Josiah Pratt* (New York, 1855): 257

JONATHAN BURKE CUTMORE

Jarrom, Joseph (b. Diseworth, Leicestershire, England, 7 Oct. 1774; d. Wisbech, Norfolk, England, 5 Sept. 1842). General Baptist New Connexion minister and theological educator. Brought up as an agricultural labourer, his only formal education was in the parish school in the winter months, but his eagerness for knowledge built on this slender base by private reading. Converted under the ministry of John Tarratt, he was baptized in the River Soar, 31 May 1795, and joined the church at Kegworth and Diseworth, which soon discovered his usefulness in Christian service and commended him for training at DAN TAYLOR's academy in London, Before he finished his course, however, he was called to the pastorate of the church at Louth, but after a year settled at Wisbech, where his ministry soon required larger premises.

He combined the pastorate with the keeping of a school, until in 1813 the New Connexion transferred their academy from London to Wisbech with Mr Jarrom as tutor, a task he discharged most effectively, penning some 16 small works of a biblical and theological nature. Heart disease and gout brought his preaching career to an effective end in 1835 though he did not resign his pastorate until 1838, and shortly thereafter his academic duties. The tribute was paid to him that he was 'a dissenter without bigotry, a controversialist without acrimony, a moralist without asceticism, a saint without hypocrisy, and a man without guile'.

BIBLIOGRAPHY
Baptist Union Report (1844)
Minutes of the 74th General Baptist Association [New Connexion], (London, 1843)
J. H. Wood, *A Condensed History of the General Baptists of the New Connexion* (London, 1847)

J. H. Y. BRIGGS

Jasper, John (b. Fluvanna Co., VA, USA, 4 July 1812; d. Richmond, VA, USA, 30 March 1901). Black Baptist minister in Virginia. John Jasper, who was always identified by both names, was considered by some to be the incomparable southern black preacher in the nineteenth century. Born a slave on a plantation in Virginia owned by the Peachy family, he eventually was moved to Richmond and became the property of a tobacco manufacturer, Samuel Hargrove. While working as a tobacco stemmer at Hargrove's factory, Jasper was converted at the age of 27. Hargrove encouraged Jasper to share his conversion with the other tobacco workers, and consequently, he always spoke highly of Hargrove and other whites.

After his conversion, Jasper began to preach, primarily in Richmond and Petersburg. He had never received any formal education but he learned to read some and spent much time reading the Bible. He gained prominence as a funeral preacher and drew large crowds whenever he spoke. He asserted, in almost every sermon, that he was a 'God-sent' man. After fifty years of slavery, 25 of them as a preacher, Jasper received his freedom. For thirty more years he continued to preach in Richmond but also travelled to other parts of Virginia and other states. At sixty years of age, Jasper started a church in Richmond. The church began with nine people and grew to over 2,000 members. Jasper led the movement to build the Sixth Mount Zion church. There were many white contributors and Jasper gave over $3,000 himself.

Jasper was known for his preaching style. William E. Hatcher, Jasper's biographer, said 'his vocabulary was poverty itself, his grammar a riot of errors, his pronunciation a dialectic wreck, his gestures wild and unmeaning, his grunts and heavings terrible to bear'. Yet, Jasper preached with a powerful eloquence that drew and captivated large integrated crowds which included prominent listeners. He was loved for his imagination and pictorial sermons that were strongly doctrinal and based on a literal reading of the Bible. Jasper received the most notoriety for his sermon, 'The Sun Do Move'. He reportedly preached the sermon 250 times and travelled as far as Philadelphia, but failed on the speaker's circuit. In the sermon Jasper chastised modern science for disagreeing with the literal meaning of the Bible that the sun moves and the earth is flat. While some post-bellum educated black preachers thought him an embarrassment, many never ceased their admiration and his congregation had perfect faith in him.

BIBLIOGRAPHY
W. E. Hatcher, *John Jasper* (New York, 1908)

C. DOUGLAS WEAVER

Jay, William (b. Tisbury, Wiltshire, England, 6 May 1769; d. Bath, Somerset, England, 27 Dec. 1853). Congregational minister and author. The son of a small freeholder and stonemason, Jay was himself apprenticed as a stonemason. He came under evangelical religious influences at a house at Tisbury that had been licensed for dissenting worship and it was there that he began to take a public part in worship. He attracted the attention of Cornelius Winter (1742–1803), the distinguished Congregational minister of Marlborough, who accepted him into his academy where Jay studied from 1785 until midsummer 1788. He first preached at Ablington when he had just turned 16 and had delivered over a thousand sermons before he became of age. Hence the appellation 'the boy preacher'. In July 1788, at the invitation of the minister, ROWLAND HILL, he preached at the fashionable Surrey Chapel and so began a series of visits that was to last for the best part of his life.

After leaving the academy in 1788 he became lay pastor at Christian Malford, near Chippenham, on a salary of £35 a year. Then he ministered in the same capacity for a year at Hope Chapel, Bristol. When Thomas Tuppen, the minister of Lady Glenorchy's new Argyle Chapel at Bath, was incapacitated by illness, Jay was persuaded to occupy his pulpit with the result that he preached the sermon at the opening of the chapel on 4 October 1789. After the death of Tuppen, Jay succeeded him and was ordained on 30 January 1791. He resigned on 31 January 1853 after a ministry of 62 years. He died at Bath before the end of the year, aged 84.

Jay was married (1) 6 January 1791, to Anne, daughter of Edward Davies, Rector of Bengeworth, Worcestershire, and later Coychurch. They had six children. She died 14 October 1845. (2) 2 September 1846, to Marianna Jane Head of Bradford. She died, 4 February 1857, aged 76.

Jay's ministry was one of the most remarkable in its century, both as regard its length and influence. Despite his early lack of social and educational advantages, he

became a preacher appreciated by all classes of people. Not without reason did JOHN FOSTER call him 'a prince amongst preachers'. His style of preaching in an age much addicted to high oratory was natural and devoid of lush rhetoric and histrionic gesture. It was his belief that the best preaching was that which combined the solemnity and substance of the old dissenting tradition with the warmth and personal appeal of the Methodist style. He was himself an exemplar of this combination. It was his earnestness, directness and simplicity that captivated huge congregations. His theology was essentially Calvinistic but he deplored sermons which indulged in long and scholastic discussions of theological niceties. He felt that those who preached such sermons were 'too orthodox to be evangelical'. He never ceased to emphasize the central doctrines of Christianity but combined sound doctrine with practical application to the spiritual condition of his hearers while emphasizing the necessity of responding in faith to the redeeming work of Christ.

Jay was also a diligent author whose more popular books ran to many editions. His printed sermons were emulated or repeated in hundreds of pulpits in Britain and the United States. He was an enthusiastic supporter of the LMS and preached the sermon at its annual meetings on five occasions. He gave his patronage also to such institutions as the RTS, the Bible Society, the Irish Evangelical Society, as well as to such causes as the Anti-Slavery Society, the Peace Society, Catholic emancipation and temperance. All in all, Jay was an extremely attractive man, a minister of rare quality, and a preacher whose influence extended far beyond the confines of Argyle Chapel.

BIBLIOGRAPHY
DNB
G. Redford and J. A. James, *The Autobiography of the Rev. William Jay* (New York, 1855)

R. TUDUR JONES

Jay, William (b. New York, 16 June 1789, d. New York, 14 Oct. 1858). Co-founder of the ABS, life director of the ATS, judge, and author. Jay was the second son of John Jay and Sarah VanBrugh Livingston. He attended Yale and entered law. In 1812, he married Hannah Augusta McVickar. By 1818, he was a judge and served almost continuously until displaced by pro-slavery Democrats in 1843.

Evangelical beliefs led him to support and write for such causes as temperance, antislavery, ABS and ATS. He early served as secretary of a Society for the Suppression of Vice. In 1816, he helped found the ABS, and was later life director of ATS. He wrote and spoke against slavery, supporting abolition on constitutional grounds and opposing colonization as immoral.

An Episcopalian, he championed evangelical causes even when that meant conflict with denominational leadership. His belief that Episcopalians should join the

ABS produced a pamphlet battle with the High Church-man John Henry Hobart. He publicly criticized Episcopalians who supported slavery using the Bible. His evangelical stance led him to oppose the Oxford Movement.

BIBLIOGRAPHY
DAB
B. Tuckerman, *William Jay and the Constitutional Movement for the Abolition of Slavery* (New York, 1893)

JOHN F. WAUKECHON

Jefferson, John Clark (b. Cornwall, England, 1760; d. Matavai, Tahiti, 25 Sept. 1807). Among the first LMS missionaries to arrive at Tahiti. In his youth Jefferson had been an actor and had been employed as a schoolmaster. He was later ordained as a Congregational minister at Fowey, Cornwall, England. Jefferson was an able man and was better educated than most of the early missionaries appointed by the LMS. His colleagues on board the *Duff* accused him of denying the faith of the Missionary Society, by holding Arminian principles rather that adhering to Calvinistic doctrines. He was excommunicated on board the ship but was soon reinstated to full fellowship. He was one of four ordained men on board the *Duff*.

Jefferson was a courageous missionary who was determined to remain on Tahiti although he had been physically abused by the islanders and in spite of the precarious nature of the mission's tenure on the island. Tahiti was Jefferson's only field of labour. Jefferson's qualities were recognized by his fellow missionaries and he served the mission as its president and its secretary. As one of the most fluent Tahitian speakers he undertook preaching tours of the island, was involved with early attempts to teach 'king' Pomare II the principles of the Christian faith. His untimely death was a great blow to the morale of the missionaries.

BIBLIOGRAPHY
N. Gunson, *Messengers of Grace* (Melbourne, 1978)
R. Lovett, *The History of the London Missionary Society 1795–1895* (London, 1899)
RMD, 4th edn (London, 1923)

R. WATCYN JAMES

Jeffrey, George (b. Leitholm, Berwickshire, Scotland, 1 Oct. 1815; d. Glasgow, 23 May 1887). United Presbyterian minister. He was educated at Edinburgh University and at the Secessionist seminary. Jeffrey was minster of Lothian Road Chapel, Edinburgh, from 1838 until his death, where he became one of the city's most popular preachers, increasing his congregation from a handful to upwards of 1,000. He was United Presbyterian moderator in 1879. Jeffrey was a member of the EA.

In 1844 he and a few fellow voluntarists, outraged at the Free Church's solicitation of support from congregations in the American slave states, threatened to withdraw from the Free Church-dominated Emancipation Society. As a consequence, in 1847 he co-founded the Free Church Anti-Slavery Society and published *The Pro-Slavery Character of the American Churches*.

SELECT WRITINGS
G. Jeffrey, *The Believer's Privilege*, memoir by A. Thomson (Edinburgh. 1888)

BIBLIOGRAPHY
Boase
C. D. Rice, *Scots Abolitionists* (Baton Rouge, LA, 1981): 129, 142

JONATHAN BURKE CUTMORE

Jenkins, Ebenezer Evans (b. Exeter, Devon, England, 10 May 1820; d. Southport, Lancashire, England, 19 July 1905). Wesleyan missionary. In 1845, the year of his ordination, Jenkins was sent to Madras as a missionary where he established the Royapettah High School and was superintendent of Wesleyan missions for southern India. He returned to England in 1865 to be superintendent of the Hackney, London circuit.

An indefatigable traveller for the Missionary Society, he attended the Evangelical Alliance Conference in New York in 1873, and toured the Far East in 1875–6, and again in 1884–5. Having been elected to the Legal Hundred in 1864, and an influential missions secretary from 1877 (to 1888), he was elected president of conference in 1880.

Jenkins, who was allied with Hugh Price Hughes in the social gospel 'forward movement', was in politics a strong Liberal, yet he strenuously resisted the identification of Methodism with any one political party. Among his published writings, most delightful are the lucid and observant overseas diary entries reproduced in his son's *Memoir*.

BIBLIOGRAPHY
DNB
J. H. Jenkins, *Ebenezer Evans Jenkins, A Memoir* (London, 1906)
G. Moon, ed., *Men and Women of the Time* (London and New York, 1891)

JONATHAN BURKE CUTMORE

Jenkins, John (b. Llangynidr, Powys, Wales, 28 Nov. 1779; d. Mynyddislwyn, Gwent, South Wales, 5 June 1853). Welsh Baptist preacher and theologian. The son of Jenkin and Mary Jenkins, adherents to the Established Church, Jenkins was drawn to the Baptist cause and immersed at Llanwenarth, Gwent, on 29 November 1795. Ordained at Llangynidr in May 1806, he moved to the Hengoed pastorate in neighbouring Glamorganshire on 14 December 1808 establishing himself, despite social and educational disadvantages, as the foremost theologian and expositor among the Welsh Baptists (see his systematic theology *Gwelediad y Palas Arian*, 1811, and his commentary on the Bible, 1819–31). He was awarded DD by Lewisburg Seminary, Pennsylvania, in 1852.

BIBLIOGRAPHY
DWB

D. DENSIL MORGAN

Jenkins, Joseph (b. Wrexham, Wales, 1743; d. Walworth, London, 21 Feb. 1819). Particular Baptist minister and essayist. The son of Evan Jenkins, Baptist minister in Wrexham, THOMAS LLEWELLYN arranged for his education in London. He showed early proficiency in Greek and Hebrew and went to Aberdeen as a [JOHN] WARD scholar. He was baptized by SAMUEL STENNETT at the Little Wild Street Church in 1766. In 1769 he exercised a pastoral ministry over an Independent church in Chester but it was not until 1773 that he was ordained to the pastorate of the Old Meeting [Baptist/Independent] in Wrexham. In 1790 he was honoured with an Edinburgh DD. The suggestion that in 1791 he served as interim president of the Bristol Academy after the death of CALEB EVANS [DWB] seems to be without foundation. Active in the Midland Baptist Association, he contributed its Circular Letter for 1792. In 1793 he moved to his first London pastorate and succeeded JOSEPH SWAIN in his lectureship at Devonshire Square and his pastorate at Walworth in 1798, serving there for twenty years. He wrote against subscription and in defence of the Baptists and the Trinitarian faith.

BIBLIOGRAPHY
DNB
DWB
J. Ivimey, *History of the English Baptists*, IV (London, 1830)
G. V. Price, *The 'Old Meeting'* (Wrexham, Wales, 1932)

J. H. Y. BRIGGS

Jennings, Samuel Kennedy (b. Essex Co., NJ, BNA, 6 June 1771; d. Baltimore, MD, USA, 19 Oct. 1854). Minister in the MEC and the MPC. He descended from a long line of faithful Independents and Presbyterians and was the son of Jacob Jennings, himself a prominent physician and minister. Samuel graduated in 1790 from Rutgers College and studied medicine under his father's direction. In 1794 he was converted, joined the MEC, and soon began preaching in Virginia. He was known for his natural, clear, and convincing style. In 1817 he went to Maryland, and was elected president of Asbury College in Baltimore in 1818. He also served for more than twenty years as a professor in the medical department of Washington University. By 1821 he was involved with others in the movement that would eventually become the MPC. During this time he was a patron and contributor to the *Wesleyan Repository* and its successor *Mutual Rights*. In 1827 he was expelled from the MEC and became one of the founders of the MPC in 1830. Between 1845 and 1853 he lived in Alabama. In 1853

he fell prey to a debilitating paralysis and returned to Baltimore, where he died the following year in his daughter's home.

BIBLIOGRAPHY
CM
EWM

STEVE HARPER

Jensen, Stephan (b. Copenhagen, Denmark, 20 May 1724; d. Nain, Labrador, 2 Aug. 1800). Moravian deacon and missionary to the Labrador Inuit. Jensen, a shipbuilder, was Lutheran before he became a member of the Moravian Church on 7 May 1769. He helped JENS HAVEN in establishing Nain in 1771, was ordained deacon on 16 April 1786, and participated in founding the Okak settlement.

BIBLIOGRAPHY
Public Archives of Canada, Ottawa, 'Catalogus der Missionare in Labrador', Records of the Moravian Mission in Labrador [1764–1944], Microfilm 511, Reels 11–12, fol. 15221–2
Kölbing

MARCELLA ROLLMANN

Jerram, Charles (b. Blidworth, Nottinghamshire, England, 17 Jan. 1770; d. Witney, Oxfordshire, 20 June 1853). Anglican clergyman; Vicar of Chobham and Rector of Witney. Tutored by T. Cursham, Rector of Blidworth, he taught in London for a while and was then enabled by the ElS to attend Magdalene College, Cambridge (1793–7) where he appreciated CHARLES SIMEON's ministry. Ordained in 1797, he served as curate at Long Sutton, Lincolnshire (1797–1805) where he was associated with the foundation of the CMS. As Curate and later Vicar of Chobham, Surrey, he successfully tutored students retaining the benefice when he ministered at St John's, Bedford Row (1824–6). In 1834 he became Rector of Witney, Oxfordshire where he was a vigorous evangelical reformer, opposed secession to dissent and withstood Tractarianism.

SELECT WRITINGS
C. Jerram, *Secession from the Church of England Considered in a Letter to a Friend* (London, 1836)

BIBLIOGRAPHY
Boase
DNB

TIMOTHY C. F. STUNT

Jersey, F(rancis) N(athaniel) (b. England, probably 1795). Primitive Methodist minister. As a youth he went to sea and was converted by WILLIAM CLOWES at Hull in 1821. A passionate evangelist, he helped open up the work in Darlington and Barnard Castle (1821) and missioned Kendal (1822) and the Furness district (1823). In the great Weardale revival of 1823 he was one of the leaders. He conducted a successful mission to Ireland in 1833–4 on behalf of the Preston Brook circuit, but shortly afterwards, while serving at Nottingham, a serious secession occurred, and though continuing to itinerate for another six years he thereafter met with little evangelistic success. He became a Baptist in 1840 and emigrated to the USA, after which no more was heard of him. A shadowy and reclusive man, 'F. N. Jersey' would reveal his Christian names only to his closest friends.

IAN SELLERS

Jervis, Charles (b. Birmingham, Warwickshire, England, baptized 6 Feb. 1782; d. Cheltenham, Gloucestershire, England, 28 Sept. 1826). Anglican clergyman. Jervis was born in Birmingham and became a scholar at Trinity College, Oxford. After ordination he was chaplain to the Duke of Cambridge and held various incumbencies including Clewer, near Windsor, Kenchester, Herefordshire and Luddenham, Kent. Jervis was probably converted through T. T. BIDDULPH, and at Windsor became a close friend of HENRY RYDER and keen supporter of the CMS.

Between 1816 and 1826 he was the Perpetual Curate of Cheltenham Parish Church and paved the way for the ministry of his successor, FRANCIS CLOSE. Jervis erected Holy Trinity Church (where G. C. GORHAM nearly became curate and to which Close was appointed) and CHARLES SIMEON's sermon prepared for its opening was undelivered (Simeon, 3, 338–51). Jervis was a cautious man of whom it was said in one funeral oration that he set forth 'zeal without enthusiasm, devotion without bigotry, and fervent piety confirmed by faith and chastened by charity.'

BIBLIOGRAPHY
A. F. Munden, 'Evangelical in the Shadows: Charles Jervis of Cheltenham', *Churchman*, 96, 2 (1982): 142–50
C. Simeon, *Horae Homileticae*, 11 vols, 3 (London, 1836)

ALAN FREDERICK MUNDEN

Jesse, William (b. England, *c.* 1739; d. West Bromwich, Staffordshire, England, 1815). Anglican clergyman; Vicar of West Bromwich. Of aristocratic stock, he was the son of William Jesse, Rector of Wellington, Somerset (1743–91). Details of his early life are obscure but in 1757 he entered Trinity College, Oxford, graduating BA in 1761. He was influenced by THOMAS HAWEIS and probably joined his evangelical club. He itinerated for Lady HUNTINGDON from 1766 until her chapels were registered as dissenting places of worship in 1781. From 1767 to 1780 he was Vicar of Hutton Cranswick, near Driffield in Yorkshire. HENRY VENN regarded him as a potential apostle of the Wolds. He was instituted to West Bromwich in 1790 on the recommendation of Lord DARTMOUTH, and in 1795 also acquired the livings of Dowles and Ribbesford in Worcestershire. His published works included lectures on Christian evidences and *Parochialia* – letters to a cleric on the discharge of parish responsibilities. These elicited an anonymous response in defence of the clergy.

A. SKEVINGTON WOOD

Jessop, William (b. Bridge Branch, DE, BNA, 22 May 1764; d. Strasburg, PA, USA, 23 Dec. 1795). Missionary of the American MEC. Jessop began to preach in 1784 five years after his conversion. He soon joined the American MEC ministry. As a foreign missionary to Nova Scotia and New Brunswick, Jessop consolidated FREEBORN GARRETTSON's earlier revival work over three tours (1787–9, 1791–3, 1794–5). In the United States he preached in Delaware, Pennsylvania, and in John Street Chapel (New York City) before succumbing to consumption. Bishop ASBURY described Jessop as, 'always solemn, and few such holy, steady men have been found among us'. His journals reveal the hardships and expectations of missionaries to Nova Scotia, while those portions concerning the United States illustrate the driving pace of itinerant preachers as well as Jessop's disdain of slavery. Jessop's life exemplified the zeal to which the American MEC owed its rapid growth.

SELECT WRITINGS
W. Jessop, [Diary 1 Jan. to 11 March 1788] MG100, 169, 27, Public Archives of Nova Scotia, Halifax
—, [Journal 1 Jan. 1790 to 12 June 1791, includes letter from John Wesley of 1 Feb. 1791] The United Library, Garrett-Evangelical Theological Seminary, Evanston, Illinois

BIBLIOGRAPHY
G. French, ed., 'The Papers of Daniel Fidler . . . 1792–1798' *The Bulletin . . . Committee on Archives of the United Church of Canada*, 12 (1959): 3–18

ALLEN B. ROBERTSON

Jesty, Thomas (b. Yeovil, Somerset, England; d. at sea, 17 Jan. 1820). CMS missionary to Sierra Leone. Jesty trained as a schoolmaster at the Central School of the National School Society before volunteering to go to Sierra Leone with the CMS. He and his wife were sent to Freetown on 29 January 1819 but he lasted less than a year and died a few days after sailing from Freetown. His wife died six months earlier in July 1819. Their willingness to serve in Sierra Leone is remarkable in view of the fate of other early CMS couples (*see* M. RENNER, P. HARTWIG, J. G. PRASSE, J. C. BARNETH, J. QUAST, C. H. MEISSNER, H. MEYER, J. H. SCHULZE and C. JOST).

BIBLIOGRAPHY
D. T. B[arry], *CMS Register of Missionaries and Native Clergy* (privately printed) (London, 1906)

DONALD M. LEWIS

Jeter, Jeremiah Bell (b. Bedford County, VA, USA, 18 July 1802; d. Richmond, VA, USA, 18 Feb. 1880). Baptist minister, editor, and denominational leader. Jeter was converted and baptized during a revival that swept through his rural community in 1821. Although he had little formal education, he soon showed himself to be a preacher of uncommon power. Ordained in 1824, Jeter went on to serve as pastor of several large congregations, including two in Richmond, Virginia: the First Baptist Church (1836–49) and the Grace Street Baptist Church (1852–70). Present in 1845 at the founding of the Southern Baptist Convention (SBC), he was the first president (1845–9) of the SBC's Foreign Mission Board, later serving as president of the board of directors of the Southern Baptist Theological Seminary in Louisville, Kentucky. Jeter's love of controversy was reflected not only in his staunch support for the Confederacy and defence of the institution of slavery but also in his most important publication, *Campbellism Examined* (1855), a critique of the views of ALEXANDER CAMPBELL and his 'Disciples'.

BIBLIOGRAPHY
DAB

GEORGE W. HARPER

Jetter, John Andrew (b. Liebenzell, Würtemburg, Germany, *c.* 1791; d. Tunbridge Wells, Kent, England, 1 Jan. 1885). Pioneer CMS missionary in India. Jetter and W. J. DEERR trained together at the Basel Mission House, studied the National School Society's system in London, spent November 1818 through April 1819 at the CMS House in Islington, and then obtained a licence to work in Bengal from the East India Company. They came to Burdwan in 1819 to work for the CMS. After a row on the ship they refused to speak to each other. Eventually DANIEL CORRIE had to intervene.

Impressed by the missions in Madras, both hoped to duplicate them in Bengal. Far from replicating C. T. E. RHENIUS's 'spirit of insubordination', as the CMS had feared, they were virtually the only Lutherans who did not disturb the Calcutta Committee. In 1820, they conducted the ordinations of ABDUL MASIH and WILLIAM BOWLEY. After friction with JOHN PEROWNE, the CMS resolved never to station German and English missionaries together.

After he married HANNAH CORTIS (another CMS missionary) in 1823 Jetter took a furlough (1824–5) and was ordained as an Anglican (deacon, 14 June 1829; priest 6 June 1830). He then sailed to Smyrna (1830) for his health, working there as a CMS agent until January 1840. From 1850 to 1856 he was incumbent of Ironbridge, Shropshire. Thereafter he travelled extensively.

BIBLIOGRAPHY
The Friend of India, 11 (1845): 451
M. A. Laird, *Missionaries and Education on Bengal 1793–1838* (Oxford, 1972)

E. M. JACKSON

Jobson, Frederick John (b. London, 6 July 1812; d. London, 4 Jan. 1881). Wesleyan minister. He was brought up in a Methodist household and as a boy was apprenticed with a view to an architectural career. His success as a local preacher led to his entering the ministry in 1834 and he quickly became distinguished as a preacher of diverse oratorical styles adapted to suit different congregations. He served three periods totalling nine years at City Road Chapel, London. He played a prominent part in the formation of the EA, wrote *Chapel and School Architecture* (1850), a very influential book in the history of Methodist church building, and *America and American Methodism* (1857). He was appointed Wesleyan book steward in 1864, and was president of the conference, 1869–70.

BIBLIOGRAPHY
B. Gregory, *The Life of F. J. Jobson*, (London, 1884)
Obituary WMM (1881)

IAN SELLERS

Jocelyn, Robert. See RODEN, the third Earl of

Jocelyn, Robert [Viscount Jocelyn] (b. London, 20 Feb. 1816; d. London, 12 Aug. 1854). British MP. Jocelyn was the eldest son of Robert Jocelyn, the third EARL OF RODEN, MP. As military secretary to Baron Saltoun in the Rifle Brigade, he visited China and wrote of his experiences in *Six Months in China* (1841). He was MP for King's Lynn (1842–54) and Secretary to the Board of Control (1845–6). A liberal Tory and moderate Protestant Constitutionalist, he supported religious toleration and free trade. He was the friend and associate of the evangelical politicians, Sir Charles Trevelyan and Sir HARRY VERNEY, and was a supporter of the CMS.

In 1842 Jocelyn married a daughter of Earl Cowper, becoming related (through his mother-in-law's remarriage) to Viscount Palmerston and Lord SHAFTESBURY. He died suddenly at Palmerston's residence, perhaps of cholera contracted at the Tower of London. Members of the East Essex Militia, just then billeted at the Tower, had complained of severe illness. As their commander, Jocelyn took up residence at the Tower to demonstrate the soundness of its environment. He died within a few days.

BIBLIOGRAPHY
GM (Sept. 1854): 297–9
Stenton

JONATHAN BURKE CUTMORE

Johns, David [christened **David Jones**]. (b. parish of Llanina, Dyfed, Wales, 1796; d. Island of Nosibé, Madagascar, 6 Aug. 1843). Pioneer LMS missionary in Madagascar. Johns studied at Neuadd-lwyd, Newtown Independent College and Gosport. He was ordained as a Congregational minister at Penrhiwgaled on 14 February 1826. He sailed for Madagascar 5 May 1826, reaching the capital, Antananarivo on 11 September. Along with DAVID JONES and DAVID GRIFFITHS he was instrumental in establishing 25 schools in and around the capital. Together the three translated the Bible into Malagasy; Johns also translated Bunyan's *Pilgrim's Progress*. Due to persecution of Christianity he left Antananarivo on 22 July 1836. Afterwards he made several visits to different parts of the island to support and rescue believers. Together with J. J. Freeman he revised the *Malagasy-English Dictionary* and wrote *A Narrative of the Persecution of Christians in Madagascar* (London, 1840).

BIBLIOGRAPHY
G. P. Griffith, *Cenhadon Cymreig* (Cardiff, 1897)
LMS Register of Missionaries 1796–1923, 4th edn (London, 1923)

IEUAN S. JONES

Johns, Henry V(an) D(yke) (b. Newcastle, DE, USA, 13 Oct. 1803; d. Baltimore, MD, USA, 22 April 1859). Protestant Episcopal clergyman. As the son of Kensey Johns (the Chancellor of Delaware), and the brother of JOHN JOHNS (Episcopal Bishop of Virginia), Henry V.D. Johns followed his family's pattern into undergraduate studies at Princeton College, but transferred to Union College, Schenectady, New York, where he graduated in 1823. He then entered General Theological Seminary, where he graduated in 1826, and was ordained deacon by Bishop William White at Emmanuel Church, Newcastle, Delaware, on 1 August 1826. After receiving priest's orders from Bishop PHILANDER CHASE, Johns organized Trinity Church in Washington, DC. In 1836, he moved to All Saints' Church, Frederick, Maryland, and then in 1837, to Baltimore, where he served as Rector of Trinity Church (1837) and St Andrew's Church (1838–43). In 1843, he moved once more to Christ Church, Cincinnati, but he was called back to Baltimore the next year to become Rector of Christ Church, which his brother had vacated after his election as Bishop of Virginia. In 1853, he organized a new parish in Baltimore, Emmanuel Church, which rose by 1858 to become first in the diocese of Maryland 'in number of communicants and with general evidences of parochial prosperity'.

Johns was renowned for his precision of expression and the compelling logic of his sermons, as well as for the forthright evangelicalism which filled them. That evangelicalism brought him into sharp and public controversy with the Bishop of Maryland, William R. Whittingham, on the occasion of Johns's institution as Rector of Christ Church, Baltimore.

Johns again clashed with Whittingham in 1850 over his High Church claims. At the Episcopal Church's General Convention of that year, Johns and ten other Maryland rectors vainly attempted to have Whittingham presented for trial. The next year, Whittingham retaliated by presenting Johns for trial for taking part in joint evangelistic services with non-Episcopalians. This charge failed, also, but it provided an important backdrop to similar clashes over ecumenical issues in the 1860s throughout the Episcopal Church, and to the dramatic

separation of the Reformed Episcopalians in 1873 under George David Cummins, who had been Johns' curate at Christ Church, Baltimore, from 1846 until 1847.

BIBLIOGRAPHY
W. F. Brand, *Life of William Rollinson Whittingham*, 1 (New York, 1883)

ALLEN C. GUELZO

Johns, John (b. Newcastle, DE, USA, 10 July 1796; d. Alexandria, VA, USA, 4 April 1876). Protestant Episcopal bishop. Son of the Chancellor and Chief Justice of Delaware, Johns graduated from the College of New Jersey (Princeton) in 1815, and spent two years at Princeton Theological Seminary before taking an MA at the college in 1818. He was ordained deacon in the following year by Bishop William White, and priest in 1820. From 1819 until 1829, he was in charge of All Saints Church, Frederick, Maryland, and then from 1829 until 1842, he served as Rector of Christ Church, Baltimore, and the Church of the Messiah, Baltimore. He was from the first noted for his 'great sweetness and flexibility of voice and precision of diction in speaking'; but even more, he was noted for his evangelical preaching 'of an humble and living faith to a crucified Saviour'. He twice narrowly missed election as bishop of the diocese of Maryland.

It was to Virginia that Johns was finally called in May 1842, as assistant bishop to the prominent evangelical Bishop of Virginia, WILLIAM MEADE. He was consecrated in the Monumental Church, Richmond, Virginia, on 13 October 1842 by Bishops ALEXANDER VIETS GRISWOLD (New England), Levi Silliman Ives (North Carolina), William R. Whittingham (Maryland) and Meade. 'He was greatly admired and much beloved in his diocese', and his support for Meade was energetic and cordial. In 1849, he undertook the added responsibility of rebuilding the College of William and Mary, serving as president without pay until 1854. He moved from there to Alexandria, Virginia, where he took up residence in the grounds of the diocesan theological seminary and provided instruction (from 1865 onwards) to the senior classes in pastoral theology and homiletics. The outbreak of the Civil War forced a temporary removal to Staunton, Virginia; and to compound his burdens, the elderly Bishop Meade died on 14 March 1862, leaving the war-torn diocese to Johns's care.

After the war, Johns returned to Alexandria, and emerged as one of the foremost opponents in the House of Bishops to the influence of the Oxford Movement. However, he equally opposed the evangelical secession movement organized by Bishop George David Cummins in 1873, and engaged one of his own proteges, James Allen Latane, in a published debate over Latane's defection to Cummins. Johns continued his steady round of episcopal visitations in his diocese up through his seventies. Those responsibilities, however, prevented him from publishing more than two dozen sermons and occasional tracts; his only sustained work was an affectionate memoir of William Meade (1847).

BIBLIOGRAPHY
E. C. Chorley, *Men and Movements in the American Episcopal Church* (New York, 1950)
W. A. R. Goodwin, *History of the Theological Seminary in Virginia and Its Historical Background*, 2 (New York, 1924)

ALLEN C. GUELZO

Johns, William   (*fl.* 1810–19). BMS missionary in India. Johns left Britain in 1810 after his friend and contemporary WILLIAM WARD invited him to join the Serampore Mission. He was medical officer in Serampore while Wallich, the famous botanist, was on furlough. In November 1813 he became the last missionary to be expelled before the renewed East India Company charter allowed missionaries into India.

Johns's very lengthy pamphlet, *The Spirit of the Serampore Mission*, was published in 1828. An important source of anecdotes about life in Serampore, it helped fuel the 'Serampore Controversy'. Like many of the 'junior brethren', Johns was totally disillusioned with Serampore. He could not abide the MARSHMANS. After failing to establish a medical practice in Serampore in 1819, and the deaths of his wife and son, he left India.

BIBLIOGRAPHY
J. C. Marshman, *The Life and Times of Carey, Marshman and Ward*, III (London, 1859)

E. M. JACKSON

Johnson, Elizabeth   [Brownhill, Mrs W.] (b. Shrewsbury, Shropshire, England, 24 Aug. 1808; d. Darlaston, Staffordshire, England, 15 Nov. 1860). Primitive Methodist itinerant preacher. Johnson attended a Wesleyan Methodist Sunday school, but when the Primitive Methodists visited the town she was converted. She very quickly began to exhort, then became a local preacher and an itinerant (1824). Her first appointment was to preach in a large casting foundry in South Wales, surely a daunting prospect for a girl of 16. She then ministered in the Oakengates, Preston-o'-the-Hill, Ramsor, Darlaston and Burton-on-Trent circuits. Johnson faced much persecution from noisy musicians, drunks and clergy during her ministry. On 17 March 1828 she married and settled in the Darlaston circuit where she worked as a local preacher and class leader. She became ill in August 1860 and died in November being survived by her husband, seven sons and three daughters. Three of her sons became mayors of Walsall (1872 and 1873; 1891; 1893) – a tribute to their upbringing.

BIBLIOGRAPHY
H. B. Kendall, *The Origin and History of the PM Church*, 2 (London, 1904?)
PMMag (1861)

E. DOROTHY GRAHAM

Johnson, Hannah   (b. Hanover; d. Sierra Leone, 1 June 1821). First CMS female missionary. Johnson and MARY BOUFFLER were the first females to be appointed in their own right as missionaries by the CMS. (Previously wives had accompanied their husbands but had not been appointed by the CMS.) Her brother was W. A. B. JOHNSON who had been serving in Sierra Leone since 1816. Apparently a schoolmistress, she sailed on 5 January 1820 for Sierra Leone with Mary Bouffler.

On 4 February 1822 she married ROBERT BECKLEY, another CMS missionary. Eight of the first ten 'female missionaries' sent out by CMS married in the field, sometimes a few months after arrival (one died *en route*; the other shortly after her arrival); in seven out of the eight cases the women were married within two years of being sent out. Given the phenomenally high death rate among the early CMS missionaries (especially in Sierra Leone), there was a supply of lonely widowers anxious for European wives.

BIBLIOGRAPHY
D. T. B[arry], *CMS Register of Missionaries and Native Clergy* (privately printed) (London, 1906)

DONALD M. LEWIS

Johnson, John   (b. Allostock, Cheshire, England, March 1706; d. Liverpool, Lancashire, England, 20 March 1791). High Calvinist Baptist minister and controversialist. Piously brought up as a General Baptist, he became minister at Byrom Street Particular Baptist Chapel, Liverpool in 1741 but his increasingly High Calvinist views, which were censured even by John Brine, soon [1747] provoked a schism and he and his followers not only founded a separate church but a separate denomination, the Johnsonian Baptists who had followers both in the north-west of England and in East Anglia. His High Calvinism notwithstanding, he was a tireless evangelist and considerable pamphleteer throughout over forty years of ministry.

BIBLIOGRAPHY
DNB
J. Ivimey, *History of the English Baptists*, III (London, 1830)
W. T. Whitley, *Baptists of North West England* (London, 1913)

J. H. Y. BRIGGS

Johnson, John   (b. Norwich, Norfolk, England, *c.* 1760; d. Manchester, 22 Sept. 1804). Countess of Huntingdon's Connexion minister. He was converted at Lady HUNTINGDON's chapel in Norwich, and sent by her to Trevecka College about 1780. He was ordained at Spa Fields chapel in London, 9 March 1783, and sent by Lady Huntingdon to Wigan to preach the Gospel in southern Lancashire. He was responsible for building chapels at Wigan and Tyldesley.

In 1791, shortly before Lady Huntingdon's death, she sent him to Georgia to put the orphan house at Bethesda in order. It had not been completely under her control since the Revolutionary War. Local supporters had been alienated by an earlier student whom she had sent out, and local politicians wished to use the lands to endow a secular school or college. Soon after his arrival at Bethesda, Lady Huntingdon died, bequeathing the lands to trustees which included Lord DARTMOUTH – not an acceptable choice for Georgians. Johnson nobly tried to resist the annexation of the property by the state, suffered temporary imprisonment in Savannah, and wrote a poem, *The Rape of Bethesda* (Charleston, SC, 1792) before returning to England.

He was imprisoned for the debt on Tyldesley Chapel on his return, but later acquired St George's Church in Manchester (which had not been consecrated) and established a congregation to which he ministered until his death. Johnson was interested in the conversion of the Jews. He is said to have preached three sermons in Hebrew for them, and also published *The Levite's Journal*.

BIBLIOGRAPHY
DNB
W. E. A. Axon, *The Annals of Manchester* (Manchester, England, 1886): 133
Johnson's journal for 1791 at Georgia Historical Society

EDWIN WELCH

Johnson, Matthew (b. Leeds, England, 1796; d. Leeds, England, 12 Jan. 1864). Protestant Methodist co-founder. Born of Wesleyan parents, Matthew became a schoolmaster and Wesleyan local preacher in Leeds. In 1827 a proposal to install an organ in the fashionable Leeds Brunswick Chapel brought to a head resentments and tensions that had long been incubating. Johnson, along with JAMES SIGSTON, led the opposition campaign and was expelled. In the ensuing uproar 1,000 members seceded in the two Leeds circuits and formed themselves into the Wesleyan Protestant Methodists, a body which was absorbed into the Wesleyan Methodist Association (WMA) in 1835. In both these bodies, Johnson played a leading role. He was president of the Protestant Methodists in 1832 and secretary five times, also four times secretary of the WMA. In 1848 he was appointed secretary of the Leeds Trade Protection Society. He contributed papers on 'Recollections of Leeds Methodism' to the *UMFC Magazine* in 1863.

E. ALAN ROSE

Johnson, Richard (b. Welton, Yorkshire, England, baptized 15 March 1755; d. London, 13 March 1827), and **Mary** [née Burton] Johnson, (b. London, *c.* 1753; d. London, 24 Jan. 1831). Church of England clergyman and first chaplain of the British colony in New South Wales, and his wife. Little is known of his early life except that at some time he attended Hull Grammar School, where he may have known WILLIAM WILBERFORCE, and that between 1780 and 1784 he was a student at Magdalene College, Cambridge. He was ordained

deacon at the end of 1783 and priest in 1784 and served two curacies, the second as assistant of the Reverend HENRY FOSTER.

Through the influence of Wilberforce and the Reverend JOHN NEWTON, Johnson was appointed chaplain to the convict fleet being prepared to set up a new penal colony in Botany Bay, Australia, a position which had been created by Pitt at Wilberforce's urging. Before sailing, Johnson married Mary Burton who accompanied him to Australia, the only officer's wife to do so in the first fleet. They sailed in May, 1787 and Johnson served with patience and devotion as the first, and for several years the only, chaplain to the new colony. His time in Sydney was marred by a bitter dispute with Francis Grose, the acting governor. Johnson resigned in 1800 and returned to England and in 1810 was appointed Rector of St Antholin's Church in London, where he served for the rest of his life.

Johnson was a firm evangelical and throughout his ministry followed the personal and pastoral principles of the evangelical wing of the Church of England. He brought faithfulness and perseverance, rather than outstanding gifts, to an extremely difficult task, and laid foundations on which others were to build. He built the first church structure on Australian soil and also began educational work in the colony. His reputation among the convicts as a Christian and as a pastor was very high, and there is no doubt that he had a genuine concern for his 'congregation'. Mary, who was also of evangelical background, served faithfully by her husband's side and was a constant support to him.

BIBLIOGRAPHY
ADB, 2: 17–19
J. Bonwick, *Australia's First Preacher* (London, 1898)
N. K. Macintosh, *Richard Johnson, Chaplain to the Colony of New South Wales: His Life and Times, 1755–1827* (Sydney, 1978)

NEIL KEITH MACINTOSH

Johnson, Samuel (b. Lichfield, Staffordshire, England, 18 Sept. 1709; d. London, 13 Dec. 1784). Writer. No single word can describe Johnson's polymorphous talents which took in poetry, plays, essays, novels, his *Dictionary* and his edition of Shakespeare, as well as his formidable conversational skills recorded at length in Boswell's biography. After a desultory education and a spell at Pembroke College, Oxford (1727–9) which he left prematurely because of poverty, Johnson was to spend most of his life in literary circles in London. He became LL D of Dublin (1765) and of Oxford (1775).

Johnson was afflicted by varying forms of ill health throughout his life and he was always deeply melancholic. A vein of what might be called Christian stoicism imbues his adaptation of Juvenal in the poem *The Vanity of Human Wishes*. With this went also a strain of self-searching and a deeply solemn sense of God. He has been aptly called a 'troubled believer' (Humphreys in Wahba, 1962).

Johnson had a terrible fear of death – and of judgment;

and it is a much argued question as to whether he underwent an evangelical conversion in the last year of his life. There appears to have been some kind of dramatic crisis on 20 February 1784, and in the remaining months of that year his letters repeatedly refer to that occasion, an event known also to others as WILLIAM COWPER's letter to JOHN NEWTON of 11 May, acknowledging the news of Johnson's conversion as 'a singular proof of the omnipotence of Grace', testifies. In his last prayer in English at the time of his last Communion on 5 December, eight days before his death, Johnson asked: 'Grant O Lord, that my whole hope and confidence may be in his merits and in thy mercy: forgive and accept my late conversion, enforce and accept my imperfect repentance . . . and make the death of thy son Jesus effectual to my redemption' (Johnson, 1958: 417–18).

SELECT WRITINGS

S. Johnson, *Diaries, Prayers and Annals*, eds E. L. McAdam with D. Hyde and M. Hyde (The Yale edition of the *Works of Samuel Johnson*, 1 [New Haven, CT, 1958])

BIBLIOGRAPHY

M. J. Quinlan, 'The Rumour of Dr Johnson's Conversion', *Review of Religion*, XII (1948): 243–61 [A sceptical view by a Jesuit critic, to which Greene's article – see following reference – is a reply]
M. Wahba, ed., *Johnsonian Studies* (Cairo, 1962) [especially A. R. Humphreys, 'Dr Johnson, Troubled Believer' and D. J. Greene, 'Dr Johnson's "Late Conversion": A Reconsideration']

ARTHUR POLLARD

Johnson, William Augustin Bernard (b. Hanover, Germany, 1788; d. at sea, 3 May 1823). CMS missionary in Sierra Leone. Johnson arrived in London in 1812 with little money or food and worked as a labourer in Whitechapel. He attended a prayer meeting at Garnon Church, Savoy, where he was convicted of his sins under the preaching of a Moravian minister, Lehmen, and he underwent a conversion experience. Shortly after this, his employer demanded that he work on Sunday, and Johnson resigned. He found some work at a sugar warehouse which, along with his wife's meagre earnings as a maid, kept the couple from extreme poverty. After a period of depression he became a member of C. STEINKOPF's German Church in the Savoy. Johnson was introduced to the CMS by a member of that congregation, W. HENRY DÜRING.

After being accepted as schoolteachers he and his wife set sail and arrived in Sierra Leone on 27 April 1816. Johnson was first appointed to Yongroo, an establishment on the Bulom coast. There he attempted to introduce the National System of Education. Johnson was moved to a small village outside Freetown called Hogbrook, shortly changed to Regent, and it became one of the success stories of the CMS mission.

From a village of a few unsettled and very ill recaptives, it grew to become one of the most economically prosperous, neatly built villages, with a very high percentage of Christians. Initially Johnson established the school, distributed rations, settled palavers, organized public works, and held morning and evening prayers daily, as well as three Sunday services. His contribution to the ministry was recognized by the CMS which allowed him, in 1817, to be ordained as a Lutheran minister, although they continually advised him not to allow so many signs of excitement and enthusiasm in his services. There had been occasions of people meeting for all night prayer meetings, fainting and crying for mercy in a manner that disturbed both the service and the CMS. Johnson established a missionary association and encouraged his communicant members to attend the special communicants' Saturday evening meeting. Regent also boasted a benefit society.

After four years Mrs Johnson suffered illness which forced her to return to London. Johnson remained; his wife returned but finally left again. Johnson returned to visit his ageing mother in Hanover, and brought his younger sister, Hannah, out to Sierra Leone with him. Finally the climate and the diseases took their toll. Almost blind and hardly able to walk, Johnson boarded ship to return to Britain in 1823, but died on the journey home.

BIBLIOGRAPHY

W. Jowett, *A Memoir of the Rev. W. A. B. Johnson* (London, 1852)
CMS Archives, University of Birmingham, England, s.v. Sierra Leone

ELIZABETH GRANT

Johnston, Sir Alexander (b. 1775; d. 1849). Colonial official, initiator and supporter of missions in Ceylon (Sri Lanka). Chief Justice in Ceylon, Johnston helped introduce Wesleyan Methodist missionaries to the island in 1814, and urged Anglican societies to do likewise. He paid for a Singhalese translation of Bishop Porteous's *Evidences of Christianity*, and for Portuguese, Tamil and Singhalese editions of the *Missionary Register*'s first issue (1813). This was planned by Bishop THOMAS COKE, whom Johnston had contacted through WILLIAM WILBERFORCE.

With Wesleyans in Colombo, where the Baptists already had a church, Johnston persuaded the Anglicans to work in Kandy. In 1817, four clergymen: SAMUEL LAMBRICK, ROBERT MAYOR (brother-in-law of CMS secretary EDWARD BICKERSTETH), BENJAMIN WARD and JOSEPH KNIGHT came to work with him.

BIBLIOGRAPHY

M. E. Gibbs, *The Anglican Church in India, 1600–1970* (Delhi, 1972)
E. Stock, *History of the Church Missionary Society*, I (London, 1900)

E. M. JACKSON

Johnston, Andrew (b. 1798; d. 24 Aug. 1862). British MP. A Scot, he was Whig MP for St Andrew's (1831–

7). He is often identified with the 'Recordite' grouping of evangelicals as opposed to those in the more moderate Claphamite tradition. He was, however, a transitional figure, as his voting and debating record shows. Johnston voted for the 1832 Reform Bill and supported factory reform and slavery abolition. He was, foremost, a defender of the established churches. He voted against the Maynooth Grant, he suggested that Catholic members should not debate church establishments, and that Jewish enfranchisement would bring an 'end to all Christianity'. To the chagrin of his constituents, he opposed the Irish Church Temporalities Bill. In debates on the Church of Scotland he railed against the 'yoke of patronage', and thus spoke for the evangelical Popular party in the denomination in which he was an elder. He is most notable, however, for championing, with Sir AND-REW AGNEW, Sabbatarian legislation. In 1834 Johnston married Priscilla Buxton, the daughter of Sir THOMAS FOWELL BUXTON. Their eldest son, Andrew Johnston (1835–1922, *Who Was Who*), also an MP, married Charlotte Trevelyan, a daughter of the Reverend G. Trevelyan, and was a member of the EA.

BIBLIOGRAPHY
Parliamentary Debates 3rd series, 5–34
Stenton

JONATHAN BURKE CUTMORE

Johnston, Bryce (b. Annan, Dumfriesshire, Scotland, 2 March 1747; d. Holywood, Dumfriesshire, Scotland, 27 April 1805). Church of Scotland minister and author. The son of a small landowner, Johnston was ordained in 1771 to the rural parish of Holywood in south-western Scotland where he remained until his death. Despite the relative obscurity of this position and his devotion to pastoral ministry, he became nationally known in several fields. As an expert in ecclesiastical law, Johnston identified with the Popular Party within the Church of Scotland, speaking at the General Assembly in opposition to patronage and in support of chapels of ease. He was also an ardent agriculturalist, publishing a technical work for the Board of Agriculture on improving farmland within his home county of Dumfries and assisting the SSPCK in purchasing and managing two estates. He welcomed the growth of new missionary societies around the turn of the century, participating in the Dumfries Missionary Society and being named a director of the LMS in 1801.

BIBLIOGRAPHY
Fasti, 2: 276
J. Johnstone, ed., *Sermons of Bryce Johnston* [with memoir] (Edinburgh, 1807)

DAVID A. CURRIE

Johnston, Robert (b. near Moffat, Dumfriesshire, Scotland, 16 Dec. 1807; d. Edinburgh, 22 March 1853). Scottish missionary in Madras. Johnston went to Madras in 1838 to join the pioneer missionary, JOHN ANDERSON, who had arrived the previous year. Both men emphasized education as the main tool of missions, following the strategy of ALEXANDER DUFF. Initially they took over the running of a school established by the congregation of St Andrews Kirk, and developed there a system of education centred on the Bible.

Two early crises threatened the continuation of the school: the so-called 'Pariah struggle', and the uproar following the baptism of the first converts. The former occurred when the families of high caste pupils withdrew their children, objecting to the presence of a few 'pariah' or Untouchable pupils. Johnston and Anderson, believing a fundamental Christian principle was involved, stuck to their guns and in due course the school was again crowded. The first three baptisms took place in 1841, and aroused a storm of controversy which for a time threatened the continuation of the school and the safety of the missionaries. The three initial converts – Rajagopaul, Venkataramaiah and Ettirajooloo – all became candidates for the ministry and were licensed in 1846 and ordained in 1851, the year that Johnston was invalided home, dying two years later.

Johnston and Anderson also established a string of 'branch schools', and a pioneering girls' school was founded. The main school later became the Madras Christian College. Johnston and all his colleagues joined the FCS at the Disruption of 1843.

BIBLIOGRAPHY
J. Braidwood, *True Yoke-Fellows in the Gospel* (London, 1862)
D. B. Forrester, *Caste and Christianity* (London, 1980)

DUNCAN FORRESTER

Johnston, William (b. Biggar, Lanarkshire, Scotland, 18 Feb. 1800; d. Edinburgh, 24 May 1874). United Presbyterian minister. Educated at Glasgow University (MA 1817) and the Secession divinity hall, he was called by Limekilns in 1823, his only charge.

His most prominent role in church councils was as convener of the Committee of Education of the newly created United Presbyterian Church from 1847. Stridently disestablishmentarian, he used the position to attack university tests and to support non-sectarian national education. Johnston was moderator in 1854. Although strongly against the proposed union between the United Presbyterian Church and the Presbyterian Church in England, he actively supported union with the Free Church. He was a member of the EA and in 1845 was president of the Total Abstinence Society of the Secession Church.

BIBLIOGRAPHY
DNB
W. Gifford, *Memorials of the Life and Work of Dr Johnston* (Edinburgh, 1876)

JONATHAN BURKE CUTMORE

Johnston, Sir William (b. Kirkhill, near Penicuik, Midlothian, Scotland, 27 Oct. 1802; d. Gorebridge, Midlothian, Scotland, 7 Feb. 1888). Businessman and Lord Provost of Edinburgh. Johnston was educated at the Edinburgh High School and apprenticed in Edinburgh as a copperplate engraver. He opened his own business in 1825. In the following year he and his brother Alexander established an engraving company that came to be known for its atlases and maps. In 1837 his firm was appointed engraver and copperplate printer to the Queen.

Johnston was very active in Edinburgh municipal affairs, as high constable and bailie of Edinburgh, as secretary and moderator to the high constables, and as a member of the dean of guild court, and of the town council. He was Lord Provost from 1848 to 1851 and in the latter year was knighted. A Free Churchman, he was a member of the Scottish Reformation Society and of the EA.

BIBLIOGRAPHY
Evangelical Christendom (London, 1847): 72
Oliver and Boyd, *Edinburgh Almanac* (Edinburgh, 1851)
Boase
DNB

JONATHAN BURKE CUTMORE

Johnstone, Francis (b. Edinburgh, 22 Sept. 1810; d. Edinburgh, 7 May 1880). Scottish Baptist minister. Born in an Edinburgh family connected with Anderson's Church and then with HALDANE's tabernacle, Francis Johnstone was educated at the High School and University of Edinburgh, and at Bradford College. After short pastorates in England he returned to Scotland as minister of the Baptist Church in Cupar in 1842. He removed to form a new church in Edinburgh in 1845, leaving for Cambridge in 1856. He went to Glasgow to another new church in 1857, and returned to build up his Edinburgh church in 1860. There he remained until his death in 1880.

Johnstone was a fervent evangelist, impatient alike with the inward looking Scotch Baptists and the carefully Calvinist Haldaneites. He was influenced by the ferment of the Disruption, and more by the teaching of JAMES MORISON and the Evangelical Union. He reformed the small Baptist Association of Scotland into the first Baptist Union in 1842. In Cupar and Edinburgh he took men into his household for training in the ministry. He established the first Baptist periodicals in Scotland, the *Evangelist* and the *Myrtle*, gathered statistics, and sent out evangelists who planted new Baptist churches. His modified Calvinism made him an object of suspicion to older leaders. In later life breaches were repaired and he lived to be president of the enduring Baptist Union of 1869.

By his writings and his energetic example, Johnstone reinvigorated the denomination and developed the work of the revival associated with the HALDANES. In so doing he prepared the way for the Awakening of 1859 and the cooperative work of Baptists.

BIBLIOGRAPHY
D. W. Bebbington, ed., *The Baptists in Scotland, A History* (Glasgow, 1988)
A. Wylie, *Jubilee Handbook, Marshall Street Baptist Church* (Edinburgh, 1896)

DEREK B. MURRAY

Jones, Abner (b. Royalton, MA, BNA, 28 April 1772; d. Exeter, NH, USA, 29 May 1841). Founder of the 'Christian Connection' in New England. Virtually self-taught, Jones was successful as a schoolteacher and Thompsonian medical practitioner. He gradually rejected the Calvinistic system and denominationalism. Jones averred, 'I will have nothing but for which I can bring, Thus saith the Lord, and, Thus it is written'. In 1801 he began an itinerant ministry of preaching and starting churches. Jones founded the first 'free Christian Church' in New England in Lyndon, Vermont, September 1801. In 1802, Jones joined forces with ELIAS SMITH. Jones and Smith organized a General Conference of Christian churches that later merged with two other restorationist groups to form the Christian Connection. Jones published one book, *Memoirs of the Life and Experience, Travels and Preaching of Abner Jones* (Exeter, NH, 1807).

BIBLIOGRAPHY
DAB
DCA
N. O. Hatch, *The Democratization of American Christianity* (New Haven, CT, 1989)
A. H. Morrill, 'Abner Jones: Founder of the "Christian Connection" in New England', in *The Centennial of Religious Journalism* (Bangor, ME, 1908): 285–96
M. T. Morrill, *A History of the Christian Denomination in America, 1794–1911* (Dayton, OH, 1912)

ANDREW L. PRATT

Jones, Absalom (b. Sussex, DE, BNA, 1746; d. Philadelphia, PA, USA, 13 Feb. 1818). Minister and founder of the African Protestant Episcopal Church of St Thomas. Born a slave, his master sent him to work in his shop in Philadelphia, where he was educated by Quakers. He saved his money and bought the freedom of himself and his wife, but continued working for his former master. In Philadelphia he became friends with RICHARD ALLEN, also a freedman, while attending St George's Methodist Church. Allen and Jones surfaced as natural leaders of the growing number of former slaves in the membership. On 17 May 1787, Allen and Jones founded the Free African Society, a non-sectarian, benevolent organization designed to aid the black community by providing fellowship, moral supervision, and a deepened black consciousness within a Methodist framework. White members of St George's Church increasingly viewed the Freed Africans with hostility, culminating in a November 1787 walkout by black members. Jones and others were interrupted and bodily removed from the sanctuary during prayers because they knelt outside their designated seating area. Remaining the leader after Allen's 1789 departure from the Free African Society, Jones and his followers moved toward Episcopalianism, founding the African Episcopal Church of St Thomas on 17 July 1794. Jones became the first black Episcopal priest in America in 1804. For the rest of his life Jones and Allen, who founded the African MEC, gave leadership to Philadelphia blacks. They worked together during the yellow fever epidemic in 1793, created the Society for the Suppression of Vice and Immorality, and led black opposition to the founding of the American Colonization Society in 1817.

BIBLIOGRAPHY

R. Allen, *The Life Experience and Gospel Labors of the Right Reverend Richard Allen* (Nashville, TN, 1960)

R. C. Boyd, *On This Rock . . .: the Mother Church of African Methodism* (Philadelphia, PA, 1982)

DANB

C. V. R. George, *Segregated Sabbaths* (New York, 1973)

ANDREW MANIS

Jones, C. Jane   See LEUPOLT, Mrs JANE C.

Jones, Charles (Colcock), Sr (b. Liberty County, GA, USA, 20 Dec. 1804; d. Liberty County, GA, USA, 16 March, 1863). Presbyterian minister and evangelist to slaves. Born into a distinguished Georgia family, Jones received his ministerial training at Andover Seminary and Princeton Theological Seminary. He pastored the First Presbyterian Church of Savannah (1831–2), while organizing the Liberty County Association for the Religious Instruction of Negroes. For all but two years from 1833 to 1848, Jones instructed and evangelized slaves in Liberty County. He then taught at Columbia Seminary (1848–50), and served as secretary of the Presbyterian Board of Domestic Missions (1850–3).

A wealthy and benevolent master who was sensitive to the psychological damage of slavery, Jones was a leading advocate and theorist of plantation missions to slaves. His writings included a widely used *Catechism of Scripture Doctrine and Practice* (1834), written for both blacks and whites, and an important historical source book, *The Religious Instruction of the Negroes, In the United States* (1842).

BIBLIOGRAPHY

E. Clarke, *Wrestlin' Jacob* (Atlanta, GA, 1979)

M. C. Sernett, *Black Religion and American Evangelicalism* (Metuchen, NJ, 1975)

W. C. Tyner, 'C. C. Jones: Mission to Slaves,' *JPH*, 55 (1977): 363–80

DAVID W. KLING

Jones, Dafydd (b. Caeo, Wales, 1711; d. Llanwrda, Wales, 30 Aug. 1777). Hymn-writer and translator of Isaac Watts. Jones was the son of a drover, Daniel John, and probably mastered the English language as he followed his father in that work. Returning from one such journey into England he was converted in Troed-rhiw-dalar. Subsequently he befriended WILLIAM WILLIAMS, and joined a remarkable band of hymn-writers from Carmarthenshire, which included MORGAN RHYS, DAVID CHARLES, John and Morgan Dafydd of Caeo, and JOHN THOMAS of Rhaeadr. Besides his original hymns published in 1763, 1764 and 1770, some seven or eight of which are included in all the denominational selections, he published translations of the Psalms and many hymns by Isaac Watts in three volumes, 1753, 1771, 1775, besides some miscellaneous poems.

BIBLIOGRAPHY

B. Jones, *Pedwar Emynydd* (Llandybie, Wales, 1948)

G. M. Roberts, *Dafydd Jones o Gaeo* (Llandysul, Wales, 1948)

R. M. JONES

Jones, David (b. White Clay Creek Hundred, New Castle, DE, BNA, 12 May 1736; d. Great Valley, Chester, PA, USA, 5 Feb. 1820). Baptist minister, army chaplain, and political activist. David Jones, the father of Horatio Gates Jones, DD (historian of the Philadelphia Association) was converted and baptized in 1758, licensed in 1761 at the Welsh Tract Church, and ordained pastor of the Freehold Church in Monmouth, New Jersey, 12 December 1766. In 1772 he made two missionary visits to the Indians north-west of the Ohio River, but met with little success. His outspoken endorsement of national independence forced him to remove in 1775 to the Great Valley Church in Chester County, Pennsylvania. His sermon, 'Defensive War in a Just Cause Sinless' was published in 1775 and inflamed war sentiment. Jones was appointed chaplain of the Pennsylvania regiment and served with uncommon distinction. After the war, Jones served as pastor and again as military chaplain in the War of 1812. His missionary zeal for the Indians directly inspired the work of EVAN JONES (no relation).

SELECT WRITINGS

D. Jones, *A Journal of Two Visits* (New York, 1865): v–xi

WADE A. HORTON

Jones, David (b. Aberceiliog, Llanllwyni, Wales, 10 July 1736; d. Manorowen, Wales, 12 Aug. 1810). Methodist cleric and revival preacher. Jones was the son of a Carmarthenshire farmer and educated at Carmarthen Grammar School. He was ordained deacon (13 August 1758) and held curacies at Tudweiliog (Gwynedd), Caldicot (Gwent) and Crudwell (Wiltshire). The influence of the Countess of Huntingdon (see SELINA HUNTINGDON) secured a living for him at Llangan (Glamorgan), where he was ordained priest in 1767. Jones ministered at Llangan for 43 years drawing hundreds from Glamorgan and beyond. His warm effective preaching greatly influenced the spiritual life of the people, and he became known as the 'Angel of Llangan'. In 1791 he built Salem Chapel at nearby Pencoed to accommodate his large congregations. He was a favourite preacher of the Countess of Huntingdon, and preached her funeral oration. The growth of the Welsh Methodist movement caused younger preachers to look to Jones for leadership out of the Established Church; but basically he was against this. He died shortly before the secession. Jones was not a leader but a preacher and evangelist, shunning the controversies of his time.

BIBLIOGRAPHY
CCH
R. B. Higham, 'The Life and Works of Rev. D. Jones Llangan' (Univ. of Wales, M.Th. Thesis, 1980)
E. Morgan, *Ministerial Record . . . D. Jones* (London, 1841)

R. B. HIGHAM

Jones, David (b. Brachodnant, Montgomeryshire, Wales, April 1785; d. Lower Dublin, PA, USA, 9 April 1833). Baptist minister and denominational organizer. Jones was an orphan who bought his passage to America in 1803 with two years of indentured service in Cincinnati. In 1805 he adopted Baptist views and then itinerated across the nation to the home of SAMUEL JONES where he received a ministerial education. In 1813 he pastored the Baptist church in Newark, New Jersey, and was a founding member of the Triennial Convention. Till his death, Jones was zealous for foreign mission causes.

BIBLIOGRAPHY
AAP

WADE A. HORTON

Jones, David (b. Neuadd-lwyd, Aberaeron, Wales, 1797; d. Port Louis, Mauritius, 1 May 1841). Pioneer LMS missionary. Jones was educated at Neuadd-lwyd and Gosport and was married to Miss Louisa Darby, at Gosport. His ordination took place at Neuadd-lwyd Independent Chapel 21 August 1817. On 9 February 1818 he sailed for Mauritius. He and THOMAS BEVAN made a short preliminary visit to Madagascar in August. He returned there with his family on 20 November, but within a few weeks their child and its mother died of fever. David Jones had to return to Port Louis to recuperate. It was there in 1821 that he married Miss Mary Ann Mabille. In the capital, Antananarivo, he found support from King Radama to establish schools. With DAVID GRIFFITHS he reduced the Malagasy language to writing and translated the Bible. Failing health and persecution of Christianity forced his return to Mauritius.

BIBLIOGRAPHY
G. P. Griffith, *Cenhadon Cymreig* (Cardiff, 1897)
LMS Register of Missionaries 1796–1923, 4th edn (London, 1923)

IEUAN S. JONES

Jones, David (b. Tanycastell, Dolwyddelan, Gwynedd, 2 June 1805; d. Treborth, near Bangor, Gwynedd, 23 June 1868). Calvinistic Methodist minister. He was the son of John and Elinor Jones and younger brother of JOHN JONES (1797–1857), Talysarn, one of Wales's most influential preachers. David had no formal education as a child but began preaching in 1826 and then attended the excellent school conducted by JOHN HUGHES (1796–1860) at Wrexham, Clwyd. He was ordained 11 June 1834 and had pastoral care of Moriah, Caernarfon, and neighbouring churches from 1832 to 1858. He was a fine preacher, dignified and substantial. His two volumes of sermons (1876, 1879) and his other published works testify to his powerful mind. He presented moderate Calvinism in a lucid, cogent and attractive form. Some of his hymns have enjoyed a continuing popularity.

BIBLIOGRAPHY
DWB
Traethodydd (Caernarfon, Wales, 1905)

R. TUDUR JONES

Jones, David Thomas (b. Wales, c. 1796; d. Llangoedmor, Wales, 26 Oct. 1844). CMS missionary and educator. Jones studied for two years at Lampeter Theological College and for three years under the tutelage of HENRY GAUNTLETT, Rector of Olney. He was ordained (deacon 22 Dec. 1822; priest 13 April 1823) by the Bishop of Gloucester and Bristol. On 31 May 1823 he was sent out to Red River to permit JOHN WEST, Hudson's Bay Company (HBC) chaplain and CMS missionary, to take a year's leave. West did not return, so Jones took charge of the new mission and established a reputation as an excellent preacher. He commissioned the construction of Middle Church (St Paul's) in 1824. During a year in England, he married Mary Lloyd in May 1829.

Upon his return to Red River, Jones organized the Red River Academy, the first school in western Canada which provided secondary instruction in English for both boys and girls. Initially the CMS was reluctant to participate so Jones financed the school privately. In 1833, the CMS finally agreed to supply one male and one female teacher. Unlike many of the missionaries in the northwest, Jones enjoyed the friendship and support of HBC officials and a broad cross-section of the community at Red River, even though most of the settlers were Presbyterians who did not share his theological views.

Mary Jones died in childbirth in 1836; the dispirited Jones returned to Great Britain with their six children two years later, selling the Red River Academy to the HBC. He withdrew from the CMS in October 1839 but continued his interest in education with a post teaching Welsh at St David's College, Lampeter. In the final year before his death, he served as rector at Llangoedmor, Wales.

BIBLIOGRAPHY
D. T. B[arry], *CMS Register of Missionaries and Native Clergy from 1804 to 1904* (privately printed) (London, 1906)
DCB

KERRY M. ABEL

Jones, Edmund (b. Aberystruth, Gwent, Wales, 1 April 1702; d. Pontypool, Gwent, Wales, 26 Nov. 1793). Congregational minister. He received hardly any formal education. He was ordained at Pen-maen Congregational Church, Gwent, in 1734 and in 1740 moved to the Transh, Pontypool, where he built Ebenezer Chapel. He and Mary (1696–1770) formed a married partnership noted for its happiness. He was the most prominent of the dissenting ministers who supported the evangelical revival. He travelled on foot incessantly to preach. He invited HOWEL HARRIS to Gwent in 1738 and remained his correspondent up to 1772. He gained a reputation for quaintness and won the sobriquet 'The Old Prophet' through his supposed ability to foretell the future. His book, *A Relation of Apparitions of Spirits* (1767, 1780, 1813) testifies to his belief in fairies and his interest in the occult, manifestations which he used to disprove deism. These idiosyncrasies, however, should not obscure his generosity, his readiness to sacrifice in the cause of the Gospel and his solid contribution to the evangelical revival.

BIBLIOGRAPHY
DWB
E. Phillips, *Edmund Jones, 'The Old Prophet'* (London, 1959)
T. Rees, *History of Protestant Nonconformity in Wales* (London, 1883): 152–4, 430–5

R. TUDUR JONES

Jones, Edward (b. Prion, Denbighshire, Wales, 19 March 1761; d. Cilcain, Wales, 27 Dec. 1836). Hymnwriter, farmer and schoolmaster. He had but little education as a child, what he had coming from the local Independent minister. At the age of 22 he attended a school in Chester for a short time. In 1787 he joined the Calvinistic Methodists. He split his early working life between keeping an English school at Prion, working in the customs house in Liverpool and farming Maes-Y-Plwm, by which name his is always identified. For a short time he was also in charge of a school in Denbigh, while for a time in 1805 he was in Chester supervising the printing of the translation of Samuel Clarke's annotated Bible into Welsh. Thereafter he looked after two other schools for a time. In 1810 there appeared a first collection of his hymns, with subsequent editions in 1820 and 1829. His sons, Daniel and John, both schoolmasters turned ministers, published a biography of their father in 1839. John (1787–1860) was Calvinistic Methodist minister in Runcorn, Cheshire, while his step-brother, Daniel (1813–46), died of fever within months of arriving in India as a missionary.

BIBLIOGRAPHY
DWB J. E. Caerwyn Williams, *Edward Jones, Maes-Y-Plwm* (Denbigh, Wales, 1962)

J. H. Y. BRIGGS

Jones, Edward (b. Ruthin, Clwyd, Wales, 9 May 1778; d. Leek, Staffordshire, England, 26 Aug. 1837). Welsh Wesleyan Methodist minister. He was the son of Edward and Anne Jones, of Bathafarn, Ruthin, and was educated at Ruthin Grammar School. He moved to Manchester to work in the cotton industry but returned in 1799 and formed a Wesleyan society at Ruthin the following year. From 1802 to 1817 he served as an itinerant minister in Wales. In 1817 he was transferred to English circuits in Wales and beyond. He married Dorothy Roberts, of Llangwyfan Hall, 4 July 1806. He made a very substantial contribution to the early work of the Wesleyans in Wales by his determined evangelism, his sincerity, his well-balanced personality and total dedication to his mission.

BIBLIOGRAPHY
DWB
H. Hones, *Hanes Wesleyaeth Gymreig* (Bangor, Wales, 1911)
A. H. Williams, *Welsh Wesleyan Methodism* (Bangor, Wales, 1935)

R. TUDUR JONES

Jones, Edward (b. USA; d. New Brompton, Chatham, Kent, England, 14 May 1865). Black American Episcopal clergyman and CMS missionary in Sierra Leone. Nothing is known of Edwards' background except that he was an American-born black who was ordained in the American Episcopal Church. Although American-born, when he joined the CMS in Sierra Leone in 1840 he was classified as one of its 'native clergy'. Apparently well educated, he served from 1840 as the principal of the CMS's Fourah Bay Institution in Freetown. Clearly, however, he had lived in Freetown for some time because in 1838 he married HANNAH NYLÄNDER (died 1839), a CMS 'female missionary', the daughter of G. R. NYLÄNDER. (Both of Nyländer's wives appear to have been black Nova Scotians.)

Jones remarried twice: in 1845 he wed someone whose last name was Wilkins (death date unknown); and (date unknown) Elizabeth Schuff (possibly German-born) who had succeeded the German-born CMS missionary, M. Sophia Hehlen, at the Hannah Braithwaite Orphan Asylum. In 1864 they settled in England.

BIBLIOGRAPHY
D. T. B[arry], *CMS Register of Missionaries And Native Clergy* (privately printed) (London, 1906)

DONALD M. LEWIS

Jones, Edward Rhys (b. Liverpool, England, *c.* 1818, d. 1899). Anglican clergyman. The eldest son of the Reverend JOHN JONES (1791–1889) of Liverpool, he had a distinguished record at Brasenose College, Oxford, achieving a first in 1839. He was Michel fellow at Queen's College (1841–3) and then a fellow at his old college (1843–51). Ordained deacon in 1841, he served his curacy in East Claydon, Buckinghamshire and was priested in 1842. He was perpetual curate first at St John's, Bethnel Green (1842–6), and then at St John's, Derby from 1847. In 1850 he was nominated by his college as Rector of St Anne's, Limehouse in London. His ministry there began with rebuilding the church which had been destroyed by fire, and he went on to build several other churches and subdivide the parish, while Bible women and charities assisted outreach to the poor of east London. From 1860 he served as 'rural dean' of Stepney. He moved to the quiet rural parish of Limpsfield in Surrey in 1870, and remained until his death, holding honourary positions as examining chaplain and Canon of the diocese of Rochester. It was a long twilight to a spectacular early ministry.

SELECT WRITINGS

E. R. Jones, *Joy in the House of God: A Sermon preached . . . on Sunday Morning April 26 1857* (London, 1857)
—, *Farewell Words at Limehouse* (London, 1870)

PETER J. LINEHAM

Jones, Evan (b. Brecknockshire, Wales, 14 May 1788; d. Tahlequah, OK, USA, 18 Aug. 1872). Missionary, abolitionist, and political advocate to the Cherokees. Jones was a Welsh Baptist schoolteacher and minister who reinforced the Baptist Mission at Valley Towns, North Carolina in 1821. After several years he assumed the position of superintendent and remained so until his retirement in 1870. He helped translate the Bible into Cherokee, opposed the 1839 removal, and was politically active as a friend and adviser to Principal Chief John Ross. It is believed that Jones was a ghost-writer of many of the memorials presented to the US Congress. He opposed slavery, encouraged temperance societies, was a pioneer of indigenous mission methods, and accompanied the Cherokees on the Trail of Tears. It is apparent that he failed to mention much of his political activity to his employers in New England, rarely worked within his budget, and at one time was acquitted of a murder charge. His work is largely responsible for the predominant Baptist populations of Oklahoma.

BIBLIOGRAPHY

W. McLoughlin, *Champions of the Cherokees* (Princeton, NJ, 1990)

WADE A. HORTON

Jones, Griffith (b. Pant-yr-efel, Carmarthenshire, Wales, baptized 1 May 1684; d. Laugharne, Carmarthenshire, Wales, 8 April 1761). Anglican clergyman and founder of the Welsh circulating schools. Jones was the youngest of four sons born to John ap Gruffydd and Elinor John of Pant-yr-efel in the parish of Pen-boyr in Carmarthenshire. Sometime during his youth, as he was tending sheep on the hillsides of Cilrhedyn, he experienced a 'heavenly call' which convinced him that God had singled him out to win souls in his native land. He entered Carmarthen Grammar School and was ordained deacon and priest in 1708. In 1716 the celebrated philanthropist Sir John Philipps appointed him Rector of Llanddowror, Carmarthenshire, a living which he held for 45 years. Even today, people still refer to him as Griffith Jones *Llanddowror*.

Long before the advent of Methodism, Jones's rousing sermons in south-west Wales attracted hundreds of hearers. Although he was a melancholic and humourless man who suffered from chronic asthma, he was a marvellously gifted preacher. Clad in his great coat and long cravat, he cut an impressive figure in the pulpit, and no Welsh cleric of his day was as highly revered and loved as he. His itinerant preaching and enthusiasm incurred the wrath of bishops but also inspired young Methodist evangelists. DANIEL ROWLAND saluted him as his spiritual father and HOWEL HARRIS, who visited him frequently to seek advice and beg favours, rarely left Llanddowror without shedding tears as he bade farewell to this 'old and much honoured soldier'. There is much to be said for the view that the soil in which Methodism sprouted had been tilled in readiness by the Rector of Llanddowror.

Jones's experience as a teacher in local charity schools convinced him that the educational scheme sponsored in Wales by the SPCK was ill-suited to the needs of poor and underprivileged Welsh-speaking people. He realized that teaching monoglot Welsh children through the medium of the English tongue was a piece of folly. In 1731, therefore, he launched a highly effective educational experiment based on circulating schools. Usually held in autumn and winter, the schools moved at three-monthly intervals from parish to parish. Adults and children attended the schools either during the day or at night, and were taught to read the Welsh Bible and the church catechism. Jones himself composed or translated over thirty Welsh books, mostly catechisms and works of piety, for use in the schools. For the first time in the history of Wales, tenant farmers, labourers and servants were given the opportunity to acquire reading skills. By 1761, 3,325 schools had been established in 1,600 different places throughout Wales. It is estimated that around 250,000 people were taught to read fluently in these schools. Jones's scheme not only helped to create a literate Welsh peasantry but also revitalized church life and gave a much needed boost to the fortunes of the Welsh language. It is significant, too, that Methodism prospered best in precisely those communities where the circulating schools were located.

When his wife, Margaret, died on 5 January 1755, Jones settled in the home of his principal patron and confidante, Madam BRIDGET BEVAN, at Laugharne, where his persistent fits of coughing and abrasive manner earned him the unfortunate nickname 'Old Peevish' in the servants' quarters. He died in 1761 and was buried in the chancel of Llanddowror Church. He was not only one of the principal benefactors of the Welsh nation but also one of the makers of modern Wales.

BIBLIOGRAPHY
DWB
G. H. Jenkins, 'An Old and Much Honoured Soldier: Griffith Jones, Llanddowror', *WelHR*, 2 (1983): 449–68
R. T. Jenkins, *Gruffydd Jones Llanddowror* (Cardiff, 1930)
T. Kelly, *Griffith Jones. Pioneer in Adult Education* (Cardiff, 1950)

GERAINT H. JENKINS

Jones, Hugh (b. Dinas Mawddwy, Merionethshire, Wales, Nov. 1749; d. Dinas Mawddwy, Merionethshire, 16 April 1825). Schoolmaster, hymn-writer and translator. He was the son of William and Elizabeth Jones of Maesglasau, between Dolgellau and Dinas Mawddwy. From 1772 he was a schoolmaster in London but returned home to help with the farming. He was one of the founding members of the Calvinistic Methodist Church at Mallwyd (1786). He continued to work as a farmer but from 1787 to 1817 he kept school at various places in Merionethshire. From 1817 until his death he devoted himself to literary work. Of twenty books which he published or edited, two were collections of his hymns. But his most substantial publication was a translation of William Whiston's English rendering of the works of Josephus.

SELECT WRITINGS
H. Jones, *Cydymaith yr Hwsmon*, ed. Henry Lewis (Caerdydd, Wales, 1949)

BIBLIOGRAPHY
DWB

R. TUDUR JONES

Jones, Humphrey Rowland (b. a Gwarcwm Bach, parish of Llancynfelyn, Dyfed, 11 Oct. 1832; d. Chilton, WI, USA, 8 May 1895). Revivalist. He was the son of Humphrey and Elizabeth Jones who emigrated to the United States in 1847 and left him behind. In 1854 the Wesleyan Methodists rejected his application to be considered a candidate for the ministry and he, too, emigrated to America. In 1855 he began to work among the Welsh in Oshkosh, Wisconsin, as a probationer with the MEC but broke his connection with that body the following year to work as a freelance evangelist, leading revival meetings in the states of Wisconsin, Illinois and New York. He returned to his home at Tre'r-ddôl, near Aberystwyth, and in June 1858 he began to conduct meetings on the principles advocated by CHARLES G. FINNEY. Large crowds attended them and considerable revival enthusiasm was displayed. These were the first manifestations of the coming of the 'Second Evangelical Awakening' to Wales. But by the end of the year DAVID MORGAN (1814–83) emerged as an even more charismatic figure than Jones and became the acknowledged leader of the revival. He disagreed with the methods of Finney and Jones's influence began to decline. He soon suffered a collapse and underwent treatment at mental hospitals in Carmarthen and (after 1871) in America. He partially recovered his health and was able to do some public work but regained none of his early influence.

BIBLIOGRAPHY
DWB
E. Evans, *Humphrey Jones a Diwygiad 1859* (National Museum of Wales Lecture, 1981)
E. Isaac, *Humphrey Jones a Diwygiad 1859* (Bala, Wales, 1930)
J. Edwin Orr, *The Second Evangelical Awakening* (London, 1949)
—, *The Fervent Prayer* (Chicago, IL, 1974)

R. TUDUR JONES

Jones, John (b. Haverfordwest, Pembrokeshire, Wales, 1721; d. Harwich, Essex, England, 10 Sept. 1785). Physician, schoolmaster, Anglican clergyman, and Methodist. Jones attended Westminster School, entered Trinity College, Oxford on 6 June 1735 as pensioner, became a scholar and graduated in both arts and medicine. He came under the influence of GEORGE WHITEFIELD and HOWELL HARRIS, and was for a time a supporter of Calvinist doctrine. But in 1746, after much heart-searching, he transferred his loyalty to JOHN WESLEY's Arminianism, and soon won much esteem in Wesley's eyes.

From 1746 to 1748 he was an assistant to Wesley in London, but in the latter year he was appointed the senior of six masters at Wesley's newly opened school in Kingswood, near Bristol. Here he stayed, during the troubled times that the school experienced in its early years, until 1758, when he again became an assistant in London. But in 1767 he left Wesley's connexion, was episcopally ordained and became first Curate then Vicar of Dovercourt and Harwich with Ramsey. He had been refused episcopal ordination several times in his early years, because, presumably, of his Methodism.

The reason for his separation from Wesley was not, however, theological or personal, but due to the onset of ill health. The two men continued in affectionate friendship, and usually agreed. Jones was always strongly opposed to separation from the Church of England.

He was plainly an important person in early Methodism, as Wesley's trusted adviser and agent, and it is extremely likely that Wesley thought of him for a time as his successor, after CHARLES WESLEY. His life story has been rescued from obscurity by A. B. Sackett (published by the Wesley Historical Society).

BIBLIOGRAPHY
A. B. Sackett, *John Jones, First After the Wesleys?* (London, 1972)

RUPERT E. DAVIES

Jones, John (b. Wales, 1737; d. 1 March 1800, St John's, Newfoundland). Royal Artillerist and later paymaster at the St John's garrison, founder of Newfoundland Congregationalism, and Congregationalist minister.

Jones, a Royal Artillerist stationed in Newfoundland since 1765, was converted from a riotous life to one of evangelical piety in a dramatic encounter at St John's, when he heard a soldier, mortally wounded in a duel, curse God. After his return to England in 1773 he was influenced by Calvinistic Dissenters and upon his return to St John's as paymaster to the garrison founded his dissenting Church of Christ at St John's in 1775. After his retirement from the army, Jones became an ordained Congregationalist minister in England and returned to St John's in July of 1779. He prevailed against the joint opposition of the Anglican clergyman and the governor and reopened his dissenting meeting house in 1780. The congregation had grown by 1794 to 400 persons and maintained a charity school for poor children. After suffering a stroke, Jones died in 1800 as a revered man in the community.

BIBLIOGRAPHY
DCB
DNLB
ENL
S. Greathead, 'The Life of the Rev. John Jones, Late of St John's, Newfoundland', *The Evangelical Magazine*, (November 1800)
St David's Presbyterian Church, *The Dissenting Church of Christ at St John's* (St John's, Canada, 1975)
H. Rollmann, 'John Jones, James O'Donel, and the Question of Religious Tolerance in Eighteenth-Century Newfoundland', *Newfoundland Quarterly* 80/1 (1984): 23–27

HANS ROLLMANN

Jones, John (b. *c*. 1783; d. Shrewsbury, Shropshire, England, 4 June 1831). Welsh Baptist minister. Twenty-one years the minister at Newtown, Montgomeryshire, he died of complications following the amputation of his hand at the early age of 48, leaving a wife and seven children, for whom Richard Ellis, a local shopkeeper, made a successful collection. Such was the shock of the town that both factories and shops closed for the day of his funeral in which thousands participated. Jones had a reconciling personality and helped the maintenance of fellowship among those who differed theologically and was an eloquent supporter of foreign missions.

BIBLIOGRAPHY
T. M. Bassett, *The Welsh Baptists* (London, 1977)
EM (1831)

J. H. Y. BRIGGS

Jones, John (b. Liverpool, 1791; d. Liverpool, 1889). Anglican clergyman. A protege of CHARLES SIMEON, Jones graduated from St John's, Cambridge in 1811 and became curate to THOMAS ROBINSON at St Mary's, Leicester. He wanted to go into the mission field but encountered parental opposition. Instead at the invitation of Sir JOHN GLADSTONE who had spent £12,000 on the building, he became first Vicar of St Andrew's, Renshaw Street, Liverpool (1816–50), serving the fashionable Abercromby Square area. He was subsequently Archdeacon of Liverpool (1855–87).

He was said to read his sermons and 'his action [was] not sufficiently masculine and energetic'. He set forth Christ as 'the only "oblation, satisfaction and atonement"', but the same source adds: 'Perhaps it would advantage his hearers, were he occasionally reminded of "the grace wherein they stand"' (McMoney, 1822–3).

BIBLIOGRAPHY
R. McMoney, ed., *The Hermes* 2 (Liverpool, England, 1822–3)
S. Nowell-Rostron, *St Andrew's, Renshaw Street* (Liverpool, England, 1915)

ARTHUR POLLARD

Jones, John (b. Dolwyddelan, Caernarfonshire, Wales, 1 March 1796; d. Talysarn, Caernarfonshire, Wales, 16 Aug. 1857). Welsh Calvinistic Methodist minister. Both John and his brother David (1805–68) became Calvinistic Methodist ministers, the latter, better known as DAVID JONES, Treborth, becoming a renowned poet and hymn-writer. Neither received any formal education apart from Sunday school, due to the impoverished circumstances of the family, made worse when the father died leaving his widow to bring up nine small children. John began to earn his living, first as a road-mender and later as a quarryman. In 1819 he was deeply affected by the Beddgelert Revival of that year and joined the Methodist society at Llangernyw, Denbighshire, where he was living at the time with a younger married sister. Two years later he began to preach and moved to work in a quarry in Trefriw in the Conwy Valley. There he began to receive instruction from EVAN EVANS ('Ieuan Glan Geirionydd'), a local schoolteacher and accomplished Welsh poet who was later ordained into the Anglican ministry.

Moving in 1823 to Talysarn in the Nantlle valley, John's reputation as a preacher began to spread far and wide. There he was to remain for the remainder of his life, becoming known throughout Wales as 'John Jones, Tal-y-sarn'. He became one of the most gifted and powerful preachers of his generation. As a preacher he typified and influenced the gradual movement which took place in Welsh Calvinistic Methodism during this period, from the exclusively doctrinal emphasis of the first two decades of the nineteenth century, to a greater emphasis on the moral and practical implications of evangelical faith by the middle of the century. His biography, by Owen Thomas, is not only a vivid portrait of the man, but an invaluable history of the religious developments and theological debates of the first half of the nineteenth century in Wales.

BIBLIOGRAPHY
DNB
DWB
O. Thomas, *Cofiant John Jones, Tal-y-Sarn* (Wrexham, Wales, 1874)

E. AP NEFYDD ROBERTS

Jones, John (Buttrick) (b. Valley Towns, NC, USA, 24 Dec. 1824; d. Denver, CO, USA, 13 June 1876). Missionary, abolitionist, political activist, and Bible translator to the Cherokees. John Jones was the son of the Reverend EVAN JONES, a Baptist minister. John Jones helped to organize the Kituwah society, an abolitionist society of Cherokee traditionalists and a political party. He was influential in the election of Lewis Downing (a Cherokee Baptist minister) to the position of principal chief. Raised bilingual, he completed the translation of the Bible into Cherokee.

BIBLIOGRAPHY
W. McLoughlin, *Champions of the Cherokees* (Princeton, NJ, 1990)

WADE A. HORTON

Jones, J(ohn) R(ichard) (b. Llanuwchllyn, Merioneth, North Wales, 13 Oct. 1765; d. Llanfrothen, Merioneth, 27 June 1822). Leader of Welsh Sandemanian Baptists. Originally a Congregationalist, Jones became convicted of the Baptist position and was immersed at Trawsfynydd on 7 June 1788 thereafter joining the Merionethshire Church whose main meeting place was at Ramoth, Llanfrothen. Ordained its minister on 4 November 1789 J. R. Jones 'of Ramoth' became, along with CHRISTMAS EVANS, the North Wales Baptists' foremost preacher. Finding the overt revivalism which by the 1790s was revitalizing the Welsh Baptist movement increasingly uncongenial, he turned to the works of the Scotsmen JOHN GLAS and ARCHIBALD MCLEAN for a cerebral version of Calvinism which emphasized the objective content rather than the subjective workings of faith. The rapidity of the movement's revivalist transformation coupled with the unbending nature of Jones's personality made a fracture inevitable, and late in 1798 he led a secession of a dozen North Wales churches to form an anti-revivalist connexion of 'Scotch' Baptists. The remainder of his career was spent serving these congregations and espousing their cause.

BIBLIOGRAPHY
DWB
J. I. Jones, *J. R. Jones o Ramoth* (Llandysul, Wales, 1966)
D. Williams, *Cofiant J. R. Jones* (Carmarthen, Wales, 1913)

D. DENSIL MORGAN

Jones, John Taylor (b. New Ipswich, NH, USA, 16 July 1802; d. Bangkok, 13 Sept. 1851). First American missionary to Siam (Thailand). Jones, educated at Brown and Amherst Colleges and then at Andover Theological Seminary and Newton Theological Institute, was inspired by the example of ADONIRAM JUDSON. Upon graduation from Newton he accepted an assignment in Burma where he served in Moulmein from February 1831 until the middle of 1833. The American Baptist mission next sent Jones and his wife, Eliza, to Bangkok where they served until their deaths.

Because the response was so much better among the Chinese, Jones concentrated his work among this immigrant population, yet he worked in the Siamese (Thai), not Chinese, language. Jones' greatest contribution is his translation and writing work in Siamese. In 1834 he published a tract entitled, 'Catechism on Geography and Astronomy', which taught new scientific knowledge as a bridge to Christian faith. By 1842 he had published a Siamese grammar and in 1844 the first edition of his 'New Testament Translated from the Greek into Siamese' was completed. Jones' language work was both exacting and colloquially appropriate. It laid the foundation for missionary work in the Siamese language.

SCOTT W. SUNQUIST

Jones, Lewis (b. Llanfihangel Geneu'r Glyn, Cardiganshire, Wales, 14 Feb. 1793; d. Almondbury, Yorkshire, England, 26 Aug. 1866). Anglican clergyman and Welsh nationalist. Educated at Ystradmeurig Grammar School, Lewis taught for some years at Clitheroe, Lancashire, before his appointment as Vicar of Almondbury, near Huddersfield, Yorkshire, in 1822. He successfully divided this huge parish into 14 separate parishes, appointing Welsh evangelical clergymen to these livings. These men formed the nucleus of the 'Association of Welsh Clergy in the West Riding of Yorkshire' which Lewis re-established in 1835 – it was formed in 1821. The five printed annual reports of 1852–6, published under such titles as *Welsh Patriotism* and *Justice to Wales*, advocated reform for the Church in Wales, Welsh speaking bishops and judges, as well as a university for Wales, and proved to be highly influential in drawing attention to these concerns.

BIBLIOGRAPHY
DWB

ROGER L. BROWN

Jones, Mary (b. Llanfihangel-y-Pennant, Merioneth, Wales, 16 Dec. 1784; d. Bryn-crug, Merioneth, Wales, 29 Dec. 1864). Weaver and folk heroine. Born the daughter of peasant weavers who were pioneer members of the local Calvinistic Methodist society, she was converted in 1793 and excelled as a pupil in the circulating schools and Sunday schools organized by THOMAS CHARLES.

In 1800 she walked over 25 miles to Bala to buy a Bible from Charles with her hard-earned savings. According to tradition her visit made a lasting impression on Charles and intensified his resolve to secure a regular supply of cheap Welsh Bibles. His appeal to that end at a meeting of the RTS in 1802 led to the formation of the BFBS in 1804. Tradition has it that Jones's efforts to obtain a Bible were related by Charles to that meeting, with great effect on those present.

In 1813 she married a fellow weaver and Methodist, Thomas Jones, and had six children. When she died, blind and widowed, in poverty and obscurity, the Bible she received from Charles (now kept in the BFBS archives in Cambridge University Library) lay at her side. Her story first appeared in book form in Welsh in 1879 and in English in 1882, and has subsequently been published in some forty languages. Mary Jones was but one of thousands in her day who made great sacrifices to obtain a Bible, but it is her story that has lived on and made her a worldwide symbol of the need for scripture distribution.

BIBLIOGRAPHY
K. M. Davies, 'Mary Jones (1784–1864)', *CCH*, 52 (1967): 74–80; 53 (1968): 27–8
D. E. Jenkins, *The Life of the Rev. Thomas Charles B.A. of Bala*, 3 vols, 2nd edn (Denbigh, Wales, 1910)
E. Williams, *To Bala for a Bible* (Bridgend, Wales, 1988)

E. WYN JAMES

Jones, Morgan (b. Troed-y-rhiw, Llywel, Breconshire, Wales, 1768; d. Tre-lech, Carmarthenshire, Wales, 23 Dec. 1835). Independent minister and a firm Calvinist. He was received into membership at Cefnarthen, 20 January 1782, and began preaching in 1786. Following a period of study in Glandwr school, where he was introduced to Latin authors and the Greek New Testament, he was ordained minister of Capel-y-Graig, Tre-lech and Capel Iwan, 13 March 1789. Under his powerful ministry the churches experienced a great spiritual awakening which resulted in a remarkable increase in membership and the formation of branch churches at Blaen-y-coed, Ffynnon-Bedr and Llwyn-yr-hwrdd. It is estimated that during his pastorate he admitted *circa* 2,400 members. He was instrumental in founding English churches in South Pembrokeshire, a Welsh church in London and in promoting the work of the Missionary Society. He published a number a short books in Welsh, including a translation of an English sermon on *The Resurrection*.

BIBLIOGRAPHY
DWB
S. Griffiths, *Cofiant y Parch Morgan Jones* (Llanelli, Wales, 1836)

E. STANLEY JOHN

Jones, Neville (b. Burton Pedwardine, Lincolnshire, England, 1809; d. Bolton, Lancashire, England, 6 Sept. 1891). Anglican clergyman. Jones was a graduate of St Catherine's College, Cambridge (BA 1832). His early ministerial career was spent in London. He was an examiner for the LCM in 1838 and incumbent of St Mark's, Whitechapel (1839–46). Subsequently he held the Brasenose College presentation of St George's, Bolton (1847–91). He was described in his London years as 'a working clergyman. Cares little . . . for parties in the church, but pursues his own course steadily. Very decidedly evangelical' (Bodleian Library, 1844).

BIBLIOGRAPHY
Al. Cant., II, iii: 605
Bodleian Library, Oxford, additional manuscript *c.* 290. 'The Principal Clergy of London classified according to their opinions . . . prepared for Mr. Delane, ed. of *The Times*' (1844)

ARTHUR POLLARD

Jones, Owen (b. Tywyn, Merionethshire, Wales, 16 Feb. 1787; d. Llanfair Caereinion, Montgomeryshire, 4 Dec. 1828). Calvinistic Methodist minister. In his youth he became involved in Sunday school work at Aberystwyth, where he experienced an unction of the Holy Spirit. In 1808 he married Mary Jones, Llanfair Caereinion, where he settled. In 1815 he became a founder member of the Borders Missionary Society, and was ordained in 1819. He is best remembered for his catechizing of Sunday schools.

BIBLIOGRAPHY
DWB
J. Hughes, *Cofiant am y diweddar Barch. Owen Jones* (Chester, England, 1830)

GORONWY PRYS OWEN

Jones, Peter (b. Burlington Heights, Upper Canada, 1 Jan. 1802; d. near Brantford, Ontario, Canada, 29 June 1856). Methodist missionary. Jones, whose Ojibwa name was Kahkewaquonaby (Sacred Feathers), was the son of surveyor Augustus Jones and Sarah Henry, a Mississauga Indian. He was baptized in the Church of England, but had little interest in religion and seemed destined for a life in the fur trade. In 1823, however, he and his sister attended a Methodist camp meeting at which he experienced a conversion. He saw Methodism as part of a programme to assist his mother's people through a difficult period of transition while their old way of life was being disrupted by European settlers. He established mission farming communities at Grand River, Credit River and on Grape Island near Belleville, Ontario. He raised funds for these ventures on extensive public speaking tours through Upper Canada, the United States and Great Britain where he met Eliza Field who became his wife in 1831. He was ordained in 1833.

Jones saw himself as a defender of both Methodism and the interests of the Ojibwa people. When the Lieutenant-Governor of Upper Canada, Sir PEREGRINE MAITLAND, attempted to convince Jones to join the Church of England and encourage the Ojibwa to do likewise, Jones refused. He also worked against the programme of another lieutenant-governor, Sir Francis Bond Head, when the latter devised a plan to ship the Indians north and out of the way of settlers in the south. In this campaign, Jones solicited the assistance of the APS in London. Jones and his wife remained active in this mission work until his death.

Jones was able to adapt Christian ideas to the needs of the native people in ways which eluded non-native missionaries. His plans to teach farming and religious ideas provided an alternative to total assimilation which was welcomed by many southern Ojibwa. After Jones' death, interest in Methodism among the Ojibwa began to wane.

BIBLIOGRAPHY
DCB, 8
D. B. Smith, *Sacred Feathers* (Toronto, 1987)

KERRY M. ABEL

Jones, Robert (b. Llanystumdwy, Caernarfonshire, Wales, 13 Jan. 1745; d. Llaniestyn, Caernarfonshire, Wales, 8 April 1829). Welsh Calvinistic Methodist exhorter, teacher and author. Having learned to read in one of the circulating schools of GRIFFITH JONES, Llanddowror, Jones (known in the annals of Calvinistic Methodism as 'Robert Jones, Rhoslan') later persuaded Madam BRIDGET BEVAN, the friend and patron of Griffith Jones, to re-establish the circulating schools in Gwynedd after their founder's death and he himself became an itinerant teacher holding schools in various parts of North Wales. In 1768 he became a Calvinistic Methodist exhorter, his preaching tours taking him throughout North and South Wales. His published works include a defence of Methodism against its persecutors (*Lleferydd yr Asyn*, 1770), a collection of hymns (*Grawnsypiau Canaan*, 1795), and his famous history of the Methodist Revival in Wales (*Drych yr Amseroedd*, 1820) which provides a firsthand account of the origins and spread of the revival. As a close friend of THOMAS CHARLES of Bala he played a significant part in persuading Charles to agree to the ordination of the first Calvinistic Methodist ministers in 1811.

BIBLIOGRAPHY
DWB
J. Elias, *Cofiant . . . R. Jones* (Llanrwst, Wales, 1834)
J. Parry and T. Gee, eds., *Y Gwyddoniadur*, 6 (Denbigh, Wales, 1889): 416–17

E. AP NEFYDD ROBERTS

Jones, Samuel (b. Glamorganshire, Wales, 14 Jan. 1735; d. 7 Feb. 1814). Baptist minister. Samuel Jones was educated at the College of Philadelphia where he earned a MA in 1762. He was instrumental to the incorporation of Rhode Island College (Brown University). A Particular Baptist, Jones became the principal pastor of Pennepek Church near Philadelphia from 1763 until his death. One of the most prominent leaders of Old School thought, he accepted the heritage of the first Great Awakening but steadfastly opposed the second, especially ANDREW FULLER and Fullerism. He wrote the Circular Letter of 1774 on the subject of the Trinity; the Circular Letter of 1783 on the problem of sin and the providence of God; the Circular Letter of 1790 against the 'leprosy of the doctrine of universal salvation'; and

the Circular Letter of 1795 on the Gospel and the extent of grace. During the first decade of the nineteenth century the 'moneyed missionary spirit' began to prevail among the Philadelphia Association despite Jones' opposition.

BIBLIOGRAPHY
C. B. Hassell and S. Hassell, *History of the Church of God* (Middletown, NY, 1886): 556–7

WADE A. HORTON

Jones, Thomas (b. England, 1729; d. Southwark, England, 6 June 1762). Junior chaplain, St Saviour's, Southwark. Little is known about his birth and upbringing. He matriculated from King's College, Cambridge, in 1746 as a sizar or poor scholar, suggesting humble parentage. Thomas Stephens, who preached his funeral sermon, was a fellow undergraduate. Jones proceeded BA (1751) and MA (1754). On 1 March 1753 he was appointed to the Collegiate Church of St Saviour, Southwark, the precursor of the present cathedral. After popular election he was nominated as one of two chaplains to the Bishop of London, Thomas Sherlock. Contacts with MARTIN MADAN and WILLIAM ROMAINE apparently led to his conversion in 1754 of which the latter gave an account. Jones had already been introduced to Lady HUNTINGDON whose counsel contributed to his spiritual awakening. He joined WHITEFIELD and WESLEY in preaching in her Park Street residence and was also in demand in London pulpits for charity sermons. His uncompromising fidelity to evangelical truth as reflected in his published sermons aroused considerable opposition, culminating in an ill-informed attack from Dr John Free, headmaster of St Olave's Grammar School. Jones remained at his post, however, and sustained his assiduous pastoral visitation, catechizing of children, and extensive Christian literature campaign. For several years he was the only beneficed evangelical clergyman in the entire London area. His pioneer ministry paved the way for the later spread and ultimate strength of Anglican evangelicalism in the capital.

BIBLIOGRAPHY
EQ 46: 174–82

A. SKEVINGTON WOOD

Jones, Thomas (b. Hafod, Cardiganshire, Wales, 2 April 1752; d. Spratton, Northamptonshire, England, 7 Jan. 1845). Evangelical cleric. Ordained in 1774, Jones served a succession of curacies in Wales and the borders, facing many difficulties because of his evangelical ministry. In 1785 CHARLES SIMEON secured him the curacy of Creaton, Northamptonshire. Appointed rector in 1829, he resigned the living in 1833. Celebrated as a preacher, the translator into Welsh of works by Richard Baxter, JOHN BERRIDGE and WILLIAM ROMAINE, a writer of numerous books and tracts, the originator of the 1799

SPCK's edition of the Welsh Bible, Jones' importance lies in his encouragement of evangelical life in England and Wales. His friendship with THOMAS CHARLES survived his attack on the 1811 Welsh Methodist ordinations, but he was not as involved in the foundation of the BFBS as is sometimes claimed.

BIBLIOGRAPHY
DNB
DWB
D. E. Jenkins, *Thomas Charles of Bala* (Denbigh, Wales, 1908–13)
J. Owen, *Memoir of the Rev. Thomas Jones* (London, 1851)

ROGER L. BROWN

Jones, Thomas (b. Pen Uchaf, Caerwys, Clwyd, Wales, Feb. 1756; d. Denbigh, Wales, 16 June 1820). Welsh Calvinistic Methodist minister. He was the son of Edward and Jane Jones, comparatively well-to-do people. He was educated at Caerwys Grammar School at the same time as Dr EDWARD WILLIAMS (1750–1813), Rotherham, and so acquired proficiency in the classics. In 1772 he joined the Methodists and became a preacher in 1783. He first met THOMAS CHARLES (1715–1814) of Bala in 1785 and was to work in the closest collaboration with him. His first published work, an elegy, appeared in 1788. He was thrice married and became one of the richest Methodist ministers in Wales. He was a diligent writer and combined wide scholarship with a courteous manner and a generous spirit. As a Church historian and theologian, he occupies the front rank in his generation. He rejected both Hyper-Calvinism and the 'New System' of his old friend Dr Edward Williams. He had long mastered the intricacies of the Welsh strict metres in poetry and was an elegant prose writer; his autobiography has long taken its place among the classics. As a denominational leader, he was wise and moderate and, next to Thomas Charles, the most influential in the Calvinistic Methodist Connexion. He was one of the first group of men to be ordained by the connexion in 1811, the act which marked the severance of the Methodists from the Anglican Church.

BIBLIOGRAPHY
I. Jones Aberystwyth, ed., *Autobiography* (1937)
Memoirs by J. Humphreys and J. Roberts (Denbigh, Wales, 1820), Jonathan Jones (Denbigh, Wales, 1897) and F. P. Jones (Denbigh, Wales, 1966)

R. TUDUR JONES

Jones, Thomas (b. Wales, *c.* 1800; d. Jamaica, 19 Aug. 1827). First CMS missionary to the West Indies. Jones and HENRY C. TAYLOR were the first CMS missionaries sent to the West Indies. They went out on 29 November 1825 to Jamaica to serve as lay catechists on the estate of J. B. Wildman. Jones lasted less than two years; he died some nine days after the death of the wife of his co-worker, Taylor. Jones's widow returned to England in 1828.

BIBLIOGRAPHY
D. T. B[arry], *CMS Register of Missionaries and Native Clergy* (privately printed) (London, 1906)

DONALD M. LEWIS

Jones, Thomas (b. Tanyffridd, Llangynyw, Berriew, Montgomeryshire (Powys), Wales. 24 Jan. 1810; d. Calcutta, India, 16 Sept. 1849). First Welsh Calvinistic Methodist missionary on the Khasi Hills (Assam), northeast India. Jones's refusal to accept the guidance of the directors of the LMS led to the formation of the Welsh Calvinistic Methodist Missionary Society. He commenced preaching in 1835, was ordained in 1840 and sailed that November for India. He and his wife arrived at Cherrapunji on 22 June 1841.

He translated Matthew's Gospel and various catechisms into Khasi. In spite of many hardships, schools were established and communities evangelized. During 1847 he became a farm manager and his connection with the society was terminated. Ill health forced him to move to Calcutta where he died. He was buried in the Scottish Cemetery. Jones was stubborn, impetuous and intolerant of the other missionaries. Nevertheless his labours paved the way for the future success of the mission.

BIBLIOGRAPHY
J. H. Morris, *Hanes Gymdeithas Genhadol Y Methodistiaid Calfinaidd Cymraeg* (Caernarfon, Wales, 1907)
E. Thomas, *Bryniau'r Glaw* (Caernarfon, Wales, 1988)
National Library of Wales, Aberystwyth, Dyfed, manuscripts pertaining to the mission

R. WATCYN JAMES

Jones, William (b. Abergavenny, Monmouthshire, England, 18 Nov. 1755; d. Broxbourne, Hertfordshire, England, 12 Oct. 1821). Anglican minister. Jones was educated at Abergavenny Grammar School and then, like so many of his compatriots, went to Jesus College, Oxford in 1773 (BA 1780). He spent some time in Jamaica as tutor to the sons of the Attorney-General (1778–80), before becoming Curate of Broxbourne and Hoddesdon (Hertfordshire) (1781–1801), eventually succeeding as vicar (1801–21) after an unsuccessful approach to become Rector of Warmley (1798). In his earlier years he expressed a deep sense of his sinful condition and he was rigorous in avoiding what he regarded as such worldly diversions as cards and dancing. He became more genial with the passing of the years, but he always retained his evangelical biblicism. In middle life he inclined to universalism, but latterly he restated his early adherence to the concept of eternal damnation. He railed against clerical magistrates, hunting and shooting parsons, and his parishioners who either failed entirely or only paid their tithes in part.

BIBLIOGRAPHY
O. F. Christie, ed., *The Diary of the Rev. William Jones* (London, 1929)

ARTHUR POLLARD

Jones, William (b. Gresford, Denbighshire, Wales, 17 June 1762; d. London, 21 Jan. 1846). Scotch Baptist pastor, author and editor. Jones was baptized in the Church of England, but as a young man joined Ecking's Baptist Church in Chester, which soon became Sandemanian in sentiment and united with MCLEAN's Scotch Baptists in 1786. In Liverpool, and from 1812 in London, Jones edited a series of journals devoted to what he termed primitive Christianity, and he was for some years an elder in Scotch Baptist churches. For a short time in 1835–6 he welcomed Campbellite teaching and contributed to the beginning of Churches of Christ in Britain. By the time of his death in 1846 he was again a Scotch Baptist, and had been nominated to a small charitable annuity by Queen Victoria. Jones wrote *A History of the Waldensians*.

SELECT WRITINGS
W. Jones, *Autobiography* (London, 1846)

BIBLIOGRAPHY
DNB
D. B. Murray, 'The Scotch Baptist Tradition in Great Britain,' *BQ*: 186–98
R. Taylor, 'English Baptist Periodicals 1790–1865', *BQ* 27 (1977): 50–82

DEREK B. MURRAY

Josenhans, Joseph Friedrich (b. Stuttgart, Germany, 9 Feb. 1812; d. Leonberg, Germany, 25 Dec. 1884). Third inspector of the Basel Mission. The son of a Leonberg Pietist businessman and co-founder of the *Deutsches Bibelanstalt* (German Bible Society), Josenhans studied theology at Tübingen. There he was influenced by the works of devout Pietists such as L. Hofacker. After university, he worked in ecclesial education at the private Christian Gymnasium at Setten (1834–6). He was appointed pastoral assistant at Stuttgart and later vicar at Backnang (where he met his wife Maria whom he married in 1840) as well as a teaching associate at the Stift at Tübingen (1836–8). He then spent a decade as a pastoral assistant in Winnenden (1839–49).

In 1849 Josenhans was named inspector of the Basel Mission succeeding C. G. BLUMHARDT (1816–38) and L. F. W. HOFFMANN (1839–50). Shortly before his appointment, Josenhans made an inspection tour of Basel Mission centres in India. From this experience he formulated plans for a more centralized, highly controlled organization. This resulted in greater efficiency but brought efforts at indigenization to a standstill. Josenhans worked to make the Basel Mission a truly international mission. For a time Josenhans edited the *Evangelisches Missionsmagazin* and *Evangelisches Heidenbote* before returning them to the care of C. G. Blumhardt's nephew, A. Ostertag.

Conflict with C. F. SPITTLER about the relation of the Basel Mission to the church in Basel and with board members about mission policy made Josenhans' tenure stormy. He resigned in 1879 to return to Leonberg. He died there in 1884.

BIBLIOGRAPHY
F. J. Josenhans, *Frauenvereine zu Leiblicher und Geistiger Versorgung Armer Verlassener und Berufsloser Jungfrauen und Witwen.* (Winnenden, Germany, 1845)
F. J. Josenhans, hrsg., *Atlas der Evangelischen Missions-Gesellschaft zu Basel* (Basel, Switzerland, 1857; 2nd edn Basel, 1859)
—, *Ausgewählte Reden* (Stuttgart, Germany, 1886)
J. Hesse, *Joseph Josenhans, ein Lebensbild* (Stuttgart, Germany, 1895)
H. Hohlwein, 'Josenhans, Joseph', *Neue Deutsche Biographie* 10 (1974): 612
P. Steiner, 'Josenhans, Joseph F.', *Allgemeine Deutsche Biographie* 50 (1905): 701–3

DAVID BUNDY

Jost, Christopher (b. Germany; d. Bullom Shore, West Africa, 28 June 1816). CMS missionary to Sierra Leone. Jost was trained as a schoolmaster and was a member of Dr CARL STEINKOPF's German-speaking Lutheran congregation in London. It would appear that he was among those who responded to the request from the CMS for German missionaries in the absence of English recruits but there is no evidence that he trained at the Berlin Mission seminary under JOHANNES JÄNICKE as had so many other German volunteers. The CMS sent him to Bullom Shore on 17 March 1816 (along with W. A. B. JOHNSON, W. H. DÜRING and J. HORTON). He died about two months after his arrival. Nothing is known of the fate of his English wife, Mary (née Stephens). The survival rate of the early CMS missionaries in Sierra Leone was appalling (*see* M. RENNER, P. HARTWIG, J. G. PRASSE, J. C. BARNETH, J. QUAST, C. H. MEISSNER, H. MEYER and J. H. SCHULZE).

BIBLIOGRAPHY
D. T. B[arry], *CMS Register of Missionaries and Native Clergy* (privately printed) (London, 1906)

DONALD M. LEWIS

Joule, James Prescott (b. Salford, near Manchester, England, 24 Dec. 1819; d. Sale, Cheshire, England, 11 Oct. 1889). Physicist and founder of the mechanical theory of heat. Joule, son of a wealthy brewer, was of independent means and spent much of his life in scientific research, alone or in collaboration with William Thomson (Kelvin). A very careful experimenter, he studied heat produced by an electric current ('Joule's Law'), established the first law of thermodynamics (conservation of energy) and determined the mechanical equivalent to heat. The present scientific unit for work and heat is named after him. Denying that energy could be annihilated he affirmed that 'power to destroy belongs to the Creator alone'. Though given to sleeping through sermons Joule went beyond his traditional Anglicanism by signing the 1865 'Declaration' affirming the congruence between science and scripture.

BIBLIOGRAPHY
D. S. L. Cardwell, *James Joule: a Biography* (Manchester, England, 1989)
DNB
DSB
C. A. Russell, *Cross-Currents* (Leicester, England, 1985)

COLIN A. RUSSELL

Jowett, Henry (b. 1756; d. Little Dunham, Norfolk, 5 Apr. 1830). Anglican clergyman and tutor. The son of Henry Jowett of Leeds, he was educated at Magdalene College, Cambridge (BA 1778; MA 1781) where he was sixth senior optime. Jowett was a fellow and tutor of his college and, with SAMUEL HEY and WILLIAM FARISH, made the college a centre of evangelical witness.

He was ordained priest in 1780. In 1792 EDWARD PARRY presented him to the living of Little Dunham, Norfolk, which he held until his death. He succeeded JOHN VENN, who had been his friend at college. He also took over Venn's tutoring of CHARLES and ROBERT GRANT – they would later attend Magdalene College – and instructed an extraordinary array of other evangelical lights, including J. W. CUNNINGHAM, F. CUNNINGHAM, H. V. ELLIOTT, A. S. THELWALL and T. P. PLATT.

BIBLIOGRAPHY
GM (October 1792): 966; (June 1796): 540; (June 1830): 648
M. Hennell, *John Venn of the Clapham Sect* (London, 1958)
J. D. Walsh, 'The Magdalene Evangelicals', *Church Quarterly Review* 159: 499–511

JONATHAN BURKE CUTMORE

Jowett, John (b. Leeds, Yorkshire, England, 1745; d. London, 14 Feb. 1800). Skinner. He was the son of Henry Jowett (1719–1810) who was converted in 1749 through JOHN WESLEY. He moved to London (*circa* 1780) and conducted a fellmongery with his brother Benjamin (grandfather of Jowett of Balliol) in Southwark. Both of them were active in the infancy of the CMS. In 1781 he worked to have W. J. ABDY appointed curate at St John Horsleydown. His other brothers were JOSEPH JOWETT, professor of civil law at Cambridge and Vicar of Wethersfield (Essex) and HENRY JOWETT, Rector of Little Dunham (Norfolk). Jowett was father of WILLIAM JOWETT, CMS missionary in the Mediterranean, and of Elizabeth, who married JOSIAH PRATT.

BIBLIOGRAPHY
C. Hole, *History of CMS* (London, 1896)

ARTHUR POLLARD

Jowett, Joseph (b. probably Leeds, England, 1752; d. Cambridge, England, 13 Nov. 1813). Professor of civil law. The son of Henry Jowett of Leeds (where he was educated), he was admitted to Trinity College, Cambridge (1769) and moved to Trinity Hall (1773) where he became assistant tutor. He became fellow and principal tutor (1775–95) and in 1782 was appointed professor of civil law. A mild and unoriginal bachelor, he was an encouragement to evangelically inclined undergraduates but a source of amusement to some of the wider community. Supported by his close friend ISAAC MILNER he opposed the election of F. WRANGHAM as a fellow of Trinity Hall. In 1795 he became Vicar of Wethersfield where he lived during long vacations.

BIBLIOGRAPHY
DNB
G. Faber, *Jowett, a Portrait with Background* (London, 1957): 50–3
D. M. Rosman, *Evangelicals and Culture* (London, 1984): 134–5
R. V. Taylor, *The Biographia Leodiensis* (London, 1865)

TIMOTHY C. F. STUNT

Jowett, William (b. London, 1787; d. Clapham, Surrey, England, 22 Feb. 1885). Anglican missionary and mission executive. Jowett was the son of JOHN JOWETT, and thus nephew of JOSEPH JOWETT and HENRY JOWETT. His sister Elizabeth married JOSIAH PRATT. He distinguished himself at Cambridge (twelfth wrangler 1810) and became a fellow of St John's. He was the first British university graduate to serve with the CMS. After studying oriental languages he was sent to Malta in 1815.

The choice of Malta for a mission was part of a strategy which saw the island as a stepping-stone not only to Mediterranean lands but also to Orthodox churches and Muslim areas of the Middle East and North Africa. Jowett was directed to collect information and to inquire about the best methods 'of propagating Christian knowledge'. He and others travelled in Greece, Egypt and Syria; Jowett helped with the publication of a modern Greek New Testament and an Amharic Bible (working with the Bible Society); and he himself, helped by his gifted wife, Martha, also a linguist, wrote and translated tracts and pamphlets. A printing press was set up in Malta. In 1820 Jowett published his highly acclaimed *Christian Researches in the Mediterranean*, and in 1824 was one of the youngest men ever to preach the CMS Annual Sermon.

He remained in Malta until 1830, returning to England and withdrawing from CMS on health grounds. Missionary tours from Malta and the distribution of tracts and scriptures continued, but there was opposition (sometimes violent) from Roman Catholic and Orthodox clergy and especially from Muslims in parts of Turkey. By 1824 a number of CMS missionaries, mainly German and Swiss trained at Basel, were established in Egypt and looking towards Abyssinia. Others were in the city of Smyrna and on the island of Syra – but the ancient Eastern churches continued to resist the hoped-for reformation.

In 1830 the Clerical Secretary of CMS, EDWARD BICKERSTETH, retired, and in 1832 Jowett replaced him. His colleague as lay secretary (administrator) was the efficient, zealous but rather narrow DANDESON COATES, and Jowett, 'pious and amiable', provided the personal and conciliatory element. He continued in the post until 1840; in those years some of the missionaries in Egypt made the first effective contacts in Ethiopia, carrying on work which in fact was possible because of the base he had established in Malta and the materials brought out by the Malta press. His linguistic work was largely carried on by German missionaries. Jowett's period in office has been overshadowed by the long and distinguished service of his successor, HENRY VENN, but he had one advantage that Venn never had – the experience of 15 years in the Mediterranean.

Jowett retired from the secretariat in 1840 and from 1840 to 1855 was the incumbent successively of St Mary Aldermanbury and of St John's, Clapham Rise. He died at Clapham at the age of 68; his wife had died in Malta in 1829. Benjamin Jowett (1817–1893), master of Balliol, was his cousin (grandson of his uncle Benjamin Jowett).

SELECT WRITINGS

W. Jowett, *Christian Researches in the Mediterranean, Syria and the Holy Land* (London, 1820)

BIBLIOGRAPHY

E. Stock, *History of the Church Missionary Society*, 3 vols (London, 1899)

JOCELYN MURRAY

Joymooni [also Jeyamuni] (*fl.* 1801). First Bengali Baptist woman. KRISHNA PAL's sister-in-law, she was the first Bengali woman to be baptized publicly (18 January 1801). She emerged from a traditional, secluded life of a 'respectable' caste to preach the Gospel on Serampore's streets.

Accompanied by other Bengali women, she travelled to Chinsurah and beyond, to visit gurus and devotees. She preached, 'One caste, one Saviour', breaking with many of the rules of 'ritual pollution'. In the recorded fragments of her conversations, she seems to have developed some original forms of spirituality, which she expressed in indigenous rather than western evangelical idioms. Several times suspended from the Serampore Church for quarrelsomeness, her enthusiasm and friendliness, nevertheless, served to encourage incoming new missionaries.

BIBLIOGRAPHY

Periodical Accounts Relative to the BMS

E. M. JACKSON

Judson, Adoniram (b. Malden, MA, USA, 9 Aug. 1788; d. near Andamen Islands, 12 April 1850). Baptist missionary. A heroic legend in his own time, Judson was America's first Baptist foreign missionary, devoted a lifetime to Christian missions in Burma, translated the Bible into Burmese and published the first English-Burmese dictionary.

Born to Congregationalist clergyman Judson and Abigail (Brown) Judson, young Judson grew up in Wenham, Braintree and Plymouth, Massachusetts, where his father held pastorates. At age 16 he entered Brown University with sophomore standing and graduated as valedictorian in 1807. After teaching in Plymouth and publishing two textbooks on grammar and mathematics, Judson spent a brief period in New York City as a sceptical, aspiring playwright.

Though unsettled about his faith, he entered the newly founded Andover Theological Seminary in 1808. There he was converted to orthodox Christianity and committed himself to overseas missionary service, a step considered unprecedented at the time. Joining with Williams College alumni (SAMUEL J. MILLS, JAMES RICHARDS, LUTHER RICE and GORDON HALL) at Andover who held similar goals, he helped found the ABCFM, a largely Congregationalist effort.

Judson married ANN (Nancy) HASSELTINE JUDSON of Bradford, Massachusetts on 5 February 1812, was ordained as a Congregational minister on 13 February and sailed for Calcutta from Salem on 19 February with the first missionary contingent to leave America for foreign fields. While *en route* to India, the Judsons adopted an immersionist view of baptism, a conviction that necessitated looking to American Baptists rather than Congregationalists for support. In response the Baptists formed in 1814 the Triennial Convention (later renamed the American Baptist Foreign Mission Society) to support their mission in Asia. When the East India Company denied them permanent residency in India, the Judsons sailed to the Isle of France in the Indian Ocean (now Mauritius) where they eventually found passage to Rangoon, Burma, their original preference for mission work.

With no European community, a hostile climate, poor inhabitants, a tyrannical government and a difficult language, Burma presented a daunting environment for preaching the Gospel. A gifted linguist, Judson, along with his wife, spent every effort to learn the language and prepare to translate the Scriptures into Burmese, a language with no capitals, no paragraphs or sentences and no breaks between words. The result was a completed Burmese Bible by 1834 and his *Dictionary, English and Burmese*, published in 1849.

The Judsons attempted various evangelistic techniques with few converts in Rangoon until they erected a *zayat* (a 20' × 20' hut with a veranda), or shelter open to all for rest, relaxation and discussion. By 1820 the Rangoon church numbered ten baptized communicants who themselves evangelized the surrounding areas. In 1824 the Judsons moved to Ava, the royal capital, in order to influence the court for more tolerance of the Christian religion. Unfortunately, a war between Burma and the

British led to a horrible 17-month imprisonment of Judson and another missionary who were accused of spying for Great Britain.

Eventually released to serve as interpreter in the peace negotiations, Judson moved his work to Maulmain after the death by fever of his wife and the loss of his only living child, a daughter, who had been born during Judson's imprisonment. In working through grief and depression, he turned increasingly to mysticism, eventually developing a spirituality that attracted many converts during his increasingly itinerant ministry.

Rejecting an offer of $3,000 per year for employment as an official interpreter for the British, Judson concentrated on preaching tours and translation work with the Burmese language, in which he became remarkably proficient. In 1834 Judson married SARAH HALL BOARDMAN, widow of missionary GEORGE DANA BOARDMAN, and herself an effective communicator of the Gospel to the Karens tribe of the Burmese interior. Animists rather than Buddhists, the Karens converted to Christianity by the thousands.

Eight children were born of Judson's second marriage, five of whom survived infancy. When Sarah Boardman Judson's health failed, the family sailed to America in 1845. The two youngest sons remained in Burma. Mrs Judson died *en route* and was buried on St Helena.

Welcomed in America as a hero, Judson travelled and spoke widely, though his voice was very weak. After a brief courtship, he married EMILY CHUBBOCK in June 1846. The marriage drew criticism because she was 29 years younger than Judson and a published novelist under the pen name, Fanny Forester.

In November 1846, the Judsons were back in Burma where a daughter was born in December 1847. In addition to preaching and supervision of the now expanded mission, Judson laboured to complete his *Dictionary, English and Burmese*. By its publication in 1849, his health failed, and in 1850 he embarked on an ocean voyage recommended to restore his strength. On 12 April 1850 Judson died on board ship and was buried at sea near the Andamen Islands. It took four months for news of his death to reach Mrs Judson. In 1851 she returned to Boston with her daughter and Judson's two sons from his second marriage. Left unfinished at Judson's death, his *Dictionary, Burmese and English* was completed by co-worker Edward A. Stevens and published in 1852.

After supplying materials to president FRANCIS WAYLAND of Brown University for his official biography of Judson, Emily Chubbock died in 1854. The well-founded church in Burma and the vigour of American sponsored foreign missions remain permanent memorials to the Judsons and their pioneering work.

BIBLIOGRAPHY
C. Anderson, *To the Golden Shore* (Valley Forge, PA, 1987)
E. Judson, *The Life of Adoniram Judson* (New York, 1883)
S. R. Warburton, *Eastward! The Story of Adoniram Judson* (New York, 1937)

F. Wayland, *A Memoir of the Life and Labors of the Rev. Adoniram Judson, DD*, 2 vols (Boston, MA, 1853)

THOMAS A. ASKEW

Judson, Ann Hasseltine (b. Bradford, MA, USA, 22 Dec. 1789; d. Burma, 24 Oct. 1826). Missionary. Judson was among the first foreign missionaries sent in 1812 by the ABCFM. After arrival in India, she and her husband were baptized by WILLIAM CAREY. Consequently, American Baptists supported the Judsons as their first foreign missionaries. Commencing mission work in Burma, Ann did evangelistic work, adopted orphan girls, and educated children. In 1824, war broke out between the British and the Burmese, and ADONIRAM JUDSON was arrested. Ann saved his life by bribing government officials, bringing food, and pressing for his freedom over the next two years. After British victory and Adoniram's release in 1826, Ann died, exhausted by persecution and family responsibilities.

With her translation of the Gospel of Matthew in 1819, Ann was the first person to translate the Bible into Thai. She translated the Books of Daniel and Jonah into Burmese and wrote a Burmese catechism. In 1823, she wrote a history of the American Baptist mission in Burma, one of the earliest volumes on an American foreign mission. Because of numerous biographies of her, she remains the most influential missionary woman in American history.

DANA L. ROBERT

Judson, Emily Chubbock (b. Eaton, NY, USA, 22 August 1817; d. Hamilton, NY, USA, 1 June 1854). Writer and Baptist missionary. The fifth child of Charles and Lavinia (Richards) Chubbock, Emily's childhood was shaped by poverty. From 1832 to 1840, she taught school, before attending the Utica Female Seminary. In 1841, she taught at Utica Seminary and in that year, published her first Sunday school book, *Charles Linn* (1841). She published three other books of the same type before beginning to write for the *New York Mirror* under the name Fanny Forester. In 1845–6, she went to Philadelphia and met ADONIRAM JUDSON. They married on 2 June 1846, and went to Burma in July. In addition to the *Memoir of Sarah B. Judson* (1848) Emily published several other books. After Adoniram's death in 1850, which was followed ten days later by the death of their second child, Emily left India with her only surviving child and two other stepchildren. Her own health failing, she returned to Hamilton, New York, where she died.

BIBLIOGRAPHY
AAP, 6: 607–20
W. H. Brackney, *The Baptists* (NY, 1988)
DAB

KAREN E. SMITH

Judson, Ephraim (b. Woodbury, CT, BNA, 5 Dec. 1737; d. Sheffield, MA, USA, 23 Feb. 1813). American Congregational minister. He was the son of Elnathan and Rebecca Judson. He graduated from Yale in 1763, and served three charges – the Second Church in Norwich, Connecticut (1771–8), and the congregations in Taunton, Massachusetts (1780–90), and in Sheffield, Massachusetts (1791–1813). He married Chloe Ellis; they had one child who bore the name of his father. He was a Jeffersonian Democrat and a Calvinist belonging to the school of SAMUEL HOPKINS. The church at Sheffield was Arminian when he arrived, but he preached his doctrines indirectly with a view to their practical application and so won over the majority of his parishioners. He was decidedly eccentric but apparently blessed with a good supply of common sense. He assisted a number of young men in their preparation for the ministry, and several of his ordination sermons were published. He was the uncle of the Baptist missionary, ADONIRAM JUDSON.

BIBLIOGRAPHY
AAP

JOHN K. LA SHELL

Judson, Sarah Hall Boardman (b. Alstead, NH, USA, 4 Nov. 1803; d. St Helena, 1 Sept. 1845). Baptist missionary. The daughter of Ralph and Abiah O. Hall, she spent her early years in Salem, Massachusetts. Early on she expressed an interest in writing religious verse and missionary work. She wrote a poem about the death of James Colman, a missionary to Burma. The poem was seen by GEORGE DANA BOARDMAN, who had volunteered to replace Colman. She and Boardman were married in 1825 and went to India as missionaries in that same year. They had three children, two of whom died in infancy. Her husband died in 1831 and she remained at their mission post. In April 1834, she married ADONIRAM JUDSON. The had eight children, three of whom died in infancy. Sarah learned the Burmese language, organized schools and translated into Burmese *The Pilgrim's Progress* as well as several tracts.

BIBLIOGRAPHY
AAP, 6: 617, 735
DAB, X
C. B. Hartley, *The Three Mrs Judsons, The Celebrated Female Missionaries* (New York, no date)

KAREN E. SMITH

Jukes, Richard (b. Clungunford, Shropshire, England, 9 Oct. 1804; d. West Bromwich, Staffordshire, England, Aug. 1867). Stonemason and bard of the Primitive Methodist poor. A commanding but neglected figure, Jukes worked six days a week as a stonemason for most of his early preaching life. Converted in 1825, he was immediately placed on the Ludlow circuit plan, although in his 32-year ministry he was to be constantly on the move around the Midlands. Described as 'a man to lay a spell upon strong men, and to win a child's heart alike', Jukes combined physical strength with tender sympathy, intelligent wisdom and grace. Officially the prolific poet and hymn-writer of the first generation of Primitive Methodists, unofficially the 'bard of the poor', Jukes wrote plain and simple hymns, which fitted precisely the revivalist mood of the time, and expressed the feelings and experiences of his audience.

BIBLIOGRAPHY
The Aldersgate Primitive Methodist Magazine (1903)

WAYNE J. JOHNSON